tchhiker's Guide to the Galaxy **Dante Alghieri** *The Divine Comedy* **Anonymous**

hts **Anonymous** *The Mabinogion* **Ludovico Arios** **Asimov**

ain M. Banks *The Culture series* **J. M. Barrie** *Gardens*

le *The Last Unicorn* **Edward Bellamy** *Looking Backward: 2000-1887* **Cyrano de**

Boulle *Planet of the Apes* **Ray Bradbury** *Fahrenheit 451* **Gerd Mjøen Brantenberg**

gar Rice Burroughs *At the Earth's Core* **Octavia E. Butler** *Kindred* **Samuel Butler**

is **Carroll** *Alice's Adventures in Wonderland* **Angela Carter** *The Bloody Chamber*

e *Blazing-World* **Miguel de Cervantes** *Don Quixote* **Michael Chabon** *The Yiddish*

athan Strange & Mr Norrell **Suzanne Collins** *The Hunger Games* **Arthur Conan**

m *of Electric Sheep?* **Jasper Fforde** *The Eyre Affair* **Cornelia Funke** *Inkheart* **Neil**

- Adventures Wonderful **William Gibson** *Necromancer* **Charlotte Perkins Gilman**

s *Klim to the World Underground* **Homer** *The Odyssey* **Robert E. Howard** *Conan*

Tove Jansson *The Moomins and the Great Flood* **Franz Kafka** *The Castle* **Stephen**

- *Land Baby* **Ann Leckie** *The Imperial Radch trilogy* **Ursula K. Le Guin** *A Wizard*

raft *The Cthulu Mythos* **Lois Lowry** *The Giver* **Thomas Malory** *Le Morte d'Arthur*

Game of Thrones **China Miéville** *The Bas-Lag cycle* **Wu Ming-Yi** *The Man with the*

ami *1Q84* **Vladimir Nabokov** *Pale Fire* **Larry Niven** *Ringworld* **Nneki Okorafor**

Gormenghast **Georges Perec** *W or the Memory of Childhood* **Terry Pratchett** *The*

he *Philosopher's Stone* **Juan Rulfo** *Pedro Páramo* **Salman Rushdie** *Two Years Eight*

n **Shakespeare** *The Tempest* **Edmund Spenser** *The Faerie Queene* **Neal Stephenson**

Edda **Jonathan Swift** *Gulliver's Travels* **Ngugi Wa Thiong'o** *Wizard of the Crow*

thur's *Court* **Jules Verne** *Twenty Thousand Leagues Under the Sea* **Kurt Vonnegut**

llace *Infinite Jest* **H. G. Wells** *The Time Machine* **Austin Tappan Wright** *Islandia*

D1374736

LITERARY WONDERLANDS

LITERARY WONDERLANDS

A Journey Through the Greatest Fictional Worlds Ever Created

General Editor Laura Miller

CONTENTS

Introduction   10

ANCIENT MYTH & LEGEND

ANONYMOUS   16
The Epic of Gilgamesh, c.1750 BCE

HOMER   18
The Odyssey, c.725–675 BCE

OVID   22
Metamorphoses, c.8

ANONYMOUS   28
Beowulf, c.700–1100

ANONYMOUS   30
The Thousand and One Nights, c.700–947

ANONYMOUS   34
The Mabinogion, 12th–14th century

SNORRI STURLUSON   36
The Prose Edda, c.1220

DANTE ALIGHIERI   40
The Divine Comedy, c.1308–21

THOMAS MALORY   44
Le Morte d'Arthur, 1485

LUDOVICO ARIOSTO   48
Orlando Furioso, c.1516/32

THOMAS MORE   52
Utopia, 1516

EDMUND SPENSER   54
The Faerie Queene, 1590–1609

WU CHENG'EN   58
Journey to the West (Xiyouji), c.1592

TOMMASO CAMPANELLA   60
The City of the Sun, 1602

MIGUEL DE CERVANTES   62
Don Quixote, 1605/15

WILLIAM SHAKESPEARE   64
The Tempest, 1611

CYRANO DE BERGERAC   68
A Voyage to the Moon, 1657

MARGARET CAVENDISH   70
*The Description of a New World,
      called The Blazing-World, 1666*

Previous page: 'Heavens. What were these?' from *The Tempest* (III:iii),
from *The Illustrated Library Shakespeare* (1890), see page 64.

2 SCIENCE & ROMANTICISM

JONATHAN SWIFT   74
Gulliver's Travels, 1726

LUDVIG HOLBERG   78
*The Journey of Niels Klim to the
World Underground*, 1741

CHARLES KINGSLEY   80
*The Water-Babies: A Fairy Tale
for a Land Baby*, 1863

LEWIS CARROLL   82
Alice's Adventures in Wonderland, 1865

JULES VERNE   88
*Twenty Thousand Leagues
Under the Sea*, 1870

SAMUEL BUTLER   94
Erewhon, 1872

RICHARD WAGNER   96
The Ring of the Nibelung, 1876

ROBERT LOUIS STEVENSON   100
Treasure Island, 1883

EDWIN A. ABBOTT   104
*Flatland: A Romance of
Many Dimensions*, 1884

EDWARD BELLAMY   106
Looking Backward: 2000–1887, 1888

MARK TWAIN   108
*A Connecticut Yankee in King Arthur's
Court*, 1889

H. G. WELLS   110
The Time Machine, 1895

L. FRANK BAUM   116
The Wonderful Wizard of Oz, 1900

3 GOLDEN AGE OF FANTASY

J. M. BARRIE   124
Peter Pan in Kensington Gardens, 1906

ARTHUR CONAN DOYLE   130
The Lost World, 1912

EDGAR RICE BURROUGHS   132
At the Earth's Core, 1914

CHARLOTTE PERKINS GILMAN   134
Herland, 1915

CECILIA MAY GIBBS   136
*Tales of Snugglepot and Cuddlepie:
    Their Adventures Wonderful*, 1918

YEVGENY ZAMYATIN   138
We, 1924

FRANZ KAFKA   140
The Castle, 1926

H. P. LOVECRAFT   144
The Cthulhu Mythos, 1928–37

ALDOUS HUXLEY   148
Brave New World, 1932

ROBERT E. HOWARD   154
Conan the Barbarian, 1932–36

VLADIMIR BARTOL   156
Alamut, 1938

JORGE LUIS BORGES   158
Tlön, Uqbar, Orbis Tertius, 1941

AUSTIN TAPPAN WRIGHT   162
Islandia, 1942

ANTOINE DE SAINT-EXUPÉRY   164
The Little Prince, 1943

TOVE JANSSON   166
The Moomins and the Great Flood, 1945

4 NEW WORLD ORDER

MERVYN PEAKE   170
Gormenghast, 1946–59

GEORGE ORWELL   174
Nineteen Eighty-Four, 1949

C. S. LEWIS   178
The Chronicles of Narnia, 1950–56

ISAAC ASIMOV   184
I, Robot, 1950

RAY BRADBURY   186
Fahrenheit 451, 1953

J. R. R. TOLKIEN   188
The Lord of the Rings, 1954–55

JUAN RULFO   192
Pedro Páramo, 1955

STANISŁAW LEM   194
Solaris, 1961

ANTHONY BURGESS   196
A Clockwork Orange, 1962

VLADIMIR NABOKOV   198
Pale Fire, 1962

PIERRE BOULLE   200
Planet of the Apes, 1963

GABRIEL GARCÍA MÁRQUEZ   204
One Hundred Years of Solitude, 1967

URSULA K. LE GUIN   206
A Wizard of Earthsea, 1968

PHILIP K. DICK   208
Do Androids Dream of Electric Sheep?, 1968

PETER S. BEAGLE   210
The Last Unicorn, 1968

KURT VONNEGUT   212
Slaughterhouse-Five, 1969

LARRY NIVEN   214
Ringworld, 1970

ITALO CALVINO   216
Invisible Cities, 1972

WILLIAM GOLDMAN   218
The Princess Bride, 1973

SAMUEL R. DELANY   220
Dhalgren, 1975

GEORGES PEREC   222
W or the Memory of Childhood, 1975

GERD MJØEN BRANTENBERG   224
Egalia's Daughters: A Satire of the Sexes, 1977

ANGELA CARTER   226
The Bloody Chamber and Other Stories, 1979

OCTAVIA E. BUTLER   230
Kindred, 1979

DOUGLAS ADAMS   232
The Hitchhiker's Guide to the Galaxy, 1979

5 THE COMPUTER AGE

STEPHEN KING 238
The Dark Tower series, 1982–2012

TERRY PRATCHETT 240
The Discworld series, 1983–2015

WILLIAM GIBSON 244
Neuromancer, 1984

MARGARET ATWOOD 248
The Handmaid's Tale, 1985

IAIN M. BANKS 252
The Culture series, 1987–2012

BERNARDO ATXAGA 254
Obabakoak, 1988

NEIL GAIMAN et al. 256
The Sandman, 1988–2015

NEAL STEPHENSON 258
Snow Crash, 1992

LOIS LOWRY 260
The Giver, 1993

PHILIP PULLMAN 262
His Dark Materials, 1995–2000

GEORGE R. R. MARTIN 264
A Game of Thrones, 1996

DAVID FOSTER WALLACE 268
Infinite Jest, 1996

J. K. ROWLING 272
Harry Potter and the Philosopher's Stone,
    1997

CHINA MIÉVILLE 276
The Bas-Lag cycle, 2000–04

JASPER FFORDE 282
The Eyre Affair, 2001

CORNELIA FUNKE 284
Inkheart, 2003

SUSANNA CLARKE 286
Jonathan Strange & Mr Norrell, 2004

DAVID MITCHELL 288
Cloud Atlas, 2004

KAZUO ISHIGURO 290
Never Let Me Go, 2005

NGŨGĨ WA THIONG'O 292
Wizard of the Crow, 2006

MICHAEL CHABON 294
The Yiddish Policemen's Union, 2007

SUZANNE COLLINS 296
The Hunger Games, 2008

HARUKI MURAKAMI 298
1Q84, 2009–10

WU MING-YI 302
The Man with the Compound Eyes, 2011

ANN LECKIE 304
The Imperial Radch trilogy, 2013–15

NNEDI OKORAFOR 306
Lagoon, 2014

SALMAN RUSHDIE 308
Two Years Eight Months and Twenty-Eight
    Nights, 2015

Contributor Biographies 310
Index 314
Credits 318

INTRODUCTION

Of all the powerful spells that fiction casts upon us – absorbing plots, believable characters, vivid language – one of the least celebrated is its ability to make us feel transported to another time and place. Most avid readers have had the experience of setting down a book and needing to shake off the sights, smells and sounds of a world they haven't actually been to, or that may not even exist. We may never have set foot in Victorian London, and we certainly haven't hiked through Middle-earth, but the writings of Arthur Conan Doyle and J. R. R. Tolkien have made those places seem more real, to millions of readers, than cities we've actually visited.

The works described in this book all conjure lands that exist only in the imagination. Some of these places – the America of David Foster Wallace's *Infinite Jest* (1996, page 268), the Japan of Haruki Murakami's *IQ84* (2009–10, page 298) – closely resemble the world we live in. Others – the Alaska of Michael Chabon's *The Yiddish Policemen's Union* (2007, page 294) and the New England of Margaret Atwood's *The Handmaid's Tale* (1985, page 248) – show us how very different our own world might have been, or could become, with only a few tweaks to the course of history. Some of these books, like Ann Leckie's *Ancillary Justice* (2013, page 304), speculate about what life might be like in the distant future, while other works, like Robert E. Howard's original *Conan the Barbarian* story series (1932–36, page 154), postulate a thrilling past that has since been irretrievably lost. Stanisław Lem's *Solaris* (1961, page 194) challenges readers to contemplate a form of intelligent life almost inconceivably alien from ourselves. Satirists like Jonathan Swift and Ngũgĩ wa Thiong'o concoct bizarre yarns about talking horses and child-bearing corpses to confront us with a pointedly familiar reflection of our own behaviours. Then there are those unfettered fantasists, ranging from Italo Calvino to Neil Gaiman, whose great gift is to offer us visions in which the imagination can be set free to roam wherever it desires.

The roots of all these books lie in humanity's oldest stories: myths, fables and folklore – the tales people made up to explain how the world came to exist and why it is the way it is. While literary criticism tends to valorise the new and the innovative, the literature of the fantastic seeks a connection to tradition, to what persists even as the world changes. The texts in the first section of this book, 'Ancient Myth & Legend', are, themselves, often attempts to preserve a fading storytelling culture; *Beowulf* (*c*.700–1100, page 28) and the *Prose Edda* (*c*.1220, page 36) were the works of Christian authors who sought to safeguard a portion of their pagan past. These books have survived in no small part because of their ability to reach across a span of centuries and speak to the inhabitants of new ages and worlds. The messy love lives of Ovid's gods and goddesses; the questing courage of Malory's Arthurian knights; the dauntless faith of Wu Cheng'en's Xuanzang – all remind us of the worst and the best of ourselves. But, along with much that is recognisable, these stories also bewitch us with the rich and strange, the miraculous, the astonishing and the awe-inspiring. The first tales human beings told each other, the ones that survive from our unrecorded past, were not about everyday life, but about the extraordinary: talking animals, wicked sorcerers, terrifying monsters and cities built of gold and jewels.

Fantastic literature has always conducted a complex dialogue with the real world. Many of us read it to escape from that world but, more often than not, this fiction aims to make us see our own lives in a new light. Allegories like *The Faerie Queene* (1590–1609, page 54) and epics like *The Divine Comedy* (*c*.1308–21, page 40) offer their readers moral instruction, even if some of those readers prefer to attend only to the lush spectacle that cloaks the lesson. In *Don Quixote* (1605/15, page 62), Miguel de Cervantes impishly used the structure of a chivalric romance to mock the conventions of the 'romance' itself, a literary genre that specialises in the wondrous. But with Thomas More's *Utopia* (1516, page 52), the most overtly didactic species of literary wonderland came into its own. In the five hundred years since it was published, utopian tales have used invented worlds and nations to critique and exhort readers to change the world. The utopian strain of fantastic literature springs not from myth but from the great age of exploration, when Europeans set out to discover (and, alas, exploit) previously unknown and unmapped parts of the globe. Travel narratives like Marco Polo's account of his journeys in Asia (*c.*1300) became immensely popular, starting in the fourteenth century, and travellers' encounters with other cultures naturally encouraged wandering Westerners to contemplate what foreigners did better or worse than the people back home.

Utopian fiction also arose from Enlightenment thinking itself. If reason and science proved themselves to be superior tools for understanding and mastering the natural world, why not apply them to the engineering of society as well? Writers would continue to produce utopian tales into the twentieth century; women, in particular, wanted to picture what a culture founded on gender equality or even female dominance might look like and, in a sense, Marxism is a utopian dream. By the nineteenth century, however, authors like Samuel Butler had turned to parodying utopian idealism. Utopias, arguably, make for dull reading, but dystopian fiction has demonstrated again and again – right up to *The Hunger Games* (page 296), a 2008 blockbuster intended for teenaged readers – its power to enthral. Some dystopias, like Yevgeny Zamyatin's *We* (1924, page 138) and Aldous Huxley's *Brave New World* (1932, page 148), are essentially works of social or political criticism – attacks on the dominant ideologies and obsessions of the modern world. Many more simply depict the age-old dilemma of a restless individual at odds with the society into which he or she was born.

Often enough, industrialisation and the rise of the mass media provoked this dissatisfaction, and writing a dystopian novel was not the only way to respond to such forces. The 'Golden Age' of fantasy, during the first sixty years or so of the twentieth century, was largely a reaction to the wholesale destruction of deeply rooted ways of life in which human beings lived in intimate relation to the natural world. Another source of anxiety was the perceived loss of long-standing folk traditions. (The Brothers Grimm first began collecting fairy tales in the early 1800s, not to compile a book for children, but as an act of ethnographic conservation.) The great, genre-defining fantasies of this period, from *The Lord of the Rings* (1954–55, page 188) to *The Chronicles of Narnia* (1950–56, page 178), were fundamentally nostalgic, celebrating a vanishing, idealised world that existed before machines and market economies defined our lives. This was also a fertile time for children's fiction, and many of the masters of the period, from J. M. Barrie to Tove Jansson, either incorporated the longing for a simpler, Arcadian idyll into their work or saturated everything they wrote with a melancholy lament for the lost innocence of childhood. Meanwhile, literary modernists like Franz Kafka and Jorge Luis Borges deployed surreal, uncanny and absurd elements in their writings as the ideal tools for portraying the metaphysical paradoxes inherent in a post-religious culture.

The last half of the twentieth century was all about questions, and few literary forms are better suited to fermenting questions than the fantastic. The wonderlands devised by Ursula K. Le Guin, Kurt Vonnegut, Vladimir Nabokov, Samuel R. Delaney and Octavia E. Butler interrogated long-held assumptions about, respectively, the primacy of European culture, modern warfare, the novel, sexuality and race. Angela Carter took perhaps the most orthodox of literary forms, the fairy tale, and turned it inside out to reveal the unspoken desires and power of women hidden within. Science fiction became more than just a vehicle for technologically enhanced adventure and began to challenge the rapidly evolving post-industrial world, and to warn us about where it is heading. A few prescient writers – William Gibson and Neal Stephenson, first and foremost – succeeded, largely, in anticipating the central role that linked computers would play in the twenty-first century. Most strikingly, by coining the term 'cyberspace', Gibson recognised that our best mental model for understanding the vast and immaterial web of communications perpetually humming all around us is spatial. The internet, we collectively decided, is a place. Much of it is made up of words. It just might be the ultimate literary wonderland.

We still haven't tired of books, though, even when they come to us via a medium constituted of bits and pixels. The wonderlands being created today and waiting to be created tomorrow will also be the work of graphic novelists, filmmakers and video-game designers, and they, in turn, will influence the many writers who have stuck with prose text in all its unadorned glory. Novelists like Salman Rushdie, Haruki Murakami and Nnedi Okorafor have raided the toolboxes of science fiction and fantasy in order to tell new stories of their own homelands. A generation of children has grown up saturated in the imaginative liberty exhibited by J. K. Rowling, as well as the trenchant social criticism of Suzanne Collins. They could not be better equipped to build the fictional ships in which all of us will sail off into the unknown, seeking the far horizon and fresh discoveries that will surpass our most extravagant dreams.

Laura Miller
New York City

Briton Rivière, *Una and the Lion* from 'The Faerie Queene', 1880, see page 54.

1 ANCIENT MYTH & LEGEND

These legends of kings, knights errant and epic adventure were the historic and poetic precursors of modern genre fiction.

ANONYMOUS

THE EPIC OF GILGAMESH

(C.1750 BCE)

*One of the earliest known works of great literature, this Babylonian poem,
which first emerged c.1750 BCE and found a stable form around 700 BCE,
details King Gilgamesh's feats of valour and vain quest for immortality.*

*The Epic of Gilgamesh was
lost to history until 150
years ago. The text is still
incomplete and under
reconstruction.*

*New fragments keep
appearing, raising the
prospect that the poem will
one day be entire again (the
tablet above was acquired
by the Sulaymaniyah
Museum, Iraq, in 2011).*

*As well as the Babylonian
poem, there are five
separate Sumerian poems
about Gilgamesh, which
may be even older.*

To the Babylonians, the legendary Gilgamesh was the mightiest hero and
greatest king of old. In telling his story the poem touches on many existential
questions, such as what it means to be mortal in an eternal world, how human
nature differs from animal and divine and the ethics of political power and
military force; these and other universal themes are what make the poem an
enduring masterpiece. The poem begins in the ancient Babylonian city of
Uruk, where Gilgamesh rules as king, but the narrative shows us imaginary
landscapes on the fringes of the known world.

Gilgamesh befriends the wild man Enkidu, and they go on an adventure in search of fame and glory. They run for many days to the Cedar Forest,
the realm of the gods, to slay its guardian, the powerful ogre Humbaba, and
plunder its timber. There were no forests in Babylonia and the landscape is
wholly imaginary – a dense and terrifying jungle that exerts a crushing force
on the heroes' strength and will. A piece of the epic reconstructed only in 2012
contains a lively description of the deafening noise that filled the forest
canopy: the squawks of birds, buzz of insects and yells of monkeys form a
cacophonous symphony to entertain the forest's guardian.

Humbaba is a king with an unfamiliar court. He is partly the personification of the eternal life-force of the ancient trees themselves, but he also
has elephantine features: his trumpeting is heard from afar, he leaves great
tracks in the undergrowth, his face is ugly with wrinkles and he has tusks.
In the episode of Humbaba and the cedars, familiar human responses react
to imposing forces of nature: terror and wonder, cupidity and remorse. The
forest is a 'Heart of Darkness' presenting contemporary moral dilemmas. May
invaders kill a ruler and steal his resources in the name of civilisation? The
episode expresses the heroes' ambivalence to the destruction of the forest. 'My
friend,' says Enkidu to Gilgamesh, 'we have reduced the forest to a wasteland;
how shall we answer our gods at home?' The gods accounted the slaughter of
Humbaba a sin, one reason why, eventually, Enkidu must die.

Enkidu's death precipitates in Gilgamesh an unbearable grief, but also
a terrible fear for himself. Must he, too, die like his friend? He travels to

Alabaster statue from Sargon II's palace at Khorsabad, Northern Iraq (eighth century BCE), supposedly depicting Gilgamesh, King of Uruk.

the ends of the earth in search of the only man known to have escaped the mortal doom that the gods laid on humankind after the great flood. The scenes are truly bizarre: a mountain-top cave whose entrance is guarded by monstrous beings, part human, part scorpion; a magic garden where trees and their fruits are precious stones; a grove where docks a ferry whose crew of stone propel it across the Waters of Death.

The poet uses imaginary landscapes to confront his hero with realities that looked unproblematic from home, things that were easier said than done. The poem's end brings the audience back to the familiar city of Uruk. Enclosed within its wall the observer can see the multifarious activities of mankind and know that, while the individual perishes, the race is eternal. To understand this simple truth, Gilgamesh had first to acquire wisdom in exotic and imaginary places.

HOMER

THE ODYSSEY (C.725–675 BCE)

One of the most celebrated and influential stories ever told, this epic poem describes Odysseus' long voyage home, beset by fantastical creatures and mythic foes in a grand evocation of the human journey through life.

The oldest known works of European literature are the Greek epics the *Iliad* and *The Odyssey*. Nothing is known for sure about their author, known from antiquity as 'Homer'. Many places have claimed the honour of his birth, including the island of Chios, a few miles off the coast of Asia Minor, but he may also have come from the mainland, in what is now Turkey. The poems were first written down in Athens in the sixth century BCE, but were orally composed probably two centuries earlier, while the events they describe – the Greek expedition against Troy and the hero Odysseus' return from it – are set in an age even older, before the fall of the great civilisations of Crete and Mycenae.

The main subject of the poem is the journey home of the Greek hero Odysseus after the fall of Troy. He is away so long (the war itself lasts ten years and the voyage another ten) that it is assumed he is dead, but his wife Penelope remains faithful and fends off an army of suitors.

Odysseus recounts eleven different adventures, as well as his long detention on the island of the nymph Calypso. The third is his encounter with the Cyclops Polyphemus. The one-eyed giant–shepherd captures the hero and his companions by trapping them with his sheep in his cave, which is closed every evening by an enormous rock. Polyphemus eats one or more of the companions every night. Odysseus and his men cannot kill the giant, because they need him to roll the stone aside in the morning; so Odysseus takes an olive branch, sharpens it, and – having given Polyphemus strong wine to make him sleep – drives it into the giant's eye. In the morning, the blinded giant rolls the stone aside to let his sheep out, and Odysseus and his men escape, clinging to the underside of the sheep as Polyphemus runs his hands over them.

In another version that must have pre-dated Homer, the giant roasts his victims on an iron spit and Odysseus uses that to blind him. This other version seems to run a little more naturally and hints of it within Homer serve to illustrate that he was not inventing the story, but repeating it, and likely conflating details from various versions as he did so.

Jacob Jordaens, *Odysseus in the Cave of Polyphemus*, 1635.

Homer not only drew upon handed-down myths, but also delved into accounts of foreign lands brought back by early Greek travellers. In Homer's time, Greeks were already familiar with the Near Eastern coastline, from Turkey to Egypt, and were probing east into the Black Sea and west across the Mediterranean to Italy and even Spain. There are traces of all these, locations suitably exaggerated and embroidered, in Odysseus' long narration, and scholars have tried for many centuries to pin down exact references.

One clear case is Odysseus' tale of 'the Lotus-eaters'. These are perfectly harmless themselves, but anyone who eats the lotus-fruit loses all interest in anything else and no longer wants to return home. There is a hint here of the traditional fairy-tale caution against eating or drinking in unknown climes, but the fruit of two kinds of lotus are eaten in both India and Egypt and Homer had probably heard of the latter. When Circe gives Odysseus sailing directions, she warns him against 'the Clashing Rocks' and says specifically that the only ship ever to traverse them was the *Argo* commanded by Jason. Homer knew, then, of the voyage of the Argonauts to find the Golden Fleece, which has often been explained as a trip into the then-unknown waters of the Black Sea, where the inhabitants used sheepskins to pan for gold.

The gods of Greek myth play a prominent and active part in Homer's imaginary world in both the *Iliad* and *The Odyssey*. Poseidon the sea-god persecutes Odysseus for blinding his son Polyphemus, and Helios the sun god troubles them, too, because Odysseus' men ate his sacred oxen. He is, however, protected by Athene, who intercedes for him with the supreme

deity Zeus, and sends her messenger Hermes to guide and advise him and his son Telemachus. Humans, nymphs, gods and goddesses interact on a basis, not of equality, but something closer to it than in later mythologies. The deities appear as a constant presence in heroic life.

Study of the Homeric poems has formed the basis of a Classical education from post-medieval Europe to the present day. Their poetic power, arguably never matched in almost 3,000 years, has had a perennial and immeasurable influence on Western art and literature. The stories have infiltrated numerous works of celebrated literature; Dante, for example, revisits the tale in *The Divine Comedy* (c.1308–21, page 40), but perhaps the greatest evocation in the twentieth century belongs to James Joyce's modernist master-piece *Ulysses*, which assigns a chapter to each adventure in *The Odyssey*.

John William Waterhouse, *Circe Offering the Cup to Ulysses*, 1891.

OVID

METAMORPHOSES (C.8)

Ovid's fifteen-book poem weaves a kaleidoscope of colourful narratives from Greek and Roman myths on the theme of change and transformation, in which the fates of both man and gods echo the never-ending mutability of life itself.

Metamorphoses contains fifteen books and covers more than 250 myths.

In CE 8 Ovid was banished from Rome and exiled to what is now Romania for reasons that remain unclear.

Metamorphoses was first printed in English by William Caxton in 1480.

Opposite: Michelangelo da Caravaggio, *Narcissus*, 1599.

Overleaf: Titian, *Perseus and Andromeda*, c.1554–56.

The *Metamorphoses* of Publius Ovidius Naso (43 BCE–CE 17/18), or Ovid, is a long Latin poem of almost 12,000 lines. It was written in the first years of the Christian era, and completed about CE 8. Each book tells stories – more than one hundred in total, casually linked and with no obvious chronological order – which together form our best surviving guide to the world of Greek and Roman mythology.

It is, however, a skewed selection, for Ovid announces that he purposefully chose stories that ended in metamorphosis or transformation. Many of these remain familiar, and have even brought words to modern language. The story of Echo and Narcissus, in Book III, tells of how the nymph Echo was punished by the goddess Juno for continually delaying her with chatter while Juno was trying to catch her husband Jupiter with other nymphs. She decreed that from then on Echo would only be able to repeat the last few words of whatever was said to her. Echo fell in love with the handsome boy Narcissus, who scorned her, and she wasted away until only her voice was left – leaving only the 'echo' we know today. Narcissus was then in turn cursed to fall in love only with himself, which he did gazing at his own reflection in a pool until he too wasted away, and his body turned into a flower – a bloom that we still call the narcissus.

These three stories show several things about the world of the *Metamorphoses*. It is a Mediterranean world, but seems much lusher, greener, and far less populated than the one we know. Events commonly take place in the forest, and by streams and pools, where gods and men hunt deer and boar. And in this world humans and divinities mix freely, along with the nymphs, fauns and goat-legged satyrs that populate the tales. Furthermore, most of the stories are love stories, and the most powerful deity in the *Metamorphoses* seems not to be Jupiter, father of gods and men, but Amor – a personification-turned-deity, who rules all the others and continually involves them in frustration, disaster or disgrace.

Many of Ovid's heroes are still the subject of film and literary adaptations today and persist as household names – and, naturally, so are the monsters

that they must defeat. Perseus must battle the snake-haired Gorgon Medusa, whose eyes can turn men to stone, a feat he follows up by rescuing the maiden Andromeda from the Godzilla-like sea-monster Cetus. Theseus defeats the bull-headed Minotaur and is also involved in the wedding feast turned bloody battle between Lapiths and Centaurs, the latter half-horse, half-man. Among the many feats of Hercules are the chaining of Cerberus, the three-headed dog who guards the gates of Hell.

The irreverence of Ovid's tales caused anger and uncertainty among pious pagans of his own time (and pious Christians in later eras); he was eventually exiled to the shores of the Black Sea by the Emperor Augustus. Another response to the *Metamorphoses*, however, was to regard the whole collection as an allegory that would teach morality, resulting in the medieval French *Ovide Moralisé*, or 'Moralised Ovid', the form in which the work was best known throughout the Middle Ages and into the Renaissance.

The overall effect of the work has been incalculable. In one form or another, often censored or allegorised, his stories became part of the school curriculum for many centuries. Chaucer's poem *The House of Fame* derives from Ovid's home of Fama (the source of all rumour), while *The Manciple's Tale* derives from the story of Phoebus and the crow. Shakespeare's poem 'Venus and Adonis' draws on several stories from the *Metamorphoses*. In *A Midsummer Night's Dream* the comic workmen attempt to put on their play of Pyramus and Thisbe before Theseus and his Amazon bride-to-be, Hippolyta.

Ovid's dramatic and provocative scenes also made him a favourite for painters, including Caravaggio, Tiepolo and Velázquez. In the sixteenth century, Titian painted *Diana and Actaeon* and *Diana and Callisto*, while in the seventeenth century Rembrandt chose *The Rape of Ganymede* and *The Abduction of Europa*. In England, in the nineteenth and early twentieth century, John Waterhouse more decorously painted *Circe* and *Thisbe*.

In later years the stories that draw on Ovid are too numerous to list, especially when mingled with second- or third-hand references. C. S. Lewis's *The Lion, the Witch and the Wardrobe* (1950, page 178) for example, mentions fauns, dryads, centaurs, the god Bacchus and the goddess Pomona. George Bernard Shaw's play *Pygmalion* (1912) – inspired by Ovid's tale of a king who fell in love with a statue – later became the 1964 musical *My Fair Lady*. And in the twenty-first century, J. K. Rowling draws heavily from Ovid's mythology in the Harry Potter series (1997–2007, see page 272): Dudley Dursley sprouts the tail of a pig, Centaurs roam the Forbidden Forest and a three-headed dog ('Fluffy') guards the Philosopher's Stone, to name but three examples.

My soul would sing of metamorphoses.
But since, o gods, you were the source of these
bodies becoming other bodies, breathe
your breath into my book of changes: may
the song I sing be seamless as its way
weaves from the world's beginning to our day. (1:1–5)

ANONYMOUS

BEOWULF (C.700–1100)

The oldest surviving epic poem in Old English centres on three battles pitting the Scandinavian hero Beowulf against monstrous giants and a dragon in a classic depiction of the ambiguous triumph of good over evil.

The full poem, more than 3,000 lines, survives as a single manuscript located in the British Library, London. Opinions on its exact age vary, but the manuscript must be approximately 1,000 years old.

There have been numerous translations of the text, including a recent well-known example by Seamus Heaney, then Nobel laureate in Literature, which won the Whitbread Book of Year Award in 1999.

The 3,000 lines of the epic poem *Beowulf* (composed in Old English between the eighth and eleventh centuries CE) are dense with meaning and give rise to multiple interpretations; some see early appreciation of Christian values, while others observe a gripping tale of pagan heroism. Its position in the canon of English literature, however, is in no small part due to the novelist and scholar J. R. R. Tolkien, who argued the poem's powerful value as a work of art to the British Academy in 1936.

Beowulf is set in southern Scandinavia around CE 400 to 600, at the start of the Dark Ages and at the heart of the Northern Heroic Age. As such, *Beowulf* is a period piece, and readers today listen in on a sophisticated tale told to a Christian Anglo-Saxon audience about their heroic pagan predecessors living in violent lands terrorised by warrior bands and (sometimes) monsters. In the world of the poem, the monstrous Grendel, his vengeful mother and the dragon are characters as real as Beowulf; for audiences more recent than the Dark Ages, these monsters remain 'fantastically real' but take on symbolic possibilities. We are told that Grendel and his mother are descendants of the biblical first murderer, Cain; and for educated Christian listeners the terrifying dragon might suggest 'that ancient serpent' described in Revelation 20:2, 'who is the devil and Satan'.

The poem also alludes to history and legends that audience members would have known well, and looks back to a time of military aristocracy when a real man is a professional warrior who serves and protects his lord, a lord who protects him in turn and equitably distributes the bloodily won loot. At the courts of King Alfred the Great (CE 849–99) or King Canute (CE 990–1035), *Beowulf* would have described a world that was still familiar, but more parochial and basic (and more bothered by monsters).

The first great battle of the poem sees Beowulf, a prince of the Geats (a northern Germanic tribe occupying part of what is now Sweden) defeat the horrifying Grendel who has terrorised a neighbouring land ruled by

King Hrothgar. After the defeat, there is much celebrating in King Hrothgar's great hall, Heorot, but Grendel's mother (never awarded her own name) wreaks a brutal attack on the hall in revenge for her son's death. Beowulf once again seeks out and slays the monster in the poem's second battle and his bravery is rewarded with gifts and celebration from Hrothgar's people. Beowulf's grand heroic actions, however, are set against a background of human betrayal and warfare that will eventually destroy Heorot and Hrothgar's dynasty.

In the final episode, fifty years later, when Beowulf is now King of the Geats, a dragon attacks his kingdom. Against good advice, Beowulf chooses to fight the dragon alone. When he falters, only one of his followers, Wiglaf, comes to his aid. At that exciting moment, the poem pauses to remind listeners of the history of Wiglaf's sword, before resuming for Beowulf to kill the dragon, which leaves him mortally wounded.

A twentieth-century interpretation of Beowulf slaying the dragon.

Wiglaf succeeds Beowulf, and in the conclusion of the poem it's clear that in addition to traditional Swedish hatred of the Geats, now made personal against Wiglaf, there is the enmity of the powerful Franks, attacked by Beowulf's predecessor. Like Beowulf's heroism and generosity, Wiglaf's will be futile; like Heorot and Hrothgar's line, the Geats are also doomed.

The poem ends as it begins, with a pagan funeral, this time Beowulf's: mourned as mild and good, a heroic warrior of the old time, striving for fame. But Beowulf's heroic deeds in life will be undone, and in any life to come he may be damned as a pagan, of all men *lofgeornost* (the last word of the poem): proudly, hence sinfully (for hard-nosed Christians), yearning for glory.

In the worlds of poem and poet, Beowulf in his doomed struggles may be the purest of heroes; in present debates about whether one can be a hero and lose and in popular cultures awash in flawed (super)heroes – for us, too, *Beowulf* remains relevant.

ANONYMOUS

THE THOUSAND AND ONE NIGHTS (C.700–947)

This vastly influential collection of folk tales was compiled more than 1,000 years ago and is framed by the narrative of King Shahriyar and the many tales told by his wife Shahrazad.

The Oriental Institute at the University of Chicago holds the earliest example of the tales in manuscript.

It is one of the oldest existing Arabic literary manuscripts. A legal document over-written on one side of the manuscript gives a likely date of CE 879.

Spellings for King Shahriyar and Shahrazad (or Shahryar and Scheherazade) vary in English transliterations, and there is still some dispute between scholars over which is more accurate.

The Thousand and One Nights, or *The Arabian Nights* (the first English translation, 1706), is a compilation of tales from many sources – Persian, Indian, Chinese and Egyptian – put together in Arabic more than a thousand years ago. It first became known in Europe when Antoine Galland published a twelve-volume French translation between 1704 and 1717. The best-known English version, by the explorer Sir Richard Burton, came out in sixteen volumes between 1885 and 1888. Two of the most famous tales in the collection, 'Aladdin's Lamp' and 'Ali Baba and the Forty Thieves', were added by Galland, who claimed to have been told them by a Syrian storyteller named Hanna Diab. They appear to be genuine Middle Eastern folk tales, so his claim is probably true, and they are now regularly added to translations.

When the collection first became known in Europe, it struck its audience as completely novel on many levels. The framing concept sees King Shahriyar, horrified by the infidelity of his wife, deciding that the only way to be safe from female betrayal is to marry a virgin every evening, and have her executed the next morning. He continues this custom until Shahrazad, or Scheherazade, the wily daughter of the king's vizier (a high official), hits on a plan. Every night she begins to tell a story, but leaves it unfinished, so that her life is spared until the next day to complete the tale, whereupon she begins another one. Often tales are inserted one inside the other, so that endings continually recede, although in the end, after a thousand and one nights (and three children) Shahrazad persuades Shahriyar to trust her and spare her life permanently.

From the start we are in a world of despotic power and cruelty, but also enormous wealth and generosity. Kings and Caliphs award thousands of gold pieces and camel-loads of treasure to deserving young men, so much money sometimes that 'no-one could count it but God'.

Wealth is abundant even on a less miraculous level, for the tales are set within the immense civilisation of medieval Islam, with its connections to Africa, India, China and Central Asia, and its great cities of Cairo, Damascus, Aleppo, Basra and above all Baghdad, home of the Caliphs, where

city markets are stuffed with goods of which Europeans in Galland's time had barely heard: quinces, peaches, jasmine from Syria, raisins of Tihama, pomegranate blooms and pistachios.

Also totally novel to Westerners, and perhaps even more influential for imitators of the *Nights*, was the cast of supernatural creatures who figure continually. Shahrazad's first tale begins with a fearsome *'ifrit*, who appears with a drawn sword to kill a merchant who has carelessly thrown away the stone of a date. Other menaces include the man-eating tomb-haunting *ghuls*, all too capable of disguising themselves as beautiful women, or even *houris*, the nymphs of the Muslim Paradise. But most prominent of all in the tales are the *jinn*, or genies, often trapped inside a lamp, bottle or ring, and when released bound to fulfil every wish of their new master. Sometimes the power that constrained them was that of the great magician Suleiman, in whom Christians could recognise the Old Testament's King Solomon, son of David.

The final and most alluring novelty for eighteenth- and nineteenth-century Western readers was the presentation of sex and love. Every king, caliph, emir and vizier has his harem of beautiful wives and concubines, graceful as gazelles, with their eunuch guards. The ladies, however, do not seem to be strictly cloistered and are as passionate for adventure as their admirers – which, of course, is what causes King Shahriyar's murderous custom. Both men and women fall in love readily and, far more than in medieval European tales, consummate their love without feelings of guilt. Although respect for the Prophet and the Koran is everywhere in *Nights*, expressed even by the *jinn* and the creatures of the sea, the characters' religious devotion contains nothing of the asceticism that often accompanies Christian piety. While women are in theory controlled and all but enslaved, their intelligence often gives them the upper hand.

The *Nights* soon became as familiar to Western children, in censored and selected forms, as 'Jack and the Beanstalk' or 'Cinderella'. Many classical authors mention them, from Stendhal to Tolstoy. Dickens makes several explicit references to them, and his London, where disguised figures walk the streets and uncover strange tales, seems a transmuted Baghdad, as is the London of Robert Louis Stevenson's *New Arabian Nights* (1882). The Brontë family was especially fond of a moralised version of some of the tales, published as *Tales of the Genii* by James Ridley in 1764.

The effect of the *Nights* on children's literature has probably been even greater than on the classics. *Aladdin* is now a staple of children's theatre, and everyone knows 'Open Sesame' and Sindbad the sailor. E. E. Nesbit's trilogy, *Five Children and It* (1902), *The Phoenix and the Carpet* (1904) and *The Story of the Amulet* (1906), uses props derived from the *Nights*, although the Psammead is her own invention. C. S. Lewis's *The Horse and His Boy* (1954) starts like a tale from the *Nights* with a poor fisherman called Arsheesh, and the hot country of Calormen to the south of Narnia, with its despotic ruler, grovelling vizier and insincerely flowery language, is a parodic version of the *Nights*'s Arabia. The world of the *Nights* is now so familiar that references to it may be third-hand, or even more indirect. It has become as much a part of Western popular culture as Middle-earth or Sherwood Forest.

As a result of its popularity *Nights* has inspired many film adaptations, including three versions of *The Thief of Baghdad* (1924, 1940, 1978), and the animated *Seventh Voyage of Sinbad* (1958). The most successful was Disney's *Aladdin* of 1992, which won two Oscars. In recent years Salman Rushdie has turned to the treasure trove of *Nights*, causing Ursula K. Le Guin to remark of his *Two Years Eight Months and Twenty-Eight Nights* (2015, page 308): 'Rushdie is our Scheherazade'.

An hour before daybreak Dinarzade awoke, and exclaimed, as
she had promised, 'My dear sister, if you are not asleep, tell me
I pray you, before the sun rises, one of your charming stories.
It is the last time that I shall have the pleasure of hearing you'.
Shahrazad did not answer her sister, but turned to the Sultan.
'Will your highness permit me to do as my sister asks?' said she.
'Willingly', he answered. So Shahrazad began …

THE MABINOGION
(12th–14th century)

A blend of Celtic mythology and Arthurian legend in eleven atmospheric tales, playing out in the forests and valleys of Wales as well as the shadowy 'otherworld', where dragons and giants roam and virtuous heroes quest for honour.

The tales of *The Mabinogion* were preserved in the *White Book of Rhydderch* (mid-thirteenth century, now in the National Library of Wales) and the *Red Book of Hergest*, (c.1382–1410, now held in the manuscript collection of Jesus College, Oxford).

Lady Charlotte Guest's (1812–95, below) translation of *The Mabinogion* became the standard for nearly a century. The first volume was published in 1838, and by 1845 the tales had appeared in seven parts.

The Mabinogion (mabbi-*nogue*-yon) is the name given to a collection of eleven medieval Welsh tales, which form our best guide to the world of early Welsh mythology. The manuscript dates from the fourteenth century, but the stories themselves were composed well before that. The meaning of *Mabinogion* is not known, and the word may be an old scribal error. It was probably intended to mean 'tales of youth', a Welsh equivalent of the French *enfances*. Some have suggested the word *mabinogi* may have meant 'tales of Maponos', the mythological Divine Son, who perhaps underlies the figure of the hero Pryderi in some of the stories.

In the world of *The Mabinogion*, myth and legend co-exist with history and reality, and they are not easy to tell apart. The geographical world of the tales looks like medieval Wales, divided into separate kingdoms such as Gwynedd, Powys and Dyfed, but this imagined Wales also contains giants, monsters and strange beasts, and is in contact with supernatural dimensions.

The society, meanwhile, is that of the medieval Welsh aristocracy – still independent and unconquered by English or Normans, proud of their native traditions as sung or told by bards – and their sense of history reaches back surprisingly far. In 'The Dream of Macsen Wledig', Macsen is thought to be the Roman general Maximus, who led his British legions into Gaul in CE 383 to fight unsuccessfully for the imperial throne. The Welsh tale makes him an Emperor of Rome, who originally came to Britain led by a vision of a beautiful Welsh princess.

Two other tales are stories of Arthurian legend. 'Culhwch and Olwen' tells how Arthur assisted his cousin Culhwch in winning the daughter of the chief giant Ysbaddaden by acquiring an extensive list of magic objects, including the blood of the Black Witch of the Valley of Grief. Both 'Culhwch' and 'The Dream of Rhonabwy' list many members of Arthur's court, including some who became widely known, such as Cei (Sir Kay), already as disobliging as he is in later stories.

Pride of place, however, must go to the four tales designated as the four 'branches' of the *mabinogi*, loosely connected by the hero Pryderi. Their

A detail from *Kilhwych* [Culhwch], *The King's Son* by Joseph Gaskin, 1901. Culhwch employs the help of his cousin Arthur in order to secure the hand of the beautiful Olwen, daughter of the chief giant Ysbaddaden.

humour and imagination set them apart from any other wonder-tales known anywhere in the world. Their characters are paradoxical: passionate but polite, wordy and taciturn, courteous but rough. Women are valued highly and treated respectfully, but when the lady Rhiannon is falsely accused of murdering her son (who will become the hero Pryderi, and has actually been carried off by a giant claw) her punishment is to sit by a mounting-block and carry visitors on her back to the court. She is later exonerated, but such vulgarities would likely have been forgotten in later courtly romance tales.

With their cast of colourful characters, high drama, philosophy and romance, it is no surprise these Celtic stories have proved an irresistible inspiration, first to French romancers and then through eight centuries of further storytellers. The stories are especially treasured in Wales as foundations of national culture. They have been retold in novelistic form several times in recent years, in Lloyd Alexander's six-volume *Chronicles of Prydain* (1964–73) and in Evangeline Walton's four-volume sequence begun with *Prince of Annwn* (1970) and re-issued as *The Mabinogion Tetralogy* in 2002. Alan Garner's *Owl Service* (1967) retells the tragic love-story of Lleu, Gronw and Blodeuwedd, with a happier ending.

SNORRI STURLUSON

THE PROSE EDDA (C.1220)

A remarkable written preservation of Norse mythology, detailing the adventures of gods, heroes, warrior kings and queens, giants, dwarves and elves. It is the most renowned and influential work of all Scandinavian literature.

Seven manuscripts of *The Prose Edda* still survive – six from the Middle Ages and one from 1666 (above).

As no manuscript is complete, *The Prose Edda* has been pieced together over many years.

A statue of Snorri Sturluson (below) by Gustav Vigeland was gifted to the Icelandic nation in 1947 by the Norwegian government, and is located at Reykholt.

Opposite: A seventeenth-century illustration depicting Odin, with his two crows, Hugin (thought) and Munin (memory).

Iceland had been Christian for two centuries by the time of Snorri Sturluson (1179–1241), and the old pagan traditions were fading. Snorri's main purpose in writing *The Prose Edda* was to provide a guide to poetic diction and allusion for future poets. He drew on and quoted older poems, both heroic and mythological, of which many survive as a group called *The Poetic Edda*.

Snorri's text describes a variety of interrelated worlds: the gods (or Æsir) live in Asgard; the giants in Jötunheim; Svartalfaheim is home to the dwarfs; Alfheim is where the 'light-elves' live; and Niflheim is a dark world of primeval chaos. The world of humans is a flat disk encircled by ocean, with girdling walls erected by the gods to keep out the giants, called *Mithgarthr* in Old Norse, usually Anglicised as Midgard. At the centre of the cosmos is the great ash-tree Yggdrasil. Its three roots extend to Asgard, to Niflheim and to the land of the frost-giants. In the ocean around Midgard lives the dreaded Midgard Serpent, also known as Iörmungand.

Perhaps the most striking thing about this Northern cosmology is its sense of grim threat. The dragon Nidhögg eternally gnaws the root of Yggdrasil. The squirrel Ratatosk runs up and down conveying messages of hate and defiance between Nidhögg at the bottom and an eagle at the top. The sun and moon move across the sky constantly pursued by two great wolves called Sköll and Hati: and one day it is expected that they will catch up. Gods and men are under constant threat from the monster-world, and this will end in Ragnarök, 'the doom of the gods', when gods and heroes will fight a final battle against the giants and the monsters – and it is known to all that they will lose, hoping only to lose gallantly and destructively.

Furthermore, the universe of *The Prose Edda* is one of moral neutrality, or even moral indifference. Humans are on the gods' side against the monsters, but no one can trust Odin, the All-Father, who betrays heroes on the battlefield in order to bring them to Valhalla and swell his armies. Thor, the thunder-god, and Frey, a god of fertility, may seem friendlier, but another lurking presence among the Æsir is the god Loki, who continually brings trouble.

Odinn

Múni

gín

þetta kÿmid Con-
tafeÿ. þargac na
þú þiodes ädur
Dÿrdka Öms ä
Jneÿ. Er Önÿ-
dú villú slöd?
sem ec Odins
Bÿ la te.

i kuerfa oc ſr. en ſi heta þicta m oſkyllt ac h̄ nea kueþ ſet
an heta h̄ tan ſtyrnir heið þyrnir leſta hrioðr við blam.
onin ſt keria himinin kalla h̄ ymiſ hauſ z erpiði z þyck
ðꝛyn hrahm auſtra veſtra noꝛꝺa ſuðra. tl ſolar z ungls
z hymtugla uız ea e uerꝛa hialm · h̄ loptz z uarbar.
eſſ ero nerti ſtundana. aulld ſękum

Vallde. fyir longu onſtarr. uetꝛ ſumar hauſt var. manoðr vika
agr nott mergin aptan. qlld arla. Snema ſipla. Iſin eyrin dag,
netꝛ igeꝛ ſ̄ahꝛel. hi eo heta nætruriar i oluiſ malumt
ge hue̅ my̅ꝛ̅. þiota helio. kallud er grima mꝛ guþu. oldeg
kalla iꝛmar par ſuepngamran ðuaar ðꝛaum
ungſi naeriz mulin mylin ny hþ atcilt
þengꝛꝛ blaz ſkyndir ſkꝛalgr ſkꝛamir.

Solseria raukull eyglon an ſkip ſym þaʒ huet lino ſtan
ſuchnſtehꝛ alpraukull. Kuing ſt keria ſol kalla h̄ a ſuer
rundul þera. ſ mana. koıu oleſ elde hın̅ꝛ z loꝛꝛ

her iꝛ̄r
iᷓuꝛ̄r
ıon mıtʒ

The other side of Norse myth, surprisingly, is its sense of (sometimes cruel) humour. Thor, with his powerful hammer, Mjöllnir, which always returns to his hand, is at once the hero and the butt of several tales. Snorri gives an extended account of the visit made by Thor and Loki to the giant Utgarda-Loki. The giant challenges Thor to an easy test of strength. He is asked to drain a drinking-horn, but fails even after three drafts; to pick a cat off the floor, but can only raise one of its paws; and to wrestle with an old woman called Elli, who forces him to one knee. Thor is humiliated, but the tests were not as they seem. The drinking horn was connected to the ocean, and Thor has just created the tides. The cat was really the Midgard Serpent, and the old woman's name, Elli, means 'Old Age', which as the Eddic poem *Hávamál* says, 'gives no-one mercy'.

Opposite: A page from a fourteenth-century illustrated manuscript of *The Prose Edda*.

Snorri tells some twenty stories of this nature in *The Prose Edda*. Richard Wagner famously re-created one of them in his four-opera cycle *Der Ring des Nibelungen* (1876, see page 96), and J. R. R. Tolkien attempted to re-create a lost original poetic version – on which he thought all others must have been based – in his posthumously published *Legend of Sigurd and Gudrún* (2009).

The fact that the legend caught the imagination of the greatest re-workers of medieval themes in both the nineteenth and twentieth centuries testifies to its abiding power. Indeed, the whole mythology of *The Prose Edda* has since become a favourite source for authors of fantasy. Tolkien's Middle-earth represents his highly eclectic re-imagining of Midgard, with elves, dwarves and other creatures, but without the pagan gods. Northern (and other) deities are brought into the contemporary American world in Neil Gaiman's *American Gods* (2003) and Joanne Harris retells the tale of the ultimate trickster in *The Gospel of Loki* (2014).

The most popular mode of modern retelling has, however, been the comic book industry. Marvel Comics have published more than 600 issues of *The Mighty Thor* since 1962, in which a modern American discovers that he is an avatar of Thor, able to move between our world and the world of Asgard. In 2011 the comic book adventures of Thor and Loki were brought to the big screen by director Kenneth Branagh, and today Northern mythology, once almost forgotten, is probably better known in the Western world than many classical or Biblical myths.

DANTE ALIGHIERI

THE DIVINE COMEDY
(C.1308–21)

Dante's epic poem is celebrated as one of the greatest and most influential works of medieval Europe. This spiritual journey takes us from the darkness of the Inferno to the mountain of Purgatory to Paradise, during which reason and faith bring moral and social chaos into order.

The Biblioteca Riccardiana in the Palazzo Medici Riccardi, Florence, Italy, holds a remarkable manuscript of the *Commedia* containing the complete text of the *Inferno, Purgatorio* and *Paradiso* written in the hand of Giovanni Boccaccio (1313–75).

Dante wrote in angry criticism of the Florentine government and was permanently exiled from the city around 1308.

La Divina Commedia (*The Divine Comedy*) was written between 1308 and the poet's death in 1321. It consists of 100 cantos, each around 140 lines, in which Dante travels successively through Hell (*Inferno*), Purgatory (*Purgatorio*) and Heaven (*Paradiso*). The work presents a medieval, Catholic image of life after death, as codified in the generations before Dante by the great theologians Thomas Aquinas and Bonaventure. Yet Dante's (*c.*1265–1321) particular vision is enriched by his classical learning: his guide through Hell and most of Purgatory is the Roman poet Virgil, who had presented a 'descent into Hell' in Book VI of his epic *Aeneid*. And throughout *The Divine Comedy* figures appear from the confused and bloody world of contemporary Italian politics, in which Dante was deeply and dangerously immersed.

Especially haunting to the imagination is Dante's description of Hell, which is famously entered through a gate marked with an inscription ending: 'Abandon all hope, you who enter here.' Beyond are nine circles in which the punishments that sinners endure are matched to their sins. The lustful are whirled forever around the Second Circle by a mighty wind. Tyrants scald forever in lakes of boiling blood in the Seventh Circle. False prophets in the Eighth Circle shuffle endlessly around, unable to see where they are going because their heads have been turned backwards on their shoulders and Flatterers forever drop filth from their mouths. The Ninth Circle is reserved for the treacherous, with the deepest division named Judecca after Judas Iscariot, the apostle who betrayed Jesus.

Not only sinners are to be found in Hell. Dante also imagines many strange creatures with roles to play there. As in Classical mythology, Charon is the ferryman who takes the souls across the river of Acheron. Minos judges each soul and wraps his tail around them, the number of coils corresponding to the circle to which they are assigned, and flings them to their place. The monstrous Geryon carries the travellers down from the Seventh Circle. With a human face, a lion's paws and a scorpion's poisonous sting in his tail, Geryon is the personification of Fraud.

Purgatory, like Hell, is organised in levels that correspond to the sins being expiated. The stiff-necked proud have their necks weighed down by stones, the envious have their eyes stitched up, the gluttonous are disciplined by thirst and hunger, the lustful learn to greet with no more than a holy kiss. The demons and monsters of Hell are, however, replaced by angel-pilots and guardian angels. Near the peak of Purgatory, Dante enters the earthly Paradise. Here, Virgil cannot enter and must return to First Circle of the virtuous heathen. Dante's guide to the celestial spheres is Beatrice, a personification of theology in the form of idealised beauty. In Heaven, finally, Dante meets those who show the virtues of their spheres. In the sphere of the Sun are the wise and the theologians, Mars has the brave commanders and Jupiter the just rulers, rising upwards to the Church Triumphant in the Eighth Sphere, the Angelic Orders in the Ninth and the Beatific Vision of the Tenth.

The vivid description and poetic craftsmanship of *The Divine Comedy* has ensured that it remains in the collective conscience today. Its influence within Western art and culture is simply immeasurable, inspiring numerous writers, from Chaucer and Milton to Balzac, T. S. Eliot and Samuel Beckett.

Joseph Anton Koch, *Dante and Virgil Riding on the Back of Geryon*, c.1821.

Overleaf: Sandro Botticelli, *The Abyss of Hell*, c.1485.

THOMAS MALORY

LE MORTE D'ARTHUR (1485)

Malory's evocative and enthralling text provides the touchstone for all later explorations of Arthurian legend, charting the ancient king's ascendancy to the throne and the adventures of the Knights of the Round Table.

If there was a historical King Arthur, he would have lived in the centuries after the withdrawal of the Romans from Britain (CE 407), a period for which we have almost no documentation. A Welsh author, writing in Latin and known as Nennius, provides an account of the king that can be dated to around 830, and Arthur is given an impressive, if bogus, biography in Geoffrey of Monmouth's *History of the Kings of Britain* written in the 1130s. The enduring legend of quests, castles and tournaments that we know so well today, however, was not cemented in the collective imagination until the fifteenth century with Sir Thomas Malory's *Le Morte d'Arthur* (written around 1469 and published in 1485).

Malory's main source was the long sequence of French prose romances known as 'the Vulgate Cycle', themselves the culmination of centuries of Arthurian invention. In Malory these monastic works were given a strong personal slant. He was not a monk, but a knight, and seems to have written the *Morte* while in prison for a whole string of violent crimes during an eventful career dating as far back as the 1430s. The extent of his guilt is unknown since his accusers could have been politically motivated – the Wars of the Roses were raging at the time, new grudges were created daily and ancient affiliations were frequently tested. The work was printed in 1485, and is one of the few medieval English works to have remained continuously familiar ever since.

Le Morte d'Arthur gives us a full account of the whole Arthurian legend, including Arthur's sinful conception, the incestuous birth of his son Mordred, Excalibur the 'sword in the stone', Merlin the magician advisor, and introduces the many Knights of the Round Table, among them Sirs Lancelot, Gawain, Geraint, Percival, Bors, Galahad and Tristan. Despite, or possibly because of, the bloody upheavals, factionism, and opportunism of the Wars of the Roses, there was a strong interest in chivalric legend and history at the time. Arthur's knights were symbolic of virtues – such as

loyalty, bravery, honour and gallantry – that were seen as being eroded by the political infighting of the Wars.

Yet there is far more to the enduring appeal of Malory's text than contemporary relevance. The tales are filled with a heady mix of prophesy, predestination, sex, danger and magic; and the bucolic English settings of streams, lakes, meadows and castles are at once both familiar and strange. In numerous stories the knights arrive at unknown castles where unusual practices and customs are the norm, their virtues are put to the test, and complexity of character is revealed.

The core of the story is the tragic, romantic triangle of Arthur, his wife Guinevere and the noble knight Sir Lancelot, which is made even more strained by the mystical presence of the Grail – the cup that, according to legend, was used by Christ at the Last Supper and in which his blood was collected at the Cross. The Grail mysteriously appears at Camelot, Arthur's

The Arming and Departure of the Knights, a tapestry based on *Le Morte d'Arthur* and designed by Edward Burne-Jones. It was woven by Morris and Co., 1895–6.

¶Here foloweth the syxth boke of the noble and worthy prynce kyng Arthur.

¶How syr Launcelot and syr Lyonell departed fro the courte for to seke auentures / ⁊ how syr Lyonell lefte syr Launcelot slepynge ⁊ was taken. Capl'm. j.

None after that the noble ⁊ worthy kyng Arthur was comen fro Rome in to Englande / all the knyghtes of the rounde table resorted vnto ⁊ kyng and made many iustes and turneymentes / ⁊ some there were that were good knyghtes / whiche encreased so in armes and worshyp that they passed all theyr felowes in prowesse ⁊ noble dedes ⁊ that was well proued on many. But in especyall it was proued on syr Launcelot du lake. For in all turneymentes and iustes and dedes of armes / bothe for lyfe and deth he passed all knyghtes ⁊ at no tyme he was neuer ouercomen but yf it were by treason or enchauntement. Syr Launcelot encreased so meruaylously in worshyp ⁊ honour / wherfore he is the first knyght ⁊ the frensshe booke maketh mencyon of / after that kynge Arthur came from Rome / Wherfore quene Gueneuer had hym in grete fauour aboue all other knyghtes / and certaynly he loued the quene agayne aboue all other ladyes and damoyselles all the dayes of his lyfe / and for her he court, and provides sustenance for a feast, beginning a series of quests by knights hoping to recover the lost vessel. Lancelot's own attempt to approach the Grail is prevented by a fiery breath and unseen hands: his sinful love for Guinevere has made him unworthy.

Lancelot's relationship with Guinevere then becomes uneasy, as if he blames her for his failure, but she continues to need him as a protector, in circumstances of increasing doubt and guilt. When Sir Mellyagaunce accuses Guinevere of adultery, Lancelot challenges him, which, given Lancelot's prowess, comes close to murder. Finally, Lancelot is caught in Guinevere's room and although he fights his way out, she is sentenced to death. In the rescue he kills his friends, Sir Gawain's brothers Gareth and Gaheris. Gawain vows eternal revenge, the Round Table breaks up, and in the confusion Mordred, Arthur's son and nephew, tries to seize the throne, leading to the Last Battle and Arthur's removal, badly wounded, to Avalon. Lancelot and Guinevere die as penitents. Malory portrays Lancelot as a man caught between love of Guinevere, loyalty to Arthur and a desperate attempt to be worthy of the Grail, in all of which endeavours he ultimately fails. The *Morte* is remarkable for its acute psychological insights, expressed in original scenes of great tension.

The legends of Arthur, Merlin, Excalibur, the Lady of the Lake and the brave and valorous knights continue to be re-told by novelists and by movie-makers. The numerous adaptations range from Mark Twain's fusion of time travel and legend *A Connecticut Yankee in King Arthur's Court* (1889, page 108), to T. H. White's *The Once and Future King* (1958), which reinterprets the story for a postwar audience, and the surreal humour of *Monty Python and the Holy Grail* (1975).

Opposite: A woodcut from Wynkyn de Worde's 1529 edition of Malory's *Le Morte d'Arthur* shows Sir Lancelot competing in a courtly tournament (coloured later).

Orlando Furioso
(c.1516/32)

A playful Renaissance fantasy that adds the theme of passionate love to the old stories of the paladins of Charlemagne, while also employing a host of enchanters, magic rings and lances, hippogriffs and sea monsters for pure imaginative entertainment.

Ludovico Ariosto was born in Reggio Emilia, but his family moved to Ferrara when he was fourteen. In 1518 Ludovico entered the service of the great patron of the arts, Duke Alfonso d'Este.

Orlando Furioso went through three major revisions or versions (1516, 1521 and 1532) before Ariosto's death in 1533.

The finished version, published in Ferrara in 1532, served as inspiration to Cervantes, Spenser and Shakespeare.

The main rival to the great cycle of Arthurian romances was the body of legends centred on Charlemagne and his paladins (his foremost knights). Their historical basis is clearer than the Arthurian stories, with the defining incident being the death of Roland, Count of Brittany, at the battle of Roncevaux Pass in 778. The stories never achieved the popularity of the Arthurian legends, and the Italian Renaissance poet Matteo Maria Boiardo (1441?–94) proposed this was because they lacked lust and passion. His long poem *Orlando Innamorato* ('Roland in Love') set out to resolve the issue, but Boiardo died leaving his work incomplete. Around ten years later, the poet Ludovico Ariosto (1474–1533) continued the story in his epic *Orlando Furioso* ('The Frenzy of Roland'), first published in 1516, with a final version in 1532.

The background for the poem is the clash between Christians and Muslims, which had continued in Spain and the Balkans up to the time of both authors. This real-world scenario, however, is overlaid with centuries of magnificent romance and magic. Keeping track of the plot is difficult because it moves at a furious pace, with one narrative thread after another being followed and dropped, frequently in cliff-hanger style. The backdrop of war is offset by honourable missions and magic props, such as the beautiful maiden Angelica's ring that defends her from enchantment; the shining shield of the magician Atlante, which strikes everyone who sees it unconscious; the magic horn of the English paladin Astolfo, which fills all hearers with terror; heroine Bradamante's invincible lance; and Atlante's winged steed the hippogriff, which Ruggiero the pagan champion rides when he rescues Angelica from the 'orc' or sea-monster to whom she is to be sacrificed in one of many damsel-in-distress sequences.

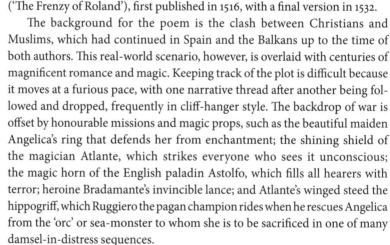

The characters' main motivations are love, lust or infatuation, but these threads are, however, perhaps less significant than the digressions. The poem is designed as pure entertainment, with a constant flow of marvels and surprises. Its world is one where anything can happen, exciting, horrifying, sexually explicit, gruesome, but above all unexpected. Characters may travel anywhere – to Cathay, Taprobane, the Moon, Hell or a Terrestrial Paradise;

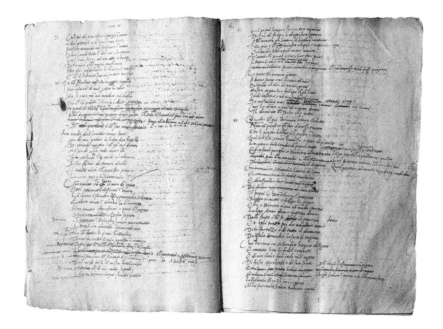

be threatened by demons and monsters, including the terrible creature born of necrophilia in Boiardo's 'Castle Cruel'; and are protected or attacked by a gallery of good and bad magicians. The author C. S. Lewis declared that the poem made for ideal convalescent reading: always amusing, light-hearted, and never too difficult or morally taxing – the ancestor of a whole modern genre of romantic fantasy.

Much of the success of *Orlando Furioso* springs from its air of free-wheeling irresponsibility, enlivened by constant sexual allusion. In 1591 Sir John Harrington translated an improper tale from canto 28 to amuse the maid-attendants of Queen Elizabeth, was caught by the Queen, and banished from court. The poem proved highly influential to Edmund Spenser's *Faerie Queene* (1590–1609, page 54) and a few years later Shakespeare would find inspiration in it for the plot of *Much Ado About Nothing* (1612). Cervantes also makes reference to *Orlando Furioso* when detailing the romances that have so enchanted *Don Quixote* (1605/15, page 62).

In the twentieth century, the poem inspired the 'Incomplete Enchanter' fantasy series written by L. S. de Camp and Fletcher Pratt (1940), in which two American academics gain the ability to travel into imaginary worlds and become magicians. In recent years the novelists Italo Calvino, Jorge Luis Borges and Salman Rushdie have all turned to Ariosto for inspiration and, more specifically, Chelsea Quinn Yarbro's *Ariosto: Ariosto Furioso, a Romance for an Alternate Renaissance* (1980), also plays with the idea of moving between worlds, including the world of the poem, an imagined Renaissance Italy, and a fantasy America.

The manuscript for *Orlando Furioso* is held by the Biblioteca Comunale Ariostea, Ferrara.

Overleaf: Jean-Auguste-Dominique Ingres, *Ruggiero Rescuing Angelica*, 1819.

THOMAS MORE

Utopia (1516)

More's vision of a faraway island where society is perfected and people live in harmony gave rise to the entire genre of Utopian fiction. Utopia, however, means 'no place', revealing the work as a criticism of the failings and corruption he observed in society.

Utopia was first published in Louvain, Belgium, in 1516.

More's learning and wit attracted the attention of King Henry VIII, who made him Lord Chancellor in 1529.

He resigned in 1532 when he refused to acknowledge the king as the head of the Church of England and was confined to the Tower of London.

He was beheaded on July 6, 1535, announcing to the crowd that he was dying as 'the King's good servant, but God's first'.

Utopia, written in 1516 by the English humanist Thomas More (1478–1535), has been so influential as to give its name to an entire literary genre, and the notion of a civilisation perfected by social engineering has fascinated writers and artists ever since. More's intentions in creating his idealised land, however, are far from straightforward.

Utopia is divided into two books. The first begins with More on official business in Antwerp, where he is introduced to Raphael Hythlodaeus. Hythlodaeus describes his travels to More and a colleague, and their talk turns to rules of governance and issues such as poverty, the death penalty and enclosure laws (where arable land is closed off and converted for more profitable sheep farming to the detriment of agricultural workers). In the end, Hythlodaeus announces abruptly that the only satisfactory arrangement is to abolish private property altogether. How this would work is then set out in Book II, as being already practised by the citizens of Utopia.

Utopia is an island around the same size as England. It has fifty-four towns, all built to the same plan. Citizens live in houses that are all the same, and every ten years they are re-allocated, so no one comes to feel ownership. Farms produce enough food to sustain the entire country. Everyone works, but only for six hours a day. Food is drawn from central stores, and like everything else, is handed over without payment. Everyone wears the same serviceable clothes, silver and gold are despised and only babies play with jewels.

Later verdicts on the Utopian system have been negative: dull, uniform, harsh and regimented. Utopians keep domestic or foreign criminals as slaves. Anyone engaging in premarital sex is sentenced to a lifetime of celibacy. Marriage is for life, and adulterers are punished by slavery. Divorce is possible, but only under strict conditions. Utopians are allowed to play, but the games described seem drearily educational. You need a passport to travel inside the country; improper documentation results in enslavement.

These monastic arrangements might have seemed more tolerable in a time when many starved to death or were hanged for theft of food, and where there was little social provision for the poor; but seen through the lens of the

twenty-first century More's island seems alarmingly totalitarian and authoritarian. More's reason for inventing *Utopia* is a question that has plagued scholars for centuries. More is aware his ideal society could never exist, since the island's name is created from the combination of the Greek words *ou*, 'no', and *topos*, 'place'. *Utopia* is satirical in places, and some of the practices in Utopia, such as euthanasia and married priests, actively contradict More's own Catholic faith. More repeatedly invites comparison between Utopia and the failings of the real world. His overriding purpose is perhaps not to provide an answer, but to ask the simple question: can we not do better than we do?

H. G. Wells tried to update More in *A Modern Utopia* (1905) and *The Shape of Things to Come* (1933), but his ideas were soon discredited by war and Stalinism. George Orwell's *Nineteen Eighty-Four* (1949, page 174) presents a kind of Communist Utopia gone horribly wrong, while Aldous Huxley's *Brave New World* (1932, page 148) satirises a consumerist technological utopia. The most thoughtful fictional comment is perhaps Ursula K. Le Guin's *The Dispossessed* (1974), which describes a community that follows many of the rules of More's Utopia, including abolition of money and private property, and which, like More's vision, was triggered by poverty and injustice. But this society is shown as beginning to crumble, unable entirely to suppress human nature.

Ambrosius Holbein (elder brother of Hans Holbein, court painter to Henry VIII) made woodcuts for an edition of *Utopia* that was published in Basel in 1518. This detail shows the island's capital Amaurotum ('Mist Town') surrounded by the river Anydrus ('Waterless'). The river's source (*Fons Anydri*) and mouth (*Ostium Anydri*) are labelled.

EDMUND SPENSER

THE FAERIE QUEENE (1590–1609)

An extended allegorical poem by one of the finest writers of Elizabethan England presents a grand vision of an Arthurian courtly landscape populated by the gods and monsters of classical and British legend.

Spenser wrote this long, but still unfinished, poem in honour of Queen Elizabeth I, but, apart from an annual pension awarded by the crown, he received little recognition during his lifetime.

He spent much of his life in Ireland as the English sought to establish rule over the country, but Irish insurgency forced him to flee in 1598 and he returned to England.

After his death in 1599 Spenser's body was interred in Poet's Corner in Westminster Abbey.

In a 1590 letter to his friend Sir Walter Raleigh, Edmund Spenser (1552–99) described how he planned for *The Faerie Queene* to comprise twenty-four books, but the project was never completed. Three books were published in London in 1590 and three more in 1596, with a part of a seventh appearing in 1609, ten years after Spenser's death. All are set in what Spenser calls a 'delightfull land of Faery', which combines the castle-studded forests of Malory's *Le Morte d'Arthur* (1485, page 44) with the enchanted whirl of Ariosto's *Orlando Furioso* (c.1516/32, page 48).

Indeed, Spenser's epic poem imitates *Orlando Furioso* in many ways: his maiden-knight Britomart closely resembles Ariosto's heroine Bradamante, and her rescue of Sir Artegall, Spenser's Knight of Justice, parallels Bradamante's rescue of the hero Ruggiero; Ariosto's fair lady Angelica, always seen in flight from would-be ravishers, is echoed by Florimell; and both romances have the same supporting cast of enchanters, giants, dragons, damsels and tournaments.

There is also a strong influence of English folklore and the Arthurian tradition. Prince Arthur (not yet king) appears in each completed book, along with, in the last of them, the Blatant Beast, modelled on Malory's Questing Beast. In his letter to Raleigh, Spenser claimed to be in the tradition of Homer and Virgil, but an even more prominent debt is owed to the Bible. The hero of Book I for example, the Red Cross Knight, is undeniably emblematic of Saint George, the patron saint of England, but, as Spenser stated in the Raleigh letter, the armour he wears is the 'armour of God' (Ephesians 6:10–18).

The Faerie Queene differs from Ariosto in its closer focus and tighter structure, imposed by Spenser's much more serious purpose. Each book has a single virtue personified by a hero or heroine (or a double hero in the form of Cambell and Triamond in Book IV), and their adventures illustrate that virtue and the potential traps that lie in store. In Book II, Sir Guyon, who personifies temperance, goes to the rescue of a young man being beaten by the lunatic Furor. Guyon struggles in the fight until his adviser, the Palmer,

But full of fire and greedy
hardiment,
The youthfull knight could
not for ought be staide,
But forth vnto the darksome
hole he went,
And looked in: his glistring
armour made
A litle glooming light, much
like a shade,
By which he saw the vgly
monster plaine …

tells him he first has to bridle the old hag, named Occasion, who accompanies Furor. The moral being that one can defeat fury by not giving it an opportunity to grow strong.

Spenser's epic is also informed by Classical mythology. The imprisonment of the beauty Florimell beneath the sea by shape-shifting god Proteus resembles the myths of Persephone or Eurydice held in the Underworld. The contemporary philosopher Francis Bacon took Proteus to represent Matter – always ripening, rotting and returning like fruit on a tree.

The Faerie Queene is remarkable for its descriptions: of the Bower of Bliss, complete with naked damsels and knights-turned-beasts; the Garden of Adonis, a place of pagan amoral fertility; the Dance of the Graces, with its pastoral setting; and the declamations of Change and Nature in the unfinished Book VII. In such colourful, sensuous settings Spenser adds new psychological and emotional depth to the charm of fantasy found in the Italian Orlando romances, as well as an insistent sense that more is meant than meets the eye.

Acrasia by John Melhuish Strudwick, 1888. The painting depicts Acrasia, the magical seductress described in Book II with an enchanted knight in the Bower of Bliss.

A study for *The Red Cross Knight* (c.1793) by John Singleton Copley, in which the knight encounters two personifications of virtue. Faith (left) holds a chalice with a serpent and Hope (right) carries a small anchor.

WU CHENG'EN

JOURNEY TO THE WEST (XIYOUJI) (C.1592)

A late sixteenth-century take on an ancient Chinese legend of dragons, bandits, demons and wizards that adds dazzling layers of comedy and profundity to spiritual wisdom.

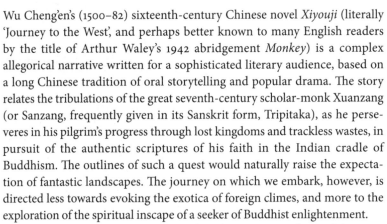

Journey to the West was originally circulated anonymously, and the subject of the text's authorship is still debated.

Centuries later, the tale was made into the television series *Monkey* in 1986, starring Masaaki Sakai in the title role, which has come to be regarded as a cult classic and still enjoys wide popularity.

Wu Cheng'en's (1500–82) sixteenth-century Chinese novel *Xiyouji* (literally 'Journey to the West', and perhaps better known to many English readers by the title of Arthur Waley's 1942 abridgement *Monkey*) is a complex allegorical narrative written for a sophisticated literary audience, based on a long Chinese tradition of oral storytelling and popular drama. The story relates the tribulations of the great seventh-century scholar-monk Xuanzang (or Sanzang, frequently given in its Sanskrit form, Tripitaka), as he perseveres in his pilgrim's progress through lost kingdoms and trackless wastes, in pursuit of the authentic scriptures of his faith in the Indian cradle of Buddhism. The outlines of such a quest would naturally raise the expectation of fantastic landscapes. The journey on which we embark, however, is directed less towards evoking the exotica of foreign climes, and more to the exploration of the spiritual inscape of a seeker of Buddhist enlightenment.

If we leap to the conclusion that this allegorisation of one of the great peregrinations of human history reflects some sort of cultural blinkers constricting the literary imagination of the 'Central Kingdom', we would be quite far from the truth. From a very early time, Chinese readers have been fascinated by the bizarre lands and creatures catalogued in works such as the 'Classic of Mountains and Seas' (*Shanhaijing*). In more recent centuries of the late-Imperial period, fictionalised accounts of expeditions to the Chinese periphery continued to cast the spell of unknown lands and peoples. Closer to home, one of the more abiding themes of the Chinese poetic imagination has long been the serendipitous discovery of hidden valleys where people live in perfect peace and harmony, far from the injurious pursuit of fame and wealth in the outside world – perhaps the best known example being Tao Yuanming's 'Peach Blossom Spring'.

In *Journey to the West*, however, primary literary interest is focused not on the imaginary worlds through which the pilgrims pass, but on the narrative figures that people these lands, both the more 'human' inhabitants – from rustic woodcutters to enlightened or benighted kings, and the demonic denizens who typically masquerade as benign rulers in order to ensnare

the unsuspecting monk. As for the lost cities or uncharted wilderness through which our heroes move, these are for the most part fully domesticated in line with the pictorial and iconographic conventions of Ming landscape. These worlds are almost always identified as 'mountains', beautiful yet forbidding venues in whose hidden fastnesses and caves there lurk a variety of maleficent forces. With the exception of the topsy-turvy 'Kingdom of Women at Xiliang' (where women assume virtually every form of male domination), we get little sense of realms in which alternative modes of existence hold sway, and – with few exceptions – all attention is focused on the evil intentions and bizarre weaponry of their demonic rulers.

One exception to this observation does materialise, however, in the full-blown literary tableau of a lost world of perfection (initially, at least) that is put before our eyes at the very start of the book. Here the narrative of the Tang monk's 'epic' journey is prefaced by a series of episodes on the pre-history of the 'Monkey King', depicting his spontaneous emergence as the insouciant founder of an enclosed paradise for his monkey-brethren on the 'Mountain of Flowers and Fruit', a land of unfettered freedom and undiminished plenty located, quite pointedly, in the 'Land of Burgeoning Pride'. It is only a matter of time, however, before the hubris of self-containment leads him to abandon his circumscribed existence and to rebel against the powers of Heaven, until he is ultimately subdued and subordinated – now in the guise of a simian figure with the monkish name Sun Wukung – to the exalted aims of a quest journey beyond the bounds of Self.

An early twentieth-century illustration showing the cunning demons of Blackwater River disguised as boatmen attempting to carry away the master Xuanzang, before Sun Wukung ('the Monkey King') comes to the rescue.

TOMMASO CAMPANELLA

THE CITY OF THE SUN (1602)

A theocratic utopia in which everything is shared. Solarians benefit from free universal education; they work only six hours daily, and live for a minimum of one hundred years.

Although written in 1602, *La Città del Sole* was first published in Frankfurt in 1623.

Campanella lived in France from October 1634 until his death, and was delighted to prepare a horoscope for the future King Louis XIV.

The child was born 5 September, 1638, the same day Campanella was born some seventy years earlier.

Dominican friar and polymath Tommaso Campanella (1568–1639) was in prison (for leading a conspiracy against Spanish rule in Naples) when he put the finishing touches to his 1,100-page utopian manifesto *Philosophia Realis* in 1602. Buried within it is an appendix entitled *La Città del Sole* (*The City of the Sun*) that was to become his best-known work. The story appears within the literary frame of a traveller's tale, a device perhaps drawn from Thomas More's *Utopia* (1516, page 52), although Campanella makes no explicit reference to the English humanist in his text, preferring instead to underline the influence and ideas of the ancient Greek philosopher Plato.

In the story, a recently returned sea captain is asked by a Grand-Master of the Knights Hospitallers (a Roman Catholic military order) to describe his visit to the faraway 'City of the Sun'. The city, explains the captain, is located on the Island of Taprobane (known to the ancient Greeks and thought to be modern-day Sri Lanka or Sumatra) and its inhabitants had fled there from India. The captain reveals an array of intricate detail about the place and its people, the Solarians, and from this we can assume that Campanella wanted his utopia to be less illusory than other examples in the genre. It is *somewhere*, and therefore not purely speculative, as was Plato's Republic, nor as brimming with negation as More's Utopia.

While some details given by the captain are rather prosaic, the most important elements – governance, education, religion and personal liberty – reflect Campanella's own views and his leanings towards astrology and numerology (for instance, we learn that the city is walled by seven heavily fortified concentric circles and each circle is dedicated to a planet). Unsurprisingly, education is a central tenet and crucial in the perfection of the inhabitants. Thus, the inner and outer walls of each circle contain illustrations of all knowledge, and this is where all children take compulsory classes from the ages of three to ten.

The city is governed by a supreme leader; a priest called Hoh. He will retain the position for life and must have a greater understanding of metaphysics and theology than anyone else. A triumvirate of three princes, each

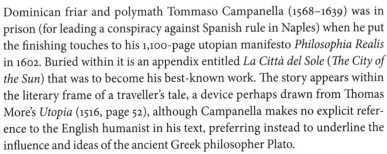

Pio Sanquirico, *Tommaso Campanella in Prison*, 1880. The Dominican friar was imprisoned for leading a conspiracy against Spanish rule in Naples, and finalised his text for *The City of the Sun* from his cell.

of whom in turn is assisted by a number of magistrates, aids Hoh in his responsibilities. First, there is Pon (power), who is charged with affairs of war and peace; next, Sin (wisdom) the 'ruler of the liberal arts, of mechanics, and of all sciences'; and finally there is Mor (love), who attends 'to the charge of the race', which means he ensures a long life for all and 'sees that men and women are so joined together that they bring forth the best offspring'.

While the seeds of dystopian alternatives lie just beneath the surface in *The City of the Sun* – ideas of proto-eugenics and totalitarianism come to mind – Campanella's text reflects important philosophical themes of equality emerging in the late Renaissance period and strives to promote intellectual freedom. The doctrine of state-controlled procreation and the view that fornication was not a sin created much of the sensation surrounding the text on its publication in 1623, and raised allegations of heresy.

DON QUIXOTE (1605/15)

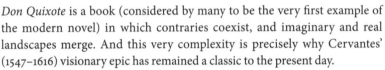

Cervantes paints a subversive portrait of imperial Spain in this epic masterpiece, charting the comic adventures of a knight deluded by legends of chivalry and romance in which the real becomes imaginary and the imaginary in turn symbolises the real.

Cervantes was christened on 9 October, 1547, but his actual birth date is unknown. It has been suggested that his first name implies he was born on Michaelmas Day, 29 September.

Since publication of the novel, 'quixotic' has become a word in its own right, meaning an impractical pursuit of rash or romantic ideals without consideration of consequences.

Volume I of *Don Quixote* was first published in Madrid by Francisco de Robles in 1605.

Don Quixote is a book (considered by many to be the very first example of the modern novel) in which contraries coexist, and imaginary and real landscapes merge. And this very complexity is precisely why Cervantes' (1547–1616) visionary epic has remained a classic to the present day.

Cervantes' writing was highly informed by his own life of travel and adventure. He was variously: a servant of an Italian Cardinal, a soldier of the Spanish empire, a prisoner in Algiers, a playwright, a poet and a tax collector. He was also detained in several Spanish prisons for financial irregularities and was far from wealthy even after the startling popularity of *Don Quixote*.

As the protagonist's name, 'Don Quixote de La Mancha', implies, the novel takes place in a real Spanish region situated south of Madrid. La Mancha is located in Castile, the area that represented dominant Christian Spain when *Don Quixote* was written, and also borders Andalusia, a southern region highly influenced by Islamic and Jewish traditions. As such, in Cervantes' hand, the landscapes of La Mancha can be seen to symbolise the multifarious ethnic identity of Spain itself. La Mancha for Don Quixote is not a place to stay, but a space in which to roam during his adventures, or 'sallies'. The descriptions given are not realistic, but symbolic and literary. For example, the caves and sierras where the Don carries out his self-imposed penance are drawn from the chivalric tradition, the beech trees against which shepherds lean as they sing and talk do not grow in La Mancha but in the pastoral poems that Cervantes parodies.

And while the real world has symbolic association for Cervantes, so does the imaginary. The Don is a character mired in delusion, driven mad by excessive reading of chivalric romances. In imitation of these legendary texts he sets out as a knight-errant seeking valour and adventure. His predicament not only satirises the impracticality of lofty or extravagant ideals, but his delusions (most famously charging at windmills, mistaking them for giants) can also be interpreted as reactions to the very real and traumatic technological transformations that were being implemented in the Castilian landscape by the ruling Habsburgs. The windmills were not at that time a traditional

feature of the Castilian landscape. On the contrary, they were monstrous new machines deployed on the windy Manchegan hills in order to drive the economy of the Habsburgs' global war. The trauma of windmills and what they represent is also powerfully and subtly expressed by the constant repetition of the word *molidos* (past participle of the verb *moler*, to grind), used to describe Don Quixote and Sancho's pitiful state almost every time they are beaten and battered – which they are frequently.

This powerful strategy of blurring the boundaries between the real and the imaginary enabled Cervantes to express his vision in times of censorship and oppression, when the truth could only circulate underground. Furthermore, his amazing capacity to turn fiction into reality and reality into fiction expanded the limits of literary expression, and showcased the highest powers of his imagination. For these reasons, among many others, *Don Quixote* is recognised as a masterpiece of literature and continues to inspire millions of writers and readers worldwide.

Honoré-Victorin Daumier, *Don Quixote and Sancho Panza*, c.1855. Daumier painted several works based on Cervantes' text. Here Don Quixote charges into the distance, while his squire Sancho Panza sits upon his donkey, drinking from a bottle.

WILLIAM SHAKESPEARE

THE TEMPEST (1611)

Shakespeare's final play centres upon an enchanted island inhabited by magician Prospero, his daughter Miranda and their servants Ariel, a sprite, and the monstrous Caliban. The drama begins with a powerful storm and a shipwrecked party interrupts the isolated idyll.

First published as part of the 'First Folio' by Edward Blount and Isaac Jaggard in 1623.

Statues of Ariel and Prospero stand outside the BBC Broadcasting House in London, symbolising the magic of radio transmission.

The 1956 film *Forbidden Planet* is a science-fiction interpretation of *The Tempest*, in which Dr. Edward Morbius and his daughter Altaira are stranded on the distant planet, Altair IV.

The Tempest begins with a ship struggling on a stormy sea, its inhabitants fearful for their lives. The storm has been conjured by the powerful magician Prospero, who is marooned nearby on a desert island with his daughter, Miranda. Along with Prospero and Miranda, the island has two other inhabitants: Caliban, described as the son of a devil and a witch, and Ariel, a sprite whom Prospero has bound into his service.

Prospero's motive is revenge for his deposition and exile at the hands of his brother Antonio, who replaced him as Duke of Milan, and Alonso, King of Naples, who supported Antonio in his coup. He arranges for Alonso's son Ferdinand to be washed ashore, followed separately by Alonso himself and various crew and companions.

Although Shakespeare's (*c.*1564–1616) island is likely located somewhere in the Mediterranean, not too far from Milan and Naples, the idea of the 'deserted' island derives from the discovery of the New World by Columbus in 1492. Shakespeare's description of the shipwreck contains ideas from an event of 1609 in which a ship, en route from England to Virginia, was thought lost in the Bermudas. In fact, all aboard eventually reached Virginia, after living easily for some months on their own 'desert island'.

To sixteenth- and seventeenth-century Europeans, the Caribbean was a land of contradictions. It was dangerous, in ways they had never encountered before, yet was fertile beyond anything they knew, and full of exotic novelties. There were other new and shocking dangers, such as hurricanes, which were first reported in English in 1555; sharks were also first mentioned around this time. (When Alonso thinks his son Ferdinand is dead, he wonders 'what strange fish Hath made his meal on thee?') Similarly, early travellers did not know quite what to make of native populations, and the New World was feared most because of its supposedly fierce and unpredictable inhabitants, often seen as devils or devil-worshippers. Furthermore, there were shocking reports of man-eating tribes. (The word 'cannibal' is first recorded in English in 1553 and comes from the same root as 'Carib', Shakespeare's own 'Caliban' looks like another deliberate variation.)

Yet Shakespeare plays with the notion of the 'native' throughout the play. When Prospero first arrived on the island, Caliban showed the magician the freshwater springs, and later he offers to show the sailors where the berries are and how to catch fish. Prospero and Miranda seem, in return, not to believe Caliban is naturally wicked and to have some kind of 'civilising mission' in mind in teaching him how to talk.

Miranda, Prospero and Ariel, English school, c.1780.

In *The Tempest*, as in many of his other plays, Shakespeare not only drew upon contemporary events, but also integrated older stories, history and fantasy. The Classical gods Juno, Iris and Ceres are referenced and a famous speech by Prospero invokes Ovid's *Metamorphoses* (*c.*8, page 22). The shipwrecked lords exclaim that after seeing Prospero's powerful display of wizardry they can easily believe in unicorns and phoenixes. Ariel functions like the mischievous spirits of English folk tales – elves and boggarts and hobgoblins. They pinch Caliban, they lead the sailors into mires and bogs, they turn will-o'-the-wisp and create fairy rings: all were likely more familiar to Shakespeare's first audience than Caribbean tales or medieval legends.

The Tempest may not contain the first 'desert island' setting in literature, but it demonstrates its enormous potential as a blank canvas for a freewheeling

Be not afeard. The isle is full of noises,
Sounds, and sweet airs, that give delight and hurt not.
Sometimes a thousand twangling instruments
Will hum about mine ears, and sometime voices
That, if I then had waked after long sleep
Will make me sleep again; and then in dreaming
The clouds methought would open and show riches
Ready to drop upon me, that when I waked
I cried to dream again. (III.ii.130–8)

mix of imagery and imagination, free from the constraints of reality. *Caliban and Ariel* in a pen-and-ink drawing by Arthur Rackham, 1899–1906. A potent notion that has inspired a wealth of literature, from Daniel Defoe's *Robinson Crusoe* (1719), Jonathan Swift's *Gulliver's Travels* (1726, page 74), R. L. Stevenson's *Treasure Island* (1883, page 100), H. G. Wells' *The Island of Dr Moreau* (1896) and even William Golding's *Lord of the Flies* (1954). In particular, J. M. Barrie's *Peter Pan* (1911), with its Lost Boys, pirates, Indians, fairies, and mermaids, all brought together in 'Never-Never Land', is particularly indebted to *The Tempest*.

As well as many famous stage productions in modern times, *The Tempest* has also been translated into various media beyond the stage. Scenes have been painted, by artists including Hogarth, Fuseli and Millais; Ariel's songs have been given new music; more than forty operas have been composed on the basis of the play; among the poems inspired by it are Browning's 'Caliban upon Setebos' (1864) and W. H. Auden's Freudian 'The Sea and the Mirror' (1944); and its television and screen adaptations are numerous.

This vast legacy of influence is one clue to the enduring importance of *The Tempest*. By creating this 'other' world, both familiar and alien, Shakespeare explored many of the most important problems that the nation faced at a period of exploration and discovery, and, prophetically, that it still faces today – race, sex, colonisation of and the experience of 'otherness'.

CYRANO DE BERGERAC

A Voyage to the Moon (1657)

Cyrano de Bergerac's fictional Moon, a paradise inhabited by natives, five humans and a Tree of Knowledge, challenged the orthodoxies of contemporary astronomy and the Christian religion.

Originally titled *L'Autre Monde: ou les États et Empires de la Lune (The Other World: or the States and Empires of the Moon)*, it was published posthumously in 1657 by Charles de Sercy.

A fictionalised account of Cyrano's life was presented in a tremendously popular 1897 play entitled *Cyrano de Bergerac* by Edmond Rostand.

Cyrano de Bergerac (1619–55) was writing his *Voyage dans la Lune*, and its sequel, *L'Histoire des États et Empires du Soleil*, not long after Rome had condemned the idea of a sun-centred universe as heretical, and one of his purposes was clearly to support the arguments of Copernicus, Kepler and Galileo. The Moon and Sun are worlds like our own, and he knows, because he has been there.

In this first-person science fiction, Cyrano's mode of transport blends old and new. His first idea is to strap bottles of dew around himself, since dew is sucked up by the Sun. This expedient only gets him as far as French-speaking Canada however, and he eventually reaches the Moon by rocket-assisted take-off, coupled with the attractive power of the Moon on the beef marrow that he has coated himself in to relieve the bruises from previous efforts.

Cyrano's main innovation is as a comic satirist. On the Moon, everything is topsy-turvy – people put their hats on and sit down to show respect, the worst punishment that can be inflicted is to be sentenced to die a natural death of old age, and the mark of a gentleman is not a sword but an erect metal phallus hung from the belt. More fancifully, the Moon people, who are eighteen feet long but walk on all fours, are separated by class in their very means of communication – conversing in music if upper class, and by gesture if lower. They have long noses, like Cyrano himself, which they can use as sundials and their currency is poetry – a sonnet buying dinners for a week. Free love is not only practised, but compulsory.

However, although comedy was possibly his main aim, Cyrano also deserves some reputation as a prophet, having foreseen the concept of the audiobook, as well as something like germ theory, with his attempt at an explanation of the nature of light. When he encounters an atheist, however, orthodoxy reasserts itself, for the atheist and Cyrano are both snatched up by a devil and carried off towards Hell. Cyrano luckily cries out 'Jesu Maria!' at which the devil drops him back on Earth. His later *History of the Sun* is a similar mix of hits and misses.

Since writing his fantastical tales of space exploration, Cyrano de Bergerac's works have been often mentioned in accounts of imaginary moon voyages (of which there are many) and in histories of science fiction. He has inspired many since, but his main influence may well be on Swift's *Gulliver's Travels* (1726, page 74) in which Gulliver, finding himself stranded in an alien land, similarly combines observation with comic surprise.

Cyrano de Bergerac first attempts to rise into outer space with the aid of birds (left) and then by balloon.

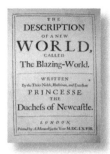

MARGARET CAVENDISH, DUCHESS OF NEWCASTLE

THE DESCRIPTION OF A NEW WORLD, CALLED THE BLAZING-WORLD (1666)

A lavish fantasy and early form of science fiction that critiques seventeenth-century scientific theories while bounding between elaborately depicted parallel worlds.

First published along with *Observations upon Experimental Philosophy*, printed by Anne Maxwell, in 1666. A second edition appeared in 1668 (above).

By the time she published *The Blazing-World*, Cavendish was already well known as a poet (*Poems and Fancies*, 1653), playwright (*Playes and Orations of Divers Sorts*, 1662), and as an essayist and philosopher (*The Worlds Olio*, 1655; *Philosophical Letters*, 1664).

Poems and Fancies (1653) includes poems on the theory of multiple worlds, and on atomic theory.

In his famous diary, Samuel Pepys records that on 30 May 1667, Margaret Cavendish (1623–74) visited the Royal Society, an unusual invitation that was a testament to her status as a wealthy, titled woman with a keen interest in science. There was of course no question of her contributing her own research or even merely joining their discussions at that time (in fact, women would have to wait until 1945 to be elected Fellows). In 1667, the idea of a woman interested in exploring scientific ideas being taken seriously could only take place in the realm of fiction.

The Blazing-World is a narrative companion to Cavendish's *Observations upon Experimental Philosophy*, a more serious critique of the latest developments in science and technology. *Observations* challenges science's claims to understand all Nature, and is critical of new technologies developed to further scientific research.

The Blazing-World begins with a young, unnamed woman, abducted aboard a ship by a merchant who desires her. They are shipwrecked in a storm, but she and a handful of the crew survive in a lifeboat. All the men succumb to the cold, leaving the woman entirely alone. After a series of encounters with Bear-men – intelligent beings who resemble bears – Fox-men, Bird-men and Satyrs, she is brought to the Emperor by mermen with green skin. The Emperor, believing the woman to be divine, marries her. The woman, hereafter designated 'the Empress', undertakes to learn all she can about her new home, and sets out to establish a number of learned societies. The bulk of the story consists of dialogues with these societies, as she seeks answers to questions about the laws of nature in the Blazing-World.

The world itself is a group of archipelagos within interconnected networks of rivers and oceans. There are numerous cities, each made out of a different kind of material, including 'some not known in our world', but all built in the style of classical Rome. The Imperial Palace in the Imperial city of Paradise is, like the city itself, made of gold and decorated with precious stones. The inhabitants are both humans and intelligent animals – each animal having its own specialised branch of learning. From the explanations given by various scientists of the learned societies, the Blazing-World either operates upon radically different laws of physics to our world, or the scientists are spectacularly incompetent, providing odd explanations for natural phenomena that were understood even in Cavendish's time.

After an extended survey of all learning, the Empress composes 'a Cabbala' – a compendium of the entirety of the esoteric knowledge. She finds her amanuensis in Cavendish herself – as 'The Duchess' – who is able to visit the Empress in 'spirit form'.

In the brief, second part of the work, the Empress learns that her native country (the fictional Kingdom of Esfi) has come under attack. The Duchess persuades the Empress to muster the forces of the Blazing-World to aid in the fight. The Empress calls her architects and engineers – who happen to be giants – to build, with the Duchess' direction, submarines to transport the forces through the gap between the Blazing-World and ours. The Empress then manages to rally the forces of her own country to victory.

The Blazing-World is one of the very first works of science fiction, and undoubtedly the only example published by a woman in the seventeenth century. Cavendish's vision of interconnected other worlds has proven influential in the development of science fiction, but her vision of a woman who effortlessly rises to absolute power through the accumulation of knowledge has been more recently embraced by scholars of feminist literature. Virginia Woolf refers to Cavendish in *A Room of One's Own* (1929); more recently Siri Hustvedt uses the text (and its title) to illustrate her story of a woman painter taking on misogyny in the New York art establishment.

An engraving by Abraham van Diepenbeeck from 1655 presents the duchess beside the accoutrements of wisdom and learning, a quill and inkwell, while above cherubs crown her with a laurel wreath.

Frontispiece to *A Connecticut Yankee in King Arthur's Court* (1889), see page 108.

2 SCIENCE & ROMANTICISM

The Industrial Revolution coincided with the heights of Gothic fantasy producing scientific miracles and a terrible fear of the unknown.

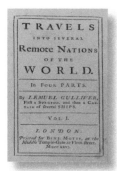

JONATHAN SWIFT

GULLIVER'S TRAVELS (1726)

This classic satire follows the adventures of Lemuel Gulliver among the miniature Lilliputians, the philosophising Houyhnhnms and the brutish Yahoos, and portrays a comic yet steely reflection of mankind.

First published in London by Benjamin Motte in 1726.

'Yahoo' has been accepted into the language as an insult meaning rude, unsophisticated and uncouth. It was this definition that led internet pioneers Jerry Yang and David Filo to adopt it as the name of their new search engine in 1994.

Opposite: Gulliver pinned to the ground by the Lilliputians, illustration from *Gulliver's Travels,* published by Nelson and Sons, 1860.

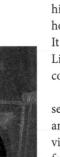

The Anglo-Irish essayist Jonathan Swift (1667–1745) is regarded today as the leading satirist in the English language, and his sardonic style is so ingrained that his name has become an adjective. The influence and import of his classic parody *Gulliver's Travels* is immeasurable and it has been continuously in print since its first publication.

The first two 'travels' of Lemuel Gulliver are mirror images of each other. In the first the inhabitants of the island of Lilliput are very small, about six inches high. In Brobdingnag they are very large, about seventy feet high; Gulliver, having once been a giant, becomes like a doll. His third voyage takes him to the flying island of Laputa, the land beneath it (Balnibarbi), the necromancers' island of Glubbdubdrib, and the kingdom of Luggnagg, with its immortal but senile 'struldbrugs'. On his fourth voyage Gulliver is marooned on the land of the Houyhnhnms, intelligent horses, which is also inhabited by the Yahoos – a dirty, dangerous and unteachable parody of humanity.

Throughout, Swift mingles marvels with satire, the latter eventually all but taking over. As a result, his first voyage has remained the best-known and the most popular for adaptations. Much of the account of the Lilliputians deals with the details of scale: how Gulliver is fed, how they try to control him, what feats he performs for the king and his court. Apart from scale, however, the land of the Lilliputians seems virtually identical with England. It has cows, sheep, horses, trees and vegetation, all scaled down like the Lilliputians themselves, and a social system that parallels and parodies Swift's contemporary Britain.

Brobdingnag gives rise to similar, if inverse, effects, with Gulliver in serious danger from mastiff-sized rats, flies as big as birds, pet cats like lions and dogs the size of elephants. Swift, moreover, seems to equate size with virtue. While the Lilliputian court is essentially ridiculous, providing in its faction-fighting a satirical image of British court-society, in Brobdingnag the satire comes from Gulliver's attempts to impress the Brobdingnagian king with his accounts of British power and skill. Even his account of gunpowder only makes the king contemptuous of the uses to which it is put.

Stephen Baghot de la Bere,
*Gulliver and the
Houyhnhnms*, 1904.

> [T]hey have no conception how a rational creature can be compelled, but only advised, or exhorted; because no person can disobey reason, without giving up his claim to being a rational creature.

Many have thought that in the third voyage Swift's satire goes well astray. The Laputians on their floating island, held aloft by a giant lodestone or magnet, respect only mathematics and music, and are totally impractical. Their subjects on the island below are even worse, having begun to imitate the Laputians and set up an 'Academy' for all kinds of ludicrous scientific experiments, distilling sunbeams from cucumbers, reconstituting dung into food and inventing a universal language that would have no words, and communicate only by things. Swift was here satirising the Royal Society, founded in 1660.

In the fourth voyage Swift's own misanthropy seems finally to have infected Gulliver. The Houyhnhnms (pronounced 'Whinnn-im' in imitation of a horse's neigh) are polite, intelligent, virtuous, while the Yahoos are unspeakably vile. At the end, Gulliver, once again returned home, can hardly bear the company of his own species, including his wife, and sits talking to his horses for hours every day. Scholarship varies as to how seriously we should take his critiques of humanity.

Gulliver's Travels has given rise to several films and TV adaptations – including the animation *Laputa: Castle in the Sky* by acclaimed Japanese director Hayao Miyazaki – and Lilliputians appear in several comic books and novels. And Swiftian concepts reappear throughout science fiction. The animated American TV series *Land of the Giants* ran from 1968–70. Laputa is remembered in James Blish's *Cities in Flight* tetralogy (1955–62), where a rogue city does what the Laputians sometimes threaten to do, and 'makes the sky fall.' The Houyhnhnms feature in John M. Myers' novel *Silverlock* (1949), and 'struldbrugs' appear at the end of Frederik Pohl's *Drunkard's Walk* (1960) as a secret society controlling human affairs.

THE JOURNEY OF NIELS KLIM TO THE WORLD UNDERGROUND (1741)

Sometimes described as the first science-fiction novel, this subterranean adventure was the first to explore ideas of a hollow Earth.

The popularity of Holberg's satirical plays earned him the sobriquet the 'Molière of the North'.

Originally published in Latin (in Germany in 1741) as *Nicolai Klimii Iter Subterraneum*. The full English title is *The Journey of Niels Klim to the World Underground, with a new theory of the Earth and the History of the previously unknown Fifth Kingdom*.

Ludvig Holberg (1684–1754) is often referred to as the 'father' of Danish and Norwegian literature – and his writing encompassed a wide range of fields. However, he is best remembered for his satirical plays and for his creation of a 'hollow Earth' in *The Journey of Niels Klim to the World Underground*.

The text recounts, as the title suggests, the adventures of one Niels Klim who, after his rope gives way while exploring a cave, falls to the centre of Earth, where a solitary planet rotates around a subterranean sun. The first adventure is set in Potu, a utopian land inhabited by intelligent and mobile trees. Since Klim's legs allow him to move faster than the trees, he is commissioned to make a tour of the entire planet of Nazar and report back to the king. The narrative turns from utopia to satire as Klim visits the different provinces of Nazar. The descriptions of these countries – inhabited by different species of trees that speak the same language as the Potuans – are very brief, and most present satirical sketches of alternative societies. In Quamso everyone is happy, healthy and bored; in Lalac, where there is no need to work, everyone is unhappy and sickly; in Kimal the citizens are wealthy, and spend their time worrying about thieves; and the 'land of Liberty' is at war.

From the inner planet of Potu, Klim travels next to the underside of the Earth's crust, carried by a giant bird. His adventures begin in the kingdom of Martinia – a country of intelligent but capricious apes preoccupied with fashion. He makes a fortune by introducing wigs to the Martinians. From social satire the book now becomes fantasy as Klim is taken on a trading voyage to the Mezandorian islands, which lie across a vast sea and are inhabited by fabulous creatures.

After a shipwreck he finds himself in a remote country inhabited not by intelligent animals or trees, but by primitive humans, who, of all the creatures of the subterranean world, 'alone were barbarous and uncivilised'. Klim sets out to redress the situation, intending that they 'would recover that dominion which Nature has given to man over all other animals'. Using his knowledge he manufactures gunpowder and conquers, one by one, all the countries of the firmament. Klim's many conquests lead him to see himself

as the 'Alexander of the Subterranean world', and he becomes a tyrant. When his subjects rebel, he is forced to flee; looking for shelter, he falls into the same hole through which he had previously fallen, thus returning to Norway.

Niels Klim is pulled from the water in a scene by Danish painter Nicolai Abraham Abildgaard.

Holberg's text is the first portrayal of a hollow Earth, but there is little evidence to suggest where this idea came from. As he is falling, Klim makes a reference to accounts of an interior realm, but without any details: 'I fell to imagining that I was sunk into the subterranean world, and that the conjectures of those men are right who hold the Earth to be hollow.' But who are 'those men' and why did they hold Earth to be hollow? Some have pointed to the astronomer Edmond Halley's 'concentric spheres' theory of the interior of the Earth (1692) – but Holberg's inner world is not a set of globes but a single planet circling an inner sun as well an inhabited inner crust – significant features of subsequent subterranean fictions, but not part of Halley's scheme. Like many other early utopias and satirical works, Holberg is indifferent to the physical details of the imaginary world. *Klim* was written at a time (1741) when the popular travel narratives of the sixteenth and seventeenth centuries had evolved into the imaginary voyages of the eighteenth century, allowing writers to visualise political and social alternatives while skirting the interdiction of speculation by passing it off as an authentic narrative.

CHARLES KINGSLEY

THE WATER-BABIES: A FAIRY TALE FOR A LAND BABY (1863)

A strange and powerful tale for children that combines imaginative exuberance, uplifting themes of redemption and contemporary ideas about evolutionary theory and contemporary child labour.

First published in 1863 by Macmillan and Co., *The Water-Babies* echoes many other fairy tales in beginning with the words 'Once upon a time'.

The book has been suggested as a trigger for the Chimney Sweepers Regulation Act of 1864.

Kingsley coined the term 'cuddly', and it was first used in *The Water-Babies*.

The Water-Babies by Charles Kingsley (1819–75) might ostensibly be a fairy tale, but this most imaginative of Victorian fables is directed at thinking adults as much as children of the period.

The hero, Tom, is that stalwart of Victorian literature: a chimney sweep. He blunders down a chimney at Harthover House and finds himself in the bedroom of Ellie, a daughter of the family. Suddenly ashamed of himself, he realises he is 'dirty' and runs away. Obsessed with the idea that he must somehow become clean, Tom throws himself, suicidal, into a nearby stream. He does not drown, but is swept down to the ocean, washed clean, and morally and physically reborn in a series of fantastic adventures, involving, among others, his bullying master Grimes and the mysterious Mother Carey. He learns valuable life lessons from Mrs Doasyouwouldbedoneby and less valuable lessons from Professor Ptthmllnsports. Finally Tom, who has undergone a literal 'sea change', is united with Ellie and goes on to grow up 'a great man of science', saved by the power of clean water.

Charles Kingsley was a clergyman, the leader of the so-called 'Muscular Christianity' movement. He perceived the mission of a clergyman as confronting social problems. The social problem that most exercised him, to the point of obsession, was sanitation. If Kingsley pictured the devil it was not horns, tail and cloven hoof, but filth. For Kingsley it was not the proverbial 'cleanliness is next to godliness', but cleanliness *was* godliness. This obsession propels the narrative of this 'not just for children' tale.

The origin of the story stems from the history of London. In 1854 the city had been ravaged by a cholera epidemic. These outbreaks happened every couple of years, and were regarded by Londoners as no more unusual than the coming of winter (which also killed thousands). The prevailing opinion thought the disease to be 'miasmic', or spread by foul air. In 1854, however, a young doctor traced the source of a recent outbreak, ascertaining that it was not, in fact, bad air but bad *water* that was responsible. Meanwhile, beneath the horse-manured and garbage-strewn streets of London, the urban engineer Joseph Bazalgette was laying down the

first effective sewage system since the Romans. Bazalgette's task was given added urgency by the famous 'Great Stink' of the summer of 1858, which was so malodorous, and lethal, that it enforced the closure of Parliament. His network of subterranean sewers ensured it would never happen again.

According to one sardonic German historian, 'the English think civilisation is soap'. Dickens certainly did. In 1850 he addressed the Metropolitan Sanitary Association: 'I can honestly declare, that all the use I have made of my eyes – or nose [laughter] ... has strengthened me in the conviction that Searching Sanitary Reform must precede all other social remedies [cheers] ... Give me my first glimpse of Heaven through a little of its light and air – give me water, help me to be clean.' Of all the persecutions of the Victorian child, chimney sweeping was the most vile. Oliver Twist narrowly escapes that fate: had he remained in the brutal employment of Gamfield (who offers five pounds for ownership of the lad) Oliver, like many others, might well have succumbed to the cancer of the scrotum or pulmonary disease – two occupational hazards. Few sweeps made it to middle age, and many did not even make it to adulthood.

'"Oh, don't hurt me!" cried Tom. "I only want to look at you; you are so handsome."' Illustration by Jessie Wilcox-Smith, created for a 1916 edition.

Pure water had another centrally important value for the nineteenth century. It symbolised Christian salvation – by the primal rite of baptism, a huge event in Christian life in the nineteenth century. The baby (what with gowns, favours, christening mugs and silver spoons) received almost as many gifts as a bride on her wedding day.

These two ideas – sanitary water supply and baptism – are fused in *The Water-Babies*. Reverend Kingsley believed, with all his soul, that social progress and fundamental religion were not contradictory. God wanted his creation to have water as pure as that in Eden. And, by God, Charles Kingsley would be at the head of those who fought for it.

LEWIS CARROLL (CHARLES LUTWIDGE DODGSON)

ALICE'S ADVENTURES IN WONDERLAND (1865)

A classic of nonsense fantasy and the curiosities it contains – a rabbit with a pocket watches, the Mad Hatter, the Cheshire Cat and the tyrannical Queen of Hearts – it has enchanted readers, young and old, for more than 150 years.

First published by Macmillan and Co. in 1865.

A stickler for perfection, the book's original illustrator, John Tenniel, insisted the first edition of two thousand copies be pulped because his exquisite designs were imperfectly reproduced.

Opposite: '"But I don't want to go among mad people," Alice remarked. "Oh, you can't help that," said the Cat: "we're all mad here. I'm mad. You're mad." "How do you know I'm mad?" said Alice. "You must be," said the Cat, "or you wouldn't have come here."' Alice meets the grinning Cheshire Cat in an illustration after Tenniel.

Reverend Charles Lutwidge Dodgson was a mathematics don at Christ Church College in Oxford, and he famously wrote *Alice's Adventures in Wonderland* for a colleague's three little girls: Ina, Alice and Edith Liddell, whom he used to take on outings on summer days to the river. He would entertain them by 'telling them stories', and luckily for the Liddell girls, he was one of the greatest (if strangest) storytellers of all time.

A novelist friend of Dodgson, Henry Kingsley (brother of Charles, author of *The Water-Babies*, 1863, page 80), read the story and was of the opinion that Alice should be given to the world at large, urging Dodgson to have it published. The unworldly Dodgson first thought of Oxford University Press, but the house rejected the manuscript as not suitable for their learned list, and further it was intimated that it would do him no good academically to publish such a work under his own name.

Eventually Dodgson was persuaded to submit the work to Macmillan and Co., Kingsley's publisher, with illustrations by John Tenniel. Dodgson came up with a pen name that suited him and his witty tale, 'Lewis Carroll'. It was a pun, inevitably – and one that his colleagues at the high table at Christ Church College doubtless had a high time puzzling out (Lewis is etymologically linked, via Latin, to 'Lutwidge'; Carroll, likewise, to 'Charles').

The two 'Alice books' (the successor to the bestselling adventures in 'Wonderland' took the little girl *Through the Looking-Glass, and What Alice Found There*) are unusual among children's literature in appealing equally to adult readers. Ideally, clever adults, who are able to appreciate the depth of Carroll's intellectualism embedded in his writing.

The tale begins with Alice lolling under a tree in high summer and failing to read her book, when she sees a white rabbit rush by:

There was nothing so *very* remarkable in that; nor did Alice think it so *very* much out of the way to hear the Rabbit say to itself, 'Oh dear! Oh dear! I shall be late' (when she thought it over afterwards, it occurred to her that she ought to have wondered at this, but at the time it all seemed quite

Alice joins the Mad Hatter, the March Hare and the Dormouse for tea in a hand-coloured etching after Tenniel.

natural); but when the Rabbit actually *took a watch out of its waistcoat-pocket*, and looked at it, and then hurried on, Alice started to her feet, for it flashed across her mind that she had never before seen a rabbit with either a waistcoat-pocket, or a watch to take out of it, and burning with curiosity, she ran across the field after it, and fortunately was just in time to see it pop down a large rabbit-hole under the hedge.

We do not need the aid of Freud to work out that this little girl, eight years out of it, is 'returning to the womb', finding herself in a mad world. Alice's way is blocked by locked doors, she eats and drinks substances that make her grow and shrink, she encounters mythical creatures like the Gryphon, extinct creatures like the Dodo, and toothy, but smiling, creatures like the Cheshire Cat. She breaks in, uninvited, on the Mad Hatter's tea party and is finally sentenced to be beheaded by the irascible Queen of Hearts (a mother figure from hell).

As the queen's playing card entourage falls on her, with decapitation in mind, Alice wakes with dead leaves brushing her face. It was spring, and now is autumn. The little girl is growing up.

'Oh my ears and whiskers, how late it's getting!' The White Rabbit checks his pocket watch.

Opposite: Alice Pleasance Liddell (1852–1934) photographed as a 'beggar maid' by Lewis Carroll.

Alice was beginning to get very tired of sitting by her sister on the bank and of having nothing to do: once or twice she had peeped into the book her sister was reading, but it had no pictures or conversations in it, 'and what is the use of a book', thought Alice, 'without pictures or conversations?'

JULES VERNE

Twenty Thousand Leagues Under the Sea (1870)

This classic tale of adventure by the 'Father of Science Fiction'
voyages through the realm of the imagination from the lost city
of Atlantis to the South Pole.

Originally serialised from 1869 to 1870, *Twenty Thousand Leagues* was first published in book form by Pierre-Jules Hetzel in 1870. An edition with illustrations by Édouard Riou and the painter Alphonse de Neuville followed in 1871.

The novel is more explicitly scientific than many of Verne's other works, such as *Journey to the Centre of the Earth* (1864), with the seemingly fantastical *Nautilus* based on the study of contemporary submarine designs.

Opposite: The view from the salon window aboard the *Nautilus*, engraving after Alphonse de Neuville (coloured later).

The narrative of *Vingt mille lieues sous les mers* (*Twenty Thousand Leagues Under the Sea*), like that of all Verne's (1828–1905) major works, is no more than a row of pegs on which to hang wild flights of his distinctive imagination. Dip anywhere into the novel and there is page after page of vivid pictorialism – see, for example, the long descriptions of submarine 'coral forests', the submerged ruins of Atlantis, the sunken galleons rotting in the Bay of Vigo. Verne was also a famously light-fingered writer. The novel's climax, detailing the attack by giant squid, is borrowed (with acknowledgement) from Victor Hugo's *Toilers of the Sea* (1866). The self-destruction of Captain Nemo and his craft in the great northern 'maelstrom' is also borrowed, from Edgar Allan Poe's story 'A Descent into the Maelstrom' (1841). However, one readily forgives these narrative larcenies, because there is so much in Verne's story that is hugely original.

Pierre Aronnax, a world-famous French marine biologist, narrates the story. On his way back from a North American expedition in March 1866, the US government recruits him to help hunt down a mysterious giant, glowing creature. Aronnax sets out on the USS *Abraham Lincoln*, accompanied by his omni-competent, urbane manservant, Conseil, and a Canadian 'king of harpooners', Ned Land, a character who seems to have walked off the pages of Herman Melville's *Moby Dick* (another source candidly plundered by Verne).

The *Abraham Lincoln* sights the mysterious, phosphorescent 'cetacean', gives chase and fires on the beast. It proves immune to artillery and turns on the ship, ramming it. Aronnax, Conseil and Land tumble into the ocean. They cling to the sides of what turns out to be not a whale but an immense metallic submarine. The trio is taken aboard and the submarine *Nautilus* is revealed to be a miracle of modern technology – electrically propelled, air conditioned and palatial in its amenities. The three captives are, however, informed that they can never leave. Ned Land takes this particularly badly and spends the whole novel plotting his escape from this 'metal prison'. Aronnax is delighted. For him it is not a prison but the world's finest laboratory. The body

of the book details their 20,000-league, nine-month voyage above and below
the oceans. The heroes finally escape by being thrown clear of the maelstrom
that sucks the craft and its crew to their destruction.

Aronnax controls the narrative, but it is Nemo, the captain of the
Nautilus, who grips the reader's imagination. Verne wanted to make the
captain a Polish aristocrat, bent on revenge against Russia for its brutal
repression of the 1863 uprising. However, he was talked out of this by his
publisher and instead Nemo was made enigmatic – a man of mystery whose
name is Latin for 'no one'. We never learn what motivates him or where
he comes from. He speaks five languages – none of which seem to be his
native tongue despite his fluency in all of them. He is sombre and gloom-
ridden by nature, but omniscient on everything he talks about. His age
is uncertain; his crew is drawn from the four corners of the earth. He is a
walking question mark. The last image Aronnax has of his captor is of Nemo
sobbing while gazing piteously at the picture of a woman and two children on
his cabin wall, as the *Nautilus* is pulled down into the maw of the maelstrom.
His wife? His mother? Aronnax will never know, nor shall we.

Twenty Thousand Leagues first appeared for French readers in instalments in the *Magasin d'Education et de Recreation*, from March 1869 to June
1870. Verne's opening sentence is: 'The year 1866 was marked by a bizarre
development.' The subsequent narrative takes the action forward to mid-1867.
This is, for a novel, a strikingly contemporary setting. Moreover, the story
references several significant current events. The name of the ship Aronnax
embarks on, the *Abraham Lincoln*, is named for the sixteenth American president assassinated only two years earlier in 1865. There was nothing new
about the idea of the submarine in 1869, but the first time submarines were
used effectively in warfare was in the American Civil War by the Confederate
Navy. They demonstrated the new crafts' immense military potential when
the forty-foot *Hunley* (with an eight-man crew and a hand-operated propel-
ler) sank the uss *Housatonic* off the coast of Charleston in 1864. Suddenly
the world took note of this new kind of weapon, which would revolutionise
warfare at sea.

These and innumerable other topicalities echo resonantly in the novel,
and they relate to that feature in fiction, immediacy, which is specifically
French rather than English or American. French popular novels tended to
appear, as did *Twenty Thousand Leagues Under the Sea*, as what were called
feuilletons – daily, weekly or bi-weekly serials in newspapers. In Britain
it was the monthly magazine and the hard-backed volume that were the
principle vehicles for novels 'of the day'. The immediacy of the French practice
goes back to the Revolution, fuelled as it was by pamphlets and newspapers
churned out by the hour by secret hand presses ('under the cloak' publications, as they were called). Verne's novel was likewise hot off the press.

With endless imagination and exhaustive detailing, Verne draws on
contemporary discovery to expand into the new and unknown, putting
forward technological, geographical and dimensional concepts to create a

The sea is everything … It is an immense desert place where man is never lonely, for he senses the weaving of Creation on every hand. It is the physical embodiment of a supernatural existence … For the sea is itself nothing but love and emotion. It is the Living Infinite, as one of your poets has said. Nature manifests herself in it, with her three kingdoms: mineral, vegetable and animal. The ocean is the vast reservoir of Nature.

world never before seen or imagined. Through this thorough and enthralling landscape, he meditates on the relationship of men with nature, with themselves and with their freedom in the modern world.

Jules Verne may not be a great prose stylist – not even his warmest admirers make that claim – but his big ideas are unsurpassed in their daring and gripping nature. No more imaginative writer ever drew his pen across the page.

SAMUEL BUTLER

Erewhon (1872)

A provocative satire on the traditions of Victorian society, which also highlights a prescient comment on the rise of machines.

First published by Trübner and Co. in 1872.

Aldous Huxley acknowledged Butler's influence on *Brave New World* (1932, page 148) and George Orwell later praised Butler, noting that at the time of its publication *Erewhon* must have required an 'imagination of a very high order to see that machinery could be dangerous as well as useful'.

Samuel Butler's (1835–1902) great dystopian satire of Victorian society may be a little more obvious than some later imagined worlds, yet *Erewhon* is still as bracing as an ice-cold shower in showing the stupidity of viewing the British Empire – or indeed any modern society – as a righteous utopia.

Butler was one of the most eloquent sceptics of his age; among his propositions were a denunciation of Christ's resurrection, and the belief that *The Odyssey* must have been written by a woman. *Erewhon* was originally published anonymously but when it met with popular success Butler claimed it as his own, and it is now best remembered for his Darwinian-inspired discussions on what we would now describe as 'artificial intelligence' and the evolution of the machine.

Erewhon, and the world it imagines, draws initially on Butler's own experience rearing sheep in New Zealand after his graduation from university. His narrator (later revealed to be called Higgs in Butler's inferior sequel, *Erewhon Revisited*, from 1901) is a young shepherd, who wonders if there is anything beyond the towering mountains that surround his farm. He embarks on a journey over perilous cliffs and a treacherous river to arrive at the unknown country of Erewhon. (Much like More's Utopia, Erewhon is a thinly veiled 'nowhere' in anagram form.)

He first encounters a circle of 'rude and barbaric' statues that elicit a terrible howl from the wind as it passes through them and cause him to collapse in fear. He is later awoken by girls tending goats who bring him to their elders. As a stranger Higgs is taken into custody, his watch removed and health assessed before being briefly imprisoned. Higgs observes that the practices and beliefs of the Erewhonians seem strangely topsy-turvy and in reverse to his own. Most intriguing is their response to the 'crime' of becoming sick, in comparison to, one might assume, more voluntary transgressions:

> if a man falls into ill health, or catches any disorder, or fails bodily in any way before he is seventy years old, he is tried before a jury of his countrymen, and if convicted is held up to public scorn … But if a man forges a

cheque, or sets his house on fire, or robs with violence from the person, or does any other such things as are criminal in our own country, he is either taken to a hospital and most carefully tended at the public expense, or if he is in good circumstances, he lets it be known to all his friends that he is suffering from a severe fit of immorality ...

Erewhonian youths attend Universities of Unreason, where nothing useful is taught; and any form of machinery is proscribed on the grounds that, if allowed to develop, the machines will take over society.

Nosnibor – who is in the process of 'recovering' from embezzling a widow and children out of all their money – takes Higgs under his wing after his release from prison, and the narrator falls in love with his daughter, Arowhena. He eventually escapes with her, and returns to the outside world by hot-air balloon. In Butler's 1901 sequel, *Erewhon Revisited*, a widowed Higgs returns to discover that following his mysterious disappearance into the sky he has become the centre of a 'Sunchild' cult. Human beings, it seems, the sceptical Butler asserts, will believe anything.

Detail from Giovanni Bellini's *Saint Jerome Reading in a Landscape,* as used to depict Butler's imaginary realm in a Penguin Classics edition of *Erewhon.*

RICHARD WAGNER

THE RING OF THE NIBELUNG
(1876)

This epic masterpiece of gods, heroes and men is arguably the most extraordinary achievement in the history of opera.

Wagner worked on the libretto and music for the four operas for nearly thirty years, from 1848 to 1874.

King Ludwig II of Bavaria demanded previews of *The Rhinegold* (1869) and *The Valkyrie* (1870) before Wagner had completed the rest of the cycle. The first complete performance of the *Ring* was at the Bayreuth Festspielhaus (specifically built to Wagner's design) from 13 to 17 August 1876.

Opposite: Arthur Rackham depicts the Valkyrie Brünnhilde riding her faithful steed Grane into the funeral pyre of her lover Siegfried, in *Siegfried and the Twilight of the Gods* (1924).

There can be very few artists more explosively divisive than Richard Wagner (1813–83). The composer's own ideas about racial supremacy and, later, the appropriation of his music by the Nazis (Adolf Hitler would claim Wagner as one of his favourite composers) have cast a dark shadow over his work. Scholars still struggle with the question of whether it is possible, or even acceptable, to separate the music from the man. And yet Wagner created some of the most celebrated music in history, and his 'Ride of the Valkyries' is arguably one of the most recognised musical themes ever written.

Wagner created both the music and the libretto (the text) for his operas, and his perception of their staged performance as a *Gesamtkunstwerk* – a 'total work of art' combining drama, music, scenery and spectacle – revolutionised the art form. His creative vision was most fully realised in the epic four-opera cycle, 'The Ring of the Nibelung' (or 'Der Ring des Nibelungen' in its original German), a masterpiece that took him nearly thirty years to write.

The 'Ring' is set in a world of Northern mythology that the composer adapted to suit his own vision. Many other writers, notably Tolkien, have found inspiration in these same sources, but Wagner's vision is original and distinctive. It is, to begin with, set on a consistently lofty plane. Wagner's main source, the Norse epic 'The Saga of the Volsungs', is a story of great heroes, but they are human, and some are known to have actually existed. Wagner's world, by contrast, is dominated by figures from mythology: the gods, the giants, the dwarfs, the Valkyries (who carry off slain warriors from the battlefield to Valhalla, Wotan's home) and the Norns (female figures who control human destiny by spinning Fate). All of these beings are mentioned, if not in 'The Saga of the Volsungs' then elsewhere in Old Norse literature, but Wagner expanded the roles of many of them and added others, notably the Rhinemaidens, who guard the Rhine's gold from which the titular magic ring is eventually forged.

As part of the *Gesamtkunstwerk,* Wagner's mythological libretto and complex characterisation are accompanied by a wealth of detailed

stage directions (which must have been difficult to follow faithfully with only nineteenth-century technology). The opening scene of the first opera, *The Rhinegold* (*Das Rheingold*), for example, is set in swirling waters, with rocks, mist, and deep gorges, from which the dwarf Alberich (the 'Nibelung' of the cycle's title) snatches the Rhinegold from the Rhinemaidens. The second scene is set outside the majestic hall of Valhalla, which the giants Fasolt and Fafner have just finished building for Wotan, chief of the gods. And so it goes on throughout the cycle, from the smoking forges of Nibelheim (where Alberich makes the magic ring), to cloud-strewn mountaintops and bird-filled forests. Wagner's capacity for epic world building knew no bounds. And yet curiously, unlike so many other world-creating artists, Wagner seems to have woven his intricate and detailed realm with the specific intention of destroying it completely.

As *The Rhinegold* continues it is revealed that, in return for building Valhalla, Wotan has promised the giants the goddess Freia (his wife Fricka's sister) as payment. Since Freia possesses the Golden Apples that keep the gods immortal, this is clearly a dangerous gamble. It appears Freia is indeed lost until Wotan's clever and resourceful assistant Loge tells of Alberich's powerful ring. The giants agree that they will return the goddess if Wotan can present the ring to them by evening.

Wotan and Loge then trick Alberich into giving up the ring, and the furious dwarf places a deadly curse upon it. Wotan attempts to keep the ring, but eventually surrenders it to the giants, whereupon the curse takes its lethal effect and Fafner beats Fasolt to death as they quarrel over the ring.

The Valkyrie (*Die Walküre*) continues the epic story, explaining that Wotan is desperate to regain the ring before Alberich does, fearing disaster for the gods. The laws of the gods, however, prevent him from seizing it back by force. It has to be done by a hero who is free from these laws, whom Wotan tries to create by siring a son, Siegmund, with Erda, the embodiment of the Earth. Siegmund, however, falls in love with his own twin sister, Sieglinde, and Wotan's wife Fricka – guardian of propriety – insists that he must die. Wotan's daughter, the Valkyrie Brünnhilde, attempts to protect Siegmund, but Wotan shatters his son's sword and Siegmund is killed by Sieglinde's husband, Hunding. Brünnhilde manages to rescue the pregnant Sieglinde and the broken sword, though the Valkyrie is punished for her disobedience by being cast into a magic sleep.

The third opera, Siegfried, centres on the eponymous hero, child of Siegmund and Sieglinde, who grows up knowing no fear. Taught by Alberich's brother, Mime, Siegfried reforges his father's sword, kills Fafner with it and recaptures the ring. He goes on to waken the sleeping Brünnhilde, and instantly falls in love with her.

The final part of the cycle, *The Twilight of the Gods* (*Götterdämmerung*), begins with the three Norns weaving the rope of Destiny. Their song reveals that the gods' time will end and that Wotan will burn Valhalla.

Wotan's scheming is finally defeated in this last instalment by Alberich's son Hagen. With a potion of oblivion he makes Siegfried forget his love for Brünnhilde, and sends him to her disguised as his half-brother Gunther. Siegfried takes back the ring and then hands Brünnhilde over to the real Gunther, but when Brünnhilde recognises the ring, which she thought had been taken by Gunther, once again on Siegfried's finger, she realises that she has been deceived and accuses Siegfried of raping her in Gunther's form. Hagen then murders Siegfried for the ring and also kills his brother.

The three Rhinemaidens from the first complete performance of Wagner's epic in 1876, played by Lilli Lehmann (Woglinde), Marie Lehmann (Wellgunde), and Minna Lammert (Flosshilde).

The ring is at last regained by Brünnhilde, who takes it with her into the funeral pyre. In the last spectacle the Rhinemaidens flood the pyre, seize the ring and drown Hagen, while in the background the gods and heroes in Valhalla are lost in flame.

Many questions arise from Wagner's complex plot. What happens in the end to Alberich? Why are the gods finally doomed along with Siegfried, when the ring is once again safe in the possession of the Rhinemaidens? The story is a fable of love and power, but the point of the fable remains an enigma. It has been interpreted as a critique of industrialisation in modern society and, conversely, as an idealisation of heroic force and individual energy.

Whatever Wagner's intention with the 'The Ring of the Nibelung', its vast world has influenced all later attempts to portray apocalyptic themes in music, literature, art and cinema. The most familiar being perhaps Francis Ford Coppola's *Apocalypse Now*, in which the 'Ride of the Valkyries' is blasted from helicopter-mounted speakers as US troops perform a bombing raid on a Vietnamese village.

ROBERT LOUIS STEVENSON

TREASURE ISLAND (1883)

One of the world's most enduring adventure stories, it is an engrossing and timeless tale of pirates, mutiny, buried treasure and 'x marks the spot'.

Stevenson's story was serialised in *Young Folks* magazine in 1881, credited to 'Captain George North'. It was first published in book form by Cassell and Company, Ltd, in 1883, without the pseudonym (see above for the first US edition, published by Roberts Brothers in 1884).

The original manuscript, like those of many of Stevenson's novels, is lost – his papers are famously scattered, having been auctioned by his family during World War I.

Opposite: Stevenson's treasure map resembles, according to the author, 'a fat dragon standing up'.

Take a poll of the greatest adventure stories ever written and the odds are that this rattling pirate tale will appear very high on the list. Robert Louis Stevenson (1850–94) – 'Louis', as friends and family called him – was no longer a young man when he finally wrote what in later life he proclaimed to be 'my first book'. Stevenson and his new wife, Fanny, had returned from California to Louis' native Edinburgh for the summer of 1880. Fanny, previously married, brought to the marriage an eleven-year-old son, Lloyd. Back in his hometown Louis was reunited with an old comrade, W. E. Henley. The two men had earlier met in a hospital where Louis was being treated for his weak lungs and Henley had just had a leg amputated. Henley is today remembered for his poem *Invictus*, with its rousing final lines: 'I am the master of my fate/I am the captain of my soul.' The character he inspired, however, has long been accepted into the collective memory.

As Stevenson admitted to Henley, after the publication of *Treasure Island*: 'It was the sight of your maimed strength and masterfulness that begot [the novel's central villain] Long John Silver ... the idea of the maimed man, ruling and dreaded by the sound, was entirely taken from you.' Wooden legs were more usually associated in the nineteenth century, not with poets, but with sea-going men. At sea, if your leg was injured, in battle or even accidentally, immediate amputation was the surest remedy. Ships had no hospital facilities and cutting the damaged limb off at once and cauterising the wound in boiling tar was the only protection against gangrene. Often the ship's cook performed the operation using kitchen knives. A piece of timber was strapped on after the wound had healed. If a hand was lost, one of the meat hooks in the ship's galley would serve as a replacement. (Captain Hook in *Peter Pan*, 1911, was directly inspired, as J. M. Barrie acknowledged, by Long John Silver.)

Doctors pronounced Edinburgh – known as 'auld reekie' because of its smog-filled air – hazardous for Stevenson's health. Fanny and Louis did not have the funds to wander far and rented a cottage in Braemar in the Highlands. The weather was 'absolutely and consistently vile' and the family was confined

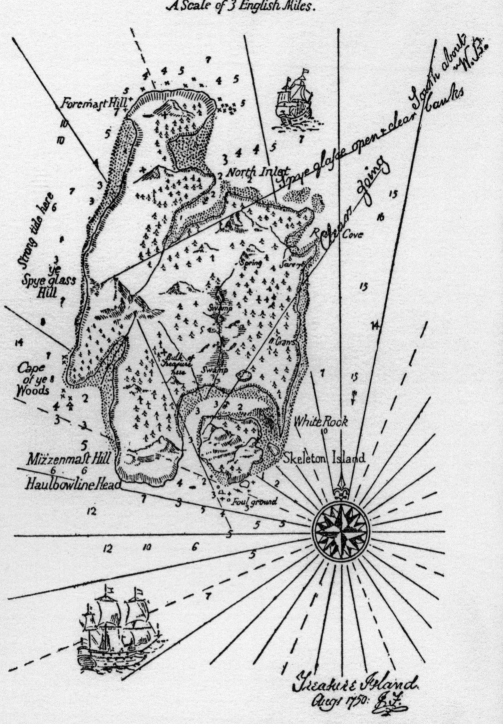

A Scale of 3 English Miles.

Treasure Island. Augt 1750

Given by above J.F. & M^r W Bones Maste of y^e Walrus Savannah this twenty July 1754 W. B.

Facsimile of Chart; latitude and longitude struck out by J. Hawkins

'"One more step, Mr Hands," said I, "and I'll blow your brains out! Dead men don't bite, you know," I added with a chuckle.' Jim wrangles in the rigging with the pirate Israel Hands.

to the house. One day, in an effort to entertain Lloyd, Stevenson painted a map of an island.

it was elaborately and (I thought) beautifully coloured; the shape of it took my fancy beyond expression; it contained harbours that pleased me like sonnets … as I paused on my map of 'Treasure Island', the future character of the book began to appear there visibly among imaginary woods … The next thing I knew I had some papers before me and was writing out a list of chapters.

The tale sprang from Stevenson's pen at the rate of a chapter every morning. Other more serious writing chores were suspended. At this stage it was entirely a domestic enterprise. Luckily, for literature and for Stevenson's career, a visitor, Dr Alexander Hay Japp, was invited to listen to the ongoing tale. One should imagine Stevenson's thrilling, Scots-accented voice as the first paragraph was read out:

I remember him as if it were yesterday, as he came plodding to the inn door, his sea-chest following behind him in a hand-barrow – a tall, strong, heavy, nut-brown man, his tarry pigtail falling over the shoulder of his soiled blue coat, his hands ragged and scarred, with black, broken nails, and the sabre cut across one cheek, a dirty, livid white.

As luck would have it, Japp was closely connected with the editor of the popular weekly comic, *Young Folks*. Based in London, the editor-proprietor was James Henderson, a fellow Scot. Why not, Japp suggested, publish the tale in *Young Folks*? It would make a welcome handful of 'jingling guineas' for the author (who was, as it happened, in dire need of funds).

Stevenson completed the history of Jim Hawkins and *Treasure Island* was duly serialised, earning its author a little under £50, and Stevenson went on to make a small fortune from subsequent reprints. *Treasure Island* also heralded the arrival of a major new talent in British fiction. The story that had begun as a domestic entertainment, recited by the fireside to while away tedious days and nights, became a classic. One cannot imagine English fiction without it.

Astonishingly, given its later popularity, *Treasure Island* was not a great success in *Young Folks*. Arguably Stevenson's story was too complex, psychologically, for the paper's juvenile readership. And perhaps, more significantly, *Treasure Island* was rather too disturbing for young readers. The murder of Tom Redruth, for example, goes well beyond the routinely spilled gore relished by Victorian children. Silver has failed to recruit the Squire's loyal man to the mutineers' cause. It is Tom's death sentence. On witnessing the brutal homicide, described gruesomely, Jim faints. And the reader, whether adult or child, also finds it hard to restrain a shudder – not least at the thought of Silver surviving, unpunished for this callous crime and rewarded with ill-gotten gold, to crack further spines that may happen to raise his ire. Whatever happened to the poetic justice that is the stock in trade of children's fiction?

Treasure Island is a richly complex work of imagination. And where did the novel's imagined world begin? With a wooden leg, bad weather and the chance visit of a stranger.

It was Silver's voice, and before I had heard a dozen words, I would not have shown myself for all the world. I lay there, trembling and listening, in the extreme of fear and curiosity, for, in those dozen words, I understood that the lives of all the honest men aboard depended on me alone.

'Down went Pew with a cry that rang high into the night.' The pirate Blind Pew is run down by tax collectors on horseback.

'A SQUARE' (EDWIN A. ABBOTT)

FLATLAND: A ROMANCE OF MANY DIMENSIONS (1884)

This short classic of science fiction describes the mathematical journeys of A Square through the varied dimensions of Spaceland, Lineland and Pointland.

First published by Seeley and Co. in 1884.

Abbott was best known in his own lifetime as an educator and theological and linguistic scholar; he authored a number of textbooks, theological treatises and even a biography of the philosopher Francis Bacon.

The story was adapted into an animated film in 2007, with the voices of Martin Sheen and Kristen Bell.

Mathematicians write interesting novels (such as Lewis Carroll's *Alice's Adventures in Wonderland*, 1865, for example, page 82). *Flatland's* author, Edwin A. Abbott (1838–1926), was a schoolteacher, a philologist, a theologian and the possessor of one of the more playfully inquiring minds of his incurably inquiring age. In *Flatland*, he produced the prototype of the allegorical science-fiction story.

The novel – if it can be called such (it reads, at times, like an extended intellectual joke) – imagines a two-dimensional (that is, flat) universe. The narrator is 'A Square', a geometric everyman. The narrative takes the form of an extended meditation on life and social mores in his single-plane universe, and sets out the fate of those who question or transgress its boundaries. Addressing his readers privileged to live in 'space', Square explains:

> Imagine a sheet of paper on which straight Lines, Triangles, Squares, Pentagons, Hexagons and other figures, instead of remaining fixed in their places, move freely about, on or in the surface, but without the power of rising above or sinking below it, very much like shadows – only hard with luminous edges – and you will then have a pretty correct notion of my country and countrymen.

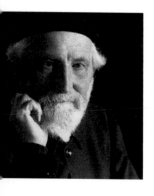

The first half of the book, especially, focuses on the rigid and hierarchical social structure of Flatland, and gives the book its reputation as a satire of Victorian social norms. The class system in Flatland is determined by the number of angles a character possesses, with many-sided polygons constituting a kind of aristocracy and isosceles triangles a working class, while regular quadrilaterals, like the narrator, are solidly middle class. Social mobility is limited and possible only for men (sons acquire additional angles with each generation), while women, who are lines only, are unable to improve their station. In addition, women, who might be mistaken for 'points' when seen head-on, are required to use separate doors and shout aloud when moving around Flatland, in order to avoid accidentally stabbing their countrymen.

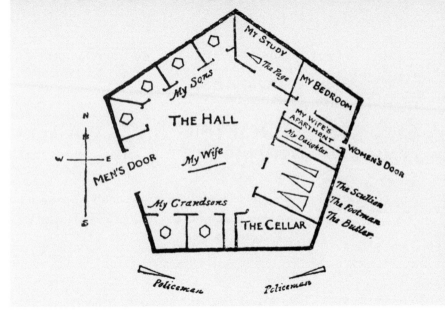

While it might seem anachronistic or heavy-handed to attribute 'feminist' consciousness to Abbott, he does seem to acknowledge his satirical intentions in the preface to a revised edition of the book, arguing that: '(until very recent times) the destinies of Women and of the masses of mankind have seldom been deemed worthy of mention and never of careful consideration.'

In the year 1999, as a new millennium dawns, Square dreams of an even less dimensional world – Lineland – where existence is unilinear (does a line have four sides, like a quadrilateral? It does if you draw it with a pencil, it doesn't in geometry. Let your mind wrestle with that).

Like the hero of H. G. Wells' story 'The Country of the Blind' (1904), Square is unable to persuade the king of Lineland that there may be worlds other than that over which he is sovereign. Mathematicians, of course, are used to people not understanding what they are talking about. Square is himself bewildered by a spherical visitor from three-dimensional Spaceland (that is, our world). Are there yet other worlds with different geometries? Pointland, where all existence is confined to a single dot, is alluded to, but Sphere himself, in his turn, refuses to countenance the possibility of fourth, fifth or higher dimensions beyond his, and our, own (though these are now a commonplace of modern physics and mathematics). Announcing his discoveries to his fellow Flatlanders, Square finds himself imprisoned for heresy. He has, so to speak, stepped over the line. Abbott's tale is dedicated, as he declares, to 'the enlargement of the imagination'. Many readers will find his imagined worlds brain-stretchers, indeed, but none the less entertaining for that.

The first cover featured a map of A. Square's house, with a wider door for the polygon males and a narrow shaft for the female lines.

EDWARD BELLAMY

LOOKING BACKWARD: 2000–1887 (1888)

*The most influential nineteenth-century 'utopia' and a book with
a political vision that inspired a network of 'Bellamy Clubs' and,
ultimately, a political party.*

First published by Ticknor
and Co. in 1888.

By 1900, *Looking Backward*
was the third best-selling
book of all time in the US,
behind *Uncle Tom's Cabin*
(1852) and *Ben-Hur: A Tale of
the Christ* (1880).

Bellamy's 'sleep and time
travel' idea was picked up by
fellow socialist H. G. Wells in
The Sleeper Awakes (1910).
Wells added the ingenious
wrinkle that, after sleeping
for one hundred years, the
sleeper awakes to discover
his savings account has
swelled to make him the
richest man in the world.

In Edward Bellamy's (1850–98) story, Julian West, a well-bred Bostonian, is
a blessed man. He has great wealth, high intellect, and, in Edith Bartlett, a
beautiful fiancée. There are two flies in Julian's ointment. One is his vague
unease regarding the huge, unfair divisions between rich and poor in 1887.
The other is an 'insomnia', worse even than Macbeth's. Julian is a happy man,
yes, but a worried man.

Street noise is particularly troublesome to Julian. He constructs a secret,
soundproof room under his house, known only to his servant, where, after
being mesmerised by a friend (in the 1880s, 'mesmerisation', or hypno-
sis, was all the rage,) Julian hopes to fall into a deep slumber. It is not to be.
So successful is the mesmerisation that Julian wakes on September 10, 2000
– 113 years into the future. He discovers that a fire destroyed his house soon
after he fell asleep and killed the servant who alone knew his master's location. No one could discover what had happened to Julian West and, after all
this time, no one cares.

Bellamy was very excited about what he called 'the rate of change' in his
world, and appended a postscript on the subject to his fable. His vision of the
future was, however, rather too accelerated; *Looking Backward*'s 'Year 2000' is
very different from that we actually experienced (the fate of many utopias –
was 1984 at all like Orwell's *Nineteen Eighty-Four*?)

Bellamy's 2000 is literally 'millennial', the perfect world at the end of time.
Julian discovers a perfect society, which has solved the problems of industrialisation by abolishing laissez-faire capitalism in favour of socialism (though
Bellamy was careful to avoid this word, freighted with negative associations for his readership). Wealth is equally distributed and private property
abolished. Everyone receives a college education and lifelong care from a
benevolent state. Work is light and rewarding and the retirement age is forty-five – life expectancy is now much higher and social ills including crime,
corruption and poverty have vanished.

Unable to return to his 'present', Julian falls in love with Edith Leete,
the great-granddaughter of his first and former love, Edith Bartlett, and

Vol. 2.   DECEMBER, 1889.   No. 1.

"THE NATIONALIZATION OF INDUSTRY AND THE PROMOTION OF THE BROTHERHOOD OF HUMANITY."—*Constitution of the Nationalist Club, Boston, Mass.*

THE
NATIONALIST

THIS EDITION . . . 35,000.

FRONTISPIECE, Pen and Ink Portrait of   .   .   EDWARD BELLAMY.

Looking Forward	*Edward Bellamy*
Now is the Time to Begin (Verse) . . .	*Frank J. Bonnelle*
The Why and Wherefore . . .	*Mrs. Abby Morton Diaz*
To Wendell Phillips (Verse)	*Henry Austin*
Politics and the People . . .	*Thaddeus B. Wakeman*
My Masterpiece (Verse)	*Arthur Macy*
A Solution of the Liquor Problem . . .	*George W. Evans*
The Poetry of Evil	*W. G. Todd*
Our Block—A Coöperative Possibility . .	*George F. Duysters*
The Key Thereof (Verse) . . .	*Mrs. Alys Hamilton Harding*
A Plan of Action	*Burnette G. Haskell*
Editorial Notes	
Remarks on Removal . . .	*John Ransom Bridge*
A Retrospect	*Cyrus F. Willard*
Goldwin Smith's "False Hopes" . . .	*Dr. William L. Faxon*

PUBLISHED BY

THE NATIONALIST EDUCATIONAL ASSOCIATION,

No. 77 BOYLSTON STREET, BOSTON, MASS.

Copyright, 1889, by Nationalist Educational Association. Entered at the Boston Post-Office as second-class matter

PRICE $1.00 A YEAR.   SINGLE NUMBERS 10 CENTS.

Bellamy ends the story with the following uplifting declaration:

> All thoughtful men agree that the present aspect of society is portentous of great changes. The only question is, whether they will be for the better or the worse. Those who believe in man's essential nobleness lean to the former view, those who believe in his essential baseness to the latter. For my part, I hold to the former opinion. *Looking Backward* was written in the belief that the Golden Age lies before us and not behind us, and is not far away.

Cover for *The Nationalist,* an American socialist magazine established by followers of Bellamy's utopian ideas, from December 1889.

Bellamy's book itself had a fairly immediate impact, becoming a national bestseller in the year after its initial release. It has stayed in print continually since first publication and spawned a huge number of sequels, as well as literary 'responses' (not consistently positive), including William Morris' utopian *News From Nowhere* (1890). In the immediate aftermath of its release, hundreds of 'Nationalist' (or 'Bellamy') clubs sprang up across the US – forums in which the novel's ideas, and their potential for realisation, were earnestly discussed. Bellamy joined the increasingly politicised movement in the early 1890s and even ran his own, short-lived magazine, *The New Nation* (previously *The Nationalist*), to disseminate the group's ideas. Financial difficulties and the increasing popularity of the People's Party (which itself later merged with the Democratic party) saw the Nationalist movement wane in the mid-1890s, but Bellamy's book – which he had, at one point, described as a 'literary fantasy, a fairy tale' – had already made its mark.

A CONNECTICUT YANKEE IN KING ARTHUR'S COURT (1889)

This satirical story imagines a very different Camelot as nineteenth-century American citizen Hank Morgan is transported to medieval England following a blow to the head.

Originally titled *A Yankee in King Arthur's Court*, the book was first published by Charles L. Webster and Co. in 1889.

Twain was inspired to write *A Connecticut Yankee* after acquiring a copy of Thomas Malory's tale of chivalrous knights *Le Morte d'Arthur* (1485, page 44).

'I am not an American. I am *the* American', is a pronouncement often mis-attributed to celebrated writer and humorist Mark Twain (he was, in fact, quoting his friend Frank Fuller), and it is easy to see why, since, among American writers, he has the firmest grasp of the national voice. But what, this most American of American writers wondered, was it to be American?

The core question, as Twain saw it, was the new country's (America) relationship with the old country (England). There was conflict as well as inheritance in the American mix. It was this contradiction that Twain set his imagination to probe in his major work of fiction, *A Connecticut Yankee in King Arthur's Court* (1889).

As the nineteenth century drew to a close, a number of writers became fascinated by the idea of time travel as a fictional device, but most, such as H. G. Wells, were happier with travel into the future than into the past. After all, if you alter the past, how can you preserve the present you have just left? Twain rode roughshod over the possible paradoxes. *A Connecticut Yankee* opens with Twain meeting a stranger who has an amazing tale to tell. Hank Morgan has returned from Camelot – King Arthur's court. This was the place where the ideals of British nobility, gentlemanliness and chivalry had been formed. It was the starting point of English civilisation.

Hank is bashed on the head with a crowbar and finds himself trans-ported from 1879 Hartford, Connecticut, to a field just outside Camelot, England, in 528. Our hero's first reaction, on being told by a passer-by where he has landed, is despair: 'I felt a mournful sinking at the heart, and muttered: "I shall never see my friends again – never, never again. They will not be born for more than thirteen hundred years yet".' Despair gives way to terror when a passing knight picks on him for a bit of lance practice.

Hank is a true American, however. He introduces himself and takes a tour of that England and is both amused and disgusted by what he sees. Merlin turns out to be fake – no more skilful than a third-rate circus magician – and England is riddled with a corrupt class system. To a freeborn Connecticut Yankee it is confusing and horrifying. Hank takes charge. What the sixth

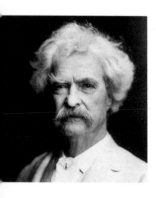

century needs, he perceives, is some good old (that's to say 'new') American know-how. Technology, industry, factories, steam power, telephones, bicycles, guns. In no time at all, wheels have replaced hooves. In no time at all he is the most important man in the country, more important indeed than the king. He assumes a title – Sir Boss.

How should we read this world? Twain's American contemporaries saw the tale as a wholly patriotic fable – its satire on the filth, servitude and superstition of 'old England'

An illustration from the first edition by Daniel Carter Beard, showing Sir Launcelot riding a penny farthing.

made their new country shine all the brighter. Twain himself seems partly to have supported this view. But, like all great works of imagination, *A Connecticut Yankee* can be read more than one way. The tale does not fit Twain's own too-neat description of a moral lesson benevolently given by an American teacher to the English people. Hank represents progress – but it is the progress of blood, iron and mass murder. In his passages of Gatling guns spitting death at the unarmed opponents, Twain is surely thinking of the American Civil War. Extraordinarily, with that strange foresight that great artists have, Twain seems to have been vouchsafed a vision of the carnage to come in 1914. It's terrible – but funny too – and very Twain.

H. G. WELLS

THE TIME MACHINE (1895)

*Popularising the concept of machinery as a means of time travel, Wells'
enduring fantasy depicts a distant future populated by frail, simple
humanoids and dark, twisted cannibals.*

First published in 1895 in
serial form in *The New
Review*. The eleventh
chapter, which appeared
in the serial, was cut from
the novel, published later
the same year by William
Heinemann.

Wells wrote several other
important works of science
fiction, including *The Island
of Doctor Moreau* (1896),
The Invisible Man (1897) and
The War of the Worlds (1897).

Opposite: Poster advertising
the 1960 MGM film
adaptation, produced and
directed by George Pal.

Who is the Shakespeare of imaginative fiction? For many it's a debate between
H. G. Wells and Jules Verne. Yet the hallmark Vernian and Wellsian narratives are different. The Frenchman's specialism was the *voyage imaginaire*
– spectacular tourism into the unexplored – conducting his travellers 20,000
leagues under the sea (see page 88), to the centre of and around Earth (in a
timetable-defying eighty days), and even to the moon. Wells' preferred style
was what he called 'scientific romances' – works of the imagination plausi-
bly anchored in the most recent discoveries of science. Imagination, for Wells,
went hand in hand with authentication, and his eye for the fictional possibilities in scientific advancements was uncanny. *The Invisible Man* was produced
barely months after Wilhelm Roentgen demonstrated the power of the X-ray
to see through flesh, *The War of the Worlds* took off from W. H. Pickering's
observations of suspiciously active 'canals' on the surface of Mars, and *The
War in the Air* followed two years after the Wright Brothers' first successful
flight at Kitty Hawk.

Where did this brilliantly imaginative populariser of the latest science
come from? H. G. Wells sprang from a generation and class liberated from
traditional servitudes by the 1870 Universal Education Act. His father was a
professional cricketer who, after injury, turned small – and unsuccessful –
shopkeeper. The family broke up when Wells was thirteen, and his mother
went to work in a large country house, where he was allowed the run of the
library. On leaving school, the young Wells served an apprenticeship in a
draper's 'emporium', which he loathed (the experience is immortalised in his
comedy *Kipps*).

Sharp as a tack, at eighteen he won a government scholarship to
the Normal School of Science where he was heavily influenced by
T. H. Huxley, the evolutionary advocate known as 'Darwin's Bulldog'.
The Origin of Species (published seven years before Wells was born)
became the young author's bible, and his belief in its infallibility would
be unshaken until his death. Huxley had introduced into the creed
the notion of 'survival of the fittest' – something ensured by eternal

struggle within and between the species. It, too, became an article of faith for the young man.

The Time Machine was Wells' first published scientific romance, and was more *voyage imaginaire* than even Verne could have devised. He wrote the story in the chance of finding a market for it. Completed at a low point in his early life, Wells remembers – in *Experiment in Autobiography* – working on it late one summer night by an open window in a meagre lodgings in Kent, England, while a disagreeable landlady grumbled at him in the darkness outside because of the excessive use of her lamp.

The Time Machine opens with a vivid paragraph, designed to hook the casually skimming reader of the magazine *The New Review* in which it was first serialised:

> The Time Traveller (for so it will be convenient to speak of him) was expounding a recondite matter to us. His grey eyes shone and twinkled, and his usually pale face was flushed and animated. The fire burned brightly, and the soft radiance of the incandescent lights in the lilies of silver caught the bubbles that flashed and passed in our glasses.

In 'The Chronic Argonauts' the traveller was given a name: Dr Nebogipfel (it translates from German as 'foggy mountain peak'). In this later incantation, rendering the traveller and his audience anonymous at their regular Thursday evening gatherings was a fine touch. His identity must, of course, be kept secret to preserve the secrecy of the time machine.

To his friends (an all-male company, of course) the traveller explains two things. First, the nature of the fourth dimension; second, the fact that he has invented a time machine to navigate it. His audience is gathered to witness his first experimental voyage, from which he will return the following Thursday. He duly returns and reports on his three journeys into the future.

The first is to the year 802,701. He discovers that evolution has gone into reverse – human kind has devolved into two contrary species: the effete Eloi, who spend their lives in a kind of Garden of Eden, doing nothing but play; and the cannibalistic Morlocks, slaving in a subterranean factory world, emerging only at night, to feast on their captors.

The Eloi live their pretty and pointless lives under a gigantic decayed Sphinx, recalling Shelley's sonnet 'Ozymandias' and the fall of civilisation. The Eloi are themselves versions of the late-nineteenth-century decadents, notably Oscar Wilde and his followers. After battling the Morlocks the traveller makes two further trips forward, witnessing the heat-death of the solar system in the sun's dying days, with nothing living in it but fungus and sinister crablike things. With this, he takes off again, never to return.

Time travel had been a favourite motif of imaginative literature long before Wells' chronic fantasies. The weak point in the scenario, however, was how you actually got into the future, or the past. A popular technique was that of Bunyan, in *The Pilgrim's Progress*:

> As I walk'd through the wilderness of this world, I lighted on a certain place where was a Den, and I laid me down in that place to sleep; and as I slept, I dreamed a Dream.

Two imaginative works that influenced *The Time Machine* use this device: Edward Bellamy's *Looking Backward* (1889, page 106) and William Morris' *News from Nowhere* (1890). Both have protagonists who fall asleep and, like Washington Irving's Rip van Winkle, mysteriously wake up in the far future. But is it the real future, or a dream future? Morris and Bellamy were proto-socialists, and congenial to young Wells, but there was something fundamentally lame in the dream-vision gimmick. While another early title for his story was 'The Time Traveller', Wells finally settled on *The Time Machine* – for him, the mechanics of the story were all-important.

But what, precisely, is the machine? Wells does not give a detailed description, other than it has a saddle and a triangular frame, and some mysterious crystals propelling it. Clearly, it is a version of the bicycle – the machine that liberated the late-Victorian slaving masses, cooped up in the urban centres of late industrial England (the next novel Wells wrote, *The Wheels of Chance* [1896] was on just this theme.) A bicycle capable of whizzing along the fourth dimension is implausible. But Wells' bejewelled roadster makes the point that, if we ever do cross the time-barrier, technology will get us there.

One direct inspiration for *The Time Machine* was an article by Simon Newcomb published in *Nature* in 1894, which the traveller mentions in his initial exposition to his friends. Newcomb, one of the country's leading mathematicians, argued that, 'as a perfectly legitimate exercise of thought' we should admit the possibility of objects existing in a fourth dimension – time. Wells undertook just such an exercise.

The other scientific validation of his story for Wells was a lecture by his mentor T. H. Huxley in 1894, who made the supremely pessimistic point that, 'our globe has been in a state of fusion, and, like the sun, is gradually cooling down … the time will come when evolution will mean an adaptation to universal winter, and all forms of life will die out … if for millions of years our globe has taken the upward road, yet some time the summit will be reached and the downward road will be commenced.' Mathematical speculation and cosmic gloom aside, *The Time Machine* is a fun adventure and reads as freshly today as it did in 1895.

Class conflict was another topic. Was society in the 1890s polarising rather than coming together? Would the working class, like the Morlocks – the exploited 'many' as Shelley called them – revenge themselves at some point in the future on the privileged 'few'? How should a socialist deal with that? Was there a solution? (The formation of the Independent Labour Party, a couple of years before was one; and one of which Wells approved.)

However, one of the problems of scientific romance is that the basic science can be demonstrably wrong. Wells' fellow novelist Israel Zangwill pointed out that the traveller, hurtling forward through time, would pass the date of his own death. Moreover, over the millennia, the steel frame of the time machine would rust. All that would arrive in 802,701 would be some bones, metal fragments and a few dulled crystals.

The science, which seemed plausible in 1895, is now not so. Humankind currently lives in an interglacial period, between ice ages. In ten thousand years or so, the elliptical orbit of the earth will bring with it another ice age – Wells saw a continuous climatic line from 1895 to 802,701, with no intervening ice ages. Nor will the sun gradually cool, as Huxley predicted, like some gigantic radiator. When its nuclear fuel is used up, it will explode into a vast fireball, not ending cosmically frozen, but fried.

Wells also avoids the biggest paradox of all. The time machine has a reverse gear. What if the traveller went into the past, met himself – or his ancestors – and changed both his and the planet's future history? Over the seven years he wrote his story, Wells toyed with a trip to the past, and actually drafted a chapter in which his traveller returns to the Pleistocene period. In the end, he decided to keep his story simple. Simple, and wonderfully imaginative, the novel has never been out of print since its first publication in 1895, and who knows, it may still be in print – and enjoyed – in 802,701.

Rod Taylor in the 1960 film
adaptation directed by
George Pal.

L. FRANK BAUM

THE WONDERFUL WIZARD OF OZ (1900)

Named 'America's greatest and best-loved home-grown fairy tale' by the Library of Congress, the ageless morality tale of Dorothy, Toto, the Scarecrow, the Tin Woodman and the Cowardly Lion continues to captivate readers young and old.

First published by George M. Hill Company in 1900.

Baum recalled taking the name for his magical kingdom from a filing cabinet in which his papers 'O–Z' were stored.

On finishing the work, Baum knew instinctively that he had created something remarkable. After writing the last page he had his pencil framed and placed over his desk under the inscription: 'With this pencil I wrote the manuscript of "The Emerald City".'

Opposite: Dorothy meets the Cowardly Lion, drawn for the first edition by W. W. Denslow.

L. Frank Baum (1856–1919; the L. stands for Lyman) was born in New York State, the son of a merchant enriched by the oil business. Baum went into journalism and published his first book for children in 1897. Thereafter, writing for the children's market was his principal activity and, in 1900, together with the illustrator W. W. Denslow (1856–1915), he produced *The Wonderful Wizard of Oz* (first entitled 'The Emerald City'). Baum later span off a series of 'Oz' sequels and was one of the first generation of American writers to adapt his work for the screen, moving himself and his family to Hollywood to do so.

Now more people have seen *The Wizard of Oz* than have read it. MGM's epoch-making film of 1939 (the eighth movie to be based on the story), however, is fairly faithful to what Baum wrote and Denslow pictured. The book was conceived and published during one of the recurrent depressions in American commercial life, and one of the points that Baum makes in his 1900 preface is that his story is 'modernised' – set in the uncomfortable present. This realism at the heart of the fantasy is something that makes it an innovative 'fairy story'.

The narrative opens on an impoverished farm, in a bleak landscape of the 'great Kansas prairies'. An orphan, Dorothy is cared for by her Uncle Henry and Auntie Em. The description of Dorothy's home is of a humble, dusty place, setting up a stark comparison to the glittering world she is to discover.

And sure enough, a cyclone does come. It carries away the rackety old house, Dorothy and her faithful dog Toto inside, transporting it to the land of the dwarfish Munchkins in the republic of Oz. From there Dorothy and Toto set off along the yellow brick road for the Emerald City, where, she understands, she will find a wizard who can help her get home to Kansas. On the way she meets up with her famous three companions: a Scarecrow, a Tin-Woodman and a (Cowardly) Lion.

After various adventures along the way, the quartet arrives at the magnificent city and is ushered into the chamber of the Great Wizard. Quickly though, they discover the him to be a fraud and a 'humbug', fed up with his

"You ought to be ashamed of yourself!"

Dorothy, the Tin Woodman,
the Scarecrow and the
Cowardly Lion make their
approach to the Emerald
City in MGM's legendary
1939 film.

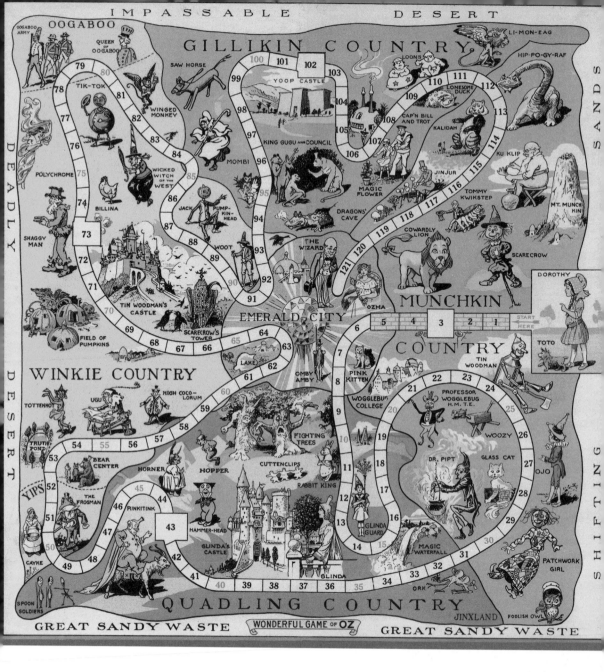

'That proves you are unusual', returned the Scarecrow; 'and I am convinced that the only people worthy of consideration in this world are the unusual ones. For the common folks are like the leaves of a tree, and live and die unnoticed'.

pretences and dreaming of his previous life as a circus clown. The Emerald City, too, is nothing but an illusion produced by the green spectacles worn by everyone who visits. The moral is clear. Help yourself – the traditional American remedy of self-improvement, which Dorothy and her companions eventually manage with some aid from the Good Witch of the South. And too, by her own efforts, Dorothy gets back to Kansas, realising that however poor it is, she loves her humble home.

Over the last half-century, in which *The Wonderful Wizard of Oz* has become one of the best-known fairy stories in the world, scholars have got to work on it. No longer it is a text for children of all ages, but evidence for the inquisitive social scientist and historian. Baum, as has been said, was writing a period of severe economic depression and he had been very impressed, in 1894, by a hunger march on the White House by 'Coxey's Army', named after the political organiser, Jacob Coxey. The unemployed, in their hundreds and sometimes thousands, marched across America to the capital. Eventually their demonstration was broken up in Washington and the leaders arrested on charges of 'trespassing on the White House lawn'.

As such, some have interpreted the phony Wizard of Oz as representing the all-talk-and-no-action President of America, William McKinley. And, on their epic march up the yellow brick road (taken to be an allusion to the gold standard, which Coxey and other populists wanted to get rid of) Dorothy, the farm girl, represents the decent working classes; the Scarecrow represents the rural poor; and the Tin Man represents the toiling masses in the factories. The Lion is harder to fit in, although various 'cowardly' leaders of the people have been proposed.

It's intriguing stuff – but not, in the end, particularly nourishing. While many things can be read into this much-loved tale of the real and unreal, the dream and nightmare, in the end they are incidental – although they do add to the charm of this perennially fascinating work of imagination.

Opposite: 'The Wonderful Game of Oz', a spin-off board game featuring all the lands and characters, which was manufactured by Parker Brothers in 1921.

3 GOLDEN AGE OF FANTASY

The early twentieth century saw a wealth of imaginary realms, from pulp space fantasies to chilling visions of a dystopian future, while the unprecedented violence of the World Wars was to alter fiction forever.

'The fairies have their tiffs with the birds.'
Illustration by Arthur Rackham from *Peter Pan in Kensington Gardens* (1910), see page 124.

PETER PAN IN KENSINGTON GARDENS (1906)

A London park becomes an after-dark wonderland, the realm of fairies, talking birds, walking trees and a little boy who can never grow up.

First published by Hodder and Stoughton in 1906.

Kensington Gardens were once the private gardens of Kensington Palace, but are today combined with Hyde Park as one of the Royal Parks of London.

J. M. Barrie wrote a number of works featuring Peter Pan: *The Little White Bird* (1902), *Peter Pan, or The Boy Who Wouldn't Grow Up* (a play from 1904), *When Wendy Grew Up* (a short play from 1908), and *Peter and Wendy* (1911), which was reprinted as *Peter Pan and Wendy*, and now usually published as simply *Peter Pan*.

Not all great stories arrive fully formed – it is in the nature of the legendary to accrue incident and resonance as time passes. So it is with Peter Pan, and the first book to bear the name of the boy who never grows up does not tell the story twenty-first century readers might expect. There is no Wendy, Neverland, Captain Hook, no pirates, crocodile, Lost Boys or Tinker Bell. There are fairies, for *Peter Pan in Kensington Gardens* is in essence a fairy story, one that turns a region of London into an after-hours wonderland.

Peter Pan in Kensington Gardens was published in 1906, by which time the character of Peter Pan was famous, being at the heart of J. M. Barrie's (1860–1937) box-office record-setting 1904 play *Peter Pan, or The Boy Who Wouldn't Grow Up*. It was through the play that the story of Peter Pan developed its most familiar form. It was there that Hook, Wendy and the rest were introduced. So then, when two years later *Peter Pan in Kensington Gardens* was published, readers might have expected a version of the play in novel form, or perhaps a sequel to the play. Instead, it was something akin to what would now be called an 'origin story'. The book was not even newly written, but had first appeared as Chapters 13–18 of Barrie's 1902 novel, *The Little White Bird*. A book extracted from a book, *Peter Pan in Kensington Gardens* is more a thematically linked series of stories and incidents than a novel.

The Little White Bird was written for adults. It is set mostly in turn-of-the-century London, around Kensington Gardens (the first US edition was published with an additional subtitle – *or Adventures in Kensington Gardens*), and is narrated by a middle-aged, ex-army officer, Captain W__. The book tells the story of the captain's friendship with six-year-old David and how the Captain brought the boy's parents together. In a touch that now seems pre-postmodern, Captain W__ refers to his own writing of the text, at the end finishing the manuscript and giving the book to David's mother.

Peter Pan in Kensington Gardens begins with a Grand Tour of the Gardens, and while this does what it promises, introducing the famous landmarks – the Broad Walk, the Round Pond, the Serpentine – by the second paragraph the text has taken already taken to whimsy. A lady sits by one of

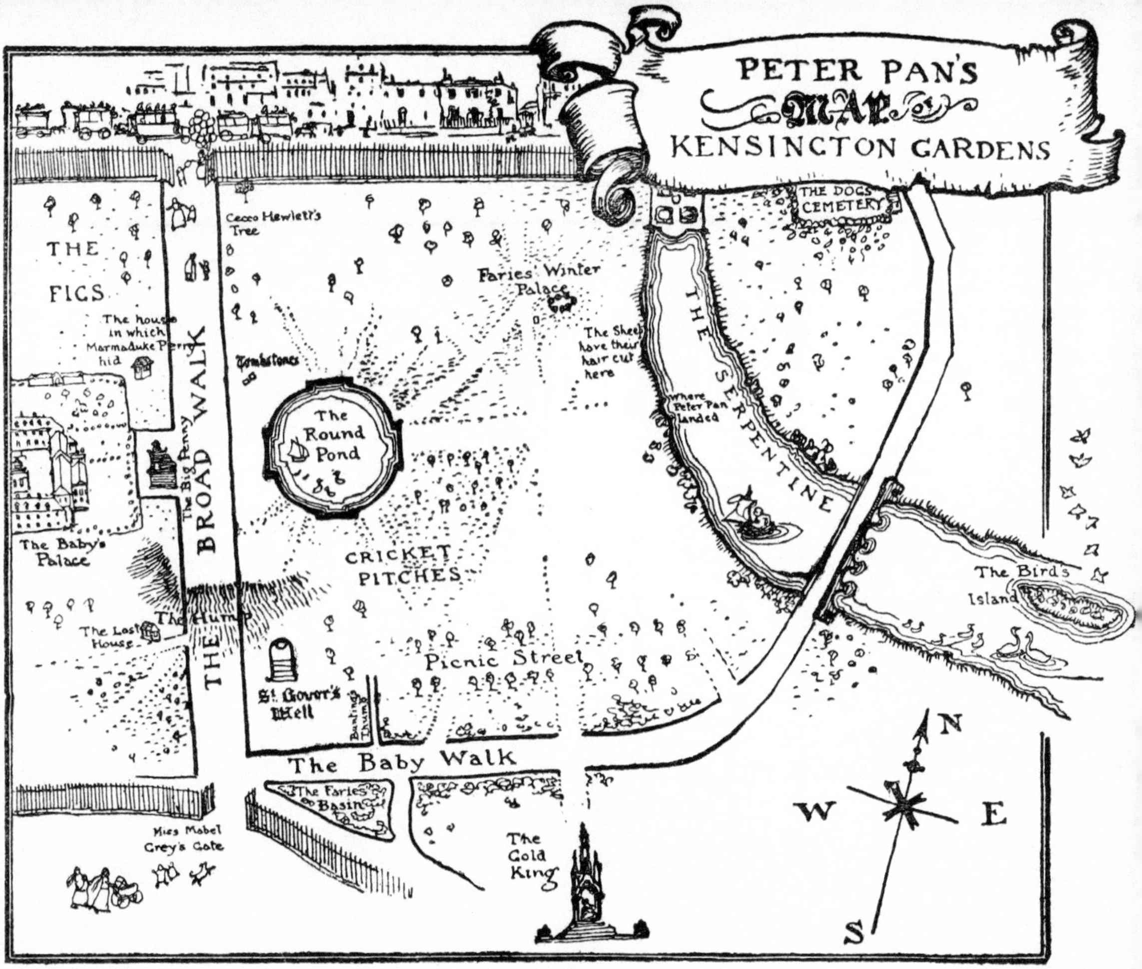
PETER PAN'S
MAP of
KENSINGTON GARDENS
THE DOGS CEMETERY
Cecco Hewlett's Tree
THE FIGS
The house in which Marmaduke Perry hid
Faries' Winter Palace
The Sheep have their hair cut here
Tombstones
THE SERPENTINE
Where Peter Pan landed
The Round Pond
THE BROAD WALK
The Big Penny
The Baby's Palace
CRICKET PITCHES
The Bird's Island
The Lost House
The Hump
Picnic Street
St. Govor's Well
The Baby Walk
The Faries' Basin
Miss Mabel Grey's Gate
The Gold King
N
W
E
S

A map from *Peter Pan in Kensington Gardens* by the illustrator of the original edition, Arthur Rackham.

the garden's gates selling balloons. She must hold on to the railings always, for if she lets go 'the balloons would lift her up, and she would be flown away'. So far in this very middle-class world in which nurses and nannies take babies for 'an airing in a perambulator', and where older children sail stick boats, she has held her position more successfully than her predecessor.

Strangely, even in the 1902 text, when Peter Pan is first mentioned, it is as if the reader already knows who he is. Writing about the notion that at night drowned stars appear in the Serpentine, Barrie first mentions his hero with the words: 'If so, Peter Pan sees them when he is sailing across the lake'. Before he is properly introduced, it is established that Peter Pan has been famous for generations, that he was as legendary then as he is to us now: 'if you ask your grandmother whether she knew about Peter Pan when she was a girl, she also says "Why, of course I did".'

In Peter's world, before children were babies they were birds, and Peter escapes at seven-days old from becoming fully human by flying out his nursery window and back to Kensington Gardens. He will never be any older, no matter how long he lives. After frightening every fairy he meets, Peter

'Autumn Fairies' by Arthur Rackham, from *Peter Pan in Kensington Gardens*.

consults with the birds, and flies to the island in the Serpentine. There is a touch of Christian allegory – the reason birds can fly and we can't is simply that they have perfect faith, and to have faith is to have wings – which rests oddly with the tale's essentially pantheist heart: Peter is a much-sanitised image of the Greek god Pan.

He sleeps by day on the island but plays by night, not entirely successfully, with whatever he finds in the gardens: a hoop, a pail, a balloon, even a perambulator 'near the entrance to the Fairy Queen's Winter Palace'. Peter comes to know the fairies well, and plays his pipe for their balls and dances. They grant him two wishes, both of which he uses to fly home. The first time he sees his mother sleeping, he almost stays. On the second occasion he resolves to stay, but finds the windows barred, 'his mother sleeping peacefully with her arm around another little boy'.

As much as Peter can never grow up, nor can he ever go home, and so he makes his world with the fairies. We are told that 'there are fairies wherever there are children. Long ago children were forbidden the Gardens, and at that time there was not a fairy in the place'. Barrie makes his fairy society a parody of the everyday world, with every rank from postman to princess represented. And while his fairies are mostly harmless, 'they never do anything useful'.

From ambulatory, sentient trees, which prefigure the Ents of *The Lord of the Rings*, to a fairy world in which love is determined by a doctor's observations of physiological reaction, *Peter Pan in Kensington Gardens* fuses fancy and satire with rich yet restricted imagination. The vision would only become unfettered when Peter took to the stage.

The book ends in darkness, with the warning that it is not safe to stay in Kensington Gardens once the gates are locked for the night. That sometimes children perish of the 'cold and dark' because Peter, riding on his goat, arrives too late to save them. In which case he digs a grave and 'erects a little tombstone'. Peter, not entirely responsible at his tender age, has been too late several times.

Opposite: Bronze statue of Peter Pan, 'the boy who never grew up', in Kensington Gardens, Hyde Park, London. J. M. Barrie commissioned Sir George Frampton to make the statue in 1902, and it was erected in Kensington Gardens in 1912.

ARTHUR CONAN DOYLE

THE LOST WORLD (1912)

Professor Challenger embarks on a suspense-filled search for prehistoric creatures in the wilds of the Amazon, but his troop soon finds itself marooned among dinosaurs and the savage ape-people.

First published by Hodder and Stoughton in 1912.

Doyle was not the first to employ dinosaurs in fiction; writers James De Mille, Jules Lermina and Frank Mackenzie Savile had all published adventure tales featuring the creatures after the first scientific descriptions of the 'megalosaurus', were published in 1824.

Doyle was inspired by the Regent's Park Zoo in London, an offshoot of the nearby Zoological Society that is terrorised by the presentation of the pterodactyl in the book.

By 1912, Arthur Conan Doyle (1859–1930) was a hugely successful author, but he felt hampered by the vast popularity of his great detective, Sherlock Holmes, and wanted to try something new. *The Lost World* is the first, and most enduringly popular, of Doyle's 'Professor Challenger' series in which the popular Victorian author aimed 'to do for the boy's book what Sherlock Holmes did for the detective tale'.

The fantasy draws on the author's own fascination with dinosaurs (iguanodon footprints had been discovered in Crowborough, Sussex, near the author's home in 1909) as well as the contemporary real-life expeditions of archaeologist and explorer Colonel Percival Harrison Fawcett. Doyle was also highly influenced by the prehistoric realms created in Jules Verne's *Journey to the Centre of the Earth* (1864), but with its introduction of the extinct giants, *The Lost World* sets the standard for all future man-meets-monster adventures.

Doyle's narrator is a brash, young journalist, Edward 'Ed' Malone of the *Daily Gazette*. Ed's Scottish editor, McArdle, sends him out to get a story on an eccentric professor who thinks he has discovered a secret valley containing prehistoric monsters. This is none other than Professor Challenger – a man notorious for physically assaulting newspaper reporters.

At a meeting of the Zoological Society, Challenger and his great opponent, the sceptical Professor Summerlee, agree to mount a scientific expedition to the Amazon and the secret valley in its remotest region. They take with them Malone and a professional explorer, the cool-headed Sir John Roxton ('the essence of the English country gentleman, the keen, alert, open-air lover of dogs and of horses'). Malone goes along too, to write the expedition up as a scoop for his paper.

The explorers travel up the great river (an area not well explored at this time) – experiencing adventures all the way – until they discover the 'lost world'. They take photographs of dinosaurs and fight a pitched battle against the 'Ape-men'. On their return home, they present their findings to the Zoological Society, which refuses to believe them, until they present some very compelling evidence:

[He] drew off the top of the case, which formed a sliding lid … An instant later, with a scratching, rattling sound, a most horrible and loathsome creature appeared from below and perched itself upon the side of the case … The face of the creature was like the wildest gargoyle that the imagination of a mad medieval builder could have conceived. It was malicious, horrible, with two small red eyes as bright as points of burning coal. Its long, savage mouth, which was held half-open, was full of a double row of shark-like teeth.

The novel retains some unpleasant descriptions of non-European ethnicity, ideas typical of Doyle's age. However, while some passages of *The Lost World* undeniably stoop to racial stereotypes by today's standards, Doyle was also an active human-rights campaigner in his day, and his book *The Crime of the Congo* (1909) exposed the merciless enforced labour inflicted on indigenous people in the Congo Free State.

Still from *The Lost World* (1925), a silent film directed by Harry O. Hoyt, which featured pioneering stop-motion special effects by Willis O'Brien, animator of the original King Kong. Doyle himself supported the film, and supposedly even used a test reel to convince an audience that dinosaurs were real in 1922.

EDGAR RICE BURROUGHS

At the Earth's Core (1914)

Prehistoric men and beasts are discovered in the subterranean world of 'Pellucidar', buried within Earth's hollow interior in a pulp classic from the creator of Tarzan and John Carter.

At the Earth's Core is the first volume in what was to become a classic pulp science-fiction series from Edgar Rice Burroughs (1875–1950), based on the subterranean world of 'Pellucidar'. Burroughs was born in Chicago in 1875 and, after being discharged from the armed forces on health grounds, took on a number of low-wage jobs throughout the 1900s to support his family. He read numerous pulp-fiction magazines and decided to try his hand at writing. His brand of science-fiction adventure story found success at the *All-Story Magazine* and allowed him to write full time, creating, in 1912, Tarzan of the Apes, the character who would make his fortune. It was his Pellucidar series, however, that pushed the boundaries of the literary imagined realm.

At the Earth's Core sees the series' hero, David Innes, a mine owner, travelling to the Sahara accompanied by Abner Perry, the inventor of a mechanical device – the 'Prospector' – used for boring deep underground. By means of their machine, the young men have discovered that the earth is actually hollow – concentrically within its sphere there is another smaller sphere, or world, called Pellucidar, lodged some five hundred miles beneath the earth's crust. Pellucidar has its own miniature sun, cosmos and geography, which are all elaborated upon in detail in subsequent instalments of the series. The description of the adventurers arrival is typical Burrovian kitsch:

> Together we stepped out to stand in silent contemplation of a landscape at once weird and beautiful. Before us a low and level shore stretched down to a silent sea. As far as the eye could reach the surface of the water was dotted with countless tiny isles – some of towering, barren, granitic rock – others resplendent in gorgeous trappings of tropical vegetation, myriad starred with the magnificent splendour of vivid blooms.

The local population, tyrannised by the all-female avian reptile Mahars who keep Pellucidarian humans for food and slavery, and the romantic involvement between Innes and Dian the Beautiful (who is attempting to escape the hated clutches of Jubal the Ugly) are all covered in this initial

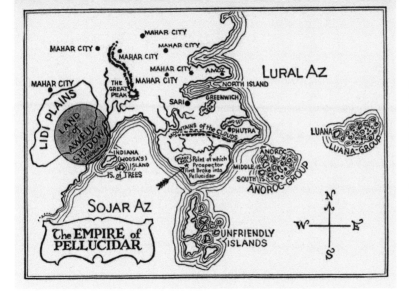

Burroughs' map of the Pellucidar Empire, which accompanied the second story in the series, *Pellucidar* (1915), and plots the many Mahar (all-female avian reptiles) cities as well as the 'Land of Awful Shadow', a region in darkness as a result of a perpetual eclipse.

incarnation, but it is cut off inconclusively. However, in the next in the series, *Pellucidar* (1915), Innes is able to trail a long telegraph wire behind the Prospector through which he relays his subsequent adventures back to the surface of Earth, and Burroughs' millions of readers.

Bizarre as it now seems, the 'hollow Earth' theory was seriously pondered by geologists of the early nineteenth century, and still held the status of folkloric belief when Burroughs was writing. The leading proponent of hollow-Earthism, John Cleves Symmes Jr. (1779–1829) urged the US government to sponsor a voyage of exploration to the centre of the earth via what he fantasised as 'the North Pole Hole' and plant the Stars and Stripes at the earth's core. It would, as modern geology informs us, need to be made of asbestos given the fiery temperatures there.

Novelists, too, had long fantasised about a world under our feet (see Ludvig Holberg's, *The Journey of Niels Klim*, 1741, page 78). Likewise, Jules Verne's *voyage imaginaire*, *A Journey to the Centre of the Earth* (1864), played with the same idea, even before Lytton and Burroughs. It, by contrast, imagined a prehistoric subterranean world, but all of these fables were inspired by the advance of geology (principally for mining) in the nineteenth century – a century fuelled by coal.

The profligacy and popularity of these novels are testimony to our never-ending fascination with what may lie beneath our feet – as wonderful as anything that may one day be found in the stars.

CHARLOTTE PERKINS GILMAN

HERLAND (1915)

Gilman's utopian novel presents an idealised world populated entirely by women, resulting in a society free from war and organised as a gigantic family.

Herland was only first published in book form in 1979 by Pantheon Books (see above).

A sequel to *Herland*, called *With Her in Ourland* (1916) describes Van and Ellador's return to Herland, after Ellador is horrified by what she finds in 'Ourland'.

Gilman was photographed (below) by Frances Benjamin Johnston, a pioneering American female photographer and photojournalist.

The country of Herland, like Arthur Conan Doyle's eponymous Lost World (1912, page 130), which was published three years earlier, is situated on an inaccessible plateau surrounded by jungle. Created by the American writer, editor and feminist activist Charlotte Perkins Gilman (1860–1935), it is a utopia of calm, tolerance and plenty, but its main distinguishing feature is its population. This fantastic land is peopled entirely by women, who reproduce asexually, and have never come into contact with men – that is, until the arrival of three male explorers. By contrasting life in Herland with the descriptions the three men offer of the world they have left behind, Gilman demonstrates the falsity of contemporary male assumptions about the intelligence, competence and, written as it was in 1915 when the campaign for women's rights was at its peak, the political capacity of women. It would be another five years before the 19th Amendment to the US Constitution gave American women the right to vote; in Britain, women over thirty were given the vote in 1918.

The women the explorers meet when they are captured after landing in Herland are 'calm, grave, wise, wholly unafraid, evidently assured and determined', and without any of the supposedly 'feminine' characteristics the explorers expect to find. They have short hair and no interest in fine clothes or decoration, and although they are horrified at displays of violence, they show no fear and assert their will over the intruders through sheer force of numbers (aided when necessary by deftly applied doses of chloroform).

The community the explorers find is organised as a single gigantic family, with property owned in common. Political authority is exercised on the basis of experience, wisdom and respect. The women are vegetarian, and are dismayed by the waste and profligacy of the world their guests describe.

Herland was originally published in serial form in *Forerunner*, a magazine edited and written by Gilman, who was a leading campaigner for the equality of women, particularly within marriage. In 1898 she had argued in her book *Women and Economics* that women needed full financial independence as well as voting rights, and her 1903 study *The Home – Its Work*

and Influence had drawn attention to the oppression that women suffered by being confined to the domestic sphere.

Charlotte Perkins Gilman addressing members of the Federation of Women's Clubs, 1916.

In *Herland*, these injustices no longer exist, and the narrator, Van, one of the three explorers, becomes completely converted to the feminist philosophy of the country. His colleague Jeff also accepts the superiority of life there, although his response is tinged with an idealistic chivalry that seems to ignore the athleticism, strength and endurance of the women he meets. However, Terry, the third explorer, is unable to accept the idea that women are as capable of ruling themselves as men.

The attitude towards sex is a major point of difference between the population of Herland and the three explorers. The women argue that the only value of sexual intercourse lies in procreation and the passing on of desirable personal characteristics to strengthen the community, while the men believe that pleasure and the expression of love are important as well. All three men marry Herland women, encouraged by the population, who believe that involving men in their community can only improve their society, but Terry, seeing himself as a 'masterful' man, provokes a crisis by attempting to force himself on his unwilling wife.

Gilman, whose life was blighted by severe bouts of depression, killed herself in 1935 after a diagnosis of terminal breast cancer. It was another forty-four years before *Herland* first appeared in book form (1979), but with its quiet and insistent irony it has now established itself as an early and influential feminist view of a peaceful and tolerant world.

CECILIA MAY GIBBS

TALES OF SNUGGLEPOT AND CUDDLEPIE: THEIR ADVENTURES WONDERFUL (1918)

A children's fantasy set in a miniature world inhabited by the 'gumnut babies' who embody the Australian native flora.

First published by Angus and Robertson in 1918.

Snugglepot and Cuddlepie was among the first generation of major illustrated children's books that were locally inspired and culture-specific to Australia and published in competition with the overseas book trade.

This book has remained in print ever since 1918 and was adapted into a ballet and a musical.

May Gibbs established a cast of bushland characters who have become central elements in Australian folklore.

The Australian bush – a wonderland or the site of unimaginable terror? Certainly, from the earliest days of white settlement, terror was the prevailing opinion. The fear of being lost in the bush, where lurking horrors from both European folklore and Aboriginal legend became wildly intertwined, haunted real life as well as the country's evolving literature. The lure of Australia's utterly novel landscape became a fatal attraction as convicts and then free settlers became lost and perished. And the epitome of the Australian image of a devouring landscape was international news with the ill-fated end to the Burke and Wills Expedition in 1861.

Nineteenth-century adventure stories set in the bush were replete with such scenarios from writers including Henry Kingsley, Marcus Clarke and Henry Lawson. And as late as 1911 a popular London publication entitled *Life in the Australian Backblocks* warned: 'The mother … knows the horrors that wait the bushed youngster. So she tells them that … in yonder scrub, there is a "bogy-man".' Only five years later, however, this threatening wonderland was to be completely inverted into a place of enchantment and fantasy.

Although May Gibbs (1877–1969) was born in England, her earliest Australian experiences as a four-year-old child who emigrated to that country with her family in 1881 became fundamental to the creation of her gumnut world. In both text and illustration her children's books established a completely original image of native flora and fauna. This enriched the country's pictorial vocabulary and made Gibbs a household name across Australia.

After sailing to London three times between 1900 and 1909 to study art, Gibbs returned to Australia in 1913 on the eve of World War I. A wartime demand for patriotic and nationalistic images helped inspire the creation of her miniature world that mirrored the human world beyond the confines and protection of the bush. Appearing on magazine covers, in syndicated comic strips and on a range of ephemera, her gumnut babies soon conquered the nation.

Gibbs then began a series of five small booklets somewhat reminiscent of Beatrix Potter. The emerging appreciation of nature education, outdoor

recreation and even conservation in Australia fostered an unprecedented demand for her work and her first full-length children's book, *Snugglepot and Cuddlepie*, added new names to the literary pantheon.

Contemporary reviews all across the British Empire were fulsome in their praise. The publisher could rightfully boast that the book was 'a link which binds together the children of the Empire'. They maintained that Australia was 'in every line and picture' in which Gibbs' 'bears, kangaroos, possums, and kookaburras have all the human virtues and weaknesses'. Like other twentieth-century creators of wonderlands such as Mervyn Peake (page 170), Gibbs added her own visual dimension to her texts that greatly solidified her creation in the public imagination.

Since Gibbs' death, her book has inspired a ballet, a musical and a series of postage stamps. The cottage she created as her home and studio looking over Sydney Harbour was saved from developers and has become as iconic to visitors as Beatrix Potter's Hilltop Farm.

Colour frontispiece by Gibbs showing the gumnut babies in the 'The Gum Blossom Ballet'.

YEVGENY ZAMYATIN

WE (1924)

Set in a futuristic, authoritarian dystopia, We *follows D-503, an engineer, who lives, perpetually observed by spies and secret police, in the vast glass conurbation of OneState, where individuality has almost all but been eradicated.*

First published in New York, in English, by E. P. Dutton in 1924.

The Russian title of the novel, *Mbl,* means 'We' in English but is, of course, also the English singular version of the word 'ours' – nicely appropriate for a novel about an individual's rebellion against the collective.

In 1921, *We* was the first work banned by Goskomizdat, the State Committee for Publishing, which functioned as the Soviet censorship bureau. Before being exiled to Paris in the 1930s, Zamyatin saw the world he predicted in 1920 coming true around him, as Stalin seized power in the USSR.

Zamyatin's dystopian novel *We* was written in 1920, but considered so incendiary the Soviet Union blocked its publication until the glasnost year of 1988. However, an unauthorised, unofficial English-language translation appeared in New York in 1924. *We* is set in a futuristic world called 'OneState' in which every aspect of life is controlled by a secret police, the Bureau of Guardians. Citizens have numbers rather than names, and live in transparent apartments so they can be observed at all times. The plot concerns a mathematician and engineer, D-503, who is helping to build a spacecraft called the *Integral*, designed to export OneState's regime to other planets. He keeps a journal in which he expresses his increasing doubts about the supposedly utopian world in which he lives.

If the world of *We* seems familiar, it is because Zamyatin established many conventions of classic dystopian fiction. Indeed, the novel was a direct inspiration for Orwell's *Nineteen Eighty-Four* (1949, page 178), Aldous Huxley's *Brave New World* (1932, page 148), and Ursula K. Le Guin's *The Dispossessed* (1974). OneState is presided over by the dictatorial 'Benefactor', citizens are surveilled at all times and every hour of life is mapped out by a schedule known as 'the Table'. Everybody dresses in light-blue overalls, eats the same synthetic food and exercises at the same time. OneState is surrounded by a vast 'Green Wall', allegedly built to keep the wilds of nature out, although we later learn that earlier a global war had killed all but 0.2 per cent of the population, and the world outside the wall is a ruined landscape. Within OneState friendships, relationships and breeding are rigorously controlled, and all sexual contact is limited to state-approved partners.

We is written in a series of short sections or 'records'. Their tone contrasts the chilly, regulated world against the often rich and moving thoughts and emotions of D-503: happy and optimistic in the beginning, and increasingly despairing as it goes on. And this contrast is also echoed in the landscape of the novel: inside the Green Wall everything is systematically ordered, with clarity and precision. Everything imprecise is banished, including human passions such as those D-503 experiences in an illegal affair with the sprightly

female 1-330, who does such illogical things as smoke cigarettes, drink alcohol and flirt.

This world might strike a reader as implausibly schematic and simplified, but Zamyatin makes it work by making schematisation the very logic of the society he portrays. It helps that his prose is vivid, colourful and evocative, and that the human dilemma of D-503 is so engagingly rendered. As such, *We* remains one of the most prophetic and powerful dystopias ever written.

Futuristic Buildings and City (detail) by Anton Brzezinski, used to illustrate the front cover of a recent Penguin Classics edition. Brzezinski (b.1946) is known to many as 'Polish Picasso', and has had a rich career in creating classic science-fiction covers.

FRANZ KAFKA

The Castle (1926)

Kafka's unfinished and ambiguous story of one man's struggle to comprehend the absurdist, labyrinthine world in which he finds himself reflects complex truths about the nature of existence.

Kafka died before finishing the novel, and it is unknown whether he intended to finish it if he had survived tuberculosis.

The book was published posthumously by Kurt Wolff in 1926, having been edited by Kafka's friend, Max Brod.

The first few chapters of the Kafka's handwritten manuscript were written in the first person and were later changed to a third-person narrator.

The Castle was the last of Kafka's three great novels, following *The Metamorphosis* (1915) and *The Trial* (1925).

Opposite: K in front of the Castle, illustration by Sam Caldwell.

The Castle, in any traditional narrative sense, goes nowhere. In the same traditional sense it is plotless. Franz Kafka (1883–1924) never finished writing it. The story breaks off mid-sentence and one could argue that, like the fallen-down 'ruins', with which romantics liked to ornament their estates, the incompleteness of *The Castle* is its reason for being. A statement is being made by its refusal to give a statement.

K. – a land surveyor – arrives at a village, somewhere in Middle Europe. His mission is to call on the Count who lives in the fog-shrouded Castle that looms, ominously, over the village. The young man has arrived at dusk and he finds himself unwelcome. Peasants glare at him and fall silent. What mystery, one wonders, awaits the visitor? What world have we entered?

Kafka wrote *The Castle* in 1922, two years before his death and three years after the Austro-Hungarian Empire fell apart with the end of World War I. The period is indisputably 'modern' – there are telephones and electric lights in the village. But where, if anywhere, is the 1914–18 cataclysm? Has it happened? Is it about to happen? Or are we in a universe where it never happens? There is no echo of the carnage to be heard in *The Castle*. Kafka has imagined the biggest event of the century out of existence.

Everything shivers with enigma. K. is a name, but no name. It is twilight – that nothing time between day and night. K. is on a bridge, suspended in the space between the outside world and the village. Fog, darkness and snow shroud the Castle. Is there anything in front of him but emptiness? And is there anything behind him? Where has K. come from? We learn in the first chapter that he has travelled for a long time from far away. What country are we in? Most of the village inhabitants have German names, but in chaotic breakdown of the Austro-Hungarian Empire in which Kafka was writing, leaves geography uncertain.

K., fatefully, crosses the bridge. At the Bridge Inn, the innkeeper grudgingly allows K. a straw mattress on the taproom floor. It stinks of beer and peasant sweat and rats run over his feet, and he is almost immediately roused

from his fitful rest by an emissary from the Castle who roughly asks what he is doing in the domain of 'Count Westwest'. Does he have the necessary 'permit'? A flustered K. declares himself to be a 'land surveyor', 'sent for by the Count'. Is he making it up?

Initially, the Castle's representative denounces K. as an impostor. Then, following a phone call, he radically changes his tune. The stranger, he now accepts, is what he claims he is. An emboldened K. goes on to say that his assistants and equipment 'are coming tomorrow by carriage'. In fact, two assistants do turn up on foot the next day, but from the Castle. They know nothing about surveying (or anything else) and have no 'instruments'. Bizarrely, K. claims to know them, identifying them as his 'old assistants' – yet he does not know their names, which, with preposterous high-handedness, he conjoins as 'Arthur'. To add further confusion, a comically inept messenger named Barnabas, is charged with arranging K.'s communications with the Castle. He does not.

The main obstacle between K. and the Castle is apparently Klamm, the Count's man-in-the-village. Klamm never speaks to anyone on business, and hastens from the room when any official matters are mentioned. He is a cartoon bureaucrat, stout, suited, with a pince-nez and smoking a Virginia cigar. Critics have noted that Klamm bears a striking similarity to photographs of Kafka's father, Hermann. K., denied access to the man himself, now seduces Klamm's current mistress, the barmaid Frieda.

Kafka was familiar with the work of Sigmund Freud and it is tempting to interpret these events and others in the novel in a Freudian reading. However, in a more romantic narrative one might call it love at first sight. After one look at K., Frieda surrenders herself to him, sealing the arrangement with a passionate coupling in the beer puddles under the counter in the taproom. Thereafter she refers to herself as his fiancée. K. informs the landlady that he intends to marry Frieda. However, the first chapter obliquely noted that K. already has a wife and child.

The 'authorities' in the Castle decide they do not require the services of a surveyor and reappoint K., in a surreal move, as a temporary school janitor. Remuneration, of an indeterminate amount, he is informed, will be forthcoming at some indefinite future point. Perhaps. K. sees it as a victory, but he promptly loses the job after robbing the school woodshed in order to keep him and Frieda warm at night.

The first half of The Castle is a quixotic quest. In its second half, it modulates into a conversation novel. The novel drifts to its end in an anticlimactic welter of talk and paralytic inaction. Finally it doesn't even have the energy to finish a sentence.

What should we make of the bewildering – at times horrific – 'imagined world' that Kafka presents in *The Castle*? In fact, one must note, he did not intend to present it at all. His deathbed instruction to his closest friend, Max Brod, was that all his manuscripts (virtually the whole of what we now have as his oeuvre) should be burned after his death, unread.

'Death' is the operative word here. *The Castle* is Kafka's terminal work – he was dying of incurable tuberculosis as he wrote it. What does a great author 'imagine' when standing on the threshold between this world and the next?

Kafka confided to Brod in September 1922 – following his return to Prague – that he would never finish the 'Castle novel'. Nevertheless, he also confided a possible ending. Were he to finish the book, it would end with the death of K. and simultaneous permission from the Castle to reside, but not legally, in the village. He is to be the perennial outsider.

However, looking at the novel through a veneer of death is only one of the many ways to interpret the text. Kafka was virtually unknown in the English-speaking world, until the first translations began to appear in the 1930s. For a couple of decades he was regarded as a wildly experimental writer, of interest only to the avant-garde. This changed with the rise of popular interest in French existentialism during the late 1940s and 1950s, which addressed the idea that 'absurdity', and ultimately meaninglessness, may be what the universe means after all. The existential philosopher Albert Camus, pictured it as the labour of Sisyphus: forever rolling a rock up a hill, only for it to roll back again. 'A first sign of the beginning of understanding', declared Camus, bleakly, 'is the wish to die'. And, if you are Kafka, burn everything you have laboured to create in life.

Many of the 'imagined worlds' described in literary wonderlands are warm, comfortable places, to which one can escape from the cold realities of everyday existence. *The Castle* imagines an even colder world than that in which most of us live but one that, as Sartre uncomfortably reminds us, is more real.

H. P. LOVECRAFT

The Cthulhu Mythos
(1928–37)

The lore and legend of Lovecraft's 'Great Old One' broke new ground in the realm of fantasy fiction, and the terrifying entity of Cthulhu has influenced generations of horror writers.

Stephen King has paid tribute to Lovecraft as the most important influence on his own early writing, and named him as the greatest horror writer of the twentieth century.

Author Michel Houellebecq has described Lovecraft's stories as 'an open slice of howling fear'.

Contemporary readers have struggled with Lovecraft's views and the overt racism in some of his work. In 2015, the World Fantasy Awards announced that it would be remodelling its award trophy (which was previously in the form of a bust of Lovecraft).

Few writers have made humanity as insignificant and powerless as the American Howard Phillips Lovecraft (1890–1937) in his horror stories of the Cthulhu Mythos. He wrote thirteen of these stories in all, which appeared between 1928 and 1941, mostly in the influential *Weird Tales* and other magazines. The last story in the sequence, *The Case of Charles Dexter Ward*, was published posthumously.

The most influential, *The Call of Cthulhu*, appeared in 1928 and established Lovecraft's conception of a vast and malevolent universe dominated by the Great Old Ones, amoral elemental deities who survived the almost inconceivably remote past – Lovecraft used the term 'vigintillions of years', a vigintillion being one with sixty-three zeros (a billion, billion, billion, billion, billion, billion, billion).

These monstrous and mysterious powers have been apparently dead for all that time but will one day – 'when the stars are right' – awaken and ravage the earth, and occasionally encounter incautious humans. Cthulhu himself, high priest to the Old Ones, has been hidden in the sunken city of R'lyeh, and bursts out when explorers open a huge carved door into a rocky cavern on a remote and uncharted island in the South Pacific.

Earth is an infinitesimally tiny part of Lovecraft's universe, but his descriptions of those specific parts in which his 'Great Old Ones' appear establish an atmosphere of mysterious horror. Whether a remote island in the South Pacific, the relatively familiar landscape of the eastern United States, or the wastes of the Antarctic, these places are suffused with an air of menace:

Great barren peaks of mystery loomed up constantly against the west as the low northern sun of noon or the still lower horizon-grazing southern sun of midnight poured its hazy reddish rays over the white snow, bluish ice and water lanes, and black bits of exposed granite slope. Through the desolate summits swept ranging, intermittent gusts of the terrible Antarctic wind; whose cadences sometimes held vague suggestions of a wild and half-sentient musical piping, with notes extending over a wide range, and

which for some subconscious mnemonic reason seemed to me disquieting and even dimly terrible. (*At the Mountains of Madness*, 1936)

A different sort of foreboding is experienced by travellers in *The Dunwich Horror* (1929):

The planted fields appear singularly few and barren; while the sparsely scattered houses wear a surprisingly uniform aspect of age, squalor, and dilapidation.

Without knowing why, one hesitates to ask directions from the gnarled solitary figures spied now and then on crumbling doorsteps or on the sloping, rock-strewn meadows. Those figures are so silent and furtive that one feels somehow confronted by forbidden things, with which it would be better to have nothing to do.

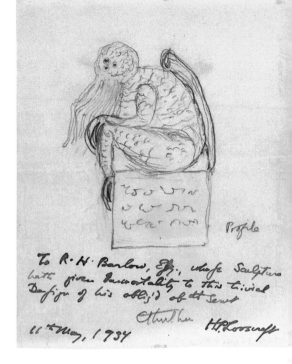

Lovecraft's own sketch of Cthulhu, drawn on a letter to fellow writer and friend, R. H. Barlow (1934).

That phrase 'without knowing why' sums up the nameless, indefinable horror of Lovecraft's work. The immense scale of the imaginary environment he created – a universe rather than simply a world – and the nightmarish, terrifying vagueness of the powers wielded by its gods, have influenced fantasy and horror writers ever since.

The gods who hold the ultimate power in Lovecraft's world have an aura of implacable evil, but are rarely presented in any physical detail. Although hideous sculptures are described at the start of *The Call of Cthulhu* depicting a monster with 'an octopus-like head whose face was a mass of feelers, a scaly, rubbery-looking body, prodigious claws on hind and fore feet, and long, narrow wings behind', the creature itself is revealed only as 'The Thing that cannot be described', with witnesses remembering just a few vague details of green, sticky, writhing slime.

Lovecraft was born in 1890 in Providence, Rhode Island, where, following the death of his father when he was eight, he was raised by his mother, maternal grandfather and two aunts. From his childhood he suffered from terrifying nightmares, which could have been the inspiration for some of his later fiction. As a small boy, he would also listen, enthralled, to tales of Gothic horror told by his grandfather.

As he grew up, there was a growing awareness among writers and the reading public in Europe and America of the terrifying malign potential of the scientific advances that were being made – H. G. Wells' *The War of the Worlds* appeared when Lovecraft was eight, and *The Gods of Pegana*, by the Anglo-Irish writer Lord Dunsany, when he was in his mid-teens. Exploration, whether in Lord Dunsany's fantasy world of Pegana or in the Antarctic in

Lovecraft's *At the Mountains of Madness* (1936) might uncover unexpected horrors. In *The Call of Cthulhu*, Lovecraft wrote:

> We live on a placid island of ignorance in the midst of black seas of infinity, and it was not meant that we should voyage far. The sciences, each straining in its own direction, have hitherto harmed us little; but some day the piecing together of dissociated knowledge will open up such terrifying vistas of reality, and of our frightful position therein, that we shall either go mad from the revelation or flee from the light into the peace and safety of a new dark age.

This idea of forbidden and dangerous knowledge is a constant theme throughout the stories.

Lovecraft maintained very close relations by letter with other horror writers of his day, including Clark Ashton Smith, Robert Bloch, who wrote *Psycho* and Robert E. Howard, the author of the Conan the Barbarian stories (1932–36, page 154). The group became known as the Lovecraft Circle, and characters, settings and other elements of Lovecraft's stories appeared occasionally in their works, with his consent. It was his publisher, August Derleth, who coined the phrase 'the Cthulhu Mythos' to popularise the stories when he published a collection in 1939, two years after Lovecraft's death.

The Mythos endures and is added to in books, magazines, video games and even in popular music. However, Lovecraft has also been the subject of controversy as contemporary readers have drawn attention to the recurring racism that is evidenced in much of his work.

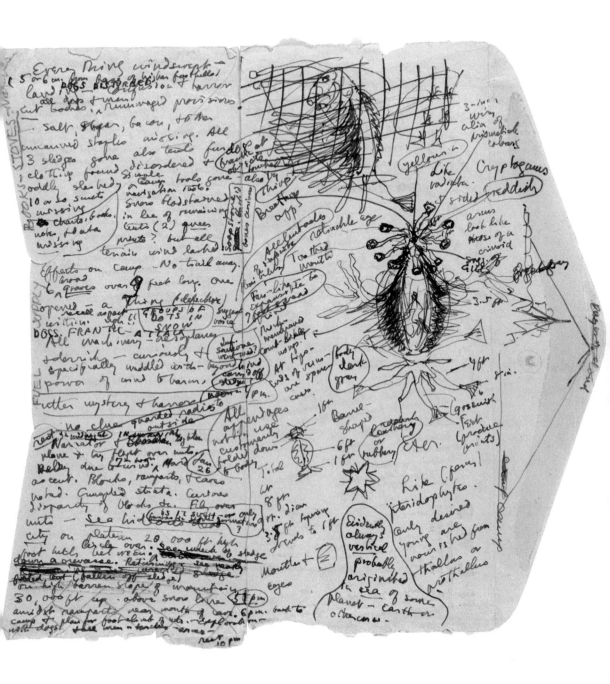

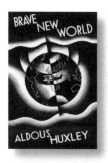

ALDOUS HUXLEY

Brave New World (1932)

Huxley's enduring masterpiece of a future world continues to shine a sombre light on the possibilities of genetic engineering and the loss of the individual in contemporary society.

First published by Chatto and Windus in 1932.

The novel is set in the year 2540, 632 years after the launch of the Model T Ford. The revered memory of the industrialist Henry Ford gives the World State the nearest thing it has to a god – 'Our Ford'.

Opposite: The Gammas, Deltas and Epsilons, the lower of the five ranked castes of Brave Alpha carry out the manual labour. Illustration by Finn Dean.

When George Orwell published *Nineteen Eighty-Four* in 1949 (page 174), he set his bleak and brutal vision of a totalitarian world less than four decades in the future, but Aldous Huxley (1894–1963) looked more than six hundred years ahead for the setting of *Brave New World*. Even so, its world remains rooted firmly in the 1930s – its main characters have the names of leading industrialists and political figures of Huxley's day, and the hypnotism, the selective breeding and the production-line lifestyle of the World State all reflect aspects of the world as Huxley knew it.

Where Orwell, writing so soon after the horrors of Nazism and Soviet Russia, famously saw the future as 'a boot stamping on a human face – for ever', Huxley presented in *Brave New World* a gentler, more insidious nightmare. There is no doubting the repressive power of the state – but though there are riot police to be called out in times of trouble, they wield nothing more brutal than feel-good drugs, anaesthetic gas and gentle words. There is no freedom of thought, but it seems hardly anybody wants it; there is no political opposition to the Resident Controller, and practically everybody accepts the status quo.

When *Brave New World* was published in 1932, the moving assembly lines of car manufacturer Henry Ford had been bringing cheap cars to the masses for twenty years or so, and in the memorable scenes in the Central London Hatchery with which the novel opens, Huxley applied this mass-production technology to human reproduction. The characters in the novel have no mothers, no fathers, no family: they, like the thousands of embryos moving sedately along the production line, were cloned and grown in bottles to fulfil their predestined roles as ruling Alphas or subservient Betas, Gammas, Deltas and Epsilons.

Thinking for oneself, passion or originality are not only deviant and sinful in the World State, but generally inconceivable: besides being created specifically for their role in society, the inhabitants, from Alpha-pluses to Epsilon-minus semi-morons, are subject to constant indoctrination and psychological manipulation to keep them malleable. Every aspect

Faceless shift workers
leaving the Ford motor
factory in Detroit,
Michigan, c.1935.

of their life is ordered by the central power – in this case, the mysterious ten Controllers.

In return, they live in a society of casual sex and hypnotic and mind-altering drugs, which are regularly distributed as a form of relaxation and escape. It is a world of absolute totalitarianism and unbridled hedonism, in which the traditional morality of Huxley's day is turned on its head: monogamy is frowned upon, the family seen as an antiquated tool of repression and the idea of motherhood considered obscene. Illness, pain and even ageing have been abolished, although sexism has apparently survived the six centuries – women, who seem to play no part in the administration of the World State, are patted dismissively on their bottoms by their bosses, and valued exclusively for the 'pneumatic' qualities of their 'firm and sunburnt flesh'. Some changes, apparently, were inconceivable for an educated man like Huxley in the early 1930s.

Huxley was born in 1894 into an impeccably middle-class family, the son of a schoolmaster – but he was an intellectual aristocrat with an impressive pedigree. His grandfather was T. H. Huxley, nicknamed 'Darwin's bulldog' for his combative defence of the theory of evolution.

Huxley, though, developed other ideas as he moved easily from Eton to Oxford. He loathed mass culture, and he believed that education should be the prerogative of those who could profit from it, by which he meant people like him. 'Universal education has created an immense class of what I may call the New Stupid', he declared dismissively. That view is clearly relevant to Huxley's vision of a world that is organised as a bizarre updating of the Hindu caste system. His grandfather had suggested that utopias could never be achieved by humans, only by insects, and it is significant that the masses in *Brave New World* are frequently described as locusts, aphids, ants and maggots.

Huxley's conception of the World State was influenced radically by his personal experiences in the US – where he shuddered at the self-conscious glitz and glamour of the film industry in California – and in the streets and factories of industrial England at the start of the Depression. The American experiment with Prohibition, just drawing to its messy close, was reflected in impractical proposals for banning soma, the drug that keeps Huxley's masses in a state of catatonic content, while the talking pictures, 'movies', were reproduced as the 'feelies', in which the audience shares not only the sights and sounds, but the smells and sensations of the characters on the screen.

The title of Huxley's novel comes from Miranda's expression of naive admiration in Shakespeare's *The Tempest* (1611, page 64), when she meets the shipwrecked courtiers wandering Prospero's island: 'Oh brave new world, that hath such people in't!' Huxley, of course, is being heavily ironic in applying that line to the World State, but if the society he described was deeply flawed, he saw no hope for humanity either in the Romantic myth of the noble savage. The 'savage' tribes living in *Brave New World's* New Mexico

reservation are without the constraints of the inhabitants of the World State, but their freedom is marked by brutality and squalor. It is only on a few remote islands that life sounds even remotely ideal. They are places where 'all the people … who've got independent ideas of their own' are exiled.

In his 1946 foreword to *Brave New World*, Huxley described this lack of a positive vision of the future in the novel as a mistake. 'Today, I feel no wish to demonstrate that sanity is impossible', he wrote. But much of the continuing power of the book derives from the implication that there is no escape from a world that, with its cultured brutality, its genetic manipulation, its psychological brainwashing and its dozy drug-and-sex culture, lies only just beyond the limits of our own experience. He said in his foreword: 'Then, I projected it six hundred years into the future: today, it seems quite possible that the horror may be upon us within a single century.' More than sixty years later, it is an uncomfortable thought.

Bernard Marx brings back John, the 'Savage', from a reservation outside World State. John becomes a society 'hit', but while touring factories and schools he becomes increasingly disturbed by what he sees. Illustration by Finn Dean.

ROBERT E. HOWARD

CONAN THE BARBARIAN
(1932–36)

The enduring hero of sword and sorcery has transcended his pulp-fiction roots and been the subject of multiple film, television, video game and comic-book adaptations.

Conan first appeared in *Weird Tales* magazine in December 1932 (above) in the story 'The Phoenix on the Sword' in which an older Conan attempts to rule the kingdom of Aquilonia and must foil an assignation plot by the 'Rebel Four'.

Howard was a friend of horror master H. P. Lovecraft (see page 144). The two authors corresponded frequently and made references to each others' works in their own writing.

In 1982 the film adaptation Conan the Barbarian brought bodybuilder and future governor of California, Arnold Schwarzenegger, his big-screen break.

To tell his stories of Conan, the wandering barbarian thief, outlaw and mercenary from the far north, the Texan writer Robert E. Howard (1906–36) travelled thousands of years back to a time before any of the known great civilisations.

Howard had already written stories set in the distant past – his first published work in the pulp magazine *Weird Tales*, 'Spear and Fang', deals with a prehistoric battle between Cro-Magnon and Neanderthal cavemen – but for his new character, he devised an entirely imaginary age of history. The stories were set in the Hyborean Age, 'between the years when the oceans drank Atlantis and the gleaming cities, and the years of the rise of the sons of Aryas' – between, that is, the mythical destruction of Atlantis and the emergence of the Indo-European races.

The fantasy world setting of Conan's adventures is one of magic and sorcery, of beautiful maidens and venomous monsters, and of strange, malevolent gods and miraculous interventions, very loosely based on a radically adapted version of Europe and North America. The Cimmerians, for instance, of whom Conan is one, have similarities with the Celtic people; far to the east is the Kingdom of Khitai, which corresponds to China; the historical Picts appear as wild savages on the fringes of civilisation; and Shem is recognisable as the area that we know as Mesopotamia, Arabia, Syria and Palestine.

In fact, the settings of the twenty-one Conan tales vary from an Arabian Nights vision of the Middle East in 'The Slithering Shadow' to an Arthurian romance-style picture of knights 'in richly wrought plate armour, coloured plumes waving above their burnished sallets'. One of Howard's main themes is the corrupting and debilitating effect of civilisation. There is no serious attempt to describe any social structure, beyond the power of various kings, counts, high priests and wizards: Conan's world is mythical and psychological rather than political.

There are several aspects of that frequently violent psychology that are troubling to a modern reader. For example, the theories of eugenics and

> Hither came Conan, the Cimmerian, black-haired, sullen-eyed, sword in hand, a thief, a reaver, a slayer, with gigantic melancholies and gigantic mirth, to tread the jewelled thrones of the Earth under his sandalled feet.
> – 'The Phoenix on the Sword'

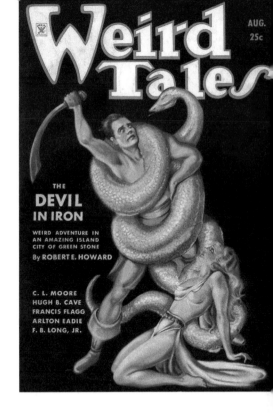

racial purity, which were popular at the time, echo throughout Howard's imagined history.

Women play a supporting role in many of the stories, generally wearing clothes that coyly do little to conceal their 'sleek limbs and ivory breasts', and occasionally whipped until they scream and writhe. Conan himself, generally a silent and terrifying man of action, occasionally grumbles like a 1930s old man about how long they take beautifying themselves.

Howard's own life was short and very ordinary. As a boy, in and around the town of Cross Plains, Texas, he idolised his sick and ailing mother and immersed himself in comics and pulp fiction. He was chronically shy and melancholy by disposition, and poured out reams of fiction and poetry through his adolescence, before his first story was accepted when he was eighteen. He lived with his parents all his life, although by the time he was twenty-five, his short stories were bringing him a growing reputation. Conan enjoyed spectacular success.

In 1936 his mother fell into a coma caused by her tuberculosis, and her nurse said she was unlikely to recover. Howard walked out to his car and shot himself in the head, dying a day before her. Conan, however, has survived not just in Howard's stories but also in comic books, television programmes, video games and films. Many of them bear little resemblance to Howard's original creation, but the 'noble savage' idea of a barbarian standing alone against the corruption of civilisation, continues to exert a powerful attraction.

Conan appears on the cover of *Weird Tales* in August 1934 wrestling a giant serpent summoned by a recently resurrected mythical demon. Although 'The Devil in Iron' is not considered one of the better early Conan stories, this cover depicts Conan as the archetypal warrior defeating a monster to save a scantily clad beauty and promises 'weird adventure in an amazing island city of Green Stone'.

VLADIMIR BARTOL

ALAMUT (1938)

A story set in the mystical world of an eleventh-century cult leader serves as an allegory of Mussolini's twentieth-century fascist state.

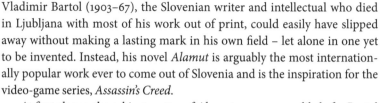

Originally published in 1938 in Slovenian, the first English edition was translated by Michael Biggins and published in 2004 by Scala House Press (their most recent edition is shown above).

Following the attacks of September 11, 2001, more than 20,000 copies were sold of a new Slovenian edition, and the book was translated into nineteen languages.

A regular refrain from the novel is 'Nothing is an absolute reality, all is permitted'.

Vladimir Bartol (1903–67), the Slovenian writer and intellectual who died in Ljubljana with most of his work out of print, could easily have slipped away without making a lasting mark in his own field – let alone in one yet to be invented. Instead, his novel *Alamut* is arguably the most internationally popular work ever to come out of Slovenia and is the inspiration for the video-game series, *Assassin's Creed*.

At first glance, the subject matter of *Alamut* appears as unlikely for Bartol as its twenty-first-century spin-off. First published in 1938 (although not translated into English until 2004), the novel is set in an eleventh-century Persian fortress, where sectarian leader Hasan ibn Sabbah, or Sayyiduna, has devised an ingenious and disturbing strategy for incentivising his troops (or 'fedayeen') to fight to the death: recreating paradise on earth.

Writing about such a challenging and alien subject required Bartol to prepare extensively. His inspiration for the tale is found in *The Travels of Marco Polo* (*c.*1300), which includes a story about a powerful Persian warlord who uses hashish and a secret garden of women to fool young men into thinking he has the power to transport them to paradise and back, and he spent ten years researching and structuring his book. He then retreated for nine months to the mountain town of Kamnik to write it, while the Anschluss proceeded just thirty miles away and Mussolini's Fascists persecuted the Slovenian population of his birthplace, Trieste.

The result is a rich and engrossing evocation of a terrifying world. In Sayyiduna's hands, the remote mountain fort of Alamut becomes a crucible in which to conduct 'an experiment in altering human nature' based on the motto that underpins his brand of Ismailism (a religious sect with roots in Islam): 'Nothing is an absolute reality; everything is permitted.' As his enemies advance to lay siege to his stronghold, the dangerously charismatic despot delves deeper into the desires and psychology of the youths under his control, steeling them to display fearlessness in the face of inevitable defeat.

Bartol's greatest achievement is that he makes Alamut almost as alluring as it is sinister. Seen through the eyes of two newcomers, young harem recruit

Halima and prospective fighter ibn Tahir, the fort is a place of mystery and delight, where misgivings flower into fear and disillusionment. Wandering Alamut's passages and secret places with Halima and ibn Tahir, peeling back layer after layer of Sayyiduna's horrific vision, we are at once charmed and appalled. As with the best action-packed computer games, the book makes us feel we are unable to look away even as we gasp.

Hasan ibn Sabbah or Sayyiduna, leader of a secretive eleventh-century cult from the Levant, demonstrates his authority by ordering one of his assassins to kill himself.

Unsurprisingly, the world of *Alamut* is often read as an allegory for the evils of Fascism. Many twenty-first-century readers also see reflections of the radicalisation of young jihadis in the novel.

Yet the eclecticism of the story's resonances and applications serve as a reminder that what Bartol criticises is not a particular ideology but the human readiness to believe and follow compelling leaders unquestioningly. As Sayyiduna himself explains, the key to his power lies in his realisation that 'people wanted fairy tales and fabrications and they were fond of the blindness they blundered through'. Knowing this enables him to control and manipulate his subjects as deftly as avatars in the virtual gaming worlds that were invented decades after Bartol committed this mesmerising and terrible world to the page.

JORGE LUIS BORGES

Tlön, Uqbar, Orbis Tertius
(1940)

*A short story incorporating many of Borges' philosophical
preoccupations, which details the creation of an alternative world
and its infiltration of our own.*

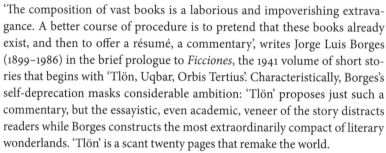

First published in Argentine
journal *Sur* in 1940, the story
appears in collection *The
Garden of Forking Paths* (later
Ficciones), first published by
Editorial Sur in 1941.

Borges was born into a
wealthy Argentine family in
Buenos Aires and his love of
literature was established at
a young age when he came
across his father's library.

Under the dictatorship of
Juan Perón during World
War II, Borges was dismissed
from his post at the Buenos
Aires library for showing
support for the Allies.

'The composition of vast books is a laborious and impoverishing extrava-
gance. A better course of procedure is to pretend that these books already
exist, and then to offer a résumé, a commentary', writes Jorge Luis Borges
(1899–1986) in the brief prologue to *Ficciones*, the 1941 volume of short stories that begins with 'Tlön, Uqbar, Orbis Tertius'. Characteristically, Borges's
self-deprecation masks considerable ambition: 'Tlön' proposes just such a
commentary, but the essayistic, even academic, veneer of the story distracts
readers while Borges constructs the most extraordinarily compact of literary
wonderlands. 'Tlön' is a scant twenty pages that remake the world.

Borges turned to fiction only shortly before his fortieth birthday, to affirm
his mental faculties in the wake of a head injury. With 'Tlön', his second story
after the accident, Borges manages to blend the 'epic destiny' he yearned
for, on the model of the many military heroes among his forebears, with
the bookishness and frailty that marked him from earliest youth. In a long
autobiographical reminiscence published in *The New Yorker* in 1970, Borges
observes that, 'if I were asked to name the chief event in my life, I should say
my father's library'. One way to understand 'Tlön' is as a singularly successful
attempt to make a library into an event.

From the start, the story blurs the lines between the literary and the literal, the figurative and real-life figures. It is dotted with the names of Borges'
contemporaries, scaffolded on his ability to reference obscure philosophical
tomes with breezy assurance – and free with its attribution of made-up quotations to both. Borges describes himself dining with his frequent collaborator
Adolfo Bioy Casares, who recalls a statement made by a heresiarch of Uqbar:
'mirrors and copulation are abominable, since they both multiply the numbers of man'. Intrigued, Borges asks for his source; Bioy points him towards
the *Anglo-American Cyclopedia*, a 'literal but delinquent' reprint of the 1902
Encyclopedia Britannica. Borges' edition makes no mention of Uqbar, but
Bioy's own copy includes four pages on Uqbar tucked into the end of Volume
XLVI. The article is vague on Uqbar's whereabouts, and largely uninspir-
ing, but piques Borges' interest with its observation that Uqbar's literature

uniformly shuns realism in favour of fantasy and takes place entirely within the imaginary regions of Mlejnas and Tlön.

Most of the remainder of the story elaborates on the fantastic, aided by Borges' discovery two years later of an entire volume of the *First Encyclopedia of Tlön*. It is 'something to be reckoned with', Borges writes, not 'a brief description of a false country', but 'a substantial fragment of the complete history of an unknown planet'. Not only the philosophical disputes, but all the rest of Tlön too, depends on Berkeleyan idealism, which holds that the physical universe does not exist other than as a projection of our minds.

Under the guise of encyclopaedic pedantry, Borges plays out numerous implications of such a stance – impugning ideas of causality and of time itself, subordinating all scientific disciplines to psychology, teasing out the scandalous 'doctrine of materialism', and, most tellingly, exploring several visions of literature that might emerge from this conceptual confluence. All books are treated as the work of one 'timeless and anonymous' author, pieces of fiction contain every permutation of a single plot, poetry eschews nominatives in favour of massive agglomerations of adjectives or verbs. 'There are famous poems', Borges notes, 'made up of one enormous word, a word which in truth forms a poetic *object*, the creation of the writer'. At length, Borges reveals that 'centuries and centuries of idealism have not failed to influence reality' in Tlön, that real objects, too, may be produced by desire or expectation. Lost items have long been rediscovered by more than one person at once; archaeologists have arrived at the methodical production of ancient artefacts, rendering the past 'no less malleable or obedient than the future'.

This unexpectedly concrete development sets up the story's final pivots: from past to future, from fantasy to reality and from poetry to prose and back again. In time, Borges learns that Bishop Berkeley himself took part in an early-seventeenth-century secret society dedicated to inventing an imaginary country. The work demands generations, and two centuries later gains the financial backing of a pugilistic American atheist millionaire who bequeaths the society his fortune on the condition that it accord itself to American audacity and create an entire planet. Members receive the complete forty-volume *First Encyclopedia of Tlön* in 1914. Then, Borges writes, 'about 1942, events began to speed up' – the fabulist qualities of the literature of an imaginary country itself situated in the literature of an imaginary country start to impinge on the real.

Borges dates the bulk of his story to 1940, reflecting the actual moment of its composition, but he appends a postscript fictitiously dated 1947, narrating Tlön's conquest of the realist precincts he has carefully woven through the rest of the tale. The specific contours of this wonderland then become more clear: that it will not lie quiescent down a rabbit-hole or over a rainbow, and that 'literary' is not in this case a contingent modifier but an absolutely essential one. This is a wonderland predicated on *poiesis* – the origin of our word 'poetry' – in its root sense in Greek: to make. Just as Tlön's poets fashion 'poetic objects' out of enormous compound words, so too does Tlön finally

insinuate its brand of poetry into the prosaic precincts of our own world. Borges is present when a compass encircled by Tlönian lettering emerges from a French packing crate in Buenos Aires, and again some months later when a dead man in rural Uruguay turns out to be in possession of a small but impossibly heavy cone made of a metal that 'does not exist in this world' – an 'image of divinity in certain religions of Tlön'.

Borges with his friend and collaborator, Adolfo Bioy Casares.

And then the world submits to Tlön, at first in decidedly literary terms: 'manuals, anthologies, summaries, literal versions, authorised reprints and pirated editions of the Master Work of Man poured and continue to pour out into the world.' Borges likens this overwhelming embrace of the 'minute and vast evidence of an ordered planet' to the widespread appeal enjoyed by 'any symmetrical system whatsoever which gave the appearance of order – dialectical materialism, anti-Semitism, Nazism' – in the 1930s. We can read the quiet resignation of the Borges character at the close, as a counterpoint to the more aggressive stance taken by Borges as author, protesting the conquests being made by actual totalitarian states even as he was writing. But we should remember, on the other hand, that Borges was indoctrinated in philosophical idealism at his father's knee and always remained fascinated by it, that many of Tlön's outré literary practices reflect conceits animating Borges' writing all along the decades.

Within the story but also beyond it, Borges makes poetic sensibility and conviction into an engine for real-world change, both narrating and subtly effecting a shift from the Enlightenment project of the Encyclopedists – to distil and record the whole of human knowledge – to the yet more radical undertaking of writing the world afresh.

AUSTIN TAPPAN WRIGHT

ISLANDIA (1942)

The story of the adventures of John Lang, a Harvard graduate who secures the position of first American consul to the utopian territory of Islandia. Rich in detail and brilliantly conceived, Wright's creation of the Karain continent is rivalled only by Tolkien's Middle-earth.

First published by Farrar and Rinehart, Inc., in 1942.

Even though Wright's sister and widow edited the text down after he died prematurely in a traffic accident in 1931, it still exceeds 900 pages.

Despite receiving little critical attention, Austin Tappan Wright's (1883–1931) *Islandia*, published posthumously, has become a cult classic and was praised by Ursula K. Le Guin for being the only utopian work that directly addressed the issues of Westernisation and 'progress'.

The novel takes place in the first years of the twentieth century when imperialism was at its peak; the maps that accompany the text – designed by Wright's geographer brother John Kirtland Wright – show Islandia as bordered by a German protectorate as well as French and British colonies. The novel is unusually detailed in its topographical descriptions. John Lang first learns of the territory through an Islandian friend at Harvard and, after learning the local language, his uncle – a prosperous businessman who sees Islandia as a potential market for American goods – negotiates him a position in the consulate. Lang's arrival dramatises the main issue of the novel: whether Islandia should open its doors to overseas trade or preserve its independence on the edge of empire. As spelled out explicitly, the country's predicament resembles that of Japan in the 1850s, which suggests Islandian independence will not last long.

Islandia appeals to Lang for being rather old-fashioned and only lightly industrialised. His travels, mostly on horseback or by boat, around the country, are leisurely paced in contrast to the tempo of American life. In the first half, Lang is gradually learning Islandian society and an essential first step is to process his perceptions of the landscape. On approaching a farm: 'the narrow road was rutted in places and with grassy patches, not in regular ridges as at home where wheeled traffic is so much, but in patches here and there, soft under the horses' feet. And quite unexpectedly we came upon three of the Islandian grey deer, with their short antlers and round bodies and long colt-like legs.' The reader is encouraged to pay attention to small differences from America and we are constantly invited to infer the better quality of life lying behind his descriptions.

Islandian society still possesses feudal elements, yet it displays greater gender equality than Lang is used to. He is initially impressed by the peaceful

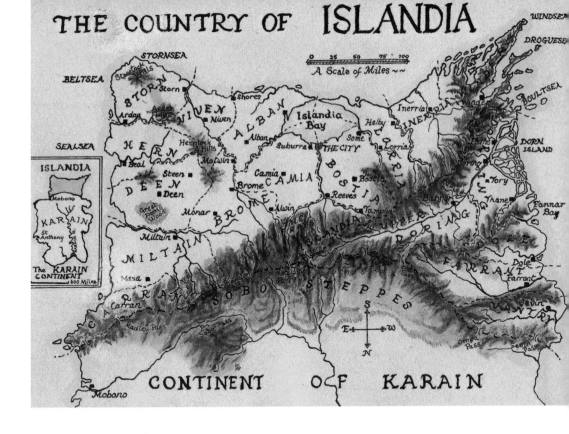

THE COUNTRY OF ISLANDIA

John Kirtland Wright's (brother of the author) map of Islandia recreated in colour by Edward Relph.

appearance of the country and also by the simplicity of dress worn by the locals. The latter greatly reduces social ritual and eases Lang's encounters with the new society. The most striking event comes when the Islandian council debates a proposal to open the country to foreign trade. Two parties have formed, the more utopian one resisting this incursion of external values, while the other camp insists that they move with the times. The council vote goes against change. This does not mean that change per se is blocked because, of course, Lang's own narrative can be read as an example of external influence.

Lang's account is divided into three phases, each revolving around a romance, but in every case the romance plot is used as a medium for cultural debate and comparison. Eventually Lang returns to America, which he sees through estranged eyes, and he finally persuades an American woman to travel with him to Islandia, marry and set up a household there. Virtually the last words of the novel are when Lang declares to his wife 'we are Islandians', but this conclusion only comes after many heated arguments over the attractions of Islandian culture.

ANTOINE DE SAINT-EXUPÉRY

THE LITTLE PRINCE (1943)

A loving lament for a friend who fell to Earth, shared the desert,
guilelessly offered parables of human truth and died in order to
return to his celestial home.

First published by Reynal
and Hitchcock, Inc., in 1943.

Le Petit Prince is the second
most widely translated book
(after *Pinocchio*, 1883) and
the third highest-selling
single work of fiction ever
(after *A Tale of Two Cities*,
1859, and *The Hobbit*, 1937).

The B612 Foundation, an
NGO conducting research to
defend Earth against
asteroid collision, is named
after the tiny home 'planet'
of Saint-Exupéry's Little
Prince. A real asteroid has
been named B612 to honour
The Little Prince and another
(Asteroid 2578) was
renamed Saint-Exupéry.

The Little Prince (published first in French as *Le Petit Prince*) is a bittersweet palimpsest that has entranced generations, deploying multiple layers of meaning to acknowledge gently the hard truths of life, leaving adults sad but hopeful, yearning for the child from the stars and his laughter. It is the best-known work of the French writer, poet and aviator Antoine de Saint-Exupéry (1900–44) and remains one of the most-translated books ever, a modern classic suggesting that the simplest things in life are the most important.

In writing *The Little Prince*, Saint-Exupéry drew on his own experiences as a pilot (he had qualified as one in 1922), including a period serving in North Africa. In 1944 during World War II he attempted a reconnaissance mission over France and never returned. In 2004 the wreckage of his plane was recovered, although the exact cause of the crash remains unknown.

The story begins with one of Saint-Exupéry's watercolours, an image copied from a 'true' jungle book the narrator read at age six. A boa constrictor coils around a 'wild beast' whose eyes bulge as the snake's mouth gapes to consume him. As a child, the narrator explains, he attempted to recreate the image; resulting in something 'grown-ups' took for a hat, but which the six-year-old clearly saw as a snake digesting an elephant. In this simple depiction of mortality Saint-Exupéry demonstrates the clash of potential meaning – which children see directly – and mundane interpretation, which blinds adults to seeing the potential. Within the narrative, however, this clash is productive: *The Little Prince* chides grown-ups, but enriches them, too.

The narrator, now an adult, has grown up to become a pilot who has crashed in a barren desert with no signs of civilisation. While he struggles to fix his plane, a young boy with golden hair and a scarf appears as if from nowhere. Over the next eight days the Little Prince tells the narrator vivid tales of his home on a faraway asteroid, his adventures on other planets and how he fell to Earth. These tales are parabolic and present culturally symbolic themes. The Little Prince tells the narrator, for example, of a man on a tiny planet who forgot to tend to his bushes. Three of the seeds should have been plucked when they began to sprout, because they were 'bad'. Instead, they

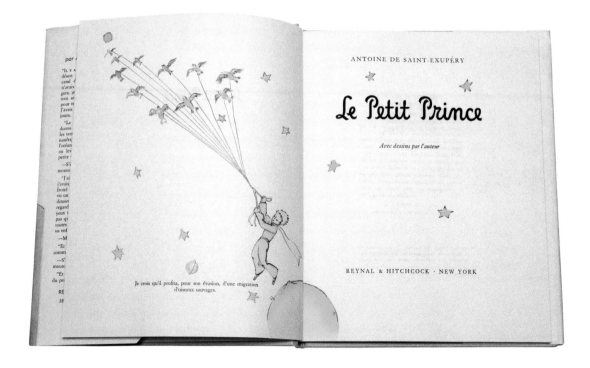

Je crois qu'il profita, pour son évasion, d'une migration
d'oiseaux sauvages.

ANTOINE DE SAINT-EXUPÉRY

Le Petit Prince

Avec dessins par l'auteur

REYNAL & HITCHCOCK · NEW YORK

Title page from the first
edition illustrated by
Saint-Exupéry.

grew to be powerful baobabs that he could not cut down, trees that sucked the life out of his planet and shattered it. 'Children', the narrator writes, recounting this story, 'Watch out for baobabs!' (We must learn for ourselves, of course, what are the baobabs in our own lives.)

This boy who fell to Earth is not an avatar of Jesus. His views, story and effect are, however, consonant with the Christian thread in Western culture: 'Unless you change and become like little children, you will never enter the kingdom of heaven' (Matthew 18:3). Furthermore, as Jesus told his doubting disciple Thomas, 'Because you have seen me, you have believed; blessed are those who have not seen and yet have believed' (John 20:29), the Little Prince tells the pilot: 'The important thing is what can't be seen'. The Little Prince does not die for his friend, however. He dies to get back to his rose, which he loves because he has tended her. Still, his home asteroid, B-612, bears the number 4 (symbolic in the Bible of Earthly completeness) multiplied by 153 (the number of miraculous fish – or souls – that Peter nets in obeying the risen Jesus [John 21:11]).

The last image of the book shows a desert landscape with only a star. The narrator asks us to let him know if we ever see this landscape, and under that star, a child. 'Don't let me go on being so sad: Send word immediately that he's come back.'

The 'grown-ups' mistook the
first drawing for a hat,
whereas a six-year-old clearly
understands it is a snake
digesting an elephant.

TOVE JANSSON

The Moomins and the Great Flood (1945)

*Jansson's much-loved tales of Moomin trolls taught generations
of children the importance of kindness and good manners,
even amid chaotic adventure.*

First published by Schildts in 1945.

In addition to the nine Moomin novels, Jansson wrote a regular comic strip featuring the Moomins. The strip was eventually taken over by her brother Lars.

Jansson also wrote novels and short stories for adults. Several of these include characters who write children's books or cartoons. One heroine of the novel *The True Deceiver* is a rich but misanthropic writer struggling to maintain control of her Moominlike creations in the face of the relentless forces of marketing and merchandising.

Tove Jansson (1914–2001), inventor of the Moomin trolls, is a Scandinavian institution, and her strange, gentle, unfailingly polite little creatures have delighted millions around the world. Jansson originally came up with the Moomins, or something very like them, in her childhood, and continued developing them when she became a professional artist and illustrator. They first appear in her adult work in political cartoons she drew for the satirical magazine *Garm*.

The first of the Moomin books published, *The Moomins and the Great Flood* (really a short story of about sixty pages), is not 'officially' part of the Moomin series. It can, however, be seen as proof of concept for the ensuing series (and the enormous franchise that they later became). The world described in the book is one in flux. The Moomins travel from forest to swamp to cliffside cave to beach, before finally being swept away by the titular flood. (They even spend the night in a candy meadow with rivers of chocolate and jam, perhaps inspiring Roald Dahl's *Charlie and the Chocolate Factory*.) The book ends with the family reuniting, and with Moominpapa announcing that he has found the perfect valley for them to build a house to live in, which serves as the setting for all future Moomin books.

And yet the world of this book (published in 1945, English translation 2005) is a great deal more civilised than we might expect. When the Moomins part from friends, Moominmama promises: 'We'll send you both a letter and tell you what happened.' Even in the midst of this wilderness, it seems, one can still rely on the mail. And after the flood, the various displaced creatures sit together around campfires, sharing their surviving utensils and making each other warm drinks, as good neighbours should. Manners, and neighbourly behaviour, are central to these books and their world, which for all its fantastic qualities, is rooted in the Finnish landscape and Swedish culture in which Tove Jansson grew up. The Moomins are earthy, eager for both diversion and comfort, and keen to have everything in its right place. The world they construct for themselves reflects these preoccupations: the Moomins' house is cosy and full of all the odds and ends that one needs to feel fully

Their tulip was glowing again, it had opened all its petals and in the midst of them stood a girl with bright blue hair that reached all the way down to her feet.

Tove Jansson's 'Map of Moomin Valley', also detailing the two floors of the Moomin family house.

at ease. Moominmama, meanwhile, never sets out on an excursion without a full meal, complete with cutlery and a butter dish, and a purse full of whatever she and her children might need to be well and happy.

The change of the seasons determines the shape and nature of the Moomin world. A later novel, *Finn Family Moomintroll* (1948, English translation 1950) takes place over a long summer, and features such quintessentially Scandinavian summer excursions as a boat trip to the islands and a night under the stars. In *Moominland Midwinter* (1957), Moomintroll wakes up unexpectedly during his hibernation, and finds the world altered and frighteningly foreign. Too-Ticky, who he finds living in the family's beach house (thus transforming it, too, into something unfamiliar), explains: 'There are such a lot of things that have no place in summer and autumn and spring. Everything that's a little shy and a little rum. Some kinds of night animals and people that don't fit in with others and that nobody really believes in. They keep out of the way all the year. And then when everything's quiet and white and the nights are long and most people are asleep – then they appear.' The world of the Moomins is simultaneously fantastic and familiar, cosy and frightening, eternal and ever-changing – a tension that explains why this series of books has resonated so powerfully with generations of children who are just starting to discover their own world.

The German city of Dresden levelled by Allied bombing between 13 and 15 February 1945. The raids and the lack of public response to them inspired Vonnegut's classic *Slaughterhouse-Five*, see page 212.

4 NEW WORLD ORDER

1946–1980

The legacy of World War II and ensuing Cold War tensions shell-shocked a generation of writers, each seeking to find a voice for the unspeakable. Feminist and postmodern writing also sought to redress tired tropes dogging the genre.

MERVYN PEAKE

GORMENGHAST (1946–59)

Peake's enduring gothic tales of the vast and crumbling Gormenghast castle and its curious inhabitants explore a dark world of age-old rituals, treachery, manipulation and murder.

Titus Groan (1946), *Gormenghast* (1950), and *Titus Alone* (1959) are the three core novels of Peake's trilogy (all published by Eyre and Spottiswoode), and Peake was making plans for a fourth, *Titus Awakes*, when he became too ill to write, around 1960.

Peake studied at the Royal Academy, London, and developed a reputation as a painter and illustrator during the pre-war years. As well as his own works he provided illustrations for *Alice's Adventures in Wonderland, The Rime of the Ancient Mariner, The Strange Case of Dr Jekyll and Mr Hyde,* and the Grimms' fairy tales.

The fantasy world of Gormenghast Castle is as hard to pin down as a nightmare. The trilogy, which Mervyn Peake (1911-68) wrote during and after World War II, describes the life of Titus Groan, heir to the ancient Earldom of Gormenghast. Parts of the story echo the unimaginable horrors Peake experienced at the end of the war, when he worked as an artist in the newly liberated Bergen-Belsen concentration camp. There is, for instance, the pitiless savagery with which some of the characters are murdered; the blind, unthinking obedience to rules and traditions that beset the castle; and the cold-hearted evil of Steerpike, who tries to seize control.

But it is impossible to make detailed comparisons, still less to see Gormenghast Castle and its massive Tower of Flints against a background of twentieth-century Europe and the Nazis. The Gothic towers of the rambling castle where Titus Groan is born – more a city than a single home, with miles of twisting, shadowy streets running through it and secret, dilapidated areas where no one ever goes – seem to place it in medieval times, as do the ancient rites read from dusty old volumes and the banquets set with gold plate and crimson goblets. Some of the characters, such as Irma Prunesquallor, with her spectacles, her hair pulled into a bun, her flower-trimmed veil and her neurotic obsessions, could be caricatures from the 1920s. In the third book, *Titus Alone* (1959), Titus journeys away from the castle among cars, skyscrapers and televisions.

Gormenghast is in a world of its own, isolated both in space and time. Nothing that happens can definitely be said to be supernatural, but an aura of magic hangs over the story. A strange tree grows horizontally out of the castle wall, its trunk so massive that Titus' two aunts, Cora and Clarice, can set a table there to have tea. The Countess of Groan, with her eerie warning, 'There is evil in the castle', seems to have a mysterious premonition of the disasters to come and, by the end, she speaks with almost supernatural knowledge as she warns the departing Titus: 'There is nowhere else. You will only tread a circle … Everything comes to Gormenghast.'

These ambiguities run throughout. Some characters, such as the Professors, are comic Dickensian figures, while Steerpike is painted with chilling psychological realism, with a terrifying, almost psychotic lack of empathy or remorse.

A page from Peake's original manuscript for *Gormenghast* showing his illustrations of Steerpike and Fuchsia Groan.

Unlike novels such as *Brave New World* (1932, page 148), *Nineteen Eighty-Four* (1949, page 174) or *Herland* (1915, page 134), *Gormenghast* presents no political warning or ideal. Rather, the literary influences on Peake's imagination are the comic vision of Dickens, the zany nonsense world of *Alice's Adventures in Wonderland* (1865, page 82) and the adventurous challenges of R. L. Stevenson's *Treasure Island* (1883, page 100). *Gormenghast* stands alone. Its world is neither magical nor realistic, neither wholly comic nor wholly tragic, neither utopia nor dystopia. Perhaps it is this shifting focus and the misty, nightmarish quality that has made *Gormenghast* so consistently popular since its publication.

The first impression of Gormenghast Castle is its sheer size, with its massive, ivy-covered walls looming over the mud huts of the Outer Dwellers huddled below. The Tower of Flints dominates everything 'like a mutilated finger from among the fists of knuckled masonry and pointed blasphemously at heaven', and the sheer Outer Wall, like a grey cliff, encloses several square miles of open ground and countless other towers, wings and passageways. The whole complex is so extensive that most of the people who live inside never venture out.

The Castle stands at the foot of the craggy Gormenghast Mountain, with the virtually impenetrable Twisted Woods and Gormenghast River at its foot. On its other three sides, marshland, quicksand and swamps stretch into the distance. This is the waterlogged, inhospitable setting for the great flood, the waters of which rise to the highest floors of the castle and nearly destroy it.

Within the castle walls, the world looks resolutely backward. Much of the fabric of the buildings is falling down, held together only by the ivy that covers it. More importantly, this atmosphere of decay extends to the people who inhabit the buildings. The ancestors of the Earl of Groan have ruled Gormenghast since time immemorial, but now the sole function of the family is to fulfil the endless, detailed and apparently ridiculous rituals and traditions recorded in old ledgers, interpreted by the Earl's Master of Ritual. This is the world, overwhelmed by the past, from which he wants to escape and over which the evil Steerpike is determined to rule.

Titus Groan, Gormenghast and *Titus Alone* have been described by the novelist Anthony Burgess as some of the most important works of the imagination to come out of the modern age. The books present a coherent fantasy world with its own bizarre rules and assumptions, but beneath the surface can be seen several aspects of Peake's own life. His father was a Christian missionary, and Peake was born in Kuling, in China's Kiang-hsi Province, spending most of his childhood in Tianjin, southeast of Beijing. Some see echoes of Imperial China in the rituals and customs of Gormenghast Castle and the Groan family, and the precipitous landscapes of Peake's birthplace, where fortified Chinese towns cling to the steep mountain slopes, are reflected in the descriptions of the castle's setting.

Furthermore, Peake spent several years before and after World War II living on the island of Sark, in the Channel Islands, from where he took some of the place-names in Gormenghast, such as the Coupée, Silvermines, Gory and Little Sark. However, probably the most significant period of his life was the time he spent drawing in the Nazi concentration camp at Bergen-Belsen in 1945. He wrote several moving and tortured poems, and the horrific sights and experiences of Belsen clearly left a dark and ineradicable impression on his imagination.

Like an earlier fantasy novel, Kenneth Grahame's *The Wind in the Willows*, *Gormenghast* demonstrates its author's anxiety about the growing demand for social equality in the first half of the twentieth century. The rule of the Groan family may be overbearing, hidebound, self-obsessed and crippled by its stultifying sense of duty to tradition for its own sake, but the aspiring new meritocracy represented by Steerpike presents a chilling alternative. In one memorable scene, Steerpike slowly pulls the legs off a beetle, murmuring to himself as he does so: 'Equality is the great thing – equality is everything.'

The three books that tell the Gormenghast story are not a true trilogy, since they were originally planned as part of a longer series intended to follow Titus throughout his life. But, by the mid-1950s, with two books completed and work on the third in hand, Peake was beginning to show early signs of Parkinson's disease. He was increasingly incapacitated both physically and mentally over the next few years, and he died in 1968, at age fifty-seven, after several years in a nursing home.

Ultimately, the world of Gormenghast defies classification – unique, fascinating, enthralling, beguiling and occasionally horrifying. It is a place of dreams, fantasies and nightmares drawn from experience.

A rare view of Gormenghast Castle over Titus's shoulder in a sketch by Peake.

GEORGE ORWELL (ERIC ARTHUR BLAIR)

NINETEEN EIGHTY-FOUR
(1949)

One of the great dystopias of the twentieth century, Orwell's bleak vision of a totalitarian near-future has spawned many imitators and its instantly recognisable ideas and terms have entered into the public consciousness.

First published by Secker and Warburg in 1949.

Nineteen Eighty-Four frequently appears in polls as one of the greatest books of the twentieth century, and its fame is so great that a 2013 edition appeared with the author's name and the book's title entirely redacted, and yet was still immediately recognisable.

Opposite: Children play beneath the ever-watchful eyes of 'Big Brother' on the set of Michael Anderson's film *1984* (Columbia, 1956).

To twenty-first-century readers, the imagined world of *Nineteen Eighty-Four* can seem over-the-top (though the surveillance state of Oceania might seem quaint by today's standards of satellite imagery and drones). In the late 1940s, however, George Orwell's (1903–50) depictions were legitimate extrapolations of very recent history, pushing contemporary trends to their grotesque ends. In 1949, it was not yet five years since the death of Adolf Hitler. Stalin still lived and ruled with a monstrous despotism that had killed millions in intentional famines, party purges ('the Great Terror'), and war crimes. The term 'socialist' had been appropriated by Hitler's 'National Socialist German Workers' Party' and 'the Union of Soviet Socialist Republics'. Hope for a benevolent Russian revolution had been betrayed. Nazism, Communism and World War II had demonstrated shocking human capacities for producing and accepting outrageous propaganda, fanatical commitment to orthodoxy, blatant rewriting of history, cynical side-switching, bureaucratic time-serving and tyranny, torture, mass enslavement, mass murder and lust for power. Orwell's bleak vision of the future was within legitimate limits of satiric exaggeration.

Nineteen Eighty-Four centres on a triangular relationship between protagonist Winston Smith, his lover Julia and O'Brien, an older male official of the ruling elite. The story is set in a near-future dystopia – although now in our past – where the major characters compete for our attention with the world of the story and its embedded satirical targets. Perhaps unfairly to *Nineteen Eighty-Four* as novel, it is the world of Orwell's imagined 1984 that has determined *Nineteen Eighty-Four*'s continuing influence, and made 'Orwellian' part of English political vocabulary.

The central setting is 'London, chief city of Airstrip One', a province of the superpower Oceania (comprising North and South America, the United Kingdom, southern Africa and Australasia). What was once the United Kingdom is now simply the airstrip nearest to Oceania's two, alternately opposing and allied, superstates of Eurasia and Eastasia. Eurasia encompasses the rest of Europe and Russia, while the boundaries of Eastasia are less

BIG BROTHER IS WATCHING YOU

defined but include modern-day China, Japan, Taiwan and Korea. Orwell's fictional divisions are a reflection of actual and forecast geopolitical alignments after World War II.

Nineteen Eighty-Four is set against the backdrop of a global nuclear and civil war that raged during the 1950s. London is barely rebuilt and is still regularly hit by 'rocket bombs'. Most people outside the ruling ministries are dirty, poor and malnourished. Oceanian society is divided into a broad-based, three-tiered pyramid, with the Party Leader, Big Brother, at the apex (although it is not known if Big Brother is dead, or even existed). Around six million members of the Inner Party (known as 'the brain of the State' and accounting for fewer than two per cent of the population) are just below him, and below them the Outer Party (comprising minor functionaries such as Smith). Below that come 'the dumb masses ... "the proles"', about eighty-five per cent of the population.

Nineteen Eighty-Four largely plays out in small, cramped spaces: Smith's squalid apartment, ministry offices and the tiny room over a shop in a 'prole' neighbourhood where Winston and Julia carry on their love affair. These confined environs are later echoed in the cells and interrogation rooms of the Ministry of Love, and climax in 'Room 101' (the ultimate torture chamber containing a prisoner's own worst nightmare, fear or phobia). The pervading claustrophobia is only briefly punctuated by a countryside scene in which Winston and Julia make love for the first time and Winston's dreams glimpses of the 'Golden Country' of his past.

Winston and Julia's room over the shop, with its apparently safe enclosure and love-bed, is also evocative of the past world surviving, tenuously, among the proles: a world of private loyalties, emotionally charged sexuality and simple decency. The room contains an old paperweight – 'a little chunk of history' the Party overlooked, a 'message from a hundred years ago' – a richly symbolic and fragile object that elegantly speaks volumes when contrasted with the massive pyramids of the Ministries. Lying in the bed with Julia in their room, Winston observes: 'The paperweight was the room he was in, and the coral was Julia's life and his own, fixed in a sort of eternity at the heart of the crystal.'

The fragile paperweight correlates with Winston and Julia's love, apparently safe enclosure, and with the world of the past; the pyramids correlate with hierarchy, bureaucracy on a monumental scale, and crushing totalitarian power. Centrally, the paperweight correlates with a past in which people could be 'governed by private loyalties' and value 'individual relationships', a world where 'a completely helpless gesture, an embrace ... could have value in itself.'

In *Nineteen Eighty-Four*, Oceania, Eurasia and Eastasia are all totalitarian states related to one another in cynical alliance or through hatred and warfare (although Julia is astute enough – more astute than Winston – to speculate that the war itself may be phony, with Oceania bombing its own

It was almost normal for people over thirty to be frightened of their own children. And with good reason, for hardly a week passed in which *The Times* did not carry a paragraph describing how some eavesdropping little sneak – 'child hero' was the phrase generally used – had overheard some compromising remark and denounced its parents to the Thought Police.

people). The only hope in the novel is the faint one of the proles' remaining human, and Winston and Julia's time of love and loyalty, a 'helpless gesture', perhaps, but one with value.

Orwell's aim with *Nineteen Eighty-Four* was to highlight the totalitarian horrors of the first half of the twentieth century and thereby help to avoid their repetition. And he has arguably achieved his aim, as evidenced by the fact that so many of the ideas within the novel – 'Big Brother is watching you', 'newspeak', 'doublethink', 'thoughtcrime', 'reality control' – have entered into common usage and remain as a warning.

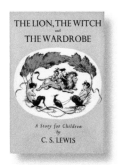

THE LION, THE WITCH and THE WARDROBE

A Story for Children
by
C. S. LEWIS

C. S. LEWIS

THE CHRONICLES OF NARNIA
(1950–56)

'Always winter and never Christmas; think of that!' C. S. Lewis'
enchanted realm beyond the wardrobe and its cast of magical
inhabitants have captivated readers of all ages for decades.

The Chronicles of Narnia were written over two years while their author nursed a dying (and querulous) old lady, coped with a binge-drinking brother and continued the work of an Oxford don specialising in medieval and Renaissance literature. The books were originally published by Geoffrey Bles and The Bodley Head, the latter publishing the final two books of the series.

As a youth, Lewis discovered Norse mythology, which impressed him as ineffably severe, melancholy and beautiful. This infatuation with what he called 'Northerness' provided common ground in his early acquaintance with J. R. R. Tolkien as fledgling dons at Oxford in the 1920s.

Born to a middle-class Anglo-Irish family in Belfast, Clive Staples Lewis (known to his friends and family as Jack), described himself as 'a product of long corridors, empty sunlit rooms, upstairs indoor silences, attics explored in solitude, distant noises of gurgling cisterns and pipes, and the noise of wind under the tiles. Also, of endless books.' His mother died when he was nine and, although he remained close to his older brother Warren for the rest of his life, his relationship with his father was difficult. With Warren, he invented an imaginary realm the boys called Boxen, populated by animals who wore clothes and discussed politics, transport, and industry. Lewis himself dismissed it as 'almost astonishingly prosaic'.

The works of Beatrix Potter and E. Nesbit made the most powerful impressions on him as a small boy, and the narration and sibling relationships of the Chronicles show how strongly Nesbit shaped his notion of what children's fiction should be. The irony and relatively sophisticated social comedy that both Nesbit and Lewis employ (for example, in the diary of the awful Eustace Scrubb in *The Voyage of the Dawn Treader*, 1952) derive from the nineteenth-century British novel – Austen and Trollope – the sort of books Lewis loved.

The critic William Empson called Lewis 'the best read man of his generation, one who read everything and remembered everything he read'. This was chiefly because he read for pleasure. Although he could be narrow-minded and intolerant, Lewis's literary criticism (rather unjustly overshadowed by his popular theological writings) shows him to be a magnanimous and sympathetic reader, always willing to meet an author halfway and forever mounting defences for Latin allegorists that no one else bothered even to know about, let alone read. (He drew the line, however, at modernism, an aesthetic movement that the conservative Lewis regarded with knee-jerk hostility.) When his oldest friend reproached him for writing letters entirely about books, Lewis replied, 'I leave to others all the sordid and uninteresting worries about so-called practical life, and share with you those joys and experiences which make that life desirable... but seriously, what can you have been

thinking about when you said 'only' books, music, etc., just as if these weren't the real things!'

The medieval literature Lewis loved and that underpinned his own work was essentially syncretic – a fusion of pagan, folkloric and Christian elements. It's a deliberately patchwork aesthetic that seeks to collect and harmonise rather than to unify and homogenise, on the principle that all the things of this world testify to the infinitely varied goodness of God. So, likewise, the talking animals, Northern European dwarves, classical fauns and Arthurian knights of Narnia all happily coexist under the banner of the lion god, Aslan. The underlying thinking is platonic – or, rather, neoplatonic: all these seemingly incompatible elements are not lies that contradict the truth and each other, but rather the many shadows that human beings have invented to conjure the one great reality we can never encounter directly in this life.

The closest model for Narnia is the Faerie Land of Edmund Spenser (see page 54), the sixteenth-century English poet whose work was Lewis' academic speciality. Like Faerie Land, and the Celtic notion of the underground kingdom of the Tuatha Dé Danann (which Lewis heard about as a boy from his Irish nurse), Narnia is a separate world that nevertheless intersects with our world at certain places and times, permitting the traffic of

The four Pevensie children (Susan, Peter, Lucy and Edmund) discover the snow-covered land of Narnia in a scene from *The Chronicles of Narnia: The Lion, the Witch and the Wardrobe* (2005) directed by Andrew Adamson and co-produced by Walden Media and Walt Disney Pictures.

people between the two. The four Pevensie children enter Narnia through an enchanted wardrobe in *The Lion, the Witch and the Wardrobe*, to find the land suffering under the tyrannous reign of the White Witch, who has cursed it to be 'always winter and never Christmas'. The siblings are enlisted by Aslan to defeat the witch, but first the lion god must sacrifice his own life to pay for the treachery of Edmund Pevensie, then be triumphantly resurrected.

In each of the other six Chronicles (with the exception of *A Horse and His Boy*), children from our world are brought over to save Narnia or Narnians. Yet, notably, surprisingly little of the action takes place in Narnia itself and, when it does, it is a Narnia gone wrong: frozen by the White Witch; its magical nature suppressed by the Telmarines in *Prince Caspian*; or sliding into corruption in the final Chronicle, *The Last Battle*. The quintessential Narnia – best captured in the fireside tales of Mr Tumnus in *The Lion, the Witch and the Wardrobe* – is almost always seen from a distance, either in space or time, or else savoured in brief snatches before the children are back to this world. This ideal Narnia is a never-ending round of pastoral revelry:

> he told about the midnight dances and how the Nymphs who lived in the
> wells and the Dryads who lived in the trees came out to dance with the

fauns; about long hunting parties after the milk white stag who could give you wishes if you caught him; about feasting and treasure seeking with the wild red Dwarves in deep mines and caverns far beneath the forest floor: and then about summer when the woods were green and old Silenus on his fat donkey would come to visit them, and sometimes Bacchus himself, and then the streams would run with wine instead of water and the whole forest would give itself up to jollification for weeks on end.

So powerful is the Arcadian resonance in these books, that most readers – including the series' most famous illustrator, Pauline Baynes – persist in seeing Narnia as a landscape of rolling hills and meadows with the occasional picturesque stand of trees. Lewis, however, described it as largely forested. Its population consists of talking beasts, larger and visibly more intelligent than ordinary 'dumb' beasts and treated by all good Narnians as free, sentient beings. Other Narnians include fauns, satyrs, dwarves (who come in 'red' and 'black' varieties), dryads and naiads (tree and water spirits), centaurs and assorted mythical creatures, ranging from minotaurs to werewolves. The magical population concurs that while Narnia is 'not men's country', it nevertheless ought to be ruled by a small elite of human beings in obedience to a decree made by Aslan at the dawn of the world (*The Magician's Nephew*, 1951).

Narnia is bordered on the west and north by rugged and sparsely inhabited mountains, and its marshy northern borders are occasionally harried by hostile, man-eating giants. To the south lies Archenland, a friendly nation populated by a feudal human society. A harsh desert separates Archenland from the vaguely Turkic empire of Calormen, whose dark-skinned and be-turbaned rulers frequently entertain imperial designs on the 'Northern barbarians'.

To the east of Narnia lies the Great Eastern Ocean, speckled with the allegorical islands visited in *The Voyage of the Dawn Treader* – the most medieval of the Chronicles and many readers' favourite. Because Narnia's world is flat, the furthest reaches of the Great Eastern Ocean abut on a wall of flowing water, beyond which is Aslan's country, home to the souls of the virtuous dead. Far beneath the surface of Narnia lies the land of Bism, whose gnome inhabitants live happily on the banks of a river of fire and pick diamonds like fruit to squeeze for their juice.

The marginal detail work on Narnia is pretty cursory; it's like an old-fashioned movie set, the facades just convincing enough to serve as a setting for the narrative at hand. Even Narnia itself is scantily shaded-in. Narnia has no major cities – just two castles and a briefly mentioned market town, Chippingford. Despite the absence of any industry or agriculture to speak of, the inhabitants have somehow obtained such commodities as a sewing machine, orange marmalade, tea and a seemingly endless supply of sausages and bacon.

A MAP OF NARNIA AND THE SURROUNDING COUNTRIES

Does this incongruity matter? Not to millions of young readers, that's for sure. Children, as a general rule, don't even detect the religious symbolism that many adults find so glaring in the Chronicles. We seldom notice the flaws in the object of our desire, and that is what Narnia is – a shimmering, delicious mirage, just out of reach. Within its elusive borders is collected every wonder that ever delighted Lewis in the thousands of books he read, every adventure he longed for, every brave prince and doughty badger, every enchanted pool and misted mountain, every mermaid and leafy-haired dryad, every spired castle and green hill. It would be a motley collection indeed if it were not unified by the intensity of his desire, which, because it is effectively a child's yearning, mysteriously preserved in the mind of a formidably well-read, middle-aged man, communicates most immediately to child readers.

That doesn't, however, make it merely childish. The desire to bring all of life's joys together in celebration is an impulse that even those who can't subscribe to Lewis's faith can nevertheless still understand and share. In the case of Narnia, it isn't the elaboration of the backdrop that casts the spell, that makes the place seem real in spite of its many absurdities, but the inexhaustible delight of the dancers who inhabit it, as well as the man who made it.

Opposite:
Pauline Baynes's map of Narnia, published in 1972 by Puffin Books.

I, ROBOT (1950)

As the science of robotics advances to an inevitable conclusion, the nine short stories of Asimov's I, Robot chronicle a remarkably prescient future history from 1998 to 2052.

First published by Gnome Press in 1950.

From robots being restricted to off-world use, to becoming indistinguishable from humans, *I, Robot* anticipates the film *Blade Runner* by decades. Asimov's book is arguably as essential to that landmark film as Philip K. Dick's *Do Androids Dream of Electric Sheep?*, upon which *Blade Runner* is officially based.

The *Oxford English Dictionary* credits Asimov with the earliest usage of the words 'robotics' and 'positronic' (although the first use of the word 'robot' belongs to Karel Čapek's 1920 play *Rossum's Universal Robots*).

Through nine stories originally published in the magazines *Astounding Science Fiction* and *Super Science Stories* between 1940 and 1950, the Russian-born American master of science fiction Isaac Asimov developed his vision of the future, our present, which now appears simultaneously naive and extraordinarily prescient. His foresight stems from an extraordinary imagination coupled to genuine facility for real science; he obtained a PhD in biochemistry in 1948 and joined the faculty of the Boston University School of Medicine.

The stories were published together in 1950 as *I, Robot* and together they present a future world of wonders, in which humanity is spread across the solar system: from flying cars, to mining operations on Mercury, to a network of interplanetary solar-power relay stations, and on to Hyper Base, where an experimental new warp drive will power a spaceship to the stars. The one unifying element to all these marvels is robots, specifically those designed by the monolithic corporation, US Robots and Mechanical Men, Inc.

Lawrence Robertson founded US Robots in 1982, the same year in which Dr Susan Calvin, the scientist who eventually becomes the company's head robot psychologist, is born. Calvin does not appear in every story, but when Asimov 'fixed up' his individual tales into a novel he devised a framing device in which the doctor, now seventy-five, is interviewed by a young journalist on the occasion of her retirement, offering the chance to reflect on her life and the intertwined history of robotics.

A handful of other characters recur through the stories – notably the troubleshooting robotics engineers Gregory Powell and Mike Donovan – but more consistent than any one character is the process of continual change realised by rapid technological progress. In the first story, set in 1998, Robbie is a humanoid metal machine who cannot speak, who serves as a companion to a little girl, Gloria. By 'Runaround', set seventeen years later, talking robots are engaged in complex mining activities on Mercury.

It is with this story that Asimov made his most inspired and enduring contribution to popular culture, codifying the 'Three Laws of Robotics'

A robot may not injure a human being or, through inaction, allow a human being to come to harm.

A robot must obey orders given it by human beings except where such orders would conflict with the First Law.

A robot must protect its own existence as long as such protection does not conflict with the First or Second Law.

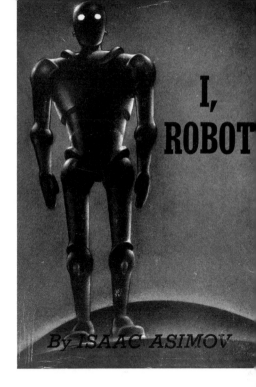

as an essential protocol to govern the increasingly sophisticated behaviour of robots and with the aim of ensuring that human safety remained paramount. Rules in place, the stories unfold as logic puzzles, with either Powell, Donovan or, later, Calvin, required to resolve a situation arising from a robot interpreting the Laws in an unanticipated way, often with dangerous consequences.

The robots have 'positronic' brains. They are conscious, but there is a tension between cybernetic 'free will' and programming. That Susan shares her name with the theologian John Calvin, who argued the individual's fate was predestined by God, does not seem coincidental. Indeed, the final story documents 'The Inevitable Conflict'.

Ultimately, for a work written through the years of World War II and the early Cold War, *I, Robot* offers a remarkably optimistic vision of a peaceful future, of a transition to a postcapitalist, post-statist global economy. Inevitably a product of its time, *I, Robot*'s future remains largely a man's world, with Calvin apparently the only successful woman, excepting a brief appearance by Madame Szegeczowska, co-coordinator of the European Region, and the fourth most powerful person in a society where all real power resides in the Machine.

The cover for the first US edition of *I, Robot* published in 1950 by Gnome Press. Opposite is shown the first UK edition (1952).

RAY BRADBURY

FAHRENHEIT 451 (1953)

A masterpiece of twentieth-century literature set in a bleak, dystopian future where literature is on the brink of extinction.

First published by Ballantine Books in 1953.

451°F is supposed to be the temperature at which book paper will begin to burn.

In December 2015, a new internet HTTP error code 451 was adopted to denote content that has been censored/blocked for legal reasons.

Ray Bradbury (1920–2012) wrote the first version of *Fahrenheit 451*, originally called 'The Fireman', in 1949, in nine days, on a rented typewriter in the basement of the library on the University of California, Los Angeles (UCLA), campus. Surrounded by books as he wrote, grabbing them at random for inspiration, Bradbury liked to say that the library had written the story for him. The novel we know as *Fahrenheit 451* was published in 1953.

Although he loved movies, the new medium of television was, in Bradbury's view, a threat both to reading and to conversation, as people spent increasing amounts of time staring at a screen in their living rooms, rather than engaging with others or exploring ideas. He imagined the results after fifty years: giant 'televisor' screens on multiple walls, social life replaced by soap-opera families, tiny 'Seashells' plugged into the ears providing a constant stream of music or chatter, and an increasing rejection of independent, critical thinking accompanying the fear of anyone being different.

Into this nightmare of bland conformity, Bradbury incorporated his personal dislikes: speed, team sports and modern art. He never learned to drive, but the citizens of his dystopia are not allowed to travel at less than fifty miles per hour, often crash and enjoy running down pedestrians. Sports have replaced books as the major part of school curricula, and are prescribed (along with easily available tranquillisers and stimulants) for anyone whose behaviour is out of line. Only abstract paintings are on display.

In a powerful reversal of the norm, firemen start fires rather than putting them out. Their job is to seek out illegal caches of books and burn them. Since the Constitutional meanings of 'happiness' and 'a free and equal society' have been corrupted to mean that all must be *made* equal in order to be happy, firemen become the guardians of society.

Guy Montag is a fireman, delighting in his destructive power until he meets a neighbour, self-described 'crazy' teenager Clarisse, who asks him 'Are you happy?' He cannot answer and begins to question his life.

Montag's boss, Captain Beatty, explains that books are so dangerous to human happiness because not one of them agrees with another. Some are

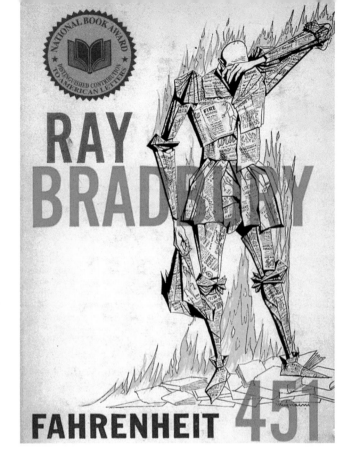

Striking cover artwork by illustrator and artist Joseph Mugnaini, a regular collaborator with Bradbury. This cover was re-released in 2003 to celebrate the book's 50th anniversary.

offensive to particular groups, some make you feel unpleasant emotions, some make you dissatisfied with your lot, others force you to ask questions – they are like loaded guns in the wrong hands. When he sees a woman refuse to be parted from her books, choosing to burn with them, Montag believes they must be the thing that is lacking in his life.

The city in *Fahrenheit 451* is unnamed, but is probably somewhere in California. The shadow of nuclear war hangs over all, yet the citizens are encouraged to believe that only 'other people' die that way. But no matter how desperate things are, there is still a ray of hope. Outside the city, living simply in the countryside, former professors, librarians and others have formed a resistance movement, not owning the banned books, but keeping them alive in their minds. They will pass the memorised texts on to their children by word of mouth, and they to their children, until the time is right for their return.

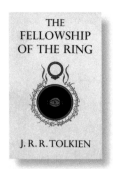

J. R. R. TOLKIEN

THE LORD OF THE RINGS
(1954–55)

Classic and incredibly detailed fantasy world of Middle-earth; created by a mild-mannered language professor as a hobby, it went on to become the most influential imaginary world ever created.

Initially published as three books by George Allen and Unwin: *The Fellowship of the Ring* (July 1954), *The Two Towers* (November 1954), and *The Return of the King* (October 1955).

The Lord of the Rings was preceded by *The Hobbit*, published as a children's book in 1937, and was intended as a sequel to it. When delivered seventeen years later, however, it was no longer a children's book and had become far longer and more ambitious. The background history to both works is contained in *The Silmarillion* (1977).

The Middle-earth of J. R. R. Tolkien's (1892–1973) *The Hobbit* and *The Lord of the Rings* is probably the best-known and most influential of all the many imaginary worlds of the twentieth century. The books have sold millions of copies in scores of languages, and yet the stories are remarkable for more than sheer numbers. Heroic fantasy existed before Tolkien, of course, but his success brought it into the mass market. Very few later authors of fantasy have escaped his imprint – even those who have tried very hard to shed it – and many have testified that it was his work that made them writers.

Tolkien's commercial and popular success is ironic because he made almost no attempt to achieve it. No one could look less like a professional author. We know, now, that he started to write a version of his personal mythology as early as 1917, but although he rewrote it continually, he made little effort to have it published for twenty years, and then met with no success. *The Hobbit* (1937) might never have seen publication if a student of Tolkien's had not mentioned it to an employee of the publisher George Allen and Unwin. When *The Hobbit* became moderately successful, Stanley Unwin asked him for a sequel. Tolkien started work on it right away, at Christmas 1937, but it was years before the sequel began to be published, in three volumes 1954–55, and by then *The Lord of the Rings* had ceased to be for children. Unwin expected the work to make a loss, but was prepared to take a chance on it – because the other side of the author's apparent amateurishness is his originality.

The Lord of the Rings is not the story of a quest, but of an anti-quest. The hero, the hobbit Frodo Baggins, is not trying to recover some lost object of power, like the Holy Grail, but to destroy forever one that he already has – the One Ring, found accidentally in the course of *The Hobbit* by his older cousin Bilbo Baggins. If the Dark Lord, Sauron, regains it, his power will become irresistible; if it is destroyed he will crumble – but the only place where the Ring can be destroyed is where it was forged, in the Cracks of Doom in the heart of Sauron's own country of Mordor. Frodo, with his companion Sam, has to get there on his own. The wars and battles that occupy

his other companions, though much more dramatic than Frodo's stealthy journey, are secondary.

Tolkien's hobbits are a race or subspecies of small humans, rarely more than four feet tall, but in almost every other respect – including behaviour and mindset – identical to the rustic English people of his own Victorian youth: cheerful, practical, unintellectual and unadventurous. They live in the Shire, very like Tolkien's home county of Worcestershire, and take no interest in the wider world of Middle-earth. It is Gandalf the wizard who decides, in *The Hobbit*, to shake them up by recommending Bilbo as a professional burglar to a company of dwarves, setting off to recover their ancestral treasures from the dragon Smaug.

The Lord of the Rings opens up far wider perspectives of space and time than *The Hobbit*, beginning with Gandalf explaining to Frodo what the Ring really is and what must be done to ensure its destruction. But a third and critical invention was there in the earlier work as well – the concept of Middle-earth. It has been rightly said that the hero of *The Lord of the Rings*

Tolkien's sketch of Orthanc, the impenetrable tower of Isengard, in an early manuscript of *The Lord of the Rings*.

is not Frodo, nor Aragorn, nor even Sam Gamgee, but Middle-earth itself. It is Middle-earth with which so many millions of readers have fallen in love. An initial feature of this mystical land is the variety of physical environment that it encompasses: the Misty Mountains, the prairies of the Riddermark, the Great River of Anduin, the Dead Marshes, but most of all, the forests: Mirkwood, the Old Forest, Fangorn Forest and Lothlórien, all different, all lovingly described.

Along with physical environments comes a variety of species. Tolkien would have been the first to acknowledge that his Middle-earth was not purely his own creation, but a re-creation, backed by his own unique professional knowledge of the lost world of early Northern fable and myth. From these tales Tolkien drew his cast of elves and dwarves, trolls and dragons, and even orcs and ents – both words that existed in Old English, and which moreover meant nothing (like hobbits) until Tolkien gave them life.

Tolkien was a Professor, first of English Language at the University of Leeds, then of Anglo-Saxon at Oxford, finally moving to the Merton Chair of English Language and Literature, also at Oxford. All his fiction is animated by his awareness of early Northern literatures – primarily, but not exclusively, Old Norse and Anglo-Saxon – and even more by his attempt to make sense of what they said, which is often said to be self-contradictory or inadequate.

It is this knowledge that gives Middle-earth one more distinctive quality, and that is its sense of great age and complex history. Tolkien's work made it almost mandatory for fantasy authors after him to include maps of their imaginary worlds, but further to this, at the end of *The Lord of the Rings* he also gave a hundred pages of history, chronicle and family tree, with carefully considered alphabets and language commentaries to boot. No one has had the resources to imitate this. As well as his vast learning, Middle-earth was, in his own mind, at least twenty years old by the time he started writing the trilogy, with already developed Elvish languages, characters and even poetic traditions – *The Lord of the Rings* is full of poems, in many modes, mostly now quite unfamiliar. But Frodo and Sam and the other hobbits, as soon as they leave the Shire, recreate the experience of modern readers as they find themselves plunged into a world with a deep sense of history, often of ancient grudge. Bilbo's dwarf-companions want revenge on Smaug the dragon, the Mines of Moria preserve the memory of the underground wars of orcs and dwarves, elves and dwarves also have old and recent enmities, the very landscape (like the English landscape) is covered with old barrows, ruined castles, memorials of forgotten people – all of them provoking a wish to know more, which is left unsatisfied. This thirst for a greater and deeper understanding of the roaming history that Tolkien created has been a major stimulus for later writers, poets, artists and even composers.

One last feature deserves to be considered as an explanation for Tolkien's extraordinary success, and that is – rather surprisingly, in view of what has just been said – his contemporary relevance. Most of Tolkien's own life was uneventful. He held one academic post after another for forty years, married the sweetheart of his teenage years, raised four children and enjoyed popular fame only in retirement. However, his early life was unremittingly sad. His father died when he was four, his mother when he was twelve. Family life was replaced for him by life at school, but many of his school friends were killed during World War I when Tolkien also saw active service at the Somme with the Lancashire Fusiliers, until he fell victim to 'trench fever', a disease probably carried by lice.

The work also carries unusual emotional depth. *The Lord of the Rings* includes a victory, but does not end with it. Frodo cannot be cured in Middle-earth, and has to leave for the Undying Lands. Not everyone can follow him. The elves, potentially immortal though they are, will die or dwindle if they stay, and if they leave will lose forever Middle-earth and the trees they love. The tree-herding ents are also doomed to species-extinction. If the dwarves and hobbits survive, it will be marginally and invisibly. Tolkien does death scenes brilliantly, even in the children's book *The Hobbit*, but even stronger than his sense of death is his sense of loss, of which death is only a part. One can lose memories as well as people, and the loss even of Gollum is sad: he had a chance to save himself before he died, but failed to take it.

Yet the counterpart of loss is determination. Tolkien's work is studded with heroes of very different types: warriors and dragon-slayers like Aragorn and Bard the Bowman or Túrin in *The Silmarillion*; Beorn the were-bear in *The Hobbit*; Théoden King charging to death and glory in *Lord of the Rings*; and, throughout, the hobbits – not very aggressive but plugging gamely and cheerfully along like overburdened soldiers in the trenches. They are heroes, too, both hobbits and soldiers. In all Tolkien's work, archaic and modern concepts interpenetrate, showing continuity beneath change, something in which he firmly believed. He brought back a whole inheritance of myth and legend in his vast world, and made it work for the present day.

JUAN RULFO

PEDRO PÁRAMO (1955)

In this hugely influential novel, Juan Preciado sets out across Mexico to the spectral town of Comala, where dream and reality, past and present and the realms of the living and dead, merge and overlap.

First published by Fondo de Cultura Económica in 1955.

Rulfo's full name was Juan Nepomuceno Carlos Pérez Rulfo Vizcaíno, and he was also a screenwriter and photographer.

He is best known for *Pedro Páramo* and a collection of short stories, *El Llano en llamas* (*The Plain in Flames*, 1953).

Although Juan Rulfo (1917–1986) authored little more than two slender volumes of fiction in his lifetime – a short novel and a collection of short stories – he remains a towering literary figure to contemporary Latin American and Mexican authors. Rulfo is largely unknown outside of Spanish-speaking countries, though authors such as Gabriel García Márquez and Jorge Luis Borges have credited him as being one of the world's greatest writers. The imaginary world Rulfo created in *Pedro Páramo* sent shock waves through the literary milieu and, although critics did not initially respond well to his work, Rulfo became a beacon to authors who were eager to engage in a type of writing that was unlike anything that came before.

Pedro Páramo uses the layering of many alternate and alternating narrative voices, flashbacks and flash-forwards, and jumps around in time. The point of view of the first-person narrator, Juan Preciado, begins us on our journey, which alternates from character to character without warning, moving between first- and third-person narration, and from the living to the dead. It leaves the reader in a permanently perplexed, dreamlike state. Rulfo's novel transports the reader to the imaginary and poignant wasteland of Comala – a journey that the reader may interpret as a descent into hell (the word itself means griddle, grill or brazier) – as Juan attempts to carry out his mother's dying wish for him to find his father. *Pedro Páramo* (the name means wasteland or barren plain) forces the reader to distinguish between the original narrator's voice, the whispers of the dead in their crypts, Pedro Páramo's frequent flashbacks to his own childhood and his love for Susana San Juan, Susana's senseless musings in life and in death, the repeated phrases of Juan Preciado's dying mother – who lauds the lush beauty of her native city, Comala – and Juan's present, voiced perceptions of the city as a deserted and burned-out wasteland.

Described as one of the most haunting works in the Spanish language, Rulfo's use of time encapsulates a way of life that was and always will be recognisable as Mexican, with its unique cultural presentation of pre- and post-revolution life. The reader is continually involved in a process of

orientation and reorientation with regard to space and time, until a sense of disorientation becomes the standard mode through which Rulfo's narrative is framed. Rulfo uses the cacophony of narrative voices to portray the community of the crypt, where people are buried nearly on top of each other (especially if they are poor), and demonstrates that the dead seem to be more concerned with the cares of the living (or of the dead when they were living). They attempt to overhear Susana San Juan speaking aloud in the sleep of death in her crypt – as a person of means, she is farther away from the rest of the buried community so that the others have to strain to hear her.

Rulfo knows that by keeping the reader disorientated in terms of causality we cannot grow comfortable with any sense of reliability in the novel. Yet the portrayal of many different narrative voices helps to create a simulacrum of the world and society. This simulacrum cannot be anything but a fantastic representation; however, the ghosts of Comala linger in our minds in the same way that a powerful event lingers in consciousness. No reader ever leaves Comala completely behind.

A scene from the film adaptation, loosely based on the novel and directed by Carlos Velo in 1967.

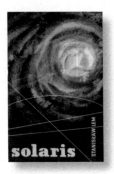

STANISŁAW LEM

SOLARIS (1961)

Lem's powerfully intelligent and influential science-fiction story asks the fundamental question of whether we can begin to understand the mysteries of the universe without first coming to understand ourselves.

First published by Wydawnictwo Ministerstwa Obrony Narodowej in 1961.

The word 'solaris' is a Latin adjective meaning 'sunny'.

It used to be believed that consciousness would always require a 'hard' or fixed system on which to run, like the pattern of neurons in the brain or the circuits of computers. Some more recent thinkers like Stuart Hameroff have theorised something more like fluid- or quantum-based consciousness, much closer to the idea Lem advances in this novel.

Polish-born Lem (1921–2006) was an astonishingly prolific and varied writer, but there are good reasons why his novel *Solaris*, published in 1961, remains his best-known work. Always restlessly intelligent and inventive, as much a philosophical thinker as a writer of fiction, many of his stories are thought-provoking on an intellectual level. But this account of explorers from Earth attempting to make contact with the radically alien intelligence represented by the planet Solaris is more than just thought-provoking: it is poetic, moving and liable to haunt your dreams.

In the novel, human space explorers have been studying the baffling world of Solaris for decades. The whole planet is covered in a globe-spanning ocean that itself seems to be conscious and intelligent, although all attempts to make contact have failed. Indeed, the ocean-world appears indifferent to humanity, and the observing scientists have been reduced to recording and cataloguing the complex phenomena that appear on the planet's fluid surface. The mental health of the space station crew is suffering, and a psychologist named Kris Kelvin is dispatched from Earth. Kelvin's wife has recently committed suicide, and when he arrives on the Solaris-orbiting space station he sees her again. Several of the crew report similar apparitions – physical manifestations of people they have lost. It seems that bombarding the planet with x-rays has caused it to respond by creating these eidolons: artificial people, gifted with minds and emotions read telepathically from the memories of the humans.

Solaris is centrally about an encounter with an almost overwhelming radical alienness and otherness. Most science-fiction aliens look rather like humans or, if they differ from us physically, we are nonetheless able to communicate and interact with them. Science fiction is full of stories of human–alien trade, or wars or intermarriage. *Solaris* is nothing like this.

Early observers of Solaris assumed, the novel tells us, 'that the thinking ocean of Solaris was a gigantic brain, prodigiously well-developed and several million years in advance of our own civilisation', which had 'long ago understood the vanity of all action and for this reason had retreated into an

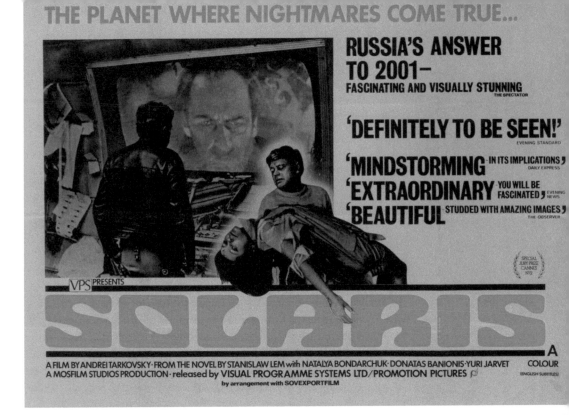

A poster for Andrei Tarkovsky's 1972 film adaptation.

unbreakable silence'. But as the novel goes on, we realise that 'the living ocean [is] active'.

Not active according to human ideas, however – it did not build cities or bridges, nor did it manufacture flying machines. Nor was it concerned with the conquest of space. It was engaged in a never-ending process of transformation, an ontological auto-metamorphosis.

That last word is key to the novel's success as a work of fiction: Solaris as imagined keeps changing, redefining itself and, therefore, redefining its human observers. This is why Lem imagines it in terms of an ocean: its consciousness is not fixed and benchmarked by static points of science, convention or ideology, the way human minds are. It is in a process of continual flux. There is no world in the whole of science fiction like it.

A CLOCKWORK ORANGE (1962)

A study of youth, violence and free will, A Clockwork Orange *creates a new language in order to build a world where children and adults are incomprehensible to each other.*

First published by Heinemann in 1962.

For many years, the UK and US editions of *A Clockwork Orange* had different endings, with the UK edition printing an extra chapter of epilogue, in which Alex matures and chooses to change his ways.

The word 'nadsat', for the youth language of the book, derives from the ending of the numerals eleven through nineteen in Russian.

A Clockwork Orange begins with a question ('What's it going to be then, eh?'), which will be repeated throughout the novel, and which will resonate differently each time it appears. It's the next sentence, though, that plunges the reader into the book's world: 'There was me, that is Alex, and my three droogs and we sat in the Korova Milkbar making up our rassoodocks what to do with the evening...' More unfamiliar words are used: *mesto, skorry, veshches, moloko, peet*. In addition, the diction is also unusual: 'the evening, a flip dark chill winter bastard though dry', 'and you may, O my brothers, have forgotten', 'admiring Bog And All His Holy Angels And Saints'.

This is 'nadsat', an argot Anthony Burgess (1917–93) invented, mostly from anglicised Russian root words. The words create not only the voice of a person, they also evoke an entire world. It becomes clear that nadsat is a language used only by certain young people. Children who speak in nadsat make themselves all but incomprehensible to adults, who speak a standard version of English. With nadsat, Burgess makes the generation gap literal.

In 1962, Anthony Burgess was already an established novelist, but *A Clockwork Orange* shot him to international fame, and particularly so after Stanley Kubrick's film adaptation was released in 1971.

A Clockwork Orange is set in what was, when the book was published in 1962, the future, but the exact date isn't clear, and the world is not significantly different from England in the 1960s. There are 'worldcast' TV shows and other items that were more speculation than reality when the book was written, but the feeling of science fiction is mostly derived from the nadsat terms, which create an alienating effect easily as strong as warp drives and ray guns in conventional science fiction.

There is also the ultraviolence. The word is Alex's own for what he and his droogs get up to. They vandalise, they assault, they rape. In Kubrick's film, the shock comes from just how much joy their sadism brings them, but in the novel the effect is somewhat different, and suggests much about this world. Alex brings girls home, plays Beethoven's *Ninth Symphony* for them, gives them drugs and rapes them. There is a similar scene in the film, but in

the book a key point is different: the girls 'couldn't have been more than ten [years old]'. After the murder that will land him in jail, Alex reveals information previously unknown: he is only fifteen years old.

The youth violence that the politicians and scientists try to solve (which renders Alex into the titular 'clockwork orange', incapable of committing any sort of aggression without being crippled by pain and nausea) is not small stuff. Alex is a monster, living a monstrous life, and such a life does not seem uncommon in this world. Whether Alex ought to be programmed against violence or left to his own free will is one of the questions the novel raises.

Alex becomes a political symbol for a group opposed to the government's plans for controlling violence. The government, too, wants to use him. Neither side consider him as a person, he is merely a symbol to be broadcast for political gain: a clockwork orange of another sort.

A Clockwork Orange is often described as depicting a dystopia, but that's not quite right. In its characters' eyes, it is a world heading that way. To the government and many citizens, the out-of-control children are leading the country towards chaos; to radicals, the government is trying to destroy free will and individuality. All we can know is that the world becomes a different one after the events of the story; in one of the first sentences of the book, Alex complains about 'things changing so skorry these days and everybody very quick to forget'. He has not forgotten, nor could he, and so he helps us remember a world we never experienced.

'The Korova Milkbar sold milk-plus, milk plus vellocet or synthemesc or drencrom, which is what we were drinking. This would sharpen you up and make you ready for a bit of the old ultra-violence'. Alex (played by Malcolm McDowell in Stanley Kubrick's 1971 film) makes his plans for the evening ahead.

VLADIMIR NABOKOV

Pale Fire (1962)

'Nabokov's most perfect novel' and a postmodern masterpiece, Pale Fire *presents a wildly original narrative structure in the form of a 999-line poem, with an extensive, and very subjective, commentary that reveals the politics and petty jealousies of academia.*

First published by G. P. Putnam's Sons in 1962.

Frequently appearing on lists of the best novels of the twentieth century, *Pale Fire* received a mixed reception, with one critic labelling it 'unreadable'.

Multifaceted and heavy with allusion to other works, *Pale Fire* also incorporates references to Nabokov's previous novels, such as *Lolita* and the eponymous hero of *Pnin*, who appears here as a minor character.

The title of John Shade's poem is taken from Shakespeare's *Timon of Athens*: 'The moon's an arrant thief, / And her pale fire she snatches from the sun.'

What can be said about *Pale Fire* to someone coming to it for the first time – someone who doesn't have all day, much less the lifetimes needed to dig down to all its different levels? To start with, it's a very fancy and very funny fairy tale, told partly by an imaginary poet and partly by an imaginary critic, who is supposedly explaining the imaginary poet's poem, but is mostly trying to shape the poem, which is a combination of fantasy and autobiography, into a reflection of his own imagination.

Pale Fire is full of tricks and mirrors and false bottoms, and also people you'd never find in your usual wonderland. Look! There's Dr Samuel Johnson! He's dressed as a suburban English professor, and pontificates in an upstate college town instead of eighteenth-century London. And then there's a trained assassin, sent from pre-Soviet Russia to kill an exiled king. When they're not turning on one another, people are turning into one another by the strange lights of *Pale Fire* – reformed and transformed, but never so you don't recognise them.

Look again at that king killer come from far away; he's reborn as a garden-variety lunatic, just escaped from the local asylum. And a closer look at that exiled monarch from a kingdom called Zembla (somewhere between Iceland and the Garden of Eden) shows a pedantic, semi-certifiably psychotic, perennially 'visiting' professor, a bizarrely and bravely unapologetic vegetarian, homosexual émigré, living in the middle of the last century, before those things were accepted.

By all accounts, the world of *Pale Fire* is hilarious. The poem 'Pale Fire', written by the imaginary poet, is a pretty good poem, although the imaginary poet (his name is Shade) would be the first to tell you it's not what a lot of people would call great the way *Paradise Lost* is great: 'Pale Fire' (and *Pale Fire*, for that matter) won't explain the mysteries of the deep to you. It won't serve up Eternity, much less promise eternal life. (That's partly why the critic – his name is Kinbote – tries to make the poem into something it isn't: an epic of his sorely missed, wholly imaginary Zembla, stocked with winter palaces and seaside dachas, 24/7 pomp and circumstance and teams of costumed young

athletes. This is Kinbote's own, his native land, all the more beloved for living only in his mind.)

About as far from Zembla or any 'kingdom by the sea' as anything could be, the poem itself makes no promise of happiness. 'Pale Fire' makes no promise to enlighten or assure, or put an end to all that ails. The poet is very imaginative – he can turn a phrase so that the most ordinary sight or sound is magically transformed into a thing of beauty and a joy, albeit not forever. This lack of 'forever' is the problem in a nutshell: it's the pain that no amount of pretending can keep out of any wonderland:

> And suddenly a festive blaze was flung
> Across five cedars, snowpatches showed,
> And a patrol car on our bumpy road
> Came to a crunching stop …

That festive blaze – police lights – is a cool transformation, but no amount of poetic dancing can keep that patrol car from its appointed round: it's come to tell the poet and his wife that their daughter has taken her own life. The pain at the heart of *Pale Fire* – the loss of the will to live, the loss of that which you love – never goes away. And the greatness of Nabokov's greatest pretending is to never pretend that it can.

This cryptic detail of messages and paperwork from a 1943 painting by Meredith Frampton was used to great effect on the cover of a recent Penguin edition of Nabokov's classic.

PIERRE BOULLE

Planet of the Apes (1963)

At once a biting satire and unsettling critique of modern civilisation and arrogance, the story of a planet ruled by primates has become one of the most well-known tales of the twentieth century.

First published by René Julliard in 1963 in French, the first English edition was translated by Xan Fielding in 1963 in the US by Vanguard Press. In the UK, the book was published as *Monkey Planet* but returned to the original title to tie in with the film franchise.

Boulle is also known for his novel, *The Bridge over the River Kwai* (1952), which was adapted into an award-winning film, garnering seven Oscars.

Opposite: Charlton Heston in the legendary film adaptation from 1968, directed by Franklin J. Schaffner and produced by Arthur P. Jacobs.

Ulysse Mérou, the central character in Pierre Boulle's 1963 satirical novel, *La Planète des Singes*, is a journalist who shares his name with the hero of Homer's *Odyssey* (*c.*725–675 BCE, page 18) Like his Greek namesake, he is a traveller – in his case journeying through deep space in the year 2500 to a planet orbiting the star Betelgeuse – and, like him, he is unexpectedly taken prisoner by strange creatures. He shows a similar degree of cunning in first winning the trust of his captors and then contriving his escape. But there the similarity with the *Odyssey* ends. While Homer concentrates on the journey that finally takes his hero home, Boulle's focus is on the world in which Ulysse and his companions find themselves.

Although Boulle puts the distance they travel at three hundred light years – less than half the actual distance to Betelgeuse – the fact that their spaceship almost reaches the speed of light means that, because of the effects of relativity, the journey takes them only two years. They land on a planet that is markedly like the one they left behind, and are so struck by the immediate similarities that they call it Soror, the Latin word for sister. However, they discover that humans in this new world have degenerated into the condition of wild animals, and apes have taken their place as the dominant species.

Even before they land, the explorers' instruments tell them that the atmosphere, like that of Earth, contains oxygen and nitrogen; although Boulle's Betelgeuse is three or four hundred times as big as the sun, the distance of the planet's orbit means that levels of radiation are also comparable. The countryside spread out below as their spaceship approaches confirms these early impressions. First, they see continents surrounded by a blue ocean. As they get nearer, there are towns with houses and tree-lined streets with cars, and a thick russet-coloured forest reminiscent of Earth's equatorial jungles.

However, it gradually becomes clear that the men and women who emerge, naked, from the jungle and finally take them prisoner have neither speech nor civilisation. When Ulysse and his companions, along with their captors, are chased through the jungle in a terrifying hunt in which many of

the humans are killed, he realises to his horror that humans and apes have changed places.

Even in the towns to which he is eventually taken by his ape captors – initially led on a chain like a pet – occasional differences from life on Earth (such as the aerial crossing places in the streets where pedestrians simply swing above the traffic) serve only to highlight the overall similarity between Soror and his home.

The gorillas, orangutans and chimpanzees who hold Ulysse captive believe that man has never evolved beyond his savage condition, because of the physical disadvantage of having only two hands, rather than the four an ape possesses. It is only later that highly controversial research comes to light, revealing that the apes actually achieved dominance by copying the achievements of a scientifically advanced but idle and feckless race of men.

There are no wars, no armies and no nations on Soror, which is ruled by a council of ministers under the leadership of a triumvirate consisting of one gorilla, one orangutan and one chimpanzee. There is also a tri-cameral parliament representing the three different species.

Long ago, the gorillas used to reign by sheer physical force, but now, at least in theory, all the different species have equal rights. In practice, despite the general ignorance of the gorillas, they remain the most powerful class, because of the cunning ways in which they manipulate the others. They also work as guards or law-enforcement, and in other roles that require physical strength, and retain a passion for hunts like the one in which Ulysse is captured and scores of other humans are killed, including one of his companions.

The orangutans – less numerous than either gorillas or chimpanzees – form a class of scientists and scholars, although Ulysse dismisses them as 'official science', unoriginal, opposed to any innovation, and content to use their highly retentive memories to learn vast amounts of information from books.

The true intellectuals are the chimpanzees, who are imbued with a powerful spirit of research, and who have been responsible for most of Soror's great discoveries. The apes have electricity, industries, motorcars and aeroplanes, but Ulysse notes that, technologically, they still lag behind the civilisation he left behind.

However, they have classical, impressionist and abstract artists, sports such as soccer and boxing, and zoos filled with various species of animals, including men, in cages. Apart from hunting, killing and imprisoning men, the apes use them for gruesome medical experiments and generally treat them with cruelty and contempt. Explaining his origins to a scientific congress on Soror, Ulysse declares:

> I come from a distant planet, from Earth, that Earth on which, by a whim
> of nature that has still to be explained, it is men who are the repositories of
> wisdom and reason … It is man who settled my planet and changed its face,

man in fact who established a civilisation so refined that in many respects,
O Monkeys, it resembles your own.

By this time, the novel has demonstrated that words such as 'wisdom',
'reason', and 'refined' are deeply ironic. The apparent similarity of the environment is a constant implied reproach as Boulle highlights the barbarity
with which animals are treated both on Soror and on Earth.

When Boulle wrote *La Planète des Singes* in 1963, he had already achieved
worldwide success with his other best-seller, *The Bridge over the River Kwai*
(1952). Both books became successful films. *The Bridge over the River Kwai*
drew directly on his time in a Japanese prisoner-of-war camp, and critics also
see echoes of these experiences in the cruel domination of humans by the ruling apes on Soror.

The original 1968 film of *The Planet of the Apes*, loosely based on the
novel, was directed by Franklin J. Schaffner, and has been followed by several
sequels, a television series, comic books and various profitable merchandising deals. A remake in 2001 was also successful, and since then there have
been *Rise of the Planet of the Apes* (2011) and *Dawn of the Planet of the Apes*
(2014). *War of the Planet of the Apes* is due for release in 2017.

Boulle, who died in 1994, criticised the original film. It lacked the subtlety and ironic bite of the novel, which ends with a surprise twist making
clear that the similarities between Earth and Soror might prove to be even
closer than the story has suggested. Where Franklin J. Schaffner was directing an action movie, Boulle had written a finely judged satire that deserves to
be judged in the tradition of Voltaire.

GABRIEL GARCÍA MÁRQUEZ

ONE HUNDRED YEARS OF SOLITUDE (1967)

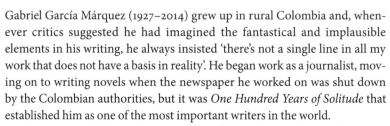

Seven generations of the Buendía family are traced in the magical and surreal location of Macondo known as 'the city of mirrors', in the South American countryside.

First published by Editorial Sudamericana in 1967.

'Gabriel García Márquez' appears as a minor character in the novel. Unlike the author, this Márquez emigrates to Paris, where he makes a living 'selling old newspapers and empty bottles'.

Márquez was awarded the Nobel Prize for Literature in 1982.

Gabriel García Márquez (1927–2014) grew up in rural Colombia and, whenever critics suggested he had imagined the fantastical and implausible elements in his writing, he always insisted 'there's not a single line in all my work that does not have a basis in reality'. He began work as a journalist, moving on to writing novels when the newspaper he worked on was shut down by the Colombian authorities, but it was *One Hundred Years of Solitude* that established him as one of the most important writers in the world.

In one sense Márquez's immensely subtle and complex novel is quite straightforward: the 'patriarch' José Arcadio Buendía, leaves Riohacha, Colombia, with his wife in search of a better life. One night, camping beside a river, he has a prophetic dream about a city made of mirrors. He decides to found this city and to call it Macondo. The novel then tells the stories of Buendía's many descendants.

There is little, however, by way of conventional narrative, beyond a list of the strange things that happen in the town, and the rise and fall of the doomed Buendía clan. Seven generations, each of which contains many individuals, makes for a crowded *dramatis personae*, but although it is possible to trace the family tree underpinning the story's many episodes, this may not be the best way of reading the text. Márquez's achievement lies in the atmosphere he creates, and the many evocative, even poetic moments of narrative intensity. Part of that atmosphere has to do with a certain intricacy, of busyness, of texture, which in turn speaks to a vision of life as rich, and complex, and involved, and endlessly surprising.

An example is the character of Colonel Aureliano Buendía, the founder's second son. The novel's famous opening sentence introduces him: 'Many years later, as he faced the firing squad, Colonel Aureliano Buendía was to remember that distant afternoon when his father took him to discover ice.' In addition to being a soldier, Aureliano is a poet and the maker of beautifully crafted golden fish. He has fathered seventeen illegitimate sons, all named Aureliano, by seventeen different women. All seventeen come to his house on the same day. Four of them decide to settle in the town, but all of them,

'Houses in Aracataca (Macondo), Colombia', c.1950. Photograph by Leo Matiz. The town in the novel, Macondo, is closely based on Márquez's childhood hometown of Aracataca, which is located near the northern Caribbean coast of Colombia. In June 2006, the town proposed a referendum to change its name to Macondo.

whether they stay or go, are murdered by mysterious assassins before they reach the age of thirty-five.

Such things are unlikely, but possible. Other aspects of the novel partake of a dream logic. Remedios the Beauty is a girl so beautiful that men break down and die at the sight of her. Apparently mentally vacant, she eventually floats off into the sky. A character called Melquíades travels to Singapore and dies, although he later returns to Macondo, declaring that he 'could not endure the solitude of death'. He then dies a second time, and is buried. All these things are treated by Márquez as if they were perfectly normal.

This last point is important, because the experience of reading the novel is not in the least whimsical, random or bizarre. On the contrary, the world Márquez creates feels exceptionally grounded and real. The textures of everyday life are precisely evoked: the weather and the landscape, infestations of red ants in the houses, the physical intensity of sexual desire.

In the end, a hurricane destroys Macondo, a fitting end for this place of South American heat and intensity, prone to floods and tempests. Márquez re-imagines his homeland as a place worked into strange shapes by the forces of individual desire and despair, by love and lust, by pride and willpower and family ties. Because those forces are so central to human life, we instinctively understand the magical logic of his City of Mirrors. *One Hundred Years of Solitude* is a foundational novel in the literary tradition known as 'magical realism' and remains to this day one of the most influential examples of this mode.

URSULA K. LE GUIN

A WIZARD OF EARTHSEA (1968)

This classic heroic journey features a young man who has to confront a frightening shadow he has released into the world in order to accept that this darkness is a part of him and to grow into his power.

A *Wizard of Earthsea* has all the vital aspects of a heroic journey, and the world in which it is set has magic as a part of daily life – it is 'a land where sorcerers come thick'. Magic is respected, its users trained to be a vital part of society, be it as healers of the sick or engineers of safe boats and ships. Earthsea has its own creation myth; it has a political system; there is an economy; a social hierarchy even where the 'wizard born' consider themselves superior; there is disease, piracy and warmongering that endangers lives; a shipping trade; smiths who work in bronze and iron; livestock and farming. There are also dragons to fear, huge ancient magical beasts that sound like an avalanche when they speak and 'have their own wisdom [and] they are an older race than man'. Earthsea is a classic example of Le Guin's (b.1929) strong world building, which is rock-solid yet never heavy-handed.

The journey of central character Ged begins in a way that is now standard for a hero's epic fantasy journey. He is a lonely young goatherd who doesn't have much, lives in a poor village, is motherless but has magical abilities greater than he can perceive. He is partly trained by his aunt who is a witch, but her skills are far less than his, and she has only a superficial understanding of the craft. Ged eventually reaches a school for wizards, where he finds himself among other young men with similar abilities. In attempting to impress them with his power, he sets free an evil that nearly kills him, one that he then has to struggle to find and face among the islands of Earthsea.

Earthsea is a large archipelago; three of the islands are named for Le Guin's children's pets, the others named in ways that sounded 'right' to her. Earthsea's civilisation is pre-industrial but literate, with an inbuilt, accepted system of magic as part of its history and culture. The magic system is such that knowing the true name of something or someone in 'Old Speech' gives you power over it or them. It is not possible to lie in true speech, so to speak a truth is to make it happen, though of course only those with powerful abilities can force such transformations, and each have repercussions. Earthsea's magic isn't without its checks and balances.

A map of Earthsea drawn by and used with permission of author Ursula K. Le Guin.

Language is important in Earthsea, and the idea of words as power and that of true names can be traced back to many real-world tribal societies and to Le Guin's interest in anthropology. The people of Earthsea are genuinely multiracial and multicultural, without any implication that the few who are of lighter skin are superior in any way. Le Guin has openly criticised the common assumption that sets much Western fantasy in a Eurocentric version of the Middle Ages. Earthsea is, in a way, the anti-Middle-earth. It's an archipelago, it is home to many people of colour, and, in it, Le Guin is more focused on the personal development of its individual residents than large-scale wars. Ged isn't in a constant battle with a large army – his battle is with his shadow self and, along the way, he must complete tasks that fade in comparison to his ultimate quest.

Magic may be a part of Earthsea's culture, but so is spirituality. Le Guin has based the spiritual systems of her world more on psychology and anthropology than on a monotheistic religious model. Through in the entire series, there is a very strong element of Taoism, especially in regard to the magical balances required. In *Wizard of Earthsea*, Ged's battle with his shadow self is clearly Jungian, though he, too, believes in the Taoist idea of Dynamic Balance. As he is taught, to light a candle is to throw a shadow.

PHILIP K. DICK

DO ANDROIDS DREAM OF ELECTRIC SHEEP? (1968)

On a post-apocalyptic Earth, a bounty hunter questions his own humanity as he attempts to 'retire' a group of renegade androids masquerading as human.

First published by Doubleday and Company, Inc., in 1968.

According to Dick, his androids were inspired by the journals of Gestapo officers he researched for his novel *The Man in the High Castle* (1960).

In an earlier, then unpublished novel, *We Can Build You* (1972), Dick wrote about the invention of androids by the Rosens, who created the first humanoid robots as replicas of important historical figures.

Dick's book was the basis for Ridley Scott's film *Blade Runner* (1982). However, many elements of the book were left out of the film.

A destroyed earth, ruined by a war for which no one can remember the reason; a planet irradiated and only just habitable; a population that has mostly migrated to off-world colonies in order to protect the genetic integrity of humanity, incentivised by the offer of an android servant, leaving a small remaining population of people on Earth to survive in the radioactive dust, living with corrupted genes and decreased intelligence; a broken, sad city filled with vacant apartment blocks – this is the anxious, depleted world of *Do Androids Dream of Electric Sheep?*

Richard Deckard is a bounty hunter who must track down and 'retire' six Nexus-6 androids, a model that has come close to passing as entirely human. These particular androids violently escaped from Mars and are attempting to hide out on Earth, settling in amid the remaining human population, who are doomed to eke out a life in clustered settlements in what were previously bustling cities. Deckard must ensure the humanoid body he kills is an android before he retires it. The only way to differentiate androids from humans is by the 'Voight-Kampff' test, which gauges the instinctual, empathic response to questions asked primarily about animals. The test isn't entirely accurate – schizophrenic humans may well fail it, too. But in a world where the care for now-endangered creatures is sacrosanct, a lack of empathy towards animals is enough to separate humans from other biological organisms created by them, no matter how lifelike they may be, or the range of emotions they display.

Do Androids Dream of Electric Sheep? is about what it means to be human, which is even more important in a post-apocalyptic world with a bleak future. The androids Deckard hunts want more than they have been allowed, and have chosen some form of independence on a ravaged planet over subservience to humans elsewhere. The humans left on Earth, on the other hand, are losing sense of their emotions, often depending on artificial mood enhancers to guide their daily behaviour. Dick's love for absurdity has to be appreciated, even in the broad, effective strokes with which he creates the world of this book – he's never without humour, even when he's writing about the steady disintegration of society and individuality.

The world of *Do Androids Dream of Electric Sheep?* is a believable, not too-far-away future, albeit one with hovercrafts and the colonisation of other planets. But this vision doesn't feel dated. Dick's future of vidphones and mood controllers is, in many ways, very much our present too. His San Francisco is a strange but believable construct – a city shrouded in dust that is slowly killing its inhabitants, residents who will do anything to own and care for live animals, almost all of which are endangered after the plagues following World War Terminus. The city is half-empty and full of vacant apartments where sinister junk known as 'kipple' collects and seems to breed overnight.

In his 1978 essay *How to Build a Universe That Doesn't Fall Apart Two Days Later*, Dick wrote of how he enjoyed creating universes that fell apart, become unhinged, unglued and how he had a secret love of chaos. 'Do not assume that order and stability are always good, in a society or in a universe', he wrote, insisting 'objects, customs, habits and ways of life must perish so that the authentic human being can live'.

During his search, Deckard finds himself face to face with Munch's *The Scream*, and Dick's description of the painting is one that perfectly describes not just the world as his reader may know it, but the taut, grim one he has created too: 'The painting showed a hairless, oppressed creature with a head like an inverted pear, its hands clapped in horror to its ears, its mouth open in a vast, soundness scream. Twisted ripples of the creature's torment, echoes of its cry, flooded out into the air surrounding it; the man or woman, whichever it was, had become contained by its own howl. It had covered its ears against its own sound . . . The creature was in isolation. Cut off by – or despite – its outcry.'

Harrison Ford plays Richard Deckard in a scene from the Warner Bros. movie *Blade Runner* (1982), directed by Ridley Scott.

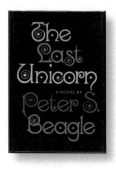

PETER S. BEAGLE

THE LAST UNICORN (1968)

Voted one of the 'All-Time Best Fantasy Novels', Beagle's novel describes a series of fairy tales through which the last unicorn must pass in search of others of her kind.

First published by Viking Press (US) and the Bodley Head (UK) in 1968, Beagle's novel has sold more than six million copies, and has been translated into more than twenty-five languages.

The Last Unicorn became an animated movie in 1982, featuring the voices of Mia Farrow, Christopher Lee, Angela Lansbury, Jeff Bridges and Alan Arkin, and an original score by American singer-songwriter Jimmy Webb.

Beagle wrote a sequel to *The Last Unicorn* entitled 'Two Hearts', which was published in *Fantasy and Science Fiction* magazine in 2005. It won both the Hugo and the Nebula award.

Peter S. Beagle's (b.1939) *The Last Unicorn* follows the titular character as she embarks on a series of episodic adventures. The unicorn's wanderings take her through a deliberately generic, if forlorn, fairyland, with indications and slight hints that it is – or is steadily becoming – the 'real' world. Although her encounters have a distinctly medieval flavour, fragments of other times and places bleed through: a glimpse of the Midgard Serpent, a passing reference to 'Anglo-Saxon folklore', and a chattering butterfly that references song lyrics and the 'A Train'.

The unicorn discovers a world where the existence of magic, including unicorns, is no longer taken for granted. Her wandering – along a long road that 'hurried to nowhere and no end' – takes her over vast distances, through lands that are either unknowable or unrecognisable in the unicorn's eyes. The feeling is mutual: as the unicorn passes through towns and villages, the residents merely see her as a white mare, if at all.

Her journey is interrupted when she is captured by Mommy Fortuna's Midnight Carnival, a bedraggled travelling show that promises 'Creatures of night, brought to light'. The show is largely illusion, with two notable exceptions: the unicorn and a harpy. The world's tentative relationship with the supernatural is on full display with the carnival. The thrill-seeking attendees simultaneously wish to glimpse 'magic', but are also reassured by the knowledge that the show is a fake. In parallel, Mommy Fortuna wrestles daily with the repercussions of having captured the uncapturable – she knows the harpy is bound to escape and that, with its departure, she will be destroyed.

The carnival is the first in a series of archetypal folkloric settings visited by the unicorn. In an outlaw-infested forest, she encounters a band of 'Merry Men' so desperate for notoriety that they've begun composing their own ballads. In a cursed village, she finds a group of wealthy burghers who – like the inhabitants of Hamelin – have traded their children for a life of comfort. In all scenarios, the unicorn finds people trying to manipulate the world by interfering with the power of

You're in the story with the rest of us now, and you must go with it, whether you will or no. If you want to find your people, if you want to become a unicorn again, then you must follow the fairy tale to King Haggard's castle, and wherever else it chooses to take you.

stories. Mommy Fortuna imprisons 'legends' in her search for power. Captain Cully, leader of the outlaws, seeks immortality by creating his own myths. The burghers strive to prevent the resolution of a curse, knowing that having it lifted will impoverish them.

It is at the crumbling castle of King Haggard, however, that the unicorn finds the truest intersection of the land's geography and her own story. Haggard and his Red Bull are behind the disappearance of the unicorns, and the unicorn's journey to find them takes her to the very heart of his dismal kingdom. Haggard's castle is a bleak location, teetering on the edge of the sea, abandoned by servants and courtiers alike.

At this point, the unicorn is transformed into a human girl. Yet, even in mortal form, she still inspires change in her surroundings. The grim atmosphere of the castle is not enough to stifle the love of the King's son for the mysterious newcomer and, despite their ominous surroundings, the remaining guardsmen and the unicorn's friends make the castle into a cosy home. Everywhere she goes, the unicorn acts as an agent of change and, despite King Haggard's best efforts, his keep is no exception.

The Last Unicorn by Rebekah Naomi Cox, 2005. Beagle has commented of Cox's work: 'unicorns look nothing at all like horned horses, and, while magically beautiful, they are also, from certain angles and under certain circumstances, just a little funny-looking. Rebekah is the only artist who has ever captured this'.

KURT VONNEGUT

Slaughterhouse-Five (1969)

Considered Vonnegut's most popular work, and inspired by his own experience of the Dresden fire-bombings, the story follows the time-travelling adventures of Billy Pilgrim, a soldier who becomes 'unstuck in time'.

First published by Delacorte in 1969.

The book has often come under censorship in the US because of its perceived vulgarity and obscene content. A film adaptation was released in 1972.

Vonnegut's other notable works include *Cat's Cradle* (1963) and *Breakfast of Champions* (1973).

On the night of 13 February, 1945, three months before the end of World War II, Kurt Vonnegut (1922–2007) was a prisoner of war, sheltering in an underground abattoir during the devastating fire-bombing of Dresden. 'Slaughterhouse-Five' (*Schlachthof-fünf*) was, ironically, shelter from the slaughter. The next morning, Vonnegut and his fellow prisoners of war were set to work excavating blackened bodies for cremation on open piles.

In the novel, Billy Pilgrim, the unheroic hero, is a POW in the same shelter as Vonnegut during the devastating fire-bombing. He, too, survives, but he goes crazy: he cannot make sense of the event.

Fiction, like history, has been generally silent about Dresden. As Hitler said: 'The victor will never be asked if he told the truth.' Vonnegut himself had almost insuperable difficulty writing his 'Dresden novel'. He had to forge an entirely new 'schizophrenic' technique, weaving realism, sci-fi schlock (little one-eyed green men from Tralfamadore, resembling toilet plungers) and slapstick social comedy into a startlingly innovative pattern.

Slaughterhouse-Five was published to huge acclaim in 1969. It shot to the top of the *New York Times* best-seller list, and has since been awarded a place in the canon of American classic fiction.

Its thesis is essentially that humankind cannot bear too much reality. Life is so horrible that only fiction can deal with it, and, crucially, the more horrible the life experience, the more fantastic the fiction. After Auschwitz, Theodore Adorno famously declared, poetry was impossible. One of the underlying contentions of *Slaughterhouse-Five* is that after Dresden, fiction, or at least realist fiction, is impossible.

A way out of this impasse was science fiction. Billy Pilgrim, a time and intergalactic traveller (or, more likely, merely nuts) ends his post-Dresden pilgrimage incarcerated no longer by Nazi Germany, but by aliens from the planet Tralfamadore.

Billy's prison is a geodesic dome (a style favoured by hippy communes in the 1960s); it is made tolerable by furniture from Sears, Roebuck (less favoured by hippies), and the presence of starlet Montana Wildhack, who is

similarly transported across space to be Billy's 'mate'. They will be earthling specimens in the Tralfamadorian national zoo.

The Tralfamadorians, like the RAF, are dangerous bombers. Billy asks his little green mentor whether earthlings will go on to destroy the universe, since they are so good at destroying their own planet? Their philosophy in the face of this inevitable doom? 'We spend eternity looking at pleasant moments – like today at the zoo.' Earthlings should learn to do the same. Forget Dresden. Enjoy Disneyland.

When Vonnegut was asked about his decision to process the horror of historical events through slapstick, black comedy and science fiction, he noted these tropes were just like the clowns in a Shakespearean tragedy: 'Trips to other planets, science fiction of an obviously kidding sort, is equivalent to bringing on the clowns every so often to lighten things up.' Yet, the novel clearly has more serious intentions. Vonnegut, in writing *Slaughterhouse-Five*, was influenced, the author acknowledged, by Joseph Heller's *Catch-22* (1961). War in *Catch-22* is conceived as a madhouse. The hero, Yossarian, can only escape the madness by being diagnosed mad himself. But to report his madness to the medical services would be to prove himself sane. This double bind is the *Catch-22* by which the military machine works. It is absurdity institutionalised, and only comedy can effectively handle it.

The other likely, but unacknowledged influence on *Slaughterhouse-Five* was Stanley Kubrick's comedy film about nuclear annihilation, *Dr. Strangelove* (1963). It's so deadly serious, you have to laugh.

The city of Dresden after the bombing. Churchill had decreed that Dresden was a strategic target. It wasn't, but was razed just the same.

LARRY NIVEN

RINGWORLD (1970)

Members of three galactic species explore an ancient artificial 'world', a vast flattened ring encircling its sun, to see if it is a threat or an opportunity, or both.

Ringworld, first published by Ballantine Books in 1970, won the Nebula Award that year, and, in 1971, both the Hugo and Locus Award.

Four sequels and four prequels extend the Ringworld narrative, and form part of Niven's wider Known Space universe, detailed across various novels and short stories.

Niven's iconic world has influenced authors including Iain M. Banks, and its engineering and physical properties have been the subject of heated debate among expert fans.

Ringworld stands as the climax to the first volumes of Larry Niven's 'Tales of Known Space' sequence. The narrative unfolds on two interacting levels. Before arriving at the Ringworld itself, readers are given back-story from earlier tales to make the complicated relationships among its cast understandable. This cast comprises two humans, the restless 200-year-old Louis Wu and the twenty-year-old Teela Brown, who has been genetically engineered to impose her good luck on events; a warrior Kzin who is deemed a coward by his civilisation for consorting with other races peaceably; and a Pierson's puppeteer, a two-headed tripodal figure described as insanely brave because of his ability to consort with dangerous alien species without fleeing from such contact. If these characterisations seem mechanical, that is, in a sense, Niven's intention.

The Ringworld itself is explored through sequences heightened by, and comprehended through, interactions among the three species, each event moving the story forward while simultaneously broadening the reader's vision of the great ring, 600 million miles around and one million miles wide, with a habitable inner surface. The lifeless outer surface is a virtually impermeable material, designed to hold the structure together, and to defend against collisions with asteroids or even planetary bodies; from beyond the ring, observers can detect in reverse the contours of the inner land: oceans cause bulges, while mountains create vast dimples gazing into the void. To contain atmosphere, the walls of the rim are one thousand miles high, and contoured in the form of mountains and ridges. Great opaque rectangular sheets between the Ringworld and its small sun slide longitudinally over the surface, which they darken into night. The habitable surface of the Ringworld is the equivalent of three million Earths.

It would have been impossible for one novel to provide a close-up conspectus of a landscape too large to comprehend, and Niven does not risk attempting to do so. The puppeteer starship the crew has travelled in is soon, therefore, incapacitated and crashes to the surface, leaving the four to

navigate in one-person, extra-vehicular scouts. All but Teela are immediately overwhelmed, and threatened, by the sheer scale of what they are, even disabled, capable of perceiving. There is no visible curvature, no horizon: all perspectives end, dizzyingly, in vanishing points. The arch of the ring is visible in the sky: if you had a million years you could walk there. Fauna is initially absent from view; nearby flora is subtly unlike Earth's, but similar enough to understand.

When the crew discover humanoid beings, they find them to have suffered a catastrophic loss of civilisation, almost certainly due to a failure in the overall power system. (There are no natural resources except for rimrock; the inhabitants of the Ringworld face the same lack of resources that would make recovery so difficult were civilisation to fall on Earth.) The novel ends in the discovery of an archaic tyranny or two. The original Ringworld engineers are nowhere to be seen, and their creation is seemingly on its last legs. The reasons for Ringworld's creation are supposititious. All we know is that a playground for trillions of people should last forever.

Engineers Chmeee and Louis investigate the enormous spacecraft parked at the spaceport on the ring walls. Illustration by Paul Marquis.

ITALO CALVINO

INVISIBLE CITIES (1972)

The merchant Marco Polo recounts impressions of fifty-five fabulous cities he has visited, or claimed to have visited, to the emperor of the Tartars, Kublai Khan.

First published by Einaudi in 1972.

The city of Leonia refashions itself every night so that its inhabitants wake to a reconfigured world. This would seem a clear inspiration for the science-fiction film *Dark City* (1998).

At one juncture, Kublai Khan himself imagines a 'city of stairs', anticipating the titular city of the first volume of Robert Jackson Bennett's *The Divine Cities* series of urban fantasy novels (2014).

If the protagonist of *Le città invisibili* (published in 1972; translated into English in 1974 and entitled *Invisible Cities*) is Italo Calvino's (1923–85) postmodern version of the real historical traveller Marco Polo, it is, as the title suggests, the places the Venetian merchant visits that are key. Calvino, a veteran of the Italian Resistance in World War II, rejected his family's Catholicism, becoming a member of the Italian Communist Party, later withdrawing from active political engagement. By nature a city dweller, he lived in Turin, Florence, Milan, Paris and Rome and once wrote, 'I always felt a New Yorker. My city is New York.'

Though the book has its roots in *The Travels of Marco Polo* (1300, the merchant's adventures as told to Rustichello da Pisa while both men were imprisoned in Genoa), Calvino's work is neither travelogue nor biography. Rather, it is a fabulous directory, preserving for posterity this fictional Marco Polo's highly unreliable accounts of distant cities as told to Kublai Khan during his sojourns in the imperial palace.

Marco's accounts are divided into nine chapters, while the metropolises themselves are, ambiguously or ironically, sorted by eleven criteria: Thin, Hidden, Continuous and Trading Cities, and Cities devoted to the Sky, Memory, Names, Eyes, Signs, Desire and the Dead.

While the chapters themselves are presented as straightforward, beautifully written accounts, it soon becomes clear that, in our world at least, these places do not, often could not, exist. Either the world of the novel is not our world, but a world of fantasy, or Calvino's Polo is a vastly accomplished fabulist, conjuring illusions to beguile, entertain, amuse or otherwise deceive the emperor for his own purposes.

An additional dimension of complexity is lent to the novel by the passages inserted between chapters, which recount the meetings between Polo and Kublai Khan. These sections are composed in a different voice, which appears to belong to a later emperor, one who understands the 'sense of emptiness which comes over us at evening', reflecting on Khan's realisation of 'the desperate moment when we discover that this empire, which had

seemed to us the sum of all wonders, is an endless, formal ruin'.

On one level *Invisible Cities* can be taken as a sly critique of the inherent untrustworthiness of travel writing, and by extension, all texts; at the literal centre point of the book Khan himself makes a rare visit, traveling to Kin-sai, a city of canals very much like Venice. Polo says, 'I should never have imagined a city like this could exist.' A little later, 'Every time I describe a city I am saying something about Venice.'

This is the heart of *Invisible Cities*, that imaginative visions can offer deeper truths than unvarnished facts. Calvino's cities are akin to Jorge Luis Borges' labyrinths and libraries. The thirteenth-century merchant reports of motorcycles, skyscrapers and radar. Marco lands in the city of Trude by plane. The city covers the world. Only the name of the airport changes.

Invisible Cities is a book with a strong heteronormative, male perspective. Women appear almost entirely as beautiful, usually unobtainable, objects of desire. Glimpsed fleetingly, they haunt the traveller's imagination, inspire him, but ultimately evade or disappoint. The cities themselves are often graced with feminine names, being called variously Cecelia, Clarice, Esmeralda or Phyllis and seem to embody the impossibility of fully knowing and possessing. Polo is always in pursuit, arriving only to leave, to travel ever onward to the next invisible city.

Isaura, the city of the thousand wells, sits over a deep, subterranean lake. Illustration by Colleen Corradi Brannigan.

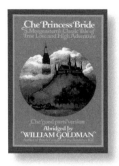

WILLIAM GOLDMAN

THE PRINCESS BRIDE (1973)

Goldman's metatextual comedy envisions a world within a world, filled with swordplay, Rodents of Unusual Size and, most of all, romance.

First published by Harcourt Brace Jovanovich in 1973.

Goldman returned to the S. Morgenstern pen name in 1983 with *The Silent Gondoliers*.

Goldman's family – his wife 'Helen' and son 'Jason' – although key figures in the introduction, are fictional. He also revisits them in the twenty-fifth anniversary edition.

The adventure of *The Princess Bride* is set primarily within the fictional European nations of Florin and Guilder, located between 'where Sweden and Germany would eventually settle'. In a tale later made popular by the classic film, the titular princess, Buttercup, is betrothed to the land's conniving prince, Humperdinck. Her childhood lover, Westley, aided by a band of talented rogues, returns from overseas in an attempt to save her from Humperdinck's clutches. Hijinks ensue.

The Princess Bride's events take place at time in history that not only doesn't exist, but is deliberately and provocatively impossible. 'A time before Europe but after Paris' is only one of the many self-contradictory explanations provided by William Goldman (b.1931). The book freely references locations such as Spain, Turkey and Scotland, but invariably and meticulously mentions that these places, and the activities therein, may or may not have existed, thus creating a sense of historicity that is, at best, utterly chaotic.

The world within the book is deliberately maddening, rife with anachronism and self-contradiction. In one breath, Goldman will note that everything in it is historically accurate, and challenge the reader to check the source against any Florinese history. Yet, at the same time, *The Princess Bride* gleefully references fire swamps, miracle men, King Bats, Blood Eagles, Sucking Squid and the immortal Rodents of Unusual Size. Florin, with its castles, forests, fleets and European neighbours is a prototypically generic Western fantasyland, littered with impossibilities.

Adding to the chaos of *The Princess Bride*, the book itself is a fictional construction. The central text comes complete with a lengthy introduction – and many interruptions – by Goldman, who sets up his version of *The Princess Bride* as an abridgement of the original by 'S. Morgenstern'. This metatextual wrapping comes complete with a fictionalised version of Goldman's own family and re-imagination of his childhood. This allows Goldman to comment on the book's themes even as he presents them, including frequent and pithy interjections from his youthful and adult selves.

Goldman states in one open aside that 'life isn't fair', and this theme is reflected through the people and the locations described in the book. Buttercup is *objectively* the most beautiful; the mighty Fezzik the strongest. Terrible things happen to deserving people, most prominently in the case of Westley's mid-book demise. Westley is faced with one unequal challenge after another: he is forced to out-brawl a giant, out-fight a 'Wizard' swordsman, out-think a genius, hide from a master huntsman and keep secrets from an uncanny interrogator. Even the geography of Florin and Guilder conspires against our heroes: ordeals range from trudging through fire swamps to falling down snow sand, to climbing the Cliffs of Insanity.

While the land in *The Princess Bride* isn't real, Goldman's conceit is that it *should* be. This is why he created a fictional and very dull history: so he could abridge it into an inspiring adventure. Similarly, the land of *The Princess Bride* is intentionally unfair – it is the triumph over the impossible that creates the romance and adventure that we require. The setting is an elaborate, improbable mechanism that exists to produce thrilling stories.

Wallace Shawn and Robin Wright Penn are forever remembered as Vizzini and Princess Buttercup in the film adaptation of *The Princess Bride* (1987).

SAMUEL R. DELANY

DHALGREN (1975)

A surprise bestseller, Dhalgren *presents an apocalyptic city outside of time,* *Bellona. What is Bellona? Each reader must decide.*

First published by Bantam Books in 1975.

In its first year of publication, *Dhalgren* went through seven printings and sold in the vicinity of half a million copies.

When editor Frederik Pohl was asked why he published *Dhalgren*, he would say, 'Because it's the first book that told me anything I didn't know about sex since *Story of O*.'

Bellona was the name of a Roman goddess of war, sometimes described as the sister or wife of Mars.

Samuel R. Delany's (b.1942) *Dhalgren* begins with the end of a sentence: 'to wound the autumnal city'. The phrase repeats throughout as a line in a mysterious notebook, puzzled over and relished. The beginning of the sentence is the final sentence of the book: 'Waiting here, away from the terrifying weaponry, out of the halls of vapour and light, beyond holland and into the hills, I have come to.' We encounter a variation on the complete sentence earlier in the book's long last section: 'I have come to wound the autumnal city: the other side of the question is a mixed metaphor if I ever heard one.' The repeated, stuttered *to* is a latch or a skip or a jump. Is the *to* of 'to wound the autumnal city' the same as the one in 'I have come to'? Should we link them, should we not? Choose your own adventure.

Delany, already an award-winning science-fiction writer, wrote *Dhalgren* from January 1969 to September 1973 between various cities. It was huge, strange and sexually explicit. On its publication in 1975, the *Los Angeles Times* critic Harlan Ellison denounced it as 'sorry compendium of pointless ramblings', while in *Galaxy* magazine, Theodore Sturgeon declared it 'the very best to come out of the science-fiction field' and compared Delany to Homer, Shakespeare and Nabokov. It became Delany's bestselling work, embraced by adventurous readers who were entranced by the city of Bellona.

Bellona is a city created by words, but not necessarily words with referents. Bellona is an idea as much as a place. When asked his purpose, the Kid, our protagonist (whose name is also not the Kid), replies, 'I want to get to Bellona and – ' His sentence doesn't finish; like so much in the book, like so much in Bellona, it is a fragment. He then restarts explaining his purpose: 'Mine's the same as everybody else's; in real life, anyway: to get through the next second, consciousness intact.'

Can anyone get through Bellona with consciousness intact? There's little evidence for it. Bellona is a place of shattered pavement, ruined buildings, ash. Its people are as wounded and mercurial as the city itself. It is a place with no time in any historical sense, a place that does not make the news:

'Very few suspect the existence of this city. It is as if not only the media but the laws of perspective themselves have redesigned knowledge and perception to pass it by.' Throughout are references to prisms, mirrors, and lenses. Bellona is all of these at one point or another.

The ashes in Bellona are not only those of buildings, but of texts. *Dhalgren* is a novel endlessly interested in writing and what has been written, in the trace that fiery writing leaves behind. Its words are other words. Fragments of countless stories, poems and books make their way through its pages, some as transients or tourists, some as lifelong citizens.

Many things happen in the novel, but there is no plot in the traditional sense, no rising and falling action, no denouement. It often seems that life in Bellona is just one thing after another, with people wandering around, having conversations, having parties, having sex, having fights. (Maybe having hallucinations, dreams, nightmares – but when reality isn't tightly fixed, how do you know you're out of your mind?) The prose and the people meander.

Why is Bellona the way it is? If this were a traditional novel we would know: there would be a neutron bomb or an invasion from space. But this is not a traditional novel. Bellona is a science-fictional effect without a science-fictional cause. If there is a cause of Bellona, or at least of Bellona's apocalypse (its time out of joint, its existence apparent only to its residents, its landscape of fires and ash), the cause is that it is a city in a novel marketed as science fiction. Bellona is an experience more than it is a place: an experience of the characters and an experience of the readers. What Bellona gives us depends on what we bring to it.

Bellona is, more than anything, a city in a novel, which is to say it is a city in the mind of whoever finds its words.

Sam Delaney

1067 Natoma Street
San Francisco, California
94103
June 14, 1969

Dear Mr Sale,

A warming letter, it was...your and Mr Pynchon's enthusiasm for a book of mine -- warming indeed!

What of mine I would most like for you to see is current work. From the brief discussion of what your magazine is looking for, what I'm working on now seems most relevant -- off (or all too possibly) chance this is simply the enthusiasm of the moment; but I would like you to take a look at the opening fifteen thousand words of the novel I am working on, Prism, Mirror, Lens.* The section forms something of a self-contained novelet.

If you can bare with me for a month while I get the various notebooks, napkin, and envelopes on which it is written together and type them neatly up ... as well as squeeze out from under some bread-and-butter deadlines.

If your schedule is terribly tight, drop me a postcard and I will condense a month into a week.

Through Marc Heafle I had heard rumour that Mr Barthelme was interested in something from me for your magazine; your conformation is a very nice thing to get in an otherwize dull Saturday morning mail.

All the best,
Samuel R. Delany

* Not in any attempt to tell you what it is about, but as a synopsis (?) of the major image: In a burning city, all but evacuated, a young man is introduced to a variety of sexual/mythical/mystical experiences.

A letter from Delany to Kirkpatrick Sale, thanking him and Thomas Pynchon for their 'enthusiasm'. He then asks Sale to 'take a look at the novel I am working on', and his brief description must allude to *Dhalgren*: 'In a burning city, all but evacuated, a young man is introduced to a variety of sexual / mythical / mystical experiences.'

GEORGES PEREC

W OR THE MEMORY OF CHILDHOOD (1975)

Perec's semi-autobiographical novel intertwines uncertain personal memories with the story of W, a fantastic, seemingly utopian island state governed through sporting competition.

First published by Editions Denoël in 1975.

Perec was a member of OuLiPo, a group that sought to impose constraints on their work to generate inspiration. Other notable members included Raymond Queneau, Harry Matthews and Italo Calvino.

Perec loved puzzles of every kind, and devised many crosswords. His most well-known book, *Life: A Users' Manual* (1978) features a vindictive jigsaw maker, and is full of hidden games for the reader.

Georges Perec (1936–82) is celebrated as one of the finest authors of his generation, and was one of the most innovative writers of the twentieth century. In Perec's work the form of the story closely reflects its themes. In *W* he intertwined autobiographical chapters about his childhood with chapters about 'W', an imaginary fascist society devoted to sports, and slowly draws the two stories together.

The autobiographical strand focuses on the author's childhood in France during World War II. Both Perec's parents died during the war; his mother was sent to Auschwitz. However, it is only in the parallel strand about the imaginary land of W that Perec is able to approach these subjects, and even here he keeps his distance from it by having this part of the book told by Gaspard Winckler. Winckler, like Perec, is an orphan, and this is one of many correspondences between the two narratives, which frequently share words, names and phrases. For Perec, it is this very overlapping that matters most, a point made by the novel's title, which in French is 'double-vé', describing the overlapping Vs that create a W. By overlapping fiction and truth, Perec intentionally generates an uncertainty about both narratives, one that paradoxically made it easier for him to face his experiences of the Holocaust.

W is located near Tierra del Fuego at the southernmost tip of South America, on a tiny island shaped 'like a sheep's head with its lower jaw distinctly out of joint'. The society of W is organised around a series of regular sporting events modelled on the Olympics. The male athletes live in villages that compete with each other, while those associated with the contests live either in giant stadiums or in the 'Fortress', which is also the seat of W's government.

In W there is no division between sports and life – its whole society claims to celebrate 'the greater glory of the Body'. But it soon becomes clear to the reader that these lofty ideals are a thin justification for a system of institutionalised cruelty. All W's athletes are permanently malnourished – only the victors are fed properly. Losers are stripped naked and attacked with sticks

> I have no childhood memories. . . . A different history, History with a capital H, had answered the questions in my stead: the war, the camps.

and riding crops, and can be condemned to death by the downturned thumb of a single spectator.

In addition to the structured humiliation and cruelty, the land of W also contains many specific parallels with the Nazi concentration camps. In W, athletes are selected for contests, just as prisoners were selected for work or extermination; novices in W have to wear a triangle on their jackets, just as Jews were forced to wear a yellow star. At the end of the book, the Fortress is revealed to contain 'piles of gold teeth, rings and spectacles' and 'stocks of poor quality soap'.

Yet for all the nightmarish excesses of Perec's imaginary land, the novel's most powerful act of imagination takes place within the autobiographical narrative. While W is clearly an imaginary land, so in many ways is Perec's memory of his childhood. He is candid about his inability to remember many aspects of it accurately, and freely admits that many of the memories he offers are implausible and distorted. These admissions and omissions, along with many intentional factual errors, obliquely highlight the novel's theme of saying something by not saying it directly – such as when Perec gives May 1945 as the date of the Japanese surrender, when it was the date of the fall of Berlin.

In *W*, Perec's greatest fantasy is not the imaginary island, but something far more ordinary. He wanted to be able to clear the dinner from the table with his mother, then to fetch his satchel and do his homework. He wanted this to be a memory.

Werner Bischof, *Children's drawing representing Adolf Hitler and a swastika, Rhone-Alpes region, Vercors,* 1945. The area was well known for its Resistance to the Nazis. This image was used to illustrate the cover of a 2013 Swedish translation, *W eller minnet av barndomen,* published by Modernista.

GERD MJØEN BRANTENBERG

Egalia's Daughters: A Satire of the Sexes (1977)

A classic text of modern feminist satire depicting a fantasy matriarchry in which wim hold the power, and the menwim are the oppressed.

Egalia's Daughters was first published by Norwegian publishers Pax in 1977.

Director of the Norwegian Author's Union from 1981 to 1983, Brantenberg was also co-organiser of four International Feminist Book Fairs between 1984 and 1992.

Brantenberg is active in the gay rights movement and was a board member of Norway's National Association for Lesbian, Gay, Bisexual and Transgender People in its early form, as the Forbundet av 1948.

Since the rise of first-wave feminism in the late nineteenth century, numerous writers have imagined worlds where women hold sway. Many, from Charlotte Perkins Gilman's *Herland* (1915, page 134), to Doris Lessing's troubling vision of an early society rent by the birth of the first male in *The Cleft* (2007), are women-only communities where life proceeds without the violence and oppression traditionally attached to patriarchal structures.

Norwegian author Gerd Mjøen Brantenberg's (b.1941) Egalia is rather different. The society depicted in *Egalia's Daughters: A Satire of the Sexes* (first published in Bokmål as *Egalias døtre* in 1977 and translated into English in 1985) is a matriarchy where gender bias is seeded into everything, right down to the words people use to describe themselves. This is a skewed mirror world of wim and menwim, sheroes and maidmen, menwim's coffee mornings and gentlewim's clubs where the powerful gather to debate the issues of the day without their housebounds worrying their pretty little heads and getting their beard bows in a twist.

Brantenberg's subversion of traditional gender inequality is ingenious and often very funny. Descriptions of the music of Womfred Womm playing in a gay club, for example, or references to the writings of eminent psychologist Sigma Floyd are guaranteed to raise a smile, as are exclamations such as 'Well I'll be a daughter of a dog!' The portrayal of the fraught process of buying a first peho – the cupping device required to hold male genitalia in place for decency's sake – is also amusing with its involved discussion of the importance of balancing tube size against strap measurements.

For all the laughs, though, readers are left in no doubt as to the seriousness of Brantenberg's intentions. Through her inverted world, she holds received wisdom up to a new, searching light and repeatedly finds it wanting. We see, for example, the holes in the arguments of those who try to use nature as a justification for the power imbalance between the sexes: in Egalia, wim use the natural order to argue it is menwim's duty to take sole responsibility for contraception, childcare, and homemaking because 'menwim engender children' and are thus 'eternally imprisoned within their own biology',

The boys said it was awkward and uncomfortable … And it was so impractical when you had to pee. First you had to loosen the waistband which held the peho in place. The waistband was fastened under the skirt, so you stood fumbling for a long time … Moreover, you had to sew a slit into each of your skirts so the peho might hang freely outside.

Gerd Brantenberg

EGALIAS DØTRE

Den utrolig morsomme satiren om landet Egalia, der kvinnene hersker og mennene undertrykkes, har lavt-lønnsjobbene, går med PH (penisholder) og legger skjegget for å behage kvinnene.

and because they are physically stronger are better suited to the demands of housework. In addition, the cruel preoccupations about body image that have boys obsessing over their figures and looks, and the abuse the young hero, Petronius, realises he has been taught to regard as normal, reveal how we internalise fear and vulnerability. Cumulatively, the novel demonstrates how apparently innocuous habits – and even the words we use – can keep human (or 'huwom') beings trapped behind the barriers to free thinking.

Alongside her robust criticism of patriarchy, however, Brantenberg works hard to avoid her book becoming an attack on the male sex. As Petronius and his 'masculinist' allies realise when they try to organise themselves to protest against Egalia's inequality, such generalisations are meaningless because 'as long as they lived in a society that was ruled and dominated by one sex, it was absurd to make use of such concepts as "menwim's nature" or "wim's nature". As long as one sex held power over the other, they would never be able to find out what differences there really were between the sexes – psychically – if there were any at all.'

The real evil in Egalia is not the notion of women having power over men (or vice versa). Instead, it is power itself.

A Norwegian paperback edition from the 1970s, featuring a crocheted 'peho', the tagline reads: 'A hilarious satire about the country of Egalia, where women rule and men are suppressed, work menial jobs, wear a PH (Penis Holder) and grow their beards to please women.'

ANGELA CARTER

THE BLOODY CHAMBER AND OTHER STORIES (1979)

A groundbreaking collection of stories about power, agency, desires and inner demons, presented as a subversive reformulation of classic fairy tales.

First published by Gollancz in 1979.

Carter sometimes called these stories 'reformulations' of fairy tales and explained that they were not 'retellings' but rather her attempt to draw out the existing latent qualities in the tales.

The 1984 film *The Company of Wolves*, directed by Neil Jordan, was based on the werewolf stories included in *The Bloody Chamber*. Carter herself was involved in writing the script.

Opposite: From 'The Tiger's Bride', in which a young woman is forced to live with a mysterious, masked man who is revealed to be a tiger. Illustration by Igor Karash.

Angela Carter (1940–92) was born as Angela Olive Stalker in the British seaside town of Eastbourne. After studying at the University of Bristol and working as a journalist, Carter began writing fiction in the 1960s.

Like that of Gabriel García Márquez, Jorge Luis Borges and Salman Rushdie, Carter's writing is often described as a 'magical realism;' a postmodern school of literature in which highly realistic and detailed settings are combined with fabulous or fantastic events.

The baroque, gothic world of *The Bloody Chamber and Other Stories* is held together almost entirely by the desires and the power of Carter's female characters. Even though they are often nameless archetypes, each are well realised in their motives and drive. Their transformative powers are what further develop the atmosphere Carter so deftly creates, with personal demons just lurking at the periphery. The idea of the beast within, a beast who will emerge whether silently or with a huge roar, but always, always just about to make its presence felt, is a powerful one – the mood of these stories is always one of something terrible, something incredible about to happen, the waiting, the knowing being very much part of the fearful excitement. The women who start off as sexual objects usually morph into something greater, taking back their agency, their power, and owning their desire.

Carter's settings for her stories may vary – from small apartments in Paris to grand castles on grim, sharp cliffs to desolate country houses to the archetypal cottage in the woods, but her worlds are all based in reality in the way any fairy tale's can be. Everything is just a little deeper, darker, more sexual – every room is a dark, lush, ornate space with secrets tucked away, while outdoors, every element of nature is pushed to its extreme. Her mise-en-scène for every story is always extravagantly theatrical and dramatic though never heavy handed, and often tender and loving camp.

But it is Carter's fabulous, rich language that is what really details the world of her stories. Her voice is bold, fearless, unabashedly lush and voluptuous. Each page rises with an orchestra of sensual colours, snarling sounds, tongues, tails, teeth and skin. Every sensation is magnified until it is almost

hallucinatory but beautiful, always beautiful, like a nightmare you don't want to wake up from. The ambience of each story itself is thick with wonder and heavy with mood, so bold, so daring, so relentlessly fearless.

Carter wrote about the importance of female heterosexuality and women taking control of their sexuality before anyone else did – these stories are erotic, but they aren't erotica – it isn't their primary purpose to titillate. Their primary purpose is to question our desires and how they define us. In understanding what she desires, Carter suggests, a woman will be able to understand who she is. And desire, of course, isn't just about sex.

Of course, sex, with its undertones of violence and control, is always present in the world of *The Bloody Chamber*. There is a constant sense of mysterious impending doom caused by dangerous desires. But female sexuality is triumphant when Carter's heroines, with their wild hearts and sharp minds accept the beast within, the wolf or tiger or lion that desire makes of them. We see them navigate marriages as wives and daughters, we see their relationships with their mothers, we watch them take power from their sexual awakenings, transform into greater beings, survive strange transmutations, live among rot and decay, struggle with gender power dynamics and manage the cruelty of their male lovers and oppressors.

These are girls and women who reclaim the night, who embrace the darkness and let it in so they can rise above it and claim the world as theirs.

Opposite: 'Bluebeard and his wife' by Gustave Dore, 1862, illustrated to accompany Charles Perrault's tale *La Barbe Bleue* (1697), the inspiration behind Carter's *The Bloody Chamber*.

OCTAVIA E. BUTLER

KINDRED (1979)

A young, black woman writer is abruptly transported from twentieth-century Los Angeles to nineteenth-century Maryland where she learns hard truths about slavery and her own family.

First published by Doubleday in 1979.

Butler received a MacArthur Fellowship, popularly known as the 'genius grant', in 1995, the first science-fiction writer to be so honoured. Her other awards included a Lifetime Achievement Award from PEN Centre West, the Langston Hughes Medal from City College of New York, two Hugos and two Nebula Awards.

Although Dana is caught when she attempts to run away, some real-life slaves had better luck. Harriet Tubman (born about 1820) escaped to Philadelphia in 1849, returned to rescue family members, and helped almost 300 slaves take the 'underground railroad' north to freedom.

Octavia E. Butler (1947–2006) began her career as a science-fiction writer in the 1970s, the only black American woman working in a genre then widely perceived to be the purview of white males. Her first three books were part of the 'Patternist' series, featuring telepathic mind control, aliens and power struggles between groups and individuals. *Kindred* was Butler's breakthrough novel and remains her best-known work: a powerful tale about race relations, which combines aspects of science fiction with the historic slave narrative.

Although it shares many common themes with her other novels, there are no psychic powers or aliens in *Kindred,* only humans shaped by social, historic and emotional forces. Its time-travel element has led to it being classified as science fiction, but because she made no attempt to provide even a pseudo-scientific justification for the time travel, Butler disagreed, calling it instead 'grim fantasy'.

Dana, the main character and narrator, has her first experience of involuntary time travel on her twenty-sixth birthday, the day she and her husband move into their first house together. One moment it is the summer of 1976, and she is in Altadena, California, unpacking books; the next, she finds herself in a green wood on the shore of a river in which a child is drowning. She plunges in and saves him, and, after a short period of confusion and danger, returns home.

Later that evening it happens again, only this time she finds herself inside a house where the same child, now about four years older, has set fire to the curtains. Once again, she saves his life. Dana learns from the boy that they are in Maryland and the year is 1815. He is Rufus Weylin – a name she knows from the family Bible. He was the father of her great-great-grandmother, Hagar. Why did no one ever mention he was white? Probably because that knowledge died with Hagar in 1880, she thinks, for she cannot deny the strange connection between them. Rufus has the power to summon her whenever his life is in danger and, for the sake of her own existence, Dana knows she must do whatever she can to keep him alive, at least until Hagar is born. But her life and liberty, as a black woman in a slave state, are constantly under threat, and

even when she manages to return to her own time, she never knows when she will be pulled back to the past by her violent, unpredictable ancestor.

Slave quarters at l'Hermitage Plantation, Frederick County, Maryland.

The world in which Dana's adventures are set is not an imaginary land, but a well-researched, realistic reconstruction of an actual place and time. The historic sections of *Kindred* take place in Talbot County, on the Eastern Shore of Maryland, between 1811 and 1832. Butler chose Maryland rather than the Deep South because it was the only state from which a slave had any realistic chance of escape, with freedom possible across the border in Pennsylvania. A native Californian like her character, Butler journeyed to Maryland to do research, to get a feeling for the physical place, in addition to reading the writings of former slaves, and many books about the history of slavery.

Butler's aim was to make readers *feel* the reality of slavery, not as mere observers of a long-ago past, but more personally, through identification with a modern character forced to live in a world as alien to her as to them – a world that, although strange to us, was at once undeniably, physically real and inescapable.

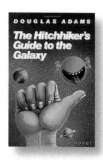

DOUGLAS ADAMS

The Hitchhiker's Guide to the Galaxy (1979)

Adams' classic series begins with the demolition of Earth to make way for a galactic freeway. Everyman Arthur Dent is saved by the freewheeling alien Ford Prefect, and so begins a hilarious and wild ride through time and space.

First published by Pan Books in 1979.

Adams was a script editor on the BBC's *Doctor Who* when he wrote the original *Hitchhiker's Guide* scripts.

The joke around the name 'Ford Prefect' is now somewhat obscure. The name refers to a make of car, manufactured from the 1940s to the 1960s, once very common on British roads, now very rare. Ford chose the name hoping to blend in, presumably because he assumed the sheer number of cars meant that they are the dominant form of life on Earth.

As a student at Cambridge University, Douglas Adams (1952–2001) became involved in the university's famous Footlights comedy club; and straight after university he wrote for the British TV shows *Monty Python's Flying Circus* and *Doctor Who*. It was while hitchhiking around Europe on a low-budget holiday in the 1970s that he got the idea of combining the surreal comedy of the Pythons with the science fiction of *Doctor Who*.

The result was the deeply funny space-opera fantasia *The Hitchhiker's Guide to the Galaxy*, which appeared in many different forms. Indeed, it might be easier to list the formats in which it *didn't* appear: it was first heard as a radio drama on BBC Radio 4 in 1978 – six half-hour episodes, broadcast late at night. Despite this low-key launch the show quickly acquired a cult following. A second six-part radio series followed in 1980, and Adams wrote two novelisations, *The Hitchhiker's Guide to the Galaxy* and *The Restaurant at the End of the Universe* (1980). A television adaptation followed in 1981, and a video-game version in 1984. There was a movie (2005), three further radio series, more novelisations, a stage adaptation, comic books and a general dissemination into fan culture.

That adaptability was key not only to its success but also to its own logic. As the *Hitchhiker's Guide* grew, its storyline proliferated in ingenious, absurd and hilarious directions, but at its heart remains a simple fish-out-of-water story of an ordinary human being named Arthur Dent. Earth is scheduled to be demolished by an unpleasant alien species called the Vogons in order to make way for a galactic hyperspace bypass. Dent – still wearing his pyjamas and dressing gown – is the only human to survive this catastrophe, having been rescued by his best friend Ford Prefect. Dent had assumed that Ford was from the English town of Guildford; in fact he was from the star Betelgeuse and had been living on Earth to research an entry on the planet for the titular encyclopedia-style guidebook.

From this bravura opening – it really does require chutzpah to *begin* a story with the end of the world – Dent and Ford embark on a peripatetic series of interstellar adventures, meeting the splendidly egotistical two-headed

Zaphod Beeblebrox, onetime president of the Galaxy and now outlaw and barfly; Marvin, a hugely intelligent but chronically depressed robot ('Marvin the Paranoid Android'); Trillian, a human woman who happened to flee Earth a few years before its end; and various others. Their adventures take them back and forth through space and time, with increasingly complicated ramifications. They visit planets teeming with life and planets abandoned to spooky ruins; they visit the headquarters of the Guide's publishers only for the entire building to be ripped from the ground and flown through space by kidnapping robots; they travel forward to the end of time itself and backward to the epoch of cavemen. At all points they actualise a very English type of inventively deadpan humour: premises are logically extrapolated into absurdity, the arbitrary cruelty of the cosmos is illustrated from the largest scale – such as the abrupt destruction of the whole of Earth and all its people – down to the smallest (Dent finds it frustratingly hard to find that beverage most essential to the English, a nice cup of tea), but disaster is always treated in a drily comic manner. There is little slapstick, no vulgarity or obscenity, and often the jokes entail quite profound metaphysical consequences. This perhaps makes Adams sound like a forbiddingly intellectual humorist, which he wasn't at all. The funniest moments in *Hitchhiker's* depend upon character and situation, and the philosophy never treads upon the jokes.

As Dent and Ford's adventures continue, they discover that Earth was not actually a regular planet, but rather a gigantic computer that had been running a program for millions of years designed to solve one of the great cosmic mysteries. This mystery is not the meaning of life, which had long ago been determined – it is '42' – but instead the meaning of the meaning of life. It is designed to determine, in other words, what the ultimate question could

The original radio cast (from left to right, David Tate, Alan Ford, Geoffrey McGivern, [Douglas Adams, behind], Mark Wing-Davey and Simon Jones).

be that might lead to the ultimate answer '42'. And by the end of the second series of the radio show, we discover what the ultimate question is; but without wishing to spoil that reveal, we can say that Adams' '42' works both as a neatly absurdist gag, and as a profound intervention into the metaphysics of meaning. What *can* the universe 'mean', if its meaning could be summed up as a two-digit number?

The appeal of *Hitchhiker's* depends upon more than its comedy, endearing though that is. The imagined world Adams creates is fascinating, varied and, above all, hospitable where fan engagement is concerned. The universe is full of the bumbling and the wisecracking but rarely with pure evil or cruelty: even the horrid Vogons compose poetry (although it is poetry so bad that reciting it is a mode of torture). Everywhere you go in Adams' imaginary cosmos there are ingenious and hilarious vignettes. Enterprising restaurateurs have created a temporal 'bubble' that sits at the very end of all time, so that diners can enjoy a sumptuous meal while watching the ultimate apocalypse in the 'Restaurant at the End of the Universe'; one planet's population has evolved into birds to avoid the need to walk on the ground, since shoes had become so expensive; humans are revealed to be the third most important life form on Earth, after dolphins and white mice. Before their first trip through hyperspace, Ford warns Arthur Dent that the experience will be 'unpleasantly like being drunk'. 'What's so unpleasant about being drunk?' Arthur asks, to which Ford replies: 'Ask a glass of water.'

It is surely the case that *Hitchhiker's* works best as a radio drama or novel, for here the imagination can engage in the least-fettered way with Adams' expertly suggestive vistas and tartly engaging characters. It has a great deal to do with the comedy of the work, a tricky matter to discuss since – as everybody knows – a joke explained is no longer funny. In fact, that's not the half of it. To excerpt examples of humour from *Hitchhiker's* does nothing to convey the calibre of the humour of Adams' world, since that humour depends so largely on the spacious, ingenious context in which it occurs. The solvent is charm, a genuinely rare quality in literature, rarer in science fiction, and impossible to fake; but a quality Douglas Adams possessed in large quantities, and with which he infuses the worlds of his creation.

In a last-ditch effort to escape a pair of missiles bearing down on them, the protagonists fire up an infinite improbability drive, turning the missiles – in an infinitely improbable way – into bowl of petunias and a sperm whale. Illustration by James Burton.

A preliminary sketch by artist John Harris for the
cover artwork for Ann Leckie's Imperial Radch
trilogy, see page 304.

5 THE COMPUTER AGE

As Cold War fears subsided and technology brought us closer to the stars, created worlds became ever more elaborate and the postmodern playfulness of the 1970s gave birth to the fantastical and parodic creations of writers such as Salman Rushdie and Terry Pratchett.

STEPHEN KING

THE DARK TOWER SERIES
(1982–2012)

In King's 'Dark Tower' universe lies one of the largest fantasy worlds ever created, and incorporates a wide variety of genres, from fantasy and science fiction to horror and the Western.

Published by Donald M. Grant between 1982 and 2012.

Robert Browning's poem 'Childe Roland to the Dark Tower Came' was an inspiration for King's best-selling series.

Although the saga appears to have come to an end, King told *Rolling Stone* magazine in October 2014: 'I'm never done with The Dark Tower. . . '

The Dark Tower series is a collection of seven novels written by Stephen King (b.1947) – an undisputed master of horror, suspense, science fiction and fantasy – and published between 1982 and 2012. The series artfully blends the traditional themes of fantasy writing with tropes of the Western. The first, and most famous, title in the series is *The Gunslinger* (1982). It nods towards the strange – set in a mysterious place called Mid-world with a desert full of demons – but for the most part, the novel is a mythical version of a classical Western narrative. There's a gunslinger, Roland Deschain, and he's going to kill somebody who is described as 'the man in black', who we'll later discover is Randall Flagg.

It is Flagg who holds the key to King's world building in the Dark Tower series, and indeed across his entire oeuvre. While *The Gunslinger* itself is a fairly straightforward book, those that followed over a thirty-year period get increasingly longer and more complicated, with massive numbers of characters, a huge world to cover, different creatures and concepts presented and even a lexicon of terms that needs to be remembered for the story to resonate properly.

Mid-world ostensibly resembles our own world. Or, rather, it's an altered facsimile of it, taking into account both King's and a wider fictional history. A town is destroyed by Captain Tripps, the virus that destroyed the world in *The Stand*; a character comes to Mid-world via Salem's Lot; a major set piece of the series takes place in *The Wizard of Oz*'s Emerald City. It's a strange and disjointed place, which, it would seem, takes in much of other literature. You get the impression that, were he able, King would have gone further with the concept of intertextuality, but much of it has to remain vague. However, some enemies (the Wolves of the Calla) are described in a way that makes it clear they're based on Marvel's Doctor Doom, and they're defeated by throwing Harry Potter's Snitches – or, in this text, sneetches – at them. The man in black is Johnny Cash, but the series' main antagonist is actually The Crimson King, one of King's favourite bands. Of course, the name of the series itself comes from Tolkien's Barad-dûr; individual books in the series take their names from T. S. Eliot and Lewis Carroll.

When, in the series' final books, the characters travel out of Mid-world and into our own reality – meeting with King himself, in a masterful piece of playful metafiction – it becomes clear that the world of the Dark Tower is everything that ever influenced King. All the fiction, cinema, music and art he sees as an influence is dragged into play, turned into an aspect of the narrative. The world is a brain map of King's creativity, and thus both entirely like and unlike anything else ever written.

The rest of King's bibliography is touched by the same influences. Randall Flagg appears in a number of King's novels, often under different names but representing the same individual; many of the characters of the Dark Tower have also appeared in other books, right from the start of King's career. It's a game, sometimes, to be reading a King novel, and trying to find out exactly how he's tied it to his masterplan.

Cover painting for the seventh and last book in the Dark Tower series by Michael Whelan, which brings to an end the saga of Roland the Gunslinger as he finally reaches the tower.

TERRY PRATCHETT

THE DISCWORLD SERIES
(1983–2015)

Pratchett's wildly popular Discworld looks, sounds and smells very much like our own, except that it is carried though space on the back of a giant turtle and populated by a host of colourful characters including bumbling heroes, Death, empowered witches and self-carrying luggage.

The series is published by several different companies, but the first title, *The Colour of Magic*, was published by Colin Smythe Ltd in 1983.

Pratchett was at one point reputed to have been the most shoplifted author in Britain.

On 12 March, 2015, the day of Terry Pratchett's death, his Twitter feed posted 'Terry took Death's arm and followed him through the doors and on to the black desert under the endless night'. Followed by 'The End'.

When Terry Pratchett's (1948–2015) first Discworld novel, *The Colour of Magic*, appeared in 1983, it employed a setting he used in an earlier science-fiction novel, *Strata* (1981). The flat, disc-shaped world was intended to parody Larry Niven's *Ringworld* (1970, page 214), but the idea stuck in his mind and he reused it as the setting for a parody of heroic fantasy. It was to prove so effective and so popular that it would serve as the world in which nearly all of his subsequent novels took place. Discworld became important as a setting that enabled Pratchett to hold a comically distorted mirror to our familiar world, allowing us to laugh while encountering often profound issues. By the time of his death in 2015, Sir Terry, as he became, was one of the most popular authors in the world, largely because the Discworld and its characters had lodged so enduringly in the minds of his readers.

From the start of the first novel we are told that the Discworld rides through space supported on the backs of four elephants who are themselves standing upon the back of a giant turtle, A'Tuin. This hints at ideas found in eastern mythologies, but it is intended to detach the Discworld from our notions of realism and to emphasise that it is a ludicrous place. Here, the turtle and elephants suggest, anything may happen because this is a realm untouched by reality. Nonetheless, while magic is the principal force on the Discworld, it operates in a similar way to the elemental forces in our own world, and is similarly theorised.

Across more than forty novels, a large cast of recurring characters appear. Rincewind, the hopeless magician, was introduced in *The Colour of Magic* (1983); Granny Weatherwax and the Witches in *Equal Rites* (1987); Death in *Mort* (1987); Vimes and the City Watch in *Guards! Guards!* (1989); and Tiffany Aching, the young witch, in an off-shoot of the Discworld series aimed at a young adult audience, in *The Wee Free Men* (2003). The novels follow a roughly chronological sequence, so that across the books we see characters develop (Vimes is promoted, Granny Weatherwax dies) and new technologies become established (steam trains are introduced in *Raising Steam* [2013]). Thus, it is a dynamic setting.

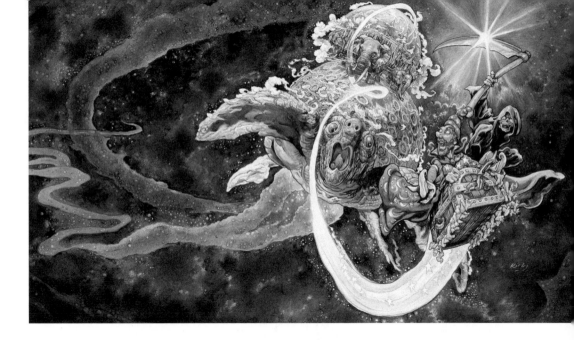

The recurring locations, the Unseen University, the capital city of Ankh-Morpork, the pub that is variously known as The Drum, The Broken Drum and The Mended Drum, all suggest a solidly realised and consistent landscape. Indeed, there is even a 'Mapp' of the city in *The Streets of Ankh-Morpork* (1993). Yet it would be a mistake to imagine that the chronology of the novels and the consistency of the settings imply that Discworld is always the same place.

In fact, as Pratchett said, the point of the Discworld series was always to 'have fun with the clichés', and each novel sets out to parody some aspect of popular culture, such as cinema (*Moving Pictures*, 1990), rock music (*Soul Music*, 1994) or journalism (*The Truth*, 2000); attitudes towards other places (Australia in *The Last Continent*, 1998); or features of modern life (the postal service in *Going Postal*, 2004). It was always necessary that the familiar should be recognisable within the books, whether global politics in *Jingo* (1997), economics in *Making Money* (2007) or conservatism in *Monstrous Regiment* (2003). Therefore, Pratchett had no hesitation in making radical changes to his setting just to suit the story being told or, more accurately, the topic being parodied. Whether it is a new island emerging in *Jingo* or a new social culture in *Pyramids*, Discworld was always and deliberately a fluid setting.

Discworld III by artist Josh Kirby. Kirby's work is unmistakeable to countless Pratchett fans, and he contributed his remarkable illustrations to each book in the series. Kirby died in 2001 and his artwork is reproduced by kind permission of his estate.

Overleaf: The Light Fantastic (1986) by Josh Kirby, showing the wizard Rincewind riding his trusty companion, the intelligent travelling chest Luggage, with Death's adopted daughter Ysabell and Discworld tourist Twoflower.

WILLIAM GIBSON

NEUROMANCER (1984)

Gibson's prescient cyberpunk novel predicts a world where technology is omnipresent and morality nowhere to be found.

First published by Ace (US) and Victor Gollancz Ltd (UK) in 1984.

Neuromancer was the first book – and only debut – to win the Hugo Award, the Nebula Award and the Philip K. Dick Award.

In 2005, *Time* magazine included it on their list of the 100 best English-language novels.

The novel popularised the term 'cyberspace', but Gibson had actually coined the word two years earlier in his short story collection *Burning Chrome*.

Neuromancer was published in 1984 and opens with a bleak, if atmospheric, description. 'The sky above the port was the colour of television, tuned to a dead channel.' Evocative and strangely haunting, this introductory line describes the world's atmosphere in a single breath – a crumbling infrastructure, overwhelmed technology; beautiful and unsettling – all packaged in Gibson's taut, neo-noir prose.

Structurally, William Gibson's (b.1948) seminal cyberpunk work flows like a particularly conspiratorial heist novel. The nominal hero, Case, is a burned-out 'cowboy', a former hacker who's been stripped of his access to cyberspace after he tried to scam a former employer. He's recruited by Molly, a physically augmented 'street samurai', and Armitage, an unstable former black-ops solider, to perform a series of raids. At first, these capers – which take place across real and virtual worlds – seem disconnected, but as the book unfolds, Case and Molly piece together not only the ultimate goal of their actions, but also the true identity – and motivation – of their employer.

Neuromancer begins at Case's lowest point – in a seedy bar in Chiba City, where he's operating, badly, as a petty criminal. A place of flickering lights and dangerous inhabitants – seemingly all back-alleys and dive bars – Chiba City is 'like a deranged experiment in Social Darwinism, designed by a bored researcher who kept one thumb permanently on the fast-forward button'. Case hustles desperately to stay alive, flitting between one errand and another, buying and selling drugs, guns, information and even organs.

The inescapable grisliness of 'Night City' is intentional – it serves as a 'deliberately unsupervised playground for technology'. Case is drawn in to the City seeking a chance to repair his ruined nervous system so he can become a hacker again. But with his money and his credit gone, he's now merely another replaceable part in its criminal ecosystem, and he's accelerating rapidly towards self-destruction.

Molly and Armitage save Case from his fate and repair his shattered system so he can hack again. But nothing in *Neuromancer* comes without a price, and now Case is beholden to his enigmatic employer. The team,

now assembled, heads to Boston-Atlanta Metropolitan Axis – the Sprawl. Although more salubrious than Night City, this series of interlinked, domed North American megacities is still far from paradise. If Chiba City is social Darwinism, the Sprawl is capitalism gone mad. The soaring towers of the all-consuming megacorporations tower over the rest of the city, a permanent reminder of who holds the power. As with Chiba City, the Sprawl is a constant hustle, but here the prize is pure profit. Both slickly suited businessmen and the surrealist street gangs target the ordinary people of the Sprawl. All have access to impressive technology, and most are addicted to the fast-paced entertainment of SimStims – exotic virtual reality that lets people share the sensations experienced by their celebrity idols.

From the heady, super-modern heights of the Sprawl, Case and Molly head to Istanbul. If Chiba City is ruthlessly carving out the future and the Sprawl is aggressively defining the 'now', Istanbul is where the past and present co-exist, albeit uneasily.

Istanbul's juxtaposition of the sleekly modern – from the airport to the interior of their hotel – and the crumbling, but inescapable past – 'crazy walls of patchwork wooden tenements' – is apparent all throughout the city. Case and Molly are joined by a corrupt member of the local secret police, indicating that the political situation is no more settled than the landscape.

From Istanbul, the crew, now accompanied by the sadistic illusionist Peter Riviera, head to *Neuromancer*'s most exotic destination, the space station Freeside. Freeside is 'Las Vegas and the Hanging Gardens of Babylon', a playground for the ultra-rich and extremely privileged. Built and completely owned by the Tessier-Ashpool family, Freeside serves as 'brothel

The dystopian underworld of Chiba City as imagined by illustrator Josh Godin.

and banking nexus, pleasure dome and free port, border town and spa'. An artificial night sky comes complete with fake constellations showing 'playing cards, the faces of glass, a top hat'. Drones and other invisible servants clean up the clutter, so the wealthy tourists can spend their time completely undisturbed.

The space station has an unusual spindle shape, which leads to complex (and not entirely consistent) gravitational effects. The bulk of Freeside is given over to a hub of hotels, casinos, night clubs and high-end shopping. The space station contains 'outdoor' elements as well, including lakes and a velodrome. Anchoring it all, filling an entire 'segment' at one end of Freeside, sits the Villa Straylight, private and impregnable, the home of the Tessier-Ashpool family. The Villa reflects the clan's philosophy: their rigid control of finance, technology and property through elaborate mechanisms. But it also captures their insanity and their decline, the hubris of their created world is dissolving into dusty relics.

Case's travels through the worlds of *Neuromancer* take him from impeccable hotels to grimy backstreets, from the physical and metaphorical depths of the underground to the heights of corporate rule. Each destination highlights a different way in which humanity relates to both technology and temporality. In Chiba City, hustlers scramble over scraps of data, selling stolen hard disks in a desperate bid to live another day. In the Sprawl, strangely immutable corporations create a rapidly accelerating cacophony of trends, products and even celebrities. In Istanbul, the past and the present are at constant war. And in the Villa Straylight, the circle completes, with the Tessier-Ashpool clan again using technology in a bid for life – cryogenics to stay young; artificial intelligence to stay financially potent. The same hustle; the same battle against the inexorable approach of time.

In the matrix, however, time does not exist – explaining, to some small degree, Case's obsession with returning to cyberspace. In *Neuromancer*, the matrix is defined loosely, often more in terms of its scale than its aesthetics. Gibson describes his vision of cyberspace as 'a consensual hallucination experienced daily by billions … a graphic representation of data abstracted from banks of every computer'. When Case jacks in – porting his consciousness into cyberspace – he leaves the physical world behind. Aches, soreness, abstract sensations like the passage of time, guilt or emotional longing: all shed when Case enters cyberspace. *Neuromancer* introduces a mechanism where Case spends much of the book 'flipping' back and forth with a VR device, reversing between the abstract vastness of cyberspace and the vigorous physicality of Molly's sensations. With every abrupt change in perception, the reader gets a fraction of what Case must feel – the shift from languorous contemplation of the universal to grubby, painful reality.

In Case's interactions with Wintermute, the Tessier-Ashpool's AI, he's transported to a realm that's indistinguishable from the real world. The AI serves up a level of stimulus that, although dreamlike, is rendered in perfect detail. The only absence is imagination: Wintermute can pull images from plugged-in minds, but can't create anything new. In this private cyberspace, Case wanders down a perfect beach in Morocco as well as locations from his own memory. The artistic detail of Wintermute's cyberspace hints at the infinite potential of technology, and its limitless future.

At the end of *Neuromancer*, the matrix reveals two additional facets. The first is that Case's quiet, personal vision – the beach placed in his mind by Wintermute – seems to take on a life of its own, complete with sentient residents. Whether these are fragments of memory or new intelligences is left unexplored. Also left unexplored is Wintermute's cryptic hint that there are other intelligences 'like it' out there – and by that, the AI indicates the Centauri System. Despite being a graphic metaphor for the transfer of data, the child of 'video games' and military software, cyberspace has extended beyond the reach of humanity – in multiple ways.

MARGARET ATWOOD

THE HANDMAID'S TALE (1985)

'God is a National Resource' in this remarkably powerful, feminist dystopian novel about a repressive American theocratic dictatorship.

First published in the UK by McClelland and Stewart, 1985.

Margaret Atwood dedicated the book to Mary Webster and Perry Miller. Mary Webster, believed by Atwood to have been one of her ancestors, was hanged as a witch in Puritan New England, but survived.

A 2015 Public Policy Polling (PPP) national survey conducted on US Republican voters found that fifty-seven per cent wanted to establish Christianity as the official national religion, and only thirty per cent were opposed to the idea, which is specifically prohibited by the Constitution.

In 1984, when Margaret Atwood began writing her dystopia set in a near-future America, she made the decision not to include technology that was not already available, nor anything human beings had not already done in some other time or place, so she could not be accused of, as she put it, 'misrepresenting the human potential for deplorable behaviour'.

The transformation of the US into a theocratic dictatorship known as the Republic of Gilead has been brought about by true believers, religious fanatics driven by a determination to establish God's kingdom on Earth, much as the Puritan settlers (who included some of Atwood's ancestors) were determined to do in seventeenth-century New England.

Prior to the beginning of the novel, fundamentalist Christian extremists assassinated the president and Congress, pinning the blame on Islamic terrorists and allowing their army to declare a state of emergency, in which the Constitution is 'temporarily' suspended, news is censored, identity cards issued, and, with the new religious rulers in place, new rules imposed. Overnight, women lose the right to have jobs, or bank accounts, or to do anything except submit to the will of their husbands. And all are subject to the rule of the Commanders of the Faith, who claim biblical authority for every act, having abolished any distinction between church and state.

The narrator of *The Handmaid's Tale* is a young woman known only as Offred – 'Of Fred' – designated as the legal concubine of a high-ranking Commander whose first name is Fred. Only a few years before, she had a name and a job, a husband and a child, friends and freedoms she took for granted. But the family left it too late to cross into Canada with fake passports, and now her husband is either dead or in detention, her daughter adopted by a childless couple. The only thing keeping Offred from being shipped off to perform slave labour in 'the Colonies' is the possibility she might bear a baby for the Commander and his wife. For another major element driving this bleak vision of the future is that from a multitude of causes – including radiation, pollution and untreated STDs – there has been a steep drop in human fertility, so women of child-bearing age and proven fertility are very valuable.

The biblical book of Genesis includes the story of Jacob, who married two sisters, Rachel and Leah. When Rachel produced no children, she told Jacob to impregnate her maid, Bilhah: 'and she shall bear upon my knees, that I may also have children by her'. Thus, under a regime that fears and mistrusts all science, preferring to find the answer to every problem through selective reading of an ancient book, the solution to childlessness, at least in the upper ranks, is to establish Rachel and Leah Centres for the indoctrination of 'handmaids' to be assigned to the households of all childless Commanders. (Naturally, the centres are not named after the handmaidens who had Jacob's children, but after his wives.)

Handmaids are recognised by their red robes, wives dress in blue ones and the 'Marthas' (designated cooks and cleaners) wear green. Illustration by Anna and Elena Balbusso.

In Gilead, society is rigidly hierarchical and divided by gender: Commanders of the Faith at the top; below them the Eyes (secret police), then Angels (soldiers), Guardians (low-level police duties), all male civilians, and all women. Women have no power of their own, and are valued only as wives and the producers of babies. Some unmarried women are assigned other roles by the state – the 'Aunts' who indoctrinate and control those who have been selected as potential surrogate mothers and 'Marthas' who work as cooks and cleaners. A few women survive by practising the oldest profession – a brothel known as Jezebel's is permitted to thrive, and the men in power take liberties forbidden to others.

If a handmaid fails to conceive after three different postings she is declared an 'Unwoman' and sent off to 'the Colonies'. This is a euphemism for forced labour camps, where lives are brutal and short. Women likewise become 'unwomen' if they refuse to submit, or the men in power have no more use for them.

Women are not the only victims of this repressive, rigidly stratified, coercively heterosexual, white dictatorship. Enemies of the state regularly tortured and then executed include Catholic priests, Quakers, doctors (if

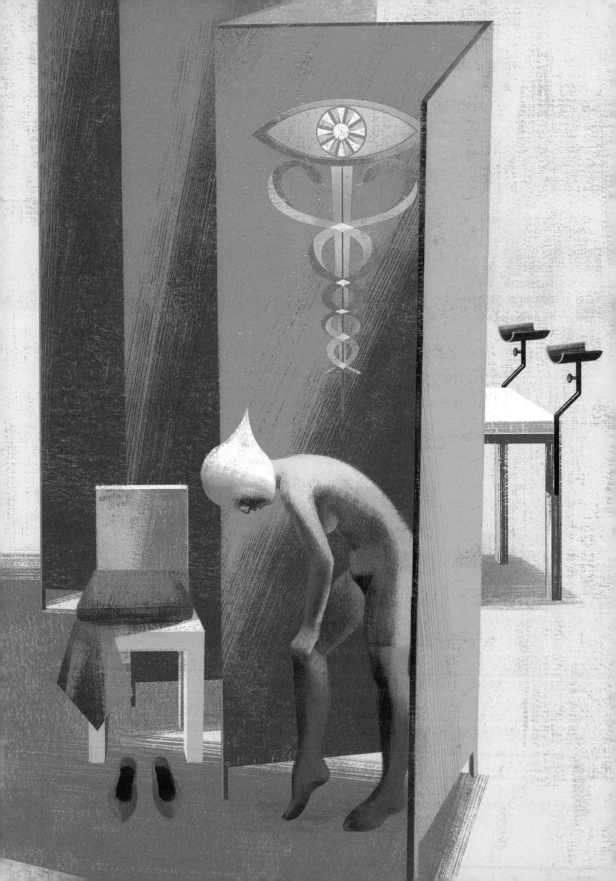

they ever performed an abortion, prescribed contraception, or are accused of having done so) and 'gender traitors'. African-Americans, called 'Children of Ham', have been resettled in distant, underpopulated areas such as North Dakota, now designated a 'National Homeland', and Jews were given a choice between conversion and emigration to Israel.

Offred's life as a handmaid is relatively easy, but deeply boring. Most of her time is spent waiting. The occasions when the Commander must attempt to impregnate her are as de-sexualised as intercourse can possibly be ('This is not recreation, even for the Commander. This is serious business. The Commander, too, is doing his duty.') and she wonders if it is worse for his wife, or for her. Her room is as bare as a prison cell, almost everything we would take for granted is classed as a luxury (hand cream) or a sin (reading). She is marked out by her red robes, as the wives are by their blue ones and the Marthas in green. Her daily walk is taken with another handmaid, and they are expected to police each other: if one tries to escape or does anything wrong, the other will be punished, too.

Although every aspect of this society is supposedly justified by the Word of God, as presented in the Bible, only the Commanders are allowed to read it, and they use it selectively, to say the least. A famous line from Karl Marx, changed to include the expected relationship between women and men, is attributed to St Paul when repeated to the handmaids-in-training: 'From each according to her ability, to each according to his needs.'

The city where Offred serves is never named, but it is evidently Cambridge, Massachusetts, home of Harvard University. The university where Margaret Atwood once studied has become the seat of oppression, a detention centre, and the site of mass executions.

Atwood has said that one of the elements that inspired her to write *The Handmaid's Tale* was a fascination with how dictatorships work ('not unusual in a person born in 1939, three months after the outbreak of World War II'). She explained: 'Nations never build apparently radical forms of government on foundations that aren't there already. The deep foundation of the US – so went my thinking – was not the comparatively recent eighteenth-century Enlightenment structures of the republic, with their talk of equality and their separation of church and state, but the heavy-handed theocracy of seventeenth-century Puritan New England, with its marked bias against women, which would need only the opportunity of a period of social chaos to reassert itself.'

During a visit to the gynaecologist, the doctor suggests the reason Offred is not yet pregnant might be because Commander is infertile. And since men are not tested, she will be blamed. As a solution he suggests that they have sex instead. Illustration by Anna and Elena Balbusso.

IAIN M. BANKS

The Culture Series (1987–2012)

The Culture is a galaxy-spanning civilisation composed of several different races (mostly human) and AIs (Artificial Intelligences, known as Minds); the Culture functions as a post-scarcity utopia.

The first four Culture books were written before Iain Banks first achieved publication with *The Wasp Factory* (1984); they were eventually published, by various companies, in the reverse order to that in which they were written.

Banks originally devised the Culture in the early 1970s while still at university. He wanted to write a story in which a bad man fought for a good cause; this would eventually become *Use of Weapons*.

Consider Phlebas is set around CE 1300; *Surface Detail* is set in 2867 CE; the whole sequence, therefore, covers a period of more than 1,500 years.

The Culture series, ten novels published between 1987 and 2012, was created by Iain M. Banks (1954–2013) as a counterpoint to the conservative American space operas. In those stories, typically, one man saves the universe, restoring order based on the American capitalist system, and operates within a militaristic society in which spaceships are modelled on naval vessels complete with the same chain of command. Banks very carefully subverts every one of those clichés.

His dynamic characters are as likely to be women as men. Even this isn't the whole story: throughout, Banks makes it clear it is easy for people to change gender, and practically all do so at least once during their life. This leads to an increase in sexual pleasure while eliminating sexual discrimination. Furthermore, most of what passes for power within the Culture is in the purview of the genderless Minds.

Nor does a lone hero save the universe. Individuals, even individual Minds, play no more than a small part in the shaping of great events, and often have no knowledge of what their precise part might have been or how successful or not it was in the grand scheme of things.

Order is not restored, because order is not threatened. Indeed, order is not an issue, since this is a universe in which change is constant. When the Culture finds itself at war (*Consider Phlebas* [1987], *Excession, Look to Windward* [2000]), for instance, the very fact of war is considered an embarrassing failure, which leaves a legacy of guilt. The Culture is a non-racist society in which everyone, human, non-human, or machine intelligence, is equal. It is based on a communist model: Banks said, 'Money is a sign of poverty. A cheque book is really a ration book.' The Culture, therefore, is a post-scarcity society that has access to all the power needed, and the technological ability to fulfil any need. Out of this has emerged an anarchist system in which there are no hierarchies, no laws and everyone is free to do as they wish. *The Player of Games* (1988) explicitly states that the only sanction against any crime is the embarrassment of it being known; but in a post-scarcity society the need for crime is largely removed.

They had no kings, no laws, no money and no property, but ... everybody lived like a prince, was well-behaved and lacked for nothing. And these people lived in peace, but they were bored, because paradise can get that way after a time.

An illustration inspired by Banks' the Culture series by Mark Brady.

The Culture is portrayed as a utopia, but this is only partly correct. On an individual level, life is utopian. People have an extended lifespan there are no constraints, no financial worries, sex is invariably wonderful and built-in drug glands provide an artificial high at a moment's notice. But such an existence can be boring without purpose, so people risk their lives in extreme sports, or become involved in the affairs of other races. On a political level, therefore, the Culture has a more imperial and less utopian aspect.

The Culture is an expression of Banks' atheistic humanism, following what Ken MacLeod calls 'pan-sentient utilitarian hedonism': the greater good leads inevitably to the greater pleasure. But again this is not straightforward. Increasingly, the novels concern the Culture's failure to Sublime, to move to the next level of being, a move equated with death or ascent to heaven. In the later novels in particular, the Culture often finds itself in conflict with religious symbols: godlike aliens, artificial hells, a demonstrably true religious book.

While outwardly fast-paced space operas are filled with dramatic action, immense artefacts and great jokes, the Culture asks profound questions about the nature of utopia and of atheism.

BERNARDO ATXAGA

OBABAKOAK (1988)

A collection of interrelated stories about life and the stories people tell, including that of the narrator's childhood in an imaginary Basque-speaking town, featuring a whirlwind of sleuthing, storytelling, and dialogue about literature and myth-making in 'big' and 'small' cultures.

First published by Editorial Erein in 1988.

Basque or Euskera is a non-IndoEuropean language of unknown origins, possibly the oldest in Europe, and is spoken in Spain, France and the US. Atxaga writes first in Basque, and translates his text into Spanish with the help of his wife.

Obabakoak launched Atxaga's career outside the Basque Country when it received the Spanish Premio Nacional de Literatura.

Critics have referred to Bernardo Atxaga (b.1951) not just as a Basque novelist, but as *the* Basque novelist, and his writing seeks to evoke his heritage without taking refuge in rose-tinted nostalgia. He was born in the small Basque-speaking village of Asteasu, near San Sebastian, at a time when Basque areas were still reeling from Franco's attempts to eradicate the culture.

In *Obabakoak* – a collection of interrelated stories based in the fictional village of Obaba – Atxaga has transformed the then-rigid borders of Basque identity into an elastic new space, both solid and transient, recognisable and unrecognisable, dark and bright, tempting, appealing and beckoning to the traveller. 'Obabakoak' means both 'of the people and things from Obaba' and 'Stories from Obaba', and the village is depicted in the stories as experienced by someone: thus, for the young or Romantic it is a 'toy valley' or *locus amoenus*; for the marginalised characters, including writers (who take shelter in primordial spaces such as woods, jungles, mountains or the outskirts), it is violent, full of threats and dark secrets.

Obaba is a small, insignificant place to most people: letters from the big city often do not reach it. Yet, Atxaga does not connect power to size. In his view, like that of a naive painter, everything exists on the same plane and has the same value. Most of the action does not take place in the town centre, but at scenic overlooks because, rather than a site to be looked upon, Obaba is a perspective from which the world is perceived. Furthermore, Obaba's borders are extremely permeable, as in a dream – a concept befitting a town whose name stems from the first words of a Basque lullaby ('*oba, oba*' means 'hush, hush') – and readers are constantly carried to unknown and unlikely places such as the Amazon jungle.

Furthermore, Atxaga establishes an unbreakable connection between landscape and storytelling. The protagonist of the first story is a geographer who recollects his childhood in Obaba. This image of geographer-writer not only promotes credibility (à la Macondo for Gabriel García Márquez, page 204, Comala for Juan Rulfo, page 192, or Yoknapatawpha County for William Faulkner) but also calls attention to the process of fiction-making,

which is omnipresent in the tales. *Obabakoak* is full of stories and rewritings ('plagiarisms', as the narrator calls them) from the works of many authors such as Borges, Kafka, Celan, Calvino, Perec, Stevenson, Dante, Axular and Cervantes.

And above everything, *Obabakoak* maps the creative process of Bernardo Atxaga. Obaba is a pool into which he dives in order to explore the childhood experiences and mysteries that constituted the humus of his creativity. Thus, his exploration in 'Childhoods' (the first section of the book) of the rich tradition of Basque beliefs from Asteasu precedes the series of narratives inspired by writers who influenced the author. The map of Atxaga's creative interior, his inner-life, shows an author who jumps over frontiers between literature and orality, Basque and non-Basque, different audiences and aesthetics – pre-, post- and modern.

The sleepy Basque-speaking village of Asteasu, near San Sebastian, the inspiration behind Obaba.

NEIL GAIMAN et al.

THE SANDMAN (1988–2015)

In this groundbreaking comic-book saga, the personification of dreams must deal with various challenges and challengers, while approaching his own inevitable fate.

The Sandman: Master of Dreams vol 2, #1 (© 1989 DC Comics) was written by Neil Gaiman and illustrated by Sam Kieth and Mike Dringenberg. Image courtesy of DC Comics.

Several minor characters from *The Sandman* have spun off into their own series and graphic novels. Gaiman himself wrote several stories about Death, who later appeared in several graphic novels by Jill Thompson.

The Sandman's version of Lucifer, who abdicates from the management of hell in the story 'Season of Mists' (issues 21–8, 1990–1), starred in his own series written by Mike Carey, which ran for 75 issues between 2000 and 2006.

The Sandman was originally a minor DC Comics superhero, the alter ego of two crime fighters, Wesley Dodds and Hector Hall. In the late 1980s DC turned to British author Neil Gaiman (b.1960) to reimagine the character as part of DC's Vertigo imprint, focusing on more mature themes and stories. Gaiman brought along his friend the artist Dave McKean, who had collaborated with the writer on some of his earlier graphic novels.

The Sandman is a story about stories, but, more importantly, it is a story in which stories shape reality, in which there is, in fact, no difference between stories and reality. In this world, cosmology (forget about geography) is shaped by personality. Though there are several fixed settings in *The Sandman*, it's quickly made clear to us that how they appear and operate is a function of the whims of people at their heart. The central character, Dream (the titular Sandman who is known by many other names including Morpheus, Oneiros and Kai'cul), is the third of seven siblings known as the 'Endless', who represent immutable powers that govern the life of every living thing in the universe. But these powers have been given bodies and personalities, which in turn shapes how they present themselves and their realms. So, for example, the oldest Endless sibling, Destiny, is always shown walking through a garden of forking paths, carrying a book from which he reads what is to come. One of Dream's younger siblings, Desire (who is both male and female), lives in a castle shaped like a giant image of her/himself, because Desire is a narcissist. Dream, meanwhile, is the only Endless who plays the role of ruler of his realm properly, complete with a castle, attendants and even a throne room, because Dream is obsessed with rules and propriety, with the supposed responsibility and demands of his office. But, as several of his siblings point out to him, what he perceives as immutable laws are merely his choices. If Dream wanted it, the world of dreams – and thus the world as a whole – could look very different.

Furthermore, Dream – usually appearing as a pale, gangly young man with a mop of unruly dark hair – is only one manifestation of himself. In *Overture* (2015), which acts as a prequel to the events of *The Sandman*, Dream encounters many other aspects of himself, the Dreams of alien races, of animals, or plants, of sentient machines and of far stranger creatures. Perhaps the only fixed point in the series is his older sister, Death, who nearly always appears as a cheerful, friendly young woman dressed in black jeans and a tank-top. But this, too, is in service of the story's tangled family drama. Death's role is to be the no-nonsense big sister who punctured Dream's self-importance and self-pity. The fact that she is also the calm, friendly face one sees at the end of it all has often been called one of the most striking and compelling aspects of Gaiman's world-building.

It's questionable whether Gaiman could have told a story in which the world is so mutable, so subject to the whims and mood-swings of fractious personalities, in any other medium but comics. The existence of pictures grounds the reader in reality where the written word alone might have left us scrambling for a foothold. The graphic medium also gives Gaiman a freedom that film or television could not have done. *The Sandman* shifts from multi-issue story arcs involving its main characters, to one-off stories whose heroes are sometimes never seen again, in which the Endless play only a supporting role; it also shifts genres, from horror to high fantasy to mythology to realist drama, in a way that only the comic-book medium can accommodate, and that is reflected in the shift in artwork styles.

A representation of the many-monikered Sandman, by J. H. Williams III who collaborated with Gaiman on the reboot *Sandman Overture* in 2013.

If *The Sandman* is a story in which the characters shape their own world (and thus write their own fate), this is not, in the end, a power reserved only for the Endless, or for stars and other cosmic beings. One of the series' recurring characters is Hob Gadling, an ordinary fourteenth-century Englishman who simply decides not to die, and continues living to the twenty-first century and perhaps even beyond. When Hob asks why Death has spared him, he is told that the choice is ultimately up to him. In the world of *The Sandman*, as in the dreams that he sends to every living creature, it is we who shape and give meaning, we who tell the story.

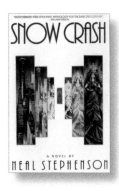

NEAL STEPHENSON

Snow Crash (1992)

In a hyper-Balkanised, ultra-franchised near-future California an African-American-Korean hacker, Hiro Protagonist, and a fifteen-year-old skateboard Kourier, Y. T., battle the ultimate cyber-conspiracy.

First published by Bantam Books in 1992.

Snow Crash has influenced mainstream culture in everything from the hyper-stylised virtual reality action sequences of *The Matrix* films to the more philosophical notions of *Inception* – an idea as a virus.

While the 1986 computer game *Habitat* first applied the Sanskrit word *avatar* in a computer or online sense, *Snow Crash* brought the term into mainstream usage. Virtual-world geography programs such as Google Earth and Nasa World Wind bear close similarities to the program Earth run in *Snow Crash*'s Metaverse.

Published in 1992, a decade after William Gibson's *Burning Chrome* and Ridley Scott's *Blade Runner* laid the ground rules for cyberpunk and US president Ronald Reagan established the conditions for a stratospheric rise of unfettered neoliberal capitalism, Neal Stephenson's (b. 1959) third novel, *Snow Crash*, appeared as a state-of-the-union interrogation of both cultural vectors. Stephenson graduated from Boston University with a BA in geography and a minor in physics, making his publishing debut in 1984. From his home in Seattle he continues to publish epic, complex novels that bring a geographer's holistic perception to entire societies and worlds.

It is the second decade of the twenty-first century, and the political impulse towards small government has reduced the US to Fedland, where loyal citizens work for a bureaucracy obsessed with micromanaging what little US territory remains. Citizens don't actually live in the US, but in LA's Burbclaves, franchised housing developments – micro-nations – protected by MetaCops Unlimited. Or else, like *Snow Crash*'s Hiro Protagonist, officially the greatest swordsman in the world, they reside in a converted container unit by the airport with Vitaly Chernobyl, lead singer of The Meltdowns.

Hiro was a co-founder of the Black Sun, the coolest place in the Metaverse, a 2K-HD-3D virtual reality world he co-coded. Now he freelances, uploading data for the Central Intelligence Corporation, an organisation formed from a merger of the CIA and the Library of Congress, for which he gets paid per view, and he delivers pizza for Uncle Enzo's CosaNostra Pizza Incorporated, through which he forms a working partnership with skate-boarding Kourier, Y. T., aka Yours Truly – aged fifteen, hip, sarcastic, sexually active and eager to further herself in a place where divisions between country and company, micro-nation and franchise are even less meaningful than the hyper-inflated dollar.

Stephenson's world flicks between a broken LA and the Metaverse, a domain of computer avatars foreshadowing Oculus Rift virtual reality and Google Earth, referencing the lightcycle races of *Tron* and anticipating the physics-defying combat of *The Matrix*. Later the action moves to The Raft, a

vast floating refugee city based around a US navy aircraft carrier under the control of megalomaniacal Texan billionaire L. Bob Rife.

At the heart of Stephenson's satirical landscape is the duel between a status quo of individuals as free-thinking agents in a free market and a vision of mind-controlled human drones created by a virus that crosses the line between biology and programming. The author explores complex theories about the neuro-linguistic origins of civilisation and organised religion, extrapolating history as a struggle between rational religions – Judaism, Christianity, Islam, all codified in a Book – and ideas as linguistic viruses capable of physically rewriting the deep structures of the brain. All this is packaged between cartoonishly violent set pieces and knowingly smart dialogue, as befits a world where anyone with their own nuke can be a sovereign state.

Infected by a baroque whirlwind of often surreally prescient ideas, protracted info dumping and James Cameron-esque cinematic spectacle, *Snow Crash* is, in its intertwining of cutting-edge technological and theological speculation as tools to interrogate the state of contemporary America, cool as snow, confrontational as crashing steel. Ironically, while Stephenson's comedic apotheosis of cyberpunk's first wave went culturally viral, his narrative has itself defeated all attempts to assimilate as the latest LA Hollywood franchise.

Graphic artist Igor Sobolevsky's 3D representation of CosaNostra Pizza Delivery Vehicle 2. Stephenson's central character, Hiro Protagonist, delivers pizza for Uncle Enzo's CosaNostra Pizza, Inc.

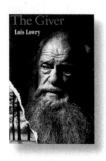

LOIS LOWRY

THE GIVER (1993)

Lowry's dystopian novel explores individuality, emotion, memory and morality in a world of 'Sameness', which assigns every person and action a time and place.

First published by Houghton Mifflin Company in 1993, *The Giver* is one of the books people most frequently tried to ban in the 1990s – for its depiction of euthanasia.

According to Lowry, the idea of exploring a world made peaceful by abolishing unsettling memories came to her through dealing with the declining faculties of her own ageing father.

The death of her older sister, Helen, at twenty-eight, inspired Lowry's first novel, *A Summer to Die* (1977).

Lowry won the Newbery Award (1990) for *Number the Stars*, about the Holocaust, as well as for *The Giver* (1994).

Aimed mainly at a young audience, *The Giver* by Lois Lowry (b.1937) explores serious themes in complex ways. Since its publication in 1993, the book has had a controversial reception: celebrated in some quarters for its perceptive exploration of the nature of authority, parents have also repeatedly demanded its removal from school libraries. Lowry herself has noted that she never thought of *The Giver* as dystopian; rather, 'it was just a story about a kid making sense of a complicated world'.

Nevertheless, the very landscape of the novel lays out the rigid values, culture and expectations of its 'Community'. Told from the viewpoint of eleven-year-old Jonas, who will become at the forthcoming 'Ceremony of Twelve' the next 'Receiver of Memories', we see his world as he has been raised to see it. Every building in the idealised, ordered Community is named according to an obvious function – Birthing Unit, Dwelling Areas, School – except one, the Annex, a small building beside the House of the Old, where Jonas will soon live. The multi-talented Jonas, unquestioningly humble in this world that eschews individuality, initially deeply approves of the order built into his landscape.

Four factors awaken Jonas. First, for reasons never explained, Jonas comes to see things 'change', first for an instant, then more persistently. Only later does he learn that the visual oddity is colour, the absence of which we, seeing through his eyes, had not noticed. Second, and less arbitrarily, Jonas has a slightly erotic dream that leads his parents, smilingly, to initiate him into the life-long regime of a pill a day to suppress 'Stirrings'. Third, through the hands-on transfer of memories from the older Receiver, now the Giver, Jonas receives knowledge of a world full not only of colour but music, joy, weather, pain, dread, agony, loss and even hills. Only then do we realise that the Community is not only grey and climate-controlled but relentlessly flat. Fourth, the Community punishes non-conformity – whether intentional, as in disobedience, or accidental, through incapacity – with 'Release'. The Giver allows Jonas to see a tape of Jonas's father, a 'Nurturer', giving Release to the less robust of identical twins, to avoid confusion in the Community. Release,

Jonas finally sees, is death by injection. Everything in his perfect world reveals itself as potentially false and cruel.

The Receiver holds all cultural memory, no matter how painful, so that others need not; however, in the rare event that the Community needs venerable wisdom to confront an unanticipated situation, the Receiver can be consulted. Keeping those memories, he lives – in the Annex – alone. When the Receiver begins to 'train' Jonas by memory transfer, the Receiver becomes the Giver. But Jonas, too, to soothe a difficult infant 'newchild' to sleep, transfers pleasant memories to him. One can be a Giver in more than one way. One can use wisdom in more than one way.

Together, the old and the young Giver devise a disruptive plan to allow Jonas individuality in 'Elsewhere', with its hills and weather, and the Community to suffer enough – from the memories that will be released by Jonas's absence – to transcend stultifying perfection.

Jonas (Brenton Thwaites) speaks with 'The Giver' (Jeff Bridges), in a 2014 film adaptation directed by Phillip Noyce.

PHILIP PULLMAN

His Dark Materials (1995–2000)

Pullman's multiverse-spanning trilogy is the story of Lyra Belacqua,
a young girl who is fated to be a second Eve, and the choices she makes
that will save or doom the worlds.

First published by Scholastic Ltd and Scholastic Ltd/ David Fickling Books (*The Amber Spyglass*) between 1995 and 2000.

Pullman has written several shorter works set in the same world: *Lyra's Oxford* (2003), *Once Upon a Time in the North* (2008) and the forthcoming *Book of Dust*.

Certain passages of *The Amber Spyglass* were cut from the US edition because their implied sexual content was considered inappropriate for a younger audience.

There have been several attempts to ban *His Dark Materials* from libraries and schools. It is the second most challenged literary work in the US.

Philip Pullman's (b.1946) *His Dark Materials* trilogy (*Northern Lights*, published in 1995 and entitled *The Golden Compass* in the US; *The Subtle Knife*, 1997; and *The Amber Spyglass*, 2000) has been a publishing phenomenon, selling more than seventeen million copies worldwide and translated into more than forty languages. The series is loved by many – both young and old – for its rich characters and the subtle complexities of its plot, as well as for its engaging re-readability. Although marketed for children and young adults, *His Dark Materials* can be read on many levels. For younger readers, it is a compelling adventure story full of new and beautiful worlds, while older readers will observe a treatise on free will and a sharp critique of religion. In Pullman's own words: 'My books are about killing God.'

The series begins in Oxford. It is not the Oxford University of our own, less obviously magical, world – for one thing, people in this alternative world are accompanied by daemons, physical manifestations of their souls in animal form – but one that is close enough that we can almost recognise it. It is this feeling of being somewhere that is almost recognisable – almost known, yet not quite home – that characterises the worlds of this series.

The Golden Compass opens with Lyra hiding in a room that is forbidden to her. She creeps into a wardrobe that is 'bigger than she'd thought' – echoing the wardrobe that leads to C. S. Lewis's Narnia (see page 178) – but Lyra's wardrobe doesn't open to a new world. Instead, it is Lyra's own curiosity and quest for knowledge that broadens her world.

When her friend Roger goes missing, she is at first comforted by the appearance of the charming Mrs Coulter – that is, until Lyra discovers that Mrs Coulter may be complicit in her friend's kidnapping. With the aid of the alethiometer, her golden compass, Lyra sets out in search for him. And as she journeys to the wildness of the North, she discovers that hers may not be the only world there is. Place is inherently tied to knowledge in this series. The witches who live in the north of Lyra's world do so because the veil between worlds is thin and their knowledge comes from this proximity. Place is also

inherently tied to perspective: 'Is this a new world?' one character asks, and is answered, 'Not to those born in it.' Things look different, depending on where they are seen.

Lyra and Pantalaimon, her daemon, meet the armoured bear, Iorek Byrnison.

The Subtle Knife (1997) begins in our world, but protagonist Will Parry soon discovers a portal to the world of Cittàgazze. Here he meets Lyra, and becomes the guardian of the subtle knife – the blade that can cut doors through universes. Yet travel between worlds is not without consequences. Each opening causes the loss of Dust, a significant elementary particle. The Church in Lyra's world sees Dust, and the knowledge that accompanies it, as a manifestation of original sin, and wishes to destroy it. But Dust, like knowledge, is necessary.

In The Amber Spyglass (2000), yet more worlds are explored. From the land of the dead to that of the elephantine mulefa, Lyra is forced to make her fated choice. But once Lyra's choice is made, the doors between the worlds must be closed – never to be opened again.

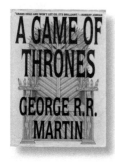

GEORGE R. R. MARTIN

A GAME OF THRONES (1996)

In the world of the Seven Kingdoms, diverse characters play the 'game of thrones', a fantastic War of the Roses that can have only one victor.

First published by Bantam Books in 1996.

A Game of Thrones, while critically acclaimed, was not a breakaway hit. Martin's epic took a while to build steam and sometimes nobody would show up to book signings.

One of Martin's strongest literary influences was Jack Vance, who wrote pulp science-fiction stories, mysteries, and space operas, among other works.

When asked about his dynamic female characters, Martin, who identifies as feminist, said: 'You know, I've always considered women to be people.'

George R. R. Martin (b.1948), dubbed by many the 'American Tolkien', published *A Game of Thrones* in 1996, during a difficult interval for fantasy literature, which was, at the time, struggling to keep up with the wise-cracking chutzpah of urban-fantasy stories. *A Game of Thrones* emerged as a link between worlds, with all the black humour and quick wit of urban fantasy, combined with the scale and drama of an epic story heavily influenced by medieval history. This heady blend of tradition and modernity made the Song of Ice and Fire series a publishing phenomenon that has been translated into over forty-five languages and spawned a hit television spin-off.

A Game of Thrones focuses on the Lord Eddard ('Ned') Stark and his family, Northern outsiders, whose aversion to politics make them essential to the reader's point of view. The novel begins, seductively, with a scene of dark magic that the reader then doubts for the next 600 pages. What were the 'Others?' How did they connect to the politics of the Seven Kingdoms, and what was the true focus of this multi-perspective story? What makes the novel so compelling is often what it leaves unsaid.

Martin's first novel divides the story geographically across the 'Seven Kingdoms:' from the frozen north and Winterfell, home of the Starks, to the seat of the Iron Throne in King's Landing and the grasslands of Essos. The latter is where Daenerys, another central character and one of the last remaining members of the noble house of Targaryen, comes of age among the Dothraki warriors. Martin's focus here on an adolescent girl – destined to become the powerful 'Mother of Dragons' – marks a distinct change from the genre's frequent interest in young male protagonists. He is working in territory that was previously staked out by feminist fantasy authors such as Mercedes Lackey and Tanya Huff, who also produced epic worlds.

Part of the adventure of reading *A Game of Thrones* lies in the way that Martin links place with perspective. Ned Stark's thoughts are always on ice and snow, his son Bran longs for the sky and Daenerys is tempered by the heat of Essos. Ever since Tolkien added runic clues to his map in *The Hobbit*, cartography has always been essential to the genre. Nowhere is this more

apparent than in *A Game of Thrones*, where ancient families, political factions and indigenous communities battle for control of overlapping territories. Along with heraldry, mapping is the chief cultural element of the Middle Ages that Martin draws upon in his creation of a mixed feudal society. Rather than romanticising these systems, *A Game of Thrones* sets out to expose the violence and corruption that underpin them.

Readers are offered glimpses of this dangerous, breathing world through a number of competing perspectives, often separated by culture and geography. Our understanding of the epic map is always incomplete. Canadian fantasy writer Guy Gavriel Kay used the same technique in his *Fionavar* trilogy, and Martin adapts this to a truly massive world. Communities whose fate depends upon mapping – such as the Wildlings, on the other side of the Wall – are often those who resist such colonial practices. Martin has cited Hadrian's Wall as an influence for his 300-mile-long, 700-foot-tall 'border', but critics such as Michail Zontos have also described it as a metaphor for the American frontier. Your perspective depends upon which side you end up on, and who draws the map around you. The diverse regions of Westeros are accompanied by living languages, developed in meticulous detail by linguist and conlanger David J. Peterson. His Dothraki language (which you can now

Lord Eddard Stark (portrayed by Sean Bean) and his family kneel before Robert Baratheon (Mark Addy), King of the Seven Kingdoms of Westeros.

take a course on) emerged from only a few words and phrases that Martin had created. What began with Tolkien's working Elvish language – immortal words – has culminated in a series of languages, even dialects, adopted by a range of cultures.

A Game of Thrones begins as an enclosed Gothic tale, then explodes outward along with the Stark family, taking advantage of its fantastic cartography. Like a darker version of the Pevensies, the Stark children grapple with a hostile landscape, whose dangers and inequalities mirror the structures of late feudalism. Magic remains within the space of the uncanny, always an undertone, while economics and the politics of lineage are the monstrous forces that keep everything turning. Bards are destitute, princesses are pawns and the maesters, like Jon Snow, 'know nothing'. Sometimes this ignores the dazzling beauty that was also present during the Middle Ages – the painting, lapidary, verse and celestial music – but Martin's focus on tragedy reminds us that this is not Disney's Middle Ages. He presents a diverse cast of characters: female translators, disabled boys, sly eunuchs and queer knights. These people set up camp in our brain, because they err, desire, betray, regret.

Critics often describe loving the series in spite of its dragons, but readers and fans alike know perfectly well that dragons are as old as storytelling itself. Rather than revitalising a genre for a new audience, *A Game of Thrones* has shown us what fantasy was always capable of, from King Arthur to the Iron Throne.

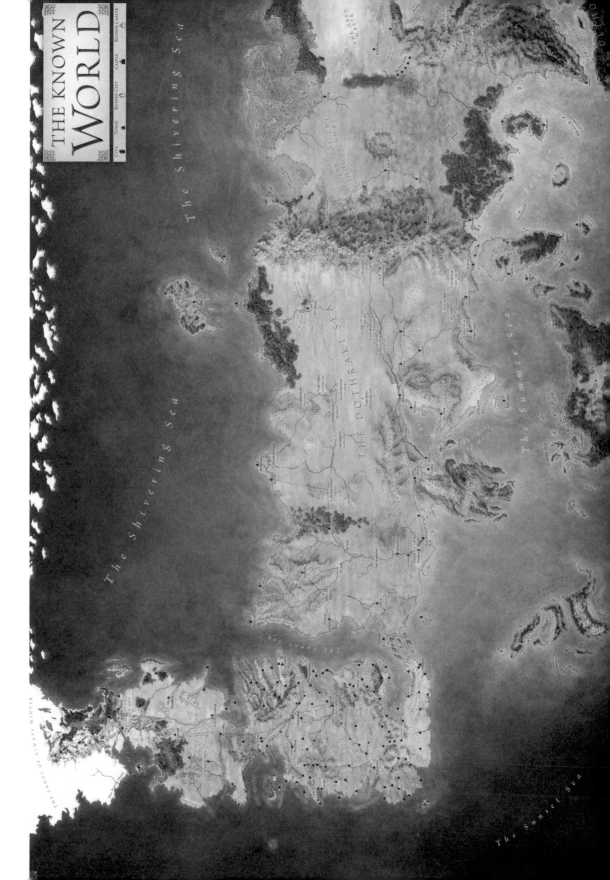

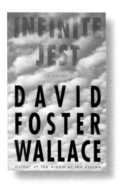

DAVID FOSTER WALLACE

INFINITE JEST (1996)

Popular entertainment dominates in David Foster Wallace's immense and complex vision of a future North America, the setting for a story that encompasses addiction, the power of advertising and tennis.

First published by Little, Brown and Company in 1996.

The book's title is taken from *Hamlet*, its working title was *A Failed Entertainment*.

Wallace wrote many non-fiction and short fiction pieces for newspapers and magazines, as well as the well-received essay collection *A Supposedly Fun Thing I'll Never Do Again* (1997), and a book of short stories titled *Brief Interviews with Hideous Men* (1999).

His last, unfinished novel, *The Pale King*, was published in 2011 and was a finalist for the 2012 Pulitzer Prize.

In the opening scene of *Infinite Jest*, Harold James Incandenza – a competitive teenage tennis player, known as 'Hal' – reflects that there's a very good chance that if he makes the finals of the WhataBurger Southwest Junior Invitational tennis tournament on Sunday he'll get to play in front of Venus Williams.

There's nothing particularly surprising about this. It's an average, ordinary scrap of novelistic detail. Why wouldn't Venus Williams be there? And why wouldn't he want to play in front of her? Except that when David Foster Wallace's (1962–2008) astounding work was published in 1996, Williams was only fifteen. She hadn't even played in her first Grand Slam tournament yet. Wallace's casual name-dropping is a bold piece of near-future prognostication, one that marks, or marked, *Infinite Jest* as what it is – a work of science fiction. Though, like all works of art set in the future, it is fated, over time, to become an alternative present instead.

The exact year in which the events of *Infinite Jest* take place is famously hard to pin down. It has been persuasively argued, based on a few carefully gleaned details, that much of the book takes place in 2009, but in the world of *Infinite Jest* years are no longer identified by numbers. The narrative is set in the era of what Wallace calls 'subsidized time', in which, every year, a corporation pays to have that year named after one of its products. So among the dates that figure in the timeline of *Infinite Jest* are the Year of the Trial-Size Dove Bar, the Year of the Whisper-Quiet Maytag Dishmaster, and most prominently (you can almost feel Wallace's glee as he types) the Year of the Depend Adult Undergarment.

Infinite Jest isn't known primarily as a work of science fiction, of course. It's better known for its extravagant, ungovernable size – 1,088 pages in paperback, counting endnotes – and its enormous literary complexity, which together have turned it into the kind of cult object that young men and women with heavy black spectacles lecture about at cocktail parties: a literary shillelagh for beating one's intellectual rivals into submission. It presents interpretive challenges as serious as James Joyce's *Ulysses* (1922), and it has

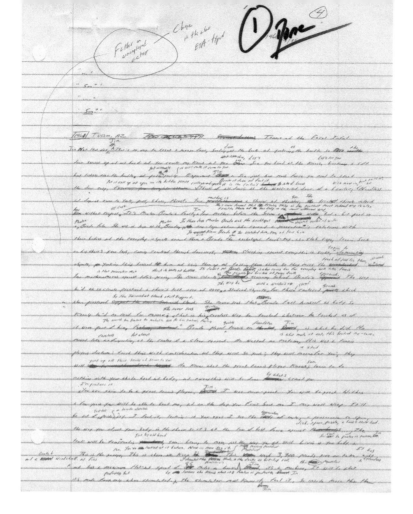

First page of a handwritten draft of *Infinite Jest*.

spawned a legion of academic papers, guides, commentaries, spreadsheets, diagrams and wikis. But the world it takes place in is not our world. *Infinite Jest* is science fiction, just well-scrubbed of any trace of science fiction's pulpy roots. Wallace came to science fiction as a crossover artist from literary fiction, working in the high-art tradition of Thomas Pynchon and Don DeLillo.

Wallace wasn't a realist, but he wasn't interested in predicting the future either. He didn't think there would actually be a Great Ohio Desert, in 1990 or ever. He wasn't a world-builder, like J. R. R. Tolkien or Frank Herbert, and he didn't need his fictional otherworlds to be plausible. Rather, time functioned for him as a solvent, a way of making reality more malleable, so that he could manipulate it and exaggerate it to express the things he wanted to express. Wallace's science fiction is a form of satire – the future is a place to play in, where he can pull aside the veil and reveal the true nature of things.

Infinite Jest has two protagonists. One is Hal, the aforementioned prodigiously intelligent seventeen-year-old who attends the Enfield Tennis Academy. The other is Don Gately, a recovering Demerol addict and reformed burglar who works at a rehabilitation clinic called Ennet House, located near the tennis academy.

Before he died, Hal's father James, who founded the tennis academy, was the patriarch of a family of eccentric prodigies reminiscent of the Glass family in J. D. Salinger's *Franny and Zooey* (1961). James Incandenza, commonly known merely as Himself, was also an avid amateur filmmaker, and he created a film so addictively entertaining that anyone watching it becomes paralyzed and can pay attention to nothing else, to the point where he or she lapses irredeemably into catatonia. 'Whoever saw it', Wallace writes, 'wanted nothing else ever in life but to see it again, and then again, and so on.' It's like the Monty Python sketch about a joke so funny that everyone who hears it dies from laughing. Before the book begins, Himself has committed suicide by sticking his head in a microwave oven.

The world of *Infinite Jest* has its own distinctive geopolitics. Under the leadership of its president, a former Las Vegas entertainer, usually referred to by Wallace as 'Johnny Gentle, Famous Crooner', the US has merged with Mexico and Canada to form a megastate called the Organization of North American Nations. (Again, check the acronym, with its sly wink to the Bible and masturbation shame: ONAN. More glee.) A large part of New England has been partitioned and written off as a massive toxic waste repository known as the 'Great Concavity'. Radioactivity from the Great Concavity has given rise to terrifying herds of feral hamsters that scour the Earth, leaving the land behind them bare of all vegetal matter.

This unstable arrangement provides the mechanism for the plot of *Infinite Jest*, to the extent that it has one. The Great Concavity runs along the border of Quebec and, inevitably, pollutants and toxins leach across the border, not to mention feral hamsters. Radical cells of Quebecois separatists oppose the Great Concavity (which they insist on referring to, by Wallacian logic, as the Great Convexity) and, by extension, ONAN as well, and they'll stop short of nothing, even terrorism, to make their opposition felt. Their weapon of choice? The fatally entertaining film created by James Incandenza, which they spend much of the book trying to get hold of. The film is called, of course, *Infinite Jest*.

Infinite Jest, the novel, is an example of literary maximalism, one of the dominant fictional modes of the 1990s; other examples include DeLillo's *Underworld* (1997) and Zadie Smith's *White Teeth* (2000). As in those works, there's a sense that Wallace is trying to import the multi-coloured, multi-layered fabric of an entire world into his novel intact, leaving nothing out. Not unlike those of *Underworld* and *White Teeth*, the world he's trying to import is one that he's also creating at the same time, detail by detail, hamster by hamster. Writing the book was a gargantuan task. 'I've never done something where I've just had to hold so many discrete pieces of information in my head at one time', he told Lipsky. 'You ever see *Johnny Mnemonic*? I mean, he gets this sort of data overload, and his ears bleed.' It would have been easier, of course, in some ways, to describe the world as it is. Certainly Wallace was up to the task: he was a first-class journalist and essayist as well as a novelist. But, at the time when he wrote *Infinite Jest*, Wallace considered realism to be all but bankrupt, and useless for what he was trying to do. Realism was too easy and familiar for the reader – not shocking enough. He wanted to jolt people out of their comfort zones, so they could make contact with real feelings and raw emotions, and see the world as it is. To do that, he paradoxically had to put them in an unreal world.

Having suffered from clinical depression for decades, Wallace committed suicide in 2008, leaving behind his fiction of another world to help the rest of us survive this one. 'Look man', Wallace once told an interviewer, 'we'd probably most of us agree that these are dark times, and stupid ones, but do we need fiction that does nothing but dramatise how dark and stupid everything is? In dark times, the definition of good art would seem to be art that locates and applies CPR to those elements of what's human and magical that still live and glow, despite the times' darkness.'

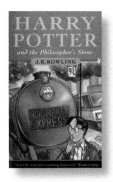

J. K. ROWLING

HARRY POTTER AND THE PHILOSOPHER'S STONE (1997)

Orphaned, unwanted Harry Potter realises his magical powers
at Hogwarts School while battling the evil wizard Voldemort,
who seeks the life-giving Philosopher's Stone.

First published by
Bloomsbury in 1997.

The Harry Potter series has
spawned multiple additional
books, including Hogwarts
textbooks, the fables read by
wizard children (*The Tales of
Beedle the Bard*), a short
online story by Rowling and
a stage play (*Harry Potter
and the Cursed Child*).

Nicholas Flamel, depicted
in *Philosopher's Stone* as a
friend of Albus Dumbledore,
was an actual fourteenth-
century scribe who gained
a posthumous reputation as
an alchemist. His house still
stands in Paris, the oldest
stone house in the city.

Harry Potter hardly needs an introduction. The series has sold more than 450 million copies worldwide and has been translated into more than seventy languages. Moreover, the world of Harry Potter extends far beyond the books themselves. The blockbuster adaptations are the second highest-grossing film series of all time, and Harry Potter pervades popular culture. From video games to board games, from fan fiction to fan sites, the Harry Potter world and characters have been used and discussed again and again. When J. K. Rowling (b.1965) wrote *Harry Potter and the Philosopher's Stone* in 1997 (published in the US as *Harry Potter and the Sorcerer's Stone*), she sparked one of the greatest and largest fandoms in history.

Perhaps the greatest appeal of the Wizarding World is that it is one both familiar and unfamiliar. Our world is translated into another, parallel world, which operated on rules sometimes similar, sometimes different. Rowling's creation expands through the seven books to reference wizards in different parts of continental Europe (and the world, in the afterlife of the Harry Potter fandom universe). However, a global presence is not necessary to be transported to a mirror image of our own universe made magical: the place is suburban England; travel is on English trains; schools have classrooms and dormitories. The familiarity of each of these locations is made fresh – sometimes strange – as the reader delights in the intersection – sometimes collision – of the wizarding and Muggle (non-wizarding) existences. The word 'utopia' does not quite apply here, but neither is this the 'dystopia' popular in contemporary fiction. The neologism 'contopia' might suit this world alongside our own, sometimes even within our own, but still functioning successfully on its own. As Hagrid explains to Harry, wizards keep their world secret because 'everyone'd be wantin' magic solutions to their problems'.

Harry actually begins his life in a wizarding home, but is ushered out of that world and into the life of Muggles with his aunt and uncle, not through a change of location or consciousness, but a traumatic event that he only remembers in dreams. Rowling at first merely suggests the happenings of that

night celebrated by every wizard in England: Voldemort has gone into hiding after spectacularly failing to kill the one-year-old Harry. As Voldemort does manage to kill his parents, Lily and James Potter, 'the boy who lived' must be hidden away in the Muggle world. He is subjected to eleven years of privation on Privet Drive with the Dursleys, who are not just aggressively Muggle (partly in response to Aunt Petunia's embarrassment over her sister's magical abilities) but also petty and mean.

As in the *Chronicles of Narnia*, readers are acquainted with the space and environment of wizard life through the eyes of a newcomer. Harry does not understand the flood of letters that are so determined to be opened only by him that hundreds of them follow the Dursleys' escape to a deserted island. The letters are the first of the adapted objects mentioned earlier. These are missives that can fly, squeeze under doors, come down chimneys and change address at will if the recipient changes locations. Sentient letters are only part of Rowling's versatile system of communication technology – owls are the major means of communication for all wizards. Simple oral instructions from their owners send owls off to carry letters and packages back and forth between wizards, anytime, anywhere. Photographs, newspaper illustrations and paintings are also forms of communication, conveniently allowing their occupants to move about and even move between frames to convey information to their viewers.

Rupert Grint, Daniel Radcliffe and Emma Watson play Ron, Harry and Hermione in Warner Bros' 2001 film adaptation.

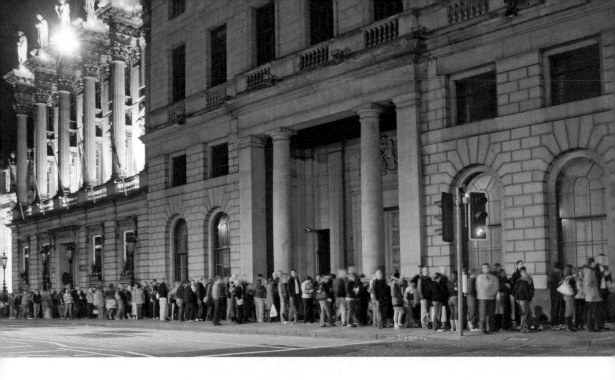

A lengthy queue snakes all the way down Prince's Street into St Andrew's Square in Rowling's adopted Edinburgh at midnight on the day of release for the seventh and last book in the series *Harry Potter and the Deathly Hallows*, July 2007.

A fundamental distinction between our existences is the markedly different capabilities of Muggles and wizards to master, and then manage, the knowledge required to make technology or magic work. We have developed complex mechanical and electronic products and systems external to our beings that control our lives probably more than we like to acknowledge. If a car coughs and stalls, many are helpless in the face of the blinking lights on the dashboard. If a computer screen is suddenly blue and blank, a visit to the electronics store is in store. Witches and wizards, trained for seven years in the magical arts, learn to control certain forces with their own minds and talents to accomplish similar tasks. We flip a switch on a flashlight; illumination springs from a wizard's wand at the sound of '*Lumos!*' After a big meal Molly Weasley waves her wand at the dirty dishes, and they quietly begin to wash themselves in the sink. A mirror does not reflect one's own face, but, as Dumbledore says to Harry, the Mirror of Erised 'shows us nothing more or less than the deepest, most desperate desire of our hearts'.

It may be assumed that the potential scope of a wizard's abilities would bestow unlimited powers, but Rowling has not resorted to that easy way out. For instance, they choose not to exercise complete magical control over their world. One question raised by magical skill is the creation of wealth: why not conjure up endless supplies of money? Some wizards are wealthier than others (the rich, haughty Malfoys versus the poor but good-hearted Weasleys), but they do not generate gold out of thin air, despite the Philosopher's Stone. Neither is the handling of their wealth what we might expect. One of Harry's first visits in the magical world is with Hagrid to Gringotts Bank, a Dickensian-looking establishment staffed by goblins so nasty they even intimidate Hagrid. We might expect wizards merely to render their money invisible, or enchant it to prevent theft. Instead, Harry enters an institutional setting organised vaguely like Muggle banks, but with special features: Gringotts sits above enchanted passages hundreds of miles beneath London, reached by a goblin driving a sort of miner's cart, with dragons guarding the most precious vaults.

This existence is imbued with magic, but is not effortless, uncomplicated, or free from evil. The world envisioned in *Philosopher's Stone* raises numerous questions addressed throughout the series: how does one negotiate with non-human creatures who also have powers? Can wizards create life? What happens if they try to control Muggle lives? To Rowling's credit, she has conceived rich possibilities, not just for plot purposes, but to explore how we interact with nature, exert power over others and cooperate in a diverse and sometimes dangerous world.

CHINA MIÉVILLE

THE BAS-LAG CYCLE (2000–04)

The seminal New Weird novels of China Miéville's mould-breaking cycle intermingle urban fantasy, steampunk, science fiction, horror and surrealism, engrossing readers with visions of wonder and grotesquery.

First published by Macmillan between 2000 and 2004.

Miéville was an avid player of Dungeons and Dragons and other roleplaying games when he was younger and still collects roleplaying bestiaries.

In addition to writing novels and short stories, Miéville also wrote the superhero comic series *Dial H* for DC Comics.

Born in Norwich, England, in 1972 and brought up in London, China Miéville has become a daring and influential voice in speculative fiction, renowned for his sweeping imaginative scope, erudite political perspectives and richly evocative prose style. His debut novel *King Rat* is a London phantasmagoria – kin to works such as Neil Gaiman's *Neverwhere* – but it was with the publication of *Perdido Street Station* in 2000 that Miéville became a literary sensation. The Arthur C. Clarke award-winning novel and the two sequels that followed, *The Scar* and *Iron Council*, together comprise the Bas-Lag cycle, a trilogy seminal to the literary movement dubbed the 'New Weird'. Looking back to the weird fiction of the early twentieth-century – a genre most closely associated with H. P. Lovecraft, but which also includes such under-appreciated luminaries as William Hope Hodgson, Clark Ashton Smith and Algernon Blackwood – the New Weird exists in what the sinister crime boss Mr Motley of *Perdido Street Station* would call 'the hybrid zone': a liminal space somewhere between existing genres, borrowing liberally from worlds too-often deemed incompatible. In Bas-Lag artificial intelligence and quantum mechanics mix with magic and monsters in a heady, hallucinogenic brew, simmering with unruly potential.

Perdido Street Station takes place entirely in the city of New Crobuzon: a churning industrial megalopolis calling to mind not only Victorian London but also Cairo, the French Quarter of New Orleans and Mervyn Peake's Gormenghast castle (see page 170). The many districts of Miéville's sprawling, baroquely described city are rendered in loving detail, from the eerie, crime-ridden slums of Bonetown, shadowed by the ribs of some centuries-dead behemoth, to the alchemical laboratories of Brock Marsh, where badger-familiars run errands for masters somewhere between scientists and sorcerers.

Magic – or thaumaturgy, as it is more generally termed in Bas-Lag – suffuses New Crobuzon's labyrinthine streets, but it is treated as a science, obeying its own distinct laws and logic, rather than an unknowable, uncontrollable mythic force.

Ruled in *Perdido Street Station* by Mayor Bentham Rudgutter, and in *Iron Council* by the coldly calculating Mayor Eliza Stem-Fulcher, New Crobuzon is a place of intrigue and everyday brutality. Though nominally a democracy, the city has strongly authoritarian leanings and rapacious colonial ambitions. Disguised militia make the city a gigantic panopticon, plain-clothes agents blending in with the crowd to ruthlessly enforce the will of their masters, while the rails radiating out from the imperialist metropole extend its power to all corners of Rohagi, Bas-Lag's most-described continent. Resistance to the oppressive Fat Sun party seethes throughout *Perdido Street Station* in the form of the righteously seditious newspaper *Runagate Rampant* and the mysterious outlaw and social bandit Jack Half-a-Prayer, only to boil over into open revolution in *Iron Council*, the most overtly political of the Bas-Lag cycle.

Two other cities feature prominently in the Bas-Lag cycle. Armada, a pirate-city fashioned from thousands of lashed-together boats, forms the setting of *The Scar*. The quasi-anarchic politics of Armada contrast markedly with the oligarchic corruption and totalitarian tendencies of New Crobuzon: here the various communities of the city jostle for power, debating which direction the flotilla should drift, which seas to sail, which targets to pick. Press-ganged captives and natives of the city co-exist uneasily, while erstwhile slaves and convicts find freedom and a new life on the waves. As in New Crobuzon, each neighbourhood of Armada possesses its own unique character, like the lucrative library-district of Booktown, the vampiric fiefdom of Dry Fall or Clockhouse Spur, the intellectuals' quarter, to name just a few. The eponymous Iron Council of the third book is similarly egalitarian, a 'perpetual train' populated by radical train labourers turned renegades, gone rogue into the wilds of Rohagi. The train-city's odyssey across the nightmarish mutant wasteland of the Catacopic Stain and other strange lands forms the heart of Iron Council.

Other cities receive only tantalising mention. There is Tesh, the City of Crawling Liquid, a place of 'moats and glass cats, and the Catoblepas Plain and merchant trawlers and tramp diplomats and the Crying Prince', an economic rival and sometimes military enemy of New Crobuzon; High Cromlech, a macabre metropolis peopled by quick and abdead in intricate castes and ruled by the embalmed thanati; The Gengris, monstrous subaquatic realm of the grindylow, a place of limb-farms and bile workshops and unthinkable weapons; Maru'ahm, with its casino-parliament and cardsharp senators; the crocodile double-city of the Brothers; Shud zar Myron zar Koni, City of Ratjinn, the Witchocracy of the Firewater Straits.

These allusions and countless others give Bas-Lag a feeling of place rarely found in fantasy fiction, a sense of depth and verisimilitude further fostered by the densely layered history Miéville hints at throughout the cycle. Never overburdening readers with heavy-handed exposition, the novels are scattered with allusions and subtle details to past events and political entities.

Overleaf: The massive conurbation of New Crobuzon. Miéville describes its sprawling districts in great detail, from the crime-ridden slums of Bonetown to the laboratories of Brock Marsh. Map by illustrator Lee Moyer.

ining Courses and Web-Based Training Courses
Prentice Hall

Multimedia Cyber Classroom and *Web-Based Training* Series

(For information regarding DEITEL™ Web-based training visit **www.ptgtraining.com**)

C++ Multimedia Cyber Classroom, 4/E

C# Multimedia Cyber Classroom

e-Business and e-Commerce Multimedia Cyber Classroom

Internet and World Wide Web Multimedia Cyber Classroom, 2/E

Java™ 2 Multimedia Cyber Classroom, 4/E

Perl Multimedia Cyber Classroom

Python Multimedia Cyber Classroom

Visual Basic® 6 Multimedia Cyber Classroom

Visual Basic® .NET Multimedia Cyber Classroom, 2/E

Wireless Internet & Mobile Business Programming Multimedia Cyber Classroom

XML Multimedia Cyber Classroom

The Complete Training Course Series

The Complete C++ Training Course, 4/E

The Complete C# Training Course

The Complete e-Business and e-Commerce Programming Training Course

The Complete Internet and World Wide Web Programming Training Course, 2/E

The Complete Java™ 2 Training Course, 4/E

The Complete Perl Training Course

The Complete Python Training Course

The Complete Visual Basic® 6 Training Course

The Complete Visual Basic® .NET Training Course, 2/E

The Complete Wireless Internet & Mobile Business Programming Training Course

The Complete XML Programming Training Course

To follow the Deitel publishing program, please register at

    www.deitel.com/newsletter/subscribe.html

for the *DEITEL™ BUZZ ONLINE* e-mail newsletter.

To communicate with the authors, send e-mail to:

    deitel@deitel.com

For information on corporate on-site seminars offered by Deitel & Associates, Inc. worldwide, visit:

    www.deitel.com

For continuing updates on Prentice Hall and Deitel publications visit:

    www.deitel.com,
    www.prenhall.com/deitel or
    www.InformIT.com/deitel

Vice President and Editorial Director, ECS: *Marcia J. Horton*
Acquisitions Editor: *Petra J. Recter*
Assistant Editor: *Sarah Burrows*
Project Manager: *Jennifer Cappello*
Vice President and Director of Production and Manufacturing, ESM: *David W. Riccardi*
Executive Managing Editor: *Vince O'Brien*
Production Editor: *Chirag Thakkar*
Director of Creative Services: *Paul Belfanti*
Creative Director: *Carole Anson*
Chapter Opener and Cover Designer: *Tamara L. Newnam, Laura Treibeck, Dr. Harvey Deitel*
Manufacturing Manager: *Trudy Pisciotti*
Manufacturing Buyer: *Lisa McDowell*
Marketing Manager: *Pamela Shaffer*
Marketing Assistant: *Barrie Reinhold*

Pearson Education Ltd.
Pearson Education Australia Pty, Ltd.
Pearson Education Singapore, Pte. Ltd.
Pearson Education North Asia Ltd.
Pearson Education Canada, Inc.
Pearson Educacion de Mexico, S.A. de C.V.
Pearson Education–Japan
Pearson Education Malaysia, Pte. Ltd.
Pearson Education, Inc., *Upper Saddle River, New Jersey*

C++

HOW TO PROGRAM

FOURTH EDITION

H. M. Deitel
Deitel & Associates, Inc.

P. J. Deitel
Deitel & Associates, Inc.

Prentice
Hall

PEARSON EDUCATION INTERNATIONAL

Trademarks

Borland and C++Builder are trademarks or registered trademarks of Borland.

DEITEL, DIVE INTO, and LIVE CODE are trademarks of Deitel and Associates, Inc.

Describe, Embarcadero's UML design tool, is a trademark of Embarcadero Technologies, Inc. and is protected by the laws of the United States and other countries.

Internet Explorer, Microsoft, Visual C++ 6, Visual C++ .NET, Visual Studio and Windows are registered trademarks of Microsoft Corporation in the United States and/or other countries.

Java and all Java-based marks are trademarks or registered trademarks of Sun Microsystems, Inc. in the United States and other countries.

Linux is a registered trademark of Linus Torvalds.

Netscape, the Netscape N and Ship's Wheel logos are registered trademarks of Netscape Communications Corporation in the U.S. and other countries.

Object Management Group, OMG, Unified Modeling Language and UML are trademarks of Object Management Group, Inc.

Rational Rose, Rational Software Corporation's UML visual modeling tool, and Rational Unified Process are registered trademarks of Rational Software Corporation in the United States and/or other countries.

Cygwin is a trademark and copyrighted work of Red Hat, Inc. in the United States and other countries.

CSS, Cascading Style Sheets Specification, and XHTML, The Extensible HyperText Markup Language, are trademarks of the World Wide Web Consortium (W3C®) and its hosts, the Massachusetts Institute of Technology (MIT), Institut National de Recherche en Informatique et en Automatique (INRIA), and Keio University (Keio).

TO

Don Kostuch:

For your steadfast commitment to excellence in teaching and writing about C++ and object technology.

Thank you for being our mentor, our colleague and our friend.

Thank you for a decade of being our most critical, yet most constructive reviewer.

It is a privilege for us to be your students.

Harvey and Paul Deitel

Contents

Preface   **xxxiv**

1   Introduction to Computers and C++ Programming   **1**

1.1	Introduction	2
1.2	What is a Computer?	4
1.3	Computer Organization	5
1.4	Evolution of Operating Systems	6
1.5	Personal Computing, Distributed Computing and Client/Server Computing	7
1.6	Machine Languages, Assembly Languages, and High-level Languages	7
1.7	History of C and C++	8
1.8	C++ Standard Library	10
1.9	Java	11
1.10	Visual Basic, Visual C++ and C#	11
1.11	Other High-level Languages	13
1.12	Structured Programming	13
1.13	The Key Software Trend: Object Technology	14
1.14	Basics of a Typical C++ Environment	15
1.15	Hardware Trends	17
1.16	History of the Internet	18
1.17	History of the World Wide Web	19
1.18	World Wide Web Consortium (W3C)	20
1.19	General Notes About C++ and This Book	20
1.20	Introduction to C++ Programming	21
1.21	A Simple Program: Printing a Line of Text	21
1.22	Another Simple Program: Adding Two Integers	26
1.23	Memory Concepts	30
1.24	Arithmetic	31

1.25	Decision Making: Equality and Relational Operators	34
1.26	Thinking About Objects: Introduction to Object Technology and the Unified Modeling Language™	40
1.27	Tour of the Book	44

2   Control Structures   **70**

2.1	Introduction	71
2.2	Algorithms	72
2.3	Pseudocode	72
2.4	Control Structures	73
2.5	**if** Selection Structure	76
2.6	**if/else** Selection Structure	77
2.7	**while** Repetition Structure	81
2.8	Formulating Algorithms: Case Study 1 (Counter-Controlled Repetition)	83
2.9	Formulating Algorithms with Top-Down, Stepwise Refinement: Case Study 2 (Sentinel-Controlled Repetition)	86
2.10	Formulating Algorithms with Top-Down, Stepwise Refinement: Case Study 3 (Nested Control Structures)	94
2.11	Assignment Operators	98
2.12	Increment and Decrement Operators	99
2.13	Essentials of Counter-Controlled Repetition	102
2.14	**for** Repetition Structure	104
2.15	Examples Using the **for** Structure	109
2.16	**switch** Multiple-Selection Structure	113
2.17	**do/while** Repetition Structure	120
2.18	**break** and **continue** Statements	122
2.19	Logical Operators	124
2.20	Confusing Equality (**==**) and Assignment (**=**) Operators	127
2.21	Structured-Programming Summary	128
2.22	[Optional Case Study] Thinking About Objects: Identifying a System's Classes from a Problem Statement	133

3   Functions   **169**

3.1	Introduction	170
3.2	Program Components in C++	170
3.3	Math Library Functions	171
3.4	Functions	173
3.5	Function Definitions	174
3.6	Function Prototypes	178
3.7	Header Files	180
3.8	Random Number Generation	182
3.9	Example: Game of Chance and Introducing **enum**	188
3.10	Storage Classes	192
3.11	Scope Rules	195
3.12	Recursion	198
3.13	Example Using Recursion: Fibonacci Series	202

3.14   Recursion vs. Iteration   206
3.15   Functions with Empty Parameter Lists   208
3.16   Inline Functions   209
3.17   References and Reference Parameters   211
3.18   Default Arguments   215
3.19   Unary Scope Resolution Operator   217
3.20   Function Overloading   219
3.21   Function Templates   222
3.22   [Optional Case Study] Thinking About Objects: Identifying a
        Class's Attributes   225

4   Arrays   252
4.1   Introduction   253
4.2   Arrays   253
4.3   Declaring Arrays   255
4.4   Examples Using Arrays   256
4.5   Passing Arrays to Functions   272
4.6   Sorting Arrays   276
4.7   Case Study: Computing Mean, Median and Mode Using Arrays   278
4.8   Searching Arrays: Linear Search and Binary Search   283
4.9   Multiple-Subscripted Arrays   289
4.10   [Optional Case Study] Thinking About Objects: Identifying the
        Operations of a Class   296

5   Pointers and Strings   319
5.1   Introduction   320
5.2   Pointer Variable Declarations and Initialization   320
5.3   Pointer Operators   322
5.4   Calling Functions by Reference   325
5.5   Using **const** with Pointers   329
5.6   Bubble Sort Using Pass-by-Reference   336
5.7   Pointer Expressions and Pointer Arithmetic   341
5.8   Relationship Between Pointers and Arrays   344
5.9   Arrays of Pointers   349
5.10   Case Study: Card Shuffling and Dealing Simulation   350
5.11   Function Pointers   355
5.12   Introduction to Character and String Processing   360
        5.12.1   Fundamentals of Characters and Strings   360
        5.12.2   String Manipulation Functions of the String-Handling Library   362
5.13   [Optional Case Study] Thinking About Objects: Collaborations
        Among Objects   370

6   Classes and Data Abstraction   404
6.1   Introduction   405
6.2   Structure Definitions   406
6.3   Accessing Structure Members   407

6.4	Implementing User-Defined Type **Time** with a C-like **struct**	408
6.5	Implementing Abstract Data Type **Time** with a **class**	411
6.6	Class Scope and Accessing Class Members	418
6.7	Separating Interface from Implementation	420
6.8	Controlling Access to Members	424
6.9	Access Functions and Utility Functions	426
6.10	Initializing Class Objects: Constructors	430
6.11	Using Default Arguments with Constructors	430
6.12	Destructors	435
6.13	When Constructors and Destructors Are Called	435
6.14	Using *Set* and *Get* Functions	439
6.15	Subtle Trap: Returning a Reference to a **private** Data Member	445
6.16	Default Memberwise Assignment	448
6.17	Software Reusability	450
6.18	[Optional Case Study) Thinking About Objects: Starting to Program the Classes for the Elevator Simulator	451

7 Classes: Part II   468

7.1	Introduction	469
7.2	**const** (Constant) Objects and **const** Member Functions	469
7.3	Composition: Objects as Members of Classes	478
7.4	**friend** Functions and **friend** Classes	485
7.5	Using the **this** Pointer	489
7.6	Dynamic Memory Management with Operators **new** and **delete**	495
7.7	**static** Class Members	497
7.8	Data Abstraction and Information Hiding	502
	7.8.1 Example: Array Abstract Data Type	504
	7.8.2 Example: String Abstract Data Type	504
	7.8.3 Example: Queue Abstract Data Type	505
7.9	Container Classes and Iterators	505
7.10	Proxy Classes	506
7.11	[Optional Case Study] Thinking About Objects: Programming the Classes for the Elevator Simulator	509

8 Operator Overloading; String and Array Objects   546

8.1	Introduction	547
8.2	Fundamentals of Operator Overloading	548
8.3	Restrictions on Operator Overloading	549
8.4	Operator Functions as Class Members vs. as **friend** Functions	550
8.5	Overloading Stream-Insertion and Stream-Extraction Operators	552
8.6	Overloading Unary Operators	555
8.7	Overloading Binary Operators	555
8.8	Case Study: **Array** Class	556
8.9	Converting between Types	568
8.10	Case Study: **String** Class	569
8.11	Overloading **++** and **--**	581

8.12   Case Study: A **Date** Class   582
8.13   Standard Library Classes **string** and **vector**   588

9   Object-Oriented Programming: Inheritance   609
9.1   Introduction   610
9.2   Base Classes and Derived Classes   611
9.3   **protected** Members   614
9.4   Relationship between Base Classes and Derived Classes   614
9.5   Case Study: Three-Level Inheritance Hierarchy   637
9.6   Constructors and Destructors in Derived Classes   642
9.7   "Uses A" and "Knows A" Relationships   648
9.8   **public**, **protected** and **private** Inheritance   648
9.9   Software Engineering with Inheritance   649
9.10   [Optional Case Study] Thinking About Objects: Incorporating
        Inheritance into the Elevator Simulation   650

10   Object-Oriented Programming: Polymorphism   662
10.1   Introduction   663
10.2   Relationships Among Objects in an Inheritance Hierarchy   664
        10.2.1   Invoking Base-Class Functions from Derived-Class Objects   665
        10.2.2   Aiming Derived-Class Pointers at Base-Class Objects   670
        10.2.3   Derived-Class Member-Function Calls via Base-Class Pointers 672
        10.2.4   Virtual Functions   673
10.3   Polymorphism Examples   679
10.4   Type Fields and **switch** Structures   680
10.5   Abstract Classes   680
10.6   Case Study: Inheriting Interface and Implementation   682
10.7   Polymorphism, Virtual Functions and Dynamic Binding "Under
        the Hood"   695
10.8   Virtual Destructors   699
10.9   Case Study: Payroll System Using Polymorphism and Run-Time
        Type Information with **dynamic_cast** and **typeid**   699

11   Templates   718
11.1   Introduction   719
11.2   Function Templates   720
11.3   Overloading Function Templates   723
11.4   Class Templates   723
11.5   Class Templates and Nontype Parameters   730
11.6   Templates and Inheritance   731
11.7   Templates and Friends   731
11.8   Templates and **static** Members   732

12   C++ Stream Input/Output   737
12.1   Introduction   739
12.2   Streams   739
        12.2.1   Classic Streams vs. Standard Streams   740

	12.2.2	**iostream** Library Header Files	740
	12.2.3	Stream Input/Output Classes and Objects	741
12.3	Stream Output		743
	12.3.1	Output of **char *** Variables	743
	12.3.2	Character Output using Member Function **put**	744
12.4	Stream Input		744
	12.4.1	**get** and **getline** Member Functions	745
	12.4.2	**istream** Member Functions **peek**, **putback** and **ignore**	748
	12.4.3	Type-Safe I/O	748
12.5	Unformatted I/O using **read**, **write** and **gcount**		748
12.6	Introduction to Stream Manipulators		749
	12.6.1	Integral Stream Base: **dec**, **oct**, **hex** and **setbase**	750
	12.6.2	Floating-Point Precision (**precision**, **setprecision**)	751
	12.6.3	Field Width (**width**, **setw**)	752
	12.6.4	Programmer-Defined Manipulators	754
12.7	Stream Format States and Stream Manipulators		755
	12.7.1	Trailing Zeros and Decimal Points (**showpoint**)	756
	12.7.2	Justification (**left**, **right** and **internal**)	757
	12.7.3	Padding (**fill**, **setfill**)	759
	12.7.4	Integral Stream Base (**dec**, **oct**, **hex**, **showbase**)	760
	12.7.5	Floating-Point Numbers; Scientific and Fixed Notation (**scientific**, **fixed**)	761
	12.7.6	Uppercase/Lowercase Control (**uppercase**)	762
	12.7.7	Specifying Boolean Format (**boolalpha**)	763
	12.7.8	Setting and Resetting the Format State via Member-Function **flags**	764
12.8	Stream Error States		766
12.9	Tying an Output Stream to an Input Stream		768
13	**Exception Handling**		**779**
13.1	Introduction		780
13.2	Exception-Handling Overview		781
13.3	Other Error-Handling Techniques		783
13.4	Simple Exception-Handling Example: Divide by Zero		784
13.5	Rethrowing an Exception		788
13.6	Exception Specifications		789
13.7	Processing Unexpected Exceptions		790
13.8	Stack Unwinding		790
13.9	Constructors, Destructors and Exception Handling		792
13.10	Exceptions and Inheritance		793
13.11	Processing **new** Failures		793
13.12	Class **auto_ptr** and Dynamic Memory Allocation		797
13.13	Standard Library Exception Hierarchy		800
14	**File Processing**		**808**
14.1	Introduction		809
14.2	The Data Hierarchy		809

14.3   Files and Streams   811
14.4   Creating a Sequential-Access File   812
14.5   Reading Data from a Sequential-Access File   816
14.6   Updating Sequential-Access Files   823
14.7   Random-Access Files   824
14.8   Creating a Random-Access File   824
14.9   Writing Data Randomly to a Random-Access File   829
14.10   Reading Data Sequentially from a Random-Access File   831
14.11   Example: A Transaction-Processing Program   834
14.12   Input/Output of Objects   841

15   Class `string` and String Stream Processing   850
15.1   Introduction   851
15.2   **string** Assignment and Concatenation   852
15.3   Comparing **string**s   855
15.4   Substrings   857
15.5   Swapping **string**s   858
15.6   **string** Characteristics   859
15.7   Finding Strings and Characters in a **string**   862
15.8   Replacing Characters in a **string**   864
15.9   Inserting Characters into a **string**   866
15.10   Conversion to C-Style **char *** Strings   867
15.11   Iterators   869
15.12   String Stream Processing   870

16   Web Programming with CGI   880
16.1   Introduction   881
16.2   HTTP Request Types   882
16.3   Multi-Tier Architecture   882
16.4   Accessing Web Servers   883
16.5   Apache HTTP Server   884
16.6   Requesting XHTML Documents   885
16.7   Introduction to CGI   885
16.8   Simple HTTP Transaction   886
16.9   Simple CGI Script   888
16.10   Sending Input to a CGI Script   895
16.11   Using XHTML Forms to Send Input   897
16.12   Other Headers   905
16.13   Case Study: An Interactive Web Page   905
16.14   Cookies   909
16.15   Server-Side Files   915
16.16   Case Study: Shopping Cart   921
16.17   Internet and Web Resources   936

17   Data Structures   942
17.1   Introduction   943
17.2   Self-Referential Classes   944

17.3	Dynamic Memory Allocation and Data Structures	945
17.4	Linked Lists	945
17.5	Stacks	960
17.6	Queues	965
17.7	Trees	969

18 Bits, Characters, Strings and Structures — 1000

18.1	Introduction	1001
18.2	Structure Definitions	1001
18.3	Initializing Structures	1003
18.4	Using Structures with Functions	1004
18.5	**typedef**	1004
18.6	Example: High-Performance Card-Shuffling and Dealing Simulation	1005
18.7	Bitwise Operators	1007
18.8	Bit Fields	1017
18.9	Character-Handling Library	1020
18.10	String-Conversion Functions	1026
18.11	Search Functions of the String-Handling Library	1031
18.12	Memory Functions of the String-Handling Library	1036

19 Preprocessor — 1053

19.1	Introduction	1054
19.2	The **#include** Preprocessor Directive	1054
19.3	The **#define** Preprocessor Directive: Symbolic Constants	1055
19.4	The **#define** Preprocessor Directive: Macros	1056
19.5	Conditional Compilation	1057
19.6	The **#error** and **#pragma** Preprocessor Directives	1058
19.7	The **#** and **##** Operators	1059
19.8	Line Numbers	1059
19.9	Predefined Symbolic Constants	1060
19.10	Assertions	1060

20 C Legacy Code Topics — 1065

20.1	Introduction	1066
20.2	Redirecting Input/Output on UNIX and DOS Systems	1066
20.3	Variable-Length Argument Lists	1067
20.4	Using Command-Line Arguments	1070
20.5	Notes on Compiling Multiple-Source-File Programs	1071
20.6	Program Termination with **exit** and **atexit**	1073
20.7	The **volatile** Type Qualifier	1075
20.8	Suffixes for Integer and Floating-Point Constants	1075
20.9	Signal Handling	1075
20.10	Dynamic Memory Allocation with **calloc** and **realloc**	1078
20.11	The Unconditional Branch: **goto**	1079
20.12	Unions	1080
20.13	Linkage Specifications	1084

21   Standard Template Library (STL)   **1090**

21.1   Introduction to the Standard Template Library (STL)   1092
       21.1.1   Introduction to Containers   1094
       21.1.2   Introduction to Iterators   1098
       21.1.3   Introduction to Algorithms   1103
21.2   Sequence Containers   1105
       21.2.1   **vector** Sequence Container   1105
       21.2.2   **list** Sequence Container   1113
       21.2.3   **deque** Sequence Container   1117
21.3   Associative Containers   1119
       21.3.1   **multiset** Associative Container   1119
       21.3.2   **set** Associative Container   1122
       21.3.3   **multimap** Associative Container   1124
       21.3.4   **map** Associative Container   1126
21.4   Container Adapters   1128
       21.4.1   **stack** Adapter   1128
       21.4.2   **queue** Adapter   1130
       21.4.3   **priority_queue** Adapter   1132
21.5   Algorithms   1133
       21.5.1   **fill**, **fill_n**, **generate** and **generate_n**   1134
       21.5.2   **equal**, **mismatch** and **lexicographical_compare**   1136
       21.5.3   **remove**, **remove_if**, **remove_copy** and
                   remove_copy_if   1138
       21.5.4   **replace**, **replace_if**, **replace_copy** and
                   replace_copy_if   1141
       21.5.5   Mathematical Algorithms   1144
       21.5.6   Basic Searching and Sorting Algorithms   1148
       21.5.7   **swap**, **iter_swap** and **swap_ranges**   1150
       21.5.8   **copy_backward**, **merge**, **unique** and **reverse**   1152
       21.5.9   **inplace_merge**, **unique_copy** and **reverse_copy**   1154
       21.5.10   Set Operations   1156
       21.5.11   **lower_bound**, **upper_bound** and **equal_range**   1160
       21.5.12   Heapsort   1162
       21.5.13   **min** and **max**   1165
       21.5.14   Algorithms Not Covered in This Chapter   1166
21.6   Class **bitset**   1168
21.7   Function Objects   1172
21.8   STL Internet and Web Resources   1175

22   Other Topics   **1183**

22.1   Introduction   1184
22.2   **const_cast** Operator   1184
22.3   **reinterpret_cast** Operator   1185
22.4   namespaces   1186
22.5   Operator Keywords   1190
22.6   **explicit** Constructors   1192

22.7   **mutable** Class Members   1197
22.8   Pointers to Class Members (**. *** and **-> ***)   1199
22.9   Multiple Inheritance   1201
22.10   Multiple Inheritance and **virtual** Base Classes   1205
22.11   Closing Remarks   1210

A   **Operator Precedence Chart**   **1214**

B   **ASCII Character Set**   **1216**

C   **Number Systems**   **1217**
C.1   Introduction   1218
C.2   Abbreviating Binary Numbers as Octal Numbers and
        Hexadecimal Numbers   1221
C.3   Converting Octal Numbers and Hexadecimal Numbers to Binary Numbers   1222
C.4   Converting from Binary, Octal or Hexadecimal to Decimal   1222
C.5   Converting from Decimal to Binary, Octal or Hexadecimal   1223
C.6   Negative Binary Numbers: Two's Complement Notation   1225

D   **C++ Internet and Web Resources**   **1230**
D.1   Resources   1230
D.2   Tutorials   1232
D.3   FAQs   1233
D.4   Visual C++   1233
D.5   Newsgroups   1233
D.6   Compilers and Development Tools   1234
D.7   Standard Template Library   1234

E   **Introduction to XHTML**   **1236**
E.1   Introduction   1237
E.2   Editing XHTML   1237
E.3   First XHTML Example   1238
E.4   Headers   1240
E.5   Linking   1242
E.6   Images   1245
E.7   Special Characters and More Line Breaks   1249
E.8   Unordered Lists   1251
E.9   Nested and Ordered Lists   1251
E.10   Basic XHTML Tables   1252
E.11   Intermediate XHTML Tables and Formatting   1257
E.12   Basic XHTML Forms   1259
E.13   More Complex XHTML Forms   1262
E.14   Internet and World Wide Web Resources   1269

F   **XHTML Special Characters**   **1274**

        Bibliography   **1275**

        Index   **1281**

Illustrations

1   Introduction to Computers and C++ Programming   1

1.1   A typical C++ environment.   16
1.2   Text-printing program.   22
1.3   Escape sequences.   24
1.4   Printing on one line with separate statements using **cout**.   25
1.5   Printing on multiple lines with a single statement using **cout**.   25
1.6   Addition program.   26
1.7   Memory location showing the name and value of variable **integer1**.   30
1.8   Memory locations after storing values for **integer1** and **integer2**.   31
1.9   Memory locations after calculating the **sum** of **integer1** and **integer2**.   31
1.10   Arithmetic operators.   31
1.11   Precedence of arithmetic operators.   33
1.12   Order in which a second-degree polynomial is evaluated.   35
1.13   Equality and relational operators.   35
1.14   Equality and relational operators .   36
1.15   Precedence and associativity of the operators discussed so far.   39

2   Control Structures   70

2.1   Sequence structure activity diagram.   73
2.2   C++ keywords.   75
2.3   **if** single-selection structure activity diagram.   77
2.4   **if/else** double-selection structure activity diagram.   78
2.5   **while** repetition structure activity diagram.   82
2.6   Class-average problem pseudocode algorithm that uses counter-controlled repetition.   83
2.7   Class-average problem with counter-controlled repetition.   84
2.8   Class-average problem pseudocode algorithm with sentinel-controlled repetition.   89

2.9   Class-average problem with sentinel-controlled repetition.   89
2.10   Examination-results problem pseudocode algorithm.   96
2.11   Nested control structures: Examination-results problem.   96
2.12   Arithmetic assignment operators.   99
2.13   Increment and decrement operators.   100
2.14   Preincrementing and postincrementing.   100
2.15   Operator precedence for the operators encountered so far in the text. 102
2.16   Counter-controlled repetition.   103
2.17   Counter-controlled repetition with the **for** structure.   104
2.18   **for** structure header components.   105
2.19   **for** repetition structure activity diagram.   108
2.20   Summation with **for**.   109
2.21   Compound interest calculations with **for**.   111
2.22   **switch** structure testing multiple letter-grade values.   114
2.23   **switch** multiple-selection structure activity diagram with
       break statements.   118
2.24   **do/while** structure.   121
2.25   **do/while** repetition structure activity diagram.   121
2.26   **break** statement exiting a **for** structure.   122
2.27   **continue** statement terminating a single iteration of a **for** structure. 123
2.28   **&&** (logical AND) operator truth table.   125
2.29   **||** (logical OR) operator truth table.   125
2.30   **!** (logical negation) operator truth table.   126
2.31   Operator precedence and associativity.   127
2.32   C++'s single-entry/single-exit sequence, selection and repetition structures. 129
2.33   Rules for forming structured programs.   130
2.34   Simplest activity diagram.   130
2.35   Repeatedly applying rule 2 of Fig. 2.33 to the simplest activity diagram. 130
2.36   Applying rule 3 of Fig. 2.33 to the simplest activity diagram.   131
2.37   Activity diagram with illegal syntax.   132
2.38   Use-case diagram for elevator system.   139
2.39   List of nouns in problem statement .   140
2.40   Representing a class in the UML.   142
2.41   Associations between classes in a class diagram.   142
2.42   Multiplicity values.   143
2.43   Full class diagram for elevator simulation.   144
2.44   Object diagram of empty building.   145

3   Functions   169
3.1   Hierarchical boss function/worker function relationship.   172
3.2   Math library functions.   172
3.3   Programmer-defined function **square**.   174
3.4   Programmer-defined **maximum** function.   177
3.5   Promotion hierarchy for built-in data types.   180
3.6   Standard library header files.   181
3.7   Shifted, scaled integers produced by **1 + rand() % 6**.   183

3.8   Rolling a six-sided die 6000 times.   184
3.9   Randomizing the die-rolling program.   186
3.10   Craps simulation.   188
3.11   Sample outputs for the craps program.   191
3.12   Scoping example.   196
3.13   Recursive evaluation of 5!.   200
3.14   Factorial calculations with a recursive function.   200
3.15   Fibonacci numbers generated with a recursive function.   202
3.16   Set of recursive calls to method **Fibonacci**.   205
3.17   Summary of recursion examples and exercises in the text.   207
3.18   Functions that take no arguments.   208
3.19   **inline** function that calculates the volume of a cube.   210
3.20   Passing arguments by value and by reference.   212
3.21   Initializing a reference.   213
3.22   Uninitialized local reference causes a syntax error.   214
3.23   Default arguments to a function.   216
3.24   Unary scope resolution operator.   217
3.25   Overloaded function definitions.   219
3.26   Name mangling to enable type-safe linkage.   221
3.27   Using a function template.   223
3.28   Descriptive words and phrases in problem statement.   225
3.29   Class diagram showing attributes.   226
3.30   Statechart diagram for classes **FloorButton** and **ElevatorButton**. 228
3.31   Statechart diagram for class **Elevator**.   228
3.32   Activity diagram that models the elevator's logic for responding to
       floor-button presses.   230
3.33   Sample program for Exercise 3.2.   237
3.34   Towers of Hanoi for the case with four disks.   247

4   Arrays   252
4.1   Array of 12 elements.   254
4.2   Operator precedence and associativity.   255
4.3   Initializing an array's elements to zeros and printing the array. 256
4.4   Initializing the elements of an array with a declaration.   257
4.5   Generating values to be placed into elements of an array.   259
4.6   Initializing and using a constant variable.   260
4.7   **const** variables must be initialized.   260
4.8   Computing the sum of the elements of an array.   261
4.9   Histogram printing program.   262
4.10   Dice-rolling program using an array instead of **switch**.   263
4.11   Student-poll-analysis program.   265
4.12   Character arrays processed as strings.   268
4.13   **static** array initialization and automatic array initialization. 270
4.14   Passing arrays and individual array elements to functions.   273
4.15   **const** type qualifier applied to an array parameter.   275
4.16   Sorting an array with bubble sort.   277

4.17   Survey data analysis program.   279
4.18   Sample run for the survey data analysis program.   282
4.19   Linear search of an array.   284
4.20   Binary search of a sorted array.   286
4.21   Double-subscripted array with three rows and four columns.   290
4.22   Initializing multidimensional arrays.   290
4.23   Double-subscripted array manipulations.   293
4.24   Verb phrases for each class in our elevator simulator.   297
4.25   Class diagram that includes attributes and operations.   298
4.26   Sequence diagram that models the steps the building repeats
        during the simulation.   300
4.27   Sequence diagram for scheduling process.   302
4.28   The 36 possible outcomes of rolling two dice.   311
4.29   Turtle graphics commands.   313
4.30   The eight possible moves of the knight.   314
4.31   The 22 squares eliminated by placing a queen in the upper-left corner.   316

5   Pointers and Strings   319
5.1   Directly and indirectly referencing a variable.   321
5.2   Graphical representation of a pointer pointing to a variable in memory.   322
5.3   Representation of **y** and **yPtr** in memory.   322
5.4   Pointer operators **&** and *****.   323
5.5   Operator precedence and associativity.   324
5.6   Pass-by-value used to cube a variable's value.   326
5.7   Pass-by-reference with a pointer argument used to cube a variable's value.   327
5.8   Pass-by-value analysis of the program of Fig. 5.6.   328
5.9   Pass-by-reference analysis (with a pointer argument) of the program
        of Fig. 5.7.   329
5.10   Converting a string to uppercase.   331
5.11   Printing a string one character at a time using a nonconstant pointer to
        constant data.   332
5.12   Attempting to modify data through a nonconstant pointer to constant data.   333
5.13   Attempting to modify a constant pointer to nonconstant data.   334
5.14   Attempting to modify a constant pointer to constant data.   335
5.15   Bubble sort with pass-by-reference.   336
5.16   **sizeof** operator when applied to an array name returns the number of
        bytes in the array.   339
5.17   **sizeof** operator used to determine standard data type sizes.   340
5.18   Array **v** and a pointer variable **vPtr** that points to **v**. 342
5.19   Pointer **vPtr** after pointer arithmetic.   342
5.20   Referencing array elements with the array name and with pointers. 345
5.21   String copying using array notation and pointer notation.   347
5.22   Graphical representation of the **suit** array.   349
5.23   Double-subscripted array representation of a deck of cards.   350
5.24   Card shuffling and dealing program.   352
5.25   Multipurpose sorting program using function pointers.   355

5.26   Array of pointers to functions.   358
5.27   String-manipulation functions of the string-handling library.   363
5.28   **strcpy** and **strncpy**.   364
5.29   **strcat** and **strncat**.   365
5.30   **strcmp** and **strncmp**.   366
5.31   **strtok**.   368
5.32   **strlen**.   370
5.33   Modified list of verb phrases for classes in the system.   371
5.34   Collaborations that occur in the elevator system.   371
5.35   Collaboration diagram for loading and unloading passengers.   373
5.36   Unshuffled **deck** array.   386
5.37   Sample shuffled **deck** array.   386
5.38   Rules for moving the tortoise and the hare.   386
5.39   Simpletron Machine Language (SML) operation codes.   388
5.40   SML Example 1.   389
5.41   SML Example 2.   389
5.42   A sample dump.   392
5.43   Double-subscripted array representation of a maze.   396
5.44   Morse code alphabet.   402

6   Classes and Data Abstraction   404

6.1   Creating a structure, setting its members and printing the structure.   408
6.2   Class **Time** definition.   411
6.3   **Time** abstract data type implementation as a class.   413
6.4   Accessing an object's data members and member functions through
        each type of object handle—the object's name, a reference to the
        object and a pointer to the object.   419
6.5   **Time** class definition.   421
6.6   **Time** class member-function definitions.   421
6.7   Program to test class **Time**.   422
6.8   **private** members of a class are not accessible outside the class.   425
6.9   **SalesPerson** class definition.   427
6.10   **SalesPerson** class member-function definitions.   428
6.11   Utility function demontration.   429
6.12   **Time** class containing a constructor with default arguments.   431
6.13   **Time** class member-function definitions including a constructor
        that takes arguments.   431
6.14   Constructor with default arguments.   433
6.15   **CreateAndDestroy** class definition.   436
6.16   **CreateAndDestroy** class member-function definitions.   437
6.17   Order in which constructors and destructors are called.   438
6.18   **Time** class definition with *set* and *get* functions.   440
6.19   **Time** class member-function definitions, including *set* and *get* functions. 441
6.20   *Set* and *get* functions manipulating an object's **private** data.   443
6.21   Returning a reference to a **private** data member.   446
6.22   Returning a reference to a **private** data member.   446

6.23	Returning a reference to a **private** data member.	447
6.24	Default memberwise assignment.	449
6.25	Class diagram that includes attributes and operations.	452
6.26	List of handles for each class.	452
6.27	**Bell** class header file.	453
6.28	**Clock** class header file.	454
6.29	**Person** class header file.	454
6.30	**Door** class header file.	455
6.31	**Light** class header file.	456
6.32	**Building** class header file.	456
6.33	**ElevatorButton** class header file.	457
6.34	**FloorButton** class header file.	458
6.35	**Scheduler** class header file.	458
6.36	**Floor** class header file.	459
6.37	**Elevator** class header file.	461

7   Classes: Part II   468

7.1	**Time** class definition with **const** member functions.	471
7.2	**Time** class member-function definitions, including **const** member functions.	471
7.3	**const** objects and **const** member functions.	473
7.4	Member initializer used to initialize a constant of a built-in data type.	475
7.5	Erroneous attempt to initialize a constant of a built-in data type by assignment.	476
7.6	**Date** class definition.	479
7.7	**Date** class member-function definitions.	480
7.8	**Employee** class definition showing composition.	481
7.9	**Employee** class member-function definitions, including constructor with a member-initializer list.	482
7.10	Member-object initializers.	483
7.11	Friends can access **private** members of a class.	486
7.12	Nonfriend/nonmember functions cannot access **private** members.	488
7.13	**this** pointer implicitly and explicitly used to access an object's members.	490
7.14	**Time** class definition modified to enable cascaded member-function calls.	491
7.15	**Time** class member-function definitions modified to enable cascaded member-function calls.	492
7.16	Cascading member-function calls.	494
7.17	**Employee** class definition with a **static** data member to track the number of **Employee** objects in memory.	498
7.18	**Employee** class member-function definitions.	499
7.19	**static** data member tracking the number of objects of a class.	501
7.20	**Implementation** class definition.	506
7.21	**Interface** class definition.	507
7.22	**Interface** class member-function definitions.	507
7.23	Implementing a proxy class.	508
7.24	Elevator simulation.	511
7.25	**Building** class header file.	511

7.26	**Building** class implementation file.	512
7.27	**Clock** class header file.	514
7.28	**Clock** class implementation file.	514
7.29	**Scheduler** class header file.	515
7.30	**Scheduler** class implementation file.	516
7.31	**Bell** class header file.	519
7.32	**Bell** class implementation file.	519
7.33	**Light** class header file.	520
7.34	**Light** class implementation file.	520
7.35	**Door** class header file.	522
7.36	**Door** class implementation file.	522
7.37	**ElevatorButton** class header file.	524
7.38	**ElevatorButton** class implementation file.	525
7.39	**FloorButton** class header file.	526
7.40	**FloorButton** class implementation file.	526
7.41	**Elevator** class header file.	528
7.42	**Elevator** class implementation file.	530
7.43	**Floor** class header file.	535
7.44	**Floor** class implementation file.	536
7.45	**Person** class header file.	538
7.46	**Person** class implementation file.	539

8   Operator Overloading; String and Array Objects   546

8.1	Operators that can be overloaded.	549
8.2	Operators that cannot be overloaded.	549
8.3	Overloaded stream-insertion and stream-extraction operators.	552
8.4	**Array** class definition with overloaded operators.	557
8.5	**Array** class member- and **friend**-function definitions.	558
8.6	**Array** class test program.	561
8.7	**String** class definition with operator overloading.	569
8.8	**String** class member-function and **friend**-function definitions.	571
8.9	**String** class test program.	574
8.10	**Date** class definition with overloaded increment operators.	582
8.11	**Date** class member- and **friend**-function definitions.	583
8.12	**Date** class test program.	586
8.13	Standard library class **string**.	588
8.14	Standard library class **vector**.	592
8.15	**Complex** class definition.	601
8.16	**Complex** class member-function definitions.	602
8.17	Complex numbers.	603
8.18	**HugeInt** class definition.	604
8.19	**HugeInt** class member-function and **friend**-function definitions.	604
8.20	Huge integers.	607

9   Object-Oriented Programming: Inheritance   609

9.1	Inheritance examples.	612
9.2	Inheritance hierarchy for university **CommunityMember**s.	613

9.3   Inheritance hierarchy for **Shape**s.   614
9.4   **Point** class header file.   615
9.5   **Point** class represents an *x–y* coordinate pair.   616
9.6   **Point** class test program.   617
9.7   **Circle** class header file.   618
9.8   **Circle** class contains an *x–y* coordinate and a radius.   619
9.9   **Circle** class test program.   621
9.10   **Circle2** class header file.   622
9.11   Private base-class data cannot be accessed from derived class.   623
9.12   **Point2** class header file.   625
9.13   **Point2** class represents an *x–y* coordinate pair as **protected** data. 625
9.14   **Circle3** class header file.   627
9.15   **Circle3** class that inherits from class **Point2**.   627
9.16   Protected base-class data can be accessed from derived class.   629
9.17   **Point3** class header file.   631
9.18   **Point3** class uses member functions to manipulate its **private** data. 632
9.19   **Circle4** class header file.   633
9.20   **Circle4** class that inherits from class **Point3**, which does not
        provide **protected** data.   634
9.21   Base-class **private** data is accessible to a derived class via **public**
        or **protected** member function inherited by the derived class.   636
9.22   **Cylinder** class header file.   638
9.23   **Cylinder** class inherits from class **Circle4** and redefines member
        function **getArea**.   639
9.24   **Point/Circle/Cylinder** hierarchy test program.   640
9.25   **Point4** class header file.   643
9.26   **Point4** base class contains a constructor and a destructor.   643
9.27   **Circle5** class header file.   644
9.28   **Circle5** class inherits from class **Point4**.   645
9.29   Constructor and destructor call order.   647
9.30   Summary of base-class member accessibility in a derived class.   649
9.31   Attributes and operations of **ElevatorButton** and **FloorButton**.   651
9.32   Class diagram incorporating inheritance into the elevator-simulator.   652
9.33   **Button** class header file.   653
9.34   **Button** class implementation file—base class for **ElevatorButton**
        and **FloorButton**.   653
9.35   **ElevatorButton** class header file.   654
9.36   **ElevatorButton** class member-function definitions.   655
9.37   **FloorButton** class header file.   656
9.38   **FloorButton** class member-function definitions.   656

10 Object-Oriented Programming: Polymorphism   662

10.1   **Point** class header file.   665
10.2   **Point** class represents an *x–y* coordinate pair.   665
10.3   **Circle** class header file.   666
10.4   **Circle** class that inherits from class **Point**.   667

10.5   Assigning addresses of base-class and derived-class objects to base-class
        and derived-class pointers.   669
10.6   Aiming a derived-class pointer at a base-class object.   671
10.7   Attempting to invoke derived-class-only functions via a base-class pointer.   672
10.8   **Point** class header file declares **print** function as **virtual**.   675
10.9   **Circle** class header file declares **print** function as **virtual**.   675
10.10   Demonstrating polymorphism by invoking a derived-class virtual
        function via a base-class pointer to a derived-class object.   676
10.11   Defining the polymorphic interface for the **Shape** hierarchy classes.   683
10.12   Abstract base class **Shape** header file.   684
10.13   Abstract base class **Shape**.   684
10.14   **Point** class header file.   685
10.15   **Point** class implementation file.   686
10.16   **Circle** class header file.   687
10.17   **Circle** class that inherits from class **Point**.   688
10.18   **Cylinder** class header file.   690
10.19   **Cylinder** class implementation file.   691
10.20   Demonstrating polymorphism via a hierarchy headed by an abstract
        base class.   692
10.21   Flow of control of a virtual function call.   697
10.22   Class hierarchy for the polymorphic employee-payroll application.   700
10.23   **Employee** class header file.   701
10.24   **Employee** class implementation file.   701
10.25   **SalariedEmployee** class header file.   703
10.26   **SalariedEmployee** class implementation file.   704
10.27   **HourlyEmployee** class header file.   705
10.28   **HourlyEmployee** class implementation file.   705
10.29   **CommissionEmployee** class header file.   707
10.30   **CommissionEmployee** class implementation file.   708
10.31   **BasePlusCommissionEmployee** class header file.   709
10.32   **BasePlusCommissionEmployee** class implementation file.   710
10.33   **Employee** class hierarchy driver program.   711

11   **Templates**   **718**
11.1   Function-template specializations of function template **printArray**.   721
11.2   Class template **Stack**.   724
11.3   Class template **Stack** test program.   726
11.4   Passing a **Stack** template object to a function template.   728

12   **C++ Stream Input/Output**   **737**
12.1   Stream-I/O template hierarchy portion.   741
12.2   Stream-I/O template hierarchy portion showing the main
        file-processing templates.   743
12.3   Printing the address stored in a **char *** variable.   743
12.4   **get**, **put** and eof member functions.   745

12.5   Input of a string using **cin** with stream extraction contrasted with
        input using **cin.get**.   746
12.6   Inputting character data with **cin** member function **getline**.   747
12.7   Unformatted I/O using the **read**, **gcount** and **write** member functions. 749
12.8   Stream manipulators **hex**, **oct**, **dec** and **setbase**.   750
12.9   Precision of floating-point values.   751
12.10   **width** member function of class **ios_base**.   753
12.11   Programmer-defined, nonparameterized stream manipulators.   754
12.12   Format-state stream manipulators from **<iostream>**.   755
12.13   Controlling the printing of trailing zeros and decimal points for **double**s. 756
12.14   Left justification and right justification with stream-manipulators
        left and **right**.   757
12.15   Printing an integer with internal spacing and plus sign.   758
12.16   Using member function **fill** and stream manipulator **setfill** to
        change the padding character for fields larger than the values being printed.   759
12.17   Stream-manipulator **showbase**.   761
12.18   Floating-point values displayed in default, scientific and fixed formats.   762
12.19   Stream manipulator **uppercase**.   763
12.20   Stream manipulators **boolalpha** and **noboolalpha**.   764
12.21   **flags** member function.   765
12.22   Testing error states.   767

13   Exception Handling   779
13.1   Exception-handling example that throws exceptions on attempts to
        divide by zero.   785
13.2   Rethrowing an exception.   788
13.3   Stack unwinding.   791
13.4   **new** returning **0** on failure.   793
13.5   **new** throwing **bad_alloc** on failure.   795
13.6   **set_new_handler** specifying the function to call when **new** fails.   797
13.7   **auto_ptr** object manages dynamically allocated memory.   798

14   File Processing   808
14.1   Data hierarchy.   810
14.2   C++'s view of a file of *n* bytes.   811
14.3   Portion of stream I/O template hierarchy.   812
14.4   Creating a sequential file.   813
14.5   File open modes.   814
14.6   End-of-file key combinations for various popular computer systems.   815
14.7   Reading and printing a sequential file.   817
14.8   Credit-inquiry program.   819
14.9   C++ view of a random-access file.   825
14.10   **ClientData** class header file.   825
14.11   **ClientData** class represents a customer's credit information.   826
14.12   Creating a random-access file sequentially.   828
14.13   Writing to a random-access file.   829

14.14 Reading a random-access file sequentially.   832
14.15 Bank-account program.   835

15   Class **string** and String Stream Processing   850

15.1   Demonstrating **string** assignment and concatenation.   853
15.2   Comparing **string**s.   855
15.3   Demonstrating **string** member function **substr**.   858
15.4   Using function **swap** to swap two **string**s.   858
15.5   Printing **string** characteristics.   859
15.6   Demonstrating the **string find** functions.   862
15.7   Demonstrating functions **erase** and **replace**.   865
15.8   Demonstrating the **string insert** member functions.   866
15.9   Converting **string**s to C-style strings and character arrays.   867
15.10 Using an iterator to output a **string**.   869
15.11 Using a dynamically allocated **ostringstream** object.   871
15.12 Demonstrating input from an **istringstream** object.   873

16   Web Programming with CGI   880

16.1   Three-tier application model.   883
16.2   Starting the Apache HTTP server.   885
16.3   Requesting **test.html** from Apache.   885
16.4   Client interacting with server and Web server.   887
16.5   First CGI script.   889
16.6   Responding to a *get* request.   891
16.7   Output of **localtime.cgi** when executed from the command line. 892
16.8   Retrieving environment variables via function **getenv**.   893
16.9   Reading input from **QUERY_STRING**.   896
16.10 XHTML form elements.   898
16.11 Using **GET** with an XHTML form.   899
16.12 Using **POST** with an XHTML form.   901
16.13 Interactive portal to create a password-protected Web page.   906
16.14 Interactive portal handler.   907
16.15 XHTML document containing a form to post data to the server   910
16.16 Writing a cookie.   911
16.17 Program to read cookies from the client's computer.   914
16.18 XHTML document to read user's contact information.   916
16.19 Creating a server-side file to store user data.   917
16.20 Contents of **clients.txt** data file.   921
16.21 Program that outputs a login page.   922
16.22 CGI script that allows users to buy a book.   929
16.23 CGI script that allows users to view their carts' content.   931
16.24 Logout program.   935
16.25 Contents of **catalog.txt**.   937

17   Data Structures   942

17.1   Two self-referential class objects linked together.   945

17.2   A graphical representation of a list.   946
17.3   **ListNode** class-template definition.   947
17.4   **List** class-template definition.   948
17.5   Manipulating a linked list.   952
17.6   Operation **insertAtFront** represented graphically.   956
17.7   Operation **insertAtBack** represented graphically.   957
17.8   Operation **removeFromFront** represented graphically.   958
17.9   Operation **removeFromBack** represented graphically.   959
17.10   **Stack** class-template definition.   961
17.11   A simple stack program.   962
17.12   **Stack** class template with a composed **List** object.   964
17.13   **Queue** class-template definition.   966
17.14   Queue-processing program.   967
17.15   A graphical representation of a binary tree.   969
17.16   A binary search tree.   970
17.17   **TreeNode** class-template definition.   970
17.18   **Tree** class-template definition.   971
17.19   Creating and traversing a binary tree.   974
17.20   A binary search tree.   976
17.21   A 15-node binary search tree.   980
17.22   Simple commands.   987
17.23   Simple program that determines the sum of two integers.   988
17.24   Simple program that finds the larger of two integers.   988
17.25   Calculate the squares of several integers.   988
17.26   Writing, compiling and executing a Simple language program.   989
17.27   SML instructions produced after the compiler's first pass.   992
17.28   Symbol table for program of Fig. 17.27.   992
17.29   Nonoptimized code from the program of Fig. 17.27.   997
17.30   Optimized code for the program of Fig. 17.27.   997

18   Bits, Characters, Strings and Structures   1000

18.1   Possible storage alignment for a variable of type **Example**, showing
        an undefined area in memory.   1003
18.2   High-performance card-shuffling and dealing simulation.   1005
18.3   Output for the high-performance card-shuffling and dealing simulation. 1007
18.4   Bitwise operators.   1008
18.5   Printing an unsigned integer in bits.   1009
18.6   Results of combining two bits with the bitwise AND operator (**&**). 1010
18.7   Bitwise AND, bitwise inclusive-OR, bitwise exclusive-OR and bitwise
        complement operators.   1011
18.8   Sample output for the program of Fig. 18.7.   1013
18.9   Combining two bits with the bitwise inclusive-OR operator (**|**). 1013
18.10   Combining two bits with the bitwise exclusive-OR operator (**^**). 1014
18.11   Bitwise shift operators.   1014
18.12   Bitwise assignment operators.   1016
18.13   Operator precedence and associativity.   1016

18.14   Bit fields used to store a deck of cards.   1017
18.15   Sample output for the program of Fig. 18.14.   1019
18.16   Character-handling library functions.   1020
18.17   Character-handling functions **isdigit**, **isalpha**, **isalnum**
        and **isxdigit**.   1021
18.18   Character-handling functions **islower**, **isupper**, **tolower**
        and **toupper**.   1023
18.19   Character-handling functions **isspace**, **iscntrl**, **ispunct**,
        isprint and **isgraph**.   1025
18.20   String-conversion functions of the general-utilities library.   1026
18.21   String-conversion function **atof**.   1027
18.22   String-conversion function **atoi**.   1027
18.23   String-conversion function **atol**.   1028
18.24   String-conversion function **strtod**.   1029
18.25   String-conversion function **strtol**.   1030
18.26   String-conversion function **strtoul**.   1030
18.27   Search functions of the string-handling library.   1031
18.28   String-search function **strchr**.   1032
18.29   String-search function **strcspn**.   1033
18.30   String-search function **strpbrk**.   1034
18.31   String-search function **strrchr**.   1034
18.32   String-search function **strspn**.   1035
18.33   String-search function **strstr**.   1036
18.34   Memory functions of the string-handling library.   1037
18.35   Memory-handling function **memcpy**.   1038
18.36   Memory-handling function **memmove**.   1038
18.37   Memory-handling function **memcmp**.   1039
18.38   Memory-handling function **memchr**.   1040
18.39   Memory-handling function **memset**.   1041

19   Preprocessor   1053
19.1   The predefined symbolic constants.   1060

20   C Legacy Code Topics   1065
20.1   The type and the macros defined in header **<cstdarg>**.   1067
20.2   Using variable-length argument lists.   1068
20.3   Using command-line arguments.   1070
20.4   Using functions **exit** and **atexit**.   1074
20.5   Signals defined in header **<csignal>**.   1076
20.6   Using signal handling.   1076
20.7   Using **goto**.   1079
20.8   Printing the value of a **union** in both member data types.   1082
20.9   Using an anonymous **union**.   1083
20.10   Sample output for Exercise 20.8.   1089

21   Standard Template Library (STL)   1090
21.1   Standard Library container classes.   1094

21.2   STL container common functions.   1095
21.3   Standard Library container header files.   1096
21.4   **typedef**s found in first-class containers.   1097
21.5   Input and output stream iterators.   1098
21.6   Iterator categories.   1100
21.7   Iterator category hierarchy.   1100
21.8   Iterator types supported by each Standard Library container.   1101
21.9   Iterator **typedef**s.   1101
21.10   Iterator operations for each type of iterator.   1102
21.11   Mutating-sequence algorithms.   1104
21.12   Non-mutating sequence algorithms.   1104
21.13   Numerical algorithms from header file **<numeric>**.   1104
21.14   Standard Library **vector** class template.   1106
21.15   Standard Library **vector** class template element-manipulation functions. 1109
21.16   STL exception types.   1112
21.17   Standard Library **list** class template.   1113
21.18   Standard Library **deque** class template.   1118
21.19   Standard Library **multiset** class template.   1120
21.20   Standard Library **set** class template.   1123
21.21   Standard Library **multimap** class template.   1124
21.22   Standard Library **map** class template.   1126
21.23   Standard Library **stack** adapter class.   1129
21.24   Standard Library **queue** adapter class templates.   1131
21.25   Standard Library **priority_queue** adapter class.   1132
21.26   Algorithms **fill**, **fill_n**, **generate** and **generate_n**.   1134
21.27   Algorithms **equal**, **mismatch** and **lexicographical_compare**.   1136
21.28   Algorithms **remove**, **remove_if**, **remove_copy** and
        remove_copy_if.   1139
21.29   Algorithms **replace**, **replace_if**, **replace_copy** and
        replace_copy_if.   1142
21.30   Mathematical algorithms of the Standard Library.   1144
21.31   Basic searching and sorting algorithms of the Standard Library.   1148
21.32   Demonstrating **swap**, **iter_swap** and **swap_ranges**.   1150
21.33   Demonstrating **copy_backward**, **merge**, **unique** and **reverse**. 1152
21.34   Demonstrating **inplace_merge**, **unique_copy** and
        reverse_copy.   1155
21.35   **set** operations of the Standard Library.   1157
21.36   Algorithms **lower_bound**, **upper_bound** and **equal_range**.   1160
21.37   Using Standard Library functions to perform a heapsort.   1163
21.38   Algorithms **min** and **max**.   1165
21.39   Algorithms not covered in this chapter.   1166
21.40   Class **bitset** and the Sieve of Eratosthenes.   1170
21.41   Function objects in the Standard Library.   1172
21.42   Binary function object.   1173

22 Other Topics   1183

22.1   Demonstrating operator **const_cast**.   1184
22.2   Demonstrating operator **reinterpret_cast**.   1186
22.3   Demonstrating the use of **namespace**s.   1187
22.4   Operator keywords as alternatives to operator symbols. 1190
22.5   Demonstrating the operator keywords.   1191
22.6   Single-argument constructors and implicit conversions—**array.h**.   1192
22.7   Single-argument constructors and implicit conversions—**array.cpp**.   1193
22.8   Single-argument constructors and implicit conversions—**fig22_08.cpp**.   1193
22.9   Demonstrating an **explicit** constructor—**array.h**.   1195
22.10 Demonstrating an **explicit** constructor—**array.cpp**.   1195
22.11 Demonstrating an **explicit** constructor—**fig22_11.cpp**.   1196
22.12 Demonstrating a **mutable** data member.   1198
22.13 Demonstrating the **.*** and **->*** operators.   1199
22.14 Demonstrating multiple inheritance—**base1.h**.   1201
22.15 Demonstrating multiple inheritance—**base2.h**.   1202
22.16 Demonstrating multiple inheritance—**derived.h**.   1202
22.17 Demonstrating multiple inheritance—**derived.cpp**.   1203
22.18 Demonstrating multiple inheritance—**fig22_18.cpp**.   1204
22.19 Multiple inheritance to form class **iostream**.   1206
22.20 Attempting to call a multiply inherited function polymorphically.   1206
22.21 Using **virtual** base classes.   1208
22.22 **namespace**s for Exercise 22.10.   1212

A Operator Precedence Chart   1214

A.1   Operator precedence chart.   1214

B ASCII Character Set   1216

B.1   ASCII character set.   1216

C Number Systems   1217

C.1   Digits of the binary, octal, decimal and hexadecimal number systems.   1219
C.2   Comparison of the binary, octal, decimal and hexadecimal number systems. 1219
C.3   Positional values in the decimal number system.   1219
C.4   Positional values in the binary number system.   1220
C.5   Positional values in the octal number system.   1220
C.6   Positional values in the hexadecimal number system.   1221
C.7   Decimal, binary, octal and hexadecimal equivalents.   1221
C.8   Converting a binary number to decimal.   1223
C.9   Converting an octal number to decimal.   1223
C.10   Converting a hexadecimal number to decimal.   1223

D C++ Internet and Web Resources   1230

E Introduction to XHTML   1236

E.1   First XHTML example.   1238

E.2   Header elements **h1** through **h6**.   1241
E.3   Linking to other Web pages.   1242
E.4   Linking to an e-mail address.   1244
E.5   Placing images in XHTML files.   1245
E.6   Using images as link anchors.   1247
E.7   Inserting special characters into XHTML.   1249
E.8   Unordered lists in XHTML.   1251
E.9   Nested and ordered lists in XHTML.   1252
E.10   XHTML table.   1255
E.11   Complex XHTML table.   1257
E.12   Simple form with hidden fields and a text box.   1260
E.13   Form with textareas, password boxes and checkboxes.   1263
E.14   Form including radio buttons and drop-down lists.   1266

F   XHTML Special Characters   1274
F.1   XHTML special characters.   1274

Preface

Welcome to ANSI/ISO Standard C++! At Deitel & Associates, we write college-level programming-language textbooks and professional books and work hard to keep our published books up-to-date with a steady flow of new editions. Writing *C++ How to Program, Fourth Edition, (4/e* for short), was a joy. This book and its support materials have everything instructors and students need for an informative, interesting, challenging and entertaining C++ educational experience. As the book goes to publication, it is compliant with the latest version of the ANSI/ISO C++ Standard (one of the most important worldwide standards for the computing community) and with object-oriented design using the latest version of the UML (Unified Modeling Language) from the Object Management Group (OMG). We tuned the writing, the pedagogy, our coding style, the book's ancillary package and even added a substantial treatment of developing Internet- and Web-based applications. We have added a comprehensive Tour of the Book section to Chapter 1. This will help instructors, students and professionals get a sense of the rich coverage the book provides of C++ object-oriented programming, object-oriented design with the UML and generic programming. If you are evaluating the book, please read the Tour of the Book now in pages 44–56.

Whether you are an instructor, a student, an experienced professional or a novice programmer, this book has much to offer. C++ is a world-class programming language for developing industrial-strength, high-performance computer applications. We carefully audited the manuscript against the ANSI/ISO C++ standard document,[1] which defines C++, and we were privileged to have as a reviewer Steve Clamage of Sun Microsystems who heads the ANSI J16 Committee responsible for evolving the C++ standard. As a result, the programs you create by studying this text should port easily to any ANSI/ISO-compliant compiler.

---

1. An electronic PDF copy of the C++ standard document, number ISO-IEC 14882-1998, is available for $18 at **webstore.ansi.org/ansidocstore/default.asp**; a paper copy is available from this site for $175.

In this Preface, we overview *C++ How to Program, 4/e*'s comprehensive suite of educational materials that help instructors maximize their students' C++ learning experience. We explain conventions we use, such as syntax coloring the code examples, "code washing" and highlighting important code segments to help focus students' attention on the key concepts introduced in each chapter. We overview the new features of *C++ How to Program, 4/e*, including our early treatment of arrays and strings as objects, an enhanced treatment of object-oriented programming, Web-application development with CGI, the enhanced elevator-simulation object-oriented design (OOD) case study with the UML, and the extensive use of UML diagrams that have been upgraded to UML version 1.4 standards.

Prentice Hall has bundled *Microsoft's Visual C++® 6 Introductory Edition* software with the text and offers a separate value-pack containing *C++ How to Program, 4/e*, with Metrowerks *CodeWarrior* for the Macintosh and Windows. We list several compilers that are available on the Web free for download. To further support novice programmers, we offer six of our new *DIVE-INTO™ Series* publications that are available free for download at **www.deitel.com**. These materials explain how to compile, execute and debug C++ programs using various popular C++ development environments.

We overview the complete package of ancillary materials available to instructors and students using *C++ How to Program, 4/e*. These include an *Instructor's Resource CD* with solutions to the book's chapter exercises and a *Test-Item File* with hundreds of multiple-choice questions and answers. Additional instructor resources are available at the book's Companion Web Site (**www.prenhall.com/deitel**), which includes a *Syllabus Manager* and customizable PowerPoint® Lecture Notes. Numerous support materials are available for students at the Companion Web Site, as well. For instructors who want to hold closed-lab sessions (or highly structured homework assignments), we provide the optional, for-sale manual, *C++ in the Lab*. This publication includes carefully constructed Prelab Activities, Lab Exercises and Postlab Activities.

This Preface also discusses *The C++ Multimedia Cyber Classroom, 4/e*, an interactive, multimedia CD-based version of the book. This learning aid provides audio "walk-throughs" of programs, animations of programs executing and hundreds of exercises and solutions. We describe how to order both the Cyber Classroom and *The Complete C++ Training Course, 4/e*, boxed product, which contains the Cyber Classroom and the textbook.

We discuss several DEITEL™ e-learning initiatives, including an explanation of Deitel content available for the *Blackboard*, *CourseCompass* and *WebCT* Course Management Systems, each of which supports *C++ How to Program, 4/e*. Premium *CourseCompass*, which offers enhanced Deitel content based on *The C++ Multimedia Cyber Classroom, 4/e*, will be available in January 2003.

C++ How to Program, 4/e, was reviewed by 52 distinguished academics and industry professionals; we list their names and affiliations so you can get a sense of how carefully this book was scrutinized. The Preface concludes with information about the authors and about Deitel & Associates, Inc. As you read this book, if you have any questions, please send an e-mail to **deitel@deitel.com**; we will respond promptly. Please visit our Web site, **www.deitel.com**, regularly and be sure to sign up for the *DEITEL™ BUZZ ONLINE* e-mail newsletter at **www.deitel.com/newsletter/subscribe**. We use the Web site and the newsletter to keep our readers current on all DEITEL™ publications and services.

Features of C++ How to Program, Fourth Edition

This book contains many features including:

Full-Color Presentation

This book is in full color to show programs and their outputs as they typically would appear on a computer screen. We syntax color all the C++ code, as do many C++ integrated-development environments and code editors. This greatly improves code readability—an especially important goal, given that this book contains over 20,000 lines of code. Our syntax-coloring conventions are as follows:

```
comments appear in green
keywords appear in dark blue
errors appear in red
constants and literal values appear in light blue
all other code appears in black
```

Code Highlighting and User-Input Highlighting

We have added extensive code highlighting. In our code walkthroughs (at Deitel, we call these "writearounds"), we have eliminated most of the "redundant" code snippets that appeared inline in the text in the *Third Edition*. We kept them in the earliest portion of the book as a pedagogic device to help novices. We want the reader to see all new code features in context, so from Chapter 3 forward, our code walkthroughs simply refer to the line numbers of the new code segments inside complete source programs. To make it easier for readers to spot the featured segments, we have highlighted them in bright yellow. This feature also helps students review the material rapidly when preparing for exams or labs. We have also highlighted in our screen dialogs all user inputs to distinguish them from program outputs.

"Code Washing"

Code washing is our term for applying comments, using meaningful identifiers, applying indentation and using vertical spacing to separate meaningful program units. This process results in programs that are much more readable and self-documenting. We have done extensive "code washing" of all the source code programs in the text, the lab manual, the ancillaries and the *Cyber Classroom*.

Early Introduction of Standard Library **string** *and* **vector** *Objects*

Object-oriented programming languages generally offer the ability to create string and array objects by instantiating them from library classes or from programmer-defined classes. It is also important for students learning C++ to become familiar with C-style, pointer-based arrays and strings, because of the massive amount of C and early C++ legacy code they will encounter in industry. In *C++ How to Program, 4/e,* we show all three means of creating strings and arrays. In Chapters 4 and 5 we show the traditional, C-like pointer-based arrays and strings, respectively. In Chapter 8, Operator Overloading, we create our own user-defined classes **Array** and **String**. At the end of Chapter 8, we introduce library classes **vector** and **string**, which we explain in detail in Chapter 15 and Chapter 21, respectively. Through Chapter 8, we favor pointer-based arrays and strings; after Chapter 8, we favor the library classes. The Chapter 15 material on **string** could be taught at any point after Chapter 8. The Chapter 21 material on **vector** (and other aspects of the STL) could also reasonably be taught after Chapter 8, although we recommend covering Chapter 11, Templates, first.

Tuned Treatment of Object-Oriented Programming in Chapters 9 and 10

This is one of the most significant improvements in this new edition. We performed a high-precision upgrade to Chapters 9 and 10. The improvements make the material clearer and more accessible to students and professionals, especially those studying object-orientation for the first time.

Redesigned Pedagogy of Chapter 9, Object-Oriented Programming: Inheritance. The new Chapter 9 carefully walks the reader through a five-example sequence that demonstrates **private** data, **protected** data and software reuse via inheritance. We begin by demonstrating a class with **private** data members and **public** member functions to manipulate that data. Next, we implement a second class with several additional capabilities. To do this, we duplicate much of the first example's code. In our third example, we begin our discussion of inheritance and software reuse—we use the class from the first example as a base class and inherit its data and functionality into a new derived class. This example introduces the inheritance mechanism and demonstrates that a derived class cannot access its base class's **private** data directly. This motivates our fourth example, in which we introduce **protected** data in the base class and demonstrate that the derived class can indeed access its base class's **protected** data. The last example in the sequence demonstrates proper software engineering by defining the base class's data as **private** and using the base class's **public** member functions (that were inherited by the derived class) to manipulate the base class's **private** data from the derived class. We follow the five-part introduction with a three-level class hierarchy that employs the software engineering techniques introduced earlier in the chapter. The chapter closes with a discussion of the three inheritance types supported by C++ and a general discussion of software engineering with inheritance.

Redesigned Pedagogy of Chapter 10, Object-Oriented Programming: Polymorphism. The new Chapter 10 builds on the inheritance concepts presented in Chapter 9 and focuses on the relationships between classes in a class hierarchy. Chapter 10 uses a four-example sequence to present the powerful processing capabilities that these relationships enable. We begin with an example that illustrates the "is-a" relationship between a derived-class object and its base-class type. This relationship enables the derived-class object to be treated as an object of its base class. We show that we are able to aim a base-class pointer at a derived-class object and invoke the base-class's functions on that object. In our second example, we demonstrate that the reverse is not true—a base-class object is not considered to be an object of its derived-class type—and we show that compiler errors occur if a program attempts to manipulate a base-class object in this manner. Our third example demonstrates that the only functions which can be invoked through a base-class pointer are those functions defined by the base class. The example shows that attempts to invoke derived-class-only functions result in error messages. The last example in the sequence introduces polymorphism with virtual functions, which enable a program to process objects of classes related by a class hierarchy as objects of their base-class type. When a virtual function is invoked via a base-class pointer (or reference), the derived-class-specific version of that function is invoked. The chapter continues with a case study on polymorphism in which we process an array of objects that all have a common abstract base class that contains the set of functions common to every class in the hierarchy. We follow this example with an in-depth discussion of how polymorphism works "under the hood." We conclude with a case study that demonstrates how a program that processes objects polymorphically can still perform type-specific processing by determining at execution time the type of the object currently being processed.

Web Applications Development with CGI

The new Chapter 16, Web Programming with CGI, has everything readers need to begin developing their own Web-based applications that will run on the Internet![2] Readers will learn how to build so-called *n*-tier applications, in which the functionality provided by each tier can be distributed to separate computers across the Internet or executed on the same computer. In particular, we build a three-tier online bookstore application. The bookstore's information is stored in the application's data tier. In industrial-strength applications, the data tier is typically a database such as Oracle, Microsoft® SQL Server or MySQL. For simplicity, we use text files and employ the file-processing techniques of Chapter 14 to access these files. The user enters requests and receives responses at the application's client tier, which is typically a computer running a Web browser such as Microsoft Internet Explorer or Netscape®. Web browsers, of course, know how to communicate with Web sites throughout the Internet. The middle tier contains both a Web server and an application-specific C++ program (e.g., our bookstore application). The Web server communicates with the C++ program (and vice versa) via the CGI (Common Gateway Interface) protocol. We use the popular Apache HTTP server as our Web server, which is available free for download from **www.apache.org**. The Web server knows how to communicate with the client tier across the Internet using the HyperText Transfer Protocol (HTTP). We discuss the crucial role of the Web server in Web programming and provide a simple example that requests a Web page from a Web server. We discuss CGI and how it allows a Web server to communicate with the top tier and CGI scripts (i.e., our C++ programs). We provide a simple example that gets the time and date from the server and renders it in a browser. In our forms-based examples we use buttons, password fields, check boxes and text fields. We present an example of an interactive portal for a travel company that displays airfares to various cities. Travel-club members can log in and view discounted airfares. We also discuss various methods of storing client-specific data, which include hidden fields (i.e., information stored in a Web page but not rendered by the Web browser) and cookies—small text files that the browser stores on the client's machine. The chapter examples conclude with an e-business case study of an online bookstore that allows users to add books to an electronic shopping cart. This case study contains several CGI scripts that interact with one another to form a complete application. The online bookstore is password protected, so users first must log in to gain access.

XHTML™

The World Wide Web Consortium (W3C) has declared HyperText Markup Language (HTML) to be a legacy technology that will undergo no further development. HTML is being replaced by the Extensible HyperText Markup Language (XHTML)—an XML-based technology that rapidly is becoming the standard for describing Web content. We use XHTML in Chapter 16, Web Programming with CGI; Appendix E presents an XHTML introduction. If you are not familiar with XHTML, please read Appendix E before reading Chapter 16.

---

2. There are other technologies for developing Web-based applications. Java™ developers use Java servlets and JavaServer™ Pages. Windows-platform developers use Active Server Pages (ASP). We chose CGI for this book, because both standard C++ and CGI are platform independent.

Unified Modeling Language™ (UML)

The Unified Modeling Language™ (UML) has become the preferred graphical modeling language for designing object-oriented systems. In *C++ How to Program, Third Edition*, we used the UML in optional sections only, and we used conventional flowchart segments and inheritance diagrams to reinforce the explanations. We have fully converted the diagrams in the book to be UML 1.4 compliant. In particular, we upgraded all the figures in the UML/OOD Elevator Simulation case study; we converted all the flowcharts in Chapter 2, Control Structures, to UML activity diagrams; and we converted all the inheritance diagrams in Chapters 9, 12, 14 and 22 to UML class diagrams.

This *Fourth Edition* carefully tunes the optional (but highly recommended) case study we present on object-oriented design using the UML. In the case study, we fully implement an elevator simulation. In the "Thinking About Objects" sections at the ends of Chapters 1–7 and 9, we present a carefully paced introduction to object-oriented design using the UML. We present a concise, simplified subset of the UML then guide the reader through a first design experience intended for the novice object-oriented designer/programmer. The case study is fully solved. It is not an exercise; rather, it is an end-to-end learning experience that concludes with a detailed walkthrough of the C++ code. In each of the first five chapters, we concentrate on the "conventional" methodology of structured programming, because the objects that we build will use these structured-program pieces. We conclude each chapter with a "Thinking About Objects" section, in which we present an introduction to object orientation using the UML. These "Thinking About Objects" sections help students develop an object-oriented way of thinking, so that they immediately can use the object-oriented programming concepts they begin learning in Chapter 6. In the first of these sections at the end of Chapter 1, we introduce basic concepts (i.e., "object think") and terminology (i.e., "object speak"). In the optional "Thinking About Objects" sections at the ends of Chapters 2–5, we consider more substantial issues, as we undertake a challenging problem with the techniques of object-oriented design (OOD). We analyze a typical problem statement that requires a system to be built, determine the objects needed to implement that system, determine the attributes these objects need to have, determine the behaviors these objects need to exhibit and specify how the objects need to interact with one another to meet the system requirements. We accomplish this even before we discuss how to write object-oriented C++ programs. In the "Thinking About Objects" sections at the ends of Chapters 6, 7 and 9, we build a C++ implementation of the object-oriented system we designed in the earlier chapters. This project enabled us to incorporate topics that we do not discuss in any other section of the book, including object interaction, an in-depth discussion of handles, the philosophy of using references vs. pointers and the use of forward declarations to avoid circular-include problems. This case study will help prepare students for the kinds of substantial projects they will encounter in industry. We employ a carefully developed, incremental object-oriented design process to produce a UML-based design for our elevator simulator. From this design, we produce a substantial working C++ implementation using key programming notions, including classes, objects, encapsulation, visibility, composition and inheritance.

More About the (Optional) Elevator Simulation Case Study

This case study was introduced in *C++ How to Program, 3/e*, and was carefully tuned for the *Fourth Edition*. We brought all the UML diagrams into compliance with version 1.4, we reorganized many of the diagrams to make them clearer, we code washed the complete

C++ solution presented in the book, and we tuned the discussions for clarity and precision. The case study was submitted to a distinguished team of OOD/UML reviewers, including leaders in the field from Rational (the creators of the UML) and the Object Management Group (responsible for maintaining and evolving the UML).

In Chapter 2, we begin the first phase of the object-oriented design (OOD) for our elevator simulator—identifying the classes needed to implement the simulator. We also introduce the UML use case, class and object diagrams and the concepts of associations, multiplicity, composition, roles and links. In Chapter 3, we determine many of the class attributes needed to implement the elevator simulator. We also introduce the UML statechart and activity diagrams and the concepts of events and actions as they relate to these diagrams. In Chapter 4, we determine many of the operations (behaviors) of the classes in the elevator simulation. We also introduce the UML sequence diagram and the concept of messages sent between objects. In Chapter 5, we determine the collaboration (sets of interactions among objects in the system) needed to implement the elevator system and represent these interactions using the UML collaboration diagram. We also include a bibliography and a list of Internet and Web resources that contain the UML 1.4 specifications and other reference materials, general resources, tutorials, FAQs, articles, whitepapers and software. In Chapter 6, we use the UML class diagram developed in previous sections to outline the C++ header files that define our classes. We also introduce the concept of handles to objects in the system, and we begin to study how to implement handles in C++. In Chapter 7, we present a complete elevator simulator C++ program (approximately 1200 lines of code) and a detailed code walkthrough. The code follows directly from the UML-based design created in previous sections and employs our best programming practices. We also discuss dynamic-memory allocation, composition, object interaction via handles, and how to use forward declarations to avoid the circular-include problem. In Chapter 9, we update the elevator simulation design and implementation to incorporate inheritance and suggest further modifications.

Standard Template Library (STL)

This might be one of the most important chapters in the book in terms of your appreciation of software reuse. The STL defines powerful, template-based, reusable components that implement many common data structures and algorithms used to process those data structures. Chapter 21 introduces the STL and discusses its three key components—containers, iterators and algorithms. STL containers are data structures capable of storing objects of any data type. We show that there are three container categories—first-class containers, adapters and near containers. STL iterators, which are similar to pointers (but much safer), are used by programs to manipulate the STL-container elements. In fact, standard arrays can be manipulated as STL containers, using standard pointers as iterators. We show that manipulating containers with iterators is convenient and provides tremendous expressive power when combined with STL algorithms—in some cases, reducing many lines of code to a single statement. STL algorithms are functions that perform common data manipulations such as searching, sorting, comparing elements (or entire data structures), etc. There are approximately 70 algorithms implemented in the STL; these include common container operations such as searching for an element, sorting elements, comparing elements, removing elements, replacing elements and many more. Most of these algorithms use iterators to access container elements. We show that each first-class container supports specific iterator types, some of which are more powerful than others. A container's supported iterator type determines whether the container can be used with a specific algorithm. Iterators encapsulate the mechanism used to access container elements. This encapsulation enables many of the STL algorithms to be applied to a variety of containers without regard for the underlying container implementation. As long as a container's iterators support the minimum requirements of the algorithm, the algorithm can process that container's elements. This also enables programmers to create algorithms that can process the elements of multiple container types. An advantage of the STL is that programmers can reuse the STL containers, iterators and algorithms to implement common data representations and manipulations. This reuse saves substantial development time and resources.

Teaching Approach

Our book is intended to be used at the introductory and intermediate levels. We have not attempted to cover every feature of the C++ standard. C++ has replaced C as the industry's high-performance systems-implementation language of choice. However, C programming continues to be an important and valuable skill, because of the enormous amount of C legacy code that must be maintained in industry. We point out pitfalls and explain procedures for dealing with them effectively. Students are highly motivated by the fact that they are learning a leading-edge language (C++) and a leading-edge programming paradigm (object-oriented programming) that will be immediately useful to them as they leave the college environment.

C++ How to Program, 4/e, contains a rich collection of examples, exercises and projects drawn from many fields and designed to provide students with a chance to solve interesting, real-world problems. The code examples in the text have been tested on multiple compilers—Microsoft Visual C++ 6, Microsoft Visual C++ .NET, two versions of Borland C++Builder and two versions of GNU C++. For the most part, the programs in the text will work on all ANSI/ISO standard-compliant compilers; we posted the few problems we found at **www.deitel.com**. When possible, we also posted the exact fixes required to enable those programs to work with a particular compiler.

The book concentrates on the principles of good software engineering and stresses program clarity. We are educators who teach edge-of-the-practice topics in industry classrooms worldwide. This text emphasizes good pedagogy.

LIVE-CODE™ *Approach*

C++ How to Program, 4/e, is loaded with numerous LIVE-CODE™ examples. Each new concept is presented in the context of a complete, working example that is immediately followed by one or more sample executions showing the program's input/output dialog. This style exemplifies the way we teach and write about programming and is the focus of our multimedia *Cyber Classrooms* and Web-based training courses. We call this method of teaching and writing the *LIVE-CODE*™ *Approach*. *We use programming languages to teach programming languages.* Reading the examples in the text is much like typing and running them on a computer.

World Wide Web Access

All of the source-code examples for *C++ How to Program, 4/e*, (and our other publications) are available on the Internet as downloads from the following Web sites:

```
www.deitel.com
www.prenhall.com/deitel
```

Registration is quick and easy and the downloads are free. We suggest downloading all the examples, then running each program as you read the corresponding text. Making changes to the examples and immediately seeing the effects of those changes is a great way to enhance your C++ learning experience.

Objectives

Each chapter begins with objectives that inform students of what to expect and gives them an opportunity, after reading the chapter, to determine whether they have met the intended objectives. The objectives serve as confidence builders.

Quotations

The chapter objectives are followed by sets of quotations. Some are humorous, some are philosophical and some offer interesting insights. We have found that students enjoy relating the quotations to the chapter material. Many of the quotations are worth a second look *after* you read the chapters.

Outline

The chapter outline enables students to approach the material in a top-down fashion. Along with the chapter objectives, the outline helps students anticipate future topics and set a comfortable and effective learning pace.

20,704 Lines of Syntax-Colored Code in 267 Example Programs (with Program Outputs)

We present C++ features in the context of complete, working C++ programs. These LIVE-CODE™ programs range in size from just a few lines of code to substantial examples containing several hundred lines of code. Each program is followed by a window containing the outputs produced when the program is run. This enables the student to confirm that the programs run as expected. Relating outputs back to the program statements that produce those outputs is an excellent way to learn and to reinforce concepts. Our programs exercise the diverse features of C++. The code is syntax colored with C++ keywords, comments and other program text each appearing in different colors. This facilitates reading the code— students especially will appreciate the syntax coloring when they read the larger programs we present. All of the examples are available on the book's CD and are free for download at **www.deitel.com**.

598 Illustrations/Figures

An abundance of charts, line drawings and program outputs is included. We have converted all flowcharts to UML activity diagrams. We also use UML class diagrams in Chapters 9, 10, 12, 14 and 22 to model the relationships between classes throughout the text.

601 Programming Tips

We have included six types of programming tip to help students focus on important aspects of program development, testing and debugging, performance and portability. We highlight hundreds of these tips as *Good Programming Practices, Common Programming Errors, Performance Tips, Portability Tips, Software Engineering Observations* and *Testing and Debugging Tips*. These tips and practices represent the best we could glean from almost six decades (combined) of programming and teaching experience. One of our students—a mathematics major—told us recently that she feels this approach is similar to the highlighting of axioms, theorems and corollaries in mathematics books, because it provides a sound basis on which to build good software.

90 Good Programming Practices

Good Programming Practices *are tips that call attention to techniques that help students produce programs that are more readable, self-documenting and easier to maintain. When we teach introductory courses to nonprogrammers, we state that the "buzzword" of each course is "clarity," and we tell the students that we will highlight (in these* Good Programming Practices) *techniques for writing programs that are clearer, more understandable and more maintainable.*

198 Common Programming Errors

Students learning a language—especially in their first programming course—tend to make certain kinds of errors frequently. Focusing on these Common Programming Errors *reduces the likelihood that students will makes the same mistakes. It also shortens long lines outside instructors' offices during office hours!*

88 Performance Tips

In our experience, teaching students to write clear and understandable programs is by far the most important goal for a first programming course. But students want to write the programs that run the fastest, use the least memory, require the smallest number of keystrokes or dazzle in other ways. Students really care about performance and they want to know what they can do to produce the most efficient programs. So we include Performance Tips *that highlight opportunities for improving program performance—making programs run faster or minimizing the amount of memory that they occupy.*

36 Portability Tips

Software development is a complex and expensive activity. Organizations that develop software must often produce versions customized to a variety of computers and operating systems. So there is a strong emphasis today on portability, i.e., on producing software that will run on a variety of computer systems with few, if any, changes. Some programmers assume that if they implement an application in standard C++, the application will be portable. This is simply not the case. Achieving portability requires careful and cautious design. There are many pitfalls. We include Portability Tips *to help students write portable code and to provide insights on how C++ achieves its high degree of portability.*

149 Software Engineering Observations

The object-oriented programming paradigm necessitates a complete rethinking of the way we build software systems. C++ is an effective language for achieving good software engineering. The Software Engineering Observations *highlight architectural and design issues, that affect the construction of software systems, especially large-scale systems. Much of what the student learns here will be useful in upper-level courses and in industry as the student begins to work with large, complex real-world systems.*

38 Testing and Debugging Tips

When we first designed this "tip type," we thought the tips would contain suggestions strictly for exposing bugs and removing them from programs. In fact, many of the tips describe aspects of C++ that prevent "bugs" from getting into programs in the first place, thus simplifying the testing and debugging process.

Summary (875 Summary bullets)

Each chapter ends with additional pedagogical devices. We present a thorough, bullet-list-style summary of the chapter. This helps the student review and reinforce key concepts. There is an average of 40 summary bullets per chapter.

Terminology (1782 Terms)

We include an alphabetized list of the important terms defined in the chapter in a *Terminology* section. Again, this serves as further reinforcement. There are, on average, 81 terms per chapter. Each term also appears in the index, so the reader can locate terms and definitions quickly.

555 Self-Review Exercises and Answers (Count Includes Separate Parts)

Extensive *Self-Review Exercises* and *Answers to Self-Review Exercises* are included for self study. This gives the student a chance to build confidence with the material and prepare to attempt the regular exercises.

800 Exercises (Solutions in Instructor's Manual; Count Includes Separate Parts)

Each chapter concludes with a substantial set of exercises including simple recall of important terminology and concepts; writing individual C++ statements; writing small portions of C++ functions and classes; writing complete C++ functions, classes and programs; and writing major term projects. The large number of exercises enables instructors to tailor their courses to the unique needs of their audiences and to vary course assignments each semester. Instructors can use these exercises to form homework assignments, short quizzes and major examinations. The solutions for the exercises are included on the *Instructor's CD* which is *available only to instructors* through their Prentice Hall representatives. **[NOTE: Please do not write to us requesting the Instructor's CD. Distribution of this ancillary is limited strictly to college professors teaching from the book. Instructors may obtain the solutions manual only from their Prentice Hall representatives.]** Students and professional readers can obtain solutions to approximately half the exercises in the book by purchasing the optional *C++ Multimedia Cyber Classroom, 4/e*. The *Cyber Classroom* offers many other valuable capabilities as well and is ideal for self study and reference. Also available is the boxed product, *The Complete C++ Training Course, 4/e*, which includes both our textbook, *C++ How to Program, 4/e*, and the *C++ Multimedia Cyber Classroom, 4/e*. All of our *Complete Training Course* products are available at bookstores and online booksellers, including **www.informIT.com**.

Approximately 5,000 Index Entries (with approximately 7,700 Page References)

We have included an extensive *Index* at the back of the book. Using this resource, readers can search for any term or concept by keyword. The *Index* is useful to people reading the book for the first time and is especially useful to professional programmers who use the book as a reference. These index entries also appear as hyperlinks in the *C++ Multimedia Cyber Classroom, 4/e*.

"Double Indexing" of All C++ LIVE-CODE™ Examples

C++ How to Program, 4/e, has 267 LIVE-CODE™ examples, which we have "double indexed." For every C++ source-code program in the book, we took the figure caption and indexed it both alphabetically and as a subindex item under "Examples." This makes it easier to find examples that are demonstrating particular features. Each of the figure captions also appears in the Illustrations section (following the Contents section) at the front of the book.

Software Included with C++ *How to Program, 4/e*

C++ How to Program, 3/e, included on its CD the Microsoft Visual C++ 6 Introductory Edition development environment. In *C++ How to Program, 4/e,* we wanted to include Microsoft's new Visual C++ .NET development environment, but Microsoft was not as yet making this software available to be included with textbooks. As soon as Microsoft does make Visual C++ .NET available, we will post information at our Web site indicating how students and professionals can obtain this software; there will be separate instructions for students and professionals. *C++ How to Program, 4/e,* includes Microsoft Visual C++ 6 Introductory Edition. A separate value-pack option also is available that contains Metrowerks CodeWarrior (ISBN# 0-13-101151-0); for more information on this option please write to **cs@prenhall.com** or **deitel@deitel.com**.

Free C++ Compilers and Trial-Edition C++ Compilers on the Web

This section overviews C++ compilers that are available for download over the Web. We discuss only those compilers that are available for free or as free-trial versions. Please keep in mind that in many cases, the trial-edition software cannot be used after the trial period has expired.

One popular organization that develops free software is the GNU Project (**www.gnu.org**), originally created to develop a free operating system similar to UNIX. GNU offers developer resources, including editors, debuggers and compilers. Many developers use the gcc (GNU Compiler Collection) compilers, available for download from **gcc.gnu.org**. This product contains compilers for C, C++, Java and other languages. The gcc compiler is a command-line compiler (i.e., it does not provide a graphical user interface). Many Linux and UNIX systems come with the gcc compiler installed. Red Hat has developed Cygwin (**www.cygwin.com**), an emulator that allows developers to use UNIX commands on Windows. Cygwin includes the gcc compiler.

Intel provides 30-day trial versions for its Windows and Linux C++ command-line compilers. The 30-day trial period also includes free customer support. Information on both compilers can be found at **developer.intel.com/software/products/global/ eval.htm**.

Borland provides a Windows-based C++ developer product called C++Builder (**www.borland.com/cbuilder/cppcomp/index.html**). The basic C++Builder compiler (a command-line compiler) is free for download. Borland also provides several versions of the C++Builder that contain graphical user interfaces (GUIs). These GUIs are more formally called integrated development environments (IDEs), and, unlike command-line compilers, enable the developer to edit, debug and test programs quickly. Using an IDE, many of the tasks that involved tedious commands can now be executed via menus and buttons. Some of these products are available on a free-trial basis. For more information on C++Builder, visit

> **www.borland.com/products/downloads/download_cbuilder.html**

For Linux developers, Borland provides the Borland Kylix development environment. The Borland Kylix Open Edition, which includes an IDE, can be downloaded from

> **www.borland.com/products/downloads/download_kylix.html**

Many of the downloads available from Borland require users to register.

The Digital Mars C++ Compiler (**www.digitalmars.com**), is available for Windows and DOS, and includes tutorials and documentation. Readers can download a command-line or IDE version of the compiler. The DJGPP C/C++ development system is available for computers running DOS. DJGPP stands for DJ's GNU Programming Platform, where DJ is for DJ Delorie, the creator of DJGPP. Information on DJGPP can be found at **www.delorie.com/djgpp**. Locations where the compiler can be downloaded at are provided at **www.delorie.com/djgpp/getting.html**.

DIVE-INTO™ *Series Tutorials for Popular C++ Environments*

We have launched our new *DIVE-INTO*™ *SERIES* of tutorials to help our readers get started with many popular C++ program-development environments. These are available free for download at **www.deitel.com/books/downloads.html**.

Currently, we have the following *DIVE-INTO*™ *SERIES* publications:

- *DIVE-INTO Microsoft® Visual C++® 6*

- *Dive-Into Microsoft® Visual C++® .NET*

- *Dive-Into Borland™ C++Builder™ Compiler* (command-line version)

- *Dive-Into Borland™ C++Builder™ Personal* (IDE version)

- *Dive-Into GNU C++ on Linux*

- *Dive-Into GNU C++ via Cygwin on Windows* (Cygwin is a UNIX emulator for Windows that includes the GNU C++ compiler.)

Each of these tutorials shows how to compile, execute and debug C++ applications in that particular compiler product. Many of these documents also provide step-by-step instructions with screenshots to help readers to install the software. Each document overviews the compiler and its online documentation.

Ancillary Package for C++ How to Program, 4/e

C++ How to Program, 4/e, has extensive ancillary materials for instructors. The *Instructor's Resource CD (IRCD)* contains the *Instructor's Manual* with solutions to the vast majority of the end-of-chapter exercises and a *Test Item File* of multiple-choice questions (approximately two per book section). In addition, we provide PowerPoint® slides containing all the code and figures in the text, and bulleted items that summarize the key points in the text. Instructors can customize the slides. The PowerPoint® slides are downloadable from **www.deitel.com** and are available as part of Prentice Hall's *Companion Web Site* (**www.prenhall.com/deitel**) for *C++ How to Program, 4/e,* which offers resources for both instructors and students. For instructors, the *Companion Web Site* offers a *Syllabus Manager*, which helps instructors plan courses interactively and create online syllabi.

Students also benefit from the functionality of the *Companion Web Site.* Book-specific resources for students include:

- Customizable PowerPoint® slides

- Example source code

- Reference materials from the book appendices (such as operator-precedence chart, character set and Web resources)

Chapter-specific resources available for students include:

- Chapter objectives

- Highlights (e.g., chapter summary)

- Outline

- Tips (e.g., *Common Programming Errors*, *Good Programming Practices*, *Portability Tips*, *Performance Tips*, *Software Engineering Observations* and *Testing and Debugging Tips*)

- Online Study Guide—contains additional short-answer self-review exercises (e.g., true/false and matching questions) with answers and provides immediate feedback to the student

Students can track their results and course performance on quizzes using the *Student Profile* feature, which records and manages all feedback and results from tests taken on the *Companion Web Site*. To access DEITEL™ *Companion Web Site*, visit **www.prenhall.com/ deitel**.

C++ in the Lab

This lab manual (full title: *C++ in the Lab, Lab Manual to Accompany C++ How to Program, Fourth Edition*; ISBN 0-13-038478-X) complements *C++ How to Program, 4/e*, and the optional *C++ Multimedia Cyber Classroom, 4/e*, by providing a series of hands-on lab assignments designed to reinforce students' understanding of lecture material. This lab manual is designed for closed laboratories, which are regularly scheduled classes supervised by an instructor. Closed laboratories provide an excellent learning environment because students can use concepts presented in class to solve carefully designed lab problems. Instructors are better able to gauge the students' understanding of the material by monitoring the students' progress in lab. This lab manual also can be used for open laboratories, homework and for self-study.

    C++ in the Lab focuses on Chapters 1–14 and 17 of *C++ How to Program, 4/e*. Each chapter in the lab manual is divided into *Prelab Activities*, *Lab Exercises* and *Postlab Activities*.[3] Each chapter contains objectives that introduce the lab's key topics and an assignment checklist that allows students to mark which exercises the instructor has assigned. Each page in the lab manual is perforated, so students can submit their answers (if required).

    Solutions to the lab manual's *Prelab Activities*, *Lab Exercises* and *Postlab Activities* are available in electronic form. Instructors can obtain these materials from their regular Prentice Hall representatives; the solutions are not available to students.

Prelab Activities

Prelab Activities are intended to be completed by students after studying each chapter in *C++ How to Program, 4/e*. *Prelab Activities* test students' understanding of the material presented

---

3. We expect few introductory classes to advance beyond Chapter 10 of this lab manual. For this reason, the labs in Chapters 11–14 and 17 do not contain the extensive sets of activities available in the previous chapters. Nevertheless, instructors will be able to conduct effective labs using the exercises we have included on these more complex topics. Instructors with special requirements should write to **deitel@deitel.com**.

in the textbook, and prepare students for the programming exercises in the lab session. (These activities may be finished before or during lab, at the instructor's discretion.) The exercises focus on important terminology and programming concepts and are effective for self-review. Prelab Activities include *Matching Exercises, Fill-in-the-Blank Exercises, Short-Answer Questions, Programming-Output Exercises* (these ask students to determine what short code segments do without actually running the program) and *Correct-the-Code Exercises* (these ask students to identify and correct all errors in short code segments).

Lab Exercises

The most important section in each chapter is the Lab Exercises. These exercises teach students how to apply the material learned in *C++ How to Program, 4/e*, and prepare them for writing C++ programs. Each lab contains one or more lab exercises and a debugging problem. The *Lab Exercises* contain the following:

- *Lab Objectives* highlight specific concepts on which the lab exercise focuses.

- *Problem Descriptions* provide the details of the exercise and hints to help students implement the program.

- *Sample Outputs* illustrate the desired program behavior, which further clarifies the problem descriptions and aids the students with writing programs.

- *Program Templates* take complete C++ programs and replace key lines of code with comments describing the missing code.

- *Problem-Solving Tips* highlight key issues that students need to consider when solving the lab exercises.

- *Follow-Up Questions and Activities* ask students to modify solutions to lab exercises, write new programs that are similar to their lab-exercise solutions or explain the implementation choices that were made when solving lab exercises.

- *Debugging Problems* consist of a blocks of code that contain syntax errors and/or logic errors. These alert students to the types of errors they are likely to encounter while programming.

Postlab Activities

Professors typically assign Postlab Activities to reinforce key concepts or to provide students with more programming experience outside the lab. Postlab Activities test the students' understanding of the Prelab and Lab Exercise material, and ask students to apply the knowledge to creating programs from scratch. The section provides two types of programming activities: coding exercises and programming challenges. Coding exercises are short and serve as review after the *Prelab Activities* and *Lab Exercises* have been completed. These exercises ask students to write programs or program segments using key concepts from the textbook. Programming challenges allow students to apply the knowledge they have gained in class to substantial programming exercises. Hints, sample outputs and/or pseudocode are provided to aid students with these problems. Students who complete the programming challenges for a chapter successfully have indeed mastered the chapter material. Answers to the programming challenges are available for download from **www.deitel.com**.

The C++ Multimedia Cyber Classroom, 4/e, and The Complete C++ Training Course, 4/e

We have updated our optional interactive multimedia version of the book—*The C++ Multimedia Cyber Classroom, 4/e* (CD for Windows®)—with considerable additional audio, including the new material on Web Programming with CGI. This resource is loaded with electronic features that are ideal for both learning and reference. The *Cyber Classroom* is packaged with the textbook at a discount in *The Complete C++ Training Course, 4/e*. If you already have the book and would like to purchase the *C++ Multimedia Cyber Classroom, 4/e*, separately, please visit **www.InformIT.com/cyberclassrooms**; the ISBN number for this product is 0-13-100253-8. Deitel™ *Cyber Classrooms* are generally available in CD and various popular Web-based training formats.

The CD provides an introduction in which the authors overview the *Cyber Classroom*'s features. The textbook's 267 LIVE-CODE™ example C++ programs truly "come alive" in the *Cyber Classroom*. If you are viewing a program and want to execute it, you simply click the lightning-bolt icon to run the program. You immediately will see the program's output. If you want to modify a program and see the effects of your changes, simply clicking the floppy-disk icon causes the source code to be "lifted off" the CD and "dropped into" one of your own directories so you can edit the code, recompile the program and try out your new version. Click the audio icon to hear one of the authors "walk you through" the code. In addition, the *Cyber Classroom* contains the full-text of *C++ How to Program, 4/e*, in fully-searchable format.

The *Cyber Classroom* also provides post-assessment exams (with answers) for each chapter in the book. These exams are powerful features that allow users to gauge their understanding of the programming concepts presented in the chapters. Each exam question hyperlinks to the section in the book from which the question was derived. This allows users to review the appropriate chapter material before or after answering the question. A chart is provided that summarizes the user's exam results by chapter.

The *Cyber Classroom* also provides navigational aids, including extensive additional hyperlinking for easy navigation. The *Cyber Classroom* is browser based, so it remembers sections that you have visited recently and allows you to move forward or backward among them. The thousands of index entries are hyperlinked to their text occurrences. Furthermore, when you key in a term using the "find" feature, the *Cyber Classroom* will locate occurrences of that term throughout the text. The Table of Contents entries are "hot," so clicking a chapter or section name takes you immediately to that chapter or section.

Students like the fact that solutions to approximately half the exercises in the book are included with the *Cyber Classroom*. Studying and running these extra programs is a nice way for students to enhance their LIVE-CODE™ learning experience.

Students and professional users of our *Cyber Classrooms* tell us that they like the interactivity and that the *Cyber Classroom* is a powerful reference tool. We received an e-mail from a person who said that he lives "in the boonies" and cannot take a live course at a university, so the *Cyber Classroom* provided a nice solution to his educational needs.

Professors tell us that their students enjoy using the *Cyber Classroom*, and consequently spend more time on the courses, mastering more of the material than in textbook-only courses. For a complete list of the available and forthcoming *Cyber Classrooms* and *Complete Training Courses*, see the *Deitel™ Series* page at the beginning of this book, the product listing and ordering information at the end of this book or visit **www.deitel.com**, **www.prenhall.com/deitel** and **www.InformIT.com/deitel**.

Course Management Systems: Blackboard™, WebCT™, CourseCompass^SM and Premium CourseCompass^SM

Selected content from the Deitels' introductory programming language *How to Program* series, including *C++ How to Program, 4/e*,[4] is available to integrate into various popular Course Management Systems, including CourseCompass, Blackboard and WebCT. An enhanced version of CourseCompass, called Premium CourseCompass, will be available for *C++ How to Program, 4/e,* in January 2003. Course Management Systems help faculty create, manage and use sophisticated Web-based educational tools and programs. Instructors can save hours of inputting data by using Deitel content, created by and for educators, for various Course Management Systems.

Blackboard, CourseCompass and WebCT offer:

- **Features to create and customize an online course**, such as areas to post course information (e.g., policies, syllabi, announcements, assignments, grades, performance evaluations and progress tracking), class and student management tools, a gradebook, reporting tools, page tracking, a calendar and assignments.

- **Communication tools** to help create and maintain interpersonal relationships between students and instructors, including chat rooms, whiteboards, document sharing, bulletin boards and private e-mail.

- **Flexible testing tools** that allow an instructor to create online quizzes and tests from questions directly linked to the text, and that grade and track results effectively. All tests can be inputted into the gradebook for efficient course management. WebCT also allows instructors to administer timed online quizzes.

- **Support materials** for instructors are available in print and online formats.

In addition to the types of tools found in Blackboard and WebCT, CourseCompass from Prentice Hall includes:

- **CourseCompass course home page**, which makes the course as easy to navigate as a book. An expandable table of contents allows instructors to view course content at a glance and to link to any section.

- **Hosting on Prentice Hall's centralized servers**, which allows course administrators to avoid separate licensing fees or server-space issues. Access to Prentice Hall technical support also is available.

- **"How Do I" online-support sections** are available for users who need help personalizing course sites, including step-by-step instructions for adding PowerPoint® slides, video and more.

- **Instructor Quick Start Guide** helps instructors create online courses using a simple, step-by-step process.

---

4. The entire text of *C++ How to Program, 4/e,* is included in the e-Book included with Premium CourseCompass.

Introducing the Premium CourseCompass Course Management System

Premium CourseCompass integrates content from a rich variety of sources, including Deitel *Cyber Classrooms*, *How to Program* books and *Companion Web Sites* with Course-Compass courseware—providing enhanced content to CourseCompass users. Premium CourseCompass includes:

- **Pre-Loaded DEITEL™ Content in a Customizable Interface**. An instructor can aggregate and customize all course materials. This feature includes the e-Book, a searchable digital version of *C++ How to Program, 4/e*, including full-color graphics and downloadable PowerPoint® slides.

- **All the Interactivity of the *Cyber Classroom*.** Students can work with code and receive the added benefit of 17+ hours of detailed audio descriptions of thousands of lines of code to help reinforce concepts. Every code example from *C++ How to Program, 4/e*, is included.

- **Abundant Self-Assessment and Complete *Test-Item File*.** Use or edit hundreds of pre-loaded assessments, or upload your own. Assessments include self-review exercises, programming exercises (half with answers included) and test questions. Instructors choose which questions to assign, and students receive immediate feedback. Instructors can collect students' work and track their progress in an on-line gradebook.

To view free online demonstrations and learn more about these Course Management Systems, that support Deitel content, visit the following Web sites:

- Blackboard: **www.blackboard.com** and **www.prenhall.com/blackboard**.

- WebCT: **www.webct.com** and **www.prenhall.com/webct**.

- CourseCompass: **www.coursecompass.com** and **www.prenhall.com/coursecompass**.

Deitel e-Learning Initiatives

e-Books and Support for Wireless Devices

Wireless devices will have an enormous role in the future of the Internet. Given recent bandwidth enhancements and the emergence of 2.5 and 3G technologies, it is projected that, within a few years, more people will access the Internet through wireless devices than through desktop computers. Deitel & Associates is committed to wireless accessibility and recently published *Wireless Internet & Mobile Business How to Program*. To fulfill the needs of a wide range of customers, we currently are developing our content both in traditional print formats and in newly developed electronic formats, such as wireless e-books so that students and professors can access content virtually anytime, anywhere. For periodic updates on these initiatives subscribe to the *Deitel™ Buzz Online* e-mail newsletter, **www.deitel.com/newsletter/subscribe.html** or visit **www.deitel.com**.

e-Matter

Deitel & Associates is partnering with Prentice Hall's parent company, Pearson PLC, and its information technology Web site, **www.InformIT.com**, to launch the DEITEL™ e-Matter series at **www.InformIT.com/deitel** in Spring 2003. This series will provide professors, students and professionals with an additional source of information on programming and software topics. e-Matter consists of stand-alone sections taken from published texts, forthcoming texts or pieces written during the Deitel research-and-development process. Developing e-Matter based on pre-publication books allows us to offer significant amounts of the material to early adopters for use in academic and corporate courses.

Deitel and InformIT Newsletters

Deitel Newsletter
Our own free newsletter, the *DEITEL™ BUZZ ONLINE*, includes commentary on industry trends and developments, links to free articles and resources from our published books and upcoming publications, product-release schedules, challenges, anecdotes, information on our corporate instructor-led training courses and more. To subscribe, visit

> **www.deitel.com/newsletter/subscribe.html**

Deitel Column in the InformIT Newsletters
Deitel & Associates, Inc., contributes articles to two free *InformIT* weekly e-mail newsletters, currently subscribed to by more than 1,000,000 IT professionals worldwide.

- *Editorial Newsletter*—Contains dozens of new articles per week on various IT topics, including programming, advanced computing, networking, business, Web development, software engineering, operating systems and more. Deitel & Associates contributes 2–3 articles per week taken from our extensive content base or from material being created during our research and development process.

- *Promotional Newsletter*—Features weekly specials and discounts on most Pearson publications. Each week a new DEITEL™ product is featured along with information about our corporate instructor-led training courses.

To subscribe, visit **www.InformIT.com**.

The New DEITEL™ Developer Series

Deitel & Associates, Inc., is making a major commitment to covering leading-edge technologies for industry software professionals through the launch of our *DEITEL™ Developer Series*. *Web Services A Technical Introduction* and *Java Web Services for Experienced Programmers* are among the first books in the series. These will be followed by *Java 2 Enterprise Edition, Java 2 Micro Edition, .NET A Technical Introduction, ASP .NET with Visual Basic .NET for Experienced Programmers, ASP .NET with C# for Experienced Programmers* and many more. Please visit **www.deitel.com** for continuous updates on all published and forthcoming *DEITEL™ Developer Series* titles.

The *DEITEL™ Developer Series* is divided into three subseries. The *A Technical Introduction* subseries provides IT managers and developers with detailed overviews of emerging technologies. The *A Programmer's Introduction* subseries is designed to teach the fundamentals of new languages and software technologies to programmers and novices from the ground up; these books discuss programming fundamentals, followed by brief introductions to more sophisticated topics. The *For Experienced Programmers* subseries is designed for seasoned developers seeking a deeper treatment of new programming languages and technologies, without the encumbrance of introductory material; the books in this subseries move quickly to in-depth coverage of the features of the programming languages and software technologies being covered.

Acknowledgments

One of the great pleasures of writing a textbook is acknowledging the efforts of many people whose names may not appear on the cover, but whose hard work, cooperation, friendship and understanding were crucial to the production of the book. Many people at Deitel & Associates, Inc. devoted long hours to this project.

- Tem Nieto, a graduate of the Massachusetts Institute of Technology and Director of Product Development at Deitel & Associates, co-authored Chapters 15, 20 and 22 and the "Building Your Own Compiler" Special Section in Chapter 17. He also contributed to the Instructor's Manual and the *C++ Multimedia Cyber Classroom, 4/e*, and developed the student lab manual, *C++ in the Lab*, and the corresponding instructor's manual.

- Ben Wiedermann, a graduate of Boston University with a degree in Computer Science, was the lead developer, programmer and writer working with Dr. Harvey M. Deitel on the UML case study in Chapters 1–7 and 9.

- Sean E. Santry, a graduate of Boston College with degrees in Computer Science and Philosophy, is Director of Software Development at Deitel & Associates. Sean worked on the coding and code walkthroughs of the UML Case Study and helped certify the technical accuracy of Chapters 2–5, 8, 9, 11, 12, 16 and 21.

- Jonathan Gadzik, a graduate of the Columbia University School of Engineering and Applied Science with a degree in Computer Science, contributed to the "Thinking About Objects" sections, the preface and Chapters 1, 9–14 and 16; Jon also updated all the UML diagrams in Chapters 2, 9, 12 and 14 to version 1.4.

- Cheryl Yaeger, a graduate of Boston University with a degree in Computer Science, is Director of .NET Development at Deitel & Associates. Cheryl helped certify the technical accuracy of Chapters 17, 19 and 20.

- Christi Kelsey, a graduate of Purdue University with a degree in Management and a minor in Information Systems, is Director of Business Development at Deitel & Associates. Christi worked on the Internet and Web Resources appendix, applied copy edits to the manuscript and contributed to the preface.

- Laura Treibick, a graduate of the University of Colorado at Boulder with a degree in Photography and Multimedia, is Director of Multimedia at Deitel & Associates. She enhanced many of the graphics throughout the text, consulted on the book-cover design and audited the index.

- Christina Courtemarche, a graduate of Boston University with a degree in Computer Science, certified Chapters 9, 11, 13 and 15 for technical accuracy.

- Betsy Duwaldt, Editorial Director at Deitel & Associates, is a graduate of Metropolitan State College of Denver with a degree in Technical Communications (Writing and Editing Emphasis). Betsy edited the Preface and Appendix D.

- Barbara Deitel applied the copy edits to the manuscript. She did this in parallel with handling her extensive financial and administrative responsibilities at Deitel & Associates.

- Abbey Deitel, a graduate of Carnegie Mellon University's Industrial Management Program and President of Deitel & Associates, recruited additional full-time employees and interns during 2002 and leased, equipped and furnished our new corporate headquarters to create the work environment in which *C++ How to Program, 4/e*, and our other Deitel 2002 publications were produced. She suggested the title for the *How to Program* series and contributed to this preface.

We would also like to thank the participants in the Deitel & Associates, Inc., College Internship Program.[5]

- Emanuel Achildiev, a sophomore in Computer Science at Northeastern University, worked on the ancillaries for Chapters 6 and 8 and tested the example programs on several platforms.

- Kalid Azad, a senior at Princeton University in Computer Science, worked on the book's ancillaries, including the PowerPoint® Instructor Lecture Notes and the Test Item File.

- Nicholas Cassie, a sophomore at Northeastern University in Computer Science, worked on the ancillary materials for Chapters 4, 10–12 and 14 and tested example programs on several C++ compilers.

- Thiago da Silva, a sophomore at Northeastern University in Computer Science, tested the programs for the entire book on many C++ compilers. He also contributed to the online *DIVE-INTO*™ support materials that demonstrate how to write, compile and debug programs with several C++ development environments.

- Mike Dos'Santos, a Computer Science major at Northeastern University, produced ancillary materials for Chapters 7, 9 and 13, and did extensive work on *C++ in the Lab*.

- Brian Foster, a sophomore at Northeastern University in Computer Science, tested the example programs on several C++ compilers. He also contributed to the online *DIVE-INTO*™ support materials that demonstrate how to write, compile and debug programs with several C++ development environments.

- Audrey Lee, a graduate of Wellesley College and a Ph.D. candidate in Computer Science at the University of Massachusetts, Amherst, worked on the book's ancillaries, including the PowerPoint® Instructor Lecture Notes, the *Companion Web Site*, the *C++ Multimedia Cyber Classroom, 4/e,* and the Test Item File.

---

5. This competitive program offers a limited number of salaried positions to Boston-area college students majoring in Computer Science, Information Technology, Marketing, Management and English. Students work at our corporate headquarters in Maynard, Massachusetts full-time in the summers and (for those attending college in the Boston area) part-time during the academic year. We also offer full-time internship positions for students interested in taking a semester off from school to gain industry experience. Regular full-time positions are available to college graduates. For more information, please contact **abbey.deitel@deitel.com** and visit our Web site, **www.deitel.com**.

- Jimmy Nguyen, a sophomore in Computer Science at Northeastern University, worked on the ancillaries for Chapters 5, 15 and 17. He also tested the book's programs on several C++ compilers.

- Matthew Rubino, a sophomore at Northeastern University in Computer Science, tested the programs on several C++ compilers. He also contributed to the online *DIVE-INTO*™ support materials.

We would like to thank one of our business colleagues who contributed to the book. Chris Poirier, an independent consultant, co-authored Chapter 16, Web Programming with CGI. Chris also is a FrameMaker Developer Kit (FDK) expert; he used this product to implement the new yellow background code-highlighting style, so crucial to enhancing the pedagogy in *C++ How to Program, 4/e*. We also would like to thank Justin Liberman who researched the URLs in Appendix D.

We are fortunate to have worked on this project with the talented and dedicated team of publishing professionals at Prentice Hall. We especially appreciate the extraordinary efforts of our Computer Science editor, Petra Recter and her boss—our mentor in publishing—Marcia Horton, Editorial Director of Prentice-Hall's Engineering and Computer Science Division. Vince O'Brien did a marvelous job managing the production of the book. Sarah Burrows managed the publication of the book's extensive ancillary package. Pamela Shaffer, Executive Marketing Manager for Computer Science, developed the book's extensive marketing program.

The *C++ Multimedia Cyber Classroom, 4/e*, was developed in parallel with *C++ How to Program, 4/e*. We sincerely appreciate the "new media" insight, savvy and technical expertise of our electronic-media editors, Mark Taub and Karen McLean. They, with project manager Mike Ruel, did a wonderful job publishing the *C++ Multimedia Cyber Classroom, 4/e*, and *The Complete C++ Training Course, 4/e*.

We owe special thanks to the creativity of Tamara Newnam (`smart_art@earthlink.net`). Tammy produced the cover and created the delightful creature who shares with you the book's programming tips. Barbara Deitel contributed the bugs' names for the front cover.

We would like to extend a special note of thanks to Steve Clamage of Sun Microsystems, the chairman of ANSI Technical Committee J16, the group responsible for developing and evolving the standard for C++. Steve's contributions to this book (and previous editions) are profound. We benefited greatly from his insightful comments and deep understanding of C++. Steve wants textbooks describing C++ to be correct and he takes time from his busy professional schedule to help us and other C++ authors "get it right." Our sincere thanks to a consummate professional.

We wish to acknowledge the efforts of our 52 *Fourth Edition* reviewers and to give a special note of thanks to Jennifer Capello of Prentice Hall, who managed this extraordinary review effort.

Fourth Edition Reviewers

Reviewers of C++ Material
Ammar Abuthuraya (Microsoft)
Richard Albright (University of Delaware)
Rob Andrews (Independent software developer)
Peter Becker (Dinkumware, Ltd.)

Carl Burnham (HostingResolve.com)
Jimmy Chen (Salt Lake Community College)
Ram Choppa (Baker Hughes)
Stephen Clamage (ANSI J16 Chair; Sun Microsystems)
Nathan Clegg (Geerbox)
Eric Crampton (Automated Trading Desk)
Timothy Culp (Harris Corporation)
Joel Davis (DinaaliSystems)
Christophe de Dinechin (Hewlett-Packard)
Vincent Drake (Borland)
Lars Marius Garshol (Ontopian)
John Godel (EPOCH Technical Services)
Ric Heishman (Northern Virginia Community College)
Anne Horton (AT&T)
James Huddleston (Independent consultant)
Rex Jaeschke (Independent consultant)
Clark Jefcoat (ProObject)
Vivek Kajale (University of Texas, Arlington)
Sam Kohn (New York Institute of Technology)
Don Kostuch (You Can C Clearly Now)
Stan Kurkovsky (Columbus State University)
Meng Lee (Co-creator of STL; Hewlett-Packard)
Sean McGrath (Propylon)
Robert Myers (Florida State University)
Ami Neiman (DeVry University—Fremont)
David Papurt (Independent contractor; C++ lecturer and author)
Garrett Pease (LearnFrame, Inc.)
Wolfgang Pelz (University of Akron)
Tom Pennings (Borland)
Prashant Rane (University of Texas)
Shailesh Ratadia (Microsoft)
Kroum Savadjiev (Purkinje Inc.)
Vicki Scott (Metrowerks, Inc.)
Richard Seabrook (Anne Arundel Community College)
Gary Sibbitts (St. Louis Community College)
Vladimir Toncar (Kerio Technologies)
Owen Urkov (Borland)
Reid Wilkes (Microsoft)

C++ How to Program, 4/e, OOD/UML Case Study Reviewers
Brian Cook (Zurich Insurance)
Ron Felice (Omniware Development)
Terry Hull (Enterprise Component Technologies, Inc.)
Don Kostuch (You Can C Clearly)
Grant Larsen (Rational Software)
Davyd Norris (Rational Software)
Kendall Scott (Independent consultant)

Cameron Skinner (Embarcadero Technologies; OMG)
Mark Taube (Raytheon)
Stephen Tockey (Construx Software; OMG)
Bing Xue (Siemens Applied Automation)

Under tight deadlines, these reviewers scrutinized every aspect of the text and made count-less suggestions for improving the accuracy and completeness of the presentation.

Contacting Deitel & Associates
We would sincerely appreciate your comments, criticisms, corrections and suggestions for improving the text. Please address all correspondence to:

deitel@deitel.com

We will respond promptly.

Errata
We will post all errata for the *Fourth Edition* at **www.deitel.com**.

Customer Support
Please direct all software and installation questions to Pearson Education Technical Support:

- By phone: 1-800-677-6337

- By email: **media.support@pearsoned.com**

- On the Web: **247.prenhall.com**

Please direct all C++ language questions to **deitel@deitel.com**.

Well, that is it for now. Welcome to the exciting world of C++, object-oriented pro-gramming, UML, generic programming with the STL and C++ Web programming with CGI. We hope you enjoy this look at contemporary computer programming. Good luck!

Dr. Harvey M. Deitel
Paul J. Deitel

About the Authors

Dr. Harvey M. Deitel, Chairman and Chief Strategy Officer (CSO) of Deitel & Associates, Inc., has 41 years experience in the computing field, including extensive industry and aca-demic experience. Dr. Deitel earned B.S. and M.S. degrees from the Massachusetts Insti-tute of Technology and a Ph.D. from Boston University. He worked on the pioneering virtual-memory operating-systems projects at IBM and MIT that developed techniques now widely implemented in systems such as UNIX, Linux and Windows XP. He has 20 years of college teaching experience, including earning tenure and serving as the Chairman of the Computer Science Department at Boston College before founding Deitel & Associ-ates, Inc., with his son, Paul J. Deitel. He and Paul are the co-authors of several dozen books and multimedia packages and they are writing many more. With translations published in Japanese, Russian, Spanish, Traditional Chinese, Simplified Chinese, Korean, French, Pol-ish, Italian, Portuguese, Greek, Urdu and Turkish, the Deitels' texts have earned international recognition. Dr. Deitel has delivered professional seminars to major corporations, government organizations and various branches of the military.

Paul J. Deitel, CEO and Chief Technical Officer of Deitel & Associates, Inc., is a graduate of the Massachusetts Institute of Technology's Sloan School of Management, where he studied Information Technology. Through Deitel & Associates, Inc., he has delivered C, C++, Java, Internet and World Wide Web courses to industry clients, including Compaq, Sun Microsystems, White Sands Missile Range, Rogue Wave Software, Boeing, Dell, Stratus, Fidelity, Cambridge Technology Partners, Open Environment Corporation, One Wave, Hyperion Software, Lucent Technologies, Adra Systems, Entergy, CableData Systems, NASA at the Kennedy Space Center, the National Severe Storm Laboratory, IBM and many other organizations. He has lectured on C++ and Java for the Boston Chapter of the Association for Computing Machinery and has taught satellite-based Java courses through a cooperative venture of Deitel & Associates, Prentice Hall and the Technology Education Network. He and his father, Dr. Harvey M. Deitel, are the world's best-selling Computer Science textbook authors.

About Deitel & Associates, Inc.

Deitel & Associates, Inc., is an internationally recognized corporate training and content-creation organization specializing in Internet/World Wide Web software technology, e-business/e-commerce software technology, object technology and computer programming languages education. The company provides instructor-led courses on Internet and World Wide Web/ programming, wireless Internet programming, object technology, and major programming languages and platforms, such as C, C++, Visual C++$^®$ .NET, Visual Basic$^®$ .NET, C#, Java, Advanced Java, XML, Perl, Python and more. The founders of Deitel & Associates, Inc., are Dr. Harvey M. Deitel and Paul J. Deitel. The company's clients include many of the world's largest computer companies, government agencies, branches of the military and business organizations. Through its 27-year publishing partnership with Prentice Hall, Deitel & Associates, Inc., publishes leading-edge programming textbooks, professional books, interactive CD-based multimedia *Cyber Classrooms*, *Complete Training Courses*, e-books, e-Matter, Web-based training courses and course management systems e-content for popular CMSs such as WebCT, Blackboard and CourseCompass. Deitel & Associates, Inc., and the authors can be reached via e-mail at:

```
deitel@deitel.com
```

To learn more about Deitel & Associates, Inc., its publications and its worldwide corporate on-site curriculum, see the last few pages of this book or visit:

```
www.deitel.com
```

Individuals wishing to purchase Deitel™ books, *Cyber Classrooms*, *Complete Training Courses* and Web-based training courses can do so through bookstores, online booksellers and:

```
www.deitel.com
www.prenhall.com/deitel
www.InformIT.com/deitel
www.InformIT.com/cyberclassrooms
```

Bulk orders by corporations and academic institutions should be placed directly with Prentice Hall. See the last few pages of this book for worldwide ordering details.

The World Wide Web Consortium (W3C)

W3C® Deitel & Associates, Inc., is a member of the *World Wide Web Consortium*
MEMBER *(W3C)*. The W3C was founded in 1994 "to develop common protocols for the evolution of the World Wide Web." As a W3C member, Deitel & Associates, Inc., holds a seat on the W3C Advisory Committee (the company's representative is our CEO, Paul Deitel). Advisory Committee members help provide "strategic direction" to the W3C through meetings held around the world. Member organizations also help develop standards recommendations for Web technologies (such as XHTML, XML and many others) through participation in W3C activities and groups. Membership in the W3C is intended for companies and large organizations. To obtain information on becoming a member of the W3C visit

> **www.w3.org/Consortium/Prospectus/Joining**

1

Introduction to Computers and C++ Programming

Objectives

- To understand basic computer-science concepts.
- To become familiar with different types of programming languages.
- To understand a typical C++ program-development environment.
- To be able to write simple computer programs in C++.
- To be able to use simple input and output statements.
- To become familiar with fundamental data types.
- To be able to use arithmetic operators.
- To understand the precedence of arithmetic operators.
- To be able to write simple decision-making statements.

High thoughts must have high language.
Aristophanes

Our life is frittered away by detail … Simplify, simplify.
Henry David Thoreau

My object all sublime
I shall achieve in time.
W. S. Gilbert

Outline

1.1	Introduction
1.2	What is a Computer?
1.3	Computer Organization
1.4	Evolution of Operating Systems
1.5	Personal Computing, Distributed Computing and Client/Server Computing
1.6	Machine Languages, Assembly Languages, and High-Level Languages
1.7	History of C and C++
1.8	C++ Standard Library
1.9	Java
1.10	Visual Basic, Visual C++ and C#
1.11	Other High-Level Languages
1.12	Structured Programming
1.13	The Key Software Trend: Object Technology
1.14	Basics of a Typical C++ Environment
1.15	Hardware Trends
1.16	History of the Internet
1.17	History of the World Wide Web
1.18	World Wide Web Consortium (W3C)
1.19	General Notes About C++ and This Book
1.20	Introduction to C++ Programming
1.21	A Simple Program: Printing a Line of Text
1.22	Another Simple Program: Adding Two Integers
1.23	Memory Concepts
1.24	Arithmetic
1.25	Decision Making: Equality and Relational Operators
1.26	Thinking About Objects: Introduction to Object Technology and the Unified Modeling Language™
1.27	Tour of the Book

Summary • Terminology • Self-Review Exercises • Answers to Self-Review Exercises • Exercises

1.1 Introduction

Welcome to C++! We have worked hard to create what we hope will be an informative, entertaining and challenging learning experience for you. C++ is a challenging language that normally is taught only to experienced programmers, so this book is unique among C++ textbooks:

- It is appropriate for technically oriented people with little or no programming experience.

- It is appropriate for experienced programmers who want a deeper treatment of the language.

How can one book appeal to both groups? The answer is that the common core of the book emphasizes achieving program *clarity* through the proven techniques of *structured programming* and *object-oriented programming*—non-programmers learn programming the right way from the beginning. We have attempted to write in a clear and straightforward manner. The book is abundantly illustrated. Perhaps most importantly, the book presents hundreds of complete working C++ programs and shows the outputs produced when those programs are run on a computer. We call this the "live-code approach." All of these example programs are provided on the CD-ROM that accompanies this book. You may also download these programs from our Web site **www.deitel.com**. The examples are also available on our interactive CD-ROM product, the *C++ Multimedia Cyber Classroom: Fourth Edition*. The Cyber Classroom contains extensive hyperlinking, audio walkthroughs of the program examples in the book, the ability to search an electronic copy of the book and answers to approximately half the exercises in this book (including short answers, small programs and many full projects). The Cyber Classroom's features and ordering information appear at the back of this book.

The first five chapters introduce the fundamentals of computers, computer programming and the C++ computer programming language. Novices who have taken our courses tell us that the material in Chapter 1–Chapter 5 presents a solid foundation for the deeper treatment of C++ in the remaining chapters. Experienced programmers typically read the first five chapters quickly then find the treatment of C++ in the remainder of the book both rigorous and challenging.

Most people are at least somewhat familiar with the exciting things computers do. Using this textbook, you will learn how to command computers to do those things. It is *software* (i.e., the instructions you write to command the computer to perform *actions* and make *decisions*) that controls computers (often referred to as *hardware*). C++ is one of today's most popular-software development languages. This text provides an introduction to programming in the version of C++ standardized in the United States through the *American National Standards Institute (ANSI)* and worldwide through the efforts of the *International Organization for Standardization (ISO).*[1]

The use of computers is increasing in almost every field of endeavor. In an era of steadily rising costs, computing costs have been decreasing dramatically because of the rapid developments in both hardware and software technology. Computers that filled large rooms and cost millions of dollars 25 to 30 years ago now are inscribed on the surfaces of silicon chips smaller than a fingernail and cost perhaps a few dollars each. Ironically, silicon is one of the most abundant materials on the earth—it is an ingredient in common sand. Silicon-chip technology has made computing so economical that hundreds of millions of general-purpose computers are in use worldwide helping people in business, industry, government and their personal lives. That number could easily double in a few years.

---

1. According to the ISO Web site (**www.iso.org/iso/en/aboutiso/introduction/ whatisISO.html**), ISO is the short name for the organization used worldwide to avoid separate acronyms for each translation of International Organization for Standardization.

Over the years, many programmers learned the programming methodology called *structured programming.* You will learn both structured programming and the exciting newer methodology, *object-oriented programming.* Why do we teach both? Object-orientation is certain to be the key programming methodology for the next decade. You will create and work with many *objects* in this course. But you will discover that the internal structure of those objects often is built best using structured-programming techniques. Also, the logic of manipulating objects occasionally is expressed best with structured programming.

There currently is a massive migration occurring from C-based systems to C++-based systems. There is a huge amount of so-called "legacy C code" in place. C has been in wide use for about a quarter of a century. Once people learn C++, they find it more powerful than C and often choose to move to C++. They begin converting their legacy systems to C++. They begin using the various C++ features generally called "C++ enhancements to C" to improve their style of writing C-like programs. Finally, they begin employing the object-oriented programming capabilities of C++ to realize the full benefits of the language.

In the first five chapters of the book you will learn structured programming in C++, the "C portion" of C++ and the "C++ enhancements to C." In the balance of the book you will learn object-oriented programming in C++. We do not want you to wait until Chapter 6, however, to begin appreciating object orientation. Therefore, each of the first five chapters concludes with a section entitled "Thinking About Objects." These sections introduce basic concepts and terminology about object-oriented programming. When we reach Chapter 6, Classes and Data Abstraction, you will be prepared to start using C++ to create objects and write object-oriented programs.

This first chapter has four parts. The first part introduces the basics of computers and computer programming. The second part gets you started immediately writing some simple C++ programs. The third part helps you start "thinking about objects." The last part tours the rest of the book.

So there you have it! You are about to start on a challenging and rewarding path. As you proceed, if you would like to communicate with us, please send email to us at

> `deitel@deitel.com`

or browse our World Wide Web site at

> `www.deitel.com`

We will respond immediately. We hope you enjoy learning with *C++ How to Program.* You may want to consider using the interactive CD-ROM version of the book called the *C++ Multimedia Cyber Classroom: Fourth Edition.* Please see the ordering instructions at the back of this book.

1.2 What is a Computer?

A *computer* is a device capable of performing computations and making logical decisions at speeds millions (even billions) of times faster than human beings can. For example, many of today's personal computers can perform a billion additions per second. A person operating a desk calculator might require a lifetime to complete the same number of calculations a powerful personal computer can perform in one second. (Points to ponder: How would you know whether the person added the numbers correctly? How would you know whether the computer added the numbers correctly?) Today's fastest *supercomputers* can perform hundreds of billions of additions per second! And trillion-instruction-per-second computers are already functioning in research laboratories!

Computers process *data* under the control of sets of instructions called *computer programs*. These computer programs guide the computer through orderly sets of actions specified by people called *computer programmers.*

A computer is comprised of various devices (such as the keyboard, screen, "mouse," disks, memory, CD-ROM and processing units) that are referred to as *hardware.* The computer programs that run on a computer are referred to as *software.* Hardware costs have been declining dramatically in recent years, to the point that personal computers have become commodities. Unfortunately, software-development costs have been rising steadily as programmers develop ever more powerful and complex applications, without significantly improved technology for software development. In this book you will learn proven software-development methods that can reduce software-development costs—structured programming, top-down stepwise refinement, functionalization, object-based programming, object-oriented programming, object-oriented design and generic programming.

1.3 Computer Organization

Regardless of differences in physical appearance, virtually every computer may be envisioned as being divided into six *logical units* or sections. These are:

1. *Input unit.* This is the "receiving" section of the computer. It obtains information (data and computer programs) from various *input devices* and places this information at the disposal of the other units so that the information may be processed. Most information is entered into computers today through keyboards and mouse devices. Information also can be entered by speaking to your computer, by scanning images and by having your computer receive information from a network, such as the Internet.

2. *Output unit.* This is the "shipping" section of the computer. It takes information that has been processed by the computer and places it on various *output devices* to make the information available for use outside the computer. Most information output from computers today is displayed on screens, printed on paper, or used to control other devices. Computers also can output their information to networks, such as the Internet.

3. *Memory unit.* This is the rapid access, relatively low-capacity "warehouse" section of the computer. It retains information that has been entered through the input unit, so the information may be made immediately available for processing when it is needed. The memory unit also retains processed information until that information can be placed on output devices by the output unit. The memory unit is often called either *memory* or *primary memory.*

4. *Arithmetic and logic unit (ALU).* This is the "manufacturing" section of the computer. It is responsible for performing calculations such as addition, subtraction, multiplication and division. It contains the decision mechanisms that allow the computer, for example, to compare two items from the memory unit to determine whether or not they are equal.

5. *Central processing unit (CPU)*. This is the "administrative" section of the computer. It is the computer's coordinator and is responsible for supervising the operation of the other sections. The CPU tells the input unit when information should be read into the memory unit, tells the ALU when information from the memory unit should be used in calculations and tells the output unit when to send information from the memory unit to certain output devices. Many of today's computers have multiple processing units and, hence, can perform many operations simultaneously—such computers are called *multiprocessors*.

6. *Secondary storage unit*. This is the long-term, high-capacity "warehousing" section of the computer. Programs or data not actively being used by the other units normally are placed on secondary storage devices (such as disks) until they are again needed, possibly hours, days, months, or even years later. Information in secondary storage takes much longer to access than information in primary memory, but the cost per unit of secondary storage is much less than the cost per unit of primary memory.

1.4 Evolution of Operating Systems

Early computers were capable of performing only one *job* or *task* at a time. This form of computer operation is often called single-user *batch processing*. The computer runs a single program at a time while processing data in groups or *batches*. In these early systems, users generally submitted their jobs to a computer center on decks of punched cards. Users often had to wait hours or even days before printouts were returned to their desks.

Software systems called *operating systems* were developed to help make it more convenient to use computers. Early operating systems managed the smooth transition between jobs. This minimized the time it took for computer operators to switch between jobs and hence increased the amount of work, or *throughput*, computers could process.

As computers became more powerful, it became evident that single-user batch processing rarely utilized the computer's resources efficiently because most of the time was spent waiting for slow input/output devices to complete their tasks. Instead, it was thought that many jobs or tasks could be made to *share* the resources of the computer to achieve better utilization. This is called *multiprogramming*. Multiprogramming involves the "simultaneous" operation of many jobs on the computer—the computer shares its resources among the jobs competing for its attention. With early multiprogramming operating systems, users still submitted jobs on decks of punched cards and waited hours or days for results.

In the 1960s, several groups in industry and the universities pioneered *timesharing* operating systems. Timesharing is a special case of multiprogramming, in which users access the computer through *terminals*, typically devices with keyboards and screens. In a typical timesharing computer system, there may be dozens or even hundreds of users sharing the computer at once. The computer actually does not run all the users simultaneously. Rather, it runs a small portion of one user's job then moves on to service the next user. The computer does this so quickly that it may provide service to each user several times per second. Thus the users' programs *appear* to be running simultaneously. An advantage of timesharing is that the user receives almost immediate responses to requests rather than having to wait long periods for results as with previous modes of computing.

1.5 Personal Computing, Distributed Computing and Client/Server Computing

In 1977, Apple Computer popularized the phenomenon of *personal computing.* Initially, it was a hobbyist's dream. Computers became economical enough for people to buy them for their own personal or business use. In 1981, IBM, the world's largest computer vendor, introduced the IBM Personal Computer. Literally overnight, personal computing became legitimate in business, industry and government organizations.

But these computers were "standalone" units—people did their work on their own machines then transported disks back and forth to share information (this is often called "sneakernet"). Although early personal computers were not powerful enough to timeshare several users, these machines could be linked together in computer networks, sometimes over telephone lines and sometimes in *local area networks (LANs)* within an organization. This led to the phenomenon of *distributed computing,* in which an organization's computing, instead of being performed strictly at some central computer installation, is distributed over networks to the sites at which the work of the organization is performed. Personal computers were powerful enough to handle the computing requirements of individual users, and to handle the basic communications tasks of passing information between one another electronically.

Today's most powerful personal computers are as powerful as the million dollar machines of just a decade ago. The most powerful desktop machines—called *workstations*—provide individual users with enormous capabilities. Information is shared easily across computer networks where some computers called *file servers* offer a common store of programs and data that may be used by *client* computers distributed throughout the network, hence the term *client/server computing.* C++ has become widely used for writing software for operating systems, for computer networking and for distributed client/server applications. Today's popular operating systems such as UNIX, Linux and Microsoft's Windows-based systems provide the kinds of capabilities discussed in this section.

1.6 Machine Languages, Assembly Languages, and High-Level Languages

Programmers write instructions in various programming languages, some directly understandable by the computer and others that require intermediate *translation* steps. Hundreds of computer languages are in use today. These may be divided into three general types:

1. Machine languages,
2. Assembly languages,
3. High-level languages.

Any computer can directly understand only its own *machine language.* Machine language is the "natural language" of a particular computer. It is defined by the hardware design of that computer. Machine languages generally consist of strings of numbers (ultimately reduced to 1s and 0s) that instruct computers to perform their most elementary operations one at a time. Machine languages are *machine-dependent,* i.e., a particular machine language can be used on only one type of computer. Machine languages are cumbersome for humans, as can be seen by the following section of a machine-language program that adds overtime pay to base pay and stores the result in gross pay.

```
+1300042774
+1400593419
+1200274027
```

As computers became more popular, it became apparent that machine-language programming was too slow, tedious and error prone. Instead of using the strings of numbers that computers could directly understand, programmers began using English-like abbreviations to represent the elementary operations of the computer. These English-like abbreviations formed the basis of *assembly languages. Translator programs* called *assemblers* were developed to convert assembly-language programs to machine language at computer speeds. The following section of an assembly-language program also adds overtime pay to base pay and stores the result in gross pay, but more clearly than its machine language equivalent:

```
LOAD    BASEPAY
ADD     OVERPAY
STORE   GROSSPAY
```

Although such code is clearer to humans, it is incomprehensible to computers until translated to machine language by assemblers.

Computer usage increased rapidly with the advent of assembly languages, but these still required many instructions to accomplish even the simplest tasks. To speed the programming process, *high-level languages* were developed in which single statements accomplish substantial tasks. Translator programs called *compilers* convert high-level language programs into machine language. High-level languages allow programmers to write instructions that look almost like everyday English and contain commonly used mathematical notations. A payroll program written in a high-level language might contain a statement such as:

```
grossPay = basePay + overTimePay
```

Obviously, high-level languages are much more desirable from the programmer's standpoint than either machine languages or assembly languages. C and C++ are among the most powerful and most widely used high-level languages.

The process of compiling a high-level language program into machine language can take a considerable amount of computer time. *Interpreter* programs were developed that can directly execute high-level language programs without the need for compiling those programs into machine language. Although compiled programs execute faster than interpreted programs, interpreters are popular in program-development environments, in which programs are changed frequently as new features are added and errors are corrected. Once a program is developed, a compiled version can be produced to run most efficiently.

1.7 History of C and C++

C++ evolved from C, which evolved from two previous programming languages, BCPL and B. BCPL was developed in 1967 by Martin Richards as a language for writing operating systems software and compilers. Ken Thompson modeled many features in his language B after their counterparts in BCPL and used B to create early versions of the UNIX operating system at Bell Laboratories in 1970 on a DEC PDP-7 computer. Both BCPL and B were "typeless" languages—every data item occupied one "word" in memory and the burden of treating a data item as a whole number or a real number, for example, was the responsibility of the programmer.

The C language was evolved from B by Dennis Ritchie at Bell Laboratories and was originally implemented on a DEC PDP-11 computer in 1972. C uses many important concepts of BCPL and B while adding data typing and other features. C initially became widely known as the development language of the UNIX operating system. Today, most operating systems are written in C and/or C++. C is now available for most computers. C is hardware independent. With careful design, it is possible to write C programs that are *portable* to most computers.

By the late 1970s, C had evolved into what now is referred to as "traditional C," "classic C," or "Kernighan and Ritchie C." The publication by Prentice-Hall in 1978 of Kernighan and Ritchie's book, *The C Programming Language,* brought wide attention to the language.

The widespread use of C with various types of computers (sometimes called *hardware platforms*) unfortunately led to many variations. These were similar, but often incompatible. This was a serious problem for program developers who needed to write portable programs that would run on several platforms. It became clear that a standard version of C was needed. In 1983, the X3J11 technical committee was created under the American National Standards Committee on Computers and Information Processing (X3) to "provide an unambiguous and machine-independent definition of the language." In 1989, the standard was approved. ANSI cooperated with the International Standards Organization (ISO) to standardize C worldwide; the joint standard document was published in 1990 and is referred to as *ANSI/ISO 9899: 1990.* Copies of this document may be ordered from ANSI. The second edition of Kernighan and Ritchie, published in 1988, reflects this version called ANSI C, a version of the language now used worldwide.

Portability Tip 1.1

Because C is a standardized, hardware-independent, widely available language, applications written in C often can be run with little or no modifications on a wide range of different computer systems.

C++, an extension of C, was developed by Bjarne Stroustrup in the early 1980s at Bell Laboratories. C++ provides a number of features that "spruce up" the C language, but more importantly, it provides capabilities for *object-oriented programming.*

There is a revolution brewing in the software community. Building software quickly, correctly and economically remains an elusive goal, and this at a time when the demand for new and more powerful software is soaring. *Objects* are essentially reusable software *components* that model items in the real world. Software developers are discovering that using a modular, object-oriented design and implementation approach can make software development groups much more productive than is possible with previous popular programming techniques, such as structured programming. Object-oriented programs are easier to understand, correct and modify.

Many other object-oriented languages have been developed, including Smalltalk, developed at Xerox's Palo Alto Research Center (PARC). Smalltalk is a pure object-oriented language—literally everything is an object. C++ is a hybrid language—it is possible to program in C++ in either a C-like style, an object-oriented style, or both.

1.8 C++ Standard Library

C++ programs consist of pieces called *classes* and *functions*. You can program each piece you may need to form a C++ program. However, most C++ programmers take advantage of the rich collections of existing classes and functions in the C++ standard library. Thus, there are really two parts to learning the C++ "world." The first is learning the C++ language itself; the second is learning how to use the classes and functions in the C++ standard library. Throughout the book, we discuss many of these classes and functions. The book by Plauger[2] is must reading for programmers who need a deep understanding of the ANSI C library functions that are included in C++, how to implement them and how to use them to write portable code. The standard class libraries generally are provided by compiler vendors. Many special-purpose class libraries are supplied by independent software vendors.

Software Engineering Observation 1.1

Use a "building block approach" to creating programs. Avoid reinventing the wheel. Use existing pieces where possible—this is called "software reuse" and it is central to object-oriented programming.

Software Engineering Observation 1.2

When programming in C++, you typically will use the following building blocks: classes and functions from the C++ standard library, classes and functions you create yourself, and classes and functions from various popular third-party libraries.

[*Note*: We include many of these *Software Engineering Observations* throughout the text to explain concepts that affect and improve the overall architecture and quality of a software system, and particularly, of large software systems. We also highlight *Good Programming Practices* (practices that can help you write programs that are clearer, more understandable, more maintainable, and easier to test and debug), *Common Programming Errors* (problems to watch for, so you do not make these errors in your programs), *Performance Tips* (techniques that help you write programs that run faster and use less memory), *Portability Tips* (techniques that help you write programs that can run, with little or no modification, on a variety of computers) and *Testing and Debugging Tips* (techniques that help you remove bugs from your programs, and more important, techniques that will help you write bug-free programs in the first place). Many of these techniques and practices are only guidelines; you will, no doubt, develop your own preferred programming style.]

The advantage of creating your own functions and classes is that you will know exactly how they work. You will be able to examine the C++ code. The disadvantage is the time-consuming and complex effort that goes into designing, developing and maintaining new functions and classes that are correct and that operate efficiently.

Performance Tip 1.1

Using standard library functions and classes instead of writing your own comparable versions can improve program performance, because this software is written carefully to perform efficiently and correctly.

Portability Tip 1.2

Using standard library functions and classes instead of writing your own can improve program portability, because this software is included in virtually all C++ implementations.

---

2. P. J. Plauger, *The Standard C Library* (Englewood Cliffs, NJ: Prentice Hall, 1992).

1.9 Java

Many people believe that the next major area in which microprocessors will have a profound impact is in intelligent consumer electronic devices. Recognizing this, Sun Microsystems funded an internal corporate research project code-named Green in 1991. The project resulted in the development of a C and C++ based language which its creator, James Gosling, called Oak after an oak tree outside his window at Sun. It was discovered later that there already was a computer language called Oak. When a group of Sun people visited a local coffee place, the name *Java* was suggested and it stuck.

But the Green project ran into some difficulties. The marketplace for intelligent consumer electronic devices was not developing as quickly as Sun had anticipated. Worse yet, a major contract for which Sun competed was awarded to another company. So the project was in danger of being canceled. By sheer good fortune, the World Wide Web exploded in popularity in 1993 and Sun people saw the immediate potential of using Java to create so-called *dynamic content* for Web pages.

Sun formally announced Java at a trade show in May 1995. Java generated immediate interest in the business community because of the phenomenal interest in the World Wide Web. Java now is used to create Web pages with dynamic and interactive content, to develop large-scale enterprise applications, to enhance the functionality of Web servers (the computers that provide the content we see in our Web browsers), to provide applications for consumer devices (such as cell phones, pagers and personal digital assistants), and more.

In 1995, we were following the development of Java by Sun Microsystems. In November 1995, we attended an Internet conference in Boston. A representative from Sun Microsystems gave a rousing presentation on Java. As the talk proceeded, it became clear to us that Java would play a significant part in the development of interactive, multimedia Web pages. But we saw immediately a much greater potential for the language.

We saw Java as a nice language for teaching first-year programming language students the essentials of graphics, images, animation, audio, video, database, networking, multithreading and collaborative computing. We went to work on the first edition of *Java How to Program* which was published in time for fall 1996 classes. *Java How to Program: Fifth Edition* was published in 2002.

In addition to its prominence in developing Internet- and intranet-based applications, Java is certain to become the language of choice for implementing software for devices that communicate over a network (such as cellular phones, pagers and personal digital assistants). Do not be surprised when your new stereo and other devices in your home will be networked together using Java technology!

1.10 Visual Basic, Visual C++ and C#

Developing Microsoft Windows-based applications in languages such as C and C++ proved to be a difficult and cumbersome process. When Bill Gates founded Microsoft Corporation, he implemented *BASIC* on several early personal computers. BASIC (Beginner's All-Purpose Symbolic Instruction Code) is a programming language developed in the mid-1960s by Professors John Kemeny and Thomas Kurtz of Dartmouth College as a language for writing simple programs. BASIC's primary purpose was to familiarize novices with programming techniques. The natural evolution from BASIC to Visual Basic was introduced in 1991 as a result of the development of the Microsoft Windows graphical user interface (GUI) in the late 1980s and the early 1990s.

Although Visual Basic is derived from the BASIC programming language, it is a distinctly different language that offers such powerful features as graphical user interfaces, event handling, access to the *Windows 32-bit Application Programming Interface (Win32 API)*, object-oriented programming and error handling. Visual Basic is one of the most popular event-driven, visual programming interfaces.

The latest version of Visual Basic, called *Visual Basic .NET,*[3] is designed for Microsoft's new programming platform, .NET. Earlier versions of Visual Basic provided object-oriented capabilities, but Visual Basic .NET offers enhanced object orientation and makes use of the powerful library of reusable software components in .NET.

Visual C++ is a Microsoft implementation of C++ that includes Microsoft's own extensions to the language. Early graphics and GUI programming with Visual C++ was implemented using the Microsoft Foundation Classes (MFC). Now, with the introduction of .NET, Microsoft provides a common library for implementing GUI, graphics, networking, multithreading and other capabilities. This library is shared among Visual Basic, Visual C++ and Microsoft's new language, C#.

The advancement of programming tools (e.g., C++ and Java) and consumer-electronic devices (e.g., cell phones) created problems and new requirements. The integration of software components from various languages proved difficult, and installation problems were common because new versions of shared components were incompatible with old software. Developers also discovered they needed Web-based applications that could be accessed and used via the Internet. As a result of mobile electronic device popularity, software developers realized that their clients were no longer restricted to desktop computers. Developers recognized the need for software that was accessible to anyone and available via almost any type of device. To address these needs, Microsoft announced its *.NET* (pronounced "dot-net") *initiative* and the *C#* (pronounced "C-Sharp") programming language.

The *.NET platform* is one over which Web-based applications can be distributed to a great variety of devices (even cell phones) and to desktop computers. The platform offers a new software-development model that allows applications created in disparate programming languages to communicate with each other. The C# programming language, developed at Microsoft by a team led by Anders Hejlsberg and Scott Wiltamuth, was designed specifically for the .NET platform as a language that would enable programmers to migrate easily to .NET. This migration is made easy due to the fact that C# has roots in C, C++ and Java, adapting the best features of each and adding new features of its own. Because C# has been built upon widely used and well-developed languages, programmers will find learning C# to be easy and enjoyable.

C# is an event-driven, fully object-oriented, visual programming language, in which programs are created using an *Integrated Development Environment (IDE)*. With the IDE, a programmer can create, run, test and debug C# programs conveniently, thereby reducing the time required to produce a working program to a fraction of the time it required without using the IDE. The process of rapidly creating an application using an IDE is referred to as *Rapid Application Development (RAD)*.

---

3. The reader interested in Visual Basic .NET may want to consider our book, *Visual Basic .NET How to Program, Second Edition*.

C# also enables a new degree of language interoperability: Software components from different languages can interact as never before. Developers can package even old software to work with new C# programs. In addition, C# applications can interact via the Internet.

1.11 Other High-Level Languages

Hundreds of high-level languages have been developed, but only a few have achieved broad acceptance. *FORTRAN* (FORmula TRANslator) was developed by IBM Corporation between 1954 and 1957 to be used for scientific and engineering applications that require complex mathematical computations. FORTRAN is still widely used, especially in engineering applications.

COBOL (COmmon Business Oriented Language) was developed in 1959 by computer manufacturers, the government and industrial computer users. COBOL is used for commercial applications that require precise and efficient manipulation of large amounts of data. By some estimates, more than half of all business software is still programmed in COBOL.

Pascal was designed at about the same time as C by Professor Niklaus Wirth and was intended for academic use. We will say more about Pascal in the next section.

1.12 Structured Programming

During the 1960s, many large software-development efforts encountered severe difficulties. Software schedules were typically late, costs greatly exceeded budgets and the finished products were unreliable. People began to realize that software development was a far more complex activity than they had imagined. Research activity in the 1960s resulted in the evolution of *structured programming*—a disciplined approach to writing programs that are clearer than unstructured programs, easier to test and debug and easier to modify. Chapter 2 discusses the principles of structured programming. Chapter 3–Chapter 5 develop many structured programs.

One of the more tangible results of this research was the development of the Pascal programming language by Niklaus Wirth in 1971. Pascal, named after the seventeenth-century mathematician and philosopher Blaise Pascal, was designed for teaching structured programming in academic environments; it rapidly became the preferred programming language in most universities. Unfortunately, the language lacks many features needed to make it useful in commercial, industrial and government applications, so it has not been widely accepted outside the universities.

The Ada programming language was developed under the sponsorship of the United States Department of Defense (DoD) during the 1970s and early 1980s. Hundreds of separate languages were being used to produce DoD's massive command-and-control software systems. DoD wanted a single language that would fulfill most of its needs. Pascal was chosen as a base, but the final Ada language is quite different from Pascal. The language was named after Lady Ada Lovelace, daughter of the poet Lord Byron. Lady Lovelace is generally credited with writing the world's first computer program in the early 1800s (for the Analytical Engine mechanical computing device designed by Charles Babbage). One important capability of Ada is called *multitasking;* this allows programmers to specify that many activities are to occur in parallel. The other widely used high-level languages we have discussed—including C and C++—generally allow the programmer to write programs that perform only one activity at a time.

1.13 The Key Software Trend: Object Technology

One of the authors, HMD, remembers the great frustration that was felt in the 1960s by software-development organizations, especially those developing large-scale projects. During his undergraduate years, HMD had the privilege of working summers at a leading computer vendor on the teams developing time-sharing, virtual memory operating systems. This was a great experience for a college student. But, in the summer of 1967, reality set in when the company "decommitted" from producing as a commercial product the particular system on which hundreds of people had been working for many years. It was difficult to get this software right. Software is "complex stuff."

Improvements to software technology did start to appear with the benefits of so-called *structured programming* (and the related disciplines of *structured systems analysis and design)* being realized in the 1970s. But it was not until the technology of object-oriented programming became widely used in the 1990s, that software developers finally felt they had the necessary tools for making major strides in the software-development process.

Actually, object technology dates back to the mid 1960s. The C++ programming language, developed at AT&T by Bjarne Stroustrup in the early 1980s, is based on two languages—C, which initially was developed at AT&T to implement the UNIX operating system in the early 1970s, and Simula 67, a simulation programming language developed in Europe and released in 1967. C++ absorbed the features of C and added Simula's capabilities for creating and manipulating objects. Neither C nor C++ was originally intended for wide use beyond the AT&T research laboratories. But grass-roots support rapidly developed for each.

What are objects and why are they special? Actually, object technology is a packaging scheme that helps us create meaningful software units. These are large and highly focussed on particular applications areas. There are date objects, time objects, paycheck objects, invoice objects, audio objects, video objects, file objects, record objects and so on. In fact, almost any noun can be reasonably represented as an object.

We live in a world of objects. Just look around you. There are cars, planes, people, animals, buildings, traffic lights, elevators, and the like. Before object-oriented languages appeared, programming languages (such as FORTRAN, Pascal, Basic and C) were focussed on actions (verbs) rather than on things or objects (nouns). Programmers living in a world of objects program primarily using verbs. This paradigm shift made it awkward to write programs. Now, with the availability of popular object-oriented languages such as Java and C++, programmers continue to live in an object-oriented world and can program in an object-oriented manner. This is a more natural process than procedural programming and has resulted in significant productivity enhancements.

A key problem with procedural programming is that the program units do not easily mirror real-world entities effectively, so these units are not particularly reusable. It is not unusual for programmers to "start fresh" on each new project and have to write similar software "from scratch." This wastes time and money as people repeatedly "reinvent the wheel." With object technology, the software entities created (called *classes*), if properly designed, tend to be much more reusable on future projects. Using libraries of reusable componentry, such as *MFC (Microsoft Foundation Classes)* and those produced by Rogue Wave and many other software development organizations, can greatly reduce the amount of effort required to implement certain kinds of systems (compared to the effort that would be required to reinvent these capabilities on new projects).

Some organizations report that software reuse is not, in fact, the key benefit they get from object-oriented programming. Rather, they indicate that object-oriented programming tends to produce software that is more understandable, better organized and easier to maintain, modify and debug. This can be significant because it has been estimated that as much as 80% of software costs are not associated with the original efforts to develop the software, but are associated with the continued evolution and maintenance of that software throughout its lifetime.

Whatever the perceived benefits of object-orientation are, it is clear that object-oriented programming will be the key programming methodology for the next several decades.

The advantage of creating your own code is that you will know exactly how it works. You will be able to examine the code. The disadvantage is the time-consuming and complex effort that goes into designing and developing new code.

Software Engineering Observation 1.3

Extensive class libraries of reusable software components are available over the Internet and the World Wide Web. Many of these libraries are available at no charge.

1.14 Basics of a Typical C++ Environment[4]

C++ systems generally consist of three parts: a program-development environment, the language and the C++ Standard Library. The following discussion explains a typical C++ program-development environment shown in Fig. 1.1.

C++ programs typically go through six phases to be executed (Fig. 1.1). These are: *edit, preprocess, compile, link, load* and *execute*.

The first phase consists of editing a file. This is accomplished with an *editor program*. The programmer types a C++ program with the editor and makes corrections if necessary. The program source file is then stored on a secondary storage device such as a disk. C++ program file names often end with the **.cpp**, **.cxx**, **.cc** or **.C** extensions (note that **C** is in uppercase). See the documentation for your C++ environment for more information on file-name extensions. Two editors widely used on UNIX systems are **vi** and **emacs**. C++ software packages for Microsoft Windows such as Borland C++, Metrowerks CodeWarrior and Microsoft Visual C++ have built-in editors that are integrated into the programming environment. We assume the reader knows how to edit a program.

Next, the programmer gives the command to *compile* the program. The compiler translates the C++ program into machine language code (also referred to as *object code*). In a C++ system, a *preprocessor* program executes automatically before the compiler's translation phase begins. The C++ preprocessor obeys commands called *preprocessor directives,* which indicate that certain manipulations are to be performed on the program before compilation. These manipulations usually include other text files to be compiled and perform various text replacements. The most common preprocessor directives are discussed in the early chapters; a detailed discussion of all the preprocessor features appears in

---

4. On our Web site at **www.deitel.com/books/downloads.html**, we provide *DEITEL™ DIVE INTO™ Series* publications to help you begin using several popular C++ development tools, including Borland® C++Builder™, Microsoft® Visual C++® 6, Microsoft® Visual C++® .NET, GNU C++ on Linux and GNU C++ on the Cygwin™ UNIX® environment for Windows®. We will make other *DIVE INTO™ Series* publications available as instructors request them.

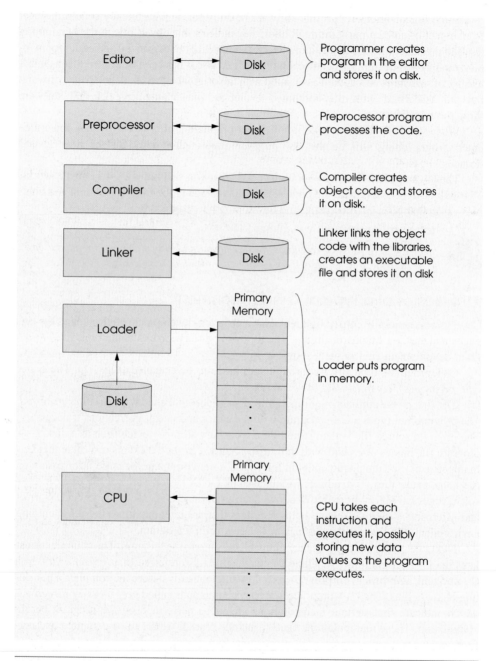

Fig. 1.1   A typical C++ environment.

Chapter 19, Preprocessor. The preprocessor is invoked by the compiler before the program is converted to machine language.

The next phase is called *linking*. C++ programs typically contain references to functions and data defined elsewhere, such as in the standard libraries or in the private libraries of groups of programmers working on a particular project. The object code produced by the C++ compiler typically contains "holes" due to these missing parts. A *linker* links the object code with the code for the missing functions to produce an *executable image* (with no missing pieces). If the program compiles and links correctly, an executable image is produced. This is the executable image of our `welcome.cpp` program.

The next phase is called *loading*. Before a program can be executed, the program must first be placed in memory. This is done by the *loader,* which takes the executable image from disk and transfers it to memory. Additional components from shared libraries that support the program are also loaded. Finally, the computer, under the control of its CPU, *executes* the program one instruction at a time.

Programs do not always work on the first try. Each of the preceding phases can fail because of various errors that we will discuss. For example, an executing program might attempt to divide by zero (an illegal operation on computers, just as it is in arithmetic). This would cause the computer to display an error message. The programmer would then return to the edit phase, make the necessary corrections and proceed through the remaining phases again to determine whether the corrections work properly.

Common Programming Error 1.1

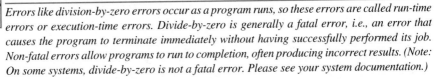
Errors like division-by-zero errors occur as a program runs, so these errors are called run-time errors or execution-time errors. Divide-by-zero is generally a fatal error, i.e., an error that causes the program to terminate immediately without having successfully performed its job. Non-fatal errors allow programs to run to completion, often producing incorrect results. (Note: On some systems, divide-by-zero is not a fatal error. Please see your system documentation.)

Most programs in C++ input and/or output data. Certain C++ functions take their input from **cin** (the *standard input stream*; pronounced "see-in") which is normally the keyboard, but **cin** can be connected to another device. Data is often output to **cout** (the *standard output stream*; pronounced "see-out") which is normally the computer screen, but **cout** can be connected to another device. When we say that a program prints a result, we normally mean that the result is displayed on a screen. Data may be output to other devices such as disks and hardcopy printers. There is also a *standard error stream* referred to as **cerr**. The **cerr** stream (normally connected to the screen) is used for displaying error messages. It is common for users to route regular output data, i.e., **cout**, to a device other than the screen while keeping **cerr** assigned to the screen, so the user can be immediately informed of errors.

1.15 Hardware Trends

The programming community thrives on the continuing stream of dramatic improvements in hardware, software and communications technologies. Every year, people generally expect to pay more for most products and services. The opposite has been the case in the computer and communications fields, especially with regard to the hardware costs of supporting these technologies. For many decades, and with no change in the foreseeable future, hardware costs have fallen rapidly, if not precipitously. This is a phenomenon of technology. Every year or two, the capacities of computers, especially the amount of memory they have in which to execute programs, *the amount of* secondary storage (such as disk storage) they have to hold programs and data over the longer term, and their processor speeds—the speeds at which computers execute their programs (i.e., do their work)—each tend to approximately double. The same has been true in the communications field with costs plummeting, especially in recent years with the enormous demand for communications bandwidth attracting tremendous competition. We know of no other fields in which technology moves so quickly and costs fall so rapidly.

When computer use exploded in the sixties and seventies, there was talk of huge improvements in human productivity that computing and communications would bring about. But these improvements did not materialize. Organizations were spending vast sums on computers and certainly employing them effectively, but without realizing the productivity gains that had been expected. It was the invention of microprocessor-chip technology and its wide deployment in the late 1970s and 1980s that laid the groundwork for the productivity improvements of the 1990s and the new millennium.

1.16 History of the Internet

In the late 1960s, one of the authors (HMD) was a graduate student at MIT. His research at MIT's Project Mac (now the Laboratory for Computer Science—the home of the World Wide Web Consortium) was funded by ARPA—the Advanced Research Projects Agency of the Department of Defense. ARPA sponsored a conference at which several dozen ARPA-funded graduate students were brought together at the University of Illinois at Urbana-Champaign to meet and share ideas. During this conference, ARPA rolled out the blueprints for networking the main computer systems of about a dozen ARPA-funded universities and research institutions. They were to be connected with communications lines operating at a then-stunning 56kb (i.e., 56,000 bits per second), this at a time when most people (of the few who could be) were connecting over telephone lines to computers at a rate of 110 bits per second. HMD vividly recalls the excitement at that conference. Researchers at Harvard talked about communication with the Univac 1108 "supercomputer" across the country at the University of Utah to handle calculations related to their computer graphics research. Many other intriguing possibilities were raised. Academic research was about to take a giant leap forward. Shortly after this conference, ARPA proceeded to implement what quickly became the *ARPAnet*, the grandparent of today's *Internet*.

Things worked out differently from what was originally planned. Rather than the primary benefit being that researchers could share each other's computers, it rapidly became clear that simply enabling the researchers to communicate quickly and easily among themselves via what became known as *electronic mail* (*e-mail*, for short) was to be the key benefit of the ARPAnet. This is true even today on the Internet with e-mail facilitating communications of all kinds among millions of people worldwide.

One of ARPA's primary goals for the network was to allow multiple users to send and receive information at the same time over the same communications paths (such as phone lines). The network operated with a technique called *packet switching* in which digital data was sent in small packages called *packets*. The packets contained data, address information, error-control information and sequencing information. The address information was used to route the packets of data to their destination. The sequencing information was used to help reassemble the packets (which—because of complex routing mechanisms—actually could arrive out of order) into their original order for presentation to the recipient. Packets of many people were intermixed on the same lines. This packet-switching technique greatly reduced transmission costs compared to the cost of dedicated communications lines.

The network was designed to operate without centralized control. This meant that if a portion of the network should fail, the remaining working portions still would be able to route packets from senders to receivers over alternate paths.

The protocols for communicating over the ARPAnet became known as *TCP—the Transmission Control Protocol*. TCP ensured that messages were routed properly from sender to receiver and that those messages arrived intact.

In parallel with the early evolution of the Internet, organizations worldwide were implementing their own networks for both intra-organization (i.e., within the organization) and inter-organization (i.e., between organizations) communication. A huge variety of networking hardware and software appeared. One challenge was to get these to intercommunicate. ARPA accomplished this with the development of *IP (the Internet Protocol)*, truly creating a "network of networks," the current architecture of the Internet. The combined set of protocols now is called *TCP/IP*.

Initially, use of the Internet was limited to universities and research institutions; then, the military became a big user. Eventually, the government allowed access to the Internet for commercial purposes. Initially, there was resentment among the research and military communities—it was felt that response times would become poor as "the net" became saturated with so many users. In fact, the exact opposite has occurred. Businesses rapidly realized that by making effective use of the Internet, they could tune their operations and offer new and better services to their clients. As a result, businesses spent vast amounts of money to develop and enhance the Internet. This generated fierce competition among the communications carriers and hardware and software suppliers to meet this demand. The result is that *bandwidth* (i.e., the information carrying capacity of communications lines) on the Internet has increased tremendously and costs have plummeted.

1.17 History of the World Wide Web

The *World Wide Web* allows computer users to locate and view multimedia-based documents (i.e., documents with text, graphics, animations, audios and/or videos) on almost any subject. Even though the Internet was developed more than three decades ago, the introduction of the *World Wide Web* was a relatively recent event. In 1990, *Tim Berners-Lee* of CERN (the European Organization for Nuclear Research) developed the World Wide Web and several communication protocols that form its backbone.

The Internet and the World Wide Web undoubtedly will be listed among the most important and profound creations of humankind. In the past, most computer applications ran on "stand-alone" computers, i.e., computers that were not connected to one another. Today's applications can be written to communicate among the world's hundreds of millions of computers. The Internet mixes computing and communications technologies. It makes our work easier. It makes information instantly and conveniently accessible worldwide. It makes it possible for individuals and small businesses to get worldwide exposure. It is changing the nature of the way business is done. People can search for the best prices on virtually any product or service. Special-interest communities can stay in touch with one another. Researchers can be made instantly aware of the latest breakthroughs worldwide. This new fourth edition of *C++ How to Program* includes Chapter 16, Web Programming with CGI. After reading this chapter, you will be able to develop computer applications that run on the World Wide Web.

1.18 World Wide Web Consortium (W3C)

In October 1994, Tim Berners-Lee founded an organization called the *World Wide Web Consortium* (*W3C*) that is devoted to developing nonproprietary, interoperable technologies for the World Wide Web. One of the W3C's primary goals is to make the Web universally accessible—regardless of disabilities, language or culture.

The W3C is also a standardization organization and is comprised of three *hosts*—the Massachusetts Institute of Technology (MIT), France's INRIA (Institut National de Recherche en Informatique et Automatique) and Keio University of Japan—and over 400 members, including Deitel & Associates, Inc. Members provide the primary financing for the W3C and help provide the strategic direction of the Consortium. To learn more about the W3C, visit **www.w3.org**.

Web technologies standardized by the W3C are called *Recommendations*. Current W3C Recommendations include *Extensible HyperText Markup Language (XHTML™)*, *Cascading Style Sheets (CSS™)* and the *Extensible Markup Language (XML)*. Recommendations are not actual software products, but documents that specify the role, syntax and rules of a technology. Before becoming a W3C Recommendation, a document passes through three major phases: *Working Draft*—which, as its name implies, specifies an evolving draft; *Candidate Recommendation*—a stable version of the document that industry can begin to implement; and *Proposed Recommendation*—a Candidate Recommendation that is considered mature (i.e., has been implemented and tested over a period of time) and is ready to be considered for W3C Recommendation status. For detailed information about the W3C Recommendation track, see "6.2 The W3C Recommendation track" at

```
www.w3.org/Consortium/Process/Process-19991111/
process.html#RecsCR
```

1.19 General Notes About C++ and This Book

C++ is a complex language. Experienced C++ programmers sometimes take pride in being able to create some weird, contorted, convoluted usage of the language. This is a poor programming practice. It makes programs more difficult to read, more likely to behave strangely, more difficult to test and debug, and more difficult to adapt to changing requirements. This book is geared for novice programmers, so we stress program *clarity*. The following is our first "good programming practice."

 **Good Programming Practice 1.1**

Write your C++ programs in a simple and straightforward manner. This is sometimes referred to as KIS ("keep it simple"). Do not "stretch" the language by trying bizarre usages.

You have heard that C and C++ are portable languages, and that programs written in C and C++ can run on many different computers. *Portability is an elusive goal.* The ANSI C standard document contains a lengthy list of portability issues and complete books have been written that discuss portability.

Portability Tip 1.3

Although it is possible to write portable programs, there are many problems among different C and C++ compilers and different computers that can make portability difficult to achieve. Writing programs in C and C++ does not guarantee portability. The programmer often will need to deal directly with compiler and computer variations.

We have done a careful walkthrough of the ANSI/ISO C++ standard document and audited our presentation against it for completeness and accuracy. However, C++ is a rich language, and there are some subtleties in the language and some advanced subjects we have not covered. If you need additional technical details on C++, we suggest that you read the C++ standard document. You can order this document from the ANSI Web site

webstore.ansi.org/ansidocstore/default.asp

The title of the document is "Information Technology – Programming Languages – C++" and its document number is INCITS/ISO/IEC 14882-1998.

We have included an extensive bibliography of books and papers on C++ and object-oriented programming. We also have included a C++ Resources appendix containing many Internet and World Wide Web sites relating to C++ and object-oriented programming.

Many features of the current versions of C++ are not compatible with older C++ implementations, so you may find that some of the programs in this text do not work on older C++ compilers.

Good Programming Practice 1.2

Read the manuals for the version of C++ you are using. Refer to these manuals frequently to be sure you are aware of the rich collection of C++ features and that you are using them correctly.

Good Programming Practice 1.3

Your computer and compiler are good teachers. If after reading your C++ language manual, you still are not sure how a feature of C++ works, experiment using a small "test program" and see what happens. Set your compiler options for "maximum warnings." Study each message that the compiler generates and correct the programs to eliminate the messages.

1.20 Introduction to C++ Programming

The C++ language facilitates a structured and disciplined approach to computer-program design. We now introduce C++ programming and present several examples that illustrate many important features of C++. Each example is analyzed one statement at a time. In Chapter 2 we present a detailed treatment of *structured programming* in C++. We then use the structured approach through Chapter 5. Beginning with Chapter 6, we study object-oriented programming in C++. Again, because of the central importance of object-oriented programming in this book, each of the first five chapters concludes with a section entitled "Thinking About Objects." These special sections introduce the concepts of object orientation and present a case study that challenges the reader to design and implement a substantial object-oriented C++ program. The complete design and implementation in C++ are included in this special sections. Even though this case study is optional, we highly recommend studying it.

1.21 A Simple Program: Printing a Line of Text

C++ uses notations that may appear strange to non-programmers. We now consider a simple program that prints a line of text. The program and its output are shown in Fig. 1.2. This program illustrates several important features of the C++ language. We consider each line of the program in detail.

```
1   // Fig. 1.2: fig01_02.cpp
2   // A first program in C++.
3   #include <iostream>
4
5   // function main begins program execution
6   int main()
7   {
8      std::cout << "Welcome to C++!\n";
9
10     return 0;   // indicate that program ended successfully
11
12  } // end function main
```

```
Welcome to C++!
```

Fig. 1.2   Text printing program.

Lines 1 and 2

```
// Fig. 1.2: fig01_02.cpp
// A first program in C++.
```

each begin with **//** indicating that the remainder of each line is a *comment*. Programmers in-sert comments to *document* programs and improve program readability. Comments also help other people read and understand your program. Comments do not cause the computer to per-form any action when the program is run. Comments are ignored by the C++ compiler and do not cause any machine-language object code to be generated. The comment **A first pro-gram in C++** describes the purpose of the program. A comment beginning with **//** is called a *single-line comment* because the comment terminates at the end of the current line. [*Note:* C++ programmers also may use C's comment style in which a comment—possibly contain-ing many lines—begins with **/*** and ends with ***/**, but this is discouraged.]

 Good Programming Practice 1.4

Every program should begin with a comment that describes the purpose of the program, au-thor, date and time. [5]

Line 3

```
#include <iostream>
```

is a *preprocessor directive,* which is a message to the C++ preprocessor. Lines that begin with **#** are processed by the preprocessor before the program is compiled. This line notifies the preprocessor to include in the program the contents of the *input/output stream header file* **<iostream>**. This file must be included for any program that outputs data to the screen or inputs data from the keyboard using C++-style stream input/output. Figure 1.2 outputs data to the screen, as we will soon see. The contents of **iostream** will be ex-plained in more detail later.

---

5. We are not showing the author, date and time in this book's programs because this information would be redundant.

Common Programming Error 1.2

Forgetting to include the `<iostream>` *file in a program that inputs data from the keyboard or outputs data to the screen causes the compiler to issue an error message.*

Line 5

```
// function main begins program execution
```

is another single-line comment indicating that program execution begins from the next line.
Line 6

```
int main()
```

is a part of every C++ program. The parentheses after **main** indicate that **main** is a program building block called a *function*. C++ programs contain one or more functions, exactly one of which must be **main**. Figure 1.2 contains only one function. C++ programs begin executing at function **main**, even if **main** is not the first function in the program. The keyword **int** to the left of **main** indicates that **main** "returns" an integer (whole number) value. We will explain what it means for a function to "return a value" when we study functions in depth in Chapter 3. For now, simply include the keyword **int** to the left of **main** in each of your programs.

The *left brace,* **{**, (line 7) must begin the *body* of every function. A corresponding *right brace,* **}**, (line 12) must end each function's body. Line 8

```
std::cout << "Welcome to C++!\n";
```

instructs the computer to print on the screen the *string* of characters contained between the quotation marks. The entire line, including **std::cout**, the **<<** *operator,* the *string* **"Welcome to C++!\n"** and the *semicolon* (**;**), is called a *statement.* Every statement must end with a semicolon (also known as the *statement terminator*). Output and input in C++ is accomplished with *streams* of characters. Thus, when the preceding statement is executed, it sends the stream of characters **Welcome to C++!** to the *standard output stream object*—**std::cout**—which is normally "connected" to the screen. We discuss **std::cout**'s many features in detail in Chapter 12, *Stream Input/Output.*

Notice that we placed **std::** before **cout**. This is required when we use the preprocessor directive **#include <iostream>**. The notation **std::cout** specifies that we are using a name, in this case **cout**, that belongs to "namespace" **std**. Namespaces are an advanced C++ feature. We discuss namespaces in depth in Chapter 22. For now, you should simply remember to include **std::** before each mention of **cout**, **cin** and **cerr** in a program. This can be cumbersome—in Fig. 1.14, we introduce the **using** statement, which will enable us to omit **std::** before each use of a namespace **std** name.

The operator **<<** is referred to as the *stream insertion operator.* When this program executes, the value to the right of the operator, the right *operand,* is inserted in the output stream. (Notice that the operator points in the direction of where the data goes.) The characters of the right operand normally print exactly as they appear between the double quotes. Notice, however, that the characters **\n** are not printed on the screen. The backslash (****) is called an *escape character.* It indicates that a "special" character is to be output. When a backslash is encountered in a string of characters, the next character is combined with the backslash to form an *escape sequence.* The escape sequence **\n** means *newline.* It causes the *cursor* (i.e., the current screen-position indicator) to move to the beginning of the next line on the screen. Some other common escape sequences are listed in Fig. 1.3.

Common Programming Error 1.3

Omitting the semicolon at the end of a statement is a   syntax error. A syntax error is caused when the compiler cannot recognize a statement. The compiler normally issues an error message to help the programmer locate and fix the incorrect statement. Syntax errors are violations of the language. Syntax errors are also called compile errors, compile-time errors, *or* compilation errors *because they appear during the compilation phase.*

Line 10

```
return 0;   // indicate that program ended successfully
```

is included at the end of every **main** function. C++ keyword **return** is one of several means we will use to *exit a function*. When the **return** statement is used at the end of **main** as shown here, the value **0** indicates that the program has terminated successfully. In Chapter 3, we discuss functions in detail and the reasons for including this statement will become clear. For now, simply include this statement in each program, or the compiler may produce a warning on some systems. The right brace, **}**, (line 12) indicates the end of function **main**.

Good Programming Practice 1.5

Many programmers make the last character printed by a function a newline (\n). This ensures that the function will leave the screen cursor positioned at the beginning of a new line. Conventions of this nature encourage software reusability—a key goal in software development environments.

Good Programming Practice 1.6

Indent the entire body of each function one level within the braces that define the body of the function. This makes the functional structure of a program stand out and helps make programs easier to read.

Good Programming Practice 1.7

Set a convention for the size of indent you prefer then uniformly apply that convention. The tab key may be used to create indents, but tab stops may vary. We recommend using either 1/4-inch tab stops or (preferably) three spaces to form a level of indent.

Escape Sequence	Description
\n	Newline. Position the screen cursor to the beginning of the next line.
\t	Horizontal tab. Move the screen cursor to the next tab stop.
\r	Carriage return. Position the screen cursor to the beginning of the current line; do not advance to the next line.
\a	Alert. Sound the system bell.
\\	Backslash. Used to print a backslash character.
\"	Double quote. Used to print a double quote character.

Fig. 1.3 Escape sequences.

Welcome to C++! can be printed several ways. For example, Fig. 1.4 uses multiple stream insertion statements (lines 8–9), yet produces identical output to the program of Fig. 1.2.[6] This works because each stream-insertion statement resumes printing where the previous statement stopped printing. The first stream insertion prints **Welcome** followed by a space and the second stream insertion begins printing on the same line immediately following the space. In general, C++ allows the programmer to express statements in a variety of ways.

A single statement can print multiple lines by using newline characters as in line 8 of Fig. 1.5. Each time the **\n** (newline) escape sequence is encountered in the output stream, the screen cursor is positioned to the beginning of the next line. To get a blank line in your output, place two newline characters back to back as in Fig. 1.5.

```cpp
1   // Fig. 1.4: fig01_04.cpp
2   // Printing a line with multiple statements.
3   #include <iostream>
4
5   // function main begins program execution
6   int main()
7   {
8       std::cout << "Welcome ";
9       std::cout << "to C++!\n";
10
11      return 0;   // indicate that program ended successfully
12
13  } // end function main
```

```
Welcome to C++!
```

Fig. 1.4   Printing on one line with separate statements using **cout**.

```cpp
1   // Fig. 1.5: fig01_05.cpp
2   // Printing multiple lines with a single statement
3   #include <iostream>
4
5   // function main begins program execution
6   int main()
7   {
8       std::cout << "Welcome\nto\n\nC++!\n";
9
10      return 0;   // indicate that program ended successfully
11
12  } // end function main
```

```
Welcome
to

C++!
```

Fig. 1.5   Printing on multiple lines with a single statement using **cout**.

6. From this point forward, we highlight in bold yellow the key features each program introduces.

1.22 Another Simple Program: Adding Two Integers

Our next program uses the input stream object **std::cin** and the *stream extraction operator*, **>>**, to obtain two integers typed by a user at the keyboard, computes the sum of these values and outputs the result using **std::cout**. Figure 1.6 shows the program and sample output.

The comments in lines 1 and 2

```
// Fig. 1.6: fig01_06.cpp
// Addition program.
```

state the name of the file and the purpose of the program. The C++ preprocessor directive

```
#include <iostream>
```

in line 3 includes the contents of the **iostream** header file in the program.

As stated earlier, every program begins execution with function **main**. The left brace marks the beginning of **main**'s body and the corresponding right brace marks the end of **main**.

```
1   // Fig. 1.6: fig01_06.cpp
2   // Addition program.
3   #include <iostream>
4
5   // function main begins program execution
6   int main()
7   {
8       int integer1;   // first number to be input by user
9       int integer2;   // second number to be input by user
10      int sum;        // variable in which sum will be stored
11
12      std::cout << "Enter first integer\n";  // prompt
13      std::cin >> integer1;                  // read an integer
14
15      std::cout << "Enter second integer\n"; // prompt
16      std::cin >> integer2;                  // read an integer
17
18      sum = integer1 + integer2;  // assign result to sum
19
20      std::cout << "Sum is " << sum << std::endl; // print sum
21
22      return 0;   // indicate that program ended successfully
23
24  } // end function main
```

```
Enter first integer
45
Enter second integer
72
Sum is 117
```

Fig. 1.6   Addition program.

Lines 8–10

```
int integer1;   // first number to be input by user
int integer2;   // second number to be input by user
int sum;        // variable in which sum will be stored
```

are *declarations*. The words **integer1**, **integer2** and **sum** are the names of *variables*. A variable is a location in the computer's memory where a value can be stored for use by a program. This declaration specifies that the variables **integer1**, **integer2** and **sum** are data of type *int*, which means that these variables will hold *integer* values, i.e., whole numbers such as 7, -11, 0, 31914. All variables must be declared with a name and a data type before they can be used in a program. Several variables of the same type may be declared in one declaration or in multiple declarations. We could have declared all three variables in one declaration as follows:

```
int integer1, integer2, sum;
```

however, this makes the program less readable and prevents us from providing comments that describe each variable's purpose in the program. If more than one name is declared in a declaration (as shown here), the names are separated by commas (**,**). This is referred to as a *comma-separated list*.

Good Programming Practice 1.8

Some programmers prefer to declare each variable on a separate line. This format allows for easy insertion of a descriptive comment next to each declaration.

We will soon discuss the data types **double** (for specifying real numbers, i.e., numbers with decimal points like 3.4, 0.0, -11.19) and **char** (for specifying character data; a **char** variable may hold only a single lowercase letter, a single uppercase letter, a single digit or a single special character like a **x**, **$**, **7**, *****, etc.).

Good Programming Practice 1.9

*Place a space after each comma (**,**) to make programs more readable.*

A variable name is any valid *identifier*. An identifier is a series of characters consisting of letters, digits and underscores (**_**) that does not begin with a digit. C++ is *case sensitive*—uppercase and lowercase letters are different, so **a1** and **A1** are different identifiers.

Portability Tip 1.4

C++ allows identifiers of any length, but your system and/or C++ implementation may impose some restrictions on the length of identifiers. Use identifiers of 31 characters or fewer to ensure portability.

Good Programming Practice 1.10

Choosing meaningful variable names helps a program to be "self-documenting," i.e., it becomes easier to understand the program simply by reading it rather than having to read manuals or use excessive comments.

Good Programming Practice 1.11

Avoid identifiers that begin with underscores and double underscores because C++ compilers may use names like that for their own purposes internally. This will prevent names you choose from being confused with names the compilers choose.

Declarations of variables can be placed almost anywhere in a function, but they must appear before their corresponding variables are used in the program. For example, in the program of Fig. 1.6, the declaration

```
int integer1;
```

could have been placed immediately before the line

```
std::cin >> integer1;
```

the declaration

```
int integer2;
```

could have been placed immediately before the line

```
std::cin >> integer2;
```

and the declaration

```
int sum;
```

could have been placed immediately before the line

```
sum = integer1 + integer2;
```

Good Programming Practice 1.12

Always place a blank line between a declaration and adjacent executable statements. This makes the declarations stand out in the program and contributes to program clarity.

Good Programming Practice 1.13

If you prefer to place declarations at the beginning of a function, separate those declarations from the executable statements in that function with one blank line to highlight where the declarations end and the executable statements begin.

Line 12

```
std::cout << "Enter first integer\n";   // prompt
```

prints the string **Enter first integer** (also known as a *string literal* or a *literal*) on the screen and positions the cursor to the beginning of the next line. This message is called a *prompt* because it tells the user to take a specific action. We like to pronounce the preceding statement as "**cout** *gets* the character string **"Enter first integer\n"**."

Line 13

```
std::cin >> integer1;                        // read an integer
```

uses the *input stream object* **cin** (of namespace **std**) and the *stream extraction operator,* **>>**, to obtain a value from the keyboard. Using the stream extraction operator with **std::cin** takes character input from the standard input stream which is usually the keyboard. We like to pronounce the preceding statement as, "**std::cin** *gives* a value to **integer1**" or simply "**std::cin** *gives* **integer1**."

When the computer executes the preceding statement, it waits for the user to enter a value for variable **integer1**. The user responds by typing an integer (as characters) then pressing the *Enter* key (sometimes called the *Return* key) to send the characters to the computer. The computer then converts the character representation of the number to an integer and assigns this number (or *value*) to the variable **integer1**. Any subsequent references to **integer1** in this program will use this same value.

The **std::cout** and **std::cin** stream objects facilitate interaction between the user and the computer. Because this interaction resembles a dialogue, it is often called *conversational computing* or *interactive computing*.

Line 15

```
std::cout << "Enter second integer\n"; // prompt
```

prints the words **Enter second integer** on the screen, then positions the cursor to the beginning of the next line. This statement prompts the user to take action. Line 16

```
std::cin >> integer2;                     // read an integer
```

obtains a value for variable **integer2** from the user.

The assignment statement in line 18

```
sum = integer1 + integer2;  // assign result to sum
```

calculates the sum of the variables **integer1** and **integer2** and assigns the result to variable **sum** using the *assignment operator* **=**. The statement is read as, "**sum** *gets* the value of **integer1 + integer2**." Most calculations are performed in assignment statements. The **=** operator and the **+** operator are called *binary operators* because they each have two *operands*. In the case of the **+** operator, the two operands are **integer1** and **integer2**. In the case of the preceding **=** operator, the two operands are **sum** and the value of the expression **integer1 + integer2**.

Good Programming Practice 1.14

Place spaces on either side of a binary operator. This makes the operator stand out and makes the program more readable.

Line 20

```
std::cout << "Sum is " << sum << std::endl; // print sum
```

displays the character string **Sum is** followed by the numerical value of variable **sum** followed by **std::endl** (**endl** is an abbreviation for "end line;" **endl** also is a name in namespace **std**)—a so-called *stream manipulator*. The **std::endl** manipulator outputs a newline then "flushes the output buffer." This simply means that, on some systems where outputs accumulate in the machine until there are enough to "make it worthwhile" to display on the screen, **std::endl** forces any accumulated outputs to be displayed at that moment.

Note that the preceding statement outputs multiple values of different types. The stream insertion operator "knows" how to output each piece of data. Using multiple stream insertion operators (**<<**) in a single statement is referred to as *concatenating, chaining* or *cascading stream insertion operations*. Thus, it is unnecessary to have multiple output statements to output multiple pieces of data.

Calculations can also be performed in output statements. We could have combined the statements at lines 18 and 20 into the statement

```
std::cout << "Sum is " << integer1 + integer2 << std::endl;
```

thus eliminating the need for the variable **sum**.

The right brace, **}**, informs the computer that the end of function **main** has been reached.

A powerful feature of C++ is that users can create their own data types (we will explore this capability in Chapter 6). Users can then "teach" C++ how to input and output values of these new data types using the **>>** and **<<** operators (this is called *operator overloading*—a topic we explore in Chapter 8).

1.23 Memory Concepts

Variable names such as **integer1**, **integer2** and **sum** actually correspond to *locations* in the computer's memory. Every variable has a *name,* a *type,* a *size* and a *value.*

In the addition program of Fig. 1.6, when the statement

```
std::cin >> integer1;
```

in line 13 is executed, the characters typed by the user are converted to an integer that is placed into a memory location to which the name **integer1** has been assigned by the C++ compiler. Suppose the user enters the number **45** as the value for **integer1**. The computer will place **45** into location **integer1** as shown in Fig. 1.7.

Whenever a value is placed in a memory location, the value overwrites the previous value in that location.

Returning to our addition program, when the statement

```
std::cin >> integer2;
```

in line 16 is executed, suppose the user enters the value **72**. This value is placed into location **integer2**, and memory appears as in Fig. 1.8. Note that these locations are not necessarily adjacent in memory.

Once the program has obtained values for **integer1** and **integer2**, it adds these values and places the sum into variable **sum**. The statement

```
sum = integer1 + integer2;
```

that performs the addition also replaces whatever value was stored in **sum**. This occurs when the calculated sum of **integer1** and **integer2** is placed into location **sum** (without regard to what value may already be in **sum**; that value is lost). After **sum** is calculated, memory appears as in Fig. 1.9. Note that the values of **integer1** and **integer2** appear exactly as they did before they were used in the calculation of **sum**. These values were used, but not destroyed, as the computer performed the calculation. Thus, when a value is read out of a memory location, the process is nondestructive.

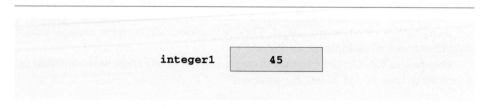

Fig. 1.7   Memory location showing the name and value of variable **integer1**.

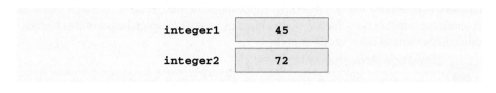

Fig. 1.8   Memory locations after storing values for **integer1** and **integer2**.

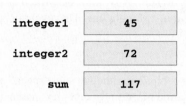

Fig. 1.9   Memory locations after calculating the **sum** of **integer1** and **integer2**.

1.24 Arithmetic

Most programs perform arithmetic calculations. Figure 1.10 summarizes the *arithmetic operators*. Note the use of various special symbols not used in algebra. The *asterisk (*)* indicates multiplication and the *percent sign (%)* is the *modulus* operator that will be discussed shortly. The arithmetic operators in Fig. 1.10 are all binary operators, i.e., operators that take two operands. For example, the expression **integer1 + integer2** contains the binary operator **+** and the two operands **integer1** and **integer2**.

Integer division (i.e., both the numerator and the denominator are integers) yields an integer quotient; for example, the expression **7 / 4** evaluates to **1** and the expression **17 / 5** evaluates to **3**. Note that any fractional part in integer division is discarded (i.e., *truncated*)— no rounding occurs.

C++ provides the *modulus operator*, **%**, that yields the remainder after integer division. The modulus operator can be used only with integer operands. The expression **x % y** yields the remainder after **x** is divided by **y**. Thus, **7 % 4** yields **3** and **17 % 5** yields **2**. In later

C++ operation	Arithmetic operator	Algebraic expression	C++ expression
Addition	+	$f + 7$	**f + 7**
Subtraction	–	$p - c$	**p - c**
Multiplication	*	bm	**b * m**
Division	/	x / y or $\dfrac{x}{y}$ or $x \div y$	**x / y**
Modulus	%	$r \bmod s$	**r % s**

Fig. 1.10   Arithmetic operators.

chapters, we discuss many interesting applications of the modulus operator, such as determining whether one number is a multiple of another (a special case of this is determining whether a number is odd or even).

 Common Programming Error 1.4

*Attempting to use the modulus operator, **%**, with non-integer operands is a syntax error.*

Arithmetic expressions in C++ must be entered into the computer in *straight-line form.* Thus, expressions such as "**a** divided by **b**" must be written as **a / b** so that all constants, variables and operators appear in a straight line. The algebraic notation

$$\frac{a}{b}$$

is generally not acceptable to compilers, although some special-purpose software packages do exist that support more natural notation for complex mathematical expressions.

Parentheses are used in C++ expressions in the same manner as in algebraic expressions. For example, to multiply **a** times the quantity **b + c** we write:

    a * (b + c)

C++ applies the operators in arithmetic expressions in a precise sequence determined by the following *rules of operator precedence,* which are generally the same as those followed in algebra:

1. Operators in expressions contained within pairs of parentheses are evaluated first. Thus, *parentheses may be used to force the order of evaluation to occur in any sequence desired by the programmer.* Parentheses are said to be at the "highest level of precedence." In cases of *nested,* or *embedded,* parentheses, the operators in the innermost pair of parentheses are applied first.

2. Multiplication, division and modulus operations are applied next. If an expression contains several multiplication, division and modulus operations, operators are applied from left to right. Multiplication, division and modulus are said to be on the same level of precedence.

3. Addition and subtraction operations are applied last. If an expression contains several addition and subtraction operations, operators are applied from left to right. Addition and subtraction also have the same level of precedence.

The rules of operator precedence enable C++ to apply operators in the correct order. When we say that certain operators are applied from left to right, we are referring to the *associativity* of the operators. For example, in the expression

    a + b + c

the addition operators (**+**) associate from left to right. We will see that some operators associate from right to left. Fig. 1.11 summarizes these rules of operator precedence. This table will be expanded as additional C++ operators are introduced. A complete precedence chart is included in the appendices.

Now let us consider several expressions in light of the rules of operator precedence. Each example lists an algebraic expression and its C++ equivalent. The following is an example of an arithmetic mean (average) of five terms:

Operator(s)	Operation(s)	Order of evaluation (precedence)
( )	Parentheses	Evaluated first. If the parentheses are nested, the expression in the innermost pair is evaluated first. If there are several pairs of parentheses "on the same level" (i.e., not nested), they are evaluated left to right.
*, /, or %	Multiplication Division Modulus	Evaluated second. If there are several, they are evaluated left to right.
+ or −	Addition Subtraction	Evaluated last. If there are several, they are evaluated left to right.

Fig. 1.11   Precedence of arithmetic operators.

Algebra: $m = \dfrac{a+b+c+d+e}{5}$

C++:   `m = ( a + b + c + d + e ) / 5;`

The parentheses are required because division has higher precedence than addition. The entire quantity **(a + b + c + d + e)** is to be divided by **5**. If the parentheses are erroneously omitted, we obtain **a + b + c + d + e / 5**, which evaluates incorrectly as

$$a + b + c + d + \frac{e}{5}$$

The following is an example of the equation of a straight line:

Algebra: $y = mx + b$

C++:   `y = m * x + b;`

No parentheses are required. The multiplication is applied first because multiplication has a higher precedence than addition.

The following example contains modulus (**%**), multiplication, division, addition and subtraction operations:

Algebra: $z = pr\%q + w/x - y$

C++:   `z  =  p  *  r  %  q  +  w  /  x  -  y;`
                   ⑥   ①   ②   ④   ③   ⑤

The circled numbers under the statement indicate the order in which C++ applies the operators. The multiplication, modulus and division are evaluated first in left-to-right order (i.e., they associate from left to right) because they have higher precedence than addition and subtraction. The addition and subtraction are applied next. These are also applied left to right.

Not all expressions with several pairs of parentheses contain nested parentheses. For example, the expression

```
a * (b + c) + c * (d + e)
```

does not contain nested parentheses. Rather, the parentheses are said to be "on the same level."

To develop a better understanding of the rules of operator precedence, consider how a second-degree polynomial is evaluated.

The circled numbers under the statement indicate the order in which C++ applies the operators. There is no arithmetic operator for exponentiation in C++, so we have represented x^2 as **x * x**. We will soon discuss the standard library function **pow** ("power") that performs exponentiation. Because of some subtle issues related to the data types required by **pow**, we defer a detailed explanation of **pow** until Chapter 3.

Common Programming Error 1.5

*Some programming languages use operators ** or ^ to represent exponentiation. C++ does not support these operators; using them results in a syntax error.*

Suppose variables **a**, **b**, **c** and **x** are initialized as follows: **a = 2, b = 3, c = 7** and **x = 5**. Figure 1.12 illustrates the order in which the operators are applied in the preceding second degree polynomial.

The preceding assignment statement can be parenthesized with unnecessary parentheses for clarity as

```
y = ( a * x * x ) + ( b * x ) + c;
```

Good Programming Practice 1.15

As in algebra, it is acceptable to place unnecessary parentheses in an expression to make the expression clearer. These redundant parentheses are commonly used to group subexpressions in a large expression to make that expression clearer. Breaking a large statement into a sequence of shorter, simpler statements also promotes clarity.

1.25 Decision Making: Equality and Relational Operators

This section introduces a simple version of C++'s *if structure* that allows a program to make a decision based on the truth or falsity of some *condition*. If the condition is met, i.e., the condition is true, the statement in the body of the **if** structure is executed. If the condition is not met, i.e., the condition is false, the body statement is not executed. We will see an example shortly.

Conditions in **if** structures can be formed by using the *equality operators* and *relational operators* summarized in Fig. 1.13. The relational operators all have the same level of precedence and associate left to right. The equality operators both have the same level of precedence, which is lower than the precedence of the relational operators. The equality operators also associate left to right.

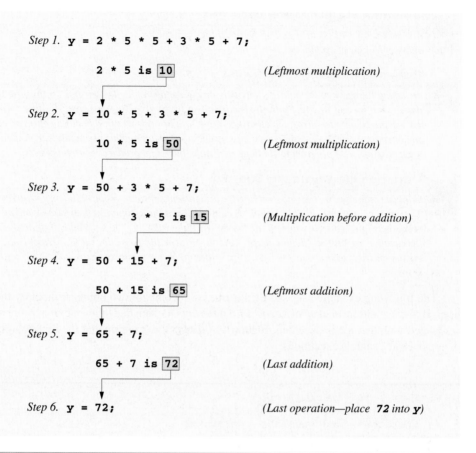

Fig. 1.12   Order in which a second-degree polynomial is evaluated.

Standard algebraic equality operator or relational operator	C++ equality or relational operator	Example of C++ condition	Meaning of C++ condition
Relational operators			
>	>	x > y	x is greater than y
<	<	x < y	x is less than y
≥	>=	x >= y	x is greater than or equal to y
≤	<=	x <= y	x is less than or equal to y
Equality operators			
=	==	x == y	x is equal to y
≠	!=	x != y	x is not equal to y

Fig. 1.13   Equality and relational operators.

Common Programming Error 1.6

A syntax error will occur if any of the operators **==**, **!=**, **>=** *and* **<=** *appears with spaces between its pair of symbols.*

Common Programming Error 1.7

Reversing the order of the pair of symbols in any of the operators **!=**, **>=** *and* **<=** *(by writing them as* **=!**, **=>** *and* **=<**, *respectively) is normally a syntax error. In some cases, writing* **!=** *as* **=!** *will not be a syntax error, but almost certainly will be a* logic error *that has an effect at execution time. A* fatal logic error *causes a program to fail and terminate prematurely. A* nonfatal logic error *allows a program to continue executing, but might produce incorrect results.*

Common Programming Error 1.8

Confusing the equality operator **==** *with the assignment operator* **=** *can result in logic errors. The equality operator should be read "is equal to," and the assignment operator should be read "gets" or "gets the value of" or "is assigned the value of." Some people prefer to read the equality operator as "double equals." As we will soon see, confusing these operators may not necessarily cause an easy-to-recognize syntax error, but may cause extremely subtle logic errors.*

The following example uses six **if** statements to compare two numbers input by the user. If the condition in any of these **if** statements is satisfied, the output statement associated with that **if** is executed. Figure 1.14 shows the program and the input/output dialogs of three sample executions.

```
1   // Fig. 1.14: fig01_14.cpp
2   // Using if statements, relational
3   // operators, and equality operators.
4   #include <iostream>
5
6   using std::cout;   // program uses cout
7   using std::cin;    // program uses cin
8   using std::endl;   // program uses endl
9
10  // function main begins program execution
11  int main()
12  {
13     int num1;   // first number to be read from user
14     int num2;   // second number to be read from user
15
16     cout << "Enter two integers, and I will tell you\n"
17          << "the relationships they satisfy: ";
18     cin >> num1 >> num2;   // read two integers
19
20     if ( num1 == num2 )
21        cout << num1 << " is equal to " << num2 << endl;
22
23     if ( num1 != num2 )
24        cout << num1 << " is not equal to " << num2 << endl;
25
```

Fig. 1.14   Equality and relational operators (Part 1 of 2.).

```
26     if ( num1 < num2 )
27         cout << num1 << " is less than " << num2 << endl;
28
29     if ( num1 > num2 )
30         cout << num1 << " is greater than " << num2 << endl;
31
32     if ( num1 <= num2 )
33         cout << num1 << " is less than or equal to "
34             << num2 << endl;
35
36     if ( num1 >= num2 )
37         cout << num1 << " is greater than or equal to "
38             << num2 << endl;
39
40     return 0;   // indicate that program ended successfully
41
42 } // end function main
```

```
Enter two integers, and I will tell you
the relationships they satisfy: 3 7
3 is not equal to 7
3 is less than 7
3 is less than or equal to 7
```

```
Enter two integers, and I will tell you
the relationships they satisfy: 22 12
22 is not equal to 12
22 is greater than 12
22 is greater than or equal to 12
```

```
Enter two integers, and I will tell you
the relationships they satisfy: 7 7
7 is equal to 7
7 is less than or equal to 7
7 is greater than or equal to 7
```

Fig. 1.14   Equality and relational operators (Part 2 of 2.).

Lines 6–8

```
using std::cout;   // program uses cout
using std::cin;    // program uses cin
using std::endl;   // program uses endl
```

are **using** *statements* that eliminate the need to repeat the **std::** prefix. Once we include these **using** statements, we can write **cout** instead of **std::cout, cin** instead of **std::cin** and **endl** instead of **std::endl**, respectively, in the remainder of the program. [*Note:* From this point forward in the book, each example contains one or more **us-ing** statements.]

Good Programming Practice 1.16

*Place **using** statements immediately after the **#include**s to which they refer.*

Lines 13–14

```
int num1;   // first number to be read from user
int num2;   // second number to be read from user
```

declare the variables used in the program. Remember that variables may be declared in one declaration or in multiple declarations.

The program uses cascaded stream-extraction operations (line 18) to input two integers. Remember that we are allowed to write **cin** (instead of **std::cin**) because of line 7. First a value is read into variable **num1**, then a value is read into variable **num2**.

The **if** structure at lines 20–21

```
if ( num1 == num2 )
    cout << num1 << " is equal to " << num2 << endl;
```

compares the values of variables **num1** and **num2** to test for equality. If the values are equal, the statement at line 21 displays a line of text indicating that the numbers are equal. If the conditions are **true** in one or more of the **if** structures starting at lines 23, 26, 29, 32 and 36, the corresponding **cout** statement displays a line of text.

Notice that each **if** structure in Fig. 1.14 has a single statement in its body and that each body is indented. Indenting the body of an **if** structure enhances program readability. In Chapter 2 we show how to specify **if** structures with multiple-statement bodies (by enclosing the body statements in a pair of braces, **{ }**).

Good Programming Practice 1.17

*Indent the statement in the body of an **if** structure to make the body of the structure more visible, thus enhancing readability.*

Good Programming Practice 1.18

There should be no more than one statement per line in a program.

Common Programming Error 1.9

*Placing a semicolon immediately after the right parenthesis after the condition in an **if** structure is often a logic error (although not a syntax error). The semicolon would cause the body of the **if** structure to be empty, so the **if** structure would perform no action, regardless of whether or not its condition is **true**. Worse yet, the original body statement of the **if** structure now would become a statement in sequence with the **if** structure and would always execute, often causing the program to produce incorrect results.*

Notice the use of spacing in Fig. 1.14. In C++ statements, *white-space* characters such as tabs, newlines and spaces are normally ignored by the compiler. (These are not ignored if they appear in strings.) So, statements may be split over several lines and may be spaced according to the programmer's preferences. It is a syntax error to split identifiers, strings (such as **"hello"**) and constants (such as the number **1000**) over several lines.

Common Programming Error 1.10

It is a syntax error to split an identifier by inserting white-space characters (e.g., writing **main** *as* **ma in)***.*

Good Programming Practice 1.19

A lengthy statement may be spread over several lines. If a single statement must be split across lines, choose breaking points that make sense such as after a comma in a comma-separated list, or after an operator in a lengthy expression. If a statement is split across two or more lines, indent all subsequent lines and left-align the group.

Figure 1.15 shows the precedence of the operators introduced in this chapter. The operators are shown top to bottom in decreasing order of precedence. Notice that all these operators, with the exception of the assignment operator **=**, associate from left to right. Addition is left associative, so an expression like **x + y + z** is evaluated as if it had been written **(x + y) + z**. The assignment operator **=** associates from right to left, so an expression such as **x = y = 0** is evaluated as if it had been written **x = (y = 0)**, which, as we will soon see, first assigns **0** to **y** then assigns the result of that assignment—**0**—to **x**.

Good Programming Practice 1.20

Refer to the operator precedence chart when writing expressions containing many operators. Confirm that the operators in the expression are performed in the order you expect. If you are uncertain about the order of evaluation in a complex expression, break the expression into smaller statements or use parentheses to force the order, exactly as you would do in an algebraic expression. Be sure to observe that some operators such as assignment (**=***) associate right to left rather than left to right.*

We have introduced many important features of C++ including printing data on the screen, inputting data from the keyboard, performing calculations and making decisions. In Chapter 2, we build on these techniques as we introduce *structured programming*. You will become more familiar with indentation techniques. We will study how to specify and vary the order in which statements are executed—this order is called *flow of control*.

Operators				Associativity	Type
( )				left to right	parentheses
*	**/**	**%**		left to right	multiplicative
+	**-**			left to right	additive
<<	**>>**			left to right	stream insertion/extraction
<	**<=**	**>**	**>=**	left to right	relational
==	**!=**			left to right	equality
=				right to left	assignment

Fig. 1.15 Precedence and associativity of the operators discussed so far.

1.26 Thinking About Objects: Introduction to Object Technology and the Unified Modeling Language™

Now we begin our introduction to object orientation. We will see that object orientation is a natural way of thinking about the world and of writing computer programs.

In each of the first five chapters we concentrate on the "conventional" methodology of structured programming, because the objects we build will be composed in part of structured-program pieces. We then end each chapter with a "Thinking About Objects" section in which we present a carefully paced introduction to object orientation. Our goal in these "Thinking About Objects" sections is to help you develop an object-oriented way of thinking, so that you can immediately put to use the knowledge of object-oriented programming that you begin to receive in Chapter 6. We also introduce you to the *Unified Modeling Language (UML)*. The UML is a graphical language that allows people who build systems (e.g., software architects, systems engineers, programmers, etc.) to represent their object-oriented designs using a common visual notation.

In this required section (Section 1.26), we introduce basic concepts (i.e., "object think") and terminology (i.e., "object speak"). In the optional "Thinking About Objects" sections at the ends of Chapters 2 through 5 we consider more substantial issues as we attack a challenging problem with the techniques of *object-oriented design (OOD)*. We analyze a simplified, example problem statement that requires a system to be built, determine the objects needed to implement the system, determine the attributes the objects need to have, determine the behaviors these objects need to exhibit and specify how the objects need to interact with one another to meet the system requirements. We do all this even before we have learned how to write object-oriented C++ programs. In the optional "Thinking About Objects" sections at the ends of Chapters 6, 7 and 9, we discuss a C++ implementation of the object-oriented system we design in the earlier chapters.

This case study will help introduce you to the practices employed in industry. Although our case study is a scaled-down version of an industry-level problem, we nevertheless cover many common industry practices. If you are a student, and your instructor does not plan on including this case study in your course, please consider covering the case study on your own time. We believe it will be well worth your while to walk through this engaging project. You will experience a solid introduction to object-oriented design with the UML, and you will sharpen your code-reading skills by touring a carefully written and well-documented 1200-line C++ program that solves the problem presented in the case study.

We begin our introduction to object orientation with some of the key terminology of object orientation. Look around you in the real world. Everywhere you look you see them—objects! People, animals, plants, cars, planes, buildings, computers, etc. Humans think in terms of objects. We have the marvelous ability of *abstraction* that enables us to view screen images as objects such as people, planes, trees and mountains, rather than as individual dots of color. We can, if we wish, think in terms of beaches rather than grains of sand, forests rather than trees and houses rather than bricks.

We might be inclined to divide objects into two categories—animate objects and inanimate objects. Animate objects are "alive" in some sense. They move around and do things. Inanimate objects, like towels, seem not to do much at all. They just kind of "sit around." All these objects, however, do have some things in common. They all have *attributes*, or *state*, like size, shape, color, weight, etc. that describe the objects. They all exhibit *behaviors*, or *operations*, (e.g., a ball rolls, bounces, inflates and deflates; a baby cries, sleeps, crawls, walks and blinks; a car accelerates, brakes and turns; a towel absorbs water; etc.) that specify what the objects do.

Humans learn about objects by studying their attributes and observing their behaviors. Different objects can have similar attributes and can exhibit similar behaviors. Comparisons can be made, for example, between babies and adults and between humans and chimpanzees. Cars, trucks, little red wagons and roller skates have much in common.

Object-oriented programming (OOP) models real-world objects with software counterparts. It takes advantage of *class* relationships where objects of a certain class—such as a class of vehicles—have similar attributes and operations. It takes advantage of *inheritance* relationships, and even *multiple inheritance* relationships where newly created classes of objects are derived by absorbing attributes and operations of existing classes and adding unique characteristics of their own. An object of class **Convertible** certainly has the characteristics of the more general class **Automobile**, but a **Convertible**'s roof goes up and down.

Object-oriented programming gives us a natural and intuitive way to view the programming process, namely, by *modeling* real-world objects, their attributes and their behaviors. OOP also provides for communication among objects. Just as people send *messages* to one another (e.g., a sergeant commanding a soldier to stand at attention), objects also communicate via messages.

OOP *encapsulates* data (attributes) and functions (operations) into packages called *objects;* the data and functions of an object are intimately tied together. Objects have the property of *information hiding.* This means that although objects may know how to communicate with each other across well-defined *interfaces,* objects normally do not know how other objects are implemented—implementation details are hidden within the objects themselves. Surely it is possible to drive a car effectively without knowing the details of how engines, transmissions and exhaust systems work internally. Indeed, driving would be much more difficult and less widespread if such understanding were required. We will see why information hiding is crucial to good software engineering, as well.

In C and other *procedural programming languages,* programming tends to be *action-oriented*; whereas in C++, programming tends to be *object-oriented.* In C, the unit of programming is the *function.* In C++, the unit of programming is the *class* from which objects are eventually *instantiated* (an OOP term for "created"). C++ classes contain functions that implement class behaviors and data that implement class attributes.

C programmers concentrate on writing functions. Programmers group actions that perform some common task into functions, and group functions to form programs. Data is certainly important in C, but the view is that data exists primarily in support of the actions that functions perform. The *verbs* in a system specification help the C programmer determine the set of functions that work together to implement the system.

C++ programmers concentrate on creating their own *user-defined types* called *classes* and *components.* Each class contains data, as well as the set of functions that manipulate that data. The data components of a class are called *data members* in C++. The function components of a class are called *member functions* in C++ (typically called *methods* in other object-oriented programming languages such as Java). Just as an instance of a built-in type such as **int** is called a *variable,* an instance of a user-defined type (i.e., a class) is called an *object.* The programmer uses built-in types (and other user defined types) as the "building blocks" for constructing user-defined types (classes). The focus of attention in C++ is on classes (from which we make objects) rather than on functions. The *nouns* in a system specification help the C++ programmer determine the set of classes from which objects are created that work together to implement the system.

Classes are to objects as blueprints are to houses. We can build many houses from one blueprint, and we can instantiate many objects from one class. Classes also can have relationships with other classes. For example, in an object-oriented design of a bank, the **BankTeller** class needs to relate to the **BankAccount** class. The simplest of these relationships is called an *association*.

We will see that software packaged as classes can be *reused* in future software systems. Groups of related classes are often packaged as reusable *components*. Just as real-estate brokers tell their clients that the three most important factors affecting the price of real estate are "location, location and location," we believe the three most important factors affecting the future of software development are "reuse, reuse and reuse."

With object-oriented technology, we build most future software by combining "standardized, interchangeable parts" called classes. This book teaches you how to "craft valuable classes" for reuse, reuse and reuse. Each class you create has the potential to become a valuable software asset that you and other programmers can use to facilitate future software-development efforts.

Introduction to Object-Oriented Analysis and Design (OOAD) and the UML

By now, you have probably written a few small programs in C++. How did you create the code for your programs? If you are like many beginning programmers, you may have turned on your computer and started typing. This approach might work for small projects, but what would you do if asked to create a software system to control a bank's automated teller machines? Such a project is too large and complex to sit down and simply start typing.

For creating the best solutions, you should follow a detailed process for obtaining an *analysis* of your project's *requirements* and developing a *design* for satisfying those requirements. You would go through this process and have its results reviewed and approved by your superiors before writing any code for your project. If this process involves analyzing and designing your system from an object-oriented point of view, it is referred to as an *object-oriented analysis and design (OOAD) process*. Experienced programmers know that no matter how simple a problem appears, time spent on analysis and design can save innumerable hours that might be lost from abandoning an ill-planned system development approach part of the way through its implementation.

OOAD is the generic term for the ideas behind the process we employ to analyze a problem and develop an approach for solving it. Small problems like the ones in these first few chapters do not require an exhaustive process. It may be sufficient to write *pseudocode* before we begin writing code. Pseudocode is an informal means of expressing program code. It is not actually a programming language, but we can use it as an "outline" to guide us as we write our code. We introduce pseudocode in Chapter 2.

Pseudocode may suffice for small problems, but as problems and the groups of people solving those problems increase in size, the techniques of OOAD become more involved. Ideally, a group should agree on a strictly defined process for solving the problem and on a uniform way of communicating the results of that process with one another. Many different OOAD processes exist; however, a language for communicating the results of any OOAD process has become widely used. This language is known as the *Unified Modeling*

Language (UML). The UML was developed in the mid-1990s, under the initial direction of a trio of software methodologists: Grady Booch, James Rumbaugh and Ivar Jacobson.

History of the UML

In the 1980s, increasing numbers of organizations began using OOP to implement their applications, and a need developed for an established process with which to approach OOAD. Many methodologists—including Booch, Rumbaugh and Jacobson—individually produced and promoted separate processes to satisfy this need. Each of these processes had their own notation, or "language" (in the form of diagrams), to convey the results of analysis and design.

By the early 1990s, different companies, and even different divisions within the same company, were using different processes and notations. Additionally, these companies wanted to use software tools that would support their particular processes. With so many processes, software vendors found it difficult to provide such tools. Clearly, standard processes and notation were needed.

In 1994, James Rumbaugh joined Grady Booch at Rational Software Corporation, and the two began working to unify their popular processes. They soon were joined by Ivar Jacobson. In 1996, the group released early versions of the UML to the software engineering community and requested feedback. Around the same time, an organization known as the *Object Management Group™ (OMG™)* invited submissions for a common modeling language. The OMG is a non-profit organization that promotes the use of object-oriented technology by issuing guidelines and specifications for object-oriented technologies. Several corporations—among them HP, IBM, Microsoft, Oracle and Rational Software— already had recognized the need for a common modeling language. These companies formed the *UML Partners* in response to the OMG's request for proposals. This consortium developed and submitted the UML version 1.1 to the OMG. The OMG accepted the proposal and, in 1997, assumed responsibility for the continuing maintenance and revision of the UML. In 2001, the OMG released the UML version 1.4 (the current version at the time this book was published). Currently, the OMG is working on version 2.0 and plans to release the new version near the end of 2002. The OMG is one of the world's largest consortia with 800 member organizations.

What is the UML?

The Unified Modeling Language is now the most widely used graphical representation scheme for modeling object-oriented systems. It has unified the various notational schemes that existed in the late 1980s. Those who design systems use the language (in the form of diagrams) to model their systems.

One of the most attractive features of the UML is its flexibility. The UML is extendable and is independent of the many OOAD processes. UML modelers can develop systems using various processes, but all developers can express those systems with one standard set of notations.

The UML is a complex, feature-rich graphical language. In our "Thinking About Objects" sections, we present a concise, simplified subset of these features. We then use this subset to guide the reader through a first design experience with the UML intended for the novice object-oriented designer/programmer. For a more complete discussion of the UML, refer to the Object Management Group's Web site (**www.omg.org**) and to the official UML 1.4 specifications document (**www.omg.org/uml**). *The Unified Modeling Language User Guide*, written by Booch, Rumbaugh and Jacobson, is the definitive tutorial to the UML. In addition, several modeling tools have emerged to enable designers to build systems via the UML. The conclusion of Section 5.13 contains links to some of these tools.

Object-oriented technology is ubiquitous in the software industry, and the UML is rapidly becoming so. Our goal in these "Thinking About Objects" sections is to encourage you to think in an object-oriented manner as early, and as often, as possible. Beginning in the "Thinking About Objects" section at the end of Chapter 2, you will apply object technology to implement a solution to a substantial problem. We hope that you find this optional project to be an enjoyable and challenging introduction to object-oriented design with the UML and to object-oriented programming.

1.27 Tour of the Book

In this section, we take a tour of the many capabilities of C++ you will study in *C++ How to Program, 4/e*.

Chapter 1—Introduction to Computers and C++ Programming—discusses what computers are, how they work and how they are programmed. It introduces the notion of structured programming and explains why these techniques have fostered a revolution in the way programs are written. The chapter gives a brief history of the development of programming languages from machine languages, to assembly languages, to high-level languages. The origin of the C++ programming language is discussed. The chapter introduces a typical C++ programming environment and gives a concise introduction to writing C++ programs. A detailed treatment of decision making and arithmetic operations in C++ is presented. We have introduced a new, more open, easier to read "look and feel" for our C++ source programs, most notably using syntax coloring to highlight keywords, comments and regular program text and to make programs more readable. We have also introduced a new background highlight to focus readers' attention on the new features presented in each program. After studying this chapter, the student will understand how to write simple, but complete, C++ programs. We discuss the explosion of interest in the Internet that has occurred with the advent of the World Wide Web. We discuss namespaces and the **using** statements. Readers plunge right into object-orientation in the "Thinking About Objects" section that introduces the basic terminology of object technology.

Chapter 2—Control Structures—introduces the notion of algorithms (procedures) for solving problems. It explains the importance of using control structures effectively in producing programs that are understandable, debuggable, maintainable and more likely to work properly on the first try. It introduces the sequence structure, selection structures (**if**, **if/else** and **switch**) and repetition structures (**while**, **do/while** and **for**). It examines repetition in detail and compares counter-controlled loops and sentinel-controlled loops. It explains the technique of top-down, stepwise refinement that is critical to the production of properly structured programs and presents the popular program design aid, pseudocode. The methods and approaches used in Chapter 2 are applicable to effective use of control structures in any programming language (not just C++). This chapter helps the student develop good programming habits in preparation for dealing with the more substantial programming tasks in the remainder of the text. The chapter concludes with a discussion of logical operators—**&&** (and), **||** (or) and **!** (not). We introduce the **static_cast** operator, which is safer than using the old-style casting C++ inherited from C. We added the "Peter Minuit" exercise, so students can see the wonders of compound interest—with the computer doing most of the work! We discuss the scoping rules for loop counters in **for**-loops. In the optional "Thinking About Objects" section, we begin the first phase of an object-oriented design (OOD) for the elevator simulator—identifying the classes needed to implement the simulator. We also introduce the UML use case, class and object diagrams and discuss the concepts of associations, multiplicity, composition, roles and links.

Chapter 3—Functions—discusses the design and construction of program modules. C++'s function-related capabilities include standard-library functions, programmer-defined functions, recursion, call-by-value and call-by-reference capabilities. The techniques presented in Chapter 3 are essential to the production of properly structured programs, especially the kinds of larger programs and software that system programmers and application programmers are likely to develop in real-world applications. The "divide and conquer" strategy is presented as an effective means for solving complex problems by dividing them into simpler interacting components. Students enjoy the treatment of random numbers and simulation, and they appreciate the discussion of the dice game of craps, which makes elegant use of control structures. The chapter offers a solid introduction to recursion and includes a table summarizing the dozens of recursion examples and exercises distributed throughout the remainder of the book. Some texts leave recursion for a chapter late in the book; we feel this topic is best covered gradually throughout the text. The extensive collection of 60 exercises at the end of the chapter includes several classic recursion problems such as the Towers of Hanoi. The chapter discusses the so-called "C++ enhancements to C," including **inline** functions, reference parameters, default arguments, the unary scope resolution operator, function overloading and function templates. The header files table introduces many of the header files that the reader will use throughout the book. In the optional "Thinking About Objects" section, we determine many of the class attributes needed to implement the elevator simulator. We also introduce the UML statechart and activity diagrams and the concepts of events and actions as they relate to these diagrams.

Chapter 4—Arrays—discusses the structuring of data into arrays, or groups, of related data items of the same type. The chapter presents numerous examples of both single-subscripted arrays and double-subscripted arrays. It is widely recognized that structuring data properly is just as important as using control structures effectively in the development of properly structured programs. Examples in the chapter investigate various common array manipulations, printing histograms, sorting data, passing arrays to functions and an introduction to the field of survey data analysis (with simple statistics). A feature of this chapter is the discussion of elementary sorting and searching techniques and the presentation of binary searching as a dramatic improvement over linear searching. The 121 end-of-chapter exercises include a variety of interesting and challenging problems, such as improved sorting techniques, the design of a simple airline-reservations system, an introduction to the concept of turtle graphics (made famous in the LOGO language) and the Knight's Tour and Eight Queens problems that introduce the notion of heuristic programming so widely employed in the field of artificial intelligence. The exercises conclude with many recursion problems including the selection sort, palindromes, linear search, binary search, the Eight Queens, printing an array, printing a string backwards and finding the minimum value in an array. This chapter still uses C-style arrays, which, as you will see in Chapter 5, are really pointers to the array contents in memory.[7] In the "Thinking About Objects" section of Chapter 4, we determine many of the operations (behaviors) of the classes in the elevator simulation. We also introduce the UML sequence diagram and the concept of messages that objects can send to each other.

Chapter 5—Pointers and Strings—presents one of the most powerful and difficult-to-master features of the C++ language—pointers. The chapter provides detailed explanations of pointer operators, call by reference, pointer expressions, pointer arithmetic, the relationship between pointers and arrays, arrays of pointers and pointers to functions. There is an intimate relationship between pointers, arrays and strings in C++, so we introduce basic string-manipulation concepts and discuss of some of the most popular string-handling functions, such as **getline** (input a line of text), **strcpy** and **strncpy** (copy a string), **strcat** and **strncat** (concatenate two strings), **strcmp** and **strncmp** (compare two strings), **strtok** ("tokenize" a string into its pieces) and **strlen** (compute the length of a string). The 134 chapter exercises include a simulation of the classic race between the tortoise and the hare, card-shuffling and dealing algorithms, recursive quicksort and recursive maze traversals. A special section entitled "Building Your Own Computer" also is included. This section explains machine-language programming and proceeds with a project involving the design and implementation of a computer simulator that allows the reader to write and run machine-language programs. This unique feature of the text will be especially useful to the reader who wants to understand how computers really work. Our students enjoy this project and often implement substantial enhancements, many of which are suggested in the exercises. In Chapter 17, another special section guides the reader through building a compiler; the machine language produced by the compiler then is executed on the machine language simulator produced in the Chapter 5 exercises. Information is communicated from the compiler to the simulator in sequential files, which we discuss in Chapter 14. A second special section includes challenging string-manipulation exercises related to text analysis, word processing, printing dates in various formats, check protection, writing the word equivalent of a check amount, Morse Code and metric-to-English conversions. The reader will want to revisit these string-manipulation exercises after studying class **string** in Chapter 15. Many people find that the topic of pointers is, by far, the most difficult part of an introductory programming course. In C and "raw C++" arrays and strings are pointers to array and string contents in memory (even function names are pointers). Studying this chapter carefully should reward you with a deep understanding of the complex topic of pointers. Again, we cover arrays and strings as full-fledged objects later in the book. In Chapter 8, we use operator overloading to craft customized **Array** and **String** classes. Chapter 8 also introduces Standard Library classes **string** and

---

7. In later chapters, we present arrays as full-fledged objects. In Chapter 8, we use the techniques of operator overloading to craft a valuable **Array** class out of which we create **Array** objects that are much more robust and pleasant to program with than the arrays of Chapter 4. We continue that discussion by introducing C++'s pre-defined **vector** class, which implements a robust array data structure. In Chapter 21, Standard Template Library (STL), we present in-depth coverage class **vector** which, when used with the iterators and algorithms discussed in Chapter 21, creates a solid treatment of arrays as full-fledged objects.

vector for manipulating strings and arrays as objects. These classes are explained in detail in Chapter 15 and Chapter 21, respectively. Chapter 5 is loaded with challenging exercises. Please be sure to try the *Special Section: Building Your Own Computer*. In the "Thinking About Objects" section, we determine many of the collaborations (interactions among objects in the system) needed to implement the elevator system and represent these collaborations using the UML collaboration diagram. We also include a bibliography and a list of Internet and World Wide Web resources that contain the UML specifications and other reference materials, general resources, tutorials, FAQs, articles, whitepapers and software.

Chapter 6—Classes and Data Abstraction—begins our discussion of object-based programming. The chapter represents a wonderful opportunity for teaching data abstraction the "right way"—through a language (C++) expressly devoted to implementing abstract data types (ADTs). In recent years, data abstraction has become a major topic in introductory computing courses. Chapter 6–Chapter 8 include a solid treatment of data abstraction. Chapter 6 discusses implementing ADTs as C++-style **class**es and why this approach is superior to using **struct**s, accessing **class** members, separating interface from implementation, using access functions and utility functions, initializing objects with constructors, destroying objects with destructors, assignment by default memberwise copy and software reusability. The chapter exercises challenge the student to develop classes for complex numbers, rational numbers, times, dates, rectangles, huge integers and playing tic-tac-toe. Students generally enjoy game-playing programs. Mathematically inclined readers will enjoy the exercises on creating class **Complex** (for complex numbers), class **Rational** (for rational numbers) and class **HugeInteger** (for arbitrarily large integers). The "Thinking About Objects" section asks you to write a class header file for each of the classes in your elevator simulator. In the "Thinking About Objects" section, we use the UML class diagram developed in previous sections to outline the C++ header files that define our classes. We also introduce the concept of handles to objects, and we begin to study how to implement handles in C++.

Chapter 7—Classes Part II—continues the study of classes and data abstraction. The chapter discusses declaring and using constant objects, constant member functions, composition—the process of building classes that have objects of other classes as members, **friend** functions and **friend** classes that have special access rights to the **private** and **protected** members of classes, the **this** pointer, which enables an object to know its own address, dynamic memory allocation, **static** class members for containing and manipulating class-wide data, examples of popular abstract data types (arrays, strings and queues), container classes and iterators. The chapter exercises ask the student to develop a savings-account class and a class for holding sets of integers. In our discussion of **const** objects, we briefly mention keyword **mutable** which, as we will see in Chapter 22, is used in a subtle manner to enable modification of "non-visible" implementation in **const** objects. We discuss dynamic memory allocation using **new** and **delete**. When **new** fails, the program terminates by default because **new** "throws an exception" in standard C++. Chapter 13 discusses catching and handling exceptions. We motivate the discussion of **static** class members with a video-game-based example. We emphasize how important it is to hide implementation details from clients of a class; then, we show **private** data in our class headers, which certainly reveals implementation. We discuss proxy classes, which provide a means of hiding implementation from clients of a class. The "Thinking About Objects" section asks you to incorporate dynamic memory management and composition into your elevator simulator. Students will enjoy the exercise creating class **IntegerSet**. This motivates the treatment of operator overloading in Chapter 8. In the "Thinking About Objects" section, we present a complete elevator simulator C++ program (approximately 1,250 lines of code) and a detailed code walkthrough. The code follows directly from the UML-based design created in previous sections and employs our good programming practices, including the proper use of **static** and **const** data members and functions. We also discuss dynamic-memory allocation, composition and object interaction via handles, and how to use forward declarations to avoid the "circular-include" problem.

Chapter 8—Operator Overloading; String and Array Objects—presents one of the most popular topics in our C++ courses. Students really enjoy this material. They find it a perfect match with the discussion of abstract data types in Chapter 6 and Chapter 7. Operator overloading enables the programmer to tell the compiler how to use existing operators with objects of new types. C++ already knows how to use these operators with objects of built-in types, such as integers, floats and characters. But suppose that we create a new **string** class—what would the plus sign mean when used between string objects? Many programmers use plus with strings to mean concatenation. In Chapter 8, the programmer will learn how to "overload" the plus sign, so when it is written between two string objects in an expression, the compiler will generate a function call to an "operator function" that will concatenate the two strings. The chapter discusses the fundamentals of operator overloading, restrictions in operator overloading, overloading with class member functions vs. with nonmember functions, overloading unary and binary operators and converting between types. A feature of the chapter is the collection of substantial case studies including an array class, a string class, a date class, a huge integer class and a complex numbers class (the last two appear with full source code in the exercises). Mathematically inclined students will enjoy creating the **polynomial** class in the exercises. This material is different from what you do in most programming languages and courses. Operator overloading is a complex topic, but an enriching one. Using operator overloading wisely helps you add that extra "polish" to your classes. The discussions of class **Array** and class **String** are particularly valuable to students who will go on to use the standard library classes **string** and **vector**, which are introduced with test programs that use **string** and **vector** to mimic the capabilities shown in the **String** and **Array** examples. Introducing **string** and **vector** here gives students valuable experience with software reuse by using existing classes, rather than "reinventing the wheel." With the techniques of Chapter 6–Chapter 8, it is possible to craft a **Date** class that, if we had been using it for the last two decades, could easily have eliminated a major portion of the so-called "Year 2000 (or Y2K) Problem." The exercises encourage the student to add operator overloading to classes **Complex**, **Rational** and **HugeInteger** to enable convenient manipulation of objects of these classes with operator symbols—as in mathematics—rather than with function calls as the student did in the Chapter 7 exercises.

Chapter 9—Object-Oriented Programming: Inheritance—introduces one of the most fundamental capabilities of object-oriented programming languages. Inheritance is a form of software reusability in which programmers create classes that absorb an existing class's data and behaviors and enhance them with new capabilities. The chapter discusses the notions of base classes and derived classes, **protected** members, **public** inheritance, **protected** inheritance, **private** inheritance, direct base classes, indirect base classes, constructors and destructors in base classes and derived classes, and software engineering with inheritance. The chapter compares inheritance ("is a" relationships) with composition ("has a" relationships) and introduces "uses-a" and "knows-a" relationships. A feature of the chapter is the example that implements a point, circle, cylinder class hierarchy. Using this "mechanical" example, we examine the relationship between base classes and derived classes, then show how derived classes use inherited data members and member functions. In the "Thinking About Objects" section, we update the elevator simulation design and implementation to incorporate inheritance. We also suggest further modifications that the student may design and implement.

Chapter 10—Object-Oriented Programming: Polymorphism—deals with another fundamental capability of object-oriented programming, namely polymorphic behavior. When many classes are related to a common base class through inheritance, each derived-class object may be treated as a base-class object. This enables programs to be written in a general manner independent of the specific types of the derived-class objects. New kinds of objects can be handled by the same program, thus making systems more extensible. Polymorphism enables programs to eliminate complex **switch** logic in favor of simpler "straight-line" logic. A screen manager of a video game, for example, can send a draw message to every object in a linked list of objects to be drawn. Each object knows how to draw itself. An object of a new class can be added to the program without modifying that program (as long as that new object also knows how to draw itself). This style of programming is typically used to implement today's popular graphical user interfaces (GUIs). The chapter discusses the mechanics of achieving polymorphic behavior via **virtual** functions. It distinguishes between abstract classes (from which objects cannot be instantiated) and concrete classes (from which objects can be instantiated). Abstract classes are useful for providing an inheritable interface to classes throughout the hierarchy. We demonstrate abstract classes and polymorphic behavior by revisiting the point, circle, cylinder hierarchy of Chapter 9. We introduce an abstract **Shape** base class, from which class **Point** inherits directly and classes **Circle** and **Cylinder** inherit indirectly. In response to this hierarchy, our professional audiences insisted that we provide a deeper explanation that shows precisely how polymorphism is implemented in C++, and hence, precisely what execution time and memory "costs" are incurred when programming with this powerful capability. We responded by developing an illustration and a precision explanation of the *vtables* (**virtual** function tables) that the C++ compiler builds automatically to support polymorphism. To conclude Chapter 10, we introduce run-time type information (RTTI) and dynamic casting, which enable a program to determine an object's type at execution time, then act on that object accordingly. We show this in the context of a more "natural" inheritance hierarchy—several classes derived from an abstract **Employee** base class, in which each employee has a common **earnings** function to calculate an employee's weekly pay. Using RTTI and dynamic casting, we give a 10% pay increase to employees of a specific type, then calculate the earnings for such employees. For all other employee types, we calculate their earnings.

Chapter 11—Templates—discusses one of the more recent additions to C++. Function templates were introduced in Chapter 3. Chapter 11 presents an additional function template example. Class templates enable the programmer to capture the essence of an abstract data type (such as a stack, an array, or a queue) and create—with minimal additional code—versions of that ADT for particular types (such as a queue of **int**, a queue of **float**, a queue of strings, etc.) and to provide specific type information as a parameter when creating an instance of that ADT. For this reason, class templates often are called parameterized types. The chapter discusses using type parameters and nontype parameters and considers the interaction among templates and other C++ concepts, such as inheritance, **friends** and **static** members. The exercises challenge the student to write a variety of function templates and class templates and to employ these in complete programs. We greatly enhance the treatment of templates in our discussion of the Standard Template Library (STL) containers, iterators and algorithms in Chapter 21.

Chapter 12—C++ Stream Input/Output—contains a comprehensive treatment of standard C++ object-oriented input/output. The chapter discusses the various I/O capabilities of C++, including output with the stream insertion operator, input with the stream-extraction operator, type-safe I/O, formatted I/O, unformatted I/O (for performance), stream manipulators for controlling the numeric base (decimal, octal, or hexadecimal), floating-point-number formatting, controlling field widths, user-defined manipulators, stream format states, stream error states, I/O of objects of user-defined types and tying output streams to input streams (to ensure that prompts appear before the user is expected to enter responses).

Chapter 13—Exception Handling—discusses how exception handling enables programmers to write programs that are robust, fault tolerant and appropriate for business-critical and mission-critical environments. The chapter discusses when exception handling is appropriate; introduces the basic capabilities of exception handling with **try** blocks, **throw** statements and **catch** blocks; indicates how and when to rethrow an exception; explains how to write an exception specification and process unexpected exceptions; and discusses the important ties between exceptions and constructors, destructors and inheritance. The exercises in this chapter show the student the diversity and power of C++'s exception-handling capabilities. We discuss rethrowing an exception, and we illustrate both ways **new** can fail when memory is exhausted. Prior to the C++ draft standard, **new** failed by returning **0**, much as **malloc** fails in C by returning a **NULL** pointer value.We show the new style of **new** failing by throwing a **bad_alloc** (bad allocation) exception. We illustrate how to use **set_new_handler** to specify a custom function to be called to deal with memory-exhaustion situations. We discuss how to use the **auto_ptr** class template to **delete** dynamically allocated memory implicitly, thus avoiding memory leaks. To conclude this chapter, we present the standard library exception hierarchy.

Chapter 14—File Processing—discusses techniques for processing text files with sequential access and random access. The chapter begins with an introduction to the data hierarchy from bits, to bytes, to fields, to records and to files. Next, we present the C++ view of files and streams. We discuss sequential-access files and build programs that show how to open and close files, how to store data sequentially in a file and how to read data sequentially from a file. We then discuss random-access files and build programs that show how to create a file for random access, how to read and write data to a file with random access and how to read data sequentially from a randomly accessed file. The fourth random-access program combines the techniques of accessing files both sequentially and randomly into a complete transaction-processing program. Students in our industry seminars have mentioned that, after studying the material on file processing, they were able to produce substantial file-processing programs that were immediately useful in their organizations. The exercises ask the student to implement a variety of programs that build and process both sequential-access files and random-access files.

Chapter 15—Class `string` and String Stream Processing—The chapter also discusses C++'s capabilities for inputting data from strings in memory and outputting data to strings in memory; these capabilities often are referred to as in-core formatting or string-stream processing. Class **string** is a required component of the standard library. We preserved the treatment of C-like strings in Chapter 5 and later for several reasons. First, it strengthens the reader's understanding of pointers. Second, for the next decade or so, C++ programmers will need to be able to read and modify the enormous amounts of C legacy code that has accumulated over the last quarter of a century—this code processes strings as pointers, as does a large portion of the C++ code that has been written in industry over the last many years. In Chapter 15 we discuss **string** assignment, concatenation and comparison. We show how to determine various **string** characteristics such as a **string**'s size, capacity and whether or not it is empty. We discuss how to resize a **string**. We consider the various *find* functions that enable us to find a substring in a **string** (searching the **string** either forwards or backwards), and we show how to find either the first occurrence or last occurrence of a character selected from a **string** of characters, and how to find the first occurrence or last occurrence of a character that is not in a selected **string** of characters. We show how to replace, erase and insert characters in a **string**. We show how to convert a **string** object to a C-style **char *** string.

Chapter 16—Web Programming with CGI—This new chapter has everything you need to begin developing your own Web-based applications that will really run on the Internet![8] You will learn how to build so-called *n*-tier applications, in which the functionality provided by each tier can be distributed to separate computers across the Internet or executed on the same computer. In particular, we build a three-tier online bookstore application. The bookstore's information is stored in the application's bottom tier, also called the data tier. In industrial-strength applications, the data tier is typically a database such as Oracle, Microsoft® SQL Server or MySQL. For simplicity, we use text files and employ the file-processing techniques of Chapter 14 to access these files. The user enters requests and receives responses at the application's top tier, also called the user-interface tier or the client tier, which is typically a computer running a popular Web browser such as Microsoft Internet Explorer or Netscape®. Web browsers, of course, know how to communicate with Web sites throughout the Internet. The middle tier, also called the business-logic tier, contains both a Web server and an application specific C++ program (e.g., our bookstore application). The Web server communicates with the C++ program (and vice versa) via the CGI (Common Gateway Interface) protocol. This program is referred to as a CGI script. We use the popular Apache Web server, which is available free for download from the Apache Web site, **www.apache.org**. Apache Installation instructions for many popular platforms, including Linux and Windows systems, are available at that site and at **www.deitel.com**

---

8. There are other technologies for developing Web-based applications. Java developers use Java servlets and JavaServer Pages. Microsoft developers use Active Server Pages (ASP). We chose CGI for this book because both standard C++ and CGI are platform independent.

and **www.prenhall.com/deitel**. The Web server knows how to talk to the client tier across the Internet using a protocol called HTTP (Hypertext Transfer Protocol). We discuss the two most popular HTTP methods for sending data to a Web server—**GET** and **POST**. We then discuss the crucial role of the Web server in Web programming and provide a simple example that requests an Extensible HyperText Markup Language (XHTML)[9] document from a Web server. We discuss CGI and how it allows a Web server to communicate with the top tier and CGI applications. We provide a simple example that gets the server's time and renders it in a browser. Other examples demonstrate how to process form-based user input via the string processing techniques introduced in Chapter 15. In our forms-based examples we use buttons, password fields, check boxes and text fields. We present an example of an interactive portal for a travel company that displays airfares to various cities. Travel-club members can log in and view discounted airfares. We also discuss various methods of storing client-specific data, which include hidden fields (i.e., information stored in a Web page but not rendered by the Web browser) and cookies—small text files that the browser stores on the client's machine. The chapter examples conclude with a case study of an online book store that allows users to add books to a shopping cart. This case study contains several CGI scripts that interact to form a complete application. The online book store is password protected, so users first must log in to gain access. The chapter's Web resources include information about the CGI specification, C++ CGI libraries and Web sites related to the Apache Web server.

    Chapter 17—Data Structures—discusses the techniques used to create and manipulate dynamic data structures. The chapter begins with discussions of self-referential classes and dynamic memory allocation, then proceeds with a discussion of how to create and maintain various dynamic data structures, including linked lists, queues (or waiting lines), stacks and trees. For each type of data structure, we present complete, working programs and show sample outputs. The chapter also helps the student master pointers. The chapter includes abundant examples that use indirection and double indirection—particularly difficult concepts. One problem when working with pointers is that students have trouble visualizing the data structures and how their nodes are linked together. We have included illustrations that show the links and the sequence in which they are created. The binary-tree example is a superb capstone for the study of pointers and dynamic data structures. This example creates a binary tree, enforces duplicate elimination and introduces recursive preorder, inorder and postorder tree traversals. Students have a genuine sense of accomplishment when they study and implement this example. They particularly appreciate seeing that the inorder traversal prints the node values in sorted order. We include a substantial collection of exercises. A highlight of the exercises is the special section "Building Your Own Compiler." The exercises walk the student through the development of an infix-to-postfix-conversion program and a postfix-expression-evaluation program. We then modify the postfix-evaluation algorithm to generate machine-language code. The compiler places this code in a file (using the techniques of Chapter 14). Students then run the machine language

---

9. XHTML is a markup language for identifying the elements of an XHTML document (Web page) so that a browser can render (i.e., display) that page on your computer screen. XHTML is a new technology designed by the World Wide Web Consortium to replace the HyperText Markup Language (HTML) as the primary means of specifying Web content. In Appendix E, we introduce XHTML.

produced by their compilers on the software simulators they built in the exercises of Chapter 5. The 47 exercises include recursively searching a list, recursively printing a list backwards, binary-tree node deletion, level-order traversal of a binary tree, printing trees, writing a portion of an optimizing compiler, writing an interpreter, inserting/deleting anywhere in a linked list, implementing lists and queues without tail pointers, analyzing the performance of binary-tree searching and sorting, implementing an indexed-list class and a supermarket simulation that uses queueing. After studying Chapter 17, the reader is prepared for the treatment of STL containers, iterators and algorithms in Chapter 21. The STL containers are pre-packaged, templatized data structures that most programmers will find sufficient for the vast majority of applications they will need to implement. STL is a giant leap forward in achieving the vision of reuse.

Chapter 18—Bits, Characters, Strings and Structures—presents a variety of important features. C++'s powerful bit-manipulation capabilities enable programmers to write programs that exercise lower-level hardware capabilities. This helps programs process bit strings, set individual bits and store information more compactly. Such capabilities, often found only in low-level assembly languages, are valued by programmers writing system software, such as operating systems and networking software. As you recall, we introduced C-style **char *** string manipulation in Chapter 5 and presented the most popular string-manipulation functions. In Chapter 18, we continue our presentation of characters and C-style **char *** strings. We present the various character-manipulation capabilities of the **<cctype>** library—these include the ability to test a character to determine whether it is a digit, an alphabetic character, an alphanumeric character, a hexadecimal digit, a lowercase letter or an uppercase letter. We present the remaining string-manipulation functions of the various string-related libraries; as always, every function is presented in the context of a complete, working C++ program. Structures in C++ are like records in other languages—they aggregate data items of various types. A feature of the chapter is its high-performance card-shuffling and dealing simulation. This is an excellent opportunity for the instructor to emphasize the quality of algorithms. The 91 exercises encourage the student to try out most of the capabilities discussed in the chapter. The feature exercise leads the student through the development of a spelling-checker program. Chapter 1–Chapter 5 and Chapter 18–Chapter 20 are mostly the "C legacy" portion of C++. In particular, this chapter presents a deeper treatment of C-like, **char *** strings for the benefit of C++ programmers who are likely to work with C legacy code. Again, Chapter 15 discusses class **string** and discusses manipulating strings as full-fledged objects.

Chapter 19—Preprocessor—provides detailed discussions of the preprocessor directives. The chapter includes more complete information on the **#include** directive, which causes a copy of a specified file to be included in place of the directive before the file is compiled and the **#define** directive that creates symbolic constants and macros. The chapter explains conditional compilation for enabling the programmer to control the execution of preprocessor directives and the compilation of program code. The **#** operator that converts its operand to a string and the **##** operator that concatenates two tokens are discussed. The various predefined preprocessor symbolic constants (**__LINE__**, **__FILE__**, **__DATE__**, **__STDC__**, **__TIME__** and **__TIMESTAMP__**) are presented. Finally, macro **assert** of the header file **<cassert>** is discussed, which is valuable in program testing, debugging, verification and validation.

Chapter 20—C Legacy-Code Topics—presents additional topics including several advanced topics not ordinarily covered in introductory courses. We show how to redirect program input to come from a file, redirect program output to be placed in a file, redirect the output of one program to be the input of another program (piping) and append the output of a program to an existing file. We develop functions that use variable-length argument lists and show how to pass command-line arguments to function **main** and use them in a program. We discuss how to compile programs whose components are spread across multiple files, register functions with **atexit** to be executed at program termination and terminate program execution with function **exit**. We also discuss the **const** and **volatile** type qualifiers, specifying the type of a numeric constant using the integer and floating-point suffixes, using the signal-handling library to trap unexpected events, creating and using dynamic arrays with **calloc** and **realloc**, using **union**s as a space-saving technique and using linkage specifications when C++ programs are to be linked with legacy C code. As the title suggests, this chapter is intended primarily for C++ programmers who will be working with C legacy code.

Chapter 21—Standard Template Library (STL)—Throughout this book, we discuss the importance of software reuse. Recognizing that many data structures and algorithms commonly were used by C++ programmers, the C++ standard committee added the Standard Template Library (STL) to the C++ Standard Library. The STL defines powerful, template-based, reusable components that implement many common data structures and algorithms used to process those data structures. The STL offers proof of concept for generic programming with templates—introduced in Chapter 11 and demonstrated in detail in Chapter 17. This chapter introduces the STL and discusses its three key components— containers (popular templatized data structures), iterators and algorithms. The STL containers are data structures capable of storing objects of any data type. We will see that there are three container categories—first-class containers, adapters and near containers. STL iterators, which have similar properties to pointers, are used by programs to manipulate the STL-container elements. In fact, standard arrays can be manipulated as STL containers, using standard pointers as iterators. We will see that manipulating containers with iterators is convenient and provides tremendous expressive power when combined with STL algorithms—in some cases, reducing many lines of code to a single statement. STL algorithms are functions that perform common data manipulations such as searching, sorting, comparing elements (or entire data structures), etc. There are approximately 70 algorithms implemented in the STL. Most of these algorithms use iterators to access container elements. We will see that each first-class container supports specific iterator types, some of which are more powerful than others. A container's supported iterator type determines whether the container can be used with a specific algorithm. Iterators encapsulate the mechanism used to access container elements. This encapsulation enables many of the STL algorithms to be applied to several containers without regard for the underlying container implementation. As long as a container's iterators support the minimum requirements of the algorithm, then the algorithm can process that container's elements. This also enables programmers to create algorithms that can process the elements of multiple different container types. Chapter 17 discusses how to implement data structures with pointers, classes and dynamic memory. Pointer-based code is complex, and the slightest omission or oversight can lead to serious memory-access violations and memory-leak errors with no compiler complaints. Implementing additional data structures such as deques, priority queues, sets, maps, etc. requires substantial additional work. In addition, if many programmers on a large project implement similar containers and algorithms for different tasks, the code becomes difficult to modify, maintain and debug. An advantage of the STL is that programmers can reuse the STL containers, iterators and algorithms to implement common data representations and manipulations. This reuse results in substantial development-time and resource savings. This chapter is meant to be an introduction to the STL. It is neither complete nor comprehensive. However, it is a friendly, accessible chapter that should convince you of the value of the STL and encourage further study. This might be one of the most important chapters in the book in terms of your appreciation of software reuse.

Chapter 22—Other Topics—is a collection of miscellaneous C++ topics. This chapter discusses two cast operators—**const_cast** and **reinterpret_cast**. These operators, along with **stat_ _cast** (Chapter 2) and **dynamic_cast** (Chapter 10), provide a more robust mechanism for converting between types than do the original cast operators C++ inherited from C. We discuss namespaces, a feature particularly crucial for software developers who build substantial systems, especially for those who build systems from class libraries. Namespaces prevent naming collisions, which can hinder such large software efforts. We discuss the operator keywords, which are useful for programmers who do not like cryptic operator symbols. The primary use of these symbols is in international markets, where certain characters are not always available on local keyboards. We discuss keyword **explicit**, which prevents the compiler from invoking conversion constructors in undesirable situations; **explicit**-conversion constructors can be invoked only through constructor syntax, not through implicit conversions. We discuss keyword **mutable**, which allows a member of a **const** object to be changed. Previously, this was accomplished by "casting away **const**-ness", which is considered a dangerous practice. We also discuss pointer-to-member operators **.*** and **->***, multiple inheritance (including the problem of "diamond inheritance") and **virtual** base classes.

Appendix A—Operator Precedence Chart—presents the complete set of C++ operator symbols, in which each operator appears on a line by itself with the operator symbol, its name and its associativity.

Appendix B—ASCII Character Set—All the programs in this book use the ASCII character set, which is presented in this appendix

Appendix C—Number Systems—discusses the binary, octal, decimal and hexadecimal number systems. It considers how to convert numbers between bases and explains the one's complement and two's complement binary representations.

Appendix D—C++ Internet and Web Resources—contains a listing of valuable C++ resources, such as demos, information about popular compilers (including "freebies"), books, articles, conferences, job banks, journals, magazines, help, tutorials, FAQs (frequently asked questions), newsgroups, Web-based courses, product news and C++ development tools.

Appendix E—Introduction to XHTML—provides an introduction to XHTML—a markup language for describing the elements of a Web page so that a browser, such as Microsoft Internet Explorer or Netscape, can render that page. The reader should be familiar with the contents of this appendix before studying Chapter 16, Web Programming with CGI. This appendix does not contain any C++ programming. Some key topics covered include incorporating text and images in an XHTML document, linking to other XHTML documents, incorporating special characters (such as copyright and trademark symbols) into an XHTML document, separating parts of an XHTML document with horizontal lines (called *horizontal rules*), presenting information in lists and tables, and collecting information from users browsing a site.

Appendix F—XHTML Special Characters—lists many commonly used XHTML special characters, called *character entity references*.

Bibliography—over 100 books and articles to encourage the student to do further reading on C++ and OOP.

Index—The book contains a comprehensive index to enable the reader to locate by keyword any term or concept throughout the text.

SUMMARY

- A computer is a device capable of performing computations and making logical decisions at speeds millions and even billions of times faster than human beings can.
- Computers process data under the control of computer programs.
- The various devices (such as the keyboard, screen, disks, memory and processing units) that comprise a computer system are referred to as hardware.
- The computer programs that run on a computer are referred to as software.
- The input unit is the "receiving" section of the computer. Most information is entered into computers today through typewriter-like keyboards.
- The output unit is the "shipping" section of the computer. Most information is output from computers today by displaying it on screens or by printing it on paper.
- The memory unit is the "warehouse" section of the computer and is often called either memory or primary memory.
- The arithmetic and logic unit (ALU) performs calculations and makes decisions.
- Programs or data not actively being used by the other units are normally placed on secondary storage devices (such as disks) until they are again needed.
- In single-user batch processing, the computer runs a single program at a time while processing data in groups or batches.
- Operating systems are software systems that make it more convenient to use computers and to get the best performance from computers.
- Multiprogramming operating systems enable the "simultaneous" operation of many jobs on the computer—the computer shares its resources among the jobs.
- Timesharing is a special case of multiprogramming in which users access the computer through terminals. The users' programs appear to be running simultaneously.
- With distributed computing, an organization's computing is distributed via networking to the sites where the work of the organization is performed.
- Servers store programs and data that may be shared by client computers distributed throughout a network, hence the term client/server computing.

- Any computer can directly understand only its own machine language. Machine languages generally consist of strings of numbers (ultimately reduced to 1s and 0s) that instruct computers to perform their most elementary operations one at a time. Machine languages are machine-dependent.

- English-like abbreviations form the basis of assembly languages. Assemblers translate assembly language programs into machine language.

- Compilers translate high-level language programs into machine language. High-level languages contain English words and conventional mathematical notations.

- Interpreter programs directly execute high-level language programs without the need for compiling those programs into machine language.

- Although compiled programs execute faster than interpreted programs, interpreters are popular in program-development environments in which programs are recompiled frequently as new features are added and errors are corrected. Once a program is developed, a compiled version can then be produced to run more efficiently.

- It is possible to write programs in C and C++ that are portable to most computers.

- FORTRAN (FORmula TRANslator) is used for mathematical applications. COBOL (COmmon Business Oriented Language) is used primarily for commercial applications that require precise and efficient manipulation of large amounts of data.

- Structured programming is a disciplined approach to writing programs that are clearer than unstructured programs, easier to test and debug and easier to modify.

- Pascal was designed for teaching structured programming in academic environments.

- Ada was developed under the sponsorship of the United States Department of Defense (DOD) using Pascal as a base.

- Multitasking allows programmers to specify parallel activities.

- All C++ systems consist of three parts: the environment, the language and the standard libraries. Library functions are not part of the C++ language itself; these functions perform operations such as popular mathematical calculations.

- C++ programs typically go through six phases to be executed: edit, preprocess, compile, link, load and execute.

- The programmer types a program with an editor and makes corrections if necessary. C++ file names typically end with the one of the extensions **.cpp**, **.cxx**, **.cc** or **.C** extension.

- A compiler translates a C++ program into machine-language code (or object code; note that this use of the term "object" is unrelated to that in "object-oriented programming").

- The preprocessor obeys preprocessor directives, which typically indicate files to be included in the file being compiled and special symbols to be replaced with program text.

- A linker links the object code with the code for missing functions to produce an executable image (with no missing pieces). If the program compiles and links correctly, an executable file is produced. This is the executable image of the program.

- A loader takes an executable image from disk and transfers it to memory.

- A computer, under the control of its CPU, executes a program one instruction at a time.

- Errors like division-by-zero errors can occur as a program runs, so these errors are called run-time errors or execution-time errors.

- Divide-by-zero is generally a fatal error, i.e., an error that causes the program to terminate immediately without having successfully performed its job. Non-fatal errors allow programs to run to completion, often producing incorrect results.

- Certain C++ functions take their input from **cin** (the standard input stream) which is normally the keyboard, but **cin** can be connected to another device. Data is output to **cout** (the standard output stream) which is normally the computer screen, but **cout** can be connected to another device.

- The standard error stream is referred to as **cerr**. The **cerr** stream (normally connected to the screen) is used for displaying error messages.

- There are many variations between different C++ implementations and different computers that make portability an elusive goal.

- C++ provides capabilities for object-oriented programming.

- Objects are essentially reusable software components that model items in the real world. Objects are made from "blueprints" called classes.

- Single-line comments begin with **//**. Programmers insert comments to document programs and improve their readability. Comments do not cause the computer to perform any action when the program is run.

- The line **#include <iostream>** tells the C++ preprocessor to include the contents of the input/output stream header file in the program. This file contains information necessary to compile programs that use **std::cin** and **std::cout** and operators **<<** and **>>**.

- C++ programs begin executing at the function **main**.

- The output stream object **std::cout**—normally connected to the screen—is used to output data. Multiple data items can be output by concatenating stream insertion (**<<**) operators.

- The input stream object **std::cin**—normally connected to the keyboard—is used to input data. Multiple data items can be input by concatenating stream extraction (**>>**) operators.

- All variables in a C++ program must be declared before they can be used.

- A variable name in C++ is any valid identifier. An identifier is a series of characters consisting of letters, digits and underscores (_). Identifiers cannot start with a digit. C++ identifiers can be any length; however, some systems and/or C++ implementations may impose some restrictions on the length of identifiers.

- C++ is case sensitive.

- Most calculations are performed in assignment statements.

- Every variable stored in the computer's memory has a name, a value, a type and a size.

- Whenever a new value is placed in a memory location, it replaces the previous value in that location. The previous value is lost.

- When a value is read from memory, the process is nondestructive, i.e., a copy of the value is read leaving the original value undisturbed in the memory location.

- C++ evaluates arithmetic expressions in a precise sequence determined by the rules of operator precedence and associativity.

- The **if** statement allows a program to make a decision when a certain condition is met. The format for an **if** statement is

```
if ( condition )
   statement ;
```

If the condition is true, the statement in the body of the **if** is executed. If the condition is not met, i.e., the condition is false, the body statement is skipped.

- Conditions in **if** statements are commonly formed by using equality operators and relational operators. The result of using these operators is always the observation of true or false.

- The statements

  ```
  using std::cout;
  using std::cin;
  using std::endl;
  ```

  are **_using_** _statements_ that eliminate the need to repeat the **std::** prefix. Once we include these **using** statements, we can write **cout** instead of **std::cout**, **cin** instead of **std::cin** and **endl** instead of **std::endl**, respectively, in the remainder of a program.

- Object-orientation is a natural way of thinking about the world and of writing computer programs.

- Objects have attributes (like size, shape, color, weight and the like) and they exhibit behaviors.

- Humans learn about objects by studying their attributes and observing their behaviors.

- Different objects can have many of the same attributes and exhibit similar behaviors.

- Object-oriented programming (OOP) models real-world objects with software counterparts. It takes advantage of class relationships where objects of a certain class have the same characteristics and behaviors. It takes advantage of inheritance relationships and even multiple inheritance relationships where newly created classes are derived by inheriting characteristics of existing classes, yet contain unique characteristics of their own.

- Object-oriented programming provides an intuitive way to view the programming process, namely by modeling real-world objects, their attributes and their behaviors.

- OOP also models communication between objects via messages.

- OOP encapsulates data (attributes) and functions (behavior) into objects.

- Objects have the property of information hiding. Although objects may know how to communicate with one another across well-defined interfaces, objects normally are not allowed to know implementation details of other objects (to eliminate unnecessary dependencies).

- Information hiding is crucial to good software engineering.

- In C and other procedural programming languages, programming tends to be action-oriented. Data is certainly important in C, but the view is that data exists primarily in support of the actions that functions perform.

- C++ programmers concentrate on creating their own user-defined types called classes. Each class contains data as well as the set of functions that manipulate the data. The data components of a class are called data members. The function components of a class are called member functions or methods.

TERMINOLOGY

// comment	association
/* ... */ comment	associativity of operators
abstraction	attribute
action	attributes of an object
action-oriented programming	behavior
analysis	behaviors of an object
ANSI/ISO standard C	binary operator
ANSI/ISO standard C++	body of a function
arithmetic and logic unit (ALU)	Booch, Grady
arithmetic operators	C
assembly language	C++
assignment operator (**=**)	C++ standard library

case sensitive
central processing unit (CPU)
cerr object
cin object
clarity
class
client/server computing
comma-separated list
comment (**//**)
compile error
compile-time error
compiler
component
computer
computer program
condition
cout object
CPU
"crafting valuable classes"
data
data member
decision
declaration
design
distributed computing
editor
encapsulate
equality operators
    == "is equal to"
    != "is not equal to"
escape character (****)
escape sequence
execution-time error
fatal error
file server
flow of control
function
hardware
high-level language
identifier
if structure
information hiding
inheritance
input device
input/output (I/O)
instantiate
int
integer (**int**)
integer division
interface

interpreter
iostream
Jacobson, Ivar
left-to-right associativity
linking
logic error
machine dependent
machine independent
machine language
main
member function
memory
memory location
message
method
modeling
multiple inheritance
modulus operator (**%**)
multiple inheritance
multiplication operator (*****)
multiprocessor
multitasking
nested parentheses
newline character (**\n**)
non-fatal error
nouns in a system specification
object
Object Management Group (OMG)
object-oriented analysis and design (OOAD)
object-oriented design (OOD)
object-oriented programming (OOP)
operand
operator
operator associativity
output device
parentheses **()**
precedence
preprocessor
primary memory
procedural programming
procedural programming language
programming language
prompt
pseudocode
Rational Software Corporation
relational operators
    < "is less than"
    <= "is less than or equal to"
    > "is greater than"
    >= "is greater than or equal to"

requirements
reserved words
requirements
reuse
right-to-left associativity
rules of operator precedence
Rumbaugh, James
run-time error
semicolon (**;**) statement terminator
software
software asset
software reusability
standard error object (**cerr**)
standard input object (**cin**)
standard output object (**cout**)
state
statement
statement terminator (**;**)
std::cerr

std::cin
std::cout
std::endl
string
structured programming
syntax error
translator program
UML Partners
Unified Modeling Language (UML)
using
using std::cerr;
using std::cin;
using std::cout;
using std::endl;
variable
variable name
variable value
verbs in a system specification
white-space characters

SELF-REVIEW EXERCISES

1.1   Fill in the blanks in each of the following:
   a) The company that popularized personal computing was _____.
   b) The computer that made personal computing legitimate in business and industry was the _____.
   c) Computers process data under the control of sets of instructions called computer _____.
   d) The six key logical units of the computer are the _____, _____, _____, _____, _____ and the _____.
   e) The three classes of languages discussed in the chapter are _____, _____ and _____.
   f) The programs that translate high-level language programs into machine language are called _____.
   g) C is widely known as the development language of the _____ operating system.
   h) The _____ language was developed by Wirth for teaching structured programming in universities.
   i) The Department of Defense developed the Ada language with a capability called _____, which allows programmers to specify that many activities can proceed in parallel.

1.2   Fill in the blanks in each of the following sentences about the C++ environment.
   a) C++ programs are normally typed into a computer using a(n) _____ program.
   b) In a C++ system, a(n) _____ program executes before the compiler's translation phase begins.
   c) The _____ program combines the output of the compiler with various library functions to produce an executable image.
   d) The _____ program transfers the executable image of a C++ program from disk to memory.

1.3   Fill in the blanks in each of the following.
  a) Every C++ program begins execution at the function _____.
  b) The _____ begins the body of every function and the _____ ends the body of every function.
  c) Every statement ends with a(n) _____.
  d) The escape sequence **\n** represents the _____ character, which causes the cursor to position to the beginning of the next line on the screen.
  e) The _____ statement is used to make decisions.

1.4   State whether each of the following is *true* or *false*. If *false*, explain why. Assume the statement **using std::cout;** is used.
  a) Comments cause the computer to print the text after the **//** on the screen when the program is executed.
  b) The escape sequence **\n** when output with **cout** causes the cursor to position to the beginning of the next line on the screen.
  c) All variables must be declared before they are used.
  d) All variables must be given a type when they are declared.
  e) C++ considers the variables **number** and **NuMbEr** to be identical.
  f) Declarations can appear almost anywhere in the body of a C++ function.
  g) The modulus operator (**%**) can be used only with integer operands.
  h) The arithmetic operators *****, **/**, **%**, **+** and **−** all have the same level of precedence.
  i) A C++ program that prints three lines of output must contain three output statements using **cout**.

1.5   Write a single C++ statement to accomplish each of the following: (Assume that **using** statements have not been used)
  a) Declare the variables **c**, **thisIsAVariable**, **q76354** and **number** to be of type **int**.
  b) Prompt the user to enter an integer. End your prompting message with a colon (**:**) followed by a space and leave the cursor positioned after the space.
  c) Read an integer from the user at the keyboard and store the value entered in integer variable **age**.
  d) If the variable **number** is not equal to **7**, print **"The variable number is not equal to 7"**.
  e) Print the message **"This is a C++ program"** on one line.
  f) Print the message **"This is a C++ program"** on two lines, in which the first line ends with **C++**.
  g) Print the message **"This is a C++ program"** with each word of the message on a separate line.
  h) Print the message **"This is a C++ program"** with each word separated from the next by a tab.

1.6   Write a statement (or comment) to accomplish each of the following: (Assume that **using** statements have been used)
  a) State that a program calculates the product of three integers.
  b) Declare the variables **x**, **y**, **z** and **result** to be of type **int**.
  c) Prompt the user to enter three integers.
  d) Read three integers from the keyboard and store them in the variables **x**, **y** and **z**.
  e) Compute the product of the three integers contained in variables **x**, **y** and **z**, and assign the result to the variable **result**.
  f) Print **"The product is "** followed by the value of the variable **result**.
  g) Return a value from **main** indicating that the program terminated successfully.

1.7   Using the statements you wrote in Exercise 1.6, write a complete program that calculates and displays the product of three integers. [*Note*: you will need to write the necessary **using** statements.]

1.8   Identify and correct the errors in each of the following statements (assume that the statement **using std::cout;** is used):

       a) `if ( c < 7 );`
            `cout << "c is less than 7\n";`
       b) `if ( c => 7 )`
            `cout << "c is equal to or greater than 7\n";`

1.9   Fill the correct "object speak" term into the blanks in each of the following:

       a) Humans can look at a TV screen and see dots of color, or they can step back and see three people sitting at a conference table; this is an example of a capability called _____.

       b) If we view a car as an object, the fact that the car is a convertible is a(n) attribute/behavior (pick one) _____ of the car.

       c) The fact that a car can accelerate or decelerate, turn left or turn right, or go forward or backward are all examples of _____ of a car object.

       d) When a new class inherits characteristics from several different existing classes, this is called _____ inheritance.

       e) Objects communicate by sending each other _____.

       f) Objects communicate with one another across well-defined _____.

       g) Each object is ordinarily not allowed to know how other objects are implemented; this property is called _____.

       h) The _____ in a system specification help the C++ programmer determine the classes that will be needed to implement the system.

       i) The data components of a class are called _____ and the function components of a class are called _____.

       j) An instance of a user-defined type is called a(n) _____.

ANSWERS TO SELF-REVIEW EXERCISES

1.1   a) Apple.   b) IBM Personal Computer.   c) programs.   d) input unit, output unit, memory unit, arithmetic and logic unit, central processing unit, secondary storage unit. e) machine languages, assembly languages, high-level languages. f) compilers. g) UNIX. h) Pascal. i) multitasking.

1.2   a) editor.   b) preprocessor.   c) linker.   d) loader.

1.3   a) **main**.   b) Left brace (**{**), right brace (**}**).   c) Semicolon.   d) newline.   e) **if**.

1.4   a) False. Comments do not cause any action to be performed when the program is executed. They are used to document programs and improve their readability.

       b) True.
       c) True.
       d) True.
       e) False. C++ is case sensitive, so these variables are unique.
       f) True.
       g) True.
       h) False. The operators *****, **/** and **%** have the same precedence, and the operators **+** and **–** have a lower precedence.
       i) False. A single output statement using cout containing multiple **\n** escape sequences can print several lines.

1.5   a) `int c, thisIsAVariable, q76354, number;`
       b) `std::cout << "Enter an integer: ";`

c) `std::cin >> age;`
d) `if ( number != 7 )`
   `    std::cout << "The variable number is not equal to 7\n";`
e) `std::cout << "This is a C++ program\n";`
f) `std::cout << "This is a C++\nprogram\n";`
g) `std::cout << "This\nis\na\nC++\nprogram\n";`
h) `std::cout << "This\tis\ta\tC++\tprogram\n";`

1.6 a) `// Calculate the product of three integers`
     b) `int x;`
        `int y;`
        `int z;`
        `int result;`
     c) `cout << "Enter three integers: ";`
     d) `cin >> x >> y >> z;`
     e) `result = x * y * z;`
     f) `cout << "The product is " << result << endl;`
     g) `return 0;`

1.7
```
// Calculate the product of three integers
#include <iostream>

using std::cout;
using std::cin;
using std::endl;

int main()
{
    int x;
    int y;
    int z;
    int result;

    cout << "Enter three integers: ";
    cin >> x >> y >> z;
    result = x * y * z;
    cout << "The product is " << result << endl;

    return 0;
} // end function main
```

1.8 a) Error: Semicolon after the right parenthesis of the condition in the **if** statement. Correction: Remove the semicolon after the right parenthesis. [*Note*: The result of this error is that the output statement will be executed whether or not the condition in the **if** statement is true.] The semicolon after the right parenthesis is considered a null (or empty) statement—a statement that does nothing. We will learn more about the null statement in the next chapter.
     b) Error: The relational operator =>. Correction: Change => to >=.

1.9 a) abstraction. b) attribute. c) behaviors. d) multiple. e) messages. f) interfaces. g) information hiding. h) nouns. i) data members; member functions or methods. j) object.

EXERCISES

1.10 Categorize each of the following items as either hardware or software:
  a) CPU
  b) C++ compiler
  c) ALU
  d) C++ preprocessor
  e) input unit
  f) an editor program

1.11 Why might you want to write a program in a machine-independent language instead of writing one in a machine-dependent language? Why might a machine-dependent language be more appropriate for writing certain types of programs?

1.12 Fill in the blanks in each of the following statements:
  a) Which logical unit of the computer receives information from outside the computer for use by the computer? _____.
  b) The process of instructing the computer to solve specific problems is called _____.
  c) What type of computer language uses English-like abbreviations for machine language instructions? _____.
  d) Which logical unit of the computer sends information that has already been processed by the computer to various devices so that the information may be used outside the computer? _____.
  e) Which logical unit of the computer retains information? _____.
  f) Which logical unit of the computer performs calculations? _____.
  g) Which logical unit of the computer makes logical decisions? _____.
  h) The level of computer language most convenient to the programmer for writing programs quickly and easily is _____.
  i) The only language a computer directly understands is called that computer's _____.
  j) Which logical unit of the computer coordinates the activities of all the other logical units? _____.

1.13 Discuss the meaning of each of the following objects:
  a) **std::cin**
  b) **std::cout**
  c) **std::cerr**

1.14 Why is so much attention today focused on object-oriented programming in general and C++ in particular?

1.15 Fill in the blanks in each of the following:
  a) _____ are used to document a program and improve its readability.
  b) The object used to print information on the screen is _____.
  c) A C++ statement that makes a decision is _____.
  d) Calculations are normally performed by _____ statements.
  e) The _____ object inputs values from the keyboard.

1.16 Write a single C++ statement or line that accomplishes each of the following:
  a) Print the message **"Enter two numbers"**.
  b) Assign the product of variables **b** and **c** to variable **a**.
  c) State that a program performs a sample payroll calculation (i.e., use text that helps to document a program).
  d) Input three integer values from the keyboard and into integer variables **a**, **b** and **c**.

1.17   State which of the following are *true* and which are *false*. If *false*, explain your answers.
    a) C++ operators are evaluated from left to right.
    b) The following are all valid variable names: **_under_bar_, m928134, t5, j7, her_sales, his_account_total, a, b, c, z, z2**.
    c) The statement **cout << "a = 5;";** is a typical example of an assignment statement.
    d) A valid C++ arithmetic expression with no parentheses is evaluated from left to right.
    e) The following are all invalid variable names: **3g, 87, 67h2, h22, 2h**.

1.18   Fill in the blanks in each of the following:
    a) What arithmetic operations are on the same level of precedence as multiplication? _____.
    b) When parentheses are nested, which set of parentheses is evaluated first in an arithmetic expression? _____.
    c) A location in the computer's memory that may contain different values at various times throughout the execution of a program is called a _____.

1.19   What, if anything, prints when each of the following C++ statements is performed? If nothing prints, then answer "nothing." Assume **x = 2** and **y = 3**.
    a) **cout << x;**
    b) **cout << x + x;**
    c) **cout << "x=";**
    d) **cout << "x = " << x;**
    e) **cout << x + y << " = " << y + x;**
    f) **z = x + y;**
    g) **cin >> x >> y;**
    h) **// cout << "x + y = " << x + y;**
    i) **cout << "\n";**

1.20   Which of the following C++ statements contain variables whose values are replaced?
    a) **cin >> b >> c >> d >> e >> f;**
    b) **p = i + j + k + 7;**
    c) **cout << "variables whose values are replaced";**
    d) **cout << "a = 5";**

1.21   Given the algebraic equation $y = ax^3 + 7$, which of the following, if any, are correct C++ statements for this equation?
    a) **y = a * x * x * x + 7;**
    b) **y = a * x * x * (x + 7);**
    c) **y = (a * x) * x * (x + 7);**
    d) **y = (a * x) * x * x + 7;**
    e) **y = a * (x * x * x) + 7;**
    f) **y = a * x * (x * x + 7);**

1.22   State the order of evaluation of the operators in each of the following C++ statements and show the value of **x** after each statement is performed.
    a) **x = 7 + 3 * 6 / 2 - 1;**
    b) **x = 2 % 2 + 2 * 2 - 2 / 2;**
    c) **x = (3 * 9 * (3 + (9 * 3 / (3))));**

1.23   Write a program that asks the user to enter two numbers, obtains the two numbers from the user and prints the sum, product, difference, and quotient of the two numbers.

1.24   Write a program that prints the numbers 1 to 4 on the same line with each pair of adjacent numbers separated by one space. Write the program using the following methods:

    a) Using one output statement with one stream insertion operator.

    b) Using one output statement with four stream insertion operators.

    c) Using four output statements.

1.25 Write a program that asks the user to enter two integers, obtains the numbers from the user, then prints the larger number followed by the words "**is larger.**" If the numbers are equal, print the message "**These numbers are equal.**"

1.26 Write a program that inputs three integers from the keyboard and prints the sum, average, product, smallest and largest of these numbers. The screen dialogue should appear as follows:

```
Input three different integers: 13 27 14
Sum is 54
Average is 18
Product is 4914
Smallest is 13
Largest is 27
```

1.27 Write a program that reads in the radius of a circle and prints the circle's diameter, circumference and area. Use the constant value 3.14159 for π. Do these calculations in output statements. [*Note*: In this chapter, we have discussed only integer constants and variables. In Chapter 3 we discuss floating-point numbers, i.e., values that can have decimal points.]

1.28 Write a program that prints a box, an oval, an arrow and a diamond as follows:

1.29 What does the following code print?

```
cout << "*\n**\n***\n****\n*****\n";
```

1.30 Write a program that reads in five integers and determines and prints the largest and the smallest integers in the group. Use only the programming techniques you learned in this chapter.

1.31 Write a program that reads an integer and determines and prints whether it is odd or even. (Hint: Use the modulus operator. An even number is a multiple of two. Any multiple of two leaves a remainder of zero when divided by 2.)

1.32 Write a program that reads in two integers and determines and prints if the first is a multiple of the second. (Hint: Use the modulus operator.)

1.33 Display the following checkerboard pattern with eight output statements, then display the same pattern using as few output statements as possible.

1.34   Distinguish between the terms fatal error and non-fatal error. Why might you prefer to experience a fatal error rather than a non-fatal error?

1.35   Here is a peek ahead. In this chapter you learned about integers and the type **int**. C++ can also represent uppercase letters, lowercase letters and a considerable variety of special symbols. C++ uses small integers internally to represent each different character. The set of characters a computer uses and the corresponding integer representations for those characters is called that computer's *character set*. You can print a character by enclosing that character in single quotes as with

```
cout << 'A';
```

You can print the integer equivalent of a character using **static_cast** as follows:

```
cout << static_cast< int >( 'A' );
```

This is called a *cast* operation (we formally introduce casts in Chapter 2). When the preceding statement executes, it prints the value 65 (on systems that use the *ASCII character set*). Write a program that prints the integer equivalents of some uppercase letters, lowercase letters, digits and special symbols. At a minimum, determine the integer equivalents of the following: **A B C a b c 0 1 2 $ * + /** and the blank character.

1.36   Write a program that inputs a five-digit number, separates the number into its individual digits and prints the digits separated from one another by three spaces each. (Hint: Use the integer division and modulus operators.) For example, if the user types in 42339 the program should print:

```
4    2    3    3    9
```

1.37   Using only the techniques you learned in this chapter, write a program that calculates the squares and cubes of the numbers from 0 to 10 and uses tabs to print the following table of values:

```
number  square  cube
0       0       0
1       1       1
2       4       8
3       9       27
4       16      64
5       25      125
6       36      216
7       49      343
8       64      512
9       81      729
10      100     1000
```

1.38 Give a brief answer to each of the following "object think" questions:

    a) Why does this text choose to discuss structured programming in detail before proceeding with an in-depth treatment of object-oriented programming?

    b) What are the typical steps (mentioned in the text) of an object-oriented design process?

    c) How is multiple inheritance exhibited by human beings?

    d) What kinds of messages do people send to one another?

    e) Objects send messages to one another across well-defined interfaces. What interfaces does a car radio (object) present to its user (a person object)?

1.39 You are probably wearing on your wrist one of the world's most common types of objects—a watch. Discuss how each of the following terms and concepts applies to the notion of a watch: object, attributes, behaviors, class, inheritance (consider, for example, an alarm clock), abstraction, modeling, messages, encapsulation, interface, information hiding, data members and member functions.

2

Control Structures

Objectives

- To understand basic problem-solving techniques.
- To be able to develop algorithms through the process of top-down, stepwise refinement.
- To be able to use the **if**, **if/else** and **switch** selection structures to choose among alternative actions.
- To be able to use the **while**, **do/while** and **for** repetition structures to execute statements in a program repeatedly.
- To understand counter-controlled repetition and sentinel-controlled repetition.
- To be able to use the increment, decrement, assignment and logical operators.
- To be able to use the **break** and **continue** program control statements.

Let's all move one place on.
Lewis Carroll

The wheel is come full circle.
William Shakespeare

Who can control his fate?
William Shakespeare

The used key is always bright.
Benjamin Franklin

Outline

2.1	Introduction
2.2	Algorithms
2.3	Pseudocode
2.4	Control Structures
2.5	`if` Selection Structure
2.6	`if/else` Selection Structure
2.7	`while` Repetition Structure
2.8	Formulating Algorithms: Case Study 1 (Counter-Controlled Repetition)
2.9	Formulating Algorithms with Top-Down, Stepwise Refinement: Case Study 2 (Sentinel-Controlled Repetition)
2.10	Formulating Algorithms with Top-Down, Stepwise Refinement: Case Study 3 (Nested Control Structures)
2.11	Assignment Operators
2.12	Increment and Decrement Operators
2.13	Essentials of Counter-Controlled Repetition
2.14	`for` Repetition Structure
2.15	Examples Using the `for` Structure
2.16	`switch` Multiple-Selection Structure
2.17	`do/while` Repetition Structure
2.18	`break` and `continue` Statements
2.19	Logical Operators
2.20	Confusing Equality (==) and Assignment (=) Operators
2.21	Structured-Programming Summary
2.22	(Optional Case Study) Thinking About Objects: Identifying a System's Classes from a Problem Statement

Summary • Terminology • Self-Review Exercises • Answers to Self-Review Exercises • Exercises

2.1 Introduction

Before writing a program to solve a particular problem, it is essential to have a thorough understanding of the problem and a carefully planned approach to solving the problem. When writing a program, it is equally essential to understand the types of building blocks that are available and to employ proven program-construction principles. This chapter discusses all of these issues in our presentation of the theory and principles of structured programming. The techniques that you will learn here are applicable to most high-level languages, including C++. When we begin our treatment of object-oriented programming in C++ in Chapter 6, we will see that the control structures we study here in Chapter 2 are helpful in building and manipulating objects.

2.2 Algorithms

Any computing problem can be solved by executing a series of actions in a specific order. A *procedure* for solving a problem in terms of

1. the *actions* to execute and

2. the *order* in which these actions execute

is called an *algorithm*. The following example demonstrates that correctly specifying the order in which the actions execute is important.

Consider the "rise-and-shine algorithm" followed by one junior executive for getting out of bed and going to work: (1) Get out of bed, (2) take off pajamas, (3) take a shower, (4) get dressed, (5) eat breakfast, (6) carpool to work.

This routine gets the executive to work well prepared to make critical decisions. Suppose that the same steps are performed in a slightly different order: (1) Get out of bed, (2) take off pajamas, (3) get dressed, (4) take a shower, (5) eat breakfast, (6) carpool to work.

In this case, our junior executive shows up for work soaking wet. Specifying the order in which statements (actions) execute in a computer program is called *program control*. This chapter investigates C++'s program-control capabilities.

2.3 Pseudocode

Pseudocode is an artificial and informal language that helps programmers develop algorithms. The pseudocode we present here is particularly useful for developing algorithms that will be converted to structured portions of C++ programs. Pseudocode is similar to everyday English; it is convenient and user friendly, although it is not an actual computer programming language.

Pseudocode does not execute on computers. Rather, pseudocode helps the programmer "think out" a program before attempting to write it in a programming language, such as C++. This chapter provides several examples of how to use pseudocode effectively in developing C++ programs.

The style of pseudocode we present consists purely of characters, so programmers can type pseudocode conveniently, using any editor program. The computer can produce a freshly printed copy of a pseudocode program on demand. A carefully prepared pseudocode program can easily be converted to a corresponding C++ program. In many cases, this requires simply replacing pseudocode statements with C++ equivalents.

Pseudocode normally describes only *executable statements*—the actions that occur after a programmer converts a program from pseudocode to C++ and the program is run on a computer. Declarations are not executable statements. For example, the declaration

```
int i;
```

tells the compiler variable **i**'s type and instructs the compiler to reserve space in memory for the variable. This declaration does not cause any action—such as input, output or a calculation—to occur when the program executes. Some programmers choose to list variables and mention their purposes at the beginning of the pseudocode representation of a program.

2.4 Control Structures

Normally, statements in a program execute one after the other in the order in which they are written. This is called *sequential execution*. Various C++ statements we will soon discuss enable the programmer to specify that the next statement to execute may be other than the next one in sequence. This is called *transfer of control*.

During the 1960s, it became clear that the indiscriminate use of transfers of control was the root of much difficulty experienced by software-development groups. The finger of blame was pointed at the **goto** *statement*, which allows the programmer to specify a transfer of control to one of a wide range of possible destinations in a program. The notion of so-called *structured programming* became almost synonymous with "*goto elimination.*"

The research of Bohm and Jacopini[1] demonstrated that programs could be written without any **goto** statements. The challenge of the era became for programmers to shift their styles to "**goto**-less programming." It was not until the 1970s that programmers started taking structured programming seriously. The results have been impressive as software development groups have reported reduced development times, more frequent on-time delivery of systems and more frequent within-budget completion of software projects. The key to these successes is that structured programs are clearer, are easier to debug, test and modify and are more likely to be bug-free in the first place.

Bohm and Jacopini's work demonstrated that all programs could be written in terms of only three *control structures*, namely, the *sequence structure*, the *selection structure* and the *repetition structure*. The sequence structure is built into C++. Unless directed otherwise, the computer executes C++ statements one after the other in the order in which they are written. The UML *activity diagram* of Fig. 2.1 illustrates a typical sequence structure in which two calculations are performed in order. C++ allows us to have as many actions as we want in a sequence structure. As we will soon see, anywhere a single action may be placed, we may place several actions in sequence.

Activity diagrams are part of the *Unified Modeling Language (UML)*—an industry standard for modeling software systems. An activity diagram models the *workflow* (also

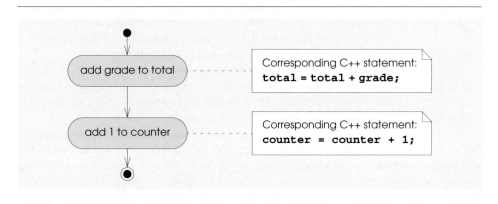

Fig. 2.1   Sequence structure activity diagram.

---

1. Bohm, C. and G. Jacopini, "Flow Diagrams, Turing Machines, and Languages with Only Two Formation Rules," *Communications of the ACM*, Vol. 9, No. 5, May 1966, pp. 336–371.

called the *activity*) of a portion of a software system. Such workflows may include a portion of an algorithm, such as the sequence structure in Fig. 2.1. Activity diagrams are composed of special-purpose symbols, such as *action-state symbols* (a rectangle with its left and right sides replaced with arcs curving outward), *diamonds* and *small circles*; these symbols are connected by *transition arrows*, which represent the flow of the activity.

Like pseudocode, activity diagrams help programmers develop and represent algorithms, although many programmers prefer pseudocode. Activity diagrams clearly show how control structures operate.

Consider the activity diagram for the sequence structure in Fig. 2.1. The activity diagram contains two *action states* that represent actions to perform. Each action state contains an *action expression*—e.g., "add grade to total" or "add 1 to counter"—that specifies a particular action to perform. Other actions might include calculations or input/output operations. The arrows in the activity diagram are called transition arrows. These arrows represent *transitions*, which indicate the order in which the actions represented by the action states occur—the program that implements the activities illustrated by the activity diagram in Fig. 2.1 first adds **grade** to **total**, then adds **1** to **counter**.

The *solid circle* located at the top of the activity diagram represents the activity's *initial state*—the beginning of the workflow before the program performs the modeled activities. The solid circle surrounded by a hollow circle that appears at the bottom of the activity diagram represents the *final state*—the end of the workflow after the program performs its activities.

Notice in Fig. 2.1 the rectangles with the upper-right corners folded over. These are called *notes* in the UML. Notes are explanatory remarks that describe the purpose of symbols in the diagram. Notes can be used in any UML diagram—not just activity diagrams. Fig. 2.1 uses UML notes to show the C++ code associated with each action state in the activity diagram. A *dotted line* connects each note with the element that the note describes. Activity diagrams normally do not show the C++ code that implements the activity. We use notes for this purpose here to illustrate how the diagram relates to C++ code.

C++ provides three types of selection structures. The **if** selection structure either performs (selects) an action if a condition (predicate) is true, or skips the action if the condition is false. The **if/else** selection structure performs an action if a condition is true, or performs a different action if the condition is false. The **switch** selection structure performs one of many different actions, depending on the value of an integer expression.

The **if** selection structure is a *single-selection structure*—it selects or ignores a single action. The **if/else** selection structure is a *double-selection structure*—it selects between two different actions. The **switch** selection structure is a *multiple-selection structure*—it selects the action to perform from many different action states.

C++ provides three types of repetition structures (also called *looping structures* or *loops*), namely **while**, **do/while** and **for**. Each of the words **if**, **else**, **switch**, **while**, **do** and **for** is a C++ *keyword*. These words are reserved by the C++ programming language to implement various features, such as C++'s control structures. Keywords must not be used as identifiers, such as variable names. Figure 2.2 contains a complete list of C++ keywords.

Common Programming Error 2.1

Using a keyword as an identifier is a syntax error.

C++ Keywords

Keywords common to the C and C++ programming languages

auto	break	case	char	const
continue	default	do	double	else
enum	extern	float	for	goto
if	int	long	register	return
short	signed	sizeof	static	struct
switch	typedef	union	unsigned	void
volatile	while			

C++ only keywords

asm	bool	catch	class	const_cast
delete	dynamic_cast	explicit	false	friend
inline	mutable	namespace	new	operator
private	protected	public	reinterpret_cast	
static_cast	template	this	throw	true
try	typeid	typename	using	virtual
wchar_t				

Fig. 2.2   C++ keywords.

Common Programming Error 2.2

Spelling a keyword with an uppercase letter is a syntax error. All of C++'s reserved keywords contain only lowercase letters.

C++ has only seven control structures: sequence, three types of selection (**if**, **if/else** and **switch**) and three types of repetition (**while**, **for** and **do/while**). Each C++ program combines as many of these control structures as is appropriate for the algorithm the program implements. As with the sequence structure of Fig. 2.1, we can model each control structure as an activity diagram. Each diagram contains an initial state and a final state, which represent a control structure's entry point and exit point, respectively. These *single-entry/single-exit control structures* make it easy to build programs—the control structures are attached to one another by connecting the exit point of one control structure to the entry point of the next. This is similar to the way a child stacks building blocks, so we call this *control-structure stacking*. We will learn shortly that there is only one other way to connect control structures—called *control-structure nesting*.

Software Engineering Observation 2.1

Any C++ program we will ever build can be constructed from only seven different types of control structures (sequence, if, if/else, switch, while, do/while and for) combined in only two ways (control-structure stacking and control-structure nesting).

2.5 if Selection Structure

Programs use selection structures to choose among alternative courses of action. For example, suppose the passing grade on an exam is 60. The pseudocode statement

> *If student's grade is greater than or equal to 60*
>   *Print "Passed"*

determines whether the condition "student's grade is greater than or equal to 60" is **true** or **false**. If the condition is **true**, then "Passed" is printed and the next pseudocode statement in order is "performed" (remember that pseudocode is not a real programming language). If the condition is **false**, the print statement is ignored and the next pseudocode statement in order is performed. Note that the second line of this selection structure is indented. Such indentation is optional, but it is highly recommended because it emphasizes the inherent structure of structured programs. When you convert your pseudocode into C++ code, the C++ compiler ignores *whitespace characters* (like blanks, tabs and newlines) used for indentation and vertical spacing.

Good Programming Practice 2.1

Consistently applying reasonable indentation conventions throughout your programs greatly improves program readability. We suggest a fixed-size tab of about 1/4 inch or three blanks per indent.

The preceding pseudocode *If* statement can be written in C++ as

```
if ( grade >= 60 )
   cout << "Passed";
```

Notice that the C++ code corresponds closely to the pseudocode. This is one of the properties of pseudocode that makes it such a useful program development tool.

Figure 2.3 illustrates the single-selection **if** structure. This activity diagram contains what is perhaps the most important symbol in an activity diagram—the diamond or *decision symbol*, which indicates that a decision is to be made. A decision symbol indicates that the workflow will continue along a path determined by the symbol's associated *guard conditions* that can be true or false. Each transition arrow emerging from a decision symbol has a guard condition (specified in square brackets above or next to the transition arrow). If a particular guard condition is true, the workflow enters the action state to which that transition arrow points. In Fig. 2.3, if the grade is greater than or equal to 60, the program prints "Passed" to the screen, then transitions to the final state of this activity. If the grade is less than 60, the program immediately transitions to the final state without displaying a message.

We learned in Chapter 1 that decisions can be based on conditions containing relational or equality operators. Actually, in C++, a decision can be based on any expression—if the expression evaluates to zero, it is treated as false; if the expression evaluates to nonzero, it is treated as true. The C++ standard provides the data type **bool** for variables that can hold only the values **true** and **false**. The values **true** and **false** are C++ keywords.

Portability Tip 2.1

*For compatibility with earlier versions of the C++ standard, the **bool** value **true** also can be represented by any nonzero value and the **bool** value **false** also can be represented as the value zero.*

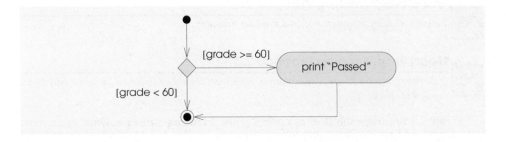

Fig. 2.3   **if** single-selection structure activity diagram.

Note that the **if** structure is a single-entry/single-exit structure. We will see that the activity diagrams for the remaining control structures also contain initial states, transition arrows, action states that indicate actions to perform, decision symbols (with associated guard conditions) that indicate decisions to be made and final states. This is consistent with the *action/decision model of programming* we have been emphasizing.

We can envision seven bins, each containing only control structures of one of the seven types. These control structures are empty. The programmer's task, then, is assembling a program from as many of each type of control structure as the algorithm demands, combining those control structures in only two possible ways (stacking or nesting), then filling in the action states and decisions with action expressions and guard conditions in a manner appropriate for the algorithm. We will discuss the variety of ways in which actions and decisions may be written.

2.6 **if/else** Selection Structure

The **if** selection structure performs an indicated action only when the condition is **true**; otherwise the action is skipped. The **if/else** selection structure allows the programmer to specify an action to perform when the condition is true and a different action to perform when the condition is false. For example, the pseudocode statement

> *If student's grade is greater than or equal to 60*
> > *Print "Passed"*
> *else*
> > *Print "Failed"*

prints *Passed* if the student's grade is greater than or equal to 60, but prints *Failed* if the student's grade is less than 60. In either case, after printing occurs, the next pseudocode statement in sequence is "performed."

The preceding pseudocode *If/else* structure can be written in C++ as

```
if ( grade >= 60 )
    cout << "Passed";
else
    cout << "Failed";
```

Note that the body of the **else** is also indented. Whatever indentation convention you choose should be applied consistently throughout your programs. It is difficult to read programs that do not obey uniform spacing conventions.

Good Programming Practice 2.2

*Indent both body statements of an **if/else** structure.*

Good Programming Practice 2.3

If there are several levels of indentation, each level should be indented the same additional amount of space.

Figure 2.4 illustrates the flow of control in the **if/else** structure. Once again, note that (besides the initial state, transition arrows and final state) the only other symbols in the activity diagram represent action states and decisions. We continue to emphasize this action/decision model of computing. Imagine again a deep bin containing as many empty double-selection structures as might be needed to build any C++ program. The programmer's job is to assemble these selection structures (by stacking and nesting) with any other control structures required by the algorithm. The programmer fills in the action states and decision symbols with action expressions and guard conditions appropriate to the algorithm.

C++ provides the *conditional operator (? :)*, which is closely related to the **if/else** structure. The conditional operator is C++'s only *ternary operator*—it takes three operands. The operands, together with the conditional operator, form a *conditional expression*. The first operand is a condition, the second operand is the value for the entire conditional expression if the condition is **true** and the third operand is the value for the entire conditional expression if the condition is **false**. For example, the output statement

```
cout << ( grade >= 60 ? "Passed" : "Failed" );
```

contains a conditional expression, **grade >= 60 ? "Passed" : "Failed"**, that evaluates to the string **"Passed"** if the condition **grade >= 60** is **true**, but evaluates to the string **"Failed"** if the condition is **false**. Thus, the statement with the conditional operator performs essentially the same as the preceding **if/else** structure. As we will see, the precedence of the conditional operator is low, so the parentheses in the preceding expression are required.

Good Programming Practice 2.4

For clarity, place conditional expressions in parentheses.

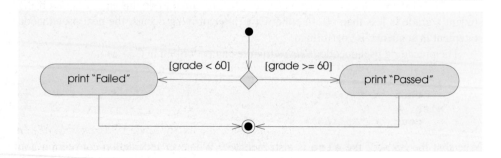

Fig. 2.4   **if/else** double-selection structure activity diagram.

The values in a conditional expression also can be actions to execute. For example, the following conditional expression also prints **"Passed"** or **"Failed"**:

grade >= 60 **? cout <<** "Passed" **: cout <<** "Failed"**;**

The preceding conditional expression is read, "If **grade** is greater than or equal to **60**, then **cout << "Passed"**; otherwise, **cout << "Failed"**." This, too, is comparable to the preceding **if/else** structure. We will see that conditional expressions can appear in some program locations where **if/else** statements cannot.

*Nested **if/else** structures* test for multiple cases by placing **if/else** selection structures inside **if/else** selection structures. For example, the following pseudocode **if/else** structure prints **A** for exam grades greater than or equal to 90, **B** for grades in the range 80 to 89, **C** for grades in the range 70 to 79, **D** for grades in the range 60 to 69 and **F** for all other grades.

> *If student's grade is greater than or equal to 90*
>   *Print "A"*
> *else*
>   *If student's grade is greater than or equal to 80*
>   *Print "B"*
>   *else*
>   *If student's grade is greater than or equal to 70*
>   *Print "C"*
>   *else*
>   *If student's grade is greater than or equal to 60*
>   *Print "D"*
>   *else*
>   *Print "F"*

This pseudocode can be written in C++ as

```
if ( grade >= 90 )          // 90 and above
   cout << "A";
else
   if ( grade >= 80 )       // 80-89
      cout << "B";
   else
      if ( grade >= 70 )    // 70-79
         cout << "C";
      else
         if ( grade >= 60 ) // 60-69
            cout << "D";
         else               // less than 60
            cout << "F";
```

If **grade** is greater than or equal to 90, the first four conditions will be **true**, but only the **cout** statement after the first test will execute. After that **cout** executes, the program skips the **else**-part of the "outer" **if/else** structure. Many C++ programmers prefer to write the preceding **if/else** structure as

```
if ( grade >= 90 )        // 90 and above
   cout << "A";
else if ( grade >= 80 )   // 80-89
   cout << "B";
else if ( grade >= 70 )   // 70-79
   cout << "C";
else if ( grade >= 60 )   // 60-69
   cout << "D";
else                      // less than 60
   cout << "F";
```

The two forms are identical except for the spacing and indentation, which the compiler ignores. The latter form is popular because it avoids deep indentation of the code to the right. Such indentation often leaves little room on a line, forcing lines to be split and decreasing program readability.

Performance Tip 2.1

*A nested **if/else** structure can perform much faster than a series of single-selection **if** structures because of the possibility of early exit after one of the conditions is satisfied.*

Performance Tip 2.2

*In a nested **if/else** structure, test the conditions that are more likely to be **true** at the beginning of the nested **if/else** structure. This will enable the nested **if/else** structure to run faster and exit earlier than will testing infrequently occurring cases first.*

The **if** selection structure expects only one statement in its body. Similarly, the **if** and **else** parts of an **if/else** structure each expect only one body statement. To include several statements in the body of an **if** or either part of an **if/else**, enclose the statements in braces (**{** and **}**). A set of statements contained within a pair of braces is called a *compound statement* or a *block*. We use the term "block" from this point forward.

Software Engineering Observation 2.2

A block can be placed anywhere in a program that a single statement can be placed.

The following example includes a block in the **else** part of an **if/else** structure.

```
if ( grade >= 60 )
   cout << "Passed.\n";
else {
   cout << "Failed.\n";
   cout << "You must take this course again.\n";
}
```

In this case, if **grade** is less than 60, the program executes both statements in the body of the **else** and prints

```
Failed.
You must take this course again.
```

Notice the braces surrounding the two statements in the **else** clause. These braces are important. Without the braces, the statement

```
cout << "You must take this course again.\n";
```

would be outside the body of the **else** part of the **if** and would execute regardless of whether the grade is less than 60.

Common Programming Error 2.3
Forgetting one or both of the braces that delimit a block can lead to syntax errors or logic errors in a program.

Good Programming Practice 2.5
*Always putting the braces in an **if/else** structure (or any control structure) helps prevent their accidental omission, especially when adding statements to an **if** or **else** clause at a later time. To avoid omitting one or both of the braces, some programmers prefer to type the beginning and ending braces of blocks before typing the individual statements within the braces.*

Just as a block can be placed anywhere a single statement can be placed, it is also possible to have no statement at all—called an *empty statement* (or a *null statement*). The empty statement is represented by placing a semicolon (**;**) where a statement would normally be.

Common Programming Error 2.4
*Placing a semicolon after the condition in an **if** structure leads to a logic error in single-selection **if** structures and a syntax error in double-selection **if/else** structures (when the **if** part contains an actual body statement).*

2.7 `while` Repetition Structure

A *repetition structure* (also called a *looping structure* or a *loop*) allows the programmer to specify that a program should repeat an action while some condition remains true. The pseudocode statement

> *While there are more items on my shopping list*
> *Purchase next item and cross it off my list*

describes the repetition that occurs during a shopping trip. The condition, "there are more items on my shopping list" is either true or false. If it is true, then the action, "Purchase next item and cross it off my list" is performed. This action will be performed repeatedly while the condition remains true. The statement contained in the ***while*** repetition structure constitutes the body of the **while**, which can be a single statement or a block. Eventually, the condition will become false (when the last item on the shopping list has been purchased and crossed off the list). At this point, the repetition terminates, and the first pseudocode statement after the repetition structure executes.

As an example of an actual **while**, consider a program segment designed to find the first power of 2 larger than 1000. Suppose the integer variable **product** has been initialized to 2. When the following **while** repetition structure finishes executing, **product** will contain the desired answer:

```
int product = 2;

while ( product <= 1000 )
   product = 2 * product;
```

When the **while** structure begins execution, the value of **product** is 2. Each repetition of the **while** structure multiplies product by 2, so **product** takes on the values 4, 8, 16, 32, 64, 128, 256, 512 and 1024 successively. When **product** becomes 1024, the **while** structure condition, **product <= 1000**, becomes **false**. This terminates the repetition—the final value of **product** is 1024. Program execution continues with the next statement after the **while**.

Common Programming Error 2.5

*Not providing, in the body of a **while** structure, an action that eventually causes the condition in the **while** to become false normally results in a logic error called an infinite loop, in which the repetition structure never terminates.*

The activity diagram of Fig. 2.5 illustrates the flow of control that corresponds to the preceding **while** structure. Once again, note that (besides the initial state, transition arrows, a final state and two notes) the only other symbols in the diagram represent an action state and a decision. This diagram also introduces the UML's *merge symbol*. The UML represents both the merge symbol and the decision symbol as diamonds. The merge symbol joins two flows of activity into one flow of activity. In this diagram, the merge symbol joins the transitions from the initial state and from the action state, so they both flow into the decision that determines whether the loop should begin executing (or continue executing). Although the UML represents decision and merge symbols with the diamond shape, the symbols can be distinguished by the number of "incoming" and "outgoing" transition arrows. A decision symbol has one transition arrow pointing to the diamond and two transition arrows pointing out from the diamond to indicate possible transitions from that point. In addition, each transition arrow pointing out of a decision symbol has a guard condition next to it. A merge symbol has two transition arrows pointing to the diamond and only one transition arrow pointing from the diamond, to indicate multiple activity flows merging to continue the activity. Note that, unlike the decision symbol, the merge symbol does not have a counterpart in C++ code.

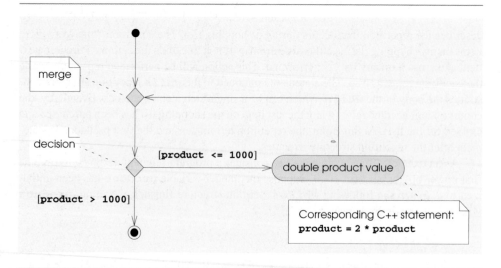

Fig. 2.5 **while** repetition structure activity diagram.

Imagine a deep bin of empty **while** structures that can be stacked and nested with other control structures to form a structured implementation of an algorithm's flow of control. The programmer fills in the action states and decision symbols with action expressions and guard conditions appropriate to the algorithm. The diagram clearly shows the repetition. The transition arrow emerging from the action state points to the merge, which transitions back to the decision that is tested each time through the loop until the guard condition **product > 1000** becomes true. Then, the **while** structure exits (reaches its final state) and control passes to the next statement in the program.

2.8 Formulating Algorithms: Case Study 1 (Counter-Controlled Repetition)

To illustrate how programmers develop algorithms, this section and Section 2.9 solve two variations of a class-averaging problem. Consider the following problem statement:

> *A class of ten students took a quiz. The grades (integers in the range 0 to 100) for this quiz are available to you. Determine the class average on the quiz.*

The class average is equal to the sum of the grades divided by the number of students. The algorithm for solving this problem on a computer must input each of the grades, calculate the average and print the result.

Let us use pseudocode to list the actions to execute and specify the order in which these actions should execute. We use *counter-controlled repetition* to input the grades one at a time. This technique uses a variable called a *counter* to control the number of times a group of statements will execute (also known as the number of *iterations* of the loop).

Counter-controlled repetition is often called *definite repetition* because the number of repetitions is known before the loop begins executing. In this example, repetition terminates when the counter exceeds 10. This section presents a pseudocode algorithm (Fig. 2.6) and the corresponding C++ program (Fig. 2.7). The next section shows how to use pseudocode to develop an algorithm.

Note the references in the algorithm to a *total* and a *counter*. A *total* is a variable used to accumulate the sum of a series of values. A *counter* is a variable used to count—in this case, to count the number of grades entered. A variable used to store a total should normally

---

Set total to zero
Set grade counter to one

While grade counter is less than or equal to ten
    Input the next grade
    Add the grade into the total
    Add one to the grade counter

Set the class average to the total divided by ten
Print the class average

Fig. 2.6   Class-average problem pseudocode algorithm that uses counter-controlled repetition.

be initialized to zero before being used in a program; otherwise, the sum would include the previous value stored in the total's memory location.

```cpp
1    // Fig. 2.7: fig02_07.cpp
2    // Class average program with counter-controlled repetition.
3    #include <iostream>
4
5    using std::cout;
6    using std::cin;
7    using std::endl;
8
9    // function main begins program execution
10   int main()
11   {
12      int total;         // sum of grades input by user
13      int gradeCounter;  // number of grade to be entered next
14      int grade;         // grade value
15      int average;       // average of grades
16
17      // initialization phase
18      total = 0;            // initialize total
19      gradeCounter = 1;     // initialize loop counter
20
21      // processing phase
22      while ( gradeCounter <= 10 ) {        // loop 10 times
23         cout << "Enter grade: ";           // prompt for input
24         cin >> grade;                      // read grade from user
25         total = total + grade;             // add grade to total
26         gradeCounter = gradeCounter + 1;   // increment counter
27      }
28
29      // termination phase
30      average = total / 10;                 // integer division
31
32      // display result
33      cout << "Class average is " << average << endl;
34
35      return 0;   // indicate program ended successfully
36
37   } // end function main
```

```
Enter grade: 98
Enter grade: 76
Enter grade: 71
Enter grade: 87
Enter grade: 83
Enter grade: 90
Enter grade: 57
Enter grade: 79
Enter grade: 82
Enter grade: 94
Class average is 81
```

Fig. 2.7   Class-average problem with counter-controlled repetition.

Lines 12–15

```
int total;       // sum of grades input by user
int gradeCounter; // number of grades entered
int grade;        // grade value
int average;      // average of grades
```

declare variables **total**, **gradeCounter**, **grade** and **average** to be of type **int**.

Notice that the preceding declarations appear in the body of function **main**. Variables declared in a function definition's body are *local variables* and can be used only from the line of their declaration in the function to the closing right brace (**}**) of the function definition. The declaration of a local variable in a function must appear before the variable is used in that function.

Lines 18–19

```
total = 0;         // clear total
gradeCounter = 1;  // initialize loop counter
```

are assignment statements that initialize **total** to **0** and **gradeCounter** to **1**.

Note that variables **total** and **gradeCounter** are initialized before they are used in a calculation. Counter variables normally are initialized to zero or one, depending on their use (we will present examples showing each of these uses). An uninitialized variable contains a *"garbage" value* (also called an *undefined value*)—the value last stored in the memory location reserved for that variable.

Common Programming Error 2.6

If a counter or total is not initialized, the results of your program probably will be incorrect. This is an example of a logic error. Most variables initially contain garbage values.

Testing and Debugging Tip 2.1

Initialize counters and totals.

Good Programming Practice 2.6

Declare each variable on a separate line to make programs more readable.

Line 22

```
while ( gradeCounter <= 10 ) {        // loop 10 times
```

indicates that the **while** structure should continue as long as **gradeCounter**'s value is less than or equal to **10**.

Lines 23–24

```
cout << "Enter grade: ";              // prompt for input
cin >> grade;                         // read grade from user
```

correspond to the pseudocode statement *"Input the next grade."* The first statement displays the prompt "**Enter grade:**" on the screen. The second statement inputs the grade value from the user. Variable **grade** was not initialized earlier in the program, because the program obtains the value for **grade** from the user during each iteration of the loop.

Next, the program updates **total** with the new **grade** entered by the user. Line 25

```
total = total + grade;              // add grade to total
```

adds **grade** to the previous value of **total** and assigns the result to **total**.

The program now is ready to increment the variable **gradeCounter** to prepare to process the next grade, then read the next grade from the user. Line 26

```
gradeCounter = gradeCounter + 1;   // increment counter
```

adds **1** to **gradeCounter**, so the condition in the **while** structure eventually will become **false** and terminate the loop.

When the loop terminates, line 30

```
average = total / 10;                      // integer division
```

assigns the results of the average calculation to variable **average**. Line 33

```
cout << "Class average is " << average << endl;
```

displays the string **"Class average is "** followed by the value of variable **average**.

Note that the averaging calculation in the program produced an integer result. Actually, the sum of the grades in this example is 817, which, when divided by 10, should yield 81.7—a number with a decimal point. We will see how to deal with such numbers (called floating-point numbers) in the next section.

In Fig. 2.7, if line 30 used **gradeCounter** rather than 10 for the calculation, the output for this program would display an incorrect value, 74.

Common Programming Error 2.7

Using a loop's counter-control variable in a calculation after the loop often causes an off-by-one-error. In a counter-controlled loop that counts up by one each time through the loop, the loop terminates when the counter-control variable's value is one higher than its last legitimate value (i.e., 11 in the case of counting from 1 to 10).

2.9 Formulating Algorithms with Top-Down, Stepwise Refinement: Case Study 2 (Sentinel-Controlled Repetition)

Let us generalize the class-average problem. Consider the following problem:

> *Develop a class-averaging program that will process an arbitrary number of grades each time the program is run.*

In the first class-average example, the problem statement specified the number of grades (10) in advance. In this example, no indication is given of how many grades the user will enter during the program's execution. The program must process an arbitrary number of grades. How can the program determine when to stop the input of grades? How will it know when to calculate and print the class average?

One way to solve this problem is to use a special value called a *sentinel value* (also called a *signal value*, a *dummy value* or a *flag value*) to indicate "end of data entry." The user types grades in until all legitimate grades have been entered. The user then types the sentinel value to indicate that the last grade has been entered. Sentinel-controlled repetition is often called *indefinite repetition* because the number of repetitions is not known before the loop begins executing.

Clearly, the sentinel value must be chosen so that it cannot be confused with an acceptable input value. Grades on a quiz are normally nonnegative integers, so –1 is an acceptable sentinel value for this problem. Thus, a run of the class-average program might process a stream of inputs such as 95, 96, 75, 74, 89 and –1. The program would then compute and print the class average for the grades 95, 96, 75, 74 and 89. Note that –1 is the sentinel value, so it should not enter into the averaging calculation.

Common Programming Error 2.8

Choosing a sentinel value that is also a legitimate data value is a logic error.

We approach the class-average program with a technique called *top-down, stepwise refinement*, a technique that is essential to the development of well-structured programs. We begin with a pseudocode representation of the *top:*

> *Determine the class average for the quiz*

The top is a single statement that conveys the overall function of the program. As such, the top is, in effect, a complete representation of a program. Unfortunately, the top (as in this case) rarely conveys a sufficient amount of detail from which to write the C++ program. So we now begin the refinement process. We divide the top into a series of smaller tasks and list these in the order in which they need to be performed. This results in the following *first refinement*.

> *Initialize variables*
> *Input, sum and count the quiz grades*
> *Calculate and print the class average*

This refinement uses only the sequence structure—the steps listed should execute in order, one after the other.

Software Engineering Observation 2.3

Each refinement, as well as the top itself, is a complete specification of the algorithm; only the level of detail varies.

Software Engineering Observation 2.4

Many programs can be divided logically into three phases: an initialization phase that initializes the program variables; a processing phase that inputs data values and adjusts program variables accordingly; and a termination phase that calculates and prints the final results.

The preceding Software Engineering Observation is often all you need for the first refinement in the top-down process. To proceed to the next level of refinement, i.e., the *second refinement*, we commit to specific variables. In this example, we need a running total of the numbers, a count of how many numbers have been processed, a variable to receive the value of each grade as it is input by the user and a variable to hold the calculated average. The pseudocode statement

> *Initialize variables*

can be refined as follows:

> *Initialize total to zero*
> *Initialize counter to zero*

Notice that only the variables *total* and *counter* need to be initialized before they are used; the variables *average* and *grade* (for the calculated average and the user input, respectively) need not be initialized, because their values will be replaced as they are calculated or input.

The pseudocode statement

> *Input, sum and count the quiz grades*

requires a repetition structure (i.e., a loop) that successively inputs each grade. We do not know in advance how many grades are to be processed, so we will use sentinel-controlled repetition. The user enters legitimate grades one at a time. After entering the last legitimate grade, the user enters the sentinel value. The program tests for the sentinel value after each grade is input and terminates the loop when the user enters the sentinel value. The second refinement of the preceding pseudocode statement is then

> *Input the first grade (possibly the sentinel)*
> *While the user has not yet entered the sentinel*
>> *Add this grade into the running total*
>> *Add one to the grade counter*
>> *Input the next grade (possibly the sentinel)*

Notice that, in pseudocode, we do not use braces around the set of statements that form the body of the *while* structure. We simply indent the statements under the *while* to show that they belong to the *while*. Again, pseudocode is only an informal program-development aid.

The pseudocode statement

> *Calculate and print the class average*

can be refined as follows:

> *If the counter is not equal to zero*
>> *Set the average to the total divided by the counter*
>> *Print the average*
> *else*
>> *Print "No grades were entered"*

Notice that we are being careful here to test for the possibility of division by zero—normally a *fatal logic error* that, if undetected, would cause the program to fail (often called *"bombing"* or *"crashing"*). The complete second refinement of the pseudocode for the class-average problem is shown in Fig. 2.8.

Common Programming Error 2.9

An attempt to divide by zero normally causes a fatal error.

Testing and Debugging Tip 2.2

When performing division by an expression whose value could be zero, explicitly test for this possibility and handle it appropriately in your program (such as by printing an error message) rather than allowing the fatal error to occur.

In Fig. 2.6 and Fig. 2.8, we include some completely blank lines and indentation in the pseudocode to make the pseudocode more readable. The blank lines separate the pseudocode algorithms into their various phases and the indentation emphasizes the bodies of the control structures.

Initialize total to zero
Initialize counter to zero

Input the first grade (possibly the sentinel)
While the user has not yet entered the sentinel
    Add this grade into the running total
    Add one to the grade counter
    Input the next grade (possibly the sentinel)

If the counter is not equal to zero
    Set the average to the total divided by the counter
    Print the average
else
    Print "No grades were entered"

Fig. 2.8   Class-average problem pseudocode algorithm with sentinel-controlled repetition.

The pseudocode algorithm in Fig. 2.8 solves the more general class-averaging problem. This algorithm was developed after only two levels of refinement. Sometimes more levels are necessary.

Software Engineering Observation 2.5

Terminate the top-down, stepwise refinement process when the pseudocode algorithm is specified in sufficient detail to be able to convert the pseudocode to C++. Normally, implementing the C++ program is then straightforward.

Figure 2.9 shows the C++ program and a sample execution. Although only integer grades are entered, the averaging calculation is likely to produce a number with a decimal point—a real number. The type **int** cannot represent real numbers. This program introduces the data type **double** to handle numbers with decimal points (also called *floating-point numbers*) and introduces a special operator called a *cast operator* to force the averaging calculation to produce a floating-point numeric result. These features are explained in detail after the program is presented.

```
1   // Fig. 2.9: fig02_09.cpp
2   // Class average program with sentinel-controlled repetition.
3   #include <iostream>
4
5   using std::cout;
6   using std::cin;
7   using std::endl;
8   using std::fixed;
```

Fig. 2.9   Class-average problem with sentinel-controlled repetition. (Part 1 of 3.)

```
9
10   #include <iomanip>           // parameterized stream manipulators
11
12   using std::setprecision;   // sets numeric output precision
13
14   // function main begins program execution
15   int main()
16   {
17      int total;           // sum of grades
18      int gradeCounter;    // number of grades entered
19      int grade;           // grade value
20
21      double average;      // number with decimal point for average
22
23      // initialization phase
24      total = 0;           // initialize total
25      gradeCounter = 0;    // initialize loop counter
26
27      // processing phase
28      // get first grade from user
29      cout << "Enter grade, -1 to end: ";   // prompt for input
30      cin >> grade;                          // read grade from user
31
32      // loop until sentinel value read from user
33      while ( grade != -1 ) {
34         total = total + grade;              // add grade to total
35         gradeCounter = gradeCounter + 1;    // increment counter
36
37         cout << "Enter grade, -1 to end: ";  // prompt for input
38         cin >> grade;                         // read next grade
39
40      } // end while
41
42      // termination phase
43      // if user entered at least one grade ...
44      if ( gradeCounter != 0 ) {
45
46         // calculate average of all grades entered
47         average = static_cast< double >( total ) / gradeCounter;
48
49         // display average with two digits of precision
50         cout << "Class average is " << setprecision( 2 )
51              << fixed << average << endl;
52
53      } // end if part of if/else
54
55      else // if no grades were entered, output appropriate message
56         cout << "No grades were entered" << endl;
57
58      return 0;   // indicate program ended successfully
59
60   } // end function main
```

Fig. 2.9   Class-average problem with sentinel-controlled repetition. (Part 2 of 3.)

```
Enter grade, -1 to end: 75
Enter grade, -1 to end: 94
Enter grade, -1 to end: 97
Enter grade, -1 to end: 88
Enter grade, -1 to end: 70
Enter grade, -1 to end: 64
Enter grade, -1 to end: 83
Enter grade, -1 to end: 89
Enter grade, -1 to end: -1
Class average is 82.50
```

Fig. 2.9   Class-average problem with sentinel-controlled repetition. (Part 3 of 3.)

In this example, we see that control structures can be stacked on top of one another (in sequence) just as a child stacks building blocks. The **while** structure (lines 33–40) is immediately followed by an **if/else** structure (lines 44–56) in sequence. Much of the code in this program is identical to the code in Fig. 2.7, so we concentrate on the new features and issues.

Line 21 declares the **double** variable **average**. This change allows us to store the class-average calculation's result as a floating-point number. Line 25 initializes the variable **gradeCounter** to **0**, because no grades have been entered yet. Remember that this program uses sentinel-controlled repetition. To keep an accurate record of the number of grades entered, the program increments variable **gradeCounter** only when the user enters a valid grade value (i.e., not the sentinel value) and the program completes the processing of the grade.

Notice that both input statements (lines 30 and 38) are preceded by an output statement that prompts the user for input.

Good Programming Practice 2.7

Prompt the user for each keyboard input. The prompt should indicate the form of the input and any special input values. For example, in a sentinel-controlled loop, the prompts requesting data entry should remind the user explicitly what the sentinel value is.

Compare the program logic for sentinel-controlled repetition in Fig. 2.9 with that of counter-controlled repetition in Fig. 2.7. In counter-controlled repetition, we read a value from the user during each pass of the **while** structure for the specified number of passes. In sentinel-controlled repetition, we read one value (line 30) before the program reaches the **while** structure. This value is used to determine whether the program's flow of control should enter the body of the **while** structure. If the **while** structure condition is **false** (i.e., the user typed the sentinel), the body of the **while** structure does not execute (no grades were entered). If, on the other hand, the condition is **true**, the body begins execution and processes the value entered by the user (i.e., adds that value to the **total** in this example). After the value is processed, the next value is input from the user before the end of the **while** structure's body. As the closing right brace (**}**) of the body is reached at line 41, execution continues with the next test of the **while** structure condition, using the new value just entered by the user to determine whether the **while** structure's body should execute again. Notice that the next value always is input from the user immediately before the

while structure condition is evaluated. This allows us to determine whether the value just entered by the user is the sentinel value *before* that value is processed (i.e., added to the **total**). If the value entered is the sentinel value, the **while** structure terminates and the value is not added to the **total**

Notice the block in the **while** loop in Fig. 2.9. Without the braces, the last three statements in the body of the loop would fall outside the loop, causing the computer to interpret this code incorrectly, as follows:

```
while ( grade != -1 )
   total = total + grade;
gradeCounter = gradeCounter + 1;
cout << "Enter grade, -1 to end: ";
cin >> grade;
```

This would cause an infinite loop if the user does not input **−1** for the first grade.

Averages do not always evaluate to integer values. Often, an average is a value that contains a fractional part, such as 7.2 or –93.541. These values are referred to as floating-point numbers and are represented in C++ by data types such as *float* and *double*. A variable of type **double** can store a value of much greater magnitude and with greater precision than **float**. For this reason, we tend to use type **double** rather than type **float** to represent floating-point values in our programs. Floating-point constants, such as **1000.0** and **.05**, are treated as type **double** by C++.

The variable **average** is declared to be of type **double** (line 21) to capture the fractional result of our calculation. However, because **total** and **gradeCounter** are both integer variables, the result of the calculation **total / gradeCounter** is an integer. Dividing two integers results in *integer division*, in which any fractional part of the calculation is lost (i.e., *truncated*). In the following statement:

```
average = total / gradeCounter;
```

the division calculation is performed first, so the fractional part of the result is lost before it is assigned to **average**. To produce a floating-point calculation with integer values, we must create temporary values that are floating-point numbers for the calculation. C++ provides the *unary cast operator* to accomplish this task. Line 47 uses the cast operator **static_cast< double >(** *operand* **)** to create a temporary floating-point copy of its operand in parentheses—**total**. Using a cast operator in this manner is called *explicit conversion*. The value stored in variable **total** is still an integer. The calculation now consists of a floating-point value (the temporary **double** version of **total**) divided by the integer **gradeCounter**.

The C++ compiler knows how to evaluate only expressions in which the data types of the operands are identical. To ensure that the operands are of the same type, the compiler performs an operation called *promotion* (also called *implicit conversion*) on selected operands. For example, in an expression containing values of data types **int** and **double**, C++ *promotes* **int** operands to **double** values. In our example, after **gradeCounter** is promoted to **double**, the calculation is performed and the result of the floating-point division is assigned to **average**. Later in this chapter, we discuss all the standard data types and their order of promotion.

Cast operators are available for any data type. The **static_cast** operator is formed by following keyword **static_cast** with angle brackets (**<** and **>**) around a data type name. The cast operator is a *unary operator*—an operator that takes only one operand. In Chapter 1, we studied the binary arithmetic operators. C++ also supports unary versions of the plus (**+**) and minus (**-**) operators, so that the programmer can write such expressions as **-7** or **+5**. Cast operators have higher precedence than other unary operators, such as unary **+** and unary **-**. This precedence is higher than that of the *multiplicative operators* *****, **/** and **%**, and lower than that of parentheses. We indicate the cast operator with the notation ***static_cast<*** *type* ***>()*** in our precedence charts.

The formatting capabilities in Fig. 2.9 are discussed here briefly and explained in depth in Chapter 12. The call **setprecision(2)** in line 50 indicates that **double** variable **average** should be printed with two digits of *precision* to the right of the decimal point (e.g., 92.37). This call is referred to as a *parameterized stream manipulator*. Programs that use these calls must contain the preprocessor directive (line 10)

```
#include <iomanip>
```

Line 12 specifies that the program uses the name **setprecision** from the **<iomanip>** header file. Note that **endl** is a *nonparameterized stream manipulator* and does not require the **<iomanip>** header file. If the precision is not specified, floating-point values are normally output with six digits of precision (i.e., the *default precision*), although we will see an exception to this in a moment.

The stream manipulator **fixed** (line 51) indicates that floating-point values should be output in so-called *fixed-point format* (as opposed to *scientific notation*, which we will discuss in Chapter 12). Specifying fixed-point formatting also forces the decimal point and trailing zeros to print, even if the value is a whole number amount, such as 88.00. Without the fixed-point formatting option, such a value prints in C++ as 88 without the trailing zeros and without the decimal point. When the preceding formatting is used in a program, the printed value is *rounded* to the indicated number of decimal positions, although the value in memory remains unaltered. For example, the values 87.946 and 67.543 are output as 87.95 and 67.54, respectively. Note that it also is possible to force a decimal point to appear by using stream-manipulator ***showpoint***. If showpoint is specified without fixed, then trailing zeros will not print. Like **endl**, stream manipulators **fixed** and **showpoint** are nonparameterized stream manipulators that do not require the **<iomanip>** header file. Both can be found in header **<iostream>**.

Common Programming Error 2.10

Using floating-point numbers in a manner that assumes they are represented exactly can lead to incorrect results. Floating-point numbers are represented only approximately by most computers.

Despite the fact that floating-point numbers are not always "100% precise," they have numerous applications. For example, when we speak of a "normal" body temperature of 98.6 we do not need to be precise to a large number of digits. When we view the temperature on a thermometer and read it as 98.6, it may actually be 98.5999473210643. The point here is that calling this number simply 98.6 is fine for most applications.

Another way floating-point numbers develop is through division. When we divide 10 by 3, the result is 3.3333333… with the sequence of 3s repeating infinitely. The computer allocates a fixed amount of space to hold such a value, so clearly the stored floating-point value can only be an approximation.

2.10 Formulating Algorithms with Top-Down, Stepwise Refinement: Case Study 3 (Nested Control Structures)

Let us work another complete problem. We will once again formulate the algorithm by using pseudocode and top-down, stepwise refinement and write a corresponding C++ program. We have seen that control structures can be stacked on top of one another (in sequence) just as a child stacks building blocks. In this case study, we will see the only other structured way control structures can be connected in C++, namely, by *nesting* of one control structure within another.

Consider the following problem statement:

A college offers a course that prepares students for the state licensing exam for real estate brokers. Last year, several of the students who completed this course took the licensing examination. Naturally, the college wants to know how well its students did on the exam. You have been asked to write a program to summarize the results. You have been given a list of these 10 students. Next to each name is written a 1 if the student passed the exam or a 2 if the student failed.

Your program should analyze the results of the exam as follows:

1. *Input each test result (i.e., a 1 or a 2). Display the message "Enter result" on the screen each time the program requests another test result.*

2. *Count the number of test results of each type.*

3. *Display a summary of the test results indicating the number of students who passed and the number of students who failed.*

4. *If more than 8 students passed the exam, print the message "Raise tuition."*

After reading the problem statement carefully, we make the following observations about the problem:

1. The program must process test results for 10 students. A counter-controlled loop will be used.

2. Each test result is a number—either a 1 or a 2. Each time the program reads a test result, the program must determine whether the number is a 1 or 2. We test for a 1 in our algorithm. If the number is not a 1, we assume that it is a 2. (Exercise 2.23 considers the consequences of this assumption.)

3. Two counters are used to keep track of the exam results—one to count the number of students who passed the exam and one to count the number of students who failed the exam.

4. After the program has processed all the results, it must decide if more than eight students passed the exam.

Let us proceed with top-down, stepwise refinement. We begin with a pseudocode representation of the top:

Analyze exam results and decide if tuition should be raised

Once again, it is important to emphasize that the top is a complete representation of the program, but several refinements are likely to be needed before the pseudocode can be evolved naturally into a C++ program.

Our first refinement is

> *Initialize variables*
> *Input the ten quiz grades and count passes and failures*
> *Print a summary of the exam results and decide if tuition should be raised*

Here, too, even though we have a complete representation of the entire program, further refinement is necessary. We now commit to specific variables. Counters are needed to record the passes and failures, a counter will be used to control the looping process and a variable is needed to store the user input. The variable in which the user input will be stored is not initialized, because its value is read from the user during each iteration of the loop.

The pseudocode statement

> *Initialize variables*

can be refined as follows:

> *Initialize passes to zero*
> *Initialize failures to zero*
> *Initialize student counter to one*

Notice that only the counters are initialized.

The pseudocode statement

> *Input the ten quiz grades and count passes and failures*

requires a loop that successively inputs the result of each exam. Here it is known in advance that there are precisely ten exam results, so counter-controlled looping is appropriate. Inside the loop (i.e., *nested* within the loop), a double-selection structure will determine whether each exam result is a pass or a failure and will increment the appropriate counter. The refinement of the preceding pseudocode statement is then

> *While student counter is less than or equal to ten*
> > *Input the next exam result*
>
> > *If the student passed*
> > > *Add one to passes*
> > *else*
> > > *Add one to failures*
>
> > *Add one to student counter*

Notice the use of blank lines to set off the *If/else* control structure to improve program readability.

The pseudocode statement

> *Print a summary of the exam results and decide if tuition should be raised*

can be refined as follows:

> *Print the number of passes*
> *Print the number of failures*
>
> *If more than eight students passed*
> > *Print "Raise tuition"*

The complete second refinement appears in Fig. 2.10. Notice that blank lines are also used to set off the *While* structure for program readability.

This pseudocode is now sufficiently refined for conversion to C++. The C++ program and two sample executions are shown in Fig. 2.11.

Lines 13–16 declare the variables used in **main** to process the examination results. Note that we have taken advantage of a feature of C++ that allows variable initialization to be incorporated into declarations (**passes** is assigned **0**, **failures** is assigned **0** and **studentCounter** is assigned **1**). Looping programs sometimes require initialization at the beginning of each repetition; such initialization normally would occur in assignment statements.

Initialize passes to zero
Initialize failures to zero
Initialize student counter to one

While student counter is less than or equal to ten
    Input the next exam result

    If the student passed
        Add one to passes
    else
        Add one to failures

    Add one to student counter

Print the number of passes
Print the number of failures

If more than eight students passed
    Print "Raise tuition"

Fig. 2.10   Examination-results problem pseudocode algorithm.

```
1   // Fig. 2.11: fig02_11.cpp
2   // Analysis of examination results.
3   #include <iostream>
4
5   using std::cout;
6   using std::cin;
7   using std::endl;
8
```

Fig. 2.11   Nested control structures: Examination-results problem. (Part 1 of 3.)

```
 9   // function main begins program execution
10   int main()
11   {
12      // initialize variables in declarations
13      int passes = 0;           // number of passes
14      int failures = 0;         // number of failures
15      int studentCounter = 1;   // student counter
16      int result;               // one exam result
17
18      // process 10 students using counter-controlled loop
19      while ( studentCounter <= 10 ) {
20
21         // prompt user for input and obtain value from user
22         cout << "Enter result (1 = pass, 2 = fail): ";
23         cin >> result;
24
25         // if result 1, increment passes; if/else nested in while
26         if ( result == 1 )          // if/else nested in while
27            passes = passes + 1;
28
29         else   // if result not 1, increment failures
30            failures = failures + 1;
31
32         // increment studentCounter so loop eventually terminates
33         studentCounter = studentCounter + 1;
34
35      } // end while
36
37      // termination phase; display number of passes and failures
38      cout << "Passed " << passes << endl;
39      cout << "Failed " << failures << endl;
40
41      // if more than eight students passed, print "raise tuition"
42      if ( passes > 8 )
43         cout << "Raise tuition " << endl;
44
45      return 0;   // successful termination
46
47   } // end function main
```

```
Enter result (1 = pass, 2 = fail): 1
Enter result (1 = pass, 2 = fail): 2
Enter result (1 = pass, 2 = fail): 2
Enter result (1 = pass, 2 = fail): 1
Enter result (1 = pass, 2 = fail): 1
Enter result (1 = pass, 2 = fail): 1
Enter result (1 = pass, 2 = fail): 2
Enter result (1 = pass, 2 = fail): 1
Enter result (1 = pass, 2 = fail): 1
Enter result (1 = pass, 2 = fail): 2
Passed 6
Failed 4
```

Fig. 2.11   Nested control structures: Examination-results problem. (Part 2 of 3.)

```
Enter result (1 = pass, 2 = fail): 1
Enter result (1 = pass, 2 = fail): 1
Enter result (1 = pass, 2 = fail): 1
Enter result (1 = pass, 2 = fail): 1
Enter result (1 = pass, 2 = fail): 2
Enter result (1 = pass, 2 = fail): 1
Enter result (1 = pass, 2 = fail): 1
Enter result (1 = pass, 2 = fail): 1
Enter result (1 = pass, 2 = fail): 1
Enter result (1 = pass, 2 = fail): 1
Passed 9
Failed 1
Raise tuition
```

Fig. 2.11   Nested control structures: Examination-results problem. (Part 3 of 3.)

Notice the **if/else** structure at lines 26–30 that is nested in the **while** structure (lines 19–35). The remainder of the program uses concepts already presented in the programs of Fig. 2.7 and Fig. 2.9.

Good Programming Practice 2.8

Initializing local variables when they are declared in functions helps avoid errors from uninitialized data.

Software Engineering Observation 2.6

Experience has shown that the most difficult part of solving a problem on a computer is developing the algorithm for the solution. Once a correct algorithm has been specified, the process of producing a working C++ program from the algorithm normally is straightforward.

Software Engineering Observation 2.7

Many experienced programmers write programs without ever using program-development tools like pseudocode. These programmers feel that their ultimate goal is to solve the problem on a computer and that writing pseudocode merely delays the production of final outputs. Although this method might work for simple and familiar problems, it can lead to serious errors in large, complex projects.

2.11 Assignment Operators

C++ provides several assignment operators (Fig. 2.12) for abbreviating assignment expressions. For example, the statement

        c = c + 3;

can be abbreviated with the *addition assignment operator* **+=** as

        c += 3;

The **+=** operator adds the value of the expression on the right of the operator to the value of the variable on the left of the operator and stores the result in the variable on the left of the operator. Any statement of the form

        variable **=** *variable operator expression*;

Assignment operator	Sample expression	Explanation	Assigns
Assume: `int c = 3, d = 5, e = 4, f = 6, g = 12;`			
`+=`	`c += 7`	`c = c + 7`	**10** to **c**
`-=`	`d -= 4`	`d = d - 4`	**1** to **d**
`*=`	`e *= 5`	`e = e * 5`	**20** to **e**
`/=`	`f /= 3`	`f = f / 3`	**2** to **f**
`%=`	`g %= 9`	`g = g % 9`	**3** to **g**

Fig. 2.12   Arithmetic assignment operators.

in which the same *variable* appears on both sides of the assignment operator and *operator* is one of the binary operators **+**, **-**, *****, **/**, or **%** (or others we will discuss later in the text), can be written in the form

> *variable operator*= *expression*;

Thus the assignment **c += 3** adds **3** to **c**. Figure 2.12 shows the arithmetic assignment operators, sample expressions using these operators and explanations.

Performance Tip 2.3

Programmers can write programs a bit faster and compilers can compile programs a bit faster when the "abbreviated" assignment operators are used. Some compilers generate code that runs faster when "abbreviated" assignment operators are used.

Performance Tip 2.4

Many of the performance tips we mention in this text result in nominal improvements, so the reader might be tempted to ignore them. When a nominal improvement is made on code that executes many times in a loop, significant performance improvement often is realized.

2.12 Increment and Decrement Operators

In addition to the arithmetic assignment operators, C++ also provides the **++** unary *increment operator* and the **--** unary *decrement operator*, which are summarized in Fig. 2.13. If a variable **c** is incremented by 1, the increment operator **++** can be used rather than the expressions **c = c + 1** or **c += 1**. If an increment or decrement operator is placed before a variable, it is referred to as the *preincrement* or *predecrement operator,* respectively. If an increment or decrement operator is placed after a variable, it is referred to as the *postincrement* or *postdecrement operator,* respectively. Preincrementing (predecrementing) a variable causes the variable to be incremented (decremented) by 1; after that, the new value of the variable is used in the expression in which it appears. Postincrementing (postdecrementing) a variable causes the current value of the variable to be used in the expression in which it appears; then, the variable value is incremented (decremented) by 1.[2]

2. For now, only a simple variable name may be used as the operand of an increment or decrement operator. We will see that these operators can be used on so-called *lvalues.*)

Operator	Called	Sample expression	Explanation
++	preincrement	++a	Increment **a** by 1, then use the new value of **a** in the expression in which **a** resides.
++	postincrement	a++	Use the current value of **a** in the expression in which **a** resides, then increment **a** by 1.
--	predecrement	--b	Decrement **b** by 1, then use the new value of **b** in the expression in which **b** resides.
--	postdecrement	b--	Use the current value of **b** in the expression in which **b** resides, then decrement **b** by 1.

Fig. 2.13   Increment and decrement operators.

Figure 2.14 demonstrates the difference between the preincrementing version and the postincrementing version of the **++** operator. Postincrementing the variable **c** causes it to be incremented after it is used in the output statement. Preincrementing the variable **c** causes it to be incremented before it is used in the output statement. The program displays the value of **c** before and after the **++** operator is used. The decrement operator (**--**) works similarly.

```cpp
1   // Fig. 2.14: fig02_14.cpp
2   // Preincrementing and postincrementing.
3   #include <iostream>
4
5   using std::cout;
6   using std::endl;
7
8   // function main begins program execution
9   int main()
10  {
11     int c;                        // declare variable
12
13     // demonstrate postincrement
14     c = 5;                        // assign 5 to c
15     cout << c << endl;            // print 5
16     cout << c++ << endl;          // print 5 then postincrement
17     cout << c << endl << endl;    // print 6
18
19     // demonstrate preincrement
20     c = 5;                        // assign 5 to c
21     cout << c << endl;            // print 5
22     cout << ++c << endl;          // preincrement then print 6
23     cout << c << endl;            // print 6
24
25     return 0;    // indicate successful termination
26
27  } // end function main
```

Fig. 2.14   Preincrementing and postincrementing. (Part 1 of 2.)

```
5
5
6

5
6
6
```

Fig. 2.14   Preincrementing and postincrementing. (Part 2 of 2.)

Good Programming Practice 2.9

Unary operators should be placed next to their operands with no intervening spaces.

The three assignment statements in Fig. 2.11

```
passes = passes + 1;
failures = failures + 1;
studentCounter = studentCounter + 1;
```

can be written more concisely with assignment operators as

```
passes += 1;
failures += 1;
studentCounter += 1;
```

with preincrement operators as

```
++passes;
++failures;
++studentCounter;
```

or with postincrement operators as

```
passes++;
failures++;
studentCounter++;
```

Note that, when incrementing (**++**) or decrementing (**--**) of a variable occurs in a statement by itself, the preincrement and postincrement forms have the same effect, and the predecrement and postdecrement forms have the same effect. It is only when a variable appears in the context of a larger expression that preincrementing the variable and postincrementing the variable have different effects (and similarly for predecrementing and postdecrementing).

Common Programming Error 2.11

*Attempting to use the increment or decrement operator on an expression other than a simple variable name, e.g., writing **++(x + 1)**, is a syntax error.*

Performance Tip 2.5

Preincrement and predecrement operate slightly faster than postincrement and postdecrement.

Figure 2.15 shows the precedence and associativity of the operators introduced to this point. The operators are shown top-to-bottom in decreasing order of precedence. The second

Operators					Associativity	Type
()					left to right	parentheses
++	--	static_cast<*type*>()			left to right	unary
++	--	+	-		right to left	unary
*	/	%			left to right	multiplicative
+	-				left to right	additive
<<	>>				left to right	insertion/extraction
<	<=	>	>=		left to right	relational
==	!=				left to right	equality
?:					right to left	conditional
=	+=	-=	*=	/=	%=	right to left	assignment

Fig. 2.15   Operator precedence for the operators encountered so far in the text.

column describes the associativity of the operators at each level of precedence. Notice that the conditional operator (**?:**), the unary operators postincrement (**++**), postdecrement (**--**), plus (**+**), minus (**-**) and casts, and the assignment operators **=**, **+=**, **-=**, ***=**, **/=** and **%=** associate from right to left. All other operators in the operator precedence chart of Fig. 2.15 associate from left to right. The third column names the various groups of operators.

2.13 Essentials of Counter-Controlled Repetition

Counter-controlled repetition requires the following:

1. the *name* of a control variable (or loop counter);
2. the *initial value* of the control variable;
3. the condition that tests for the *final value* of the control variable (i.e., whether looping should continue);
4. the *increment* (or *decrement*) by which the control variable is modified each time through the loop.

Consider the simple program in Fig. 2.16, which prints the numbers from 1 to 10. The declaration at line 11 *names* the control variable (**counter**), declares it to be an integer, reserves space for it in memory and sets it to an *initial value* of **1**. Declarations that require initialization are, in effect, executable statements. In C++, it is more precise to call a declaration that also reserves memory—as the preceding declaration does—a *definition*.

The declaration and initialization of **counter** also could have been accomplished with the statements

```
int counter;
counter = 1;
```

We use both methods of initializing variables.

```
1   // Fig. 2.16: fig02_16.cpp
2   // Counter-controlled repetition.
3   #include <iostream>
4
5   using std::cout;
6   using std::endl;
7
8   // function main begins program execution
9   int main()
10  {
11     int counter = 1;              // initialization
12
13     while ( counter <= 10 ) {     // repetition condition
14        cout << counter << endl;   // display counter
15        ++counter;                 // increment
16
17     } // end while
18
19     return 0;   // indicate successful termination
20
21  } // end function main
```

```
1
2
3
4
5
6
7
8
9
10
```

Fig. 2.16   Counter-controlled repetition.

Line 15 *increments* the loop counter by 1 each time the loop is performed. The loop-continuation condition (line 13) in the **while** structure determines whether the value of the control variable is less than or equal to **10** (the last value for which the condition is **true**). Note that the body of this **while** executes even when the control variable is **10**. The loop terminates when the control variable is greater than **10** (i.e., **counter** becomes **11**).

Figure 2.16 can be made more concise by initializing **counter** to **0** and by replacing the **while** structure with

```
while ( ++counter <= 10 )
   cout << counter << endl;
```

This code saves a statement, because the incrementing is done directly in the **while** condition before the condition is tested. Also, this code eliminates the braces around the body of the **while**, because the **while** now contains only one statement. Coding in such a condensed fashion takes some practice and can lead to programs that are more difficult to read, debug, modify and maintain.

Common Programming Error 2.12

Floating-point values are approximate, so controlling counting loops with floating-point variables can result in imprecise counter values and inaccurate tests for termination.

Testing and Debugging Tip 2.3

Control counting loops with integer values.

Good Programming Practice 2.10

Indent the statements in the body of each control structure.

Good Programming Practice 2.11

Put a blank line before and after each control structure to make it stand out in the program.

Good Programming Practice 2.12

Too many levels of nesting can make a program difficult to understand. As a general rule, try to avoid using more than three levels of indentation.

Good Programming Practice 2.13

Vertical spacing above and below control structures, and indentation of the bodies of control structures within the control-structure headers, give programs a two-dimensional appearance that greatly improves readability.

2.14 **for** Repetition Structure

The ***for*** *repetition structure* handles all the details of counter-controlled repetition. To illustrate the power of **for**, let us rewrite the program of Fig. 2.16. The result is shown in Fig. 2.17.

```
1   // Fig. 2.17: fig02_17.cpp
2   // Counter-controlled repetition with the for structure.
3   #include <iostream>
4
5   using std::cout;
6   using std::endl;
7
8   // function main begins program execution
9   int main()
10  {
11     // Initialization, repetition condition and incrementing
12     // are all included in the for structure header.
13
14     for ( int counter = 1; counter <= 10; counter++ )
15        cout << counter << endl;
16
17     return 0;   // indicate successful termination
18
19  } // end function main
```

Fig. 2.17 Counter-controlled repetition with the **for** structure. (Part 1 of 2.)

Fig. 2.17   Counter-controlled repetition with the **for** structure. (Part 2 of 2.)

When the **for** structure begins executing, the control variable **counter** is declared and initialized to 1. Then, the loop-continuation condition **counter <= 10** is checked. The initial value of **counter** is 1, so the condition is satisfied and the body statement prints the value of **counter**, namely 1. Then, the expression **counter++** increments control variable **counter** and the loop begins again with the loop-continuation test. The control variable is now equal to 2, so the final value is not exceeded and the program performs the body statement again. This process continues until the control variable **counter** is incremented to 11—this causes the loop-continuation test to fail and repetition to terminate. The program continues by performing the first statement after the **for** structure (in this case, the **return** statement at line 17).

Figure 2.18 takes a closer look at the **for** structure of Fig. 2.17. Notice that the **for** structure "does it all"—it specifies each of the items needed for counter-controlled repetition with a control variable. If there is more than one statement in the body of the **for**, braces are required to enclose the body of the loop.

Notice that Fig. 2.17 uses the loop-continuation condition **counter <= 10**. If the programmer incorrectly wrote **counter < 10**, then the loop would execute only 9 times. This is a common logic error called an *off-by-one error*.

Common Programming Error 2.13

*Using an incorrect relational operator or using an incorrect final value of a loop counter in the condition of a **while** or **for** structure can cause off-by-one errors.*

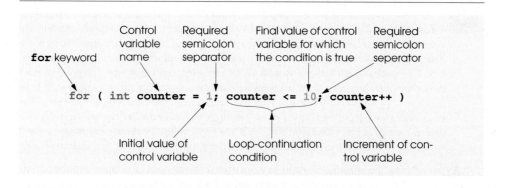

Fig. 2.18   **for** structure header components.

Good Programming Practice 2.14

*Using the final value in the condition of a **while** or **for** structure and using the **<=** relational operator helps avoid off-by-one errors. For example, in a loop that prints the values 1 to 10, the loop-continuation condition should be **counter <= 10** rather than **counter < 10** (which is an off-by-one error) or **counter < 11** (which is nevertheless correct). Many programmers prefer so-called* zero-based counting, *in which, to count 10 times,* **counter** *would be initialized to zero and the loop-continuation test would be* **counter < 10**.

The general format of the **for** structure is

```
for ( initialization; loopContinuationCondition; increment )
    statement
```

where the *initialization* expression initializes the loop's control variable, *loopContinuationCondition* is the condition that determines whether the loop should continue executing (this condition contains the final value of the control variable for which the condition is true) and *increment* increments the control variable. In most cases, the **for** structure can be represented by an equivalent **while** structure, as follows:

```
initialization;
while ( loopContinuationCondition ) {
    statement
    increment;
}
```

There is an exception to this rule, which we will discuss in Section 2.18.

If the *initialization* expression in the **for** structure header declares the control variable (i.e., the control variable's type is specified before the variable name), the control variable can be used only in the body of the **for** structure—the control variable will be unknown outside the **for** structure. This restricted use of the control variable name is known as the variable's *scope*. The scope of a variable specifies where it can be used in a program. Scope is discussed in detail in Chapter 3, "Functions."

Common Programming Error 2.14

*When the control variable of a **for** structure is defined in the initialization section of the **for** structure header, using the control variable after the body of the structure is a syntax error.*

Portability Tip 2.2

*In the C++ standard, the scope of the control variable declared in the initialization section of a **for** structure differs from the scope in older C++ compilers. In pre-standard compilers, the scope of the control variable does not terminate at the end of the block defining the body of the **for** structure; rather, the scope terminates at the end of the block that encloses the **for** structure. C++ code created with pre-standard C++ compilers can break when compiled on standard-compliant compilers. If you are working with pre-standard compilers and you want to be sure your code will work with standard-compliant compilers, there are two defensive programming strategies that can be used to prevent this problem: either declare control variables with different names in every **for** structure, or, if you prefer to use the same name for the control variable in several **for** structures, define the control variable before the first **for** structure.*

As we will see, the *initialization* and *increment* expressions can be comma-separated lists of expressions. The commas, as used in these expressions, are *comma operators*, which guarantee that lists of expressions evaluate from left to right. The comma operator has the lowest precedence of all C++ operators. The value and type of a comma-separated list of expressions is the value and type of the rightmost expression in the list. The comma operator most often is used in **for** structures. Its primary application is to enable the programmer to use multiple initialization expressions and/or multiple increment expressions. For example, there may be several control variables in a single **for** structure that must be initialized and incremented.

Good Programming Practice 2.15

*Place only expressions involving the control variables in the initialization and increment sections of a **for** structure. Manipulations of other variables should appear either before the loop (if they should execute only once, like initialization statements) or in the loop body (if they should execute once per repetition, like incrementing or decrementing statements).*

The three expressions in the **for** structure header are optional. If the *loopContinuationCondition* is omitted, C++ assumes that the loop-continuation condition is true, thus creating an infinite loop. One might omit the *initialization* expression if the control variable is initialized earlier in the program. One might omit the *increment* expression if the increment is calculated by statements in the body of the **for** or if no increment is needed. The increment expression in the **for** structure acts as a stand-alone statement at the end of the body of the **for**. Therefore, the expressions

```
counter = counter + 1
counter += 1
++counter
counter++
```

are all equivalent as the **for** structure increment. Many programmers prefer **counter++**, because **for** loops evaluate the increment expression after the loop body executes. The postincrementing form therefore seems more natural. The variable being incremented here does not appear in a larger expression, so both preincrementing and postincrementing actually have the same effect. The two semicolons in the **for** structure header are required.

Common Programming Error 2.15

*Using commas instead of the two required semicolons in a **for** header is a syntax error.*

Common Programming Error 2.16

*Placing a semicolon immediately to the right of the right parenthesis of a **for** header makes the body of that **for** structure an empty statement. Normally, this is a logic error.*

Software Engineering Observation 2.8

*Placing a semicolon immediately after a **for** header is sometimes used to create a so-called delay loop. Such a **for** loop with an empty body still loops the indicated number of times, doing nothing other than the counting. For example, you might use a delay loop to slow down a program that is producing outputs on the screen too quickly for you to read them.*

The initialization, loop-continuation condition and increment expressions of a **for** structure can contain arithmetic expressions. For example, assume that **x = 2** and **y = 10**. If **x** and **y** are not modified in the loop body, the statement

```
for ( int j = x; j <= 4 * x * y; j += y / x )
```

is equivalent to the statement

```
for ( int j = 2; j <= 80; j += 5 )
```

The "increment" of a **for** structure can be negative, in which case it is really a decrement and the loop actually counts downwards (as shown in Section 2.15).

If the loop-continuation condition is initially false, the body of the **for** structure is not performed. Instead, execution proceeds with the statement following the **for**.

Frequently, the control variable is printed or used in calculations in the body of a **for** structure, but this is not required. It is common to use the control variable for controlling repetition while never mentioning it in the body of the **for** structure.

Testing and Debugging Tip 2.4

*Although the value of the control variable can be changed in the body of a **for** loop, avoid doing so, because this practice can lead to subtle logic errors.*

The **for** structure's activity diagram is similar to that of the **while** structure's. Figure 2.19 shows the activity diagram of the **for** structure in Fig. 2.17. The diagram makes it clear that the initialization occurs once before the loop-continuation test evaluates the first time, and that incrementing occurs each time *after* the body statement executes. Note that (besides an initial state, transition arrows, a merge, a final state and several notes) the diagram contains only action states and a decision. Imagine, again, that the programmer has a bin of empty **for** structures—as many as needed to form a structured implementation of an algorithm. The programmer fills in the action states and decision symbols with action expressions and guard conditions appropriate to the algorithm.

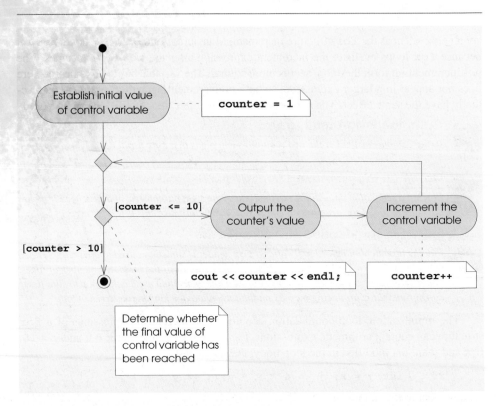

Fig. 2.19   **for** repetition structure activity diagram.

2.15 Examples Using the `for` Structure

The following examples show methods of varying the control variable in a **for** structure. In each case, we write the appropriate **for** structure header. Note the change in the relational operator for loops that decrement the control variable.

a) Vary the control variable from **1** to **100** in increments of **1**.

```
for ( int i = 1; i <= 100; i++ )
```

b) Vary the control variable from **100** to **1** in increments of **-1** (decrements of **1**).

```
for ( int i = 100; i >= 1; i-- )
```

c) Vary the control variable from **7** to **77** in steps of **7**.

```
for ( int i = 7; i <= 77; i += 7 )
```

d) Vary the control variable from **20** to **2** in steps of **-2**.

```
for ( int i = 20; i >= 2; i -= 2 )
```

e) Vary the control variable over the following sequence of values: **2, 5, 8, 11, 14, 17, 20**.

```
for ( int j = 2; j <= 20; j += 3 )
```

f) Vary the control variable over the following sequence of values: **99, 88, 77, 66, 55, 44, 33, 22, 11, 0**.

```
for ( int j = 99; j >= 0; j -= 11 )
```

 Common Programming Error 2.17

*Not using the proper relational operator in the loop-continuation condition of a loop that counts downwards (such as incorrectly using **i <= 1** in a loop counting down to 1) is usually a logic error that will yield incorrect results when the program runs.*

The next two examples provide simple applications of the **for** structure. The program of Fig. 2.20 uses the **for** structure to sum all the even integers from **2** to **100**. Each iteration of the loop (lines 14–15) adds the current value of the control variable **number** to variable **sum**.

```
1   // Fig. 2.20: fig02_20.cpp
2   // Summation with for.
3   #include <iostream>
4
5   using std::cout;
6   using std::endl;
7
8   // function main begins program execution
9   int main()
10  {
```

Fig. 2.20   Summation with **for**. (Part 1 of 2.)

```
11      int sum = 0;                            // initialize sum
12
13      // sum even integers from 2 through 100
14      for ( int number = 2; number <= 100; number += 2 )
15          sum += number;                      // add number to sum
16
17      cout << "Sum is " << sum << endl;   // output sum
18      return 0;                           // successful termination
19
20   } // end function main
```

```
Sum is 2550
```

Fig. 2.20   Summation with **for**. (Part 2 of 2.)

Note that the body of the **for** structure in Fig. 2.20 actually could be merged into the rightmost portion of the **for** header, by using the comma operator as follows:

```
for ( int number = 2;                   // initialization
        number <= 100;                  // continuation condition
        sum += number, number += 2 )    // total and increment
    ; // empty body
```

Good Programming Practice 2.16

*Although statements preceding a **for** and statements in the body of a **for** often can be merged into the **for** header, doing so can make the program more difficult to read, maintain, modify and debug.*

Good Programming Practice 2.17

Limit the size of control structure headers to a single line, if possible.

The next example computes compound interest using the **for** structure. Consider the following problem statement:

> *A person invests $1000.00 in a savings account yielding 5 percent interest. Assuming that all interest is left on deposit in the account, calculate and print the amount of money in the account at the end of each year for 10 years. Use the following formula for determining these amounts:*
>
> $$a = p (1 + r)^n$$
>
> *where*
> > *p is the original amount invested (i.e., the principal),*
> > *r is the annual interest rate,*
> > *n is the number of years and*
> > *a is the amount on deposit at the end of the nth year.*

This problem involves a loop that performs the indicated calculation for each of the 10 years the money remains on deposit. The solution is shown in Fig. 2.21.

The **for** structure (lines 31–40) executes its body 10 times, varying a control variable from 1 to 10 in increments of 1. C++ does not include an exponentiation operator, so we use the *standard library function* **pow** (line 34) for this purpose. The function **pow(x, y)** calculates the value of **x** raised to the **y**th power. In this example, the algebraic expression $(1 + r)^n$ is written as **pow(1.0 + rate, year)** where variable **rate** represents r and variable **year** represents n. Function **pow** takes two arguments of type **double** and returns a **double** value.

This program will not compile without including header file **<cmath>** (line 15). Function **pow** requires two **double** arguments. Note that **year** is an integer. Header **<cmath>**[3] includes information that tells the compiler to convert the value of **year** to a temporary **double** representation before calling the function. This information is contained in **pow**'s *function prototype*. Function prototypes are explained in Chapter 3. Chapter 3 also provides a summary of other math library functions.

Common Programming Error 2.18

*In general, forgetting to include the appropriate header file when using standard library functions (e.g., **<cmath>** in a program that uses math library functions) is a syntax error.*

```
1   // Fig. 2.21: fig02_21.cpp
2   // Calculating compound interest.
3   #include <iostream>
4
5   using std::cout;
6   using std::endl;
7   using std::ios;
8   using std::fixed;
9
10  #include <iomanip>
11
12  using std::setw;
13  using std::setprecision;
14
15  #include <cmath>   // enables program to use function pow
16
17  // function main begins program execution
18  int main()
19  {
20     double amount;               // amount on deposit
21     double principal = 1000.0;   // starting principal
22     double rate = .05;           // interest rate
23
24     // output table column heads
25     cout << "Year" << setw( 21 ) << "Amount on deposit" << endl;
26
```

Fig. 2.21   Compound interest calculations with **for**. (Part 1 of 2.)

---

3. All functions in the C++ Standard Library are part of namespace **std**. For this reason, Fig. 2.21 should include a **using** statement for function **pow**. A portion of the C++ standard library consists of functions, such as pow, that were absorbed into C++ from the C programming language. Some compilers will not compile **using** statements for those functions. However, most compilers will compile programs that do not provide **using** statements for such functions. To support a wider range of compilers, we do not provide **using** statements for C library functions. Another way to fix this problem would be to use the old-style C header file **<math.h>** rather than the C++ standard version of that header (**<cmath>**). However, we made the decision to use only standard C++ header files throughout this book.

```
27    // set floating-point number format
28    cout << fixed << setprecision( 2 );
29
30    // calculate amount on deposit for each of ten years
31    for ( int year = 1; year <= 10; year++ ) {
32
33        // calculate new amount for specified year
34        amount = principal * pow( 1.0 + rate, year );
35
36        // output one table row
37        cout << setw( 4 ) << year
38             << setw( 21 ) << amount << endl;
39
40    } // end for
41
42    return 0;    // indicate successful termination
43
44 } // end function main
```

```
Year    Amount on deposit
 1          1050.00
 2          1102.50
 3          1157.63
 4          1215.51
 5          1276.28
 6          1340.10
 7          1407.10
 8          1477.46
 9          1551.33
10          1628.89
```

Fig. 2.21   Compound interest calculations with **for**. (Part 2 of 2.)

Lines 20–22 declare **double** variables **amount**, **principal** and **rate**. We have done this for simplicity because we are dealing with fractional parts of dollars, and we need a type that allows decimal points in its values. Unfortunately, this can cause trouble. Here is a simple explanation of what can go wrong when using **float** or **double** to represent dollar amounts (assuming **setprecision(2)** is used to specify two digits of precision when printing): Two dollar amounts stored in the machine could be 14.234 (which prints as 14.23) and 18.673 (which prints as 18.67). When these amounts are added, they produce the internal sum 32.907 which prints as 32.91. Thus your printout could appear as

```
  14.23
+ 18.67
-------
  32.91
```

but a person adding the individual numbers as printed would expect the sum 32.90! You have been warned!

Good Programming Practice 2.18

*Do not use variables of type **float** or **double** to perform monetary calculations. The imprecision of floating-point numbers can cause errors that result in incorrect monetary values. In* *the exercises, we explore the use of integers to perform monetary calculations. [Note: Some third-party vendors sell C++ class libraries that perform precise monetary calculations.]*

The output statement at line 28 before the **for** loop and the output statement at lines 37–38 in the **for** loop combine to print the values of the variables **year** and **amount** with the formatting specified by the parameterized stream manipulators **setprecision** and **setw** and the nonparameterized stream manipulator **fixed**. The call **setw(4)** specifies that the next value output should appear in a *field width* of 4—i.e., **cout** prints the value with at least 4 character positions. If the value to be output is less than 4 character positions wide, the value is *right justified* in the field by default. If the value to be output is more than 4 character positions wide, the field width is extended to accommodate the entire value. To indicate that values should be output *left justified,* simply output non-parameterized stream manipulator **left** (found in header **<iostream>**).

The other formatting in the output statements indicates that variable **amount** is printed as a fixed-point value with a decimal point (specified in line 28 with the stream manipulator **fixed**) right-justified in a field of 21 character positions (specified in line 38 with **setw(21)**) and two digits of precision to the right of the decimal point (specified in line 28 with manipulator **setprecision(2)**). We placed the stream manipulator **fixed** and **setprecision** in a **cout** before the **for** loop because these settings remain in effect until they are changed. Thus, they do not need to be applied during each iteration of the loop. However, the field width specified with **setw** applies only to the next value output. We discuss the powerful input/output formatting capabilities of C++ in detail in Chapter 12.

Note that the calculation **1.0 + rate**, which appears as an argument to the **pow** function, is contained in the body of the **for** statement. In fact, this calculation produces the same result during each iteration of the loop, so repeating the calculation is wasteful. This calculation should be performed once before the loop.

Performance Tip 2.6

Avoid placing expressions whose values do not change inside loops—but, even if you do, many of today's sophisticated optimizing compilers will automatically place such expressions outside loops in the generated machine-language code.

Performance Tip 2.7

Many compilers contain optimization features that improve the code you write, but it is still better to write good code from the start.

For fun, be sure to try our Peter Minuit problem in the Exercise 2.65. This problem demonstrates the wonders of compound interest.

2.16 **switch** Multiple-Selection Structure

We have discussed the **if** single-selection structure and the **if/else** double-selection structure. Occasionally, an algorithm will contain a series of decisions in which a variable or expression is tested separately for each of the constant integral values it can assume and different actions are taken. C++ provides the **switch** multiple-selection structure to handle such decision making.

The **switch** structure consists of a series of **case** labels and an optional **default** case. The program in Fig. 2.22 uses **switch** to count the number of each different letter grade that students earned on an exam.

```
1   // Fig. 2.22: fig02_22.cpp
2   // Counting letter grades.
3   #include <iostream>
4
5   using std::cout;
6   using std::cin;
7   using std::endl;
8
9   // function main begins program execution
10  int main()
11  {
12     int grade;        // one grade
13     int aCount = 0;   // number of As
14     int bCount = 0;   // number of Bs
15     int cCount = 0;   // number of Cs
16     int dCount = 0;   // number of Ds
17     int fCount = 0;   // number of Fs
18
19     cout << "Enter the letter grades." << endl
20          << "Enter the EOF character to end input." << endl;
21
22     // loop until user types end-of-file key sequence
23     while ( ( grade = cin.get() ) != EOF ) {
24
25        // determine which grade was input
26        switch ( grade ) {  // switch structure nested in while
27
28           case 'A':        // grade was uppercase A
29           case 'a':        // or lowercase a
30              ++aCount;     // increment aCount
31              break;        // necessary to exit switch
32
33           case 'B':        // grade was uppercase B
34           case 'b':        // or lowercase b
35              ++bCount;     // increment bCount
36              break;        // exit switch
37
38           case 'C':        // grade was uppercase C
39           case 'c':        // or lowercase c
40              ++cCount;     // increment cCount
41              break;        // exit switch
42
43           case 'D':        // grade was uppercase D
44           case 'd':        // or lowercase d
45              ++dCount;     // increment dCount
46              break;        // exit switch
47
48           case 'F':        // grade was uppercase F
49           case 'f':        // or lowercase f
50              ++fCount;     // increment fCount
51              break;        // exit switch
52
```

Fig. 2.22   **switch** structure testing multiple letter-grade values. (Part 1 of 2.)

```
53              case '\n':        // ignore newlines,
54              case '\t':        // tabs,
55              case ' ':         // and spaces in input
56                 break;         // exit switch
57
58              default:          // catch all other characters
59                 cout << "Incorrect letter grade entered."
60                      << " Enter a new grade." << endl;
61                 break;         // optional; will exit switch anyway
62
63           } // end switch
64
65        } // end while
66
67        // output summary of results
68        cout << "\n\nTotals for each letter grade are:"
69             << "\nA: " << aCount    // display number of A grades
70             << "\nB: " << bCount    // display number of B grades
71             << "\nC: " << cCount    // display number of C grades
72             << "\nD: " << dCount    // display number of D grades
73             << "\nF: " << fCount    // display number of F grades
74             << endl;
75
76        return 0;  // indicate successful termination
77
78     } // end function main
```

```
Enter the letter grades.
Enter the EOF character to end input.
a
B
c
C
A
d
f
C
E
Incorrect letter grade entered. Enter a new grade.
D
A
b
^Z


Totals for each letter grade are:
A: 3
B: 2
C: 3
D: 2
F: 1
```

Fig. 2.22 **switch** structure testing multiple letter-grade values. (Part 2 of 2.)

In the program, the user enters letter grades for a class. Inside the **while** header, at line 23, the parenthesized assignment **(grade = cin.get())** executes first. The **cin.get()** function reads one character from the keyboard and stores that character in integer variable **grade**. We explain the dot notation used in **cin.get()** in Chapter 6, Classes and Data Abstraction. Characters normally are stored in variables of type *char*; however, an important feature of C++ is that characters can be stored in any integer data type because they are represented as 1-byte integers in the computer. Thus, we can treat a character either as an integer or as a character, depending on its use. For example, the statement

```
cout << "The character (" << 'a' << ") has the value "
     << static_cast< int > ( 'a' ) << endl;
```

prints the character **a** and its integer value as follows:

```
The character (a) has the value 97
```

The integer 97 is the character's numerical representation in the computer. Many computers today use the *ASCII (American Standard Code for Information Interchange) character set*, in which 97 represents the lowercase letter **'a'**. A list of the ASCII characters and their decimal values is presented in Appendix B.

Assignment statements as a whole have the value that is assigned to the variable on the left side of the **=**. Thus, the value of the assignment expression **grade = cin.get()** is the same as the value returned by **cin.get()** and assigned to the variable **grade**.

The fact that assignment statements have values can be useful for initializing several variables to the same value. For example,

```
a = b = c = 0;
```

first evaluates the assignment **c = 0** (because the **=** operator associates from right to left). The variable **b** is then assigned the value of the assignment **c = 0** (which is 0). Then, the variable **a** is assigned the value of the assignment **b = (c = 0)** (which is also 0). In the program, the value of the assignment **grade = cin.get()** is compared with the value of **EOF** (a symbol whose acronym stands for "end-of-file"). We use **EOF** (which normally has the value –1) as the sentinel value. *However, you do not type the value –1, nor do you type the letters EOF as the sentinel value.* Rather, you type a system-dependent keystroke combination that means "end-of-file" to indicate that you have no more data to enter. **EOF** is a symbolic integer constant defined in the **<iostream>** header file. If the value assigned to **grade** is equal to **EOF**, the program terminates. We have chosen to represent the characters entered into this program as **int**s, because **EOF** has an integer value.

On UNIX systems and many others, end-of-file is entered by typing the sequence

> *<ctrl-d>*

on a line by itself. This notation means to simultaneously press both the **ctrl** key and the **d** key. On other systems such as Microsoft Windows, end-of-file can be entered by typing

> *<ctrl-z>*

[*Note:* In some cases, you must press *Enter* after the preceding key sequence. Also, the characters **^Z** sometimes appear on the screen to represent end-of-file, as is shown in Fig. 2.22.]

Portability Tip 2.3

The keystroke combinations for entering end-of-file are system dependent.

Portability Tip 2.4

*Testing for the symbolic constant **EOF** rather than –1 makes programs more portable. The ANSI standard states that **EOF** is a negative integral value (but not necessarily –1). Thus, **EOF** could have different values on different systems.*

In this program, the user enters grades at the keyboard. When the user presses the *Enter* (or *Return*) key, the characters are read by the **cin.get()** function, one character at a time. If the character entered is not end-of-file, the flow of control enters the **switch** structure. The keyword **switch** is followed by the variable name **grade** in parentheses. This is called the *controlling expression*. The **switch** structure compares the value of this expression with each of the **case** *labels* in the order they appear in the **switch**. Assume the user enters the letter **C** as a grade. The program compares **C** to each **case** in the **switch**. If a match occurs (**case 'C':**), the statements for that **case** execute. For the letter **C**, the program increments **cCount** by **1** and the **switch** structure exits immediately with the **break** statement. Note that, unlike other control structures, it is not necessary to enclose a multiple-statement **case** in braces.

The **break** statement causes program control to proceed with the first statement after the **switch** structure. The **break** statement is used because the **case**s in a **switch** statement otherwise would run together. If **break** is not used anywhere in a **switch** structure, then, each time a match occurs in the structure, the statements for all the remaining **case**s execute. (This feature is sometimes useful when performing the same actions for several **case**s, as the program of Fig. 2.22 does for the lowercase and uppercase versions of the same letter.) If no match occurs, the **default** case is executed and an error message is printed.

Each **case** can have one or more actions. The **switch** selection structure is different from all other control structures in that braces are not required around multiple actions in a **case** of a **switch**. Figure 2.23 shows the activity diagram for the general **switch** multiple-selection structure. A majority of **switch** structures use a **break** in each **case** to terminate the **switch** structure after processing the **case**. Figure 2.23 emphasizes this by including **break** statements in the activity diagram. Without the **break** statement, control would not transition to the end of the **switch** structure after a **case** is processed. Instead, control would transition to the next **case**'s actions.

The diagram makes it clear that the **break** statement at the end of a **case** causes control to exit the **switch** structure immediately. Again, note that (besides an initial state, transition arrows and a final state) the diagram contains action states and decisions. Also, note that the diagram uses merge symbols to merge the transitions from the **break** statements to the final state.

Imagine, again, that the programmer has a bin of empty **switch** structures—as many as needed to stack and nest with other control structures to form a structured implementation of an algorithm. The programmer fills in the action states and decision symbols with action expressions and guard conditions appropriate to the algorithm. Note that, although nested control structures are common, it is rare to find nested **switch** structures in a program.

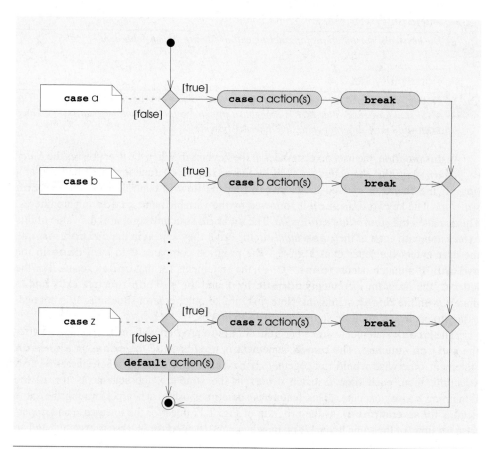

Fig. 2.23   **switch** multiple-selection structure activity diagram with **break** statements.

Common Programming Error 2.19

*Forgetting a **break** statement when one is needed in a **switch** structure is a logic error.*

Common Programming Error 2.20

*Omitting the space between the word **case** and the integral value being tested in a **switch** structure can cause a logic error. For example, writing **case3:** instead of writing **case 3:** simply creates an unused label. We will say more about this in Chapter 20. In this situation, the **switch** structure will not perform the appropriate actions when the **switch**'s controlling expression has a value of 3.*

Good Programming Practice 2.19

*Provide a **default** case in **switch** statements. Cases not tested explicitly in a **switch** statement without a **default** case are ignored. Including a **default** case focuses the programmer on the need to process exceptional conditions. There are situations in which no **default** processing is needed. Although the **case** clauses and the **default** case clause in a **switch** structure can occur in any order, it is a good programming practice to place the **default** clause last.*

Good Programming Practice 2.20

In a **switch** *structure that lists the* **default** *clause last, the* **default** *clause does not require a* **break** *statement. Some programmers include this* **break** *for clarity and for symmetry with other cases.*

In the **switch** structure of Fig. 2.22, lines 53–56 cause the program to skip newline, tab and blank characters. Reading characters one at a time can cause some problems. To have the program read the characters, they must be sent to the computer by pressing the *Enter key* on the keyboard. This places a newline character in the input after the character we wish to process. Often, this newline character must be specially processed to make the program work correctly. By including the preceding cases in our **switch** structure, we prevent the error message in the **default** case from being printed each time a newline, tab or space is encountered in the input.

Common Programming Error 2.21

Not processing newline and other whitespace characters in the input when reading characters one at a time can cause logic errors.

Note that several case labels listed together (such as **case 'D': case 'd':** in Fig. 2.22) simply means that the same set of actions is to occur for each of the cases.

When using the **switch** structure, remember that it can be used only for testing a *constant integral expression*—any combination of character constants and integer constants that evaluates to a constant integer value. A character constant is represented as the specific character in single quotes such as **'A'**. An integer constant is simply an integer value. Also, each **case** label can specify only one constant integral expression.

Common Programming Error 2.22

Specifying an expression (e.g., **a + b***) in a* **switch** *structure's* **case** *label is a syntax error.*

In our discussion of object-oriented programming in Chapter 6–Chapter 10, we present a more elegant way to implement **switch** logic. We will use a technique called polymorphism to create programs that are often clearer, more concise, easier to maintain and easier to extend than programs that use **switch** logic.

C++ has flexible data type sizes. Different applications, for example, might need integers of different sizes. C++ provides several data types to represent integers. The range of integer values for each type depends on the particular computer's hardware. In addition to the types **int** and **char**, C++ provides the types **short** (an abbreviation of **short int**) and **long** (an abbreviation of **long int**). The minimum range of values for **short** integers is -32,768 to 32,767. For the vast majority of integer calculations, **long** integers are sufficient. The minimum range of values for **long** integers is –2,147,483,648 to 2,147,483,647. On most computers, **int**s are equivalent either to **short** or to **long**. The range of values for an **int** is at least the same as the range for **short** integers and no larger than the range for **long** integers. The data type **char** can be used to represent any of the characters in the computer's character set. The data type **char** also can be used to represent small integers.

Portability Tip 2.5

Because **int***s vary in size between systems, use* **long** *integers if you expect to process integers outside the range –32,768 to 32,767 and you would like to run the program on several different computer systems.*

Performance Tip 2.8

In performance-oriented situations where memory is at a premium, it might be desirable to use smaller integer sizes.

Performance Tip 2.9

Using smaller integer sizes can result in a slower program if the machine's instructions for manipulating them are not as efficient as those for the natural-size integers.

Common Programming Error 2.23

*Providing identical case labels in a **switch** structure is a syntax error.*

2.17 do/while Repetition Structure

The **do/while** repetition structure is similar to the **while** structure. In the **while** structure, the loop-continuation condition test occurs at the beginning of the loop before the body of the loop executes. The **do/while** structure tests the loop-continuation condition *after* the loop body executes; therefore, the loop body executes at least once. When a **do/while** terminates, execution continues with the statement after the **while** clause. Note that it is not necessary to use braces in the **do/while** structure if there is only one statement in the body; however, most programmers include the braces to avoid confusion between the **while** and **do/while** structures. For example,

```
while ( condition )
```

normally is regarded as the header to a **while** structure. A **do/while** with no braces around the single statement body appears as

```
do
    statement
while ( condition );
```

which can be confusing. The last line—**while(** *condition* **);**—might be misinterpreted by the reader as a **while** structure containing an empty statement. Thus, the **do/while** with one statement is often written as follows to avoid confusion:

```
do {
    statement
} while ( condition );
```

Good Programming Practice 2.21

*Always including braces in a **do/while** structure helps eliminate ambiguity between the **while** structure and the **do/while** structure containing one statement.*

Figure 2.24 uses a **do/while** structure to print the numbers from 1 to 10. Note that the program preincrements the control variable **counter** in the loop-continuation test. Also, note the use of the braces to enclose the single-statement body of the **do/while** structure.

```
1   // Fig. 2.24: fig02_24.cpp
2   // Using the do/while repetition structure.
3   #include <iostream>
4
5   using std::cout;
6   using std::endl;
7
8   // function main begins program execution
9   int main()
10  {
11     int counter = 1;              // initialize counter
12
13     do {
14        cout << counter << "   ";   // display counter
15     } while ( ++counter <= 10 );   // end do/while
16
17     cout << endl;
18
19     return 0;    // indicate successful termination
20
21  } // end function main
```

```
1   2   3   4   5   6   7   8   9   10
```

Fig. 2.24   **do/while** structure.

Figure 2.25 contains the activity diagram for the **do/while** structure. This diagram makes it clear that the loop-continuation condition does not evaluate until after the loop performs the action state at least once. Again, note that (besides an initial state, transition arrows, a final state and a note) the diagram contains only an action state and a decision. Imagine, again, that the programmer has access to a bin of empty **do/while** repetition structures—as many as the programmer might need to stack and nest with other control structures to form a structured implementation of an algorithm. The programmer fills in the action states and decision symbols with action expressions and guard conditions appropriate to the algorithm.

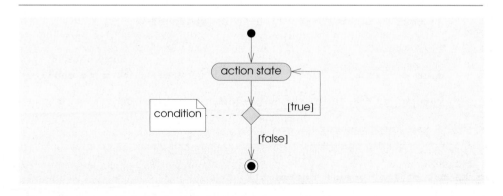

Fig. 2.25   **do/while** repetition structure activity diagram.

2.18 `break` and `continue` Statements

The **break** and **continue** statements alter the flow of control. The **break** statement, when executed in a **while**, **for**, **do/while** or **switch** structure, causes immediate exit from that structure. Program execution continues with the first statement after the structure. Common uses of the **break** statement are to escape early from a loop or to skip the remainder of a **switch** structure (as in Fig. 2.22). Figure 2.26 demonstrates the **break** statement (line 19) in a **for** repetition structure. When the **if** structure detects that **x** is **5**, **break** executes. This terminates the **for** structure and the program continues with the **cout** after the **for**. The loop body executes fully only four times. Note that the control variable **x** in this program is defined outside the **for** structure header. This is because we intend to use the control variable both in the body of the loop and after the loop completes its execution.

```cpp
1   // Fig. 2.26: fig02_26.cpp
2   // Using the break statement in a for structure.
3   #include <iostream>
4
5   using std::cout;
6   using std::endl;
7
8   // function main begins program execution
9   int main()
10  {
11
12      int x;   // x declared here so it can be used after the loop
13
14      // loop 10 times
15      for ( x = 1; x <= 10; x++ ) {
16
17          // if x is 5, terminate loop
18          if ( x == 5 )
19              break;              // break loop only if x is 5
20
21          cout << x << " ";    // display value of x
22
23      } // end for
24
25      cout << "\nBroke out of loop when x became " << x << endl;
26
27      return 0;   // indicate successful termination
28
29  } // end function main
```

```
1 2 3 4
Broke out of loop when x became 5
```

Fig. 2.26   **break** statement exiting a **for** structure.

The **continue** statement, when executed in a **while**, **for** or **do/while** structure, skips the remaining statements in the body of that structure and proceeds with the next iteration of the loop. In **while** and **do/while** structures, the loop-continuation test evaluates immediately after the **continue** statement executes. In the **for** structure, the increment expression executes, then the loop-continuation test evaluates. Earlier, we stated that the **while** structure could be used in most cases to represent the **for** structure. The one exception occurs when the increment expression in the **while** structure follows the **continue** statement. In this case, the increment does not execute before the program tests the repetition-continuation condition and the **while** does not execute in the same manner as the **for**. Figure 2.27 uses the **continue** statement (line 16) in a **for** structure to skip the output statement in the structure and begin the next iteration of the loop.

Good Programming Practice 2.22

*Some programmers feel that **break** and **continue** violate structured programming. The effects of these statements can be achieved by structured programming techniques we soon will learn, so these programmers do not use **break** and **continue**.*

```cpp
1   // Fig. 2.27: fig02_27.cpp
2   // Using the continue statement in a for structure.
3   #include <iostream>
4
5   using std::cout;
6   using std::endl;
7
8   // function main begins program execution
9   int main()
10  {
11     // loop 10 times
12     for ( int x = 1; x <= 10; x++ ) {
13
14        // if x is 5, continue with next iteration of loop
15        if ( x == 5 )
16           continue;          // skip remaining code in loop body
17
18        cout << x << " ";    // display value of x
19
20     } // end for structure
21
22     cout << "\nUsed continue to skip printing the value 5"
23          << endl;
24
25     return 0;              // indicate successful termination
26
27  } // end function main
```

```
1 2 3 4 6 7 8 9 10
Used continue to skip printing the value 5
```

Fig. 2.27   **continue** statement terminating a single iteration of a **for** structure.

Performance Tip 2.10

*The **break** and **continue** statements, when used properly, perform faster than do the cor-responding structured techniques.*

Software Engineering Observation 2.9

There is a tension between achieving quality software engineering and achieving the best-performing software. Often, one of these goals is achieved at the expense of the other. For all but the most performance-intensive situations, apply the following rule of thumb: First, make your code simple and correct; then make it fast and small, but only if necessary.

2.19 Logical Operators

So far we have studied only *simple conditions*, such as **counter <= 10**, **total > 1000** and **number != sentinelValue**. We expressed these conditions in terms of the relational operators **>**, **<**, **>=** and **<=**, and the equality operators **==** and **!=**. Each decision tested precisely one condition. To test multiple conditions while making a decision, we performed these tests in separate statements or in nested **if** or **if/else** structures.

C++ provides *logical operators* that are used to form more complex conditions by combining simple conditions. The logical operators are **&&** *(logical AND)*, **||** *(logical OR)* and **!** *(logical NOT*, also called *logical negation)*.

Suppose we wish to ensure that two conditions are *both* **true** before we choose a certain path of execution. In this case, we can use the logical **&&** operator as follows:

```
if ( gender == 1 && age >= 65 )
    ++seniorFemales;
```

This **if** structure contains two simple conditions. The condition **gender == 1** is used here to determine whether a person is a female. The condition **age >= 65** determines whether a person is a senior citizen. The simple condition to the left of the **&&** operator evaluates first, because the precedence of **==** is higher than the precedence of **&&**. If necessary, the simple condition to the right of the **&&** operator evaluates next, because the precedence of **>=** is higher than the precedence of **&&**. As we will discuss shortly, the right side of a logical AND expression evaluates only if the left side is **true**. The **if** structure then considers the combined condition

```
gender == 1 && age >= 65
```

This condition is **true** if and only if both of the simple conditions are **true**. Finally, if this combined condition is indeed **true**, the statement in the **if** structure's body increments the count of **seniorFemales**. If either of the simple conditions are **false** (or both are), then the program skips the incrementing and proceeds to the statement following the **if**. The preceding combined condition can be made more readable by adding redundant parentheses

```
( gender == 1 ) && ( age >= 65 )
```

Common Programming Error 2.24

*Although **3 < x < 7** is a mathematically correct condition, it does not evaluate as you might expect in C++. Use **(3 < x && x < 7)** to get the proper evaluation in C++.*

Figure 2.28 summarizes the **&&** operator. The table shows all four possible combinations of **false** and **true** values for *expression1* and *expression2*. Such tables are often called *truth tables*. C++ evaluates to **false** or **true** all expressions that include relational operators, equality operators and/or logical operators.

Now let us consider the **||** (logical OR) operator. Suppose we wish to ensure at some point in a program that either *or* both of two conditions are **true** before we choose a certain path of execution. In this case, we use the **||** operator, as in the following program segment:

```
if ( semesterAverage >= 90 || finalExam >= 90 )
    cout << "Student grade is A" << endl;
```

This preceding condition also contains two simple conditions. The simple condition **semesterAverage >= 90** evaluates to determine whether the student deserves an "A" in the course because of a solid performance throughout the semester. The simple condition **finalExam >= 90** evaluates to determine whether the student deserves an "A" in the course because of an outstanding performance on the final exam. The **if** structure then considers the combined condition

```
semesterAverage >= 90 || finalExam >= 90
```

and awards the student an "A" if either or both of the simple conditions are **true**. Note that the message "**Student grade is A**" prints unless both of the simple conditions are **false**. Figure 2.29 is a truth table for the logical OR operator (**||**).

expression1	expression2	expression1 && expression2
false	false	false
false	true	false
true	false	false
true	true	true

Fig. 2.28   **&&** (logical AND) operator truth table.

expression1	expression2	expression1 || expression2
false	false	false
false	true	true
true	false	true
true	true	true

Fig. 2.29   **||** (logical OR) operator truth table.

The **&&** operator has a higher precedence than the | | operator. Both operators associate from left to right. An expression containing **&&** or | | operators evaluates only until truth or falsehood is known. Thus, evaluation of the expression

```
gender == 1 && age >= 65
```

stops immediately if **gender** is not equal to **1** (i.e., the entire expression is **false**) and continues if **gender** is equal to **1** (i.e., the entire expression could still be **true** if the condition **age >= 65** is **true**). This performance feature for the evaluation of logical AND and logical OR expressions is called *short-circuit evaluation.*

Performance Tip 2.11

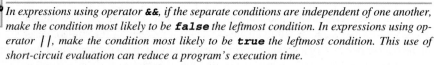

In expressions using operator **&&***, if the separate conditions are independent of one another, make the condition most likely to be* **false** *the leftmost condition. In expressions using operator* | |*, make the condition most likely to be* **true** *the leftmost condition. This use of short-circuit evaluation can reduce a program's execution time.*

C++ provides the **!** (logical negation) operator to enable a programmer to "reverse" the meaning of a condition. Unlike the **&&** and | | binary operators, which combine two conditions, the unary logical negation operator has only a single condition as an operand. The unary logical negation operator is placed before a condition when we are interested in choosing a path of execution if the original condition (without the logical negation operator) is **false**, such as in the following program segment:

```
if ( !( grade == sentinelValue ) )
    cout << "The next grade is " << grade << endl;
```

The parentheses around the condition **grade == sentinelValue** are needed because the logical negation operator has a higher precedence than the equality operator. Figure 2.30 is a truth table for the logical negation operator.

In most cases, the programmer can avoid using logical negation by expressing the condition with an appropriate relational or equality operator. For example, the preceding **if** structure also can be written as follows:

```
if ( grade != sentinelValue )
    cout << "The next grade is " << grade << endl;
```

This flexibility often can help a programmer express a condition in a more "natural" or convenient manner.

Figure 2.31 shows the precedence and associativity of the C++ operators introduced to this point. The operators are shown from top to bottom, in decreasing order of precedence.

expression	! expression
false	true
true	false

Fig. 2.30   **!** (logical negation) operator truth table.

Operators					Associativity	Type
( )					left to right	parentheses
++	--	static_cast<*type*>()			left to right	unary
++	--	+	-	!	right to left	unary
*	/	%			left to right	multiplicative
+	-				left to right	additive
<<	>>				left to right	insertion/extraction
<	<=	>	>=		left to right	relational
==	!=				left to right	equality
&&					left to right	logical AND
||					left to right	logical OR
?:					right to left	conditional
=	+=	-=	*=	/=	%=	right to left	assignment
,					left to right	comma

Fig. 2.31   Operator precedence and associativity.

2.20 Confusing Equality (==) and Assignment (=) Operators

There is one type of error that C++ programmers, no matter how experienced, tend to make so frequently that we felt it required a separate section. That error is accidentally swapping the operators **==** (equality) and **=** (assignment). What makes these swaps so damaging is the fact that they ordinarily do not cause syntax errors. Rather, statements with these errors tend to compile correctly and the programs run to completion, probably generating incorrect results through run-time logic errors. [*Note:* Some compilers issue a warning when **=** is used in a context where **==** normally is expected.]

There are two aspects of C++ that cause these problems. One is that any expression that produces a value can be used in the decision portion of any control structure. If the value of the expression is zero, it is treated as **false**, and if the value is nonzero, it is treated as **true**. The second is that C++ assignments produce a value—namely, the value assigned to the variable on the left side of the assignment operator. For example, suppose we intend to write

```
if ( payCode == 4 )
    cout << "You get a bonus!" << endl;
```

but we accidentally write

```
if ( payCode = 4 )
    cout << "You get a bonus!" << endl;
```

The first **if** structure properly awards a bonus to the person whose **paycode** is equal to 4. The second **if** structure—the one with the error—evaluates the assignment expression in the **if** condition to the constant 4. Any nonzero value is interpreted as **true**, so the condition in this **if** structure is always **true** and the person always receives a bonus regardless of what the actual paycode is! Even worse, the paycode has been modified when it was only supposed to be examined!

Common Programming Error 2.25

*Using operator **==** for assignment and using operator **=** for equality are logic errors.*

Testing and Debugging Tip 2.5

*Programmers normally write conditions such as **x == 7** with the variable name on the left and the constant on the right. By reversing these so that the constant is on the left and the variable name is on the right, as in **7 == x**, the programmer who accidentally replaces the **==** operator with **=** will be protected by the compiler. The compiler treats this as a syntax error because only a variable name can be placed on the left-hand side of an assignment statement. This will prevent the potential devastation of a run-time logic error.*

Variable names are said to be *lvalues* (for "left values") because they can be used on the left side of an assignment operator. Constants are said to be *rvalues* (for "right values") because they can be used on only the right side of an assignment operator. Note that *lvalues* can also be used as *rvalues*, but not vice versa.

There is another equally unpleasant situation. Suppose the programmer wants to assign a value to a variable with a simple statement like

```
x = 1;
```

but instead writes

```
x == 1;
```

Here, too, this is not a syntax error. Rather, the compiler simply evaluates the conditional expression. If **x** is equal to **1**, the condition is **true** and the expression evaluates to the value **true**. If **x** is not equal to **1**, the condition is **false** and the expression evaluates to the value **false**. Regardless of the expression's value, there is no assignment operator, so the value simply is lost. The value of **x** remains unaltered, probably causing an execution-time logic error. Unfortunately, we do not have a handy trick available to help you with this problem!

Testing and Debugging Tip 2.6

*Use your text editor to search for all occurrences of **=** in your program and check that you have the correct operator in each place.*

2.21 Structured-Programming Summary

Just as architects design buildings by employing the collective wisdom of their profession, so should programmers design programs. Our field is younger than architecture is and our collective wisdom is considerably sparser. We have learned that structured programming produces programs that are easier than unstructured programs to understand, test, debug, modify, and even prove correct in a mathematical sense.

Figure 2.32 uses activity diagrams to summarize C++'s control structures. The initial and final states indicate the single entry point and the single exit point of each control structure. Arbitrarily connecting individual symbols in an activity diagram can lead to unstructured programs. Therefore, the programming profession has chosen a limited set of control structures that can be combined in only two simple ways to build structured programs.

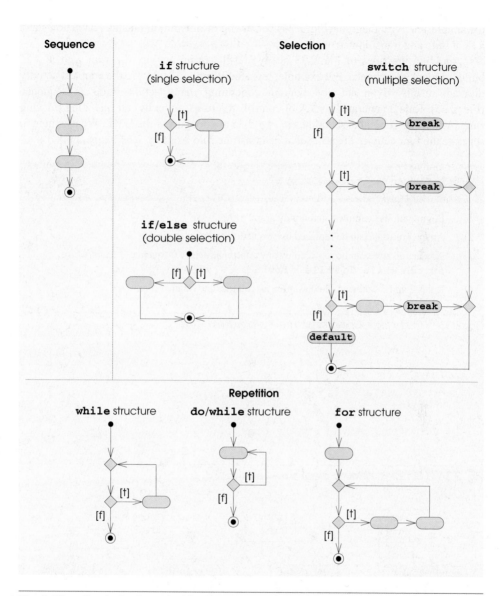

Fig. 2.32   C++'s single-entry/single-exit sequence, selection and repetition structures.

For simplicity, only single-entry/single-exit control structures are used—there is only one way to enter and only one way to exit each control structure. Connecting control structures in sequence to form structured programs is simple—the final state of one control structure is connected to the initial state of the next control structure—that is, the control structures are placed one after another in a program. We have called this "control-structure stacking." The rules for forming structured programs also allow for control structures to be nested.

Figure 2.33 shows the rules for forming structured programs. The rules assume that action states may be used to indicate any action. The rules also assume that we begin with the simplest activity diagram (Fig. 2.34) consisting of only an initial state, an action state, a final state and transition arrows.

Applying the rules of Fig. 2.33 always results in an activity diagram with a neat, building-block appearance. For example, repeatedly applying rule 2 to the simplest activity diagram results in an activity diagram containing many action states in sequence (Fig. 2.35). Rule 2 generates a stack of control structures, so let us call rule 2 the *stacking rule*. [*Note:* The vertical dashed lines in Fig. 2.35 are not part of the UML. We use them to separate the four activity diagrams that demonstrate rule 2 of Fig. 2.33 being applied.]

Rules for Forming Structured Programs

1) Begin with the "simplest activity diagram" (Fig. 2.34).

2) Any action state can be replaced by two action states in sequence.

3) Any action state can be replaced by any control structure (sequence, **if**, **if/else**, **switch**, **while**, **do/while** or **for**).

4) Rules 2 and 3 can be applied as often as you like and in any order.

Fig. 2.33   Rules for forming structured programs.

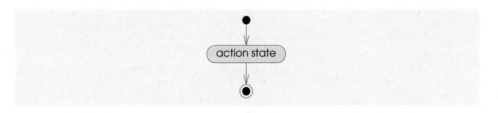

Fig. 2.34   Simplest activity diagram.

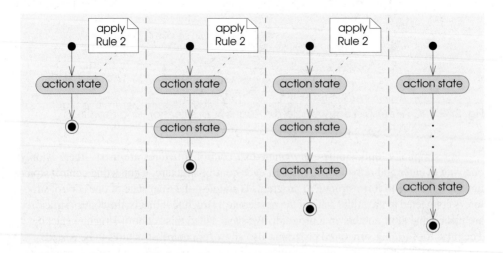

Fig. 2.35   Repeatedly applying rule 2 of Fig. 2.33 to the simplest activity diagram.

Rule 3 is called the *nesting rule*. Repeatedly applying rule 3 to the simplest activity diagram results in an activity diagram with neatly nested control structures. For example, in Fig. 2.36, the action state in the simplest activity diagram is replaced with a double-selection (**if/else**) structure. Then rule 3 is applied again to the action states in the double-selection structure, replacing each of these action states with a double-selection structure. The dashed action-state symbols around each of the double-selection structures represent the action state that was replaced in the original simplest activity diagram. [*Note:* The

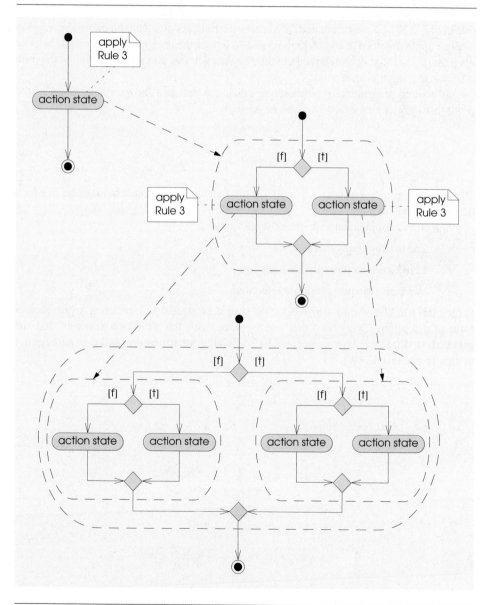

Fig. 2.36   Applying rule 3 of Fig. 2.33 to the simplest activity diagram.

dashed arrows and dashed action state symbols shown in Fig. 2.36 are not part of the UML. They are used here as pedagogic devices to illustrate that any action state may be replaced with a control structure.]

Rule 4 generates larger, more involved and more deeply nested structures. The diagrams that emerge from applying the rules in Fig. 2.33 constitute the set of all possible activity diagrams and hence the set of all possible structured programs. The beauty of the structured approach is that we use only seven simple single-entry/single-exit control structures and assemble them in only two simple ways.

If the rules in Fig. 2.33 are followed, an activity diagram with illegal syntax (such as that in Fig. 2.37) cannot be created. If you are uncertain about whether a particular diagram is legal, apply the rules of Fig. 2.33 in reverse to reduce the diagram to the simplest activity diagram. If the diagram is reducible to the simplest activity diagram, the original diagram is structured; otherwise, it is not.

Structured programming promotes simplicity. Bohm and Jacopini have given us the result that only three forms of control are needed:

- Sequence
- Selection
- Repetition

The sequence structure is trivial. Simply list the statements to execute in the order in which they should execute.

Selection is implemented in one of three ways:

- **if** structure (single selection)
- **if/else** structure (double selection)
- **switch** structure (multiple selection)

In fact, it is straightforward to prove that the simple **if** structure is sufficient to provide any form of selection—everything that can be done with the **if/else** structure and the **switch** structure can be implemented by combining **if** structures (although perhaps not as clearly and efficiently).

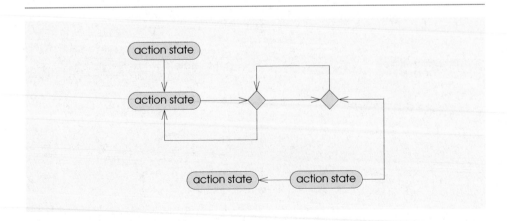

Fig. 2.37   Activity diagram with illegal syntax.

Repetition is implemented in one of three ways:

- **while** structure
- **do/while** structure
- **for** structure

It is straightforward to prove that the **while** structure is sufficient to provide any form of repetition. Everything that can be done with the **do/while** structure and the **for** structure can be done with the **while** structure (although perhaps not as smoothly).

Combining these results illustrates that any form of control ever needed in a C++ program can be expressed in terms of the following:

- sequence
- **if** structure (selection)
- **while** structure (repetition)

and that these control structures can be combined in only two ways—stacking and nesting. Indeed, structured programming promotes simplicity.

This chapter discussed how to compose programs from control structures containing action states and decisions. In Chapter 3, we will introduce another program-structuring unit called the *function*. We will learn to compose large programs by combining functions that, in turn, are composed of control structures. We also will discuss how functions promote software reusability. In Chapter 6, we will introduce C++'s other program-structuring unit, called the *class*. We then create objects from classes and proceed with our treatment of object-oriented programming. Now, we continue our introduction to object technology by introducing a problem that the reader will attack with the techniques of object-oriented design.

2.22 (Optional Case Study) Thinking About Objects: Identifying a System's Classes from a Problem Statement[4]

Now we begin our optional, object-oriented design/implementation case study. These "Thinking About Objects" sections at the ends of this and the next several chapters ease you into object orientation by examining an elevator-simulation case study. This case study provides you with a substantial, carefully paced, complete design and implementation experience. In Chapter 2–Chapter 5, we perform the various steps of an object-oriented design (OOD), using the UML. In Chapter 6, Chapter 7 and Chapter 9, we implement the elevator simulator, using the techniques of object-oriented programming (OOP) in C++. We present this case study in a fully solved format. This is not an exercise; rather, it is an end-to-end learning experience that concludes with a detailed walkthrough of the C++ code. We have provided this case study so you can become accustomed to the kinds of substantial problems that are attacked in industry.

Problem Statement

A company intends to build a two-floor office building and equip it with an elevator. The company wants you to develop an object-oriented *software simulator* in C++ that models the operation of the elevator to determine whether the elevator suits the company's needs.

---

4. The terminology for the optional "Thinking About Objects" sections appears at the end of the terminology section for each chapter.

Your simulator should include a clock that begins with its time, in seconds, set to zero. The clock ticks (increments the time by one) every second, but it does not keep track of hours and minutes. Your simulator also should include a scheduler that begins the day by scheduling two times randomly: the time when a person first steps onto floor 1 and presses the button on that floor to summon the elevator, and the time when a person first steps onto floor 2 and presses the button on that floor to summon the elevator. Each of these times is a random integer in the range from 5 to 20 seconds, inclusive (i.e., 5, 6, 7, …, 20). [*Note:* We discuss how to schedule random times in Chapter 3.] When the clock time equals the earlier of these two times, the scheduler creates a person, who then walks onto the appropriate floor and presses the floor button. [*Note:* It is possible that these two randomly scheduled times will be identical, in which case people step onto both floors and press both floor buttons at the same time.] The floor button illuminates, indicating that it has been pressed. [*Note:* The illumination of the floor button occurs automatically when the button is pressed and needs no programming; the light built into the button turns off automatically when the button is reset.] At the beginning of the simulation, the elevator starts the day waiting with its door closed on floor 1. To conserve energy, the elevator moves only when necessary. The elevator alternates directions between moving up and moving down.

For simplicity, the elevator and each of the floors have a capacity of one person. The scheduler first verifies that a floor is unoccupied before creating a person to walk onto that floor. If the floor is occupied, the scheduler delays creating the person by one second (thus allowing the elevator an opportunity to pick up the person and move to the floor). After a person walks onto a floor, the scheduler creates the next random time (between 5 and 20 seconds into the future) for a person to walk onto that floor and press the floor button.

When the elevator arrives at a floor, it resets the elevator button and sounds the elevator bell (which is inside the elevator). The elevator then signals its arrival to the floor. The floor, in response, resets the floor button and turns on the floor's elevator-arrival light. The elevator then opens its door. [*Note:* The door on the floor opens automatically with the elevator door and needs no programming.] The elevator's passenger, if there is one, exits the elevator, and a person, if there is one waiting on that floor, enters the elevator. Although each floor has a capacity of one person, assume there is enough room on each floor for a person to wait on that floor while the elevator's passenger exits.

A person entering the elevator presses the elevator button, which illuminates (automatically, without programming) when pressed and turns off when the elevator arrives on the floor and resets the elevator button. [*Note:* Because the building has only two floors, only one elevator button is necessary; this button notifies the elevator to move to the other floor.] Next, the elevator closes its door and begins moving to the other floor. When the elevator arrives at a floor, if a person does not enter the elevator and the floor button on the other floor has not been pressed, the elevator closes its door and remains on that floor until another person presses a button on a floor.

For simplicity, assume that all the activities that happen, from when the elevator reaches a floor until the elevator closes its door, take zero time. [*Note:* Although these activities take zero time, they still occur sequentially; e.g., the elevator door must open before the passenger exits the elevator.] The elevator takes five seconds to move from one floor to the other. Once per second, the simulator provides the time to the scheduler and to the elevator. The scheduler and elevator use the time to determine what actions each must take at that particular time, (e.g., the scheduler might determine that it is time to create a person, and the elevator, if moving, might determine that it is time to arrive at its destination floor).

The simulator should display messages on the screen that describe the activities that occur in the system. These include a person pressing a floor button, the elevator arriving on a floor, the clock ticking, a person entering the elevator, etc. The output should resemble the following (which is a 30-second sample):

```
*** ELEVATOR SIMULATION BEGINS ***

TIME: 1
elevator at rest on floor 1

TIME: 2
elevator at rest on floor 1

TIME: 3
elevator at rest on floor 1

TIME: 4
elevator at rest on floor 1

TIME: 5
scheduler creates person 1
person 1 steps onto floor 2
person 1 presses floor button on floor 2
floor 2 button summons elevator
(scheduler schedules next person for floor 2 at time 11)
elevator begins moving up to floor 2 (arrives at time 10)

TIME: 6
scheduler creates person 2
person 2 steps onto floor 1
person 2 presses floor button on floor 1
floor 1 button summons elevator
(scheduler schedules next person for floor 1 at time 24)
elevator moving up

TIME: 7
elevator moving up

TIME: 8
elevator moving up

TIME: 9
elevator moving up

TIME: 10
elevator arrives on floor 2
elevator resets its button
elevator rings its bell
floor 2 resets its button
floor 2 light turns on
elevator opens its door on floor 2
```

```
person 1 enters elevator from floor 2
person 1 presses elevator button
elevator button tells elevator to prepare to leave
floor 2 light turns off
elevator closes its door on floor 2
elevator begins moving down to floor 1 (arrives at time 15)

TIME: 11
scheduler creates person 3
person 3 steps onto floor 2
person 3 presses floor button on floor 2
floor 2 button summons elevator
(scheduler schedules next person for floor 2 at time 27)
elevator moving down

TIME: 12
elevator moving down

TIME: 13
elevator moving down

TIME: 14
elevator moving down

TIME: 15
elevator arrives on floor 1
elevator resets its button
elevator rings its bell
floor 1 resets its button
floor 1 light turns on
elevator opens its door on floor 1
person 1 exits elevator on floor 1
person 2 enters elevator from floor 1
person 2 presses elevator button
elevator button tells elevator to prepare to leave
floor 1 light turns off
elevator closes its door on floor 1
elevator begins moving up to floor 2 (arrives at time 20)

TIME: 16
elevator moving up

TIME: 17
elevator moving up

TIME: 18
elevator moving up

TIME: 19
elevator moving up

TIME: 20
elevator arrives on floor 2
elevator resets its button
```

```
elevator rings its bell
floor 2 resets its button
floor 2 light turns on
elevator opens its door on floor 2
person 2 exits elevator on floor 2
person 3 enters elevator from floor 2
person 3 presses elevator button
elevator button tells elevator to prepare to leave
floor 2 light turns off
elevator closes its door on floor 2
elevator begins moving down to floor 1 (arrives at time 25)

TIME: 21
elevator moving down

TIME: 22
elevator moving down

TIME: 23
elevator moving down

TIME: 24
scheduler creates person 4
person 4 steps onto floor 1
person 4 presses floor button on floor 1
floor 1 button summons elevator
(scheduler schedules next person for floor 1 at time 43)
elevator moving down

TIME: 25
elevator arrives on floor 1
elevator resets its button
elevator rings its bell
floor 1 resets its button
floor 1 light turns on
elevator opens its door on floor 1
person 3 exits elevator on floor 1
person 4 enters elevator from floor 1
person 4 presses elevator button
elevator button tells elevator to prepare to leave
floor 1 light turns off
elevator closes its door on floor 1
elevator begins moving up to floor 2 (arrives at time 30)

TIME: 26
elevator moving up

TIME: 27
scheduler creates person 5
person 5 steps onto floor 2
person 5 presses floor button on floor 2
floor 2 button summons elevator
(scheduler schedules next person for floor 2 at time 47)
elevator moving up
```

```
TIME: 28
elevator moving up

TIME: 29
elevator moving up

TIME: 30
elevator arrives on floor 2
elevator resets its button
elevator rings its bell
floor 2 resets its button
floor 2 light turns on
elevator opens its door on floor 2
person 4 exits elevator on floor 2
person 5 enters elevator from floor 2
person 5 presses elevator button
elevator button tells elevator to prepare to leave
floor 2 light turns off
elevator closes its door on floor 2
elevator begins moving down to floor 1 (arrives at time 35)

*** ELEVATOR SIMULATION ENDS ***
```

Our goal (over these "Thinking About Objects" sections in Chapter 2–Chapter 7 and in Chapter 9) is to implement a working software simulator that models the operation of the elevator for the number of seconds entered by the simulator user.

Analyzing and Designing the System

In this and the next several "Thinking About Objects" sections, we perform the steps of an object-oriented design process for the elevator system. The UML is designed for use with any OOAD process—many such processes exist. One popular method is the *Rational Unified Process*™ developed by Rational Software Corporation. For this case study, we present our own, simplified design process for your first OOD/UML experience.

Before we begin, we must examine the nature of simulations. A simulation consists of two portions. One contains all the elements that belong to the world we want to simulate. These elements include the elevator, the door, the floors, the buttons and the lights. We refer to these elements collectively as the *model*. The other portion contains all the elements needed to simulate this world. These elements include the clock and the scheduler. We refer to these elements collectively as the *controller*. We keep these two portions in mind as we design our system.

Use-Case Diagrams

When developers begin a project, they rarely start with a detailed problem statement, such as the one we have provided at the beginning of this section (Section 2.22). This document and others usually are the result of the *object-oriented analysis* (OOA) phase. In this phase, you interview the people who want you to build the system and the people who eventually will use the system. You use the information gained in these interviews to compile a list of *system requirements*. These requirements guide you and your fellow developers as you design the system. In our case study, the problem statement contains a summary of the system requirements for the elevator system. The output of the analysis phase is intended to specify clearly *what* the system is supposed to do. The output of the design phase is intended to specify *how* the system should be constructed to do what is needed.

The UML provides the *use-case diagram* to facilitate the process of requirements gathering. The use-case diagram models the interactions between the system's external clients and the *use cases* of the system. Each use case represents a different capability that the system provides to its clients. For example, in an automated-teller-machine system, the bank customer interacts with the system through the use cases "Withdraw funds," "Deposit funds" and "Query account."

Figure 2.38 shows the use-case diagram for the elevator system. The stick figure represents an *actor*. An actor defines the roles that an external entity, such as a person or another system, plays when interacting with the system. The only actors in our system are the people who want to ride the elevator. We therefore model one actor called "Person." The actor's "name" appears underneath the stick figure.

The *system box* (i.e., the enclosing rectangle in the figure) contains the use cases for the system. A fully formed use-case diagram does not require a system box. However, the UML allows the designer the option to include a system box whose title provides more information about the system. In our example, the box is labeled "Elevator System." This title shows that *this use-case diagram focuses on the behaviors of the system we want to simulate* (i.e., the elevator transporting people), *as opposed to the behaviors of the simulation* (i.e., creating people and scheduling arrivals).

The UML models each use case as an oval. In our simple system, external entities use the elevator for only one purpose: to move to another floor. The system provides only one capability to its users; therefore, "Move to another floor" is the only use case in our elevator system.

The use-case diagram acts as a key form of communication between the client and the system builders. As the system evolves, the use-case diagram helps ensure that all the clients' needs are met. The goal of the use-case diagram is to show the kinds of interactions users have with a system without providing the details of those interactions. Our case study contains only one use case. In larger systems, use-case diagrams are indispensable tools that help system designers remain focused on satisfying the users' needs.

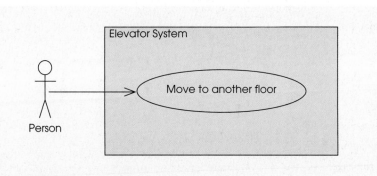

Fig. 2.38   Use-case diagram for elevator system.

Identifying the Classes in a System

The next step of our OOD process is to *identify the classes* in our problem. We eventually describe these classes in a formal way and implement them in C++. (We begin implementing the elevator simulator in C++ in Chapter 6.) First, we review the problem statement and locate all the *nouns*; with high likelihood, these represent most of the classes (or instances of classes) necessary to implement the elevator simulator. Figure 2.39 is a list of these nouns.

We extract only the nouns that perform important duties in our system. For this reason, we omit the following:

- company
- simulator
- time
- energy
- capacity

List of nouns in the problem statement

company

building

elevator

simulator

clock

time

scheduler

person

floor 1

floor button

floor 2

elevator door

energy

capacity

elevator button

elevator bell

floor's elevator arrival light

person waiting on a floor

elevator's passenger

Fig. 2.39 List of nouns in problem statement .

We do not need to model "company" as a class, because the company is not part of the simulation; the company simply wants us to model the elevator. The "simulator" is our entire C++ program, not necessarily an individual class. The "time" is a property of the clock, not an entity itself. We do not model "energy" in our simulation, and "capacity" is a property of the elevator and of the floor—not a separate entity.

We determine the classes for our system by filtering the remaining nouns into categories. To do this, we can analyze the noun phrases for similarity. For example, the noun phrases "floor 1" and "floor 2" each refer to a floor. From these two noun phrases, we infer that our system should have some way of representing a building's floor. We therefore create a category called "floor." We create all the following categories by combining like noun phrases from the remaining items in Fig. 2.39

- building
- elevator
- clock
- scheduler
- person (person waiting on a floor, elevator's passenger)
- floor (floor 1, floor 2)
- floor button
- elevator button
- bell
- light
- door

These categories are likely to be the classes we need to implement our system. Notice that we create one category for the buttons on the floors and one category for the button on the elevator. The two types of buttons perform different duties in our simulation—the buttons on the floors summon the elevator, and the button in the elevator notifies the elevator to begin moving to the other floor. In Chapter 9, we explore how to describe the similarities between the two types of buttons, while keeping their differences separate.

We now can model the classes in our system, using these categories. By convention, we capitalize class names. If the name of a class contains more than one word, we concatenate the words and capitalize each word (e.g., **MultipleWordName**). Using this convention, we create classes **Elevator**, **Clock**, **Scheduler**, **Person**, **Floor**, **Door**, **Building**, **FloorButton**, **ElevatorButton**, **Bell** and **Light**. We construct our system, using all these classes as building blocks. Before we begin building the system, however, we must gain a better understanding of how the classes relate to one another.

Class Diagrams

The UML enables us to model the classes in the elevator system and their relationships, via the *class diagram*. Figure 2.40 shows how to represent a class with the UML. Here, we model class **Elevator**. In a class diagram, each class is modeled as a rectangle. The UML allows us to divide each rectangle into three parts. The top part contains the name of the class.

Fig. 2.40   Representing a class in the UML.

The middle part contains the class's *attributes* (i.e., the properties a class possesses). We discuss attributes in the "Thinking About Objects" section at the end of Chapter 3. The bottom contains the class's *operations* (i.e., the services a class provides to other classes). We discuss operations in the "Thinking About Objects" section at the end of Chapter 4.

Classes can relate to one another via *associations*. Figure 2.41 shows how classes **Building**, **Elevator** and **Floor** relate to one another. Notice that we have not divided the rectangles in this diagram into three sections. The UML allows the *suppression* of class symbols in this manner to create more readable diagrams.

In this class diagram, a solid line that connects classes represents an association—a simple relationship among classes. The numbers along the lines near the class rectangles express *multiplicity* values. Multiplicity values indicate *how many* objects of a class participate in the association. From the diagram, we see that two objects of class **Floor** participate in an association with one object of class **Building**. Therefore, class **Building** has a *one-to-two* relationship with class **Floor**; we also can say that class **Floor** has a *two-to-one relationship* with class **Building**. The diagram also models a   *one-to-one* relationship between classes **Building** and **Elevator**. Using the UML, we can model many types of multiplicity. Figure 2.42 shows common multiplicity values and how to represent them.

An association can be named. For example, the word "Services" above the line connecting classes **Floor** and **Elevator** describes that association—the arrow shows the direction of the association. This part of the diagram reads: "One object of class **Elevator** services two objects of class **Floor**."

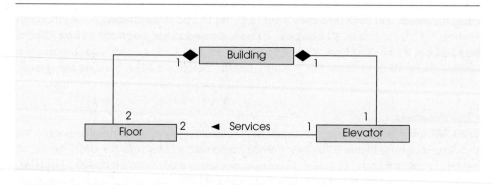

Fig. 2.41   Associations between classes in a class diagram.

The solid diamond attached to the association lines of class **Building** indicates that class **Building** has a *composition* relationship with classes **Floor** and **Elevator**. Composition implies a whole/part relationship. The class that has the composition symbol (the solid diamond) on its end of the association line is the whole (i.e., class **Building**); the class on the other end of the association line is the part (i.e., classes **Floor** and **Elevator**). [5]

Figure 2.43 shows the full class diagram for the elevator system. All the classes we created are modeled, as are the relationships between these classes. [*Note:* In Chapter 9, we expand our class diagram by using the object-oriented concept of *inheritance*.]

Class **Building** is represented near the top of the diagram and is composed of four classes, including **Clock** and **Scheduler**. These two classes compose the controller portion of the simulation. The composite relationship between class **Building** and classes **Clock** and **Scheduler** represents a design decision on our part. We consider class **Building** to be part of both the model and the controller portions of our simulation. In our design, we give class **Building** the responsibility of running the simulation. Class **Building** also is composed of class **Elevator** and class **Floor** (notice the one-to-two relationship between class **Building** and class **Floor**).

Classes **Floor** and **Elevator** are modeled near the bottom of the diagram. Class **Floor** is composed of one object each of classes **Light** and **FloorButton**. Class **Elevator** is composed of one object each of class **ElevatorButton**, class **Door** and class **Bell**. Notice that we model the composite objects of classes **Floor** and **Elevator** differently from the way we model the composite objects of class **Building**. Whereas class **Building** has a separate diamond symbol for each composite relationship, classes **Floor** and **Building** have one diamond symbol whose line branches into three composite objects. The two representations are equivalent. The way we represent composition for classes **Elevator** and **Floor** allows us to make the diagram more readable by reducing the number of symbols.

Symbol	Meaning
0	None.
1	One.
m	An integer value.
0..1	Zero or one.
m..n	At least *m*, but not more than *n*.
*	Any non-negative integer.
0..*	Zero or more (identical to the value *****)
1..*	One or more

Fig. 2.42   Multiplicity values.

---

5. According to the UML 1.4 specifications, classes in a composition relationship observe the following three properties: 1) only one class in the relationship may represent the whole (i.e., the diamond can be placed on only one end of the association line); 2) composition implies coincident lifetimes of the parts with the whole, and the whole is responsible for the creation and destruction of its parts; 3) a part may belong to only one whole at a time, although the part may be removed and attached to another whole, which then assumes responsibility for the part.

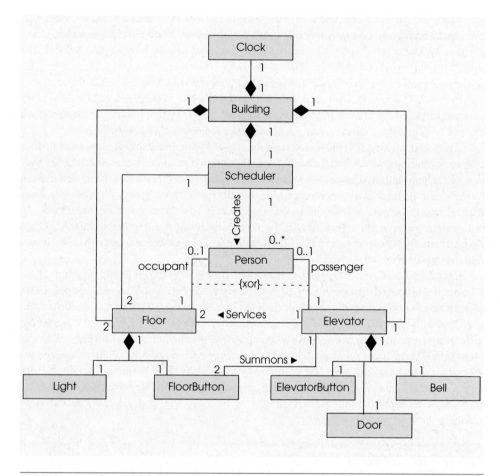

Fig. 2.43   Full class diagram for elevator simulation.

The classes involved in an association also can have *roles*. Roles help clarify the relationship between two classes. For example, class **Person** plays the "occupant" role in its association with class **Floor** (because the person occupies the floor while waiting for the elevator). Class **Person** plays the "passenger" role in its association with class **Elevator**. In a class diagram, the name of a class's role is placed on either side of the association line, near the class's rectangle. Each class in an association can play a different role.

The association between class **Person** and class **Floor** indicates that zero or one objects of class **Person** can relate to an object of class **Floor**. Zero or one objects of class **Person** also can relate to an object of class **Elevator**. The dashed line that bridges these two association lines indicates a *constraint* on the relationship between classes **Person**, **Floor** and **Elevator**. The constraint indicates that an object of class **Person** can participate in a relationship with an object of class **Floor** or with an object of class **Elevator**, but not with both objects at the same time. The notation for this relationship is the word "xor" (which stands for "exclusive or") placed inside braces.[6] The association between class **Scheduler** and class **Person** states that one object of class **Scheduler** creates zero or more objects of class **Person**.

Object Diagrams

The UML also defines *object diagrams*, which are similar to class diagrams except that they model objects and *links*. Links are simple relationships between objects—associations are to classes as links are to objects. Like class diagrams, object diagrams model the structure of the system. Object diagrams present a snapshot of the structure while the system is running—this provides information about which objects participate in the system at a specific point in time. Modelers do not use object diagrams often. The UML specification states that object diagrams often are used to model examples of data structures (i.e., objects that store collections of data and provide operations for manipulating data). A modeler also might use an object diagram to model a complex configuration of interrelated objects. We present an example of an object diagram in this section to introduce the diagram's syntax. When modelling a system, it is not necessary to include every type of diagram—the modeler should provide enough information so that the system may be implemented.

Figure 2.44 models a snapshot of the system when no one is in the building (i.e., no objects of class **Person** exist in the system at this point in time). Object names usually are written in the form: **objectName : ClassName**. The first word in an object name is not capitalized, but subsequent words are. All object names in an object diagram are underlined. We omit the object name for some of the objects in the diagram (e.g., objects of class **FloorButton**). In large systems, many names of objects can be used in the model. This can cause cluttered, hard-to-read diagrams. If the name of a particular object is unknown, or if it is not necessary to include the name (i.e., we care about only the type of the object), we may omit the object name. In this instance, we display only the colon and the class name.

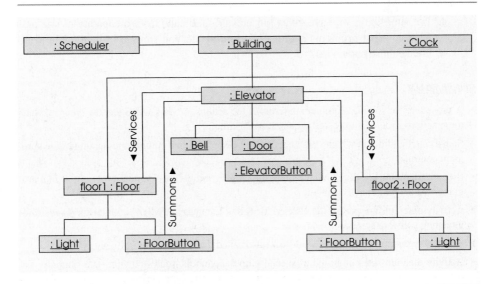

Fig. 2.44   Object diagram of empty building.

---

6. Constraints in UML diagrams can be written with the *Object Constraint Language* (*OCL*). The OCL was created so that modelers could express constraints on a system in a clearly defined way. To learn more, visit **www-4.ibm.com/software/ad/standards/ocl.html**.

Now we have identified the classes for this system (although we might discover others in later phases of the design process). We also have examined the system's use case. In the "Thinking About Objects" section at the end of Chapter 3, we use this knowledge to examine how the system changes over time. As we expand our knowledge, we will discover new information that enables us to describe our classes in greater depth.

Notes

1. We discuss how to implement randomness in the next chapter (Chapter 3), where we study random-number generation. Random-number generation helps simulate random processes, such as coin tossing and dice rolling. It also helps simulate people arriving at random to use the elevator.

2. Because the real world is so object-oriented, it is quite natural for you to pursue this project, even though you have not yet formally studied object orientation.

Questions

1. How might you decide whether the elevator is able to handle the expected traffic volume?

2. Why might it be more complicated to implement a three-story (or taller) building?

3. It is common for large buildings to have many elevators. We will see in Chapter 6 that, once we have created one elevator object, it is easy to create as many as we want. What problems and/or opportunities do you foresee in having several elevators, each of which may pick up and discharge passengers at every floor in a large building?

4. For simplicity, we have given our elevator and each floor a capacity of one passenger. What problems and/or opportunities do you foresee in being able to increase these capacities?

SUMMARY

- A procedure for solving a problem in terms of the actions to be executed and the order in which these actions should be executed is called an algorithm.

- Specifying the order in which statements are to be executed in a computer program is called program control.

- Pseudocode helps the programmer "think out" a program before attempting to write it in a programming language such as C++.

- Activity diagrams are part of the Unified Modeling Language (UML)—an industry standard for modeling software systems.

- An activity diagram models the workflow (also called the activity) of a software system.

- Activity diagrams are composed of special-purpose symbols, such as action-state symbols, diamonds and small circles; these symbols are connected by transition arrows that represent the flow of the activity.

- Like pseudocode, activity diagrams help programmers develop and represent algorithms, although many programmers prefer pseudocode.

- An action state is represented as parallel horizontal lines connected at each end with convex arcs. The action expression appears inside the action state.

- The arrows in the activity diagram are called transition arrows. These arrows model transitions, which indicate the order in which the action states are performed.
- The solid circle located at the top of the activity diagram represents the initial state—the beginning of the workflow before the program performs the modeled activity.
- The solid circle surrounded by a hollow circle that appears at the bottom of the activity diagram represents the final state—the end of the workflow after the program performs the activity.
- Rectangles with the upper-right corners folded over are called notes in the UML. Notes are explanatory remarks that describe the purpose of symbols in the diagram. A dotted line connects each note with the element that the note describes.
- Declarations are messages to the compiler telling it the names and attributes of variables and telling it to reserve space for variables.
- The most important symbol in an activity diagram—the diamond or decision symbol—indicates that a decision is to be made. A decision symbol indicates that the workflow will continue along a path determined by the associated guard conditions that can be true or false. Each transition arrow emerging from a decision symbol has a guard condition (specified in square brackets above or next to the transition arrow). If a particular guard condition is true, the workflow enters the action state to which that transition arrow points.
- A selection structure is used to choose among alternative courses of action.
- The **if** selection structure executes an indicated action only when the condition is true.
- The **if/else** selection structure specifies separate actions to be executed when the condition is true and when the condition is false.
- Whenever more than one statement is to be executed where normally only a single statement is expected, these statements must be enclosed in braces forming a block (or compound statement). A block can be placed anywhere a single statement can be placed.
- Placing a semicolon (**;**) where a statement would normally be specifies an empty statement.
- A repetition structure specifies that an action is to be repeated while some condition remains true.
- The format for the **while** repetition structure is

    > **while (** *condition* **)**
    >   *statement*

- A value that contains a fractional part is referred to as a floating-point number and is represented approximately by data types such as **float** or **double**.
- The unary cast operator **static_cast< double >( )** creates a temporary floating-point copy of its operand.
- C++ provides the arithmetic assignment operators **+=**, **-=**, ***=**, **/=** and **%=**, which help abbreviate certain common expressions.
- C++ provides the increment (**++**) and decrement (**--**) operators to increment or decrement a variable by 1. If the operator is prefixed to the variable, the variable is incremented or decremented by 1 first, then used in its expression. If the operator is postfixed to the variable, the variable is used in its expression, then incremented or decremented by 1.
- A loop is a group of instructions the computer executes repeatedly until a terminating condition is satisfied. Two forms of repetition are counter-controlled repetition and sentinel-controlled repetition.
- A loop counter is used to count repetitions for a group of instructions. It is incremented (or decremented), usually by 1, each time the group of instructions is performed.
- Sentinel values generally are used to control repetition when the precise number of repetitions is not known in advance and the loop includes statements that obtain data each time the loop is per-

formed. A sentinel value is entered after all valid data items have been supplied to the program. Sentinels should be different from valid data items.

- The **for** repetition structure handles all the details of counter-controlled repetition. The general format of the **for** structure is

      for (*initialization*; *loopContinuationCondition*; *increment*)
          statement

  where *initialization* initializes the loop's control variable, *loopContinuationCondition* is the is the condition that determines whether the loop should continue executing and *increment* increments the control variable.

- The **do/while** repetition structure tests the loop-continuation condition at the end of the loop, so the body of the loop will be executed at least once. The format for the **do/while** structure is

      do
          statement
      while (*condition*);

- The **break** statement, when executed in one of the repetition structures (**for**, **while** and **do/while**), causes immediate exit from the structure.

- The **continue** statement, when executed in one of the repetition structures (**for**, **while** and **do/while**), skips any remaining statements in the body of the structure and proceeds with the next iteration of the loop. In a **while** or **do/while** structure, execution continues with the next evaluation of the condition. In a **for** structure, execution continues with the increment expression in the **for** structure header.

- The **switch** statement handles a series of decisions in which a particular variable or expression is tested for values it can assume and different actions are taken. In most programs, it is necessary to include a **break** statement after the statements for each **case**. Several **case**s can execute the same statements by listing the **case** labels together before the statements. The **switch** structure can test only constant integral expressions. It is not necessary to enclose a multiple-statement **case** in braces.

- On UNIX systems and many others, end-of-file is entered by typing the sequence

      <ctrl-d>

  on a line by itself. On Windows, end-of-file is entered by typing

      <ctrl-z>

  possibly followed by pressing the *Enter* key.

- Logical operators can be used to form complex conditions by combining conditions. The logical operators are **&&**, **||** and **!**—logical AND, logical OR and logical NOT (negation), respectively.

- When used as a condition, any nonzero value implicitly converts to **true**; 0 (zero) implicitly converts to **false**.

TERMINOLOGY

! operator	action
&& operator	action/decision model
|| operator	action expression
++ operator	action state
-- operator	action-state symbol
?: operator	activity

activity diagram
algorithm
arithmetic assignment operators:
    +=, -=, *=, /= and **%=**
ASCII character set
block
body of a loop
bool
break
case label
cast operator
char
cin.get() function
compound statement
conditional operator (**?:**)
continue
control structure
counter-controlled repetition
decision
decision symbol
decrement operator (**--**)
default case in **switch**
definite repetition
definition
delay loop
do/while repetition structure
double
double-selection structure
empty statement (**;**)
EOF
false
fatal error
field width
final state
fixed
fixed-point format
float
for repetition structure
garbage value
if selection structure
if/else selection structure
increment operator (**++**)
indefinite repetition
infinite loop
initialization
initial state
integer division
keyword
left
logic error

logical AND (**&&**)
logical negation (**!**)
logical operators
logical OR (**||**)
long
loop counter
loop-continuation condition
lvalue ("left value")
merge symbol
multiple-selection structure
nested control structures
nonfatal error
note
off-by-one error
parameterized stream manipulator
postdecrement operator
postincrement operator
pow function
predecrement operator
preincrement operator
pseudocode
repetition
rvalue ("right value")
selection
sentinel value
sequential execution
setprecision stream manipulator
setw stream manipulator
short
showpoint
single-entry/single-exit control structures
single-selection structure
stacked control structures
static_cast< *type* **>()**
structured programming
switch selection structure
syntax error
ternary operator
top-down, stepwise refinement
transfer of control
transition arrow
true
UML (Unified Modeling Language)
unary operator
undefined value
Unified Modeling Language (UML)
while repetition structure
whitespace characters
zero-based counting

Terminology for Optional "Thinking About Objects" Section

actor	Rational Unified Process
association	rectangle symbol in UML class diagram
association name	role
class diagram	software simulator
composition	solid diamond symbol in UML class and
constraint	object diagram
controller portion of a simulation	solid line symbol in UML class and
link	object diagram
model portion of a simulation	static structure of a system
multiplicity	system box
Object Constraint Language (OCL)	system requirements
object diagram	two-to-one relationship
object-oriented analysis (OOA)	use case
object-oriented analysis and design (OOAD)	use case diagram
object-oriented design (OOD)	"what vs. how"
one-to-one relationship	xor
one-to-two relationship	

SELF-REVIEW EXERCISES

Exercise 2.1–Exercise 2.10 correspond to Section 2.1–Section 2.12.
Exercise 2.11–Exercise 2.13 correspond to Section 2.13–Section 2.21.

2.1   Answer each of the following questions.
  a) All programs can be written in terms of three types of control structures: _____, _____ and _____.
  b) The _____selection structure is used to execute one action when a condition is **true** or a different action when that condition is **false**.
  c) Repeating a set of instructions a specific number of times is called _____ repetition.
  d) When it is not known in advance how many times a set of statements will be repeated, a _____value can be used to terminate the repetition.

2.2   Write four different C++ statements that each add 1 to integer variable **x**.

2.3   Write C++ statements to accomplish each of the following:
  a) In one statement, assign the sum of the current value of **x** and **y** to **z** and increment the value of **x**.
  b) Determine whether the value of the variable **count** is greater than 10. If it is, print "**Count is greater than 10**."
  c) Decrement the variable **x** by 1, then subtract it from the variable **total**.
  d) Calculate the remainder after **q** is divided by **divisor** and assign the result to **q**. Write this statement two different ways.

2.4   Write a C++ statement to accomplish each of the following tasks.
  a) Declare variables **sum** and **x** to be of type **int**.
  b) Initialize variable **x** to **1**.
  c) Initialize variable **sum** to **0**.
  d) Add variable **x** to variable **sum** and assign the result to variable **sum**.
  e) Print **"The sum is: "** followed by the value of variable **sum**.

2.5   Combine the statements that you wrote in Exercise 2.4 into a program that calculates and prints the sum of the integers from 1 to 10. Use the **while** structure to loop through the calculation and increment statements. The loop should terminate when the value of **x** becomes 11.

2.6   State the values of each variable after the calculation is performed. Assume that, when each statement begins executing, all variables have the integer value 5.

a) `product *= x++;`
b) `quotient /= ++x;`

2.7   Write single C++ statements that do the following:

a) Input integer variable **x** with **cin** and **>>**.
b) Input integer variable **y** with **cin** and **>>**.
c) Initialize integer variable **i** to **1**.
d) Initialize integer variable **power** to **1**.
e) Multiply variable **power** by **x** and assign the result to **power**.
f) Increment variable **i** by **1**.
g) Determine whether **i** is less than or equal to **y**.
h) Output integer variable **power** with **cout** and **<<**.

2.8   Write a C++ program that uses the statements in Exercise 2.7 to calculate **x** raised to the **y** power. The program should have a **while** repetition structure.

2.9   Identify and correct the errors in each of the following:

a)
```
while ( c <= 5 ) {
    product *= c;
    ++c;
```
b) `cin << value;`
c)
```
if ( gender == 1 )
    cout << "Woman" << endl;
else;
    cout << "Man" << endl;
```

2.10   What is wrong with the following **while** repetition structure?

```
while ( z >= 0 )
    sum += z;
```

2.11   State whether the following are true or false. If the answer is false, explain why.

a) The **default** case is required in the **switch** selection structure.
b) The **break** statement is required in the default case of a **switch** selection structure to exit the structure properly.
c) The expression (**x > y && a < b**) is **true** if either the expression **x > y** is **true** or the expression **a < b** is **true**.
d) An expression containing the **||** operator is **true** if either or both of its operands are **true**.

2.12   Write a C++ statement or a set of C++ statements to accomplish each of the following:

a) Sum the odd integers between 1 and 99 using a **for** structure. Assume the integer variables **sum** and **count** have been declared.
b) Print the value **333.546372** in a field width of **15** characters with precisions of **1, 2** and **3**. Print each number on the same line. Left-justify each number in its field. What three values print?
c) Calculate the value of **2.5** raised to the power **3** using function **pow**. Print the result with a precision of **2** in a field width of **10** positions. What prints?
d) Print the integers from 1 to 20 using a **while** loop and the counter variable **x**. Assume that the variable **x** has been declared, but not initialized. Print only 5 integers per line. Hint: Use the calculation **x % 5**. When the value of this is 0, print a newline character; otherwise, print a tab character.
e) Repeat Exercise 2.12 (d) using a **for** structure.

2.13   Find the error(s) in each of the following code segments and explain how to correct it (them).

a) ```
x = 1;
while (x <= 10);
    x++;
}
```

b) ```
for ( y = .1; y != 1.0; y += .1 )
    cout << y << endl;
```

c) ```
switch (n) {
    case 1:
        cout << "The number is 1" << endl;
    case 2:
        cout << "The number is 2" << endl;
        break;
    default:
        cout << "The number is not 1 or 2" << endl;
        break;
}
```

d) The following code should print the values 1 to 10.
```
n = 1;
while (n < 10)
    cout << n++ << endl;
```

## ANSWERS TO SELF-REVIEW EXERCISES

2.1    a) Sequence, selection and repetition.   b) **if/else**.   c) Counter-controlled or definite.
d) Sentinel, signal, flag or dummy.

2.2    ```
x = x + 1;
x += 1;
++x;
x++;
```

2.3   a) ```z = x++ + y;```
b) ```
if (count > 10)
    cout << "Count is greater than 10" << endl;
```
c) ```total -= --x;```
d) ```
q %= divisor;
q = q % divisor;
```

2.4   a) ```int sum, x;```
b) ```x = 1;```
c) ```sum = 0;```
d) ```sum += x;```
   or
   ```sum = sum + x;```
e) ```cout << "The sum is: " << sum << endl;```

2.5   See the following code:

```
1  // Ex. 2.5: ex02_05.cpp
2  // Calculate the sum of the integers from 1 to 10.
3  #include <iostream>
4
```
```

```
5    using std::cout;
6    using std::endl;
7
8    // function main begins program execution
9    int main()
10   {
11      int sum;                // stores sum of integers 1 to 10
12      int x;                  // counter
13
14      x = 1;                  // count from 1
15      sum = 0;                // initialize sum
16
17      while ( x <= 10 ) {
18         sum += x;            // add x to sum
19         ++x;                 // increment x
20
21      } // end while
22
23      cout << "The sum is: " << sum << endl;
24
25      return 0;   // indicate successful termination
26
27   } // end function main
```

2.6   a) **product = 25, x = 6;**
      b) **quotient = 0, x = 6;**

2.7   a) **cin >> x;**
      b) **cin >> y;**
      c) **i = 1;**
      d) **power = 1;**
      e) **power *= x;**
         or
         power = power * x;
      f) **++i;**
      g) **if (i <= y)**
      h) **cout << power << endl;**

2.8   See the following code:

```
1    // Ex. 2.8: ex02_08.cpp
2    // Raise x to the y power.
3    #include <iostream>
4
5    using std::cout;
6    using std::cin;
7    using std::endl;
8
9    // function main begins program execution
10   int main()
11   {
12      int x;        // base
13      int y;        // exponent
```

```
14    int i;        // counts from 1 to y
15    int power;    // used to calculate x raised to power y
16
17    i = 1;        // initialize i to begin counting from 1
18    power = 1;    // initialize power
19
20    cout << "Enter base as an integer: ";    // prompt for base
21    cin >> x;                                 // input base
22
23    // prompt for exponent
24    cout << "Enter exponent as an integer: ";
25    cin >> y;                                 // input exponent
26
27    // count from 1 to y and multiply power by x each time
28    while ( i <= y ) {
29       power *= x;
30       ++i;
31
32    } // end while
33
34    cout << power << endl;   // display result
35
36    return 0;                // indicate successful termination
37
38 } // end function main
```

2.9   a) Error: Missing the closing right brace of the **while** body.
Correction: Add closing right brace after the statement **++c;**.

b) Error: Used stream insertion instead of stream extraction.
Correction: Change **<<** to **>>**.

c) Error: Semicolon after **else** results in a logic error. The second output statement will always be executed.
Correction: Remove the semicolon after **else**.

2.10   The value of the variable **z** is never changed in the **while** structure. Therefore, if the loop-continuation condition **(z >= 0)** is **true**, an infinite loop is created. To prevent the infinite loop, **z** must be decremented so that it eventually becomes less than 0.

2.11   a) False. The **default** case is optional. If no default action is needed, then there is no need for a **default** case.

b) False. The **break** statement is used to exit the **switch** structure. The **break** statement is not required when the **default** case is the last case.

c) False. When using the **&&** operator, both of the relational expressions must be **true** for the entire expression to be **true**.

d) True.

2.12   a) **sum = 0;**
```
for ( count = 1; count <= 99; count += 2 )
   sum += count;
```
b) **cout << fixed << left**
```
        << setprecision( 1 ) << setw( 15 ) << 333.546372
        << setprecision( 2 ) << setw( 15 ) << 333.546372
        << setprecision( 3 ) << setw( 15 ) << 333.546372
        << endl;
```

Output is:
```
333.5                333.55              333.546
```
c) `cout << fixed << setprecision( 2 )`
   `      << setw( 10 ) << pow( 2.5, 3 )`
   `      << endl;`

Output is:
```
        15.63
```
d) `x = 1;`

```
while ( x <= 20 ) {
   cout << x;

   if ( x % 5 == 0 )
      cout << endl;
   else
      cout << '\t';

   x++;
}
```
e) `for ( x = 1; x <= 20; x++ ) {`
```
   cout << x;

   if ( x % 5 == 0 )
      cout << endl;
   else
      cout << '\t';
}
```

or

```
for ( x = 1; x <= 20; x++ )

   if ( x % 5 == 0 )
      cout << x << endl;
   else
      cout << x << '\t';
```

2.13 a) Error: The semicolon after the **while** header causes an infinite loop.
Correction: Replace the semicolon by a **{**, or remove both the **;** and the **}**.

b) Error: Using a floating-point number to control a **for** repetition structure.
Correction: Use an integer and perform the proper calculation in order to get the values you desire.

```
for ( y = 1; y != 10; y++ )
   cout << ( static_cast< double >( y ) / 10 ) << endl;
```

c) Error: Missing **break** statement in the statements for the first **case**.
Correction: Add a **break** statement at the end of the statements for the first **case**. Note that this is not an error if the programmer wants the statement of **case 2:** to execute every time the **case 1:** statement executes.

d) Error: Improper relational operator used in the while repetition-continuation condition.
Correction: Use **<=** rather than **<**, or change **10** to **11**.

EXERCISES

Exercise 2.14–Exercise 2.38 correspond to Section 2.1–Section 2.12.
Exercise 2.39–Exercise 2.63 correspond to Section 2.13–Section 2.21.

2.14   Identify and correct the error(s) in each of the following:

a)
```cpp
if ( age >= 65 );
    cout << "Age is greater than or equal to 65" << endl;
else
    cout << "Age is less than 65 << endl";
```

b)
```cpp
if ( age >= 65 )
    cout << "Age is greater than or equal to 65" << endl;
else;
    cout << "Age is less than 65 << endl";
```

c)
```cpp
int x = 1, total;

while ( x <= 10 ) {
    total += x;
    ++x;
}
```

d)
```cpp
While ( x <= 100 )
    total += x;
    ++x;
```

e)
```cpp
while ( y > 0 ) {
    cout << y << endl;
    ++y;
}
```

2.15   What does the following program print?

```cpp
1   // Ex. 2.15: ex02_15.cpp
2   // What does this program print?
3   #include <iostream>
4
5   using std::cout;
6   using std::endl;
7
8   // function main begins program execution
9   int main()
10  {
11      int y;          // declare y
12      int x = 1;      // initialize x
13      int total = 0;  // initialize total
14
15      while ( x <= 10 ) {     // loop 10 times
16          y = x * x;          // perform calculation
17          cout << y << endl;  // output result
18          total += y;         // add y to total
19          ++x;                // increment counter x
20
21      } // end while
22
23      cout << "Total is " << total << endl;  // display result
```

```
24
25      return 0;   // indicate successful termination
26
27  } // end function main
```

For Exercises 2.16 to 2.19, perform each of these steps:

   a) Read the problem statement.
   b) Formulate the algorithm using pseudocode and top-down, stepwise refinement.
   c) Write a C++ program.
   d) Test, debug and execute the C++ program.

2.16 Drivers are concerned with the mileage obtained by their automobiles. One driver has kept track of several tankfuls of gasoline by recording miles driven and gallons used for each tankful. Develop a C++ program that uses a **while** structure to input the miles driven and gallons used for each tankful. The program should calculate and display the miles per gallon obtained for each tankful. After processing all input information, the program should calculate and print the combined miles per gallon obtained for all tankfuls.

```
Enter the gallons used (-1 to end): 12.8
Enter the miles driven: 287
The miles / gallon for this tank was 22.421875

Enter the gallons used (-1 to end): 10.3
Enter the miles driven: 200
The miles / gallon for this tank was 19.417475

Enter the gallons used (-1 to end): 5
Enter the miles driven: 120
The miles / gallon for this tank was 24.000000

Enter the gallons used (-1 to end): -1

The overall average miles/gallon was 21.601423
```

2.17 Develop a C++ program that will determine whether a department-store customer has exceeded the credit limit on a charge account. For each customer, the following facts are available:

   a) Account number (an integer)
   b) Balance at the beginning of the month
   c) Total of all items charged by this customer this month
   d) Total of all credits applied to this customer's account this month
   e) Allowed credit limit

The program should use a **while** structure to input each of these facts, calculate the new balance (= beginning balance + charges – credits) and determine whether the new balance exceeds the customer's credit limit. For those customers whose credit limit is exceeded, the program should display the customer's account number, credit limit, new balance and the message "Credit limit exceeded."

```
Enter account number (-1 to end): 100
Enter beginning balance: 5394.78
Enter total charges: 1000.00
Enter total credits: 500.00
Enter credit limit: 5500.00
Account:      100
Credit limit: 5500.00
Balance:      5894.78
Credit Limit Exceeded.

Enter account number (-1 to end): 200
Enter beginning balance: 1000.00
Enter total charges: 123.45
Enter total credits: 321.00
Enter credit limit: 1500.00

Enter account number (-1 to end): 300
Enter beginning balance: 500.00
Enter total charges: 274.73
Enter total credits: 100.00
Enter credit limit: 800.00

Enter account number (-1 to end): -1
```

2.18   One large chemical company pays its salespeople on a commission basis. The salespeople receive $200 per week plus 9 percent of their gross sales for that week. For example, a salesperson who sells $5000 worth of chemicals in a week receives $200 plus 9 percent of $5000, or a total of $650. Develop a C++ program that uses a **while** structure to input each salesperson's gross sales for last week and calculate and display that salesperson's earnings. Process one salesperson's figures at a time.

```
Enter sales in dollars (-1 to end): 5000.00
Salary is: $650.00

Enter sales in dollars (-1 to end): 6000.00
Salary is: $740.00

Enter sales in dollars (-1 to end): 7000.00
Salary is: $830.00

Enter sales in dollars (-1 to end): -1
```

2.19   Develop a C++ program that uses a **while** structure to determine the gross pay for each of several employees. The company pays "straight-time" for the first 40 hours worked by each employee and pays "time-and-a-half" for all hours worked in excess of 40 hours. You are given a list of the employees of the company, the number of hours each employee worked last week and the hourly rate of each employee. Your program should input this information for each employee and should determine and display the employee's gross pay.

```
Enter hours worked (-1 to end): 39
Enter hourly rate of the worker ($00.00): 10.00
Salary is $390.00

Enter hours worked (-1 to end): 40
Enter hourly rate of the worker ($00.00): 10.00
Salary is $400.00

Enter hours worked (-1 to end): 41
Enter hourly rate of the worker ($00.00): 10.00
Salary is $415.00

Enter hours worked (-1 to end): -1
```

2.20   The process of finding the largest number (i.e., the maximum of a group of numbers) is used frequently in computer applications. For example, a program that determines the winner of a sales contest would input the number of units sold by each salesperson. The salesperson who sells the most units wins the contest. Write a pseudocode program, then a C++ program that uses a **while** structure to determine and print the largest number of 10 numbers input by the user. Your program should use three variables, as follows:

> **counter:**   A counter to count to 10 (i.e., to keep track of how many numbers have been input and to determine when all 10 numbers have been processed).
>
> **number:**   The current number input to the program.
>
> **largest:**   The largest number found so far.

2.21   Write a C++ program that uses a **while** structure and the tab escape sequence **\t** to print the following table of values:

N	10*N	100*N	1000*N
1	10	100	1000
2	20	200	2000
3	30	300	3000
4	40	400	4000
5	50	500	5000

2.22   Using an approach similar to that in Exercise 2.20, find the *two* largest values among the 10 numbers. [*Note:* You must input each number only once.]

2.23   The examination-results program of Fig. 2.11 assumes that any value input by the user that is not a 1 must be a 2. Modify Fig. 2.11 to validate its inputs. On any input, if the value entered is other than 1 or 2, keep looping until the user enters a correct value.

2.24   What does the following program print?

```
1   // Ex. 2.25: ex02_25.cpp
2   // What does this program print?
3   #include <iostream>
4
```

```
5   using std::cout;
6   using std::endl;
7
8   // function main begins program execution
9   int main()
10  {
11      int count = 1;              // initialize count
12
13      while ( count <= 10 ) {    // loop 10 times
14
15          // output line of text
16          cout << ( count % 2 ? "****" : "++++++++" )
17              << endl;
18          ++count;                // increment count
19
20      } // end while
21
22      return 0;    // indicate successful termination
23
24  } // end function main
```

2.25 What does the following program print?

```
1   // Ex. 2.25: ex_02_25.cpp
2   // What does this program print?
3   #include <iostream>
4
5   using std::cout;
6   using std::endl;
7
8   // function main begins program execution
9   int main()
10  {
11      int row = 10;    // initialize row
12      int column;      // declare column
13
14      while ( row >= 1 ) {    // loop until row < 1
15          column = 1;    // set column to 1 as iteration begins
16
17          while ( column <= 10 ) {                // loop 10 times
18              cout << ( row % 2 ? "<" : ">" );    // output
19              ++column;                           // increment column
20
21          } // end inner while
22
23          --row;             // decrement row
24          cout << endl;      // begin new output line
25
26      } // end outer while
27
28      return 0;  // indicate successful termination
29
30  } // end function main
```

2.32   Write a program that prints the powers of the integer 2, namely 2, 4, 8, 16, 32, 64, etc. Your **while** loop should not terminate (i.e., you should create an infinite loop). What happens when you run this program?

2.33   Write a program that reads the radius of a circle (as a **double** value) and computes and prints the diameter, the circumference and the area. Use the value 3.14159 for π.

2.34   What is wrong with the following statement? Provide the correct statement to accomplish what the programmer was probably trying to do.

```
cout << ++( x + y );
```

2.35   Write a program that reads three nonzero **double** values and determines and prints whether they could represent the sides of a triangle.

2.36   Write a program that reads three nonzero integers and determines and prints whether they could be the sides of a right triangle.

2.37   A company wants to transmit data over the telephone, but is concerned that its phones could be tapped. All of the data are transmitted as four-digit integers. The company has asked you to write a program that encrypts the data so that it can be transmitted more securely. Your program should read a four-digit integer and encrypt it as follows: Replace each digit by *(the sum of that digit plus 7) modulus 10*. Then, swap the first digit with the third, swap the second digit with the fourth and print the encrypted integer. Write a separate program that inputs an encrypted four-digit integer and decrypts it to form the original number.

2.38   The factorial of a nonnegative integer n is written $n!$ (pronounced "*n* factorial") and is defined as follows:

$$n! = n \cdot (n - 1) \cdot (n - 2) \cdot \ldots \cdot 1 \quad \text{(for values of } n \text{ greater than to 1)}$$

and

$$n! = 1 \quad \text{(for } n = 0 \text{ or } n = 1\text{)}.$$

For example, $5! = 5 \cdot 4 \cdot 3 \cdot 2 \cdot 1$, which is 120. Use **while** structures in each of the following:
   a) Write a program that reads a nonnegative integer and computes and prints its factorial.
   b) Write a program that estimates the value of the mathematical constant e by using the formula:

$$e = 1 + \frac{1}{1!} + \frac{1}{2!} + \frac{1}{3!} + \ldots$$

   c) Write a program that computes the value of e^x by using the formula

$$e^x = 1 + \frac{x}{1!} + \frac{x^2}{2!} + \frac{x^3}{3!} + \ldots$$

2.39   Find the error(s) in each of the following:
   a)
```
For ( x = 100, x >= 1, x++ )
    cout << x << endl;
```
   b) The following code should print whether integer **value** is odd or even:

```
switch ( value % 2 ) {
   case 0:
      cout << "Even integer" << endl;
   case 1:
      cout << "Odd integer" << endl;
}
```

c) The following code should output the odd integers from 19 to 1:

```
for ( x = 19; x >= 1; x += 2 )
    cout << x << endl;
```

d) The following code should output the even integers from 2 to 100:

```
counter = 2;

do {
    cout << counter << endl;
    counter += 2;
} While ( counter < 100 );
```

2.40 Write a program that uses a **for** structure to sum a sequence of integers. Assume that the first integer read specifies the number of values remaining to be entered. Your program should read only one value per input statement. A typical input sequence might be

5 100 200 300 400 500

where the **5** indicates that the subsequent **5** values are to be summed.

2.41 Write a program that uses a **for** structure to calculate and print the average of several integers. Assume the last value read is the sentinel **9999**. A typical input sequence might be

10 8 11 7 9 9999

indicating that the program should calculate the average of all the values preceding **9999**.

2.42 What does the following program do?

```
1   // Ex. 2.42: ex02_42.cpp
2   // What does this program print?
3   #include <iostream>
4
5   using std::cout;
6   using std::cin;
7   using std::endl;
8
9   // function main begins program execution
10  int main()
11  {
12      int x;  // declare x
13      int y;  // declare y
14
15      // prompt user for input
16      cout << "Enter two integers in the range 1-20: ";
17      cin >> x >> y;  // read values for x and y
18
19      for ( int i = 1; i <= y; i++ ) {    // count from 1 to y
20
21          for ( int j = 1; j <= x; j++ )  // count from 1 to x
22              cout << '@';                 // output @
23
24          cout << endl;                    // begin new line
25
26      } // end outer for
```

```
27
28       return 0;   // indicate successful termination
29
30   } // end function main
```

2.43   Write a program that uses a **for** structure to find the smallest of several integers. Assume that the first value read specifies the number of values remaining and that the first number is not one of the integers to compare.

2.44   Write a program that uses a **for** structure to calculate and print the product of the odd integers from 1 to 15.

2.45   The *factorial* function is used frequently in probability problems. Using the definition of factorial in Exercise 2.38, write a program that uses **for** structures to evaluate the factorials of the integers from 1 to 5. Print the results in tabular format. What difficulty might prevent you from calculating the factorial of 20?

2.46   Modify the compound-interest program of Section 2.15 to repeat its steps for the interest rates 5 percent, 6 percent, 7 percent, 8 percent, 9 percent and 10 percent. Use a **for** loop to vary the interest rate.

2.47   Write a program that uses **for** structures to print the following patterns separately, one below the other. Use **for** loops to generate the patterns. All asterisks (*) should be printed by a single statement of the form **cout << '*';** (this causes the asterisks to print side by side). [*Hint:* The last two patterns require that each line begin with an appropriate number of blanks. *Extra credit:* Combine your code from the four separate problems into a single program that prints all four patterns side by side by making clever use of nested **for** loops.]

```
(A)              (B)                (C)                (D)
*                **********         **********                  *
**               *********          *********                  **
***              ********           ********                  ***
****             *******            *******                  ****
*****            ******             ******                  *****
******           *****              *****                  ******
*******          ****               ****                  *******
********          ***                ***                  ********
*********          **                 **                  *********
**********          *                  *                  **********
```

2.48   One interesting application of computers is the drawing of graphs and bar charts (sometimes called "histograms"). Write a program that reads five numbers (each between 1 and 30). For each number read, your program should print a line containing that number of adjacent asterisks. For example, if your program reads the number seven, it should print *******.

2.49   A mail order house sells five different products whose retail prices are: product 1 — $2.98, product 2—$4.50, product 3—$9.98, product 4—$4.49 and product 5—$6.87. Write a program that reads a series of pairs of numbers as follows:
  a) Product number
  b) Quantity sold for one day

Your program should use a **switch** statement to help determine the retail price for each product. Your program should calculate and display the total retail value of all products sold last week.

2.50   Modify the program of Fig. 2.22 so that it calculates the grade-point average for the class. A grade of 'A' is worth 4 points, 'B' is worth 3 points, etc.

2.51   Modify the program in Fig. 2.21 so it uses only integers to calculate the compound interest. [*Hint:* Treat all monetary amounts as integral numbers of pennies. Then "break" the result into its dollar portion and cents portion by using the division and modulus operations. Insert a period.]

2.52   Assume **i = 1, j = 2, k = 3** and **m = 2**. What does each of the following statements print? Are the parentheses necessary in each case?

```
a) cout << ( i == 1 ) << endl;
b) cout << ( j == 3 ) << endl;
c) cout << ( i >= 1 && j < 4 ) << endl;
d) cout << ( m <= 99 && k < m ) << endl;
e) cout << ( j >= i || k == m ) << endl;
f) cout << ( k + m < j || 3 - j >= k ) << endl;
g) cout << ( !m ) << endl;
h) cout << ( !( j - m ) ) << endl;
i) cout << ( !( k > m ) ) << endl;
```

2.53   Write a program that prints a table of the binary, octal and hexadecimal equivalents of the decimal numbers in the range 1 through 256. If you are not familiar with these number systems, read Appendix C first.

2.54   Calculate the value of π from the infinite series

$$\pi = 4 - \frac{4}{3} + \frac{4}{5} - \frac{4}{7} + \frac{4}{9} - \frac{4}{11} + \cdots$$

Print a table that shows the value of π approximated by 1 term of this series, by two terms, by three terms, etc. How many terms of this series do you have to use before you first get 3.14? 3.141? 3.1415? 3.14159?

2.55   (*Pythagorean Triples*) A right triangle can have sides that are all integers. A set of three integer values for the sides of a right triangle is called a Pythagorean triple. These three sides must satisfy the relationship that the sum of the squares of two of the sides is equal to the square of the hypotenuse. Find all Pythagorean triples for **side1**, **side2** and **hypotenuse** all no larger than 500. Use a triple-nested **for**-loop that tries all possibilities. This is an example of *brute force* computing. You will learn in more advanced computer-science courses that there are many interesting problems for which there is no known algorithmic approach other than sheer brute force.

2.56   A company pays its employees as managers (who receive a fixed weekly salary), hourly workers (who receive a fixed hourly wage for up to the first 40 hours they work and "time-and-a-half"—1.5 times their hourly wage—for overtime hours worked), commission workers (who receive $250 plus 5.7% of their gross weekly sales), or pieceworkers (who receive a fixed amount of money per item for each of the items they produce—each pieceworker in this company works on only one type of item). Write a program to compute the weekly pay for each employee. You do not know the number of employees in advance. Each type of employee has its own pay code: Managers have pay-code 1, hourly workers have code 2, commission workers have code 3 and pieceworkers have code 4. Use a **switch** to compute each employee's pay according to that employee's paycode. Within the **switch**, prompt the user (i.e., the payroll clerk) to enter the appropriate facts your program needs to calculate each employee's pay according to that employee's paycode.

2.57   (*De Morgan's Laws*) In this chapter, we discussed the logical operators **&&**, **||** and **!**. De Morgan's Laws can sometimes make it more convenient for us to express a logical expression. These laws state that the expression **!**(*condition1* **&&** *condition2*) is logically equivalent to the expression (**!***condition1* **||** **!***condition2*). Also, the expression **!**(*condition1* **||** *condition2*) is logically equivalent to the expression (**!***condition1* **&&** **!***condition2*). Use De Morgan's Laws to write equivalent expressions for each of the following, then write a program to show that the original expression and the new expression in each case are equivalent:

    a) `!( x < 5 ) && !( y >= 7 )`
    b) `!( a == b ) || !( g != 5 )`
    c) `!( ( x <= 8 ) && ( y > 4 ) )`
    d) `!( ( i > 4 ) || ( j <= 6 ) )`

2.58 Write a program that prints the following diamond shape. You may use output statements that print either a single asterisk (`*`) or a single blank. Maximize your use of repetition (with nested **for** structures) and minimize the number of output statements.

```
    *
   ***
  *****
 *******
*********
 *******
  *****
   ***
    *
```

2.59 Modify the program you wrote in Exercise 2.58 to read an odd number in the range 1 to 19 to specify the number of rows in the diamond. Your program should then display a diamond of the appropriate size.

2.60 A criticism of the **break** statement and the **continue** statement is that each is unstructured. Actually **break** statements and **continue** statements can always be replaced by structured statements, although doing so can be awkward. Describe in general how you would remove any **break** statement from a loop in a program and replace that statement with some structured equivalent. (Hint: The **break** statement leaves a loop from within the body of the loop. The other way to leave is by failing the loop-continuation test. Consider using in the loop-continuation test a second test that indicates "early exit because of a 'break' condition.") Use the technique you developed here to remove the break statement from the program of Fig. 2.26.

2.61 What does the following program segment do?

```
 1   for ( i = 1; i <= 5; i++ ) {
 2
 3      for ( j = 1; j <= 3; j++ ) {
 4
 5         for ( k = 1; k <= 4; k++ )
 6            cout << '*';
 7
 8         cout << endl;
 9
10      } // end inner for
11
12      cout << endl;
13
14   } // end outer for
```

2.62   Describe in general how you would remove any **continue** statement from a loop in a program and replace that statement with some structured equivalent. Use the technique you developed here to remove the **continue** statement from the program of Fig. 2.27.

2.63   *("The Twelve Days of Christmas" Song)* Write a program that uses repetition and **switch** structures to print the song "The Twelve Days of Christmas." One **switch** structure should be used to print the day (i.e., "First," "Second," etc.). A separate **switch** structure should be used to print the remainder of each verse. Visit the Web site **www.12days.com/library/carols/12daysofxmas.htm** for the complete lyrics to the song.

2.64   [*Note:* This exercise corresponds to Section 2.22, "Thinking About Objects."] Describe in 200 words or fewer what an automobile is and does. List the nouns and verbs separately. In the text, we stated that each noun might correspond to an object that will need to be built to implement a system, in this case a car. Pick five of the objects you listed, and, for each, list several attributes and several behaviors. Describe briefly how these objects interact with one another and other objects in your description. You have just performed several of the key steps in a typical object-oriented design.

2.65   *(Peter Minuit Problem)* Legend has it that, in 1626, Peter Minuit purchased Manhattan for $24.00 in barter. Did he make a good investment? To answer this question, modify the compound interest program of Fig. 2.21 to begin with a principal of $24.00 and to calculate the amount of interest on deposit if that money had been kept on deposit until this year (376 years through 2002). Run the program with the interest rates 5%, 6%, 7%, 8%, 9% and 10% to observe the wonders of compound interest.

3

Functions

Objectives

- To understand how to construct programs modularly from pieces called functions.
- To be able to create new functions.
- To understand the mechanisms used to pass information between functions.
- To introduce simulation techniques using random number generation.
- To understand how the visibility of identifiers is limited to specific regions of programs.
- To understand how to write and use functions that call themselves.

Form ever follows function.
Louis Henri Sullivan

E pluribus unum.
(One composed of many.)
Virgil

O! call back yesterday, bid time return.
William Shakespeare

Call me Ishmael.
Herman Melville

When you call me that, smile.
Owen Wister

Outline

3.1	Introduction
3.2	Program Components in C++
3.3	Math Library Functions
3.4	Functions
3.5	Function Definitions
3.6	Function Prototypes
3.7	Header Files
3.8	Random Number Generation
3.9	Example: Game of Chance and Introducing **enum**
3.10	Storage Classes
3.11	Scope Rules
3.12	Recursion
3.13	Example Using Recursion: Fibonacci Series
3.14	Recursion vs. Iteration
3.15	Functions with Empty Parameter Lists
3.16	Inline Functions
3.17	References and Reference Parameters
3.18	Default Arguments
3.19	Unary Scope Resolution Operator
3.20	Function Overloading
3.21	Function Templates
3.22	(Optional Case Study) Thinking About Objects: Identifying a Class's Attributes

Summary • Terminology • Self-Review Exercises • Answers to Self-Review Exercises • Exercises

3.1 Introduction

Most computer programs that solve real-world problems are much larger than the programs presented in the first few chapters. Experience has shown that the best way to develop and maintain a large program is to construct it from smaller pieces or components, each of which is more manageable than the original program. This technique is called *divide and conquer*. This chapter describes many key features of the C++ language that facilitate the design, implementation, operation and maintenance of large programs.

3.2 Program Components in C++

Modules in C++ are called *functions* and *classes*. C++ programs are typically written by combining new functions the programmer writes with "pre-packaged" functions available in the C++ *standard library* and by combining new classes the programmer writes with "pre-packaged" classes available in various class libraries. In this chapter, we concentrate on functions; we discuss classes in detail beginning with Chapter 6.

The C++ standard library provides a rich collection of functions for performing common mathematical calculations, string manipulations, character manipulations, input/output, error checking and many other useful operations. This makes the programmer's job easier, because these functions provide many of the capabilities programmers need. The C++ standard library functions are provided as part of the C++ programming environment.

Software Engineering Observation 3.1

Use the online documentation for your compiler to familiarize yourself with the rich collection of functions and classes in the C++ standard library.

Software Engineering Observation 3.2

Avoid reinventing the wheel. When possible, use C++ standard library functions instead of writing new functions. This reduces program development time.

Portability Tip 3.1

Using the functions in the C++ standard library helps make programs more portable.

Performance Tip 3.1

Do not try to rewrite existing library routines to make them more efficient. You usually will not be able to increase the performance of these routines and you may introduce errors.

Programmers can write functions to define specific tasks that could be used at many points in a program. These are sometimes referred to as *programmer-defined functions*. The actual statements defining the function are written only once, and these statements are hidden from other functions.

A function is *invoked* (i.e., made to perform its designated task) by a *function call*. The function call specifies the function name and provides information (as *arguments*) that the called function needs to do its job. A common analogy for this is the hierarchical form of management. A boss (the *calling function* or *caller*) asks a worker (the *called function*) to perform a task and *return* (i.e., report back) the results when the task is done. The boss function does not know *how* the worker function performs its designated tasks. The worker might call other worker functions; the boss will be unaware of this. We will soon see how this "hiding" of implementation details promotes good software engineering. Figure 3.1 illustrates function **main** communicating with several worker functions in a hierarchical manner. Note that **worker1** acts as a boss function to **worker4** and **worker5**. Relationships among functions can be other than the hierarchical structure shown in this figure.

3.3 Math Library Functions

Math library functions allow the programmer to perform certain common mathematical calculations. We use various math library functions here to introduce the concept of functions. We discuss many other C++ standard library functions throughout the book.

Functions normally are called by writing the name of the function, followed by a left parenthesis, followed by the *argument* (or a comma-separated list of arguments) of the function, followed by a right parenthesis. For example, a programmer desiring to calculate and print the square root of **900.0** might write

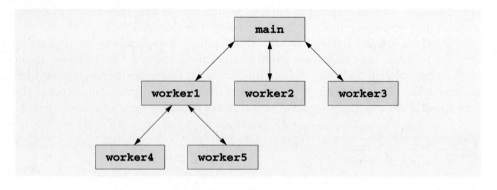

Fig. 3.1   Hierarchical boss function/worker function relationship.

```
cout << sqrt( 900.0 );
```

When this statement executes, math library function **sqrt** is called to calculate the square root of the number contained in the parentheses (**900.0**). The number **900.0** is the *argument* of function **sqrt**. The preceding statement would print **30**. Function **sqrt** takes an argument of type **double** and returns a result of type **double**. All functions in the math library return the data type **double**. To use the math library functions, include the header file **<cmath>**.[1]

Common Programming Error 3.1

Forgetting to include the math header file when using math library functions is a syntax error.

Function arguments can be constants, variables, or expressions. If **c1 = 13.0**, **d = 3.0** and **f = 4.0**, then the statement

```
cout << sqrt( c1 + d * f );
```

calculates and prints the square root of **13.0 + 3.0 * 4.0 = 25.0**, namely **5**. Note that C++ ordinarily does not print trailing zeros or the decimal point in a floating-point number that has no fractional part.

Some math library functions are summarized in Fig. 3.2. In the figure, the variables **x** and **y** are of type **double**.

Method	Description	Example
ceil(x)	rounds x to the smallest integer not less than x	**ceil(9.2)** is **10.0** **ceil(-9.8)** is **-9.0**
cos(x)	trigonometric cosine of x (x in radians)	**cos(0.0)** is **1.0**

Fig. 3.2   Math library functions. (Part 1 of 2.)

---

1. The standard library actually provides multiple versions of these functions that work with each floating-point data type (**float**, **double** and **long double**).

Method	Description	Example
exp(x)	exponential function e^x	**exp(** 1.0 **)** is **2.71828** **exp(** 2.0 **)** is **7.38906**
fabs(x)	absolute value of x	**fabs(** 5.1 **)** is **5.1** **fabs(** 0.0 **)** is **0.0** **fabs(** -8.76 **)** is **8.76**
floor(x)	rounds x to the largest integer not greater than x	**floor(** 9.2 **)** is **9.0** **floor(** -9.8 **)** is **-10.0**
fmod(x, y)	remainder of x/y as a floating-point number	**fmod(** 13.657, 2.333 **)** is **1.992**
log(x)	natural logarithm of x (base e)	**log(** 2.718282 **)** is **1.0** **log(** 7.389056 **)** is **2.0**
log10(x)	logarithm of x (base 10)	**log10(** 10.0 **)** is **1.0** **log10(** 100.0 **)** is **2.0**
pow(x, y)	x raised to power y (x^y)	**pow(** 2, 7 **)** is **128** **pow(** 9, .5 **)** is **3**
sin(x)	trigonometric sine of x (x in radians)	**sin(** 0.0 **)** is **0**
sqrt(x)	square root of x	**sqrt(** 900.0 **)** is **30.0** **sqrt(** 9.0 **)** is **3.0**
tan(x)	trigonometric tangent of x (x in radians)	**tan(** 0.0 **)** is **0**

Fig. 3.2   Math library functions. (Part 2 of 2.)

3.4 Functions

Functions allow the programmer to modularize a program. All variables defined in function definitions are *local variables*—they are known only in the function in which they are defined. Most functions have a list of *parameters* that provide the means for communicating information between functions. A function's parameters are also local variables of that function.

Software Engineering Observation 3.3

*In programs containing many functions, **main** should be implemented as a group of calls to functions that perform the bulk of the program's work.*

There are several motivations for "functionalizing" a program. The divide-and-conquer approach makes program development more manageable. Another motivation is *software reusability*—using existing functions as building blocks to create new programs. Software reusability is a major factor in object-oriented programming. With good function naming and definition, programs can be created from standardized functions that accomplish specific tasks, rather than being built by using customized code. Another motivation is to avoid repeating code in a program. Packaging code as a function allows the code to be executed from different locations in a program simply by calling the function.

Software Engineering Observation 3.4

Each function should be limited to performing a single, well-defined task, and the function name should effectively express that task. This promotes software reusability.

Software Engineering Observation 3.5

If you cannot choose a concise name that expresses what the function does, it is possible that your function is attempting to perform too many diverse tasks. It is usually best to break such a function into several smaller functions. Then the original function can call the smaller functions to perform the complete task.

3.5 Function Definitions

Each program we have presented consisted of function **main** calling standard library functions to accomplish its tasks. We now consider how programmers write their own customized functions.

Consider a program, with a programmer-defined function **square**, that calculates and displays the squares of the integers from 1 to 10 (Fig. 3.3).

```cpp
1   // Fig. 3.3: fig03_03.cpp
2   // Creating and using a programmer-defined function.
3   #include <iostream>
4
5   using std::cout;
6   using std::endl;
7
8   int square( int );    // function prototype
9
10  int main()
11  {
12     // loop 10 times and calculate and output
13     // square of x each time
14     for ( int x = 1; x <= 10; x++ )
15        cout << square( x ) << " ";   // function call
16
17     cout << endl;
18
19     return 0;  // indicates successful termination
20
21  } // end main
22
23  // square function definition returns square of an integer
24  int square( int y )   // y is a copy of argument to function
25  {
26     return y * y;      // returns square of y as an int
27
28  } // end function square
```

```
1   4   9   16   25   36   49   64   81   100
```

Fig. 3.3   Programmer-defined function **square**.

Function **square** is *invoked* or *called* in **main** with the expression **square(x)** in line 15. The parentheses **( )** in the function call are an operator in C++ that causes the function to be called. Function **square** (lines 24–28) receives a copy of the value of argument **x** and stores it in the *parameter* **y**. Then **square** calculates **y * y** (line 26). Function **square** passes the result back to the point in **main** where **square** was invoked (line 15) and displays the result. Note that the function call does not change the value of **x**. The **for** repetition structure repeats this process for each of the values 1 through 10.

The definition of **square** (lines 24–28) shows that it uses integer parameter **y**. Keyword **int** preceding the function name indicates that **square** returns an integer result. The **return** statement in **square** (line 26) passes the result of the calculation back to the calling function.

Line 8 is a *function prototype*. The data type **int** in parentheses informs the compiler that function **square** expects an integer value from the caller. The data type **int** to the left of the function name **square** informs the compiler that **square** returns an integer result to the caller. The compiler refers to the function prototype to check that calls to **square** contain the correct number and types of arguments and that the arguments are in the correct order. In addition, the compiler uses the prototype to ensure that the data type returned by the function can be used correctly in the expression that called the function. If the arguments passed to a function do not match the types specified in the function's prototype, the compiler attempts to convert the arguments to the types specified in the prototype. Section 3.6 discusses the rules for these conversions. The function prototype is not required if the definition of the function appears before the function's first use in the program. In such a case, the function header also acts as the function prototype. If lines 24–28 in Fig. 3.3 appeared before **main**, the function prototype on line 8 would be unnecessary. Function prototypes are discussed in detail in Section 3.6.

The format of a function definition is as follows:

return-value-type function-name **(** *parameter-list* **)**
{
    declarations and statements
}

The *function-name* is any valid identifier. The *return-value-type* is the data type of the result returned from the function to the caller. *Return-value-type* **void** indicates that a function does not return a value.

Common Programming Error 3.2

Forgetting to return a value from a function that is supposed to return a value is a syntax error.

Common Programming Error 3.3

*Returning a value from a function whose return type has been declared **void** is a syntax error.*

The *parameter-list* is a comma-separated list containing the declarations of the parameters received by the function when it is called. If a function does not receive any values, *parameter-list* is **void** or simply left empty. A type must be listed explicitly for each parameter in the parameter list of a function.

Common Programming Error 3.4

Declaring function parameters of the same type, such as **float x, y** *instead of* **float x, float y***, is a syntax error.*

Common Programming Error 3.5

Placing a semicolon after the right parenthesis enclosing the parameter list of a function definition is a syntax error.

Common Programming Error 3.6

Defining a function parameter again as a local variable in the function is a syntax error.

Good Programming Practice 3.1

To avoid ambiguity, do not use the same names for the arguments passed to a function and the corresponding parameters in the function definition.

The *declarations* and *statements* in braces form the *function body* also called a block or compound statement. Variables can be declared in any block, and blocks can be nested. *A function cannot be defined inside another function.*

Common Programming Error 3.7

Defining a function inside another function is a syntax error.

Good Programming Practice 3.2

Place a blank line between function definitions to separate the functions and enhance program readability.

Good Programming Practice 3.3

Choosing meaningful function names and meaningful parameter names makes programs more readable and helps avoid excessive use of comments.

Software Engineering Observation 3.6

Try to keep functions small. Regardless of how long a function is, it should perform one task well. Small functions promote software reusability.

Software Engineering Observation 3.7

Programs should be written as collections of small functions. This makes programs easier to write, debug, maintain and modify.

Software Engineering Observation 3.8

A function requiring a large number of parameters might be performing too many tasks. Consider dividing the function into smaller functions that perform the separate tasks.

Common Programming Error 3.8

It is a syntax error if the function prototype, function header and function calls do not all agree in the number, type and order of arguments and parameters and in the return-value type.

There are three ways to return control to the point at which a function was invoked. If the function does not return a result, control returns when the program reaches the function-ending right brace, or by executing the statement

```
        return;
```

If the function does return a result, the statement

```
        return expression;
```

evaluates *expression* and returns the value of *expression* to the caller.

Our second example (Fig. 3.4) uses a programmer-defined function **maximum** to determine and return the largest of three floating-point numbers.

```cpp
1   // Fig. 3.4: fig03_04.cpp
2   // Finding the maximum of three floating-point numbers.
3   #include <iostream>
4
5   using std::cout;
6   using std::cin;
7   using std::endl;
8
9   double maximum( double, double, double ); // function prototype
10
11  int main()
12  {
13      double number1;
14      double number2;
15      double number3;
16
17      cout << "Enter three floating-point numbers: ";
18      cin >> number1 >> number2 >> number3;
19
20      // number1, number2 and number3 are arguments to
21      // the maximum function call
22      cout << "Maximum is: "
23          << maximum( number1, number2, number3 ) << endl;
24
25      return 0;  // indicates successful termination
26
27  } // end main
28
29  // function maximum definition;
30  // x, y and z are parameters
31  double maximum( double x, double y, double z )
32  {
33      double max = x;    // assume x is largest
34
35      if ( y > max )     // if y is larger,
36          max = y;       // assign y to max
37
38      if ( z > max )     // if z is larger,
39          max = z;       // assign z to max
40
41      return max;        // max is largest value
42
43  } // end function maximum
```

Fig. 3.4   Programmer-defined **maximum** function. (Part 1 of 2.)

```
Enter three floating-point numbers: 99.32 37.3 27.1928
Maximum is: 99.32
```

```
Enter three floating-point numbers: 1.1 3.333 2.22
Maximum is: 3.333
```

```
Enter three floating-point numbers: 27.9 14.31 88.99
Maximum is: 88.99
```

Fig. 3.4   Programmer-defined **maximum** function. (Part 2 of 2.)

The program prompts the user to input three floating-point numbers (line 15), then inputs the numbers (line 16). Next, the program calls function **maximum** (line 21), passing the numbers as arguments. Function **maximum** determines the largest value, then the **return** statement (line 39) returns that value to the point at which function **main** invoked **maximum** (line 21). Then the **cout** statement (lines 20–21) outputs the returned value. [*Note:* The commas used in line 21 to separate the arguments to function **maximum** are not comma operators as discussed in Section 2.14. The comma operator guarantees that its operands are evaluated left to right; however, the order of evaluation of a function's arguments is not defined.]

3.6 Function Prototypes

One of the most important features of C++ is the *function prototype*. A function prototype tells the compiler the name of a function, the type of data returned by that function, the number of parameters that function expects to receive, the types of those parameters and the order in which the parameters of those types are expected. The compiler uses function prototypes to validate function calls. Early versions of the C programming language did not perform this kind of checking, so it was possible to call C functions with incorrect arguments and compilers would not detect the errors. Such calls could result in fatal execution-time errors or nonfatal errors that caused subtle logic errors that were difficult to detect. Function prototypes correct this deficiency. The header files we include in C++ programs contain function prototypes (and other information), which enable the compiler to ensure that a program uses functions correctly.

Software Engineering Observation 3.9

*Function prototypes are required in C++. Use **#include** preprocessor directives to obtain function prototypes for the standard library functions from the header files for the appropriate libraries (e.g., the prototype for math function **sqrt** is in header file **<cmath>**; a list of standard library header files appears in Section 3.7). Also use **#include** to obtain header files containing function prototypes used by you or your group members.*

Common Programming Error 3.9

Forgetting the semicolon at the end of a function prototype is a syntax error.

Common Programming Error 3.10

A function call that does not match the function prototype is a syntax error.

Common Programming Error 3.11

Forgetting a function prototype when a function is not defined before it is first invoked is a syntax error.

The function prototype for function **maximum** at line 9 of Fig. 3.4 states that **maximum** takes three arguments of type **double** and returns a result of type **double**. Notice that this function prototype is the same as the header of the function definition of **maximum**, except the names of the parameters (**x**, **y** and **z**) are not included.

Good Programming Practice 3.4

Although parameter names in function prototypes are optional, many programmers use these names for documentation purposes.

The portion of a function prototype that includes the name of the function and the types of its arguments is called the *function signature* or simply the *signature*. The function signature does not include the function return type.

Common Programming Error 3.12

When compiling a function definition, it is an error if the return type and signature in the function prototype and the function definition disagree.

As an example of the preceding Common Programming Error, in Fig. 3.4, if the function prototype had been written

```
void maximum( double, double, double );
```

the compiler would report an error, because the **void** return type in the function prototype would differ from the **double** return type in the function header.

Another important feature of function prototypes is the *argument coercion*—i.e., forcing arguments to the appropriate types specified by the parameter declarations. For example, a program can call the math library function **sqrt** with an integer argument even though the function prototype in **<cmath>** specifies a **double** argument and the function still works correctly. The statement

```
cout << sqrt( 4 );
```

correctly evaluates **sqrt(4)** and prints the value **2**. The function prototype causes the compiler to convert the integer argument **4** to the **double** value **4.0** before the value is passed to **sqrt**.

In general, argument values that do not correspond precisely to the parameter types in the function prototype are converted to the proper type before the function is called. These conversions can lead to incorrect results if C++'s *promotion rules* are not followed. The promotion rules specify how to convert between types without losing data. In our earlier **sqrt** example, an **int** can be converted to a **double** without changing its value. However, a **double** converted to an **int** truncates the fractional part of the **double** value. Converting large integer types to small integer types (e.g., **long** to **short**) also can result in changed values.

The promotion rules apply to expressions containing values of two or more data types; such expressions are also referred to as *mixed-type expressions*. The type of each value in a mixed-type expression is promoted to the "highest" type in the expression (actually a temporary version of each value is created and used for the expression—the original values remain unchanged). Promotion also occurs when the type of an argument to a function does not match the parameter type specified in the function definition. Figure 3.5 lists the built-in data types in order from "highest type" to "lowest type."

Converting values to lower types can result in incorrect values. Therefore, a value can be converted to a lower type only by explicitly assigning the value to a variable of lower type or by using a cast operator (see Section 2.9). Function argument values are converted to the parameter types in a function prototype as if they are being assigned directly to variables of those types. If our **square** function that uses an integer parameter (Fig. 3.3) is called with a floating-point argument, the argument is converted to **int** (a lower type) and **square** usually returns an incorrect value. For example, **square(4.5)** would return **16**, not **20.25**.

Common Programming Error 3.13

Converting from a higher data type in the promotion hierarchy to a lower type can change the data value.

3.7 Header Files

The C++ standard library is divided into many portions, each with its own *header file*. The header files contain the function prototypes for the related functions that form each portion of the library. The header files also contain definitions of various data types and constants needed by those functions. Figure 3.6 lists some common C++ standard library header files, most of which are discussed later in the book. The term "macro" that is used several times in Fig. 3.6 is discussed in detail in Chapter 19, Preprocessor. Header file names ending in

Data types	
long double	
double	
float	
unsigned long int	(synonymous with unsigned long)
long int	(synonymous with long)
unsigned int	(synonymous with unsigned)
int	
unsigned short int	(synonymous with unsigned short)
short int	(synonymous with short)
unsigned char	
char	
bool	(false becomes 0, true becomes 1)

Fig. 3.5   Promotion hierarchy for built-in data types.

.h are "old-style" header files that have been superseded by the C++ standard library header files.[2]

Standard library header file	Explanation
<cassert>	Contains macros for adding diagnostics that aid program debugging. This replaces header file **<assert.h>** from pre-standard C++.
<cctype>	Contains function prototypes for functions that test characters for certain properties, and function prototypes for functions that can be used to convert lowercase letters to uppercase letters and vice versa. This header file replaces header file **<ctype.h>**.
<cfloat>	Contains the floating-point size limits of the system. This header file replaces header file **<float.h>**.
<climits>	Contains the integral size limits of the system. This header file replaces header file **<limits.h>**.
<cmath>	Contains function prototypes for math library functions. This header file replaces header file **<math.h>**.
<cstdio>	Contains function prototypes for the C-style standard input/output library functions and information used by them. This header file replaces header file **<stdio.h>**.
<cstdlib>	Contains function prototypes for conversions of numbers to text, text to numbers, memory allocation, random numbers and various other utility functions. This header file replaces header file **<stdlib.h>**.
<cstring>	Contains function prototypes for C-style string processing functions. This header file replaces header file **<string.h>**.
<ctime>	Contains function prototypes and types for manipulating the time and date. This header file replaces header file **<time.h>**.
<iostream>	Contains function prototypes for the C++ standard input and standard output functions. This header file replaces header file **<iostream.h>**.
<iomanip>	Contains function prototypes for stream manipulators that format of streams of data. This header file replaces header file **<iomanip.h>**.
<fstream>	Contains function prototypes for functions that perform input from files on disk and output to files on disk (discussed in Chapter 14). This header file replaces header file **<fstream.h>**.
<utility>	Contains classes and functions that are used by many standard library header files.

Fig. 3.6   Standard library header files. (Part 1 of 2.)

---

2. The programmer can create custom header files. Programmer-defined header file names often end in **.h**, **.hpp** or **.hxx**. A program includes a programmer-defined header file by using the **#include** preprocessor directive. For example, the header file **square.h** can be included in our program by the directive **#include "square.h"** in the program file. Note that programmer-defined header files normally are enclosed in quotes (**""**) rather than angle brackets (**<>**). Section 6.7 and Section 19.2 present additional information on including programmer-defined header files.

Standard library header file	Explanation
`<vector>`, `<list>`, `<deque>`, `<queue>`, `<stack>`, `<map>`, `<set>`, `<bitset>`	These header files contain classes that implement the standard library containers. Containers store data during a program's execution. We discuss these header files in Chapter 21, Standard Template Library (STL).
`<functional>`	Contains classes and functions used by standard library algorithms.
`<memory>`	Contains classes and functions used by the standard library to allocate memory to the standard library containers.
`<iterator>`	Contains classes for accessing data in the standard library containers.
`<algorithm>`	Contains functions for manipulating data in standard library containers.
`<exception>`, `<stdexcept>`	These header files contain classes that are used for exception handling (discussed in Chapter 13, Exception Handling).
`<string>`	Contains the definition of class **string** from the standard library (discussed in Chapter 15, Strings).
`<sstream>`	Contains function prototypes for functions that perform input from strings in memory and output to strings in memory (discussed in Chapter 15).
`<locale>`	Contains classes and functions normally used by stream processing to process data in the natural form for different languages (e.g., monetary formats, sorting strings, character presentation, etc.).
`<limits>`	Contains classes for defining the numerical data type limits on each computer platform.
`<typeinfo>`	Contains classes for run-time type identification (determining data types at execution time).

Fig. 3.6   Standard library header files. (Part 2 of 2.)

3.8 Random Number Generation

We now take a brief and, it is hoped, entertaining diversion into a popular programming application, namely simulation and game playing. In this and the next section, we develop a nicely structured game-playing program that includes multiple functions. The program uses most of the control structures and concepts discussed to this point.

There is something in the air of a gambling casino that invigorates every person—from the high-rollers at the plush mahogany-and-felt craps tables to the quarter-poppers at the one-armed bandits. It is the *element of chance,* the possibility that luck will convert a pocketful of money into a mountain of wealth. The element of chance can be introduced into computer applications by using the standard library function **rand**.

Consider the following statement:

```
i = rand();
```

The function **rand** generates an unsigned integer between 0 and **RAND_MAX** (a symbolic constant defined in the **<cstdlib>** header file). The value of **RAND_MAX** must be at least 32767—the maximum positive value for a two-byte (16-bit) integer. If **rand** truly produces integers at random, every number between 0 and **RAND_MAX** has an equal *chance* (or *probability*) of being chosen each time **rand** is called.

The range of values produced directly by **rand** often is different than what a specific application requires. For example, a program that simulates coin tossing might require only 0 for "heads" and 1 for "tails." A program that simulates rolling a six-sided die would require random integers in range 1 to 6. A program that randomly predicts the next type of spaceship (out of four possibilities) that will fly across the horizon in a video game might require random integers in the range 1 through 4.

To demonstrate **rand**, let us develop a program (Fig. 3.7) to simulate 20 rolls of a six-sided die and print the value of each roll. The function prototype for the **rand** function can be found in **<cstdlib>**. To produce integers in the range 0 to 5, we use the modulus operator (**%**) with **rand** as follows:

```
rand() % 6
```

```
1   // Fig. 3.7: fig03_07.cpp
2   // Shifted, scaled integers produced by 1 + rand() % 6.
3   #include <iostream>
4
5   using std::cout;
6   using std::endl;
7
8   #include <iomanip>
9
10  using std::setw;
11
12  #include <cstdlib>      // contains function prototype for rand
13
14  int main()
15  {
16     // loop 20 times
17     for ( int counter = 1; counter <= 20; counter++ ) {
18
19        // pick random number from 1 to 6 and output it
20        cout << setw( 10 ) << ( 1 + rand() % 6 );
21
22        // if counter divisible by 5, begin new line of output
23        if ( counter % 5 == 0 )
24           cout << endl;
25
26     } // end for structure
27
28     return 0;   // indicates successful termination
29
30  } // end main
```

6	6	5	5	6
5	1	1	5	3
6	6	2	4	2
6	2	3	4	1

Fig. 3.7   Shifted, scaled integers produced by **1 + rand() % 6**.

This is called *scaling*. The number 6 is called the *scaling factor*. We then *shift* the range of numbers produced by adding 1 to our previous result. Figure 3.7 confirms that the results are in the range 1 to 6.

To show that the numbers produced by function **rand** occur with approximately equal likelihood, Fig. 3.8 simulates 6000 rolls of a die. Each integer in the range 1 to 6 should appear approximately 1000 times. This is confirmed by the output window at the end of Fig. 3.8.

```
1   // Fig. 3.8: fig03_08.cpp
2   // Roll a six-sided die 6000 times.
3   #include <iostream>
4
5   using std::cout;
6   using std::endl;
7
8   #include <iomanip>
9
10  using std::setw;
11
12  #include <cstdlib>    // contains function prototype for rand
13
14  int main()
15  {
16     int frequency1 = 0;
17     int frequency2 = 0;
18     int frequency3 = 0;
19     int frequency4 = 0;
20     int frequency5 = 0;
21     int frequency6 = 0;
22     int face;  // represents one roll of the die
23
24     // loop 6000 times and summarize results
25     for ( int roll = 1; roll <= 6000; roll++ ) {
26        face = 1 + rand() % 6;   // random number from 1 to 6
27
28        // determine face value and increment appropriate counter
29        switch ( face ) {
30
31           case 1:          // rolled 1
32              ++frequency1;
33              break;
34
35           case 2:          // rolled 2
36              ++frequency2;
37              break;
38
39           case 3:          // rolled 3
40              ++frequency3;
41              break;
42
```

Fig. 3.8   Rolling a six-sided die 6000 times. (Part 1 of 2.)

```
43            case 4:            // rolled 4
44                ++frequency4;
45                break;
46
47            case 5:            // rolled 5
48                ++frequency5;
49                break;
50
51            case 6:            // rolled 6
52                ++frequency6;
53                break;
54
55            default:           // invalid value
56                cout << "Program should never get here!";
57
58        } // end switch
59
60    } // end for
61
62    // display results in tabular format
63    cout << "Face" << setw( 13 ) << "Frequency"
64         << "\n   1" << setw( 13 ) << frequency1
65         << "\n   2" << setw( 13 ) << frequency2
66         << "\n   3" << setw( 13 ) << frequency3
67         << "\n   4" << setw( 13 ) << frequency4
68         << "\n   5" << setw( 13 ) << frequency5
69         << "\n   6" << setw( 13 ) << frequency6 << endl;
70
71    return 0;  // indicates successful termination
72
73 } // end main
```

Face	Frequency
1	1003
2	1017
3	983
4	994
5	1004
6	999

Fig. 3.8   Rolling a six-sided die 6000 times. (Part 2 of 2.)

As the program output shows, we can simulate the rolling of a six-sided die by scaling and shifting the values produced by **rand**. Note that the program should never get to the **default** case provided in the **switch** structure, because the **switch**'s controlling expression (**face**) always has values in the range 1–6; however, we provide the **default** case as a matter of good practice. After we study arrays in Chapter 4, we show how to replace the entire **switch** structure in Fig. 3.8 elegantly with a single-line statement.

Testing and Debugging Tip 3.1

*Provide a **default** case in a **switch** to catch errors even if you are absolutely, positively certain that you have no bugs!*

Executing the program of Fig. 3.7 again produces

```
        6          6          5          5          6
        5          1          1          5          3
        6          6          2          4          2
        6          2          3          4          1
```

Notice that the program prints exactly the same sequence of values shown in Fig. 3.7. How can these be random numbers? Ironically, this repeatability is an important characteristic of function **rand**. When debugging a simulation program, this repeatability is essential for proving that corrections to the program work properly.

Function **rand** actually generates *pseudo-random numbers*. Calling **rand** repeatedly produces a sequence of numbers that appears to be random. However, the sequence repeats itself each time the program executes. Once a program has been thoroughly debugged, it can be conditioned to produce a different sequence of random numbers for each execution. This is called *randomizing* and is accomplished with the standard library function **srand**. Function **srand** takes an **unsigned** integer argument and *seeds* the **rand** function to produce a different sequence of random numbers for each execution of the program.

Figure 3.9 demonstrates function **srand**. The program uses the data type **unsigned**, which is short for **unsigned int**. An **int** is stored in at least two bytes of memory and can have positive and negative values. A variable of type **unsigned int** is also stored in at least two bytes of memory. A two-byte **unsigned int** can have only nonnegative values in the range 0–65535. A four-byte **unsigned int** can have only nonnegative values in the range 0–4294967295. Function **srand** takes an **unsigned int** value as an argument. The function prototype for the **srand** function is in header file **<cstdlib>**.

```cpp
1   // Fig. 3.9: fig03_09.cpp
2   // Randomizing die-rolling program.
3   #include <iostream>
4
5   using std::cout;
6   using std::cin;
7   using std::endl;
8
9   #include <iomanip>
10
11  using std::setw;
12
13  // contains prototypes for functions srand and rand
14  #include <cstdlib>
15
16  // main function begins program execution
17  int main()
18  {
```

Fig. 3.9   Randomizing the die-rolling program. (Part 1 of 2.)

```
19      unsigned seed;
20
21      cout << "Enter seed: ";
22      cin >> seed;
23      srand( seed );   // seed random number generator
24
25      // loop 10 times
26      for ( int counter = 1; counter <= 10; counter++ ) {
27
28         // pick random number from 1 to 6 and output it
29         cout << setw( 10 ) << ( 1 + rand() % 6 );
30
31         // if counter divisible by 5, begin new line of output
32         if ( counter % 5 == 0 )
33            cout << endl;
34
35      } // end for
36
37      return 0;   // indicates successful termination
38
39   } // end main
```

```
Enter seed: 67
         6         1         4         6         2
         1         6         1         6         4
```

```
Enter seed: 432
         4         6         3         1         6
         3         1         5         4         2
```

```
Enter seed: 67
         6         1         4         6         2
         1         6         1         6         4
```

Fig. 3.9   Randomizing the die-rolling program. (Part 2 of 2.)

Let us run the program several times and observe the results. Notice that the program produces a *different* sequence of random numbers each time it executes, provided that the user enters a different seed during each execution.

If we wish to randomize without the need for entering a seed each time, we may use a statement like

```
srand( time( 0 ) );
```

This causes the computer to read its clock to obtain the value for the seed. Function **time** (with the argument **0** as written in the preceding statement) returns the current "calendar time" in seconds. This value is converted to an **unsigned** integer and used as the seed to the random number generator. The function prototype for **time** is in **<ctime>**.

Common Programming Error 3.14

*Calling function **srand** more than once in a program restarts the pseudo-random-number sequence and can affect the randomness of the numbers produced by **rand**.*

The values produced directly by **rand** are always in the range

$$0 \leq \textbf{rand()} \leq \text{RAND\_MAX}$$

Previously, we demonstrated how to write a single statement to simulate the rolling of a six-sided die with the statement

```
face = 1 + rand() % 6;
```

which always assigns an integer (at random) to variable **face** in the range $1 \leq \textbf{face} \leq 6$. Note that the width of this range (i.e., the number of consecutive integers in the range) is 6 and the starting number in the range is 1. Referring to the preceding statement, we see that the width of the range is determined by the number used to scale **rand** with the modulus operator (i.e., 6), and the starting number of the range is equal to the number (i.e., 1) that is added to the expression **rand % 6**. We can generalize this result as

number = *shiftingValue* + **rand()** % *scalingFactor*;

where *shiftingValue* is equal to the first number in the desired range of consecutive integers and *scalingFactor* is equal to the width of the desired range of consecutive integers. The exercises show that it is possible to choose integers at random from sets of values other than ranges of consecutive integers.

Common Programming Error 3.15

*Using **srand** in place of **rand** to attempt to generate random numbers is a syntax error—function **srand** does not return a value.*

3.9 Example: Game of Chance and Introducing **enum**

One of the most popular games of chance is a dice game known as "craps," which is played in casinos and back alleys worldwide. The rules of the game are straightforward:

> *A player rolls two dice. Each die has six faces. These faces contain 1, 2, 3, 4, 5 and 6 spots. After the dice have come to rest, the sum of the spots on the two upward faces is calculated. If the sum is 7 or 11 on the first roll, the player wins. If the sum is 2, 3 or 12 on the first roll (called "craps"), the player loses (i.e., the "house" wins). If the sum is 4, 5, 6, 8, 9 or 10 on the first roll, then that sum becomes the player's "point." To win, you must continue rolling the dice until you "make your point." The player loses by rolling a 7 before making the point.*

The program in Fig. 3.10 simulates the game of craps. Figure 3.11 shows several sample executions.

```
1   // Fig. 3.10: fig03_10.cpp
2   // Craps.
3   #include <iostream>
4
```

Fig. 3.10 Craps simulation. (Part 1 of 3.)

```
 5   using std::cout;
 6   using std::endl;
 7
 8   // contains function prototypes for functions srand and rand
 9   #include <cstdlib>
10
11   #include <ctime>     // contains prototype for function time
12
13   int rollDice( void );   // function prototype
14
15   int main()
16   {
17      // enumeration constants represent game status
18      enum Status { CONTINUE, WON, LOST };
19
20      int sum;
21      int myPoint;
22
23      Status gameStatus;   // can contain CONTINUE, WON or LOST
24
25      // randomize random number generator using current time
26      srand( time( 0 ) );
27
28      sum = rollDice();    // first roll of the dice
29
30      // determine game status and point based on sum of dice
31      switch ( sum ) {
32
33         // win on first roll
34         case 7:
35         case 11:
36            gameStatus = WON;
37            break;
38
39         // lose on first roll
40         case 2:
41         case 3:
42         case 12:
43            gameStatus = LOST;
44            break;
45
46         // remember point
47         default:
48            gameStatus = CONTINUE;
49            myPoint = sum;
50            cout << "Point is " << myPoint << endl;
51            break;                  // optional
52
53      } // end switch
54
55      // while game not complete ...
56      while ( gameStatus == CONTINUE ) {
57         sum = rollDice();          // roll dice again
```

Fig. 3.10   Craps simulation. (Part 2 of 3.)

```
58
59              // determine game status
60              if ( sum == myPoint )          // win by making point
61                 gameStatus = WON;
62              else
63                 if ( sum == 7 )             // lose by rolling 7
64                    gameStatus = LOST;
65
66        } // end while
67
68        // display won or lost message
69        if ( gameStatus == WON )
70           cout << "Player wins" << endl;
71        else
72           cout << "Player loses" << endl;
73
74        return 0;   // indicates successful termination
75
76    } // end main
77
78    // roll dice, calculate sum and display results
79    int rollDice( void )
80    {
81       int die1;
82       int die2;
83       int workSum;
84
85       die1 = 1 + rand() % 6;   // pick random die1 value
86       die2 = 1 + rand() % 6;   // pick random die2 value
87       workSum = die1 + die2;   // sum die1 and die2
88
89       // display results of this roll
90       cout << "Player rolled " << die1 << " + " << die2
91            << " = " << workSum << endl;
92
93       return workSum;          // return sum of dice
94
95    } // end function rollDice
```

Fig. 3.10   Craps simulation. (Part 3 of 3.)

In the rules of the game, notice that the player must roll two dice on the first roll, and must do the same on all subsequent rolls. We define function **rollDice** (lines 79–95) to roll the dice and compute and print their sum. Function **rollDice** is defined once, but it is called from two places (lines 28 and 57) in the program. Interestingly, **rollDice** takes no arguments, so we have indicated **void** in the parameter list. Function **rollDice** does return the sum of the two dice, so return type **int** is indicated in the function prototype (line 13) and function header (line 79).

The game is reasonably involved. The player may win or lose on the first roll, or may win or lose on any subsequent roll. The program uses variable **gameStatus** to keep track of this. Variable **gameStatus** is declared to be of new type **Status**. Line 18 creates a *user-defined type* called an *enumeration*. An enumeration, introduced by the keyword

```
Player rolled 2 + 5 = 7
Player wins
```

```
Player rolled 6 + 6 = 12
Player loses
```

```
Player rolled 3 + 3 = 6
Point is 6
Player rolled 5 + 3 = 8
Player rolled 4 + 5 = 9
Player rolled 2 + 1 = 3
Player rolled 1 + 5 = 6
Player wins
```

```
Player rolled 1 + 3 = 4
Point is 4
Player rolled 4 + 6 = 10
Player rolled 2 + 4 = 6
Player rolled 6 + 4 = 10
Player rolled 2 + 3 = 5
Player rolled 2 + 4 = 6
Player rolled 1 + 1 = 2
Player rolled 4 + 4 = 8
Player rolled 4 + 3 = 7
Player loses
```

Fig. 3.11   Sample outputs for the craps program.

enum and followed by a *type name* (in this case, **Status**), is a set of integer constants represented by identifiers. The values of these *enumeration constants* start at **0**, unless specified otherwise, and increment by **1**. In the preceding enumeration, the constant **CONTINUE** has the value 0, **WON** has the value 1 and **LOST** has the value 2. The identifiers in an **enum** must be unique, but separate enumeration constants can have the same integer value.

Good Programming Practice 3.5

Capitalize the first letter of an identifier used as a user-defined type name.

Good Programming Practice 3.6

Use only uppercase letters in the names of enumeration constants. This makes these constants stand out in a program and reminds the programmer that enumeration constants are not variables.

Variables of user-defined type **Status** can be assigned only one of the three values declared in the enumeration. When the game is won, the program sets variable **gameStatus** to **WON** (lines 36 and 61). When the game is lost, the program sets variable

gameStatus to **LOST** (lines 43 and 64). Otherwise, the program sets variable **gameStatus** to **CONTINUE** to indicate that the dice must be rolled again.

Good Programming Practice 3.7

Using enumerations rather than integer constants can make programs clearer and more maintainable. If you need to change the value of an enumeration constant, it can be changed once in the enumeration declaration.

Common Programming Error 3.16

Assigning the integer equivalent of an enumeration constant to a variable of the enumeration type is a syntax error.

Common Programming Error 3.17

After an enumeration constant has been defined, attempting to assign another value to the enumeration constant is a syntax error.

Another popular enumeration is

```
enum Months { JAN = 1, FEB, MAR, APR, MAY, JUN, JUL, AUG,
    SEP, OCT, NOV, DEC };
```

which creates user-defined type **Months** with enumeration constants representing the months of the year. The first value in the preceding enumeration is explicitly set to **1**, so the remaining values increment from **1**, resulting in the values **1** through **12**. Any enumeration constant can be assigned an integer value in the enumeration definition, and subsequent enumeration constants each have a value 1 higher than the preceding constant in the list.

After the first roll, if the game is won or lost, the program skips the body of the **while** structure (lines 56–66) because **gameStatus** is not equal to **CONTINUE**. The program proceeds to the **if/else** structure at lines 69–72, which prints "**Player wins**" if **gameStatus** is equal to **WON** and "**Player loses**" if **gameStatus** is equal to **LOST**.

After the first roll, if the game is not over, the program saves the **sum** in **myPoint** (line 49). Execution proceeds with the **while** structure because **gameStatus** is equal to **CONTINUE**. During each iteration of the **while**, the program calls **rollDice** to produce a new **sum**. If **sum** matches **myPoint**, the program sets **gameStatus** to **WON** (line 61), the **while**-test fails, the **if/else** structure prints "**Player wins**" and execution terminates. If **sum** is equal to **7**, the program sets **gameStatus** to **LOST** (line 64), the **while**-test fails, the **if/else** structure prints "**Player loses**" and execution terminates.

Note the interesting use of the various program-control mechanisms we have discussed. The craps program uses two functions—**main** and **rollDice**—and the **switch**, **while**, **if/else** and nested **if/else** structures. In the exercises, we investigate various interesting characteristics of the game of craps.

3.10 Storage Classes

The programs of Chapter 1 through Chapter 3 use identifiers for variable names. The attributes of variables include name, type, size and value. This chapter also uses identifiers as names for programmer-defined functions. Actually, each identifier in a program has other attributes, including *storage class*, *scope* and *linkage*.

C++ provides five *storage-class specifiers: **auto**, **register**, **extern**, **mutable** and **static***. An identifier's storage-class specifier helps determine its storage class and linkage. This section discusses storage-class specifiers **auto**, **register**, **extern** and **static**. Storage-class specifier **mutable** (discussed in detail in Chapter 22) is used exclusively with C++ user-defined types called *classes* (introduced in Chapter 6 and Chapter 7).

An identifier's *storage class* determines the period during which that identifier exists in memory. Some identifiers exist briefly, some are repeatedly created and destroyed and others exist for the entire execution of a program. This section discusses two storage classes: *static* and *automatic*.

An identifier's *scope* is where the identifier can be referenced in a program. Some identifiers can be referenced throughout a program; others can be referenced from only limited portions of a program. Section 3.11 discusses the scope of identifiers.

An identifier's *linkage* determines for a multiple-source-file program (a topic we begin investigating in Chapter 6) whether an identifier is known only in the current source file or in any source file with proper declarations.

The storage-class specifiers can be split into two storage classes: *automatic storage class* and *static storage class*. Keywords **auto** and **register** are used to declare variables of the automatic storage class. Such variables are created when program execution enters the block in which they are defined, they exist while the block is active and they are destroyed when the program exits the block.

Only local variables of a function can be of automatic storage class. A function's local variables and parameters normally are of automatic storage class. The storage class specifier **auto** explicitly declares variables of automatic storage class. For example, the following declaration indicates that **double** variables **x** and **y** are local variables of automatic storage class—they exist only in the body of the function in which the definition appears:

```
auto double x, y;
```

Local variables are of automatic storage class by default, so keyword **auto** rarely is used. For the remainder of the text, we refer to variables of automatic storage class simply as automatic variables.

Performance Tip 3.2

Automatic storage is a means of conserving memory because automatic storage class variables exist in memory only when the block in which they are defined is executing.

Software Engineering Observation 3.10

Automatic storage is an example of the principle of least privilege. Why have variables stored in memory and accessible when they are not needed?

Data in the machine-language version of a program are normally loaded into registers for calculations and other processing.

Performance Tip 3.3

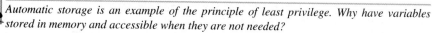

*The storage-class specifier **register** can be placed before an automatic variable declaration to suggest that the compiler maintain the variable in one of the computer's high-speed hardware registers rather than in memory. If intensely used variables such as counters or totals can be maintained in hardware registers, the overhead of repeatedly loading the variables from memory into the registers and storing the results back into memory can be eliminated.*

Common Programming Error 3.18

Using multiple storage-class specifiers for an identifier is a syntax error. Only one storage-class specifier can be applied to an identifier. For example, if you include **register***, do not also include* **auto***.*

The compiler might ignore **register** declarations. For example, there might not be a sufficient number of registers available for the compiler to use. The following declaration *suggests* that the integer variable **counter** be placed in one of the computer's registers; regardless of whether the compiler does this, **counter** is initialized to 1:

```
register int counter = 1;
```

The **register** keyword can be used only with local variables and function parameters.

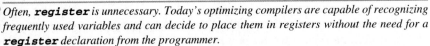 **Performance Tip 3.4**

Often, **register** *is unnecessary. Today's optimizing compilers are capable of recognizing frequently used variables and can decide to place them in registers without the need for a* **register** *declaration from the programmer.*

Keywords **extern** and **static** declare identifiers for variables and functions of the static storage class. Such variables exist from the point at which the program begins execution. For static-storage class variables, storage is allocated and initialized once when the program begins execution. For static-storage class functions, the name of the function exists when the program begins execution. However, even though the variables and the function names exist from the start of program execution, this does not mean that these identifiers can be used throughout the program. Storage class and scope (where a name can be used) are separate issues, as we will see in Section 3.11.

There are two types of identifiers with static storage class—external identifiers (such as *global variables* and function names) and local variables declared with the storage class specifier **static**. Global variables are created by placing variable declarations outside any function definition. Global variables retain their values throughout the execution of the program. Global variables and functions can be referenced by any function that follows their declarations or definitions in the source file. Global variables and function names default to storage-class specifier **extern**.

 Software Engineering Observation 3.11

Declaring a variable as global rather than local allows unintended side effects to occur when a function that does not need access to the variable accidentally or maliciously modifies it. In general, use of global variables should be avoided except in certain situations with unique performance requirements.

Software Engineering Observation 3.12

Variables used only in a particular function should be declared as local variables in that function rather than as global variables.

Local variables declared with the keyword **static** are still known only in the function in which they are defined, but, unlike automatic variables, **static** local variables retain their values when the function returns to its caller. The next time the function is called, the **static** local variables contain the values they had when the function last completed execution. The following statement declares local variable **count** to be **static** and to be initialized to 1:

level computer science courses. This section and the next present simple examples of recursion. This book contains an extensive treatment of recursion. Figure 3.17 (at the end of Section 3.14) summarizes the recursion examples and exercises in the book.

We first consider recursion conceptually, then we examine two programs containing recursive functions. Recursive problem-solving approaches have a number of elements in common. A recursive function is called to solve a problem. The function actually knows how to solve only the simplest case(s), or so-called *base case(s)*. If the function is called with a base case, the function simply returns a result. If the function is called with a more complex problem, the function divides the problem into two conceptual pieces—a piece that the function knows how to do and a piece that the function does not know how to do. To make recursion feasible, the latter piece must resemble the original problem, but be a slightly simpler or slightly smaller version of the original problem. This new problem looks like the original problem, so the function launches (calls) a fresh copy of itself to work on the smaller problem—this is referred to as a *recursive call* and is also called the *recursion step*. The recursion step often includes the keyword **return**, because its result will be combined with the portion of the problem the function knew how to solve to form a result that will be passed back to the original caller, possibly **main**.

The recursion step executes while the original call to the function is still open, i.e., it has not yet finished executing. The recursion step can result in many more such recursive calls as the function keeps dividing each new subproblem with which the function is called into two conceptual pieces. In order for the recursion to eventually terminate, each time the function calls itself with a slightly simpler version of the original problem, this sequence of smaller and smaller problems must eventually converge on the base case. At that point, the function recognizes the base case and returns a result to the previous copy of the function, and a sequence of returns ensues all the way up the line until the original function call eventually returns the final result to **main**. All of this sounds quite exotic compared to the kind of conventional problem solving we have been using to this point. As an example of these concepts at work, let us write a recursive program to perform a popular mathematical calculation.

The factorial of a nonnegative integer *n,* written *n!* (and pronounced "*n* factorial"), is the product

$$n \cdot (n-1) \cdot (n-2) \cdot \ldots \cdot 1$$

with 1! equal to 1, and 0! defined to be 1. For example, 5! is the product $5 \cdot 4 \cdot 3 \cdot 2 \cdot 1$, which is equal to 120.

The factorial of an integer, **number**, greater than or equal to 0, can be calculated *iteratively* (nonrecursively) by using **for** as follows:

```
factorial = 1;

for ( int counter = number; counter >= 1; counter-- )
    factorial *= counter;
```

A recursive definition of the factorial function is arrived at by observing the following relationship:

$$n! = n \cdot (n-1)!$$

For example, 5! is clearly equal to 5 * 4! as is shown by the following:

$$5! = 5 \cdot 4 \cdot 3 \cdot 2 \cdot 1$$
$$5! = 5 \cdot (4 \cdot 3 \cdot 2 \cdot 1)$$
$$5! = 5 \cdot (4!)$$

The evaluation of 5! would proceed as shown in Fig. 3.13. Figure 3.13(a) shows how the succession of recursive calls proceeds until 1! is evaluated to be 1, which terminates the recursion. Figure 3.13(b) shows the values returned from each recursive call to its caller until the final value is calculated and returned.

The program of Fig. 3.14 uses recursion to calculate and print the factorials of the integers 0–10. (The choice of the data type **unsigned long** is explained momentarily.) The recursive function **factorial** (lines 27–37) first determines whether the terminating condition **number <= 1** (line 30) is true. If **number** is indeed less than or equal to 1, function **factorial** returns 1 (line 31), no further recursion is necessary and the function terminates. If **number** is greater than 1, line 35 expresses the problem as the product of **number** and a recursive call to **factorial** evaluating the factorial of **number - 1**. Note that **factorial(number - 1)** is a slightly simpler problem than the original calculation **factorial(number)**.

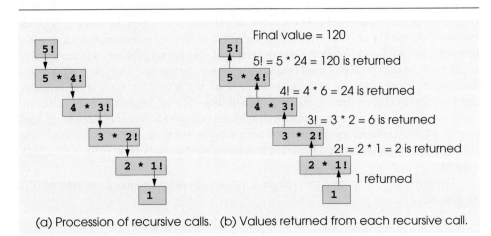

(a) Procession of recursive calls.   (b) Values returned from each recursive call.

Fig. 3.13   Recursive evaluation of 5!.

```
1   // Fig. 3.14: fig03_14.cpp
2   // Recursive factorial function.
3   #include <iostream>
4
5   using std::cout;
6   using std::endl;
7
8   #include <iomanip>
9
10  using std::setw;
```

Fig. 3.14   Factorial calculations with a recursive function. (Part 1 of 2.)

```
11
12   unsigned long factorial( unsigned long ); // function prototype
13
14   int main()
15   {
16       // Loop 10 times. During each iteration, calculate
17       // factorial( i ) and display result.
18       for ( int i = 0; i <= 10; i++ )
19           cout << setw( 2 ) << i << "! = "
20                << factorial( i ) << endl;
21
22       return 0;  // indicates successful termination
23
24   } // end main
25
26   // recursive definition of function factorial
27   unsigned long factorial( unsigned long number )
28   {
29       // base case
30       if ( number <= 1 )
31           return 1;
32
33       // recursive step
34       else
35           return number * factorial( number - 1 );
36
37   } // end function factorial
```

```
  0! = 1
  1! = 1
  2! = 2
  3! = 6
  4! = 24
  5! = 120
  6! = 720
  7! = 5040
  8! = 40320
  9! = 362880
 10! = 3628800
```

Fig. 3.14   Factorial calculations with a recursive function. (Part 2 of 2.)

Function **factorial** has been declared to receive a parameter of type **unsigned long** and return a result of type **unsigned long**. This is shorthand notation for **unsigned long int**. The C++ language specification requires that a variable of type **unsigned long int** be stored in at least four bytes (32 bits); thus, it can hold a value in the range 0 to at least 4294967295. (The data type **long int** is also stored in at least four bytes and can hold a value at least in the range –2147483648 to 2147483647.) As can be seen in Fig. 3.14, factorial values become large quickly. We chose the data type **unsigned long** so that the program can calculate factorials greater than 7! on computers with small (such as two-byte) integers. Unfortunately, function **factorial** produces

5 55555555555555555 5555555555

large values so quickly that even **unsigned long** does not help us compute many factorial values before the size of an **unsigned long** variable is exceeded.

The exercises explore using variables of data type **double** to calculate factorials of larger numbers. This points to a weakness in most programming languages, namely, that the languages are not easily extended to handle the unique requirements of various applications. As we will see in the section of the book on object-oriented programming, C++ is an extensible language that allows us to create arbitrarily large integers if we wish.

Common Programming Error 3.20

Either omitting the base case, or writing the recursion step incorrectly so that it does not converge on the base case, causes "infinite" recursion, eventually exhausting memory. This is analogous to the problem of an infinite loop in an iterative (nonrecursive) solution.

3.13 Example Using Recursion: Fibonacci Series

The Fibonacci series

0, 1, 1, 2, 3, 5, 8, 13, 21, …

begins with 0 and 1 and has the property that each subsequent Fibonacci number is the sum of the previous two Fibonacci numbers.

The series occurs in nature and, in particular, describes a form of spiral. The ratio of successive Fibonacci numbers converges on a constant value of 1.618…. This number, too, repeatedly occurs in nature and has been called the *golden ratio* or the *golden mean*. Humans tend to find the golden mean aesthetically pleasing. Architects often design windows, rooms, and buildings whose length and width are in the ratio of the golden mean. Postcards are often designed with a golden mean length/width ratio.

The Fibonacci series can be defined recursively as follows:

fibonacci(0) = 0
fibonacci(1) = 1
fibonacci(n) = fibonacci($n-1$) + fibonacci($n-2$)

The program of Fig. 3.15 calculates the nth Fibonacci number recursively by using function **fibonacci**. Notice that Fibonacci numbers tend to become large quickly. Therefore, we chose the data type **unsigned long** for the parameter type and the return type in function **fibonacci**. Figure 3.15 shows 11 executions of the program.

```
1   // Fig. 3.15: fig03_15.cpp
2   // Recursive fibonacci function.
3   #include <iostream>
4
5   using std::cout;
6   using std::cin;
7   using std::endl;
8
9   unsigned long fibonacci( unsigned long ); // function prototype
10
```

Fig. 3.15   Fibonacci numbers generated with a recursive function. (Part 1 of 3.)

```
11   int main()
12   {
13      unsigned long result, number;
14
15      // obtain integer from user
16      cout << "Enter an integer: ";
17      cin >> number;
18
19      // calculate fibonacci value for number input by user
20      result = fibonacci( number );
21
22      // display result
23      cout << "Fibonacci(" << number << ") = " << result << endl;
24
25      return 0;   // indicates successful termination
26
27   } // end main
28
29   // recursive definition of function fibonacci
30   unsigned long fibonacci( unsigned long n )
31   {
32      // base case
33      if ( n == 0 || n == 1 )
34         return n;
35
36      // recursive step
37      else
38         return fibonacci( n - 1 ) + fibonacci( n - 2 );
39
40   } // end function fibonacci
```

```
Enter an integer: 0
Fibonacci(0) = 0
```

```
Enter an integer: 1
Fibonacci(1) = 1
```

```
Enter an integer: 2
Fibonacci(2) = 1
```

```
Enter an integer: 3
Fibonacci(3) = 2
```

```
Enter an integer: 4
Fibonacci(4) = 3
```

Fig. 3.15   Fibonacci numbers generated with a recursive function. (Part 2 of 3.)

```
Enter an integer: 5
Fibonacci(5) = 5
```

```
Enter an integer: 6
Fibonacci(6) = 8
```

```
Enter an integer: 10
Fibonacci(10) = 55
```

```
Enter an integer: 20
Fibonacci(20) = 6765
```

```
Enter an integer: 30
Fibonacci(30) = 832040
```

```
Enter an integer: 35
Fibonacci(35) = 9227465
```

Fig. 3.15   Fibonacci numbers generated with a recursive function. (Part 3 of 3.)

The call to **fibonacci** (line 20) from **main** is not a recursive call, but all subsequent calls to **fibonacci** are recursive. Each time the program invokes **fibonacci** (lines 30–40), the function immediately tests the base case to determine whether **n** is equal to **0** or **1** (line 33). If this is true, line 34 returns **n**. Interestingly, if **n** is greater than 1, the recursion step (line 38) generates *two* recursive calls, each is for a slightly simpler problem than the original call to **fibonacci**. Figure 3.16 shows how function **fibonacci** would evaluate **fibonacci(3)**.

This figure raises some interesting issues about the order in which C++ compilers will evaluate the operands of operators. This is a different issue from the order in which operators are applied to their operands, namely, the order dictated by the rules of operator precedence. Figure 3.16 shows that evaluating **fibonacci(3)** causes two recursive calls, namely, **fibonacci(2)** and **fibonacci(1)**. But in what order are these calls made?

Most programmers simply assume the that operands are evaluated left to right. The C++ language does not specify the order in which the operands of most operators (including **+**) are to be evaluated. Therefore, the programmer must make no assumption about the order in which these calls execute. The calls could in fact execute **fibonacci(2)** first, then **fibonacci(1)**, or the calls could execute in the reverse order, **fibonacci(1)**, then **fibonacci(2)**. In this program and in most other programs, it turns out the final result would be the same. However, in some programs the evaluation of an operand can have *side effects* (changes to data values) that could affect the final result of the expression.

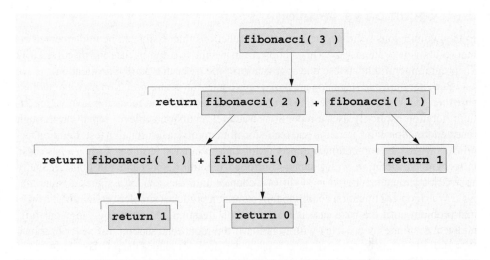

Fig. 3.16   Set of recursive calls to method **Fibonacci**.

The C++ language specifies the order of evaluation of the operands of only four operators—namely, **&&**, **||**, the comma (**,**) operator and **?:**. The first three of these are binary operators whose two operands are guaranteed to be evaluated left to right. The last operator is C++'s only ternary operator. Its leftmost operand is always evaluated first; if the leftmost operand evaluates to nonzero (true), the middle operand evaluates next and the last operand is ignored; if the leftmost operand evaluates to zero (false), the third operand evaluates next and the middle operand is ignored.

Common Programming Error 3.21
*Writing programs that depend on the order of evaluation of the operands of operators other than **&&**, **||**, **?:** and the comma (**,**) operator can lead to logic errors.*

Portability Tip 3.2
*Programs that depend on the order of evaluation of the operands of operators other than **&&**, **||**, **?:** and the comma (**,**) operator can function differently on systems with different compilers.*

A word of caution is in order about recursive programs like the one we use here to generate Fibonacci numbers. Each level of recursion in function **fibonacci** has a doubling effect on the number of function calls, i.e., the number of recursive calls that are required to calculate the nth Fibonacci number is on the order of 2^n. This rapidly gets out of hand. Calculating only the 20th Fibonacci number would require on the order of 2^{20} or about a million calls, calculating the 30th Fibonacci number would require on the order of 2^{30} or about a billion calls, and so on. Computer scientists refer to this as *exponential complexity*. Problems of this nature humble even the world's most powerful computers! Complexity issues in general, and exponential complexity in particular, are discussed in detail in the upper-level computer science curriculum course generally called "Algorithms."

Performance Tip 3.5
Avoid Fibonacci-style recursive programs that result in an exponential "explosion" of calls.

3.14 Recursion vs. Iteration

In the two previous sections, we studied two functions that easily can be implemented either recursively or iteratively. This section compares the two approaches and discusses why the programmer might choose one approach over the other in a particular situation.

Both iteration and recursion are based on a control structure: Iteration uses a repetition structure; recursion uses a selection structure. Both iteration and recursion involve repetition: Iteration explicitly uses a repetition structure; recursion achieves repetition through repeated function calls. Iteration and recursion both involve a termination test: Iteration terminates when the loop-continuation condition fails; recursion terminates when a base case is recognized. Iteration with counter-controlled repetition and recursion both gradually approach termination: Iteration modifies a counter until the counter assumes a value that makes the loop-continuation condition fail; recursion produces simpler versions of the original problem until the base case is reached. Both iteration and recursion can occur infinitely: An infinite loop occurs with iteration if the loop-continuation test never becomes false; infinite recursion occurs if the recursion step does not reduce the problem during each recursive call in a manner that converges on the base case.

Recursion has many negatives. It repeatedly invokes the mechanism, and consequently the overhead, of function calls. This can be expensive in both processor time and memory space. Each recursive call causes another copy of the function (actually only the function's variables) to be created; this can consume considerable memory. Iteration normally occurs within a function, so the overhead of repeated function calls and extra memory assignment is omitted. So why choose recursion?

Software Engineering Observation 3.13

Any problem that can be solved recursively can also be solved iteratively (nonrecursively). A recursive approach is normally chosen in preference to an iterative approach when the recursive approach more naturally mirrors the problem and results in a program that is easier to understand and debug. Another reason to choose a recursive solution is that an iterative solution is not apparent.

Performance Tip 3.6

Avoid using recursion in performance situations. Recursive calls take time and consume additional memory.

Common Programming Error 3.22

Accidentally having a nonrecursive function call itself, either directly or indirectly (through another function), is a logic error.

Most programming textbooks introduce recursion much later than we have done here. We feel that recursion is a sufficiently rich and complex topic that it is better to introduce it earlier and spread the examples over the remainder of the text. Figure 3.17 summarizes the recursion examples and exercises in the text.

Let us reconsider some observations that we make repeatedly throughout the book. Good software engineering is important. High performance is important. Unfortunately, these goals are often at odds with one another. Good software engineering is key to making more manageable the task of developing the larger and more complex software systems we need. High performance in these systems is key to realizing the systems of the future that will place ever greater computing demands on hardware. Where do functions fit in here?

Chapter	Recursion Examples and Exercises
Chapter 3	Factorial function
	Fibonacci function
	Greatest common divisor
	Sum of two integers
	Multiply two integers
	Raising an integer to an integer power
	Towers of Hanoi
	Printing keyboard inputs in reverse
	Visualizing recursion
Chapter 4	Sum the elements of an array
	Print an array
	Print an array backwards
	Print a string backwards
	Determine whether a string is a palindrome
	Minimum value in an array
	Selection sort
	Eight Queens
	Linear search
	Binary search
Chapter 5	Quicksort
	Maze traversal
	Printing backwards a string input at the keyboard
Chapter 17	Linked-list insert
	Linked-list delete
	Search a linked list
	Print a linked list backwards
	Binary tree insert
	Preorder traversal of a binary tree
	Inorder traversal of a binary tree
	Postorder traversal of a binary tree

Fig. 3.17 Summary of recursion examples and exercises in the text.

Software Engineering Observation 3.14

Functionalizing programs in a neat, hierarchical manner promotes good software engineering, but it has a price.

Performance Tip 3.7

A heavily functionalized program—as compared to a monolithic (i.e., one-piece) program without functions—makes potentially large numbers of function calls that can slow down a program's execution speed. However, monolithic programs are difficult to program, test, debug, maintain and evolve.

So functionalize your programs judiciously, always keeping in mind the delicate balance between performance and good software engineering.

3.15 Functions with Empty Parameter Lists

In C++, an empty parameter list is specified by writing either **void** or nothing at all in parentheses. The prototype

```
void print();
```

specifies that function **print** does not take arguments and does not return a value. Figure 3.18 demonstrates both ways to declare and use functions that do not take arguments.

Software Engineering Observation 3.15

Always provide function prototypes, even though it is possible to omit them when functions are defined before they are used (in which case the first line of the function definition acts as the function prototype as well). Providing the prototypes avoids tying the code to the order in which functions are defined (which can easily change as a program evolves).

```
1   // Fig. 3.18: fig03_18.cpp
2   // Functions that take no arguments.
3   #include <iostream>
4
5   using std::cout;
6   using std::endl;
7
8   void function1();        // function prototype
9   void function2( void );  // function prototype
10
11  int main()
12  {
13     function1();  // call function1 with no arguments
14     function2();  // call function2 with no arguments
15
16     return 0;     // indicates successful termination
17
18  } // end main
19
20  // function1 uses an empty parameter list to specify that
21  // the function receives no arguments
22  void function1()
23  {
24     cout << "function1 takes no arguments" << endl;
25
26  } // end function1
```

Fig. 3.18   Functions that take no arguments. (Part 1 of 2.)

```
27
28    // function2 uses a void parameter list to specify that
29    // the function receives no arguments
30    void function2( void )
31    {
32        cout << "function2 also takes no arguments" << endl;
33
34    } // end function2
```

```
function1 takes no arguments
function2 also takes no arguments
```

Fig. 3.18   Functions that take no arguments. (Part 2 of 2.)

Portability Tip 3.3

The meaning of an empty function parameter list in C++ is dramatically different than in C. In C, it means all argument checking is disabled (i.e., the function call can pass any arguments it wants). In C++, it means that the function takes no arguments. Thus, C programs using this feature might report syntax errors when compiled in C++.

Common Programming Error 3.23

C++ programs do not compile unless function prototypes are provided for every function or each function is defined before it is called.

3.16 Inline Functions

Implementing a program as a set of functions is good from a software engineering standpoint, but function calls involve execution-time overhead. C++ provides *inline functions* to help reduce function-call overhead—especially for small functions. The qualifier **inline** before a function's return type in the function definition "advises" the compiler to generate a copy of the function's code in place (when appropriate) to avoid a function call. The trade-off is that multiple copies of the function code are inserted in the program (often making the program larger) rather than having a single copy of the function to which control is passed each time the function is called. The compiler can ignore the **inline** qualifier and typically does so for all but the smallest functions.

Software Engineering Observation 3.16

*Any change to an **inline** function could require all clients of the function to be recompiled. This can be significant in some program-development and maintenance situations.*

Good Programming Practice 3.9

*The **inline** qualifier should be used only with small, frequently used functions.*

Performance Tip 3.8

*Using **inline** functions can reduce execution time, but often increases program size.*

Figure 3.19 uses **inline** function **cube** (lines 14–18) to calculate the volume of a cube of side **side**. Keyword **const** in the parameter list of function **cube** (line 14) tells the compiler that the function does not modify variable **side**. This ensures that the value of **side** is not changed by the function when the calculation is performed. Keyword **const** is discussed in detail in Chapter 4, Chapter 5 and Chapter 7.

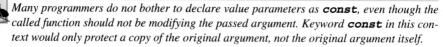

Software Engineering Observation 3.17

*Many programmers do not bother to declare value parameters as **const**, even though the called function should not be modifying the passed argument. Keyword **const** in this context would only protect a copy of the original argument, not the original argument itself.*

```cpp
1   // Fig. 3.19: fig03_19.cpp
2   // Using an inline function to calculate.
3   // the volume of a cube.
4   #include <iostream>
5
6   using std::cout;
7   using std::cin;
8   using std::endl;
9
10  // Definition of inline function cube. Definition of function
11  // appears before function is called, so a function prototype
12  // is not required. First line of function definition acts as
13  // the prototype.
14  inline double cube( const double side )
15  {
16     return side * side * side;   // calculate cube
17
18  } // end function cube
19
20  int main()
21  {
22     cout << "Enter the side length of your cube: ";
23
24     double sideValue;
25
26     cin >> sideValue;
27
28     // calculate cube of sideValue and display result
29     cout << "Volume of cube with side "
30          << sideValue << " is " << cube( sideValue ) << endl;
31
32     return 0;   // indicates successful termination
33
34  } // end main
```

```
Enter the side length of your cube: 3.5
Volume of cube with side 3.5 is 42.875
```

Fig. 3.19   **inline** function that calculates the volume of a cube.

```
 4
 5   using std::cout;
 6   using std::endl;
 7
 8   int main()
 9   {
10      int x = 3;
11      int &y;        // Error: y must be initialized
12
13      cout << "x = " << x << endl << "y = " << y << endl;
14      y = 7;
15      cout << "x = " << x << endl << "y = " << y << endl;
16
17      return 0;  // indicates successful termination
18
19   } // end main
```

Borland C++ command-line compiler error message:

```
Error E2304 Fig03_22.cpp 11: Reference variable 'y' must be
    initialized in function main()
```

Microsoft Visual C++ compiler error message:

```
D:\cpphtp4_examples\ch03\Fig03_22.cpp(11) : error C2530: 'y' :
    references must be initialized
```

Fig. 3.22   Uninitialized local reference causes a syntax error. (Part 2 of 2.)

3.18 Default Arguments

It is not uncommon for a program to invoke a function repeatedly with the same argument value for a particular parameter. In such cases, the programmer can specify that such an argument is a *default argument,* and the programmer can provide a default value for that argument. When a program omits a default argument in a function call, the compiler rewrites the function call and inserts the default value of that argument to be passed as an argument to the function call.

Default arguments must be the rightmost (trailing) arguments in a function's parameter list. When one is calling a function with two or more default arguments, if an omitted argument is not the rightmost argument in the argument list, then all arguments to the right of that argument also must be omitted. Default arguments should be specified with the first occurrence of the function name—typically, in the function prototype. Default values can be constants, global variables or function calls. Default arguments also can be used with **inline** functions.

Figure 3.23 demonstrates using default arguments in calculating the volume of a box. The function prototype for **boxVolume** (line 9) specifies that all three arguments have been given default values of **1**. Note that the default values should be defined only in the function prototype. Also note that we provided variable names in the function prototype for readability. As always, variable names are not required in function prototypes.

```cpp
1   // Fig. 3.23: fig03_23.cpp
2   // Using default arguments.
3   #include <iostream>
4
5   using std::cout;
6   using std::endl;
7
8   // function prototype that specifies default arguments
9   int boxVolume( int length = 1, int width = 1, int height = 1 );
10
11  int main()
12  {
13     // no arguments--use default values for all dimensions
14     cout << "The default box volume is: " << boxVolume();
15
16     // specify length; default width and height
17     cout << "\n\nThe volume of a box with length 10,\n"
18        << "width 1 and height 1 is: " << boxVolume( 10 );
19
20     // specify length and width; default height
21     cout << "\n\nThe volume of a box with length 10,\n"
22        << "width 5 and height 1 is: " << boxVolume( 10, 5 );
23
24     // specify all arguments
25     cout << "\n\nThe volume of a box with length 10,\n"
26        << "width 5 and height 2 is: " << boxVolume( 10, 5, 2 )
27        << endl;
28
29     return 0;  // indicates successful termination
30
31  } // end main
32
33  // function boxVolume calculates the volume of a box
34  int boxVolume( int length, int width, int height )
35  {
36     return length * width * height;
37
38  } // end function boxVolume
```

```
The default box volume is: 1

The volume of a box with length 10,
width 1 and height 1 is: 10

The volume of a box with length 10,
width 5 and height 1 is: 50

The volume of a box with length 10,
width 5 and height 2 is: 100
```

Fig. 3.23   Default arguments to a function.

The first call to **boxVolume** (line 14) specifies no arguments, thus using all three default values. The second call (line 18) passes a **length** argument, thus using default values for the **width** and **height** arguments. The third call (line 22) passes arguments for **length** and **width**, thus using a default value for the **height** argument. The last call (line 26) passes arguments for **length**, **width** and **height**, thus using no default values. Note that any arguments passed to the function explicitly are assigned to the function's parameters from left to right. Therefore, when **boxVolume** receives one argument, the function assigns the value of that argument to its **length** parameter (i.e., the leftmost parameter in the parameter list). When **boxVolume** receives two arguments, the function assigns the values of those arguments to its **length** and **width** parameters in that order. Finally, when **boxVolume** receives all three arguments, the function assigns the values of those arguments to its **length**, **width** and **height** parameters, respectively.

Good Programming Practice 3.10

Using default arguments can simplify writing function calls. However, some programmers feel that explicitly specifying all arguments is clearer. If the default values for a function change, the program may not yield the desired results.

Common Programming Error 3.28

Specifying and attempting to use a default argument that is not a rightmost (trailing) argument (while not simultaneously defaulting all the rightmost arguments) is a syntax error.

3.19 Unary Scope Resolution Operator

It is possible to declare local and global variables of the same name. C++ provides the *unary scope resolution operator (::)* to access a global variable when a local variable of the same name is in scope. The unary scope resolution operator cannot be used to access a local variable of the same name in an outer block. A global variable can be accessed directly without the unary scope resolution operator if the name of the global variable is not the same as the name of a local variable in scope. In Chapter 6, we discuss the use of the *binary scope resolution operator* with classes.

Figure 3.24 demonstrates the unary scope resolution operator with local and global variables of the same name. To emphasize that the local and global versions of constant variable **PI** are distinct, the program declares one variable **double** and one **float**.

```
1   // Fig. 3.24: fig03_24.cpp
2   // Using the unary scope resolution operator.
3   #include <iostream>
4
5   using std::cout;
6   using std::endl;
7
8   #include <iomanip>
9
10  using std::setprecision;
11
12  // define global constant PI
13  const double PI = 3.14159265358979;
```

Fig. 3.24   Unary scope resolution operator. (Part 1 of 2.)

```
14
15   int main()
16   {
17      // define local constant PI
18      const float PI = static_cast< float >( ::PI );
19
20      // display values of local and global PI constants
21      cout << setprecision( 20 )
22          << "  Local float value of PI = " << PI
23          << "\nGlobal double value of PI = " << ::PI << endl;
24
25      return 0;   // indicates successful termination
26
27   } // end main
```

Borland C++ command-line compiler output:

```
  Local float value of PI = 3.141592741012573242
Global double value of PI = 3.141592653589790007
```

Microsoft Visual C++ compiler output:

```
  Local float value of PI = 3.141592741012573232
Global double value of PI = 3.14159265358979
```

Fig. 3.24   Unary scope resolution operator. (Part 2 of 2.)

Using the unary scope resolution operator (**::**) with a given variable name is optional when the only variable with that name is a global variable.

Common Programming Error 3.29

*It is a syntax error to use the unary scope resolution operator (**::**) to access a global variable if a global variable of that name does not exist.*

Common Programming Error 3.30

*It is an error to attempt to use the unary scope resolution operator (**::**) to access a non-global variable in an outer block—it is a syntax error if no global variable with that name exists; it is a logic error if a global variable with that name exists (because the unary scope resolution operator will cause the program to refer to the global variable when, in fact, you are trying to improperly access the non-global variable in the outer block).*

Always using the unary scope resolution operator (**::**) to refer to global variables makes programs clearer, easier to modify and avoids subtle errors.

Good Programming Practice 3.11

*Always using the unary scope resolution operator (**::**) to refer to global variables makes programs easier to read and understand, because it makes it clear that you are intending to access a global variable rather than a non-global variable.*

Software Engineering Observation 3.20

*Always using the unary scope resolution operator (**::**) to refer to global variables makes programs easier to modify by reducing the risk of name collisions with non-global variables.*

Testing and Debugging Tip 3.2

Always using the unary scope resolution operator (: :) to refer to a global variable eliminates possible logic errors that might occur if a non-global variable hides the global variable.

Testing and Debugging Tip 3.3

Avoid using variables of the same name for different purposes in a program. Although this is allowed in various circumstances, it can lead to errors.

3.20 Function Overloading

C++ enables several functions of the same name to be defined, as long as these functions have different sets of parameters (at least as far as the parameter types or the number of parameters or the order of the parameter types are concerned). This capability is called *function overloading*. When an overloaded function is called, the C++ compiler selects the proper function by examining the number, types and order of the arguments in the call. Function overloading is commonly used to create several functions of the same name that perform similar tasks, but on different data types. For example, many functions in the math library are overloaded for different numeric data types.[4]

Good Programming Practice 3.12

Overloading functions that perform closely related tasks can make programs more readable and understandable.

Figure 3.25 uses overloaded **square** functions to calculate the square of an **int** (lines 9–14) and the square of a **double** (lines 17–22). In function **main**, line 26 invokes the **int** version of function **square** by passing the literal value **7**. C++ treats whole number literal values as type **int** by default. Similarly, line 27 invokes the **double** version of function **square** by passing the literal value **7.5**, which C++ treats as a **double** value by default. In each case, the compiler chooses the proper function to call based on the type of the argument. The last two lines of the output window confirm that the proper function was called in each case.

Overloaded functions are distinguished by their *signatures*—a signature is a combination of a function's name and its parameter types (in order). The compiler encodes each function identifier with the number and types of its parameters (sometimes referred to as *name mangling* or *name decoration*) to enable *type-safe linkage*. Type-safe linkage ensures that the proper overloaded function is called and that the types of the arguments conform to the types of the parameters.

```
1   // Fig. 3.25: fig03_25.cpp
2   // Using overloaded functions.
3   #include <iostream>
4
5   using std::cout;
6   using std::endl;
```

Fig. 3.25   Overloaded function definitions. (Part 1 of 2.)

---

4. The C++ standard requires **float**, **double** and **long double** overloaded versions of the math library functions discussed in Section 3.3.

```
7
8     // function square for int values
9     int square( int x )
10    {
11       cout << "Called square with int argument: " << x << endl;
12       return x * x;
13
14    } // end int version of function square
15
16    // function square for double values
17    double square( double y )
18    {
19       cout << "Called square with double argument: " << y << endl;
20       return y * y;
21
22    } // end double version of function square
23
24    int main()
25    {
26       int intResult = square( 7 );          // calls int version
27       double doubleResult = square( 7.5 ); // calls double version
28
29       cout << "\nThe square of integer 7 is " << intResult
30            << "\nThe square of double 7.5 is " << doubleResult
31            << endl;
32
33       return 0;  // indicates successful termination
34
35    } // end main
```

```
Called square with int argument: 7
Called square with double argument: 7.5

The square of integer 7 is 49
The square of double 7.5 is 56.25
```

Fig. 3.25   Overloaded function definitions. (Part 2 of 2.)

Figure 3.26 was compiled on the Borland C++ compiler. Rather than showing the execution output of the program (as we normally would), we show the mangled function names produced in assembly language by Borland C++. Each mangled name begins with **@** followed by the function name. The function name is then separated from the mangled parameter list by **$q**. In the parameter list for function **nothing2** (line 25), **c** represents a **char**, **i** represents an **int**, **pf** represents a **float *** (i.e., a pointer[5] to a **float**) and **pd** represents a **double ***. In the parameter list for function **nothing1**, **i** represents an **int**, **f** represents a **float**, **c** represents a **char** and **pi** represents an **int ***. The two

---

5. Some of the function parameters and function return types in this example are declared with types that include the ***** character. This indicates that the parameter or return value is a pointer. Pointers are discussed in Chapter 5. We use them here only to show how a variety of types are encoded to enable function overloading.

square functions are distinguished by their parameter lists; one specifies **d** for double and the other specifies **i** for **int**. The return types of the functions are not specified in the mangled names. Overloaded functions can have different return types, but must have different parameter lists. Note that function name mangling is compiler specific. Also note that function **main** is not mangled, because it cannot be overloaded.

Common Programming Error 3.31

Creating overloaded functions with identical parameter lists and different return types is a syntax error.

```
1   // Fig. 3.26: fig03_26.cpp
2   // Name mangling.
3
4   // function square for int values
5   int square( int x )
6   {
7      return x * x;
8   }
9
10  // function square for double values
11  double square( double y )
12  {
13     return y * y;
14  }
15
16  // function that receives arguments of types
17  // int, float, char and int *
18  void nothing1( int a, float b, char c, int *d )
19  {
20     // empty function body
21  }
22
23  // function that receives arguments of types
24  // char, int, float * and double *
25  char *nothing2( char a, int b, float *c, double *d )
26  {
27     return 0;
28  }
29
30  int main()
31  {
32     return 0;  // indicates successful termination
33
34  } // end main
```

```
_main
@nothing2$qcipfpd
@nothing1$qifcpi
@square$qd
@square$qi
```

Fig. 3.26   Name mangling to enable type-safe linkage.

The compiler uses only the parameter lists to distinguish between functions of the same name. Overloaded functions need not have the same number of parameters. Programmers should use caution when overloading functions with default parameters, because this may cause ambiguity.

Common Programming Error 3.32

A function with default arguments omitted might be called identically to another overloaded function; this is a syntax error. For example, having in a program both a function that explicitly takes no arguments and a function of the same name that contains all default arguments results in a syntax error when an attempt is made to use that function name in a call passing no arguments. The compiler does not know which version of the function to choose.

In Chapter 8, we discuss how to overload operators to define how they should operate on objects of user-defined data types. (In fact, we have been using many overloaded operators to this point, including the stream insertion operator **<<** and the stream extraction operator **>>**. We say more about overloading **<<** and **>>** in Chapter 8.) Section 3.21 introduces function templates for automatically generating overloaded functions that perform identical tasks on different data types.

3.21 Function Templates

Overloaded functions are normally used to perform similar operations that involve different program logic on different data types. If the program logic and operations are identical for each data type, overloading may be performed more compactly and conveniently by using *function templates*. The programmer writes a single function template definition. Given the argument types provided in calls to this function, C++ automatically generates separate *function-template specializations* to handle each type of call appropriately. Thus, defining a single function template defines a whole family of solutions.

All function template definitions begin with the **template** keyword followed by a list of *formal type parameters* to the function template enclosed in angle brackets (**<** and **>**). Every formal type parameter is preceded by keyword **typename** or keyword **class** (which are synonyms). The formal type parameters are placeholders for built-in types or user-defined types. These placeholders are used to specify the types of the arguments to the function, to specify the return type of the function and to declare variables within the body of the function definition. The function definition follows and is defined like any other function, using the formal type parameters as placeholders for actual data types.

The following function template definition is also used in Fig. 3.27 (lines 10–23):

```
template < class T >   // or template < typename T >
T maximum( T value1, T value2, T value3 )
{
   T max = value1;

   if ( value2 > max )
      max = value2;

   if ( value3 > max )
      max = value3;

   return max;

} // end function template maximum
```

This function template declares a single formal type parameter **T** as a placeholder for the type of the data to be tested by function **maximum**. When the compiler detects a **maximum** invocation in the program source code, the type of the data passed to **maximum** is substituted for **T** throughout the template definition, and C++ creates a complete function for determining the maximum of three values of the specified data type. Then the newly created function is compiled. Thus, templates are a means of code generation. In Fig. 3.27, three functions are created as a result of the calls in lines 35, 45 and 55—one expects three **int** values, one expects three **double** values and one expects three **char** values. The specialization created for type **int** replaces each occurrence of **T** with **int** as follows:

```
int maximum( int value1, int value2, int value3 )
{
    int max = value1;

    if ( value2 > max )
        max = value2;

    if ( value3 > max )
        max = value3;

    return max;

} // end function template maximum
```

The name of a type parameter must be unique in the formal parameter list of a particular template definition. Figure 3.27 demonstrates the **maximum** template function to determine the largest of three **int** values, three **double** values and three **char** values.

```
1    // Fig. 3.27: fig03_27.cpp
2    // Using a function template.
3    #include <iostream>
4
5    using std::cout;
6    using std::cin;
7    using std::endl;
8
9    // definition of function template maximum
10   template < class T >   // or template < typename T >
11   T maximum( T value1, T value2, T value3 )
12   {
13       T max = value1;
14
15       if ( value2 > max )
16           max = value2;
17
18       if ( value3 > max )
19           max = value3;
20
21       return max;
22
23   } // end function template maximum
```

Fig. 3.27   Using a function template. (Part 1 of 2.)

```
24
25   int main()
26   {
27      // demonstrate maximum with int values
28      int int1, int2, int3;
29
30      cout << "Input three integer values: ";
31      cin >> int1 >> int2 >> int3;
32
33      // invoke int version of maximum
34      cout << "The maximum integer value is: "
35           << maximum( int1, int2, int3 );
36
37      // demonstrate maximum with double values
38      double double1, double2, double3;
39
40      cout << "\n\nInput three double values: ";
41      cin >> double1 >> double2 >> double3;
42
43      // invoke double version of maximum
44      cout << "The maximum double value is: "
45           << maximum( double1, double2, double3 );
46
47      // demonstrate maximum with char values
48      char char1, char2, char3;
49
50      cout << "\n\nInput three characters: ";
51      cin >> char1 >> char2 >> char3;
52
53      // invoke char version of maximum
54      cout << "The maximum character value is: "
55           << maximum( char1, char2, char3 )
56           << endl;
57
58      return 0;  // indicates successful termination
59
60   } // end main
```

```
Input three integer values: 1 2 3
The maximum integer value is: 3

Input three double values: 3.3 2.2 1.1
The maximum double value is: 3.3

Input three characters: A C B
The maximum character value is: C
```

Fig. 3.27   Using a function template. (Part 2 of 2.)

Common Programming Error 3.33

*Not placing either keyword **class** or keyword **typename** before every formal type param-*
*eter of a function template (e.g., < **class S, class T** >) is a syntax error.*

3.22 (Optional Case Study) Thinking About Objects: Identifying a Class's Attributes

In the "Thinking About Objects" section at the end of Chapter 2, we began the first phase of an object-oriented design (OOD) for our elevator simulator—identifying the classes needed to implement the simulator. We began by listing the nouns in the problem statement, and we created a separate class for each category of nouns that performs an important duty in the elevator simulation. We then represented the classes and their relationships in a UML class diagram. Classes have *attributes* and *operations*. A class's attributes are implemented in C++ programs as data; whereas a class's operations are implemented as functions. In this section, we determine many of the class attributes needed to implement the elevator simulator. In Chapter 4, we determine the operations. In Chapter 5, we concentrate on the interactions and sets of interactions (often called *collaborations*), among the objects in the elevator simulator.

Consider the attributes of some real-world objects. A person's attributes include height and weight. A radio's attributes include its station setting, its volume setting and whether it is set to AM or FM. A car's attributes include its speed and mileage readings, the amount of gas in its tank, what gear it is in, etc. A personal computer's attributes include manufacturer (e.g., Apple, IBM or Dell), processor speed, main-memory size (which can be expressed in megabytes), hard-disk size (which can be expressed in gigabytes), etc.

Attributes describe classes. An object's attribute values help differentiate that object from other objects in the system. We can identify the attributes of the classes in our system by looking for descriptive words and phrases in the problem statement. For each descriptive word or phrase, we create an attribute and assign that attribute to a class. We also create attributes to represent any data that a class may need. For example, class **Scheduler** needs to know the times to create the next person to step onto each of the floors. Figure 3.28 is a table that lists the words or phrases from the problem statement that describe each class.

Class	Descriptive words and phrases
Elevator	starts the day waiting...on floor 1 of the building alternates direction: moving up and moving down capacity of 1 takes 5 seconds to move from one floor to the other elevator moving
Clock	begins the day set to time 0
Scheduler	creates the next random time for a person to walk onto a floor (between 5 and 20 seconds later)
Person	person number (as indicated in the sample output)
Floor	capacity of 1 is unoccupied/occupied
FloorButton	has been pressed/reset
ElevatorButton	has been pressed/reset

Fig. 3.28 Descriptive words and phrases in problem statement. (Part 1 of 2.)

Class	Descriptive words and phrases
Door	door shut/door open
Bell	none in problem statement
Light	light off/on
Building	none in problem statement

Fig. 3.28 Descriptive words and phrases in problem statement. (Part 2 of 2.)

Note that classes **Bell** and **Building** list no attributes. As we progress through this case study, we continue to add, modify and delete information about each class in our system.

Figure 3.29 is a class diagram that lists some of the attributes for each class in our system—we create these attributes from the descriptive words and phrases in Fig. 3.28. In the UML class diagram, we place a class's attributes in the middle compartment of the class's rectangle. Consider the following attribute of class **Elevator**:

   capacity : Integer = 1

This listing contains three pieces of information about the attribute. The attribute has a *name*—**capacity**. The attribute also has a *type*—**Integer**. The UML defines data types (e.g., **Integer**, **String**, **Boolean**) that we can use to indicate what kind of value a certain attribute may take. When we implement the system in a particular language, we choose language-specific data types that match those suggested by the UML diagram.

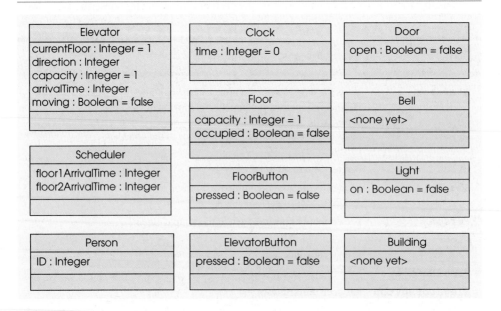

Fig. 3.29 Class diagram showing attributes.

We also can indicate an *initial value* for each attribute. The **capacity** attribute has an initial value of **1**. If the designer does not know the initial value of a particular attribute at design time, the UML diagram need show only its name and type (separated by a colon). For example, the **floor1ArrivalTime** attribute of class **Scheduler** is of type **Integer**. Here we show no initial value, because the value of this attribute is a random number that we do not know; the scheduler determines this value at execution time. For now, we do not overly concern ourselves with the types or initial values of the attributes. We include only the information we can glean from the problem statement.

Statechart Diagrams

Objects in a system can have *states*. States describe the condition of an object (e.g., the values of the object's attributes) at a given point in time. *Statechart diagrams* (also called *state* diagrams) give us a way to express how, and under what conditions, the objects in a system change state.

Figure 3.30 is a statechart diagram that models the states of an object of class **Floor-Button** or of class **ElevatorButton**. Each state in a statechart diagram is represented as a rounded rectangle that contains the state's name. A solid circle with an attached arrowhead points to the *initial state* (i.e., the "Not pressed" state). An object's initial state is the default state of the object after it has been created. The arrows indicate *transitions* between states. An object can transition from one state to another in response to an *event*. For example, objects of classes **FloorButton** and **ElevatorButton** change from the "Not pressed" state to the "Pressed" state in response to a "button press" event. In a statechart diagram, we place the name of the event that causes a transition near the line that corresponds to that transition. (We can include more information about events, as in Fig. 3.31.)

Figure 3.31 shows the statechart diagram for an object of class **Elevator**. The elevator has three possible states: "Waiting," "Servicing Floor" (i.e., the elevator is stopped on a floor, but is busy resetting the elevator button or communicating with the floor, etc.) and "Moving." The elevator begins in the "Waiting" state. Events that trigger transitions are indicated next to the appropriate transition lines.

Let us examine the events in this statechart diagram. The text

elevator button press

tells us that the "elevator button press" event causes the elevator to transition from the "Servicing Floor" state to the "Moving" state. The *guard condition* in square brackets states that the transition occurs only if the elevator needs to move. The complete event text states that the elevator transitions from the "Servicing Floor" state to the "Moving" state in response to the "elevator button press" event. Similarly, the elevator transitions from the "Waiting" state to the "Servicing Floor" state when a person presses a button on the elevator's current floor.

The text next to the transition line from the "Waiting" state to the "Moving" state indicates that this transition occurs in the event of a floor button press (if the button is pressed on the other floor). The forward slash (*/*) indicates that an *action* accompanies this state change. The elevator performs the action of calculating and setting the time at which it will arrive at the other floor.[6]

---

6. In a real-world elevator system, a sensor on the elevator might cause it to stop on a floor. In our elevator simulator, we know that the elevator takes five seconds to move from one floor to another. Thus, in our simulation, the elevator can simply schedule its own arrival to a floor, and the elevator stops at that scheduled time.

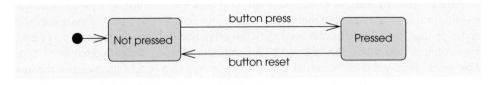

Fig. 3.30 Statechart diagram for classes **FloorButton** and
ElevatorButton.

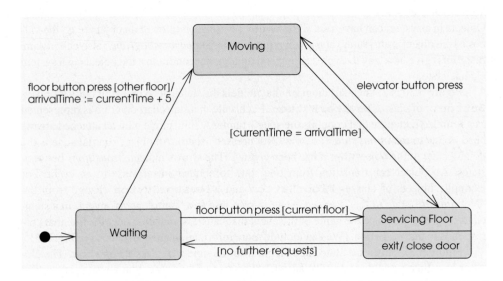

Fig. 3.31 Statechart diagram for class **Elevator**.

A state transition also can occur on the event that a certain condition is true. The text

[currentTime = arrivalTime]

indicates that the elevator transitions from the "Moving" state to the "Servicing Floor" state when the current time of the simulation becomes equal to the time at which the elevator is scheduled to arrive on a floor.

The text that accompanies the transition line from the "Servicing Floor" state to the "Waiting" state indicates that the elevator enters the "Waiting" state from the "Servicing Floor" state on the condition that no further requests for the elevator's service exist.[7]

An object also can perform actions while in a particular state (e.g., the "Servicing Floor" state in Fig. 3.31). We model these actions by splitting the appropriate state into two compartments. The top compartment contains the state name, and the bottom compartment contains the state actions. The UML defines special *action-labels* that describe the conditions under which certain actions may take place. One such action-label is called *exit*. The

---

7. In a real-world elevator system, the elevator probably transitions between these states after a certain amount of time expires. We want to program a simulator, but we do not want to concern ourselves with the details of how the elevator "knows" when no further requests for its services exist. Therefore, we say that the elevator changes state in the event that no more requests exist.

exit action indicates an action that is performed when the object exits a state. Other action-labels include the *entry* action-label (which describes an action performed when an object enters the state) and the *do* action-label (which describes an ongoing action performed while an object is in the state). In our model, the elevator must perform the "close door" action when it exits the "Servicing Floor" state. If the elevator needs to move, it must first close its door. If the elevator has no more requests (i.e., button presses) to satisfy, it closes its door and enters the "Waiting" state.

Activity Diagrams

The *activity diagram* is a variation of the statechart diagram. The activity diagram focuses on the actions that an object performs; in other words, the activity diagram models what an object does during its lifetime. We first introduced activity diagrams in Chapter 2, where we used them to model control structures. In this section, we focus on the diagram's more conventional use, which is to model the "internal work flow" of an object.

The statechart diagram in the previous figure (Fig. 3.31) conveys no information about the internal logic that the elevator employs to decide if it needs to move. The activity diagram in Fig. 3.32 adds to the information presented in the statechart diagram by modeling the actions the elevator performs in response to a request for service.

An *action state* is represented as two parallel lines connected by convex segments. Each action state contains an *action-expression* that describes an action the object can perform. A solid line with an arrowhead, called a transition, connects two action states. After an object performs an action, the object follows the transition to the next action state in the diagram and performs the corresponding action. As with statechart diagrams, the solid circle indicates the initial state of the diagram. A solid circle surrounded by another circle (sometimes called a "bull's-eye") represents the *final state* of an activity diagram. The action in an activity diagram begins at the initial state and follows transitions to the various action states until the action terminates by following a transition to the final state.

The sequence of actions modeled in Fig. 3.32 occurs whenever a floor button is pressed (i.e., if either of the floor's buttons are currently in the "Pressed" state). When this condition is true, the elevator must make a decision (represented by the diamond). The elevator can transition to one of many action states at this point, based on certain conditions. Each transition extending from the diamond represents the choice of one of these different action states. A guard condition placed next to each transition indicates under what circumstances that transition will occur.

In our diagram, the elevator performs one of four different activities when a button is pressed. If the elevator is in motion (i.e., in the "Moving" state) and if the elevator has not arrived at its destination floor (i.e., **currentTime** is less than **arrivalTime**), the elevator cannot immediately perform any more activities. In this case, the sequence of actions on the current path terminates. If the elevator has arrived at its destination floor (i.e., **currentTime** equals **arrivalTime**), then the elevator stops moving, resets the elevator button, rings the bell and opens the door on the destination floor.

If the floor button is pressed on the elevator's current floor, the elevator resets its button, rings its bell and opens its door. If the button on the elevator's current floor is not pressed, the elevator must first close its door, move to the other floor and then stop at the other floor before it can service the other floor. Notice that the UML models the merging of decision paths (e.g., see just above the final state) with another small diamond symbol. After the elevator opens its door, the sequence of actions terminates.

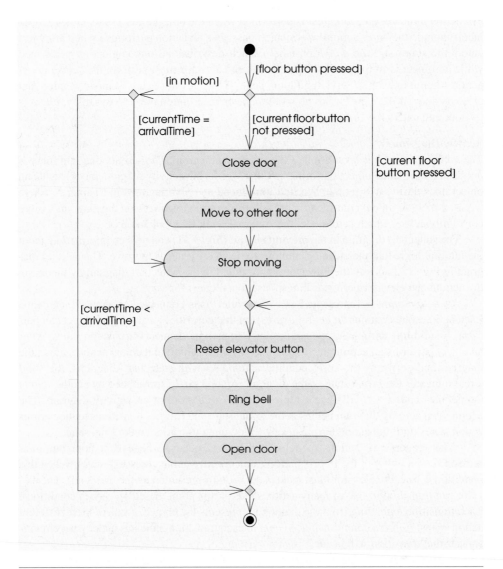

Fig. 3.32 Activity diagram that models the elevator's logic for responding to floor-button presses.

Conclusion

In this "Thinking About Objects" section, we expanded our knowledge of the classes in our system (as we continue to do in the next several chapters), and we represented this new knowledge in our class diagram. We also used statechart and activity diagrams to gain more information about how the system's objects change over time and how the objects perform their tasks. Even though we have not yet discussed the details of object-oriented programming in C++, we already have a significant amount of information about our system. In the "Thinking About Objects" sections at the ends of Chapter 4 and Chapter 5, we determine the operations associated with our classes and how our classes interact with one another.

Note

In this chapter, we discussed how to implement "randomness." The statement

```
arrivalTime = currentTime + ( 5 + rand() % 16 );
```

can be used to randomly schedule the next arrival of a person on a floor.

SUMMARY

- The best way to develop and maintain a large program is to divide it into several smaller program modules, each of which is more manageable than the original program. Modules are written in C++ as classes and functions.

- A function is invoked by a function call. The function call mentions the function by name and provides information (as arguments) that the called function needs to perform its task.

- The purpose of information hiding is for functions to have access only to the information they need to complete their tasks. This is a means of implementing the principle of least privilege, one of the most important principles of good software engineering.

- Data type **double** is a floating-point type like **float**. A variable of type **double** can store a value of much greater magnitude and precision than **float** can store.

- Each argument of a function may be a constant, a variable, or an expression.

- A local variable is known only in a function definition. Functions are not allowed to know the implementation details of any other function (including local variables).

- The general format for a function definition is

  > *return-value-type function-name* **(** *parameter-list* **)**
  > **{**
  >   *declarations and statements*
  > **}**

  The *return-value-type* states the type of the value returned to the calling function. If a function does not return a value, the *return-value-type* is declared as **void**. The *function-name* is any valid identifier. The *parameter-list* is a comma-separated list containing the declarations of the variables that will be passed to the function. If a function does not receive any values, *parameter-list* is declared as **void** (or simply as empty parentheses). The *function-body* is the set of declarations and statements that constitutes the function.

- The arguments passed to a function should match in number, type and order with the parameters in the function definition.

- When a program encounters a function call, control is transferred from the point of invocation to the called function, the function is executed and control returns to the caller.

- A called function can return control to the caller in one of three ways. If the function does not return a value, control is returned when the function-ending right brace is reached or by executing the statement

  ```
  return;
  ```

  If the function does return a value, the statement

  ```
  return expression;
  ```

  returns the value of *expression*.

- A function prototype declares the return type of the function and declares the number, the types and the order of the parameters the function expects to receive.

- Function prototypes enable the compiler to verify that functions are called correctly.
- The compiler ignores variable names mentioned in the function prototype.
- Each standard library has a corresponding header file containing the function prototypes for all the functions in that library, as well as definitions of symbolic constants needed by those functions.
- When an argument is passed by value, a copy of the variable's value is made, and the copy is passed to the called function. Changes to the copy in the called function do not affect the original variable's value.
- Function **rand** generates an integer between 0 and **RAND_MAX** (defined to be at least 32767).
- Values produced by **rand** can be scaled and shifted to produce values in a specific range.
- To randomize the output of **rand**, use the standard library function **srand**.
- The function prototypes for **rand** and **srand** are contained in **<cstdlib>**.
- To randomize without the need for entering a seed each time, use **srand(time(0))**. Function **time** normally returns "calendar time" in seconds. Function **time**'s prototype is located in header **<ctime>**.
- The general equation for scaling and shifting a random number is

    number = *shiftingValue* + **rand()** % *scalingFactor*;

  where *shiftingValue* is equal to the first number in the desired range of consecutive integers and *scalingFactor* is equal to the width of the desired range of consecutive integers.
- An enumeration, introduced by the keyword **enum** and followed by a type name, is a set of integer constants represented by identifiers.
- The values of enumeration constants start at **0**, unless specified otherwise, and increment by **1**.
- The identifiers in an **enum** must be unique, but separate enumeration constants can have the same integer value.
- Any enumeration constant can be assigned an integer value in the enumeration definition.
- Each variable identifier has the attributes storage class, scope and linkage.
- C++ provides storage-class specifiers **auto**, **register**, **extern**, **mutable** and **static**.
- An identifier's storage class determines when that identifier exists in memory.
- An identifier's scope is where the identifier can be referenced in a program.
- An identifier's linkage determines for a multiple-source-file program that an identifier is known either only in the current source file or in any source file with proper declarations.
- Variables of automatic storage class are created when the block in which they are defined is entered, exist while the block is active and are destroyed when the block is exited. A function's local variables are of automatic storage class by default.
- The storage-class specifier **register** can be placed before an automatic variable declaration to suggest that the compiler maintain the variable in one of the computer's high-speed hardware registers. The compiler might ignore **register** declarations. Keyword **register** can be used only with variables of the automatic storage class.
- Keywords **extern** and **static** declare identifiers for static storage class variables and functions.
- Static storage class variables are allocated and initialized when the program begins execution.
- Two types of identifiers have static storage class—external identifiers and local variables declared with the storage-class specifier **static**.
- Global variables are created by placing variable declarations outside any function definition, and they retain their values throughout the execution of the program.

- Local variables declared **static** retain their values when the function in which they are declared is exited.

- All numeric variables of static storage class are initialized to zero if they are not explicitly initialized by the programmer.

- Identifier scopes include function scope, file scope, block scope and function-prototype scope.

- Labels are the only identifiers with function scope. Labels can be used anywhere in the function in which they appear, but cannot be referenced outside the function body.

- An identifier declared outside any function has file scope. Such an identifier is "known" from the point at which the identifier is declared until the end of the file.

- Identifiers declared inside a block have block scope. Block scope ends at the terminating right brace (**}**) of the block.

- Local variables have block scope, as do function parameters, which are considered to be local variables.

- Any block can contain variable declarations. When blocks are nested and an identifier in an outer block has the same name as an identifier in an inner block, the identifier in the outer block is "hidden" until the inner block terminates.

- The only identifiers with function-prototype scope are those used in a function prototype's parameter list.

- A recursive function is a function that calls itself either directly or indirectly.

- If a recursive function is called with a base case, the function simply returns a result. If the function is called with a more complex problem, the function divides the problem into two conceptual pieces—a piece that the function knows how to do and a slightly smaller version of the original problem. Because this new problem looks like the original problem, the function launches a recursive call to work on the smaller problem.

- For recursion to terminate, each time the recursive function calls itself with a slightly simpler version of the original problem, the sequence of smaller and smaller problems must converge on the base case. When the function recognizes the base case, the result is returned to the previous function call, and a sequence of returns ensues all the way up the line until the original call of the function eventually returns the final result.

- The C++ standard does not specify the order in which the operands of most operators are to be evaluated. C++ specifies the order of evaluation of the operands of the operators **&&**, **||**, the comma (**,**) operator and **?:**. The first three are binary operators whose operands are evaluated left to right. The last operator is C++'s only ternary operator. Its leftmost operand evaluates first; if it evaluates to nonzero (true), the middle operand evaluates next, and the last operand is ignored; if it evaluates to zero (false), the third operand evaluates next, and the middle operand is ignored.

- Both iteration and recursion are based on a control structure: Iteration uses a repetition structure; recursion uses a selection structure.

- Both iteration and recursion involve repetition: Iteration explicitly uses a repetition structure; recursion achieves repetition through repeated function calls.

- Both iteration and recursion involve a termination test: Iteration terminates when the loop-continuation condition fails; recursion terminates when a base case is recognized.

- Iteration and recursion can occur infinitely: An infinite loop occurs with iteration if the loop-continuation test never becomes false; infinite recursion occurs if the recursion step does not reduce the problem in a manner that converges on the base case.

- Recursion repeatedly invokes the mechanism, and consequently the overhead, of function calls. This can be expensive in both processor time and memory space.

- C++ programs do not compile unless a function prototype is provided for every function or a function is defined before it is first called.

- A function that does not return a value is declared with a **void** return type. An attempt to return a value from the function or to use the result of the function invocation in the calling function is a syntax error.

- An empty parameter list is specified with empty parentheses or **void** in parentheses.

- Inline functions eliminate function-call overhead. The programmer uses the keyword **inline** to advise the compiler to generate function code in line to minimize function calls. The compiler could choose to ignore **inline**.

- C++ offers a direct form of pass-by-reference using reference parameters. To indicate that a function parameter is passed by reference, follow the parameter's type in the function prototype by an **&**. In the function call, mention the variable by name and to pass it by reference. In the called function, mentioning the variable by its local name actually refers to the original variable in the calling function. Thus, the original variable can be modified directly by the called function.

- Reference variables can be created for local use as aliases for other variables within a function. Reference variables must be initialized in their declarations, and they cannot be reassigned as aliases to other variables. Once a reference variable is declared as an alias for another variable, all operations performed on the alias actually are performed on the variable.

- C++ allows the programmer to specify default arguments to functions. If a default argument is omitted in a call to a function, the default value of that argument is used. Default arguments must be the rightmost (trailing) arguments in a function's parameter list. Default arguments should be specified with the first occurrence of the function name. Default values can be constants, global variables, or function calls.

- The unary scope resolution operator (**::**) enables a program to access a global variable when a local variable of the same name is in scope.

- It is possible to define several functions with the same name, but with different parameter types. This is called function overloading. When an overloaded function is called, the compiler selects the proper function by examining the number and types of arguments in the call.

- Overloaded functions can have different return values and must have different parameter lists. Two functions differing only by return type result in a compilation error.

- Function templates enable the creation of functions that perform the same operations on different data types, but the function template is defined only once.

TERMINOLOGY

ampersand (**&**) suffix	coercion of arguments
argument in a function call	component
auto storage-class specifier	**const**
automatic storage	constant variable
automatic storage class	dangling reference
automatic variable	default function argument
base case in recursion	divide and conquer
block scope	**enum**
C++ standard library	enumeration
call a function	enumeration constant
called function	**extern** storage-class specifier
caller	factorial function
calling function	file scope

function

function call

function declaration

function definition

function overloading

function prototype

function scope

function signature

function template

function-template specialization

global variable

header file

infinite recursion

information hiding

inline function

invoke a function

iteration

linkage

linkage specification

local variable

math library functions

mixed-type expression

modular program

mutable storage-class specifier

name decoration

name mangling

named constant

optimizing compiler

overloading

parameter in a function definition

pass-by-reference

pass-by-value

principle of least privilege

programmer-defined function

promotion hierarchy

rand function

random number generation

randomize

RAND_MAX symbolic constant

read-only variable

recursion

recursive call

recursive function

reference parameter

reference type

register storage-class specifier

return

return value type

scaling

scope

shifting

side effect

signature

simulation

software engineering

software reusability

srand function

standard library header files

static storage-class specifier

static storage duration

static variable

storage-class specifier

storage class

template

time function

type-safe linkage

typename

unary scope resolution operator (**::**)

unsigned

void

Terminology for Optional "Thinking About Objects" Section

action

action state

action-expression

action-label

activity diagram

Boolean

decision

diamond

do action-label

entry action-label

event

exit action-label

final state

guard condition

initial state

Integer

rounded rectangle

solid circle

state

statechart diagram

String

transitions

SELF-REVIEW EXERCISES

3.1   Answer each of the following:
   a) Program components in C++ are called _____ and_____.
   b) A function is invoked with a _____.
   c) A variable that is known only within the function in which it is defined is called a
       _____.
   d) The _____ statement in a called function passes the value of an expression back to
       the calling function.
   e) The keyword _____ is used in a function header to indicate that a function does not
       return a value or to indicate that a function contains no parameters.
   f) The _____ of an identifier is the portion of the program in which the identifier can
       be used.
   g) The three ways to return control from a called function to a caller are _____,
       _____ and _____.
   h) A _____ allows the compiler to check the number, types and order of the arguments
       passed to a function.
   i) Function _____ is used to produce random numbers.
   j) Function _____ is used to set the random number seed to randomize a program.
   k) The storage-class specifiers are **mutable**, _____, _____, _____ and _____.
   l) Variables declared in a block or in the parameter list of a function are assumed to be of
       storage class _____ unless specified otherwise.
   m) Storage-class specifier _____ is a recommendation to the compiler to store a vari-
       able in one of the computer's registers.
   n) A variable declared outside any block or function is a _____ variable.
   o) For a local variable in a function to retain its value between calls to the function, it must
       be declared with the _____ storage-class specifier.
   p) The four possible scopes of an identifier are _____, _____, _____ and _____.
   q) A function that calls itself either directly or indirectly (i.e., through another function) is
       a _____ function.
   r) A recursive function typically has two components: One that provides a means for the
       recursion to terminate by testing for a _____ case and one that expresses the prob-
       lem as a recursive call for a slightly simpler problem than the original call.
   s) In C++, it is possible to have various functions with the same name that operate on dif-
       ferent types or numbers of arguments. This is called function _____.
   t) The _____ enables access to a global variable with the same name as a variable in
       the current scope.
   u) The _____ qualifier is used to declare read-only variables.
   v) A function _____ enables a single function to be defined to perform a task on many
       different data types.

3.2   For the program in Fig. 3.33, state the scope (either function scope, file scope, block scope
or function-prototype scope) of each of the following elements:
   a) The variable **x** in **main**.
   b) The variable **y** in **cube**.
   c) The function **cube**.
   d) The function **main**.
   e) The function prototype for **cube**.
   f) The identifier **y** in the function prototype for **cube**.

3.3   Write a program that tests whether the examples of the math library function calls shown in
Fig. 3.2 actually produce the indicated results.

```
1   // Exercise 3.2: ex03_02.cpp
2   #include <iostream>
3
4   using std::cout;
5   using std::endl;
6
7   int cube( int y );   // function prototype
8
9   int main()
10  {
11     int x;
12
13     // loop 10 times, calculate cube of x and output results
14     for ( x = 1; x <= 10; x++ )
15        cout << cube( x ) << endl;
16
17     return 0;   // indicates successful termination
18
19  } // end main
20
21  // definition of function cube
22  int cube( int y )
23  {
24     return y * y * y;
25  }
```

Fig. 3.33   Sample program for Exercise 3.2.

3.4   Give the function header for each of the following functions:
   a) Function **hypotenuse** that takes two double-precision, floating-point arguments, **side1** and **side2**, and returns a double-precision, floating-point result.
   b) Function **smallest** that takes three integers, **x**, **y** and **z**, and returns an integer.
   c) Function **instructions** that does not receive any arguments and does not return a value. (*Note:* Such functions are commonly used to display instructions to a user.)
   d) Function **intToDouble** that takes an integer argument, **number**, and returns a double-precision, floating-point result.

3.5   Give the function prototype for each of the following:
   a) The function described in Exercise 3.4a.
   b) The function described in Exercise 3.4b.
   c) The function described in Exercise 3.4c.
   d) The function described in Exercise 3.4d.

3.6   Write a declaration for each of the following:
   a) Integer **count** that should be maintained in a register. Initialize **count** to **0**.
   b) Double-precision, floating-point variable **lastVal** that is to retain its value between calls to the function in which it is defined.
   c) External integer **number**, whose scope should be restricted to the remainder of the file in which it is defined.

3.7   Find the error in each of the following program segments, and explain how the error can be corrected (see also Exercise 3.53):
   a) `int g( void ) {`
         `cout << "Inside function g" << endl;`

```
         int h( void )
         {
             cout << "Inside function h" << endl;
         }
      }
b)  int sum( int x, int y )
    {
        int result;

        result = x + y;
    }
c)  int sum( int n )
    {
        if ( n == 0 )
            return 0;
        else
            n + sum( n - 1 );
    }
d)  void f( double a );
    {
        float a;
        cout << a << endl;
    }
e)  void product( void )
    {
        int a;
        int b;
        int c;
        int result;
        cout << "Enter three integers: ";
        cin >> a >> b >> c;
        result = a * b * c;
        cout << "Result is " << result;
        return result;
    }
```

3.8   Why would a function prototype contain a parameter type declaration such as **double &**?

3.9   (True/False) All arguments to function calls in C++ are passed by value.

3.10   Write a complete program that prompts the user for the radius of a sphere, and calculates and prints the volume of that sphere. Use an **inline** function **sphereVolume** that returns the result of the following expression: **(4.0 / 3.0) * 3.14159 * pow(radius, 3)**.

ANSWERS TO SELF-REVIEW EXERCISES

3.1   a) functions, classes. b) function call. c) local variable. d) **return**. e) **void**. f) scope. g) **return;**, **return** *expression;* or encounter the closing right brace of a function. h) function prototype. i) **rand**. j) **srand**. k) **auto, register, extern, static**. l) **auto**. m) **register**. n) global. o) **static**. p) function scope, file scope, block scope, function-prototype scope. q) recursive. r) base. s) overloading. t) unary scope resolution operator (**::**). u) **const**. v) template.

3.2   a) Block scope. b) Block Scope. c) File scope. d) File scope. e) File scope. f) Function-prototype scope.

3.3   See the following program:

```cpp
1   // Exercise 3.3: ex03_03.cpp
2   // Testing the math library functions.
3   #include <iostream>
4
5   using std::cout;
6   using std::endl;
7   using std::fixed;
8
9   #include <iomanip>
10
11  using std::setprecision;
12
13  #include <cmath>
14
15  int main()
16  {
17     cout << fixed << setprecision( 1 );
18
19     cout << "sqrt(" << 900.0 << ") = " << sqrt( 900.0 )
20          << "\nsqrt(" << 9.0 << ") = " << sqrt( 9.0 );
21     cout << "\nexp(" << 1.0 << ") = " << setprecision( 6 )
22          << exp( 1.0 ) << "\nexp(" << setprecision( 1 ) << 2.0
23          << ") = " << setprecision( 6 ) << exp( 2.0 );
24     cout << "\nlog(" << 2.718282 << ") = " << setprecision( 1 )
25          << log( 2.718282 )
26          << "\nlog(" << setprecision( 6 ) << 7.389056 << ") = "
27          << setprecision( 1 ) << log( 7.389056 );
28     cout << "\nlog10(" << 1.0 << ") = " << log10( 1.0 )
29          << "\nlog10(" << 10.0 << ") = " << log10( 10.0 )
30          << "\nlog10(" << 100.0 << ") = " << log10( 100.0 ) ;
31     cout << "\nfabs(" << 13.5 << ") = " << fabs( 13.5 )
32          << "\nfabs(" << 0.0 << ") = " << fabs( 0.0 )
33          << "\nfabs(" << -13.5 << ") = " << fabs( -13.5 );
34     cout << "\nceil(" << 9.2 << ") = " << ceil( 9.2 )
35          << "\nceil(" << -9.8 << ") = " << ceil( -9.8 );
36     cout << "\nfloor(" << 9.2 << ") = " << floor( 9.2 )
37          << "\nfloor(" << -9.8 << ") = " << floor( -9.8 );
38     cout << "\npow(" << 2.0 << ", " << 7.0 << ") = "
39          << pow( 2.0, 7.0 ) << "\npow(" << 9.0 << ", "
40          << 0.5 << ") = " << pow( 9.0, 0.5 );
41     cout << setprecision( 3 ) << "\nfmod("
42          << 13.675 << ", " << 2.333 << ") = "
43          << fmod( 13.675, 2.333 ) << setprecision( 1 );
44     cout << "\nsin(" << 0.0 << ") = " << sin( 0.0 );
45     cout << "\ncos(" << 0.0 << ") = " << cos( 0.0 );
46     cout << "\ntan(" << 0.0 << ") = " << tan( 0.0 ) << endl;
47
48     return 0;  // indicates successful termination
49
50  } // end main
```

```
sqrt(900.0) = 30.0
sqrt(9.0) = 3.0
exp(1.0) = 2.718282
exp(2.0) = 7.389056
log(2.718282) = 1.0
log(7.389056) = 2.0
log10(1.0) = 0.0
log10(10.0) = 1.0
log10(100.0) = 2.0
fabs(13.5) = 13.5
fabs(0.0) = 0.0
fabs(-13.5) = 13.5
ceil(9.2) = 10.0
ceil(-9.8) = -9.0
floor(9.2) = 9.0
floor(-9.8) = -10.0
pow(2.0, 7.0) = 128.0
pow(9.0, 0.5) = 3.0
fmod(13.675, 2.333) = 2.010
sin(0.0) = 0.0
cos(0.0) = 1.0
tan(0.0) = 0.0
```

3.4 a) `double hypotenuse( double side1, double side2 )`
   b) `int smallest( int x, int y, int z )`
   c) `void instructions( void )  // in C++ (void) can be written ()`
   d) `double intToDouble( int number )`

3.5 a) `double hypotenuse( double, double );`
   b) `int smallest( int, int, int );`
   c) `void instructions( void ); // in C++ (void) can be written ()`
   d) `double intToDouble( int );`

3.6 a) `register int count = 0;`
   b) `static double lastVal;`
   c) `static int number;`
   Note: This would appear outside any function definition.

3.7 a) Error: Function **h** is defined in function **g**.
   Correction: Move the definition of **h** out of the definition of **g**.
   b) Error: The function is supposed to return an integer, but does not.
   Correction: Delete variable `result` and place the following statement in the function:

   `return x + y;`

   c) Error: The result of **n** + **sum(n - 1)** is not returned; **sum** returns an improper result.
   Correction: Rewrite the statement in the **else** clause as

   `return n + sum( n - 1 );`

   d) Errors: Semicolon after the right parenthesis that encloses the parameter list, and re-defining the parameter **a** in the function definition.
   Corrections: Delete the semicolon after the right parenthesis of the parameter list, and delete the declaration `float a;`.

e) Error: The function returns a value when it is not supposed to.
   Correction: Eliminate the **return** statement.

3.8   This creates a reference parameter of type "reference to **double**" that enables the function to modify the original variable in the calling function.

3.9   False. C++ enables pass-by-reference using reference parameters (and pointers, as we discuss in Chapter 5).

3.10   See the following program:

```cpp
1   // Exercise 3.10: ex03_10.cpp
2   // Inline function that calculates the volume of a sphere.
3   #include <iostream>
4
5   using std::cout;
6   using std::cin;
7   using std::endl;
8
9   #include <cmath>
10
11  // define global constant PI
12  const double PI = 3.14159;
13
14  // calculates volume of a sphere
15  inline double sphereVolume( const double radius )
16  {
17     return 4.0 / 3.0 * PI * pow( radius, 3 );
18
19  } // end inline function sphereVolume
20
21  int main()
22  {
23     double radiusValue;
24
25     // prompt user for radius
26     cout << "Enter the length of the radius of your sphere: ";
27     cin >> radiusValue;   // input radius
28
29     // use radiusValue to calculate volume of sphere
30     // and display result
31     cout << "Volume of sphere with radius " << radiusValue
32          << " is " << sphereVolume( radiusValue ) << endl;
33
34     return 0;   // indicates successful termination
35
36  } // end main
```

EXERCISES

3.11   Show the value of **x** after each of the following statements is performed:
   a) **x = fabs(7.5)**
   b) **x = floor(7.5)**

c) **x** = **fabs(** 0.0 **)**
d) **x** = **ceil(** 0.0 **)**
e) **x** = **fabs(** -6.4 **)**
f) **x** = **ceil(** -6.4 **)**
g) **x** = **ceil(-fabs(** -8 + **floor(** -5.5 **)))**

3.12   A parking garage charges a $2.00 minimum fee to park for up to three hours. The garage charges an additional $0.50 per hour for each hour *or part thereof* in excess of three hours. The maximum charge for any given 24-hour period is $10.00. Assume that no car parks for longer than 24 hours at a time. Write a program that calculates and prints the parking charges for each of three customers who parked their cars in this garage yesterday. You should enter the hours parked for each customer. Your program should print the results in a neat tabular format and should calculate and print the total of yesterday's receipts. The program should use the function **calculateCharges** to determine the charge for each customer. Your outputs should appear in the following format:

```
Car        Hours        Charge
1           1.5          2.00
2           4.0          2.50
3          24.0         10.00
TOTAL      29.5         14.50
```

3.13   An application of function **floor** is rounding a value to the nearest integer. The statement

y = **floor(** **x** + .5 **);**

rounds the number **x** to the nearest integer and assigns the result to **y**. Write a program that reads several numbers and uses the preceding statement to round each of these numbers to the nearest integer. For each number processed, print both the original number and the rounded number.

3.14   Function **floor** can be used to round a number to a specific decimal place. The statement

y = **floor(** **x** * 10 + .5 **)** / 10**;**

rounds **x** to the tenths position (the first position to the right of the decimal point). The statement

y = **floor(** **x** * 100 + .5 **)** / 100**;**

rounds **x** to the hundredths position (the second position to the right of the decimal point). Write a program that defines four functions to round a number **x** in various ways:
a) **roundToInteger(number)**
b) **roundToTenths(number)**
c) **roundToHundredths(number)**
d) **roundToThousandths(number)**

For each value read, your program should print the original value, the number rounded to the nearest integer, the number rounded to the nearest tenth, the number rounded to the nearest hundredth and the number rounded to the nearest thousandth.

3.15   Answer each of the following questions:
a) What does it mean to choose numbers "at random?"
b) Why is the **rand** function useful for simulating games of chance?
c) Why would you randomize a program by using **srand**? Under what circumstances is it desirable not to randomize?
d) Why is it often necessary to scale or shift the values produced by **rand**?
e) Why is computerized simulation of real-world situations a useful technique?

```
22        // output contents of array n in tabular format
23        for ( int j = 0; j < 10; j++ )
24           cout << setw( 7 ) << j << setw( 13 ) << n[ j ] << endl;
25
26        return 0;   // indicates successful termination
27
28     } // end main
```

```
Element        Value
      0            0
      1            0
      2            0
      3            0
      4            0
      5            0
      6            0
      7            0
      8            0
      9            0
```

Fig. 4.3   Initializing an array's elements to zeros and printing the array. (Part 2 of 2.)

Initializing an Array in a Declaration with an Initializer List

The elements of an array also can be initialized in the array declaration by following the declaration with an equals sign and a comma-separated list (enclosed in braces) of *initializers.* The program in Fig. 4.4 uses an *initializer list* to initialize an integer array with 10 values (line 15) and prints the array in tabular format (lines 17–21).

```
1    // Fig. 4.4: fig04_04.cpp
2    // Initializing an array with a declaration.
3    #include <iostream>
4
5    using std::cout;
6    using std::endl;
7
8    #include <iomanip>
9
10   using std::setw;
11
12   int main()
13   {
14       // use initializer list to initialize array n
15       int n[ 10 ] = { 32, 27, 64, 18, 95, 14, 90, 70, 60, 37 };
16
17       cout << "Element" << setw( 13 ) << "Value" << endl;
18
19       // output contents of array n in tabular format
20       for ( int i = 0; i < 10; i++ )
21          cout << setw( 7 ) << i << setw( 13 ) << n[ i ] << endl;
22
```

Fig. 4.4   Initializing the elements of an array with a declaration. (Part 1 of 2.)

```
23        return 0;   // indicates successful termination
24
25   }  // end main
```

```
Element           Value
      0              32
      1              27
      2              64
      3              18
      4              95
      5              14
      6              90
      7              70
      8              60
      9              37
```

Fig. 4.4 Initializing the elements of an array with a declaration. (Part 2 of 2.)

If there are fewer initializers than elements in the array, the remaining array elements are initialized to zero. For example, the elements of the array **n** in Fig. 4.3 could have been initialized to zero with the declaration

```
int n[ 10 ] = { 0 };
```

The declaration explicitly initializes the first element to zero and implicitly initializes the remaining nine elements to zero, because there are fewer initializers than elements in the array. Remember that automatic arrays are not implicitly initialized to zero. The programmer must at least initialize the first element to zero with an initializer list for the remaining elements to be implicitly set to zero. The initialization method shown in Fig. 4.3 can be performed repeatedly as a program executes, whereas an initializer list can be used only when an array is declared and has its effect only at compile time.

If the array size is omitted from a declaration with an initializer list, the compiler determines the number of elements in the array by counting the number of elements in the initializer list. For example,

```
int n[] = { 1, 2, 3, 4, 5 };
```

creates a five-element array.

Performance Tip 4.1

If, instead of initializing an array with execution-time assignment statements, you initialize the array at compile time with an array initializer list, your program will execute faster.

If the array size and an initializer list are specified in an array declaration, the number of initializers must be less than or equal to the array size. The array declaration

```
int n[ 5 ] = { 32, 27, 64, 18, 95, 14 };
```

causes a syntax error, because there are six initializers and only five array elements.

Common Programming Error 4.2

Providing more initializers in an array initializer list than there are elements in the array is a syntax error.

Common Programming Error 4.3

Forgetting to initialize the elements of an array whose elements should be initialized is a logic error.

Specifying an Array's Size with a Constant Variable and Initializing Array Elements with Calculations

The program in Fig. 4.5 initializes the elements of a 10-element array **s** to the integers **2**, **4**, **6**, …, **20** (lines 19–20) and prints the array in tabular format (lines 21–26). These numbers are generated (line 20) by multiplying each successive value of the loop counter by **2** and adding **2**.

Line 15 uses the **const** qualifier to declare a so-called *constant variable*[1] **array-Size** with the value **10**. Constant variables must be initialized with a constant expression when they are declared and cannot be modified thereafter (as shown in Fig. 4.6 and Fig. 4.7). Constant variables are also called *named constants* or *read-only variables*.

```
1   // Fig. 4.5: fig04_05.cpp
2   // Initialize array s to the even integers from 2 to 20.
3   #include <iostream>
4
5   using std::cout;
6   using std::endl;
7
8   #include <iomanip>
9
10  using std::setw;
11
12  int main()
13  {
14     // constant variable can be used to specify array size
15     const int arraySize = 10;
16
17     int s[ arraySize ];   // array s has 10 elements
18
19     for ( int i = 0; i < arraySize; i++ )   // set the values
20        s[ i ] = 2 + 2 * i;
21
22     cout << "Element" << setw( 13 ) << "Value" << endl;
23
24     // output contents of array s in tabular format
25     for ( int j = 0; j < arraySize; j++ )
26        cout << setw( 7 ) << j << setw( 13 ) << s[ j ] << endl;
27
28     return 0;   // indicates successful termination
29
30  } // end main
```

Fig. 4.5   Generating values to be placed into elements of an array. (Part 1 of 2.)

---

1. Note that the term "constant variable" is an oxymoron—a contradiction in terms like "jumbo shrimp" or "freezer burn." Please send your favorite oxymorons to our e-mail address listed in the Preface. Thanks!

Element	Value
0	2
1	4
2	6
3	8
4	10
5	12
6	14
7	16
8	18
9	20

Fig. 4.5   Generating values to be placed into elements of an array. (Part 2 of 2.)

```
1   // Fig. 4.6: fig04_06.cpp
2   // Using a properly initialized constant variable.
3   #include <iostream>
4
5   using std::cout;
6   using std::endl;
7
8   int main()
9   {
10      const int x = 7;  // initialized constant variable
11
12      cout << "The value of constant variable x is: "
13           << x << endl;
14
15      return 0;  // indicates successful termination
16
17   } // end main
```

```
The value of constant variable x is: 7
```

Fig. 4.6   Initializing and using a constant variable.

```
1   // Fig. 4.7: fig04_07.cpp
2   // A const object must be initialized.
3
4   int main()
5   {
6      const int x;  // Error: x must be initialized
7
8      x = 7;        // Error: cannot modify a const variable
9
10     return 0;     // indicates successful termination
11
12   } // end main
```

Fig. 4.7   **const** variables must be initialized. (Part 1 of 2.)

```
d:\cpphtp4_examples\ch04\Fig04_07.cpp(6) : error C2734: 'x' :
   const object must be initialized if not extern
d:\cpphtp4_examples\ch04\Fig04_07.cpp(8) : error C2166:
   l-value specifies const object
```

Fig. 4.7   **const** variables must be initialized. (Part 2 of 2.)

Common Programming Error 4.4

Assigning a value to a constant variable in an executable statement is a syntax error.

Constant variables can be placed anywhere a constant expression is expected. In Fig. 4.5, constant variable **arraySize** specifies the size of array **s** in line 17.

Common Programming Error 4.5

Only constants can be used to declare the size of automatic and static arrays. Not using a constant for this purpose is a syntax error.

Using constant variables to specify array sizes makes programs more *scalable*. In Fig. 4.5, the first **for** loop could fill a 1000-element array by simply changing the value of **arraySize** in its declaration from **10** to **1000**. If the constant variable **arraySize** had not been used, we would have to change lines 17, 19 and 25 of the program to scale the program to handle 1000 array elements. As programs get larger, this technique becomes more useful for writing clearer, easier-to-modify programs.

Software Engineering Observation 4.1

Defining the size of each array as a constant variable instead of a literal constant makes programs more scalable.

Good Programming Practice 4.2

Defining the size of an array as a constant variable instead of a literal constant makes programs clearer. This technique eliminates so-called magic numbers. *For example, repeatedly mentioning the size 10 in array-processing code for a 10-element array gives the number 10 an artificial significance and can unfortunately confuse the reader when the program includes other 10s that have nothing to do with the array size.*

Summing the Elements of an Array
The program in Fig. 4.8 sums the values contained in the 10-element integer array **a**. Line 18 in the **for** loop does the totaling. The values being supplied as initializers for array **a** also could be read into the program from the user at the keyboard, or from a file on disk (see Chapter 14, File Processing). For example, the **for** structure

```
for ( int j = 0; j < arraySize; j++ )
   cin >> a[ j ];
```

reads one value at a time from the keyboard and stores the value in element **a[j]**.

```
1   // Fig. 4.8: fig04_08.cpp
2   // Compute the sum of the elements of the array.
3   #include <iostream>
```

Fig. 4.8   Computing the sum of the elements of an array. (Part 1 of 2.)

```
4
5   using std::cout;
6   using std::endl;
7
8   int main()
9   {
10     const int arraySize = 10;
11
12     int a[ arraySize ] = { 1, 2, 3, 4, 5, 6, 7, 8, 9, 10 };
13
14     int total = 0;
15
16     // sum contents of array a
17     for ( int i = 0; i < arraySize; i++ )
18        total += a[ i ];
19
20     cout << "Total of array element values is " << total << endl;
21
22     return 0;  // indicates successful termination
23
24  } // end main
```

```
Total of array element values is 55
```

Fig. 4.8   Computing the sum of the elements of an array. (Part 2 of 2.)

Graphing Array Element Values with Histograms

Figure 4.9 reads numbers from an array and graphs the information in the form of a bar chart, or histogram—each number is printed (lines 22–23) followed by a bar consisting of that many asterisks (lines 25–26). The nested **for** loop (lines 25–26) actually draws the bars. Note the use of **endl** (line 28) to end a histogram bar and begin a new line of output.

Common Programming Error 4.6

*Although it is possible to use the same control variable in a **for** loop and a second **for** loop nested inside, this is normally a logic error.*

```
1   // Fig. 4.9: fig04_09.cpp
2   // Histogram printing program.
3   #include <iostream>
4
5   using std::cout;
6   using std::endl;
7
8   #include <iomanip>
9
10  using std::setw;
11
12  int main()
13  {
14     const int arraySize = 10;
```

Fig. 4.9   Histogram printing program. (Part 1 of 2.)

```
15      int n[ arraySize ] = { 19, 3, 15, 7, 11, 9, 13, 5, 17, 1 };
16
17      cout << "Element" << setw( 13 ) << "Value"
18          << setw( 17 ) << "Histogram" << endl;
19
20      // for each element of array n, output a bar in histogram
21      for ( int i = 0; i < arraySize; i++ ) {
22         cout << setw( 7 ) << i << setw( 13 )
23             << n[ i ] << setw( 9 );
24
25         for ( int j = 0; j < n[ i ]; j++ )       // print one bar
26            cout << '*';
27
28         cout << endl;   // start next line of output
29
30      } // end outer for structure
31
32      return 0;   // indicates successful termination
33
34   } // end main
```

```
Element          Value        Histogram
      0             19         *******************
      1              3         ***
      2             15         ***************
      3              7         *******
      4             11         ***********
      5              9         *********
      6             13         *************
      7              5         *****
      8             17         *****************
      9              1         *
```

Fig. 4.9   Histogram printing program. (Part 2 of 2.)

Rolling a Die 6000 Times and Summarizing the Results in an Array

Chapter 3 stated that we would show a more elegant version of the dice-rolling program of Fig. 3.8. The problem was to roll a single six-sided die 6000 times to test whether the random-number generator evenly distributes the random numbers it produces. An array version of this program is shown in Fig. 4.10. Line 24 replaces the **switch** structure in Fig. 3.8. The calculation **1 + rand() % 6** produces a random integer between **1** and **6** inclusive, which determines the subscript of the array element that corresponds to a particular side of the die. For example, if the calculation produces the value **3**, line 24 increments **frequency[3]**).

```
1   // Fig. 4.10: fig04_10.cpp
2   // Roll a six-sided die 6000 times.
3   #include <iostream>
4
5   using std::cout;
6   using std::endl;
```

Fig. 4.10   Dice-rolling program using an array instead of **switch**. (Part 1 of 2.)

```
7
8    #include <iomanip>
9
10   using std::setw;
11
12   #include <cstdlib>
13   #include <ctime>
14
15   int main()
16   {
17      const int arraySize = 7;
18      int frequency[ arraySize ] = { 0 };
19
20      srand( time( 0 ) );  // seed random-number generator
21
22      // roll die 6000 times
23      for ( int roll = 1; roll <= 6000; roll++ )
24         ++frequency[ 1 + rand() % 6 ]; // replaces 20-line switch
25                                         // of Fig. 3.8
26
27      cout << "Face" << setw( 13 ) << "Frequency" << endl;
28
29      // output frequency elements 1-6 in tabular format
30      for ( int face = 1; face < arraySize; face++ )
31         cout << setw( 4 ) << face
32              << setw( 13 ) << frequency[ face ] << endl;
33
34      return 0;  // indicates successful termination
35
36   } // end main
```

```
Face     Frequency
   1          1003
   2          1004
   3           999
   4           980
   5          1013
   6          1001
```

Fig. 4.10   Dice-rolling program using an array instead of **switch**. (Part 2 of 2.)

Using Arrays to Summarize Survey Results

Our next example (Fig. 4.11) uses arrays to summarize the results of data collected in a survey. Consider the following problem statement:

> *Forty students were asked to rate the quality of the food in the student cafeteria on a scale of 1 to 10 (1 meaning awful and 10 meaning excellent). Place the 40 responses in an integer array and summarize the results of the poll.*

This is a typical array application. We wish to summarize the number of responses of each value (i.e., 1 through 10). Array **responses** is a 40-element array of the students' responses. We use an 11-element array **frequency** to count the number of occurrences of each response. We ignore the first element, **frequency[0]**, because it is more logical to have the response value 1 increment element **frequency[1]** than element

frequency[0]. This allows us to use each response value directly as a subscript on the **frequency** array.

Good Programming Practice 4.3

Strive for program clarity. It is sometimes worthwhile to trade off the most efficient use of memory or processor time in favor of writing clearer programs.

Performance Tip 4.2

Sometimes performance considerations far outweigh clarity considerations.

```cpp
1   // Fig. 4.11: fig04_11.cpp
2   // Student poll program.
3   #include <iostream>
4
5   using std::cout;
6   using std::endl;
7
8   #include <iomanip>
9
10  using std::setw;
11
12  int main()
13  {
14     // define array sizes
15     const int responseSize = 40;    // size of array responses
16     const int frequencySize = 11;   // size of array frequency
17
18     // place survey responses in array responses
19     int responses[ responseSize ] = { 1, 2, 6, 4, 8, 5, 9, 7, 8,
20        10, 1, 6, 3, 8, 6, 10, 3, 8, 2, 7, 6, 5, 7, 6, 8, 6, 7,
21        5, 6, 6, 5, 6, 7, 5, 6, 4, 8, 6, 8, 10 };
22
23     // initialize frequency counters to 0
24     int frequency[ frequencySize ] = { 0 };
25
26     // for each answer, select value of an element of array
27     // responses and use that value as subscript in array
28     // frequency to determine element to increment
29     for ( int answer = 0; answer < responseSize; answer++ )
30        ++frequency[ responses[answer] ];
31
32     // display results
33     cout << "Rating" << setw( 17 ) << "Frequency" << endl;
34
35     // output frequencies in tabular format
36     for ( int rating = 1; rating < frequencySize; rating++ )
37        cout << setw( 6 ) << rating
38             << setw( 17 ) << frequency[ rating ] << endl;
39
40     return 0;  // indicates successful termination
41
42  } // end main
```

Fig. 4.11   Student-poll-analysis program. (Part 1 of 2.)

Rating	Frequency
1	2
2	2
3	2
4	2
5	5
6	11
7	5
8	7
9	1
10	3

Fig. 4.11   Student-poll-analysis program. (Part 2 of 2.)

The first **for** loop (lines 29–30) takes the responses one at a time from the array **responses** and increments one of the 10 counters (**frequency[1]** through **frequency[10]**) in the **frequency** array. Line 30 is the key statement in the loop. This statement increments the appropriate **frequency** counter, depending on the value of **responses[answer]**. For example, when counter **answer** is **0**, the value of **responses[answer]** (line 19) is **1**, so the program actually interprets the statement **++frequency[responses[answer]];** as

        ++frequency[1];

which increments array element one. When **answer** is **1**, **responses[answer]** (line 19) is **2**, so **++frequency[responses[answer]];** is interpreted as

        ++frequency[2];

which increments array element two. When **answer** is **2**, **responses[answer]** (line 19) is **6**, so **++frequency[responses[answer]];** is interpreted as

        ++frequency[6];

which increments array element six, and so on. Note that regardless of the number of responses processed in the survey, only an 11-element array is required (ignoring element zero) to summarize the results. If the data contained invalid values such as 13, the program would attempt to add **1** to **frequency[13]**. This would be outside the bounds of the array. *C++ has no array bounds checking to prevent the computer from referring to an element that does not exist.* Thus, an executing program can walk off either end of an array without warning. The programmer should ensure that all array references remain within the bounds of the array.

Common Programming Error 4.7

Referring to an element outside the array bounds is an execution-time logic error. It is not a syntax error.

Testing and Debugging Tip 4.1

When looping through an array, the array subscript should never go below 0 and should always be less than the total number of elements in the array (one less than the size of the array). Make sure that the loop-terminating condition prevents accessing elements outside this range.

Testing and Debugging Tip 4.2

Programs should validate the correctness of all input values to prevent erroneous information from affecting a program's calculations.

Portability Tip 4.1

The (normally serious) effects of referencing elements outside the array bounds are system dependent. Often this results in changes to the value of an unrelated variable or a fatal error that terminates program execution.

C++ is an extensible language. In Chapter 8, we will extend C++ by implementing an array as a user-defined type with a class. Our new array definition will enable us to perform many operations that are not standard for C++'s built-in arrays. For example, we will be able to compare arrays directly, assign one array to another, input and output entire arrays with **cin** and **cout**, initialize arrays when they are created, prevent access to out-of-range array elements and change the range of subscripts (and even their subscript type) so that the first element of an array is not required to be element 0.

Testing and Debugging Tip 4.3

When we study classes (Chapter 6 through Chapter 8), we will see how to develop a "smart array," which checks that all subscript references are in bounds at run time. Using such smart data types helps eliminate bugs.

Using Character Arrays to Store and Manipulate Strings

To this point, we have discussed only integer arrays. However, arrays may be of any type. We now introduce storing character strings in character arrays. (Chapter 5 discusses strings in more detail.) The only string-processing capability shown to this point is outputting a string with **cout** and **<<**. A string such as "**hello**" is really an array of characters. Character arrays that represent strings have several unique features.

A character array can be initialized using a string literal. For example, the declaration

```
char string1[] = "first";
```

initializes the elements of array **string1** to the individual characters in the string literal **"first"**. The size of array **string1** in the preceding declaration is determined by the compiler based on the length of the string. It is important to note that the string **"first"** contains five characters *plus* a special string termination character called the *null character*. Thus, array **string1** actually contains six elements. The character constant representation of the null character is **'\0'** (backslash followed by zero). All strings end with this character. A character array representing a string should always be declared large enough to hold the number of characters in the string and the terminating null character.

Character arrays also can be initialized with individual character constants in an initializer list. The preceding declaration is equivalent to the more tedious form

```
char string1[] = { 'f', 'i', 'r', 's', 't', '\0' };
```

Note the use of single quotes to delineate each character constant. Also, note that we explicitly provided the terminating null character as the last initializer value. Without it, this array would simply represent an array of characters, not a string. As we discuss in Chapter 5, not providing a terminating null character for a string can be problematic.

Because a string is an array of characters, we can access individual characters in a string directly with array subscript notation. For example, **string1[0]** is the character **'f'**, **string1[3]** is the character **'s'** and **string1[5]** is the null character.

We also can input a string directly into a character array from the keyboard using **cin** and **>>**. For example, the declaration

    char string2[20];

creates a character array capable of storing a string of 19 characters and a terminating null character. The statement

    cin >> string2;

reads a string from the keyboard into **string2** and appends the null character to the end of the string input by the user. Note in the preceding statement that only the name of the array is supplied; no information about the size of the array is provided. It is the programmer's responsibility to ensure that the array into which the string is read is capable of holding any string the user types at the keyboard. By default, **cin** reads characters from the keyboard until the first whitespace character is encountered—regardless of the array size. Thus, inputting data with **cin** and **>>** can insert data beyond the end of the array (see Section 5.12 for information on preventing insertion beyond the end of a **char** array).

Common Programming Error 4.8

Not providing **cin >>** *with a character array large enough to store a string typed at the keyboard can result in loss of data in a program and other serious run-time errors.*

A character array representing a null-terminated string can be output with **cout** and **<<**. The statement

    cout << string2 << endl;

prints the array **string2**. Note that **cout <<**, like **cin >>**, does not care how large the character array is. The characters of the string are output until a terminating null character is encountered. [*Note:* **cin** and **cout** assume that character arrays should be processed as strings terminated by null characters; **cin** and **cout** do not provide similar input and output processing capabilities for other array types.]

Figure 4.12 demonstrates initializing a character array with a string literal, reading a string into a character array, printing a character array as a string and accessing individual characters of a string.

```
1   // Fig. 4_12: fig04_12.cpp
2   // Treating character arrays as strings.
3   #include <iostream>
4
5   using std::cout;
6   using std::cin;
7   using std::endl;
8
```

Fig. 4.12   Character arrays processed as strings. (Part 1 of 2.)

```
 9   int main()
10   {
11      char string1[ 20 ],                      // reserves 20 characters
12      char string2[] = "string literal"; // reserves 15 characters
13
14      // read string from user into array string2
15      cout << "Enter the string \"hello there\": ";
16      cin >> string1;   // reads "hello" [space terminates input]
17
18      // output strings
19      cout << "string1 is: " << string1
20          << "\nstring2 is: " << string2;
21
22      cout << "\nstring1 with spaces between characters is:\n";
23
24      // output characters until null character is reached
25      for ( int i = 0; string1[ i ] != '\0'; i++ )
26         cout << string1[ i ] << ' ';
27
28      cin >> string1;   // reads "there"
29      cout << "\nstring1 is: " << string1 << endl;
30
31      return 0;   // indicates successful termination
32
33   } // end main
```

```
Enter the string "hello there": hello there
string1 is: hello
string2 is: string literal
string1 with spaces between characters is:
h e l l o
string1 is: there
```

Fig. 4.12   Character arrays processed as strings. (Part 2 of 2.)

Lines 25–26 of Fig. 4.12 use a **for** structure to loop through the **string1** array and print the individual characters separated by spaces. The condition in the **for** structure, **string1[i] != '\0'**, is true until the loop encounters the terminating null character of the string.

Static Local Arrays and Automatic Local Arrays

Chapter 3 discussed the storage class specifier **static**. A **static** local variable in a function definition exists for the duration of the program, but is visible only in the function body.

Performance Tip 4.3

*We can apply **static** to a local array declaration so the array is not created and initialized each time the program calls the function, and the array is not destroyed each time the function terminates in the program. This can improve performance, especially when using large arrays.*

A program initializes **static** arrays when the program begins execution. If a **static** array is not initialized explicitly by the programmer, each element of that array is initialized to zero by the compiler when the array is created.

Figure 4.13 demonstrates function **staticArrayInit** (lines 27–45) with a **static** local array (line 30) and function **automaticArrayInit** (lines 48–66) with an automatic local array (line 51).

```cpp
1   // Fig. 4.13: fig04_13.cpp
2   // Static arrays are initialized to zero.
3   #include <iostream>
4
5   using std::cout;
6   using std::endl;
7
8   void staticArrayInit( void );      // function prototype
9   void automaticArrayInit( void );   // function prototype
10
11  int main()
12  {
13     cout << "First call to each function:\n";
14     staticArrayInit();
15     automaticArrayInit();
16
17     cout << "\n\nSecond call to each function:\n";
18     staticArrayInit();
19     automaticArrayInit();
20     cout << endl;
21
22     return 0;  // indicates successful termination
23
24  } // end main
25
26  // function to demonstrate a static local array
27  void staticArrayInit( void )
28  {
29     // initializes elements to 0 first time function is called
30     static int array1[ 3 ];
31
32     cout << "\nValues on entering staticArrayInit:\n";
33
34     // output contents of array1
35     for ( int i = 0; i < 3; i++ )
36        cout << "array1[" << i << "] = " << array1[ i ] << "   ";
37
38     cout << "\nValues on exiting staticArrayInit:\n";
39
40     // modify and output contents of array1
41     for ( int j = 0; j < 3; j++ )
42        cout << "array1[" << j << "] = "
43             << ( array1[ j ] += 5 ) << "   ";
44
45  } // end function staticArrayInit
```

Fig. 4.13   **static** array initialization and automatic array initialization. (Part 1 of 2.)

```
46
47   // function to demonstrate an automatic local array
48   void automaticArrayInit( void )
49   {
50      // initializes elements each time function is called
51      int array2[ 3 ] = { 1, 2, 3 };
52
53      cout << "\n\nValues on entering automaticArrayInit:\n";
54
55      // output contents of array2
56      for ( int i = 0; i < 3; i++ )
57         cout << "array2[" << i << "] = " << array2[ i ] << "  ";
58
59      cout << "\nValues on exiting automaticArrayInit:\n";
60
61      // modify and output contents of array2
62      for ( int j = 0; j < 3; j++ )
63         cout << "array2[" << j << "] = "
64              << ( array2[ j ] += 5 ) << "  ";
65
66   } // end function automaticArrayInit
```

```
First call to each function:

Values on entering staticArrayInit:
array1[0] = 0  array1[1] = 0  array1[2] = 0
Values on exiting staticArrayInit:
array1[0] = 5  array1[1] = 5  array1[2] = 5

Values on entering automaticArrayInit:
array2[0] = 1  array2[1] = 2  array2[2] = 3
Values on exiting automaticArrayInit:
array2[0] = 6  array2[1] = 7  array2[2] = 8

Second call to each function:

Values on entering staticArrayInit:
array1[0] = 5  array1[1] = 5  array1[2] = 5
Values on exiting staticArrayInit:
array1[0] = 10  array1[1] = 10  array1[2] = 10

Values on entering automaticArrayInit:
array2[0] = 1  array2[1] = 2  array2[2] = 3
Values on exiting automaticArrayInit:
array2[0] = 6  array2[1] = 7  array2[2] = 8
```

Fig. 4.13   **static** array initialization and automatic array initialization. (Part 2 of 2.)

Function **staticArrayInit** is called twice (lines 14 and 18). The **static** local array is initialized to zero by the compiler the first time the function is called. The function prints the array, adds 5 to each element and prints the array again. The second time the function is called, the **static** array contains the modified values stored during the first function call. Function **automaticArrayInit** also is called twice (lines 15 and 19). The

elements of the automatic local array are initialized (line 51) with the values 1, 2 and 3. The function prints the array, adds 5 to each element and prints the array again. The second time the function is called, the array elements are reinitialized to 1, 2 and 3. The array has automatic storage class, so the array is recreated during each call to **automaticArrayInit**.

Common Programming Error 4.9

*Assuming that elements of a function's local **static** array are initialized to zero every time the function is called can lead to logic errors in a program.*

4.5 Passing Arrays to Functions

To pass an array argument to a function, specify the name of the array without any brackets. For example, if array **hourlyTemperatures** has been declared as

```
int hourlyTemperatures[ 24 ];
```

the function call

```
modifyArray( hourlyTemperatures, 24 );
```

passes array **hourlyTemperatures** and its size to function **modifyArray**. When passing an array to a function, the array size is normally passed as well, so the function can process the specific number of elements in the array. (Otherwise, we would need to build this knowledge into the called function itself or, worse yet, place the array size in a global variable.) In Chapter 8, when we introduce our own **Array** class, we will build the size of the array into the user-defined type—every **Array** object that we create will "know" its own size. Thus, when we pass an **Array** object into a function, we no longer will have to pass the size of the array as an argument.

C++ passes arrays to functions using simulated pass-by-reference—the called functions can modify the element values in the callers' original arrays. The value of the name of the array is the address in the computer's memory of the first element of the array. Because the starting address of the array is passed, the called function knows precisely where the array is stored in memory. Therefore, when the called function modifies array elements in its function body, it is modifying the actual elements of the array in their original memory locations.

Performance Tip 4.4

Passing arrays by simulated pass-by-reference makes sense for performance reasons. If arrays were passed by value, a copy of each element would be passed. For large, frequently passed arrays, this would be time consuming and would require considerable storage for the copies of the array elements.

Software Engineering Observation 4.2

It is possible to pass an array by value (by using a simple trick we explain in Chapter 18)—this is rarely done.

Although entire arrays are passed by simulated pass-by-reference, individual array elements are passed by value exactly as simple variables are. Such simple single pieces of data are called *scalars* or *scalar quantities*. To pass an element of an array to a function, use the subscripted name of the array element as an argument in the function call. In Chapter 3, we

showed how to pass scalars (i.e., individual variables and array elements) by reference with references. In Chapter 5, we show how to pass scalars by reference with pointers.

For a function to receive an array through a function call, the function's parameter list must specify that the function expects to receive an array. For example, the function header for function **modifyArray** might be written as

```
void modifyArray( int b[], int arraySize )
```

indicating that **modifyArray** expects to receive the address of an array of integers in parameter **b** and the number of array elements in parameter **arraySize**. The size of the array is not required between the array brackets. If it is included, the compiler ignores it. Because C++ uses pass-by-reference to pass arrays to functions, when the called function uses the array name **b**, it will in fact be referring to the actual array in the caller (i.e., array **hourlyTemperatures** discussed at the beginning of this section).

Note the strange appearance of the function prototype for **modifyArray**

```
void modifyArray( int [], int );
```

This prototype could have been written

```
void modifyArray( int anyArrayName[], int anyVariableName );
```

but as we learned in Chapter 3, C++ compilers ignore variable names in prototypes. Remember, the prototype tells the compiler the number of arguments and the types of each argument (in the order in which the arguments are expected to appear).

The program in Fig. 4.14 demonstrates the difference between passing an entire array and passing an array element. Lines 24–25 print the five original elements of integer array **a**. Line 30 passes **a** and its size to function **modifyArray** (lines 55–61), which multiplies each of **a**'s elements by 2 (through parameter **b**). Then, lines 35–36 print array **a** again in **main**. As the output shows, the elements of **a** are indeed modified by **modifyArray**. Next, line 41 prints the value of **a[3]**, then line 44 passes element **a[3]** to function **modifyElement** (lines 65–71), which multiplies its argument by 2 and prints the new value. Note that when line 47 again prints **a[3]** in **main**, the value has not been modified, because individual array elements are passed by value.

There may be situations in your programs in which a function should not be allowed to modify array elements. Because arrays are always passed by simulated pass-by-reference, modification of values in an array is difficult to control. C++ provides the type qualifier **const** that can be used to prevent modification of array values in a function. When a function specifies an array parameter that is preceded by the **const** qualifier, the elements

```
1   // Fig. 4.14: fig04_14.cpp
2   // Passing arrays and individual array elements to functions.
3   #include <iostream>
4
5   using std::cout;
6   using std::endl;
7
8   #include <iomanip>
```

Fig. 4.14   Passing arrays and individual array elements to functions. (Part 1 of 3.)

```
 9
10   using std::setw;
11
12   void modifyArray( int [], int );   // appears strange
13   void modifyElement( int );
14
15   int main()
16   {
17      const int arraySize = 5;                    // size of array a
18      int a[ arraySize ] = { 0, 1, 2, 3, 4 };  // initialize a
19
20      cout << "Effects of passing entire array by reference:"
21           << "\n\nThe values of the original array are:\n";
22
23      // output original array
24      for ( int i = 0; i < arraySize; i++ )
25         cout << setw( 3 ) << a[ i ];
26
27      cout << endl;
28
29      // pass array a to modifyArray by reference
30      modifyArray( a, arraySize );
31
32      cout << "The values of the modified array are:\n";
33
34      // output modified array
35      for ( int j = 0; j < arraySize; j++ )
36         cout << setw( 3 ) << a[ j ];
37
38      // output value of a[ 3 ]
39      cout << "\n\n\n"
40           << "Effects of passing array element by value:"
41           << "\n\nThe value of a[3] is " << a[ 3 ] << '\n';
42
43      // pass array element a[ 3 ] by value
44      modifyElement( a[ 3 ] );
45
46      // output value of a[ 3 ]
47      cout << "The value of a[3] is " << a[ 3 ] << endl;
48
49      return 0;  // indicates successful termination
50
51   } // end main
52
53   // in function modifyArray, "b" points to
54   // the original array "a" in memory
55   void modifyArray( int b[], int sizeOfArray )
56   {
57      // multiply each array element by 2
58      for ( int k = 0; k < sizeOfArray; k++ )
59         b[ k ] *= 2;
60
61   } // end function modifyArray
```

Fig. 4.14   Passing arrays and individual array elements to functions. (Part 2 of 3.)

```
62
63    // in function modifyElement, "e" is a local copy of
64    // array element a[ 3 ] passed from main
65    void modifyElement( int e )
66    {
67       // multiply parameter by 2
68       cout << "Value in modifyElement is "
69            << ( e *= 2 ) << endl;
70
71    } // end function modifyElement
```

```
Effects of passing entire array by reference:

The values of the original array are:
   0   1   2   3   4
The values of the modified array are:
   0   2   4   6   8


Effects of passing array element by value:

The value of a[3] is 6
Value in modifyElement is 12
The value of a[3] is 6
```

Fig. 4.14   Passing arrays and individual array elements to functions. (Part 3 of 3.)

of the array become constant in the function body, and any attempt to modify an element of the array in the function body results in a compiler error. This enables the programmer to correct a program so it does not attempt to modify array elements.

Figure 4.15 demonstrates the **const** qualifier. Function **tryToModifyArray** (lines 24–30) is defined with parameter **const int b[]**, which specifies that array **b** is constant and cannot be modified. Each of the three attempts by the function to modify array **b**'s elements (lines 26–28) results in the compiler error "**Cannot modify a const object**." Note that compiler error messages vary between compilers. The **const** qualifier will be discussed again in Chapter 7.

```
1    // Fig. 4.15: fig04_15.cpp
2    // Demonstrating the const type qualifier.
3    #include <iostream>
4
5    using std::cout;
6    using std::endl;
7
8    void tryToModifyArray( const int [] );  // function prototype
9
10   int main()
11   {
12      int a[] = { 10, 20, 30 };
13
14      tryToModifyArray( a );
```

Fig. 4.15   **const** type qualifier applied to an array parameter. (Part 1 of 2.)

```
15
16        cout << a[ 0 ] << ' ' << a[ 1 ] << ' ' << a[ 2 ] << '\n';
17
18        return 0;   // indicates successful termination
19
20    } // end main
21
22    // In function tryToModifyArray, "b" cannot be used
23    // to modify the original array "a" in main.
24    void tryToModifyArray( const int b[] )
25    {
26        b[ 0 ] /= 2;      // error
27        b[ 1 ] /= 2;      // error
28        b[ 2 ] /= 2;      // error
29
30    } // end function tryToModifyArray
```

```
d:\cpphtp4_examples\ch04\Fig04_15.cpp(26) : error C2166:
   l-value specifies const object
d:\cpphtp4_examples\ch04\Fig04_15.cpp(27) : error C2166:
   l-value specifies const object
d:\cpphtp4_examples\ch04\Fig04_15.cpp(28) : error C2166:
   l-value specifies const object
```

Fig. 4.15   **const** type qualifier applied to an array parameter. (Part 2 of 2.)

Common Programming Error 4.10

Forgetting that arrays are passed by reference, and hence can be modified, may result in logic errors.

Software Engineering Observation 4.3

Applying the **const** *type qualifier to an array parameter in a function definition to prevent the original array from being modified in the function body is another example of the principle of least privilege. Functions should not be given the capability to modify an array unless it is absolutely necessary.*

4.6 Sorting Arrays

Sorting data (i.e., placing the data into some particular order such as ascending or descending) is one of the most important computing applications. A bank sorts all checks by account number so that it can prepare individual bank statements at the end of each month. Telephone companies sort their lists of accounts by last name and, within that, by first name to make it easy to find phone numbers. Virtually every organization must sort some data and, in many cases, massive amounts of data. Sorting data is an intriguing problem that has attracted some of the most intense research efforts in the field of computer science. In this chapter, we discuss the simplest known sorting scheme. In the exercises and in Chapter 17, we investigate more complex schemes that yield superior performance.

Performance Tip 4.5

Sometimes, simple algorithms perform poorly. Their virtue is that they are easy to write, test and debug. More complex algorithms are sometimes needed to realize maximum performance.

The program in Fig. 4.16 sorts the values of the 10-element array **a** into ascending order. The technique we use is called the *bubble sort,* or the *sinking sort*, because the smaller values gradually "bubble" their way upward to the top of the array like air bubbles rising in water, while the larger values sink to the bottom of the array. The bubble sort makes several passes through the array. On each pass, successive pairs of elements are compared. If a pair is in increasing order (or the values are identical), we leave the values as they are. If a pair is in decreasing order, their values are swapped in the array.

```cpp
1   // Fig. 4.16: fig04_16.cpp
2   // This program sorts an array's values into ascending order.
3   #include <iostream>
4
5   using std::cout;
6   using std::endl;
7
8   #include <iomanip>
9
10  using std::setw;
11
12  int main()
13  {
14     const int arraySize = 10;  // size of array a
15     int a[ arraySize ] = { 2, 6, 4, 8, 10, 12, 89, 68, 45, 37 };
16     int hold;  // temporary location used to swap array elements
17
18     cout << "Data items in original order\n";
19
20     // output original array
21     for ( int i = 0; i < arraySize; i++ )
22        cout << setw( 4 ) << a[ i ];
23
24     // bubble sort
25     // loop to control number of passes
26     for ( int pass = 0; pass < arraySize - 1; pass++ )
27
28        // loop to control number of comparisons per pass
29        for ( int j = 0; j < arraySize - 1; j++ )
30
31           // compare side-by-side elements and swap them if
32           // first element is greater than second element
33           if ( a[ j ] > a[ j + 1 ] ) {
34              hold = a[ j ];
35              a[ j ] = a[ j + 1 ];
36              a[ j + 1 ] = hold;
37
38           } // end if
39
40     cout << "\nData items in ascending order\n";
41
42     // output sorted array
43     for ( int k = 0; k < arraySize; k++ )
44        cout << setw( 4 ) << a[ k ];
```

Fig. 4.16   Sorting an array with bubble sort. (Part 1 of 2.)

```
45
46      cout << endl;
47
48      return 0;  // indicates successful termination
49
50  } // end main
```

```
Data items in original order
   2    6    4    8   10   12   89   68   45   37
Data items in ascending order
   2    4    6    8   10   12   37   45   68   89
```

Fig. 4.16   Sorting an array with bubble sort. (Part 2 of 2.)

First the program compares **a[0]** with **a[1]**, then **a[1]** with **a[2]**, then **a[2]** with **a[3]**, and so on until it completes the pass by comparing **a[8]** to **a[9]**. Although there are 10 elements, only nine comparisons are performed. Because of the manner in which bubble sort performs the successive comparisons, a large value can move down the array many positions on a single pass, but a small value can move up only one position. On the first pass, the largest value is guaranteed to sink to the bottom element of the array, **a[9]**. On the second pass, the second largest value is guaranteed to sink to **a[8]**. On the ninth pass, the ninth largest value sinks to **a[1]**. This leaves the smallest value in **a[0]**, so only nine passes are needed to sort a 10-element array.

The sorting is performed by the nested **for** loop (lines 26–38). If a swap is necessary, it is performed by lines 34–36 in which the extra variable **hold** temporarily stores one of the two values being swapped. The swap cannot be performed with only the two assignments

```
a[ j ] = a[ j + 1 ];
a[ j + 1 ] = a[ j ];
```

If, for example, **a[j]** is **7** and **a[j + 1]** is **5**, after the first assignment both values will be **5**, and the value **7** will be lost; hence the need for the extra variable **hold**.

The chief virtue of the bubble sort is that it is easy to program, however, it runs slowly. This becomes apparent when sorting large arrays. In the exercises, we will develop more efficient versions of the bubble sort and investigate some far more efficient sorts than the bubble sort. More advanced courses investigate sorting and searching in greater depth.

4.7 Case Study: Computing Mean, Median and Mode Using Arrays

We now consider a larger example. Computers are commonly used to compile and analyze the results of surveys and opinion polls. The program in Fig. 4.17 uses array **response** (lines 29–39) initialized with 99 responses to a survey. The program represents the size of this array with constant variable **responseSize**. Each of the responses is a number from 1 to 9. The program computes the mean, median and mode of the 99 values.

The mean is the arithmetic average of the 99 values. Function **mean** (lines 51–73) totals the 99 elements (lines 58–59) and divides the result by 99 (line 70) to compute the mean.

```
1    // Fig. 4.17: fig04_17.cpp
2    // This program introduces the topic of survey data analysis.
3    // It computes the mean, median, and mode of the data.
4    #include <iostream>
5
6    using std::cout;
7    using std::endl;
8    using std::fixed;
9    using std::showpoint;
10
11   #include <iomanip>
12
13   using std::setw;
14   using std::setprecision;
15
16   void mean( const int [], int );
17   void median( int [], int );
18   void mode( int [], int [], int );
19   void bubbleSort( int[], int );
20   void printArray( const int[], int );
21
22   int main()
23   {
24      const int responseSize = 99;  // size of array responses
25
26      int frequency[ 10 ] = { 0 };  // initialize array frequency
27
28      // initialize array responses
29      int response[ responseSize ] =
30              { 6, 7, 8, 9, 8, 7, 8, 9, 8, 9,
31                7, 8, 9, 5, 9, 8, 7, 8, 7, 8,
32                6, 7, 8, 9, 3, 9, 8, 7, 8, 7,
33                7, 8, 9, 8, 9, 8, 9, 7, 8, 9,
34                6, 7, 8, 7, 8, 7, 9, 8, 9, 2,
35                7, 8, 9, 8, 9, 8, 9, 7, 5, 3,
36                5, 6, 7, 2, 5, 3, 9, 4, 6, 4,
37                7, 8, 9, 6, 8, 7, 8, 9, 7, 8,
38                7, 4, 4, 2, 5, 3, 8, 7, 5, 6,
39                4, 5, 6, 1, 6, 5, 7, 8, 7 };
40
41      // process responses
42      mean( response, responseSize );
43      median( response, responseSize );
44      mode( frequency, response, responseSize );
45
46      return 0;  // indicates successful termination
47
48   } // end main
49
50   // calculate average of all response values
51   void mean( const int answer[], int arraySize )
52   {
53      int total = 0;
```

Fig. 4.17   Survey data analysis program. (Part 1 of 4.)

```
54
55       cout << "********\n  Mean\n********\n";
56
57       // total response values
58       for ( int i = 0; i < arraySize; i++ )
59          total += answer[ i ];
60
61       // format and output results
62       cout << fixed << setprecision( 4 );
63
64       cout << "The mean is the average value of the data\n"
65            << "items. The mean is equal to the total of\n"
66            << "all the data items divided by the number\n"
67            << "of data items (" << arraySize
68            << "). The mean value for\nthis run is: "
69            << total << " / " << arraySize << " = "
70            << static_cast< double >( total ) / arraySize
71            << "\n\n";
72
73    } // end function mean
74
75    // sort array and determine median element's value
76    void median( int answer[], int size )
77    {
78       cout << "\n********\n Median\n********\n"
79            << "The unsorted array of responses is";
80
81       printArray( answer, size );  // output unsorted array
82
83       bubbleSort( answer, size );  // sort array
84
85       cout << "\n\nThe sorted array is";
86       printArray( answer, size );  // output sorted array
87
88       // display median element
89       cout << "\n\nThe median is element " << size / 2
90            << " of\nthe sorted " << size
91            << " element array.\nFor this run the median is "
92            << answer[ size / 2 ] << "\n\n";
93
94    } // end function median
95
96    // determine most frequent response
97    void mode( int freq[], int answer[], int size )
98    {
99       int largest = 0;     // represents largest frequency
100      int modeValue = 0;   // represents most frequent response
101
102      cout << "\n********\n  Mode\n********\n";
103
104      // initialize frequencies to 0
105      for ( int i = 1; i <= 9; i++ )
106         freq[ i ] = 0;
```

Fig. 4.17   Survey data analysis program. (Part 2 of 4.)

```
107
108       // summarize frequencies
109       for ( int j = 0; j < size; j++ )
110          ++freq[ answer[ j ] ];
111
112       // output headers for result columns
113       cout << "Response" << setw( 11 ) << "Frequency"
114             << setw( 19 ) << "Histogram\n\n" << setw( 55 )
115             << "1    1    2    2\n" << setw( 56 )
116             << "5    0    5    0    5\n\n";
117
118       // output results
119       for ( int rating = 1; rating <= 9; rating++ ) {
120          cout << setw( 8 ) << rating << setw( 11 )
121             << freq[ rating ] << "                ";
122
123          // keep track of mode value and largest fequency value
124          if ( freq[ rating ] > largest ) {
125             largest = freq[ rating ];
126             modeValue = rating;
127
128          } // end if
129
130          // output histogram bar representing frequency value
131          for ( int k = 1; k <= freq[ rating ]; k++ )
132             cout << '*';
133
134          cout << '\n';   // begin new line of output
135
136       } // end outer for
137
138       // display the mode value
139       cout << "The mode is the most frequent value.\n"
140             << "For this run the mode is " << modeValue
141             << " which occurred " << largest << " times." << endl;
142
143 } // end function mode
144
145 // function that sorts an array with bubble sort algorithm
146 void bubbleSort( int a[], int size )
147 {
148    int hold;   // temporary location used to swap elements
149
150    // loop to control number of passes
151    for ( int pass = 1; pass < size; pass++ )
152
153       // loop to control number of comparisons per pass
154       for ( int j = 0; j < size - 1; j++ )
155
156          // swap elements if out of order
157          if ( a[ j ] > a[ j + 1 ] ) {
158             hold = a[ j ];
159             a[ j ] = a[ j + 1 ];
```

Fig. 4.17   Survey data analysis program. (Part 3 of 4.)

```
160                  a[ j + 1 ] = hold;
161
162              } // end if
163
164  } // end function bubbleSort
165
166  // output array contents (20 values per row)
167  void printArray( const int a[], int size )
168  {
169     for ( int i = 0; i < size; i++ ) {
170
171        if ( i % 20 == 0 )   // begin new line every 20 values
172           cout << endl;
173
174        cout << setw( 2 ) << a[ i ];
175
176     } // end for
177
178  } // end function printArray
```

Fig. 4.17   Survey data analysis program. (Part 4 of 4.)

The median is the "middle value." Function **median** (lines 76–94) determines the median by calling **bubbleSort** (line 83) to sort array **response** and picking the middle element (line 92), **answer[size / 2]**, of the sorted array. Note that when there is an even number of elements, the median should be calculated as the average of the two middle elements. Function **median** does not provide this capability. Lines 81 and 86 call **print-Array** (lines 167–178) to output array **response** before and after its elements are sorted.

The mode is the most frequent value among the 99 responses. Function **mode** (lines 97–143) counts the responses of each type then selects the value with the greatest count (lines 119–136). This version of function **mode** does not handle a tie (see Exercise 4.14). Function **mode** also produces a histogram to aid in determining the mode graphically. Fig. 4.18 contains a sample execution of this program. This example demonstrates most of the common manipulations required in array problems, including passing arrays to functions.

```
*******
  Mean
*******
The mean is the average value of the data
items. The mean is equal to the total of
all the data items divided by the number
of data items (99). The mean value for
this run is: 681 / 99 = 6.8788
```

(continued top of next page)

Fig. 4.18   Sample run for the survey data analysis program. (Part 1 of 2.)

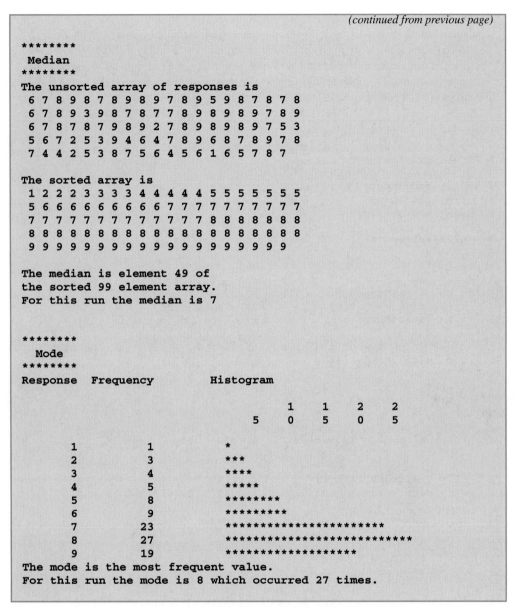

(continued from previous page)

```
********
 Median
********
The unsorted array of responses is
  6 7 8 9 8 7 8 9 8 9 7 8 9 5 9 8 7 8 7 8
  6 7 8 9 3 9 8 7 8 7 7 8 9 8 9 8 9 7 8 9
  6 7 8 7 8 7 9 8 9 2 7 8 9 8 9 8 9 7 5 3
  5 6 7 2 5 3 9 4 6 4 7 8 9 6 8 7 8 9 7 8
  7 4 4 2 5 3 8 7 5 6 4 5 6 1 6 5 7 8 7

The sorted array is
  1 2 2 2 3 3 3 3 4 4 4 4 4 5 5 5 5 5 5 5
  5 6 6 6 6 6 6 6 6 6 6 7 7 7 7 7 7 7 7 7
  7 7 7 7 7 7 7 7 7 7 7 7 7 8 8 8 8 8 8 8
  8 8 8 8 8 8 8 8 8 8 8 8 8 8 8 8 8 8 8 8
  9 9 9 9 9 9 9 9 9 9 9 9 9 9 9 9 9 9 9

The median is element 49 of
the sorted 99 element array.
For this run the median is 7


********
  Mode
********
Response  Frequency      Histogram

                                   1     1     2     2
                              5    0     5     0     5

         1          1        *
         2          3        ***
         3          4        ****
         4          5        *****
         5          8        *******
         6          9        *********
         7          23       ***********************
         8          27       ***************************
         9          19       *******************
The mode is the most frequent value.
For this run the mode is 8 which occurred 27 times.
```

Fig. 4.18   Sample run for the survey data analysis program. (Part 2 of 2.)

4.8 Searching Arrays: Linear Search and Binary Search

Often, a programmer will be working with large amounts of data stored in arrays. It may be necessary to determine whether an array contains a value that matches a certain *key value*. The process of finding a particular element of an array is called *searching*. In this section, we discuss two searching techniques—the simple *linear search* technique and the more complex, yet more efficient, *binary search* technique. Exercise 4.33 and Exercise 4.34 at the end of this chapter ask you to implement recursive versions of the linear search and the binary search.

Linear Search

The linear search (Fig. 4.19, lines 39–48) compares each element of an array with a *search key*. Because the array is not in any particular order, it is just as likely that the value will be found in the first element as the last. On average, therefore, the program must compare the search key with half the elements of the array. To determine that a value is not in the array, the program must compare the search key to every element in the array.

```cpp
1   // Fig. 4.19: fig04_19.cpp
2   // Linear search of an array.
3   #include <iostream>
4
5   using std::cout;
6   using std::cin;
7   using std::endl;
8
9   int linearSearch( const int [], int, int );  // prototype
10
11  int main()
12  {
13     const int arraySize = 100;  // size of array a
14     int a[ arraySize ];         // create array a
15     int searchKey;              // value to locate in a
16
17     for ( int i = 0; i < arraySize; i++ )  // create some data
18        a[ i ] = 2 * i;
19
20     cout << "Enter integer search key: ";
21     cin >> searchKey;
22
23     // attempt to locate searchKey in array a
24     int element = linearSearch( a, searchKey, arraySize );
25
26     // display results
27     if ( element != -1 )
28        cout << "Found value in element " << element << endl;
29     else
30        cout << "Value not found" << endl;
31
32     return 0;  // indicates successful termination
33
34  } // end main
35
36  // compare key to every element of array until location is
37  // found or until end of array is reached; return subscript of
38  // element if key or -1 if key not found
39  int linearSearch( const int array[], int key, int sizeOfArray )
40  {
41     for ( int j = 0; j < sizeOfArray; j++ )
42
43        if ( array[ j ] == key )  // if found,
44           return j;              // return location of key
45
```

Fig. 4.19   Linear search of an array. (Part 1 of 2.)

```
46        return -1;  // key not found
47
48  }  // end function linearSearch
```

```
Enter integer search key: 36
Found value in element 18
```

```
Enter integer search key: 37
Value not found
```

Fig. 4.19   Linear search of an array. (Part 2 of 2.)

Binary Search

The linear searching method works well for small arrays or for unsorted arrays. However, for large arrays, linear searching is inefficient. If the array is sorted, the high-speed binary search technique can be used.

The binary search algorithm eliminates one-half of the elements in the array being searched after each comparison. The algorithm locates the middle element of the array and compares it with the search key. If they are equal, the search key is found, and the array subscript of that element is returned. Otherwise, the problem is reduced to searching one-half of the array. If the search key is less than the middle element of the array, the first half of the array is searched; otherwise, the second half of the array is searched. If the search key is not the middle element in the specified subarray (piece of the original array), the algorithm is repeated on one-quarter of the original array. The search continues until the search key is equal to the middle element of a subarray or until the subarray consists of one element that is not equal to the search key (i.e., the search key is not found).

In a worst-case scenario, searching an array of 1023 elements will take only 10 comparisons using a binary search. Repeatedly dividing 1024 by 2 (because after each comparison, we are able to eliminate half of the array) yields the values 512, 256, 128, 64, 32, 16, 8, 4, 2 and 1. The number 1024 (2^{10}) is divided by 2 only 10 times to get the value 1. Dividing by 2 is equivalent to one comparison in the binary search algorithm. An array of 1048575 (2^{20}) elements takes a maximum of 20 comparisons to find the search key. An array of one billion elements takes a maximum of 30 comparisons to find the search key. This is a tremendous increase in performance over the linear search that required comparing the search key to an average of half the elements in the array. For a one-billion-element array, this is a difference between an average of 500 million comparisons and a maximum of 30 comparisons! The maximum number of comparisons needed for the binary search of any sorted array can be determined by finding the first power of 2 greater than the number of elements in the array.

Performance Tip 4.6

The tremendous performance gains of the binary search over the linear search do not come without a price. Sorting an array is an expensive operation compared with searching an entire array once for one item. The overhead of sorting an array becomes worthwhile when the array will need to be searched many times at high speed.

Figure 4.20 presents the iterative version of function **binarySearch** (lines 48–81).
The function receives five arguments—an integer array **b**, an integer **searchKey**, the
low array subscript, the **high** array subscript and the **size** of the array. If the search key
does not match the middle element of a subarray, the **low** subscript or **high** subscript is
adjusted so a smaller subarray can be searched. In lines 63–76, if the search key is less than

```
1   // Fig. 4.20: fig04_20.cpp
2   // Binary search of an array.
3   #include <iostream>
4
5   using std::cout;
6   using std::cin;
7   using std::endl;
8
9   #include <iomanip>
10
11  using std::setw;
12
13  // function prototypes
14  int binarySearch( const int [], int, int, int, int );
15  void printHeader( int );
16  void printRow( const int [], int, int, int, int );
17
18  int main()
19  {
20     const int arraySize = 15;    // size of array a
21     int a[ arraySize ];          // create array a
22     int key;                     // value to locate in a
23
24     for ( int i = 0; i < arraySize; i++ )   // create some data
25        a[ i ] = 2 * i;
26
27     cout << "Enter a number between 0 and 28: ";
28     cin >> key;
29
30     printHeader( arraySize );
31
32     // search for key in array a
33     int result =
34        binarySearch( a, key, 0, arraySize - 1, arraySize );
35
36     // display results
37     if ( result != -1 )
38        cout << '\n' << key << " found in array element "
39             << result << endl;
40     else
41        cout << '\n' << key << " not found" << endl;
42
43     return 0;  // indicates successful termination
44
45  } // end main
46
```

Fig. 4.20   Binary search of a sorted array. (Part 1 of 4.)

```
47   // function to perform binary search of an array
48   int binarySearch( const int b[], int searchKey, int low,
49      int high, int size )
50   {
51      int middle;
52
53      // loop until low subscript is greater than high subscript
54      while ( low <= high ) {
55
56         // determine middle element of subarray being searched
57         middle = ( low + high ) / 2;
58
59         // display subarray used in this loop iteration
60         printRow( b, low, middle, high, size );
61
62         // if searchKey matches middle element, return middle
63         if ( searchKey == b[ middle ] )   // match
64            return middle;
65
66         else
67
68            // if searchKey less than middle element,
69            // set new high element
70            if ( searchKey < b[ middle ] )
71               high = middle - 1;   // search low end of array
72
73            // if searchKey greater than middle element,
74            // set new low element
75            else
76               low = middle + 1;    // search high end of array
77      }
78
79      return -1;   // searchKey not found
80
81   } // end function binarySearch
82
83   // print header for output
84   void printHeader( int size )
85   {
86      cout << "\nSubscripts:\n";
87
88      // output column heads
89      for ( int j = 0; j < size; j++ )
90         cout << setw( 3 ) << j << ' ';
91
92      cout << '\n';   // start new line of output
93
94      // output line of - characters
95      for ( int k = 1; k <= 4 * size; k++ )
96         cout << '-';
97
98      cout << endl;   // start new line of output
```

Fig. 4.20   Binary search of a sorted array. (Part 2 of 4.)

```
99
100  } // end function printHeader
101
102  // print one row of output showing the current
103  // part of the array being processed
104  void printRow( const int b[], int low, int mid,
105     int high, int size )
106  {
107     // loop through entire array
108     for ( int m = 0; m < size; m++ )
109
110        // display spaces if outside current subarray range
111        if ( m < low || m > high )
112           cout << "    ";
113
114        // display middle element marked with a *
115        else
116
117           if ( m == mid )              // mark middle value
118              cout << setw( 3 ) << b[ m ] << '*';
119
120           // display other elements in subarray
121           else
122              cout << setw( 3 ) << b[ m ] << ' ';
123
124     cout << endl;  // start new line of output
125
126  } // end function printRow
```

```
Enter a number between 0 and 28: 6

Subscripts:
   0   1   2   3   4   5   6   7   8   9  10  11  12  13  14
-----------------------------------------------------------------
   0   2   4   6   8  10  12  14* 16  18  20  22  24  26  28
   0   2   4   6*  8  10  12

6 found in array element 3
```

```
Enter a number between 0 and 28: 25

Subscripts:
   0   1   2   3   4   5   6   7   8   9  10  11  12  13  14
-----------------------------------------------------------------
   0   2   4   6   8  10  12  14* 16  18  20  22  24  26  28
                              16  18  20  22* 24  26  28
                                              24  26* 28
                                              24*

25 not found
```

Fig. 4.20   Binary search of a sorted array. (Part 3 of 4.)

```
Enter a number between 0 and 28: 8

Subscripts:
   0   1   2   3   4   5   6   7   8   9  10  11  12  13  14
--------------------------------------------------------------
   0   2   4   6   8  10  12  14* 16  18  20  22  24  26  28
   0   2   4   6*  8  10  12
                   8  10* 12
                   8*

8 found in array element 4
```

Fig. 4.20   Binary search of a sorted array. (Part 4 of 4.)

the middle element, the **high** subscript is set to **middle - 1** (line 71), and the search continue on the elements from **low** to **middle - 1**. If the search key is greater than the middle element, the **low** subscript is set to **middle + 1** (line 76), and the search continues on the elements from **middle + 1** to **high**. The program uses an array of 15 elements. The first power of 2 greater than the number of elements in this array is 16 (2^4), so the binary search requires a maximum of 4 comparisons to find the search key. Function **printHeader** (lines 84–100) prints the array subscripts across the top of the output and function **printRow** (lines 104–126) outputs each subarray during the binary search process. The middle element in each subarray is marked with an asterisk (*****) to indicate the element with which the search key is compared.

4.9 Multiple-Subscripted Arrays

Arrays in C++ can have multiple subscripts. A common use of multiple-subscripted arrays is to represent *tables* of values consisting of information arranged in *rows* and *columns*. To identify a particular table element, we must specify two subscripts: The first (by convention) identifies the element's row, and the second (by convention) identifies the element's column.

Tables or arrays that require two subscripts to identify a particular element are called *double-subscripted arrays*. Note that multiple-subscripted arrays can have more than two subscripts. Figure 4.21 illustrates a double-subscripted array, **a**. The array contains three rows and four columns, so it is said to be a 3-by-4 array. In general, an array with *m* rows and *n* columns is called an *m-by-n array*.

Every element in array **a** is identified in Fig. 4.21 by an element name of the form **a[i][j]**; **a** is the name of the array, and **i** and **j** are the subscripts that uniquely identify each element in **a**. Notice that the names of the elements in the first row all have a first subscript of **0**; the names of the elements in the fourth column all have a second subscript of **3**.

Common Programming Error 4.11

*Referencing a double-subscripted array element **a[x][y]** incorrectly as **a[x, y]** is an error. Actually, **a[x, y]** is treated as **a[y]**, because C++ evaluates the expression **x, y** (containing a comma operator) simply as **y** (the last of the comma-separated expressions).*

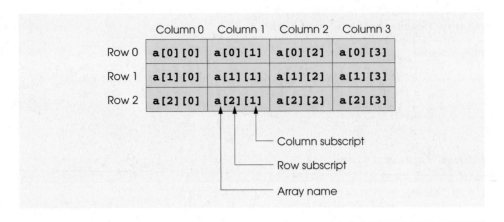

Fig. 4.21   Double-subscripted array with three rows and four columns.

A multiple-subscripted array can be initialized in its declaration much like a single subscripted array. For example, a double-subscripted array **b[2][2]** could be declared and initialized with

```
int b[ 2 ][ 2 ] = { { 1, 2 }, { 3, 4 } };
```

The values are grouped by row in braces. So, **1** and **2** initialize **b[0][0]** and **b[0][1]**, and **3** and **4** initialize **b[1][0]** and **b[1][1]**. If there are not enough initializers for a given row, the remaining elements of that row are initialized to **0**. Thus, the declaration

```
int b[ 2 ][ 2 ] = { { 1 }, { 3, 4 } };
```

initializes **b[0][0]** to **1**, **b[0][1]** to **0**, **b[1][0]** to **3** and **b[1][1]** to **4**.

Fig. 4.22 demonstrates initializing double-subscripted arrays in declarations. Lines 12–14 declare three arrays, each with two rows and three columns.

```cpp
1   // Fig. 4.22: fig04_22.cpp
2   // Initializing multidimensional arrays.
3   #include <iostream>
4
5   using std::cout;
6   using std::endl;
7
8   void printArray( int [][ 3 ] );
9
10  int main()
11  {
12      int array1[ 2 ][ 3 ] = { { 1, 2, 3 }, { 4, 5, 6 } };
13      int array2[ 2 ][ 3 ] = { 1, 2, 3, 4, 5 };
14      int array3[ 2 ][ 3 ] = { { 1, 2 }, { 4 } };
15
```

Fig. 4.22   Initializing multidimensional arrays. (Part 1 of 2.)

```
16        cout << "Values in array1 by row are:" << endl;
17        printArray( array1 );
18
19        cout << "Values in array2 by row are:" << endl;
20        printArray( array2 );
21
22        cout << "Values in array3 by row are:" << endl;
23        printArray( array3 );
24
25        return 0;  // indicates successful termination
26
27    } // end main
28
29    // function to output array with two rows and three columns
30    void printArray( int a[][ 3 ] )
31    {
32       for ( int i = 0; i < 2; i++ ) {    // for each row
33
34          for ( int j = 0; j < 3; j++ )    // output column values
35             cout << a[ i ][ j ] << ' ';
36
37          cout << endl;  // start new line of output
38
39       } // end outer for structure
40
41    } // end function printArray
```

```
Values in array1 by row are:
1 2 3
4 5 6
Values in array2 by row are:
1 2 3
4 5 0
Values in array3 by row are:
1 2 0
4 0 0
```

Fig. 4.22   Initializing multidimensional arrays. (Part 2 of 2.)

The declaration of **array1** (line 12) provides six initializers in two sublists. The first sublist initializes the first row of the array to the values 1, 2 and 3; and the second sublist initializes the second row of the array to the values 4, 5 and 6. If the braces around each sublist are removed from the **array1** initializer list, the compiler initializes the elements of the first row followed by the elements of the second row.

The declaration of **array2** (line 13) provides five initializers. The initializers are assigned to the first row and then the second row. Any elements that do not have an explicit initializer are initialized to zero, so **array2[1][2]** is initialized to zero.

The declaration of **array3** (line 14) provides three initializers in two sublists. The sublist for the first row explicitly initializes the first two elements of the first row to 1 and 2; the third element is implicitly initialized to zero. The sublist for the second row explicitly initializes the first element to 4 and implicitly initializes the last two elements to zero.

The program calls function **printArray** to output each array's elements. Notice that the function definition (lines 30–41) specifies the parameter **int a[][3]**. When we receive a single-subscripted array as an argument to a function, the array brackets are empty in the function's parameter list. The size of the first subscript of a multiple-subscripted array is not required either, but all subsequent subscript sizes are required. The compiler uses these sizes to determine the locations in memory of elements in multiple-subscripted arrays. All array elements are stored consecutively in memory, regardless of the number of subscripts. In a double-subscripted array, the first row is stored in memory followed by the second row. In a double-subscripted array, each row is a single-subscripted array. To locate an element in a particular row, the function must know exactly how many elements are in each row so it can skip the proper number of memory locations when accessing the array. Thus, when accessing **a[1][2]**, the function knows to skip the first row's three elements in memory to get to the second row (row 1). Then, the function accesses the third element of that row (element 2).

Many common array manipulations use **for** repetition structures. For example, the following **for** structure sets all the elements in the third row of array **a** in Fig. 4.21 to zero:

```
for ( column = 0; column < 4; column++ )
    a[ 2 ][ column ] = 0;
```

We specified the *third* row, and therefore we know that the first subscript is always **2**—**0** is the first row subscript and **1** is the second row subscript. The **for** loop varies only the second subscript (i.e., the column subscript). The preceding **for** structure is equivalent to the following assignment statements:

```
a[ 2 ][ 0 ] = 0;
a[ 2 ][ 1 ] = 0;
a[ 2 ][ 2 ] = 0;
a[ 2 ][ 3 ] = 0;
```

The following nested **for** structure determines the total of all the elements in array **a**:

```
total = 0;

for ( row = 0; row < 3; row++ )

    for ( column = 0; column < 4; column++ )

        total += a[ row ][ column ];
```

The **for** structure totals the elements of the array one row at a time. The outer **for** structure begins by setting **row** (i.e., the row subscript) to **0**, so the elements of the first row may be totaled by the inner **for** structure. The outer **for** structure then increments **row** to **1**, so the elements of the second row can be totaled. Then, the outer **for** structure increments **row** to **2**, so the elements of the third row can be totaled. When the nested **for** structure terminates, **total** contains the sum of all the array elements.

The program of Fig. 4.23 performs several other common array manipulations on 3-by-4 array **studentGrades**. Each row of the array represents a student, and each column represents a grade on one of the four exams the students took during the semester. The array manipulations are performed by four functions. Function **minimum** (lines 56–69) determines the lowest grade of any student for the semester. Function **maximum** (lines 72–85) determines the highest grade of any student for the semester. Function **average** (lines 88–98) determines a particular student's semester average. Function **printArray** (lines 101–118) outputs the double-subscripted array in a neat, tabular format.

```cpp
1    // Fig. 4.23: fig04_23.cpp
2    // Double-subscripted array example.
3    #include <iostream>
4
5    using std::cout;
6    using std::endl;
7    using std::fixed;
8    using std::left;
9
10   #include <iomanip>
11
12   using std::setw;
13   using std::setprecision;
14
15   const int students = 3;   // number of students
16   const int exams = 4;      // number of exams
17
18   // function prototypes
19   int minimum( int [][ exams ], int, int );
20   int maximum( int [][ exams ], int, int );
21   double average( int [], int );
22   void printArray( int [][ exams ], int, int );
23
24   int main()
25   {
26      // initialize student grades for three students (rows)
27      int studentGrades[ students ][ exams ] =
28         { { 77, 68, 86, 73 },
29           { 96, 87, 89, 78 },
30           { 70, 90, 86, 81 } };
31
32      // output array studentGrades
33      cout << "The array is:\n";
34      printArray( studentGrades, students, exams );
35
36      // determine smallest and largest grade values
37      cout << "\n\nLowest grade: "
38           << minimum( studentGrades, students, exams )
39           << "\nHighest grade: "
40           << maximum( studentGrades, students, exams ) << '\n';
41
42      cout << fixed << setprecision( 2 );
43
44      // calculate average grade for each student
45      for ( int person = 0; person < students; person++ )
46         cout << "The average grade for student " << person
47              << " is "
48              << average( studentGrades[ person ], exams )
49              << endl;
50
51      return 0;  // indicates successful termination
52
53   } // end main
```

Fig. 4.23   Double-subscripted array manipulations. (Part 1 of 3.)

```
54
55   // find minimum grade
56   int minimum( int grades[][ exams ], int pupils, int tests )
57   {
58      int lowGrade = 100; // initialize to highest possible grade
59
60      for ( int i = 0; i < pupils; i++ )
61
62         for ( int j = 0; j < tests; j++ )
63
64            if ( grades[ i ][ j ] < lowGrade )
65               lowGrade = grades[ i ][ j ];
66
67      return lowGrade;
68
69   } // end function minimum
70
71   // find maximum grade
72   int maximum( int grades[][ exams ], int pupils, int tests )
73   {
74      int highGrade = 0;   // initialize to lowest possible grade
75
76      for ( int i = 0; i < pupils; i++ )
77
78         for ( int j = 0; j < tests; j++ )
79
80            if ( grades[ i ][ j ] > highGrade )
81               highGrade = grades[ i ][ j ];
82
83      return highGrade;
84
85   } // end function maximum
86
87   // determine average grade for particular student
88   double average( int setOfGrades[], int tests )
89   {
90      int total = 0;
91
92      // total all grades for one student
93      for ( int i = 0; i < tests; i++ )
94         total += setOfGrades[ i ];
95
96      return static_cast< double >( total ) / tests;   // average
97
98   } // end function maximum
99
100  // Print the array
101  void printArray( int grades[][ exams ], int pupils, int tests )
102  {
103     // set left justification and output column heads
104     cout << left << "                    [0]   [1]   [2]   [3]";
105
```

Fig. 4.23   Double-subscripted array manipulations. (Part 2 of 3.)

```
106    // output grades in tabular format
107    for ( int i = 0; i < pupils; i++ ) {
108
109       // output label for row
110       cout << "\nstudentGrades[" << i << "] ";
111
112       // output one grades for one student
113       for ( int j = 0; j < tests; j++ )
114          cout << setw( 5 ) << grades[ i ][ j ];
115
116    } // end outer for
117
118 } // end function printArray
```

```
The array is:
                 [0]   [1]   [2]   [3]
studentGrades[0] 77    68    86    73
studentGrades[1] 96    87    89    78
studentGrades[2] 70    90    86    81

Lowest grade: 68
Highest grade: 96
The average grade for student 0 is 76.00
The average grade for student 1 is 87.50
The average grade for student 2 is 81.75
```

Fig. 4.23   Double-subscripted array manipulations. (Part 3 of 3.)

Functions **minimum**, **maximum** and **printArray** each receive three arguments—
the **studentGrades** array (called **grades** in each function), the number of students
(rows of the array) and the number of exams (columns of the array). Each function loops
through array **grades** using nested **for** structures. The following nested **for** structure is
from function **minimum** (lines 60–65):

```
for ( i = 0; i < pupils; i++ )

    for ( j = 0; j < tests; j++ )

        if ( grades[ i ][ j ] < lowGrade )
            lowGrade = grades[ i ][ j ];
```

The outer **for** structure begins by setting **i** (i.e., the row subscript) to **0**, so the elements
of the first row can be compared with variable **lowGrade** in the body of the inner **for**
structure. The inner **for** structure loops through the four grades of a particular row and
compares each grade with **lowGrade**. If a grade is less than **lowGrade**, **lowGrade** is
set to that grade. The outer **for** structure then increments the row subscript to **1**. The elements of the second row are compared with variable **lowGrade**. The outer **for** structure
then increments the row subscript to **2**. The elements of the third row are compared with
variable **lowGrade**. When execution of the nested structure is complete, **lowGrade** contains the smallest grade in the double-subscripted array. Function **maximum** works similarly to function **minimum**.

Function **average** (lines 88–98) takes two arguments—a single-subscripted array of test results for a particular student and the number of test results in the array. When **average** is called (line 48), the first argument is **studentGrades[student]**, which specifies that a particular row of the double-subscripted array **studentGrades** is to be passed to **average**. For example, the argument **studentGrades[1]** represents the four values (a single-subscripted array of grades) stored in the second row of the double-subscripted array **studentGrades**. A double-subscripted array could be considered an array with elements that are single-subscripted arrays. Function **average** calculates the sum of the array elements, divides the total by the number of test results and returns the floating-point result.

4.10 (Optional Case Study) Thinking About Objects: Identifying the Operations of a Class

In the "Thinking About Objects" sections at the ends of Chapter 2 and Chapter 3, we performed the first few steps of an object-oriented design for our elevator simulator. In Chapter 2, we identified the classes we need to implement, and we created a class diagram that models the structure of our system. In Chapter 3, we determined many of the attributes of our classes and we investigated the possible states of class **Elevator** and represented them in a statechart diagram. We also modeled in an activity diagram the logic the elevator uses to respond to button presses.

In this section, we concentrate on determining the class operations (or behaviors) needed to implement the elevator simulator. One object interacts with a second object by invoking the second object's operations. In Chapter 5, we further investigate the interactions between objects in our system.

An *operation* of a class is a service that the class provides to "clients" (users) of that class. Let us consider the operations of some real-world classes. A radio's operations include setting its station and volume (typically invoked by a listener adjusting the radio's controls). A car's operations include accelerating (which may be invoked by pressing the accelerator pedal), decelerating (which may be invoked by pressing the brake pedal), turning and shifting gears.

Objects ordinarily do not perform their operations spontaneously. Rather, a receiving object (often called a *server object*) performs an operation when the object receives a *message* from a sending object (often called a *client object*). In this section, we identify many of the operations the classes offer in our system.

We can derive many of the operations of each class directly from the problem statement. To do so, we examine the verbs and verb phrases from the problem statement. We then relate each of these phrases to a particular class in our system. Many of the verb phrases in the table in Fig. 4.24 help determine the operations of our classes.

To create operations from these verb phrases, we examine the verb phrases listed with each class. The "moves" verb listed with class **Elevator** refers to the activity in which the elevator moves between floors. Should "moves" be an operation of class **Elevator**? No message tells the elevator to move; rather, the elevator decides to move in response to a button press based on the condition that the door is closed. Therefore, "moves" does not correspond to an operation. The "arrives at a floor" phrase also is not an operation, because the elevator itself decides when to arrive on the floor, based on the time.

Class	Verb phrases
Elevator	moves, arrives at a floor, resets the elevator button, sounds the elevator bell, signals its arrival to a floor, opens its door, closes its door
Clock	ticks every second
Scheduler	randomly schedules times, creates a person, verifies that a floor is unoccupied, delays creating a person by one second
Person	steps onto floor, presses floor button, presses elevator button, enters elevator, exits elevator
Floor	resets floor button, turns off light, turns on light
FloorButton	summons elevator
ElevatorButton	signals elevator to move
Door	(opening of door) signals person to exit elevator, (opening of door) signals person to enter elevator
Bell	none in problem statement
Light	none in problem statement
Building	none in problem statement

Fig. 4.24 Verb phrases for each class in our elevator simulator.

These choices represent a decision on our part to differentiate between *public* (client-accessible) function of a class and *private* (client-inaccessible) functions. A public function corresponds to an operation—a client invokes an object's operation by calling the object's corresponding public function. A private function corresponds to self-initiated activities (such as the elevator deciding to move)—we do not consider such a function to be an operation. Beginning in Chapter 6, we discuss how to use C++ to designate a class member as public (meaning a client can access the member) or private (meaning a client cannot access the member).

Now we return to the verb phrases so we can determine the operations our classes should provide. The "resets elevator button" phrase implies that the elevator sends a message to the elevator button notifying the button to reset. Therefore, class **ElevatorButton** needs an operation to provide this service to the elevator. We place this operation in the bottom compartment of class **ElevatorButton** in our class diagram (Fig. 4.25). We represent the name of an operation as a function name, such as:

resetButton()

The operation name is written first, followed by parentheses containing a comma-separated list of the parameters that the operation takes (in this case, none). If we know the return type of the operation, a colon follows the parameter list, followed by the operation's return type. If the operation does not return a value (i.e., the operation has return type **void**), we omit the colon and return type. Note that most of our operations appear to have no parameters and no return type; this might change as our design and implementation processes proceed.

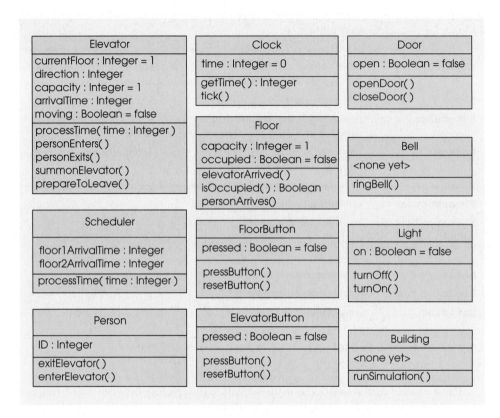

Fig. 4.25   Class diagram that includes attributes and operations.

From the "sounds the elevator bell" phrase listed with class **Elevator**, we conclude that class **Bell** should have an operation that provides a service for ringing. We list the **ringBell** operation under class **Bell**.

When the elevator arrives at a floor, it "signals its arrival to a floor," and the floor responds by performing its various activities (i.e., resetting the floor button and turning on the light). Therefore, class **Floor** needs an operation that provides this service. We call this operation **elevatorArrived** and place the operation name in the bottom compartment of class **Floor** in Fig. 4.25.

The remaining two verb phrases for class **Elevator** state that the elevator needs to open and close its door. Therefore, class **Door** needs to provide these operations. We place the **openDoor** and **closeDoor** operations in the bottom compartment of class **Door**.

Class **Clock** lists the phrase "ticks every second." This phrase brings up an interesting point. Certainly "getting the time" is an operation that the clock provides, so we must decide whether the ticking of the clock also is an operation.

The problem statement indicates that the scheduler must know the current time to decide whether the scheduler should create a person on a floor. The elevator needs the time value to decide whether it is time to arrive at a floor. We also decided that the **Building** class bears the responsibility for running the simulation and for passing the time to the scheduler and to the elevator. We now begin to see how our simulation operates. The operation of our simulation is becoming clearer. The building repeats the following steps once per second for the duration of the simulation:

1. Get the time from the clock.

2. Give the time to the scheduler so that the scheduler can create a person, if necessary.

3. Give the time to the elevator so that the elevator can decide to arrive at a floor, if the elevator is moving.

We decided that the building has full responsibility for running all parts of the simulation. Therefore, the building also must increment the clock once per second; then the time should be passed to the scheduler and the elevator.

This leads us to create operations **getTime** and **tick**, and to list them under class **Clock**. Operation **getTime** returns as an integer the value of the clock's **time** attribute. In the preceding items 2 and 3, we see the phrases "Give the time to the scheduler" and "Give the time to the elevator." Thus we can add operation **processTime** to classes **Scheduler** and **Elevator**. We also can add operation **runSimulation** to class **Building**.

Class **Scheduler** lists the verb phrases "randomly schedules times" and "delays creating a person by one second." The scheduler decides to perform these actions itself and does not provide these services to clients. Therefore, these two phrases do not correspond to operations, but instead may be private functions.

The phrase "creates a person" listed with class **Scheduler** presents a special case. Although we can model an object of class **Scheduler** sending a "create" message, an object of class **Person** cannot respond to a "create" message because that object does not yet exist. In this case, the creation of objects is left to implementation details and is not represented as an operation of a class. We discuss the creation of objects when we discuss implementation in Chapter 7.

The phrase "verifies that a floor is unoccupied" implies that class **Floor** must provide a service that reports whether the floor is occupied. The operation of this service should return **true** if the floor is occupied and **false** if not. We place the operation

isOccupied( ) : Boolean

in the bottom compartment of class **Floor**.

Class **Person** lists the phrase "steps onto floor." We might therefore imagine a message called **personArrives**, which a **Person** object sends to a **Floor** when the person first enters the simulation. For this reason, we place the **personArrives** message under class **Floor** in Fig. 4.25. For the "presses floor button" and "presses elevator button" verb phrases, we include the **pressButton** operation under classes **FloorButton** and **ElevatorButton**. The "enters elevator" and "exits elevator" phrases listed with class **Person** suggest that class **Elevator** needs operations that correspond to these actions.

Class **Floor** also lists "resets floor button" in its verb phrases column, so we place the appropriate **resetButton** operation under class **FloorButton**. Class **Floor** also lists "turns off light" and "turns on light," so we create the **turnOff** and **turnOn** operations and include them under class **Light**.

The "summons elevator" phrase listed under class **FloorButton** implies that class **Elevator** needs a **summonElevator** operation. The phrase "signals elevator to move" listed with class **ElevatorButton** implies that class **Elevator** needs to provide a "move" service. Before the elevator can move, however, the elevator must close its door. Therefore, a **prepareToLeave** operation, wherein the elevator performs the necessary actions before moving, seems a more appropriate choice to list under class **Elevator**.

The phrases listed with class **Door** imply that the door sends a message to a person to tell the person to exit or enter the elevator. We create two operations for class **Person** to cover these behaviors—**exitElevator** and **enterElevator**.

For now we do not concern ourselves too much with the parameters or return types; we attempt to gain only a basic understanding of the operations of each class. As we continue our design process, the number of operations belonging to each class might vary—we might find that additional operations are needed or that some current operations are unnecessary.

Sequence Diagrams

We can use the UML *sequence diagram* (Fig. 4.26) to model the steps from the preceding discussion that the building repeats during the simulation. The sequence diagram focuses on how messages are sent among objects over time.

Each object is represented by a rectangle at the top of the diagram. The name of the object is placed inside the rectangle. We write object names in the sequence diagram using the convention we introduced with the object diagram in the "Thinking About Objects" section at the end of Chapter 2 (Fig. 2.44). The dashed line that extends vertically from an object's rectangle is that object's *lifeline*. This lifeline represents the progression of time. Actions happen along an object's lifeline in chronological order from top to bottom—an action near the top of a lifeline happens before an action near the bottom.

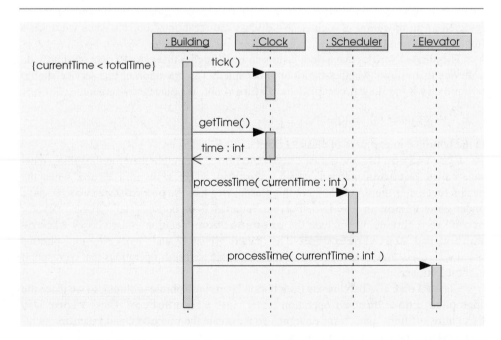

Fig. 4.26   Sequence diagram that models the steps the building repeats during the simulation.

A message between two objects in a sequence diagram is represented as a line with an arrowhead that extends from the object sending that message to the object receiving that message. The message invokes the corresponding operation in the receiving object. The arrowhead points to the lifeline of the object receiving the message. The name of the message appears above the message line and should include any parameters being passed. For example, the object of class **Building** sends the **processTime** message to the object of class **Elevator**. The name of the message appears above the message line, and the name of the parameter (**currentTime**) appears inside parentheses to the right of the message; each parameter name is followed by a colon and the parameter type.

If an object returns the flow of control or if an object returns a value, a return message (represented as a dashed line with an arrowhead) extends from the object returning control to the object that initially sent the message. For example, the object of class **Clock** returns **time** in response to the **getTime** message received from the object of class **Building**. We also could use the notation

     time := getTime()

for the **getTime** message that the **Building** object sends to the **Clock** object. In this case, we would omit the return message, because the original message notation contained information about how the **Building** obtains the return value.

If a message call returns no value, the flow of control returns to the calling object when the called object's activation ends. In this case, we may omit the dashed return message (as in the **tick** and **processTime** messages in Fig. 4.26).

The rectangles along the objects' lifelines—called *activations*—each represent the duration of an activity. An activation is initiated when an object receives a message and is denoted by a rectangle on that object's lifeline. The height of the rectangle corresponds to the duration of the activity or activities initiated by the message—the longer the duration of the activity, the taller the rectangle.

The text to the far left of the diagram in Fig. 4.26 indicates a timing constraint. While the current time is less than the total simulation time (**currentTime < totalTime**), the objects continue sending messages to one another in the sequence modeled in the diagram.

Figure 4.27 models how the scheduler handles the time and creates people to walk onto floors. For this diagram, we assume the scheduler has scheduled a person to walk onto each of the two floors at a time that matches the time supplied by the building. Let us follow the flow of messages through this sequence diagram.

The object of class **Building** first sends the **processTime** message to the object of class **Scheduler**, passing the current time. The **Scheduler** object then must decide whether to create a person on the first floor (represented by the **floor1** object of class **Floor**). The problem statement tells us that the scheduler first must verify that the floor is unoccupied before the scheduler can create a person on that floor. The **Scheduler** object therefore sends an **isOccupied** message to the **floor1** object.

The **floor1** object returns either **true** or **false** (indicated by the dashed return message line and the **bool** type). At this point, the **Scheduler** object's lifeline splits into two parallel lifelines to represent each possible sequence of messages that the object can send, based on the value returned by object **floor1**. An object's lifeline can split into two or more lifelines to indicate the *conditional execution of activities*. A condition must be supplied for each lifeline. The new lifeline(s) run parallel to the main lifeline, and the lifelines may converge at some later point.

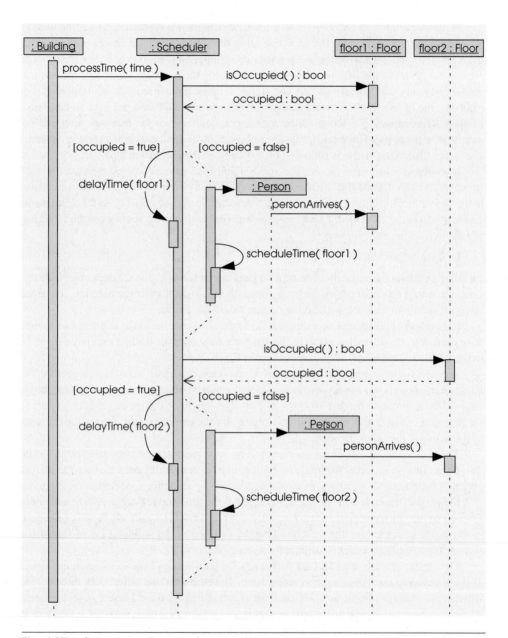

Fig. 4.27   Sequence diagram for scheduling process.

If the **floor1** object returns **true** (i.e., the floor is occupied), the **Scheduler** calls its own **delayTime** function, passing a parameter indicating that the **floor1** arrival time needs to be rescheduled. This function is not an operation of class **Scheduler**, because it is not invoked by another object. The **delayTime** function is instead a private activity that object **Scheduler** performs inside an operation. Notice that when the **Scheduler** object sends a message to itself (i.e., invokes one of its own member functions), the activation bar for that message is centered on the edge of the current activation bar.

If the **floor1** object returns **false** (i.e., the floor is unoccupied), the **Scheduler** object creates an object of class **Person**. To denote object creation in a sequence diagram, we place the created object's rectangle at a vertical position that corresponds to the time at which the object is created. A large "X" at the end of an object's lifeline denotes the destruction of that object. [Note: Our sequence diagram does not model the destruction of any objects of class **Person**; therefore, no "X" appears in the diagram. We discuss creating and destroying objects dynamically, using C++'s **new** and **delete** operators, in Chapter 7.]

After the **Scheduler** creates the object of class **Person**, the person next must step onto the first floor. Therefore, the new **Person** object sends a **personArrives** message to the **floor1** object. This message notifies the **floor1** object that a person is stepping onto the floor.

After the **Scheduler** object has created an object of class **Person**, it schedules a new arrival for **floor1**. The **Scheduler** object invokes its own **scheduleTime** function, and the activation bar for this call is centered on the right of the current activation bar. The **scheduleTime** function is not an operation, but rather an activity that class **Scheduler** performs inside an operation. At this point, the two lifelines converge. The **Scheduler** object then handles the second floor in the same manner as the first. When the scheduler has finished with **floor2**, control returns to the **Building** object.

Conclusion
In this section, we discussed the operations of classes and introduced the UML sequence diagram to illustrate these operations. In the "Thinking About Objects" section at the end of Chapter 5, we examine how objects in a system interact with one another to accomplish specific tasks.

SUMMARY

- C++ can store lists of values in arrays. An array is a group of consecutive memory locations that are related by the fact that they all have the same name and the same type. To refer to a particular location or element within the array, we specify the name of the array and the subscript. The subscript indicates the number of elements from the beginning of the array.

- A subscript may be an integer or an integer expression. Subscript expressions are evaluated to determine the particular element of the array.

- It is important to note the difference when referring to the seventh element of the array as opposed to array element seven. The seventh element has a subscript of **6**, while array element seven has a subscript of **7** (actually the eighth element of the array). This is a source of "off-by-one" errors.

- The elements of an array can be initialized by declaration, by assignment and by input.

- When initializing an array with an initializer list, if there are fewer initializers than elements in the array, the remaining elements are initialized to zero.

- C++ does not prevent referencing elements beyond the bounds of an array.

- An array of type **char** can be used to store a character string.

- A character array can be initialized using a string literal.

- All strings end with the null character (**'\0'**).

- Character arrays can be initialized with character constants in an initializer list.

- Individual characters in a string stored in an array can be accessed directly using array subscript notation.

- To pass an array to a function, the name of the array is passed. To pass a single element of an array to a function, simply pass the name of the array followed by the subscript (contained in square brackets) of the particular element.

- Arrays are passed to functions using simulated pass-by-reference—the called functions can modify the element values in the callers' original arrays. The value of the name of the array is the address in the computer's memory of the first element of the array. Because the starting address of the array is passed, the called function knows precisely where the array is stored in memory.

- To receive an array argument, the function's parameter list must specify that an array will be received. The size of the array is not required in the brackets for a single-subscripted array parameter.

- C++ provides the type qualifier **const** that enables programs to prevent modification of array values in a function. When an array parameter is preceded by the **const** qualifier, the elements of the array become constant in the function body, and any attempt to modify an element of the array in the function body is a compiler error.

- An array can be sorted using the bubble-sort technique. Several passes of the array are made. On each pass, successive pairs of elements are compared. If a pair is in order (or the values are identical), it is left as is. If a pair is out of order, the values are swapped. For small arrays, the bubble sort is acceptable, but for larger arrays it is inefficient compared to other more sophisticated sorting algorithms.

- The linear search compares each element of an array with a search key. If the array is not in any particular order, it is just as likely that the value will be found in the first element as the last. On average, therefore, the program will have to compare the search key with half the elements of the array. The linear searching method works well for small arrays and is acceptable for unsorted arrays.

- The binary search requires a sorted array. Binary search eliminates from consideration half the elements in the array after each comparison by locating the middle element of the array and comparing it with the search key. If they are equal, the search key is found, and the array subscript of that element is returned. Otherwise, the problem is reduced to searching one-half of the array. In a worst-case scenario, searching an array of 1023 elements will take only 10 comparisons using a binary search. One billion elements requires a maximum of 30 comparisons.

- Arrays may be used to represent tables of values consisting of information arranged in rows and columns. To identify a particular element of a table, two subscripts are specified. The first (by convention) identifies the row in which the element is contained, and the second (by convention) identifies the column in which the element is contained. Tables or arrays that require two subscripts to identify a particular element are called double-subscripted arrays.

- When we receive a single-subscripted array as an argument to a function, the array brackets are empty in the function's parameter list. The size of the first subscript of a multiple-subscripted array is not required either, but all subsequent subscript sizes are required. The compiler uses these sizes to determine the locations in memory of elements in multiple-subscripted arrays.

- To pass one row of a double-subscripted array to a function that receives a single-subscripted array, simply pass the name of the array followed by the first subscript.

TERMINOLOGY

`a[ i ]`	array initializer list
`a[ i ][ j ]`	binary search of an array
array	bounds checking

bubble sort
column subscript
constant variable
const type qualifier
declare an array
double-subscripted array
element of an array
initialize an array
initializer
initializer list
linear search of an array
magic number
m-by-*n* array
multiple-subscripted array
name of an array
named constant
null character (**'\0'**)
off-by-one error
passing arrays to functions
pass-by-reference

pass of a bubble sort
position number
row subscript
scalability
scalar
search an array
search key
simulated pass-by-reference
single-subscripted array
sinking sort
sort an array
square brackets **[]**
string
subscript
table of values
value of an element
"walk off" an array
zeroth element
tabular format
temporary area for exchange of values

Terminology for Optional "Thinking About Objects" Section

activation rectangle in UML sequence diagram
behavior
client object
conditional execution of activities
dotted line with arrowhead in UML
    sequence diagram
duration of activity
flow of messages in UML sequence diagram
line with solid arrowhead in UML
    sequence diagram
message
object lifeline in UML sequence diagram

object rectangle in UML sequence diagram
operation
public function
private function
return message
return type of an operation
sequence diagram
server object
service that an object provides
simulation loop
splitting an object's lifeline
verb phrase in a problem statement

SELF-REVIEW EXERCISES

4.1   Answer each of the following:
    a) Lists and tables of values can be stored in _____.
    b) The elements of an array are related by the fact that they have the same _____ and
        _____.
    c) The number used to refer to a particular element of an array is called its _____.
    d) A _____ should be used to declare the size of an array, because it makes the program more scalable.
    e) The process of placing the elements of an array in order is called _____ the array.
    f) The process of determining if an array contains a certain key value is called _____ the array.
    g) An array that uses two subscripts is referred to as a _____ array.

4.2   State whether the following are *true* or *false*. If the answer is *false*, explain why.
    a) An array can store many different types of values.
    b) An array subscript should normally be of data type **float**.

c) If there are fewer initializers in an initializer list than the number of elements in the array, the remaining elements are initialized to the last value in the list of initializers.

d) It is an error if an initializer list contains more initializers than there are elements in the array.

e) An individual array element that is passed to a function and modified in that function will contain the modified value when the called function completes execution.

4.3   Answer the following questions regarding an array called **fractions**:

a) Define a constant variable **arraySize** initialized to 10.

b) Declare an array with **arraySize** elements of type **double**, and initialize the elements to **0**.

c) Name the fourth element of the array.

d) Refer to array element 4.

e) Assign the value **1.667** to array element 9.

f) Assign the value **3.333** to the seventh element of the array.

g) Print array elements 6 and 9 with two digits of precision to the right of the decimal point, and show the output that is actually displayed on the screen.

h) Print all the elements of the array using a **for** repetition structure. Define the integer variable **i** as a control variable for the loop. Show the output.

4.4   Answer the following questions regarding an array called **table**:

a) Declare the array to be an integer array and to have 3 rows and 3 columns. Assume that the constant variable **arraySize** has been defined to be 3.

b) How many elements does the array contain?

c) Use a **for** repetition structure to initialize each element of the array to the sum of its subscripts. Assume that the integer variables **i** and **j** are declared as control variables.

d) Write a program segment to print the values of each element of array **table** in tabular format with 3 rows and 3 columns. Assume that the array was initialized with the declaration

```
int table[ arraySize ][ arraySize ] =
   { { 1, 8 }, { 2, 4, 6 }, { 5 } };
```

and the integer variables **i** and **j** are declared as control variables. Show the output.

4.5   Find the error in each of the following program segments and correct the error:

a) `#include <iostream>;`

b) `arraySize = 10;   // arraySize was declared const`

c) Assume that `int b[ 10 ] = { 0 };`
```
for ( int i = 0; i <= 10; i++ )
   b[ i ] = 1;
```

d) Assume that `int a[ 2 ][ 2 ] = { { 1, 2 }, { 3, 4 } };`
```
a[ 1, 1 ] = 5;
```

ANSWERS TO SELF-REVIEW EXERCISES

4.1   a) arrays.   b) name, type.   c) subscript (or index).   d) constant variable.   e) sorting. f) searching. g) double-subscripted.

4.2   a) False. An array can store only values of the same type.

b) False. An array subscript should be an integer or an integer expression.

c) False. The remaining elements are initialized to zero.

d) True.

e) False. Individual elements of an array are passed by call-by-value. If the entire array is passed to a function, then any modifications will be reflected in the original.

4.3   a) `const int arraySize = 10;`

b) `double fractions[ arraySize ] = { 0.0 };`

c) `fractions[ 3 ]`

d) `fractions[ 4 ]`

e) `fractions[ 9 ] = 1.667;`

f) `fractions[ 6 ] = 3.333;`

g) `cout << fixed << setprecision( 2 );`

   `cout << fractions[ 6 ] << ' ' << fractions[ 9 ] << endl;`

   Output: **3.33 1.67**.

h) `for ( int i = 0; i < arraySize; i++ )`

     `cout << "fractions[" << i << "] = " << fractions[ i ]`

       `<< endl;`

Output:

```
fractions[ 0 ] = 0.0
fractions[ 1 ] = 0.0
fractions[ 2 ] = 0.0
fractions[ 3 ] = 0.0
fractions[ 4 ] = 0.0
fractions[ 5 ] = 0.0
fractions[ 6 ] = 3.333
fractions[ 7 ] = 0.0
fractions[ 8 ] = 0.0
fractions[ 9 ] = 1.667
```

4.4   a) `int table[ arraySize ][ arraySize ];`

b) Nine.

c) `for ( i = 0; i < arraySize; i++ )`

     `for ( j = 0; j < arraySize; j++ )`

       `table[ i ][ j ] = i + j;`

d) `cout << "     [0]   [1]   [2]" << endl;`

   `for ( int i = 0; i < arraySize; i++ ) {`

     `cout << '[' << i << "] ";`

     `for ( int j = 0; j < arraySize; j++ )`

       `cout << setw( 3 ) << table[ i ][ j ] << "   ";`

     `cout << endl;`

Output:

	[0]	[1]	[2]
[0]	1	8	0
[1]	2	4	6
[2]	5	0	0

4.5   a) Error: Semicolon at end of **#include** preprocessor directive.

   Correction: Eliminate semicolon.

b) Error: Assigning a value to a constant variable using an assignment statement.

   Correction: Assign a value to the constant variable in a **const int arraySize** declaration.

c) Error: Referencing an array element outside the bounds of the array (**b[10]**).

   Correction: Change the final value of the control variable to **9**.

d) Error: Array subscripting done incorrectly.

   Correction: Change the statement to **a[1][1] = 5;**

EXERCISES

4.6   Fill in the blanks in each of the following:

   a) The names of the four elements of array **p** (**int p[4];**) are _____, _____, _____ and _____.

   b) Naming an array, stating its type and specifying the number of elements in the array is called _____ the array.

   c) In a double-subscripted array, the first subscript (by convention) identifies the _____ of an element, and the second subscript (by convention) identifies the _____ of an element.

   d) An *m-by-n* array contains _____ rows, _____ columns and _____ elements.

   e) The name of the element in row 3 and column 5 of array **d** is _____.

4.7   State which of the following are true and which are false; for those that are false, explain why they are false.

   a) To refer to a particular location or element within an array, we specify the name of the array and the value of the particular element.

   b) An array declaration reserves space for the array.

   c) To indicate that 100 locations should be reserved for integer array **p**, the programmer writes the declaration

```
p[ 100 ];
```

   d) A C++ program that initializes the elements of a 15-element array to zero must contain at least one **for** structure.

   e) A C++ program that totals the elements of a double-subscripted array must contain nested **for** structures.

4.8   Write C++ statements to accomplish each of the following:

   a) Display the value of the seventh element of character array **f**.

   b) Input a value into element 4 of single-subscripted floating-point array **b**.

   c) Initialize each of the 5 elements of single-subscripted integer array **g** to **8**.

   d) Total and print the elements of floating-point array **c** of 100 elements.

   e) Copy array **a** into the first portion of array **b**. Assume **double a[11], b[34];**

   f) Determine and print the smallest and largest values contained in 99-element floating-point array **w**.

4.9   Consider a 2-by-3 integer array **t**.

   a) Write a declaration for **t**.

   b) How many rows does **t** have?

   c) How many columns does **t** have?

   d) How many elements does **t** have?

   e) Write the names of all the elements in the second row of **t**.

   f) Write the names of all the elements in the third column of **t**.

   g) Write a single statement that sets the element of **t** in row 1 and column 2 to zero.

   h) Write a series of statements that initialize each element of **t** to zero. Do not use a loop.

   i) Write a nested **for** structure that initializes each element of **t** to zero.

   j) Write a statement that inputs the values for the elements of **t** from the terminal.

   k) Write a series of statements that determine and print the smallest value in array **t**.

   l) Write a statement that displays the elements of the first row of **t**.

   m) Write a statement that totals the elements of the fourth column of **t**.

   n) Write a series of statements that prints the array **t** in neat, tabular format. List the column subscripts as headings across the top and list the row subscripts at the left of each row.

4.10   Use a single-subscripted array to solve the following problem. A company pays its salespeople on a commission basis. The salespeople receive $200 per week plus 9 percent of their gross sales for that week. For example, a salesperson who grosses $5000 in sales in a week receives $200 plus 9 percent of $5000, or a total of $650. Write a program (using an array of counters) that determines how many of the salespeople earned salaries in each of the following ranges (assume that each salesperson's salary is truncated to an integer amount):

    a) $200–$299
    b) $300–$399
    c) $400–$499
    d) $500–$599
    e) $600–$699
    f) $700–$799
    g) $800–$899
    h) $900–$999
    i) $1000 and over

4.11   The bubble sort presented in Fig. 4.16 is inefficient for large arrays. Make the following simple modifications to improve the performance of the bubble sort:

    a) After the first pass, the largest number is guaranteed to be in the highest-numbered element of the array; after the second pass, the two highest numbers are "in place," and so on. Instead of making nine comparisons on every pass, modify the bubble sort to make eight comparisons on the second pass, seven on the third pass, and so on.
    b) The data in the array may already be in the proper order or near-proper order, so why make nine passes if fewer will suffice? Modify the sort to check at the end of each pass if any swaps have been made. If none have been made, then the data must already be in the proper order, so the program should terminate. If swaps have been made, then at least one more pass is needed.

4.12   Write single statements that perform the following single-subscripted array operations:

    a) Initialize the 10 elements of integer array **counts** to zero.
    b) Add 1 to each of the 15 elements of integer array **bonus**.
    c) Read 12 values for **double** array **monthlyTemperatures** from the keyboard.
    d) Print the 5 values of integer array **bestScores** in column format.

4.13   Find the error(s) in each of the following statements:

    a) Assume that: `char str[ 5 ];`

        `cin >> str;      // User types "hello"`

    b) Assume that: `int a[ 3 ];`

        `cout << a[ 1 ] << " " << a[ 2 ] << " " << a[ 3 ] << endl;`

    c) `double f[ 3 ] = { 1.1, 10.01, 100.001, 1000.0001 };`
    d) Assume that: `double d[ 2 ][ 10 ];`

        `d[ 1, 9 ] = 2.345;`

4.14   Modify the program of Fig. 4.17 so function **mode** is capable of handling a tie for the mode value. Also modify function **median** so the two middle elements are averaged in an array with an even number of elements.

4.15   Use a single-subscripted array to solve the following problem. Read in 20 numbers, each of which is between 10 and 100, inclusive. As each number is read, print it only if it is not a duplicate of a number already read. Provide for the "worst case" in which all 20 numbers are different. Use the smallest possible array to solve this problem.

4.16   Label the elements of 3-by-5 double-subscripted array **sales** to indicate the order in which they are set to zero by the following program segment:

```
for ( row = 0; row < 3; row++ )

    for ( column = 0; column < 5; column++ )
        sales[ row ][ column ] = 0;
```

4.17   Write a program that simulates the rolling of two dice. The program should use **rand** to roll the first die and should use **rand** again to roll the second die. The sum of the two values should then be calculated. [*Note:* Each die can show an integer value from 1 to 6, so the sum of the two values will vary from 2 to 12, with 7 being the most frequent sum and 2 and 12 being the least frequent sums.] Fig. 4.28 shows the 36 possible combinations of the two dice. Your program should roll the two dice 36,000 times. Use a single-subscripted array to tally the numbers of times each possible sum appears. Print the results in a tabular format. Also, determine if the totals are reasonable (i.e., there are six ways to roll a 7, so approximately one sixth of all the rolls should be 7).

4.18   What does the following program do?

```cpp
1   // Ex. 4.18: ex04_18.cpp
2   // What does this program do?
3   #include <iostream>
4
5   using std::cout;
6   using std::endl;
7
8   int whatIsThis( int [], int );   // function prototype
9
10  int main()
11  {
12      const int arraySize = 10;
13      int a[ arraySize ] = { 1, 2, 3, 4, 5, 6, 7, 8, 9, 10 };
14
15      int result = whatIsThis( a, arraySize );
16
17      cout << "Result is " << result << endl;
18
19      return 0;  // indicates successful termination
20
21  } // end main
22
23  // What does this function do?
24  int whatIsThis( int b[], int size )
25  {
26      // base case
27      if ( size == 1 )
28          return b[ 0 ];
29
30      // recursive step
31      else
32          return b[ size - 1 ] + whatIsThis( b, size - 1 );
33
34  } // end function whatIsThis
```

	1	2	3	4	5	6
1	2	3	4	5	6	7
2	3	4	5	6	7	8
3	4	5	6	7	8	9
4	5	6	7	8	9	10
5	6	7	8	9	10	11
6	7	8	9	10	11	12

Fig. 4.28 The 36 possible outcomes of rolling two dice.

4.19 Modify the program of Fig. 3.10 to play 1000 games of craps. The program should keep track of the statistics and answer the following questions:

a) How many games are won on the 1st roll, 2nd roll, …, 20th roll, and after the 20th roll?
b) How many games are lost on the 1st roll, 2nd roll, …, 20th roll, and after the 20th roll?
c) What are the chances of winning at craps? (*Note:* You should discover that craps is one of the fairest casino games. What do you suppose this means?)
d) What is the average length of a game of craps?
e) Do the chances of winning improve with the length of the game?

4.20 (*Airline Reservations System*) A small airline has just purchased a computer for its new automated reservations system. You have been asked to program the new system. You are to write a program to assign seats on each flight of the airline's only plane (capacity: 10 seats).

Your program should display the following menu of alternatives—**`Please type 1 for "First Class"`** and **`Please type 2 for "Economy"`**. If the person types **`1`**, your program should assign a seat in the first class section (seats 1-5). If the person types **`2`**, your program should assign a seat in the economy section (seats 6-10). Your program should print a boarding pass indicating the person's seat number and whether it is in the first class or economy section of the plane.

Use a single-subscripted array to represent the seating chart of the plane. Initialize all the elements of the array to 0 to indicate that all seats are empty. As each seat is assigned, set the corresponding elements of the array to 1 to indicate that the seat is no longer available.

Your program should, of course, never assign a seat that has already been assigned. When the first class section is full, your program should ask the person if it is acceptable to be placed in the economy section (and vice versa). If yes, then make the appropriate seat assignment. If no, then print the message **`"Next flight leaves in 3 hours."`**

4.21 What does the following program do?

```
// Ex. 4.21: ex04_21.cpp
// What does this program do?
#include <iostream>

using std::cout;
using std::endl;

void someFunction( int [], int, int );  // function prototype
```

```
9
10   int main()
11   {
12      const int arraySize = 10;
13      int a[ arraySize ] = { 1, 2, 3, 4, 5, 6, 7, 8, 9, 10 };
14
15      cout << "The values in the array are:" << endl;
16      someFunction( a, 0, arraySize );
17      cout << endl;
18
19      return 0;  // indicates successful termination
20
21   } // end main
22
23   // What does this function do?
24   void someFunction( int b[], int current, int size )
25   {
26      if ( current < size ) {
27         someFunction( b, current + 1, size );
28         cout << b[ current ] << "   ";
29      }
30
31   } // end function someFunction
```

4.22   Use a double-subscripted array to solve the following problem. A company has four sales-people (1 to 4) who sell five different products (1 to 5). Once a day, each salesperson passes in a slip for each different type of product sold. Each slip contains the following:

a) The salesperson number

b) The product number

c) The total dollar value of that product sold that day

Thus, each salesperson passes in between 0 and 5 sales slips per day. Assume that the information from all of the slips for last month is available. Write a program that will read all this information for last month's sales and summarize the total sales by salesperson by product. All totals should be stored in the double-subscripted array **sales**. After processing all the information for last month, print the results in tabular format with each of the columns representing a particular salesperson and each of the rows representing a particular product. Cross total each row to get the total sales of each product for last month; cross total each column to get the total sales by salesperson for last month. Your tabular printout should include these cross totals to the right of the totaled rows and to the bottom of the totaled columns.

4.23   (*Turtle Graphics*) The Logo language, which is particularly popular among personal comput-er users, made the concept of *turtle graphics* famous. Imagine a mechanical turtle that walks around the room under the control of a C++ program. The turtle holds a pen in one of two positions, up or down. While the pen is down, the turtle traces out shapes as it moves; while the pen is up, the turtle moves about freely without writing anything. In this problem, you will simulate the operation of the turtle and create a computerized sketchpad as well.

Use a 20-by-20 array **floor** that is initialized to zeros. Read commands from an array that contains them. Keep track of the current position of the turtle at all times and whether the pen is cur-rently up or down. Assume that the turtle always starts at position 0,0 of the floor with its pen up. The set of turtle commands your program must process are shown in Fig. 4.29.

Suppose that the turtle is somewhere near the center of the floor. The following "program" would draw and print a 12-by-12 square and end with the pen in the up position:

Command	Meaning
1	Pen up
2	Pen down
3	Turn right
4	Turn left
5,10	Move forward 10 spaces (or a number other than 10)
6	Print the 20-by-20 array
9	End of data (sentinel)

Fig. 4.29   Turtle graphics commands.

```
2
5,12
3
5,12
3
5,12
3
5,12
1
6
9
```

As the turtle moves with the pen down, set the appropriate elements of array **floor** to **1**'s. When the **6** command (print) is given, wherever there is a **1** in the array, display an asterisk or some other character you choose. Wherever there is a zero, display a blank. Write a program to implement the turtle graphics capabilities discussed here. Write several turtle graphics programs to draw interesting shapes. Add other commands to increase the power of your turtle graphics language.

4.24   (*Knight's Tour*) One of the more interesting puzzlers for chess buffs is the Knight's Tour problem. The question is this: Can the chess piece called the knight move around an empty chessboard and touch each of the 64 squares once and only once? We study this intriguing problem in depth here.

The knight makes L-shaped moves (over two in one direction and then over one in a perpendicular direction). Thus, from a square in the middle of an empty chessboard, the knight can make eight different moves (numbered 0 through 7) as shown in Fig. 4.30.

    a) Draw an 8-by-8 chessboard on a sheet of paper and attempt a Knight's Tour by hand. Put a **1** in the first square you move to, a **2** in the second square, a **3** in the third, etc. Before starting the tour, estimate how far you think you will get, remembering that a full tour consists of 64 moves. How far did you get? Was this close to your estimate?

    b) Now let us develop a program that will move the knight around a chessboard. The board is represented by an 8-by-8 double-subscripted array **board**. Each of the squares is initialized to zero. We describe each of the eight possible moves in terms of both their horizontal and vertical components. For example, a move of type 0, as shown in Fig. 4.30, consists of moving two squares horizontally to the right and one square vertically upward. Move 2 consists of moving one square horizontally to the left and two squares vertically upward. Horizontal moves to the left and vertical moves upward are indicated with negative numbers. The eight moves may be described by two single-subscripted arrays, **horizontal** and **vertical**, as follows:

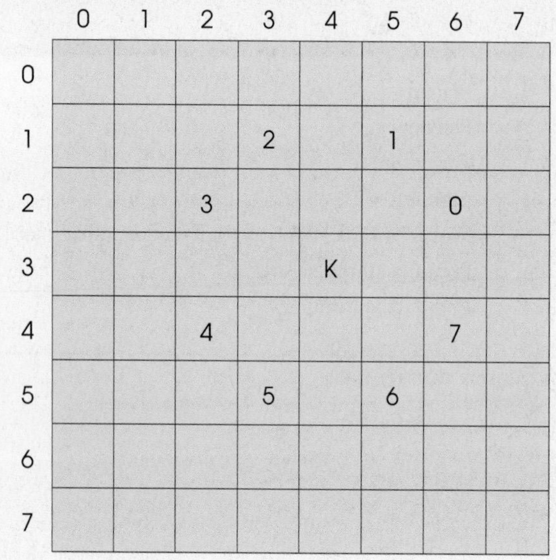

Fig. 4.30   The eight possible moves of the knight.

```
horizontal[ 0 ] = 2
horizontal[ 1 ] = 1
horizontal[ 2 ] = -1
horizontal[ 3 ] = -2
horizontal[ 4 ] = -2
horizontal[ 5 ] = -1
horizontal[ 6 ] = 1
horizontal[ 7 ] = 2

vertical[ 0 ] = -1
vertical[ 1 ] = -2
vertical[ 2 ] = -2
vertical[ 3 ] = -1
vertical[ 4 ] = 1
vertical[ 5 ] = 2
vertical[ 6 ] = 2
vertical[ 7 ] = 1
```

Let the variables **currentRow** and **currentColumn** indicate the row and column of the knight's current position. To make a move of type **moveNumber**, where **moveNumber** is between 0 and 7, your program uses the statements

```
currentRow += vertical[ moveNumber ];
currentColumn += horizontal[ moveNumber ];
```

Keep a counter that varies from **1** to **64**. Record the latest count in each square the knight moves to. Remember to test each potential move to see if the knight has already visited that square, and, of course, test every potential move to make sure that the knight does not land off the chessboard. Now write a program to move the knight around the chessboard. Run the program. How many moves did the knight make?

c) After attempting to write and run a Knight's Tour program, you have probably developed some valuable insights. We will use these to develop a *heuristic* (or strategy) for moving the knight. Heuristics do not guarantee success, but a carefully developed heuristic greatly improves the chance of success. You may have observed that the outer squares are more troublesome than the squares nearer the center of the board. In fact, the most troublesome, or inaccessible, squares are the four corners.

Intuition may suggest that you should attempt to move the knight to the most troublesome squares first and leave open those that are easiest to get to, so when the board gets congested near the end of the tour, there will be a greater chance of success.

We may develop an "accessibility heuristic" by classifying each of the squares according to how accessible they are and then always moving the knight to the square (within the knight's L-shaped moves, of course) that is most inaccessible. We label a double-subscripted array **accessibility** with numbers indicating from how many squares each particular square is accessible. On a blank chessboard, each center square is rated as **8**, each corner square is rated as **2** and the other squares have accessibility numbers of **3**, **4** or **6** as follows:

```
2   3   4   4   4   4   3   2
3   4   6   6   6   6   4   3
4   6   8   8   8   8   6   4
4   6   8   8   8   8   6   4
4   6   8   8   8   8   6   4
4   6   8   8   8   8   6   4
3   4   6   6   6   6   4   3
2   3   4   4   4   4   3   2
```

Now write a version of the Knight's Tour program using the accessibility heuristic. At any time, the knight should move to the square with the lowest accessibility number. In case of a tie, the knight may move to any of the tied squares. Therefore, the tour may begin in any of the four corners. (*Note:* As the knight moves around the chessboard, your program should reduce the accessibility numbers as more and more squares become occupied. In this way, at any given time during the tour, each available square's accessibility number will remain equal to precisely the number of squares from which that square may be reached.) Run this version of your program. Did you get a full tour? Now modify the program to run 64 tours, one starting from each square of the chessboard. How many full tours did you get?

d) Write a version of the Knight's Tour program which, when encountering a tie between two or more squares, decides what square to choose by looking ahead to those squares reachable from the "tied" squares. Your program should move to the square for which the next move would arrive at a square with the lowest accessibility number.

4.25 (*Knight's Tour: Brute-Force Approaches*) In Exercise 4.24, we developed a solution to the Knight's Tour problem. The approach used, called the "accessibility heuristic," generates many solutions and executes efficiently.

As computers continue increasing in power, we will be able to solve more problems with sheer computer power and relatively unsophisticated algorithms. This is the "brute force" approach to problem solving.

a) Use random-number generation to enable the knight to walk around the chessboard (in its legitimate L-shaped moves, of course) at random. Your program should run one tour and print the final chessboard. How far did the knight get?

b) Most likely, the preceding program produced a relatively short tour. Now modify your program to attempt 1000 tours. Use a single-subscripted array to keep track of the number of tours of each length. When your program finishes attempting the 1000 tours, it should print this information in neat tabular format. What was the best result?

c) Most likely, the preceding program gave you some "respectable" tours, but no full tours. Now "pull all the stops out" and simply let your program run until it produces a full tour. (*Caution:* This version of the program could run for hours on a powerful computer.) Once again, keep a table of the number of tours of each length, and print this table when the first full tour is found. How many tours did your program attempt before producing a full tour? How much time did it take?

d) Compare the brute-force version of the Knight's Tour with the accessibility-heuristic version. Which required a more careful study of the problem? Which algorithm was more difficult to develop? Which required more computer power? Could we be certain (in advance) of obtaining a full tour with the accessibility heuristic approach? Could we be certain (in advance) of obtaining a full tour with the brute-force approach? Argue the pros and cons of brute-force problem solving in general.

4.26 (*Eight Queens*) Another puzzler for chess buffs is the Eight Queens problem. Simply stated: Is it possible to place eight queens on an empty chessboard so that no queen is "attacking" any other, i.e., no two queens are in the same row, the same column, or along the same diagonal? Use the thinking developed in Exercise 4.24 to formulate a heuristic for solving the Eight Queens problem. Run your program. (*Hint:* It is possible to assign a value to each square of the chessboard indicating how many squares of an empty chessboard are "eliminated" if a queen is placed in that square. Each of the corners would be assigned the value 22, as in Fig. 4.31.) Once these "elimination numbers" are placed in all 64 squares, an appropriate heuristic might be: Place the next queen in the square with the smallest elimination number. Why is this strategy intuitively appealing?

4.27 (*Eight Queens: Brute-Force Approaches*) In this exercise, you will develop several brute-force approaches to solving the Eight Queens problem introduced in Exercise 4.26.

a) Solve the Eight Queens exercise, using the random brute-force technique developed in Exercise 4.25.

b) Use an exhaustive technique, i.e., try all possible combinations of eight queens on the chessboard.

c) Why do you suppose the exhaustive brute-force approach may not be appropriate for solving the Knight's Tour problem?

d) Compare and contrast the random brute-force and exhaustive brute-force approaches in general.

4.28 (*Knight's Tour: Closed-Tour Test*) In the Knight's Tour, a full tour occurs when the knight makes 64 moves touching each square of the chess board once and only once. A closed tour occurs when the 64th move is one move away from the location in which the knight started the tour. Modify the Knight's Tour program you wrote in Exercise 4.24 to test for a closed tour if a full tour has occurred.

Fig. 4.31   The 22 squares eliminated by placing a queen in the upper-left corner.

4.29   (*The Sieve of Eratosthenes*) A prime integer is any integer that is evenly divisible only by itself and 1. The Sieve of Eratosthenes is a method of finding prime numbers. It operates as follows:

    a) Create an array with all elements initialized to 1 (true). Array elements with prime subscripts will remain 1. All other array elements will eventually be set to zero.

    b) Starting with array subscript 2, every time an array element is found whose value is 1, loop through the remainder of the array and set to zero every element whose subscript is a multiple of the subscript for the element with value 1. For array subscript 2, all elements beyond 2 in the array that are multiples of 2 will be set to zero (subscripts 4, 6, 8, 10, etc.); for array subscript 3, all elements beyond 3 in the array that are multiples of 3 will be set to zero (subscripts 6, 9, 12, 15, etc.); and so on.

When this process is complete, the array elements that are still set to one indicate that the subscript is a prime number. These subscripts can then be printed. Write a program that uses an array of 1000 elements to determine and print the prime numbers between 2 and 999. Ignore element 0 of the array.

4.30   (*Bucket Sort*) A bucket sort begins with a single-subscripted array of positive integers to be sorted and a double-subscripted array of integers with rows subscripted from 0 to 9 and columns subscripted from 0 to $n-1$, where n is the number of values in the array to be sorted. Each row of the double-subscripted array is referred to as a bucket. Write a function **bucketSort** that takes an integer array and the array size as arguments and performs as follows:

    a) Place each value of the single-subscripted array into a row of the bucket array based on the value's ones digit. For example, 97 is placed in row 7, 3 is placed in row 3 and 100 is placed in row 0. This is called a "distribution pass."

    b) Loop through the bucket array row by row, and copy the values back to the original array. This is called a "gathering pass." The new order of the preceding values in the single-subscripted array is 100, 3 and 97.

    c) Repeat this process for each subsequent digit position (tens, hundreds, thousands, etc.).

On the second pass, 100 is placed in row 0, 3 is placed in row 0 (because 3 has no tens digit) and 97 is placed in row 9. After the gathering pass, the order of the values in the single-subscripted array is 100, 3 and 97. On the third pass, 100 is placed in row 1, 3 is placed in row zero and 97 is placed in row zero (after the 3). After the last gathering pass, the original array is now in sorted order.

Note that the double-subscripted array of buckets is 10 times the size of the integer array being sorted. This sorting technique provides better performance than a bubble sort, but requires much more memory. The bubble sort requires space for only one additional element of data. This is an example of the space–time trade-off: The bucket sort uses more memory than the bubble sort, but performs better. This version of the bucket sort requires copying all the data back to the original array on each pass. Another possibility is to create a second double-subscripted bucket array and repeatedly swap the data between the two bucket arrays.

RECURSION EXERCISES

4.31   (*Selection Sort*) A selection sort searches an array looking for the smallest element in the array. Then, the smallest element is swapped with the first element of the array. The process is repeated for the subarray beginning with the second element of the array. Each pass of the array results in one element being placed in its proper location. This sort performs comparably to the bubble sort—for an array of n elements, $n-1$ passes must be made, and for each subarray, $n-1$ comparisons must be made to find the smallest value. When the subarray being processed contains one element, the array is sorted. Write recursive function **selectionSort** to perform this algorithm.

4.32   (*Palindromes*) A palindrome is a string that is spelled the same way forwards and backwards. Some examples of palindromes are "radar," "able was i ere i saw elba" and (if blanks are ignored) "a man a plan a canal panama." Write a recursive function **testPalindrome** that returns **true** if the string stored in the array is a palindrome, and **false** otherwise. The function should ignore spaces and punctuation in the string.

4.33   (*Linear Search*) Modify the program in Fig. 4.19 to use recursive function **linearSearch** to perform a linear search of the array. The function should receive an integer array and the size of the array as arguments. If the search key is found, return the array subscript; otherwise, return –1.

4.34   (*Binary Search*) Modify the program of Fig. 4.20 to use a recursive function **binary-Search** to perform the binary search of the array. The function should receive an integer array and the starting subscript and ending subscript as arguments. If the search key is found, return the array subscript; otherwise, return –1.

4.35   (*Eight Queens*) Modify the Eight Queens program you created in Exercise 4.26 to solve the problem recursively.

4.36   (*Print an array*) Write a recursive function **printArray** that takes an array and the size of the array as arguments and returns nothing. The function should stop processing and return when it receives an array of size zero.

4.37   (*Print a string backwards*) Write a recursive function **stringReverse** that takes a character array containing a string as an argument, prints the string backwards and returns nothing. The function should stop processing and return when the terminating null character is encountered.

4.38   (*Find the minimum value in an array*) Write a recursive function **recursiveMinimum** that takes an integer array and the array size as arguments and returns the smallest element of the array. The function should stop processing and return when it receives an array of 1 element.

5

Pointers and Strings

Objectives

- To be able to use pointers.
- To be able to use pointers to pass arguments to functions by reference.
- To understand the close relationships among pointers, arrays and strings.
- To understand the use of pointers to functions.
- To be able to declare and use arrays of strings.

Addresses are given to us to conceal our whereabouts.
Saki (H. H. Munro)

By indirections find directions out.
William Shakespeare

Many things, having full reference
To one consent, may work contrariously.
William Shakespeare

You will find it a very good practice always to verify your references, sir!
Dr. Routh

You can't trust code that you did not totally create yourself. (Especially code from companies that employ people like me.)
Ken Thompson

Outline

5.1   Introduction
5.2   Pointer Variable Declarations and Initialization
5.3   Pointer Operators
5.4   Calling Functions by Reference
5.5   Using const with Pointers
5.6   Bubble Sort Using Pass-by-Reference
5.7   Pointer Expressions and Pointer Arithmetic
5.8   Relationship Between Pointers and Arrays
5.9   Arrays of Pointers
5.10   Case Study: Card Shuffling and Dealing Simulation
5.11   Function Pointers
5.12   Introduction to Character and String Processing
        5.12.1 Fundamentals of Characters and Strings
        5.12.2 String Manipulation Functions of the String-Handling Library
5.13   (Optional Case Study) Thinking About Objects: Collaborations
        Among Objects

*Summary • Terminology • Self-Review Exercises • Answers to Self-Review Exercises • Exercises •
Special Section: Building Your Own Computer • More Pointer Exercises • String-Manipulation
Exercises • Special Section: Advanced String-Manipulation Exercises • A Challenging String-
Manipulation Project*

5.1 Introduction

This chapter discusses one of the most powerful features of the C++ programming language, the pointer. Pointers are among C++'s most difficult capabilities to master. In Chapter 3, we saw that references can be used to perform pass-by-reference. Pointers enable programs to simulate pass-by-reference and to create and manipulate dynamic data structures (i.e., data structures that can grow and shrink), such as linked lists, queues, stacks and trees. This chapter explains basic pointer concepts. This chapter also reinforces the intimate relationship among arrays, pointers and strings and includes a substantial collection of string-processing exercises.

Chapter 6 examines the use of pointers with structures and classes. In Chapter 9 and Chapter 10, we will see that the so-called "polymorphic processing" of object-oriented programming is performed with pointers and references. Chapter 17 presents examples of creating and using dynamic data structures.

The view of arrays and strings as pointers derives from C. Later in the book, we will discuss arrays and strings as full-fledged objects.

5.2 Pointer Variable Declarations and Initialization

Pointer variables contain memory addresses as their values. Normally, a variable directly contains a specific value. A pointer, on the other hand, contains the address of a variable that contains a specific value. In this sense, a variable name *directly* references a value, and a pointer *indirectly* references a value (Fig. 5.1). Referencing a value through a pointer is often called *indirection*. Note that diagrams typically represent a pointer as an arrow from the variable that contains an address to the variable located at that address in memory.

Pointers, like any other variables, must be declared before they can be used. For example, the declaration

```
int *countPtr, count;
```

declares the variable **countPtr** to be of type **int *** (i.e., a pointer to an **int** value) and is read, "**countPtr** is a pointer to **int**" or "**countPtr** points to an object of type **int**." Also, variable **count** in the preceding declaration is declared to be an **int**, not a pointer to an **int**. The ***** in the declaration applies only to **countPtr**. Each variable being declared as a pointer must be preceded by an asterisk (*****). For example, the declaration

```
double *xPtr, *yPtr;
```

indicates that both **xPtr** and **yPtr** are pointers to **double** values. When ***** appears in a declaration, it is not an operator; rather, it indicates that the variable being declared is a pointer. Pointers can be declared to point to objects of any data type.

Common Programming Error 5.1

*Assuming that the ***** used to declare a pointer distributes to all variable names in a declaration's comma-separated list of variables can lead to errors. Each pointer must be declared with the ***** prefixed to the name.*

Good Programming Practice 5.1

*Although it is not a requirement, including the letters **Ptr** in pointer variable names makes it clear that these variables are pointers and that they must be handled appropriately.*

Pointers should be initialized either when they are declared or in an assignment statement. A pointer may be initialized to **0**, **NULL** or an address. A pointer with the value **0** or **NULL** points to nothing. Symbolic constant **NULL** is defined in header file **<iostream>** (and in several other standard library header files) to represent the value **0**. Initializing a

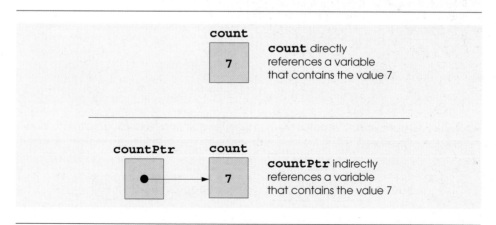

Fig. 5.1   Directly and indirectly referencing a variable.

pointer to **NULL** is equivalent to initializing a pointer to **0**, but in C++, **0** is used by convention. When **0** is assigned, it is converted to a pointer of the appropriate type. The value **0** is the only integer value that can be assigned directly to a pointer variable without casting the integer to a pointer type first. Assigning a variable's address to a pointer is discussed in Section 5.3.

Testing and Debugging Tip 5.1

Initialize pointers to prevent pointing to unknown or uninitialized areas of memory.

5.3 Pointer Operators

The *address operator* (**&**) is a unary operator that returns the memory address of its operand. For example, assuming the declarations

```
int y = 5;
int *yPtr;
```

the statement

```
yPtr = &y;
```

assigns the address of the variable **y** to pointer variable **yPtr**. Then variable **yPtr** is said to "point to" **y**. Now, **yPtr** indirectly references variable **y**'s value. Note that the **&** in the preceding assignment statement is not the same as the **&** in a reference variable declaration, which is always preceded by a data-type name.

Figure 5.2 shows a schematic representation of memory after the preceding assignment. In the figure, we show the "pointing relationship" by drawing an arrow from the box that represents the pointer **yPtr** in memory to the box that represents the variable **y** in memory.

Figure 5.3 shows another representation of the pointer in memory, assuming that integer variable **y** is stored at location **600000** and that pointer variable **yPtr** is stored at location **500000**. The operand of the address operator must be an *lvalue* (i.e., something to which a value can be assigned, such as a variable name); the address operator cannot be applied to constants or to expressions that do not result in references.

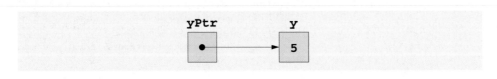

Fig. 5.2   Graphical representation of a pointer pointing to a variable in memory.

Fig. 5.3   Representation of **y** and **yPtr** in memory.

Operators						Associativity	Type
*	/	%				left to right	multiplicative
+	−					left to right	additive
<<	>>					left to right	insertion/extraction
<	<=	>	>=			left to right	relational
==	!=					left to right	equality
&&						left to right	logical AND
||						left to right	logical OR
?:						right to left	conditional
=	+=	−=	*=	/=	%=	right to left	assignment
,						left to right	comma

Fig. 5.5   Operator precedence and associativity. (Part 2 of 2.)

5.4 Calling Functions by Reference

There are three ways in C++ to pass arguments to a function—*pass-by-value, pass-by-reference with reference arguments* and *pass-by-reference with pointer arguments*. Chapter 3 compared and contrasted pass-by-value and pass-by-reference with reference arguments. This chapter concentrates on pass-by-reference with pointer arguments.

As we saw in Chapter 3, **return** can be used to return one value from a called function to a caller (or to return control from a called function without passing back a value). We also saw that arguments can be passed to a function using reference arguments. Such arguments enable the function to modify the original values of the arguments (thus, more than one value can be "returned" from a function). Reference arguments also enable programs to pass large data objects to a function and avoid the overhead of passing the objects by value (which, of course, requires making a copy of the object). Pointers, like references, also can be used to modify one or more variables in the caller or to pass pointers to large data objects to avoid the overhead of passing the objects by value.

In C++, programmers can use pointers and the indirection operator to simulate pass-by-reference (exactly as pass-by-reference is accomplished in C programs, because C does not have references). When calling a function with arguments that should be modified, the addresses of the arguments are passed. This is normally accomplished by applying the address operator (**&**) to the name of the variable whose value will be modified.

As we saw in Chapter 4, arrays are not passed using operator **&**, because the name of the array is the starting location in memory of the array (i.e., an array name is already a pointer). The name of an array is equivalent to **&arrayName[0]**. When the address of a variable is passed to a function, the indirection operator (*****) can be used in the function to form a synonym (i.e., an alias or a nickname) for the name of the variable—this in turn can be used to modify the value of the variable at that location in the caller's memory.

Figure 5.6 and Fig. 5.7 present two versions of a function that cubes an integer—**cubeByValue** and **cubeByReference**. Figure 5.6 passes variable **number** by value to function **cubeByValue** (line 17). Function **cubeByValue** (lines 26–30) cubes its argument and passes the new value back to **main** using a **return** statement (line 28). The new value is assigned to **number** in **main**. Note that you have the opportunity to examine the result of the function call before modifying variable **number**'s value. For example, in this program, we could have stored the result of **cubeByValue** in another variable, examined its value and assigned the result to **number** after determining whether the returned value was reasonable.

Figure 5.7 passes the variable **number** to function **cubeByReference** using pass-by-reference with a pointer argument (line 18)—the address of **number** is passed to the function. Function **cubeByReference** (lines 27–31) specifies parameter **nPtr** (a pointer to **int**) to receive its argument. The function dereferences the pointer and cubes the value to which **nPtr** points (line 29). This changes the value of **number** in **main**.

Common Programming Error 5.5

Not dereferencing a pointer when it is necessary to do so to obtain the value to which the pointer points is an error.

```cpp
1   // Fig. 5.6: fig05_06.cpp
2   // Cube a variable using pass-by-value.
3   #include <iostream>
4
5   using std::cout;
6   using std::endl;
7
8   int cubeByValue( int );    // prototype
9
10  int main()
11  {
12      int number = 5;
13
14      cout << "The original value of number is " << number;
15
16      // pass number by value to cubeByValue
17      number = cubeByValue( number );
18
19      cout << "\nThe new value of number is " << number << endl;
20
21      return 0;   // indicates successful termination
22
23  } // end main
24
25  // calculate and return cube of integer argument
26  int cubeByValue( int n )
27  {
28      return n * n * n; // cube local variable n and return result
29
30  } // end function cubeByValue
```

```
The original value of number is 5
The new value of number is 125
```

Fig. 5.6   Pass-by-value used to cube a variable's value.

```cpp
1   // Fig. 5.7: fig05_07.cpp
2   // Cube a variable using pass-by-reference
3   // with a pointer argument.
4   #include <iostream>
5
6   using std::cout;
7   using std::endl;
8
9   void cubeByReference( int * );    // prototype
10
11  int main()
12  {
13     int number = 5;
14
15     cout << "The original value of number is " << number;
16
17     // pass address of number to cubeByReference
18     cubeByReference( &number );
19
20     cout << "\nThe new value of number is " << number << endl;
21
22     return 0;  // indicates successful termination
23
24  } // end main
25
26  // calculate cube of *nPtr; modifies variable number in main
27  void cubeByReference( int *nPtr )
28  {
29     *nPtr = *nPtr * *nPtr * *nPtr;  // cube *nPtr
30
31  } // end function cubeByReference
```

```
The original value of number is 5
The new value of number is 125
```

Fig. 5.7   Pass-by-reference with a pointer argument used to cube a variable's value.

A function receiving an address as an argument must define a pointer parameter to receive the address. For example, the header for function **cubeByReference** (line 27) specifies that **cubeByReference** receives the address of an **int** variable (i.e., a pointer to an **int**) as an argument, stores the address locally in **nPtr** and does not return a value.

The function prototype for **cubeByReference** (line 9) contains **int *** in parentheses. As with other variable types, it is not necessary to include names of pointer parameters in function prototypes. Parameter names included for documentation purposes are ignored by the compiler.

Figure 5.8 and Fig. 5.9 analyze graphically the execution of the programs in Fig. 5.6 and Fig. 5.7, respectively.

Software Engineering Observation 5.1

Use pass-by-value to pass arguments to a function unless the caller explicitly requires that the called function modify the value of the argument variable in the caller's environment. This is another example of the principle of least privilege.

Before **main** calls **cubeByValue**:

```
int main()                        number
{
    int number = 5;                 5
    number = cubeByValue( number );
}
```

```
int cubeByValue( int n )
{
    return n * n * n;
}
                                n
                          undefined
```

After **cubeByValue** receives the call:

```
int main()                        number
{
    int number = 5;                 5
    number = cubeByValue( number );
}
```

```
int cubeByValue( int n )
{
    return n * n * n;
}
                                n
                                5
```

After **cubeByValue** cubes parameter **n** and before **cubeByValue** returns to **main**:

```
int main()                        number
{
    int number = 5;                 5
    number = cubeByValue( number );
}
```

```
int cubeByValue( int n )
{            125
    return n * n * n;
}
                                n
                                5
```

After **cubeByValue** returns to **main** and before assigning the result to **number**:

```
int main()                        number
{
    int number = 5;                 5
             125
    number = cubeByValue( number );
}
```

```
int cubeByValue( int n )
{
    return n * n * n;
}
                                n
                          undefined
```

After **main** completes the assignment to **number**:

```
int main()                        number
{
    int number = 5;                125
       125          125
    number = cubeByValue( number );
}
```

```
int cubeByValue( int n )
{
    return n * n * n;
}
                                n
                          undefined
```

Fig. 5.8   Pass-by-value analysis of the program of Fig. 5.6.

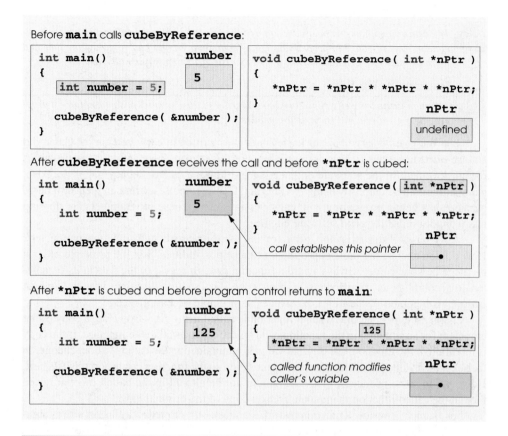

Fig. 5.9   Pass-by-reference analysis (with a pointer argument) of the program of Fig. 5.7.

In the function header and in the prototype for a function that expects a single-subscripted array as an argument, the pointer notation in the parameter list of **cubeByReference** may be used. The compiler does not differentiate between a function that receives a pointer and a function that receives a single-subscripted array. This, of course, means that the function must "know" when it is receiving an array or simply a single variable for which it is to perform pass-by-reference. When the compiler encounters a function parameter for a single-subscripted array of the form **int b[]**, the compiler converts the parameter to the pointer notation **int * const b** (pronounced "**b** is a constant pointer to an integer"—**const** pointers are explained in Section 5.5). Both forms of declaring a function parameter as a single-subscripted array are interchangeable.

5.5 Using **const** with Pointers

The **const** *qualifier* enables the programmer to inform the compiler that the value of a particular variable should not be modified.

Software Engineering Observation 5.2

*The **const** qualifier can be used to enforce the principle of least privilege. Using the principle of least privilege to properly design software can greatly reduce debugging time and improper side effects and can make a program easier to modify and maintain.*

Portability Tip 5.2

*Although **const** is well defined in ANSI C and C++, some compilers do not enforce it properly. So a good rule is, "know your compiler."*

Over the years, a large base of legacy code was written in early versions of C that did not use **const**, because it was not available. For this reason, there are great opportunities for improvement in the software engineering of old (also called "legacy") C code. Also, many programmers currently using ANSI C and C++ do not use **const** in their programs, because they began programming in early versions of C. These programmers are missing many opportunities for good software engineering.

Many possibilities exist for using (or not using) **const** with function parameters. How do you choose the most appropriate of these possibilities? Let the principle of least privilege be your guide. Always award a function enough access to the data in its parameters to accomplish its specified task, but no more. This section discusses how to combine **const** with pointer declarations to enforce the principle of least privilege.

Chapter 3 explained that when a function is called using pass-by-value, a copy of the argument (or arguments) in the function call is made and passed to the function. If the copy is modified in the function, the original value is maintained in the caller without change. In many cases, a value passed to a function is modified so the function can accomplish its task. However, in some instances, the value should not be altered in the called function, even though the called function manipulates only a copy of the original value.

For example, consider a function that takes a single-subscripted array and its size as arguments and subsequently prints the array. Such a function should loop through the array and output each array element individually. The size of the array is used in the function body to determine the highest subscript of the array so the loop can terminate when the printing completes. The size of the array does not change in the function body, so it should be declared **const**. Of course, because the array is only being printed, it, too, should be declared **const**.

Software Engineering Observation 5.3

*If a value does not (or should not) change in the body of a function to which it is passed, the parameter should be declared **const** to ensure that it is not accidentally modified.*

If an attempt is made to modify a **const** value, a warning or an error is issued, depending on the particular compiler.

Software Engineering Observation 5.4

Only one value can be returned to the caller when pass-by-value is used. To modify multiple values in a calling function, several arguments can be passed by reference.

Good Programming Practice 5.2

Before using a function, check its function prototype to determine the parameters that it can modify.

There are four ways to pass a pointer to a function: a nonconstant pointer to nonconstant data (Fig. 5.10), a nonconstant pointer to constant data (Fig. 5.11 and Fig. 5.12), a constant pointer to non-constant data (Fig. 5.13) and a constant pointer to constant data (Fig. 5.14). Each combination provides a different level of access privileges.

Nonconstant Pointer to Nonconstant Data

The highest access is granted by a nonconstant pointer to nonconstant data—the data can be modified through the dereferenced pointer, and the pointer can be modified to point to other data. Declarations for nonconstant pointers to nonconstant data do not include **const**. Such a pointer can be used to receive a string in a function that changes the pointer value to process (and possibly modify) each character in the string. In Fig. 5.10, function **convertToUppercase** (lines 27–38) declares parameter **sPtr** (line 27) to be a non-constant pointer to nonconstant data. The function processes the string **phrase** one character at a time (lines 29–36). Function **islower** (line 31) takes a character argument and returns true if the character is a lowercase letter and false otherwise. Characters in the range **'a'** through **'z'** are converted to their corresponding uppercase letters by function **toupper** (line 32); others remain unchanged. Function **toupper** takes one character as an argument. If the character is a lowercase letter, the corresponding uppercase letter is returned; otherwise, the original character is returned. Function **toupper** and function **islower** are part of the character handling library **<cctype>**. (See Chapter 18, Bits, Characters, Strings and Structures.) After processing one character, line 34 increments **sPtr** by 1. When operator **++** is applied to a pointer that points to an array, the memory address stored in the pointer is modified to point to the next element of the array (in this case, the next character in the string). Adding one to a pointer is one valid operation in *pointer arithmetic*, which is covered in detail in Section 5.7 and Section 5.8.

```
1   // Fig. 5.10: fig05_10.cpp
2   // Converting lowercase letters to uppercase letters
3   // using a non-constant pointer to non-constant data.
4   #include <iostream>
5
6   using std::cout;
7   using std::endl;
8
9   #include <cctype>     // prototypes for islower and toupper
10
11  void convertToUppercase( char * );
12
13  int main()
14  {
15     char phrase[] = "characters and $32.98";
16
17     cout << "The phrase before conversion is: " << phrase;
18     convertToUppercase( phrase );
19     cout << "\nThe phrase after conversion is:  "
20          << phrase << endl;
21
22     return 0;  // indicates successful termination
23
24  } // end main
25
```

Fig. 5.10   Converting a string to uppercase. (Part 1 of 2.)

```
26   // convert string to uppercase letters
27   void convertToUppercase( char *sPtr )
28   {
29      while ( *sPtr != '\0' ) {    // current character is not '\0'
30
31         if ( islower( *sPtr ) )   // if character is lowercase,
32            *sPtr = toupper( *sPtr );   // convert to uppercase
33
34         ++sPtr;   // move sPtr to next character in string
35
36      } // end while
37
38   } // end function convertToUppercase
```

```
The phrase before conversion is: characters and $32.98
The phrase after conversion is:  CHARACTERS AND $32.98
```

Fig. 5.10   Converting a string to uppercase. (Part 2 of 2.)

Nonconstant Pointer to Constant Data

A nonconstant pointer to constant data is a pointer that can be modified to point to any data item of the appropriate type, but the data to which it points cannot be modified through that pointer. Such a pointer might be used to receive an array argument to a function that will process each element of the array, but should not be allowed to modify the data. For example, function **printCharacters** (lines 25–30 of Fig. 5.11) declares parameter **sPtr** (line 25) to be of type **const char ***. The declaration is read from right to left as "**sPtr** is a pointer to a character constant." The body of the function uses a **for** structure (lines 27–28) to output each character in the string until the null character is encountered. After each character is printed, pointer **sPtr** is incremented to point to the next character in the string.

```
1    // Fig. 5.11: fig05_11.cpp
2    // Printing a string one character at a time using
3    // a non-constant pointer to constant data.
4    #include <iostream>
5
6    using std::cout;
7    using std::endl;
8
9    void printCharacters( const char * );
10
11   int main()
12   {
13      char phrase[] = "print characters of a string";
14
15      cout << "The string is:\n";
16      printCharacters( phrase );
17      cout << endl;
18
```

Fig. 5.11   Printing a string one character at a time using a nonconstant pointer to constant data. (Part 1 of 2.)

```
19       return 0;   // indicates successful termination
20
21   } // end main
22
23   // sPtr cannot modify the character to which it points,
24   // i.e., sPtr is a "read-only" pointer
25   void printCharacters( const char *sPtr )
26   {
27      for ( ; *sPtr != '\0'; sPtr++ )     // no initialization
28         cout << *sPtr;
29
30   } // end function printCharacters
```

```
The string is:
print characters of a string
```

Fig. 5.11   Printing a string one character at a time using a nonconstant pointer to constant data. (Part 2 of 2.)

Figure 5.12 demonstrates the syntax error messages produced when attempting to compile a function that receives a nonconstant pointer to constant data, then tries to use that pointer to modify the data.

```
1    // Fig. 5.12: fig05_12.cpp
2    // Attempting to modify data through a
3    // non-constant pointer to constant data.
4
5    void f( const int * );   // prototype
6
7    int main()
8    {
9       int y;
10
11      f( &y );     // f attempts illegal modification
12
13      return 0;   // indicates successful termination
14
15   } // end main
16
17   // xPtr cannot modify the value of the variable
18   // to which it points
19   void f( const int *xPtr )
20   {
21      *xPtr = 100;   // error: cannot modify a const object
22
23   } // end function f
```

```
d:\cpphtp4_examples\ch05\Fig05_12.cpp(21) : error C2166:
   l-value specifies const object
```

Fig. 5.12   Attempting to modify data through a nonconstant pointer to constant data.

As we know, arrays are aggregate data types that store related data items of the same type under one name. Chapter 6 discusses another form of aggregate data type called a *structure* (sometimes called a *record* in other languages). A structure can store data items of different data types under one name (e.g., storing information about each employee of a company). When a function is called with an array as an argument, the array is passed to the function by reference. However, structures are always passed by value—a copy of the entire structure is passed. This requires the execution-time overhead of making a copy of each data item in the structure and storing it on the function call stack (the place where the local automatic variables used in the function call are stored while the function is executing). When structure data must be passed to a function, we can use a pointer to constant data (or a reference to constant data) to get the performance of pass-by-reference and the protection of pass-by-value. When a pointer to a structure is passed, only a copy of the address at which the structure is stored must be made; the structure itself is not copied. On a machine with four-byte addresses, a copy of four bytes of memory is made rather than a copy of a possibly large structure.

Performance Tip 5.1

Pass large objects such as structures using pointers to constant data, or references to constant data, to obtain the performance benefits of pass-by-reference.

Software Engineering Observation 5.5

Pass large objects such as structures using pointers to constant data, or references to constant data, to obtain the security of pass-by-value.

Constant Pointer to Nonconstant Data

A constant pointer to nonconstant data is a pointer that always points to the same memory location; the data at that location can be modified through the pointer. This is the default for an array name. An array name is a constant pointer to the beginning of the array. All data in the array can be accessed and changed by using the array name and array subscripting. A constant pointer to nonconstant data can be used to receive an array as an argument to a function that accesses array elements using array subscript notation. Pointers that are declared **const** must be initialized when they are declared. (If the pointer is a function parameter, it is initialized with a pointer that is passed to the function.) The program of Fig. 5.13 attempts to modify a constant pointer. Line 12 declares pointer **ptr** to be of type **int * const**. The declaration in the figure is read from right to left as "**ptr** is a constant pointer to an integer." The pointer is initialized with the address of integer variable **x**. Line 15 attempts to assign the address of **y** to **ptr**, but the compiler generates an error message. Note that no error occurs when line 14 assigns the value **7** to ***ptr**—the nonconstant value to which **ptr** points can be modified using **ptr**.

```
1   // Fig. 5.13: fig05_13.cpp
2   // Attempting to modify a constant pointer to
3   // non-constant data.
4
5   int main()
6   {
7       int x, y;
8
```

Fig. 5.13   Attempting to modify a constant pointer to nonconstant data. (Part 1 of 2.)

```
9       // ptr is a constant pointer to an integer that can
10      // be modified through ptr, but ptr always points to the
11      // same memory location.
12      int * const ptr = &x;
13
14      *ptr = 7;   // allowed: *ptr is not const
15      ptr = &y;   // error: ptr is const; cannot assign new address
16
17      return 0;   // indicates successful termination
18
19   } // end main
```

```
d:\cpphtp4_examples\ch05\Fig05_13.cpp(15) : error C2166:
   1-value specifies const object
```

Fig. 5.13   Attempting to modify a constant pointer to nonconstant data. (Part 2 of 2.)

 Common Programming Error 5.6

Not initializing a pointer that is declared **const** *is a syntax error.*

Constant Pointer to Constant Data

The least amount of access privilege is granted by a constant pointer to constant data. Such a pointer always points to the same memory location, and the data at that memory location cannot be modified using the pointer. This is how an array should be passed to a function that only reads the array, using array subscript notation, and does not modify the array. The program of Fig. 5.14 declares pointer variable **ptr** to be of type **const int * const** (line 15). This declaration is read from right to left as "**ptr** is a constant pointer to an integer constant." The figure shows the error messages generated when an attempt is made to modify the data to which **ptr** points (line 19) and when an attempt is made to modify the address stored in the pointer variable (line 20). Note that no errors occur when the program attempts to dereference **ptr**, or when the program attempts to output the value to which **ptr** points (line 17), because neither the pointer nor the data it points to is being modified in this statement.

```
1   // Fig. 5.14: fig05_14.cpp
2   // Attempting to modify a constant pointer to constant data.
3   #include <iostream>
4
5   using std::cout;
6   using std::endl;
7
8   int main()
9   {
10      int x = 5, y;
11
12      // ptr is a constant pointer to a constant integer.
13      // ptr always points to the same location; the integer
14      // at that location cannot be modified.
```

Fig. 5.14   Attempting to modify a constant pointer to constant data. (Part 1 of 2.)

```
15    const int *const ptr = &x;
16
17    cout << *ptr << endl;
18
19    *ptr = 7;   // error: *ptr is const; cannot assign new value
20    ptr = &y;   // error: ptr is const; cannot assign new address
21
22    return 0;   // indicates successful termination
23
24  } // end main
```

```
d:\cpphtp4_examples\ch05\Fig05_14.cpp(19) : error C2166:
   l-value specifies const object
d:\cpphtp4_examples\ch05\Fig05_14.cpp(20) : error C2166:
   l-value specifies const object
```

Fig. 5.14   Attempting to modify a constant pointer to constant data. (Part 2 of 2.)

5.6 Bubble Sort Using Pass-by-Reference

Let us modify the bubble sort program of Fig. 4.16 to use two functions—**bubbleSort** and **swap** (Fig. 5.15). Function **bubbleSort** (lines 40–52) performs the sort of the array. Function **bubbleSort** calls function **swap** (line 50) to exchange the array elements **array[k]** and **array[k + 1]**. Remember that C++ enforces information hiding between functions, so **swap** does not have access to individual array elements in **bubbleSort**. Because **bubbleSort** *wants* **swap** to have access to the array elements to be swapped, **bubbleSort** passes each of these elements by reference to **swap**—the address of each array element is passed explicitly. Although entire arrays are passed by reference, individual array elements are scalars and are ordinarily passed by value. Therefore, **bubbleSort** uses the address operator (**&**) on each array element in the **swap** call (line 50 to effect pass-by-reference). Function **swap** (lines 56–62) receives **&array[k]** in pointer variable **element1Ptr**. Information hiding prevents **swap** from "knowing" the name **array[k]**, but **swap** can use ***element1Ptr** as a synonym for **array[k]**. Thus, when **swap** references ***element1Ptr**, it is actually referencing **array[k]** in **bubbleSort**. Similarly, when **swap** references ***element2Ptr**, it is actually referencing **array[k + 1]** in **bubbleSort**.

```
1   // Fig. 5.15: fig05_15.cpp
2   // This program puts values into an array, sorts the values into
3   // ascending order and prints the resulting array.
4   #include <iostream>
5
6   using std::cout;
7   using std::endl;
8
9   #include <iomanip>
10
```

Fig. 5.15   Bubble sort with pass-by-reference. (Part 1 of 3.)

```cpp
11   using std::setw;
12
13   void bubbleSort( int *, const int );    // prototype
14   void swap( int * const, int * const );  // prototype
15
16   int main()
17   {
18      const int arraySize = 10;
19      int a[ arraySize ] = { 2, 6, 4, 8, 10, 12, 89, 68, 45, 37 };
20
21      cout << "Data items in original order\n";
22
23      for ( int i = 0; i < arraySize; i++ )
24         cout << setw( 4 ) << a[ i ];
25
26      bubbleSort( a, arraySize );  // sort the array
27
28      cout << "\nData items in ascending order\n";
29
30      for ( int j = 0; j < arraySize; j++ )
31         cout << setw( 4 ) << a[ j ];
32
33      cout << endl;
34
35      return 0;  // indicates successful termination
36
37   } // end main
38
39   // sort an array of integers using bubble sort algorithm
40   void bubbleSort( int *array, const int size )
41   {
42      // loop to control passes
43      for ( int pass = 0; pass < size - 1; pass++ )
44
45         // loop to control comparisons during each pass
46         for ( int k = 0; k < size - 1; k++ )
47
48            // swap adjacent elements if they are out of order
49            if ( array[ k ] > array[ k + 1 ] )
50               swap( &array[ k ], &array[ k + 1 ] );
51
52   } // end function bubbleSort
53
54   // swap values at memory locations to which
55   // element1Ptr and element2Ptr point
56   void swap( int * const element1Ptr, int * const element2Ptr )
57   {
58      int hold = *element1Ptr;
59      *element1Ptr = *element2Ptr;
60      *element2Ptr = hold;
61
62   } // end function swap
```

Fig. 5.15   Bubble sort with pass-by-reference. (Part 2 of 3.)

```
Data items in original order
   2    6    4    8   10   12   89   68   45   37
Data items in ascending order
   2    4    6    8   10   12   37   45   68   89
```

Fig. 5.15   Bubble sort with pass-by-reference. (Part 3 of 3.)

Even though **swap** is not allowed to use the statements

```
hold = array[ k ];
array[ k ] = array[ k + 1 ];
array[ k + 1 ] = hold;
```

precisely the same effect is achieved by

```
int hold = *element1Ptr;
*element1Ptr = *element2Ptr;
*element2Ptr = hold;
```

in the **swap** function of Fig. 5.15.

Several features of function **bubbleSort** should be noted. The function header (line 40) declares **array** as **int *array**, rather than **int array[]**, to indicate that function **bubbleSort** receives a single-subscripted array as an argument (again, these notations are interchangeable). Parameter **size** is declared **const** to enforce the principle of least privilege. Although parameter **size** receives a copy of a value in **main** and modifying the copy cannot change the value in **main**, **bubbleSort** does not need to alter **size** to accomplish its task. The array size remains fixed during the execution of **bubbleSort**. Therefore, **size** is declared **const** to ensure that it is not modified. If the size of the array is modified during the sorting process, the sorting algorithm will not run correctly.

Note that function **bubbleSort** receives the size of the array as a parameter, because the function must know the size of the array to sort the array. When an array is passed to a function, the memory address of the first element of the array is received by the function. The array size must be passed separately to the function.

By defining function **bubbleSort** so it receives the array size as a parameter, we enable the function to be used by any program that sorts single-subscripted **int** arrays of arbitrary size. The size of the array could have been programmed directly into the function. This would restrict the use of the function to an array of a specific size and reduce the function's reusability. Only programs processing single-subscripted **int** arrays of the specific size "hard coded" into the function could use the function.

Software Engineering Observation 5.6

When passing an array to a function, also pass the size of the array (rather than building into the function knowledge of the array size). This helps make the function more general. General functions are often reusable in many programs.

C++ provides the *unary operator **sizeof*** to determine the size of an array (or of any other data type, variable or constant) in bytes during program compilation. When applied to the name of an array, as in Fig. 5.16 (line 16), the **sizeof** operator returns the total number of bytes in the array as a value of type **size_t** (which is usually **unsigned int**). The computer we used to compile this program stores variables of type **double** in 8 bytes of memory, and **array** is declared to have 20 elements, so **array** uses 160 bytes in memory.

When applied to a pointer parameter (line 28) in a function that receives an array as an argument, the **sizeof** operator returns the size of the pointer in bytes (4), not the size of the array.

Common Programming Error 5.7

*Using the **sizeof** operator in a function to find the size in bytes of an array parameter results in the size in bytes of a pointer, not the size in bytes of the array.*

The number of elements in an array also can be determined using the results of two **sizeof** operations. For example, consider the following array declaration:

```
double realArray[ 22 ];
```

If variables of data type **double** are stored in eight bytes of memory, array **realArray** contains a total of 176 bytes. To determine the number of elements in the array, the following expression can be used:

```
sizeof realArray / sizeof( double )
```

```cpp
1   // Fig. 5.16: fig05_16.cpp
2   // Sizeof operator when used on an array name
3   // returns the number of bytes in the array.
4   #include <iostream>
5
6   using std::cout;
7   using std::endl;
8
9   size_t getSize( double * );   // prototype
10
11  int main()
12  {
13     double array[ 20 ];
14
15     cout << "The number of bytes in the array is "
16          << sizeof( array );
17
18     cout << "\nThe number of bytes returned by getSize is "
19          << getSize( array ) << endl;
20
21     return 0;  // indicates successful termination
22
23  } // end main
24
25  // return size of ptr
26  size_t getSize( double *ptr )
27  {
28     return sizeof( ptr );
29
30  } // end function getSize
```

```
The number of bytes in the array is 160
The number of bytes returned by getSize is 4
```

Fig. 5.16 **sizeof** operator when applied to an array name returns the number of bytes in the array.

The expression determines the number of bytes in array **realArray** and divides that value by the number of bytes used in memory to store a **double** value; the result is the number of elements in **realArray**.

The program of Fig. 5.17 uses the **sizeof** operator to calculate the number of bytes used to store each of the standard data types.

Portability Tip 5.3

*The number of bytes used to store a particular data type may vary between systems. When writing programs that depend on data type sizes, and that will run on several computer systems, use **sizeof** to determine the number of bytes used to store the data types.*

```cpp
1   // Fig. 5.17: fig05_17.cpp
2   // Demonstrating the sizeof operator.
3   #include <iostream>
4
5   using std::cout;
6   using std::endl;
7
8   int main()
9   {
10      char c;
11      short s;
12      int i;
13      long l;
14      float f;
15      double d;
16      long double ld;
17      int array[ 20 ];
18      int *ptr = array;
19
20      cout << "sizeof c = " << sizeof c
21           << "\tsizeof(char) = " << sizeof( char )
22           << "\nsizeof s = " << sizeof s
23           << "\tsizeof(short) = " << sizeof( short )
24           << "\nsizeof i = " << sizeof i
25           << "\tsizeof(int) = " << sizeof( int )
26           << "\nsizeof l = " << sizeof l
27           << "\tsizeof(long) = " << sizeof( long )
28           << "\nsizeof f = " << sizeof f
29           << "\tsizeof(float) = " << sizeof( float )
30           << "\nsizeof d = " << sizeof d
31           << "\tsizeof(double) = " << sizeof( double )
32           << "\nsizeof ld = " << sizeof ld
33           << "\tsizeof(long double) = " << sizeof( long double )
34           << "\nsizeof array = " << sizeof array
35           << "\nsizeof ptr = " << sizeof ptr
36           << endl;
37
38      return 0;  // indicates successful termination
39
40   } // end main
```

Fig. 5.17   **sizeof** operator used to determine standard data type sizes. (Part 1 of 2.)

```
sizeof c = 1      sizeof(char) = 1
sizeof s = 2      sizeof(short) = 2
sizeof i = 4      sizeof(int) = 4
sizeof l = 4      sizeof(long) = 4
sizeof f = 4      sizeof(float) = 4
sizeof d = 8      sizeof(double) = 8
sizeof ld = 8     sizeof(long double) = 8
sizeof array = 80
sizeof ptr = 4
```

Fig. 5.17   **sizeof** operator used to determine standard data type sizes. (Part 2 of 2.)

Operator **sizeof** can be applied to any variable name, type name or constant value. When **sizeof** is applied to a variable name (which is not an array name) or a constant value, the number of bytes used to store the specific type of variable or constant is returned. Note that the parentheses used with **sizeof** are required only if a type name is supplied as its operand. The parentheses used with **sizeof** are not required when **sizeof**'s operand is a variable name or constant. Remember that **sizeof** is an operator, not a function, and that it has its effect at compile time, not execution time.

Common Programming Error 5.8

*Omitting the parentheses in a **sizeof** operation when the operand is a type name is a syntax error.*

Performance Tip 5.2

*Because **sizeof** is a compile-time unary operator, not an execution-time operator, using **sizeof** does not negatively impact execution performance.*

Testing and Debugging Tip 5.2

*To avoid errors associated with omitting the parentheses around the operand of operator **sizeof**, many programmers include parentheses around every **sizeof** operand.*

5.7 Pointer Expressions and Pointer Arithmetic

Pointers are valid operands in arithmetic expressions, assignment expressions and comparison expressions. However, not all the operators normally used in these expressions are valid with pointer variables. This section describes the operators that can have pointers as operands and how these operators are used with pointers.

Several arithmetic operations may be performed on pointers. A pointer may be incremented (**++**) or decremented (**--**), an integer may be added to a pointer (**+** or **+=**), an integer may be subtracted from a pointer (**-** or **-=**) or one pointer may be subtracted from another.

Assume that array **int v[5]** has been declared and that its first element is at location **3000** in memory. Assume that pointer **vPtr** has been initialized to point to **v[0]** (i.e., that the value of **vPtr** is **3000**). Figure 5.18 diagrams this situation for a machine with four-byte integers. Note that **vPtr** can be initialized to point to array **v** with either of the following statements:

```
vPtr = v;
vPtr = &v[ 0 ];
```

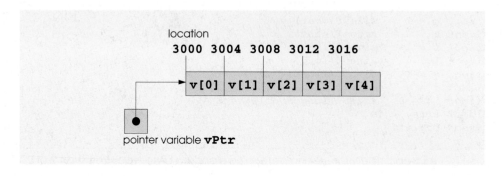

Fig. 5.18   Array **v** and a pointer variable **vPtr** that points to **v**.

 Portability Tip 5.4

Most computers today have two-byte or four-byte integers. Some of the newer machines use eight-byte integers. Because the results of pointer arithmetic depend on the size of the objects a pointer points to, pointer arithmetic is machine dependent.

In conventional arithmetic, the addition **3000 + 2** yields the value **3002**. This is normally not the case with pointer arithmetic. When an integer is added to, or subtracted from, a pointer, the pointer is not simply incremented or decremented by that integer, but by that integer times the size of the object to which the pointer refers. The number of bytes depends on the object's data type. For example, the statement

```
vPtr += 2;
```

would produce **3008** (**3000 + 2 * 4**), assuming that an **int** is stored in four bytes of memory. In the array **v**, **vPtr** would now point to **v[2]** (Fig. 5.19). If an integer is stored in two bytes of memory, then the preceding calculation would result in memory location **3004** (**3000 + 2 * 2**). If the array were of a different data type, the preceding statement would increment the pointer by twice the number of bytes it takes to store an object of that data type. When performing pointer arithmetic on a character array, the results will be consistent with regular arithmetic, because each character is one byte long.

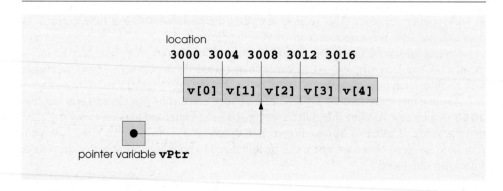

Fig. 5.19   Pointer **vPtr** after pointer arithmetic.

If **vPtr** had been incremented to **3016**, which points to **v[4]**, the statement

```
vPtr -= 4;
```

would set **vPtr** back to **3000**—the beginning of the array. If a pointer is being incremented or decremented by one, the increment (**++**) and decrement (**--**) operators can be used. Each of the statements

```
++vPtr;
vPtr++;
```

increments the pointer to point to the next element of the array. Each of the statements

```
--vPtr;
vPtr--;
```

decrements the pointer to point to the previous element of the array.

Pointer variables pointing to the same array may be subtracted from one another. For example, if **vPtr** contains the location **3000** and **v2Ptr** contains the address **3008**, the statement

```
x = v2Ptr - vPtr;
```

would assign to **x** the number of array elements from **vPtr** to **v2Ptr**, in this case, **2**. Pointer arithmetic is meaningless unless performed on a pointer that points to an array. We cannot assume that two variables of the same type are stored contiguously in memory unless they are adjacent elements of an array.

Common Programming Error 5.9

Using pointer arithmetic on a pointer that does not refer to an array of values is a logic error.

Common Programming Error 5.10

Subtracting or comparing two pointers that do not refer to elements of the same array is a logic error.

Common Programming Error 5.11

Using pointer arithmetic to increment or decrement a pointer such that the pointer refers to an element past the end of the array or before the beginning of the array is normally a logic error.

A pointer can be assigned to another pointer if both pointers are of the same type. Otherwise, a cast operator must be used to convert the value of the pointer on the right of the assignment to the pointer type on the left of the assignment. The exception to this rule is the pointer to **void** (i.e., **void ***), which is a generic pointer capable of representing any pointer type. All pointer types can be assigned to a pointer of type **void *** without casting. However, a pointer of type **void *** cannot be assigned directly to a pointer of another type—the pointer of type **void *** must first be cast to the proper pointer type.

A **void *** pointer cannot be dereferenced. For example, the compiler "knows" that a pointer to **int** refers to four bytes of memory on a machine with four-byte integers, but a pointer to **void** simply contains a memory address for an unknown data type—the precise number of bytes to which the pointer refers is not known by the compiler. The compiler must know the data type to determine the number of bytes to be dereferenced for a particular pointer. For a pointer to **void**, this number of bytes cannot be determined from the type.

Common Programming Error 5.12

*Assigning a pointer of one type to a pointer of another (other than **void ***) without casting the first pointer to the type of the second pointer is a syntax error.*

Common Programming Error 5.13

*All operations on a **void *** pointer are syntax errors, except comparing **void *** pointers with other pointers, casting **void *** pointers to valid pointer types and assigning addresses to **void *** pointers.*

Pointers can be compared using equality and relational operators. Comparisons using relational operators are meaningless unless the pointers point to members of the same array. Pointer comparisons compare the addresses stored in the pointers. A comparison of two pointers pointing to the same array could show, for example, that one pointer points to a higher numbered element of the array than the other pointer does. A common use of pointer comparison is determining whether a pointer is 0 (i.e., the pointer does not point to anything).

5.8 Relationship Between Pointers and Arrays

Arrays and pointers are intimately related in C++ and may be used *almost* interchangeably. An array name can be thought of as a constant pointer. Pointers can be used to do any operation involving array subscripting.

Assume the following declarations:

```
int b[ 5 ];
int *bPtr;
```

Because the array name (without a subscript) is a pointer to the first element of the array, we can set **bPtr** to the address of the first element in array **b** with the statement

```
bPtr = b;
```

This is equivalent to taking the address of the first element of the array as follows:

```
bPtr = &b[ 0 ];
```

Array element **b[3]** can alternatively be referenced with the pointer expression

```
*( bPtr + 3 )
```

The **3** in the preceding expression is the *offset* to the pointer. When the pointer points to the beginning of an array, the offset indicates which element of the array should be referenced, and the offset value is identical to the array subscript. The preceding notation is referred to as *pointer/offset notation*. The parentheses are necessary, because the precedence of ***** is higher than the precedence of **+**. Without the parentheses, the above expression would add **3** to the value of the expression ***bPtr** (i.e., **3** would be added to **b[0]**, assuming that **bPtr** points to the beginning of the array). Just as the array element can be referenced with a pointer expression, the address

```
&b[ 3 ]
```

can be written with the pointer expression

    bPtr + 3

The array name can be treated as a pointer and used in pointer arithmetic. For example, the expression

    *(b + 3)

also refers to the array element **b[3]**. In general, all subscripted array expressions can be written with a pointer and an offset. In this case, pointer/offset notation was used with the name of the array as a pointer. Note that the preceding expression does not modify the array name in any way; **b** still points to the first element in the array.

Pointers can be subscripted exactly as arrays can. For example, the expression

    bPtr[1]

refers to the array element **b[1]**; this expression uses *pointer/subscript notation*.

Remember that an array name is essentially a constant pointer; it always points to the beginning of the array. Thus, the expression

    b += 3

is invalid, because it attempts to modify the value of the array name with pointer arithmetic.

Common Programming Error 5.14

Although array names are pointers to the beginning of the array and pointers can be modified in arithmetic expressions, array names cannot be modified in arithmetic expressions, because array names are constant pointers.

Good Programming Practice 5.3

For clarity, use array notation instead of pointer notation when manipulating arrays.

Figure 5.20 uses the four notations discussed in this section for referring to array elements—array subscript notation, pointer/offset notation with the array name as a pointer, pointer subscript notation and pointer/offset notation with a pointer—to print the four elements of the integer array **b**.

```
1   // Fig. 5.20: fig05_20.cpp
2   // Using subscripting and pointer notations with arrays.
3
4   #include <iostream>
5
6   using std::cout;
7   using std::endl;
8
9   int main()
10  {
```

Fig. 5.20   Referencing array elements with the array name and with pointers. (Part 1 of 3.)

```
11        int b[] = { 10, 20, 30, 40 };
12        int *bPtr = b;    // set bPtr to point to array b
13
14        // output array b using array subscript notation
15        cout << "Array b printed with:\n"
16             << "Array subscript notation\n";
17
18        for ( int i = 0; i < 4; i++ )
19           cout << "b[" << i << "] = " << b[ i ] << '\n';
20
21        // output array b using the array name and
22        // pointer/offset notation
23        cout << "\nPointer/offset notation where "
24             << "the pointer is the array name\n";
25
26        for ( int offset1 = 0; offset1 < 4; offset1++ )
27           cout << "*(b + " << offset1 << ") = "
28                << *( b + offset1 ) << '\n';
29
30        // output array b using bPtr and array subscript notation
31        cout << "\nPointer subscript notation\n";
32
33        for ( int j = 0; j < 4; j++ )
34           cout << "bPtr[" << j << "] = " << bPtr[ j ] << '\n';
35
36        cout << "\nPointer/offset notation\n";
37
38        // output array b using bPtr and pointer/offset notation
39        for ( int offset2 = 0; offset2 < 4; offset2++ )
40           cout << "*(bPtr + " << offset2 << ") = "
41                << *( bPtr + offset2 ) << '\n';
42
43        return 0;  // indicates successful termination
44
45     } // end main
```

```
Array b printed with:

Array subscript notation
b[0] = 10
b[1] = 20
b[2] = 30
b[3] = 40

Pointer/offset notation where the pointer is the array name
*(b + 0) = 10
*(b + 1) = 20
*(b + 2) = 30
*(b + 3) = 40
```
(Continued on top of next page)

Fig. 5.20   Referencing array elements with the array name and with pointers. (Part 2 of 3.)

```
                                              (Continued from previous page)
Pointer subscript notation
bPtr[0] = 10
bPtr[1] = 20
bPtr[2] = 30
bPtr[3] = 40

Pointer/offset notation
*(bPtr + 0) = 10
*(bPtr + 1) = 20
*(bPtr + 2) = 30
*(bPtr + 3) = 40
```

Fig. 5.20   Referencing array elements with the array name and with pointers. (Part 3 of 3.)

To further illustrate the interchangeability of arrays and pointers, let us look at the two string copying functions—**copy1** and **copy2**—in the program of Fig. 5.21. Both functions copy a string into a character array. After a comparison of the function prototypes for **copy1** and **copy2**, the functions appear identical (because of the interchangeability of arrays and pointers). These functions accomplish the same task, but they are implemented differently.

```cpp
1   // Fig. 5.21: fig05_21.cpp
2   // Copying a string using array notation
3   // and pointer notation.
4   #include <iostream>
5
6   using std::cout;
7   using std::endl;
8
9   void copy1( char *, const char * );   // prototype
10  void copy2( char *, const char * );   // prototype
11
12  int main()
13  {
14     char string1[ 10 ];
15     char *string2 = "Hello";
16     char string3[ 10 ];
17     char string4[] = "Good Bye";
18
19     copy1( string1, string2 );
20     cout << "string1 = " << string1 << endl;
21
22     copy2( string3, string4 );
23     cout << "string3 = " << string3 << endl;
24
25     return 0;   // indicates successful termination
26
27  } // end main
```

Fig. 5.21   String copying using array notation and pointer notation. (Part 1 of 2.)

```
28
29   // copy s2 to s1 using array notation
30   void copy1( char *s1, const char *s2 )
31   {
32      for ( int i = 0; ( s1[ i ] = s2[ i ] ) != '\0'; i++ )
33         ;    // do nothing in body
34
35   } // end function copy1
36
37   // copy s2 to s1 using pointer notation
38   void copy2( char *s1, const char *s2 )
39   {
40      for ( ; ( *s1 = *s2 ) != '\0'; s1++, s2++ )
41         ;    // do nothing in body
42
43   } // end function copy2
```

```
string1 = Hello
string3 = Good Bye
```

Fig. 5.21   String copying using array notation and pointer notation. (Part 2 of 2.)

Function **copy1** (lines 30–35) uses array subscript notation to copy the string in **s2** to the character array **s1**. The function declares an integer counter variable **i** to use as the array subscript. The **for** structure header (line 32) performs the entire copy operation—its body is the empty statement. The header specifies that **i** is initialized to zero and incremented by one on each iteration of the loop. The condition in the **for**, **(s1[i] = s2[i]) != '\0'**, performs the copy operation character by character from **s2** to **s1**. When the null character is encountered in **s2**, it is assigned to **s1**, and the loop terminates, because the null character is equal to **'\0'**. Remember that the value of an assignment statement is the value assigned to its left operand.

Function **copy2** (lines 38–43) uses pointers and pointer arithmetic to copy the string in **s2** to the character array **s1**. Again, the **for** structure header (line 40) performs the entire copy operation. The header does not include any variable initialization. As in function **copy1**, the condition **(*s1 = *s2) != '\0'** performs the copy operation. Pointer **s2** is dereferenced, and the resulting character is assigned to the dereferenced pointer **s1**. After the assignment in the condition, the loop increments both pointers, so they point to the next element of array **s1** and the next character of string **s2**, respectively. When the loop encounters the null character in **s2**, the null character is assigned to the dereferenced pointer **s1** and the loop terminates. Note that the "increment portion" of this **for** structure has two increment expressions separated by a comma operator.

The first argument to both **copy1** and **copy2** must be an array large enough to hold the string in the second argument. Otherwise, an error may occur when an attempt is made to write into a memory location beyond the bounds of the array. Also, note that the second parameter of each function is declared as **const char *** (a pointer to a character constant—i.e., a constant string). In both functions, the second argument is copied into the first argument—characters are copied from the second argument one at a time, but the characters are never modified. Therefore, the second parameter is declared to point to a constant value to enforce the principle of least privilege—neither function needs to modify the second argument, so neither function is allowed to modify the second argument.

5.9 Arrays of Pointers

Arrays may contain pointers. A common use of such a data structure is to form an array of strings, referred to simply as a *string array*. Each entry in the array is a string, but in C++ a string is essentially a pointer to its first character, so each entry in an array of strings is actually a pointer to the first character of a string. Consider the declaration of string array **suit** that might be useful in representing a deck of cards:

```
const char *suit[ 4 ] =
    { "Hearts", "Diamonds", "Clubs", "Spades" };
```

The **suit[4]** portion of the declaration indicates an array of four elements. The **char ＊** portion of the declaration indicates that each element of array **suit** is of type "pointer to **char**." The four values to be placed in the array are **"Hearts"**, **"Diamonds"**, **"Clubs"** and **"Spades"**. Each of these is stored in memory as a null-terminated character string that is one character longer than the number of characters between quotes. The four strings are seven, nine, six and seven characters long, respectively. Although it appears as though these strings are being placed in the **suit** array, only pointers are actually stored in the array, as shown in Fig. 5.22. Each pointer points to the first character of its corresponding string. Thus, even though the **suit** array is fixed in size, it provides access to character strings of any length. This flexibility is one example of C++'s powerful data structuring capabilities.

The suit strings could be placed into a double-subscripted array in which each row represents one suit and each column represents one of the letters of a suit name. Such a data structure must have a fixed number of columns per row, and that number must be as large as the largest string. Therefore, considerable memory is wasted when a large number of strings is stored with most strings shorter than the longest string. We use arrays of strings to help represent a deck of cards in the next section.

String arrays are commonly used with *command-line arguments* that are passed to function **main** when a program begins execution. Such arguments follow the program name when a program is executed from the command line. A typical use of command-line

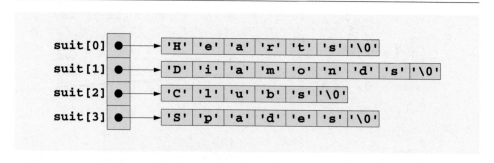

Fig. 5.22   Graphical representation of the **suit** array.

arguments is to pass options to a program. For example, from the command line on a Windows computer, the user can type

```
dir /P
```

to list the contents of the current directory and pause after each screen of information. When the **dir** command executes, the option **/P** is passed to **dir** as a command-line argument. Such arguments are placed in a string array that **main** receives as an argument. We discuss command-line arguments in Section 20.4.

5.10 Case Study: Card Shuffling and Dealing Simulation

This section uses random-number generation to develop a card shuffling and dealing simulation program. This program can then be used to implement programs that play specific card games. To reveal some subtle performance problems, we have intentionally used suboptimal shuffling and dealing algorithms. In the exercises, we develop more efficient algorithms.

Using the top-down, stepwise-refinement approach, we develop a program that will shuffle a deck of 52 playing cards and then deal each of the 52 cards. The top-down approach is particularly useful in attacking larger, more complex problems than we have seen in the early chapters.

We use a 4-by-13 double-subscripted array **deck** to represent the deck of playing cards (Fig. 5.23). The rows correspond to the suits—row 0 corresponds to hearts, row 1 to diamonds, row 2 to clubs and row 3 to spades. The columns correspond to the face values of the cards—columns 0 through 9 correspond to faces ace through 10, respectively, and columns 10 through 12 correspond to jack, queen and king, respectively. We shall load string array **suit** with character strings representing the four suits and string array **face** with character strings representing the 13 face values.

This simulated deck of cards may be shuffled as follows. First the array **deck** is initialized to zeros. Then, a **row** (0–3) and a **column** (0–12) are each chosen at random. The number 1 is inserted in array element **deck[row][column]** to indicate that this card is going to be the first one dealt from the shuffled deck. This process continues with the numbers 2, 3, …, 52 being randomly inserted in the **deck** array to indicate which cards are

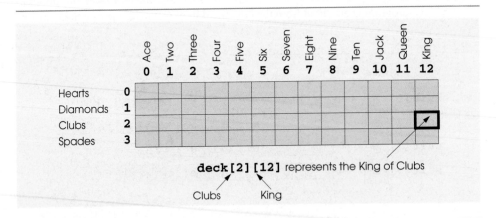

Fig. 5.23   Double-subscripted array representation of a deck of cards.

to be placed second, third, ..., and 52nd in the shuffled deck. As the **deck** array begins to fill with card numbers, it is possible that a card will be selected twice (i.e., **deck[row][column]** will be nonzero when it is selected). This selection is simply ignored, and other **row**s and **column**s are repeatedly chosen at random until an unselected card is found. Eventually, the numbers 1 through 52 will occupy the 52 slots of the **deck** array. At this point, the deck of cards is fully shuffled.

This shuffling algorithm could execute for an indefinitely long period if cards that have already been shuffled are repeatedly selected at random. This phenomenon is known as *indefinite postponement*. In the exercises, we discuss a better shuffling algorithm that eliminates the possibility of indefinite postponement.

Performance Tip 5.3

Sometimes algorithms that emerge in a "natural" way can contain subtle performance problems such as indefinite postponement. Seek algorithms that avoid indefinite postponement.

To deal the first card, we search the array for **deck[row][column]** matching **1**. This is accomplished with a nested **for** structure that varies **row** from 0 to 3 and **column** from 0 to 12. What card does that slot of the array correspond to? The **suit** array has been preloaded with the four suits, so to get the suit, we print the character string **suit[row]**. Similarly, to get the face value of the card, we print the character string **face[column]**. We also print the character string **" of "**. Printing this information in the proper order enables us to print each card in the form **"King of Clubs"**, **"Ace of Diamonds"** and so on.

Let us proceed with the top-down, stepwise-refinement process. The top is simply

>   *Shuffle and deal 52 cards*

Our first refinement yields

>   *Initialize the suit array*
>   *Initialize the face array*
>   *Initialize the deck array*
>   *Shuffle the deck*
>   *Deal 52 cards*

"Shuffle the deck" may be expanded as follows:

>   *For each of the 52 cards*
>   *Place card number in randomly selected unoccupied slot of deck*

"Deal 52 cards" may be expanded as follows:

>   *For each of the 52 cards*
>   *Find card number in deck array and print face and suit of card*

Incorporating these expansions yields our complete second refinement:

>   *Initialize the suit array*
>   *Initialize the face array*
>   *Initialize the deck array*
>
>   *For each of the 52 cards*
>   *Place card number in randomly selected unoccupied slot of deck*
>
>   *For each of the 52 cards*
>   *Find card number in deck array and print face and suit of card*

"Place card number in randomly selected unoccupied slot of deck" may be expanded as follows:

> *Choose slot of deck randomly*
>
> *While chosen slot of deck has been previously chosen*
> > *Choose slot of deck randomly*
>
> *Place card number in chosen slot of deck*

"Find card number in deck array and print face and suit of card" may be expanded as follows:

> *For each slot of the deck array*
> > *If slot contains card number*
> > > *Print the face and suit of the card*

Incorporating these expansions yields our third refinement:

> *Initialize the suit array*
> *Initialize the face array*
> *Initialize the deck array*
>
> *For each of the 52 cards*
> > *Choose slot of deck randomly*
> >
> > *While slot of deck has been previously chosen*
> > > *Choose slot of deck randomly*
> >
> > *Place card number in chosen slot of deck*
>
> *For each of the 52 cards*
> > *For each slot of deck array*
> > > *If slot contains desired card number*
> > > > *Print the face and suit of the card*

This completes the refinement process. Figure 5.24 contains the card shuffling and dealing program and a sample execution. Note the output formatting (lines 81–84) used in function **deal**. The output statement causes the face to be output right justified in a field of five characters and the suit to be output left justified in a field of eight characters. The output is printed in two-column format—if the card being output is in the first column (line 84), a tab is output after the card to move to the second column; otherwise, a newline is output.

```
1   // Fig. 5.24: fig05_24.cpp
2   // Card shuffling dealing program.
3   #include <iostream>
4
5   using std::cout;
6   using std::left;
7   using std::right;
8
9   #include <iomanip>
10
11  using std::setw;
12
```

Fig. 5.24 Card shuffling and dealing program. (Part 1 of 3.)

```cpp
13   #include <cstdlib>   // prototypes for rand and srand
14   #include <ctime>     // prototype for time
15
16   // prototypes
17   void shuffle( int [][ 13 ] );
18   void deal( const int [][ 13 ], const char *[], const char *[] );
19
20   int main()
21   {
22      // initialize suit array
23      const char *suit[ 4 ] =
24         { "Hearts", "Diamonds", "Clubs", "Spades" };
25
26      // initialize face array
27      const char *face[ 13 ] =
28         { "Ace", "Deuce", "Three", "Four",
29           "Five", "Six", "Seven", "Eight",
30           "Nine", "Ten", "Jack", "Queen", "King" };
31
32      // initialize deck array
33      int deck[ 4 ][ 13 ] = { 0 };
34
35      srand( time( 0 ) );             // seed random-number generator
36
37      shuffle( deck );
38      deal( deck, face, suit );
39
40      return 0;   // indicates successful termination
41
42   } // end main
43
44   // shuffle cards in deck
45   void shuffle( int wDeck[][ 13 ] )
46   {
47      int row;
48      int column;
49
50      // for each of the 52 cards, choose slot of deck randomly
51      for ( int card = 1; card <= 52; card++ ) {
52
53         // choose new random location until unoccupied slot found
54         do {
55            row = rand() % 4;
56            column = rand() % 13;
57         } while ( wDeck[ row ][ column ] != 0 ); // end do/while
58
59         // place card number in chosen slot of deck
60         wDeck[ row ][ column ] = card;
61
62      } // end for
63
64   } // end function shuffle
```

Fig. 5.24   Card shuffling and dealing program. (Part 2 of 3.)

```
65
66    // deal cards in deck
67    void deal( const int wDeck[][ 13 ], const char *wFace[],
68              const char *wSuit[] )
69    {
70       // for each of the 52 cards
71       for ( int card = 1; card <= 52; card++ )
72
73          // loop through rows of wDeck
74          for ( int row = 0; row <= 3; row++ )
75
76             // loop through columns of wDeck for current row
77             for ( int column = 0; column <= 12; column++ )
78
79                // if slot contains current card, display card
80                if ( wDeck[ row ][ column ] == card ) {
81                   cout << setw( 5 ) << right << wFace[ column ]
82                      << " of " << setw( 8 ) << left
83                      << wSuit[ row ]
84                      << ( card % 2 == 0 ? '\n' : '\t' );
85
86                } // end if
87
88    } // end function deal
```

```
  Nine of Spades         Seven of Clubs
  Five of Spades         Eight of Clubs
Queen of Diamonds        Three of Hearts
  Jack of Spades          Five of Diamonds
  Jack of Diamonds       Three of Diamonds
Three of Clubs            Six of Clubs
  Ten of Clubs           Nine of Diamonds
  Ace of Hearts         Queen of Hearts
Seven of Spades         Deuce of Spades
  Six of Hearts         Deuce of Clubs
  Ace of Clubs          Deuce of Diamonds
 Nine of Hearts         Seven of Diamonds
  Six of Spades         Eight of Diamonds
  Ten of Spades          King of Hearts
 Four of Clubs            Ace of Spades
  Ten of Hearts          Four of Spades
Eight of Hearts         Eight of Spades
 Jack of Hearts           Ten of Diamonds
 Four of Diamonds        King of Diamonds
Seven of Hearts          King of Spades
Queen of Spades          Four of Hearts
 Nine of Clubs            Six of Diamonds
Deuce of Hearts          Jack of Clubs
 King of Clubs          Three of Spades
Queen of Clubs           Five of Clubs
 Five of Hearts           Ace of Diamonds
```

Fig. 5.24   Card shuffling and dealing program. (Part 3 of 3.)

There is also a weakness in the dealing algorithm. Once a match is found, even if it is found on the first try, the two inner **for** structures continue searching the remaining elements of **deck** for a match. In the exercises, we correct this deficiency.

5.11 Function Pointers

A pointer to a function contains the address of the function in memory. In Chapter 4, we saw that an array name is really the address in memory of the first element of the array. Similarly, a function name is really the starting address in memory of the code that performs the function's task. Pointers to functions can be passed to functions, returned from functions, stored in arrays and assigned to other function pointers.

Multipurpose Bubble Sort Using Function Pointers
To illustrate the use of pointers to functions, Fig. 5.25 modifies the bubble sort program of Fig. 5.15. Figure 5.25 consists of **main** (lines 19–57) and the functions **bubble** (lines 61–74), **swap** (lines 78–84), **ascending** (lines 88–92) and **descending** (lines 96–100). Function **bubble** receives a pointer to a function—either function **ascending** or function **descending**—as an argument in addition to an integer array and the size of the array. Functions **ascending** and **descending** determine the sorting order. The program prompts the user to choose whether the array should be sorted in ascending order or in descending order. If the user enters 1, a pointer to function **ascending** is passed to function **bubble** (line 38), causing the array to be sorted into increasing order. If the user enters 2, a pointer to function **descending** is passed to function **bubble** (line 45), causing the array to be sorted into decreasing order.

```
1   // Fig. 5.25: fig05_25.cpp
2   // Multipurpose sorting program using function pointers.
3   #include <iostream>
4
5   using std::cout;
6   using std::cin;
7   using std::endl;
8
9   #include <iomanip>
10
11  using std::setw;
12
13  // prototypes
14  void bubble( int [], const int, bool (*)( int, int ) );
15  void swap( int * const, int * const );
16  bool ascending( int, int );
17  bool descending( int, int );
18
19  int main()
20  {
21     const int arraySize = 10;
22     int order;
23     int counter;
24     int a[ arraySize ] = { 2, 6, 4, 8, 10, 12, 89, 68, 45, 37 };
```

Fig. 5.25 Multipurpose sorting program using function pointers. (Part 1 of 3.)

```
25
26      cout << "Enter 1 to sort in ascending order,\n"
27           << "Enter 2 to sort in descending order: ";
28      cin >> order;
29      cout << "\nData items in original order\n";
30
31      // output original array
32      for ( counter = 0; counter < arraySize; counter++ )
33         cout << setw( 4 ) << a[ counter ];
34
35      // sort array in ascending order; pass function ascending
36      // as an argument to specify ascending sorting order
37      if ( order == 1 ) {
38         bubble( a, arraySize, ascending );
39         cout << "\nData items in ascending order\n";
40      }
41
42      // sort array in descending order; pass function descending
43      // as an agrument to specify descending sorting order
44      else {
45         bubble( a, arraySize, descending );
46         cout << "\nData items in descending order\n";
47      }
48
49      // output sorted array
50      for ( counter = 0; counter < arraySize; counter++ )
51         cout << setw( 4 ) << a[ counter ];
52
53      cout << endl;
54
55      return 0;   // indicates successful termination
56
57  } // end main
58
59  // multipurpose bubble sort; parameter compare is a pointer to
60  // the comparison function that determines sorting order
61  void bubble( int work[], const int size,
62              bool (*compare)( int, int ) )
63  {
64      // loop to control passes
65      for ( int pass = 1; pass < size; pass++ )
66
67         // loop to control number of comparisons per pass
68         for ( int count = 0; count < size - 1; count++ )
69
70            // if adjacent elements are out of order, swap them
71            if ( (*compare)( work[ count ], work[ count + 1 ] ) )
72               swap( &work[ count ], &work[ count + 1 ] );
73
74  } // end function bubble
75
```

Fig. 5.25   Multipurpose sorting program using function pointers. (Part 2 of 3.)

```
76   // swap values at memory locations to which
77   // element1Ptr and element2Ptr point
78   void swap( int * const element1Ptr, int * const element2Ptr )
79   {
80      int hold = *element1Ptr;
81      *element1Ptr = *element2Ptr;
82      *element2Ptr = hold;
83
84   } // end function swap
85
86   // determine whether elements are out of order
87   // for an ascending order sort
88   bool ascending( int a, int b )
89   {
90      return b < a;     // swap if b is less than a
91
92   } // end function ascending
93
94   // determine whether elements are out of order
95   // for a descending order sort
96   bool descending( int a, int b )
97   {
98      return b > a;     // swap if b is greater than a
99
100  } // end function descending
```

```
Enter 1 to sort in ascending order,
Enter 2 to sort in descending order: 1

Data items in original order
   2    6    4    8   10   12   89   68   45   37
Data items in ascending order
   2    4    6    8   10   12   37   45   68   89
```

```
Enter 1 to sort in ascending order,
Enter 2 to sort in descending order: 2

Data items in original order
   2    6    4    8   10   12   89   68   45   37
Data items in descending order
  89   68   45   37   12   10    8    6    4    2
```

Fig. 5.25   Multipurpose sorting program using function pointers. (Part 3 of 3.)

The following parameter appears in the function header for **bubble**:

```
bool ( *compare )( int, int )
```

This tells **bubble** to expect a parameter that is a pointer to a function that receives two integer parameters and returns a **bool** result. Parentheses are needed around ***compare** to indicate that **compare** is a pointer to a function. If we had not included the parentheses, the declaration would have been

```
bool *compare( int, int )
```

which declares a function that receives two integers as parameters and returns a pointer to a **bool** value.

The corresponding parameter in the function prototype of **bubble** is

```
bool (*)( int, int )
```

Note that only types have been included. However, for documentation purposes, the programmer can include names that the compiler will ignore.

The function passed to **bubble** is called in line 71 as follows:

```
( *compare )( work[ count ], work[ count + 1 ] )
```

Just as a pointer to a variable is dereferenced to access the value of the variable, a pointer to a function is dereferenced to execute the function.

The call to the function could have been made without dereferencing the pointer, as in

```
compare( work[ count ], work[ count + 1 ] )
```

which uses the pointer directly as the function name. We prefer the first method of calling a function through a pointer, because it explicitly illustrates that **compare** is a pointer to a function that is dereferenced to call the function. The second method of calling a function through a pointer makes it appear as though **compare** is the name of an actual function in the program. This may be confusing to a user of the program who would like to see the definition of function **compare** and finds that it is never defined in the file.

Arrays of Pointers to Functions

One use of function pointers is in menu-driven systems. The program prompts a user to select an option (e.g., from 1 to 5) from a menu. Each option is serviced by a different function. Pointers to each function are stored in an array of pointers to functions. In this case, all the functions to which the array points must have the same return type and same parameter types. The user's choice is used as a subscript into the array of function pointers, and the pointer in the array is used to call the function.

Figure 5.26 provides a generic example of the mechanics of declaring and using an array of pointers to functions. Three functions are defined—**function1**, **function2** and **function3**—that each take an integer argument and do not return a value. Line 18 stores pointers to these three functions in array **f**. The declaration is read beginning in the leftmost set of parentheses as, "**f** is an array of three pointers to functions that each take an **int** as an argument and return **void**." The array is initialized with the names of the three functions (which, again, are pointers). When the user enters a value between 0 and 2, the value is used as the subscript into the array of pointers to functions. Line 30 invokes one of the functions in array **f**. In the call, **f[choice]** selects the pointer at location **choice** in the array. The pointer is dereferenced to call the function, and **choice** is passed as the argument to the function. Each function prints its argument's value and its function name to indicate that the function is called correctly. In the exercises, you will develop a menu-driven system.

```
1   // Fig. 5.26: fig05_26.cpp
2   // Demonstrating an array of pointers to functions.
```

Fig. 5.26   Array of pointers to functions. (Part 1 of 3.)

```
3    #include <iostream>
4
5    using std::cout;
6    using std::cin;
7    using std::endl;
8
9    // function prototypes
10   void function1( int );
11   void function2( int );
12   void function3( int );
13
14   int main()
15   {
16      // initialize array of 3 pointers to functions that each
17      // take an int argument and return void
18      void (*f[ 3 ])( int ) = { function1, function2, function3 };
19
20      int choice;
21
22      cout << "Enter a number between 0 and 2, 3 to end: ";
23      cin >> choice;
24
25      // process user's choice
26      while ( choice >= 0 && choice < 3 ) {
27
28         // invoke function at location choice in array f
29         // and pass choice as an argument
30         (*f[ choice ])( choice );
31
32         cout << "Enter a number between 0 and 2, 3 to end: ";
33         cin >> choice;
34      }
35
36      cout << "Program execution completed." << endl;
37
38      return 0;   // indicates successful termination
39
40   } // end main
41
42   void function1( int a )
43   {
44      cout << "You entered " << a
45           << " so function1 was called\n\n";
46
47   } // end function1
48
49   void function2( int b )
50   {
51      cout << "You entered " << b
52           << " so function2 was called\n\n";
53
54   } // end function2
55
```

Fig. 5.26   Array of pointers to functions. (Part 2 of 3.)

```
56   void function3( int c )
57   {
58      cout << "You entered " << c
59          << " so function3 was called\n\n";
60
61   } // end function3
```

```
Enter a number between 0 and 2, 3 to end: 0
You entered 0 so function1 was called

Enter a number between 0 and 2, 3 to end: 1
You entered 1 so function2 was called

Enter a number between 0 and 2, 3 to end: 2
You entered 2 so function3 was called

Enter a number between 0 and 2, 3 to end: 3
Program execution completed.
```

Fig. 5.26   Array of pointers to functions. (Part 3 of 3.)

5.12 Introduction to Character and String Processing

In this section, we introduce some common standard library functions that facilitate string processing. The techniques discussed here are appropriate for developing text editors, word processors, page layout software, computerized typesetting systems and other kinds of text-processing software. We use pointer-based strings here. Chapter 8 introduces strings as full-fledged objects, and Chapter 15 explains strings as full-fledged objects in detail.

5.12.1 Fundamentals of Characters and Strings

Characters are the fundamental building blocks of C++ source programs. Every program is composed of a sequence of characters that—when grouped together meaningfully—is interpreted by the compiler as a series of instructions used to accomplish a task. A program may contain *character constants*. A character constant is an integer value represented as a character in single quotes. The value of a character constant is the integer value of the character in the machine's character set. For example, `'z'` represents the integer value of `z` (122 in the ASCII character set; see Appendix B), and `'\n'` represents the integer value of newline (10 in the ASCII character set).

A string is a series of characters treated as a single unit. A string may include letters, digits and various *special characters* such as +, -, *, / and $. *String literals,* or *string constants,* in C++ are written in double quotation marks as follows:

`"John Q. Doe"`	(a name)
`"9999 Main Street"`	(a street address)
`"Maynard, Massachusetts"`	(a city and state)
`"(201) 555-1212"`	(a telephone number)

A string in C++ is an array of characters ending in the *null character ('\0'),* which specifies where the string terminates in memory. A string is accessed via a pointer to the first character in the string. The value of a string is the (constant) address of its first character. Thus, in C++, it is appropriate to say that *a string is a constant pointer*—in fact, a pointer to the string's first character. In this sense, strings are like arrays, because an array name is also a (constant) pointer to its first element.

A string may be assigned in a declaration to either a character array or a variable of type **char ***. The declarations

```
char color[] = "blue";
const char *colorPtr = "blue";
```

each initialize a variable to the string **"blue"**. The first declaration creates a five-element array **color** containing the characters **'b'**, **'l'**, **'u'**, **'e'** and **'\0'**. The second declaration creates pointer variable **colorPtr** that points to the letter **b** in the string **"blue"** somewhere in memory.

 Portability Tip 5.5

*When a variable of type **char *** is initialized with a string literal, some compilers may place the string in a location in memory where the string cannot be modified. If a string literal must be modified in a program, it should be stored in a character array to ensure modifiability on all systems.*

The declaration **char color[] = "blue";** could also be written

```
char color[] = { 'b', 'l', 'u', 'e', '\0' };
```

When declaring a character array to contain a string, the array must be large enough to store the string and its terminating null character. The preceding declaration determines the size of the array, based on the number of initializers provided in the initializer list.

 Common Programming Error 5.15

Not allocating sufficient space in a character array to store the null character that terminates a string is an error.

 Common Programming Error 5.16

Creating or using a "string" that does not contain a terminating null character is an error.

 Testing and Debugging Tip 5.3

When storing a string of characters in a character array, be sure that the array is large enough to hold the largest string that will be stored. C++ allows strings of any length to be stored. If a string is longer than the character array in which it is to be stored, characters beyond the end of the array will overwrite data in memory following the array.

A string can be stored in an array using stream extraction with **cin**. For example, the following statement can be used to store a string to character array **word[20]**:

```
cin >> word;
```

The string entered by the user is stored in **word**. The preceding statement reads characters until a whitespace character or end-of-file indicator is encountered. Note that the string should be no longer than 19 characters to leave room for the terminating null character. The **setw** stream manipulator introduced in Chapter 2 can be used to ensure that the string read into **word** does not exceed the size of the array. For example, the statement

```
cin >> setw( 20 ) >> word;
```

specifies that **cin** should read a maximum of 19 characters into array **word** and save the 20th location in the array to store the terminating null character for the string. The **setw** stream manipulator applies only to the next value being input.

In some cases, it is desirable to input an entire line of text into an array. For this purpose, C++ provides the function **cin.getline**. The **cin.getline** function takes three arguments—a character array in which the line of text will be stored, a length and a delimiter character. For example, the program segment

```
char sentence[ 80 ];
cin.getline( sentence, 80, '\n' );
```

declares array **sentence** of 80 characters and reads a line of text from the keyboard into the array. The function stops reading characters when the delimiter character **'\n'** is encountered, when the end-of-file indicator is entered or when the number of characters read so far is one less than the length specified in the second argument. (The last character in the array is reserved for the terminating null character.) If the delimiter character is encountered, it is read and discarded. The third argument to **cin.getline** has **'\n'** as a default value, so the preceding function call could have been written as follows:

```
cin.getline( sentence, 80 );
```

Chapter 12, Stream Input/Output, provides a detailed discussion of **cin.getline** and other input/output functions.

Common Programming Error 5.17

Processing a single character as a string can lead to a fatal runtime error. A string is a pointer—probably a respectably large integer. However, a character is a small integer (ASCII values range 0–255). On many systems, this causes an error, because low memory addresses are reserved for special purposes such as operating system interrupt handlers—so "access violations" occur.

Common Programming Error 5.18

Passing a string as an argument to a function when a character is expected is a syntax error.

5.12.2 String Manipulation Functions of the String-Handling Library

The string-handling library provides many useful functions for manipulating string data, comparing strings, searching strings for characters and other strings, tokenizing strings (separating strings into logical pieces) and determining the length of strings. This section presents some common string-manipulation functions of the string-handling library (from the C++ standard library). The functions are summarized in Fig. 5.27. The prototypes for these functions are located in header file **<cstring>**.

Note that several functions in Fig. 5.27 contain parameters with data type **size_t**. This type is defined in the header file **<cstring>** to be an unsigned integral type such as **unsigned int** or **unsigned long**.

Common Programming Error 5.19

*Forgetting to include the **<cstring>** header file when using functions from the string handling library causes compilation errors.*

Function prototype	Function description

`char *strcpy( char *s1, const char *s2 );`

Copies the string **s2** into the character array **s1**. The value of **s1** is returned.

`char *strncpy( char *s1, const char *s2, size_t n );`

Copies at most **n** characters of the string **s2** into the character array **s1**. The value of **s1** is returned.

`char *strcat( char *s1, const char *s2 );`

Appends the string **s2** to the string **s1**. The first character of **s2** overwrites the terminating null character of **s1**. The value of **s1** is returned.

`char *strncat( char *s1, const char *s2, size_t n );`

Appends at most **n** characters of string **s2** to string **s1**. The first character of **s2** overwrites the terminating null character of **s1**. The value of **s1** is returned.

`int strcmp( const char *s1, const char *s2 );`

Compares the string **s1** with the string **s2**. The function returns a value of zero, less than zero or greater than zero if **s1** is equal to, less than or greater than **s2**, respectively.

`int strncmp( const char *s1, const char *s2, size_t n );`

Compares up to **n** characters of the string **s1** with the string **s2**. The function returns zero, less than zero or greater than zero if the **n**-character portion of **s1** is equal to, less than or greater than the corresponding **n**-character portion of **s2**, respectively.

`char *strtok( char *s1, const char *s2 );`

A sequence of calls to **strtok** breaks string **s1** into "tokens"—logical pieces such as words in a line of text—delimited by characters contained in string **s2**. The first call contains **s1** as the first argument, and subsequent calls to continue tokenizing the same string contain **NULL** as the first argument. A pointer to the current token is returned by each call. If there are no more tokens when the function is called, **NULL** is returned.

`size_t strlen( const char *s );`

Determines the length of string **s**. The number of characters preceding the terminating null character is returned.

Fig. 5.27   *String-manipulation functions of the string-handling library.*

Copying Strings with **strcpy** *and* **strncpy**

Function **strcpy** copies its second argument—a string—into its first argument—a character array that must be large enough to store the string and its terminating null character, (which is also copied). Function **strncpy** is equivalent to **strcpy**, except that **strncpy** specifies the number of characters to be copied from the string into the array. Note that function **strncpy** does not necessarily copy the terminating null character of its second argument—a terminating null character is written only if the number of characters to be copied is at least one more than the length of the string. For example, if **"test"** is the second argument, a terminating null character is written only if the third argument to **strncpy** is at least **5** (four characters in **"test"** plus one terminating null character). If the third argument is larger than **5**, null characters are appended to the array until the total number of characters specified by the third argument is written.

Common Programming Error 5.20

*Not appending a terminating null character to the first argument of a **strncpy** (in a statement after the **strncpy** call) when the third argument is less than or equal to the length of the string in the second argument can cause fatal run-time errors.*

Figure 5.28 uses **strcpy** (line 16) to copy the entire string in array **x** into array **y** and uses **strncpy** (line 22) to copy the first **14** characters of array **x** into array **z**. Line 23 appends a null character (**'\0'**) to array **z**, because the call to **strncpy** in the program does not write a terminating null character. (The third argument is less than the string length of the second argument plus one.)

```
1    // Fig. 5.28: fig05_28.cpp
2    // Using strcpy and strncpy.
3    #include <iostream>
4
5    using std::cout;
6    using std::endl;
7
8    #include <cstring>    // prototypes for strcpy and strncpy
9
10   int main()
11   {
12      char x[] = "Happy Birthday to You";
13      char y[ 25 ];
14      char z[ 15 ];
15
16      strcpy( y, x );  // copy contents of x into y
17
18      cout << "The string in array x is: " << x
19           << "\nThe string in array y is: " << y << '\n';
20
21      // copy first 14 characters of x into z
22      strncpy( z, x, 14 );  // does not copy null character
23      z[ 14 ] = '\0';       // append '\0' to z's contents
24
25      cout << "The string in array z is: " << z << endl;
26
27      return 0;  // indicates successful termination
28
29   } // end main
```

```
The string in array x is: Happy Birthday to You
The string in array y is: Happy Birthday to You
The string in array z is: Happy Birthday
```

Fig. 5.28   **strcpy** and **strncpy**.

Concatenating Strings with *strcat* and *strncat*

Function **strcat** appends its second argument (a string) to its first argument (a character array containing a string). The first character of the second argument replaces the null character (**'\0'**) that terminates the string in the first argument. The programmer must ensure that the array used to store the first string is large enough to store the combination of the first string, the second string and the terminating null character (copied from the second string). Function **strncat** appends a specified number of characters from the second string to the first string and appends a terminating null character to the result. The program of Fig. 5.29 demonstrates function **strcat** (lines 18 and 29) and function **strncat** (line 24).

Comparing Strings with *strcmp* and *strncmp*

Figure 5.30 compares three strings using **strcmp** (lines 22, 24 and 25) and **strncmp** (lines 28, 29 and 31). Function **strcmp** compares its first string argument with its second string argument character by character. The function returns zero if the strings are equal, a

```cpp
1   // Fig. 5.29: fig05_29.cpp
2   // Using strcat and strncat.
3   #include <iostream>
4
5   using std::cout;
6   using std::endl;
7
8   #include <cstring>    // prototypes for strcat and strncat
9
10  int main()
11  {
12     char s1[ 20 ] = "Happy ";
13     char s2[] = "New Year ";
14     char s3[ 40 ] = "";
15
16     cout << "s1 = " << s1 << "\ns2 = " << s2;
17
18     strcat( s1, s2 );  // concatenate s2 to s1
19
20     cout << "\n\nAfter strcat(s1, s2):\ns1 = " << s1
21          << "\ns2 = " << s2;
22
23     // concatenate first 6 characters of s1 to s3
24     strncat( s3, s1, 6 );  // places '\0' after last character
25
26     cout << "\n\nAfter strncat(s3, s1, 6):\ns1 = " << s1
27          << "\ns3 = " << s3;
28
29     strcat( s3, s1 );  // concatenate s1 to s3
30     cout << "\n\nAfter strcat(s3, s1):\ns1 = " << s1
31          << "\ns3 = " << s3 << endl;
32
33     return 0;  // indicates successful termination
34
35  } // end main
```

Fig. 5.29   **strcat** and **strncat**. (Part 1 of 2.)

```
s1 = Happy
s2 = New Year

After strcat(s1, s2):
s1 = Happy New Year
s2 = New Year

After strncat(s3, s1, 6):
s1 = Happy New Year
s3 = Happy

After strcat(s3, s1):
s1 = Happy New Year
s3 = Happy Happy New Year
```

Fig. 5.29   **strcat** and **strncat**. (Part 2 of 2.)

negative value if the first string is less than the second string and a positive value if the first
string is greater than the second string. Function **strncmp** is equivalent to **strcmp**, except that **strncmp** compares up to a specified number of characters. Function **strncmp**
stops comparing characters if it reaches the null character in one of its string arguments.
The program prints the integer value returned by each function call.

```
1   // Fig. 5.30: fig05_30.cpp
2   // Using strcmp and strncmp.
3   #include <iostream>
4
5   using std::cout;
6   using std::endl;
7
8   #include <iomanip>
9
10  using std::setw;
11
12  #include <cstring>   // prototypes for strcmp and strncmp
13
14  int main()
15  {
16     char *s1 = "Happy New Year";
17     char *s2 = "Happy New Year";
18     char *s3 = "Happy Holidays";
19
20     cout << "s1 = " << s1 << "\ns2 = " << s2
21          << "\ns3 = " << s3 << "\n\nstrcmp(s1, s2) = "
22          << setw( 2 ) << strcmp( s1, s2 )
23          << "\nstrcmp(s1, s3) = " << setw( 2 )
24          << strcmp( s1, s3 ) << "\nstrcmp(s3, s1) = "
25          << setw( 2 ) << strcmp( s3, s1 );
26
```

Fig. 5.30   **strcmp** and **strncmp**. (Part 1 of 2.)

```
27      cout << "\n\nstrncmp(s1, s3, 6) = " << setw( 2 )
28           << strncmp( s1, s3, 6 ) << "\nstrncmp(s1, s3, 7) = "
29           << setw( 2 ) << strncmp( s1, s3, 7 )
30           << "\nstrncmp(s3, s1, 7) = "
31           << setw( 2 ) << strncmp( s3, s1, 7 ) << endl;
32
33      return 0;  // indicates successful termination
34
35   } // end main
```

```
s1 = Happy New Year
s2 = Happy New Year
s3 = Happy Holidays

strcmp(s1, s2) =  0
strcmp(s1, s3) =  1
strcmp(s3, s1) = -1

strncmp(s1, s3, 6) =  0
strncmp(s1, s3, 7) =  1
strncmp(s3, s1, 7) = -1
```

Fig. 5.30   **strcmp** and **strncmp**. (Part 2 of 2.)

Common Programming Error 5.21

*Assuming that **strcmp** and **strncmp** return one (a true value) when their arguments are equal is a logic error. Both functions return zero (C++'s false value) for equality. Therefore, when testing two strings for equality, the result of the **strcmp** or **strncmp** function should be compared with zero to determine whether the strings are equal.*

To understand just what it means for one string to be "greater than" or "less than" another string, consider the process of alphabetizing a series of last names. The reader would, no doubt, place "Jones" before "Smith," because the first letter of "Jones" comes before the first letter of "Smith" in the alphabet. But the alphabet is more than just a list of 26 letters—it is an ordered list of characters. Each letter occurs in a specific position within the list. "Z" is more than just a letter of the alphabet; "Z" is specifically the 26th letter of the alphabet.

How does the computer know that one letter comes before another? All characters are represented inside the computer as numeric codes; when the computer compares two strings, it actually compares the numeric codes of the characters in the strings.

In an effort to standardize character representations, most computer manufacturers have designed their machines to utilize one of two popular coding schemes—*ASCII* or *EBCDIC*. ASCII stands for "American Standard Code for Information Interchange," and EBCDIC stands for "Extended Binary Coded Decimal Interchange Code." There are other coding schemes, but these two are the most popular.

ASCII and EBCDIC are called *character codes,* or *character sets.* Most readers of this book will be using desktop or notebook computers that use the ASCII character set. IBM mainframe computers use the EBCDIC character set. As Internet and World Wide Web usage becomes pervasive, the newer Unicode character set is growing rapidly in popularity. For more information on Unicode, visit **www.unicode.org**. String and character manipulations actually involve the manipulation of the appropriate numeric codes and not the characters themselves. This explains the interchangeability of characters and small integers in C++. Since it is meaningful to say that one numeric code is greater than, less than or equal to another numeric code, it becomes possible to relate various characters or strings to one another by referring to the character codes. Appendix B contains the ASCII character codes.

Portability Tip 5.6

The internal numeric codes used to represent characters may be different on different computers, because these computers may use different character sets.

Portability Tip 5.7

Do not explicitly test for ASCII codes, as in **if (rating == 65)***; rather, use the corresponding character constant, as in* **if (rating == 'A')***.*

Tokenizing a String with **strtok**

Function **strtok** breaks a string into a series of *tokens*. A token is a sequence of characters separated by *delimiting characters* (usually spaces or punctuation marks). For example, in a line of text, each word can be considered a token, and the spaces separating the words can be considered delimiters.

Multiple calls to **strtok** are required to break a string into tokens (assuming that the string contains more than one token). The first call to **strtok** contains two arguments, a string to be tokenized and a string containing characters that separate the tokens (i.e., delimiters). Line 19 in Fig. 5.31 assigns to **tokenPtr** a pointer to the first token in **sentence**. The second argument, **" "**, indicates that tokens in **sentence** are separated by spaces. Function **strtok** searches for the first character in **sentence** that is not a delimiting character (space). This begins the first token. The function then finds the next delimiting character in the string and replaces it with a null (**'\0'**) character. This terminates the current token. Function **strtok** saves a pointer to the next character following the token in **sentence** and returns a pointer to the current token.

```
1   // Fig. 5.31: fig05_31.cpp
2   // Using strtok.
3   #include <iostream>
4
5   using std::cout;
6   using std::endl;
7
8   #include <cstring>   // prototype for strtok
9
10  int main()
11  {
12     char sentence[] = "This is a sentence with 7 tokens";
13     char *tokenPtr;
14
15     cout << "The string to be tokenized is:\n" << sentence
16          << "\n\nThe tokens are:\n\n";
17
```

Fig. 5.31 **strtok**. (Part 1 of 2.)

```
18      // begin tokenization of sentence
19      tokenPtr = strtok( sentence, " " );
20
21      // continue tokenizing sentence until tokenPtr becomes NULL
22      while ( tokenPtr != NULL ) {
23         cout << tokenPtr << '\n';
24         tokenPtr = strtok( NULL, " " );   // get next token
25
26      } // end while
27
28      cout << "\nAfter strtok, sentence = " << sentence << endl;
29
30      return 0;   // indicates successful termination
31
32   } // end main
```

```
The string to be tokenized is:
This is a sentence with 7 tokens

The tokens are:

This
is
a
sentence
with
7
tokens

After strtok, sentence = This
```

Fig. 5.31 **strtok**. (Part 2 of 2.)

Subsequent calls to **strtok** to continue tokenizing **sentence** contain **NULL** as the first argument (line 24). The **NULL** argument indicates that the call to **strtok** should continue tokenizing from the location in **sentence** saved by the last call to **strtok**. Note that **strtok** maintains this saved information in a manner that is not visible to the programmer. If no tokens remain when **strtok** is called, **strtok** returns **NULL**. The program of Fig. 5.31 uses **strtok** to tokenize the string **"This is a sentence with 7 tokens"**. The program prints each token on a separate line. Line 28 outputs **sentence** after tokenization. Note that **strtok** modifies the input string; therefore, a copy of the string should be made if the program requires the original after the calls to **strtok**. When **sentence** is output after tokenization, note that only the word "**This**" prints, because **strtok** replaced each blank in **sentence** with a null character (**'\0'**) during the tokenization process.

Common Programming Error 5.22

*Not realizing that **strtok** modifies the string being tokenized and then attempting to use that string as if it were the original unmodified string is a logic error.*

Determining String Lengths

Function **strlen** takes a string as an argument and returns the number of characters in the string—the terminating null character is not included in the length. The program of Fig. 5.32 demonstrates function **strlen**.

```
1   // Fig. 5.32: fig05_32.cpp
2   // Using strlen.
3   #include <iostream>
4
5   using std::cout;
6   using std::endl;
7
8   #include <cstring>    // prototype for strlen
9
10  int main()
11  {
12     char *string1 = "abcdefghijklmnopqrstuvwxyz";
13     char *string2 = "four";
14     char *string3 = "Boston";
15
16     cout << "The length of \"" << string1
17          << "\" is " << strlen( string1 )
18          << "\nThe length of \"" << string2
19          << "\" is " << strlen( string2 )
20          << "\nThe length of \"" << string3
21          << "\" is " << strlen( string3 ) << endl;
22
23     return 0;   // indicates successful termination
24
25  } // end main
```

```
The length of "abcdefghijklmnopqrstuvwxyz" is 26
The length of "four" is 4
The length of "Boston" is 6
```

Fig. 5.32   strlen.

5.13 (Optional Case Study) Thinking About Objects: Collaborations Among Objects

This is the last of our object-oriented design sections before we begin our study of C++ object-oriented programming in Chapter 6. After we discuss the interactions among objects in this section and discuss creating classes and objects in Chapter 6, we begin coding the elevator simulator in C++. To complete the elevator simulator, we also use the C++ techniques discussed in Chapter 7 and Chapter 9. We have included at the end of this section a list of Internet and World Wide Web UML resources and a bibliography of UML references.

In the "Thinking About Objects" section at the end of Chapter 4, we began to investigate how objects interact by discussing how a **Scheduler** object interacts with other objects to schedule a person to step onto a floor. In this section, we concentrate on the interactions among other objects in the system. When two or more objects communicate with one another to accomplish a task, they interact with one another by sending and receiving messages.

When two objects interact, a message sent by one object invokes an operation of the second object (just as pressing down the accelerator pedal in a car signals the car to "go faster" and pressing the brake pedal signals the car to "go slower"). In the "Thinking About Objects" section at the end of Chapter 4, we determined many of the operations of the classes in our system. In this section, we concentrate on the messages that invoke these operations.

Figure 5.33 is the table of classes and verb phrases from Section 4.10. We removed all the verb phrases that do not correspond to a message sent between two objects. (For example, we eliminate "moves" in the **Elevator** because the **Elevator** sends this message to itself.) The remaining phrases are likely to correspond to the interactions between objects in our system. We associate the phrases "provides the time to the scheduler" and "provides the time to the elevator" with class **Building**, because we decided in Chapter 4 that the building controls the simulation. We associate the phrases "increments the clock time" and "gets the time from the clock" with class **Building** for the same reason.

　　　We examine the list of verbs to determine the interactions in our system. For example, class **Elevator** lists the phrase "resets the elevator button." To accomplish this task, an object of class **Elevator** must send the **resetButton** message to an object of class **ElevatorButton**, invoking the **resetButton** operation of that class. Figure 5.34 lists all the interactions that can be gleaned from our table of verb phrases.

Class	Verb phrases
Elevator	resets the elevator button, sounds the elevator bell, signals its arrival to a floor, opens its door, closes its door
Clock	none in problem statement
Scheduler	verifies that a floor is unoccupied
Person	steps onto a floor, presses floor button, presses elevator button, enters elevator, exits elevator
Floor	resets floor button, turns off light, turns on light
FloorButton	summons elevator
ElevatorButton	signals elevator to prepare to leave
Door	(opening of door) signals person to exit elevator, (opening of door) signals person to enter elevator
Bell	none in problem statement
Light	none in problem statement
Building	increments the clock time, gets the time from the clock, provides the time to the scheduler, provides the time to the elevator

Fig. 5.33　Modified list of verb phrases for classes in the system.

An object of class	Sends the message	To an object of class
Elevator	**resetButton**	**ElevatorButton**
	ringBell	**Bell**
	elevatorArrived	**Floor**
	openDoor	**Door**
	closeDoor	**Door**

Fig. 5.34　Collaborations that occur in the elevator system. (Part 1 of 2.)

An object of class	Sends the message	To an object of class
Clock	-----	-----
Scheduler	stepOntoFloor	Person
	isOccupied	Floor
Person	pressButton	FloorButton
	pressButton	ElevatorButton
	passengerEnters	Elevator
	passengerExits	Elevator
	personArrives	Floor
Floor	resetButton	FloorButton
	turnOff	Light
	turnOn	Light
FloorButton	summonElevator	Elevator
ElevatorButton	prepareToLeave	Elevator
Door	exitElevator	Person
	enterElevator	Person
Bell	-----	-----
Light	-----	-----
Building	tick	Clock
	getTime	Clock
	processTime	Scheduler
	processTime	Elevator

Fig. 5.34   Collaborations that occur in the elevator system. (Part 2 of 2.)

Collaboration Diagrams

Now let us consider the objects that must interact so that people in our simulation can enter and exit the elevator when it arrives on a floor. A *collaboration* consists of a collection of objects that work together to perform a task. The UML enables us to model such objects, and their interactions, with *collaboration diagrams*. Collaboration diagrams and sequence diagrams both provide information about how objects interact, but each diagram emphasizes different information. Sequence diagrams emphasize *when* interactions occur. Collaboration diagrams emphasize *which objects participate* in the interactions and the relationships among those objects.

Figure 5.35 shows a collaboration diagram that models the interaction among objects in our system as objects of class **Person** enter and exit the elevator. The collaboration begins when the elevator arrives on a floor. As in a sequence diagram, an object in a collaboration diagram is represented as a rectangle that encloses the object's name.

Interacting objects are connected with solid lines, and objects pass messages to one another along these lines in the direction shown by the arrows. Each message's name and a *message number* appear next to the corresponding arrow.

The *sequence of messages* in a collaboration diagram progresses in numerical order from least to greatest. In this diagram, the numbering starts with message **1**. When the elevator

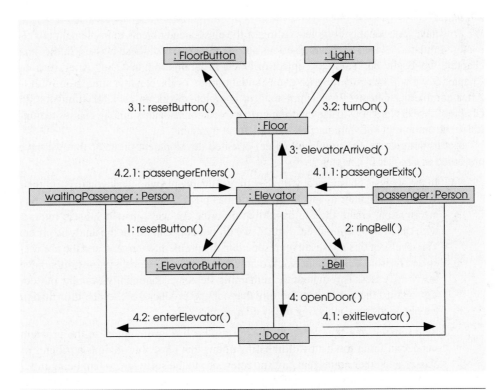

Fig. 5.35　Collaboration diagram for loading and unloading passengers.

arrives at a floor, the first thing it does is send this message (**resetButton**) to the elevator button to reset the button. The elevator then sends the **ringBell** message (message 2) to the bell. Then the elevator notifies the floor of its arrival (message 3), so that the floor can reset its button and turn on its light (messages 3.1 and 3.2, respectively).

After the floor has reset its button and turned on its light, the elevator opens its door (message 4). At this point, the door sends the **exitElevator** message (message 4.1) to the **passenger** object.[1] The **passenger** object notifies the elevator of its intent to exit via the **passengerExits** message (message 4.1.1).

After the person riding the elevator has exited, the person waiting on the floor (the **waitingPassenger** object) can enter the elevator. Notice that the door sends the **enterElevator** message (message 4.2) to the **waitingPassenger** object after the **passenger** object sends the **passengerExits** message to the elevator (message 4.1.1). This sequence ensures that a person on the floor waits for an elevator passenger to exit before the person on the floor enters the elevator. The **waitingPassenger** object enters the elevator via the **passengerEnters** message (message 4.2.1). Determining the sequence of these messages and modeling them with a diagram will aid us as we implement the various classes in our system.

1.　In the real world, a person riding on the elevator waits until the door opens before exiting the elevator. We must model this behavior; therefore, we have the door send a message to the **passenger** object in the elevator. This message represents a visual cue to the person in the elevator. When the person receives the cue, the person can exit the elevator.

Summary

We now have a reasonably complete listing of the classes and objects to implement our elevator simulator, as well as the interactions among the objects of these classes. In the next chapter, we begin our study of object-oriented programming in C++. After reading Chapter 6, we will be ready to write a substantial portion of the elevator simulator in C++. After completing Chapter 7, we implement a complete, working elevator simulator. In Chapter 9, we discuss how to use inheritance to exploit commonality among classes to minimize the amount of software needed to implement a system.

Let us summarize our simplified object-oriented development process[2] that we have presented in Chapter 2–Chapter 5:

1. In the analysis phase, meet with the clients (the people who want you to build their system) and gather as much information as possible about the system. With this information, create the use cases that describe the ways in which users interact with the system. (In our case study, we do not concentrate on the analysis phase. The results of this phase are represented in the problem statement, and the use cases derive from this statement.) We note again that real-world systems often have many use cases. Throughout the remaining steps, we continually evaluate our design against the use cases to be sure that our end product matches the information we obtained from analyzing the system requirements.

2. Begin identifying the classes in the system by listing the nouns in the problem statement. Filter the list by eliminating nouns that represent obvious attributes of classes and other nouns that have no relevance to the software system being modeled. Create a class diagram that models the classes in the system and their relationships (associations).

3. Extract the attributes of each class from the problem statement by listing words and phrases that describe each class in the system.

4. Learn more about the dynamic nature of the system. Create statechart diagrams to learn how the objects in the system change over time.

5. Examine verbs and verb phrases associated with each class. Use these phrases to extract the operations of the classes in our system. Activity diagrams can help model the details of these operations.

6. Examine the interactions among various objects. Use sequence and collaboration diagrams to model these interactions. Add attributes and operations to the classes as the design process reveals the need for them.

7. At this point, our design probably still has a few missing pieces. These will become apparent as we begin to implement our elevator simulator in C++ in the "Thinking About Objects" section at the end of Chapter 6.

---

2. We created this basic OOD process to introduce readers to object-oriented design using the UML. Readers who wish to pursue this topic in more depth can study the more formal and detailed Rational Unified Process. For more information on this software-design methodology, we recommend reading *The Rational Unified Process: An Introduction (2nd Edition)* by Philippe Kruchten and *The Unified Software Develpment Process* by Ivar Jacobson, Grady Booch and James Rumbaugh. For online resources, visit **www.therationaledge.com**, which contains numerous articles on this process.

UML Resources on the Internet and World Wide Web
The following is a collection of Internet and World Wide Web resources for the UML. These include the UML 1.4 specification and other reference materials, general resources, tutorials, FAQs, articles, whitepapers and software.

References

www.omg.org
This is the Object Management Group (OMG) site. The OMG is responsible for overseeing maintenance and future revisions of the UML. The site contains information about the UML and other object-oriented technologies.

www.rational.com
Rational Software Corporation developed the UML. Its Web site contains information about the UML and the creators of the UML—Grady Booch, James Rumbaugh and Ivar Jacobson.

www.omg.org/technology/documents/formal/uml.htm
This site contains the official UML 1.4 specification.

www.rational.com/uml/resources/quick/index.jtmpl
Rational Software Corporation's UML quick-reference guide can be found at this site.

www.holub.com/class/uml/uml.html
This site provides a detailed UML quick-reference card with additional commentary.

softdocwiz.com/UML.htm
Kendall Scott, an author of several UML resources, maintains a UML dictionary at this site.

Resources

www.omg.org/uml/
This site contains the OMG UML resource page.

www.rational.com/uml/index.jsp
Rational Software Corporation's UML resource page

www.platinum.com/corp/uml/uml.htm
UML Partners member Platinum Technology maintains this UML resource site.

www.cetus-links.org/oo_uml.html
This site contains hundreds of links to other UML sites, including information, tutorials and software.

www.embarcadero.com/support/uml_central.asp
This site contains links to several UML-related items, including references, tutorials and articles.

www.devx.com/uml
This site contains a wealth of UML information, including articles and links to news groups and to other sites.

www.celigent.com/uml
This site contains general information and links to important sites on the Web.

www.methods-tools.com/cgi-bin/DiscussionUML.cgi
This site provides access to several UML discussion groups.

www.pols.co.uk/usecasezone/index.htm
This site provides resources and articles about applying use cases.

www.ics.uci.edu/pub/arch/uml/uml_books_and_tools.html
This site contains links to information about books on the UML, as well as a list of tools that support UML notation.

home.earthlink.net/~salhir
Sinan Si Alhir, author of *UML in a Nutshell*, maintains this site; it includes links to many UML resources.

www.rational.com/products/rup/index.jsp
This is the main site for the Rational Unified Process (RUP), Rational's OOAD methodology.

www.cetus-links.org/oo_ooa_ood_methods.html
This site contains links to many software development methodologies, including RUP, Extreme Programming, the Booch methodology and many more.

Software

www.rational.com/products/rose/index.jsp
This site is the home page for Rational Software Corporation's UML visual modeling tool, Rational Rose.™ You can download a trial version from this location and use it free for a limited time.

www.sparxsystems.com.au/ea.htm
Sparx Systems offers Enterprise Architect, a UML OOAD tool. The professional version provides code generation and reverse-engineering support for C++, Java and C#, among others.

www.visualobject.com
Visual Object Modelers has created a visual UML modeling tool. You can download a limited demonstration version from this Web site and use it free for a limited time.

www.embarcadero.com/downloads/download.asp
Embarcadero provides Desribe™ Enterprise, a UML design tool.

www.microgold.com/version2/stage/product.html
Microgold Software, Inc. has created *With*Class, a software design application that supports the UML notation.

dir.lycos.com/Computers/Software/Object_Oriented/Methodologies/ UML/Tools
This site lists dozens of UML modeling tools and their home pages.

www.methods-tools.com/tools/modeling.html
This site contains a listing of many object modeling tools, including those that support the UML.

Articles and Whitepapers

www.omg.org/news/pr99/UML_2001_CACM_Oct99_p29-Kobryn.pdf
This article, written by Cris Kobryn, explores the past, present and future of the UML.

www.db.informatik.uni-bremen.de/umlbib
The UML Bibliography provides names and authors of many UML-related articles. You can search articles by author or title.

www.ratio.co.uk/white.html
You can read a whitepaper that outlines a process for OOAD using the UML at this site. The paper also includes some implementation in C++.

www.conallen.com/whitepapers/webapps/ModelingWebApplications.htm
This site contains a case study that models Web applications using the UML.

www.sdmagazine.com
The Software Development Magazine Online site has a repository of many articles on the UML. You can search by subject or browse article titles.

FAQs

www.rational.com/uml/gstart/faq.jsp
This is the location of Rational Software Corporation's UML FAQ.

www.jguru.com/faq
Enter UML in the search box to access a this site's UML FAQ.

Bibliography

Alhir, S. *UML in a Nutshell*. Cambridge: O'Reily & Associates, Inc., 1998.

Booch, G., Rumbaugh, J. and Jacobson, I. *The Unified Modeling Language User Guide*. Reading, MA: Addison-Wesley, 1999.

Firesmith, D.G., and Henderson-Sellers, B. "Clarifying Specialized Forms of Association in UML and OML." *Journal of Object-Oriented Programming* May 1998: 47–50.

Fowler, M., and Scott, K. *UML Distilled: Applying the Standard Object Modeling Language*. Reading, MA: Addison-Wesley, 1997.

Johnson, L.J. "Model Behavior." *Enterprise Development* May 2000: 20–28.

McLaughlin, M., and A. Moore. "Real-Time Extensions to the UML." *Dr. Dobb's Journal* December 1998: 82–93.

Melewski, D. "UML Gains Ground." *Application Development Trends* October 1998: 34–44.

Melewski, D. "UML: Ready for Prime Time?" *Application Development Trends* November 1997: 30–44.

Melewski, D. "Wherefore and what now, UML?" *Application Development Trends* December 1999: 61–68.

Muller, P. *Instant UML*. Birmingham, UK: Wrox Press Ltd, 1997.

Perry, P. "UML Steps to the Plate." *Application Development Trends* May 1999: 33–36.

Rumbaugh, J., Jacobson, I. and Booch, G. *The Unified Modeling Language Reference Manual*. Reading, MA: Addison-Wesley, 1999.

Schmuller, J. *Sam's Teach Yourself UML in 24 Hours*. Indianapolis: Macmillan Computer Publishing, 1999.

The Unified Modeling Language Specification: Version 1.4. Framingham, MA: Object Management Goup (OMG), 2001.

SUMMARY

- Pointers are variables that contain as their values addresses of other variables.
- The declaration

    ```
    int *ptr;
    ```

    declares **ptr** to be a pointer to a variable of type **int** and is read, "**ptr** is a pointer to **int**." The ***** as used here in a declaration indicates that the variable is a pointer.

- There are three values that can be used to initialize a pointer: **0**, **NULL** or an address of an object of the same type. Initializing a pointer to **0** and initializing that same pointer to **NULL** are identical—**0** is the convention in C++.

- The only integer that can be assigned to a pointer without casting is zero.

- The **&** (address) operator returns the memory address of its operand.

- The operand of the address operator must be a variable name (or another *lvalue*); the address operator cannot be applied to constants or to expressions that do not return a reference.

- The `*` operator, referred to as the indirection (or dereferencing) operator, returns a synonym, alias or nickname for the name of the object that its operand points to in memory. This is called dereferencing the pointer.

- When calling a function with an argument that the caller wants the called function to modify, the address of the argument may be passed. The called function then uses the indirection operator (`*`) to dereference the pointer and modify the value of the argument in the calling function.

- A function receiving an address as an argument must have a pointer as its corresponding parameter.

- The `const` qualifier enables the programmer to inform the compiler that the value of a particular variable cannot be modified through the specified identifier. If an attempt is made to modify a `const` value, the compiler issues either a warning or an error, depending on the particular compiler.

- There are four ways to pass a pointer to a function—a nonconstant pointer to nonconstant data, a nonconstant pointer to constant data, a constant pointer to nonconstant data and a constant pointer to constant data.

- The value of the array name is the address of (a pointer to) the array's first element.

- To pass a single element of an array by reference using pointers, pass the address of the specific array element.

- C++ provides unary operator `sizeof` to determine the size of an array (or of any other data type, variable or constant) in bytes at compile time.

- When applied to the name of an array, the `sizeof` operator returns the total number of bytes in the array as an integer.

- The arithmetic operations that may be performed on pointers are incrementing (`++`) a pointer, decrementing (`--`) a pointer, adding (`+` or `+=`) an integer to a pointer, subtracting (`-` or `-=`) an integer from a pointer and subtracting one pointer from another.

- When an integer is added or subtracted from a pointer, the pointer is incremented or decremented by that integer times the size of the object to which the pointer refers.

- Pointer arithmetic operations should only be performed on contiguous portions of memory such as an array. All elements of an array are stored contiguously in memory.

- Pointers can be assigned to one another if both pointers are of the same type. Otherwise, a cast must be used. The exception to this is a `void *` pointer, which is a generic pointer type that can hold pointer values of any type. Pointers to `void` can be assigned pointers of other types. A `void *` pointer can be assigned to a pointer of another type only with an explicit type cast.

- The only valid operations on a `void *` pointer are comparing `void *` pointers with other pointers, assigning addresses to `void *` pointers and casting `void *` pointers to valid pointer types.

- Pointers can be compared using the equality and relational operators. Comparisons using relational operators are meaningful only if the pointers point to members of the same array.

- Pointers that point to arrays can be subscripted exactly as array names can.

- An array name is equivalent to a constant pointer to the first element of the array.

- In pointer/offset notation, if the pointer points to the first element of the array, the offset is the same as an array subscript.

- All subscripted array expressions can be written with a pointer and an offset, using either the name of the array as a pointer or using a separate pointer that points to the array.

- Arrays may contain pointers.

- A pointer to a function is the address where the code for the function resides.

- Pointers to functions can be passed to functions, returned from functions, stored in arrays and assigned to other pointers.

- A common use of function pointers is in so-called menu-driven systems. The function pointers are used to select which function to call for a particular menu item.

- Function **strcpy** copies its second argument—a string—into its first argument—a character array. The programmer must ensure that the target array is large enough to store the string and its terminating null character.

- Function **strncpy** is equivalent to **strcpy**, except that a call to **strncpy** specifies the number of characters to be copied from the string into the array. The terminating null character will be copied only if the number of characters to be copied is at least one more than the length of the string.

- Function **strcat** appends its second string argument—including the terminating null character—to its first string argument. The first character of the second string replaces the null (**'\0'**) character of the first string. The programmer must ensure that the target array used to store the first string is large enough to store both the first string and the second string.

- Function **strncat** is equivalent to **strcat**, except that a call to **strncat** appends a specified number of characters from the second string to the first string. A terminating null character is appended to the result.

- Function **strcmp** compares its first string argument with its second string argument character by character. The function returns zero if the strings are equal, a negative value if the first string is less than the second string and a positive value if the first string is greater than the second string.

- Function **strncmp** is equivalent to **strcmp**, except that **strncmp** compares a specified number of characters. If the number of characters in one of the strings is less than the number of characters specified, **strncmp** compares characters until the null character in the shorter string is encountered.

- A sequence of calls to **strtok** breaks a string into tokens that are separated by characters contained in a second string argument. The first call specifies the string to be tokenized as the first argument, and subsequent calls to continue tokenizing the same string specify **NULL** as the first argument. The function returns a pointer to the current token from each call. If there are no more tokens when **strtok** is called, **NULL** is returned.

- Function **strlen** takes a string as an argument and returns the number of characters in the string—the terminating null character is not included in the length of the string.

TERMINOLOGY

add a pointer and an integer

address operator (**&**)

appending strings to other strings

array of pointers

array of strings

ASCII

<cctype>

character code

character constant

character pointer

character set

comparing strings

const

constant pointer

constant pointer to constant data

constant pointer to nonconstant data

copying strings

<cstring>

decrement a pointer

delimiter

dereference a pointer

dereferencing operator (*****)

directly reference a variable

EBCDIC

function pointer

increment a pointer

indefinite postponement

indirection

indirection operator (*****)

indirectly reference a variable

initialize a pointer

islower

length of a string	`strcat`
literal	`strcmp`
nonconstant pointer to constant data	`strcpy`
nonconstant pointer to nonconstant data	string
NULL pointer	string concatenation
numeric code of a character	string constant
offset	string literal
pass-by-reference	string processing
pass-by-value	`strlen`
pointer	`strncat`
pointer arithmetic	`strncmp`
pointer assignment	`strncpy`
pointer comparison	`strtok`
pointer expression	subtracting an integer from a pointer
pointer/offset notation	subtracting two pointers
pointer subscripting	token
pointer to a function	tokenizing strings
pointer to **void** (**void ***)	`toupper`
pointer types	**void *** (pointer to **void**)
principle of least privilege	word processing
`sizeof`	

Terminology for Optional "Thinking About Objects" Section

collaboration	rectangle symbol in UML
collaboration diagram	collaboration diagram
interaction	sequence of messages
message	solid line with arrowhead symbol in UML
numbers in UML collaboration diagram	collaboration diagram
objects that participate in interaction	when interactions occur

SELF-REVIEW EXERCISES

5.1   Answer each of the following:
a) A pointer is a variable that contains as its value the _____ of another variable.
b) The three values that can be used to initialize a pointer are _____, _____ and _____.
c) The only integer that can be assigned directly to a pointer is _____.

5.2   State whether the following are *true* or *false*. If the answer is *false*, explain why.
a) The address operator **&** can be applied only to constants and to expressions.
b) A pointer that is declared to be of type **void** can be dereferenced.
c) Pointers of different types may not be assigned to one another without a cast operation.

5.3   For each of the following, write C++ statements that perform the specified task. Assume that double-precision, floating-point numbers are stored in eight bytes and that the starting address of the array is at location 1002500 in memory. Each part of the exercise should use the results of previous parts where appropriate.
a) Declare an array of type **double** called **numbers** with 10 elements, and initialize the elements to the values **0.0**, **1.1**, **2.2**, ..., **9.9**. Assume that the symbolic constant **SIZE** has been defined as **10**.
b) Declare a pointer **nPtr** that points to a variable of type **double**.
c) Use a **for** structure to print the elements of array **numbers** using array subscript notation. Print each number with one position of precision to the right of the decimal point.

d) Write two separate statements that each assign the starting address of array **numbers** to the pointer variable **nPtr**.

e) Use a **for** structure to print the elements of array **numbers** using pointer/offset notation with pointer **nPtr**.

f) Use a **for** structure to print the elements of array **numbers** using pointer/offset notation with the array name as the pointer.

g) Use a **for** structure to print the elements of array **numbers** using pointer/subscript notation with pointer **nPtr**.

h) Refer to the fourth element of array **numbers** using array subscript notation, pointer/offset notation with the array name as the pointer, pointer subscript notation with **nPtr** and pointer/offset notation with **nPtr**.

i) Assuming that **nPtr** points to the beginning of array **numbers**, what address is referenced by **nPtr + 8**? What value is stored at that location?

j) Assuming that **nPtr** points to **numbers[5]**, what address is referenced by **nPtr** after **nPtr -= 4** is executed? What is the value stored at that location?

5.4 For each of the following, write a single statement that performs the specified task. Assume that floating-point variables **number1** and **number2** have been declared and that **number1** has been initialized to **7.3**. Assume that variable **ptr** is of type **char ***. Assume that arrays **s1** and **s2** are each 100-element **char** arrays that are initialized with string literals.

a) Declare the variable **fPtr** to be a pointer to an object of type **double**.

b) Assign the address of variable **number1** to pointer variable **fPtr**.

c) Print the value of the object pointed to by **fPtr**.

d) Assign the value of the object pointed to by **fPtr** to variable **number2**.

e) Print the value of **number2**.

f) Print the address of **number1**.

g) Print the address stored in **fPtr**. Is the value printed the same as the address of **number1**?

h) Copy the string stored in array **s2** into array **s1**.

i) Compare the string in **s1** with the string in **s2**, and print the result.

j) Append the first 10 characters from the string in **s2** to the string in **s1**.

k) Determine the length of the string in **s1**, and print the result.

l) Assign to **ptr** the location of the first token in **s2**. The tokens delimiters are commas (**,**).

5.5 Perform the task specified by each of the following statements:

a) Write the function header for a function called **exchange** that takes two pointers to double-precision, floating-point numbers **x** and **y** as parameters and does not return a value.

b) Write the function prototype for the function in part (a).

c) Write the function header for a function called **evaluate** that returns an integer and that takes as parameters integer **x** and a pointer to function **poly**. Function **poly** takes an integer parameter and returns an integer.

d) Write the function prototype for the function in part (c).

e) Write two statements that each initialize character array **vowel** with the string of vowels, **"AEIOU"**.

5.6 Find the error in each of the following program segments. Assume the following declarations and statements:

```
int *zPtr;          // zPtr will reference array z
int *aPtr = 0;
void *sPtr = 0;
int number;
int z[ 5 ] = { 1, 2, 3, 4, 5 };

sPtr = z;
```

a) `++zPtr;`

b) `// use pointer to get first value of array`
   `number = zPtr;`

c) `// assign array element 2 (the value 3) to number`
   `number = *zPtr[ 2 ];`

d) `// print entire array z`
   `for ( int i = 0; i <= 5; i++ )`
   `   cout << zPtr[ i ] << endl;`

e) `// assign the value pointed to by sPtr to number`
   `number = *sPtr;`

f) `++z;`

g) `char s[ 10 ];`
   `cout << strncpy( s, "hello", 5 ) << endl;`

h) `char s[ 12 ];`
   `strcpy( s, "Welcome Home" );`

i) `if ( strcmp( string1, string2 ) )`
   `     cout << "The strings are equal" << endl;`

5.7   What (if anything) prints when each of the following statements is performed? If the statement contains an error, describe the error and indicate how to correct it. Assume the following variable declarations:

```
char s1[ 50 ] = "jack";
char s2[ 50 ] = "jill";
char s3[ 50 ];
```

a) `cout << strcpy( s3, s2 ) << endl;`

b) `cout << strcat( strcat( strcpy( s3, s1 ), " and " ), s2 )`
   `     << endl;`

c) `cout << strlen( s1 ) + strlen( s2 ) << endl;`

d) `cout << strlen( s3 ) << endl;`

ANSWERS TO SELF-REVIEW EXERCISES

5.1   a) address. b) **0**, **NULL**, an address. c) **0**.

5.2   a) False. The operand of the address operator must be an *lvalue*; the address operator cannot be applied to constants or to expressions that do not result in references.

         b) False. A pointer to **void** cannot be dereferenced. Such a pointer does not have a type that enables the compiler to determine the number of bytes of memory to dereference.

         c) False. Pointers of any type can be assigned to **void** pointers. Pointers of type **void** can be assigned to pointers of other types only with an explicit type cast.

5.3   a) `double numbers[ SIZE ] =`
   `     { 0.0, 1.1, 2.2, 3.3, 4.4, 5.5, 6.6, 7.7, 8.8, 9.9 };`

         b) `double *nPtr;`

         c) `cout << fixed << showpoint << setprecision( 1 );`
   `for ( int i = 0; i < SIZE; i++ )`
   `   cout << numbers[ i ] << ' ';`

         d) `nPtr = numbers;`
   `nPtr = &numbers[ 0 ];`

         e) `cout << fixed << showpoint << setprecision( 1 );`
   `for ( int j = 0; j < SIZE; j++ )`
   `   cout << *( nPtr + j ) << ' ';`

```
f)  cout << fixed << showpoint << setprecision( 1 );
    for ( int k = 0; k < SIZE; k++ )
        cout << *( numbers + k ) << ' ';
g)  cout << fixed << showpoint << setprecision( 1 );
    for ( int m = 0; m < SIZE; m++ )
        cout << nPtr[ m ] << ' ';
h)  numbers[ 3 ]
    *( numbers + 3 )
    nPtr[ 3 ]
    *( nPtr + 3 )
```

i) The address is **1002500 + 8 * 8 = 1002564**. The value is **8.8**.

j) The address of **numbers[5]** is **1002500 + 5 * 8 = 1002540**.
    The address of **nPtr -= 4** is **1002540 - 4 * 8 = 1002508**.
    The value at that location is **1.1**.

5.4
```
a)  double *fPtr;
b)  fPtr = &number1;
c)  cout << "The value of *fPtr is " << *fPtr << endl;
d)  number2 = *fPtr;
e)  cout << "The value of number2 is " << number2 << endl;
f)  cout << "The address of number1 is " << &number1 << endl;
g)  cout << "The address stored in fPtr is " << fPtr << endl;
```
    Yes, the value is the same.
```
h)  strcpy( s1, s2 );
i)  cout << "strcmp(s1, s2) = " << strcmp( s1, s2 ) << endl;
j)  strncat( s1, s2, 10 );
k)  cout << "strlen(s1) = " << strlen( s1 ) << endl;
l)  ptr = strtok( s2, "," );
```

5.5
```
a)  void exchange( double *x, double *y )
b)  void exchange( double *, double * );
c)  int evaluate( int x, int (*poly)( int ) )
d)  int evaluate( int, int (*)( int ) );
e)  char vowel[] = "AEIOU";
    char vowel[] = { 'A', 'E', 'I', 'O', 'U', '\0' };
```

5.6 a) Error: **zPtr** has not been initialized.
        Correction: Initialize **zPtr** with **zPtr = z;**

     b) Error: The pointer is not dereferenced.
        Correction: Change the statement to **number = *zPtr;**

     c) Error: **zPtr[2]** is not a pointer and should not be dereferenced.
        Correction: Change ***zPtr[2]** to **zPtr[2]**.

     d) Error: Referring to an array element outside the array bounds with pointer subscripting.
        Correction: Change the relational operator in the **for** structure to **<** to prevent walking
        off the end of the array.

     e) Error: Dereferencing a **void** pointer.
        Correction: To dereference the **void** pointer, it must first be cast to an integer pointer.
        Change the preceding statement to **number = *((int *) sPtr);**

     f) Error: Trying to modify an array name with pointer arithmetic.
        Correction: Use a pointer variable instead of the array name to accomplish pointer arith-
        metic, or subscript the array name to refer to a specific element.

     g) Error: Function **strncpy** does not write a terminating null character to array **s**, because
        its third argument is equal to the length of the string **"hello"**.

Correction: Make **6** the third argument of **strncpy** or assign **'\0'** to **s[5]** to ensure that the terminating null character is added to the string.

h) Error: Character array **s** is not large enough to store the terminating null character.
Correction: Declare the array with more elements.

i) Error: Function **strcmp** will return 0 if the strings are equal; therefore, the condition in the **if** structure will be false, and the output statement will not be executed.
Correction: Explicitly compare the result of **strcmp** with **0** in the condition of the **if** structure.

5.7   a) **jill**
           b) **jack and jill**
           c) **8**
           d) **13**

EXERCISES

5.8   State whether the following are *true* or *false*. If *false*, explain why.
   a) Two pointers that point to different arrays cannot be compared meaningfully.
   b) Because the name of an array is a pointer to the first element of the array, array names can be manipulated in precisely the same manner as pointers.

5.9   For each of the following, write C++ statements that perform the specified task. Assume that unsigned integers are stored in two bytes and that the starting address of the array is at location 1002500 in memory.
   a) Declare an array of type **unsigned int** called **values** with five elements, and initialize the elements to the even integers from 2 to 10. Assume that the symbolic constant **SIZE** has been defined as **5**.
   b) Declare a pointer **vPtr** that points to an object of type **unsigned int**.
   c) Use a **for** structure to print the elements of array **values** using array subscript notation.
   d) Write two separate statements that assign the starting address of array **values** to pointer variable **vPtr**.
   e) Use a **for** structure to print the elements of array **values** using pointer/offset notation.
   f) Use a **for** structure to print the elements of array **values** using pointer/offset notation with the array name as the pointer.
   g) Use a **for** structure to print the elements of array **values** by subscripting the pointer to the array.
   h) Refer to the fifth element of **values** using array subscript notation pointer/offset notation with the array name as the pointer, pointer subscript notation and pointer/offset notation.
   i) What address is referenced by **vPtr + 3**? What value is stored at that location?
   j) Assuming that **vPtr** points to **values[4]**, what address is referenced by **vPtr -= 4**? What value is stored at that location?

5.10   For each of the following, write a single statement that performs the specified task. Assume that **long** integer variables **value1** and **value2** have been declared and that **value1** has been initialized to **200000**.
   a) Declare the variable **longPtr** to be a pointer to an object of type **long**.
   b) Assign the address of variable **value1** to pointer variable **longPtr**.
   c) Print the value of the object pointed to by **longPtr**.
   d) Assign the value of the object pointed to by **longPtr** to variable **value2**.
   e) Print the value of **value2**.
   f) Print the address of **value1**.
   g) Print the address stored in **longPtr**. Is the value printed the same as **value1**'s address?

5.11   Perform the task specified by each of the following statements:

    a) Write the function header for function **zero** that takes a long integer array parameter **bigIntegers** and does not return a value.

    b) Write the function prototype for the function in part (a).

    c) Write the function header for function **add1AndSum** that takes an integer array parameter **oneTooSmall** and returns an integer.

    d) Write the function prototype for the function described in part (c).

Note: Exercise 5.12 through Exercise 5.15 are reasonably challenging. Once you have solved these problems, you ought to be able to implement most popular card games.

5.12   Modify the program in Fig. 5.24 so that the card dealing function deals a five-card poker hand. Then write functions to accomplish each of the following:

    a) Determine whether the hand contains a pair.

    b) Determine whether the hand contains two pairs.

    c) Determine whether the hand contains three of a kind (e.g., three jacks).

    d) Determine whether the hand contains four of a kind (e.g., four aces).

    e) Determine whether the hand contains a flush (i.e., all five cards of the same suit).

    f) Determine whether the hand contains a straight (i.e., five cards of consecutive face values).

5.13   Use the functions developed in Exercise 5.12 to write a program that deals two five-card poker hands, evaluates each hand and determines which is the better hand.

5.14   Modify the program developed in Exercise 5.13 so that it can simulate the dealer. The dealer's five-card hand is dealt "face down" so the player cannot see it. The program should then evaluate the dealer's hand, and, based on the quality of the hand, the dealer should draw one, two or three more cards to replace the corresponding number of unneeded cards in the original hand. The program should then reevaluate the dealer's hand. [*Caution:* This is a difficult problem!]

5.15   Modify the program developed in Exercise 5.14 so that it handles the dealer's hand, but the player is allowed to decide which cards of the player's hand to replace. The program should then evaluate both hands and determine who wins. Now use this new program to play 20 games against the computer. Who wins more games, you or the computer? Have one of your friends play 20 games against the computer. Who wins more games? Based on the results of these games, make appropriate modifications to refine your poker-playing program. [*Note:* This, too, is a difficult problem.] Play 20 more games. Does your modified program play a better game?

5.16   In the card-shuffling and dealing program of Fig. 5.24, we intentionally used an inefficient shuffling algorithm that introduced the possibility of indefinite postponement. In this problem, you will create a high-performance shuffling algorithm that avoids indefinite postponement.

    Modify Fig. 5.24 as follows. Initialize the **deck** array as shown in Fig. 5.36. Modify the **shuffle** function to loop row-by-row and column-by-column through the array, touching every element once. Each element should be swapped with a randomly selected element of the array. Print the resulting array to determine whether the deck is satisfactorily shuffled (as in Fig. 5.37, for example). You may want your program to call the **shuffle** function several times to ensure a satisfactory shuffle.

    Note that although the approach in this problem improves the shuffling algorithm, the dealing algorithm still requires searching the **deck** array for card 1, then card 2, then card 3 and so on. Worse yet, even after the dealing algorithm locates and deals the card, the algorithm continues searching through the remainder of the deck. Modify the program of Fig. 5.24 so that once a card is dealt, no further attempts are made to match that card number, and the program immediately proceeds with dealing the next card.

Unshuffled **deck** array												
	0	1	2	3	4	5	6	7	8	9	10	11	12
0	1	2	3	4	5	6	7	8	9	10	11	12	13
1	14	15	16	17	18	19	20	21	22	23	24	25	26
2	27	28	29	30	31	32	33	34	35	36	37	38	39
3	40	41	42	43	44	45	46	47	48	49	50	51	52

Fig. 5.36   Unshuffled **deck** array.

Sample shuffled **deck** array												
	0	1	2	3	4	5	6	7	8	9	10	11	12
0	19	40	27	25	36	46	10	34	35	41	18	2	44
1	13	28	14	16	21	30	8	11	31	17	24	7	1
2	12	33	15	42	43	23	45	3	29	32	4	47	26
3	50	38	52	39	48	51	9	5	37	49	22	6	20

Fig. 5.37   Sample shuffled **deck** array.

5.17   (*Simulation: The Tortoise and the Hare*) In this exercise, you will re-create the classic race of the tortoise and the hare. You will use random-number generation to develop a simulation of this memorable event.

Our contenders begin the race at "square 1" of 70 squares. Each square represents a possible position along the race course. The finish line is at square 70. The first contender to reach or pass square 70 is rewarded with a pail of fresh carrots and lettuce. The course weaves its way up the side of a slippery mountain, so occasionally the contenders lose ground.

There is a clock that ticks once per second. With each tick of the clock, your program should adjust the position of the animals according to the rules in Fig. 5.38.

Animal	Move type	Percentage of the time	Actual move
Tortoise	Fast plod	50%	3 squares to the right
	Slip	20%	6 squares to the left
	Slow plod	30%	1 square to the right
Hare	Sleep	20%	No move at all
	Big hop	20%	9 squares to the right
	Big slip	10%	12 squares to the left
	Small hop	30%	1 square to the right
	Small slip	20%	2 squares to the left

Fig. 5.38   Rules for moving the tortoise and the hare.

Use variables to keep track of the positions of the animals (i.e., position numbers are 1–70). Start each animal at position 1 (i.e., the "starting gate"). If an animal slips left before square 1, move the animal back to square 1.

Generate the percentages in the preceding table by producing a random integer i in the range $1 \le i \le 10$. For the tortoise, perform a "fast plod" when $1 \le i \le 5$, a "slip" when $6 \le i \le 7$ or a "slow plod" when $8 \le i \le 10$. Use a similar technique to move the hare.

Begin the race by printing

    BANG !!!!!
    AND THEY'RE OFF !!!!!

For each tick of the clock (i.e., each repetition of a loop), print a 70-position line showing the letter **T** in the tortoise's position and the letter **H** in the hare's position. Occasionally, the contenders land on the same square. In this case, the tortoise bites the hare and your program should print **OUCH!!!** beginning at that position. All print positions other than the **T**, the **H** or the **OUCH!!!** (in case of a tie) should be blank.

After printing each line, test if either animal has reached or passed square 70. If so, print the winner and terminate the simulation. If the tortoise wins, print **TORTOISE WINS!!! YAY!!!** If the hare wins, print **Hare wins. Yuch.** If both animals win on the same clock tick, you may want to favor the turtle (the "underdog"), or you may want to print **It's a tie**. If neither animal wins, perform the loop again to simulate the next tick of the clock. When you are ready to run your program, assemble a group of fans to watch the race. You'll be amazed how involved the audience gets!

SPECIAL SECTION: BUILDING YOUR OWN COMPUTER

In the next several problems, we take a temporary diversion away from the world of high-level-language programming. We "peel open" a computer and look at its internal structure. We introduce machine-language programming and write several machine-language programs. To make this an especially valuable experience, we then build a computer (using software-based *simulation*) on which you can execute your machine-language programs!

5.18 (*Machine-Language Programming*) Let us create a computer we will call the Simpletron. As its name implies, it is a simple machine, but, as we will soon see, a powerful one as well. The Simpletron runs programs written in the only language it directly understands, that is, Simpletron Machine Language, or SML for short.

The Simpletron contains an *accumulator*—a "special register" in which information is put before the Simpletron uses that information in calculations or examines it in various ways. All information in the Simpletron is handled in terms of *words*. A word is a signed four-digit decimal number, such as **+3364**, **–1293**, **+0007**, **–0001**, etc. The Simpletron is equipped with a 100-word memory and these words are referenced by their location numbers **00, 01, …, 99**.

Before running an SML program, we must *load,* or place, the program into memory. The first instruction (or statement) of every SML program is always placed in location **00**. The simulator will start executing at this location.

Each instruction written in SML occupies one word of the Simpletron's memory; thus, instructions are signed four-digit decimal numbers. Assume that the sign of an SML instruction is always plus, but the sign of a data word may be either plus or minus. Each location in the Simpletron's memory may contain an instruction, a data value used by a program or an unused (and hence undefined) area of memory. The first two digits of each SML instruction are the *operation code* that specifies the operation to be performed. SML operation codes are shown in Fig. 5.39.

The last two digits of an SML instruction are the *operand*—the address of the memory location containing the word to which the operation applies.

Operation code	Meaning
Input/output operations:	
`const int READ = 10;`	Read a word from the keyboard into a specific location in memory.
`const int WRITE = 11;`	Write a word from a specific location in memory to the screen.
Load and store operations:	
`const int LOAD = 20;`	Load a word from a specific location in memory into the accumulator.
`const int STORE = 21;`	Store a word from the accumulator into a specific location in memory.
Arithmetic operations:	
`const int ADD = 30;`	Add a word from a specific location in memory to the word in the accumulator (leave result in accumulator).
`const int SUBTRACT = 31;`	Subtract a word from a specific location in memory from the word in the accumulator (leave result in accumulator).
`const int DIVIDE = 32;`	Divide a word from a specific location in memory into the word in the accumulator (leave result in accumulator).
`const int MULTIPLY = 33;`	Multiply a word from a specific location in memory by the word in the accumulator (leave result in accumulator).
Transfer-of-control operations:	
`const int BRANCH = 40;`	Branch to a specific location in memory.
`const int BRANCHNEG = 41;`	Branch to a specific location in memory if the accumulator is negative.
`const int BRANCHZERO = 42;`	Branch to a specific location in memory if the accumulator is zero.
`const int HALT = 43;`	Halt—the program has completed its task.

Fig. 5.39   Simpletron Machine Language (SML) operation codes.

Now let us consider two simple SML programs. The first SML program (Fig. 5.40) reads two numbers from the keyboard and computes and prints their sum. The instruction **+1007** reads the first number from the keyboard and places it into location **07** (which has been initialized to zero). Instruction **+1008** reads the next number into location **08**. The *load* instruction, **+2007**, places (copies) the first number into the accumulator, and the *add* instruction, **+3008**, adds the second number to the number in the accumulator. *All SML arithmetic instructions leave their results in the accumulator.* The *store* instruction, **+2109**, places (copies) the result back into memory location **09**. Then the *write* instruction, **+1109**, takes the number and prints it (as a signed four-digit decimal number). The *halt* instruction, **+4300**, terminates execution.

Location	Number	Instruction
00	+1007	(Read A)
01	+1008	(Read B)
02	+2007	(Load A)
03	+3008	(Add B)
04	+2109	(Store C)
05	+1109	(Write C)
06	+4300	(Halt)
07	+0000	(Variable A)
08	+0000	(Variable B)
09	+0000	(Result C)

Fig. 5.40   SML Example 1.

The SML program in Fig. 5.41 reads two numbers from the keyboard, then determines and prints the larger value. Note the use of the instruction **+4107** as a conditional transfer of control, much the same as C++'s **if** statement.

Now write SML programs to accomplish each of the following tasks:

   a) Use a sentinel-controlled loop to read positive numbers and compute and print their sum. Terminate input when a negative number is entered.
   b) Use a counter-controlled loop to read seven numbers, some positive and some negative, and compute and print their average.
   c) Read a series of numbers, and determine and print the largest number. The first number read indicates how many numbers should be processed.

Location	Number	Instruction
00	+1009	(Read A)
01	+1010	(Read B)
02	+2009	(Load A)
03	+3110	(Subtract B)
04	+4107	(Branch negative to **07**)
05	+1109	(Write A)
06	+4300	(Halt)
07	+1110	(Write B)
08	+4300	(Halt)
09	+0000	(Variable A)
10	+0000	(Variable B)

Fig. 5.41   SML Example 2.

5.19   (*Computer Simulator*) It may at first seem outrageous, but in this problem, you are going to build your own computer. No, you will not be soldering components together. Rather, you will use the powerful technique of *software-based simulation* to create a *software model* of the Simpletron. You will not be disappointed. Your Simpletron simulator will turn the computer you are using into a Simpletron, and you actually will be able to run, test and debug the SML programs you wrote in Exercise 5.18.

When you run your Simpletron simulator, it should begin by printing

```
*** Welcome to Simpletron! ***

*** Please enter your program one instruction ***
*** (or data word) at a time. I will type the ***
*** location number and a question mark (?).  ***
*** You then type the word for that location. ***
*** Type the sentinel -99999 to stop entering ***
*** your program. ***
```

Your program should simulate the Simpletron's memory with a single-subscripted, 100-element array **memory**. Now assume that the simulator is running, and let us examine the dialog as we enter the program of Example 2 of Exercise 5.18:

```
00 ? +1009
01 ? +1010
02 ? +2009
03 ? +3110
04 ? +4107
05 ? +1109
06 ? +4300
07 ? +1110
08 ? +4300
09 ? +0000
10 ? +0000
11 ? -99999

*** Program loading completed ***
*** Program execution begins  ***
```

Note that the numbers to the right of each **?** in the preceding dialog represent the SML program instructions input by the user.

The SML program has now been placed (or loaded) into array **memory**. Now the Simpletron executes your SML program. Execution begins with the instruction in location **00** and, like C++, continues sequentially, unless directed to some other part of the program by a transfer of control.

Use variable **accumulator** to represent the accumulator register. Use variable **counter** to keep track of the location in memory that contains the instruction being performed. Use variable **operationCode** to indicate the operation currently being performed (i.e., the left two digits of the instruction word). Use variable **operand** to indicate the memory location on which the current instruction operates. Thus, **operand** is the rightmost two digits of the instruction currently being performed. Do not execute instructions directly from memory. Rather, transfer the next instruction to be performed from memory to a variable called **instructionRegister**. Then "pick off" the left two digits and place them in **operationCode**, and "pick off" the right two digits and place them in **operand**. When Simpletron begins execution, the special registers are all initialized to zero.

Now let us "walk through" the execution of the first SML instruction, **+1009** in memory location **00**. This is called an *instruction execution cycle*.

The **counter** tells us the location of the next instruction to be performed. We *fetch* the contents of that location from **memory** by using the C++ statement

```
instructionRegister = memory[ counter ];
```

The operation code and operand are extracted from the instruction register by the statements

```
operationCode = instructionRegister / 100;
operand = instructionRegister % 100;
```

Now, the Simpletron must determine that the operation code is actually a *read* (versus a *write*, a *load*, etc.). A **switch** differentiates among the 12 operations of SML.

In the **switch** structure, the behavior of various SML instructions is simulated as follows (we leave the others to the reader):

read:	`cin >> memory[ operand ];`
load:	`accumulator = memory[ operand ];`
add:	`accumulator += memory[ operand ];`
branch:	We will discuss the branch instructions shortly.
halt:	This instruction prints the message
	`*** Simpletron execution terminated ***`

The *halt* instruction also causes the Simpletron to print the name and contents of each register, as well as the complete contents of memory. Such a printout is often called a *computer dump* (and, no, a computer dump is not a place where old computers go). To help you program your dump function, a sample dump format is shown in Fig. 5.42. Note that a dump after executing a Simpletron program would show the actual values of instructions and data values at the moment execution terminated. To format numbers with their sign as shown in the dump, use stream manipulator **showpos**. To disable the display of the sign use stream manipulator **noshowpos**. For numbers that have fewer than four digits, you can format numbers with leading zeros between the sign and the value by using the following statement before outputting the value:

```
cout << setfill( '0' ) << internal;
```

Parameterized stream manipulator **setfill** (from header **<iomanip>**) specifies the fill character that will appear between the sign and the value when a number is displayed with a field width of five characters, but does not have four digits. (One position in the field width is reserved for the sign.) Stream manipulator **internal** indicates that the fill characters should appear between the sign and the numeric value.

Let us proceed with the execution of our program's first instruction—**+1009** in location **00**. As we have indicated, the **switch** structure simulates this by performing the C++ statement

```
cin >> memory[ operand ];
```

A question mark (**?**) should be displayed on the screen before the **cin** statement executes to prompt the user for input. The Simpletron waits for the user to type a value and press the *Enter* key. The value is then read into location **09**.

At this point, simulation of the first instruction is complete. All that remains is to prepare the Simpletron to execute the next instruction. The instruction just performed was not a transfer of control, so we need merely increment the instruction counter register as follows:

```
++counter;
```

This completes the simulated execution of the first instruction. The entire process (i.e., the instruction execution cycle) begins anew with the fetch of the next instruction to execute.

```
REGISTERS:
accumulator           +0000
counter                  00
instructionRegister   +0000
operationCode            00
operand                  00

MEMORY:
        0       1       2       3       4       5       6       7       8       9
 0  +0000   +0000   +0000   +0000   +0000   +0000   +0000   +0000   +0000   +0000
10  +0000   +0000   +0000   +0000   +0000   +0000   +0000   +0000   +0000   +0000
20  +0000   +0000   +0000   +0000   +0000   +0000   +0000   +0000   +0000   +0000
30  +0000   +0000   +0000   +0000   +0000   +0000   +0000   +0000   +0000   +0000
40  +0000   +0000   +0000   +0000   +0000   +0000   +0000   +0000   +0000   +0000
50  +0000   +0000   +0000   +0000   +0000   +0000   +0000   +0000   +0000   +0000
60  +0000   +0000   +0000   +0000   +0000   +0000   +0000   +0000   +0000   +0000
70  +0000   +0000   +0000   +0000   +0000   +0000   +0000   +0000   +0000   +0000
80  +0000   +0000   +0000   +0000   +0000   +0000   +0000   +0000   +0000   +0000
90  +0000   +0000   +0000   +0000   +0000   +0000   +0000   +0000   +0000   +0000
```

Fig. 5.42   A sample dump.

Now let us consider how to simulate the branching instructions (i.e., the transfers of control). All we need to do is adjust the value in the instruction counter appropriately. Therefore, the unconditional branch instruction (**40**) is simulated in the **switch** as

```
counter = operand;
```

The conditional "branch if accumulator is zero" instruction is simulated as

```
if ( accumulator == 0 )
   counter = operand;
```

At this point, you should implement your Simpletron simulator and run each of the SML programs you wrote in Exercise 5.18. You may embellish SML with additional features and provide for these in your simulator.

Your simulator should check for various types of errors. During the program loading phase, for example, each number the user types into the Simpletron's **memory** must be in the range **-9999** to **+9999**. Your simulator should use a **while** loop to test that each number entered is in this range and, if not, keep prompting the user to reenter the number until the user enters a correct number.

During the execution phase, your simulator should check for various serious errors, such as attempts to divide by zero, attempts to execute invalid operation codes, accumulator overflows (i.e., arithmetic operations resulting in values larger than **+9999** or smaller than **-9999**) and the like. Such serious errors are called *fatal errors*. When a fatal error is detected, your simulator should print an error message such as

```
*** Attempt to divide by zero ***
*** Simpletron execution abnormally terminated ***
```

and should print a full computer dump in the format we have discussed previously. This will help the user locate the error in the program.

MORE POINTER EXERCISES

5.20   Modify the card-shuffling and dealing program of Fig. 5.24 so the shuffling and dealing operations are performed by the same function (**shuffleAndDeal**). The function should contain one nested looping structure that is similar to function **shuffle** in Fig. 5.24.

5.21   What does this program do?

```cpp
// Ex. 5.21: ex05_21.cpp
// What does this program do?
#include <iostream>

using std::cout;
using std::cin;
using std::endl;

void mystery1( char *, const char * );   // prototype

int main()
{
   char string1[ 80 ];
   char string2[ 80 ];

   cout << "Enter two strings: ";
   cin >> string1 >> string2;
   mystery1( string1, string2 );
   cout << string1 << endl;

   return 0;   // indicates successful termination

} // end main

// What does this function do?
void mystery1( char *s1, const char *s2 )
{
   while ( *s1 != '\0' )
      ++s1;

   for ( ; *s1 = *s2; s1++, s2++ )
      ;    // empty statement

} // end function mystery1
```

5.22   What does this program do?

```cpp
// Ex. 5.22: ex05_22.cpp
// What does this program do?
#include <iostream>

using std::cout;
using std::cin;
using std::endl;

int mystery2( const char * );   // prototype
```

```
10
11   int main()
12   {
13      char string1[ 80 ];
14
15      cout << "Enter a string: ";
16      cin >> string1;
17      cout << mystery2( string1 ) << endl;
18
19      return 0;  // indicates successful termination
20
21   } // end main
22
23   // What does this function do?
24   int mystery2( const char *s )
25   {
26      int x;
27
28      for ( x = 0; *s != '\0'; s++ )
29         ++x;
30
31      return x;
32
33   } // end function mystery2
```

5.23   Find the error in each of the following segments. If the error can be corrected, explain how.

```
a) int *number;
   cout << number << endl;
```

```
b) double *realPtr;
   long *integerPtr;
   integerPtr = realPtr;
```

```
c) int * x, y;
   x = y;
```

```
d) char s[] = "this is a character array";
   for ( ; *s != '\0'; s++)
      cout << *s << ' ';
```

```
e) short *numPtr, result;
   void *genericPtr = numPtr;
   result = *genericPtr + 7;
```

```
f) double x = 19.34;
   double xPtr = &x;
   cout << xPtr << endl;
```

```
g) char *s;
   cout << s << endl;
```

5.24   (*Quicksort*) In the examples and exercises of Chapter 4, we discussed the sorting techniques of the bubble sort, bucket sort and selection sort. We now present the recursive sorting technique called Quicksort. The basic algorithm for a single-subscripted array of values is as follows:

a) *Partitioning Step:* Take the first element of the unsorted array and determine its final location in the sorted array (i.e., all values to the left of the element in the array are less than the element, and all values to the right of the element in the array are greater than the element). We now have one element in its proper location and two unsorted subarrays.

b) *Recursive Step:* Perform step 1 on each unsorted subarray.

Each time step 1 is performed on a subarray, another element is placed in its final location of the sorted array, and two unsorted subarrays are created. When a subarray consists of one element, that subarray must be sorted; therefore, that element is in its final location.

The basic algorithm seems simple enough, but how do we determine the final position of the first element of each subarray? As an example, consider the following set of values (the element in bold is the partitioning element—it will be placed in its final location in the sorted array):

37 2 6 4 89 8 10 12 68 45

a) Starting from the rightmost element of the array, compare each element with **37** until an element less than **37** is found. Then swap **37** and that element. The first element less than **37** is 12, so **37** and 12 are swapped. The values now reside in the array as follows:

12 2 6 4 89 8 10 **37** 68 45

Element 12 is in italics to indicate that it was just swapped with **37**.

b) Starting from the left of the array, but beginning with the element after 12, compare each element with **37** until an element greater than **37** is found. Then swap **37** and that element. The first element greater than **37** is 89, so **37** and 89 are swapped. The values now reside in the array as follows:

12 2 6 4 **37** 8 10 89 68 45

c) Starting from the right, but beginning with the element before 89, compare each element with **37** until an element less than **37** is found. Then swap **37** and that element. The first element less than **37** is 10, so **37** and 10 are swapped. The values now reside in the array as follows:

12 2 6 4 10 8 **37** 89 68 45

d) Starting from the left, but beginning with the element after 10, compare each element with **37** until an element greater than **37** is found. Then swap **37** and that element. There are no more elements greater than **37**, so when we compare **37** with itself, we know that **37** has been placed in its final location of the sorted array.

Once the partition has been applied to the array, there are two unsorted subarrays. The subarray with values less than 37 contains 12, 2, 6, 4, 10 and 8. The subarray with values greater than 37 contains 89, 68 and 45. The sort continues with both subarrays being partitioned in the same manner as the original array.

Based on the preceding discussion, write recursive function **quickSort** to sort a single-subscripted integer array. The function should receive as arguments an integer array, a starting subscript and an ending subscript. Function **partition** should be called by **quickSort** to perform the partitioning step.

5.25   (*Maze Traversal*) The grid of hashes (**#**) and dots (**.**) in Fig. 5.43 is a double-subscripted array representation of a maze. In the double-subscripted array, the hashes (**#**) represent the walls of the maze and the dots represent squares in the possible paths through the maze. Moves can be made only to a location in the array that contains a dot.

There is a simple algorithm for walking through a maze that guarantees finding the exit (assuming that there is an exit). If there is not an exit, you will arrive at the starting location again. Place your right hand on the wall to your right and begin walking forward. Never remove your hand from the wall. If the maze turns to the right, you follow the wall to the right. As long as you do not remove your hand from the wall, eventually you will arrive at the exit of the maze. There may be a shorter path than the one you have taken, but you are guaranteed to get out of the maze if you follow the algorithm.

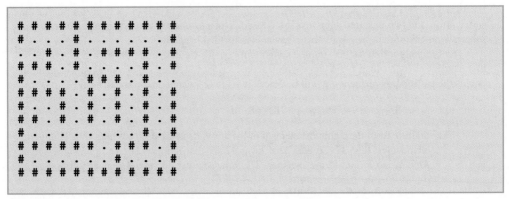

Fig. 5.43   *Double-subscripted array representation of a maze.*

Write recursive function **mazeTraverse** to walk through the maze. The function should receive as arguments a 12-by-12 character array representing the maze and the starting location of the maze. As **mazeTraverse** attempts to locate the exit from the maze, it should place the character **X** in each square in the path. The function should display the maze after each move so the user can watch as the maze is solved.

5.26   (*Generating Mazes Randomly*) Write a function **mazeGenerator** that takes as an argument a double-subscripted 12-by-12 character array and randomly produces a maze. The function should also provide the starting and ending locations of the maze. Try your function **mazeTraverse** from Exercise 5.25 using several randomly generated mazes.

5.27   (*Mazes of Any Size*) Generalize functions **mazeTraverse** and **mazeGenerator** of Exercise 5.25 and Exercise 5.26 to process mazes of any width and height.

5.28   (*Arrays of Pointers to Functions*) Rewrite the program of Fig. 4.23 to use a menu-driven interface. The program should offer the user five options as follows (these should be displayed on the screen):

```
Enter a choice:
   0   Print the array of grades
   1   Find the minimum grade
   2   Find the maximum grade
   3   Print the average on all tests for each student
   4   End program
```

One restriction on using arrays of pointers to functions is that all the pointers must have the same type. The pointers must be to functions of the same return type that receive arguments of the same type. For this reason, the functions in Fig. 4.23 must be modified so they each return the same type and take the same parameters. Modify functions **minimum** and **maximum** to print the minimum or maximum value and return nothing. For option 3, modify function **average** of Fig. 4.23 to output the average for each student (not a specific student). Function **average** should return nothing and take the same parameters as **printArray**, **minimum** and **maximum**. Store the pointers to the four functions in array **processGrades**, and use the choice made by the user as the subscript into the array for calling each function.

5.29   (*Modifications to the Simpletron Simulator*) In Exercise 5.19, you wrote a software simulation of a computer that executes programs written in Simpletron Machine Language (SML). In this exercise, we propose several modifications and enhancements to the Simpletron Simulator. In Exercise 17.26 and Exercise 17.27, we propose building a compiler that converts programs written in a high-level programming language (a variation of BASIC) to SML. Some of the following modifications and enhancements may be required to execute the programs produced by the compiler. (*Note:* Some modifications may conflict with others and therefore must be done separately.)

a) Extend the Simpletron Simulator's memory to contain 1000 memory locations to enable the Simpletron to handle larger programs.

b) Allow the simulator to perform modulus calculations. This requires an additional Simpletron Machine Language instruction.

c) Allow the simulator to perform exponentiation calculations. This requires an additional Simpletron Machine Language instruction.

d) Modify the simulator to use hexadecimal values rather than integer values to represent Simpletron Machine Language instructions.

e) Modify the simulator to allow output of a newline. This requires an additional Simpletron Machine Language instruction.

f) Modify the simulator to process floating-point values in addition to integer values.

g) Modify the simulator to handle string input. [*Hint:* Each Simpletron word can be divided into two groups, each holding a two-digit integer. Each two-digit integer represents the ASCII decimal equivalent of a character. Add a machine-language instruction that will input a string and store the string beginning at a specific Simpletron memory location. The first half of the word at that location will be a count of the number of characters in the string (i.e., the length of the string). Each succeeding half-word contains one ASCII character expressed as two decimal digits. The machine-language instruction converts each character into its ASCII equivalent and assigns it to a half-word.]

h) Modify the simulator to handle output of strings stored in the format of part (g). [*Hint:* Add a machine-language instruction that will print a string beginning at a certain Simpletron memory location. The first half of the word at that location is a count of the number of characters in the string (i.e., the length of the string). Each succeeding half-word contains one ASCII character expressed as two decimal digits. The machine-language instruction checks the length and prints the string by translating each two-digit number into its equivalent character.]

i) Modify the simulator to include instruction **SML_DEBUG** that prints a memory dump after each instruction executes. Give **SML_DEBUG** an operation code of **44**. The word **+4401** turns on debug mode, and **+4400** turns off debug mode.

5.30 What does this program do?

```
1   // Ex. 5.30: ex05_30.cpp
2   // What does this program do?
3   #include <iostream>
4
5   using std::cout;
6   using std::cin;
7   using std::endl;
8
9   bool mystery3( const char *, const char * );  // prototype
10
11  int main()
12  {
13     char string1[ 80 ], string2[ 80 ];
14
```

```
15        cout << "Enter two strings: ";
16        cin >> string1 >> string2;
17        cout << "The result is "
18             << mystery3( string1, string2 ) << endl;
19
20        return 0;   // indicates successful termination
21
22   } // end main
23
24   // What does this function do?
25   bool mystery3( const char *s1, const char *s2 )
26   {
27        for ( ; *s1 != '\0' && *s2 != '\0'; s1++, s2++ )
28
29             if ( *s1 != *s2 )
30                  return false;
31
32        return true;
33
34   } // end function mystery3
```

STRING-MANIPULATION EXERCISES

5.31   Write a program that uses function **strcmp** to compare two strings input by the user. The program should state whether the first string is less than, equal to or greater than the second string.

5.32   Write a program that uses function **strncmp** to compare two strings input by the user. The program should input the number of characters to compare. The program should state whether the first string is less than, equal to or greater than the second string.

5.33   Write a program that uses random-number generation to create sentences. The program should use four arrays of pointers to **char** called **article**, **noun**, **verb** and **preposition**. The program should create a sentence by selecting a word at random from each array in the following order: **article**, **noun**, **verb**, **preposition**, **article** and **noun**. As each word is picked, it should be concatenated to the previous words in an array that is large enough to hold the entire sentence. The words should be separated by spaces. When the final sentence is output, it should start with a capital letter and end with a period. The program should generate 20 such sentences.

The arrays should be filled as follows: The **article** array should contain the articles **"the"**, **"a"**, **"one"**, **"some"** and **"any"**; the **noun** array should contain the nouns **"boy"**, **"girl"**, **"dog"**, **"town"** and **"car"**; the **verb** array should contain the verbs **"drove"**, **"jumped"**, **"ran"**, **"walked"** and **"skipped"**; the **preposition** array should contain the prepositions **"to"**, **"from"**, **"over"**, **"under"** and **"on"**.

After completing the program, modify it to produce a short story consisting of several of these sentences. (How about the possibility of a random term-paper writer!)

5.34   *(Limericks)* A limerick is a humorous five-line verse in which the first and second lines rhyme with the fifth, and the third line rhymes with the fourth. Using techniques similar to those developed in Exercise 5.33, write a C++ program that produces random limericks. Polishing this program to produce good limericks is a challenging problem, but the result will be worth the effort!

5.35   Write a program that encodes English language phrases into pig Latin. Pig Latin is a form of coded language often used for amusement. Many variations exist in the methods used to form pig Latin phrases. For simplicity, use the following algorithm: To form a pig-Latin phrase from an English-language phrase, tokenize the phrase into words with function **strtok**. To translate each English word into a pig-Latin word, place the first letter of the English word at the end of the English word and add the letters "**ay**." Thus, the word "**jump**" becomes "**umpjay**," the word "**the**" becomes "**hetay**" and the word "**computer**" becomes "**omputercay**." Blanks between words remain as blanks. Assume that the English phrase consists of words separated by blanks, there are no punctuation marks and all words have two or more letters. Function **printLatinWord** should display each word. (*Hint:* Each time a token is found in a call to **strtok**, pass the token pointer to function **printLatinWord** and print the pig-Latin word.)

5.36   Write a program that inputs a telephone number as a string in the form **(555) 555-5555**. The program should use function **strtok** to extract the area code as a token, the first three digits of the phone number as a token, and the last four digits of the phone number as a token. The seven digits of the phone number should be concatenated into one string. Both the area code and the phone number should be printed.

5.37   Write a program that inputs a line of text, tokenizes the line with function **strtok** and outputs the tokens in reverse order.

5.38   Use the string comparison functions discussed in Section 5.12.2 and the techniques for sorting arrays developed in Chapter 4 to write a program that alphabetizes a list of strings. Use the names of 10 or 15 towns in your area as data for your program.

5.39   Write two versions of each string copy and string concatenation function in Fig. 5.27. The first version should use array subscripting, and the second should use pointers and pointer arithmetic.

5.40   Write two versions of each string comparison function in Fig. 5.27. The first version should use array subscripting, and the second version should use pointers and pointer arithmetic.

5.41   Write two versions of function **strlen** in Fig. 5.27. The first version should use array subscripting, and the second version should use pointers and pointer arithmetic.

SPECIAL SECTION: ADVANCED STRING-MANIPULATION EXERCISES

The preceding exercises are keyed to the text and designed to test the reader's understanding of fundamental string-manipulation concepts. This section includes a collection of intermediate and advanced string-manipulation exercises. The reader should find these problems challenging, yet enjoyable. The problems vary considerably in difficulty. Some require an hour or two of program writing and implementation. Others are useful for lab assignments that might require two or three weeks of study and implementation. Some are challenging term projects.

5.42   (*Text Analysis*) The availability of computers with string-manipulation capabilities has resulted in some rather interesting approaches to analyzing the writings of great authors. Much attention has been focused on whether William Shakespeare ever lived. Some scholars believe there is substantial evidence indicating that Christopher Marlowe or other authors actually penned the masterpieces attributed to Shakespeare. Researchers have used computers to find similarities in the writings of these two authors. This exercise examines three methods for analyzing texts with a computer.

   a) Write a program that reads several lines of text from the keyboard and prints a table indicating the number of occurrences of each letter of the alphabet in the text. For example, the phrase

   To be, or not to be: that is the question:

   contains one "a," two "b's," no "c's," etc.

   b) Write a program that reads several lines of text and prints a table indicating the number of one-letter words, two-letter words, three-letter words, etc., appearing in the text. For example, the phrase

   Whether 'tis nobler in the mind to suffer

contains the following word lengths and occurrences:

Word length	Occurrences
1	0
2	2
3	1
4	2 (including `'tis`)
5	0
6	2
7	1

c) Write a program that reads several lines of text and prints a table indicating the number of occurrences of each different word in the text. The first version of your program should include the words in the table in the same order in which they appear in the text. For example, the lines

> **To be, or not to be: that is the question:**
> **Whether 'tis nobler in the mind to suffer**

contain the words "to" three times, the word "be" two times, the word "or" once, etc. A more interesting (and useful) printout should then be attempted in which the words are sorted alphabetically.

5.43   *(Word Processing)* One important function in word-processing systems is *type justification*—the alignment of words to both the left and right margins of a page. This generates a professional-looking document that gives the appearance of being set in type rather than prepared on a typewriter. Type justification can be accomplished on computer systems by inserting blank characters between each of the words in a line so that the rightmost word aligns with the right margin.

Write a program that reads several lines of text and prints this text in type-justified format. Assume that the text is to be printed on 8-1/2-inch-wide paper and that one-inch margins are to be allowed on both the left and right sides of the printed page. Assume that the computer prints 10 characters to the horizontal inch. Therefore, your program should print 6-1/2 inches of text, or 65 characters per line.

5.44   *(Printing Dates in Various Formats)* Dates are commonly printed in several different formats in business correspondence. Two of the more common formats are

> **07/21/1955**
> **July 21, 1955**

Write a program that reads a date in the first format and prints that date in the second format.

5.45   *(Check Protection)* Computers are frequently employed in check-writing systems such as payroll and accounts payable applications. Many strange stories circulate regarding weekly paychecks being printed (by mistake) for amounts in excess of $1 million. Weird amounts are printed by computerized check-writing systems, because of human error or machine failure. Systems designers build controls into their systems to prevent such erroneous checks from being issued.

Another serious problem is the intentional alteration of a check amount by someone who intends to cash a check fraudulently. To prevent a dollar amount from being altered, most computerized check-writing systems employ a technique called *check protection.*

Checks designed for imprinting by computer contain a fixed number of spaces in which the computer may print an amount. Suppose that a paycheck contains eight blank spaces in which the computer is supposed to print the amount of a weekly paycheck. If the amount is large, then all eight of those spaces will be filled, for example,

```
1,230.60      (check amount)
--------
12345678      (position numbers)
```

On the other hand, if the amount is less than $1000, then several of the spaces would ordinarily be left blank. For example,

```
   99.87
--------
12345678
```

contains three blank spaces. If a check is printed with blank spaces, it is easier for someone to alter the amount of the check. To prevent a check from being altered, many check-writing systems insert *leading asterisks* to protect the amount as follows:

```
***99.87
--------
12345678
```

Write a program that inputs a dollar amount to be printed on a check and then prints the amount in check-protected format with leading asterisks if necessary. Assume that nine spaces are available for printing an amount.

5.46   *(Writing the Word Equivalent of a Check Amount)* Continuing the discussion of the previous example, we reiterate the importance of designing check-writing systems to prevent alteration of check amounts. One common security method requires that the check amount be written both in numbers and "spelled out" in words. Even if someone is able to alter the numerical amount of the check, it is extremely difficult to change the amount in words.

Write a program that inputs a numeric check amount and writes the word equivalent of the amount. Your program should be able to handle check amounts as large as $99.99. For example, the amount 112.43 should be written as

ONE HUNDRED TWELVE and 43/100

5.47   *(Morse Code)* Perhaps the most famous of all coding schemes is the Morse code, developed by Samuel Morse in 1832 for use with the telegraph system. The Morse code assigns a series of dots and dashes to each letter of the alphabet, each digit and a few special characters (such as period, comma, colon and semicolon). In sound-oriented systems, the dot represents a short sound, and the dash represents a long sound. Other representations of dots and dashes are used with light-oriented systems and signal-flag systems.

Separation between words is indicated by a space, or, quite simply, the absence of a dot or dash. In a sound-oriented system, a space is indicated by a short period of time during which no sound is transmitted. The international version of the Morse code appears in Fig. 5.44.

Write a program that reads an English-language phrase and encodes the phrase into Morse code. Also write a program that reads a phrase in Morse code and converts the phrase into the English-language equivalent. Use one blank between each Morse-coded letter and three blanks between each Morse-coded word.

Character	Code	Character	Code
A	.-	T	-
B	-...	U	..-
C	-.-.	V	...-
D	-..	W	.--
E	.	X	-..-
F	..-.	Y	-.--
G	--.	Z	--..
H	....		
I	..	*Digits*	
J	.---	1	.----
K	-.-	2	..---
L	.-..	3	...--
M	--	4	....-
N	-.	5	.....
O	---	6	-....
P	.--.	7	--...
Q	--.-	8	---..
R	.-.	9	----.
S	...	0	-----

Fig. 5.44   Morse code alphabet.

5.48   *(A Metric Conversion Program)* Write a program that will assist the user with metric conversions. Your program should allow the user to specify the names of the units as strings (i.e., centimeters, liters, grams, etc., for the metric system and inches, quarts, pounds, etc., for the English system) and should respond to simple questions such as

```
"How many inches are in 2 meters?"
"How many liters are in 10 quarts?"
```

Your program should recognize invalid conversions. For example, the question

```
"How many feet in 5 kilograms?"
```

is not meaningful, because **"feet"** are units of length, while **"kilograms"** are units of weight.

A CHALLENGING STRING-MANIPULATION PROJECT

5.49   *(A Crossword Puzzle Generator)* Most people have worked a crossword puzzle, but few have ever attempted to generate one. Generating a crossword puzzle is a difficult problem. It is suggested here as a string-manipulation project requiring substantial sophistication and effort. There are many issues that the programmer must resolve to get even the simplest crossword puzzle generator program working. For example, how does one represent the grid of a crossword puzzle inside the computer?

Should one use a series of strings, or should double-subscripted arrays be used? The programmer needs a source of words (i.e., a computerized dictionary) that can be directly referenced by the program. In what form should these words be stored to facilitate the complex manipulations required by the program? The really ambitious reader will want to generate the "clues" portion of the puzzle in which the brief hints for each "across" word and each "down" word are printed for the puzzle worker. Merely printing a version of the blank puzzle itself is not a simple problem.

6

Classes and Data Abstraction

Objectives

- To understand the software engineering concepts of encapsulation and data hiding.
- To understand the notions of data abstraction and abstract data types (ADTs).
- To be able to create C++ ADTs, namely, classes.
- To understand how to create, use and destroy class objects.
- To be able to control access to object data members and member functions.
- To begin to appreciate the value of object orientation.

My object all sublime
I shall achieve in time.
W. S. Gilbert

Is it a world to hide virtues in?
William Shakespeare

Your public servants serve you right.
Adlai Stevenson

Private faces in public places
Are wiser and nicer
Than public faces in private places.
W. H. Auden

Outline

6.1	**Introduction**
6.2	**Structure Definitions**
6.3	**Accessing Structure Members**
6.4	**Implementing User-Defined Type `Time` with a C-like `struct`**
6.5	**Implementing Abstract Data `Time` Type with a `class`**
6.6	**Class Scope and Accessing Class Members**
6.7	**Separating Interface from Implementation**
6.8	**Controlling Access to Members**
6.9	**Access Functions and Utility Functions**
6.10	**Initializing Class Objects: Constructors**
6.11	**Using Default Arguments with Constructors**
6.12	**Destructors**
6.13	**When Constructors and Destructors Are Called**
6.14	**Using *Set* and *Get* Functions**
6.15	**Subtle Trap: Returning a Reference to a `private` Data Member**
6.16	**Default Memberwise Assignment**
6.17	**Software Reusability**
6.18	**(Optional Case Study) Thinking About Objects: Starting to Program the Classes for the Elevator Simulator**

Summary • Terminology • Self-Review Exercises • Answers to Self-Review Exercises • Exercises

6.1 Introduction

Now we begin our introduction to object orientation in C++. Why have we deferred object-oriented programming in C++ until Chapter 6? The answer is that the objects we will build will be composed in part of structured program pieces, so we needed to establish a basis in structured programming first.

Through our "Thinking About Objects" sections at the ends of Chapter 1 through Chapter 5, we have introduced the basic concepts (i.e., "object think") and terminology (i.e., "object speak") of object-oriented programming in C++. In these special sections, we also discussed the techniques of *object-oriented design (OOD)*: We analyzed a typical problem statement that required a system (an elevator simulator) to be built, determined what classes were needed to implement the system, determined what attributes objects of these classes needed to have, determined what behaviors objects of these classes needed to exhibit and specified how the objects needed to interact with one another to accomplish the overall goals of the system.

Let us briefly review some key concepts and terminology of object orientation. Object-oriented programming (OOP) *encapsulates* data (attributes) and functions (behavior) into packages called *classes*; the data and functions of a class are intimately tied together. A class is like a blueprint. Out of a blueprint, a builder can build a house. Out of a class, a programmer can create an object. One blueprint can be reused many times to make many houses. One class can be reused many times to make many objects of the same class. In Section 6.5, we define class **Time** that can be used to create many **Time** objects (e.g., **wakeupTime**, **breakfastTime**, **lunchTime**, **dinnerTime**, **bedTime**, etc.).

Classes have the property of *information hiding*. This means that although class objects may know how to communicate with one another across well-defined *interfaces,* classes normally are not allowed to know how other classes are implemented—implementation details are hidden within the classes themselves. Surely it is possible to drive a car effectively without knowing the details of how engines, transmissions and exhaust systems work internally. We will see why information hiding is so crucial to good software engineering.

In C and other *procedural programming languages*, programming tends to be *action-oriented*, whereas ideally in C++ programming is *object-oriented*. In C, the unit of programming is the *function*. In C++, the unit of programming is the *class* from which objects are eventually *instantiated* (i.e., created).

C programmers concentrate on writing functions. Groups of actions that perform some task are formed into functions, and functions are grouped to form programs. Data are certainly important in C, but the view is that data exist primarily in support of the actions that functions perform. The *verbs* in a system specification help the C programmer determine the set of functions that will work together to implement the system.

C++ programmers concentrate on creating their own *user-defined types* called *classes*. Classes are also referred to as *programmer-defined types*. Each class contains data as well as the set of functions that manipulate the data. The data components of a class are called *data members*. The function components of a class are called *member functions* (or *methods* in other object-oriented languages). Just as an instance of a built-in type such as **int** is called a *variable*, an instance of a user-defined type (i.e., a class) is called an *object*. In the C++ community, the terms variable and object are often used interchangeably. The focus of attention in C++ is on classes rather than functions. The *nouns* in a system specification help the C++ programmer determine the set of classes that will be used to create the objects that will work together to implement the system.

Classes in C++ are a natural evolution of the C notion of **struct**. Before proceeding with the specifics of developing classes in C++, we discuss structures, and we build a user-defined type based on a C-style structure. In subsequent sections, the weaknesses we expose in this approach will help motivate the notion of a class.

6.2 Structure Definitions

Structures are *aggregate data types*—that is, they can be built using elements of other types including other **struct**s. Consider the following structure definition:

```
struct Time {
    int hour;      // 0-23 (24-hour clock format)
    int minute;    // 0-59
    int second;    // 0-59

}; // end struct Time
```

Keyword ***struct*** introduces the structure definition. The identifier **Time** is the *structure tag* that names the structure definition and is used to declare variables of the *structure type*. In this example, the new type name is **Time**. The names declared in the braces of the structure definition are the structure's *members*. Members of the same structure must have unique names, but two different structures may contain members of the same name without conflict. Each structure definition must end with a semicolon. The preceding explanation is valid for classes also; as we will soon see, structures and classes are quite similar in C++.

The definition of **Time** contains three members of type **int**—**hour**, **minute** and **second**. Structure members can be of any type, and one structure can contain members of many different types. A structure cannot, however, contain an instance of itself. For example, a member of type **Time** cannot be declared in the structure definition for **Time**. A pointer to another **Time** structure, however, can be included. A structure containing a member that is a pointer to the same structure type is referred to as a *self-referential structure*. Self-referential structures are useful for forming linked data structures such as linked lists, queues, stacks and trees, as we will see in Chapter 17.

The preceding structure definition does not reserve any space in memory; rather, the definition creates a new data type that is used to declare variables. Structure variables are declared like variables of other types. The declarations

```
Time timeObject;              // object of class Time
Time timeArray[ 10 ];         // array of Time objects
Time *timePtr = &timeObject;  // pointer to a Time object
Time &timeRef = timeObject;   // reference to a Time object
```

declare **timeObject** to be a variable of type **Time**, **timeArray** to be an array with 10 elements of type **Time**, **timePtr** to be a pointer to a **Time** object that is initialized with the address of **timeObject** and **timeRef** to be a reference to a **Time** object that is initialized with **timeObject**.

6.3 Accessing Structure Members

Members of a structure (or of a class) are accessed using the *member access operators*— the *dot operator* (**.**) and the *arrow operator* (**->**). The dot operator accesses a structure or class member via the variable name for the object or via a reference to the object. For example, to print member **hour** of **timeObject**, use the statement

```
cout << timeObject.hour;
```

To print member **hour** of the **Time** object referenced by **timeRef**, use the statement

```
cout << timeRef.hour;
```

The arrow operator—which consists of a minus sign (**-**) and a greater than sign (**>**) with no intervening whitespace—accesses a structure member or class member via a pointer to an object. Assume that the pointer **timePtr** has been declared to point to a **Time** object, and that the address of **timeObject** has been assigned to **timePtr**. To print member **hour** of **timeObject** with pointer **timePtr**, use the statement

```
cout << timePtr->hour;
```

The expression **timePtr->hour** is equivalent to **(*timePtr).hour**, which dereferences the pointer and accesses the member **hour** using the dot operator. The parentheses are needed here because the dot operator (**.**) has a higher precedence than the pointer dereferencing operator (*****). The arrow operator and dot operator, along with parentheses and brackets (**[ ]**), have the second highest operator precedence (after the scope resolution operator introduced in Chapter 3); these operators associate from left to right.

 Common Programming Error 6.1

The expression **(*timePtr).hour** *refers to the* **hour** *member of the* **struct** *pointed to by* **timePtr**. *Operator* **.** *has a higher precedence than* *****, *so omitting the parentheses would cause the expression to be evaluated as if parenthesized as* ***(timePtr.hour)**. *This would be a syntax error because with a pointer you must use the arrow operator to refer to a member.*

6.4 Implementing User-Defined Type **Time** with a C-like **struct**

Figure 6.1 creates the user-defined structure type **Time** (lines 14–19) with three integer members: **hour**, **minute** and **second**. The program defines a single **Time** structure called **dinnerTime** (line 26) and uses the dot operator to initialize the structure members with the values **18** for **hour**, **30** for **minute** and **0** for **second** (lines 28–30). Line 33 then prints the time in universal format (also called 24-hour clock format), and line 35 prints the time in standard format (i.e., 12-hour clock format). Note that functions **print-Universal** (lines 50–56) and **printStandard** (lines 59–67) receive references to constant **Time** objects. This causes the **Time** objects to be passed to the print functions by reference—thus eliminating the copying overhead associated with passing structure objects to functions by value—and using **const** prevents the **Time** objects from being modified by the print functions. Also, note that functions **printUniversal** and **printStandard** use parameterized stream manipulator **setfill** to specify the *fill character* that is displayed when an integer is output in a field width larger than the number of digits in the value. By default, the fill characters appear before the digits in the number. In this example, if the **minute** value is 2, it will be displayed as 02. If the number being output fills the specified field width, the fill character will not be displayed. Note that once the fill character is specified with **setfill**, it applies for all subsequent fields being printed. This is in contrast to **setw**, which only applies to the next field being printed.

```
1   // Fig. 6.1: fig06_01.cpp
2   // Create a structure, set its members, and print it.
3   #include <iostream>
4
5   using std::cout;
6   using std::endl;
7
8   #include <iomanip>
9
10  using std::setfill;
11  using std::setw;
```

Fig. 6.1   Creating a structure, setting its members and printing the structure. (Part 1 of 3.)

```
12
13   // structure definition
14   struct Time {
15      int hour;       // 0-23 (24-hour clock format)
16      int minute;     // 0-59
17      int second;     // 0-59
18
19   }; // end struct Time
20
21   void printUniversal( const Time & );   // prototype
22   void printStandard( const Time & );    // prototype
23
24   int main()
25   {
26      Time dinnerTime;         // variable of new type Time
27
28      dinnerTime.hour = 18;    // set hour member of dinnerTime
29      dinnerTime.minute = 30;  // set minute member of dinnerTime
30      dinnerTime.second = 0;   // set second member of dinnerTime
31
32      cout << "Dinner will be held at ";
33      printUniversal( dinnerTime );
34      cout << " universal time,\nwhich is ";
35      printStandard( dinnerTime );
36      cout << " standard time.\n";
37
38      dinnerTime.hour = 29;    // set hour to invalid value
39      dinnerTime.minute = 73;  // set minute to invalid value
40
41      cout << "\nTime with invalid values: ";
42      printUniversal( dinnerTime );
43      cout << endl;
44
45      return 0;
46
47   } // end main
48
49   // print time in universal-time format
50   void printUniversal( const Time &t )
51   {
52      cout << setfill( '0' ) << setw( 2 ) << t.hour << ":"
53           << setw( 2 ) << t.minute << ":"
54           << setw( 2 ) << t.second;
55
56   } // end function printUniversal
57
58   // print time in standard-time format
59   void printStandard( const Time &t )
60   {
61      cout << ( ( t.hour == 0 || t.hour == 12 ) ?
62                 12 : t.hour % 12 ) << ":" << setfill( '0' )
63           << setw( 2 ) << t.minute << ":"
```

Fig. 6.1   Creating a structure, setting its members and printing the structure. (Part 2 of 3.)

```
64              << setw( 2 ) << t.second
65              << ( t.hour < 12 ? " AM" : " PM" );
66
67  } // end function printStandard
```

```
Dinner will be held at 18:30:00 universal time,
which is 6:30:00 PM standard time.

Time with invalid values: 29:73:00
```

Fig. 6.1   Creating a structure, setting its members and printing the structure. (Part 3 of 3.)

Performance Tip 6.1

By default, structures are passed by value. To avoid the overhead of copying a structure, pass the structure by reference.

Software Engineering Observation 6.1

To avoid the overhead of pass-by-value yet still gain the benefit that the caller's original data are protected from modification, pass large-size arguments as **const** *references.*

There are drawbacks to creating new data types with structures in this manner. Initialization is not specifically required, so it is possible to have uninitialized data and the consequent problems. Even if the data are initialized, they might not be initialized correctly. Invalid values can be assigned to the members of a structure (as we did in Fig. 6.1) because the program has direct access to the data. In lines 38–39, for example, the program was easily able to assign bad values to the **hour** and **minute** members of the **Time** object **dinnerTime**.

If the programmer changes the implementation of the **struct** (e.g., the time could be represented as the number of seconds since midnight), all programs that use the **struct** must be changed accordingly. This is because the programmer directly manipulates the data representation. There is no "interface" to the data representation to ensure that the programmer uses the data type's services correctly and to ensure that the data remains in a consistent state.

Software Engineering Observation 6.2

It is important to write programs that are understandable and easy to maintain. Change is the rule rather than the exception. Programmers should anticipate that their code will be modified. As we will see, classes can facilitate program modifiability.

There are other problems associated with C-style structures. In C, structures cannot be printed as a unit; rather, their members must be printed and formatted one at a time. A function could be written to print the members of a structure in some appropriate format. Chapter 8, Operator Overloading; String and Array Objects, illustrates how to overload the **<<** operator to enable objects of a structure type or class type to be printed easily. In C, structures may not be compared in their entirety; they must be compared member by member. Chapter 8 also illustrates how to overload equality operators and relational operators to compare objects of (C++) structure and class types.

The next section reimplements our **Time** structure as a C++ class and demonstrates some of the advantages of creating so-called *abstract data types* as classes. We will see that classes and structures can be used almost identically in C++. The difference between the two is in the default accessibility associated with the members of each. This will be explained shortly.

6.5 Implementing Abstract Data Type **Time** with a **class**

Classes enable the programmer to model objects that have *attributes* (represented as *data members*) and *behaviors* or *operations* (represented as *member functions*). Types containing data members and member functions are defined in C++ using the keyword **class**.

Member functions are sometimes called *methods* in other object-oriented programming languages and are invoked in response to *messages* sent to an object. A message corresponds to a member-function call sent from one object to another or sent from a function to an object.

Once a class has been defined, the class name is now a type name, which can be used to declare objects of that class. Figure 6.2 contains a simple definition for class **Time**.

Our **Time** class definition begins with the keyword **class** (line 1). The *body* of the class definition is delineated with left and right braces (**{** and **}**) at lines 1 and 14. The class definition terminates with a semicolon (line 14). Like the **Time** structure definition in Fig. 6.1, our **Time** class definition contains the three integer members **hour, minute** and **second** (lines 10–12).

Common Programming Error 6.2

Forgetting the semicolon at the end of a class (or structure) definition is a syntax error.

The remaining parts of the class definition are new. The **public:** and **private:** labels (lines 3 and 9) are called *member access specifiers*. Any data member or member function declared after member access specifier **public** (and before the next member access specifier) is accessible wherever an object of class **Time** is in scope. Any data member or member function declared after member access specifier **private** (and before the next member access specifier) is accessible only to member functions of the class.

```
1    class Time {
2
3    public:
4        Time();                        // constructor
5        void setTime( int, int, int ); // set hour, minute, second
6        void printUniversal();         // print universal-time format
7        void printStandard();          // print standard-time format
8
9    private:
10       int hour;      // 0 - 23 (24-hour clock format)
11       int minute;    // 0 - 59
12       int second;    // 0 - 59
13
14   }; // end class Time
```

Fig. 6.2   Class **Time** definition.

Member access specifiers are always followed by a colon (**:**) and can appear multiple times and in any order in a class definition. For the remainder of the text, when we refer to the member access specifiers **public** and **private** in our discussions of programs, we will omit the colons as we did in this sentence. Chapter 9 introduces a third member access specifier, **protected**, as we study inheritance and the part it plays in object-oriented programming.

The class definition contains prototypes for the following four member functions after the **public** member access specifier—**Time**, **setTime**, **printUniversal** and **printStandard**. These are the *public member functions* of the class (also known as the *public services, public behaviors* or *interface* of the class). These functions will be used by *clients* (i.e., portions of a program that are users) of the class to manipulate the class's data. We will soon see that classes can have non-**public** member functions as well. The data members of the class support the delivery of the *services* the class provides to the clients of the class with its member functions. These services allow the client code to interact with an object of the class.

Good Programming Practice 6.1

*For clarity and readability, use each member access specifier only once in a class definition. Place **public** members first where they are easy to locate.*

Notice the member function with the same name as the class; it is called a *constructor* function of that class. A constructor is a special member function that initializes the data members of a class object. A class's constructor is called when a program creates an object of that class. We will see that it is common to have several constructors for a class; this is accomplished through function overloading. Note that no return type can be specified for the constructor.

Common Programming Error 6.3

Specifying a return type or a return value for a constructor is a syntax error.

The three integer members appear after the **private** member access specifier. This indicates that these data members of the class are accessible only to member functions—and, as we will see in the next chapter, "friends"—of the class. Thus, class **Time**'s data members can be accessed only by the four functions whose prototypes appear in the class definition. Normally, data members are listed in the **private** portion of a class and member functions are listed in the **public** portion. It is possible to have **private** member functions and **public** data, as we will see later; using **public** data is uncommon and is considered poor software engineering.

Once the class has been defined, it can be used as a type in object, array, pointer and reference declarations as follows:

```
Time sunset;                    // object of type Time
Time arrayOfTimes[ 5 ],         // array of Time objects
Time &dinnerTime = sunset;      // reference to a Time object
Time *timePtr = &dinnerTime,    // pointer to a Time object
```

The class name becomes a new type specifier. There can be many objects of a class, just as there can be many variables of a type such as **int**. The programmer can create new class types as needed. This is one reason why C++ is said to be an *extensible language*.

Figure 6.3 uses class **Time** (defined at lines 14–27). Line 68 instantiates a single object of class **Time** called **t**. When the object is instantiated, the **Time** constructor (lines 31–35) is called to initialize each **private** data member to **0**. Then, lines 72 and 75 print the time in universal and standard formats to confirm that the members were initialized properly. Line 77 sets a new time by calling member function **setTime**, and lines 81 and 84 print the time again in both formats. Line 86 attempts use **setTime** to set the data members to invalid values. Function **setTime** recognizes this and sets the invalid values to 0 to maintain the object in a consistent state. Finally, lines 91 and 94 print the time again in both formats.

```
1   // Fig. 6.3: fig06_03.cpp
2   // Time class.
3   #include <iostream>
4
5   using std::cout;
6   using std::endl;
7
8   #include <iomanip>
9
10  using std::setfill;
11  using std::setw;
12
13  // Time abstract data type (ADT) definition
14  class Time {
15
16  public:
17     Time();                          // constructor
18     void setTime( int, int, int ); // set hour, minute, second
19     void printUniversal();          // print universal-time format
20     void printStandard();           // print standard-time format
21
22  private:
23     int hour;      // 0 - 23 (24-hour clock format)
24     int minute;    // 0 - 59
25     int second;    // 0 - 59
26
27  }; // end class Time
28
29  // Time constructor initializes each data member to zero and
30  // ensures all Time objects start in a consistent state
31  Time::Time()
32  {
33     hour = minute = second = 0;
34
35  } // end Time constructor
36
37  // set new Time value using universal time, perform validity
38  // checks on the data values and set invalid values to zero
39  void Time::setTime( int h, int m, int s )
40  {
41     hour = ( h >= 0 && h < 24 ) ? h : 0;
```

Fig. 6.3   **Time** abstract data type implementation as a class. (Part 1 of 3.)

```
42          minute = ( m >= 0 && m < 60 ) ? m : 0;
43          second = ( s >= 0 && s < 60 ) ? s : 0;
44
45      } // end function setTime
46
47      // print Time in universal format
48      void Time::printUniversal()
49      {
50          cout << setfill( '0' ) << setw( 2 ) << hour << ":"
51               << setw( 2 ) << minute << ":"
52               << setw( 2 ) << second;
53
54      } // end function printUniversal
55
56      // print Time in standard format
57      void Time::printStandard()
58      {
59          cout << ( ( hour == 0 || hour == 12 ) ? 12 : hour % 12 )
60               << ":" << setfill( '0' ) << setw( 2 ) << minute
61               << ":" << setw( 2 ) << second
62               << ( hour < 12 ? " AM" : " PM" );
63
64      } // end function printStandard
65
66      int main()
67      {
68          Time t;   // instantiate object t of class Time
69
70          // output Time object t's initial values
71          cout << "The initial universal time is ";
72          t.printUniversal();    // 00:00:00
73
74          cout << "\nThe initial standard time is ";
75          t.printStandard();     // 12:00:00 AM
76
77          t.setTime( 13, 27, 6 );   // change time
78
79          // output Time object t's new values
80          cout << "\n\nUniversal time after setTime is ";
81          t.printUniversal();    // 13:27:06
82
83          cout << "\nStandard time after setTime is ";
84          t.printStandard();     // 1:27:06 PM
85
86          t.setTime( 99, 99, 99 );  // attempt invalid settings
87
88          // output t's values after specifying invalid values
89          cout << "\n\nAfter attempting invalid settings:"
90               << "\nUniversal time: ";
91          t.printUniversal();    // 00:00:00
92
93          cout << "\nStandard time: ";
94          t.printStandard();     // 12:00:00 AM
```

Fig. 6.3   **Time** abstract data type implementation as a class. (Part 2 of 3.)

```
95        cout << endl;
96
97        return 0;
98
99    } // end main
```

```
The initial universal time is 00:00:00
The initial standard time is 12:00:00 AM

Universal time after setTime is 13:27:06
Standard time after setTime is 1:27:06 PM

After attempting invalid settings:
Universal time: 00:00:00
Standard time: 12:00:00 AM
```

Fig. 6.3   **Time** abstract data type implementation as a class. (Part 3 of 3.)

Note that the data members **hour**, **minute** and **second** (lines 23–25) are preceded by the **private** member access specifier (line 22). A class's **private** data members normally are not accessible outside the class. (Again, we will see in Chapter 7 that friends of a class may access the class's **private** members.) The philosophy here is that the data representation used within the class is of no concern to the class's clients. For example, it would be perfectly reasonable for the class to represent the time internally as the number of seconds since midnight. Clients could use the same **public** member functions and get the same results without being aware of this. In this sense, the implementation of a class is said to be *hidden* from its clients. Such *information hiding* promotes program modifiability and simplifies the client's perception of a class.

Software Engineering Observation 6.3

Clients of a class use the class without knowing the internal details of how the class is implemented. If the class implementation changes (to improve performance, for example), provided the class's interface remains constant, the class's client source code need not change (although the client code will need to be re-linked). This makes it much easier to modify systems.

In Fig. 6.3, the **Time** constructor (lines 31–35) initializes the data members to 0 (i.e., the universal time equivalent of 12 AM). This ensures that the object is in a consistent state when it is created. Invalid values cannot be stored in the data members of a **Time** object because the constructor is called when the **Time** object is created and all subsequent attempts by a client to modify the data members are scrutinized by function **setTime**.

Software Engineering Observation 6.4

Member functions are usually shorter than functions in non-object-oriented programs because the data stored in data members have ideally been validated by a constructor or by member functions that store new data. Because the data are already in the object, the member function calls often have no arguments or at least have fewer arguments than typical function calls in non-object-oriented languages. Thus, the calls are shorter, the function definitions are shorter and the function prototypes are shorter.

Note that the data members of a class cannot be initialized where they are declared in the class body. These data members should be initialized by the class's constructor, or they can be assigned values by *set* functions (such as **setTime** in lines 39–45 of Fig. 6.3).

Common Programming Error 6.4

Attempting to initialize a data member of a class explicitly in the class definition is a syntax error.

A function with the same name as the class, but preceded with a *tilde character (~)* is called the *destructor* of that class. (This example does not explicitly include a destructor, so the C++ implementation "plugs one in" for you.)\ The destructor does "termination housekeeping" on each class object before the system reclaims the memory for the object. Destructors cannot take arguments and hence cannot be overloaded. We will discuss constructors and destructors in more detail later in this chapter and in Chapter 7.

Software Engineering Observation 6.5

Clients have access to a class's interface, but should not have access to a class's implementation.

The class definition contains declarations of the class's data members and the class's member functions. The member function declarations are the function prototypes we discussed in earlier chapters. Member functions can be defined inside a class, but it is good software engineering to define these functions outside the class definition.

Software Engineering Observation 6.6

Declaring member functions inside a class definition (via their function prototypes) and defining those member functions outside that class definition separates the interface of a class from its implementation. This promotes good software engineering. Clients of a class cannot see the implementation of that class's member functions and need not recompile if that implementation changes.

Note the use of *binary scope resolution operator (: :)* in each member-function definition (lines 31, 39, 48 and 57) following the class definition in Fig. 6.3. Once a class is defined and its member functions are declared, the member functions must be defined. For each member function defined after its corresponding class definition, the function name is preceded by the class name and the binary scope resolution operator (**: :**). This "ties" the member name to the class name to uniquely identify the functions of a particular class.

Common Programming Error 6.5

When defining a class's member functions outside that class, omitting the class name and scope resolution operator on the function name is an error.

Even though a member function declared in a class definition may be defined outside that class definition (and "tied" to the class via the binary scope resolution operator), that member function is still within that *class's scope*, i.e., its name is known only to other members of the class unless referred to via an object of the class, a reference to an object of the class or a pointer to an object of the class. We will say more about class scope shortly.

If a member function is defined in the body of a class definition, the C++ compiler attempts to inline calls to the member function. Member functions defined outside a class definition can be inlined by explicitly using keyword **inline**. Remember that the compiler reserves the right not to inline any function.

Performance Tip 6.2

Defining a small member function inside the class definition inlines the member function (if the compiler chooses to do so). This can improve performance.

Software Engineering Observation 6.7

Defining a small member function inside the class definition does not promote the best software engineering because clients of the class will be able to see the implementation of the function and the client code must be recompiled if the function definition changes.

Software Engineering Observation 6.8

Only the simplest and most stable member functions (i.e., the implementation is unlikely to change) should be defined in the class header.

It is interesting that the **printUniversal** and **printStandard** member functions take no arguments. This is because these member functions implicitly know that they are to print the data members of the particular **Time** object for which they are invoked. This makes member function calls more concise than conventional function calls in procedural programming.

Testing and Debugging Tip 6.1

The fact that member function calls generally take either no arguments or substantially fewer arguments than conventional function calls in non-object-oriented languages reduces the likelihood of passing the wrong arguments, the wrong types of arguments or the wrong number of arguments.

Software Engineering Observation 6.9

Using an object-oriented programming approach can often simplify function calls by reducing the number of parameters to be passed. This benefit of object-oriented programming derives from the fact that encapsulating data members and member functions within an object gives the member functions the right to access the data members.

Classes simplify programming because the client (or user of the class object) need only be concerned with the operations encapsulated or embedded in the object. Such operations are usually designed to be client oriented rather than implementation oriented. Clients need not be concerned with a class's implementation (although the client, of course, wants a correct and efficient implementation). Interfaces do change, but less frequently than implementations. When an implementation changes, implementation-dependent code must change accordingly. Hiding the implementation eliminates the possibility of other program parts becoming dependent on the details of the class implementation.

Often, classes do not have to be created "from scratch." Rather, they can include objects of other classes as members or they may be *derived* from other classes that provide attributes and behaviors the new classes can use. Such *software reuse* can greatly enhance programmer productivity. Including class objects as members of other classes is called *composition* (or *aggregation*) and is discussed in Chapter 7. Deriving new classes from existing classes is called *inheritance* and is discussed in Chapter 9.

Software Engineering Observation 6.10

A central theme of this book is "reuse, reuse, reuse." We will carefully discuss a number of techniques for "polishing" classes to encourage reuse. We focus on "crafting valuable classes" and creating valuable "software assets."

People new to object-oriented programming often express concern at the fact that objects must be quite large because they contain data and functions. Logically, this is true—the programmer may think of objects as containing data and functions. Physically, however, this is not true.

Performance Tip 6.3

Objects contain only data, so objects are much smaller than if they also contained functions. Applying operator **sizeof** *to a class name or to an object of that class will report only the size of the class's data. The compiler creates one copy (only) of the member functions separate from all objects of the class. All objects of the class share this one copy of the member functions. Each object, of course, needs its own copy of the class's data because these data can vary among the objects. The function code is nonmodifiable (also called* reentrant code *or* pure procedure*) and, hence, can be shared among all objects of one class.*

6.6 Class Scope and Accessing Class Members

A class's data members (variables declared in the class definition) and member functions (functions declared in the class definition) belong to that *class's scope*. Nonmember functions are defined at *file scope*.

Within a class's scope, class members are immediately accessible by all of that class's member functions and can be referenced by name. Outside a class's scope, class members are referenced through one of the *handles* on an object—an object name, a reference to an object or a pointer to an object. [We will see in Chapter 7 that an implicit handle is inserted by the compiler on every reference to a data member or member function from within an object.]

Member functions of a class can be overloaded, but only by other member functions of that class. To overload a member function, simply provide in the class definition a prototype for each version of the overloaded function, and provide a separate function definition for each version of the function.

Variables declared in a member function have *function scope*—they are known only to that function. If a member function defines a variable with the same name as a variable with class scope, the class-scope variable is hidden by the function-scope variable in the function scope. Such a hidden variable can be accessed by preceding the variable name with the class name followed by the scope resolution operator (**::**). Hidden global variables can be accessed with the unary scope resolution operator (see Chapter 3).

The operators used to access class members are identical to the operators used to access structure members. The *dot member selection operator (**.**)* is preceded by an object's name or with a reference to an object to access the object's members. The *arrow member selection operator (**->**)* is preceded by a pointer to an object to access that object's members.

Figure 6.4 uses a simple class called **Count** (lines 11–21) with **public** data member **x** of type **int** (line 14) and **public** member function **print** (lines 16–19) to illustrate accessing the members of a class with the member selection operators. Lines 25–27 create three variables related to type **Count**—**counter** (a **Count** object), **counterRef** (a reference to a **Count** object) and **counterPtr** (a pointer to a **Count** object). Variable **counterRef** refers to **counter**, and variable **counterPtr** points to **counter**. It is important to note that class **Count** declares data member **x** as **public** here simply to demonstrate how **public** members are accessed off handles (i.e., a name, a reference or a pointer). As we have stated, data typically are made **private**, as we will do in most subsequent examples. Beginning in Chapter 9, Inheritance, we will sometimes make data **protected**. In lines 30–31 and 34–35, note that the program can access member variable **x** and invoke member function **print** by using the name of the object (**counter**) or a reference to the object (**counterRef**) together with the dot (**.**) member selection operator. Similarly, lines 38–39 demonstrate that the program can access member variable **x** and invoke member function **print** by using a pointer (**countPtr**) and the arrow (**->**) member selection operator.

```cpp
1   // Fig. 6.4: fig06_04.cpp
2   // Demonstrating the class member access operators . and ->
3   //
4   // CAUTION: IN FUTURE EXAMPLES WE AVOID PUBLIC DATA!
5   #include <iostream>
6
7   using std::cout;
8   using std::endl;
9
10  // class Count definition
11  class Count {
12
13  public:
14     int x;
15
16     void print()
17     {
18        cout << x << endl;
19     }
20
21  }; // end class Count
22
23  int main()
24  {
25     Count counter;                  // create counter object
26     Count *counterPtr = &counter;  // create pointer to counter
27     Count &counterRef = counter;   // create reference to counter
28
29     cout << "Assign 1 to x and print using the object's name: ";
30     counter.x = 1;          // assign 1 to data member x
31     counter.print();        // call member function print
32
33     cout << "Assign 2 to x and print using a reference: ";
34     counterRef.x = 2;       // assign 2 to data member x
35     counterRef.print();     // call member function print
36
37     cout << "Assign 3 to x and print using a pointer: ";
38     counterPtr->x = 3;      // assign 3 to data member x
39     counterPtr->print();    // call member function print
40
41     return 0;
42
43  } // end main
```

```
Assign 1 to x and print using the object's name: 1
Assign 2 to x and print using a reference: 2
Assign 3 to x and print using a pointer: 3
```

Fig. 6.4   Accessing an object's data members and member functions through each type of object handle—the object's name, a reference to the object and a pointer to the object.

6.7 Separating Interface from Implementation

One of the fundamental principles of good software engineering is to separate interface from implementation. This makes it easier to modify programs. As far as clients of a class are concerned, changes in the class's implementation do not affect the client as long as the class's interface originally provided to the client remains unchanged.

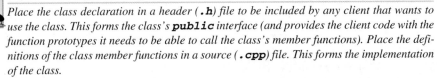

Software Engineering Observation 6.11

*Place the class declaration in a header (`.h`) file to be included by any client that wants to use the class. This forms the class's **public** interface (and provides the client code with the function prototypes it needs to be able to call the class's member functions). Place the definitions of the class member functions in a source (`.cpp`) file. This forms the implementation of the class.*

Software Engineering Observation 6.12

Clients of a class do not need access to the class's source code in order to use the class. The clients do, however, need to be able to link to the class's object code (i.e., the compiled version of the class). This encourages independent software vendors (ISVs) to provide class libraries for sale or license. The ISVs provide in their products only the header files and the object modules. No proprietary information is revealed—as would be the case if source code were provided. The C++ user community benefits by having more ISV-produced class libraries available.

Actually, things are not quite this rosy. Header files do contain some portions of the implementation and hints about others. Inline member functions, for example, need to be in a header file, so that when the compiler compiles a client, the client can include the **inline** function definition in place. A class's **private** members are listed in the class definition in the header file, so these members are visible to clients even though the clients may not access the **private** members. In Chapter 7, we show how to use a so-called *proxy class* to hide even the **private** data of a class from clients of the class.

Software Engineering Observation 6.13

Information important to the interface to a class should be included in the header file. Information that will be used only internally in the class and will not be needed by clients of the class should be included in the unpublished source file. This is yet another example of the principle of least privilege.

The next program (Fig. 6.5–Fig. 6.7) demonstrates separating interface from implementation by splitting Fig. 6.3 into multiple files, a good software engineering convention that we follow in the majority of the code examples throughout the rest of this book. When building a C++ program, each class definition is normally placed in a *header file,* and that class's member-function definitions are placed in a *source-code file* of the same base name (by convention). The header files are included (via **#include**) in each file in which the class is used, and the source-code file is compiled and linked with the file containing the main program. See your compiler's documentation to determine how to compile and link programs consisting of multiple source files.

The program consists of the header file **time1.h** (Fig. 6.5) in which class **Time** is defined, the source file **time1.cpp** (Fig. 6.6) in which the member functions of class **Time** are defined and the source file **fig06_07.cpp** (Fig. 6.7) in which function **main** is defined. The output for this program is identical to the output of Fig. 6.3.

```
1   // Fig. 6.5: time1.h
2   // Declaration of class Time.
3   // Member functions are defined in time1.cpp
4
5   // prevent multiple inclusions of header file
6   #ifndef TIME1_H
7   #define TIME1_H
8
9   // Time abstract data type definition
10  class Time {
11
12  public:
13     Time();                        // constructor
14     void setTime( int, int, int ); // set hour, minute, second
15     void printUniversal();         // print universal-time format
16     void printStandard();          // print standard-time format
17
18  private:
19     int hour;      // 0 - 23 (24-hour clock format)
20     int minute;    // 0 - 59
21     int second;    // 0 - 59
22
23  }; // end class Time
24
25  #endif
```

Fig. 6.5   **Time** class definition.

```
1   // Fig. 6.6: time1.cpp
2   // Member-function definitions for class Time.
3   #include <iostream>
4
5   using std::cout;
6
7   #include <iomanip>
8
9   using std::setfill;
10  using std::setw;
11
12  // include definition of class Time from time1.h
13  #include "time1.h"
14
15  // Time constructor initializes each data member to zero.
16  // Ensures all Time objects start in a consistent state.
17  Time::Time()
18  {
19     hour = minute = second = 0;
20
21  } // end Time constructor
22
```

Fig. 6.6   **Time** class member-function definitions. (Part 1 of 2.)

```
23    // Set new Time value using universal time. Perform validity
24    // checks on the data values. Set invalid values to zero.
25    void Time::setTime( int h, int m, int s )
26    {
27       hour = ( h >= 0 && h < 24 ) ? h : 0;
28       minute = ( m >= 0 && m < 60 ) ? m : 0;
29       second = ( s >= 0 && s < 60 ) ? s : 0;
30
31    } // end function setTime
32
33    // print Time in universal format
34    void Time::printUniversal()
35    {
36       cout << setfill( '0' ) << setw( 2 ) << hour << ":"
37            << setw( 2 ) << minute << ":"
38            << setw( 2 ) << second;
39
40    } // end function printUniversal
41
42    // print Time in standard format
43    void Time::printStandard()
44    {
45       cout << ( ( hour == 0 || hour == 12 ) ? 12 : hour % 12 )
46            << ":" << setfill( '0' ) << setw( 2 ) << minute
47            << ":" << setw( 2 ) << second
48            << ( hour < 12 ? " AM" : " PM" );
49
50    } // end function printStandard
```

Fig. 6.6   **Time** class member-function definitions. (Part 2 of 2.)

```
1     // Fig. 6.7: fig06_07.cpp
2     // Program to test class Time.
3     // NOTE: This file must be compiled with time1.cpp.
4     #include <iostream>
5
6     using std::cout;
7     using std::endl;
8
9     // include definition of class Time from time1.h
10    #include "time1.h"
11
12    int main()
13    {
14       Time t;   // instantiate object t of class Time
15
16       // output Time object t's initial values
17       cout << "The initial universal time is ";
18       t.printUniversal();   // 00:00:00
19       cout << "\nThe initial standard time is ";
20       t.printStandard();    // 12:00:00 AM
21
```

Fig. 6.7   Program to test class **Time**. (Part 1 of 2.)

```
22        t.setTime( 13, 27, 6 );   // change time
23
24        // output Time object t's new values
25        cout << "\n\nUniversal time after setTime is ";
26        t.printUniversal();    // 13:27:06
27        cout << "\nStandard time after setTime is ";
28        t.printStandard();     // 1:27:06 PM
29
30        t.setTime( 99, 99, 99 );  // attempt invalid settings
31
32        // output t's values after specifying invalid values
33        cout << "\n\nAfter attempting invalid settings:"
34             << "\nUniversal time: ";
35        t.printUniversal();    // 00:00:00
36        cout << "\nStandard time: ";
37        t.printStandard();     // 12:00:00 AM
38        cout << endl;
39
40        return 0;
41
42   } // end main
```

```
The initial universal time is 00:00:00
The initial standard time is 12:00:00 AM

Universal time after setTime is 13:27:06
Standard time after setTime is 1:27:06 PM

After attempting invalid settings:
Universal time: 00:00:00
Standard time: 12:00:00 AM
```

Fig. 6.7   Program to test class **Time**. (Part 2 of 2.)

Note that line 13 of **time1.cpp** and line 10 of **fig06_07.cpp** both include header file **time1.h**. Also note, that the name of the header file is enclosed in quotes (**" "**) rather than angle brackets (**<>**). Normally, programmer-defined header files are placed in the same directory as the files that include the header files. When the preprocessor encounters a header file name in quotes, it assumes that the header file is in the same directory as the file in which the **#include** directive appears. If the preprocessor cannot find the header file in the current directory, it searches for the header file in the same location as the header files of the C++ Standard Library. When the preprocessor encounters a header file name in angle brackets, it simply assumes that the header is part of the C++ Standard Library and does not look in the local directory. In **time1.cpp**, the compiler uses the information in **time1.h** to ensure that the member function headers are defined correctly and that the member functions use the class's data correctly. In **fig06_07.cpp**, the compiler uses the information in **time1.h** to ensure that the client code (i.e., **main**) creates and manipulates the **Time** object correctly. For example, to create **Time** object **t** in line 14, the compiler must know the size of a **Time** class object. Recall that only an object's data is in the object—the member functions are stored elsewhere. By including **time.h** in line 10, we give the compiler access to the information it needs (Fig. 6.5, lines 19–21) to determine the size of a **Time** class object.

In Fig. 6.5, note that the class definition is enclosed in the following preprocessor code (lines 5–7 and 25):

```
// prevent multiple inclusions of header file
#ifndef TIME1_H
#define TIME1_H
   ...
#endif
```

When we build larger programs, other definitions and declarations will also be placed in header files. The preceding preprocessor directives prevent the code between **#ifndef** (which means "if not defined") and **#endif** from being included if the name **TIME1_H** has been defined. If the header has not been included previously in a file, the name **TIME1_H** is defined by the **#define** directive and the header file statements are included. If the header has been included previously, **TIME1_H** is defined already and the header file is not included again. Attempts to include a header file multiple times (inadvertently) typically occur in large programs with many header files that may themselves include other header files. [*Note:* The convention we use for the symbolic constant name in the preprocessor directives is simply the header file name with the underscore character replacing the period.]

Testing and Debugging Tip 6.2

*Use **#ifndef**, **#define** and **#endif** preprocessor directives to prevent header files from being included more than once in a program.*

Good Programming Practice 6.2

*Use the name of the header file with the period replaced by an underscore in the **#ifndef** and **#define** preprocessor directives of a header file.*

6.8 Controlling Access to Members

The member access specifiers **public** and **private** (and **protected**, as we will see in Chapter 9) control access to a class's data members and member functions. The default access mode for classes is **private** so all members after the class header and before the first member access specifier are **private**. After each member access specifier, the mode that was invoked by that member access specifier applies until the next member access specifier or until the terminating right brace (**}**) of the class definition. The member access specifiers **public**, **private** and **protected** may be repeated, but such usage is rare and can be confusing.

A class's **private** members can be accessed only by member functions (and friends, as we will see in Chapter 7) of that class. The **public** members of a class may be accessed by any function in the program that holds a handle on an object of that class.

Common Programming Error 6.6

*An attempt by a function, which is not a member of a particular class (or a friend of that class), to access a **private** member of that class is a compiler error.*

Software Engineering Observation 6.14

*Each element of a class should have **private** visibility unless it can be proven that the element needs **public** visibility.*

Figure 6.8 demonstrates that **private** class members are not accessible outside the class. When this program is compiled, the compiler generates two errors stating that the **private** member specified in each statement is not accessible. Figure 6.8 includes **time1.h** from Fig. 6.5 and is compiled with **time1.cpp** from Fig. 6.6.

Good Programming Practice 6.3

*If you choose to list the **private** members first in a class definition, explicitly use the **private** member access specifier despite the fact that **private** is assumed by default. This improves program clarity.*

Good Programming Practice 6.4

*Despite the fact that the **public** and **private** member access specifiers may be repeated and intermixed, list all the **public** members of a class first in one group and then list all the **private** members in another group. This focuses the client's attention on the class's **public** interface, rather than on the class's implementation.*

A client of a class may be a member function of another class or it may be a global function (i.e., a C-like "loose" or "free" function in the file, such as **main**, that is not a member function of any class).

```
1   // Fig. 6.8: fig06_08.cpp
2   // Demonstrate errors resulting from attempts
3   // to access private class members.
4   #include <iostream>
5
6   using std::cout;
7
8   // include definition of class Time from time1.h
9   #include "time1.h"
10
11  int main()
12  {
13     Time t;   // create Time object
14
15
16     t.hour = 7;  // error: 'Time::hour' is not accessible
17
18     // error: 'Time::minute' is not accessible
19     cout << "minute = " << t.minute;
20
21     return 0;
22
23  } // end main
```

```
D:\cpphtp4_examples\ch06\Fig6_06\Fig06_06.cpp(16) : error C2248:
   'hour' : cannot access private member declared in class 'Time'
D:\cpphtp4_examples\ch06\Fig6_06\Fig06_06.cpp(19) : error C2248:
   'minute' : cannot access private member declared in class 'Time'
```

Fig. 6.8   **private** members of a class are not accessible outside the class.

Access to members of a class may be implicitly set to **private** by default, or explicitly set to **public**, **protected** (as we will see in Chapter 9) or **private**. The default access for **struct** members is **public**. Access to members of a **struct** also can be explicitly set to **public**, **protected** or **private** and can be implicitly set to **public** by default.

Just because class data is **private** does not necessarily mean that clients cannot effect changes to that data. The data can be changed by member functions or friends of that class. As we will see, these functions should be designed to ensure the integrity of the data.

Access to a class's **private** data should be carefully controlled by the use of member functions, called *access functions* (also called *accessor methods*). For example, to allow clients to read the value of **private** data, the class can provide a *get* function. To enable clients to modify **private** data, the class can provide a *set* function. Such modification would seem to violate the notion of **private** data. But a *set* member function can provide data validation capabilities (such as range checking) to ensure that the value is set properly. A *set* function can also translate between the form of the data used in the interface and the form used in the implementation. For example, a client might view a **Time** as having hour, minute and second components, but class **Time** might represent the time as the number of seconds since midnight. A *get* function need not expose the data in "raw" format; rather, the *get* function can edit the data and limit the view of the data the client will see.

Software Engineering Observation 6.15

*Keep all the data members of a class **private**. Provide **public** member functions to set the values of **private** data members and to get the values of **private** data members. This architecture helps hide the implementation of a class from its clients, which reduces bugs and improves program modifiability.*

Software Engineering Observation 6.16

*The class designer need not provide set or get functions for each **private** data item; these capabilities should be provided only when appropriate. If a service is useful to the client code, that service should be provided in the class's **public** interface.*

Testing and Debugging Tip 6.3

*Making the data members of a class **private** and the member functions of the class **public** facilitates debugging because problems with data manipulations are localized to either the class's member functions or the friends of the class.*

6.9 Access Functions and Utility Functions

Not all member functions need be made **public** to serve as part of the interface of a class. Some member functions remain **private** and serve as *utility functions* to the other functions of the class (and to friends of the class).

Software Engineering Observation 6.17

*Member functions tend to fall into a number of different categories—get functions that read and return the value of **private** data members; functions that set the value of **private** data members; functions that implement the services of the class; functions that perform various mechanical chores for the class such as initializing class objects, assigning class objects, converting between classes and built-in types (or between classes and other classes) and handling memory for class objects.*

Access functions can read or display data. Another common use for access functions is to test the truth or falsity of conditions—such functions are often called *predicate functions*. An example of a predicate function would be an **isEmpty** function for any container class—a class capable of holding many objects—such as a linked list, a stack or a queue. A program would test **isEmpty** before attempting to read another item from the container object. An **isFull** predicate function might test a container class object to determine whether it has no additional room. Useful predicate functions for our **Time** class might be **isAM** and **isPM**.

The program of Fig. 6.9–Fig. 6.11 demonstrates the notion of a *utility function* (also called a *helper function*). A utility function is not part of a class's **public** interface; rather, it is a **private** member function that supports the operation of the class's **public** member functions. Utility functions are not intended to be used by clients of a class.

Class **SalesPerson** (Fig. 6.9) declares an array of 12 monthly sales figures (line 17) and the prototypes for the class's constructor and member functions that manipulate the array.

In Fig. 6.10, the **SalesPerson** constructor (lines 18–23) initializes array **sales** to zero. The **public** member function **setSales** (lines 41–50) sets the elements of array **sales** to user-supplied values. The **public** member function **printAnnualSales** (lines 53–59) prints the total sales for the last 12 months. The **private** utility function **totalAnnualSales** (lines 62–71) totals the 12 monthly sales figures for the benefit of **printAnnualSales**. Member function **printAnnualSales** edits the sales figures into dollar amount format.

In Fig. 6.11, notice that the application's **main** function includes only a simple sequence of member function calls—there are no control structures. The logic of manipulating the **sales** array is completely encapsulated in class **SalesPerson**'s member functions.

```
1   // Fig. 6.9: salesp.h
2   // SalesPerson class definition.
3   // Member functions defined in salesp.cpp.
4   #ifndef SALESP_H
5   #define SALESP_H
6
7   class SalesPerson {
8
9   public:
10      SalesPerson();                  // constructor
11      void getSalesFromUser();        // input sales from keyboard
12      void setSales( int, double );   // set sales for a month
13      void printAnnualSales();        // summarize and print sales
14
15   private:
16      double totalAnnualSales();      // utility function
17      double sales[ 12 ];             // 12 monthly sales figures
18
19   }; // end class SalesPerson
20
21   #endif
```

Fig. 6.9 **SalesPerson** class definition.

```cpp
1   // Fig. 6.10: salesp.cpp
2   // Member functions for class SalesPerson.
3   #include <iostream>
4
5   using std::cout;
6   using std::cin;
7   using std::endl;
8   using std::fixed;
9
10  #include <iomanip>
11
12  using std::setprecision;
13
14  // include SalesPerson class definition from salesp.h
15  #include "salesp.h"
16
17  // initialize elements of array sales to 0.0
18  SalesPerson::SalesPerson()
19  {
20     for ( int i = 0; i < 12; i++ )
21        sales[ i ] = 0.0;
22
23  } // end SalesPerson constructor
24
25  // get 12 sales figures from the user at the keyboard
26  void SalesPerson::getSalesFromUser()
27  {
28     double salesFigure;
29
30     for ( int i = 1; i <= 12; i++ ) {
31        cout << "Enter sales amount for month " << i << ": ";
32        cin >> salesFigure;
33        setSales( i, salesFigure );
34
35     } // end for
36
37  } // end function getSalesFromUser
38
39  // set one of the 12 monthly sales figures; function subtracts
40  // one from month value for proper subscript in sales array
41  void SalesPerson::setSales( int month, double amount )
42  {
43     // test for valid month and amount values
44     if ( month >= 1 && month <= 12 && amount > 0 )
45        sales[ month - 1 ] = amount; // adjust for subscripts 0-11
46
47     else // invalid month or amount value
48        cout << "Invalid month or sales figure" << endl;
49
50  } // end function setSales
51
```

Fig. 6.10   **SalesPerson** class member-function definitions. (Part 1 of 2.)

```
52   // print total annual sales (with help of utility function)
53   void SalesPerson::printAnnualSales()
54   {
55      cout << setprecision( 2 ) << fixed
56         << "\nThe total annual sales are: $"
57         << totalAnnualSales() << endl; // call utility function
58
59   } // end function printAnnualSales
60
61   // private utility function to total annual sales
62   double SalesPerson::totalAnnualSales()
63   {
64      double total = 0.0;                // initialize total
65
66      for ( int i = 0; i < 12; i++ )    // summarize sales results
67         total += sales[ i ];
68
69      return total;
70
71   } // end function totalAnnualSales
```

Fig. 6.10   **SalesPerson** class member-function definitions. (Part 2 of 2.)

Software Engineering Observation 6.18

A phenomenon of object-oriented programming is that once a class is defined, creating and manipulating objects of that class usually involves issuing only a simple sequence of member function calls—few, if any, control structures are needed. By contrast, it is common to have control structures in the implementation of a class's member functions.

```
1    // Fig. 6.11: fig06_11.cpp
2    // Demonstrating a utility function.
3    // Compile this program with salesp.cpp
4
5    // include SalesPerson class definition from salesp.h
6    #include "salesp.h"
7
8    int main()
9    {
10      SalesPerson s;              // create SalesPerson object s
11
12      s.getSalesFromUser();  // note simple sequential code; no
13      s.printAnnualSales();  // control structures in main
14
15      return 0;
16
17   } // end main
```

Fig. 6.11   Utility function demontration. (Part 1 of 2.)

```
Enter sales amount for month 1: 5314.76
Enter sales amount for month 2: 4292.38
Enter sales amount for month 3: 4589.83
Enter sales amount for month 4: 5534.03
Enter sales amount for month 5: 4376.34
Enter sales amount for month 6: 5698.45
Enter sales amount for month 7: 4439.22
Enter sales amount for month 8: 5893.57
Enter sales amount for month 9: 4909.67
Enter sales amount for month 10: 5123.45
Enter sales amount for month 11: 4024.97
Enter sales amount for month 12: 5923.92

The total annual sales are: $60120.59
```

Fig. 6.11   Utility function demontration. (Part 2 of 2.)

6.10 Initializing Class Objects: Constructors

When a class object is created, its members can be initialized by a *constructor* function of that class. A constructor is a special member function with the same name as the class and no return data type. The programmer provides the constructor, which is then invoked each time an object of that class is created (instantiated). Constructors may be overloaded to provide a variety of means for initializing objects of a class. Data members can be initialized in a constructor of the class or their values may be *set* later after the object is created. However, it is a good software engineering practice to ensure that an object is fully initialized before the client code invokes the object's member functions. In general, you should not rely on the client code to ensure that an object gets initialized properly.

Good Programming Practice 6.5

When appropriate (almost always), provide a constructor to ensure that every object is properly initialized with meaningful values. Pointer data members, in particular, should be initialized to some legitimate pointer value or to 0.

Testing and Debugging Tip 6.4

Every member function (and friend) that modifies the **private** *data members of an object should ensure that the data remains in a consistent state.*

When an object of a class is declared, *initializers* can be provided in parentheses to the right of the object name and before the semicolon. These initializers are passed as arguments to the class's constructor. In the next section, Fig. 6.14 demonstrates these implicit *constructor calls*. [*Note:* Although programmers normally do not call constructors, programmers can still provide data that get passed to constructors as arguments.]

6.11 Using Default Arguments with Constructors

The program of Fig. 6.12–Fig. 6.14 enhances class **Time** to demonstrate how arguments are implicitly passed to a constructor. The constructor defined in **time1.cpp** (Fig. 6.6) initialized **hour**, **minute** and **second** to **0** (i.e., midnight in universal time). Like other functions, constructors can specify default arguments. Line 13 of Fig. 6.12 declares the

Time constructor to include default arguments, specifying a default value of zero for each argument passed to the constructor. In Fig. 6.13, lines 17–21 define the new version of the **Time** constructor that receives values for parameters **hr**, **min** and **sec** that will be used to initalize **private** data members **hour**, **minute** and **second**, respectively. By specifying default arguments for the constructor, even if no values are provided in a constructor call, the object is still guaranteed to be initialized to a consistent state. A programmer-supplied constructor that defaults all its arguments (or explicitly requires no arguments) is called a *default constructor*—i.e., a constructor that can be invoked with no arguments. There can be only one default constructor per class.

In Fig. 6.13, line 19 of the constructor calls member function **setTime** with the values passed to the constructor (or the default values) to ensure that the value supplied for **hour** is in the range 0–23, and that the values for **minute** and **second** are each in the range 0–59. If a value is out of range, that value is set to zero by **setTime** (to ensure that each data member remains in a consistent state).

```
1   // Fig. 6.12: time2.h
2   // Declaration of class Time.
3   // Member functions defined in time2.cpp.
4
5   // prevent multiple inclusions of header file
6   #ifndef TIME2_H
7   #define TIME2_H
8
9   // Time abstract data type definition
10  class Time {
11
12  public:
13     Time( int = 0, int = 0, int = 0); // default constructor
14     void setTime( int, int, int ); // set hour, minute, second
15     void printUniversal();          // print universal-time format
16     void printStandard();           // print standard-time format
17
18  private:
19     int hour;     // 0 - 23 (24-hour clock format)
20     int minute;   // 0 - 59
21     int second;   // 0 - 59
22
23  }; // end class Time
24
25  #endif
```

Fig. 6.12   **Time** class containing a constructor with default arguments.

```
1   // Fig. 6.13: time2.cpp
2   // Member-function definitions for class Time.
3   #include <iostream>
4
5   using std::cout;
```

Fig. 6.13   **Time** class member-function definitions including a constructor that takes arguments. (Part 1 of 2.)

```
6
7   #include <iomanip>
8
9   using std::setfill;
10  using std::setw;
11
12  // include definition of class Time from time2.h
13  #include "time2.h"
14
15  // Time constructor initializes each data member to zero;
16  // ensures all Time objects start in a consistent state
17  Time::Time( int hr, int min, int sec )
18  {
19     setTime( hr, min, sec );   // validate and set time
20
21  } // end Time constructor
22
23  // set new Time value using universal time, perform validity
24  // checks on the data values and set invalid values to zero
25  void Time::setTime( int h, int m, int s )
26  {
27     hour = ( h >= 0 && h < 24 ) ? h : 0;
28     minute = ( m >= 0 && m < 60 ) ? m : 0;
29     second = ( s >= 0 && s < 60 ) ? s : 0;
30
31  } // end function setTime
32
33  // print Time in universal format
34  void Time::printUniversal()
35  {
36     cout << setfill( '0' ) << setw( 2 ) << hour << ":"
37          << setw( 2 ) << minute << ":"
38          << setw( 2 ) << second;
39
40  } // end function printUniversal
41
42  // print Time in standard format
43  void Time::printStandard()
44  {
45     cout << ( ( hour == 0 || hour == 12 ) ? 12 : hour % 12 )
46          << ":" << setfill( '0' ) << setw( 2 ) << minute
47          << ":" << setw( 2 ) << second
48          << ( hour < 12 ? " AM" : " PM" );
49
50  } // end function printStandard
```

Fig. 6.13   **Time** class member-function definitions including a constructor that takes arguments. (Part 2 of 2.)

Note that the **Time** constructor could be written to include the same statements as member function **setTime**. This may be slightly more efficient because the extra call to **setTime** would be eliminated. However, coding the **Time** constructor and member function **setTime** identically would make maintenance of this program more difficult. If the implementation of member function **setTime** were to change, the implementation of the

Time constructor would have to change accordingly. Having the **Time** constructor call **setTime** directly requires any changes to the implementation of **setTime** to be made only once. This reduces the likelihood of errors when altering the implementation. Also, the performance of the **Time** constructor can be enhanced by explicitly declaring the constructor **inline** or by defining the constructor in the class definition (which implicitly inlines the function definition).

Software Engineering Observation 6.19

If a member function of a class already provides all or part of the functionality required by a constructor (or other member function) of the class, call that member function from the constructor (or other member function). This simplifies the maintenance of the code and reduces the likelihood of an error if the implementation of the code is modified. As a general rule: Avoid repeating code.

Software Engineering Observation 6.20

Declare default function argument values only in the function prototype within the class definition in the header file.

Software Engineering Observation 6.21

Any change to the default argument values of a function requires the client code to be recompiled. If it is likely that the default argument values will change, use overloaded functions instead. Thus, if the implementation of a member function changes, the client code need not be recompiled.

Function **main** in Fig. 6.14 initializes five **Time** objects—one with all three arguments defaulted in the constructor call (line 13), one with one argument specified (line 14), one with two arguments specified (line 15), one with three arguments specified (line 16) and one with three invalid arguments specified (line 17). Then the program displays each object in universal-time and standard-time formats.

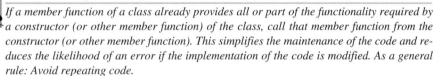

```
1   // Fig. 6.14: fig06_14.cpp
2   // Demonstrating a default constructor for class Time.
3   #include <iostream>
4
5   using std::cout;
6   using std::endl;
7
8   // include definition of class Time from time2.h
9   #include "time2.h"
10
11  int main()
12  {
13      Time t1;                    // all arguments defaulted
14      Time t2( 2 );               // minute and second defaulted
15      Time t3( 21, 34 );          // second defaulted
16      Time t4( 12, 25, 42 );      // all values specified
17      Time t5( 27, 74, 99 );      // all bad values specified
18
```

Fig. 6.14   Constructor with default arguments. (Part 1 of 2.)

```
19        cout << "Constructed with:\n\n"
20            << "all default arguments:\n  ";
21        t1.printUniversal();   // 00:00:00
22        cout << "\n  ";
23        t1.printStandard();    // 12:00:00 AM
24
25        cout << "\n\nhour specified; default minute and second:\n  ";
26        t2.printUniversal();   // 02:00:00
27        cout << "\n  ";
28        t2.printStandard();    // 2:00:00 AM
29
30        cout << "\n\nhour and minute specified; default second:\n  ";
31        t3.printUniversal();   // 21:34:00
32        cout << "\n  ";
33        t3.printStandard();    // 9:34:00 PM
34
35        cout << "\n\nhour, minute, and second specified:\n  ";
36        t4.printUniversal();   // 12:25:42
37        cout << "\n  ";
38        t4.printStandard();    // 12:25:42 PM
39
40        cout << "\n\nall invalid values specified:\n  ";
41        t5.printUniversal();   // 00:00:00
42        cout << "\n  ";
43        t5.printStandard();    // 12:00:00 AM
44        cout << endl;
45
46        return 0;
47
48    } // end main
```

```
Constructed with:

all default arguments:
  00:00:00
  12:00:00 AM

hour specified; default minute and second:
  02:00:00
  2:00:00 AM

hour and minute specified; default second:
  21:34:00
  9:34:00 PM

hour, minute, and second specified:
  12:25:42
  12:25:42 PM

all invalid values specified:
  00:00:00
  12:00:00 AM
```

Fig. 6.14   Constructor with default arguments. (Part 2 of 2.)

If the programmer does not explicitly define at least one constructor for a class, the compiler implicitly creates a default constructor. Such a constructor does not perform any initialization of fundamental-type variables (e.g., **int**s, **double**s, pointers, etc.), so when the object is created, it is not guaranteed to be in a consistent state.[1]

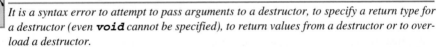

Software Engineering Observation 6.22

It is possible for a class not to have a default constructor—this occurs if the programmer defines at least one constructor that receives arguments and the programmer does not explicitly define a default constructor.

6.12 Destructors

A *destructor* is another type of special member function of a class. The name of the destructor for a class is the *tilde (~)* character followed by the class name. This naming convention has intuitive appeal, because as we will see in a later chapter, the tilde operator is the bitwise complement operator, and, in a sense, the destructor is the complement of the constructor.

A class's destructor is called when an object is destroyed. This occurs, for example, as an automatic object is destroyed when program execution leaves the scope in which that object was instantiated. The destructor itself does not actually destroy the object—it performs *termination housekeeping* before the system reclaims the object's memory so that memory may be reused to hold new objects.

A destructor receives no parameters and returns no value. A class may have only one destructor—destructor overloading is not allowed.

Common Programming Error 6.7

*It is a syntax error to attempt to pass arguments to a destructor, to specify a return type for a destructor (even **void** cannot be specified), to return values from a destructor or to overload a destructor.*

Even though destructors have not been provided for the classes presented so far, every class has a destructor. If the programmer does not explicitly provide a destructor, the compiler creates an "empty" destructor.[2] In Chapter 8, we will build destructors appropriate for classes whose objects contain dynamically allocated memory (e.g., for arrays and strings) or use other system resources (e.g., files on disk). [We discuss how to dynamically allocate and deallocate memory in Chapter 7.]

Software Engineering Observation 6.23

As we will see throughout the remainder of the book, constructors and destructors have much greater prominence in C++ and object-oriented programming than is possible to convey after only our brief introduction here.

6.13 When Constructors and Destructors Are Called

Constructors and destructors are called implicitly by the compiler. The order in which these function calls occur depends on the order in which execution enters and leaves the scopes where the objects are instantiated. Generally, destructor calls are made in the reverse order

---

1. We will see that such a constructor can, in fact, initialize portions of objects created through composition (Chapter 7) and inheritance (Chapter 9).
2. We will see that such an implicitly created destructor does, in fact, perform important operations on objects that are created through composition (Chapter 7) and inheritance (Chapter 9).

of the corresponding constructor calls. However, as we will see in Fig. 6.17, the storage classes of objects can alter the order in which destructors are called.

Constructors are called for objects defined in global scope before any other function (including **main**) in that file begins execution (although the order of execution of global object constructors between files is not guaranteed). The corresponding destructors are called when **main** terminates or function **exit** is called. Destructors are not called for global objects if the program terminates with a call to function **abort**. (See Chapter 20 for more information on functions **exit** and **abort**.)

The constructor for an automatic local object is called when execution reaches the point where that object is defined—the corresponding destructor is called when execution leaves the object's scope (i.e., the block in which that object is defined is exited). Constructors and destructors for automatic objects are called each time the objects enter and leave scope. Destructors are not called for automatic objects if the program terminates with a call to function **exit** or function **abort**.

The constructor for a **static** local object is called only once when execution first reaches the point where the object is defined—the corresponding destructor is called when **main** terminates or the program calls function **exit**. Global and **static** objects are destroyed in the reverse order of their creation. Destructors are not called for **static** objects if the program terminates with a call to function **abort**.

The program of Fig. 6.15–Fig. 6.17 demonstrates the order in which constructors and destructors are called for objects of class **CreateAndDestroy** (Fig. 6.15 and Fig. 6.16) of various storage classes in several scopes. Each object of class **CreateAndDestroy** contains an integer (**data**) and a string (**message**) that are used in the program's output to identify the object. This mechanical example is purely for pedagogic purposes. For this reason, line 27 of the destructor in Fig. 6.16 determines whether the object being destroyed has a **data** value **1** or **6** and, if so, outputs a newline character. This line helps make the program's output easier to follow.

```
1   // Fig. 6.15: create.h
2   // Definition of class CreateAndDestroy.
3   // Member functions defined in create.cpp.
4   #ifndef CREATE_H
5   #define CREATE_H
6
7   class CreateAndDestroy {
8
9   public:
10     CreateAndDestroy( int, char * );    // constructor
11     ~CreateAndDestroy();                // destructor
12
13   private:
14     int objectID;
15     char *message;
16
17   }; // end class CreateAndDestroy
18
19   #endif
```

Fig. 6.15   **CreateAndDestroy** class definition.

```
1    // Fig. 6.16: create.cpp
2    // Member-function definitions for class CreateAndDestroy
3    #include <iostream>
4
5    using std::cout;
6    using std::endl;
7
8    // include CreateAndDestroy class definition from create.h
9    #include "create.h"
10
11   // constructor
12   CreateAndDestroy::CreateAndDestroy(
13       int objectNumber, char *messagePtr )
14   {
15       objectID = objectNumber;
16       message = messagePtr;
17
18       cout << "Object " << objectID << "   constructor runs   "
19           << message << endl;
20
21   } // end CreateAndDestroy constructor
22
23   // destructor
24   CreateAndDestroy::~CreateAndDestroy()
25   {
26       // the following line is for pedagogic purposes only
27       cout << ( objectID == 1 || objectID == 6 ? "\n" : "" );
28
29       cout << "Object " << objectID << "   destructor runs   "
30           << message << endl;
31
32   } // end ~CreateAndDestroy destructor
```

Fig. 6.16   **CreateAndDestroy** class member-function definitions.

The program of Fig. 6.17 defines object **first** (line 15) in global scope. Its constructor is actually called before any statements in **main** execut,e and its destructor is called at program termination after the destructors for all other objects have run.

Function **main** (lines 17–36) declares three objects. Objects **second** (line 21) and **fourth** (line 30) are local automatic objects, and object **third** (lines 23–24) is a **static** local object. The constructor for each of these objects is called when execution reaches the point where that object is declared. The destructors for objects **fourth** then **second** are called (i.e., the reverse of the order in which their constructors were called) when execution reaches the end of **main**. Because object **third** is **static**, it exists until program termination. The destructor for object **third** is called before the destructor for global object **first**, but after all other objects are destroyed.

Function **create** (lines 39–53) declares three objects—**fifth** (line 43) and **seventh** (lines 48–49) are local automatic objects, and **sixth** (lines 45–46) is a **static** local object. The destructors for objects **seventh** then **fifth** are called (i.e., the reverse of the order in which their constructors were called) when **create** terminates. Because **sixth** is **static**, it exists until program termination. The destructor for **sixth** is called before the destructors for **third** and **first**, but after all other objects are destroyed.

```cpp
1   // Fig. 6.17: fig06_17.cpp
2   // Demonstrating the order in which constructors and
3   // destructors are called.
4   #include <iostream>
5
6   using std::cout;
7   using std::endl;
8
9   // include CreateAndDestroy class definition from create.h
10  #include "create.h"
11
12  void create( void );    // prototype
13
14  // global object
15  CreateAndDestroy first( 1, "(global before main)" );
16
17  int main()
18  {
19     cout << "\nMAIN FUNCTION: EXECUTION BEGINS" << endl;
20
21     CreateAndDestroy second( 2, "(local automatic in main)" );
22
23     static CreateAndDestroy third(
24        3, "(local static in main)" );
25
26     create();   // call function to create objects
27
28     cout << "\nMAIN FUNCTION: EXECUTION RESUMES" << endl;
29
30     CreateAndDestroy fourth( 4, "(local automatic in main)" );
31
32     cout << "\nMAIN FUNCTION: EXECUTION ENDS" << endl;
33
34     return 0;
35
36  } // end main
37
38  // function to create objects
39  void create( void )
40  {
41     cout << "\nCREATE FUNCTION: EXECUTION BEGINS" << endl;
42
43     CreateAndDestroy fifth( 5, "(local automatic in create)" );
44
45     static CreateAndDestroy sixth(
46        6, "(local static in create)" );
47
48     CreateAndDestroy seventh(
49        7, "(local automatic in create)" );
50
51     cout << "\nCREATE FUNCTION: EXECUTION ENDS\" << endl;
52
53  } // end function create
```

Fig. 6.17   Order in which constructors and destructors are called. (Part 1 of 2.)

```
Object 1    constructor runs    (global before main)

MAIN FUNCTION: EXECUTION BEGINS
Object 2    constructor runs    (local automatic in main)
Object 3    constructor runs    (local static in main)

CREATE FUNCTION: EXECUTION BEGINS
Object 5    constructor runs    (local automatic in create)
Object 6    constructor runs    (local static in create)
Object 7    constructor runs    (local automatic in create)

CREATE FUNCTION: EXECUTION ENDS
Object 7    destructor runs     (local automatic in create)
Object 5    destructor runs     (local automatic in create)

MAIN FUNCTION: EXECUTION RESUMES
Object 4    constructor runs    (local automatic in main)

MAIN FUNCTION: EXECUTION ENDS
Object 4    destructor runs     (local automatic in main)
Object 2    destructor runs     (local automatic in main)
Object 6    destructor runs     (local static in create)
Object 3    destructor runs     (local static in main)

Object 1    destructor runs     (global before main)
```

Fig. 6.17   Order in which constructors and destructors are called. (Part 2 of 2.)

6.14 Using *Set* and *Get* Functions

A class's **private** data members can be accessed only by member functions (and friends) of the class. A typical manipulation might be the adjustment of a customer's bank balance (e.g., a **private** data member of a class **BankAccount**) by a member function **computeInterest**.

Classes often provide **public** member functions to allow clients of the class to *set* (i.e., write) or *get* (i.e., read) the values of **private** data members. These functions need not be called *set* and *get* specifically, but they often are. More specifically, a member function that *sets* data member **interestRate** might be named **setInterestRate**, and a member function that *gets* the **interestRate** might be named **getInterestRate**. Get functions are also commonly called "query" functions.

It may seem that providing both *set* and *get* capabilities is essentially the same as making the data members **public**. This is yet another subtlety of C++ that makes the language so desirable for software engineering. If a data member is **public**, then the data member can be read or written at will by any function in the program. If a data member is **private**, a **public** *get* function would certainly seem to allow other functions to read the data at will. However, the *get* function could control the format in which the data is returned to the client. A **public** *set* function could—and most likely would—carefully scrutinize any attempt to modify the value of the data member. This would ensure that the new value is appropriate for that data item, i.e., the data item remains in a consistent state. For example, an attempt to *set* the day of the month to 37 could be rejected, an attempt to *set* a person's weight to zero or a negative value could be rejected, an attempt to *set* a numeric quantity to an alphabetic value could be rejected, an attempt to *set* a grade on an exam to 185 (when the proper range is zero to 100) could be rejected, etc.

Software Engineering Observation 6.24

Making data members **private** *and controlling access, especially write access, to those data members through* **public** *member functions helps ensure data integrity.*

Testing and Debugging Tip 6.5

The benefits of data integrity are not automatic simply because data members are made **private**—*the programmer must provide appropriate validity checking. C++ does, however, provide a framework in which programmers can design better programs in a convenient manner.*

Software Engineering Observation 6.25

Member functions that set *the values of private data should verify that the intended new values are proper; if they are not, the* set *functions should place the* **private** *data members into an appropriate state.*

The client of a class should be notified when an attempt is made to assign an invalid value to a data member. A class's *set* functions are often written to return values indicating that an attempt was made to assign invalid data to an object of the class. This enables clients of the class to test the return values of *set* functions to determine whether the object they are manipulating is a valid object and to take appropriate action if the object is not valid.

The program of Fig. 6.18–Fig. 6.20 enhances class **Time** (Fig. 6.18 and Fig. 6.19) to include *set* and *get* functions for the **private** data members **hour**, **minute** and **second**. The new member-function definitions appear in Fig. 6.19. The *set* functions (defined at lines 34–38, 41–45 and 48–52) strictly control the setting of the data members. Attempts to *set* any data member to an incorrect value cause the data member to be set to zero (thus leaving the data member in a consistent state). Each *get* function (defined at lines 55–59, 62–66 and 69–73) simply returns the appropriate data member's value.

```
1   // Fig. 6.18: time3.h
2   // Declaration of class Time.
3   // Member functions defined in time3.cpp
4
5   // prevent multiple inclusions of header file
6   #ifndef TIME3_H
7   #define TIME3_H
8
9   class Time {
10
11  public:
12     Time( int = 0, int = 0, int = 0 );  // default constructor
13
14     // set functions
15     void setTime( int, int, int );  // set hour, minute, second
16     void setHour( int );   // set hour
17     void setMinute( int ); // set minute
18     void setSecond( int ); // set second
19
```

Fig. 6.18   **Time** class definition with *set* and *get* functions. (Part 1 of 2.)

```
20      // get functions
21      int getHour();          // return hour
22      int getMinute();        // return minute
23      int getSecond();        // return second
24
25      void printUniversal();  // output universal-time format
26      void printStandard();   // output standard-time format
27
28   private:
29      int hour;               // 0 - 23 (24-hour clock format)
30      int minute;             // 0 - 59
31      int second;             // 0 - 59
32
33   }; // end clas Time
34
35   #endif
```

Fig. 6.18   **Time** class definition with *set* and *get* functions. (Part 2 of 2.)

```
1    // Fig. 6.19: time3.cpp
2    // Member-function definitions for Time class.
3    #include <iostream>
4
5    using std::cout;
6
7    #include <iomanip>
8
9    using std::setfill;
10   using std::setw;
11
12   // include definition of class Time from time3.h
13   #include "time3.h"
14
15   // constructor function to initialize private data;
16   // calls member function setTime to set variables;
17   // default values are 0 (see class definition)
18   Time::Time( int hr, int min, int sec )
19   {
20      setTime( hr, min, sec );
21
22   } // end Time constructor
23
24   // set hour, minute and second values
25   void Time::setTime( int h, int m, int s )
26   {
27      setHour( h );
28      setMinute( m );
29      setSecond( s );
30
31   } // end function setTime
32
```

Fig. 6.19   **Time** class member-function definitions, including *set* and *get* functions.
            (Part 1 of 3.)

```
33  // set hour value
34  void Time::setHour( int h )
35  {
36     hour = ( h >= 0 && h < 24 ) ? h : 0;
37
38  } // end function setHour
39
40  // set minute value
41  void Time::setMinute( int m )
42  {
43     minute = ( m >= 0 && m < 60 ) ? m : 0;
44
45  } // end function setMinute
46
47  // set second value
48  void Time::setSecond( int s )
49  {
50     second = ( s >= 0 && s < 60 ) ? s : 0;
51
52  } // end function setSecond
53
54  // return hour value
55  int Time::getHour()
56  {
57     return hour;
58
59  } // end function getHour
60
61  // return minute value
62  int Time::getMinute()
63  {
64     return minute;
65
66  } // end function getMinute
67
68  // return second value
69  int Time::getSecond()
70  {
71     return second;
72
73  } // end function getSecond
74
75  // print Time in universal format
76  void Time::printUniversal()
77  {
78     cout << setfill( '0' ) << setw( 2 ) << hour << ":"
79          << setw( 2 ) << minute << ":"
80          << setw( 2 ) << second;
81
82  } // end function printUniversal
83
```

Fig. 6.19   **Time** class member-function definitions, including *set* and *get* functions. (Part 2 of 3.)

```
84   // print Time in standard format
85   void Time::printStandard()
86   {
87      cout << ( ( hour == 0 || hour == 12 ) ? 12 : hour % 12 )
88           << ":" << setfill( '0' ) << setw( 2 ) << minute
89           << ":" << setw( 2 ) << second
90           << ( hour < 12 ? " AM" : " PM" );
91
92   } // end function printStandard
```

Fig. 6.19   **Time** class member-function definitions, including *set* and *get* functions. (Part 3 of 3.)

In Fig. 6.20, function **main** (lines 13–45) first uses the *set* functions to *set* the data members of **Time** object **t** to valid values (lines 18–20), then uses the *get* functions to retrieve the values for output (lines 24–26). Next the *set* functions attempt to *set* the **hour** and **second** members to invalid values (lines 29 and 31) and the **minute** member to a valid value (line 30). Then the program uses the *get* functions to retrieve the values for output (lines 36–38). The output confirms that invalid values cause the data members to be *set* to zero. Finally, the program *set*s the time to **11:58:00** (line 40) and increments the minute value by 3 with a call to function **incrementMinutes** (line 41). Function **increment-Minutes** (lines 48–67) is a nonmember function that uses the *get* and *set* member functions to increment the **minute** member of a **Time** object. Although this works, it incurs the performance burden of issuing multiple function calls. In the next chapter, we discuss the notion of friend functions as a means of eliminating this performance burden.

Software Engineering Observation 6.26

Because C++ is a hybrid language, it is possible to have a mix of two types of function calls in one program and often back to back—C-like calls that pass primitive data or objects to functions and C++ calls that pass functions (or messages) to objects.

Common Programming Error 6.8

A constructor can call other member functions of the class such as set *or* get *functions, but because the constructor is initializing the object, the data members may not yet be in a consistent state. Using data members before they have been properly initialized can cause logic errors.*

```
1    // Fig. 6.20: fig06_20.cpp
2    // Demonstrating the Time class set and get functions
3    #include <iostream>
4
5    using std::cout;
6    using std::endl;
7
8    // include definition of class Time from time3.h
9    #include "time3.h"
10
11   void incrementMinutes( Time &, const int );  // prototype
12
```

Fig. 6.20   *Set* and *get* functions manipulating an object's **private** data. (Part 1 of 3.)

```cpp
13   int main()
14   {
15       Time t;                  // create Time object
16
17       // set time using individual set functions
18       t.setHour( 17 );         // set hour to valid value
19       t.setMinute( 34 );       // set minute to valid value
20       t.setSecond( 25 );       // set second to valid value
21
22       // use get functions to obtain hour, minute and second
23       cout << "Result of setting all valid values:\n"
24            << "  Hour: " << t.getHour()
25            << "  Minute: " << t.getMinute()
26            << "  Second: " << t.getSecond();
27
28       // set time using individual set functions
29       t.setHour( 234 );        // invalid hour set to 0
30       t.setMinute( 43 );       // set minute to valid value
31       t.setSecond( 6373 );     // invalid second set to 0
32
33       // display hour, minute and second after setting
34       // invalid hour and second values
35       cout << "\n\nResult of attempting to set invalid hour and"
36            << " second:\n Hour: " << t.getHour()
37            << "  Minute: " << t.getMinute()
38            << "  Second: " << t.getSecond() << "\n\n";
39
40       t.setTime( 11, 58, 0 );     // set time
41       incrementMinutes( t, 3 );   // increment t's minute by 3
42
43       return 0;
44
45   } // end main
46
47   // add specified number of minutes to a Time object
48   void incrementMinutes( Time &tt, const int count )
49   {
50       cout << "Incrementing minute " << count
51            << " times:\nStart time: ";
52       tt.printStandard();
53
54       for ( int i = 0; i < count; i++ ) {
55           tt.setMinute( ( tt.getMinute() + 1 ) % 60 );
56
57           if ( tt.getMinute() == 0 )
58               tt.setHour( ( tt.getHour() + 1 ) % 24);
59
60           cout << "\nminute + 1: ";
61           tt.printStandard();
62
63       } // end for
64
65       cout << endl;
```

Fig. 6.20 *Set* and *get* functions manipulating an object's **private** data. (Part 2 of 3.)

```
66
67   } // end function incrementMinutes
```

```
Result of setting all valid values:
  Hour: 17   Minute: 34   Second: 25

Result of attempting to set invalid hour and second:
  Hour: 0   Minute: 43   Second: 0

Incrementing minute 3 times:
Start time: 11:58:00 AM
minute + 1: 11:59:00 AM
minute + 1: 12:00:00 PM
minute + 1: 12:01:00 PM
```

Fig. 6.20   *Set* and *get* functions manipulating an object's **private** data. (Part 3 of 3.)

Using *set* functions is certainly important from a software engineering standpoint because they can perform validity checking. Both *set* and *get* functions have another important software engineering advantage.

Software Engineering Observation 6.27

*Accessing **private** data through* set *and* get *member functions not only protects the data members from receiving invalid values, but it also insulates clients of the class from the representation of the data members. Thus, if the representation of the data changes for some reason (typically to reduce the amount of storage required or to improve performance), only the member functions need to change—the clients need not change as long as the interface provided by the member functions remains the same. The clients will, however, need to be re-linked.*

Software Engineering Observation 6.28

The presence of get *methods in a class sometimes suggests that the client code using a class is implementing services (i.e., functions) that the class should provide. If a class's client provides a service that could be used by other clients, that service should be a member of the class, not part of the client. For example, if function **incrementMinutes** in Fig. 6.18 might be used by other clients, it should be defined as a member of class **Time**. Exercise 6.8 asks you to implement as a member of class **Time** a **tick** function that can be used by any client of class **Time** to add one second to the time.*

6.15 Subtle Trap: Returning a Reference to a **private** Data Member

A reference to an object is an alias for the *name* of the object and, hence, may be used on the left side of an assignment statement. In this context, the reference makes a perfectly acceptable *lvalue* that can receive a value. One way to use this capability (unfortunately!) is to have a **public** member function of a class return a non-**const** reference to a **private** data member of that class.

The program of Fig. 6.21–Fig. 6.23 uses a simplified **Time** class (Fig. 6.21 and Fig. 6.22) to demonstrate returning a reference to a **private** data member with member function **badSetHour** (declared in Fig. 6.21 at line 16 and defined in Fig. 6.22 at lines 34–40). Such a return actually makes a call to member function **badSetHour** an alias for

private data member **hour**! The function call can be used in any way that the **private** data member can be used, including as an *lvalue* in an assignment statement, thus enabling clients of the class to clobber the class's **private** data at will!

```
1   // Fig. 6.21: time4.h
2   // Declaration of class Time.
3   // Member functions defined in time4.cpp
4
5   // prevent multiple inclusions of header file
6   #ifndef TIME4_H
7   #define TIME4_H
8
9   class Time {
10
11  public:
12     Time( int = 0, int = 0, int = 0 );
13     void setTime( int, int, int );
14     int getHour();
15
16     int &badSetHour( int );   // DANGEROUS reference return
17
18  private:
19     int hour;
20     int minute;
21     int second;
22
23  }; // end class Time
24
25  #endif
```

Fig. 6.21   Returning a reference to a **private** data member.

```
1   // Fig. 6.22: time4.cpp
2   // Member-function definitions for Time class.
3
4   // include definition of class Time from time4.h
5   #include "time4.h"
6
7   // constructor function to initialize private data;
8   // calls member function setTime to set variables;
9   // default values are 0 (see class definition)
10  Time::Time( int hr, int min, int sec )
11  {
12     setTime( hr, min, sec );
13
14  } // end Time constructor
15
16  // set values of hour, minute and second
17  void Time::setTime( int h, int m, int s )
18  {
19     hour = ( h >= 0 && h < 24 ) ? h : 0;
```

Fig. 6.22   Returning a reference to a **private** data member. (Part 1 of 2.)

```
20        minute = ( m >= 0 && m < 60 ) ? m : 0;
21        second = ( s >= 0 && s < 60 ) ? s : 0;
22
23   } // end function setTime
24
25   // return hour value
26   int Time::getHour()
27   {
28      return hour;
29
30   } // end function getHour
31
32   // POOR PROGRAMMING PRACTICE:
33   // Returning a reference to a private data member.
34   int &Time::badSetHour( int hh )
35   {
36      hour = ( hh >= 0 && hh < 24 ) ? hh : 0;
37
38      return hour;  // DANGEROUS reference return
39
40   } // end function badSetHour
```

Fig. 6.22   Returning a reference to a **private** data member. (Part 2 of 2.)

Figure 6.23 declares **Time** object **t** (line 14) and reference **hourRef** (line 17), which is assigned the reference returned by the call **t.badSetHour(20)**. Line 19 displays the value of the alias **hourRef**. Next, line 22 uses the alias to set the value of **hour** to 30 (an invalid value) and line 24 displays the value returned by function **getHour** to show that assigning a value to **hourRef** actually modifies the **private** data in the **Time** object **t**. Finally, line 28 uses the **badSetHour** function call itself as an *lvalue* and assigns 74 (another invalid value) to the reference returned by the function. Line 33 again displays the value returned by function **getHour** to show that assigning a value to the result of the function call in line 28 modifies the **private** data in the **Time** object **t**.

```
1    // Fig. 6.23: fig06_23.cpp
2    // Demonstrating a public member function that
3    // returns a reference to a private data member.
4    #include <iostream>
5
6    using std::cout;
7    using std::endl;
8
9    // include definition of class Time from time4.h
10   #include "time4.h"
11
12   int main()
13   {
14      Time t;
15
16      // store in hourRef the reference returned by badSetHour
17      int &hourRef = t.badSetHour( 20 );
```

Fig. 6.23   Returning a reference to a **private** data member. (Part 1 of 2.)

```
18
19        cout << "Hour before modification: " << hourRef;
20
21        // use hourRef to set invalid value in Time object t
22        hourRef = 30;
23
24        cout << "\nHour after modification: " << t.getHour();
25
26        // Dangerous: Function call that returns
27        // a reference can be used as an lvalue!
28        t.badSetHour( 12 ) = 74;
29
30        cout << "\n\n*********************************\n"
31             << "POOR PROGRAMMING PRACTICE!!!!!!!!\n"
32             << "badSetHour as an lvalue, Hour: "
33             << t.getHour()
34             << "\n*********************************" << endl;
35
36        return 0;
37
38    } // end main
```

```
Hour before modification: 20
Hour after modification: 30


*********************************
POOR PROGRAMMING PRACTICE!!!!!!!!
badSetHour as an lvalue, Hour: 74
*********************************
```

Fig. 6.23   Returning a reference to a **private** data member. (Part 2 of 2.)

Testing and Debugging Tip 6.6

Never have a **public** *member function return a non-***const*** reference (or a pointer) to a* **private** *data member. Returning such a reference violates the encapsulation of the class. In fact, returning any reference or pointer to* **private** *data makes the client code dependent on the representation of the class's data. So, returning pointers or references to* **private** *data is a dangerous practice that should be avoided.*

6.16 Default Memberwise Assignment

The assignment operator (**=**) can be used to assign an object to another object of the same type. By default, such assignment is performed by *memberwise assignment*—each member of the object on the right of the assignment operator is assigned individually to the same member in the object on the left of the assignment operator. Line 49 of Fig. 6.24 uses default memberwise assignment to assign the values of **Date** object **date1** to **Date** object **date2**. In this case, the **month** member of **date1** is assigned to the **month** member of **date2**, the **day** member of **date1** is assigned to the **day** member of **date2** and the **year** member of **date1** is assigned to the **year** member of **date2**. [*Note:* Memberwise assignment can cause serious problems when used with a class whose data members contain pointers to dynamically allocated storage; in Chapter 8, we will discuss these problems and show how to deal with them.]

```cpp
1    // Fig. 6.24: fig06_24.cpp
2    // Demonstrating that class objects can be assigned
3    // to each other using default memberwise assignment.
4    #include <iostream>
5
6    using std::cout;
7    using std::endl;
8
9    // class Date definition
10   class Date {
11
12   public:
13      Date( int = 1, int = 1, int = 1990 ); // default constructor
14      void print();
15
16   private:
17      int month;
18      int day;
19      int year;
20
21   }; // end class Date
22
23   // Date constructor with no range checking
24   Date::Date( int m, int d, int y )
25   {
26      month = m;
27      day = d;
28      year = y;
29
30   } // end Date constructor
31
32   // print Date in the format mm-dd-yyyy
33   void Date::print()
34   {
35      cout << month << '-' << day << '-' << year;
36
37   } // end function print
38
39   int main()
40   {
41      Date date1( 7, 4, 2002 );
42      Date date2;  // date2 defaults to 1/1/1990
43
44      cout << "date1 = ";
45      date1.print();
46      cout << "\ndate2 = ";
47      date2.print();
48
49      date2 = date1;   // default memberwise assignment
50
```

Fig. 6.24   Default memberwise assignment. (Part 1 of 2.)

```
51        cout << "\n\nAfter default memberwise assignment, date2 = ";
52        date2.print();
53        cout << endl;
54
55        return 0;
56
57   } // end main
```

```
date1 = 7-4-2002
date2 = 1-1-1990

After default memberwise assignment, date2 = 7-4-2002
```

Fig. 6.24   Default memberwise assignment. (Part 2 of 2.)

Objects may be passed as function arguments and may be returned from functions. Such passing and returning is performed using pass-by-value by default—a copy of the object is passed or returned. In such cases, C++ creates a new object and uses a *copy constructor* to copy the original object's values into the new object. For each class, the compiler provides a default copy constructor that copies each member of the original object into the corresponding member of the new object. Like memberwise assignment, copy constructors can cause serious problems when used with a class whose data members contain pointers to dynamically allocated storage. Chapter 8 discusses how programmers can define a customized copy constructor that properly copies objects containing pointers to dynamic memory.

Performance Tip 6.4

*Passing an object by value is good from a security standpoint because the called function has no access to the original object in the caller, but pass-by-value can degrade performance when making a copy of a large object. An object can be passed by reference by passing either a pointer or a reference to the object. Pass-by-reference offers good performance, but is weaker from a security standpoint because the called function is given access to the original object. Pass-by-**const**-reference is a safe, good-performing alternative.*

6.17 Software Reusability

People who write object-oriented programs concentrate on implementing useful classes. There is a tremendous motivation to capture and catalog classes so that they can be accessed by large segments of the programming community. Many substantial *class libraries* exist and others are being developed worldwide. Software is increasingly being constructed from existing, well-defined, carefully tested, well-documented, portable, high-performance, widely available components. This kind of software reusability speeds the development of powerful, high-quality software. *Rapid applications development (RAD)* through the mechanisms of reusable componentry has become an important field.

Significant problems must be solved, however, before the full potential of software reusability can be realized. We need cataloging schemes, licensing schemes, protection mechanisms to ensure that master copies of classes are not corrupted, description schemes so that designers of new systems can determine whether existing objects meet their needs, browsing mechanisms to determine what classes are available and how closely they meet software developer requirements and the like. Many interesting research and development problems need to be solved. There is great motivation to solve these problems because the potential value of their solutions is enormous.

In this chapter, we began our presentation of object-based programming. We showed how to extend C++ by creating user-defined types called classes, then explained how to create and use objects of those classes in programs. We presented many common class features, including **public** and **private** class members, constructors, destructors, and *set* and *get* functions. In Chapter 7, we present additional object-based programming features, including **const** class members, **const** objects, composition, friendship, dynamic memory allocation and **static** class members.

6.18 (Optional Case Study) Thinking About Objects: Starting to Program the Classes for the Elevator Simulator

In the "Thinking About Objects" sections in Chapter 1–Chapter 5, we introduced the fundamentals of object orientation and developed an object-oriented design for an elevator simulator. In the body of Chapter 6, we introduced the details of programming with C++ classes. We now begin implementing our object-oriented design in C++. In this section, we use our UML class diagram to outline the C++ header files that define our classes.

Implementation: Visibility

In the body of Chapter 6, we introduced the access specifiers **public** and **private**. Before we create the class header files, we first must consider which elements from our class diagram should be **public** and which elements should be **private**.

In Chapter 6, we discussed how data members generally should be **private**. We also must consider what visibility member functions should have. The operations of a class are its member functions. These operations must be invoked by clients of that class; therefore, the member functions that correspond to operations should be **public**. In the UML, **public** visibility is indicated by placing a plus sign (+) before a particular element (i.e., a member function or a data member); a minus sign (–) indicates **private** visibility. Member functions that correspond to an action that an object initiates itself should be **private**. Figure 6.25 shows our updated class diagram with visibility notations included. (Note that we have added the **personArrives** operation to class **Floor** from our sequence diagram in Fig. 4.27, as well as several other members that we discuss throughout this section.) As we write the C++ header files for the classes in our system, we place the items designated with "**+**" into the **public** sections and items designated with "**-**" into the **private** sections of the class declarations.

Implementation: Handles

For an object of class A to communicate with an object of class B, the class A object must have a *handle* to the class B object. This means that either the class A object must know the name of the class B object, or the class A object must hold a reference (Section 3.17) or a pointer (Chapter 5) to the class B object.[3] Figure 5.34 contained a list of interactions among objects in our system. Objects of the classes in the left column of the table need handles to objects of the classes in the right column, to send messages to those objects. Figure 6.26 lists the handles for each class based on the information displayed in the table from Fig. 5.34.

---

3. In situations where the name of the class B object is not available to the class A object, we prefer references over pointers (where appropriate), because references are inherently safer than pointers.

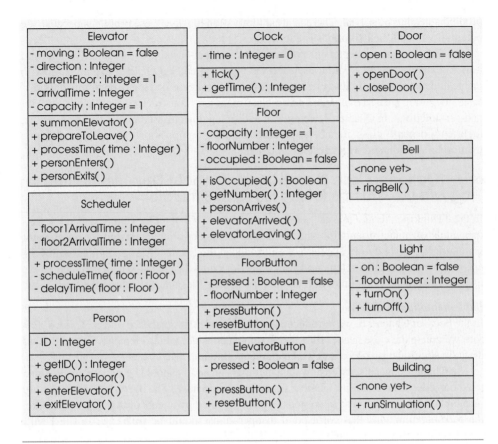

Fig. 6.25   Class diagram that includes attributes and operations.

In the body of Chapter 6, we discussed how to implement handles in C++ as references and pointers to objects. These references then become attributes (data) of the class. Until we discuss composition in Chapter 7, we cannot represent every item from Fig. 6.26 in our class header files. We discuss these special cases shortly.

Class	Handles
Elevator	ElevatorButton, Bell, Floor, Door
Clock	
Scheduler	Person, Floor
Person	FloorButton, ElevatorButton, Elevator, Floor
Floor	FloorButton, Light
FloorButton	Elevator
ElevatorButton	Elevator

Fig. 6.26   List of handles for each class. (Part 1 of 2.)

Class	Handles
Door	Person
Bell	
Light	
Building	Clock, Scheduler, Elevator

Fig. 6.26 List of handles for each class. (Part 2 of 2.)

Implementation: Class Header Files

Now that we have discussed programming C++ classes, we are ready to begin writing the code for our elevator simulator. In this section, we examine the header files for each class in our system. In the "Thinking About Objects" section at the end of Chapter 7, we present the complete, working C++ code for the simulator. In Chapter 9, we modify that code to incorporate inheritance.

To demonstrate the order in which constructors and destructors run, we include a constructor and destructor for each of our classes that displays messages indicating that these functions are running. We include the constructor and destructor prototypes in our header files; we include their implementations in the **.cpp** files presented in Chapter 7.

Figure 6.27 lists the header file for class **Bell**. Working from our class diagram (Fig. 6.25), we declare a constructor (line 9), a destructor (line 10) and the member function **ringBell** (line 11); each of these member functions has **public** visibility. We have identified no other **public** or **private** elements for this class, so our header file is complete.

Figure 6.28 lists the header file for class **Clock**. We include a constructor and destructor (lines 9–10) and the **public** member functions **tick()** and **getTime()** (lines 11–12) from Fig. 6.25. We implement the **time** attribute by declaring a **private** data member **time** of type **int** (line 15). An object of class **Building** invokes the **Clock**'s **getTime** member function to obtain the current value of **time** and invokes the **tick** member function to increment **time**.

```
1   // Fig. 6.27: bell.h
2   // Bell class definition.
3   #ifndef BELL_H
4   #define BELL_H
5
6   class Bell {
7
8   public:
9      Bell();              // constructor
10     ~Bell();             // destructor
11     void ringBell();     // ring the bell
12
13   }; // end class Bell
14
15   #endif // BELL_H
```

Fig. 6.27 **Bell** class header file.

```
1   // Fig. 6.28: clock.h
2   // Clock class definition.
3   #ifndef CLOCK_H
4   #define CLOCK_H
5
6   class Clock {
7
8   public:
9      Clock();              // constructor
10     ~Clock();             // destructor
11     void tick();          // increment clock by one second
12     int getTime();        // returns clock's current time
13
14  private:
15     int time;             // clock's time
16
17  }; // end class Clock
18
19  #endif // CLOCK_H
```

Fig. 6.28   **Clock** class header file.

The header file for class **Person** (Fig. 6.29) contains a constructor declaration (line 9) with one **int** parameter, which identifies the person's arrival floor number. A **Person** object uses this value for output purposes. Line 18 declares attribute **ID**, and lines 13–15 declare operations **stepOntoFloor**, **enterElevator** and **exitElevator** from our class diagram (Fig. 6.25). Line 11 declares member function **getID** that returns the person's **ID** number. We use this operation to keep track of the people in our simulation.

```
1   // Fig. 6.29: person.h
2   // Person class definition.
3   #ifndef PERSON_H
4   #define PERSON_H
5
6   class Person {
7
8   public:
9      Person( int );        // constructor
10     ~Person();            // destructor
11     int getID();          // returns person's ID
12
13     void stepOntoFloor();
14     void enterElevator();
15     void exitElevator();
16
17  private:
18     int ID;               // person's unique ID #
19
20  }; // end class Person
21
22  #endif // PERSON_H
```

Fig. 6.29   **Person** class header file.

Objects of class **Person** are not created at the beginning of the simulation—the scheduler creates them dynamically and randomly as the simulation runs. For this reason, we must implement class **Person** differently from the implementation of other classes in our system. After we discuss how to create objects dynamically in Chapter 7, we add significant elements to the header file for class **Person**.

Figure 6.30 lists the header file for class **Door**. Lines 11–12 declare a constructor and a destructor, and lines 14–15 declare the **public** member functions **openDoor** and **closeDoor**. Line 18 declares the **private** class data member **open**. The table in Fig. 6.26 states that class **Door** needs a handle to class **Person**. However, because objects of class **Person** are created dynamically in our system, we are unsure at this point how to implement handles to objects of class **Person**. We discuss this in Chapter 7.

We list the header file for class **Light** in Fig. 6.31. The information from the class diagram in Fig. 6.25 leads us to declare **public** member functions **turnOn** and **turnOff** (lines 11–12) and **private** data member **on** of type **bool** (line 15). In this header file, we also include the ability to distinguish between different objects of the same class. For example, we know that the simulation contains two objects of class **Light**: One object belongs to the first floor, and the other object belongs to the second floor. We want to distinguish between these objects for output purposes, so we must assign a name to each. Therefore, we declare **int** attribute **floorNumber** in the **private** section of the class declaration (line 16). We also add an **int** parameter to the constructor (line 9), for initializing each **Light** object's floor number.

Figure 6.32 lists the header file for class **Building**. The **public** section of the class declaration includes a constructor (line 9), a destructor (line 10) and member function **runSimulation** (line 11) from Fig. 6.25. When we first identified operation **runSimulation** in Chapter 4, we did not know what object would invoke the function to begin the

```
1   // Fig. 6.30: door.h
2   // Door class definition.
3   #ifndef DOOR_H
4   #define DOOR_H
5
6   class Elevator;   // forward declaration
7
8   class Door {
9
10  public:
11     Door();        // constructor
12     ~Door();       // destructor
13
14     void openDoor();
15     void closeDoor();
16
17  private:
18     bool open;     // open or closed
19
20  };
21
22  #endif // DOOR_H
```

Fig. 6.30   **Door** class header file.

```
1   // Fig. 6.31: light.h
2   // Light class definition.
3   #ifndef LIGHT_H
4   #define LIGHT_H
5
6   class Light {
7
8   public:
9      Light( int );      // constructor
10     ~Light();          // destructor
11     void turnOn();     // turns light on
12     void turnOff();    // turns light off
13
14  private:
15     bool on;           // true if on; false if off
16     int floorNumber;   // floor number that contains light
17
18  }; // end class Light
19
20  #endif // LIGHT_H
```

Fig. 6.31 **Light** class header file.

simulation. Now that we have discussed classes in C++, we know that a **Building** object needs to be declared in **main**, which invokes member function **runSimulation**.

We also choose to include a parameter of type **int** in the **runSimulation** declaration. The **Building** object runs the elevator simulation for the number of seconds specified by this parameter. The table in Fig. 6.26 indicates that class **Building** needs handles to its composite objects. We cannot implement these handles at this point, because we have not discussed composition. Therefore, we delay the implementation of the component objects of class **Building** until Chapter 7 (see the comments in lines 14–18 in Fig. 6.32).

```
1   // Fig. 6.32: building.h
2   // Building class definition.
3   #ifndef BUILDING_H
4   #define BUILDING_H
5
6   class Building {
7
8   public:
9      Building();                   // constructor
10     ~Building();                  // destructor
11     void runSimulation( int );    // controls simulation
12
13  private:
14     // In Chapter 7, we show how to include:
15     //    one object of class Clock
16     //    one object of class Scheduler
17     //    one object of class Elevator
18     //    two objects of class Floor
```

Fig. 6.32 **Building** class header file. (Part 1 of 2.)

```
19
20   }; // end class Building
21
22   #endif // BUILDING_H
```

Fig. 6.32 **Building** class header file. (Part 2 of 2.)

Figure 6.33 lists the header file for class **ElevatorButton**. We declare the **pressed** attribute (line 18), the **pressButton** (line 14) and **resetButton** (line 15) member functions (from the class diagram in Fig. 6.25) and the constructor and destructor (lines 11–12). Figure 6.26 states that class **ElevatorButton** needs a handle to the elevator. In line 21, we include this handle (notice that we use a reference to implement the handle). In Chapter 7, we discuss how to send messages to the elevator using this reference.

A reference must be initialized when it is declared, but we are not allowed to assign a value to class data member in the header file. Therefore, a reference must be initialized in the constructor; we include an **Elevator** reference as a parameter to the constructor in line 11.

Line 6 is a *forward declaration* of class **Elevator**. The forward declaration allows us to declare a reference to an object of class **Elevator** without needing to include the header file for class **Elevator** in the header file for class **ElevatorButton**.[4]

```
 1   // Fig. 6.33: elevatorButton.h
 2   // ElevatorButton class definition.
 3   #ifndef ELEVATORBUTTON_H
 4   #define ELEVATORBUTTON_H
 5
 6   class Elevator;   // forward declaration
 7
 8   class ElevatorButton {
 9
10   public:
11      ElevatorButton( Elevator & );   // constructor
12      ~ElevatorButton();              // destructor
13
14      void pressButton();             // press the button
15      void resetButton();             // reset the button
16
17   private:
18      bool pressed;                   // state of button
19
20      // reference to elevator containing this button
21      Elevator &elevatorRef;
22
23   }; // end class ElevatorButton
24
25   #endif // ELEVATORBUTTON_H
```

Fig. 6.33 **ElevatorButton** class header file.

---

4. Using the forward declaration (where possible) instead of including the full header file helps avoid a preprocessor problem called a *circular include*. We discuss the circular include problem in more detail in Chapter 7.

Figure 6.34 lists the header file for class **FloorButton**. This header file is identical to the header file for class **ElevatorButton**, except that line 18 declares a **private** data member **floorNumber** of type **int**. Objects of class **FloorButton** need to know to which floor they belong for simulator-output purposes. The floor number is declared as a constructor parameter for initialization purposes (line 11).

Figure 6.35 lists the header file for class **Scheduler**. Lines 25–26 declare class **Scheduler**'s **private** data members, which correspond to the attributes we identified (Fig. 6.25). In line 13, we declare the **public** member function **processTime**, which corresponds to the operation we identified in Section 4.10.

```
1   // Fig. 6.34: floorButton.h
2   // FloorButton class definition.
3   #ifndef FLOORBUTTON_H
4   #define FLOORBUTTON_H
5
6   class Elevator;  // forward declaration
7
8   class FloorButton {
9
10  public:
11      FloorButton( int, Elevator & );  // constructor
12      ~FloorButton();                  // destructor
13
14      void pressButton();  // press the button
15      void resetButton();  // reset the button
16
17  private:
18      int floorNumber;     // button's floor number
19      bool pressed;        // button state
20
21      // reference to elevator used to notify summon
22      // elevator to floor
23      Elevator &elevatorRef;
24
25  }; // end class FloorButton
26
27  #endif // FLOORBUTTON_H
```

Fig. 6.34 **FloorButton** class header file.

```
1   // Fig. 6.35: scheduler.h
2   // Scheduler class definition.
3   #ifndef SCHEDULER_H
4   #define SCHEDULER_H
5
6   class Floor;                              // forward declaration
7
8   class Scheduler {
9
```

Fig. 6.35 **Scheduler** class header file. (Part 1 of 2.)

```
10    public:
11       Scheduler( Floor &, Floor & );    // constructor
12       ~Scheduler();                     // destructor
13       void processTime( int );          // set scheduler's time
14
15    private:
16       // schedule arrival to a floor
17       void scheduleTime( Floor & );
18
19       // delay arrival to a floor
20       void delayTime( Floor & );
21
22       Floor &floor1Ref;
23       Floor &floor2Ref;
24
25       int floor1ArrivalTime;
26       int floor2ArrivalTime;
27
28    }; // end class Scheduler
29
30    #endif // SCHEDULER_H
```

Fig. 6.35   **Scheduler** class header file. (Part 2 of 2.)

Lines 17 and 20 declare the functions we identified in the sequence diagram of Fig. 4.27. Each of these functions takes as a parameter a reference to an object of class **Floor**. Note that we did not list these functions as operations (i.e., **public** member functions), because client objects do not invoke these methods. Instead, only class **Scheduler** uses these methods to perform its own internal actions. Therefore, we place these methods in the **private** section of the class declaration.

Lines 22–23 declare the handles identified in Fig. 6.26. Again, we implement each handle as a reference to an object of class **Floor**. Class **Scheduler** needs these handles for sending the **isOccupied** message to the two floors in the simulation (see diagram in Fig. 4.27). Line 6 makes a forward declaration of class **Floor** so that we may declare the references.

Figure 6.36 contains the header file for class **Floor**. We declare the **public** member function **elevatorArrived** (line 21), function **isOccupied** (line 14) and function **personArrives** (line 18) from Fig. 6.25. We also declare the **public** member function **elevatorLeaving** in line 24. We include this member function so that the elevator can notify the floor when the elevator prepares to leave. The elevator invokes the **elevatorLeaving** operation, and the floor responds by turning off its light.

```
1    // Fig. 7.30: floor.h
2    // Floor class definition.
3    #ifndef FLOOR_H
4    #define FLOOR_H
5
6    class Elevator;    // forward declaration
7    class Person;      // forward declaration
```

Fig. 6.36   **Floor** class header file. (Part 1 of 2.)

```
8
9    class Floor {
10
11   public:
12      Floor( int, Elevator & );  // constructor
13      ~Floor();                  // destructor
14      bool isOccupied();         // return true if floor occupied
15      int getNumber();           // return floor's number
16
17      // pass a handle to new person coming on floor
18      void personArrives();
19
20      // notify floor that elevator has arrived
21      void elevatorArrived();
22
23      // notify floor that elevator is leaving
24      void elevatorLeaving();
25
26      // declaration of FloorButton component (see Chapter 7)
27
28   private:
29      int floorNumber;         // the floor's number
30      Elevator &elevatorRef;   // reference to elevator
31      bool occupied;           // true if person is on floor
32
33      // declaration of Light component (see Chapter 7)
34
35   }; // end class Floor
36
37   #endif // FLOOR_H
```

Fig. 6.36   **Floor** class header file. (Part 2 of 2.)

In line 29, we include a **private floorNumber** data member in the class—we include this value for output purposes, just as we did with the **floorNumber** data member of class **FloorButton**. We include a parameter of type **int** in the constructor declaration (line 12), so the constructor can initialize that data member. We do not need to declare the **capacity** attribute; instead, we write our code to ensure that only one person may be on a floor at a time. We also declare the handle to class **Elevator** (line 30) identified in Fig. 6.26. We defer declaration of the component members of class **Floor** (see lines 26 and 33) until Chapter 7.

We list the header file for class **Elevator** in Fig. 6.37. In the **public** section of the header file, we declare the **summonElevator** (line 13), **prepareToLeave** (line 14) and **processTime** (line 15) operations listed in Fig. 6.25. To differentiate between people who wait on the floor and people who ride in the elevator, we rename the last two operations listed under class **Elevator**. We call these operations **passengerEnters** (line 16) and **passengerExits** (line 17), and we declare them in the **public** section of the header file. We also declare a reference to each of the two floors (lines 27–28); the constructor (line 11) initializes these references.

In the **private** section of the header file, we declare the **moving**, **direction**, **currentFloor** and **arrivalTime** attributes (lines 22–25) from Fig. 6.25. We do not

```
1   // Fig. 7.28: elevator.h
2   // Elevator class definition.
3   #ifndef ELEVATOR_H
4   #define ELEVATOR_H
5
6   class Floor;    // forward declaration
7
8   class Elevator {
9
10  public:
11      Elevator( Floor &, Floor & );    // constructor
12      ~Elevator();                     // destructor
13      void summonElevator( int );      // request to service floor
14      void prepareToLeave( bool );     // prepare to leave
15      void processTime( int );         // give time to elevator
16      void passengerEnters();          // board a passenger
17      void passengerExits();           // exit a passenger
18
19      // declaration of ElevatorButton component (see Chapter 7)
20
21  private:
22      bool moving;                     // elevator state
23      int direction;                   // current direction
24      int currentFloor;                // current location
25      int arrivalTime;                 // time to arrive at a floor
26
27      Floor &floor1Ref;                // reference to floor1
28      Floor &floor2Ref;                // reference to floor2
29
30      // declaration of Door component (see Chapter 7)
31      // declaration of Bell component (see Chapter 7)
32
33  }; // end class Elevator
34
35  #endif // ELEVATOR_H
```

Fig. 6.37   **Elevator** class header file.

need to declare the **capacity** attribute; instead, we write our code to ensure that only one person may be inside the elevator at a time.

Conclusion

In the next "Thinking About Objects" section (Section 7.11), we present the full C++ code for our elevator simulation. We use the concepts presented in the next chapter to implement composite relationships, dynamic creation of objects of class **Person** and **static** and **const** data members and functions. In Section 9.10, we use inheritance to further improve our object-oriented elevator simulator design and implementation.

SUMMARY

- Structures are aggregate data types built using data of other types.

- Keyword **struct** introduces a structure definition. The body of a structure is delineated by braces (**{** and **}**). Every structure definition must end with a semicolon.

- A structure tag name can be used to declare variables of a structure type.
- Structure definitions do not reserve space in memory; they create new data types that are used to declare variables.
- Members of a structure or a class are accessed using the member access operators—the dot operator (**.**) and the arrow operator (**->**). The dot operator accesses a structure member via the object's variable name or a reference to the object. The arrow operator accesses a structure member via a pointer to the object.
- Drawbacks to creating new data types with C-like **struct**s are the possibility of having uninitialized data; improper initialization; all programs using a **struct** must be changed if the **struct** implementation changes and no protection is provided to ensure that data are kept in a consistent state with proper data values.
- Classes enable the programmer to model objects with attributes and behaviors. Class types can be defined in C++ using the keywords **class** and **struct**, but keyword **class** is preferred.
- The class name can be used as a type name to declare objects of that class.
- Class definitions begin with the keyword **class**. The body of the class definition is delineated with braces (**{** and **}**). Class definitions terminate with a semicolon.
- Any data member or member function declared after **public** in a class is accessible to any function with access to an object of the class.
- Any data member or member function declared after **private** is accessible only to friends and other members of the same class.
- Member access specifiers always end with a colon (**:**) and can appear multiple times and in any order in a class definition.
- The implementation of a class should be hidden from its clients.
- A constructor is a special member function with the same name as the class and no return data type; it is used to initialize the members of objects of that class. The constructor is called implicitly when an object of that class is instantiated.
- The function with the same name as the class, but preceded with a tilde character (~) is called a destructor.
- The set of **public** member functions of a class is called the class's interface or **public** interface.
- When a member function is defined outside the class definition, the function name must be preceded by the class name and the binary scope resolution operator (**::**).
- Member functions defined using the scope-resolution operator outside a class definition are within that class's scope.
- Member functions defined in a class definition are implicitly declared **inline**. The compiler reserves the right not to **inline** any function.
- Calling member functions is more concise than calling functions in procedural programming because most data used by the member function is directly accessible in the object.
- Within a class's scope, class members may be referenced simply by their names. Outside a class's scope, class members are referenced through either an object name, a reference to an object or a pointer to an object.
- Member selection operators **.** and **->** are used to access class members.
- Class definitions are normally placed in header files and member-function definitions are normally placed in source-code files of the same base name.
- The default access mode for classes is **private** so that all members after the class header and before the first member access specifier are **private**.

- A class's **public** members present a view of the services the class provides to the class's clients.

- Access to a class's **private** data can be carefully controlled via member functions called access functions. If a class wants to allow clients to read **private** data, the class can provide a *get* function. To enable clients to modify **private** data, the class can provide a *set* function.

- Data members of a class are normally made **private** and member functions of a class are normally made **public**. Some member functions may be **private** and serve as utility functions to the other functions of the class.

- Data members cannot be initialized in a class definition. They must be initialized in a constructor, or their values may be *set* after their object is created.

- Constructors can be overloaded.

- Once a class object is properly initialized, all member functions that manipulate the object should ensure that the object remains in a consistent state.

- When an object of a class is declared, initializers can be provided. These initializers are passed to the class's constructor.

- Constructors can specify default arguments.

- If no constructor is defined for a class, the compiler creates a default constructor. A default constructor supplied by the compiler does not perform any initialization of fundamental-type variables; so when an object of the class is created, the object is not guaranteed to be in a consistent state.

- The destructor of an automatic object is called when the object goes out of scope (i.e., execution leaves the block in which the object was defined). The destructor itself does not actually destroy the object, but it does perform termination housekeeping before the system reclaims the object's storage.

- Destructors do not receive parameters and do not return values. A class may have only one destructor. (Destructors cannot be overloaded.)

- The assignment operator (**=**) is used to assign an object to another object of the same type. Such assignment is normally performed by default memberwise assignment. Memberwise assignment is not ideal for all classes.

- For each class that does not define its own copy constructor, the compiler provides a default copy constructor that copies each member of the original object into the corresponding member of the new object.

TERMINOLOGY

abstract data type (ADT)
access function
arrow member-selection operator (**->**)
attribute
behavior
binary scope resolution operator (**::**)
class
class definition
class member-selection operator (**.**)
class scope
client of a class
consistent state for a data member
constructor
copy constructor
data member
data type

default constructor
destructor
dot member-selection operator (**.**)
encapsulation
extensibility
file scope
get function
global object
header file
helper function
implementation of a class
information hiding
initialize a class object
inline a member function
instance of a class
instantiate an object of a class

interface to a class

member access control

member access specifiers

member function

member-selection operators (**.** and **->**)

memberwise assignment

message

nonmember function

non-**static** local object

object

object-oriented design (OOD)

object-oriented programming (OOP)

predicate function

principle of least privilege

private

procedural programming

programmer-defined type

protected

proxy class

public

public interface of a class

query function

rapid applications development (RAD)

reusable code

scope resolution operator (**::**)

self-referential structure

services of a class

set function

software reusability

source-code file

static local object

structure

tilde (**~**) in destructor name

unary scope resolution operator (**::**)

user-defined type

utility function

Terminology for Optional "Thinking About Objects" Section

"+" symbol for **public** visibility

"–" symbol for **private** visibility

circular include problem

forward declaration

handle

public visibility

private visibility

references vs. pointers

visibility

SELF-REVIEW EXERCISES

6.1   Fill in the blanks in each of the following:

    a) Keyword _____ introduces a structure definition.

    b) Class members are accessed via the _____ operator in conjunction with the name of an object (or reference to an object) of the class or via the _____ operator in conjunction with a pointer to an object of the class.

    c) Class members specified as _____ are accessible only to member functions of the class and friends of the class.

    d) A _____ is a special member function used to initialize the data members of a class.

    e) The default access for members of a class is _____.

    f) A _____ function is used to assign values to **private** data members of a class.

    g) _____ can be used to assign an object of a class to another object of the same class.

    h) Member functions of a class are normally made _____ and data members of a class are normally made _____.

    i) A _____ function is used to retrieve values of **private** data of a class.

    j) The set of **public** member functions of a class is referred to as the class's _____.

    k) A class implementation is said to be hidden from its clients or _____.

    l) The keywords _____ and _____ can be used to introduce a class definition.

    m) Class members specified as _____ are accessible anywhere an object of the class is in scope.

6.2   Find the error(s) in each of the following and explain how to correct it:

    a) Assume the following prototype is declared in class **Time**:

```
void ~Time( int );
```

b) The following is a partial definition of class **Time**:

```
class Time {

public:
    // function prototypes

private:
    int hour = 0;
    int minute = 0;
    int second = 0;

}; // end class Time
```

c) Assume the following prototype is declared in class **Employee**:

```
int Employee( const char *, const char * );
```

ANSWERS TO SELF-REVIEW EXERCISES

6.1   a) **struct**. b) dot (**.**), arrow (**->**). c) **private**. d) constructor. e) **private**. f) *set*.
g) Default memberwise assignment (performed by the assignment operator). h) **public, private**. i) *get*. j) interface. k) encapsulated. l) **class, struct**. m) **public**.

6.2   a) Error: Destructors are not allowed to return values or take arguments.
        Correction: Remove the return type **void** and the parameter **int** from the declaration.
      b) Error: Members cannot be explicitly initialized in the class definition.
        Correction: Remove the explicit initialization from the class definition and initialize the data members in a constructor.
      c) Error: Constructors are not allowed to return values.
        Correction: Remove the return type **int** from the declaration.

EXERCISES

6.3   What is the purpose of the scope resolution operator?

6.4   Compare and contrast the notions of **struct** and **class** in C++.

6.5   Provide a constructor that is capable of using the current time from the **time()** function—declared in the C++ Standard Library header **<ctime>**—to initialize an object of the **Time** class.

6.6   Create a class called **Complex** for performing arithmetic with complex numbers. Write a program to test your class.
        Complex numbers have the form

```
realPart + imaginaryPart * i
```

where *i* is

Use **double** variables to represent the **private** data of the class. Provide a constructor that enables an object of this class to be initialized when it is declared. The constructor should contain default values in case no initializers are provided. Provide **public** member functions for each of the following:
      a) Adding two **Complex** numbers: The real parts are added together and the imaginary parts are added together.

b) Subtracting two **Complex** numbers: The real part of the right operand is subtracted from the real part of the left operand, and the imaginary part of the right operand is subtracted from the imaginary part of the left operand.

c) Printing **Complex** numbers in the form **(a, b),** where **a** is the real part and **b** is the imaginary part.

6.7   Create a class called **Rational** for performing arithmetic with fractions. Write a program to test your class.

Use integer variables to represent the **private** data of the class—the **numerator** and the **denominator**. Provide a constructor that enables an object of this class to be initialized when it is declared. The constructor should contain default values in case no initializers are provided and should store the fraction in reduced form. For example, the fraction

$$\frac{2}{4}$$

would be stored in the object as 1 in the **numerator** and 2 in the **denominator**. Provide **public** member functions that perform each of the following tasks:

a) Adding two **Rational** numbers. The result should be stored in reduced form.

b) Subtracting two **Rational** numbers. The result should be stored in reduced form.

c) Multiplying two **Rational** numbers. The result should be stored in reduced form.

d) Dividing two **Rational** numbers. The result should be stored in reduced form.

e) Printing **Rational** numbers in the form **a/b**, where **a** is the numerator and **b** is the denominator.

f) Printing **Rational** numbers in floating-point format.

6.8   Modify the **Time** class of Fig. 6.18 to include a **tick** member function that increments the time stored in a **Time** object by one second. The **Time** object should always remain in a consistent state. Write a program that tests the **tick** member function in a loop that prints the time in standard format during each iteration of the loop to illustrate that the **tick** member function works correctly. Be sure to test the following cases:

a) Incrementing into the next minute.

b) Incrementing into the next hour.

c) Incrementing into the next day (i.e., 11:59:59 PM to 12:00:00 AM).

6.9   Modify the **Date** class of Fig. 6.24 to perform error checking on the initializer values for data members **month, day** and **year**. Also, provide a member function **nextDay** to increment the day by one. The **Date** object should always remain in a consistent state. Write a program that tests function **nextDay** in a loop that prints the date during each iteration to illustrate that **nextDay** works correctly. Be sure to test the following cases:

a) Incrementing into the next month.

b) Incrementing into the next year.

6.10   Combine the modified **Time** class of Exercise 6.8 and the modified **Date** class of Exercise 6.9 into one class called **DateAndTime**. (In Chapter 9, we will discuss inheritance, which will enable us to accomplish this task quickly without modifying the existing class definitions.) Modify the **tick** function to call the **nextDay** function if the time increments into the next day. Modify function **printStandard** and **printUniversal** to output the date and time. Write a program to test the new class **DateAndTime**. Specifically, test incrementing the time into the next day.

6.11   Modify the *set* functions in the program of Fig. 6.18 to return appropriate error values if an attempt is made to *set* a data member of an object of class **Time** to an invalid value. Write a program that tests your new version of class **Time**. Display error messages when *set* methods return error values.

6.12   Create a class **Rectangle** with attributes **length** and **width**, each of which defaults to 1. Provide member functions that calculate the **perimeter** and the **area** of the rectangle. Also, provide *set* and *get* functions for the **length** and **width** attributes. The *set* functions should verify that **length** and **width** are each floating-point numbers larger than 0.0 and less than 20.0.

6.13   Create a more sophisticated **Rectangle** class than the one you created in Exercise 6.12. This class stores only the Cartesian coordinates of the four corners of the rectangle. The constructor calls a *set* function that accepts four sets of coordinates and verifies that each of these is in the first quadrant with no single *x* or *y* coordinate larger than 20.0. The *set* function also verifies that the supplied coordinates do, in fact, specify a rectangle. Provide member functions that calculate the **length**, **width**, **perimeter** and **area**. The length is the larger of the two dimensions. Include a predicate function **square** that determines whether the rectangle is a square.

6.14   Modify class **Rectangle** from Exercise 6.13 to include a **draw** function that displays the rectangle inside a 25-by-25 box enclosing the portion of the first quadrant in which the rectangle resides. Include a **setFillCharacter** function to specify the character out of which the body of the rectangle will be drawn. Include a **setPerimeterCharacter** function to specify the character that will be used to draw the border of the rectangle. If you feel ambitious, you might include functions to scale the size of the rectangle, rotate it, and move it around within the designated portion of the first quadrant.

6.15   Create a class **HugeInteger** that uses a 40-element array of digits to store integers as large as 40 digits each. Provide member functions **input**, **output**, **add** and **substract**. For comparing **HugeInteger** objects, provide functions **isEqualTo**, **isNotEqualTo**, **isGreaterThan**, **isLessThan**, **isGreaterThanOrEqualTo** and **isLessThanOrEqualTo**—each of these is a "predicate" function that simply returns **true** if the relationship holds between the two huge integers and returns **false** if the relationship does not hold. Also, provide a predicate function **isZero**. If you feel ambitious, provide member functions **multiply**, **divide** and **modulus**.

6.16   Create a class **TicTacToe** that will enable you to write a complete program to play the game of tic-tac-toe. The class contains as **private** data a 3-by-3 double-subscripted array of integers. The constructor should initialize the empty board to all zeros. Allow two human players. Wherever the first player moves, place a 1 in the specified square. Place a 2 wherever the second player moves. Each move must be to an empty square. After each move, determine whether the game has been won or is a draw. If you feel ambitious, modify your program so that the computer makes the moves for one of the players. Also, allow the player to specify whether he or she wants to go first or second. If you feel exceptionally ambitious, develop a program that will play three-dimensional tic-tac-toe on a 4-by-4-by-4 board. (*Caution*: This is an extremely challenging project that could take many weeks of effort!)

7

Classes: Part II

Objectives

- To be able to specify **const** (constant) objects and **const** member functions.
- To understand the purpose of **friend** functions and **friend** classes.
- To understand the use of the **this** pointer.
- To be able to create and destroy objects dynamically.
- To understand how to use **static** data members and member functions.
- To understand the concept of a container class.
- To understand the notion of iterator classes that walk through the elements of container classes.

But what, to serve our private ends,
Forbids the cheating of our friends?
Charles Churchill

Instead of this absurd division into sexes they ought to class
people as static and dynamic.
Evelyn Waugh

This above all: to thine own self be true.
William Shakespeare

Have no friends not equal to yourself.
Confucius

Outline

7.1   Introduction

7.2   **const** (Constant) Objects and **const** Member Functions

7.3   Composition: Objects as Members of Classes

7.4   **friend** Functions and **friend** Classes

7.5   Using the **this** Pointer

7.6   Dynamic Memory Management with Operators **new** and **delete**

7.7   **static** Class Members

7.8   Data Abstraction and Information Hiding

    7.8.1   Example: Array Abstract Data Type

    7.8.2   Example: String Abstract Data Type

    7.8.3   Example: Queue Abstract Data Type

7.9   Container Classes and Iterators

7.10   Proxy Classes

7.11   (Optional Case Study) Thinking About Objects: Programming the Classes for the Elevator Simulator

Summary • Terminology • Self-Review Exercises • Answers to Self-Review Exercises • Exercises

7.1 Introduction

In this chapter, we continue our study of classes and data abstraction. We discuss many more advanced topics and lay the groundwork for the discussion of classes and operator overloading in Chapter 8. The discussion in Chapter 6–Chapter 8 encourages programmers to use objects, what we call *object-based programming (OBP)*. Then, Chapter 9–Chapter 10 introduce inheritance and polymorphism—the techniques of truly *object-oriented programming (OOP)*. In this chapter, we use the pointer-based strings we introduced in Chapter 5 to help the reader master pointers and prepare for the professional world in which the reader will see a great deal of C legacy code implemented over the last two decades. In Chapter 8, we introduce strings as full-fledged class objects. Chapter 15 explains strings as full-fledged class objects in detail. Thus, the reader will become familiar with the two most prevalent methods of creating and manipulating strings in C++.

7.2 const (Constant) Objects and const Member Functions

We have emphasized the *principle of least privilege* as one of the most fundamental principles of good software engineering. Let us see how this principle applies to objects.

Some objects need to be modifiable and some do not. The programmer may use keyword **const** to specify that an object is not modifiable and that any attempt to modify the object should result in a compiler error. The statement

```
const Time noon( 12, 0, 0 );
```

declares a **const** object **noon** of class **Time** and initializes it to 12 noon.

*Declaring an object as **const** helps enforce the principle of least privilege. Attempts to modify the object are caught at compile time rather than causing execution-time errors.*

Software Engineering Observation 7.2

*Using **const** is crucial to proper class design, program design and coding.*

Performance Tip 7.1

*Declaring variables and objects **const** is not only an effective software engineering practice, it can improve performance as well. Today's sophisticated optimizing compilers can perform certain optimizations on constants that cannot be performed on variables.*

C++ compilers disallow member function calls for **const** objects unless the member functions themselves are also declared **const**. This is true even for *get* member functions that do not modify the object. In addition, the compiler does not allow member functions declared **const** to modify the object.

A function is specified as **const** *both* in its prototype and in its definition by inserting the keyword **const** after the function's parameter list and, in the case of the function definition, before the left brace that begins the function body.

Common Programming Error 7.1

*Defining as **const** a member function that modifies a data member of an object is a compiler error.*

Common Programming Error 7.2

*Defining as **const** a member function that calls a non-**const** member function of the class on the same instance of the class is a compiler error.*

Common Programming Error 7.3

*Invoking a non-**const** member function on a **const** object is a compiler error.*

Software Engineering Observation 7.3

*A **const** member function can be overloaded with a non-**const** version. The choice of which overloaded member function to use is made by the compiler based on whether the object is **const**.*

An interesting problem arises for constructors and destructors, each of which typically modifies objects. The **const** declaration is not allowed for constructors and destructors. A constructor must be allowed to modify an object so that the object can be initialized properly. A destructor must be able to perform its termination housekeeping chores before an object's memory is reclaimed by the system.

Common Programming Error 7.4

*Attempting to declare a constructor or destructor **const** is a syntax error.*

Defining and Using const Member Functions

The program of Fig. 7.1–Fig. 7.3 modifies class **Time** of Fig. 6.18–Fig. 6.19 by making its *get* functions and **printUniversal** function **const**. In the header file **time5.h**

(Fig. 7.1), lines 19–21 and 24 now include keyword **const** after each function's parameter list. The corresponding definition of each function in Fig. 7.2 (lines 55, 62, 69 and 76, respectively) also specifies keyword **const** after each function's parameter list.

```
1   // Fig. 7.1: time5.h
2   // Definition of class Time.
3   // Member functions defined in time5.cpp.
4   #ifndef TIME5_H
5   #define TIME5_H
6
7   class Time {
8
9   public:
10     Time( int = 0, int = 0, int = 0 );  // default constructor
11
12     // set functions
13     void setTime( int, int, int );  // set time
14     void setHour( int );            // set hour
15     void setMinute( int );          // set minute
16     void setSecond( int );          // set second
17
18     // get functions (normally declared const)
19     int getHour() const;            // return hour
20     int getMinute() const;          // return minute
21     int getSecond() const;          // return second
22
23     // print functions (normally declared const)
24     void printUniversal() const;    // print universal time
25     void printStandard();           // print standard time
26
27   private:
28     int hour;    // 0 - 23 (24-hour clock format)
29     int minute;  // 0 - 59
30     int second;  // 0 - 59
31
32   }; // end class Time
33
34   #endif
```

Fig. 7.1   **Time** class definition with **const** member functions.

```
1   // Fig. 7.2: time5.cpp
2   // Member-function definitions for class Time.
3   #include <iostream>
4
5   using std::cout;
6
7   #include <iomanip>
8
```

Fig. 7.2   **Time** class member-function definitions, including **const** member functions. (Part 1 of 3.)

```
9    using std::setfill;
10   using std::setw;
11
12   // include definition of class Time from time5.h
13   #include "time5.h"
14
15   // constructor function to initialize private data;
16   // calls member function setTime to set variables;
17   // default values are 0 (see class definition)
18   Time::Time( int hour, int minute, int second )
19   {
20      setTime( hour, minute, second );
21
22   } // end Time constructor
23
24   // set hour, minute and second values
25   void Time::setTime( int hour, int minute, int second )
26   {
27      setHour( hour );
28      setMinute( minute );
29      setSecond( second );
30
31   } // end function setTime
32
33   // set hour value
34   void Time::setHour( int h )
35   {
36      hour = ( h >= 0 && h < 24 ) ? h : 0;
37
38   } // end function setHour
39
40   // set minute value
41   void Time::setMinute( int m )
42   {
43      minute = ( m >= 0 && m < 60 ) ? m : 0;
44
45   } // end function setMinute
46
47   // set second value
48   void Time::setSecond( int s )
49   {
50      second = ( s >= 0 && s < 60 ) ? s : 0;
51
52   } // end function setSecond
53
54   // return hour value
55   int Time::getHour() const
56   {
57      return hour;
58
59   } // end function getHour
60
```

Fig. 7.2   **Time** class member-function definitions, including **const** member
functions. (Part 2 of 3.)

```
61   // return minute value
62   int Time::getMinute() const
63   {
64      return minute;
65
66   } // end function getMinute
67
68   // return second value
69   int Time::getSecond() const
70   {
71      return second;
72
73   } // end function getSecond
74
75   // print Time in universal format
76   void Time::printUniversal() const
77   {
78      cout << setfill( '0' ) << setw( 2 ) << hour << ":"
79           << setw( 2 ) << minute << ":"
80           << setw( 2 ) << second;
81
82   } // end function printUniversal
83
84   // print Time in standard format
85   void Time::printStandard() // note lack of const declaration
86   {
87      cout << ( ( hour == 0 || hour == 12 ) ? 12 : hour % 12 )
88           << ":" << setfill( '0' ) << setw( 2 ) << minute
89           << ":" << setw( 2 ) << second
90           << ( hour < 12 ? " AM" : " PM" );
91
92   } // end function printStandard
```

Fig. 7.2   **Time** class member-function definitions, including **const** member functions. (Part 3 of 3.)

Figure 7.3 instantiates two **Time** objects—non-**const** object **wakeUp** (line 10) and **const** object **noon** (line 11). The program attempts to invoke non-**const** member functions **setHour** (line 16) and **printStandard** (line 23) on the **const** object **noon**. In each case, the compiler generates an error message. The program also illustrates the three other member-function-call combinations on objects—a non-**const** member function on a non-**const** object (line 14), a **const** member function on a non-**const** object (line 18) and a **const** member function on a **const** object (lines 20–21). The error messages generated for non-**const** member functions called on a **const** object are shown in the output window.

```
1   // Fig. 7.3: fig07_03.cpp
2   // Attempting to access a const object with
3   // non-const member functions.
4
5   // include Time class definition from time5.h
6   #include "time5.h"
```

Fig. 7.3   **const** objects and **const** member functions. (Part 1 of 2.)

```
7
8    int main()
9    {
10      Time wakeUp( 6, 45, 0 );       // non-constant object
11      const Time noon( 12, 0, 0 );   // constant object
12
13                                  // OBJECT        MEMBER FUNCTION
14      wakeUp.setHour( 18 );       // non-const    non-const
15
16      noon.setHour( 12 );         // const        non-const
17
18      wakeUp.getHour();           // non-const    const
19
20      noon.getMinute();           // const        const
21      noon.printUniversal();      // const        const
22
23      noon.printStandard();       // const        non-const
24
25      return 0;
26
27   } // end main
```

```
d:\cpphtp4_examples\ch07\fig07_01\fig07_01.cpp(16) : error C2662:
   'setHour' : cannot convert 'this' pointer from 'const class Time'
   to 'class Time &'
        Conversion loses qualifiers
d:\cpphtp4_examples\ch07\fig07_01\fig07_01.cpp(23) : error C2662:
   'printStandard' : cannot convert 'this' pointer from 'const class
   Time' to 'class Time &'
        Conversion loses qualifiers
```

Fig. 7.3   **const** objects and **const** member functions. (Part 2 of 2.)

Notice that even though a constructor must be a non-**const** member function (Fig. 7.2, lines 18–22), it can still be used to initialize a **const** object (Fig. 7.3, line 11). The definition of the **Time** constructor (Fig. 7.2, lines 18–22) shows that the **Time** constructor calls another non-**const** member function—**setTime** (lines 25–31)—to perform the initialization of a **Time** object. Invoking a non-**const** member function from the constructor call as part of the initialization of a **const** object is allowed. The "**const**ness" of a **const** object is enforced from the time the constructor completes initialization of the object until that object's destructor is called.

Software Engineering Observation 7.4

*A **const** object cannot be modified by assignment so it must be initialized. When a data member of a class is declared **const**, a member initializer must be used to provide the constructor with the initial value of the data member for an object of the class.*

Also notice that line 23 in Fig. 7.3 generates a compiler error even though member function **printStandard** of class **Time** does not modify the object on which it is invoked. The fact that a function does not modify an object is not sufficient to indicate a **const** member function—the function must explicitly be declared **const**.

Initializing a **const** *Data Member with a Member Initializer*

Figure 7.4 introduces using *member initializer syntax*. All data members *can* be initialized using member initializer syntax, but **const** data members and data members that are references *must* be initialized using member initializers. Later in this chapter, we will see that member objects must be initialized this way as well. In Chapter 9 when we study inheritance, we will see that base-class portions of derived classes also must be initialized this way.

```cpp
1  // Fig. 7.4: fig07_04.cpp
2  // Using a member initializer to initialize a
3  // constant of a built-in data type.
4  #include <iostream>
5
6  using std::cout;
7  using std::endl;
8
9  class Increment {
10
11 public:
12    Increment( int c = 0, int i = 1 );  // default constructor
13
14    void addIncrement()
15    {
16       count += increment;
17
18    } // end function addIncrement
19
20    void print() const;      // prints count and increment
21
22 private:
23    int count;
24    const int increment;     // const data member
25
26 }; // end class Increment
27
28 // constructor
29 Increment::Increment( int c, int i )
30    : count( c ),        // initializer for non-const member
31      increment( i )    // required initializer for const member
32 {
33    // empty body
34
35 } // end Increment constructor
36
37 // print count and increment values
38 void Increment::print() const
39 {
40    cout << "count = " << count
41         << ", increment = " << increment << endl;
42
43 } // end function print
44
```

Fig. 7.4   Member initializer used to initialize a constant of a built-in data type. (Part 1 of 2.)

```
45    int main()
46    {
47        Increment value( 10, 5 );
48
49        cout << "Before incrementing: ";
50        value.print();
51
52        for ( int j = 0; j < 3; j++ ) {
53            value.addIncrement();
54            cout << "After increment " << j + 1 << ": ";
55            value.print();
56        }
57
58        return 0;
59
60    } // end main
```

```
Before incrementing: count = 10, increment = 5
After increment 1: count = 15, increment = 5
After increment 2: count = 20, increment = 5
After increment 3: count = 25, increment = 5
```

Fig. 7.4   Member initializer used to initialize a constant of a built-in data type. (Part 2 of 2.)

The constructor definition (lines 29–35) uses a *member initializer list* to initialize class **Increment**'s data members—non-**const** integer **count** and **const** integer **increment**. Member initializers appear between a constructor's parameter list and the left brace that begins the constructor's body. The member initializer list is separated from the parameter list with a colon (**:**). Lines 30–31 show the member initializer list. Each member initializer consists of the data member name followed by parentheses containing the member's initial value. In this example, **count** is initialized with the value of constructor parameter **c** and **increment** is initialized with the value of constructor parameter **i**. Note that multiple member initializers are separated by commas. Also, note that the member initializer list executes before the body of the constructor executes.

Figure 7.5 illustrates the compiler errors for a program that attempts to initialize **const** data member **increment** with an assignment statement (line 32) in the **Increment** constructor's body rather than with a member initializer. Note that line 31 does not generate an error message, because **count** is not declared **const**—only **const** data members must be initialized using member initializers.

```
1    // Fig. 7.5: fig07_05.cpp
2    // Attempting to initialize a constant of
3    // a built-in data type with an assignment.
4    #include <iostream>
5
6    using std::cout;
7    using std::endl;
```

Fig. 7.5   Erroneous attempt to initialize a constant of a built-in data type by assignment. (Part 1 of 3.)

```
8
9    class Increment {
10
11   public:
12      Increment( int c = 0, int i = 1 );   // default constructor
13
14      void addIncrement()
15      {
16         count += increment;
17
18      } // end function addIncrement
19
20      void print() const;        // prints count and increment
21
22   private:
23      int count;
24      const int increment;       // const data member
25
26   }; // end class Increment
27
28   // constructor
29   Increment::Increment( int c, int i )
30   {                    // Constant member 'increment' is not initialized
31      count = c;        // allowed because count is not constant
32      increment = i;    // ERROR: Cannot modify a const object
33
34   } // end Increment constructor
35
36   // print count and increment values
37   void Increment::print() const
38   {
39      cout << "count = " << count
40           << ", increment = " << increment << endl;
41
42   } // end function print
43
44   int main()
45   {
46      Increment value( 10, 5 );
47
48      cout << "Before incrementing: ";
49      value.print();
50
51      for ( int j = 0; j < 3; j++ ) {
52         value.addIncrement();
53         cout << "After increment " << j + 1 << ": ";
54         value.print();
55      }
56
57      return 0;
58
59   } // end main
```

Fig. 7.5   Erroneous attempt to initialize a constant of a built-in data type by assignment. (Part 2 of 3.)

```
D:\cpphtp4_examples\ch07\Fig07_03\Fig07_03.cpp(30) : error C2758:
   'increment' : must be initialized in constructor base/member
   initializer list
         D:\cpphtp4_examples\ch07\Fig07_03\Fig07_03.cpp(24) :
            see declaration of 'increment'
D:\cpphtp4_examples\ch07\Fig07_03\Fig07_03.cpp(32) : error C2166:
   l-value specifies const object
```

Fig. 7.5   Erroneous attempt to initialize a constant of a built-in data type by assignment. (Part 3 of 3.)

Common Programming Error 7.5

*Not providing a member initializer for a **const** data member is a syntax error.*

Software Engineering Observation 7.5

*Constant data members (**const** objects and **const** "variables") and data members declared as references must be initialized with member initializer syntax; assignments in the constructor body are not allowed.*

Note that function **print** (lines 37–42) is declared **const**. It is reasonable, yet strange, to label this function **const** because a program probably will never have a **const Increment** object. However, it is possible that a program will have a **const** reference to an **Increment** object or a pointer to **const** that points to an **Increment** object. Typically, this occurs when objects of class **Increment** are passed to functions or returned from functions. In these cases, only the **const** member functions of class **Increment** can be called through the reference or pointer.

Software Engineering Observation 7.6

*Declare as **const** all of a class's member functions that do not modify the object in which they operate. Occasionally, this will be an anomaly because you will have no intention of creating **const** objects of that class or accessing objects of that class through **const** references or pointers to **const**. Declaring such member functions **const** does offer a benefit though. If the member function inadvertently modifies the object, the compiler will issue an error message.*

Testing and Debugging Tip 7.1

Languages like C++ are "moving targets" as they evolve. More keywords are likely to be added to the language. Avoid using "loaded" words like "object" as identifiers. Even though "object" is not currently a keyword in C++, it could become one; therefore, future compiling with new compilers could break existing code.

7.3 Composition: Objects as Members of Classes

An **AlarmClock** object needs to know when it is supposed to sound its alarm, so why not include a **Time** object as a member of the **AlarmClock** class? Such a capability is called *composition*. A class can have objects of other classes as members.

Software Engineering Observation 7.7

The most common form of software reusability is composition, in which a class has objects of other classes as members.

When an object is created, its constructor is called automatically. Previously, we saw how to pass arguments to the constructor of an object we created in **main**. This section shows how an object's constructor can pass arguments to member-object constructors, which is accomplished via member initializers. Member objects are constructed in the order in which they are declared in a class definition (not in the order they are listed in the constructor's member initializer list) and before their enclosing class objects (sometimes called *host objects*) are constructed.

The program of Fig. 7.6–Fig. 7.10 uses class **Date** (Fig. 7.6–Fig. 7.7) and class **Employee** (Fig. 7.8–Fig. 7.9) to demonstrate objects as members of other objects. The definition of class **Employee** (Fig. 7.8) contains private data members **firstName**, **lastName**, **birthDate** and **hireDate**. Members **birthDate** and **hireDate** are **const** objects of class **Date**, which contains **private** data members **month**, **day** and **year**. The **Employee** constructor's header (Fig. 7.9, lines 17–20) specifies that the constructor receives four parameters (**fname**, **lname**, **dateOfBirth** and **dateOfHire**). The first two parameters are used in the constructor's body to initialize the character arrays **firstName** and **lastName**. The last two parameters are passed via member initializers to the constructor for class **Date**. The colon (**:**) in the header separates the member initializers from the parameter list. The member initializers specify the **Employee** constructor parameters being passed to the constructors of the member **Date** objects. Parameter **dateOfBirth** is passed to object **birthDate**'s constructor (Fig. 7.9, line 19), and parameter **dateOfHire** is passed to object **hireDate**'s constructor (Fig. 7.9, line 20). Again, member initializers are separated by commas. As you study class **Date** (Fig. 7.6), notice that the class does not provide a constructor that receives a parameter of type **Date**. So, how is the member initializer list in class **Employee**'s constructor able to initialize the **birthDate** and **hireDate** objects by passing **Date** object's to their **Date** constructors? As we mentioned in Chapter 6, the compiler provides each class with a default copy constructor that copies each member of the constructor's argument object into the corresponding member of the object being initialized. Chapter 8 discusses how programmers can define customized copy constructors.

```
1   // Fig. 7.6: date1.h
2   // Date class definition.
3   // Member functions defined in date1.cpp
4   #ifndef DATE1_H
5   #define DATE1_H
6
7   class Date {
8
9   public:
10     Date( int = 1, int = 1, int = 1900 ); // default constructor
11     void print() const;  // print date in month/day/year format
12     ~Date();  // provided to confirm destruction order
13
14   private:
15     int month;  // 1-12 (January-December)
16     int day;    // 1-31 based on month
17     int year;   // any year
```

Fig. 7.6   **Date** class definition. (Part 1 of 2.)

```
18
19      // utility function to test proper day for month and year
20      int checkDay( int ) const;
21
22   }; // end class Date
23
24   #endif
```

Fig. 7.6   Date class definition. (Part 2 of 2.)

```
1    // Fig. 7.7: date1.cpp
2    // Member-function definitions for class Date.
3    #include <iostream>
4
5    using std::cout;
6    using std::endl;
7
8    // include Date class definition from date1.h
9    #include "date1.h"
10
11   // constructor confirms proper value for month; calls
12   // utility function checkDay to confirm proper value for day
13   Date::Date( int mn, int dy, int yr )
14   {
15      if ( mn > 0 && mn <= 12 )  // validate the month
16         month = mn;
17
18      else {                     // invalid month set to 1
19         month = 1;
20         cout << "Month " << mn << " invalid. Set to month 1.\n";
21      }
22
23      year = yr;                 // should validate yr
24      day = checkDay( dy );      // validate the day
25
26      // output Date object to show when its constructor is called
27      cout << "Date object constructor for date ";
28      print();
29      cout << endl;
30
31   } // end Date constructor
32
33   // print Date object in form month/day/year
34   void Date::print() const
35   {
36      cout << month << '/' << day << '/' << year;
37
38   } // end function print
39
```

Fig. 7.7   Date class member-function definitions. (Part 1 of 2.)

```
40   // output Date object to show when its destructor is called
41   Date::~Date()
42   {
43      cout << "Date object destructor for date ";
44      print();
45      cout << endl;
46
47   } // end destructor ~Date
48
49   // utility function to confirm proper day value based on
50   // month and year; handles leap years, too
51   int Date::checkDay( int testDay ) const
52   {
53      static const int daysPerMonth[ 13 ] =
54         { 0, 31, 28, 31, 30, 31, 30, 31, 31, 30, 31, 30, 31 };
55
56      // determine whether testDay is valid for specified month
57      if ( testDay > 0 && testDay <= daysPerMonth[ month ] )
58         return testDay;
59
60      // February 29 check for leap year
61      if ( month == 2 && testDay == 29 &&
62         ( year % 400 == 0 ||
63            ( year % 4 == 0 && year % 100 != 0 ) ) )
64         return testDay;
65
66      cout << "Day " << testDay << " invalid. Set to day 1.\n";
67
68      return 1;   // leave object in consistent state if bad value
69
70   } // end function checkDay
```

Fig. 7.7 **Date** class member-function definitions. (Part 2 of 2.)

```
1   // Fig. 7.8: employee1.h
2   // Employee class definition.
3   // Member functions defined in employee1.cpp.
4   #ifndef EMPLOYEE1_H
5   #define EMPLOYEE1_H
6
7   // include Date class definition from date1.h
8   #include "date1.h"
9
10  class Employee {
11
12  public:
13     Employee(
14        const char *, const char *, const Date &, const Date & );
15
16     void print() const;
17     ~Employee();   // provided to confirm destruction order
18
```

Fig. 7.8 **Employee** class definition showing composition. (Part 1 of 2.)

```
19   private:
20      char firstName[ 25 ];
21      char lastName[ 25 ];
22      const Date birthDate;    // composition: member object
23      const Date hireDate;     // composition: member object
24
25   }; // end class Employee
26
27   #endif
```

Fig. 7.8   **Employee** class definition showing composition. (Part 2 of 2.)

```
1    // Fig. 7.9: employee1.cpp
2    // Member-function definitions for class Employee.
3    #include <iostream>
4
5    using std::cout;
6    using std::endl;
7
8    #include <cstring>        // strcpy and strlen prototypes
9
10   #include "employee1.h"   // Employee class definition
11   #include "date1.h"        // Date class definition
12
13   // constructor uses member initializer list to pass initializer
14   // values to constructors of member objects birthDate and
15   // hireDate [Note: This invokes the so-called "default copy
16   // constructor" which the C++ compiler provides implicitly.]
17   Employee::Employee( const char *first, const char *last,
18      const Date &dateOfBirth, const Date &dateOfHire )
19      : birthDate( dateOfBirth ),  // initialize birthDate
20        hireDate( dateOfHire )     // initialize hireDate
21   {
22      // copy first into firstName and be sure that it fits
23      int length = strlen( first );
24      length = ( length < 25 ? length : 24 );
25      strncpy( firstName, first, length );
26      firstName[ length ] = '\0';
27
28      // copy last into lastName and be sure that it fits
29      length = strlen( last );
30      length = ( length < 25 ? length : 24 );
31      strncpy( lastName, last, length );
32      lastName[ length ] = '\0';
33
34      // output Employee object to show when constructor is called
35      cout << "Employee object constructor: "
36           << firstName << ' ' << lastName << endl;
37
38   } // end Employee constructor
39
```

Fig. 7.9   **Employee** class member-function definitions, including constructor with a member-initializer list. (Part 1 of 2.)

```
40  // print Employee object
41  void Employee::print() const
42  {
43     cout << lastName << ", " << firstName << "\nHired: ";
44     hireDate.print();
45     cout << "  Birth date: ";
46     birthDate.print();
47     cout << endl;
48
49  } // end function print
50
51  // output Employee object to show when its destructor is called
52  Employee::~Employee()
53  {
54     cout << "Employee object destructor: "
55          << lastName << ", " << firstName << endl;
56
57  } // end destructor ~Employee
```

Fig. 7.9   **Employee** class member-function definitions, including constructor with a member-initializer list. (Part 2 of 2.)

Figure 7.10 creates two **Date** objects (lines 12–13) and passes them as arguments to the constructor of the **Employee** object created on line 14. Line 17 outputs the **Employee** object's data. When each **Date** object is created in lines 12–13, the **Date** constructor defined at lines 13–31 of Fig. 7.7 displays a line of output to show that the constructor was called (see the first two lines of the sample output). [*Note:* Line 14 causes two additional **Date** constructor calls that do not appear in the program's output. When each of the **Employee**'s **Date** member object's is initialized in the **Employee** constructor's member initializer list, the default copy constructor for class **Date** is called. This constructor is defined implicitly by the compiler and does not contain any output statements to demonstrate when it is called. We discuss copy constructors and default copy constructors in detail in Chapter 8.]

```
1   // Fig. 7.10: fig07_10.cpp
2   // Demonstrating composition--an object with member objects.
3   #include <iostream>
4
5   using std::cout;
6   using std::endl;
7
8   #include "employee1.h"  // Employee class definition
9
10  int main()
11  {
12     Date birth( 7, 24, 1949 );
13     Date hire( 3, 12, 1988 );
14     Employee manager( "Bob", "Jones", birth, hire );
15
16     cout << '\n';
```

Fig. 7.10   Member-object initializers. (Part 1 of 2.)

```
17        manager.print();
18
19        cout << "\nTest Date constructor with invalid values:\n";
20        Date lastDayOff( 14, 35, 1994 );  // invalid month and day
21        cout << endl;
22
23        return 0;
24
25    } // end main
```

```
Date object constructor for date 7/24/1949
Date object constructor for date 3/12/1988
Employee object constructor: Bob Jones

Jones, Bob
Hired: 3/12/1988  Birth date: 7/24/1949

Test Date constructor with invalid values:
Month 14 invalid. Set to month 1.
Day 35 invalid. Set to day 1.
Date object constructor for date 1/1/1994

Date object destructor for date 1/1/1994
Employee object destructor: Jones, Bob
Date object destructor for date 3/12/1988
Date object destructor for date 7/24/1949
Date object destructor for date 3/12/1988
Date object destructor for date 7/24/1949
```

Fig. 7.10   Member-object initializers. (Part 2 of 2.)

Class **Date** and class **Employee** each include a destructor (lines 41–47 of Fig. 7.7 and lines 52–57 of Fig. 7.9, respectively) that prints a message when an object of its class is destroyed. This enables us to confirm in the program output that objects are constructed from the inside out and destructed in the reverse order from the outside in (i.e., the **Date** member objects are destroyed after the **Employee** object that contains them). Notice the last four lines in the output of Fig. 7.10. The last two lines are the outputs of the **Date** destructor running on **Date** objects **hire** (line 13) and **birth** (line 12), respectively. These outputs confirm that the three objects created in **main** are destructed in the reverse of the order in which they were constructed. (The **Employee** destructor output is five lines from the bottom.) The fourth and third lines from the bottom of the output window show the destructors running for the **Employee**'s member objects **hireDate** (Fig. 7.8, line 23) and **birthDate** (Fig. 7.8, line 22). These outputs confirm that the **Employee** object is destructed from the outside in—i.e., the **Employee** destructor runs first (output shown five lines from the bottom of the output window), then the member objects are destructed in the reverse order from which they were constructed. Again, the outputs in Fig. 7.10 did not show the constructors running for these objects because these were the default copy constructors provided by the C++ compiler.

A member object does not need to be initialized explicitly through a member initializer. If a member initializer is not provided, the member object's default constructor will be called implicitly. Values, if any, established by the default constructor can be overridden by *set* functions. However, for complex initialization, this approach may require significant additional work and time.

Common Programming Error 7.6

A compiler error occurs if a member object is not initialized with a member initializer and the member object's class does not provide a default constructor (i.e., the member object's class defines one or more constructors, but none is a default constructor).

Performance Tip 7.2

Initialize member objects explicitly through member initializers. This eliminates the overhead of "doubly initializing" member objects—once when the member object's default constructor is called and again when set *functions are called in the constructor body (or later) to initialize the member object.*

Software Engineering Observation 7.8

If a class member is an object of another class, making that member object public does not violate the encapsulation and hiding of that member object's private members.

In line 28 of Fig. 7.7, notice the call to **Date** member function **print**. Many member functions of classes in C++ require no arguments. This is because each member function contains an implicit handle (in the form of a pointer) to the object on which it operates. We discuss the implicit pointer, which is represented by keyword **this**, in Section 7.5.

Class **Employee** uses two 25-character arrays (Fig. 7.8, lines 20–21) to represent the first and last name of the **Employee**. These arrays may waste space for names shorter than 24 characters. (Remember, one character in each array is for the terminating null character, **'\0'**, of the string.)\ Also, names longer than 24 characters must be truncated to fit in these fixed-size arrays. Section 7.7 presents another version of class **Employee** that dynamically creates the exact amount of space required to hold the first and last name. The simplest way to do this would be to use two **string** objects to represent the names. Standard library class **string** is introduced in Chapter 8 and discussed in detail in Chapter 15.

7.4 `friend` Functions and `friend` Classes

A ***friend*** *function* of a class is defined outside that class's scope, yet has the right to access the non-**public** members of the class. Standalone functions or entire classes may be declared to be friends of another class.

Using **friend** functions can enhance performance. This section presents a mechanical example of how a **friend** function works. Later in the book, **friend** functions are used to overload operators for use with class objects and to create iterator classes. Objects of an iterator class can successively select items or perform an operation on items in a container class (see Section 7.9) object. Objects of container classes can store items. Using friends is often appropriate when a member function cannot be used for certain operations as we will see in Chapter 8.

To declare a function as a friend of a class, precede the function prototype in the class definition with keyword **friend**. To declare all member functions of class **ClassTwo** as friends of class **ClassOne**, place a declaration of the form

```
friend class ClassTwo;
```

in the definition of class **ClassOne**.

Software Engineering Observation 7.9

Even though the prototypes for friend functions appear in the class definition, friends are not member functions.

Software Engineering Observation 7.10

Member access notions of **private**, **protected** *and* **public** *are not relevant to* **friend** *declarations, so* **friend** *declarations can be placed anywhere in a class definition.*

Good Programming Practice 7.1

Place all friendship declarations first inside the class definition's body and do not precede them with any member-access specifier.

Friendship is granted, not taken—i.e., for class B to be a friend of class A, class A must explicitly declare that class B is its friend. Also, friendship is neither symmetric nor transitive, i.e., if class A is a friend of class B, and class B is a friend of class C, you cannot infer that class B is a friend of class A (again, friendship is not symmetric), that class C is a friend of class B, or that class A is a friend of class C (again, friendship is not transitive).

Software Engineering Observation 7.11

Some people in the OOP community feel that "friendship" corrupts information hiding and weakens the value of the object-oriented design approach. In this text, we show several examples of the responsible use of friendship.

Figure 7.11 defines friend function **setX** to set the **private** data member **x** of class **Count**. Note that the **friend** declaration (line 10) appears first (by convention) in the class definition, even before **public** member functions are declared. Again, this friend declaration can appear anywhere in the class.

```
1   // Fig. 7.11: fig07_11.cpp
2   // Friends can access private members of a class.
3   #include <iostream>
4
5   using std::cout;
6   using std::endl;
7
8   // Count class definition
9   class Count {
10     friend void setX( Count &, int ); // friend declaration
11
12  public:
13
14     // constructor
15     Count()
16        : x( 0 )   // initialize x to 0
17     {
18        // empty body
19
20     } // end Count constructor
21
```

Fig. 7.11   Friends can access **private** members of a class. (Part 1 of 2.)

```
22         // output x
23         void print() const
24         {
25             cout << x << endl;
26
27         } // end function print
28
29     private:
30         int x;   // data member
31
32     }; // end class Count
33
34     // function setX can modify private data of Count
35     // because setX is declared as a friend of Count
36     void setX( Count &c, int val )
37     {
38         c.x = val;   // legal: setX is a friend of Count
39
40     } // end function setX
41
42     int main()
43     {
44         Count counter;          // create Count object
45
46         cout << "counter.x after instantiation: ";
47         counter.print();
48
49         setX( counter, 8 );   // set x with a friend
50
51         cout << "counter.x after call to setX friend function: ";
52         counter.print();
53
54         return 0;
55
56     } // end main
```

```
counter.x after instantiation: 0
counter.x after call to setX friend function: 8
```

Fig. 7.11   Friends can access **private** members of a class. (Part 2 of 2.)

Function **setX** (lines 36–40) is a C-style, standalone function—it is not a member function of class **Count**. For this reason, when **setX** is invoked for object **counter**, line 49 passes **counter** as an argument to **setX** rather than using a handle (such as the name of the object) to call the function, as in

```
counter.setX( 8 );
```

As we mentioned, Fig. 7.11 is a mechanical example of using the **friend** construct. It would normally be appropriate to define function **setX** as a member function of class **Count**.

The program of Fig. 7.12 demonstrates the error messages produced by the compiler when nonfriend function **cannotSetX** (lines 37–41) is called to modify **private** data member **x**.

```cpp
1   // Fig. 7.12: fig07_12.cpp
2   // Non-friend/non-member functions cannot access
3   // private data of a class.
4   #include <iostream>
5
6   using std::cout;
7   using std::endl;
8
9   // Count class definition
10  // (note that there is no friendship declaration)
11  class Count {
12
13  public:
14
15     // constructor
16     Count()
17        : x( 0 )  // initialize x to 0
18     {
19        // empty body
20
21     } // end Count constructor
22
23     // output x
24     void print() const
25     {
26        cout << x << endl;
27
28     } // end function print
29
30  private:
31     int x;  // data member
32
33  }; // end class Count
34
35  // function tries to modify private data of Count,
36  // but cannot because function is not a friend of Count
37  void cannotSetX( Count &c, int val )
38  {
39     c.x = val;  // ERROR: cannot access private member in Count
40
41  } // end function cannotSetX
42
43  int main()
44  {
45     Count counter;               // create Count object
46
47     cannotSetX( counter, 3 ); // cannotSetX is not a friend
```

Fig. 7.12   Nonfriend/nonmember functions cannot access **private** members. (Part 1 of 2.)

```
48
49      return 0;
50
51   } // end main
```

```
D:\cpphtp4_examples\ch07\Fig07_12\Fig07_12.cpp(39) : error C2248:
   'x' : cannot access private member declared in class 'Count'
       D:\cpphtp4_examples\ch07\Fig07_12\Fig07_12.cpp(31) :
          see declaration of 'x'
```

Fig. 7.12   Nonfriend/nonmember functions cannot access **private** members.
(Part 2 of 2.)

It is possible to specify overloaded functions as friends of a class. Each overloaded
function intended to be a friend must be explicitly declared in the class definition as a friend
of the class.

7.5 Using the `this` Pointer

We have seen that an object's member functions can manipulate the object's data. How do
member functions know which object's data members to manipulate? Every object has access to its own address through a pointer called **this** (a C++ keyword). An object's **this**
pointer is not part of the object itself—i.e., the size of the memory occupied by the **this**
pointer is not reflected in the result of a **sizeof** operation on the object. Rather, the **this**
pointer is passed into the object (by the compiler) as an implicit argument to each of the
object's non-**static** member function calls (**static** members are discussed in
Section 7.7).

Objects use the **this** pointer implicitly (as we have done to this point) or explicitly to
reference their data members and member functions. The type of the **this** pointer depends
on the type of the object and whether the member function in which **this** is used is
declared **const**. For example, in a nonconstant member function of class **Employee**, the
this pointer has type **Employee * const** (a constant pointer to a non-constant
Employee object). In a constant member function of the class **Employee**, the **this**
pointer has the data type **const Employee * const** (a constant pointer to a constant
Employee object).

Our first example in this section shows implicit and explicit use of the **this** pointer;
later in this chapter and in Chapter 8, we show some substantial and subtle examples of
using **this**. Every non-**static** member function has access to the **this** pointer that
points to the object for which the member function is being invoked.

Performance Tip 7.3

*For economy of storage, only one copy of each member function exists per class, and this
member function is invoked by every object of that class. Each object, on the other hand, has
its own copy of the class's data members.*

Implicitly and Explicitly Using the `this` Pointer to Access an Object's Data Members
Figure 7.13 demonstrates the implicit and explicit use of the **this** pointer to enable a
member function of class **Test** to print the **private** data **x** of a **Test** object.

```
1    // Fig. 7.13: fig07_13.cpp
2    // Using the this pointer to refer to object members.
3    #include <iostream>
4
5    using std::cout;
6    using std::endl;
7
8    class Test {
9
10   public:
11      Test( int = 0 );      // default constructor
12      void print() const;
13
14   private:
15      int x;
16
17   }; // end class Test
18
19   // constructor
20   Test::Test( int value )
21      : x( value )  // initialize x to value
22   {
23      // empty body
24
25   } // end Test constructor
26
27   // print x using implicit and explicit this pointers;
28   // parentheses around *this required
29   void Test::print() const
30   {
31      // implicitly use this pointer to access member x
32      cout << "       x = " << x;
33
34      // explicitly use this pointer to access member x
35      cout << "\n  this->x = " << this->x;
36
37      // explicitly use dereferenced this pointer and
38      // the dot operator to access member x
39      cout << "\n(*this).x = " << ( *this ).x << endl;
40
41   } // end function print
42
43   int main()
44   {
45      Test testObject( 12 );
46
47      testObject.print();
48
49      return 0;
50
51   } // end main
```

Fig. 7.13   **this** pointer implicitly and explicitly used to access an object's members.
(Part 1 of 2.)

```
        x = 12
   this->x = 12
(*this).x = 12
```

Fig. 7.13   **this** pointer implicitly and explicitly used to access an object's members.
(Part 2 of 2.)

For illustration purposes, member function **print** (lines 29–41) first prints **x** by using
the **this** pointer implicitly (line 32)—only the name of the data member is specified. Then
print uses two different notations to access **x** through the **this** pointer—the arrow operator (**->**) off the **this** pointer (line 35) and the dot operator (**.**) off the dereferenced **this**
pointer (line 39).

Note the parentheses around ***this** (line 39) when used with the dot member selection operator (**.**). The parentheses are required because the dot operator has higher precedence than the ***** operator. Without the parentheses, the expression ***this.x** would be
evaluated as if it were parenthesized as *** (this.x)**, which is a syntax error because the
dot operator cannot be used with a pointer.

Common Programming Error 7.7

*Attempting to use the member-selection operator (**.**) with a pointer to an object is a syntax
error—the dot member-selection operator may be used only with an object's name or with a
reference to an object.*

One interesting use of the **this** pointer is to prevent an object from being assigned to
itself. As we will see in Chapter 8, self-assignment can cause serious errors when the object
contains pointers to dynamically allocated storage.

*Using the **this** Pointer to Enable Cascaded Function Calls*

Another use of the **this** pointer is to enable *cascaded member-function calls* in which
multiple functions are invoked in the same statement. The program of Fig. 7.14–Fig. 7.16
modifies class **Time**'s *set* functions **setTime**, **setHour**, **setMinute** and **setSec-
ond** such that each returns a reference to a **Time** object to enable cascaded member-function calls. Notice in Fig. 7.15 that the last statement in the body of each of these member
functions returns ***this** (lines 30, 39, 48 and 57).

```
1   // Fig. 7.14: time6.h
2   // Cascading member function calls.
3
4   // Time class definition.
5   // Member functions defined in time6.cpp.
6   #ifndef TIME6_H
7   #define TIME6_H
8
9   class Time {
10
11  public:
12      Time( int = 0, int = 0, int = 0 );   // default constructor
```

Fig. 7.14   **Time** class definition modified to enable cascaded member-function
calls. (Part 1 of 2.)

```
13
14       // set functions
15       Time &setTime( int, int, int ); // set hour, minute, second
16       Time &setHour( int );       // set hour
17       Time &setMinute( int );     // set minute
18       Time &setSecond( int );     // set second
19
20       // get functions (normally declared const)
21       int getHour() const;        // return hour
22       int getMinute() const;      // return minute
23       int getSecond() const;      // return second
24
25       // print functions (normally declared const)
26       void printUniversal() const;  // print universal time
27       void printStandard() const;   // print standard time
28
29    private:
30       int hour;    // 0 - 23 (24-hour clock format)
31       int minute;  // 0 - 59
32       int second;  // 0 - 59
33
34    }; // end class Time
35
36    #endif
```

Fig. 7.14   **Time** class definition modified to enable cascaded member-function calls. (Part 2 of 2.)

```
1     // Fig. 7.15: time6.cpp
2     // Member-function definitions for Time class.
3     #include <iostream>
4
5     using std::cout;
6
7     #include <iomanip>
8
9     using std::setfill;
10    using std::setw;
11
12    #include "time6.h"   // Time class definition
13
14    // constructor function to initialize private data;
15    // calls member function setTime to set variables;
16    // default values are 0 (see class definition)
17    Time::Time( int hr, int min, int sec )
18    {
19        setTime( hr, min, sec );
20
21    } // end Time constructor
22
```

Fig. 7.15   **Time** class member-function definitions modified to enable cascaded member-function calls. (Part 1 of 3.)

```
23   // set values of hour, minute, and second
24   Time &Time::setTime( int h, int m, int s )
25   {
26      setHour( h );
27      setMinute( m );
28      setSecond( s );
29
30      return *this;   // enables cascading
31
32   } // end function setTime
33
34   // set hour value
35   Time &Time::setHour( int h )
36   {
37      hour = ( h >= 0 && h < 24 ) ? h : 0;
38
39      return *this;    // enables cascading
40
41   } // end function setHour
42
43   // set minute value
44   Time &Time::setMinute( int m )
45   {
46      minute = ( m >= 0 && m < 60 ) ? m : 0;
47
48      return *this;    // enables cascading
49
50   } // end function setMinute
51
52   // set second value
53   Time &Time::setSecond( int s )
54   {
55      second = ( s >= 0 && s < 60 ) ? s : 0;
56
57      return *this;    // enables cascading
58
59   } // end function setSecond
60
61   // get hour value
62   int Time::getHour() const
63   {
64      return hour;
65
66   } // end function getHour
67
68   // get minute value
69   int Time::getMinute() const
70   {
71      return minute;
72
73   } // end function getMinute
74
```

Fig. 7.15   **Time** class member-function definitions modified to enable cascaded member-function calls. (Part 2 of 3.)

```
75   // get second value
76   int Time::getSecond() const
77   {
78      return second;
79
80   } // end function getSecond
81
82   // print Time in universal format
83   void Time::printUniversal() const
84   {
85      cout << setfill( '0' ) << setw( 2 ) << hour << ":"
86           << setw( 2 ) << minute << ":"
87           << setw( 2 ) << second;
88
89   } // end function printUniversal
90
91   // print Time in standard format
92   void Time::printStandard() const
93   {
94      cout << ( ( hour == 0 || hour == 12 ) ? 12 : hour % 12 )
95           << ":" << setfill( '0' ) << setw( 2 ) << minute
96           << ":" << setw( 2 ) << second
97           << ( hour < 12 ? " AM" : " PM" );
98
99   } // end function printStandard
```

Fig. 7.15   **Time** class member-function definitions modified to enable cascaded member-function calls. (Part 3 of 3.)

The program of Fig. 7.16 creates **Time** object **t** (line 12), then uses it in cascaded member-function calls (lines 15 and 27). Why does the technique of returning ***this** as a reference work? The dot operator (**.**) associates from left to right, so line 15 first evaluates **t.setHour(18)** then returns a reference to object **t** as the value of this function call. The remaining expression is then interpreted as

    t.setMinute(30).setSecond(22);

The **t.setMinute(30)** call executes and returns a reference to the object **t**. The remaining expression is interpreted as

    t.setSecond(22);

```
1    // Fig. 7.16: fig07_16.cpp
2    // Cascading member function calls with the this pointer.
3    #include <iostream>
4
5    using std::cout;
6    using std::endl;
7
8    #include "time6.h"  // Time class definition
9
```

Fig. 7.16   Cascading member-function calls. (Part 1 of 2.)

```
10   int main()
11   {
12      Time t;
13
14      // cascaded function calls
15      t.setHour( 18 ).setMinute( 30 ).setSecond( 22 );
16
17      // output time in universal and standard formats
18      cout << "Universal time: ";
19      t.printUniversal();
20
21      cout << "\nStandard time: ";
22      t.printStandard();
23
24      cout << "\n\nNew standard time: ";
25
26      // cascaded function calls
27      t.setTime( 20, 20, 20 ).printStandard();
28
29      cout << endl;
30
31      return 0;
32
33   } // end main
```

```
Universal time: 18:30:22
Standard time: 6:30:22 PM

New standard time: 8:20:20 PM
```

Fig. 7.16   Cascading member-function calls. (Part 2 of 2.)

Line 27 also uses cascading. The calls must appear in the order shown in line 27, because **printStandard** as defined in the class does not return a reference to **t**. Placing the call to **printStandard** before the call to **setTime** in line 27 results in a syntax error. Chapter 8 presents several practical examples of using cascaded function calls. One such example is using **<<** with **cout** to output multiple values in a single statement.

7.6 Dynamic Memory Management with Operators *new* and *delete*

C++ enables programmers to control the allocation and deallocation of memory in a program for any built-in or user-defined type. This is known as *dynamic memory management* and is performed with operators *new* and *delete*. In standard C++, a program that uses dynamic memory management should include standard header **<new>**, which provides access to the standard version of operator **new**.

Consider the following declaration and statement:

```
Time *timePtr;
timePtr = new Time;
```

Operator **new** creates an object of the proper size for type **Time**, calls the default constructor for the object and returns a pointer of the type specified to the right of operator **new** (i.e., a **Time ***). Note that **new** can be used to dynamically allocate any primitive type (such as **int** or **double**) or class type. If **new** is unable to find space in memory for the object, it indicates that an error occurred by "throwing" an "exception."[1] Chapter 13, Exception Handling, discusses how to deal with **new** failures in the context of the ANSI/ISO C++ standard. In particular, we will show how to "catch" the exception thrown by **new** and deal with it. When a program does not "catch" an exception, the program terminates immediately.

To destroy a dynamically allocated object and free the space for the object, use the **delete** operator as follows:

```
delete timePtr;
```

The preceding statement first calls the destructor for the object to which **timePtr** points, then deallocates the memory associated with the object. After the preceding statement, the memory can be reused by the system to allocate other objects.

C++ allows you to provide an *initializer* for a newly created object, as in

```
double *ptr = new double( 3.14159 );
```

which initializes a newly created **double** object to **3.14159** and assigns the resulting pointer to **ptr**. The same syntax can be used to specify a comma-separated list of arguments to the constructor of an object. For example,

```
Time *timePtr = new Time( 12, 0, 0 );
```

initializes a newly created **Time** object to 12 PM and assigns the resulting pointer to **timePtr**.

Operator **new** can be used to allocate arrays dynamically. For example, a 10-element integer array can be allocated and assigned to **gradesArray** as follows:

```
int *gradesArray = new int[ 10 ];
```

which declares pointer **gradesArray** and assigns it a pointer to the first element of a dynamically allocated 10-element array of integers. To delete this dynamically allocated array, use the statement

```
delete [] gradesArray;
```

The preceding statement deallocates the array to which **gradesArray** points. If the pointer in the preceding statement points to an array of objects, the statement first calls the destructor for every object in the array, then deallocates the memory. If the preceding statement did not include the square brackets (**[]**) and **gradesArray** pointed to an array of objects, only the first object in the array would receive a destructor call. [*Note:* We use dynamic memory in the example of Section 7.7.]

---

1. Operator **new** returns a **0** pointer in versions of C++ prior to the ANSI/ISO standard. This version of operator **new** is the default version in most C++ compilers to maintain backwards compatibility with older C++ programs. We use the standard version of operator **new** in header **<new>** throughout this book.

Common Programming Error 7.8

*Using **delete** instead of **delete []** for arrays of objects can lead to runtime logic errors. To ensure that every object in the array receives a destructor call, always delete memory allocated as an array with operator **delete []**. Similarly, always delete memory allocated as an individual element with operator **delete**.*

7.7 static Class Members

Each object of a class has its own copy of all the data members of the class. In certain cases, only one copy of a variable should be shared by all objects of a class. A ***static*** *class variable* is used for these and other reasons. A **static** class variable represents "class-wide" information (i.e., a property of the class, not a property of a specific object of the class). The declaration of a **static** member begins with keyword **static**.

Let us motivate the need for **static** class-wide data with a video game example. Suppose that we have a video game with **Martian**s and other space creatures. Each **Martian** tends to be brave and willing to attack other space creatures when the **Martian** is aware that there are at least five **Martian**s present. If fewer than five are present, each **Martian** becomes cowardly. So each **Martian** needs to know the **martianCount**. We could endow each instance of class **Martian** with **martianCount** as a data member. If we do, every **Martian** will have a separate copy of the data member. Every time we create a new **Martian**, we will have to update the data member **martianCount** in all **Martian** objects. Doing this would require every **Martian** object to have, or have access to, handles to all other **Martian** objects in memory. This wastes space with the redundant copies and wastes time in updating the separate copies. Instead, we declare **martianCount** to be **static**. This makes **martianCount** class-wide data. Every **Martian** can see **martianCount** as if it were a data member of the **Martian**, but only one copy of the **static** variable **martianCount** is maintained by C++. This saves space. We save time by having the **Martian** constructor increment **static** variable **martianCount** and having the **Martian** destructor decrement **martianCount**. Because there is only one copy, we do not have to increment separate copies of **martianCount** for each **Martian** object.

Performance Tip 7.4

*Use **static** data members to save storage when a single copy of the data will suffice.*

Although **static** data members may seem like global variables, **static** data members have class scope. Also, **static** members can be declared **public**, **private** or **protected**. Each **static** data member *must* be initialized *once* (and only once) at file scope (i.e., not in the body of the class definition). A class's **private** and **protected** **static** members must be accessed through **public** member functions of the class or through **friend**s of the class. A class's **static** members exist even when no objects of that class exist. To access a **public static** class member when no objects of the class exist, simply prefix the class name and the binary scope resolution operator (**::**) to the name of the data member (such notation also works where there are objects of the class). For example, if our preceding variable **martianCount** is **public**, it can be accessed with the expression **Martian::martianCount** when there are no **Martian** objects.

A class's **public static** class members can be accessed through any object of that class. To access a **private** or **protected static** class member when no objects of the class exist, a **public static** member function must be provided and the function must be called by prefixing its name with the class name and binary scope resolution operator.

The program of Fig. 7.17–Fig. 7.19 demonstrates a **private static** data member called **count** (Fig. 7.17, line 22) and a **public static** member function called **get-Count** (Fig. 7.17, line 15). In Fig. 7.18, line 14 defines and initializes the data member **count** to zero at file scope and lines 18–22 define **static** function **getCount**. Data member **count** maintains a count of the number of objects of class **Employee** that have been instantiated. When objects of class **Employee** exist, member **count** can be referenced through any member function of an **Employee** object—in Fig. 7.18, **count** is referenced by both line 35 in the constructor and line 51 in the destructor.

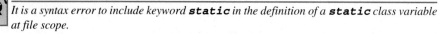

Common Programming Error 7.9

It is a syntax error to include keyword **static** *in the definition of a* **static** *class variable at file scope.*

In Fig. 7.18, note the use of operator **new** (lines 29 and 32) in the **Employee** constructor to dynamically allocate the correct amount of memory for members **firstName** and **lastName**. If operator **new** is unable to fulfill the request for memory for one or both of these character arrays, the program will terminate immediately. In Chapter 13, we will provide a better mechanism for dealing with cases in which **new** is unable to allocate memory.

```
1   // Fig. 7.17: employee2.h
2   // Employee class definition.
3   #ifndef EMPLOYEE2_H
4   #define EMPLOYEE2_H
5
6   class Employee {
7
8   public:
9      Employee( const char *, const char * );  // constructor
10     ~Employee();                              // destructor
11     const char *getFirstName() const;  // return first name
12     const char *getLastName() const;   // return last name
13
14     // static member function
15     static int getCount();  // return # objects instantiated
16
17   private:
18      char *firstName;
19      char *lastName;
20
21      // static data member
22      static int count;  // number of objects instantiated
23
24   }; // end class Employee
25
26   #endif
```

Fig. 7.17   **Employee** class definition with a **static** data member to track the number of **Employee** objects in memory.

```cpp
1   // Fig. 7.18: employee2.cpp
2   // Member-function definitions for class Employee.
3   #include <iostream>
4
5   using std::cout;
6   using std::endl;
7
8   #include <new>            // C++ standard new operator
9   #include <cstring>        // strcpy and strlen prototypes
10
11  #include "employee2.h"  // Employee class definition
12
13  // define and initialize static data member
14  int Employee::count = 0;
15
16  // define static member function that returns number of
17  // Employee objects instantiated
18  int Employee::getCount()
19  {
20     return count;
21
22  } // end static function getCount
23
24  // constructor dynamically allocates space for
25  // first and last name and uses strcpy to copy
26  // first and last names into the object
27  Employee::Employee( const char *first, const char *last )
28  {
29     firstName = new char[ strlen( first ) + 1 ];
30     strcpy( firstName, first );
31
32     lastName = new char[ strlen( last ) + 1 ];
33     strcpy( lastName, last );
34
35     ++count;   // increment static count of employees
36
37     cout << "Employee constructor for " << firstName
38          << ' ' << lastName << " called." << endl;
39
40  } // end Employee constructor
41
42  // destructor deallocates dynamically allocated memory
43  Employee::~Employee()
44  {
45     cout << "~Employee() called for " << firstName
46          << ' ' << lastName << endl;
47
48     delete [] firstName;   // recapture memory
49     delete [] lastName;    // recapture memory
50
51     --count;   // decrement static count of employees
52
53  } // end destructor ~Employee
```

Fig. 7.18   **Employee** class member-function definitions. (Part 1 of 2.)

```
54
55   // return first name of employee
56   const char *Employee::getFirstName() const
57   {
58      // const before return type prevents client from modifying
59      // private data; client should copy returned string before
60      // destructor deletes storage to prevent undefined pointer
61      return firstName;
62
63   } // end function getFirstName
64
65   // return last name of employee
66   const char *Employee::getLastName() const
67   {
68      // const before return type prevents client from modifying
69      // private data; client should copy returned string before
70      // destructor deletes storage to prevent undefined pointer
71      return lastName;
72
73   } // end function getLastName
```

Fig. 7.18   **Employee** class member-function definitions. (Part 2 of 2.)

Also note in Fig. 7.18 that the implementations of functions **getFirstName** (lines 56–63) and **getLastName** (lines 66–73) return constant character pointers to the caller. In this implementation, if the client wishes to retain a copy of the first name or last name, the client is responsible for copying the dynamically allocated memory in the **Employee** object after obtaining the constant character pointer from the object. It is also possible to implement **getFirstName** and **getLastName** so the client is required to pass a character array and the size of the array to each function. Then the functions could copy the first or last name into the character array provided by the client. Once again, class **string** could be used here to return a copy of a **string** object to the caller.

Figure 7.19 uses function **getCount** to determine the number of **Employee** objects currently instantiated. Note that when there are no objects instantiated in the program, the **Employee::getCount()** function call is issued (lines 15 and 36). However, when there are objects instantiated, function **getCount** can be called through either of the objects as shown in the statement at lines 20–21, which uses pointer **e1Ptr** to invoke function **getCount**. Note that using **e2Ptr->getCount()** or **Employee::get-Count()** in line 21 would produce the same result, because **getCount** always accesses the same **static** member **count**.

Software Engineering Observation 7.12

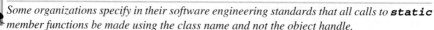

Some organizations specify in their software engineering standards that all calls to **static** *member functions be made using the class name and not the object handle.*

A member function may be declared **static** if it does not access non-**static** class data members and member functions of the class. Unlike non-**static** member functions, a **static** member function does not have a **this** pointer, because **static** data members and **static** member functions exist independent of any objects of a class.

```
 1   // Fig. 7.19: fig07_19.cpp
 2   // Driver to test class Employee.
 3   #include <iostream>
 4
 5   using std::cout;
 6   using std::endl;
 7
 8   #include <new>              // C++ standard new operator
 9
10   #include "employee2.h"  // Employee class definition
11
12   int main()
13   {
14      cout << "Number of employees before instantiation is "
15          << Employee::getCount() << endl;    // use class name
16
17      Employee *e1Ptr = new Employee( "Susan", "Baker" );
18      Employee *e2Ptr = new Employee( "Robert", "Jones" );
19
20      cout << "Number of employees after instantiation is "
21          << e1Ptr->getCount();
22
23      cout << "\n\nEmployee 1: "
24          << e1Ptr->getFirstName()
25          << " " << e1Ptr->getLastName()
26          << "\nEmployee 2: "
27          << e2Ptr->getFirstName()
28          << " " << e2Ptr->getLastName() << "\n\n";
29
30      delete e1Ptr;    // recapture memory
31      e1Ptr = 0;       // disconnect pointer from free-store space
32      delete e2Ptr;    // recapture memory
33      e2Ptr = 0;       // disconnect pointer from free-store space
34
35      cout << "Number of employees after deletion is "
36          << Employee::getCount() << endl;
37
38      return 0;
39
40   } // end main
```

```
Number of employees before instantiation is 0
Employee constructor for Susan Baker called.
Employee constructor for Robert Jones called.
Number of employees after instantiation is 2

Employee 1: Susan Baker
Employee 2: Robert Jones

~Employee() called for Susan Baker
~Employee() called for Robert Jones
Number of employees after deletion is 0
```

Fig. 7.19   **static** data member tracking the number of objects of a class.

Common Programming Error 7.10

*Using the **this** pointer in a **static** member function is a syntax error.*

Common Programming Error 7.11

*Declaring a **static** member function **const** is a syntax error.*

Software Engineering Observation 7.13

*A class's **static** data members and **static** member functions exist and can be used even if no objects of that class have been instantiated.*

Lines 17–18 of Fig. 7.19 use operator **new** to dynamically allocate two **Employee** objects. Remember that the program will terminate immediately if it is unable to allocate one or both of these objects. When each **Employee** object is allocated, its constructor is called. When **delete** is used at lines 30 and 32 to deallocate the two **Employee** objects, each object's destructor is called.

Good Programming Practice 7.2

*After deleting dynamically allocated memory, set the pointer that referred to that memory to **0**. This disconnects the pointer from the previously allocated space on the free store.*

7.8 Data Abstraction and Information Hiding

Classes normally hide their implementation details from the clients of the classes. This is called *information hiding*. As an example of information hiding, let us consider a data structure called a *stack*.

Think of a stack in terms of a pile of dishes. When a dish is placed on the pile, it is always placed at the top (referred to as *pushing onto the stack*); when a dish is removed from the pile, it is always removed from the top (referred to as *popping off the stack*). Stacks are known as *last-in, first-out (LIFO) data structures*—the last item pushed (inserted) on the stack is the first item popped (removed) from the stack.

The programmer may create a stack class and hide from its clients the implementation of the stack. Stacks can easily be implemented with arrays (or linked lists; see Chapter 17, Data Structures). A client of a stack class need not know how the stack is implemented. The client simply requires that when data items are placed in the stack, the data items will be recalled in last-in, first-out order. Describing the functionality of a class independent of its implementation is called *data abstraction*, and C++ classes define so-called *abstract data types (ADTs)*. Although users may happen to know the details of how a class is implemented, users should not write code that depends on these details. This means that the implementation of a particular class (such as one that implements a stack and its operations of *push* and *pop*) can be altered or replaced without affecting the rest of the system, as long as the interface to that class does not change.

The job of a high-level language is to create a view convenient for programmers to use. There is no single accepted standard view—that is one reason why there are so many programming languages. Object-oriented programming in C++ presents yet another view.

Most programming languages emphasize actions. In these languages, data exists in support of the actions programs need to take. Data is viewed as being "less interesting" than actions, anyway. Data is "crude." There are only a few built-in data types, and it is difficult for programmers to create their own new data types.

This view changes with C++ and the object-oriented style of programming. C++ elevates the importance of data and its behavior. The primary activity in C++ is creating new types (i.e., classes) and expressing the interactions among objects of those types.

To move in this direction, the programming-languages community needed to formalize some notions about data. The formalization we consider is the notion of abstract data types (ADTs). ADTs receive as much attention today as structured programming did over the last two decades. ADTs do not replace structured programming. Rather, they provide an additional formalization that can further improve the program-development process.

What is an abstract data type? Consider the built-in type **int**. What comes to mind is the notion of an integer in mathematics, but **int** on a computer is not precisely what an integer is in mathematics. In particular, computer **int**s are normally quite limited in size. For example, **int** on a 32-bit machine may be limited approximately to the range –2 billion to +2 billion. If the result of a calculation falls outside this range, an "overflow" error occurs and the machine responds in some machine-dependent manner, including the possibility of "quietly" producing an incorrect result. Mathematical integers do not have this problem. So the notion of a computer **int** is really only an approximation to the notion of a real-world integer. The same is true with **double**.

Even **char** is an approximation; **char** values are normally eight-bit patterns of ones and zeros; these patterns look nothing like the characters they represent such as a capital **Z**, a lowercase **z**, a dollar sign (**$**), a digit (**5**), and so on. Values of type **char** on most computers are quite limited compared with the range of real-world characters. The seven-bit ASCII character set (Appendix B) provides for 128 different character values. This is inadequate for representing languages such as Japanese and Chinese that require thousands of characters. As Internet and World Wide Web usage becomes pervasive, the newer Unicode character set is growing rapidly in popularity due to its ability to represent most languages.[2]

The point is that even the built-in data types provided with programming languages like C++ are really only approximations or models of real-world concepts and behaviors. We have taken **int** for granted until this point, but now you have a new perspective to consider. Types like **int**, **double**, **char** and others are all examples of abstract data types. They are essentially ways of representing real-world notions to some satisfactory level of precision within a computer system.

An abstract data type actually captures two notions, namely, a *data representation* and the *operations* that are allowed on those data. For example, the notion of **int** defines addition, subtraction, multiplication, division and modulus operations (among others) in C++, but division by zero is undefined; and these allowed operations perform in a manner sensitive to machine parameters such as the fixed word size of the underlying computer system. Another example is the notion of negative integers, whose operations and data representation are clear, but the operation of taking the square root of a negative integer is undefined. In C++, the programmer uses classes to implement abstract data types and their services. We create our own stack class in Chapter 11, Templates, and we study the standard library **stack** class in Chapter 21, Standard Template Library (STL).

---

2. For more information on Unicode, visit **www.unicode.org**.

7.8.1 Example: Array Abstract Data Type

We discussed arrays in Chapter 4. An array is not much more than a pointer and some space in memory. This primitive capability is acceptable for performing array operations if the programmer is cautious and undemanding. There are many operations that would be nice to perform with arrays, but that are not built into C++. With C++ classes, the programmer can develop an array ADT that is preferable to "raw" arrays. The array class can provide many helpful new capabilities such as

- subscript range checking

- an arbitrary range of subscripts instead of having to start with 0

- array assignment

- array comparison

- array input/output

- arrays that know their sizes

- arrays that expand dynamically to accommodate more elements.

We create our own array class with many of these capabilities in Chapter 8, and we introduce the standard library class **vector** with many of these capabilities in Chapter 8 as well. Chapter 21 explains class **vector** in detail.

C++ has a small set of built-in types. Classes extend the base programming language.

Software Engineering Observation 7.14

The programmer is able to create new types through the class mechanism. These new types can be designed to be used as conveniently as the built-in types. Thus, C++ is an extensible language. *Although the language is easy to extend with these new types, the base language itself is not changeable.*

New classes created in C++ environments can be proprietary to an individual, to small groups or to companies. Classes can also be placed in standard class libraries intended for wide distribution. ANSI (the American National Standards Institute) and ISO (the International Organization for Standardization) have developed a standard version of C++ that includes a standard class library. The reader who learns C++ and object-oriented programming will be ready to take advantage of the new kinds of rapid, component-oriented software development made possible with increasingly abundant and rich libraries.

7.8.2 Example: String Abstract Data Type

C++ is an intentionally sparse language that provides programmers with only the raw capabilities needed to build a broad range of systems (consider it a tool for making tools). The language is designed to minimize performance burdens. C++ is appropriate for both applications programming and systems programming—the latter places extraordinary performance demands on programs. Certainly, it would have been possible to include a string data type among C++'s built-in data types. Instead, the language was designed to include mechanisms for creating and implementing string abstract data types through classes. In Chapter 8, we will develop our own **String** ADT and introduce the standard library class **string** as well. We discuss in detail in Chapter 15.

7.8.3 Example: Queue Abstract Data Type

Each of us stands in line from time to time. A waiting line is also called a *queue*. We wait in line at the supermarket checkout counter, we wait in line to get gasoline, we wait in line to board a bus, we wait in line to pay a highway toll and students know all too well about waiting in line during registration to get the courses they want. Computer systems use many waiting lines internally, so we need to write programs that simulate what queues are and do.

A queue is a good example of an abstract data type. A queue offers well-understood behavior to its clients. Clients put things in a queue one at a time—using an *enqueue* operation—and the clients get those things back one at a time on demand—using a *dequeue* operation. Conceptually, a queue can become infinitely long. A real queue, of course, is finite. Items are returned from a queue in *first-in, first-out (FIFO)* order—the first item inserted in the queue is the first item removed from the queue.

The queue hides an internal data representation that somehow keeps track of the items currently waiting in line, and it offers a set of operations to its clients, namely, *enqueue* and *dequeue*. The clients are not concerned about the implementation of the queue. Clients merely want the queue to operate "as advertised." When a client enqueues a new item, the queue should accept that item and place it internally in some kind of first-in, first-out data structure. When the client wants the next item from the front of the queue, the queue should remove the item from its internal representation and should deliver the item to the outside world (i.e., to the *client* of the queue) in FIFO order (i.e., the item that has been in the queue the longest should be the next one returned by the next *dequeue* operation).

The queue ADT guarantees the integrity of its internal data structure. Clients may not manipulate this data structure directly. Only the queue member functions have access to its internal data. Clients may cause only allowable operations to be performed on the data representation; operations not provided in the ADT's public interface are rejected in some appropriate manner. This could mean issuing an error message, terminating execution or simply ignoring the operation request.

We create our own queue class in Chapter 17, Data Structures, and we study the standard library **queue** class in Chapter 21, Standard Template Library (STL).

7.9 Container Classes and Iterators

Among the most popular types of classes are *container classes* (also called *collection classes*), i.e., classes designed to hold collections of objects. Container classes commonly provide services such as insertion, deletion, searching, sorting, testing an item to determine whether it is a member of the collection. Arrays, stacks, queues, trees and linked lists are examples of container classes; we studied arrays in Chapter 4 and we will study each of these other data structures in Chapter 17 and Chapter 21.

It is common to associate *iterator objects*—or more simply *iterators*—with container classes. An iterator is an object that returns the next item of a collection (or performs some action on the next item of a collection). Once an iterator for a class has been written, obtaining the next element from the class can be expressed simply. Just as a book being shared by several people could have several bookmarks in it at once, a container class can have several iterators operating on it at once. Each iterator maintains its own "position" information. We will discuss containers and iterators in detail in Chapter 21.

7.10 Proxy Classes

Sometimes, it is desirable to hide the implementation details of a class to prevent access to proprietary information (including private data) and proprietary program logic in a class. Providing clients of your class with a *proxy class* that knows only the public interface to your class enables the clients to use your class's services without giving the client access to your class's implementation details.

Implementing a proxy class requires several steps, which we demonstrate in Fig. 7.20–Fig. 7.23. First, we create the class definition for the class that contains the proprietary implementation we would like to hide. Our example class, which we call **Implementation**, is shown in Fig. 7.20. The proxy class **Interface** is shown in Fig. 7.21–Fig. 7.22. The test program and sample output are shown in Fig. 7.23.

Class **Implementation** (Fig. 7.20) provides a single **private** data member called **value** (the data we would like to hide from the client), a constructor to initialize **value** and functions **setValue** and **getValue**.

```
1   // Fig. 7.20: implementation.h
2   // Header file for class Implementation
3
4   class Implementation {
5
6   public:
7
8      // constructor
9      Implementation( int v )
10        : value( v )  // initialize value with v
11     {
12        // empty body
13
14     } // end Implementation constructor
15
16     // set value to v
17     void setValue( int v )
18     {
19        value = v;  // should validate v
20
21     } // end function setValue
22
23     // return value
24     int getValue() const
25     {
26        return value;
27
28     } // end function getValue
29
30   private:
31      int value;
32
33   }; // end class Implementation
```

Fig. 7.20 **Implementation** class definition.

We create a proxy class definition called **Interface** (Fig. 7.21) with an identical public interface (except for the names of the constructor and destructor) to that of class **Implementation**. The only private member of the proxy class is a pointer to an object of class **Implementation**. Using a pointer in this manner allows us to hide the implementation details of class **Implementation** from the client. Notice that the only mention in class **Interface** of the proprietary **Implementation** class is in the pointer declaration (line 17). When a class definition (such as class **Interface**) uses only a pointer or reference to an object of another class (such as to an object of class **Implementation**), the class header file for that other class (which would ordinarily reveal the **private** data of that class) is not required to be included with **#include**. You can simply declare that other class as a data type with a *forward class declaration* (line 4) before the type is used in the file.

The member function implementation file for proxy class **Interface** (Fig. 7.22) is the only file that includes the header file **implementation.h** (line 4) containing class **Implementation**. The file **interface.cpp** (Fig. 7.22) is provided to the client as a precompiled object code file along with the header file **interface.h** that includes the function prototypes of the services provided by the proxy class. Because file **interface.cpp** is made available to the client only as object code, the client is not able to see the interactions between the proxy class and the proprietary class (lines 8, 17, 24 and 31).

```
1    // Fig. 7.21: interface.h
2    // Header file for interface.cpp
3
4    class Implementation;        // forward class declaration
5
6    class Interface {
7
8    public:
9       Interface( int );
10      void setValue( int );   // same public interface as
11      int getValue() const;   // class Implementation
12      ~Interface();
13
14   private:
15
16      // requires previous forward declaration (line 4)
17      Implementation *ptr;
18
19   }; // end class Interface
```

Fig. 7.21   **Interface** class definition.

```
1    // Fig. 7.22: interface.cpp
2    // Definition of class Interface
3    #include "interface.h"       // Interface class definition
4    #include "implementation.h"  // Implementation class definition
5
```

Fig. 7.22   **Interface** class member-function definitions. (Part 1 of 2.)

```
6    // constructor
7    Interface::Interface( int v )
8       : ptr ( new Implementation( v ) )  // initialize ptr
9    {
10      // empty body
11
12   } // end Interface constructor
13
14   // call Implementation's setValue function
15   void Interface::setValue( int v )
16   {
17      ptr->setValue( v );
18
19   } // end function setValue
20
21   // call Implementation's getValue function
22   int Interface::getValue() const
23   {
24      return ptr->getValue();
25
26   } // end function getValue
27
28   // destructor
29   Interface::~Interface()
30   {
31      delete ptr;
32
33   } // end destructor ~Interface
```

Fig. 7.22   **Interface** class member-function definitions. (Part 2 of 2.)

Figure 7.23 tests class **Interface**. Notice that only the header file for **Interface** is included in **main** (line 8)—there is no mention of the existence of a separate class called **Implementation**. Thus, the client never sees the **private** data of class **Implementation**, nor can the client code become dependent on the **Implementation** code.

```
1    // Fig. 7.23: fig07_23.cpp
2    // Hiding a class's private data with a proxy class.
3    #include <iostream>
4
5    using std::cout;
6    using std::endl;
7
8    #include "interface.h"  // Interface class definition
9
10   int main()
11   {
12      Interface i( 5 );
13
14      cout << "Interface contains: " << i.getValue()
15           << " before setValue" << endl;
```

Fig. 7.23   Implementing a proxy class. (Part 1 of 2.)

```
16
17      i.setValue( 10 );
18
19      cout << "Interface contains: " << i.getValue()
20           << " after setValue" << endl;
21
22      return 0;
23
24  } // end main
```

```
Interface contains: 5 before setValue
Interface contains: 10 after setValue
```

Fig. 7.23   Implementing a proxy class. (Part 2 of 2.)

7.11 (Optional Case Study) Thinking About Objects: Programming the Classes for the Elevator Simulator

In the "Thinking About Objects" sections at the ends of Chapter 2 through Chapter 5, we designed our elevator simulator. In Chapter 6, we began programming the simulator in C++. In the body of Chapter 7, we discussed the remaining C++ capabilities that we need to implement a complete, working elevator simulator. We discussed dynamic object management, using **new** and **delete** to create and destroy objects, respectively. We also discussed composition, a capability that allows us to create classes that contain objects of other classes as data members. Composition enables us to create a **Building** class that contains a **Scheduler** object, a **Clock** object, an **Elevator** object and two **Floor** objects; an **Elevator** class that contains one object each of classes **ElevatorButton**, **Door** and **Bell**; and a **Floor** class that contains **FloorButton** and **Light** objects. We also discussed how to use **static** class members, **const** class members and member-initialization syntax in constructors. In this section, we continue implementing our elevator system in C++ using these techniques. At the end of this section, we present a complete elevator simulator in C++ (almost 1300 lines of code) and a detailed code walkthrough. In Section 9.10, we complete our elevator-simulator case study by incorporating inheritance into the elevator simulator; at that point, we present only the additional C++ code that we use to implement the inheritance.

Overview of the Elevator Simulation Implementation

Our elevator simulation is controlled by an object of class **Building**, which contains two objects of class **Floor** and one object each of classes **Elevator**, **Clock** and **Scheduler**. This composite relationship was shown in the UML class diagram of Fig. 2.43. The clock keeps track of the current simulation time in seconds, and the building increments the clock once every second. The scheduler is responsible for scheduling the arrival of people on each floor.

The sequence diagram we presented in Fig. 4.27 models the scheduler's behavior. After each clock tick, the building updates the scheduler with the current time (via member function **processTime** of class **Scheduler**). The scheduler checks this time against the next scheduled arrival times for people on each floor. If a person is scheduled to arrive on a floor, the scheduler determines whether the floor is unoccupied by calling member function **isOccupied** of class **Floor**. If this call returns **true**, then a person currently is waiting on the floor. In this case, the scheduler invokes its **delayTime** function to delay for one second the next time a person may arrive on that floor.

If the floor is unoccupied (i.e., the call returns **false**), the scheduler creates an object of class **Person**, and that person steps onto the appropriate floor. The person then invokes member function **pressButton** of class **FloorButton**. The floor button, in turn, invokes member function **summonElevator** of class **Elevator**.

The building also updates the elevator with the current time in seconds after each clock tick. The activity diagram we presented in Fig. 3.32 models some of the elevator's behavior. Upon receiving the updated time, the elevator first checks its current state (either "moving" or "not moving"). If the elevator is moving between floors, but is not scheduled to arrive at a floor at that time, the elevator outputs its direction of motion to the screen. If the elevator is moving, and the current time matches the next scheduled arrival time, the elevator stops, resets its elevator button, rings its bell and notifies the floor that the elevator has arrived (via member function **elevatorArrived** of class **Floor**). In response, the floor resets its floor button and turns on its light. The elevator opens its door, which causes the floor's door to open, allowing the elevator passenger to exit and allowing the person on the floor to enter. The elevator then closes its door, which causes the floor's door to close, and determines whether the other floor needs service. If the other floor needs service, the elevator begins moving to that floor.

If the elevator is not moving when it receives the updated time from the building, the elevator determines which floors need its service. If the current floor needs service (i.e., a person has pressed a button on the elevator's current floor), the elevator rings its bell, notifies the floor that the elevator has arrived and opens the elevator door. The person on the floor enters the elevator and presses the elevator button to start the elevator moving to the other floor. If the other floor needs service (i.e., a person has pressed a button on the other floor), the elevator begins moving to that floor.

Elevator Simulation Implementation

In the preceding "Thinking About Objects" sections, we gathered information about our system. We used this information to create an object-oriented design of our elevator simulation, and we used the UML to represent this design. We now have discussed all the C++ object-oriented programming technology required to implement a working simulation. The remainder of this section contains our C++ implementation and a detailed code walkthrough.

Our main program (Fig. 7.24) first prompts the user to enter the length of time for which the simulation should run and inputs that value (lines 15–16). The call to **cin.ignore** (line 17) instructs the **cin** stream to ignore the return character the user types after the integer at run time. This removes the return character from the input stream. We do this to help the program user view the output. In particular, class **Building**'s **runSimulation** function (Fig. 7.26, lines 30–50) contains a loop that waits for the user to press the *Enter* key (Fig. 7.26, line 46) to execute the next iteration of the loop. This enables the user to study the output, then tell the program when to continue executing. When the user initially enters the duration of the simulation, the user types an integer representing the simulation length and presses the *Enter* key to submit the value to the program. Both the integer value and the return character that represents the *Enter* key are sent into the program. However, only the integer value the user typed is actually read by line 16—the return character remains in the input waiting to be read. Without the call to **cin.ignore** at line

17, the statement at line 46 of Fig. 7.26 would read that return character, thus preventing the user from studying the first part of the program's output and preventing the user from telling the program when to execute the next iteration of the loop.

Next, the main program creates the **building** object (line 19) and invokes its **run-Simulation** member function (line 24), passing as an argument the duration specified by the user. The driver also prints out messages to the user when the simulation begins (lines 21–22) and ends (line 26).

According to our class diagram (Fig. 2.43), class **Building** is composed of objects from several other classes. The **Building** header file (Fig. 7.25) reflects this composition in lines 19–23. Class **Building** is composed of two **Floor** objects (**floor1** and **floor2**), an **Elevator** object (**elevator**), a **Clock** object (**clock**) and a **Scheduler** object (**scheduler**).

```
1   // Fig. 7.24: elevatorSimulation.cpp
2   // Driver for the simulation.
3   #include <iostream>
4
5   using std::cout;
6   using std::cin;
7   using std::endl;
8
9   #include "building.h"   // Building class definition
10
11  int main()
12  {
13      int duration;   // length of simulation in seconds
14
15      cout << "Enter run time: ";
16      cin >> duration;
17      cin.ignore();          // ignore return char
18
19      Building building;   // create the building
20
21      cout << endl << "*** ELEVATOR SIMULATION BEGINS ***"
22           << endl << endl;
23
24      building.runSimulation( duration );   // start simulation
25
26      cout << "*** ELEVATOR SIMULATION ENDS ***" << endl;
27
28      return 0;
29
30  } // end main
```

Fig. 7.24   Elevator simulation.

```
1   // Fig. 7.25: building.h
2   // Building class definition.
3   #ifndef BUILDING_H
4   #define BUILDING_H
```

Fig. 7.25   **Building** class header file. (Part 1 of 2.)

```
5
6   #include "elevator.h"    // Elevator class definition
7   #include "floor.h"       // Floor class definition
8   #include "clock.h"       // Clock class definition
9   #include "scheduler.h"   // Scheduler class definition
10
11  class Building {
12
13  public:
14     Building();                  // constructor
15     ~Building();                 // destructor
16     void runSimulation( int );   // controls simulation
17
18  private:
19     Floor floor1;                // floor1 object
20     Floor floor2;                // floor2 object
21     Elevator elevator;           // elevator object
22     Clock clock;                 // clock object
23     Scheduler scheduler;         // scheduler object
24
25  }; // end class Building
26
27  #endif // BUILDING_H
```

Fig. 7.25   **Building** class header file. (Part 2 of 2.)

Figure 7.26 shows the implementation file for class **Building**. Lines 12–20 define
the class's constructor. Its member-initialization list (lines 13–16) calls the constructors for
several of the objects that compose class **Building**. Arguments **Floor::FLOOR1** and
Floor::FLOOR2 (in lines 13–14) are constants defined in class **Floor**.

```
1   // Fig. 7.26: building.cpp
2   // Member-function definitions for class Building.
3   #include <iostream>
4
5   using std::cout;
6   using std::cin;
7   using std::endl;
8
9   #include "building.h"   // Building class definition
10
11  // constructor
12  Building::Building()
13     : floor1( Floor::FLOOR1, elevator ),
14       floor2( Floor::FLOOR2, elevator ),
15       elevator( floor1, floor2 ),
16       scheduler( floor1, floor2 )
17  {
18     cout << "building constructed" << endl;
19
20  } // end Building constructor
```

Fig. 7.26   **Building** class implementation file. (Part 1 of 2.)

```
21
22    // destructor
23    Building::~Building()
24    {
25       cout << "building destructed" << endl;
26
27    } // end destructor ~Building
28
29    // function to control simulation
30    void Building::runSimulation( int totalTime )
31    {
32       int currentTime = 0;
33
34       while ( currentTime < totalTime ) {
35          clock.tick();                       // increment time
36          currentTime = clock.getTime();   // get new time
37          cout << "TIME: " << currentTime << endl;
38
39          // process person arrivals for currentTime
40          scheduler.processTime( currentTime );
41
42          // process elevator events for currentTime
43          elevator.processTime( currentTime );
44
45          // wait for Enter key press, so user can view output
46          cin.get();
47
48       } // end while
49
50    } // end function runSimulation
```

Fig. 7.26   **Building** class implementation file. (Part 2 of 2.)

The primary functionality of class **Building** is in its **runSimulation** member function (lines 30–50), which loops until the specified amount of time has passed. On each iteration, the **Building** instructs the **clock** to increment its time by one second by sending **clock** the **tick** message (line 35). Then the **Building** retrieves the time from the **clock** by calling member function **getTime** (line 36). The **currentTime** is then sent via the **processTime** messages to the **scheduler** and the **elevator** (lines 40 and 43, respectively). Finally, we add a call to **cin.get** (line 46) to allow the user to view the simulation output, before pressing the *Enter* key to view the simulation results for the next tick of the clock. Note that without the **cin.ignore** statement at line 17 in Fig. 7.24, the first time the **cin.get** statement executes, it would read the return character the user typed to submit the simulation length to the program and the loop would continue immediately with its next iteration.

Class **Clock** (Fig. 7.27–Fig. 7.28) is not composed of any other objects. An object of class **Clock** can receive messages to increment **time** through member function **tick**. The current time is made available to other objects through member function **getTime**. Notice that function **getTime** is **const**, because it does not modify an object of class **Clock**.

```
1   // Fig. 7.27: clock.h
2   // Clock class definition.
3   #ifndef CLOCK_H
4   #define CLOCK_H
5
6   class Clock {
7
8   public:
9      Clock();              // constructor
10     ~Clock();             // destructor
11     void tick();          // increment clock by one second
12     int getTime() const;  // returns clock's current time
13
14  private:
15     int time;             // clock's time
16
17  }; // end class Clock
18
19  #endif // CLOCK_H
```

Fig. 7.27 **Clock** class header file.

```
1   // Fig. 7.28: clock.cpp
2   // Member-function definitions for class Clock.
3   #include <iostream>
4
5   using std::cout;
6   using std::endl;
7
8   #include "clock.h"  // Clock class definition
9
10  // constructor
11  Clock::Clock()
12     : time( 0 )  // initialize time to 0
13  {
14     cout << "clock constructed" << endl;
15
16  } // end Clock constructor
17
18  // destructor
19  Clock::~Clock()
20  {
21     cout << "clock destructed" << endl;
22
23  } // end destructor ~Clock
24
25  // increment time by 1
26  void Clock::tick()
27  {
28     time++;
29
30  } // end function tick
```

Fig. 7.28 **Clock** class implementation file. (Part 1 of 2.)

```
31
32   // return current time
33   int Clock::getTime() const
34   {
35      return time;
36
37   } // end function getTime
```

Fig. 7.28   Clock class implementation file. (Part 2 of 2.)

Class **Scheduler** (Fig. 7.29) creates objects of class **Person** at randomly generated times and places these objects on the appropriate floors. The public interface lists member function **processTime** (line 13), which takes as its argument the current time. The header file also lists several private utility functions (which we discuss momentarily) that perform the tasks required by member function **processTime**. These functions do not appear in the UML diagram of Fig. 6.25; rather, we create these functions as we implement the class, to help divide the scheduler's tasks into more manageable pieces.

```
1    // Fig. 7.29: scheduler.h
2    // Scheduler class definition.
3    #ifndef SCHEDULER_H
4    #define SCHEDULER_H
5
6    class Floor;                          // forward declaration
7
8    class Scheduler {
9
10   public:
11      Scheduler( Floor &, Floor & );    // constructor
12      ~Scheduler();                     // destructor
13      void processTime( int );          // set scheduler's time
14
15   private:
16      // schedule arrival to a floor
17      void scheduleTime( const Floor & );
18
19      // delay arrival to a floor
20      void delayTime( const Floor & );
21
22      // create new person; place on floor
23      void createNewPerson( Floor & );
24
25      // handle person arrival on a floor
26      void handleArrivals( Floor &, int );
27
28      int currentClockTime;
29
30      Floor &floor1Ref;
31      Floor &floor2Ref;
32
```

Fig. 7.29   Scheduler class header file. (Part 1 of 2.)

```
33        int floor1ArrivalTime;
34        int floor2ArrivalTime;
35
36    }; // end class Scheduler
37
38    #endif // SCHEDULER_H
```

Fig. 7.29   **Scheduler** class header file. (Part 2 of 2.)

Figure 7.30 shows the implementation file for class **Scheduler**. Member function **processTime** (lines 69–79) delegates most of its responsibilities to smaller utility functions within the class. Class **Scheduler**'s constructor (lines 17–29) first seeds the pseudo-random-number generator (line 22) with a number based on the computer's current system time. This causes the random-number generator to produce a different series of numbers each time the program executes. The constructor then calls utility function **scheduleTime** (defined at lines 39–52) for each of the two floors (lines 26–27). This member function calculates a pseudo-random arrival time (in this case, a random number in the range 5 to 20, inclusive) for the first **Person** object that the **Scheduler** creates on each floor.

```
1    // Fig. 7.30: scheduler.cpp
2    // Member-function definitions for class Scheduler.
3    #include <iostream>
4
5    using std::cout;
6    using std::endl;
7
8    #include <new>
9    #include <cstdlib>
10   #include <ctime>
11
12   #include "scheduler.h"  // Scheduler class definition
13   #include "floor.h"      // Floor class definition
14   #include "person.h"     // Person class definition
15
16   // constructor
17   Scheduler::Scheduler( Floor &firstFloor, Floor &secondFloor )
18      : currentClockTime( 0 ),
19        floor1Ref( firstFloor ),
20        floor2Ref( secondFloor )
21   {
22      srand( time( 0 ) ); // seed random number generator
23      cout << "scheduler constructed" << endl;
24
25      // schedule first arrivals for floor 1 and floor 2
26      scheduleTime( floor1Ref );
27      scheduleTime( floor2Ref );
28
29   } // end Scheduler constructor
30
```

Fig. 7.30   **Scheduler** class implementation file. (Part 1 of 3.)

```
31   // destructor
32   Scheduler::~Scheduler()
33   {
34      cout << "scheduler destructed" << endl;
35
36   } // end Scheduler destructor
37
38   // schedule arrival on a floor
39   void Scheduler::scheduleTime( const Floor &floor )
40   {
41      int floorNumber = floor.getNumber();
42      int arrivalTime = currentClockTime + ( 5 + rand() % 16 );
43
44      floorNumber == Floor::FLOOR1 ?
45         floor1ArrivalTime = arrivalTime :
46         floor2ArrivalTime = arrivalTime;
47
48      cout << "(scheduler schedules next person for floor "
49         << floorNumber << " at time " << arrivalTime << ')'
50         << endl;
51
52   } // end function scheduleTime
53
54   // reschedule arrival on a floor
55   void Scheduler::delayTime( const Floor &floor )
56   {
57      int floorNumber = floor.getNumber();
58
59      int arrivalTime = ( floorNumber == Floor::FLOOR1 ) ?
60         ++floor1ArrivalTime : ++floor2ArrivalTime;
61
62      cout << "(scheduler delays next person for floor "
63         << floorNumber << " until time " << arrivalTime << ')'
64         << endl;
65
66   } // end function delayTime
67
68   // give time to scheduler
69   void Scheduler::processTime( int time )
70   {
71      currentClockTime = time;   // record time
72
73      // handle arrivals on floor 1
74      handleArrivals( floor1Ref, currentClockTime );
75
76      // handle arrivals on floor 2
77      handleArrivals( floor2Ref, currentClockTime );
78
79   } // end function processTime
80
81   // create new person and place it on specified floor
82   void Scheduler::createNewPerson( Floor &floor )
83   {
```

Fig. 7.30   **Scheduler** class implementation file. (Part 2 of 3.)

```
84      int destinationFloor =
85         floor.getNumber() == Floor::FLOOR1 ?
86            Floor::FLOOR2 : Floor::FLOOR1;
87
88      // create new person
89      Person *newPersonPtr = new Person( destinationFloor );
90
91      cout << "scheduler creates person "
92         << newPersonPtr->getID() << endl;
93
94      // place person on proper floor
95      newPersonPtr->stepOntoFloor( floor );
96
97      scheduleTime( floor ); // schedule next arrival
98
99   } // end function createNewPerson
100
101  // handle arrivals for a specified floor
102  void Scheduler::handleArrivals( Floor &floor, int time )
103  {
104      int floorNumber = floor.getNumber();
105
106      int arrivalTime = ( floorNumber == Floor::FLOOR1 ) ?
107         floor1ArrivalTime : floor2ArrivalTime;
108
109      if ( arrivalTime == time ) {
110
111         if ( floor.isOccupied() )         // if floor occupied,
112            delayTime( floor );            // delay arrival
113
114         else                              // otherwise,
115            createNewPerson( floor );      // create new person
116
117      } // end outer if
118
119  } // end function handleArrivals
```

Fig. 7.30   **Scheduler** class implementation file. (Part 3 of 3.)

In our simulation, the **building** updates the **scheduler** every second with the current time via the **scheduler**'s **processTime** member function (lines 69–79). The sequence diagram in Fig. 4.27 modeled the sequence of activities that occur in response to the **processTime** message, and our implementation reflects this model. When member function **processTime** is invoked, lines 74 and 77 call utility function **handle-Arrivals** (lines 102–119) for each floor. This utility function compares the current **time** (as provided by **building**) to the next scheduled arrival time for the given floor (line 109). If the current time matches the arrival time for this floor, and if a person currently occupies a floor (line 111), line 112 calls utility function **delayTime** to delay the next scheduled arrival by one second. If a person does not occupy the floor, the **scheduler** invokes utility function **createNewPerson** (line 115), which creates an object of class **Person** by using the **new** operator (line 89). The **scheduler** then sends this object of class **Person** the **stepOntoFloor** message (line 95). Once the person has stepped onto the floor, the **scheduler** calls utility function **scheduleTime** (line 97) to determine the next time the scheduler should create a person.

We have examined the implementation for all the classes that compose the controller portion of the simulation; we now examine the classes that compose the model portion of the simulation. Class **Bell** (Fig. 7.31), like class **Clock**, is not composed of other objects. Class **Bell**'s public interface consists of a constructor, a destructor and member function **ringBell**. The implementations of these functions (Fig. 7.32) output messages to the screen.

```cpp
1   // Fig. 7.31: bell.h
2   // Bell class definition.
3   #ifndef BELL_H
4   #define BELL_H
5
6   class Bell {
7
8   public:
9      Bell();                // constructor
10     ~Bell();               // destructor
11     void ringBell() const; // ring the bell
12
13  }; // end class Bell
14
15  #endif // BELL_H
```

Fig. 7.31   **Bell** class header file.

```cpp
1   // Fig. 7.32: bell.cpp
2   // Member-function definitions for class Bell.
3   #include <iostream>
4
5   using std::cout;
6   using std::endl;
7
8   #include "bell.h"  // Bell class definition
9
10  // constructor
11  Bell::Bell()
12  {
13     cout << "bell constructed" << endl;
14
15  } // end Bell constructor
16
17  // destructor
18  Bell::~Bell()
19  {
20     cout << "bell destructed" << endl;
21
22  } // end destructor ~Bell
23
```

Fig. 7.32   **Bell** class implementation file. (Part 1 of 2.)

```
24   // ring bell
25   void Bell::ringBell() const
26   {
27      cout << "elevator rings its bell" << endl;
28
29   } // end function ringBell
```

Fig. 7.32   Bell class implementation file. (Part 2 of 2.)

Class **Light** (Fig. 7.33–Fig. 7.34) exposes two member functions, a constructor and a destructor in its public interface. Member function **turnOn** turns on the light by setting data member **on** to **true** (Fig. 7.34, lines 29–38). Member function **turnOff** (Fig. 7.34, lines 41–50) turns off the light off by setting data member **on** to **false**.

```
1    // Fig. 7.33: light.h
2    // Light class definition.
3    #ifndef LIGHT_H
4    #define LIGHT_H
5
6    class Light {
7
8    public:
9       Light( int );      // constructor
10      ~Light();          // destructor
11
12      void turnOn();     // turns light on
13      void turnOff();    // turns light off
14
15   private:
16      bool on;                    // true if on; false if off
17      const int floorNumber;      // floor number that contains light
18
19   }; // end class Light
20
21   #endif // LIGHT_H
```

Fig. 7.33   Light class header file.

```
1    // Fig. 7.34: light.cpp
2    // Member-function definitions for class Light.
3    #include <iostream>
4
5    using std::cout;
6    using std::endl;
7
8    #include "light.h"  // Light class definition
9
10   // constructor
11   Light::Light( int number )
12      : on( false ),
13        floorNumber( number )
```

Fig. 7.34   Light class implementation file. (Part 1 of 2.)

```
14  {
15      cout << "floor " << floorNumber << " light constructed"
16          << endl;
17
18  } // end Light constructor
19
20  // destuctor
21  Light::~Light()
22  {
23      cout << "floor " << floorNumber
24          << " light destructed" << endl;
25
26  } // end destructor ~Light
27
28  // turn light on
29  void Light::turnOn()
30  {
31      if ( !on ) {  // if light not on, turn it on
32          on = true;
33          cout << "floor " << floorNumber
34              << " light turns on" << endl;
35
36      } // end if
37
38  } // end function turnOn
39
40  // turn light off
41  void Light::turnOff()
42  {
43      if ( on ) {  // if light is on, turn it off
44          on = false;
45          cout << "floor " << floorNumber
46              << " light turns off" << endl;
47
48      } // end if
49
50  } // end function turnOff
```

Fig. 7.34   **Light** class implementation file. (Part 2 of 2.)

Class **Door** (Fig. 7.35–Fig. 7.36) plays an important role in our elevator simulation. The **door** object signals the elevator passenger to leave and signals the person who waits on the floor to enter the **elevator**. Class **Door** member function **openDoor** (Fig. 7.36, lines 29–54) enables these events to occur. Member function **openDoor** takes four arguments. The first is a pointer to the object of class **Person** that occupies the **elevator**. The second is a pointer to the object of class **Person** that waits on the floor. The remaining arguments are references to objects of class **Floor** and class **Elevator**, respectively.

An **Elevator** is composed of several objects, one of which is a **Door**; to implement this composition, the header file for class **Elevator** must contain the line

```
#include "door.h"
```

Class **Door** uses a reference to an object of class **Elevator** (Fig. 7.35, line 17). To use this reference, class **Door** could include the header file for class **Elevator** with the line

```
1   // Fig. 7.35: door.h
2   // Door class definition.
3   #ifndef DOOR_H
4   #define DOOR_H
5
6   class Person;      // forward declaration
7   class Floor;       // forward declaration
8   class Elevator;    // forward declaration
9
10  class Door {
11
12  public:
13     Door();         // constructor
14     ~Door();        // destructor
15
16     void openDoor( Person * const,            // opens door
17        Person * const, Floor &, Elevator & );
18     void closeDoor( const Floor & );          // closes door
19
20  private:
21     bool open;      // open or closed
22
23  };
24
25  #endif // DOOR_H
```

Fig. 7.35   **Door** class header file.

```
#include "elevator.h"
```

Thus, the header file for class **Elevator** would include the header file for class **Door** and vice versa. Some preprocessors would not be able to resolve such **#include** directives and would produce a fatal error because of this *circular include problem.*

Rather than including the entire **Elevator** header file, we place only a forward declaration of class **Elevator** in the header file for class **Door** (Fig. 7.35, line 8). The forward declaration signifies that the header file contains pointers or references to objects of class **Elevator**, but that the definition of class **Elevator** lies outside the header file. Notice that we also make forward declarations to classes **Person** and **Floor** (lines 6–7), so we may use these classes in the prototype for member function **openDoor**.

Figure 7.36 lists the implementation file for class **Door**. In lines 9–11, we include the header files for classes **Person**, **Floor** and **Elevator**. These **#include** directives correspond to our forward declarations in the **Door** header file. The included header files contain the function prototypes needed to invoke the member functions of these classes.

```
1   // Fig. 7.36: door.cpp
2   // Member-function definitions for class Door.
3   #include <iostream>
4
5   using std::cout;
6   using std::endl;
```

Fig. 7.36   **Door** class implementation file. (Part 1 of 3.)

```
 7
 8    #include "door.h"        // Door class definition
 9    #include "person.h"      // Person class definition
10    #include "floor.h"       // Floor class definition
11    #include "elevator.h"    // Elevator class definition
12
13    // constructor
14    Door::Door()
15       : open( false )  // initialize open to false
16    {
17       cout << "door constructed" << endl;
18
19    } // end Door constructor
20
21    // destructor
22    Door::~Door()
23    {
24       cout << "door destructed" << endl;
25
26    } // end destructor ~Door
27
28    // open the door
29    void Door::openDoor( Person * const passengerPtr,
30       Person * const nextPassengerPtr, Floor &currentFloor,
31       Elevator &elevator )
32    {
33       if ( !open ) {  // if door is not open, open door
34          open = true;
35
36          cout << "elevator opens its door on floor "
37               << currentFloor.getNumber() << endl;
38
39          // if passenger is in elevator, tell person to leave
40          if ( passengerPtr != 0 ) {
41             passengerPtr->exitElevator( currentFloor, elevator );
42             delete passengerPtr; // passenger leaves simulation
43
44          } // end if
45
46          // if passenger waiting to enter elevator,
47          // tell passenger to enter
48          if ( nextPassengerPtr != 0 )
49             nextPassengerPtr->enterElevator(
50                elevator, currentFloor );
51
52       } // end outer if
53
54    } // end function openDoor
55
56    // close the door
57    void Door::closeDoor( const Floor &currentFloor )
58    {
59       if ( open ) {  // if door is open, close door
```

Fig. 7.36   **Door** class implementation file. (Part 2 of 3.)

```
60          open = false;
61          cout << "elevator closes its door on floor "
62               << currentFloor.getNumber() << endl;
63
64       } // end if
65
66   } // end function closeDoor
```

Fig. 7.36   **Door** class implementation file. (Part 3 of 3.)

When member function **openDoor** (lines 29–54) is called, it first determines whether the **door** already is open. If it is not open, the **door** determines whether the pointer to the person on the **elevator** (**passengerPtr**) is zero (line 40). If this pointer is nonzero, then a passenger is in the **elevator** and needs to exit. The **exitElevator** message (line 41) notifies the **person** to exit the **elevator**. The **door** deletes (via the **delete** operator) the **Person** object that was riding the **elevator** (line 42). This removes the person from the simulation.

Once the passenger has exited the **elevator**, the door determines whether the pointer to the **Person** object waiting on the floor (**nextPassengerPtr**) is not equal to zero (line 48). If so, a person is waiting to enter the **elevator**. The person enters the **elevator** by calling member function **enterElevator** of class **Person** (lines 49–50). **Door** member function **closeDoor** (lines 57–66) closes the **Door** if it is open.

Person objects use an object of class **ElevatorButton** (Fig. 7.37–Fig. 7.38) to start the **elevator** moving to the other floor. Member function **pressButton** (Fig. 7.38, lines 28–35) first sets the elevator button's **pressed** attribute to **true**, then sends the **prepareToLeave** message to the **elevator**. Member function **reset-Button** (lines 38–42) sets the **pressed** attribute to **false**.

```
1   // Fig. 7.37: elevatorButton.h
2   // ElevatorButton class definition.
3   #ifndef ELEVATORBUTTON_H
4   #define ELEVATORBUTTON_H
5
6   class Elevator;   // forward declaration
7
8   class ElevatorButton {
9
10  public:
11     ElevatorButton( Elevator & );   // constructor
12     ~ElevatorButton();              // destructor
13
14     void pressButton();            // press the button
15     void resetButton();            // reset the button
16
17  private:
18     bool pressed;                  // state of button
19
```

Fig. 7.37   **ElevatorButton** class header file. (Part 1 of 2.)

```
20      // reference to elevator containing this button
21      Elevator &elevatorRef;
22
23   }; // end class ElevatorButton
24
25   #endif // ELEVATORBUTTON_H
```

Fig. 7.37   **ElevatorButton** class header file. (Part 2 of 2.)

```
 1   // Fig. 7.38: elevatorButton.cpp:
 2   // Member-function definitions for class ElevatorButton.
 3   #include <iostream>
 4
 5   using std::cout;
 6   using std::endl;
 7
 8   #include "elevatorButton.h"  // ElevatorButton class definition
 9   #include "elevator.h"        // Elevator class definition
10
11   // constructor
12   ElevatorButton::ElevatorButton( Elevator &elevatorHandle )
13      : pressed( false ),
14        elevatorRef( elevatorHandle )
15   {
16      cout << "elevator button constructed" << endl;
17
18   } // end ElevatorButton constructor
19
20   // destructor
21   ElevatorButton::~ElevatorButton()
22   {
23      cout << "elevator button destructed" << endl;
24
25   } // end destructor ~ElevatorButton
26
27   // press button and signal elevator to prepare to leave floor
28   void ElevatorButton::pressButton()
29   {
30      pressed = true;
31      cout << "elevator button tells elevator to prepare to leave"
32           << endl;
33      elevatorRef.prepareToLeave( true );
34
35   } // end function pressButton
36
37   // reset button
38   void ElevatorButton::resetButton()
39   {
40      pressed = false;
41
42   } // end function resetButton
```

Fig. 7.38   **ElevatorButton** class implementation file.

Class **FloorButton** (Fig. 7.39–Fig. 7.40) exposes the same member functions as class **ElevatorButton** through its public interface. Member function **pressButton** summons the **elevator** via the **summonElevator** message. Member function **resetButton** resets a floor button.

```cpp
1   // Fig. 7.39: floorButton.h
2   // FloorButton class definition.
3   #ifndef FLOORBUTTON_H
4   #define FLOORBUTTON_H
5
6   class Elevator;   // forward declaration
7
8   class FloorButton {
9
10  public:
11      FloorButton( int, Elevator & );   // constructor
12      ~FloorButton();                    // destructor
13
14      void pressButton();   // press the button
15      void resetButton();   // reset the button
16
17  private:
18      const int floorNumber;   // button's floor number
19      bool pressed;            // button state
20
21      // reference to elevator used to summon
22      // elevator to floor
23      Elevator &elevatorRef;
24
25  }; // end class FloorButton
26
27  #endif // FLOORBUTTON_H
```

Fig. 7.39   FloorButton class header file.

```cpp
1   // Fig. 7.40: floorButton.cpp
2   // Member-function definitions for class FloorButton.
3   #include <iostream>
4
5   using std::cout;
6   using std::endl;
7
8   #include "floorButton.h"
9   #include "elevator.h"
10
11  // constructor
12  FloorButton::FloorButton( int floor, Elevator &elevatorHandle )
13      : floorNumber( floor ),
14        pressed( false ),
15        elevatorRef( elevatorHandle )
16  {
```

Fig. 7.40   FloorButton class implementation file. (Part 1 of 2.)

```
17      cout << "floor " << floorNumber << " button constructed"
18          << endl;
19
20   } // end FloorButton constructor
21
22   // destructor
23   FloorButton::~FloorButton()
24   {
25      cout << "floor " << floorNumber << " button destructed"
26          << endl;
27
28   } // end destructor ~FloorButton
29
30   // press the button
31   void FloorButton::pressButton()
32   {
33      pressed = true;
34      cout << "floor " << floorNumber
35          << " button summons elevator" << endl;
36
37      // call elevator to this floor
38      elevatorRef.summonElevator( floorNumber );
39
40   } // end function pressButton
41
42   // reset button
43   void FloorButton::resetButton()
44   {
45      pressed = false;
46
47   } // end function resetButton
```

Fig. 7.40   **FloorButton** class implementation file. (Part 2 of 2.)

The header file for class **Elevator** (Fig. 7.41) is the most complex in our simulation. Class **Elevator** exposes five member functions, a constructor and a destructor in its public interface. Member function **processTime** (line 21) allows the building to send the updated clock **time** to the **elevator**. Member function **summonElevator** (line 19) allows a **Person** object to send a message to the **elevator** to request its service. Member functions **passengerEnters** (line 22) and **passengerExits** (line 23) enable passengers to enter and exit the **elevator**. Member function **prepareToLeave** (line 20) enables the **elevator** to perform any necessary tasks (e.g., closing the door, turning off the light) before the **elevator** begins moving to another floor. We declare object **elevatorButton** (line 27) as **public**, so that an object of class **Person** can access the **elevatorButton** directly. A person does not interact with the bell or the door. Therefore, we declare the **door** (line 56) and **bell** (line 57) objects in the **private** section of the class definition.

Lines 32–35 declare utility functions. Class **Elevator** also declares three **private static const** constants (lines 39–41). We declare these constants as **static**, because they contain information that all objects of class **Elevator** share. Note that these constants are initialized at file scope in lines 14–16 of Fig. 7.42.

```
1   // Fig. 7.41: elevator.h
2   // Elevator class definition.
3   #ifndef ELEVATOR_H
4   #define ELEVATOR_H
5
6   #include "elevatorButton.h"
7   #include "door.h"
8   #include "bell.h"
9
10  class Floor;    // forward declaration
11  class Person;   // forward declaration
12
13  class Elevator {
14
15  public:
16     Elevator( Floor &, Floor & );   // constructor
17     ~Elevator();                     // destructor
18
19     void summonElevator( int );      // request to service floor
20     void prepareToLeave( bool );     // prepare to leave
21     void processTime( int );    // give current time to elevator
22     void passengerEnters( Person * const ); // board a passenger
23     void passengerExits();           // exit a passenger
24
25     // public object accessible to client code with
26     // access to Elevator object
27     ElevatorButton elevatorButton;
28
29  private:
30
31     // utility functions
32     void processPossibleArrival();
33     void processPossibleDeparture();
34     void arriveAtFloor( Floor & );
35     void move();
36
37     // static constants that represent time required to travel
38     // between floors and directions of the elevator
39     static const int ELEVATOR_TRAVEL_TIME;
40     static const int UP;
41     static const int DOWN;
42
43     // data members
44     int currentBuildingClockTime;   // current time
45     bool moving;                    // elevator state
46     int direction;                 // current direction
47     int currentFloor;              // current location
48     int arrivalTime;               // time to arrive at a floor
49     bool floor1NeedsService;       // floor1 service flag
50     bool floor2NeedsService;       // floor2 service flag
51
52     Floor &floor1Ref;              // reference to floor1
53     Floor &floor2Ref;              // reference to floor2
```

Fig. 7.41   **Elevator** class header file. (Part 1 of 2.)

```
54        Person *passengerPtr;              // pointer to passenger
55
56        Door door;                         // door object
57        Bell bell;                         // bell object
58
59    }; // end class Elevator
60
61    #endif // ELEVATOR_H
```

Fig. 7.41   **Elevator** class header file. (Part 2 of 2.)

Lines 44–50 of the **Elevator** header file contain additional private data members. Note that lines 52–53 declare reference handles to the objects of class **Floor**, whereas line 54 declares a pointer for the passenger object. We use a pointer for the passenger object, because this handle changes every time an object of class **Person** enters or leaves the **elevator**. We prefer reference handles for the objects of class **Floor**, because each handle always refers to the same floor.

Throughout this design process, we used the UML to model many of the activities and collaborations associated with class **Elevator** (see Fig. 3.31, Fig. 3.32 and Fig. 5.35). Figure 7.42 provides class **Elevator**'s implementation of these models. The **Elevator** constructor has an extensive member initializer list (lines 20–30). Recall from Fig. 7.37 that an object of class **ElevatorButton** requires a handle to an object of class **Elevator** as an argument to its constructor. We provide this handle in our member initialization list by dereferencing the **elevator**'s **this** pointer (line 20).[3]

The **Elevator** destructor (lines 37–42) uses the **delete** operator to reclaim memory from the **passengerPtr** data member. We include this line so our program can release memory if the elevator has a passenger at the time the simulation terminates. Although it is not necessary to release the memory in this way when the program ends, it is a good practice to explicitly delete any memory that the program creates with operator **new**. If the elevator has a passenger, data member **passengerPtr** points to an object of class **Person**. In this case, the memory for that object is reclaimed. If the elevator does not have a passenger, then **passengerPtr** has the value **0**. When a program uses the **delete** operator on a **0** (null) pointer, the program does not perform any action for that instruction and instead moves on to the next instruction; this is often referred to as a "no op" (no operation).

The **building** invokes member function **processTime** (lines 45–59) of class **Elevator**, passing as a parameter the current simulation **time**. This member function updates the **currentBuildingClockTime** data member with the current simulation **time** (line 47), then checks the value of the **moving** data member (line 49). If the **elevator** is moving, line 50 invokes its **processPossibleArrival** utility function. If the **elevator** is not moving, line 53 invokes utility function **processPossible-Departure**. If the **elevator** determines that it does not need to move, lines 55–57

---

3. Some compilers generate a warning on this line, because the **elevator** object has not yet been initialized. However, the address of the object has been determined by the compiler at this point, which is the only information that the **ElevatorButton** constructor requires for initialization.

output a message to the screen indicating that the elevator is at rest on the **current-Floor**.

Function **processPossibleArrival** (lines 62–89) determines whether the **elevator** should stop moving by comparing the **currentBuildingClockTime** to the calculated **arrivalTime** (line 65). If it is time for the **elevator** to arrive at a particular floor, the **elevator** updates **currentFloor** (lines 67–69) and **direction** (lines 71–72). Then lines 78–79 call utility function **arriveAtFloor** to perform the necessary tasks upon arrival (e.g., ring bell, open door).

Utility function **processPossibleDeparture** (lines 92–116) determines whether the **elevator** should move to another floor. Lines 95–102 decide which floor needs the **elevator**'s service. If the current floor needs service, the **elevator** calls its **arriveAtFloor** utility function for the current floor (lines 106–107). If the other floor needs service, the **elevator** calls its **prepareToLeave** utility function (line 114) and moves to the other floor.

```cpp
1   // Fig. 7.42: elevator.cpp
2   // Member-function definitions for class Elevator.
3   #include <iostream>
4
5   using std::cout;
6   using std::endl;
7
8   #include "elevator.h"   // Elevator class definition
9   #include "person.h"     // Person class definition
10  #include "floor.h"      // Floor class definition
11
12  // constants that represent time required to travel
13  // between floors and directions of the elevator
14  const int Elevator::ELEVATOR_TRAVEL_TIME = 5;
15  const int Elevator::UP = 0;
16  const int Elevator::DOWN = 1;
17
18  // constructor
19  Elevator::Elevator( Floor &firstFloor, Floor &secondFloor )
20     : elevatorButton( *this ),
21       currentBuildingClockTime( 0 ),
22       moving( false ),
23       direction( UP ),
24       currentFloor( Floor::FLOOR1 ),
25       arrivalTime( 0 ),
26       floor1NeedsService( false ),
27       floor2NeedsService( false ),
28       floor1Ref( firstFloor ),
29       floor2Ref( secondFloor ),
30       passengerPtr( 0 )
31  {
32     cout << "elevator constructed" << endl;
33
34  } // end Elevator constructor
```

Fig. 7.42   **Elevator** class implementation file. (Part 1 of 5.)

```
35
36   // destructor
37   Elevator::~Elevator()
38   {
39      delete passengerPtr;
40      cout << "elevator destructed" << endl;
41
42   } // end destructor ~Elevator
43
44   // give time to elevator
45   void Elevator::processTime( int time )
46   {
47      currentBuildingClockTime = time;
48
49      if ( moving )   // elevator is moving
50         processPossibleArrival();
51
52      else            // elevator is not moving
53         processPossibleDeparture();
54
55      if ( !moving )
56         cout << "elevator at rest on floor "
57              << currentFloor << endl;
58
59   } // end function processTime
60
61   // when elevator is moving, determine if it should stop
62   void Elevator::processPossibleArrival()
63   {
64      // if elevator arrives at destination floor
65      if ( currentBuildingClockTime == arrivalTime ) {
66
67         currentFloor =   // update current floor
68            ( currentFloor == Floor::FLOOR1 ?
69              Floor::FLOOR2 : Floor::FLOOR1 );
70
71         direction =      // update direction
72            ( currentFloor == Floor::FLOOR1 ? UP : DOWN );
73
74         cout << "elevator arrives on floor "
75              << currentFloor << endl;
76
77         // process arrival at currentFloor
78         arriveAtFloor( currentFloor == Floor::FLOOR1 ?
79            floor1Ref : floor2Ref );
80
81         return;
82
83      } // end if
84
85      // elevator still moving
86      cout << "elevator moving "
87           << ( direction == UP ? "up" : "down" ) << endl;
```

Fig. 7.42   **Elevator** class implementation file. (Part 2 of 5.)

```
88
89    } // end function processPossibleArrival
90
91    // determine whether elevator should move
92    void Elevator::processPossibleDeparture()
93    {
94       // this floor needs service?
95       bool currentFloorNeedsService =
96          currentFloor == Floor::FLOOR1 ?
97             floor1NeedsService : floor2NeedsService;
98
99       // other floor needs service?
100      bool otherFloorNeedsService =
101         currentFloor == Floor::FLOOR1 ?
102            floor2NeedsService : floor1NeedsService;
103
104      // service this floor (if needed)
105      if ( currentFloorNeedsService ) {
106         arriveAtFloor( currentFloor == Floor::FLOOR1 ?
107            floor1Ref : floor2Ref );
108
109         return;
110      }
111
112      // service other floor (if needed)
113      if ( otherFloorNeedsService )
114         prepareToLeave( true );
115
116   } // end function processPossibleDeparture
117
118   // arrive at a particular floor
119   void Elevator::arriveAtFloor( Floor& arrivalFloor )
120   {
121      moving = false;    // reset state
122
123      cout << "elevator resets its button" << endl;
124      elevatorButton.resetButton();
125
126      bell.ringBell();
127
128      // notify floor that elevator has arrived
129      Person *floorPersonPtr = arrivalFloor.elevatorArrived();
130
131      door.openDoor(
132         passengerPtr, floorPersonPtr, arrivalFloor, *this );
133
134      // this floor needs service?
135      bool currentFloorNeedsService =
136         currentFloor == Floor::FLOOR1 ?
137            floor1NeedsService : floor2NeedsService;
138
```

Fig. 7.42   **Elevator** class implementation file. (Part 3 of 5.)

```
139     // other floor needs service?
140     bool otherFloorNeedsService =
141        currentFloor == Floor::FLOOR1 ?
142           floor2NeedsService : floor1NeedsService;
143
144     // if this floor does not need service
145     // prepare to leave for the other floor
146     if ( !currentFloorNeedsService )
147        prepareToLeave( otherFloorNeedsService );
148
149     else   // otherwise, reset service flag
150        currentFloor == Floor::FLOOR1 ?
151           floor1NeedsService = false: floor2NeedsService = false;
152
153  } // end function arriveAtFloor
154
155  // request service from elevator
156  void Elevator::summonElevator( int floor )
157  {
158     // set appropriate servicing flag
159     floor == Floor::FLOOR1 ?
160        floor1NeedsService = true : floor2NeedsService = true;
161
162  } // end function summonElevator
163
164  // accept a passenger
165  void Elevator::passengerEnters( Person * const personPtr )
166  {
167     // board passenger
168     passengerPtr = personPtr;
169
170     cout << "person " << passengerPtr->getID()
171          << " enters elevator from floor "
172          << currentFloor << endl;
173
174  } // end function passengerEnters
175
176  // notify elevator that passenger is exiting
177  void Elevator::passengerExits()
178  {
179     passengerPtr = 0;
180
181  } // end function passengerExits
182
183  // prepare to leave a floor
184  void Elevator::prepareToLeave( bool leaving )
185  {
186     // get reference to current floor
187     Floor &thisFloor =
188        currentFloor == Floor::FLOOR1 ? floor1Ref : floor2Ref;
189
190     // notify floor that elevator may be leaving
191     thisFloor.elevatorLeaving();
```

Fig. 7.42   **Elevator** class implementation file. (Part 4 of 5.)

```
192
193    door.closeDoor( thisFloor );
194
195    if ( leaving )  // leave, if necessary
196       move();
197
198 } // end function prepareToLeave
199
200 // go to other floor
201 void Elevator::move()
202 {
203    moving = true;  // change state
204
205    // schedule arrival time
206    arrivalTime = currentBuildingClockTime +
207       ELEVATOR_TRAVEL_TIME;
208
209    cout << "elevator begins moving "
210         << ( direction == DOWN ? "down " : "up " )
211         << "to floor "
212         << ( direction == DOWN ? '1' : '2' )
213         << " (arrives at time " << arrivalTime << ')'
214         << endl;
215
216 } // end function move
```

Fig. 7.42   **Elevator** class implementation file. (Part 5 of 5.)

Utility function **arriveAtFloor** (lines 119–153) performs all tasks for the **elevator** upon arrival at a particular floor. This utility function first stops the **elevator** by setting the **moving** member variable to **false** (line 121), then resets the **elevatorButton** (line 124) and rings the **bell** (line 126). Line 129 declares a temporary pointer to an object of class **Person**, which stores a handle to a **Person** object that might be waiting on the floor. This pointer receives the return value of the call to the floor's **elevatorArrived** member function.

The **elevator** opens its **door** by calling member function **openDoor** of class **Door** passing as parameters handles to the current passenger, to the person waiting on the floor, to the floor on which the **elevator** has arrived and to the **elevator** itself (lines 131–132). The **elevator** again determines whether either floor needs service (lines 135–142). If the current floor does not need service, the **elevator** prepares to leave for the other floor (line 147). The **elevator** leaves if the other floor needs service; otherwise, the **elevator** resets the service flag for the current floor (lines 150–151).

Member function **summonElevator** (lines 156–162) allows other objects (i.e., the **FloorButton** objects) to request service from the **elevator**. When invoked, **summonElevator** takes a floor number as an argument and sets the appropriate service flag to **true** (lines 159–160).

Member function **passengerEnters** (lines 165–174) takes as an argument a pointer to an object of class **Person** and updates the **elevator**'s **passengerPtr** handle to point to the new passenger (line 168). Member function **passengerExits** (lines 177–181) sets the **passengerPtr** handle to zero, thus indicating that the passenger has left the **elevator**.

Member function **prepareToLeave** (184–198) takes an argument of type **bool** that indicates whether the **elevator** should leave the current floor. The **elevator** notifies the current floor of the **elevator**'s departure by sending the floor an **elevatorLeaving** message (line 191). The **elevator** closes its **door** (line 193), then determines whether it should leave the floor (line 195). If the **elevator** should move, it calls utility function **move** (line 196). Utility function **move** (lines 201–216) sets the **moving** data member to **true** (line 203), then calculates the arrival time for the **elevator** at its destination by adding the **static const** value **ELEVATOR_TRAVEL_TIME** to the current time (lines 206–207). Finally, the **elevator** outputs the direction of travel, the destination floor and the scheduled **arrivalTime** (lines 209–214).

Class **Floor** (Fig. 7.43) contains a mixture of ways to associate other objects with **Floor** objects. First, we use a reference as a handle to the **elevator** (line 42)—this is appropriate, because this handle always refers to the same **elevator**. We also have a pointer as a handle to a **Person** object (line 43)—this handle changes every time a person walks onto the floor or leaves the floor to enter the **elevator**. Class **Floor** defines composite objects, including a **public floorButton** object (line 38) and a **private light** object (line 44). We declare the **floorButton** as **public** so objects of class **Person** can access the **floorButton** object directly. A person generally does not have permission to interact with the light on a floor. Therefore, we declare the **light** object as **private**. Class **Floor** also defines the **static const** data members **FLOOR1** and **FLOOR2** (lines 33–34). We use these constants in place of actual floor numbers; we initialize these **static const** data members at file scope in the implementation file (Fig. 7.44, lines 14–15).

```
1   // Fig. 7.43: floor.h
2   // Floor class definition.
3   #ifndef FLOOR_H
4   #define FLOOR_H
5
6   #include "floorButton.h"
7   #include "light.h"
8
9   class Elevator;   // forward declaration
10  class Person;     // forward declaration
11
12  class Floor {
13
14  public:
15     Floor( int, Elevator & ); // constructor
16     ~Floor();                 // destructor
17     bool isOccupied() const;  // return true if floor occupied
18     int getNumber() const;    // return floor's number
19
20     // pass a handle to new person coming on floor
21     void personArrives( Person * const );
22
```

Fig. 7.43 **Floor** class header file. (Part 1 of 2.)

```
23         // notify floor that elevator has arrived
24         Person *elevatorArrived();
25
26         // notify floor that elevator is leaving
27         void elevatorLeaving();
28
29         // notify floor that person is leaving floor
30         void personBoardingElevator();
31
32         // static constants representing floor numbers
33         static const int FLOOR1;
34         static const int FLOOR2;
35
36         // public FloorButton object accessible to
37         // any client code with access to a Floor
38         FloorButton floorButton;
39
40      private:
41         const int floorNumber;     // the floor's number
42         Elevator &elevatorRef;     // reference to elevator
43         Person *occupantPtr;       // pointer to person on floor
44         Light light;               // light object
45
46      }; // end class Floor
47
48      #endif // FLOOR_H
```

Fig. 7.43   **Floor** class header file. (Part 2 of 2.)

Figure 7.44 contains the implementation for class **Floor**. The destructor (lines 30–35) reclaims memory of a **Person** object waiting on a floor at the time of simulation termination. Member function **isOccupied** (lines 38–42) returns a **bool** value that indicates whether a person is waiting on the floor. To determine whether a person is waiting, line 40 tests whether **occupantPtr** is zero. If **occupantPtr** is zero, then no person is waiting on the floor. Member function **getNumber** (lines 45–49) returns the value of the **floorNumber** member variable. Member function **personArrives** (lines 52–56) receives a pointer to the **Person** object walking onto the floor and assigns it to **private** data member **occupantPtr**.

```
1     // Fig. 7.44: floor.cpp
2     // Member-function definitions for class Floor.
3     #include <iostream>
4
5     using std::cout;
6     using std::endl;
7
8     #include "floor.h"       // Floor class definition
9     #include "person.h"      // Person class definition
10    #include "elevator.h"    // Elevator class definition
11    #include "door.h"        // Door class definition
```

Fig. 7.44   **Floor** class implementation file. (Part 1 of 3.)

```
12
13   // static constants that represent the floor numbers
14   const int Floor::FLOOR1 = 1;
15   const int Floor::FLOOR2 = 2;
16
17   // constructor
18   Floor::Floor( int number, Elevator &elevatorHandle )
19      : floorButton( number, elevatorHandle ),
20        floorNumber( number ),
21        elevatorRef( elevatorHandle ),
22        occupantPtr ( 0 ),
23        light( floorNumber )
24   {
25      cout << "floor " << floorNumber << " constructed" << endl;
26
27   } // end Floor constructor
28
29   // destructor
30   Floor::~Floor()
31   {
32      delete occupantPtr;
33      cout << "floor " << floorNumber << " destructed" << endl;
34
35   } // end destructor ~Floor
36
37   // determine whether floor is occupied
38   bool Floor::isOccupied() const
39   {
40      return ( occupantPtr != 0 );
41
42   } // end function isOccupied
43
44   // return this floor's number
45   int Floor::getNumber() const
46   {
47      return floorNumber;
48
49   } // end function getNumber
50
51   // person arrives on floor
52   void Floor::personArrives( Person * const personPtr )
53   {
54      occupantPtr = personPtr;
55
56   } // end function personArrives
57
58   // notify floor that elevator has arrived
59   Person *Floor::elevatorArrived()
60   {
61      cout << "floor " << floorNumber
62           << " resets its button" << endl;
63
64      floorButton.resetButton();
```

Fig. 7.44   **Floor** class implementation file. (Part 2 of 3.)

```
65          light.turnOn();
66
67          return occupantPtr;
68
69      } // end function elevatorArrived
70
71      // tell floor that elevator is leaving
72      void Floor::elevatorLeaving()
73      {
74          light.turnOff();
75
76      } // end function elevatorLeaving
77
78      // notifies floor that person is leaving
79      void Floor::personBoardingElevator()
80      {
81          occupantPtr = 0;   // person no longer on floor
82
83      } // end function personBoardingElevator
```

Fig. 7.44   **Floor** class implementation file. (Part 3 of 3.)

Member function **elevatorArrived** (lines 59–69) resets the **floorButton** object of the **floor** (line 64), turns on the **light** (line 65) and returns the **occupantPtr** handle (line 67). Member function **elevatorLeaving** (lines 72–76) turns off the **light**. Member function **personBoardingElevator** (lines 79–83) sets the **occupantPtr** to zero to indicate that the person left the floor and entered the elevator.

The elements of class **Person**'s header file (Fig. 7.45) should appear familiar at this point. Member function **getID** (line 14) returns the **Person** object's unique **ID**. The **stepOntoFloor**, **enterElevator** and **exitElevator** member functions (lines 16–18) form the remainder of the **Person**'s public interface. We use a **private static** class variable **personCount** (line 21) to store the number of objects of class **Person** that the **scheduler** has created. We also declare the **ID** and **destinationFloor** attributes (lines 22–23) as **private const** data members.

```
1   // Fig. 7.45: person.h
2   // Person class definition.
3   #ifndef PERSON_H
4   #define PERSON_H
5
6   class Floor;     // forward declaration
7   class Elevator;  // forward declaration
8
9   class Person {
10
11  public:
12      Person( int );       // constructor
13      ~Person();           // destructor
14      int getID() const;   // returns person's ID
15
```

Fig. 7.45   **Person** class header file. (Part 1 of 2.)

```
16        void stepOntoFloor( Floor & );
17        void enterElevator( Elevator &, Floor & );
18        void exitElevator( const Floor &, Elevator & ) const;
19
20     private:
21        static int personCount;      // total number of people
22        const int ID;                // person's unique ID #
23        const int destinationFloor;  // destination floor #
24
25     }; // end class Person
26
27     #endif // PERSON_H
```

Fig. 7.45   **Person** class header file. (Part 2 of 2.)

The implementation of class **Person** (Fig. 7.46) first initializes **static** member **personCount** to **0** (line 13). A **Person** object uses this member to generate an ID number. The constructor (lines 16–22) takes an **int** that represents the destination floor for the **Person** object and displays a message indicating that the person is being constructed. We use this value in our simulation outputs. The destructor (lines 25–29) displays a message to indicate that a **Person** object is being destroyed.

```
1     // Fig. 7.46: person.cpp
2     // Member-function definitions for class Person.
3     #include <iostream>
4
5     using std::cout;
6     using std::endl;
7
8     #include "person.h"     // Person class definition
9     #include "floor.h"      // Floor class definition
10    #include "elevator.h"   // Elevator class definition
11
12    // initialize static member personCount
13    int Person::personCount = 0;
14
15    // constructor
16    Person::Person( int destFloor )
17       : ID( ++personCount ),
18         destinationFloor( destFloor )
19    {
20       cout << "person " << ID << " constructed" << endl;
21
22    } // end Person constructor
23
24    // destructor
25    Person::~Person()
26    {
27       cout << "(person " << ID << " destructor invoked)" << endl;
28
29    } // end destructor ~Person
```

Fig. 7.46   **Person** class implementation file. (Part 1 of 2.)

```
30
31   // return person's ID number
32   int Person::getID() const
33   {
34      return ID;
35
36   } // end function getID
37
38   // person walks onto a floor
39   void Person::stepOntoFloor( Floor& floor )
40   {
41      // notify floor person is coming
42      cout << "person " << ID << " steps onto floor "
43           << floor.getNumber() << endl;
44      floor.personArrives( this );
45
46      // press button on floor
47      cout << "person " << ID
48           << " presses floor button on floor "
49           << floor.getNumber() << endl;
50      floor.floorButton.pressButton();
51
52   } // end function stepOntoFloor
53
54   // person enters elevator
55   void Person::enterElevator( Elevator &elevator, Floor &floor )
56   {
57      floor.personBoardingElevator();    // person leaves floor
58
59      elevator.passengerEnters( this ); // person enters elevator
60
61      // press button on elevator
62      cout << "person " << ID
63           << " presses elevator button" << endl;
64      elevator.elevatorButton.pressButton();
65
66   } // end function enterElevator
67
68   // person exits elevator
69   void Person::exitElevator(
70      const Floor &floor, Elevator &elevator ) const
71   {
72      cout << "person " << ID << " exits elevator on floor "
73           << floor.getNumber() << endl;
74      elevator.passengerExits();
75
76   } // end function exitElevator
```

Fig. 7.46   **Person** class implementation file. (Part 2 of 2.)

Member function **stepOntoFloor** (lines 39–52) first notifies the floor that the person has arrived, via a **personArrives** message (line 44). The person then calls **floorButton**'s **pressButton** method (line 50), which summons the **elevator**.

Member function **enterElevator** (line 55–66) first notifies the floor that the person is boarding the **elevator**, via the **personBoardingElevator** message (line 57). The person sends the **passengerEnters** message to notify the **elevator** that the person is entering (line 59). The person then sends the **pressButton** message to the **elevatorButton** object (line 64). This message notifies the **elevator** to move to the other floor. Member function **exitElevator** (lines 69–76) outputs a message, indicating that the person is exiting the **elevator**, then sends the **passengerExits** message to the **elevator** (line 74).

We have completed a working implementation of the elevator simulation from the design we created throughout the previous chapters. Chapter 8 does not contain a "Thinking About Objects" section. In Chapter 9, we discuss inheritance in C++, then show how our simulation can benefit from using this capability.

SUMMARY

- Keyword **const** prevents an identifier from being used to modify an object.
- The C++ compiler disallows non-**const** member function calls on **const** objects.
- An attempt by a **const** member function to modify an object of its class is a compiler error.
- A **const** member function is specified as **const** in both its declaration and its definition.
- A **const** member function may be overloaded with a non-**const** version. The compiler chooses which overloaded member function to use based on whether the object, reference or pointer used to invoke the function has been declared **const**.
- A **const** object must be initialized.
- Member initializers must be provided in the constructor of a class when that class contains **const** data members.
- Member objects are constructed in the order in which they are listed in the class definition and before their enclosing class objects are constructed.
- If a member initializer is not provided for a member object, the member object's default constructor is called.
- A **friend** function of a class is a function defined outside that class and that has the right to access all members of the class.
- Friendship declarations can be placed anywhere in the class definition.
- The **this** pointer is used implicitly to reference both the non-**static** member functions and non-**static** data members of an object.
- Each non-**static** member function has access to its object's address via the **this** keyword.
- The **this** pointer can be used explicitly.
- Operator **new** allocates space for an object, runs the object's constructor and returns a pointer of the correct type. The program terminates immediately if it is unable to allocate the requested memory. To free the space for this object, use operator **delete**.
- An array of objects can be allocated dynamically with **new** as in

```
int *ptr = new int[ 100 ];
```

which allocates an array of 100 integers and assigns the starting location of the array to **ptr**. The preceding array of integers is deleted with the statement

```
delete [] ptr;
```

- A **static** data member represents "class-wide" information (i.e., a property of the class, not an object). The declaration of a **static** member begins with keyword **static**.
- **static** data members have class scope.
- **static** members of a class can be accessed through an object of that class or through the class name using the scope resolution operator (if the member is **public**).
- A member function may be declared **static** if it does not access non-**static** class members. Unlike non-**static** member functions, a **static** member function has no **this** pointer, because **static** data members and **static** member functions exist independent of any objects of a class.
- Classes normally hide their implementation details from the clients of the classes. This is called information hiding.
- Stacks are known as last-in, first-out (LIFO) data structures—the last item pushed (inserted) on a stack is the first item popped (removed) from that stack.
- Describing the functionality of a class independent of its implementation is called data abstraction and C++ classes define so-called abstract data types (ADTs).
- C++ elevates the importance of data. The primary activity in C++ is creating new data types (i.e., classes) and expressing the interactions among objects of those data types.
- Abstract data types are ways of representing real-world notions to some satisfactory level of precision within a computer system.
- An abstract data type actually captures two notions—a data representation and the operations that are allowed on that data.
- C++ is an extensible language. Although the language is easy to extend with new types, the base language itself is not changeable.
- C++ is an intentionally sparse language that provides programmers with only the raw capabilities needed to build a broad range of systems. C++ is designed to minimize performance burdens.
- Items are returned from a queue in first-in, first-out (FIFO) order—the first item inserted in the queue is the first item removed from the queue.
- Container classes (also called collection classes) are designed to hold collections of objects. Container classes commonly provide services such as insertion, deletion, searching, sorting, testing an item for membership in the collection and the like.
- It is common to associate iterators with container classes. An iterator is an object that returns the next item of a collection (or performs some action on the next item of a collection).
- Providing clients of your class with a proxy class that knows only the public interface to your class enables the clients to use your class's services without giving the client access to your class's implementation details.
- The only private member of the proxy class is a pointer to an object of the class whose private data we would like to hide.
- When a class definition uses only a pointer or reference to another class, the class header file for that other class (which would ordinarily reveal the private data of that class) is not required to be included with **#include**. You can simply declare that other class as a data type with a forward class declaration before the type is used in the file.
- The implementation file containing the member functions for a proxy class is the only file that includes the header file for the class whose private data we would like to hide.
- The implementation file containing the member functions for the proxy class is provided to the client as a precompiled object code file along with the header file that includes the function prototypes of the services provided by the proxy class.

TERMINOLOGY

abstract data type (ADT)	forward class declaration
binary scope resolution operator (**::**)	**friend** class
cascading member-function calls	**friend** function
class scope	host object
composition	iterator
const member function	last-in, first-out (LIFO)
const object	member-access specifiers
constructor	member initializer
container	member object
copy constructor	member object constructor
data representation	**new** operator
default constructor	**new []** operator
default copy constructor	object-based programming
default destructor	operations in an ADT
delete operator	*pop* (stack operation)
delete[] operator	proxy class
dequeue (queue operation)	*push* (stack operation)
destructor	queue abstract data type
dynamic objects	stack abstract data type
enqueue (queue operation)	**static** data member
extensible language	**static** member function
first-in, first-out (FIFO)	**this** pointer

Terminology for Optional "Thinking About Objects" Section

circular include problem	forward reference

SELF-REVIEW EXERCISES

7.1 Fill in the blanks in each of the following:

a) _____ must be used to initialize constant members of a class.

b) A nonmember function must be declared as a _____ of a class to have access to that class's private data members.

c) The _____ operator dynamically allocates memory for an object of a specified type and returns a _____ to that type.

d) A constant object must be _____; it cannot be modified after it is created.

e) A _____ data member represents class-wide information.

f) An object's non-static member functions have access to a "self pointer" to the object called the _____ pointer.

g) The keyword _____ specifies that an object or variable is not modifiable after it is initialized.

h) If a member initializer is not provided for a member object of a class, the object's _____ is called.

i) A member function can be declared **static** if it does not access _____ class members.

j) Member objects are constructed _____ their enclosing class object.

k) The _____ operator reclaims memory previously allocated by **new**.

7.2 Find the errors in the following class and explain how to correct them:

```
class Example {
public:
```

```
   Example( int y = 10 )
      : data( y )
   {
      // empty body
   }

   int getIncrementedData() const
   {
      return ++data;
   }

   static int getCount()
   {
      cout << "Data is " << data << endl;
      return count;
   }
private:
   int data;
   static int count;

}; // end class Example
```

ANSWERS TO SELF-REVIEW EXERCISES

7.1   a) member initializer. b) **friend**. c) **new**, pointer. d) initialized. e) **static**. f) **this**.
g) **const**. h) default constructor. i) non-**static**. j) before. k) **delete**.

7.2   Error: The class definition for **Example** has two errors. The first occurs in function **get-
IncrementedData**. The function is declared **const**, but it modifies the object.
Correction: To correct the first error, remove the **const** keyword from the definition of
getIncrementedData.
Error: The second error occurs in function **getCount**. This function is declared **static**,
so it is not allowed to access any non-**static** member of the class.
Correction: To correct the second error, remove the output line from the **getCount** definition.

EXERCISES

7.3   Compare and contrast dynamic memory allocation and deallocation operators **new**, **new []**,
delete and **delete []**.

7.4   Explain the notion of friendship in C++. Explain the negative aspects of friendship as described in the text.

7.5   Can a correct **Time** class definition include both of the following constructors? If not, explain why not.

```
Time( int h = 0, int m = 0, int s = 0 );
Time();
```

7.6   What happens when a return type, even **void**, is specified for a constructor or destructor?

7.7   Modify class **Date** in Fig. 7.6 to have the following capabilities:
a) Output the date in multiple formats such as

```
DDD YYYY
MM/DD/YY
June 14, 1992
```

b) Use overloaded constructors to create **Date** objects initialized with dates of the formats
in part (a).

c) Create a **Date** constructor that reads the system date using the standard library functions of the **<ctime>** header and sets the **Date** members. (See your compiler's reference documentation or **www.cplusplus.com/ref/ctime/index.html** for information on the functions in header **<ctime>**).

In Chapter 8, we will be able to create operators for testing the equality of two dates and for comparing dates to determine whether one date is prior to, or after, another.

7.8   Create a **SavingsAccount** class. Use a **static** data member to contain the **annualInterestRate** for each of the savers. Each member of the class contains a **private** data member **savingsBalance** indicating the amount the saver currently has on deposit. Provide a **calculateMonthlyInterest** member function that calculates the monthly interest by multiplying the **balance** by **annualInterestRate** divided by 12; this interest should be added to **savingsBalance**. Provide a **static** member function **modifyInterestRate** that sets the **static annualInterestRate** to a new value. Write a driver program to test class **SavingsAccount**. Instantiate two different **savingsAccount** objects, **saver1** and **saver2**, with balances of $2000.00 and $3000.00, respectively. Set **annualInterestRate** to 3%. Then calculate the monthly interest, and print the new balances for each of the savers. Then set the **annualInterestRate** to 4%, and calculate the next month's interest and print the new balances for each of the savers.

7.9   Create class **IntegerSet** for which each object can hold integers in the range 0 through 100. A set is represented internally as an array of ones and zeros. Array element **a[i]** is 1 if integer i is in the set. Array element **a[j]** is 0 if integer j is not in the set. The default constructor initializes a set to the so-called "empty set," i.e., a set whose array representation contains all zeros.

Provide member functions for the common set operations. For example, provide a **unionOfSets** member function that creates a third set that is the set-theoretic union of two existing sets (i.e., an element of the third set's array is set to 1 if that element is 1 in either or both of the existing sets, and an element of the third set's array is set to 0 if that element is 0 in each of the existing sets).

Provide an **intersectionOfSets** member function which creates a third set which is the set-theoretic intersection of two existing sets (i.e., an element of the third set's array is set to 0 if that element is 0 in either or both of the existing sets, and an element of the third set's array is set to 1 if that element is 1 in each of the existing sets).

Provide an **insertElement** member function that inserts a new integer k into a set (by setting **a[k]** to 1). Provide a **deleteElement** member function that deletes integer m (by setting **a[m]** to 0).

Provide a **printSet** member function that prints a set as a list of numbers separated by spaces. Print only those elements that are present in the set (i.e., their position in the array has a value of 1). Print **---** for an empty set.

Provide an **isEqualTo** member function that determines whether two sets are equal.

Provide an additional constructor that receives an array of integers and the size of that array and uses the array to initialize a set object.

Now write a driver program to test your **IntegerSet** class. Instantiate several **IntegerSet** objects. Test that all your member functions work properly.

7.10   It would be perfectly reasonable for the **Time** class of Fig. 7.14–Fig. 7.15 to represent the time internally as the number of seconds since midnight rather than the three integer values **hour**, **minute** and **second**. Clients could use the same public methods and get the same results. Modify the **Time** class of Fig. 7.14 to implement the **Time** as the number of seconds since midnight and show that there is no visible change in functionality to the clients of the class.

Operator Overloading;
String and Array Objects

Objectives

- To understand how to redefine (overload) operators to work with new abstract data types (ADTs).
- To understand how to convert objects from one class to another class.
- To learn when to, and when not to, overload operators.
- To create **Array**, **String** and **Date** classes that demonstrate operator overloading.

The whole difference between construction and creation is exactly this: that a thing constructed can only be loved after it is constructed; but a thing created is loved before it exists.
Gilbert Keith Chesterton

The die is cast.
Julius Caesar

Our doctor would never really operate unless it was necessary. He was just that way. If he didn't need the money, he wouldn't lay a hand on you.
Herb Shriner

Outline

8.1   Introduction

8.2   Fundamentals of Operator Overloading

8.3   Restrictions on Operator Overloading

8.4   Operator Functions as Class Members vs. as `friend` Functions

8.5   Overloading Stream-Insertion and Stream-Extraction Operators

8.6   Overloading Unary Operators

8.7   Overloading Binary Operators

8.8   Case Study: `Array` Class

8.9   Converting between Types

8.10   Case Study: `String` Class

8.11   Overloading ++ and --

8.12   Case Study: A `Date` Class

8.13   Standard Library Classes `string` and `vector`

Summary • Terminology • Self-Review Exercises • Answers to Self-Review Exercises • Exercises

8.1 Introduction

In Chapter 6 and Chapter 7, we introduced the basics of C++ classes and the notion of abstract data types (ADTs). Manipulations on objects were accomplished by sending messages (in the form of member-function calls) to the objects. This function-call notation is cumbersome for certain kinds of classes (such as mathematical classes). Also, many common manipulations are performed with operators (e.g., input and output). We can use C++'s rich set of built-in operators to specify object common manipulations. This chapter shows how to enable C++'s operators to work with objects—a process called *operator overloading*. It is straightforward and natural to extend C++ with these new capabilities, but it does also require great care.

One example of an overloaded operator built into C++ is operator **<<**, which is used both as the stream-insertion operator and as the bitwise left-shift operator. Similarly, **>>** is also overloaded; it is used both as the stream-extraction operator and as the bitwise right-shift operator. [*Note:* The bitwise left-shift and bitwise right-shift operators are discussed in detail in Chapter 18.] Both of these operators are overloaded in the C++ class library. The C++ language itself overloads **+** and **-**. These operators perform differently, depending on their context in integer arithmetic, floating-point arithmetic and pointer arithmetic.

C++ enables the programmer to overload most operators to be sensitive to the context in which they are used—the compiler generates the appropriate code based on the context. Some operators are overloaded frequently, especially the assignment operator and various arithmetic operators such as **+** and **-**. The jobs performed by overloaded operators can also be performed by explicit function calls, but operator notation is often clearer and more familiar to programmers.

We discuss when to, and when not to, use operator overloading. We show how to overload operators, and we present several complete programs using overloaded operators. This chapter ends with examples of C++'s standard library classes **string** and **vector**, each of which provides many overloaded operators.

8.2 Fundamentals of Operator Overloading

C++ programming is a type-sensitive and type-focused process. Programmers can use built-in types and can define new types. The built-in types can be used with C++'s rich collection of operators. Operators provide programmers with a concise notation for expressing manipulations of objects of built-in types.

Programmers can use operators with user-defined types as well. Although C++ does not allow new operators to be created, it does allow most existing operators to be overloaded so that, when these operators are used with objects, the operators have meaning appropriate to those objects. This is one of C++'s most powerful features.

Software Engineering Observation 8.1

Operator overloading contributes to C++'s extensibility, one of the language's most appealing attributes.

Good Programming Practice 8.1

Use operator overloading when it makes a program clearer than accomplishing the same operations with explicit function calls.

Good Programming Practice 8.2

Overloaded operators should mimic the functionality of their built-in counterparts—for example, the + operator should be overloaded to perform addition, not subtraction. Avoid excessive or inconsistent use of operator overloading, as this can make a program cryptic and difficult to read.

Although operator overloading sounds like an exotic capability, most programmers implicitly use overloaded operators regularly. For example, the addition operator (**+**) operates quite differently on integers, floats and doubles. But addition nevertheless works fine with variables of type **int**, **float**, **double** and a number of other built-in types, because the addition operator (**+**) has been overloaded in the C++ language itself.

Operators are overloaded by writing a function definition (with a header and body) as you normally would, except that the function name now becomes the keyword **operator** followed by the symbol for the operator being overloaded. For example, the function name **operator+** would be used to overload the addition operator (**+**).

To use an operator on class objects, that operator *must* be overloaded—with two exceptions. The assignment operator (**=**) may be used with every class without explicit overloading. The default behavior of the assignment operator is a *memberwise assignment* of the data members of the class. We will soon see that such default memberwise assignment is dangerous for classes with pointer members; we will explicitly overload the assignment operator for such classes. The address operator (**&**) may also be used with objects of any class without overloading; it simply returns the address of the object in memory. The address operator can also be overloaded.

Overloading is especially appropriate for mathematical classes. These often require that a substantial set of operators be overloaded to ensure consistency with the way these mathematical classes are handled in the real world. For example, it would be unusual to overload only addition for a complex number class, because other arithmetic operators are also commonly used with complex numbers.

The point of operator overloading is to provide the same concise and familiar expressions for user-defined types that C++ provides with its rich collection of operators for built-in types. Operator overloading is not automatic, however; the programmer must write operator-overloading functions to perform the desired operations. Sometimes these functions are best made member functions; sometimes they are best as **friend** functions; occasionally they can be made non-member, non-**friend** functions. We discuss these issues throughout the chapter.

8.3 Restrictions on Operator Overloading

Most of C++'s operators can be overloaded. These are shown in Fig. 8.1. Figure 8.2 shows the operators that cannot be overloaded.

Common Programming Error 8.1

Attempting to overload a non-overloadable operator is a syntax error.

The precedence of an operator cannot be changed by overloading. This can lead to awkward situations in which an operator is overloaded in a manner for which its fixed precedence is inappropriate. However, parentheses can be used to force the order of evaluation of overloaded operators in an expression.

The associativity of an operator (i.e., whether the operator is applied right-to-left or left-to-right) cannot be changed by overloading.

It is not possible to change the "arity" of an operator (i.e., the number of operands an operator takes): Overloaded unary operators remain unary operators; overloaded binary

Operators that can be overloaded							
+	-	*	/	%	^	&	|
~	!	=	<	>	+=	-=	*=
/=	%=	^=	&=	|=	<<	>>	>>=
<<=	==	!=	<=	>=	&&	||	++
--	->*	,	->	[]	()	new	delete
new[]	delete[]						

Fig. 8.1   Operators that can be overloaded.

Operators that cannot be overloaded			
.	.*	::	?:

Fig. 8.2   Operators that cannot be overloaded.

operators remain binary operators. C++'s only ternary operator (**? :**) cannot be overloaded. Operators **&**, *****, **+** and **-** all have both unary and binary versions; these unary and binary versions can each be overloaded.

Common Programming Error 8.2

Attempting to change the "arity" of an operator via operator overloading is a syntax error.

It is not possible to create new operators; only existing operators can be overloaded. Unfortunately, this prevents the programmer from using popular notations like the ****** operator used in some other programming languages for exponentiation.

Common Programming Error 8.3

Attempting to create new operators via operator overloading is a syntax error.

The meaning of how an operator works on objects of built-in types cannot be changed by operator overloading. The programmer cannot, for example, change the meaning of how **+** adds two integers. Operator overloading works only with objects of user-defined types or with a mixture of an object of a user-defined type and an object of a built-in type.

Common Programming Error 8.4

Attempting to modify how an operator works with objects of built-in types is a syntax error.

Software Engineering Observation 8.2

At least one argument of an operator function must be an object or reference of a user-defined type. This prevents programmers from changing how operators work on built-in types.

Overloading an assignment operator and an addition operator to allow statements like

```
object2 = object2 + object1;
```

does not imply that the **+=** operator is also overloaded to allow statements such as

```
object2 += object1;
```

Such behavior can be achieved only by explicitly overloading operator **+=** for that class.

Common Programming Error 8.5

Assuming that overloading an operator such as **+** *overloads related operators such as* **+=** *or that overloading* **==** *overloads a related operator like* **!=** *can lead to errors. Operators can be overloaded only explicitly; there is no implicit overloading.*

8.4 Operator Functions as Class Members vs. as `friend` Functions

Operator functions can be member functions or non-member functions; non-member functions are often made friends for performance reasons. Member functions use the **this** pointer implicitly to obtain one of their class object arguments (the left operand for binary operators). Parameters for both operands of a binary operator must be explicitly listed in a non-member function call.

When overloading **()**, **[]**, **->** or any of the assignment operators, the operator over-loading function must be declared as a class member. For the other operators, the operator overloading functions can be non-member functions.

Whether an operator function is implemented as a member function or as a non-member function, the operator is still used the same way in expressions. So which implementation is best?

When an operator function is implemented as a member function, the leftmost (or only) operand must be an object (or a reference to an object) of the operator's class. If the left operand must be an object of a different class or a built-in type, this operator function must be implemented as a non-member function (as we will do in Section 8.5 when over-loading **<<** and **>>** as the stream-insertion and stream-extraction operators, respectively). A non-member operator function needs to be a **friend** if that function must access **private** or **protected** members of that class directly.

The overloaded **<<** operator must have a left operand of type **ostream &** (such as the object **cout** in the expression **cout << classObject**), so it must be a non-member function. Similarly, the overloaded **>>** operator must have a left operand of type **istream &** (such as the object **cin** in the expression **cin >> classObject**), so it, too, must be a non-member function. Also, each of these overloaded operator functions may require access to the **private** data members of the class object being output or input, so these overloaded operator functions can be made **friend** functions of the class for performance reasons.

Performance Tip 8.1

*It is possible to overload an operator as a non-member, non-friend function, but such a function requiring access to a class's **private** or **protected** data would need to use set or get functions provided in that class's **public** interface. The overhead of calling these functions could cause poor performance, so these functions can be inlined to improve performance.*

Operator member functions of a specific class are called only when the left operand of a binary operator is specifically an object of that class, or when the single operand of a unary operator is an object of that class.

Another reason why one might choose a non-member function to overload an operator is to enable the operator to be commutative. For example, suppose we have an object, **number**, of type **long int**, and an object **bigInteger1**, of class **HugeInteger** (a class in which integers may be arbitrarily large rather than being limited by the machine word size of the underlying hardware; class **HugeInteger** is developed in the chapter exercises). The addition operator (**+**) produces a temporary **HugeInteger** object as the sum of a **HugeInteger** and a **long int** (as in the expression **bigInteger1 + number**), or as the sum of a **long int** and a **HugeInteger** (as in the expression **number + bigInteger1**). Thus, we require the addition operator to be commutative (exactly as it is normally). The problem is that the class object must appear on the left of the addition operator if that operator is to be overloaded as a member function. So, we over-load the operator as a non-member **friend** function to allow the **HugeInteger** to appear on the right of the addition. Function **operator+**, which deals with the **HugeInteger** on the left, can still be a member function. Remember that a non-member function need not necessarily be a **friend** if appropriate *set* and *get* functions exist in the class's **public** interface.

8.5 Overloading Stream-Insertion and Stream-Extraction Operators

C++ is able to input and output the built-in data types using the stream-extraction operator **>>** and the stream-insertion operator **<<**. These operators are overloaded (in the class libraries provided with C++ compilers) to process each built-in data type, including pointers and C-like **char *** strings. The stream-insertion and stream-extraction operators also can be overloaded to perform input and output for user-defined types. Figure 8.3 demonstrates overloading the stream-extraction and stream-insertion operators to handle data of a user-defined telephone number class called **PhoneNumber**. This program assumes telephone numbers are input correctly.

```
1   // Fig. 8.3: fig08_03.cpp
2   // Overloading the stream-insertion and
3   // stream-extraction operators.
4   #include <iostream>
5
6   using std::cout;
7   using std::cin;
8   using std::endl;
9   using std::ostream;
10  using std::istream;
11
12  #include <iomanip>
13
14  using std::setw;
15
16  // PhoneNumber class definition
17  class PhoneNumber {
18     friend ostream &operator<<( ostream&, const PhoneNumber & );
19     friend istream &operator>>( istream&, PhoneNumber & );
20
21  private:
22     char areaCode[ 4 ];   // 3-digit area code and null
23     char exchange[ 4 ];   // 3-digit exchange and null
24     char line[ 5 ];       // 4-digit line and null
25
26  }; // end class PhoneNumber
27
28  // overloaded stream-insertion operator; cannot be
29  // a member function if we would like to invoke it with
30  // cout << somePhoneNumber;
31  ostream &operator<<( ostream &output, const PhoneNumber &num )
32  {
33     output << "(" << num.areaCode << ") "
34            << num.exchange << "-" << num.line;
35
36     return output;       // enables cout << a << b << c;
37
38  } // end function operator<<
39
```

Fig. 8.3   Overloaded stream-insertion and stream-extraction operators. (Part 1 of 2.)

```
40   // overloaded stream-extraction operator; cannot be
41   // a member function if we would like to invoke it with
42   // cin >> somePhoneNumber;
43   istream &operator>>( istream &input, PhoneNumber &num )
44   {
45      input.ignore();                    // skip (
46      input >> setw( 4 ) >> num.areaCode; // input area code
47      input.ignore( 2 );                 // skip ) and space
48      input >> setw( 4 ) >> num.exchange; // input exchange
49      input.ignore();                    // skip dash (-)
50      input >> setw( 5 ) >> num.line;    // input line
51
52      return input;     // enables cin >> a >> b >> c;
53
54   } // end function operator>>
55
56   int main()
57   {
58      PhoneNumber phone; // create object phone
59
60      cout << "Enter phone number in the form (123) 456-7890:\n";
61
62      // cin >> phone invokes operator>> by implicitly issuing
63      // the non-member function call operator>>( cin, phone )
64      cin >> phone;
65
66      cout << "The phone number entered was: " ;
67
68      // cout << phone invokes operator<< by implicitly issuing
69      // the non-member function call operator<<( cout, phone )
70      cout << phone << endl;
71
72      return 0;
73
74   } // end main
```

```
Enter phone number in the form (123) 456-7890:
(800) 555-1212
The phone number entered was: (800) 555-1212
```

Fig. 8.3   Overloaded stream-insertion and stream-extraction operators. (Part 2 of 2.)

The stream-extraction operator function **operator>>** (lines 43–54) takes **istream** reference **input** and **PhoneNumber** reference **num** as arguments and returns an **istream** reference. Operator function **operator>>** inputs phone numbers of the form

```
(800) 555-1212
```

into objects of class **PhoneNumber**. When the compiler sees the expression

```
cin >> phone
```

in line 64, the compiler generates the non-member function call

```
operator>>( cin, phone );
```

When this call executes, reference parameter **input** becomes an alias for **cin** and reference parameter **num** becomes an alias for **phone** (line 43). The operator function reads as strings the three parts of the telephone number into the **areaCode** (line 46), **exchange** (line 48) and **line** (line 50) members of the referenced **PhoneNumber** object (parameter **num** in the operator function and object **phone** in **main**). Stream manipulator **setw** limits the number of characters read into each character array. Remember that, when used with **cin**, **setw** restricts the number of characters read to one less than its argument (i.e., **setw(4)** allows three characters to be read and saves one position for a terminating null character). The parentheses, space and dash characters are skipped by calling **istream** member function **ignore** (lines 45, 47 and 49), which discards the specified number of characters in the input stream (one character by default). Function **operator>>** returns **istream** reference **input** (i.e., **cin**). This enables input operations on **PhoneNumber** objects to be cascaded with input operations on other **PhoneNumber** objects or on objects of other data types. For example, a program can input two **PhoneNumber** objects in one statement as follows:

```
cin >> phone1 >> phone2;
```

First, the expression **cin >> phone1** executes by making the non-member function call

```
operator>>( cin, phone1 );
```

This call would then return a reference to **cin** as the value of **cin >> phone1**, so the remaining portion of the expression would be interpreted simply as **cin >> phone2**. This would execute by making the non-member function call

```
operator>>( cin, phone2 );
```

The stream-insertion operator function (lines 31–38) takes an **ostream** reference (**output**) and a **const PhoneNumber** reference (**num**) as arguments and returns an **ostream** reference. Function **operator<<** displays objects of type **PhoneNumber**. When the compiler sees the expression

```
cout << phone
```

in line 70, the compiler generates the non-member function call

```
operator<<( cout, phone );
```

Function **operator<<** displays the parts of the telephone number as strings, because they are stored in string format.

Note that the functions **operator>>** and **operator<<** are declared in **class PhoneNumber** as non-member, **friend** functions (lines 18–19). These operators must be non-members because the object of class **PhoneNumber** appears in each case as the right operand of the operator; the class operand must appear on the left of the operator to enables us to overload that operator as a member function of that class. Overloaded input and output operators are declared as friends if they need to access non-**public** class members directly for performance reasons. Also note that the **PhoneNumber** reference in function **operator<<**'s parameter list (line 31) is **const** (because the **PhoneNumber** will simply be output) and the **PhoneNumber** reference in function **operator>>**'s parameter list (line 43) is non-**const** (because the **PhoneNumber** object must be modified to store the input telephone number in the object).

Software Engineering Observation 8.3

New input/output capabilities for user-defined types can be added to C++ without modifying C++'s standard input/output library classes. This is another example of the extensibility of the C++ programming language.

8.6 Overloading Unary Operators

A unary operator for a class can be overloaded as a non-**static** member function with no arguments or as a non-member function with one argument; that argument must be either an object of the class or a reference to an object of the class. Member functions that implement overloaded operators must be non-**static** so that they can access the non-**static** data in each object of the class. Remember that **static** member functions only can access **static** data members of the class.

Later in this chapter, we will overload unary operator **!** to test whether an object of the **String** class we create (Section 8.10) is empty and return a **bool** result. When overloading a unary operator such as **!** as a non-**static** member function with no arguments, if **s** is a **String** class object or a reference to a **String** class object, when the compiler sees the expression **!s**, the compiler generates the call **s.operator!()**. The operand **s** is the class object for which the **String** class member function **operator!** is being invoked. The function is declared in the class definition as follows:

```
class String {
public:
   bool operator!() const;
   ...
};
```

A unary operator such as **!** may be overloaded as a non-member function with one argument in two different ways—either with an argument that is an object (this requires a copy of the object, so the side effects of the function are not applied to the original object), or with an argument that is a reference to an object (no copy of the original object is made, so all side effects of this function are applied to the original object). If **s** is a **String** class object (or a reference to a **String** class object), then **!s** is treated as if the call **operator!(s)** had been written, invoking the non-member **friend** function of class **String** declared as follows:

```
class String {
   friend bool operator!( const String & );
   ...
};
```

8.7 Overloading Binary Operators

A binary operator can be overloaded as a non-**static** member function with one argument or as a non-member function with two arguments (one of those arguments must be either a class object or a reference to a class object).

Later in this chapter, we will overload **+=** to indicate concatenation of two string objects. When overloading binary operator **+=** as a non-**static** member function of a **String** class with one argument, if **y** and **z** are **String**-class objects, then **y += z** is treated as if **y.operator+=(z)** had been written, invoking the **operator+=** member function declared below

```
class String {
public:
   const String &operator+=( const String & );
   ...
};
```

If binary operator **+=** is to be overloaded as a non-member function, it must take two arguments—one of which must be a class object or a reference to a class object. If **y** and **z** are **String**-class objects or references to **String**-class objects, then **y += z** is treated as if the call **operator+=(y, z)** had been written in the program, invoking non-member friend function **operator+=** declared as follows:

```
class String {
   friend const String &operator+=(
      String &, const String & );
   ...
};
```

8.8 Case Study: **Array** Class

Array notation in C++ is just an alternative to pointers, so arrays have great potential for errors. For example, a program can easily "walk off" either end of an array, because C++ does not check whether subscripts fall outside the range of an array. Arrays of size n must number their elements 0, ..., $n - 1$; alternate subscript ranges are not allowed. An entire non-**char** array cannot be input or output at once; each array element must be read or written individually. Two arrays cannot be meaningfully compared with equality operators or relational operators (because the array names are simply pointers to where the arrays begin in memory and, of course, two arrays will always be at different memory locations). When an array is passed to a general-purpose function designed to handle arrays of any size, the size of the array must be passed as an additional argument. One array cannot be assigned to another with the assignment operator(s) (because array names are **const** pointers and a constant pointer cannot be used on the left side of an assignment operator). These and other capabilities certainly seem like "naturals" for dealing with arrays, but C++ does not provide such capabilities. However, C++ does provide the means to implement such array capabilities through the mechanisms of class development and operator overloading.

In this example, we create an array class that performs range checking to ensure that subscripts remain within the bounds of the array. The class allows one array object to be assigned to another with the assignment operator. Objects of this array class know their size, so the size does not need to be passed separately as an argument when passing an array to a function. Entire arrays can be input or output with the stream-extraction and stream-insertion operators, respectively. Array comparisons can be made with the equality operators **==** and **!=**.

This example will sharpen your appreciation of data abstraction. You will probably want to suggest many enhancements to this array class. Class development is an interesting, creative and intellectually challenging activity—always with the goal of "crafting valuable classes."

The program of Fig. 8.4–Fig. 8.6 demonstrates class **Array** and its overloaded operators. First we walk through the driver program in **main** (Fig. 8.6). Then we consider the class definition (Fig. 8.4) and each of the class's member-function and **friend**-function definitions (Fig. 8.5).

```
1   // Fig. 8.4: array1.h
2   // Array class for storing arrays of integers.
3   #ifndef ARRAY1_H
4   #define ARRAY1_H
5
6   #include <iostream>
7
8   using std::ostream;
9   using std::istream;
10
11  class Array {
12     friend ostream &operator<<( ostream &, const Array & );
13     friend istream &operator>>( istream &, Array & );
14
15  public:
16     Array( int = 10 );         // default constructor
17     Array( const Array & );    // copy constructor
18     ~Array();                  // destructor
19     int getSize() const;       // return size
20
21     // assignment operator
22     const Array &operator=( const Array & );
23
24     // equality operator
25     bool operator==( const Array & ) const;
26
27     // inequality operator; returns opposite of == operator
28     bool operator!=( const Array &right ) const
29     {
30        return ! ( *this == right ); // invokes Array::operator==
31
32     } // end function operator!=
33
34     // subscript operator for non-const objects returns lvalue
35     int &operator[]( int );
36
37     // subscript operator for const objects returns rvalue
38     const int &operator[]( int ) const;
39
40  private:
41     int size; // array size
42     int *ptr; // pointer to first element of array
43
44  }; // end class Array
45
46  #endif
```

Fig. 8.4 **Array** class definition with overloaded operators.

```cpp
1    // Fig 8.5: array1.cpp
2    // Member function definitions for class Array
3    #include <iostream>
4
5    using std::cout;
6    using std::cin;
7    using std::endl;
8
9    #include <iomanip>
10
11   using std::setw;
12
13   #include <new>          // C++ standard "new" operator
14
15   #include <cstdlib>      // exit function prototype
16
17   #include "array1.h"     // Array class definition
18
19   // default constructor for class Array (default size 10)
20   Array::Array( int arraySize )
21   {
22      // validate arraySize
23      size = ( arraySize > 0 ? arraySize : 10 );
24
25      ptr = new int[ size ]; // create space for array
26
27      for ( int i = 0; i < size; i++ )
28         ptr[ i ] = 0;                 // initialize array
29
30   } // end Array default constructor
31
32   // copy constructor for class Array;
33   // must receive a reference to prevent infinite recursion
34   Array::Array( const Array &arrayToCopy )
35      : size( arrayToCopy.size )
36   {
37      ptr = new int[ size ]; // create space for array
38
39      for ( int i = 0; i < size; i++ )
40         ptr[ i ] = arrayToCopy.ptr[ i ];  // copy into object
41
42   } // end Array copy constructor
43
44   // destructor for class Array
45   Array::~Array()
46   {
47      delete [] ptr;  // reclaim array space
48
49   } // end destructor
50
51   // return size of array
52   int Array::getSize() const
53   {
```

Fig. 8.5   **Array** class member- and **friend**-function definitions. (Part 1 of 4.)

```
54       return size;
55
56    } // end function getSize
57
58    // overloaded assignment operator;
59    // const return avoids: ( a1 = a2 ) = a3
60    const Array &Array::operator=( const Array &right )
61    {
62       if ( &right != this ) {   // check for self-assignment
63
64          // for arrays of different sizes, deallocate original
65          // left-side array, then allocate new left-side array
66          if ( size != right.size ) {
67             delete [] ptr;          // reclaim space
68             size = right.size;      // resize this object
69             ptr = new int[ size ];  // create space for array copy
70
71          } // end inner if
72
73          for ( int i = 0; i < size; i++ )
74             ptr[ i ] = right.ptr[ i ];   // copy array into object
75
76       } // end outer if
77
78       return *this;    // enables x = y = z, for example
79
80    } // end function operator=
81
82    // determine if two arrays are equal and
83    // return true, otherwise return false
84    bool Array::operator==( const Array &right ) const
85    {
86       if ( size != right.size )
87          return false;    // arrays of different sizes
88
89       for ( int i = 0; i < size; i++ )
90
91          if ( ptr[ i ] != right.ptr[ i ] )
92             return false; // arrays are not equal
93
94       return true;        // arrays are equal
95
96    } // end function operator==
97
98    // overloaded subscript operator for non-const Arrays
99    // reference return creates an lvalue
100   int &Array::operator[]( int subscript )
101   {
102      // check for subscript out of range error
103      if ( subscript < 0 || subscript >= size ) {
104         cout << "\nError: Subscript " << subscript
105            << " out of range" << endl;
106
```

Fig. 8.5   **Array** class member- and **friend**-function definitions. (Part 2 of 4.)

```
107        exit( 1 );   // terminate program; subscript out of range
108
109     } // end if
110
111     return ptr[ subscript ]; // reference return
112
113 } // end function operator[]
114
115 // overloaded subscript operator for const Arrays
116 // const reference return creates an rvalue
117 const int &Array::operator[]( int subscript ) const
118 {
119     // check for subscript out of range error
120     if ( subscript < 0 || subscript >= size ) {
121         cout << "\nError: Subscript " << subscript
122             << " out of range" << endl;
123
124         exit( 1 );   // terminate program; subscript out of range
125
126     } // end if
127
128     return ptr[ subscript ]; // const reference return
129
130 } // end function operator[]
131
132 // overloaded input operator for class Array;
133 // inputs values for entire array
134 istream &operator>>( istream &input, Array &a )
135 {
136     for ( int i = 0; i < a.size; i++ )
137         input >> a.ptr[ i ];
138
139     return input;    // enables cin >> x >> y;
140
141 } // end function
142
143 // overloaded output operator for class Array
144 ostream &operator<<( ostream &output, const Array &a )
145 {
146     int i;
147
148     // output private ptr-based array
149     for ( i = 0; i < a.size; i++ ) {
150         output << setw( 12 ) << a.ptr[ i ];
151
152         if ( ( i + 1 ) % 4 == 0 ) // 4 numbers per row of output
153             output << endl;
154
155     } // end for
156
157     if ( i % 4 != 0 )   // end last line of output
158         output << endl;
159
```

Fig. 8.5   **Array** class member- and **friend**-function definitions. (Part 3 of 4.)

```
160       return output;    // enables cout << x << y;
161
162  } // end function operator<<
```

Fig. 8.5   **Array** class member- and **friend**-function definitions. (Part 4 of 4.)

```
1    // Fig. 8.6: fig08_06.cpp
2    // Array class test program.
3    #include <iostream>
4
5    using std::cout;
6    using std::cin;
7    using std::endl;
8
9    #include "array1.h"
10
11   int main()
12   {
13       Array integers1( 7 );  // seven-element Array
14       Array integers2;       // 10-element Array by default
15
16       // print integers1 size and contents
17       cout << "Size of array integers1 is "
18            << integers1.getSize()
19            << "\nArray after initialization:\n" << integers1;
20
21       // print integers2 size and contents
22       cout << "\nSize of array integers2 is "
23            << integers2.getSize()
24            << "\nArray after initialization:\n" << integers2;
25
26       // input and print integers1 and integers2
27       cout << "\nInput 17 integers:\n";
28       cin >> integers1 >> integers2;
29
30       cout << "\nAfter input, the arrays contain:\n"
31            << "integers1:\n" << integers1
32            << "integers2:\n" << integers2;
33
34       // use overloaded inequality (!=) operator
35       cout << "\nEvaluating: integers1 != integers2\n";
36
37       if ( integers1 != integers2 )
38          cout << "integers1 and integers2 are not equal\n";
39
40       // create array integers3 using integers1 as an
41       // initializer; print size and contents
42       Array integers3( integers1 );  // calls copy constructor
43
44       cout << "\nSize of array integers3 is "
45            << integers3.getSize()
46            << "\nArray after initialization:\n" << integers3;
```

Fig. 8.6   **Array** class test program. (Part 1 of 3.)

```
47
48      // use overloaded assignment (=) operator
49      cout << "\nAssigning integers2 to integers1:\n";
50      integers1 = integers2;  // note target is smaller
51
52      cout << "integers1:\n" << integers1
53          << "integers2:\n" << integers2;
54
55      // use overloaded equality (==) operator
56      cout << "\nEvaluating: integers1 == integers2\n";
57
58      if ( integers1 == integers2 )
59          cout << "integers1 and integers2 are equal\n";
60
61      // use overloaded subscript operator to create rvalue
62      cout << "\nintegers1[5] is " << integers1[ 5 ];
63
64      // use overloaded subscript operator to create lvalue
65      cout << "\n\nAssigning 1000 to integers1[5]\n";
66      integers1[ 5 ] = 1000;
67      cout << "integers1:\n" << integers1;
68
69      // attempt to use out-of-range subscript
70      cout << "\nAttempt to assign 1000 to integers1[15]" << endl;
71      integers1[ 15 ] = 1000;  // ERROR: out of range
72
73      return 0;
74
75  } // end main
```

```
Size of array integers1 is 7
Array after initialization:
            0           0           0           0
            0           0           0

Size of array integers2 is 10
Array after initialization:
            0           0           0           0
            0           0           0           0
            0           0

Input 17 integers:
1 2 3 4 5 6 7 8 9 10 11 12 13 14 15 16 17

After input, the arrays contain:
integers1:
            1           2           3           4
            5           6           7
integers2:
            8           9          10          11
           12          13          14          15
           16          17
```
(continued next page)

Fig. 8.6   **Array** class test program. (Part 2 of 3.)

```
Evaluating: integers1 != integers2
integers1 and integers2 are not equal

Size of array integers3 is 7
Array after initialization:
            1               2               3               4
            5               6               7

Assigning integers2 to integers1:
integers1:
            8               9              10              11
           12              13              14              15
           16              17
integers2:
            8               9              10              11
           12              13              14              15
           16              17

Evaluating: integers1 == integers2
integers1 and integers2 are equal

integers1[5] is 13

Assigning 1000 to integers1[5]
integers1:
            8               9              10              11
           12            1000              14              15
           16              17

Attempt to assign 1000 to integers1[15]

Error: Subscript 15 out of range
```

Fig. 8.6   **Array** class test program. (Part 3 of 3.)

The program begins by instantiating two objects of class **Array**—**integers1** (line 13) with seven elements, and **integers2** (line 14) with the default **Array** size—10 elements (specified by the **Array** default constructor's prototype in Fig. 8.4, line 16). Lines 17–19 use member function **getSize** to determine the size of **integers1** and output **integers1**, using the **Array** overloaded stream-insertion operator. The sample output confirms that the array elements were initialized correctly to zeros by the constructor. Next, lines 22–24 output the size of array **integers2** and output **integers2**, using the **Array** overloaded stream-insertion operator.

Line 27 prompts the user to input 17 integers. Line 28 uses the **Array** overloaded stream-extraction operator to read these values into both arrays. The first seven values are stored in **integers1** and the remaining 10 values are stored in **integers2**. Lines 30–32 output the two arrays with the **Array** stream-insertion operator to confirm that the input was performed correctly.

Line 37 tests the overloaded inequality operator by evaluating the condition

```
integers1 != integers2
```

The program output shows that the arrays indeed are not equal.

Line 42 instantiates a third **Array** called **integers3** and initializes it with a copy of **Array integers1**. This invokes the **Array** *copy constructor* to copy the elements of **integers1** into **integers3**. We discuss the details of the copy constructor shortly.

Lines 44–46 output the size of **integers3** and output **integers3**, using the **Array** overloaded stream-insertion operator to confirm that the array elements were initialized correctly by the copy constructor.

Next, line 50 tests the overloaded assignment operator (=) by assigning **integers2** to **integers1**. Lines 52–53 print both **Array** objects to confirm that the assignment was successful. Note that **integers1** originally held 7 integers and was resized to hold a copy of the 10 elements in **integers2**. As we will see, the overloaded assignment operator performs this resizing operation in a manner that is transparent to the client code.

Next, line 58 uses the overloaded equality operator (==) to confirm that objects **integers1** and **integers2** are indeed identical after the assignment.

Line 62 uses the overloaded subscript operator to refer to **integers1[5]**—an in-range element of **integers1**. This subscripted name is used as an *rvalue* to print the value stored in **integers1[5]**. Line 66 uses **integers1[5]** as an *lvalue* on the left side of an assignment statement to assign a new value, **1000**, to element **5** of **integers1**. We will see that **operator[]** returns a reference to use as the *lvalue* after the operator confirms that **5** is a valid subscript for **integers1**.

Line 71 attempts to assign the value **1000** to **integers1[15]**—an out-of-range element. In this example, **operator[]** determines that the subscript is out of range, prints a message and terminates the program.

Interestingly, the array subscript operator **[]** is not restricted for use only with arrays; it can be used to select elements from other kinds of container classes, such as linked lists, strings and dictionaries. Also, when defining **operator[]** functions, subscripts no longer have to be integers—characters, strings, floats or even objects of user-defined classes also could be used.

Now that we have seen how this program operates, let us walk through the class header (Fig. 8.4). As we refer to each member function in the header, we discuss that function's implementation in Fig. 8.5. Lines 41–42 represent the **private** data members of class **Array**. Each **Array** object consists of a **size** member indicating the number of elements in the array and an **int** pointer—**ptr**—that points to the dynamically allocated array of integers managed by **Array** object.

Lines 12–13 of the header file declare the overloaded stream-insertion operator and the overloaded stream-extraction operator to be friends of class **Array**. When the compiler sees an expression like **cout << arrayObject**, it invokes non-member function **operator<<** with the call

```
operator<<( cout, arrayObject )
```

When the compiler sees an expression like **cin >> arrayObject**, it invokes non-member function **operator>>** with the call

```
operator>>( cin, arrayObject )
```

We note again that these stream-insertion and stream-extraction operator functions cannot be members of class **Array**, because the **Array** object is always mentioned on the right side of a stream-insertion operator and a stream-extraction operator. If these operator functions were to be members of class **Array**, the following awkward statements would be used to output and input an **Array**:

```
arrayObject << cout;
arrayObject >> cin;
```

Such statements would be confusing to most C++ programmers, who are familiar with **cout** and **cin** appearing as the left operands of **<<** and **>>**, respectively.

Function **operator<<** (defined in Fig. 8.5, lines 144–162) prints the number of elements indicated by **size** from the integer array to which **ptr** points. Function **operator>>** (defined in Fig. 8.5, lines 134–141) inputs directly into the array to which **ptr** points. Each of these operator functions returns an appropriate reference to enable cascaded output or input statements, respectively. Note that each of these functions has access to an **Array**'s **private** data because these functions are declared as friends of class **Array**. Also, note that class **Array**'s **getSize** and **operator[]** functions could be used by **operator<<** and **operator>>**, in which case these operator functions would not need to be friends of class **Array**. However, the additional function calls might increase execution-time overhead.

Line 16 of the header file declares the default constructor for the class and specifies a default size of 10 elements. When the compiler sees a declaration like line 13 in Fig. 8.6, it invokes class **Array**'s default constructor (remember that the default constructor in this example actually receives a single **int** argument that has a default value of 10). The default constructor (defined in Fig. 8.5, lines 20–30) validates and assigns the argument to data member **size**, uses **new** to obtain the memory for the internal representation of this array and assigns the pointer returned by **new** to data member **ptr**. Then the constructor uses a **for** loop to initialize all the elements of the array to zero. It is possible to have an **Array** class that does not initialize its members if, for example, these members are to be read at some later time; but this is considered to be a poor programming practice. **Array**s, and objects in general, should be maintained at all times in a properly initialized and consistent state.

Line 17 of the header file declares a *copy constructor* (defined in Fig. 8.5, lines 34–42) that initializes an **Array** by making a copy of an existing **Array** object. Such copying must be done carefully to avoid the pitfall of leaving both **Array** objects pointing to the same dynamically allocated memory. This is exactly the problem that would occur with default memberwise assignment, if the compiler is allowed to define a default copy constructor for this class. Copy constructors are invoked whenever a copy of an object is needed, such as in passing an object by value to a function, returning an object by value from a function or initializing an object with a copy of another object of the same class. The copy constructor is called in a declaration when an object of class **Array** is instantiated and initialized with another object of class **Array**, as in the declaration on line 42 of Fig. 8.6.

Common Programming Error 8.6

Note that the copy constructor must receive its argument pass-by-reference, not pass-by-value. Otherwise, the copy constructor call results in infinite recursion (a fatal logic error) because, for pass-by-value, a copy of the object passed to the copy constructor must be made. Remember that any time a copy of an object is required, the class's copy constructor is called. If the copy constructor receives its argument by value, the copy constructor would call itself recursively to make a copy of its argument!

The copy constructor for **Array** (Fig. 8.5, line 35) uses a member initializer to copy the **size** of the initializer array into data member **size**, uses **new** (line 37) to obtain the memory for the internal representation of this array and assigns the pointer returned by **new** to data member **ptr**.[1] Then the copy constructor uses a **for** loop to copy all the elements of the initializer array into the new array object.

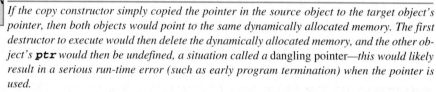

Common Programming Error 8.7

If the copy constructor simply copied the pointer in the source object to the target object's pointer, then both objects would point to the same dynamically allocated memory. The first destructor to execute would then delete the dynamically allocated memory, and the other object's **ptr** *would then be undefined, a situation called a* dangling pointer—*this would likely result in a serious run-time error (such as early program termination) when the pointer is used.*

Line 18 of the header file declares the destructor for the class (defined in Fig. 8.5, lines 45–49). The destructor is invoked when an object of class **Array** goes out of scope. The destructor uses **delete []** to reclaim the memory allocated dynamically by **new** in the constructor. Line 19 declares function **getSize** (defined in Fig. 8.5, lines 52–56) that returns the size of the array.

Line 22 of the header file declares the overloaded assignment operator function for the class. When the compiler sees the expression **integers1 = integers2** in line 50 of Fig. 8.6, the compiler invokes member function **operator=** with the call

```
integers1.operator=( integers2 )
```

The implementation of member function **operator=** (Fig. 8.5, lines 60–80) tests for *self-assignment* (line 62) in which an object of class **Array** is being assigned to itself. When **this** is equal to the address of the **right** operand, a self-assignment is being attempted, so the assignment is skipped (i.e., the object already is itself; in a moment we will see why self-assignment is dangerous). If it is not a self-assignment, then the member function determines whether the sizes of the two arrays are identical (line 66); in that case, the original array of integers in the left-side **Array** object is not reallocated. Otherwise, **operator=** uses **delete** (line 67) to reclaim the memory originally allocated to the target array, copies the **size** of the source array to the **size** of the target array (line 68), uses **new** to allocate memory for the target array and places the pointer returned by **new** into the array's **ptr** member.[2] Then the **for** loop at lines 73–74 copies the array elements from the source array to the target array. Regardless of whether this is a self-assignment, the member function returns the current object (i.e., ***this** at line 78) as a constant reference; this enables cascaded **Array** assignments such as **x = y = z**. If self-assignment occurs, and function **operator=** did not test for this case, **operator=** would delete the dynamic memory associated with the **Array** object before the assignment is complete. This would leave **ptr** pointing to memory that has been deallocated, which can lead to fatal runtime errors.

Software Engineering Observation 8.4

A constructor, a destructor, an overloaded assignment operator and a copy constructor are usually provided as a group for any class that uses dynamically allocated memory.

1. Note that **new** could fail to obtain the needed memory. We deal with **new** failures in Chapter 13, Exception Handling.
2. Once again, **new** could fail. We discuss **new** failures in Chapter 13.

Common Programming Error 8.8

Not providing an overloaded assignment operator and a copy constructor for a class when objects of that class contain pointers to dynamically allocated memory is a logic error.

Software Engineering Observation 8.5

*It is possible to prevent one object of a class from being assigned to another. This is done by declaring the assignment operator as a **private** member of the class.*

Software Engineering Observation 8.6

*It is possible to prevent class objects from being copied; to do this, simply make both the overloaded assignment operator and the copy constructor of that class **private**.*

Line 25 of the header file declares the overloaded equality operator (**==**) for the class. When the compiler sees the expression **integers1 == integers2** in line 58 of Fig. 8.6, the compiler invokes member function **operator==** with the call

```
integers1.operator==( integers2 )
```

Member function **operator==** (defined in Fig. 8.5, lines 84–96) immediately returns **false** if the **size** members of the arrays are not equal. Otherwise, **operator==** compares each pair of elements. If they are all equal, the function returns **true**. The first pair of elements to differ causes the function to return **false** immediately.

Lines 28–32 of the header file define the overloaded inequality operator (**!=**) for the class. Member function **operator!=** uses the overloaded **operator==** function to determine whether one **Array** is equal to another, then returns the opposite of that result. Writing **operator!=** in this manner enables the programmer to reuse **operator==**, which reduces the amount of code that must be written in the class. Also, note that the full function definition for **operator!=** is in the **Array** header file. This allows the compiler to inline the definition of **operator!=** to eliminate the overhead of the extra function call.

Lines 35 and 38 of the header file declare two overloaded subscript operators (defined in Fig. 8.5 at lines 100–113 and 117–130, respectively). When the compiler sees the expression **integers1[5]** (Fig. 8.6, line 62), the compiler invokes the appropriate overloaded **operator[]** member function by generating the call

```
integers1.operator[]( 5 )
```

The compiler creates a call to the **const** version of **operator[]** (Fig. 8.5, lines 117–130) when the subscript operator is used on a **const Array** object. For example, if **const** object **z** is instantiated with the statement

```
const Array z( 5 );
```

then the **const** version of **operator[]** is required to execute a statement such as

```
cout << z[ 3 ] << endl;
```

Remember, a program can invoke only the **const** member functions of a **const** object.

Each definition of **operator[]** determines whether the subscript it receives as an argument is in range. If it is not, each function prints an error message and terminates the program with a call to function **exit** (header **<cstdlib>**).[3] If the subscript is in range, the appropriate element of the array is returned as a reference so that it may be used as an *lvalue* (for example, on the left side of an assignment statement) for the non-**const** version of **c**, or an *rvalue* for the **const** version of **operator[]**.

8.9 Converting between Types

Most programs process information of a variety of types. Sometimes all the operations "stay within a type." For example, adding an integer to an integer produces an integer (as long as the result is not too large to be represented as an integer). It is often necessary, however, to convert data of one type to data of another type. This can happen in assignments, in calculations, in passing values to functions and in returning values from functions. The compiler knows how to perform certain conversions among built-in types. Programmers can use cast operators to force conversions among built-in types.

But what about user-defined types? The compiler cannot know in advance how to convert among user-defined types, and between user-defined types and built-in types, so the programmer must specify this. Such conversions can be performed with *conversion constructors*—single-argument constructors that turn objects of other types (including built-in types) into objects of a particular class. In Section 8.10, we use a conversion constructor to convert ordinary **char *** strings into **String** class objects.

A *conversion operator* (also called a *cast operator*) can be used to convert an object of one class into an object of another class or into an object of a built-in type. Such a conversion operator must be a non-**static** member function; this kind of conversion operator cannot be a **friend** function. The function prototype

```
A::operator char *() const;
```

declares an overloaded cast operator function for converting an object of user-defined type **A** into a temporary **char *** object. An overloaded *cast operator function* does not specify a return type—the return type is the type to which the object is being converted. If **s** is a class object, when the compiler sees the expression **(char *) s**, the compiler generates the call **s.operator char *()**. The operand **s** is the class object **s** for which the member function **operator char *** is being invoked.

Overloaded cast-operator functions can be defined for converting objects of user-defined types into built-in types or into objects of other user-defined types. The prototypes

```
A::operator int() const;
A::operator OtherClass() const;
```

declare overloaded cast operator functions that can convert an object of user-defined type **A** into an integer or into an object of user-defined type **OtherClass**, respectively.

One of the nice features of cast operators and conversion constructors is that, when necessary, the compiler can call these functions implicitly to create temporary objects. For example, if an object **s** of a user-defined **String** class appears in a program at a location where an ordinary **char *** is expected, such as

```
cout << s;
```

---

3. Note that it is more appropriate when a subscript is out of range to "throw an exception" indicating the out-of-range subscript. Then the program can "catch" that exception, process it and possibly continue execution. See Chapter 13 for more information on exceptions.

the compiler can call the overloaded cast-operator function **operator char *** to convert the object into a **char *** and use the resulting **char *** in the expression. With this cast operator provided for our **String** class, the stream-insertion operator does not have to be overloaded to output a **String** using **cout**.

Common Programming Error 8.9

Unfortunately, the compiler might use implicit conversions in cases that you do not expect, resulting in ambiguous expressions that generate compilation errors or resulting in execution-time logic errors.

8.10 Case Study: **String** Class

As a capstone exercise to our study of overloading, we will build our own **String** class to handle the creation and manipulation of strings (Fig. 8.7–Fig. 8.9). The C++ standard library provides a similar, more robust class **string** as well. We present an example of the standard class **string** in Section 8.13 and study class **string** in detail in Chapter 15. For now, we will make extensive use of operator overloading to craft our own class **String**.

First, we present the header file for class **String**. We discuss the private data used to represent **String** objects. Then we walk through the class's public interface, discussing each of the services the class provides. We discuss the member-function definitions for the class **String**. For each of the overloaded operator functions, we show the code in the driver program that invokes the overloaded operator function, and we provide an explanation of how the overloaded operator function works.

Now let us walk through the **String** class header file in Fig. 8.7. We begin with the internal representation of a **String**. Lines 63–64 declare the **private** data members of the class. Our **String** class has a **length** field, which represents the number of characters in the string, not including the null character at the end of the character string, and has a pointer **sPtr** that points to the dynamically allocated memory representing the character string.

```
1   // Fig. 8.7: string1.h
2   // String class definition.
3   #ifndef STRING1_H
4   #define STRING1_H
5
6   #include <iostream>
7
8   using std::ostream;
9   using std::istream;
10
11  class String {
12     friend ostream &operator<<( ostream &, const String & );
13     friend istream &operator>>( istream &, String & );
14
15  public:
16     String( const char * = "" ); // conversion/default ctor
17     String( const String & );    // copy constructor
```

Fig. 8.7   **String** class definition with operator overloading. (Part 1 of 2.)

```
18      ~String();                          // destructor
19
20      const String &operator=( const String & );   // assignment
21      const String &operator+=( const String & );  // concatenation
22
23      bool operator!() const;                       // is String empty?
24      bool operator==( const String & ) const;  // test s1 == s2
25      bool operator<( const String & ) const;   // test s1 < s2
26
27      // test s1 != s2
28      bool operator!=( const String & right ) const
29      {
30         return !( *this == right );
31
32      } // end function operator!=
33
34      // test s1 > s2
35      bool operator>( const String &right ) const
36      {
37         return right < *this;
38
39      } // end function operator>
40
41      // test s1 <= s2
42      bool operator<=( const String &right ) const
43      {
44         return !( right < *this );
45
46      } // end function operator <=
47
48      // test s1 >= s2
49      bool operator>=( const String &right ) const
50      {
51         return !( *this < right );
52
53      } // end function operator>=
54
55      char &operator[]( int );              // subscript operator
56      const char &operator[]( int ) const; // subscript operator
57
58      String operator()( int, int );        // return a substring
59
60      int getLength() const;                // return string length
61   private:
62      int length;  // string length
63      char *sPtr;  // pointer to start of string
64
65      void setString( const char * );  // utility function
66
67   }; // end class String
68
69   #endif
70
```

Fig. 8.7   String class definition with operator overloading. (Part 2 of 2.)

```
1    // Fig. 8.8: string1.cpp
2    // Member function definitions for class String.
3    #include <iostream>
4
5    using std::cout;
6    using std::endl;
7
8    #include <iomanip>
9
10   using std::setw;
11
12   #include <new>            // C++ standard "new" operator
13
14   #include <cstring>        // strcpy and strcat prototypes
15   #include <cstdlib>        // exit prototype
16
17   #include "string1.h"  // String class definition
18
19   // conversion constructor converts char * to String
20   String::String( const char *s )
21      : length( strlen( s ) )
22   {
23      cout << "Conversion constructor: " << s << '\n';
24      setString( s );          // call utility function
25
26   } // end String conversion constructor
27
28   // copy constructor
29   String::String( const String &copy )
30      : length( copy.length )
31   {
32      cout << "Copy constructor: " << copy.sPtr << '\n';
33      setString( copy.sPtr ); // call utility function
34
35   } // end String copy constructor
36
37   // destructor
38   String::~String()
39   {
40      cout << "Destructor: " << sPtr << '\n';
41      delete [] sPtr;          // reclaim string
42
43   } // end ~String destructor
44
45   // overloaded = operator; avoids self assignment
46   const String &String::operator=( const String &right )
47   {
48      cout << "operator= called\n";
49
50      if ( &right != this ) {        // avoid self assignment
51         delete [] sPtr;             // prevents memory leak
52         length = right.length;      // new String length
```

Fig. 8.8   **String** class member-function and **friend**-function definitions. (Part 1 of 4.)

```
53            setString( right.sPtr );        // call utility function
54        }
55
56        else
57           cout << "Attempted assignment of a String to itself\n";
58
59        return *this;    // enables cascaded assignments
60
61   } // end function operator=
62
63   // concatenate right operand to this object and
64   // store in this object.
65   const String &String::operator+=( const String &right )
66   {
67      size_t newLength = length + right.length;    // new length
68      char *tempPtr = new char[ newLength + 1 ];   // create memory
69
70      strcpy( tempPtr, sPtr );                      // copy sPtr
71      strcpy( tempPtr + length, right.sPtr );       // copy right.sPtr
72
73      delete [] sPtr;        // reclaim old space
74      sPtr = tempPtr;        // assign new array to sPtr
75      length = newLength;    // assign new length to length
76
77      return *this;    // enables cascaded calls
78
79   } // end function operator+=
80
81   // is this String empty?
82   bool String::operator!() const
83   {
84      return length == 0;
85
86   } // end function operator!
87
88   // is this String equal to right String?
89   bool String::operator==( const String &right ) const
90   {
91      return strcmp( sPtr, right.sPtr ) == 0;
92
93   } // end function operator==
94
95   // is this String less than right String?
96   bool String::operator<( const String &right ) const
97   {
98      return strcmp( sPtr, right.sPtr ) < 0;
99
100  } // end function operator<
101
102  // return reference to character in String as lvalue
103  char &String::operator[]( int subscript )
104  {
```

Fig. 8.8   **String** class member-function and **friend**-function definitions. (Part 2 of 4.)

```
105    // test for subscript out of range
106    if ( subscript < 0 || subscript >= length ) {
107       cout << "Error: Subscript " << subscript
108          << " out of range" << endl;
109
110       exit( 1 );  // terminate program
111    }
112
113    return sPtr[ subscript ];  // creates lvalue
114
115 } // end function operator[]
116
117 // return reference to character in String as rvalue
118 const char &String::operator[]( int subscript ) const
119 {
120    // test for subscript out of range
121    if ( subscript < 0 || subscript >= length ) {
122       cout << "Error: Subscript " << subscript
123          << " out of range" << endl;
124
125       exit( 1 );  // terminate program
126    }
127
128    return sPtr[ subscript ];  // creates rvalue
129
130 } // end function operator[]
131
132 // return a substring beginning at index and
133 // of length subLength
134 String String::operator()( int index, int subLength )
135 {
136    // if index is out of range or substring length < 0,
137    // return an empty String object
138    if ( index < 0 || index >= length || subLength < 0 )
139       return "";  // converted to a String object automatically
140
141    // determine length of substring
142    int len;
143
144    if ( ( subLength == 0 ) || ( index + subLength > length ) )
145       len = length - index;
146    else
147       len = subLength;
148
149    // allocate temporary array for substring and
150    // terminating null character
151    char *tempPtr = new char[ len + 1 ];
152
153    // copy substring into char array and terminate string
154    strncpy( tempPtr, &sPtr[ index ], len );
155    tempPtr[ len ] = '\0';
156
```

Fig. 8.8   **String** class member-function and **friend**-function definitions. (Part 3 of 4.)

```
157    // create temporary String object containing the substring
158    String tempString( tempPtr );
159    delete [] tempPtr;   // delete temporary array
160
161    return tempString;   // return copy of the temporary String
162
163 } // end function operator()
164
165 // return string length
166 int String::getLength() const
167 {
168    return length;
169
170 } // end function getLenth
171
172 // utility function called by constructors and operator=
173 void String::setString( const char *string2 )
174 {
175    sPtr = new char[ length + 1 ]; // allocate memory
176    strcpy( sPtr, string2 );        // copy literal to object
177
178 } // end function setString
179
180 // overloaded output operator
181 ostream &operator<<( ostream &output, const String &s )
182 {
183    output << s.sPtr;
184
185    return output;    // enables cascading
186
187 } // end function operator<<
188
189 // overloaded input operator
190 istream &operator>>( istream &input, String &s )
191 {
192    char temp[ 100 ];    // buffer to store input
193
194    input >> setw( 100 ) >> temp;
195    s = temp;          // use String class assignment operator
196
197    return input;     // enables cascading
198
199 } // end function operator>>
```

Fig. 8.8   **String** class member-function and **friend**-function definitions. (Part 4 of 4.)

```
1    // Fig. 8.9: fig08_09.cpp
2    // String class test program.
3    #include <iostream>
4
```

Fig. 8.9   **String** class test program. (Part 1 of 4.)

```
 5    using std::cout;
 6    using std::endl;
 7
 8    #include "string1.h"
 9
10    int main()
11    {
12       String s1( "happy" );
13       String s2( " birthday" );
14       String s3;
15
16       // test overloaded equality and relational operators
17       cout << "s1 is \"" << s1 << "\"; s2 is \"" << s2
18            << "\"; s3 is \"" << s3 << '\"'
19            << "\n\nThe results of comparing s2 and s1:"
20            << "\ns2 == s1 yields "
21            << ( s2 == s1 ? "true" : "false" )
22            << "\ns2 != s1 yields "
23            << ( s2 != s1 ? "true" : "false" )
24            << "\ns2 >  s1 yields "
25            << ( s2 > s1 ? "true" : "false" )
26            << "\ns2 <  s1 yields "
27            << ( s2 < s1 ? "true" : "false" )
28            << "\ns2 >= s1 yields "
29            << ( s2 >= s1 ? "true" : "false" )
30            << "\ns2 <= s1 yields "
31            << ( s2 <= s1 ? "true" : "false" );
32
33       // test overloaded String empty (!) operator
34       cout << "\n\nTesting !s3:\n";
35
36       if ( !s3 ) {
37          cout << "s3 is empty; assigning s1 to s3;\n";
38          s3 = s1;  // test overloaded assignment
39          cout << "s3 is \"" << s3 << "\"";
40       }
41
42       // test overloaded String concatenation operator
43       cout << "\n\ns1 += s2 yields s1 = ";
44       s1 += s2;  // test overloaded concatenation
45       cout << s1;
46
47       // test conversion constructor
48       cout << "\n\ns1 += \" to you\" yields\n";
49       s1 += " to you";  // test conversion constructor
50       cout << "s1 = " << s1 << "\n\n";
51
52       // test overloaded function call operator () for substring
53       cout << "The substring of s1 starting at\n"
54            << "location 0 for 14 characters, s1(0, 14), is:\n"
55            << s1( 0, 14 ) << "\n\n";
56
```

Fig. 8.9   **String** class test program. (Part 2 of 4.)

```
57      // test substring "to-end-of-String" option
58      cout << "The substring of s1 starting at\n"
59          << "location 15, s1(15, 0), is: "
60          << s1( 15, 0 ) << "\n\n";  // 0 is "to end of string"
61
62      // test copy constructor
63      String *s4Ptr = new String( s1 );
64      cout << "\n*s4Ptr = " << *s4Ptr << "\n\n";
65
66      // test assignment (=) operator with self-assignment
67      cout << "assigning *s4Ptr to *s4Ptr\n";
68      *s4Ptr = *s4Ptr;   // test overloaded assignment
69      cout << "*s4Ptr = " << *s4Ptr << '\n';
70
71      // test destructor
72      delete s4Ptr;
73
74      // test using subscript operator to create lvalue
75      s1[ 0 ] = 'H';
76      s1[ 6 ] = 'B';
77      cout << "\ns1 after s1[0] = 'H' and s1[6] = 'B' is: "
78          << s1 << "\n\n";
79
80      // test subscript out of range
81      cout << "Attempt to assign 'd' to s1[30] yields:" << endl;
82      s1[ 30 ] = 'd';        // ERROR: subscript out of range
83
84      return 0;
85
86  } // end main
```

```
Conversion constructor: happy
Conversion constructor:  birthday
Conversion constructor:
s1 is "happy"; s2 is " birthday"; s3 is ""

The results of comparing s2 and s1:
s2 == s1 yields false
s2 != s1 yields true
s2 >  s1 yields false
s2 <  s1 yields true
s2 >= s1 yields false
s2 <= s1 yields true

Testing !s3:
s3 is empty; assigning s1 to s3;
operator= called
s3 is "happy"

s1 += s2 yields s1 = happy birthday

s1 += " to you" yields
Conversion constructor:  to you
Destructor:  to you
s1 = happy birthday to you                    (continued next page)
```

Fig. 8.9   **String** class test program. (Part 3 of 4.)

```
Conversion constructor: happy birthday
Copy constructor: happy birthday
Destructor: happy birthday
The substring of s1 starting at
location 0 for 14 characters, s1(0, 14), is:
happy birthday

Destructor: happy birthday
Conversion constructor: to you
Copy constructor: to you
Destructor: to you
The substring of s1 starting at
location 15, s1(15, 0), is: to you

Destructor: to you
Copy constructor: happy birthday to you

*s4Ptr = happy birthday to you

assigning *s4Ptr to *s4Ptr
operator= called
Attempted assignment of a String to itself
*s4Ptr = happy birthday to you
Destructor: happy birthday to you

s1 after s1[0] = 'H' and s1[6] = 'B' is: Happy Birthday to you

Attempt to assign 'd' to s1[30] yields:
Error: Subscript 30 out of range
```

Fig. 8.9 **String** class test program. (Part 4 of 4.)

Lines 12–13 declare the overloaded stream-insertion operator function **operator<<** (defined in Fig. 8.8, lines 181–187) and the overloaded stream-extraction operator function **operator>>** (defined in Fig. 8.8, lines 190–199) as friends of the class. The implementation of **operator<<** is straightforward. Note that **operator>>** restricts the total number of characters that can be read into array **temp** to 99 with **setw** (line 194); the 100th position is saved for the string's terminating null character. [*Note:* We did not have this restriction for **operator>>** in class **Array** (Fig. 8.4–Fig. 8.5), because that class's **operator>>** read one array element at a time and stopped reading values when the end of the array was reached. Object **cin** does not know how to do this by default for input of character arrays.] Also, note the use of **operator=** (line 195) to assign the C-style string **temp** to the **String** object to which **s** refers. This statement invokes the conversion constructor to create a temporary **String** object containing the C-style string; the temporary **String** is then assigned to **s**.

Line 16 declares a *conversion constructor*. This constructor (defined in Fig. 8.8, lines 20–26) takes a **const char *** argument (that defaults to the empty string; Fig. 8.7, line 16) and initializes a **String** object containing that same character string. Any *single-argument constructor* can be thought of as a conversion constructor. As we will see, such constructors are helpful when we are doing any **String** operation using **char *** arguments. The conversion constructor can convert a **char *** string into a **String** object, which can then be assigned to the target **String** object. The availability of this conversion constructor means that it is not necessary to supply an overloaded assignment operator for specifically assigning character strings to **String** objects. The compiler invokes the conversion constructor to create a temporary **String** object containing the character string; then the overloaded assignment operator is invoked to assign the temporary **String** object to another **String** object.

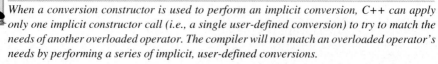

Software Engineering Observation 8.7

When a conversion constructor is used to perform an implicit conversion, C++ can apply only one implicit constructor call (i.e., a single user-defined conversion) to try to match the needs of another overloaded operator. The compiler will not match an overloaded operator's needs by performing a series of implicit, user-defined conversions.

The **String** conversion constructor could be invoked in such a declaration as **String s1("happy")**. The conversion constructor calculates the length of its character-string argument and assigns it to data-member **length** in the member-initializer list. Then, line 24 of the conversion constructor calls utility function **setString** (defined in Fig. 8.8, lines 173–178), which uses **new** to allocate a sufficient amount of memory to **private** data member **sPtr** and uses **strcpy** to copy the character string into the memory to which **sPtr** points.[4]

Line 17 in the header file declares a copy constructor (defined in Fig. 8.8, lines 29–35) that initializes a **String** object by making a copy of an existing **String** object. As with our class **Array** (Fig. 8.4–Fig. 8.5), such copying must be done carefully to avoid the pitfall in which both **String** objects point to the same dynamically allocated memory. The copy constructor operates similarly to the conversion constructor, except that it simply copies the **length** member from the source **String** object to the target **String** object. Note that the copy constructor calls **setString** to create new space for the target object's internal character string. If it simply copied the **sPtr** in the source object to the target object's **sPtr**, then both objects would point to the same dynamically allocated memory. The first destructor to execute would then delete the dynamically allocated memory and the other object's **sPtr** would then be undefined (i.e., **sPtr** would be a dangling pointer), a situation likely to cause a serious run-time error.

Line 18 of Fig. 8.7 declares the **String** destructor (defined in Fig. 8.8, lines 38–43). The destructor uses **delete []** to reclaim the dynamic memory to which **sPtr** points.

Line 20 declares the overloaded assignment operator function **operator=** (defined in Fig. 8.8, lines 46–61). When the compiler sees an expression like **string1 = string2**, the compiler generates the function call

      string1.operator=(string2);

The overloaded assignment operator function **operator=** tests for self-assignment. If this is a self-assignment, the function does not need to change the object. If this test were omitted, the function would immediately delete the space in the target object and thus lose

---

4. There is a subtle issue in the implementation of this conversion constructor. As implemented, if a null pointer (i.e., **0**) is passed to the constructor, the program will fail. The proper way to implement this constructor would be to detect whether the constructor argument is a null pointer, then "throw an exception." Chapter 13 discusses how we can make classes more robust in this manner. Also, note that a null pointer (**0**) is not the same as the empty string (**""**). A null pointer is a pointer that does not point to anything. An empty string is an actual string that contains only a null character (**'\0'**).

Line 58 of Fig
lines 134–163). W
integer parameters
from the **String**
the operator simpl
string is selected t
String object c
the compiler gen
When this call ex
returns a copy of t

Overloading t
trarily long and co
purposes. One suc
tion: Instead of us
as in **a[b][c**
enable the notatio
static member
object of class **St**

Line 60 in Fig
which returns the

At this point,
window and check
attention to the im
objects throughou
program that can
arguments. Howe
modify and debug

8.11 Overlo

The increment and
postdecrement—c
tween the prefix v

To overload
usage, each overl
piler will be able
overloaded exactl

Suppose, for
compiler sees the
function call

    d1.opera

The prototype for

    Date &op

If the preincr
the compiler sees

the character string, such that the pointer would no longer be pointing to valid data—a classic example of a dangling pointer. If there is no self-assignment, the function deletes the memory and copies the **length** field of the source object to the target object. Then **operator=** calls **setString** to create new space for the target object and copy the character string from the source object to the target object. Whether or not this is a self-assignment, **operator=** returns ***this** to enable cascaded assignments.

Line 21 of Fig. 8.7 declares the overloaded string-concatenation operator **+=** (defined in Fig. 8.8, lines 65–79). When the compiler sees the expression **s1 += s2** (line 44 of Fig. 8.9), the compiler generates the member-function call **s1.operator+=(s2)**. Function **operator+=** calculates the combined length of the concatenated string and stores it in local variable **newLength**, then creates a temporary pointer (**tempPtr**) and allocates a new character array in which the concatenated string will be stored. Next, **operator+=** uses **strcpy** to copy the original character strings from **sPtr** and **right.sPtr** into the memory to which **tempPtr** points. Note that the location into which **strcpy** will copy the first character of **right.sPtr** is determined by the pointer-arithmetic calculation **tempPtr + length**. This calculation indicates that the first character of **right.sPtr** should be placed at location **length** in the array to which **tempPtr** points. Next, **operator+=** uses **delete []** to reclaim the space occupied by this object's original character string, assigns **tempPtr** to **sPtr** so that this **String** object points to the new character string, assigns **newLength** to **length** so that this **String** object contains the new string length and returns ***this** as a **const String &** to enable cascading of **+=** operators.

Do we need a second overloaded concatenation operator to allow concatenation of a **String** and a **char ***? No. The **const char *** conversion constructor converts a C-style string into a temporary **String** object, which then matches the existing overloaded concatenation operator. This is exactly what the compiler does when it encounters line 49 in Fig. 8.9. Again, C++ can perform such conversions only one level deep to facilitate a match. C++ can also perform an implicit compiler-defined conversion between built-in types before it performs the conversion between a built-in type and a class. Note that, when a temporary **String** object is created in this case, the conversion constructor and the destructor are called (see the output resulting from line 49, **s1 += " to you"**, in Fig. 8.9). This is an example of function-call overhead that is hidden from the client of the class when temporary class objects are created and destroyed during implicit conversions. Similar overhead is generated by copy constructors in call-by-value parameter passing and in returning class objects by value.

Performance Tip 8.2

*Overloading the **+=** concatenation operator with an additional version that takes a single argument of type **const char *** executes more efficiently than having only a version that takes a **String** argument. Without the **const char *** version of the **+=** operator, a **const char *** argument would first be converted to a **String** object with class **String**'s conversion constructor, then the **+=** operator that receives a **String** argument would be called to perform the concatenation.*

Software Engineering Observation 8.8

Using implicit conversions with overloaded operators, rather than overloading operators for many different operand types, often requires less code, which makes a class easier to modify, maintain and debug.

Line 23 of F
82–86). This op
example, when t

string1

This function si
Lines 24–2
lines 89–93) and
class **String**.
loading the **==** c
the compiler ger

string

which returns **t**
tion **strcmp** (fr
Many C++ prog
plement others. S
in terms of **ope**
tor>= (implen
determine wheth
erator functions
these definition

Softwa

By imple
grammer

Lines 55–5
Fig. 8.8, lines 10
for **const Str**
piler generates t
priate version
implementation
the subscript is c
with a call to **e**
returns a **char**
used as an *lvalue*
sion of **operat**
object; this **cha**

Testing

Returnin
String
('\0') c

---

5. Note that it is
   the out-of-ran
   continue exec
   exception han

```
operator++( d1 )
```

The prototype for this operator function would be declared in the **Date** class as

```
friend Date &operator++( Date & );
```

Overloading the postincrementing operator presents a challenge, because the compiler must be able to distinguish between the signatures of the overloaded preincrement and postincrement operator functions. The convention that has been adopted in C++ is that, when the compiler sees the postincrementing expression **d1++**, it generates the member-function call

```
d1.operator++( 0 )
```

The prototype for this function is

```
Date operator++( int )
```

The argument **0** is strictly a "dummy value" that enables the compiler to distinguish between the preincrement and postincrement operator functions.

If the postincrementing is implemented as a non-member function, then, when the compiler sees the expression **d1++**, the compiler generates the function call

```
operator++( d1, 0 )
```

The prototype for this function would be

```
friend Date operator++( Date &, int );
```

Once again, the **0** argument is used by the compiler to distinguish between the preincrement and postincrement operators implemented as non-member functions. Note that the postincrement operator returns **Date** objects by value, whereas the preincrement operator returns **Date** objects by reference, because the postincrement operator typically returns a temporary object that contains the original value of the object before the increment occurred. C++ treats such objects as *rvalues*, which cannot be used on the left side of an assignment. The preincrement operator returns the actual incremented object with its new value. Such an object can be used as an *lvalue* in a continuing expression.

Everything stated in this section for overloading preincrement and postincrement operators applies to overloading predecrement and postdecrement operators. Next, we examine a **Date** class with overloaded preincrement and postincrement operators.

8.12 Case Study: A Date Class

The program of Fig. 8.10–Fig. 8.12 demonstrates a **Date** class. The class uses overloaded preincrement and postincrement operators to add 1 to the day in a **Date** object, while causing appropriate increments to the month and year if necessary.

```
1   // Fig. 8.10: date1.h
2   // Date class definition.
3   #ifndef DATE1_H
4   #define DATE1_H
5   #include <iostream>
```

Fig. 8.10   **Date** class definition with overloaded increment operators. (Part 1 of 2.)

```
 6
 7  using std::ostream;
 8
 9  class Date {
10     friend ostream &operator<<( ostream &, const Date & );
11
12  public:
13     Date( int m = 1, int d = 1, int y = 1900 ); // constructor
14     void setDate( int, int, int ); // set the date
15
16     Date &operator++();                // preincrement operator
17     Date operator++( int );            // postincrement operator
18
19     const Date &operator+=( int ); // add days, modify object
20
21     bool leapYear( int ) const;    // is this a leap year?
22     bool endOfMonth( int ) const;  // is this end of month?
23
24  private:
25     int month;
26     int day;
27     int year;
28
29     static const int days[];       // array of days per month
30     void helpIncrement();          // utility function
31
32  }; // end class Date
33
34  #endif
```

Fig. 8.10   **Date** class definition with overloaded increment operators. (Part 2 of 2.)

```
 1  // Fig. 8.11: date1.cpp
 2  // Date class member function definitions.
 3  #include <iostream>
 4  #include "date1.h"
 5
 6  // initialize static member at file scope;
 7  // one class-wide copy
 8  const int Date::days[] =
 9     { 0, 31, 28, 31, 30, 31, 30, 31, 31, 30, 31, 30, 31 };
10
11  // Date constructor
12  Date::Date( int m, int d, int y )
13  {
14     setDate( m, d, y );
15
16  } // end Date constructor
17
18  // set month, day and year
19  void Date::setDate( int mm, int dd, int yy )
20  {
```

Fig. 8.11   **Date** class member- and **friend**-function definitions. (Part 1 of 3.)

```
21       month = ( mm >= 1 && mm <= 12 ) ? mm : 1;
22       year = ( yy >= 1900 && yy <= 2100 ) ? yy : 1900;
23
24       // test for a leap year
25       if ( month == 2 && leapYear( year ) )
26          day = ( dd >= 1 && dd <= 29 ) ? dd : 1;
27       else
28          day = ( dd >= 1 && dd <= days[ month ] ) ? dd : 1;
29
30    } // end function setDate
31
32    // overloaded preincrement operator
33    Date &Date::operator++()
34    {
35       helpIncrement();
36
37       return *this;  // reference return to create an lvalue
38
39    } // end function operator++
40
41    // overloaded postincrement operator; note that the dummy
42    // integer parameter does not have a parameter name
43    Date Date::operator++( int )
44    {
45       Date temp = *this;  // hold current state of object
46       helpIncrement();
47
48       // return unincremented, saved, temporary object
49       return temp;    // value return; not a reference return
50
51    } // end function operator++
52
53    // add specified number of days to date
54    const Date &Date::operator+=( int additionalDays )
55    {
56       for ( int i = 0; i < additionalDays; i++ )
57          helpIncrement();
58
59       return *this;    // enables cascading
60
61    } // end function operator+=
62
63    // if the year is a leap year, return true;
64    // otherwise, return false
65    bool Date::leapYear( int testYear ) const
66    {
67       if ( testYear % 400 == 0 ||
68          ( testYear % 100 != 0 && testYear % 4 == 0 ) )
69          return true;   // a leap year
70       else
71          return false;  // not a leap year
72
73    } // end function leapYear
```

Fig. 8.11   **Date** class member- and **friend**-function definitions. (Part 2 of 3.)

```
74
75   // determine whether the day is the last day of the month
76   bool Date::endOfMonth( int testDay ) const
77   {
78      if ( month == 2 && leapYear( year ) )
79         return testDay == 29; // last day of Feb. in leap year
80      else
81         return testDay == days[ month ];
82
83   } // end function endOfMonth
84
85   // function to help increment the date
86   void Date::helpIncrement()
87   {
88      // day is not end of month
89      if ( !endOfMonth( day ) )
90         ++day;
91
92      else
93
94         // day is end of month and month < 12
95         if ( month < 12 ) {
96            ++month;
97            day = 1;
98         }
99
100        // last day of year
101        else {
102           ++year;
103           month = 1;
104           day = 1;
105        }
106
107  } // end function helpIncrement
108
109  // overloaded output operator
110  ostream &operator<<( ostream &output, const Date &d )
111  {
112     static char *monthName[ 13 ] = { "", "January",
113        "February", "March", "April", "May", "June",
114        "July", "August", "September", "October",
115        "November", "December" };
116
117     output << monthName[ d.month ] << ' '
118           << d.day << ", " << d.year;
119
120     return output;   // enables cascading
121
122  } // end function operator<<
```

Fig. 8.11   **Date** class member- and **friend**-function definitions. (Part 3 of 3.)

The **Date** header file (Fig. 8.10) specifies that **Date**'s public interface includes an overloaded stream-insertion operator (line 10), a default constructor (line 13), a **setDate** function (line 14), an overloaded preincrement operator (line 16), an overloaded postincrement operator (line 17), an overloaded **+=** addition assignment operator (line 19), a function to test for leap years (line 21) and a function to determine whether a day is the last day of the month (line 22).

The driver program in **main** (Fig. 8.12) creates three **Date** objects—**d1** is initialized by default to January 1, 1900; **d2** is initialized to December 27, 1992; and **d3** is initialized to an invalid date. The **Date** constructor (defined in Fig. 8.11, lines 12–16) calls **setDate** to validate the month, day and year specified. An invalid month is set to 1, an invalid year is set to 1900 and an invalid day is set to 1.

Lines 16–17 of the driver program output each of the constructed **Date** objects, using the overloaded stream-insertion operator (defined in Fig. 8.11, lines 110–122). Line 19 of the driver program uses overloaded operator **+=** to add seven days to **d2**. Line 21 uses function **setDate** to set **d3** to February 28, 1992. Next, line 25 creates a **Date** object, **d4**, which is initialized with the date July 13, 2002. Then line 29 increments **d4** by 1 with the overloaded preincrement operator. Lines 27–30 output **d4** before and after the preincrement operation to confirm that it worked correctly. Finally, line 34 increments **d4** with the overloaded postincrement operator. Lines 32–35 output **d4** before and after the postincrement operation to confirm that it worked correctly.

```
1   // Fig. 8.12: fig08_12.cpp
2   // Date class test program.
3   #include <iostream>
4
5   using std::cout;
6   using std::endl;
7
8   #include "date1.h"   // Date class definition
9
10  int main()
11  {
12     Date d1;   // defaults to January 1, 1900
13     Date d2( 12, 27, 1992 );
14     Date d3( 0, 99, 8045 );   // invalid date
15
16     cout << "d1 is " << d1 << "\nd2 is " << d2
17          << "\nd3 is " << d3;
18
19     cout << "\n\nd2 += 7 is " << ( d2 += 7 );
20
21     d3.setDate( 2, 28, 1992 );
22     cout << "\n\n  d3 is " << d3;
23     cout << "\n++d3 is " << ++d3;
24
25     Date d4( 7, 13, 2002 );
26
27     cout << "\n\nTesting the preincrement operator:\n"
28          << "  d4 is " << d4 << '\n';
29     cout << "++d4 is " << ++d4 << '\n';
30     cout << "  d4 is " << d4;
```

Fig. 8.12   **Date** class test program. (Part 1 of 2.)

```
31
32          cout << "\n\nTesting the postincrement operator:\n"
33               << "  d4 is " << d4 << '\n';
34          cout << "d4++ is " << d4++ << '\n';
35          cout << "  d4 is " << d4 << endl;
36
37          return 0;
38
39   } // end main
```

```
d1 is January 1, 1900
d2 is December 27, 1992
d3 is January 1, 1900

d2 += 7 is January 3, 1993

  d3 is February 28, 1992
++d3 is February 29, 1992

Testing the preincrement operator:
  d4 is July 13, 2002
++d4 is July 14, 2002
  d4 is July 14, 2002

Testing the postincrement operator:
  d4 is July 14, 2002
d4++ is July 14, 2002
  d4 is July 15, 2002
```

Fig. 8.12   **Date** class test program. (Part 2 of 2.)

Overloading the preincrementing operator is straightforward. The preincrementing operator (defined in Fig. 8.11, lines 33–39) calls utility function **helpIncrement** (defined in Fig. 8.11, lines 86–107) to increment the date. This function deals with "wraparounds" or "carries" that occur when we increment the last day of the month. These carries require incrementing the month. If the month is already 12, then the year must also be incremented. Function **helpIncrement** uses function **endOfMonth** to increment the day correctly.

The overloaded preincrement operator returns a reference to the current **Date** object (i.e., the one that was just incremented). This occurs because the current object, ***this**, is returned as a **Date &**. This enables a preincremented **Date** object to be used as an *lvalue*, which is how the built-in preincrement operator works for primitive types.

Overloading the postincrement operator (defined in Fig. 8.11, lines 43–51) is trickier. To emulate the effect of the postincrement, we must return an unincremented copy of the **Date** object. On entry to **operator++**, we save the current object (***this**) in **temp** (line 45). Next, we call **helpIncrement** to increment the current **Date** object. Then, line 49 returns the unincremented copy of the object previously stored in **temp**. Note that this function cannot return a reference to the local **Date** object **temp**, because a local variable is destroyed when the function in which it is declared exits. Thus, declaring the return type to this function as **Date &** would return a reference to an object that no longer exists. Returning a reference (or a pointer) to a local variable is a common error for which most compilers will issue a warning.

8.13 Standard Library Classes `string` and `vector`

In Chapter 6 and Chapter 7, we introduced the features of object-based programming in C++. A key observation from these chapters is that we can build a software entity called a class, from which we can create objects in programs. In this chapter, we learned that we can build a **String** class (Fig. 8.7–Fig. 8.9) that is better than the C-style, **char *** strings that C++ absorbed from C. We also learned that we can build an **Array** class (Fig. 8.4–Fig. 8.6) that is better than the C-style, pointer-based arrays that C++ absorbed from C.

Building good, useful and reusable classes such as **String** and **Array** takes work. However, once such classes are tested and debugged, they can be reused by you, your colleagues, your company, many companies, an entire industry or even many industries (if they are placed in public or for-sale libraries). The designers of C++ did exactly that, building classes *string* and *vector* (which represents a dynamically-resizable array) into standard C++. These classes are available to anyone building applications with C++.

To close this chapter, we redo our **String** (Fig. 8.7–Fig. 8.9) and **Array** (Fig. 8.4–Fig. 8.6) examples, using the standard C++ **string** and **vector** classes. We rework our **String** example to demonstrate similar functionality provided by standard class **string**. Similarly, we rework our **Array** example to demonstrate similar functionality provided by standard class **vector**. The notations that the **vector** example uses might be unfamiliar to you, because **vector**s use template notation. Recall that Section 3.21 discussed function templates. In Chapter 11, we discuss class templates. For now, you should feel comfortable using class **vector** by mimicking the syntax in the example we show in this section. You will deepen your understanding as we study class templates in Chapter 11. Chapter 15 presents class **string** in detail, and Chapter 21 presents class **vector** (and several other standard C++ container classes) in detail.

Standard Library Class `string`

The program of Fig. 8.13 reimplements the program of Fig. 8.9, using standard class **string**. As you will see in this example, standard class **string** provides all the functionality of our class **String** presented in Fig. 8.7–Fig. 8.8. Standard class **string** is defined in header **<string>** (line 8) and belongs to namespace **std** (line 10). Chapter 15 discusses the full functionality of standard class **string**.

```
1   // Fig. 8.13: fig08_13.cpp
2   // Standard library string class test program.
3   #include <iostream>
4
5   using std::cout;
6   using std::endl;
7
8   #include <string>
9
10  using std::string;
11
12  int main()
13  {
14      string s1( "happy" );
15      string s2( " birthday" );
```

Fig. 8.13   Standard library class **string**. (Part 1 of 4.)

```
16        string s3;
17
18        // test overloaded equality and relational operators
19        cout << "s1 is \"" << s1 << "\"; s2 is \"" << s2
20             << "\"; s3 is \"" << s3 << '\"'
21             << "\n\nThe results of comparing s2 and s1:"
22             << "\ns2 == s1 yields "
23             << ( s2 == s1 ? "true" : "false" )
24             << "\ns2 != s1 yields "
25             << ( s2 != s1 ? "true" : "false" )
26             << "\ns2 >  s1 yields "
27             << ( s2 > s1 ? "true" : "false" )
28             << "\ns2 <  s1 yields "
29             << ( s2 < s1 ? "true" : "false" )
30             << "\ns2 >= s1 yields "
31             << ( s2 >= s1 ? "true" : "false" )
32             << "\ns2 <= s1 yields "
33             << ( s2 <= s1 ? "true" : "false" );
34
35        // test string member function empty
36        cout << "\n\nTesting s3.empty():\n";
37
38        if ( s3.empty() ) {
39           cout << "s3 is empty; assigning s1 to s3;\n";
40           s3 = s1;  // assign s1 to s3
41           cout << "s3 is \"" << s3 << "\"";
42        }
43
44        // test overloaded string concatenation operator
45        cout << "\n\ns1 += s2 yields s1 = ";
46        s1 += s2;  // test overloaded concatenation
47        cout << s1;
48
49        // test overloaded string concatenation operator
50        // with C-style string
51        cout << "\n\ns1 += \" to you\" yields\n";
52        s1 += " to you";
53        cout << "s1 = " << s1 << "\n\n";
54
55        // test string member function substr
56        cout << "The substring of s1 starting at location 0 for\n"
57             << "14 characters, s1.substr(0, 14), is:\n"
58             << s1.substr( 0, 14 ) << "\n\n";
59
60        // test substr "to-end-of-string" option
61        cout << "The substring of s1 starting at\n"
62             << "location 15, s1.substr(15), is:\n"
63             << s1.substr( 15 ) << '\n';
64
65        // test copy constructor
66        string *s4Ptr = new string( s1 );
67        cout << "\n*s4Ptr = " << *s4Ptr << "\n\n";
68
```

Fig. 8.13   Standard library class **string**. (Part 2 of 4.)

```
69        // test assignment (=) operator with self-assignment
70        cout << "assigning *s4Ptr to *s4Ptr\n";
71        *s4Ptr = *s4Ptr;
72        cout << "*s4Ptr = " << *s4Ptr << '\n';
73
74        // test destructor
75        delete s4Ptr;
76
77        // test using subscript operator to create lvalue
78        s1[ 0 ] = 'H';
79        s1[ 6 ] = 'B';
80        cout << "\ns1 after s1[0] = 'H' and s1[6] = 'B' is: "
81             << s1 << "\n\n";
82
83        // test subscript out of range with string member function "at"
84        cout << "Attempt to assign 'd' to s1.at( 30 ) yields:" << endl;
85        s1.at( 30 ) = 'd';       // ERROR: subscript out of range
86
87        return 0;
88
89    } // end main
```

```
s1 is "happy"; s2 is " birthday"; s3 is ""

The results of comparing s2 and s1:
s2 == s1 yields false
s2 != s1 yields true
s2 >  s1 yields false
s2 <  s1 yields true
s2 >= s1 yields false
s2 <= s1 yields true

Testing s3.empty():
s3 is empty; assigning s1 to s3;
s3 is "happy"

s1 += s2 yields s1 = happy birthday

s1 += " to you" yields
s1 = happy birthday to you

The substring of s1 starting at location 0 for
14 characters, s1.substr(0, 14), is:
happy birthday

The substring of s1 starting at
location 15, s1.substr(15), is:
to you

*s4Ptr = happy birthday to you

assigning *s4Ptr to *s4Ptr
*s4Ptr = happy birthday to you

s1 after s1[0] = 'H' and s1[6] = 'B' is: Happy Birthday to you
```
                                                    (continued next page)

Fig. 8.13   Standard library class **string**. (Part 3 of 4.)

```
Attempt to assign 'd' to s1.at( 30 ) yields:

abnormal program termination
```

Fig. 8.13   Standard library class **string**. (Part 4 of 4.)

Lines 14–16 create three **string** objects—**s1** is initialized with the literal **"happy"**, **s2** is initialized with the literal **" birthday"** and **s3** uses the default string constructor to create an empty **string**. Lines 19–20 output these three objects, using **cout** and operator **<<**, which the **string** class designers overloaded to handle **string** objects. Then lines 21–33 show the results of comparing **s2** to **s1** by using class **string**'s overloaded equality and relational operators.

Our class **String** (Fig. 8.7–Fig. 8.8) provided an overloaded **operator!** that tested a **String** to determine whether it was empty. Standard class **string** does not provide this functionality as an overloaded operator; instead, it provides member function **empty**, which we demonstrate on line 38. Member function **empty** returns **true** if the **string** is empty; otherwise, it returns **false**.

Line 40 demonstrates class **string**'s overloaded assignment operator by assigning **s1** to **s3**. Line 41 outputs **s3** to demonstrate that the assignment worked correctly.

Line 46 demonstrates class **string**'s overloaded **+=** operator for string concatenation. In this case, the contents of **s2** are appended to **s1**. Then line 47 outputs the resulting string that is stored in **s1**. Line 52 demonstrates that a C-style string literal can be appended to a **string** object by using operator **+=**. Line 53 displays the result.

Our class **String** (Fig. 8.7–Fig. 8.8) provided overloaded **operator()** to obtain substrings. Standard class **string** does not provide this functionality as an overloaded operator; instead, it provides member function **substr** (lines 58 and 63). The call to **substr** in line 58 obtains a 14-character substring (specified by the second argument) of **s1** starting at position 0 (specified by the first argument).The call to **substr** in line 63 obtains a substring starting from position 15 of **s1**. When the second argument is not specified, **substr** returns the remainder of the **string** on which it is called.

Line 66 dynamically allocates a **string** object and initializes it with a copy of **s1**. This results in a call to class **string**'s copy constructor. Line 71 uses class **string**'s overloaded **=** operator to demonstrate that it handles self-assignment properly.

Lines 78–79 used class **string**'s overloaded **[]** operator to create *lvalues* that enable new characters to replace existing characters in **s1**. Line 81 outputs the new value of **s1**. In our class **String** (Fig. 8.7–Fig. 8.8), the overloaded **[]** operator performed bounds checking to determine whether the subscript it received as an argument was a valid subscript in the string. If the subscript was invalid, the operator printed an error message and terminated the program. Standard class **string**'s overloaded **[]** operator does not perform any bounds checking. Therefore, the programmer must ensure that operations using standard class **string**'s overloaded **[]** operator do not accidentally manipulate elements outside the bounds of the **string**. Standard class **string** does provide bounds checking in its member function **at**, which "throws an exception" if its argument is an invalid subscript. By default, this causes a C++ program to terminate.[6] If the subscript is valid, func-

---

6. Chapter 13, Exception Handling, demonstrates how to build more robust programs that "catch" such exceptions when they occur and enable the program to continue executing.

tion **at** returns the character at the specified location as an *lvalue* or an *rvalue*, depending on the context in which the call appears. Line 85 demonstrates a call to function **at** with an invalid subscript.

Standard Library Class `vector`

The program of Fig. 8.14 reimplements the program of Fig. 8.6, using standard class **vector**. As the next example demonstrates, standard class **vector** provides many of the same features as our class **Array** presented in Fig. 8.4–Fig. 8.6. Standard class **vector** is defined in header **<vector>** (line 13) and belongs to namespace **std** (line 15). Two features that class **vector** does not provide are overloaded operators **>>** and **<<** for input and output, respectively. So, Fig. 8.14 defines functions **outputVector** (lines 98–111) and **inputVector** (lines 114–119), which mimic the overloaded **operator<<** and **operator>>** functions provided in Fig. 8.4–Fig. 8.5 for our **Array** class. Chapter 21 discusses the full functionality of standard class **vector**.

```cpp
1  // Fig. 8.14: fig08_14.cpp
2  // Demonstrating standard library class vector.
3  #include <iostream>
4
5  using std::cout;
6  using std::cin;
7  using std::endl;
8
9  #include <iomanip>
10
11 using std::setw;
12
13 #include <vector>
14
15 using std::vector;
16
17 void outputVector( const vector< int > & );
18 void inputVector( vector< int > & );
19
20 int main()
21 {
22    vector< int > integers1( 7 );    // 7-element vector< int >
23    vector< int > integers2( 10 );   // 10-element vector< int >
24
25    // print integers1 size and contents
26    cout << "Size of vector integers1 is "
27         << integers1.size()
28         << "\nvector after initialization:\n";
29    outputVector( integers1 );
30
```

Fig. 8.14   Standard library class **vector**. (Part 1 of 4.)

```
31      // print integers2 size and contents
32      cout << "\nSize of vector integers2 is "
33           << integers2.size()
34           << "\nvector after initialization:\n";
35      outputVector( integers2 );
36
37      // input and print integers1 and integers2
38      cout << "\nInput 17 integers:\n";
39      inputVector( integers1 );
40      inputVector( integers2 );
41
42      cout << "\nAfter input, the vectors contain:\n"
43           << "integers1:\n";
44      outputVector( integers1 );
45      cout << "integers2:\n";
46      outputVector( integers2 );
47
48      // use overloaded inequality (!=) operator
49      cout << "\nEvaluating: integers1 != integers2\n";
50
51      if ( integers1 != integers2 )
52         cout << "integers1 and integers2 are not equal\n";
53
54      // create vector integers3 using integers1 as an
55      // initializer; print size and contents
56      vector< int > integers3( integers1 );   // copy constructor
57
58      cout << "\nSize of vector integers3 is "
59           << integers3.size()
60           << "\nvector after initialization:\n";
61      outputVector( integers3 );
62
63
64      // use overloaded assignment (=) operator
65      cout << "\nAssigning integers2 to integers1:\n";
66      integers1 = integers2;
67
68      cout << "integers1:\n";
69      outputVector( integers1 );
70      cout << "integers2:\n";
71      outputVector( integers1 );
72
73      // use overloaded equality (==) operator
74      cout << "\nEvaluating: integers1 == integers2\n";
75
76      if ( integers1 == integers2 )
77         cout << "integers1 and integers2 are equal\n";
78
79      // use overloaded subscript operator to create rvalue
80      cout << "\nintegers1[5] is " << integers1[ 5 ];
81
82      // use overloaded subscript operator to create lvalue
83      cout << "\n\nAssigning 1000 to integers1[5]\n";
```

Fig. 8.14   Standard library class **vector**. (Part 2 of 4.)

```
84        integers1[ 5 ] = 1000;
85        cout << "integers1:\n";
86        outputVector( integers1 );
87
88        // attempt to use out of range subscript
89        cout << "\nAttempt to assign 1000 to integers1.at( 15 )"
90             << endl;
91        integers1.at( 15 ) = 1000;  // ERROR: out of range
92
93        return 0;
94
95     } // end main
96
97     // output vector contents
98     void outputVector( const vector< int > &array )
99     {
100       for ( int i = 0; i < array.size(); i++ ) {
101          cout << setw( 12 ) << array[ i ];
102
103          if ( ( i + 1 ) % 4 == 0 ) // 4 numbers per row of output
104             cout << endl;
105
106       } // end for
107
108       if ( i % 4 != 0 )
109          cout << endl;
110
111    } // end function outputVector
112
113    // input vector contents
114    void inputVector( vector< int > &array )
115    {
116       for ( int i = 0; i < array.size(); i++ )
117          cin >> array[ i ];
118
119    } // end function inputVector
```

```
Size of vector integers1 is 7
vector after initialization:
          0           0           0           0
          0           0           0

Size of vector integers2 is 10
vector after initialization:
          0           0           0           0
          0           0           0           0
          0           0

Input 17 integers:
1 2 3 4 5 6 7 8 9 10 11 12 13 14 15 16 17
```

(continued next page)

Fig. 8.14   Standard library class **vector**. (Part 3 of 4.)

```
After input, the vectors contain:
integers1:
           1           2           3           4
           5           6           7
integers2:
           8           9          10          11
          12          13          14          15
          16          17

Evaluating: integers1 != integers2
integers1 and integers2 are not equal

Size of vector integers3 is 7
vector after initialization:
           1           2           3           4
           5           6           7

Assigning integers2 to integers1:
integers1:
           8           9          10          11
          12          13          14          15
          16          17
integers2:
           8           9          10          11
          12          13          14          15
          16          17

Evaluating: integers1 == integers2
integers1 and integers2 are equal

integers1[5] is 13

Assigning 1000 to integers1[5]
integers1:
           8           9          10          11
          12        1000          14          15
          16          17

Attempt to assign 1000 to integers1.at( 15 )

abnormal program termination
```

Fig. 8.14 Standard library class **vector**. (Part 4 of 4.)

Lines 22–23 create two **vector** objects that store values of type **int**—**integers1** contains seven elements, and **integers2** contains 10 elements. By default, all the elements of each **vector** object are set to 0. Note that **vector**s can be defined to store any data type, by replacing **int** in **vector< int >** with the appropriate data type. This notation, which specifies the type stored in the **vector**, is similar to the template notation that Section 3.21 introduced with function templates. Again, Chapter 11 discusses this syntax in detail.

Line 27 uses **vector** member function *size* to obtain the size of **integers1**. Line 29 passes **integers1** to function **outputVector** (lines 98–111), which uses **vector**'s overloaded **[]** operator to obtain the value in each element of the **vector** as an *rvalue* that can be used for output. Lines 33 and 35 perform the same tasks for **integers2**.

Lines 39–40 pass **integers1** and **integers2** to function **inputVector** (lines 114–119) to read values for each **vector**'s elements from the user. Function **inputVector** uses **vector**'s overloaded **[]** operator to obtain *lvalues* that can be used to store the input values in each element of the **vector**.

Line 51 demonstrates class **vector**'s overloaded **!=** operator, which determines whether the contents of two **vector**s are not equal and returns **true** if they are not; otherwise, the operator returns **false**.

Line 56 creates a **vector** object (**integers3**) and initializes it with a copy of **integers1**. This invokes class **vector**'s copy constructor to perform the copy operation. Lines 59 and 61 output the size and contents of **integers3** to demonstrate that it was initialized correctly.

Line 66 uses **vector**'s overloaded **=** operator to assign **integers2** to **integers1**. Lines 69 and 71 output the contents of both objects to show that they now contain identical values. Line 76 then compares **integers1** to **integers2** with **vector**'s overloaded **==** operator to determine whether the contents of the two objects are equal after the assignment on line 66 (which they are).

Lines 80 and 84 use **vector**'s overloaded **[]** operator to obtain a **vector** element as an *rvalue* and as an *lvalue*, respectively. As is the case with standard class **string**'s overloaded **[]** operator, class **vector**'s overloaded **[]** does not perform any bounds checking. Therefore, the programmer must ensure that operations using **vector**'s overloaded **[]** operator do not accidentally manipulate elements outside the bounds of the **vector**. Standard class **vector** also provides bounds checking in its member function **at**, which "throws an exception" if its argument is an invalid subscript. By default, this causes a C++ program to terminate. If the subscript is valid, function **at** returns the element at the specified location as an *lvalue* or an *rvalue*, depending on the context in which the call appears. Line 91 demonstrates a call to function **at** with an invalid subscript.

In this chapter, we demonstrated how to make our classes more robust by defining overloaded operators that enable programmers to treat objects of our classes as if they are built-in C++ data types. In addition, we demonstrate two standard C++ classes—**string** and **vector**—that make extensive use of overloaded operators to create robust, reusable classes that can replace C-style, pointer-based strings and arrays. In the next chapter, we continue our discussion of classes by introducing a form of software reuse called inheritance. We will see that classes often share common attributes and behaviors. In such cases, it is possible to define those attributes and behaviors in a common "base" class and "inherit" those capabilities into new class definitions.

SUMMARY

- Operator **<<** is used for multiple purposes in C++—as the stream-insertion operator and as the left-shift operator. This is an example of operator overloading. Similarly, **>>** is also overloaded; it is used both as the stream-extraction operator and as the right-shift operator.

- C++ enables the programmer to overload most operators to be sensitive to the context in which they are used. The compiler generates the appropriate code based on the operator's use.

- Operator overloading contributes to C++'s extensibility.

- To overload an operator, write a function definition; the function name must be the keyword **operator** followed by the symbol for the operator being overloaded.

- To use an operator on class objects, that operator *must* be overloaded—with two exceptions. The assignment operator (**=**) may be used with two objects of the same class to perform a default memberwise assignment without overloading. The address operator (**&**) also can be used with objects of any class without overloading; it returns the address of the object in memory.

- Operator overloading provides the same concise expressive power for user-defined types that C++ provides with its rich collection of operators that work on built-in types.

- The precedence and associativity of an operator cannot be changed by overloading.

- It is not possible to change the number of operands an operator takes: Overloaded unary operators remain unary operators; overloaded binary operators remain binary operators. C++'s only ternary operator, **?:**, cannot be overloaded.

- It is not possible to create symbols for new operators; only existing operators may be overloaded.

- The meaning of how an operator works on built-in types cannot be changed by overloading.

- The C++ standard specifies that overloaded operators **()**, **[]**, **->** and any assignment operator must be members of the class for which they are overloaded.

- For operators other than **()**, **[]**, **->** and the assignment operators, overloaded operator functions can be member functions or non-member functions.

- When an operator function is implemented as a member function, the leftmost operand must be a class object (or a reference to a class object) of the operator's class.

- If the left operand must be an object of a different class, this operator function must be implemented as a non-member function.

- Operator member functions are called only when the left operand of a binary operator is an object of that class, or when the single operand of a unary operator is an object of that class.

- One might choose a non-member function to overload an operator to enable the operator to be commutative.

- A unary operator can be overloaded as a non-**static** member function with no arguments or as a non-member function with one argument; that argument must be either an object of a user-defined type or a reference to an object of a user-defined type.

- A binary operator can be overloaded as a non-**static** member function with one argument or as a non-member function with two arguments (one of those arguments must be either a class object or a reference to a class object).

- Array-subscript operator **[]** is not restricted for use only with arrays; it can be used to select elements from other kinds of container classes, such as linked lists, strings and dictionaries. Also, with overloading, subscripts no longer have to be integers; characters or strings could be used, for example.

- A copy constructor is used to initialize an object with another object of the same class. Copy constructors are also invoked whenever a copy of an object is needed, such as in passing an object by value to a function and returning an object by value from a function. In a copy constructor, the parameter type must be a reference.

- The compiler does not know how to convert between user-defined types and built-in types—the programmer must explicitly specify how such conversions are to occur. Such conversions can be performed with conversion constructors (i.e., single-argument constructors) that simply turn objects of other types into objects of a particular class.

- A conversion operator (or cast operator) can be used to convert an object of one class into an object of another class or into an object of a built-in type. Such a conversion operator must be a non-**static** member function; this kind of conversion operator cannot be a **friend** function.

- A conversion constructor is a single-argument constructor used to convert the argument into an object of the constructor's class. The compiler can call such a constructor implicitly.

- The assignment operator is the operator most frequently overloaded. It is normally used to assign an object to another object of the same class, but, through the use of conversion constructors, it can also be used to assign between different classes.

- If an overloaded assignment operator is not defined, assignment is still allowed, but it defaults to a memberwise assignment of each data member. In some cases this is acceptable. For objects that contain pointers to dynamically allocated memory, memberwise assignment results in two different objects pointing to the same memory. When the destructor for either of these objects is called, the dynamic memory is released. If the other object then refers to that memory, the result is undefined.

- To overload the increment operator to allow both preincrement and postincrement usage, each overloaded operator function must have a distinct signature, so that the compiler will be able to determine which version of **++** is intended. The prefix versions are overloaded exactly as is any other prefix unary operator. Providing a unique signature to the postincrement operator function is achieved by providing a second argument—which must be of type **int**. Actually, the user does not supply a value for this special integer argument. It is there simply to help the compiler distinguish between prefix and postfix versions of increment and decrement operators.

- Standard class **string** is defined in header **<string>** and belongs to namespace **std**.

- Class **string** provides many overloaded operators, including equality, relational, assignment, addition assignment (for concatenation) and subscript operators.

- Class **string** provides member function **empty**, which returns **true** if the **string** is empty; otherwise, it returns **false**.

- Standard class **string** member function **substr** obtains a substring of a length specified by the second argument, starting at the position 0 specified by the first argument. When the second argument is not specified, **substr** returns the remainder of the **string** on which it is called.

- Class **string**'s overloaded **[]** operator does not perform any bounds checking. Therefore, the programmer must ensure that operations using standard class **string**'s overloaded **[]** operator do not accidentally manipulate elements outside the bounds of the **string**.

- Standard class **string** provides bounds checking with member function **at**, which "throws an exception" if its argument is an invalid subscript. By default, this causes a C++ program to terminate. If the subscript is valid, function **at** returns the character at the specified location as an *lvalue* or an *rvalue*, depending on the context in which the call appears.

- A **vector** can be defined to store any data type.

- Class **vector**'s member function **size** returns the number of elements in the **vector**.

- Class **vector** defines overloaded equality and inequality operators to determine whether the contents of two **vector** are equal.

- Class **vector**'s overloaded **[]** operator returns a **vector** element as an *rvalue* or an *lvalue*, depending on the context. As is the case with standard class **string**'s overloaded **[]** operator, class **vector**'s overloaded **[]** does not perform any bounds checking. Therefore, the programmer must ensure that operations using **vector**'s overloaded **[]** operator do not accidentally manipulate elements outside the bounds of the **vector**.

- Standard class **vector** also provides bounds checking in its member function **at**, which "throws an exception" if its argument is an invalid subscript. By default, this causes a C++ program to terminate. If the subscript is valid, function **at** returns the element at the specified location as an *lvalue* or an *rvalue*, depending on the context in which the call appears.

TERMINOLOGY

at member function of **string**
at member function of **vector**

cascaded overloaded operators
cast-operator function

class **Array**
class **Date**
class **PhoneNumber**
class **String**
conversion constructor
conversion function
conversion operator
conversions between built-in types and classes
conversions between class types
copy constructor
dangling pointer
default memberwise assignment
default memberwise copy
empty member function of **string**
explicit type conversions (with casts)
friend overloaded operator function
function-call operator
implicit type conversions
memory leak
non-overloadable operators
operator char *
operator int
operator keyword
operator overloading
operator!
operator!=
operator()
operator+
operator++
operator++(int)
operator+=
operator<
operator<<
operator<=
operator=
operator==
operator>

operator>=
operator>>
operator[]
operators implemented as functions
overloadable operators
overloaded **!** operator
overloaded **!=** operator
overloaded **()** operator
overloaded **+** operator
overloaded **++** operator
overloaded **++(int)** operator
overloaded **+=** operator
overloaded **<** operator
overloaded **<<** operator
overloaded **<=** operator
overloaded **==** operator
overloaded **>** operator
overloaded **>=** operator
overloaded **>>** operator
overloaded assignment (**=**) operator
overloaded **[]** operator
overloading
overloading a binary operator
overloading a unary operator
postfix unary-operator overloading
prefix unary-operator overloading
self-assignment
single-argument constructor
size member function of **vector**
substr member function of **string**
string (standard C++ class)
string concatenation
substring
user-defined conversion
user-defined type
vector (standard C++ class)

SELF-REVIEW EXERCISES

8.1   Fill in the blanks in each of the following:

a) Suppose **a** and **b** are integer variables and we form the sum **a + b**. Now suppose **c** and **d** are floating-point variables and we form the sum **c + d**. The two **+** operators here are clearly being used for different purposes. This is an example of _____.

b) Keyword _____ introduces an overloaded-operator function definition.

c) To use operators on class objects, they must be overloaded, with the exception of operators _____ and _____.

d) The _____, _____ and _____ of an operator cannot be changed by overloading the operator.

8.2   Explain the multiple meanings of the operators **<<** and **>>** in C++.

```
13
14   private:
15      double real;        // real part
16      double imaginary;   // imaginary part
17
18   }; // end class Complex
19
20   #endif
```

Fig. 8.15 **Complex** class definition. (Part 2 of 2.)

```
1    // Fig. 8.16: complex1.cpp
2    // Complex class member function definitions.
3    #include <iostream>
4
5    using std::cout;
6
7    #include "complex1.h"  // Complex class definition
8
9    // constructor
10   Complex::Complex( double realPart, double imaginaryPart )
11      : real( realPart ),
12        imaginary( imaginaryPart )
13   {
14      // empty body
15
16   } // end Complex constructor
17
18   // addition operator
19   Complex Complex::operator+( const Complex &operand2 ) const
20   {
21      return Complex( real + operand2.real,
22         imaginary + operand2.imaginary );
23
24   } // end function operator+
25
26   // subtraction operator
27   Complex Complex::operator-( const Complex &operand2 ) const
28   {
29      return Complex( real - operand2.real,
30         imaginary - operand2.imaginary );
31
32   } // end function operator-
33
34   // display a Complex object in the form: (a, b)
35   void Complex::print() const
36   {
37      cout << '(' << real << ", " << imaginary << ')';
38
39   } // end function print
```

Fig. 8.16 **Complex** class member-function definitions.

```cpp
1   // Fig. 8.17: fig08_17.cpp
2   // Complex class test program.
3   #include <iostream>
4
5   using std::cout;
6   using std::endl;
7
8   #include "complex1.h"
9
10  int main()
11  {
12     Complex x;
13     Complex y( 4.3, 8.2 );
14     Complex z( 3.3, 1.1 );
15
16     cout << "x: ";
17     x.print();
18     cout << "\ny: ";
19     y.print();
20     cout << "\nz: ";
21     z.print();
22
23     x = y + z;
24     cout << "\n\nx = y + z:\n";
25     x.print();
26     cout << " = ";
27     y.print();
28     cout << " + ";
29     z.print();
30
31     x = y - z;
32     cout << "\n\nx = y - z:\n";
33     x.print();
34     cout << " = ";
35     y.print();
36     cout << " - ";
37     z.print();
38     cout << endl;
39
40     return 0;
41
42  } // end main
```

```
x: (0, 0)
y: (4.3, 8.2)
z: (3.3, 1.1)

x = y + z:
(7.6, 9.3) = (4.3, 8.2) + (3.3, 1.1)

x = y - z:
(1, 7.1) = (4.3, 8.2) - (3.3, 1.1)
```

Fig. 8.17 Complex numbers.

8.16   A machine with 32-bit integers can represent integers in the range of approximately -2 billion to +2 billion. This fixed-size restriction is rarely troublesome, but there are applications in which we would like to be able to use a much wider range of integers. This is what C++ was built to do, namely, create powerful new data types. Consider class **HugeInt** of Fig. 8.18–Fig. 8.20. Study the class carefully, then answer the following:

a) Describe precisely how it operates.
b) What restrictions does the class have?
c) Overload the ***** multiplication operator.
d) Overload the **/** division operator.
e) Overload all the relational and equality operators.

```cpp
1   // Fig. 8.18: hugeint1.h
2   // HugeInt class definition.
3   #ifndef HUGEINT1_H
4   #define HUGEINT1_H
5
6   #include <iostream>
7
8   using std::ostream;
9
10  class HugeInt {
11     friend ostream &operator<<( ostream &, const HugeInt & );
12
13  public:
14     HugeInt( long = 0 );        // conversion/default constructor
15     HugeInt( const char * );    // conversion constructor
16
17     // addition operator; HugeInt + HugeInt
18     HugeInt operator+( const HugeInt & );
19
20     // addition operator; HugeInt + int
21     HugeInt operator+( int );
22
23     // addition operator;
24     // HugeInt + string that represents large integer value
25     HugeInt operator+( const char * );
26
27  private:
28     short integer[ 30 ];
29
30  }; // end class HugeInt
31
32  #endif
```

Fig. 8.18   **HugeInt** class definition.

```cpp
1   // Fig. 8.19: hugeint1.cpp
2   // HugeInt member-function and friend-function definitions.
3
4   #include <cctype>       // isdigit function prototype
```

Fig. 8.19   **HugeInt** class member-function and **friend**-function definitions. (Part 1 of 3.)

```
 5    #include <cstring>        // strlen function prototype
 6
 7    #include "hugeint1.h"   // HugeInt class definition
 8
 9    // default constructor; conversion constructor that converts
10    // a long integer into a HugeInt object
11    HugeInt::HugeInt( long value )
12    {
13       // initialize array to zero
14       for ( int i = 0; i <= 29; i++ )
15          integer[ i ] = 0;
16
17       // place digits of argument into array
18       for ( int j = 29; value != 0 && j >= 0; j-- ) {
19          integer[ j ] = value % 10;
20          value /= 10;
21
22       } // end for
23
24    } // end HugeInt default/conversion constructor
25
26    // conversion constructor that converts a character string
27    // representing a large integer into a HugeInt object
28    HugeInt::HugeInt( const char *string )
29    {
30       // initialize array to zero
31       for ( int i = 0; i <= 29; i++ )
32          integer[ i ] = 0;
33
34       // place digits of argument into array
35       int length = strlen( string );
36
37       for ( int j = 30 - length, k = 0; j <= 29; j++, k++ )
38
39          if ( isdigit( string[ k ] ) )
40             integer[ j ] = string[ k ] - '0';
41
42    } // end HugeInt conversion constructor
43
44    // addition operator; HugeInt + HugeInt
45    HugeInt HugeInt::operator+( const HugeInt &op2 )
46    {
47       HugeInt temp;    // temporary result
48       int carry = 0;
49
50       for ( int i = 29; i >= 0; i-- ) {
51          temp.integer[ i ] =
52             integer[ i ] + op2.integer[ i ] + carry;
53
54          // determine whether to carry a 1
55          if ( temp.integer[ i ] > 9 ) {
56             temp.integer[ i ] %= 10;   // reduce to 0-9
```

Fig. 8.19   HugeInt class member-function and **friend**-function definitions. (Part 2 of 3.)

```
57              carry = 1;
58
59          } // end if
60
61          // no carry
62          else
63              carry = 0;
64       }
65
66       return temp;   // return copy of temporary object
67
68    } // end function operator+
69
70    // addition operator; HugeInt + int
71    HugeInt HugeInt::operator+( int op2 )
72    {
73       // convert op2 to a HugeInt, then invoke
74       // operator+ for two HugeInt objects
75       return *this + HugeInt( op2 );
76
77    } // end function operator+
78
79    // addition operator;
80    // HugeInt + string that represents large integer value
81    HugeInt HugeInt::operator+( const char *op2 )
82    {
83       // convert op2 to a HugeInt, then invoke
84       // operator+ for two HugeInt objects
85       return *this + HugeInt( op2 );
86
87    } // end operator+
88
89    // overloaded output operator
90    ostream& operator<<( ostream &output, const HugeInt &num )
91    {
92       int i;
93
94       for ( i = 0; ( num.integer[ i ] == 0 ) && ( i <= 29 ); i++ )
95          ; // skip leading zeros
96
97       if ( i == 30 )
98          output << 0;
99       else
100
101          for ( ; i <= 29; i++ )
102             output << num.integer[ i ];
103
104       return output;
105
106    } // end function operator<<
```

Fig. 8.19 **HugeInt** class member-function and **friend**-function definitions. (Part 3 of 3.)

```
1    // Fig. 8.20: fig08_20.cpp
2    // HugeInt test program.
3    #include <iostream>
4
5    using std::cout;
6    using std::endl;
7
8    #include "hugeint1.h"
9
10   int main()
11   {
12      HugeInt n1( 7654321 );
13      HugeInt n2( 7891234 );
14      HugeInt n3( "99999999999999999999999999999" );
15      HugeInt n4( "1" );
16      HugeInt n5;
17
18      cout << "n1 is " << n1 << "\nn2 is " << n2
19           << "\nn3 is " << n3 << "\nn4 is " << n4
20           << "\nn5 is " << n5 << "\n\n";
21
22      n5 = n1 + n2;
23      cout << n1 << " + " << n2 << " = " << n5 << "\n\n";
24
25      cout << n3 << " + " << n4 << "\n= " << ( n3 + n4 )
26           << "\n\n";
27
28      n5 = n1 + 9;
29      cout << n1 << " + " << 9 << " = " << n5 << "\n\n";
30
31      n5 = n2 + "10000";
32      cout << n2 << " + " << "10000" << " = " << n5 << endl;
33
34      return 0;
35
36   } // end main
```

```
n1 is 7654321
n2 is 7891234
n3 is 99999999999999999999999999999
n4 is 1
n5 is 0

7654321 + 7891234 = 15545555

99999999999999999999999999999 + 1
= 100000000000000000000000000000

7654321 + 9 = 7654330

7891234 + 10000 = 7901234
```

Fig. 8.20   Huge integers.

8.17   Create a class **RationalNumber** (fractions) with the following capabilities:

a) Create a constructor that prevents a 0 denominator in a fraction, reduces or simplifies fractions that are not in reduced form and avoids negative denominators.

b) Overload the addition, subtraction, multiplication and division operators for this class.

c) Overload the relational and equality operators for this class.

8.18   Study the C string-handling library functions and implement each of the functions as part of class **String** (Fig. 8.7–Fig. 8.8). Then, use these functions to perform text manipulations.

8.19   Develop class **Polynomial**. The internal representation of a **Polynomial** is an array of terms. Each term contains a coefficient and an exponent. The term

$$2x^4$$

has the coefficient 2 and the exponent 4. Develop a complete class containing proper constructor and destructor functions as well as *set* and *get* functions. The class should also provide the following overloaded operator capabilities:

a) Overload the addition operator (**+**) to add two **Polynomials**.

b) Overload the subtraction operator (**-**) to subtract two **Polynomials**.

c) Overload the assignment operator to assign one **Polynomial** to another.

d) Overload the multiplication operator (*****) to multiply two **Polynomials**.

e) Overload the addition assignment operator (**+=**), the subtraction assignment operator (**-=**), and the multiplication assignment operator (***=**).

8.20   The program of Fig. 8.3 contains the comment

```
// overloaded stream-insertion operator; cannot be
// a member function if we would like to invoke it with
// cout << somePhoneNumber;
```

Actually, it can be a member function of class **PhoneNumber** if we were willing to invoke it in either of the following ways:

```
somePhoneNumber.operator<<( cout );
```

or

```
somePhoneNumber << cout;
```

Rewrite the program of Fig. 8.3 with the overloaded stream-insertion **operator<<** as a member function and try the two preceding statements in the program to demonstrate that they work.

Object-Oriented Programming: Inheritance

Objectives

- To be able to create classes by inheriting from existing classes.
- To understand how inheritance promotes software reusability.
- To understand the notions of base classes and derived classes.
- To understand the **protected** member-access modifier.
- To understand the use of constructors and destructors in inheritance hierarchies.

Say not you know another entirely, till you have divided an inheritance with him.
Johann Kasper Lavater

This method is to define as the number of a class the class of all classes similar to the given class.
Bertrand Russell

A deck of cards was built like the purest of hierarchies, with every card a master to those below it, a lackey to those above it.
Ely Culbertson

Good as it is to inherit a library, it is better to collect one.
Augustine Birrell

Save base authority from others' books.
William Shakespeare

Outline	
9.1	**Introduction**
9.2	**Base Classes and Derived Classes**
9.3	**`protected` Members**
9.4	**Relationship between Base Classes and Derived Classes**
9.5	**Case Study: Three-Level Inheritance Hierarchy**
9.6	**Constructors and Destructors in Derived Classes**
9.7	**"Uses A" and "Knows A" Relationships**
9.8	**`public`, `protected` and `private` Inheritance**
9.9	**Software Engineering with Inheritance**
9.10	**(Optional Case Study) Thinking About Objects: Incorporating Inheritance into the Elevator Simulation**

Summary • Terminology • Self-Review Exercises • Answers to Self-Review Exercises • Exercises

9.1 Introduction

In this chapter, we begin our discussion of object-oriented programming (OOP) by introducing one of its main features—*inheritance*. Inheritance is a form of software reusability in which programmers create classes that absorb an existing class's data and behaviors and enhance them with new capabilities. Software reusability saves time during program development. It also encourages the reuse of proven and debugged high-quality software, which increases the likelihood that a system will be implemented effectively.

When creating a class, instead of writing completely new data members and member functions, the programmer can designate that the new class should *inherit* the members of an existing class. This existing class is called the *base class*, and the new class is referred to as the *derived class*. (Other programming languages, such as Java™, refer to the base class as the *superclass* and the derived class as the *subclass*.) A derived class represents a more specialized group of objects. Typically, a derived class contains behaviors inherited from its base class plus additional behaviors. As we will see, a derived class can also customize behaviors inherited from the base class. A *direct base class* is the base class from which a derived class explicitly inherits. An *indirect base class* is inherited from two or more levels up the *class hierarchy*. In the case of *single inheritance,* a class is derived from one base class. C++ also supports *multiple inheritance*, in which a derived class inherits from multiple (possibly unrelated) base classes. Single inheritance is straightforward—we show several examples that should enable the reader to become proficient quickly. Multiple inheritance can be complex and error prone. We cover multiple inheritance in Chapter 22.

C++ offers three kinds of inheritance—**public**, **protected** and **private**. In this chapter, we concentrate on **public** inheritance and briefly explain the other two kinds. In Chapter 17, we show how **private** inheritance can be used as an alternative to composition. The third form, **protected** inheritance, is rarely used. With **public** inheritance, every object of a derived class is also an object of that derived class's base class. However, base-class objects are not objects of their derived classes. For example, all cars are vehicles, but not all vehicles are cars. As we continue our study of object-oriented programming in Chapter 9 and Chapter 10, we take advantage of this relationship to perform some interesting manipulations.

Experience in building software systems indicates that significant portions of code deal with closely related special cases. When programmers are preoccupied with special cases, the details can obscure the "big picture." With object-oriented programming, programmers focus on the commonalities among objects in the system, rather than on the special cases. This process is called *abstraction*.

We distinguish between the *"is-a" relationship* and the *"has-a" relationship*. The "is-a" relationship represents inheritance. In an "is-a" relationship, an object of a derived class also can be treated as an object of its base class—for example, a car *is a* vehicle, so any properties and behaviors of a vechicle are also properties of a car. By contrast, the "has-a" relationship stands for composition. (Composition was discussed in Chapter 7.) In a "has-a" relationship, an object contains one or more objects of other classes as members—for example, a car *has a* steering wheel.

Derived-class member functions might require access to base-class data members and member functions. A derived class can access the non-**private** members of its base class. Base-class members that should not be accessible to the member functions of derived classes should be declared **private** in the base class. A derived class can effect state changes in **private** base-class members, but only through non-**private** member functions provided in the base class and inherited into the derived class.

Software Engineering Observation 9.1

*Member functions of a derived class cannot directly access **private** members of their class's base class.*

Software Engineering Observation 9.2

*If a derived class could access its base class's **private** members, classes that inherit from that derived class could access that data as well. This would propagate access to what should be **private** data, and the benefits of information hiding would be lost.*

One problem with inheritance is that a derived class can inherit data members and member functions it does not need or should not have. It is the class designer's responsibility to ensure that the capabilities provided by a class are appropriate for future derived classes. Even when a base-class member function is appropriate for a derived class, the derived class often requires that member function to behave in a manner specific to the derived class. In such cases, the base-class member function can be redefined in the derived class with an appropriate implementation.

9.2 Base Classes and Derived Classes

Often, an object of one class "is an" object of another class, as well. For example, in geometry, a rectangle *is a* quadrilateral (as are squares, parallelograms and trapezoids). Thus, in C++, class **Rectangle** can be said to *inherit* from class **Quadrilateral**. In this context, class **Quadrilateral** is a base class, and class **Rectangle** is a derived class. A rectangle *is a* specific type of quadrilateral, but it is incorrect to claim that a quadrilateral *is a* rectangle—the quadrilateral could be a parallelogram or some other shape. Figure 9.1 lists several simple examples of base classes and derived classes.

Base class	Derived classes
Student	GraduateStudent UndergraduateStudent
Shape	Circle Triangle Rectangle
Loan	CarLoan HomeImprovementLoan MortgageLoan
Employee	Faculty Staff
Account	CheckingAccount SavingsAccount

Fig. 9.1   Inheritance examples.

Because every derived-class object "is an" object of its base class, and one base class can have many derived classes, the set of objects represented by a base class typically is larger than the set of objects represented by any of its derived classes. For example, the base class **Vehicle** represents all vehicles, including cars, trucks, boats, bicycles and so on. By contrast, derived class **Car** represents a smaller, more-specific subset of all vehicles.

Inheritance relationships form tree-like hierarchical structures. A base class exists in a hierarchical relationship with its derived classes. Although classes can exist independently, once they are employed in inheritance relationships, they become affiliated with other classes. A class becomes either a base class, supplying data and behaviors to other classes, or a derived class, inheriting its data and behaviors from other classes.

Let us develop a simple inheritance hierarchy. A university community has thousands of members. These members consist of employees, students and alumni. Employees are either faculty members or staff members. Faculty members are either administrators (such as deans and department chairpersons) or teachers. This organizational structure yields the inheritance hierarchy depicted in Fig. 9.2. Note that this inheritance hierarchy could contain many other classes. For example, students can be graduate or undergraduate students. Undergraduate students can be freshmen, sophomores, juniors and seniors. Each arrow in the hierarchy represents an "is-a" relationship. For example, as we follow the arrows in this class hierarchy, we can state "an **Employee** *is a* **CommunityMember**" and "a **Teacher** *is a* **Faculty** member." **CommunityMember** is the *direct base class* of **Employee**, **Student** and **Alumnus**. In addition, **CommunityMember** is an *indirect base class* of all the other classes in the diagram. Starting from the bottom of the diagram, the reader can follow the arrows and apply the *is-a* relationship to the topmost base class. For example, an **Administrator** *is a* **Faculty** member, *is an* **Employee** and *is a* **Community-Member**. Note that some administrators also teach classes, so we have used multiple inheritance to form class **AdministratorTeacher**.

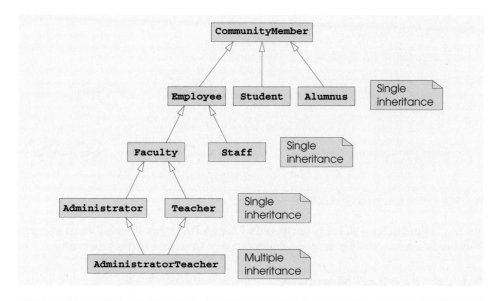

Fig. 9.2   Inheritance hierarchy for university **CommunityMember**s.

Another inheritance hierarchy is the **Shape** hierarchy of Fig. 9.3. To specify that class **TwoDimensionalShape** is derived from (or inherits from) class **Shape**, class **TwoDimensionalShape** could be defined in C++ as follows:

```
class TwoDimensionalShape : public Shape
```

This is an example of ***public*** *inheritance* and is the most commonly used type of inheritance. We also will discuss ***private*** *inheritance* and ***protected*** *inheritance* (Section 9.8). With **public** inheritance, **private** members of a base class are not accessible directly from that class's derived classes, but these **private** base-class members are still inherited. All other base-class members retain their original member access when they become members of the derived class (e.g., **public** members of the base class become **public** members of the derived class, and, as we will soon see, **protected** members of the base class become **protected** members of the derived class). Through these inherited base-class members, the derived class can manipulate **private** members of the base class (if these inherited members provide such functionality in the base class). Note that **friend** functions are not inherited.

Inheritance is not appropriate for every class relationship. In Chapter 7, we discussed the *has-a* relationship, in which classes have members that are objects of other classes. Such relationships create classes by composition of existing classes. For example, given the classes **Employee**, **BirthDate** and **TelephoneNumber**, it is improper to say that an **Employee** *is a* **BirthDate** or that an **Employee** *is a* **TelephoneNumber**. However, it is appropriate to say that an **Employee** *has a* **BirthDate** and that an **Employee** *has a* **TelephoneNumber**.

It is possible to treat base-class objects and derived-class objects similarly; their commonalities are expressed in the members of the base class. Objects of all classes derived from a common base class can be treated as objects of that base class (i.e., such objects have

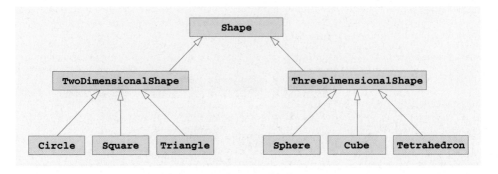

Fig. 9.3   Inheritance hierarchy for **Shape**s.

an "is-a" relationship with the base class). In Chapter 10, Object-Oriented Programming: Polymorphism, we consider many examples that take advantage of this relationship.

9.3 **protected** Members

Chapter 7 discussed **public** and **private** member-access specifiers. A base class's **public** members are accessible anywhere that the program has a handle (i.e., a name, reference or pointer) to an object of that base class or one of its derived classes. A base class's **private** members are accessible only within the body of that base class and the **friend**s of that base class. In this section, we introduce an additional member-access specifier: *protected*.

Using **protected** access offers an intermediate level of protection between **public** and **private** access. A base class's **protected** members can be accessed by members and **friend**s of that base class and by members and **friend**s of any classes derived from that base class.

Derived-class member functions can refer to **public** and **protected** members of the base class simply by using the member names. When a derived-class member function redefines a base-class member function, the base-class member can be accessed from the derived class by preceding the base-class member name with the base-class name and the binary scope resolution operator (**::**). We discuss accessing redefined members of the base class in Section 9.4.

9.4 Relationship between Base Classes and Derived Classes

In this section, we use a point/circle inheritance hierarchy[1] to discuss the relationship between a base class and a derived class. We divide our discussion of the point/circle relationship into several parts. First, we create class **Point**, which contains as **private** data an x–y coordinate pair. Then, we create class **Circle**, which contains as **private** data an x–y coordinate pair (representing the location of the center of the circle) and a radius. We

---

1. The point/circle relationship may seem unnatural when we say that a circle "is a" point. This example teaches what is sometimes called *structural inheritance* and focuses on the "mechanics" of inheritance and how a base class and a derived class relate to one another. In the exercises and in Chapter 10, we present more natural inheritance examples.

do not use inheritance to create class **Circle**; rather, we construct the class by writing every line of code the class requires. Next, we create a separate **Circle2** class, which inherits directly from class **Point** (i.e., class **Circle2** "is a" **Point** but also contains a radius) and attempts to access class **Point**'s **private** members—this results in compilation errors, because the derived class does not have access to the base class's **private** data. We then show that if **Point**'s data is declared as **protected**, a **Circle3** class that inherits from class **Point2** can access that data. For this purpose, we define class **Point2** with **protected** data. Both the inherited and noninherited **Circle** classes contain identical functionality, but we show how the inherited **Circle3** class is easier to create and manage. After discussing the convenience of using **protected** data, we set the **Point** data back to **private** in class **Point3** (to enforce good software engineering), then show how a separate **Circle4** class (which inherits from class **Point3**) can use **Point3** member functions to manipulate **Point3**'s **private** data.

Creating a Point Class

Let us first examine **Point**'s class definition (Fig. 9.4–Fig. 9.5). The **Point** header file (Fig. 9.4) specifies class **Point**'s **public** services, which include a constructor (line 9) and member functions **setX** and **getX** (lines 11–12), **setY** and **getY** (lines 14–15) and **print** (line 17). The **Point** header file specifies data members **x** and **y** as **private** (lines 20–21), so objects of other classes cannot access **x** and **y** directly. Technically, even if **Point**'s data members **x** and **y** were made **public**, **Point** could never maintain an invalid state—a **Point** object's **x** and **y** data members could never contain invalid values, because the *x–y* coordinate plane is infinite in both directions. In general, however, declar-

```
1   // Fig. 9.4: point.h
2   // Point class definition represents an x-y coordinate pair.
3   #ifndef POINT_H
4   #define POINT_H
5
6   class Point {
7
8   public:
9      Point( int = 0, int = 0 ); // default constructor
10
11     void setX( int );          // set x in coordinate pair
12     int getX() const;          // return x from coordinate pair
13
14     void setY( int );          // set y in coordinate pair
15     int getY() const;          // return y from coordinate pair
16
17     void print() const;        // output Point object
18
19  private:
20     int x;  // x part of coordinate pair
21     int y;  // y part of coordinate pair
22
23  }; // end class Point
24
25  #endif
```

Fig. 9.4   **Point** class header file.

ing data members as **private** and providing non-**private** member functions to manipulate and validate the data members enforces good software engineering. [*Note*: The **Point** constructor definition purposely does not use member-initializer syntax in the first several examples of this section, so that we can demonstrate how **private** and **protected** specifiers affect member access in derived classes. As shown in Fig. 9.5, lines 12–13, we assign values to the data members in the constructor body. Later in this section, we will return to using member-initializer lists in the constructors.]

```cpp
1   // Fig. 9.5: point.cpp
2   // Point class member-function definitions.
3   #include <iostream>
4
5   using std::cout;
6
7   #include "point.h"   // Point class definition
8
9   // default constructor
10  Point::Point( int xValue, int yValue )
11  {
12     x = xValue;
13     y = yValue;
14
15  } // end Point constructor
16
17  // set x in coordinate pair
18  void Point::setX( int xValue )
19  {
20     x = xValue; // no need for validation
21
22  } // end function setX
23
24  // return x from coordinate pair
25  int Point::getX() const
26  {
27     return x;
28
29  } // end function getX
30
31  // set y in coordinate pair
32  void Point::setY( int yValue )
33  {
34     y = yValue; // no need for validation
35
36  } // end function setY
37
38  // return y from coordinate pair
39  int Point::getY() const
40  {
41     return y;
42
43  } // end function getY
44
```

Fig. 9.5   **Point** class represents an *x–y* coordinate pair. (Part 1 of 2.)

```
45   // output Point object
46   void Point::print() const
47   {
48      cout << '[' << x << ", " << y << ']';
49
50   } // end function print
```

Fig. 9.5   **Point** class represents an *x*–*y* coordinate pair. (Part 2 of 2.)

Figure 9.6 tests class **Point**. Line 12 instantiates object **point** of class **Point** and passes **72** as the *x*-coordinate value and **115** as the *y*-coordinate value to the constructor. Lines 15–16 use **point**'s **getX** and **getY** member functions to retrieve these values, then output the values. Lines 18–19 invoke **point**'s member functions **setX** and **setY** to change the values for **point**'s **x** and **y** data members. Line 23 then calls **point**'s **print** member function to display the new *x*- and *y*-coordinate values.

```
1    // Fig. 9.6: pointtest.cpp
2    // Testing class Point.
3    #include <iostream>
4
5    using std::cout;
6    using std::endl;
7
8    #include "point.h"  // Point class definition
9
10   int main()
11   {
12      Point point( 72, 115 );      // instantiate Point object
13
14      // display point coordinates
15      cout << "X coordinate is " << point.getX()
16           << "\nY coordinate is " << point.getY();
17
18      point.setX( 10 ); // set x-coordinate
19      point.setY( 10 ); // set y-coordinate
20
21      // display new point value
22      cout << "\n\nThe new location of point is ";
23      point.print();
24      cout << endl;
25
26      return 0;  // indicates successful termination
27
28   } // end main
```

```
X coordinate is 72
Y coordinate is 115

The new location of point is [10, 10]
```

Fig. 9.6   **Point** class test program.

Creating a **Circle** *Class Without Using Inheritance*

We now discuss the second part of our introduction to inheritance by creating and testing (a completely new) class **Circle** (Fig. 9.7–Fig. 9.8), which contains an *x–y* coordinate pair (indicating the center of the circle) and a radius. The **Circle** header file (Fig. 9.7) specifies class **Circle**'s **public** services, which include the **Circle** constructor (line 11), member functions **setX** and **getX** (lines 13–14), **setY** and **getY** (lines 16–17), **setRadius** and **getRadius** (lines 19–20), **getDiameter** (line 22), **getCircumference** (line 23), **getArea** (line 24) and **print** (line 26). Lines 29–31 declare members **x**, **y** and **radius** as **private** data. These data members and member functions encapsulate all necessary features of a circle. In Section 9.5, we show how this encapsulation enables us to reuse and extend this class.

Figure 9.9 tests class **Circle**. Line 17 instantiates object **circle** of class **Circle**, passing **37** as the *x*-coordinate value, **43** as the *y*-coordinate value and **2.5** as the radius value to the constructor. Lines 20–22 use member functions **getX**, **getY** and **getRadius**

```
1   // Fig. 9.7: circle.h
2   // Circle class contains x-y coordinate pair and radius.
3   #ifndef CIRCLE_H
4   #define CIRCLE_H
5
6   class Circle {
7
8   public:
9
10      // default constructor
11      Circle( int = 0, int = 0, double = 0.0 );
12
13      void setX( int );          // set x in coordinate pair
14      int getX() const;          // return x from coordinate pair
15
16      void setY( int );          // set y in coordinate pair
17      int getY() const;          // return y from coordinate pair
18
19      void setRadius( double );  // set radius
20      double getRadius() const;  // return radius
21
22      double getDiameter() const;      // return diameter
23      double getCircumference() const; // return circumference
24      double getArea() const;          // return area
25
26      void print() const;        // output Circle object
27
28   private:
29      int x;          // x-coordinate of Circle's center
30      int y;          // y-coordinate of Circle's center
31      double radius;  // Circle's radius
32
33   }; // end class Circle
34
35   #endif
```

Fig. 9.7   **Circle** class header file.

```cpp
1   // Fig. 9.8: circle.cpp
2   // Circle class member-function definitions.
3   #include <iostream>
4
5   using std::cout;
6
7   #include "circle.h"   // Circle class definition
8
9   // default constructor
10  Circle::Circle( int xValue, int yValue, double radiusValue )
11  {
12     x = xValue;
13     y = yValue;
14     setRadius( radiusValue );
15
16  } // end Circle constructor
17
18  // set x in coordinate pair
19  void Circle::setX( int xValue )
20  {
21     x = xValue; // no need for validation
22
23  } // end function setX
24
25  // return x from coordinate pair
26  int Circle::getX() const
27  {
28     return x;
29
30  } // end function getX
31
32  // set y in coordinate pair
33  void Circle::setY( int yValue )
34  {
35     y = yValue; // no need for validation
36
37  } // end function setY
38
39  // return y from coordinate pair
40  int Circle::getY() const
41  {
42     return y;
43
44  } // end function getY
45
46  // set radius
47  void Circle::setRadius( double radiusValue )
48  {
49     radius = ( radiusValue < 0.0 ? 0.0 : radiusValue );
50
51  } // end function setRadius
52
```

Fig. 9.8　**Circle** class contains an *x–y* coordinate and a radius. (Part 1 of 2.)

```
53   // return radius
54   double Circle::getRadius() const
55   {
56      return radius;
57
58   } // end function getRadius
59
60   // calculate and return diameter
61   double Circle::getDiameter() const
62   {
63      return 2 * radius;
64
65   } // end function getDiameter
66
67   // calculate and return circumference
68   double Circle::getCircumference() const
69   {
70      return 3.14159 * getDiameter();
71
72   } // end function getCircumference
73
74   // calculate and return area
75   double Circle::getArea() const
76   {
77      return 3.14159 * radius * radius;
78
79   } // end function getArea
80
81   // output Circle object
82   void Circle::print() const
83   {
84      cout << "Center = [" << x << ", " << y << ']'
85           << "; Radius = " << radius;
86
87   } // end function print
```

Fig. 9.8   **Circle** class contains an *x–y* coordinate and a radius. (Part 2 of 2.)

to retrieve **circle**'s values, then display. Lines 24–26 invoke **circle**'s **setX**, **setY** and **setRadius** member functions to change the *x–y* coordinates and the radius, respectively. Member function **setRadius** (Fig. 9.8, lines 47–51) ensures that data member **radius** cannot be assigned a negative value (i.e., a circle cannot have a negative radius). Line 30 of Fig. 9.9 calls **circle**'s **print** member function to display its *x*-coordinate, *y*-coordinate and radius. Lines 36–42 call **circle**'s **getDiameter**, **getCircumference** and **getArea** member functions to display **circle**'s diameter, circumference and area, respectively.

For class **Circle** (Fig. 9.7–Fig. 9.8), note that much of the code is similar, if not identical, to the code in class **Point** (Fig. 9.4–Fig. 9.5). For example, the declaration in class **Circle** of **private** data members **x** and **y** and member functions **setX**, **getX**, **setY** and **getY** are identical to those of class **Point**. In addition, the **Circle** constructor and member function **print** are almost identical to those of class **Point**, except that they also manipulate the **radius**. The other additions to class **Circle** are **private** data member **radius** and member functions **setRadius**, **getRadius**, **getDiameter**, **get-Circumference** and **getArea**.

```cpp
1   // Fig. 9.9: circletest.cpp
2   // Testing class Circle.
3   #include <iostream>
4
5   using std::cout;
6   using std::endl;
7   using std::fixed;
8
9   #include <iomanip>
10
11  using std::setprecision;
12
13  #include "circle.h"   // Circle class definition
14
15  int main()
16  {
17     Circle circle( 37, 43, 2.5 );   // instantiate Circle object
18
19     // display point coordinates
20     cout << "X coordinate is " << circle.getX()
21          << "\nY coordinate is " << circle.getY()
22          << "\nRadius is " << circle.getRadius();
23
24     circle.setX( 2 );              // set new x-coordinate
25     circle.setY( 2 );              // set new y-coordinate
26     circle.setRadius( 4.25 );  // set new radius
27
28     // display new point value
29     cout << "\n\nThe new location and radius of circle are\n";
30     circle.print();
31
32     // display floating-point values with 2 digits of precision
33     cout << fixed << setprecision( 2 );
34
35     // display Circle's diameter
36     cout << "\nDiameter is " << circle.getDiameter();
37
38     // display Circle's circumference
39     cout << "\nCircumference is " << circle.getCircumference();
40
41     // display Circle's area
42     cout << "\nArea is " << circle.getArea();
43
44     cout << endl;
45
46     return 0;  // indicates successful termination
47
48  } // end main
```

Fig. 9.9   **Circle** class test program. (Part 1 of 2.)

```
X coordinate is 37
Y coordinate is 43
Radius is 2.5

The new location and radius of circle are
Center = [2, 2]; Radius = 4.25
Diameter is 8.50
Circumference is 26.70
Area is 56.74
```

Fig. 9.9   Circle class test program. (Part 2 of 2.)

It appears that we literally copied code from class **Point**, pasted this code into class **Circle**, then modified class **Circle** to include a radius and member functions that manipulate the radius. This "copy-and-paste" approach is often error prone and time consuming. Worse yet, it can result in many physical copies of the code existing throughout a system, creating a code-maintenance nightmare. Is there a way to "absorb" the attributes and behaviors of one class in a way that makes them part of other classes without duplicating code? In the next several examples, we answer that question using a more elegant class construction approach emphasizing the benefits of inheritance.

Point/Circle Hierarchy Using Inheritance
Now we create and test class **Circle2** (Fig. 9.10–Fig. 9.11), which inherits data members **x** and **y** and member functions **setX**, **getX**, **setY** and **getY** from class **Point** (Fig. 9.4–Fig. 9.5). An object of class **Circle2** "is a" **Point** (because inheritance absorbs the capabilities of class **Point**), but, as evidenced by the class **Circle2** header file, also contains data member **radius** (Fig. 9.10, line 25). The colon (**:**) in line 8 of the class definition indicates inheritance. Keyword **public** indicates the type of inheritance. As a derived class (formed with **public** inheritance), **Circle2** inherits all the members of class **Point**, except for the constructor. Thus, the public services of **Circle2** include the **Circle2** constructor (line 13)—each class provides its own constructors that are specific to the class—the **public** member functions inherited from class **Point**; member functions **setRadius** and **getRadius** (lines 15–16); and member functions **getDiameter**, **getCircumference**, **getArea** and **print** (lines 18–22).

```
1   // Fig. 9.10: circle2.h
2   // Circle2 class contains x-y coordinate pair and radius.
3   #ifndef CIRCLE2_H
4   #define CIRCLE2_H
5
6   #include "point.h"   // Point class definition
7
8   class Circle2 : public Point {
9
10  public:
11
12      // default constructor
13      Circle2( int = 0, int = 0, double = 0.0 );
```

Fig. 9.10   Circle2 class header file. (Part 1 of 2.)

```
14
15      void setRadius( double );    // set radius
16      double getRadius() const;    // return radius
17
18      double getDiameter() const;        // return diameter
19      double getCircumference() const;   // return circumference
20      double getArea() const;            // return area
21
22      void print() const;          // output Circle2 object
23
24  private:
25      double radius;   // Circle2's radius
26
27  }; // end class Circle2
28
29  #endif
```

Fig. 9.10   Circle2 class header file. (Part 2 of 2.)

Figure 9.11 shows the member-function implementations for class **Circle2**. The constructor (lines 10–16) should set the *x–y* coordinate to a specific value, so lines 12–13 attempt to assign parameter values to **x** and **y** directly. The compiler generates syntax errors for lines 12 and 13 (and line 56, where **Circle2**'s **print** member function attempts to use the values of **x** and **y** directly), because the derived class **Circle2** is not allowed to access base class **Point**'s **private** data members **x** and **y**. As you can see, C++ rigidly enforces restrictions on accessing **private** data members, so that even a derived class (which is closely related to its base class) cannot access the base class's **private** data.

```
1   // Fig. 9.11: circle2.cpp
2   // Circle2 class member-function definitions.
3   #include <iostream>
4
5   using std::cout;
6
7   #include "circle2.h"    // Circle2 class definition
8
9   // default constructor
10  Circle2::Circle2( int xValue, int yValue, double radiusValue )
11  {
12      x = xValue;
13      y = yValue;
14      setRadius( radiusValue );
15
16  } // end Circle2 constructor
17
18  // set radius
19  void Circle2::setRadius( double radiusValue )
20  {
21      radius = ( radiusValue < 0.0 ? 0.0 : radiusValue );
22
23  } // end function setRadius
```

Fig. 9.11   Private base-class data cannot be accessed from derived class. (Part 1 of 3.)

```
24
25   // return radius
26   double Circle2::getRadius() const
27   {
28      return radius;
29
30   } // end function getRadius
31
32   // calculate and return diameter
33   double Circle2::getDiameter() const
34   {
35      return 2 * radius;
36
37   } // end function getDiameter
38
39   // calculate and return circumference
40   double Circle2::getCircumference() const
41   {
42      return 3.14159 * getDiameter();
43
44   } // end function getCircumference
45
46   // calculate and return area
47   double Circle2::getArea() const
48   {
49      return 3.14159 * radius * radius;
50
51   } // end function getArea
52
53   // output Circle2 object
54   void Circle2::print() const
55   {
56      cout << "Center = [" << x << ", " << y << ']'
57          << "; Radius = " << radius;
58
59   } // end function print
```

```
C:\cpphtp4\examples\ch09\CircleTest\circle2.cpp(12) : error C2248:
'x' : cannot access private member declared in class 'Point'
        C:\cpphtp4\examples\ch09\circletest\point.h(20) :
        see declaration of 'x'

C:\cpphtp4\examples\ch09\CircleTest\circle2.cpp(13) : error C2248:
'y' : cannot access private member declared in class 'Point'
        C:\cpphtp4\examples\ch09\circletest\point.h(21) :
        see declaration of 'y'

C:\cpphtp4\examples\ch09\CircleTest\circle2.cpp(56) : error C2248:
'x' : cannot access private member declared in class 'Point'
        C:\cpphtp4\examples\ch09\circletest\point.h(20) :
        see declaration of 'x'
```

(continued next page)

Fig. 9.11 Private base-class data cannot be accessed from derived class. (Part 2 of 3.)

```
C:\cpphtp4\examples\ch09\CircleTest\circle2.cpp(56) : error C2248:
'y' : cannot access private member declared in class 'Point'
        C:\cpphtp4\examples\ch09\circletest\point.h(21) :
        see declaration of 'y'
```

Fig. 9.11   Private base-class data cannot be accessed from derived class. (Part 3 of 3.)

Point/Circle Hierarchy Using protected Data

To enable class **Circle2** to access **Point** data members **x** and **y** directly, we can declare those members as **protected** in the base class. As we discussed in Section 9.3, a base class's **protected** members can be accessed by members and **friend**s of the base class and by members and **friend**s of any classes derived from that base class. Class **Point2** (Fig. 9.12–Fig. 9.13) is a modification of class **Point** (Fig. 9.4–Fig. 9.5) that declares data members **x** and **y** as **protected** (Fig. 9.12, lines 19–21) rather than **private**. Other than the class name change (and, hence, the constructor name change) to **Point2**, the member-function implementations in Fig. 9.13 are identical to those in Fig. 9.5.

```
1   // Fig. 9.12: point2.h
2   // Point2 class definition represents an x-y coordinate pair.
3   #ifndef POINT2_H
4   #define POINT2_H
5
6   class Point2 {
7
8   public:
9       Point2( int = 0, int = 0 ); // default constructor
10
11      void setX( int );    // set x in coordinate pair
12      int getX() const;    // return x from coordinate pair
13
14      void setY( int );    // set y in coordinate pair
15      int getY() const;    // return y from coordinate pair
16
17      void print() const;  // output Point2 object
18
19  protected:
20      int x;  // x part of coordinate pair
21      int y;  // y part of coordinate pair
22
23  }; // end class Point2
24
25  #endif
```

Fig. 9.12   **Point2** class header file.

```
1   // Fig. 9.13: point2.cpp
2   // Point2 class member-function definitions.
3   #include <iostream>
```

Fig. 9.13   **Point2** class represents an *x-y* coordinate pair as **protected** data. (Part 1 of 2.)

```
4
5   using std::cout;
6
7   #include "point2.h"   // Point2 class definition
8
9   // default constructor
10  Point2::Point2( int xValue, int yValue )
11  {
12     x = xValue;
13     y = yValue;
14
15  } // end Point2 constructor
16
17  // set x in coordinate pair
18  void Point2::setX( int xValue )
19  {
20     x = xValue; // no need for validation
21
22  } // end function setX
23
24  // return x from coordinate pair
25  int Point2::getX() const
26  {
27     return x;
28
29  } // end function getX
30
31  // set y in coordinate pair
32  void Point2::setY( int yValue )
33  {
34     y = yValue; // no need for validation
35
36  } // end function setY
37
38  // return y from coordinate pair
39  int Point2::getY() const
40  {
41     return y;
42
43  } // end function getY
44
45  // output Point2 object
46  void Point2::print() const
47  {
48     cout << '[' << x << ", " << y << ']';
49
50  } // end function print
```

Fig. 9.13   **Point2** class represents an x-y coordinate pair as **protected** data. (Part 2 of 2.)

Class **Circle3** (Fig. 9.14–Fig. 9.15) is a modification of class **Circle2** (Fig. 9.10–Fig. 9.11) that inherits from class **Point2** rather than from class **Point**. Because class **Circle3** inherits from class **Point2**, objects of class **Circle3** can access inherited data members that were declared **protected** in class **Point2** (i.e., data members **x** and **y**). As a result, the compiler does not generate errors when compiling the **Circle3** constructor and **print** member function definitions in Fig. 9.15 (lines 10–16 and 54–59, respectively). This shows the special privileges that a derived class is granted to access **protected** base-class data members. Objects of a derived class also can access **protected** members in any of that derived class's indirect base classes.

```cpp
1   // Fig. 9.14: circle3.h
2   // Circle3 class contains x-y coordinate pair and radius.
3   #ifndef CIRCLE3_H
4   #define CIRCLE3_H
5
6   #include "point2.h"  // Point2 class definition
7
8   class Circle3 : public Point2 {
9
10  public:
11
12     // default constructor
13     Circle3( int = 0, int = 0, double = 0.0 );
14
15     void setRadius( double );   // set radius
16     double getRadius() const;   // return radius
17
18     double getDiameter() const;       // return diameter
19     double getCircumference() const;  // return circumference
20     double getArea() const;           // return area
21
22     void print() const;       // output Circle3 object
23
24  private:
25     double radius;  // Circle3's radius
26
27  }; // end class Circle3
28
29  #endif
```

Fig. 9.14　Circle3 class header file.

```cpp
1   // Fig. 9.15: circle3.cpp
2   // Circle3 class member-function definitions.
3   #include <iostream>
4
5   using std::cout;
6
7   #include "circle3.h"   // Circle3 class definition
8
9   // default constructor
10  Circle3::Circle3( int xValue, int yValue, double radiusValue )
11  {
12     x = xValue;
```

Fig. 9.15　Circle3 class that inherits from class **Point2**. (Part 1 of 2.)

```
13        y = yValue;
14        setRadius( radiusValue );
15
16   } // end Circle3 constructor
17
18   // set radius
19   void Circle3::setRadius( double radiusValue )
20   {
21      radius = ( radiusValue < 0.0 ? 0.0 : radiusValue );
22
23   } // end function setRadius
24
25   // return radius
26   double Circle3::getRadius() const
27   {
28      return radius;
29
30   } // end function getRadius
31
32   // calculate and return diameter
33   double Circle3::getDiameter() const
34   {
35      return 2 * radius;
36
37   } // end function getDiameter
38
39   // calculate and return circumference
40   double Circle3::getCircumference() const
41   {
42      return 3.14159 * getDiameter();
43
44   } // end function getCircumference
45
46   // calculate and return area
47   double Circle3::getArea() const
48   {
49      return 3.14159 * radius * radius;
50
51   } // end function getArea
52
53   // output Circle3 object
54   void Circle3::print() const
55   {
56      cout << "Center = [" << x << ", " << y << ']'
57           << "; Radius = " << radius;
58
59   } // end function print
```

Fig. 9.15   `Circle3` class that inherits from class `Point2`. (Part 2 of 2.)

Class **Circle3** does not inherit class **Point2**'s constructor. However, class **Circle3**'s constructor (lines 10–16) calls class **Point2**'s constructor implicitly. In fact, the first task of any derived-class constructor is to call its direct base class's constructor, either implicitly or explicitly. (The syntax for calling a base-class constructor is discussed later in this section.) If the code does not include an explicit call to the base-class constructor, an implicit call is made to the base class's default constructor. Even though lines 12–13 set **x** and **y** values explicitly, the constructor first calls the **Point2** default constructor, which initializes these data members to their default **0** values. Thus, **x** and **y** each are initialized twice. We will fix this performance problem in the next examples.

Figure 9.16 performs identical tests on class **Circle3** as those that Fig. 9.9 performed on class **Circle** (Fig. 9.7–Fig. 9.8). Note that the outputs of the two programs are identical. We created class **Circle** without using inheritance and created class **Circle3** using inheritance; however, both classes provide the same functionality. Note that the code listing for class **Circle3** (i.e., the header and implementation files), which is 88 lines, is considerably shorter than the code listing for class **Circle**, which is 122 lines, because class **Circle3** absorbs part of its functionality from **Point2**, whereas class **Circle** does not absorb any functionality. Also, there is now only one copy of the point functionality mentioned in class **Point2**. This makes the code easier to debug, maintain and modify, because the point-related code exists only in the files of Fig. 9.12–Fig. 9.13.

```
1   // Fig. 9.16: circletest3.cpp
2   // Testing class Circle3.
3   #include <iostream>
4
5   using std::cout;
6   using std::endl;
7   using std::fixed;
8
9   #include <iomanip>
10
11  using std::setprecision;
12
13  #include "circle3.h"  // Circle3 class definition
14
15  int main()
16  {
17     Circle3 circle( 37, 43, 2.5 ); // instantiate Circle3 object
18
19     // display point coordinates
20     cout << "X coordinate is " << circle.getX()
21          << "\nY coordinate is " << circle.getY()
22          << "\nRadius is " << circle.getRadius();
23
24     circle.setX( 2 );           // set new x-coordinate
25     circle.setY( 2 );           // set new y-coordinate
26     circle.setRadius( 4.25 );   // set new radius
27
28     // display new point value
29     cout << "\n\nThe new location and radius of circle are\n";
30     circle.print();
31
32     // display floating-point values with 2 digits of precision
33     cout << fixed << setprecision( 2 );
34
```

Fig. 9.16   Protected base-class data can be accessed from derived class. (Part 1 of 2.)

```
35        // display Circle3's diameter
36        cout << "\nDiameter is " << circle.getDiameter();
37
38        // display Circle3's circumference
39        cout << "\nCircumference is " << circle.getCircumference();
40
41        // display Circle3's area
42        cout << "\nArea is " << circle.getArea();
43
44        cout << endl;
45
46        return 0;  // indicates successful termination
47
48    } // end main
```

```
X coordinate is 37
Y coordinate is 43
Radius is 2.5

The new location and radius of circle are
Center = [2, 2]; Radius = 4.25
Diameter is 8.50
Circumference is 26.70
Area is 56.74
```

Fig. 9.16   Protected base-class data can be accessed from derived class. (Part 2 of 2.)

In this example, we declared base-class data members as **protected**, so that derived classes could modify their values directly. The use of **protected** data members allows for a slight increase in performance, because we avoid incurring the overhead of a call to a *set* or *get* member function. However, such performance increases are often negligible compared to the optimizations compilers can perform. It is better to use **private** data to encourage proper software engineering. Your code will be easier to maintain, modify and debug.

Using **protected** data members creates two major problems. First, the derived-class object does not have to use a member function to set the value of the base-class's **protected** data member. Therefore, a derived-class object easily can assign an illegal value to the **protected** data member, thus leaving the object in an invalid state. For example, if we were to declare **Circle3**'s data member **radius** as **protected**, a derived-class object (e.g., **Cylinder**) could then assign a negative value to **radius**. The second problem with using **protected** data members is that derived-class member functions are more likely to be written to depend on the base-class implementation. In practice, derived classes should depend only on the base-class services (i.e., non-**private** member functions) and not on the base-class implementation. With **protected** data members in the base class, if the base-class implementation changes, we may need to modify all derived classes of that base class. For example, if for some reason we were to change the names of data members **x** and **y** to **xCoordinate** and **yCoordinate**, then we would have to do so for all occurrences in which a derived class references these base-class data members directly. In such a case, the software is said to be *fragile* or *brittle*, because a small change in the base class can "break" derived-class implementation. The programmer should be able to change the base-class implementation freely, while still providing the same services to derived classes. (Of course, if the base-class services change, we must reimplement our derived classes, but good object-oriented design attempts to prevent this.)

Software Engineering Observation 9.3

*It is appropriate to use the **protected** access specifier when a base class should provide a service (i.e., a member function) only to its derived classes and should not provide the service to other clients.*

Software Engineering Observation 9.4

*Declaring base-class data members **private** (as opposed to declaring them **protected**) enables programmers to change the base-class implementation without having to change derived-class implementations.*

Testing and Debugging Tip 9.1

*When possible, avoid including **protected** data members in a base class. Rather, include non-**private** member functions that access **private** data members, ensuring that the object maintains a consistent state.*

Point/Circle Hierarchy Using private Data

We now reexamine our point/circle hierarchy example once more; this time, attempting to use the best software-engineering practices. Class **Point3** (Fig. 9.17–Fig. 9.18) declares data members **x** and **y** as **private** (Fig. 9.17, lines 19–21) and exposes member functions **setX**, **getX**, **setY**, **getY** and **print** for manipulating these values. In the constructor implementation (Fig. 9.18, lines 10–15), note that member initializers are used (line 11) to specify the values of members **x** and **y**. We show how derived-class **Circle4** (Fig. 9.19–Fig. 9.20) can invoke non-**private** base-class member functions (**setX**, **getX**, **setY** and **getY**) to manipulate these data members.

Software Engineering Observation 9.5

When possible, use member functions to alter and obtain the values of data members, even if those values can be modified directly. A set member function can prevent attempts to assign inappropriate values to the data member, and a get member function can help control the presentation of the data to clients.

Performance Tip 9.1

Using a member function to access a data member's value can be slightly slower than accessing the data directly. However, attempting to optimize programs by referencing data directly often is unnecessary, because the compiler optimizes the programs implicitly. Today's so-called "optimizing compilers" are carefully designed to perform many optimizations implicitly, even if the programmer does not write what appears to be the most optimal code. A good rule is, "Do not second-guess the compiler."

```
1   // Fig. 9.17: point3.h
2   // Point3 class definition represents an x-y coordinate pair.
3   #ifndef POINT3_H
4   #define POINT3_H
5
6   class Point3 {
7
```

Fig. 9.17   Point3 class header file. (Part 1 of 2.)

```
8   public:
9      Point3( int = 0, int = 0 ); // default constructor
10
11     void setX( int );    // set x in coordinate pair
12     int getX() const;    // return x from coordinate pair
13
14     void setY( int );    // set y in coordinate pair
15     int getY() const;    // return y from coordinate pair
16
17     void print() const;  // output Point3 object
18
19  private:
20     int x;   // x part of coordinate pair
21     int y;   // y part of coordinate pair
22
23  }; // end class Point3
24
25  #endif
```

Fig. 9.17   **Point3** class header file. (Part 2 of 2.)

```
1   // Fig. 9.18: point3.cpp
2   // Point3 class member-function definitions.
3   #include <iostream>
4
5   using std::cout;
6
7   #include "point3.h"    // Point3 class definition
8
9   // default constructor
10  Point3::Point3( int xValue, int yValue )
11     : x( xValue ), y( yValue )
12  {
13     // empty body
14
15  } // end Point3 constructor
16
17  // set x in coordinate pair
18  void Point3::setX( int xValue )
19  {
20     x = xValue; // no need for validation
21
22  } // end function setX
23
24  // return x from coordinate pair
25  int Point3::getX() const
26  {
27     return x;
28
29  } // end function getX
30
```

Fig. 9.18   **Point3** class uses member functions to manipulate its **private** data. (Part 1 of 2.)

```
31  // set y in coordinate pair
32  void Point3::setY( int yValue )
33  {
34     y = yValue; // no need for validation
35
36  } // end function setY
37
38  // return y from coordinate pair
39  int Point3::getY() const
40  {
41     return y;
42
43  } // end function getY
44
45  // output Point3 object
46  void Point3::print() const
47  {
48     cout << '[' << getX() << ", " << getY() << ']';
49
50  } // end function print
```

Fig. 9.18   **Point3** class uses member functions to manipulate its **private** data. (Part 2 of 2.)

Class **Circle4** (Fig. 9.19–Fig. 9.20) has several changes to its member function implementations (Fig. 9.20) that distinguish it from class **Circle3** (Fig. 9.14–Fig. 9.15). Class **Circle4**'s constructor (lines 10–15) introduces *base-class initializer syntax* (line 11), which uses a member initializer to pass arguments to the base-class (**Point3**) constructor. C++ actually requires a derived-class constructor to call its base-class constructor to initialize the base-class data members that are inherited into the derived class. Line 11 accomplishes this task by invoking the **Point3** constructor by name. Values **xValue** and **yValue** are passed from the **Circle4** constructor to the **Point3** constructor to initialize base-class members **x** and **y**. If the **Circle** constructor did not invoke the **Point** constructor explicitly, the default **Point** constructor would be invoked implicitly with the default values for **x** and **y** (i.e., 0 and 0). If class **Point3** did not provide a default constructor, the compiler would issue a syntax error.

Common Programming Error 9.1

It is a syntax error if a derived-class constructor calls one of its base-class constructors with arguments that do not match exactly the number and types of parameters specified in one of the base-class constructor definitions.

In Fig. 9.15, class **Circle3**'s constructor actually initialized base-class members **x** and **y** twice. First, class **Point2**'s constructor was called implicitly with the default values **x** and **y**, then class **Circle3**'s constructor assigned values to **x** and **y** in its body.

```
1  // Fig. 9.19: circle4.h
2  // Circle4 class contains x-y coordinate pair and radius.
3  #ifndef CIRCLE4_H
4  #define CIRCLE4_H
```

Fig. 9.19   **Circle4** class header file. (Part 1 of 2.)

```
5
6   #include "point3.h"   // Point3 class definition
7
8   class Circle4 : public Point3 {
9
10  public:
11
12     // default constructor
13     Circle4( int = 0, int = 0, double = 0.0 );
14
15     void setRadius( double );   // set radius
16     double getRadius() const;   // return radius
17
18     double getDiameter() const;        // return diameter
19     double getCircumference() const;   // return circumference
20     double getArea() const;            // return area
21
22     void print() const;        // output Circle4 object
23
24  private:
25     double radius;   // Circle4's radius
26
27  }; // end class Circle4
28
29  #endif
```

Fig. 9.19   **Circle4** class header file. (Part 2 of 2.)

```
1   // Fig. 9.20: circle4.cpp
2   // Circle4 class member-function definitions.
3   #include <iostream>
4
5   using std::cout;
6
7   #include "circle4.h"   // Circle4 class definition
8
9   // default constructor
10  Circle4::Circle4( int xValue, int yValue, double radiusValue )
11     : Point3( xValue, yValue )  // call base-class constructor
12  {
13     setRadius( radiusValue );
14
15  } // end Circle4 constructor
16
17  // set radius
18  void Circle4::setRadius( double radiusValue )
19  {
20     radius = ( radiusValue < 0.0 ? 0.0 : radiusValue );
21
22  } // end function setRadius
23
```

Fig. 9.20   **Circle4** class that inherits from class **Point3**, which does not provide **protected** data. (Part 1 of 2.)

```
24   // return radius
25   double Circle4::getRadius() const
26   {
27      return radius;
28
29   } // end function getRadius
30
31   // calculate and return diameter
32   double Circle4::getDiameter() const
33   {
34      return 2 * getRadius();
35
36   } // end function getDiameter
37
38   // calculate and return circumference
39   double Circle4::getCircumference() const
40   {
41      return 3.14159 * getDiameter();
42
43   } // end function getCircumference
44
45   // calculate and return area
46   double Circle4::getArea() const
47   {
48      return 3.14159 * getRadius() * getRadius();
49
50   } // end function getArea
51
52   // output Circle4 object
53   void Circle4::print() const
54   {
55      cout << "Center = ";
56      Point3::print();            // invoke Point3's print function
57      cout << "; Radius = " << getRadius();
58
59   } // end function print
```

Fig. 9.20 `Circle4` class that inherits from class `Point3`, which does not provide `protected` data. (Part 2 of 2.)

Performance Tip 9.2

In a derived-class constructor, initializing member objects and invoking base-class constructors explicitly in the member initializer list can prevent duplicate initialization in which a default constructor is called, then data members are modified again in the body of the derived-class constructor.

In addition to the changes discusses so far, member functions **getDiameter** (Fig. 9.20, lines 32–36), **getArea** (lines 46–50) and **print** (lines 53–59) each invoke member function **getRadius** to obtain the radius value, rather than accessing the **radius** directly. If we decide to rename data member **radius**, only the bodies of functions **setRadius** and **getRadius** will need to change.

Class **Circle4**'s **print** function (Fig. 9.20, lines 53–59) redefines class **Point3**'s **print** member function (Fig. 9.18, lines 46–50). Class **Circle4**'s version displays the

private data members **x** and **y** of class **Point3** by calling base-class **Point3**'s **print** function with the expression **Point3::print()** (line 56). Note the syntax used to invoke a redefined base-class member function from a derived class—place the base-class name and the binary scope-resolution operator (**::**) before the base-class member-function name. This member-function invocation is a good software engineering practice: Recall that *Software Engineering Observation* 6.19 stated that, if an object's member function performs the actions needed by another object, call that member function rather than duplicating its code body. By having **Circle4**'s **print** function invoke **Point3**'s **print** function to perform part of the task of printing a **Circle4** object (i.e., to display the *x*- and *y*-coordinate values), we avoid duplicating code and reduce code-maintenance problems.

Common Programming Error 9.2

When a base-class member function is redefined in a derived class, the derived-class version often calls the base-class version to do additional work. Failure to use the **::** *reference (prefixed with the name of the base class) when referencing the base class's member function causes infinite recursion, because the derived-class member function would then call itself.*

Common Programming Error 9.3

Including a base-class member function with a different signature in the derived class hides the base-class version of the function. Attempts to call the base-class version through the **public** *interface of a derived-class object result in compilation errors.*

Figure 9.21 performs identical manipulations on a **Circle4** object as did Fig. 9.9 and Fig. 9.16 on objects of classes **Circle** and **Circle3**, respectively. Although each "circle" class behaves identically, class **Circle4** is the best engineered. Using inheritance, we have efficiently and effectively constructed a well-engineered class.

```
1   // Fig. 9.21: circletest4.cpp
2   // Testing class Circle4.
3   #include <iostream>
4
5   using std::cout;
6   using std::endl;
7   using std::fixed;
8
9   #include <iomanip>
10
11  using std::setprecision;
12
13  #include "circle4.h"   // Circle4 class definition
14
15  int main()
16  {
17     Circle4 circle( 37, 43, 2.5 ); // instantiate Circle4 object
18
19     // display point coordinates
20     cout << "X coordinate is " << circle.getX()
21          << "\nY coordinate is " << circle.getY()
22          << "\nRadius is " << circle.getRadius();
```

Fig. 9.21   Base-class **private** data is accessible to a derived class via **public** or **protected** member function inherited by the derived class. (Part 1 of 2.)

```
23
24      circle.setX( 2 );        // set new x-coordinate
25      circle.setY( 2 );        // set new y-coordinate
26      circle.setRadius( 4.25 );   // set new radius
27
28      // display new circle value
29      cout << "\n\nThe new location and radius of circle are\n";
30      circle.print();
31
32      // display floating-point values with 2 digits of precision
33      cout << fixed << setprecision( 2 );
34
35      // display Circle4's diameter
36      cout << "\nDiameter is " << circle.getDiameter();
37
38      // display Circle4's circumference
39      cout << "\nCircumference is " << circle.getCircumference();
40
41      // display Circle4's area
42      cout << "\nArea is " << circle.getArea();
43
44      cout << endl;
45
46      return 0;   // indicates successful termination
47
48  } // end main
```

```
X coordinate is 37
Y coordinate is 43
Radius is 2.5

The new location and radius of circle are
Center = [2, 2]; Radius = 4.25
Diameter is 8.50
Circumference is 26.70
Area is 56.74
```

Fig. 9.21   Base-class **private** data is accessible to a derived class via **public** or **protected** member function inherited by the derived class. (Part 2 of 2.)

9.5 Case Study: Three-Level Inheritance Hierarchy

Let us consider a more substantial inheritance example involving a three-level point/circle–cylinder hierarchy. In Section 9.4, we developed classes **Point3** (Fig. 9.17–Fig. 9.18) and **Circle4** (Fig. 9.19–Fig. 9.20). Now, we present an example in which we derive class **Cylinder** from class **Circle4**.

The first class that we use in our case study is class **Point3** (Fig. 9.17–Fig. 9.18). We declared **Point3**'s data members as **private**. Class **Point3** also contains member functions **setX**, **getX**, **setY** and **getY** for accessing **x** and **y**, and member function **print** for displaying the *x–y* coordinate pair on the standard output.

We also use class **Circle4** (Fig. 9.19–Fig. 9.20), which inherits from class **Point3**. Class **Circle4** contains functionality from class **Point3** and provides member function **setRadius**, which ensures that the **radius** data member cannot hold a negative value, and member functions **getRadius**, **getDiameter**, **getCircumference**, **getArea** and **print**. Derived classes of class **Circle4** (such as class **Cylinder**, which we introduce momentarily) should redefine these member functions as necessary to provide implementations specific to the derived class. For example, a circle has an area that is calculated by the formula, πr^2, in which r represents the circle's radius. However, a cylinder has a surface area that is calculated by the formula, $(2\pi r^2) + (2\pi rh)$, in which r represents the cylinder's radius and h represents the cylinder's height. Therefore, class **Cylinder** should redefine member function **getArea** to include this calculation.

Figure 9.22–Fig. 9.23 present class **Cylinder**, which inherits from class **Circle4**. The **Cylinder** header file (Fig. 9.22) specifies that a **Cylinder** has a **height** (line 23) and specifies class **Cylinder**'s **public** services, which include inherited **Circle4** member functions (line 8) **setRadius**, **getRadius**, **getDiameter**, **getCircumference**, **getArea** and **print**; indirectly inherited **Point3** member functions **setX**, **getX**, **setY** and **getY**; the **Cylinder** constructor (line 13); and **Cylinder** member functions **setHeight**, **getHeight**, **getArea**, **getVolume** and **print** (lines 15–20). Member functions **getArea** and **print** redefine the member functions with the same names that are inherited from class **Circle4**.

Figure 9.23 shows class **Cylinder**'s member-function implementations. Member function **getArea** (lines 33–38) redefines member function **getArea** of class **Circle4** to calculate surface area. Member function **print** (lines 48–53) redefines member function **print** of class **Circle4** to display the text representation of the cylinder to the standard

```cpp
1  // Fig. 9.22: cylinder.h
2  // Cylinder class inherits from class Circle4.
3  #ifndef CYLINDER_H
4  #define CYLINDER_H
5
6  #include "circle4.h"  // Circle4 class definition
7
8  class Cylinder : public Circle4 {
9
10 public:
11
12    // default constructor
13    Cylinder( int = 0, int = 0, double = 0.0, double = 0.0 );
14
15    void setHeight( double );  // set Cylinder's height
16    double getHeight() const;  // return Cylinder's height
17
18    double getArea() const;    // return Cylinder's area
19    double getVolume() const;  // return Cylinder's volume
20    void print() const;        // output Cylinder
21
22 private:
23    double height;  // Cylinder's height
24
25 }; // end class Cylinder
26
27 #endif
```

Fig. 9.22 Cylinder class header file.

output. Class **Cylinder** also includes member function **getVolume** (lines 41–45) to calculate the cylinder's volume.

Figure 9.24 is a **CylinderTest** application that tests class **Cylinder**. Line 18
instantiates a **Cylinder** object called **cylinder**. Lines 21–24 use **cylinder**'s

```cpp
1   // Fig. 9.23: cylinder.cpp
2   // Cylinder class inherits from class Circle4.
3   #include <iostream>
4
5   using std::cout;
6
7   #include "cylinder.h"    // Cylinder class definition
8
9   // default constructor
10  Cylinder::Cylinder( int xValue, int yValue, double radiusValue,
11     double heightValue )
12     : Circle4( xValue, yValue, radiusValue )
13  {
14     setHeight( heightValue );
15
16  } // end Cylinder constructor
17
18  // set Cylinder's height
19  void Cylinder::setHeight( double heightValue )
20  {
21     height = ( heightValue < 0.0 ? 0.0 : heightValue );
22
23  } // end function setHeight
24
25  // get Cylinder's height
26  double Cylinder::getHeight() const
27  {
28     return height;
29
30  } // end function getHeight
31
32  // redefine Circle4 function getArea to calculate Cylinder area
33  double Cylinder::getArea() const
34  {
35     return 2 * Circle4::getArea() +
36        getCircumference() * getHeight();
37
38  } // end function getArea
39
40  // calculate Cylinder volume
41  double Cylinder::getVolume() const
42  {
43     return Circle4::getArea() * getHeight();
44
45  } // end function getVolume
46
```

Fig. 9.23   **Cylinder** class inherits from class **Circle4** and redefines member
function **getArea**. (Part 1 of 2.)

```
47    // output Cylinder object
48    void Cylinder::print() const
49    {
50       Circle4::print();
51       cout << "; Height = " << getHeight();
52
53    } // end function print
```

Fig. 9.23 **Cylinder** class inherits from class **Circle4** and redefines member function **getArea**. (Part 2 of 2.)

member functions **getX**, **getY**, **getRadius** and **getHeight** to obtain information about **cylinder**, because **CylinderTest** cannot reference the **private** data members of class **Cylinder** directly. Lines 26–29 use member functions **setX**, **setY**, **setRadius** and **setHeight** to reset **cylinder**'s *x–y* coordinates (we assume the cylinder's *x–y* coordinates specify the position of the center of its bottom on the *x–y* plane), radius and height. Class **Cylinder** can use class **Point3**'s **setX**, **getX**, **setY** and **getY** member functions, because class **Cylinder** inherits them indirectly from class **Point3**. (Class **Cylinder** inherits member functions **setX**, **getX**, **setY** and **getY** directly from class **Circle4**, which inherited them directly from class **Point3**.) Line 33 invokes **cylinder**'s **print** member function to display the text representation of object **cylinder**. Lines 39 and 43 invoke member functions **getDiameter** and **getCircumference** of the **cylinder** object—because class **Cylinder** inherits these functions from class **Circle4**, these member functions, exactly as defined in **Circle4**, are invoked. Lines 46 and 49 invoke member functions **getArea** and **getVolume** to determine the surface area and volume of **cylinder**.

```
1     // Fig. 9.24: cylindertest.cpp
2     // Testing class Cylinder.
3     #include <iostream>
4
5     using std::cout;
6     using std::endl;
7     using std::fixed;
8
9     #include <iomanip>
10
11    using std::setprecision;
12
13    #include "cylinder.h"  // Cylinder class definition
14
15    int main()
16    {
17       // instantiate Cylinder object
18       Cylinder cylinder( 12, 23, 2.5, 5.7 );
19
20       // display point coordinates
21       cout << "X coordinate is " << cylinder.getX()
22            << "\nY coordinate is " << cylinder.getY()
```

Fig. 9.24 **Point/Circle/Cylinder** hierarchy test program. (Part 1 of 2.)

```
23                    << "\nRadius is " << cylinder.getRadius()
24                    << "\nHeight is " << cylinder.getHeight();
25
26       cylinder.setX( 2 );           // set new x-coordinate
27       cylinder.setY( 2 );           // set new y-coordinate
28       cylinder.setRadius( 4.25 );   // set new radius
29       cylinder.setHeight( 10 );     // set new height
30
31       // display new cylinder value
32       cout << "\n\nThe new location and radius of circle are\n";
33       cylinder.print();
34
35       // display floating-point values with 2 digits of precision
36       cout << fixed << setprecision( 2 );
37
38       // display cylinder's diameter
39       cout << "\n\nDiameter is " << cylinder.getDiameter();
40
41       // display cylinder's circumference
42       cout << "\nCircumference is "
43           << cylinder.getCircumference();
44
45       // display cylinder's area
46       cout << "\nArea is " << cylinder.getArea();
47
48       // display cylinder's volume
49       cout << "\nVolume is " << cylinder.getVolume();
50
51       cout << endl;
52
53       return 0;  // indicates successful termination
54
55   } // end main
```

```
X coordinate is 12
Y coordinate is 23
Radius is 2.5
Height is 5.7

The new location and radius of circle are
Center = [2, 2]; Radius = 4.25; Height = 10

Diameter is 8.50
Circumference is 26.70
Area is 380.53
Volume is 567.45
```

Fig. 9.24   **Point/Circle/Cylinder** hierarchy test program. (Part 2 of 2.)

Using the point/circle/cylinder example, we have shown the use and benefits of inheritance. We were able to develop classes **Circle4** and **Cylinder** much more quickly by using inheritance than if we had developed these classes "from scratch." Inheritance avoids duplicating code and the associated code-maintenance problems.

9.6 Constructors and Destructors in Derived Classes

As we explained in the previous section, instantiating a derived-class object begins a chain of constructor calls in which the derived-class constructor, before performing its own tasks, invokes its direct base class's constructor either explicitly or implicitly. Similarly, if the base class were derived from another class, the base-class constructor would be required to invoke the constructor of the next class up in the hierarchy, and so on. The last constructor called in the chain is defined in the class at the base of the inheritance hierarchy (for example, class **Point3**, in the **Point3/Circle4/Cylinder** hierarchy), whose body actually finishes executing first. The original derived-class constructor's body finishes executing last. Each base-class constructor initializes the base-class data members that the derived-class object inherits. For example, again consider the **Point3/Circle4/Cylinder** hierarchy from Fig. 9.18, Fig. 9.20 and Fig. 9.23. When a program creates a **Cylinder** object, the **Cylinder** constructor is called. That constructor calls **Circle4**'s constructor, which in turn calls **Point3**'s constructor. The **Point3** constructor initializes the *x*–*y* coordinates of the **Cylinder** object. When **Point3**'s constructor completes execution, it returns control to **Circle4**'s constructor, which initializes the **Cylinder** object's radius. When **Circle4**'s constructor completes execution, it returns control to **Cylinder**'s constructor, which initializes the **Cylinder** object's height.

Software Engineering Observation 9.6

When a program creates a derived-class object, the derived-class constructor immediately calls the base-class constructor, the base-class constructor's body executes, then the derived-class constructor's body executes.

When a derived-class object is destroyed, the program then calls that object's destructor. This begins a chain of destructor calls in which the derived-class destructor and the destructors of the direct and indirect base classes execute in reverse of the order in which the constructors executed. When a derived-class object's destructor is called, the destructor performs its task, then invokes the destructor of the next base class in the hierarchy. This process repeats until the destructor of the final base class at the top of the hierarchy is called. Then the object is removed from memory.

Software Engineering Observation 9.7

Suppose that we create an object of a derived class where both the base class and the derived class contain objects of other classes. When an object of that derived class is created, first the constructors for the base class's member objects execute, then the base-class constructor executes, then the constructors for the derived class's member objects execute, then the derived class's constructor executes. Destructors are called in the reverse of the order in which their corresponding constructors are called.

Base-class constructors, destructors and assignment operators are not inherited by derived classes. Derived-class constructors and assignment operators, however, can call base-class constructors and assignment operators.

Our next example revisits the point/circle hierarchy by defining class **Point4** (Fig. 9.25–Fig. 9.26) and class **Circle5** (Fig. 9.27–Fig. 9.28) that contain constructors and destructors, each of which prints a message when it is invoked.

Class **Point4** (Fig. 9.25–Fig. 9.26) contains the features from class **Point** (Fig. 9.4–Fig. 9.5). We modified the constructor (lines 11–18 of Fig. 9.26) and included a destructor (lines 21–27), each of which outputs a line of text upon its invocation.

```
1   // Fig. 9.25: point4.h
2   // Point4 class definition represents an x-y coordinate pair.
3   #ifndef POINT4_H
4   #define POINT4_H
5
6   class Point4 {
7
8   public:
9      Point4( int = 0, int = 0 ); // default constructor
10     ~Point4();                   // destructor
11
12     void setX( int );    // set x in coordinate pair
13     int getX() const;    // return x from coordinate pair
14
15     void setY( int );    // set y in coordinate pair
16     int getY() const;    // return y from coordinate pair
17
18     void print() const;  // output Point3 object
19
20  private:
21     int x;  // x part of coordinate pair
22     int y;  // y part of coordinate pair
23
24  }; // end class Point4
25
26  #endif
```

Fig. 9.25   Point4 class header file.

```
1   // Fig. 9.26: point4.cpp
2   // Point4 class member-function definitions.
3   #include <iostream>
4
5   using std::cout;
6   using std::endl;
7
8   #include "point4.h"   // Point4 class definition
9
10  // default constructor
11  Point4::Point4( int xValue, int yValue )
12     : x( xValue ), y( yValue )
13  {
14     cout << "Point4 constructor: ";
15     print();
16     cout << endl;
17
18  } // end Point4 constructor
19
20  // destructor
21  Point4::~Point4()
22  {
23     cout << "Point4 destructor: ";
```

Fig. 9.26   Point4 base class contains a constructor and a destructor. (Part 1 of 2.)

```
24        print();
25        cout << endl;
26
27   } // end Point4 destructor
28
29   // set x in coordinate pair
30   void Point4::setX( int xValue )
31   {
32        x = xValue; // no need for validation
33
34   } // end function setX
35
36   // return x from coordinate pair
37   int Point4::getX() const
38   {
39        return x;
40
41   } // end function getX
42
43   // set y in coordinate pair
44   void Point4::setY( int yValue )
45   {
46        y = yValue; // no need for validation
47
48   } // end function setY
49
50   // return y from coordinate pair
51   int Point4::getY() const
52   {
53        return y;
54
55   } // end function getY
56
57   // output Point4 object
58   void Point4::print() const
59   {
60        cout << '[' << getX() << ", " << getY() << ']';
61
62   } // end function print
```

Fig. 9.26   **Point4** base class contains a constructor and a destructor. (Part 2 of 2.)

Class **Circle5** (Fig. 9.27–Fig. 9.28) contains features from class **Circle4** (Fig. 9.19–Fig. 9.20). We modified the constructor (lines 11–20 of Fig. 9.28) and included a destructor (lines 23–29), each of which outputs a line of text upon its invocation.

```
1    // Fig. 9.27: circle5.h
2    // Circle5 class contains x-y coordinate pair and radius.
3    #ifndef CIRCLE5_H
4    #define CIRCLE5_H
```

Fig. 9.27   **Circle5** class header file. (Part 1 of 2.)

```
5
6    #include "point4.h"  // Point4 class definition
7
8    class Circle5 : public Point4 {
9
10   public:
11
12      // default constructor
13      Circle5( int = 0, int = 0, double = 0.0 );
14
15      ~Circle5();                    // destructor
16      void setRadius( double );      // set radius
17      double getRadius() const;      // return radius
18
19      double getDiameter() const;        // return diameter
20      double getCircumference() const;   // return circumference
21      double getArea() const;            // return area
22
23      void print() const;           // output Circle5 object
24
25   private:
26      double radius;   // Circle5's radius
27
28   }; // end class Circle5
29
30   #endif
```

Fig. 9.27   **Circle5** class header file. (Part 2 of 2.)

```
1    // Fig. 9.28: circle5.cpp
2    // Circle5 class member-function definitions.
3    #include <iostream>
4
5    using std::cout;
6    using std::endl;
7
8    #include "circle5.h"    // Circle5 class definition
9
10   // default constructor
11   Circle5::Circle5( int xValue, int yValue, double radiusValue )
12      : Point4( xValue, yValue )  // call base-class constructor
13   {
14      setRadius( radiusValue );
15
16      cout << "Circle5 constructor: ";
17      print();
18      cout << endl;
19
20   } // end Circle5 constructor
```

Fig. 9.28   **Circle5** class inherits from class **Point4**. (Part 1 of 2.)

```
21
22   // destructor
23   Circle5::~Circle5()
24   {
25       cout << "Circle5 destructor: ";
26       print();
27       cout << endl;
28
29   } // end Circle5 destructor
30
31   // set radius
32   void Circle5::setRadius( double radiusValue )
33   {
34       radius = ( radiusValue < 0.0 ? 0.0 : radiusValue );
35
36   } // end function setRadius
37
38   // return radius
39   double Circle5::getRadius() const
40   {
41       return radius;
42
43   } // end function getRadius
44
45   // calculate and return diameter
46   double Circle5::getDiameter() const
47   {
48       return 2 * getRadius();
49
50   } // end function getDiameter
51
52   // calculate and return circumference
53   double Circle5::getCircumference() const
54   {
55       return 3.14159 * getDiameter();
56
57   } // end function getCircumference
58
59   // calculate and return area
60   double Circle5::getArea() const
61   {
62       return 3.14159 * getRadius() * getRadius();
63
64   } // end function getArea
65
66   // output Circle5 object
67   void Circle5::print() const
68   {
69       cout << "Center = ";
70       Point4::print();       // invoke Point4's print function
71       cout << "; Radius = " << getRadius();
72
73   } // end function print
```

Fig. 9.28   Circle5 class inherits from class Point4. (Part 2 of 2.)

Figure 9.29 demonstrates the order in which constructors and destructors are called for objects of classes that are part of an inheritance hierarchy. Function **main** (lines 11–29) begins by instantiating a **Point4** object (line 15) in a separate block inside **main** (lines 13–17). The object goes in and out of scope immediately (the end of the block is reached as soon

```cpp
1   // Fig. 9.29: fig09_29.cpp
2   // Display order in which base-class and derived-class
3   // constructors are called.
4   #include <iostream>
5
6   using std::cout;
7   using std::endl;
8
9   #include "circle5.h"  // Circle5 class definition
10
11  int main()
12  {
13     { // begin new scope
14
15        Point4 point( 11, 22 );
16
17     } // end scope
18
19     cout << endl;
20     Circle5 circle1( 72, 29, 4.5 );
21
22     cout << endl;
23     Circle5 circle2( 5, 5, 10 );
24
25     cout << endl;
26
27     return 0;  // indicates successful termination
28
29  } // end main
```

```
Point4 constructor: [11, 22]
Point4 destructor: [11, 22]

Point4 constructor: [72, 29]
Circle5 constructor: Center = [72, 29]; Radius = 4.5

Point4 constructor: [5, 5]
Circle5 constructor: Center = [5, 5]; Radius = 10

Circle5 destructor: Center = [5, 5]; Radius = 10
Point4 destructor: [5, 5]
Circle5 destructor: Center = [72, 29]; Radius = 4.5
Point4 destructor: [72, 29]
```

Fig. 9.29　Constructor and destructor call order.

as the object is created), so both the **Point4** constructor and destructor are called. Next, line 20 instantiates **Circle5** object **circle1**. This invokes the **Point4** constructor to perform output with values passed from the **Circle5** constructor, then performs the output specified in the **Circle5** constructor. Line 23 then instantiates **Circle5** object **circle2**. Again, the **Point4** and **Circle5** constructors are both called. Note that, in each case, the body of the **Point4** constructor is executed before the body of the **Circle5** constructor executes. When the end of **main** is reached, the destructors are called for objects **circle1** and **circle2**. But, because destructors are called in the reverse order of their corresponding constructors, the **Circle5** destructor and **Point4** destructor are called (in that order) for object **circle2**, then the **Circle5** and **Point4** destructors are called (in that order) for object **circle1**.

9.7 "Uses A" and "Knows A" Relationships

Inheritance and composition encourage software reuse by creating classes that take advantage of functionality and data defined in existing classes. There are other ways to use the services of classes. Although a person object is not a car and a person object does not contain a car, a person object certainly *uses a* car. A function *uses* an object simply by calling a non-**private** member function of that object using a pointer, reference or the object name itself.

An object can be *aware of* another object. Knowledge networks frequently have such relationships. One object can contain a pointer handle or a reference handle to another object to be aware of that object. In this case, one object is said to have a *knows a* relationship with the other object; this is sometimes called an *association*.

9.8 `public`, `protected` and `private` Inheritance

When deriving a class from a base class, the base class may be inherited through **public**, **protected** or **private** inheritance. Use of **protected** and **private** inheritance is rare and each should be used only with great care; we normally use **public** inheritance in this book. (Chapter 17 demonstrates **private** inheritance as an alternative to composition.) Figure 9.30 summarizes for each type of inheritance the accessibility of base-class members in a derived class. The first column contains the base-class member-access specifiers.

When deriving a class from a **public** base class, **public** members of the base class become **public** members of the derived class and **protected** members of the base class become **protected** members of the derived class. A base class's **private** members are never accessible directly from a derived class, but can be accessed through calls to the **public** and **protected** members of the base class.

When deriving from a **protected** base class, **public** and **protected** members of the base class become **protected** members of the derived class. When deriving from a **private** base class, **public** and **protected** members of the base class become **private** members (e.g., the functions become utility functions) of the derived class. **Private** and **protected** inheritance are not *is-a* relationships.

Base-class member-access specifier	Type of inheritance		
	public inheritance	**protected** inheritance	**private** inheritance
public	**public** in derived class. Can be accessed directly by non-**static** member functions, **friend** functions and nonmember functions.	**protected** in derived class. Can be accessed directly by non-**static** member functions and **friend** functions.	**private** in derived class. Can be accessed directly by non-**static** member functions and **friend** functions.
protected	**protected** in derived class. Can be accessed directly by non-**static** member functions and **friend** functions.	**protected** in derived class. Can be accessed directly by non-**static** member functions and **friend** functions'.	**private** in derived class. Can be accessed directly by non-**static** member functions and **friend** functions.
private	Hidden in derived class. Can be accessed by non-**static** member functions and **friend** functions through **public** or **protected** member functions of the base class.	Hidden in derived class. Can be accessed by non-**static** member functions and **friend** functions through **public** or **protected** member functions of the base class.	Hidden in derived class. Can be accessed by non-**static** member functions and **friend** functions through **public** or **protected** member functions of the base class.

Fig. 9.30   Summary of base-class member accessibility in a derived class.

9.9 Software Engineering with Inheritance

In this section, we discuss the use of inheritance to customize existing software. When we use inheritance to create a new class from an existing one, the new class inherits the data members and member functions of the existing class. We can customize the new class to meet our needs by including additional members and by redefining base-class members. This is done in C++ without the derived-class programmer accessing the base class's source code. The derived class must be able to link to the base class's object code. This powerful capability is attractive to independent software vendors (ISVs). ISVs can develop proprietary classes for sale or license and make these classes available to users in object-code format. Users then can derive new classes from these library classes rapidly and without accessing the ISVs' proprietary source code. All the ISVs need to supply with the object code are the header files.

Sometimes, it is difficult for students to appreciate the scope of problems faced by designers who work on large-scale software projects in industry. People experienced with such projects say that effective software reuse improves the software-development process. Object-oriented programming facilitates software reuse, thus shortening development times.

The availability of substantial and useful class libraries delivers the maximum benefits of software reuse through inheritance. Interest in class libraries is growing exponentially. Just as shrink-wrapped software produced by independent software vendors became an explosive-growth industry with the arrival of the personal computer, so, too, is the creation and sale of class libraries. Application designers build their applications with these libraries, and library designers are being rewarded by having their libraries included with the applications. The standard C++ libraries that are shipped with C++ compilers tend to be rather general purpose and limited in scope. However, there is massive worldwide commitment to the development of class libraries for a huge variety of applications arenas.

Software Engineering Observation 9.8

At the design stage in an object-oriented system, the designer often determines that certain classes are closely related. The designer should "factor out" common attributes and behaviors and place these in a base class. Then use inheritance to form derived classes, endowing them with capabilities beyond those inherited from the base class.

Software Engineering Observation 9.9

The creation of a derived class does not affect its base class's source code. Inheritance preserves the integrity of a base class.

Software Engineering Observation 9.10

Just as designers of non-object-oriented systems should avoid proliferation of functions, designers of object-oriented systems should avoid proliferation of classes. Proliferation of classes creates management problems and can hinder software reusability, because it becomes difficult for a client to locate the most appropriate class of a huge class library. The alternative is to create fewer classes that provide more substantial functionality, but such classes might provide too much functionality.

Performance Tip 9.3

If classes produced through inheritance are larger than they need to be (i.e., contain too much functionality), memory and processing resources might be wasted. Inherit from the class whose functionality is "closest" to what is needed.

Reading derived-class definitions can be confusing, because inherited members are not shown physically in the derived class, but nevertheless are present in the derived classes. A similar problem exists when documenting derived-class members.

In this chapter, we introduced inheritance—the ability to create classes by absorbing an existing class's data members and member functions, and embellishing these with new capabilities. In Chapter 10, we build upon our discussion of inheritance by introducing *polymorphism*—an object-oriented technique that enables us to write programs that handle, in a more general manner, a wide variety of classes related by inheritance. After studying Chapter 10, you will be familiar with classes, encapsulation, inheritance and polymorphism—the most crucial aspects of object-oriented programming.

9.10 (Optional Case Study) Thinking About Objects: Incorporating Inheritance into the Elevator Simulation

We now examine our simulation design to decide whether it might benefit from inheritance. In the previous "Thinking About Objects" sections, we have been treating **Elevator-Button** and **FloorButton** as separate classes. In fact, these classes have much in common; each is a *kind of* a button. To apply inheritance, we first look for commonality between these classes. We then extract this commonality, place it into base class **Button** and derive classes **ElevatorButton** and **FloorButton** from **Button**.

Let us now examine the similarities between classes **ElevatorButton** and **FloorButton**. Figure 9.31 shows the attributes and operations of both classes, as declared in their header files from Chapter 7 (Fig. 7.37 and Fig. 7.39, respectively). The classes have in common one attribute (**pressed**) and two operations (**pressButton** and **resetButton**). We place these three elements in base-class **Button**, then **ElevatorButton** and **FloorButton** inherit the attributes and operations of **Button**. In our previous implementation, **ElevatorButton** and **FloorButton** each declared a reference to an object of class **Elevator**—class **Button** also should contain this reference.

Figure 9.32 shows our modified elevator simulator design, which incorporates inheritance. Class **Floor** is composed of one object of class **FloorButton** and one object of class **Light**. In addition, class **Elevator** is composed of one object of class **ElevatorButton**, one object of class **Door** and one object of class **Bell**. A solid line with a hollow arrowhead extends from each of the derived classes to the base class—this line indicates that classes **FloorButton** and **ElevatorButton** inherit from class **Button**.

One question remains: Should the derived classes redefine any of the base-class member functions? If we compare the public member functions of each class (Fig. 7.38 and Fig. 7.40), we notice that the **resetButton** member function is identical for both classes. This function does not need to be redefined. However, the implementation of member function **pressButton** differs for each class. Class **ElevatorButton** contains the **pressButton** code

```
pressed = true;
cout << "elevator button tells elevator to prepare to leave"
    << endl;
elevatorRef.prepareToLeave( true );
```

whereas class **FloorButton** contains this different **pressButton** code

```
pressed = true;
cout << "floor " << floorNumber
    << " button summons elevator" << endl;
elevatorRef.summonElevator( floorNumber );
```

The first line of each block of code is identical, but the remaining sections are different. Therefore, each derived class must redefine the base-class **Button** member function **pressButton**.

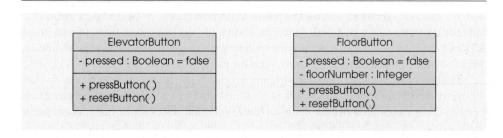

Fig. 9.31   Attributes and operations of classes **ElevatorButton** and **FloorButton**.

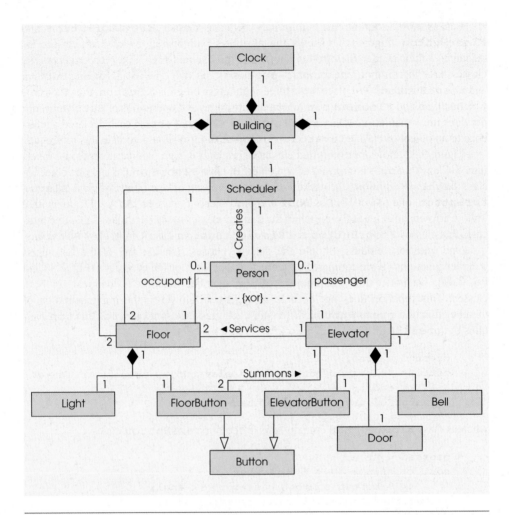

Fig. 9.32   Class diagram incorporating inheritance into the elevator-simulator.

Figure 9.33 lists the header file for the base class **Button**.[2] We declare **public** member functions **pressButton** and **resetButton** (lines 13–14) and **private** data member **pressed** of type **bool** (line 22). Notice the declaration of the reference to an **Elevator** object in line 19 and the corresponding parameter to the constructor in line 11. We show how to initialize the reference when we discuss the code for the derived classes.

The derived classes perform two different actions. Class **ElevatorButton** invokes the **prepareToLeave** member function of class **Elevator**; class **FloorButton** invokes the **summonElevator** member function. Thus, both classes need access to the

---

2. The benefit of encapsulation is that no other files in our elevator simulation need to be changed. We simply substitute the new **elevatorButton** and **floorButton** header and implementation files for the old ones and add the files for class **Button**.

elevatorRef data member of the base class; however, this data member should not be available to non-**Button** objects. Therefore, we place the **elevatorRef** data member in the **protected** section of **Button**. Only base-class member functions directly manipulate data member **pressed**, so we declare this data member as **private**. Derived classes do not need to access **pressed** directly.

Figure 9.34 lists the implementation file for class **Button**. Line 12 in the constructor initializes the reference to the elevator. The constructor and destructor display messages indicating that they are running, and the **pressButton** and **resetButton** member functions manipulate **private** data member **pressed**.

```cpp
1   // Fig. 9.33: button.h
2   // Definition for class Button.
3   #ifndef BUTTON_H
4   #define BUTTON_H
5
6   class Elevator;                 // forward declaration
7
8   class Button {
9
10  public:
11     Button( Elevator & );        // constructor
12     ~Button();                   // destructor
13     void pressButton();          // sets button on
14     void resetButton();          // resets button off
15
16  protected:
17
18     // reference to button's elevator
19     Elevator &elevatorRef;
20
21  private:
22     bool pressed;                // state of button
23
24  }; // end class Button
25
26  #endif // BUTTON_H
```

Fig. 9.33 **Button** class header file.

```cpp
1   // Fig. 9.34: button.cpp
2   // Member function definitions for class Button.
3   #include <iostream>
4
5   using std::cout;
6   using std::endl;
7
8   #include "button.h"  // Button class definition
9
```

Fig. 9.34 **Button** class implementation file—base class for **ElevatorButton** and **FloorButton**. (Part 1 of 2.)

```
10   // constructor
11   Button::Button( Elevator &elevatorHandle )
12      : elevatorRef( elevatorHandle ), pressed( false )
13   {
14      cout << "button constructed" << endl;
15
16   } // end Button constructor
17
18   // destructor
19   Button::~Button()
20   {
21      cout << "button destructed" << endl;
22
23   } // end Button destructor
24
25   // press button
26   void Button::pressButton()
27   {
28      pressed = true;
29
30   } // end function pressButton
31
32   // reset button
33   void Button::resetButton()
34   {
35      pressed = false;
36
37   } // end function resetButton
```

Fig. 9.34   **Button** class implementation file—base class for **ElevatorButton** and **FloorButton**. (Part 2 of 2.)

Figure 9.35 contains the header file for class **ElevatorButton**. Line 8 indicates that the class inherits from class **Button**. This inheritance means that class **Elevator-Button** contains the protected **elevatorRef** data member and the public **press-Button** and **resetButton** member functions of the base class. In line 13, we provide a function prototype for **pressButton** to signal our intent to redefine that member function in the **.cpp** file. We discuss the **pressButton** implementation momentarily.

The constructor takes as a parameter a reference to class **Elevator** (line 11). We discuss the necessity for this parameter when we discuss the class's implementation. Notice, however, that we do not need to include a forward declaration of class **Elevator** in the derived class, because the base-class header file contains the forward reference.

```
1    // Fig. 9.35: elevatorButton.h
2    // ElevatorButton class definition.
3    #ifndef ELEVATORBUTTON_H
4    #define ELEVATORBUTTON_H
5
6    #include "button.h"  // Button class definition
```

Fig. 9.35   **ElevatorButton** class header file. (Part 1 of 2.)

```
 7
 8   class ElevatorButton : public Button {
 9
10   public:
11      ElevatorButton( Elevator & );   // constructor
12      ~ElevatorButton();              // destructor
13      void pressButton();             // press the button
14
15   }; // end class ElevatorButton
16
17   #endif // ELEVATORBUTTON_H
```

Fig. 9.35   **ElevatorButton** class header file. (Part 2 of 2.)

Figure 9.36 lists the implementation file of class **ElevatorButton**. The class constructors and destructors display messages to indicate that these functions are executing. Line 13 passes the **Elevator** reference to the base-class constructor.

```
 1   // Fig. 9.36: elevatorButton.cpp:
 2   // Member-function definitions for class ElevatorButton.
 3   #include <iostream>
 4
 5   using std::cout;
 6   using std::endl;
 7
 8   #include "elevatorButton.h"   // ElevatorButton class definition
 9   #include "elevator.h"         // Elevator class definition
10
11   // constructor
12   ElevatorButton::ElevatorButton( Elevator &elevatorHandle )
13      : Button( elevatorHandle )
14   {
15      cout << "elevator button constructed" << endl;
16
17   } // end ElevatorButton constructor
18
19   // destructor
20   ElevatorButton::~ElevatorButton()
21   {
22      cout << "elevator button destructed" << endl;
23
24   } // end ~ElevatorButton destructor
25
26   // press button and signal elevator to prepare to leave floor
27   void ElevatorButton::pressButton()
28   {
29      Button::pressButton();
30      cout << "elevator button tells elevator to prepare to leave"
31         << endl;
32      elevatorRef.prepareToLeave( true );
33
34   } // end function pressButton
```

Fig. 9.36   **ElevatorButton** class member-function definitions.

Member function **pressButton** first calls the **pressButton** member function (line 29) in base class **Button**; this call sets to **true** the **pressed** attribute of class **Button**. Line 32 notifies the elevator to move to the other floor by passing **true** to member function **prepareToLeave**.

Figure 9.37 lists the header file for class **FloorButton**. The only difference between this file and the header file for class **ElevatorButton** is the addition in line 16 of the **floorNumber** data member. We use this data member to distinguish the floors in the simulation output messages. The constructor declaration includes a parameter of type **int** (line 11), so the **FloorButton** object can initialize attribute **floorNumber**.

Figure 9.38 shows the implementation of class **FloorButton**. Lines 13–14 pass the **Elevator** reference to the base-class constructor and initialize the **floorNumber** data member. The constructor (lines 12–19) and destructor (lines 22–27) output appropriate messages, using data member **floorNumber**. The redefined **pressButton** member function (lines 30–39) first calls member function **pressButton** (line 32) in the base class, then invokes the elevator's **summonElevator** member function (line 37), passing **floorNumber** to indicate the floor that summoned the elevator.

```
1  // Fig. 9.37: floorButton.h
2  // FloorButton class definition.
3  #ifndef FLOORBUTTON_H
4  #define FLOORBUTTON_H
5
6  #include "button.h"  // Button class definition
7
8  class FloorButton : public Button {
9
10 public:
11    FloorButton( int, Elevator & );  // constructor
12    ~FloorButton();                  // destructor
13    void pressButton();              // press the button
14
15 private:
16    const int floorNumber;  // button's floor number
17
18 }; // end class FloorButton
19
20 #endif // FLOORBUTTON_H
```

Fig. 9.37   **FloorButton** class header file.

```
1  // Fig. 9.38: floorButton.cpp
2  // Member-function definitions for class FloorButton.
3  #include <iostream>
4
5  using std::cout;
6  using std::endl;
7
8  #include "floorButton.h"
9  #include "elevator.h"
```

Fig. 9.38   **FloorButton** class member-function definitions. (Part 1 of 2.)

```
10
11    // constructor
12    FloorButton::FloorButton( int floor, Elevator &elevatorHandle )
13       : Button( elevatorHandle ),
14         floorNumber( floor )
15    {
16       cout << "floor " << floorNumber << " button constructed"
17            << endl;
18
19    } // end FloorButton constructor
20
21    // destructor
22    FloorButton::~FloorButton()
23    {
24       cout << "floor " << floorNumber << " button destructed"
25            << endl;
26
27    } // end ~FloorButton destructor
28
29    // press the button
30    void FloorButton::pressButton()
31    {
32       Button::pressButton();
33       cout << "floor " << floorNumber
34            << " button summons elevator" << endl;
35
36       // call elevator to this floor
37       elevatorRef.summonElevator( floorNumber );
38
39    } // end function pressButton
```

Fig. 9.38   **FloorButton** class member-function definitions. (Part 2 of 2.)

We now have completed the implementation for the elevator-simulator case study that we have been developing since Chapter 2. One significant architectural opportunity remains. You might have noticed that classes **Button**, **Door** and **Light** have much in common. Each of these classes contains a "state" attribute and corresponding "set on" and "set off" operations. Class **Bell** also bears some similarity to these other classes. Object-oriented thinking tells us that we should place commonalities in one or more base classes, from which we should then use inheritance to form appropriate derived classes. We leave this implementation to the reader as an exercise. We suggest that you begin by modifying the class diagram in Fig. 9.32. [*Hint*: **Button**, **Door** and **Light** are essentially "toggle" classes—they each have "state," "set on" and "set off" capabilities; **Bell** is a "thinner" class, with only a single operation and no state.]

We sincerely hope that this elevator simulation case study was a challenging and meaningful experience for you. We employed a carefully developed, incremental object-oriented process to produce a UML-based design for our elevator simulator. From this design, we produced a substantial working C++ implementation using key programming notions, including classes, objects, encapsulation, visibility, composition and inheritance.

In the remaining chapters of the book, we present many additional key C++ technologies. We would be grateful if you would take a moment to send your comments, criticisms and suggestions for improving this case study to us at **deitel@deitel.com**.

SUMMARY

- Software reuse reduces program-development time.

- The direct base class of a derived class is the base class from which the derived class inherits (specified by the class name to the right of the **:** in the first line of a class definition). An indirect base class of a derived class is two or more levels up the class hierarchy from that derived class.

- With single inheritance, a class is derived from one base class. With multiple inheritance, a class is derived from more than one direct base class.

- A derived class can include its own data members and member functions, so a derived class is often larger than its base class.

- A derived class is more specific than its base class and represents a smaller group of objects.

- Every object of a derived class is also an object of that class's base class. However, a base-class object is not an object of that class's derived classes.

- Derived-class member functions can access protected base-class members directly.

- An "is-a" relationship represents inheritance. In an "is-a" relationship, an object of a derived class also can be treated as an object of its base class.

- A "has-a" relationship represents composition. In a "has-a" relationship, a class object contains one or more objects of other classes as members.

- A derived class cannot access the private members of its base class directly; allowing this would violate the encapsulation of the base class. A derived class can, however, access the public and protected members of its base class directly.

- When a base-class member function is inappropriate for a derived class, that member function can be redefined in the derived class with an appropriate implementation.

- Single-inheritance relationships form tree-like hierarchical structures—a base class exists in a hierarchical relationship with its derived classes.

- It is possible to treat base-class objects and derived-class objects similarly; the commonality shared between the object types is expressed in the data members and member functions of the base class.

- A base class's public members are accessible anywhere that the program has a handle to an object of that base class or to an object of one of that base class's derived classes.

- A base class's private members are accessible only within the definition of that base class or from friends of that class.

- A base class's protected members have an intermediate level of protection between public and private access. A base class's protected members can be accessed by members and friends of that base class and by members and friends of any classes derived from that base class.

- Unfortunately, protected data members often yield two major problems. First, the derived-class object does not have to use a *set* function to change the value of the base-class's protected data. Second, derived-class member functions are more likely to depend on base-class implementation details.

- When a derived-class member function redefines a base-class member function, the base-class member function can be accessed from the derived class by preceding the base-class member function name with the base-class name and the scope resolution operator (**::**).

- When an object of a derived class is instantiated, the base class's constructor is called immediately (either explicitly or implicitly) to initialize the base-class data members in the derived-class object (before the derived-class data members are initialized).

- Declaring data members **private**, while providing non-private member functions to manipulate and perform validation checking on this data, enforces good software engineering.

- When a derived-class object is destroyed, the destructors are called in the reverse order of the constructors—first the derived-class destructor is called, then the base-class destructor is called.

- When deriving a class from a base class, the base class may be declared as either **public**, **protected** or **private**.

- When deriving a class from a **public** base class, **public** members of the base class become **public** members of the derived class, and **protected** members of the base class become **protected** members of the derived class.

- When deriving a class from a **protected** base class, **public** and **protected** members of the base class become **protected** members of the derived class.

- When deriving a class from a **private** base class, **public** and **protected** members of the base class become **private** members of the derived class.

- "Knows a" relationships are examples of objects containing pointers or references to other objects so they can be aware of those objects.

TERMINOLOGY

abstraction
association
base class
base-class constructor
base-class default constructor
base-class destructor
base-class initializer
class hierarchy
composition
customize software
derived class
derived-class constructor
derived-class destructor
direct base class
friend of a base class
friend of a derived class
has-a relationship
hierarchical relationship
indirect base class
infinite recursion error

inheritance
is-a relationship
knows-a relationship
member access control
member class
member object
multiple inheritance
object-oriented programming (OOP)
private base class
private inheritance
protected base class
protected inheritance
protected keyword
protected member of a class
public base class
public inheritance
redefine a base-class member function
single inheritance
software reusability
uses-a relationship

SELF-REVIEW EXERCISES

9.1   Fill in the blanks in each of the following statements:

a)   _____ is a form of software reusability in which new classes absorb the data and behaviors of existing classes and embellish these classes with new capabilities.

b)   A base class's _____ members can be accessed only in the base-class definition or in derived-class definitions.

c) In a(n) _____ relationship, an object of a derived class also can be treated as an object of its base class.

d) In a(n) _____ relationship, a class object has one or more objects of other classes as members.

e) In single inheritance, a class exists in a(n) _____ relationship with its derived classes.

f) A base class's _____ members are accessible anywhere that the program has a handle to an object of that base class or to an object of one of its derived classes.

g) A base class's **protected** access members have a level of protection between those of **public** and _____ access.

h) C++ provides for _____, which allows a derived class to inherit from many base classes, even if these base classes are unrelated.

i) When an object of a derived class is instantiated, the base class's _____ is called implicitly or explicitly to do any necessary initialization of the base-class data members in the derived-class object.

j) When deriving a class from a base class with **public** inheritance, **public** members of the base class become _____ members of the derived class, and **protected** members of the base class become _____ members of the derived class.

k) When deriving a class from a base class with **protected** inheritance, **public** members of the base class become _____ members of the derived class, and **protected** members of the base class become _____ members of the derived class.

9.2 State whether each of the following is *true* or *false*. If *false*, explain why.
a) It is possible to treat base-class objects and derived-class objects similarly.
b) Base-class constructors are not inherited by derived classes.
c) A "has-a" relationship is implemented via inheritance.
d) A **Car** class has an "is a" relationship with its **SteeringWheel** and **Brakes**.
e) Inheritance encourages the reuse of proven high-quality software.

ANSWERS TO SELF-REVIEW EXERCISES

9.1   a) Inheritance. b) **protected**. c) "is-a" or inheritance. d) "has-a" or composition or aggregation. e) hierarchical. f) **public**. g) **private**. h) multiple inheritance. i) constructor. j) **public**, **protected**. k) **protected**, **protected**.

9.2   a) True. b) True. c) False. A "has-a" relationship is implemented via composition. An "is-a" relationship is implemented via inheritance. d) False. This is an example of a "has–a" relationship. Class **Car** has an "is–a" relationship with class **Vehicle**. e) True.

EXERCISES

9.3   Many programs written with inheritance could be written with composition instead, and vice versa. Rewrite classes **Point3**, **Circle4** and **Cylinder** to use composition, rather than inheritance. After you do this, assess the relative merits of the two approaches for the **Point3**, **Circle4**, **Cylinder** problem, as well as for object-oriented programs in general. Which approach is more natural, why?

9.4   Some programmers prefer not to use **protected** access because it breaks the encapsulation of the base class. Discuss the relative merits of using **protected** access vs. using **private** access in base classes.

9.5   Rewrite the case study in Section 9.5 as a **Point**, **Square**, **Cube** program. Do this two ways—once via inheritance and once via composition.

9.6   Write an inheritance hierarchy for class **Quadrilateral**, **Trapezoid**, **Parallelogram**, **Rectangle** and **Square**. Use **Quadrilateral** as the base class of the hierarchy. Make the hierarchy as deep (i.e., as many levels) as possible. The **private** data of **Quadrilateral** should be the *x–y* coordinate pairs for the four endpoints of the **Quadrilateral**.

9.7   Modify classes **Point3**, **Circle4** and **Cylinder** to contain destructors. Then modify the program of Fig. 9.29 to demonstrate the order in which constructors and destructors are invoked in this hierarchy.

9.8   Write down all the shapes you can think of—both two dimensional and three dimensional—and form those shapes into a shape hierarchy. Your hierarchy should have base class **Shape** from which class **TwoDimensionalShape** and class **ThreeDimensionalShape** are derived. Once you have developed the hierarchy, define each of the classes in the hierarchy. We will use this hierarchy in the exercises of Chapter 10 to process all shapes as objects of base-class **Shape**. (This technique, called polymorphism, is the subject of Chapter 10.)

10

Object-Oriented Programming: Polymorphism

Objectives

- To understand the concept of polymorphism.
- To understand how to declare and use **virtual** functions to effect polymorphism.
- To distinguish between abstract and concrete classes.
- To learn how to declare pure **virtual** functions to create abstract classes.
- To appreciate how polymorphism makes systems extensible and maintainable.
- To understand how C++ implements **virtual** functions and dynamic binding "under the hood."
- To understand how to use run-time type information (RTTI) and operators **typeid** and **dynamic_cast**.

One Ring to rule them all, One Ring to find them,
One Ring to bring them all and in the darkness bind them.
John Ronald Reuel Tolkien

The silence often of pure innocence
Persuades when speaking fails.
William Shakespeare

General propositions do not decide concrete cases.
Oliver Wendell Holmes

A philosopher of imposing stature doesn't think in a vacuum.
Even his most abstract ideas are, to some extent, conditioned
by what is or is not known in the time when he lives.
Alfred North Whitehead

Outline

10.1   **Introduction**

10.2   **Relationships Among Objects in an Inheritance Hierarchy**

   10.2.1   **Invoking Base-Class Functions from Derived-Class Objects**

   10.2.2   **Aiming Derived-Class Pointers at Base-Class Objects**

   10.2.3   **Derived-Class Member-Function Calls via Base-Class Pointers**

   10.2.4   **Virtual Functions**

10.3   **Polymorphism Examples**

10.4   **Type Fields and `switch` Structures**

10.5   **Abstract Classes**

10.6   **Case Study: Inheriting Interface and Implementation**

10.7   **Polymorphism, Virtual Functions and Dynamic Binding "Under the Hood"**

10.8   **Virtual Destructors**

10.9   **Case Study: Payroll System Using Polymorphism and Run-Time Type Information with `dynamic_cast` and `typeid`**

Summary • Terminology • Self-Review Exercises • Answers to Self-Review Exercises • Exercises

10.1 Introduction

In Chapter 6 and Chapter 7, we discussed object-based programming and its component technologies—classes, objects, encapsulation and data abstraction. Chapter 9 focused on a key object-oriented programming (OOP) technology—inheritance. In Chapter 10, we continue our study of OOP by explaining and demonstrating *polymorphism* with inheritance hierarchies. Polymorphism enables us to "program in the general" rather than "program in the specific." In particular, polymorphism enables us to write programs that process objects of classes that are part of the same class hierarchy as if they are all objects of the hierarchy's base class. As we will soon see, polymorphism works off base-class pointer handles and base-class reference handles, but not off name handles.

This chapter has several key parts. We begin with a sequence of small, focused examples that lead up to an understanding of *virtual functions* and *dynamic binding*—polymorphism's two underlying technologies. We then present a case study that revisits Chapter 9's **Point**-**Circle**-**Cylinder** hierarchy. In the case study, we define a common "interface" (i.e., set of functionality) for all the classes in the hierarchy. This common functionality among shapes is defined in a so-called *abstract base class*, **Shape**, from which class **Point** inherits directly and classes **Circle** and **Cylinder** inherit indirectly.

A key feature of this chapter is its detailed discussion of polymorphism, virtual functions and dynamic binding "under the hood," in which we use an elegant diagram to explain how polymorphism works in C++.

We then present a more "natural" **Employee** class hierarchy. We develop a simple payroll system for this hierarchy in which every employee has a common earnings function to calculate the employee's weekly pay. These earnings functions vary by employee type—**SalariedEmployee**s are paid a fixed weekly salary regardless of the number of hours worked, **HourlyEmployee**s are paid by the hour and receive overtime pay, **CommissionEmployee**s receive a percentage of their sales and **BasePlusCommissionEmployee**s receive a base salary plus a percentage of their sales. We show how to process each employee "in the general" by invoking its **earnings** function off a base-class pointer.

Occasionally, when performing polymorphic processing, it is necessary to program "in the specific." Our **Employee** case study demonstrates the powerful capabilities of *run-time type information (RTTI)* and *dynamic casting*, which enable a program to determine the type of an object at execution time and act on that object accordingly. In the case study, we use these capabilities to determine whether a particular employee object is a **BasePlusCommissionEmployee**, then give that employee a 10% bonus on his or her base salary.

With polymorphism, it is possible to design and implement systems that are easily extensible. New classes can be added with little or no modification to the generic portions of the program, as long as those classes are part of the inheritance hierarchy that the program processes generically. The only parts of a program that must be altered to accommodate new classes are those program components that require direct knowledge of the new classes that the programmer adds to the hierarchy.

10.2 Relationships Among Objects in an Inheritance Hierarchy

Section 9.4 created a point-circle class hierarchy, in which class **Circle** inherited from class **Point**. The Chapter 9 examples manipulated **Point** and **Circle** objects by using the names of those objects to invoke their member functions. We now examine the relationships among classes in a hierarchy. The next several sections present a series of examples that demonstrate how base-class and derived-class pointers can be aimed at base-class and derived-class objects, and how those pointers can be used to invoke member functions that manipulate those objects. Later in the chapter, we demonstrate that we can get polymorphic behavior off base-class references as well.

In Section 10.2.1, we assign the address of a derived-class object to a base-class pointer, then show how invoking a function via the base-class pointer will invoke the base-class functionality—i.e., the type of the handle determines which function is called. In Section 10.2.2, we assign the address of a base-class object to a derived-class pointer, which results in a compilation error. We discuss the error message and investigate why the compiler does not allow such an assignment. In Section 10.2.3, we assign the address of a a derived-class object to the base-class pointer, then examine how a base-class pointer can be used to invoke only the base-class functionality—when we attempt to invoke derived-class functions through the base-class pointer, compilation errors occur. Finally, in Section 10.2.4, we introduce virtual functions and polymorphism by declaring a base-class function as **virtual**—we then assign a derived-class object to the base-class pointer and use that pointer to invoke derived-class functionality.

A key concept in these examples is to demonstrate that an object of a derived class can be treated as an object of its base class. This enables various interesting manipulations. For example, a program can create an array of base-class pointers that point to objects of many derived-class types. This is allowed despite the fact that the derived-class objects are of different data types, because each derived-class object *is an* object of its base class. However, a base-class object is not an object of any of its derived classes. For example, a **Point** is not a

Circle in the hierarchy defined in Chapter 9—a **Point** does not have a **radius** data member and does not have member functions **setRadius**, **getRadius** and **area**. The *is–a* relationship applies only from a derived-class to its direct and indirect base classes.

10.2.1 Invoking Base-Class Functions from Derived-Class Objects

The example in Fig. 10.1–Fig. 10.5 demonstrates three ways to aim base-class pointers and derived-class pointers at base-class objects and derived-class objects. The first two are straightforward—we aim a base-class pointer at base-class object, and we aim a derived-class pointer at a derived-class object. Then, we demonstrate the relationship between derived classes and base classes (i.e., the *is–a* relationship) by aiming a base-class pointer at a derived-class object.

Class **Point** (Fig. 10.1–Fig. 10.2), which we discussed in Chapter 9, represents an *x–y* coordinate pair. Class **Circle** (Fig. 10.3–Fig. 10.4), which we also discussed in Chapter 9, represents a circle and inherits from class **Point**. Each **Circle** object "is a" **Point** that also has a radius. Class **Circle**'s **print** member function (lines 53–59 of Fig. 10.4) redefines class **Point**'s **print** member function (lines 46–50 of Fig. 10.2) to display the center coordinate of the circle and the radius value.

```
1   // Fig. 10.1: point.h
2   // Point class definition represents an x-y coordinate pair.
3   #ifndef POINT_H
4   #define POINT_H
5
6   class Point {
7
8   public:
9      Point( int = 0, int = 0 ); // default constructor
10
11     void setX( int );   // set x in coordinate pair
12     int getX() const;   // return x from coordinate pair
13
14     void setY( int );   // set y in coordinate pair
15     int getY() const;   // return y from coordinate pair
16
17     void print() const;   // output Point object
18
19  private:
20     int x;   // x part of coordinate pair
21     int y;   // y part of coordinate pair
22
23  }; // end class Point
24
25  #endif
```

Fig. 10.1 **Point** class header file.

```
1   // Fig. 10.2: point.cpp
2   // Point class member-function definitions.
3   #include <iostream>
```

Fig. 10.2 **Point** class represents an *x–y* coordinate pair. (Part 1 of 2.)

```
4
5    using std::cout;
6
7    #include "point.h"   // Point class definition
8
9    // default constructor
10   Point::Point( int xValue, int yValue )
11      : x( xValue ), y( yValue )
12   {
13      // empty body
14
15   } // end Point constructor
16
17   // set x in coordinate pair
18   void Point::setX( int xValue )
19   {
20      x = xValue; // no need for validation
21
22   } // end function setX
23
24   // return x from coordinate pair
25   int Point::getX() const
26   {
27      return x;
28
29   } // end function getX
30
31   // set y in coordinate pair
32   void Point::setY( int yValue )
33   {
34      y = yValue; // no need for validation
35
36   } // end function setY
37
38   // return y from coordinate pair
39   int Point::getY() const
40   {
41      return y;
42
43   } // end function getY
44
45   // output Point object
46   void Point::print() const
47   {
48      cout << '[' << getX() << ", " << getY() << ']';
49
50   } // end function print
```

Fig. 10.2 **Point** class represents an *x–y* coordinate pair. (Part 2 of 2.)

```
1    // Fig. 10.3: circle.h
2    // Circle class contains x-y coordinate pair and radius.
```

Fig. 10.3 **Circle** class header file. (Part 1 of 2.)

```
3   #ifndef CIRCLE_H
4   #define CIRCLE_H
5
6   #include "point.h"  // Point class definition
7
8   class Circle : public Point {
9
10  public:
11
12     // default constructor
13     Circle( int = 0, int = 0, double = 0.0 );
14
15     void setRadius( double );   // set radius
16     double getRadius() const;   // return radius
17
18     double getDiameter() const;      // return diameter
19     double getCircumference() const; // return circumference
20     double getArea() const;          // return area
21
22     void print() const;             // output Circle object
23
24  private:
25     double radius;  // Circle's radius
26
27  }; // end class Circle
28
29  #endif
```

Fig. 10.3   Circle class header file. (Part 2 of 2.)

```
1   // Fig. 10.4: circle.cpp
2   // Circle class member-function definitions.
3   #include <iostream>
4
5   using std::cout;
6
7   #include "circle.h"    // Circle class definition
8
9   // default constructor
10  Circle::Circle( int xValue, int yValue, double radiusValue )
11     : Point( xValue, yValue )  // call base-class constructor
12  {
13     setRadius( radiusValue );
14
15  } // end Circle constructor
16
17  // set radius
18  void Circle::setRadius( double radiusValue )
19  {
20     radius = ( radiusValue < 0.0 ? 0.0 : radiusValue );
21
22  } // end function setRadius
```

Fig. 10.4   Circle class that inherits from class **Point**. (Part 1 of 2.)

```
23
24   // return radius
25   double Circle::getRadius() const
26   {
27      return radius;
28
29   } // end function getRadius
30
31   // calculate and return diameter
32   double Circle::getDiameter() const
33   {
34      return 2 * getRadius();
35
36   } // end function getDiameter
37
38   // calculate and return circumference
39   double Circle::getCircumference() const
40   {
41      return 3.14159 * getDiameter();
42
43   } // end function getCircumference
44
45   // calculate and return area
46   double Circle::getArea() const
47   {
48      return 3.14159 * getRadius() * getRadius();
49
50   } // end function getArea
51
52   // output Circle object
53   void Circle::print() const
54   {
55      cout << "center = ";
56      Point::print();   // invoke Point's print function
57      cout << "; radius = " << getRadius();
58
59   } // end function print
```

Fig. 10.4   **Circle** class that inherits from class **Point**. (Part 2 of 2.)

In Fig. 10.5, lines 19–20 create a **Point** object and a pointer to a **Point** object; lines 22–23 create a **Circle** object and a pointer to a **Circle** object. Lines 31 and 33 use each object's name (**point** and **circle**, respectively) to invoke each object's **print** member function. Line 36 assigns the address of base-class object **point** to base-class pointer **pointPtr**, which line 40 uses to invoke member function **print** on that **Point** object. This invokes the version of **print** defined in base class **Point**. Similarly, line 44 assigns the address of derived-class object **circle** to derived-class pointer **circlePtr**, which line 48 uses to invoke member function **print** on that **Circle** object. This invokes the version of **print** defined in derived class **Circle**. Line 51 then assigns the address of derived-class object **circle** to base-class pointer **pointPtr**, which line 55 uses to invoke member function **print**. The C++ compiler allows this "crossover" because an object of a derived class "is an" object of its base class. However, despite the fact that the base class **Point** pointer points to a derived-class **Circle** object, the base class **Point**'s **print** member function is invoked (rather than **Circle**'s **print** function). As evidenced by the output of each **print** member-function invocation in this program, the invoked functionality depends on the type of the handle (i.e., the pointer or reference type) used to invoke the function, not the type of the object to which the handle points. (In Section 10.2.4, when we introduce **virtual** functions, we demonstrate that it is possible to invoke the object type's functionality, rather than invoke the handle type's functionality. We will see that this is crucial to implementing polymorphic behavior—the key topic of this chapter.)

```cpp
1   // Fig. 10.5: fig10_05.cpp
2   // Aiming base-class and derived-class pointers at base-class
3   // and derived-class objects, respectively.
4   #include <iostream>
5
6   using std::cout;
7   using std::endl;
8   using std::fixed;
9
10  #include <iomanip>
11
12  using std::setprecision;
13
14  #include "point.h"    // Point class definition
15  #include "circle.h"   // Circle class definition
16
17  int main()
18  {
19      Point point( 30, 50 );
20      Point *pointPtr = 0;      // base-class pointer
21
22      Circle circle( 120, 89, 2.7 );
23      Circle *circlePtr = 0;  // derived-class pointer
24
25      // set floating-point numeric formatting
26      cout << fixed << setprecision( 2 );
27
28      // output objects point and circle
29      cout << "Print point and circle objects:"
30          << "\nPoint: ";
31      point.print();    // invokes Point's print
32      cout << "\nCircle: ";
33      circle.print();   // invokes Circle's print
34
35      // aim base-class pointer at base-class object and print
36      pointPtr = &point;
37      cout << "\n\nCalling print with base-class pointer to "
38          << "\nbase-class object invokes base-class print "
39          << "function:\n";
40      pointPtr->print();   // invokes Point's print
```

Fig. 10.5 Assigning addresses of base-class and derived-class objects to base-class and derived-class pointers. (Part 1 of 2.)

```
41
42      // aim derived-class pointer at derived-class object
43      // and print
44      circlePtr = &circle;
45      cout << "\n\nCalling print with derived-class pointer to "
46           << "\nderived-class object invokes derived-class "
47           << "print function:\n";
48      circlePtr->print();   // invokes Circle's print
49
50      // aim base-class pointer at derived-class object and print
51      pointPtr = &circle;
52      cout << "\n\nCalling print with base-class pointer to "
53           << "derived-class object\ninvokes base-class print "
54           << "function on that derived-class object:\n";
55      pointPtr->print();   // invokes Point's print
56      cout << endl;
57
58      return 0;
59
60  } // end main
```

```
Print point and circle objects:
Point: [30, 50]
Circle: center = [120, 89]; radius = 2.70

Calling print with base-class pointer to
base-class object invokes base-class print function:
[30, 50]

Calling print with derived-class pointer to
derived-class object invokes derived-class print function:
center = [120, 89]; radius = 2.70

Calling print with base-class pointer to derived-class object
invokes base-class print function on that derived-class object:
[120, 89]
```

Fig. 10.5   Assigning addresses of base-class and derived-class objects to base-class and derived-class pointers. (Part 2 of 2.)

10.2.2 Aiming Derived-Class Pointers at Base-Class Objects

In Section 10.2.1, we assigned the address of a derived-class object to a base-class pointer and explained that the C++ compiler allows this assignment, because a derived-class object *is a* base-class object. Now, we take the opposite approach in Fig. 10.6, as we aim a derived-class pointer at a base-class object. [*Note*: This program uses classes **Point** and **Circle** of Fig. 10.1–Fig. 10.4.] Line 8 creates a **Point** object, and line 9 creates a **Circle** pointer. Line 12 attempts to assign the address of base-class object **point** to **circlePtr**, but the C++ compiler generates an error. The compiler prevents this assignment, because a **Point** is not a **Circle**. Consider the consequences if the compiler were to allow this assignment. Through a **Circle** pointer, we can invoke a **Circle** member function, such as

setRadius, for the object to which the pointer points (i.e., the base-class object **point**). However, the **Point** object does not provide a **setRadius** member function, nor does it provide a **radius** data member to set. This could lead to problems, because member function **setRadius** would assume that there is a **radius** data member to set at its "usual location" in a **Circle** object. Because this memory does not belong to the **Point** object, member function **setRadius** might overwrite other important data in memory that belongs to a different object.

It turns out that the C++ compiler does allow this assignment if we explicitly cast the address of the base-class object to the derived-class pointer type, which we discuss in greater detail in Section 10.9. After having contemplated its potential consequences, you may wonder why you ever would want to perform this assignment. In programs that process base-class and derived-class objects using base-class pointers, only functions defined in the base class can be invoked via the base-class pointers. Casting base-class pointers to derived-class pointers (also known as *downcasting*) enables a program to invoke derived-class functionality to perform derived-class-specific operations on derived-class objects.

Common Programming Error 10.1

Assigning the address of a base-class object to a derived-class pointer (without an explicit cast) is a syntax error.

Software Engineering Observation 10.1

If the address of a derived-class object has been assigned to a pointer of one of its direct or indirect base classes, it is acceptable to cast that base-class pointer back to a pointer of the derived-class type. In fact, this must be done to send that derived-class object messages that do not appear in the base class. [Note: We sometimes use the term "message" synonymously with "function call."]

```
1   // Fig. 10.6: fig10_06.cpp
2   // Aiming a derived-class pointer at a base-class object.
3   #include "point.h"    // Point class definition
4   #include "circle.h"   // Circle class definition
5
6   int main()
7   {
8      Point point( 30, 50 );
9      Circle *circlePtr = 0;
10
11     // aim derived-class pointer at base-class object
12     circlePtr = &point;  // Error: a Point is not a Circle
13
14     return 0;
15
16  } // end main
```

```
C:\cpphtp4\examples\ch10\fig10_06\Fig10_06.cpp(12) : error C2440:
'=' : cannot convert from 'class Point *' to 'class Circle *'
       Types pointed to are unrelated; conversion requires
       reinterpret_cast, C-style cast or function-style cast
```

Fig. 10.6   Aiming a derived-class pointer at a base-class object.

10.2.3 Derived-Class Member-Function Calls via Base-Class Pointers

Off a derived-class pointer, the compiler allows us to invoke all derived-class member functions. Thus, if a derived-class pointer is aimed at a base-class object, and an attempt is made to access a derived-class-only member function, errors will almost certainly occur. So we saw in Section 10.2.2 that aiming a derived-class pointer at a base-class object is a compiler error.

Figure 10.7 discusses the consequences of invoking a derived-class member function off a base-class pointer. [*Note*: We are once again using classes **Point** and **Circle** of Fig. 10.1–Fig. 10.4.] Line 9 creates **pointPtr**—a pointer to a **Point** object—and line 10 creates a **Circle** object. Line 13 aims **pointPtr** at derived-class object **circle**. Recall from Section 10.2.1 that the C++ compiler allows this, because a **Circle** "is a" **Point** (in the sense that **Circle** objects contain all the functionality of **Point** objects). Lines 17–21 invoke base-class member functions **getX**, **getY**, **setX**, **setY** and **print** off the base-class pointer. We know that **pointPtr** is aimed at a **Circle** object, so in

```
1   // Fig. 10.7: fig10_07.cpp
2   // Attempting to invoke derived-class-only member functions
3   // through a base-class pointer.
4   #include "point.h"   // Point class definition
5   #include "circle.h"  // Circle class definition
6
7   int main()
8   {
9      Point *pointPtr = 0;
10     Circle circle( 120, 89, 2.7 );
11
12     // aim base-class pointer at derived-class object
13     pointPtr = &circle;
14
15     // invoke base-class member functions on derived-class
16     // object through base-class pointer
17     int x = pointPtr->getX();
18     int y = pointPtr->getY();
19     pointPtr->setX( 10 );
20     pointPtr->setY( 10 );
21     pointPtr->print();
22
23     // attempt to invoke derived-class-only member functions
24     // on derived-class object through base-class pointer
25     double radius = pointPtr->getRadius();
26     pointPtr->setRadius( 33.33 );
27     double diameter = pointPtr->getDiameter();
28     double circumference = pointPtr->getCircumference();
29     double area = pointPtr->getArea();
30
31     return 0;
32
33  } // end main
```

Fig. 10.7   Attempting to invoke derived-class-only functions via a base-class pointer. (Part 1 of 2.)

```
C:\cpphtp4\examples\ch10\fig10_07\fig10_07.cpp(25) : error C2039:
'getRadius' : is not a member of 'Point'
        C:\cpphtp4\examples\ch10\fig10_07\point.h(6) :
        see declaration of 'Point'

C:\cpphtp4\examples\ch10\fig10_07\fig10_07.cpp(26) : error C2039:
'setRadius' : is not a member of 'Point'
        C:\cpphtp4\examples\ch10\fig10_07\point.h(6) :
        see declaration of 'Point'

C:\cpphtp4\examples\ch10\fig10_07\fig10_07.cpp(27) : error C2039:
'getDiameter' : is not a member of 'Point'
        C:\cpphtp4\examples\ch10\fig10_07\point.h(6) :
        see declaration of 'Point'

C:\cpphtp4\examples\ch10\fig10_07\fig10_07.cpp(28) : error C2039:
'getCircumference' : is not a member of 'Point'
        C:\cpphtp4\examples\ch10\fig10_07\point.h(6) :
        see declaration of 'Point'

C:\cpphtp4\examples\ch10\fig10_07\fig10_07.cpp(29) : error C2039:
'getArea' : is not a member of 'Point'
        C:\cpphtp4\examples\ch10\fig10_07\point.h(6) :
        see declaration of 'Point'
```

Fig. 10.7   Attempting to invoke derived-class-only functions via a base-class pointer. (Part 2 of 2.)

lines 25–29, we attempt to invoke **Circle** member functions **getRadius, setRadius, getDiameter, getCircumference** and **getArea**. The C++ compiler generates errors on each of these lines, because these are not member functions of base-class **Point**. The handle can invoke only those functions that are members of that handle's associated class type. (In this case, off a **Point ***, we can invoke only **Point** member functions **getX, getY, setX, setY** and **print**.)

10.2.4 Virtual Functions

In Section 10.2.1, we aimed a base-class **Point** pointer at a derived-class **Circle** object, then invoked member function **print** through that pointer. Recall that the data type of the handle determined which class's functionality to invoke. In that case, the **Point** pointer invoked **Point** member function **print** on the **Circle**, despite the fact that the pointer was aimed at a **Circle** that has its own proper **print** function. Now, with **virtual** functions, the type of the object being pointed to, not the type of the handle, determines which version of a **virtual** function to invoke.

First, we consider why **virtual** functions are useful. Suppose that a set of shape classes such as **Circle, Triangle, Rectangle, Square**, etc., are all derived from base class **Shape**. In object-oriented programming, each of these classes might be endowed with the ability to draw itself via a function **draw**. Although each class has its own **draw** function, the function for each shape is quite different. When drawing a shape, whatever that shape may be, it would be nice to be able to treat all these shapes generically as objects of the base class **Shape**. Then to draw any shape, we could use a base-class **Shape** pointer to invoke function **draw** and let the program determine *dynamically* (i.e., at run time) which derived-class **draw** function to use, based on the type of the object to which the base-class **Shape** pointer points at any given time.

To enable this kind of behavior, we declare **draw** in the base class as a *virtual function*, and we *override* **draw** in each of the derived classes to draw the appropriate shape. From an implementation perspective, overriding a function is no different than redefining one (which is the approach we have been using until now). An overridden function in a derived class has the same signature as the function it overrides in its base class. If we do not declare the base-class function as **virtual**, we can redefine that function. By contrast, if we declare the base-class function as **virtual**, we can override that function. We declare a **virtual** function by preceding the function's prototype with the keyword **virtual** in the base class. For example,

```
virtual void draw() const;
```

would appear in base class **Shape**. The preceding prototype declares that function **draw** is a constant **virtual** function that takes no arguments and returns nothing.

Software Engineering Observation 10.2

*Once a function is declared **virtual**, it remains **virtual** all the way down the inheritance hierarchy from that point, even if that function is not explicitly declared **virtual** when a class overrides it.*

Good Programming Practice 10.1

*Even though certain functions are implicitly **virtual** because of a declaration made higher in the class hierarchy, explicitly declare these functions **virtual** at every level of the hierarchy to promote program clarity.*

Testing and Debugging Tip 10.1

*When a programmer browses a class hierarchy to locate a class to reuse, it is possible that a function in that class will exhibit **virtual** function behavior even though it is not explicitly declared **virtual**. This happens when the class inherits a **virtual** function from its base class, and it can lead to subtle logic errors. Such errors can be avoided by explicitly declaring all **virtual** functions **virtual**.*

Software Engineering Observation 10.3

*When a derived class chooses not to override a **virtual** function from its base class, the derived class simply inherits its base class' **virtual** function implementation.*

If the program invokes a **virtual** function through a base-class pointer to a derived-class object (e.g., **shapePtr->draw()**), the program will choose the correct derived-class **draw** function dynamically based on the object type—not the pointer type. Choosing the appropriate function to call at execution time is known as *dynamic binding*.

When a **virtual** function is called by referencing a specific object by name and using the dot member-selection operator (e.g., **squareObject.draw()**), the function invocation is resolved at compile time (this is called *static binding*) and the **virtual** function that is called is the one defined for (or inherited by) the class of that particular object. Thus, dynamic binding with virtual functions occurs only off pointer (and, as we will soon see, reference) handles.

Now that we have discussed the motivation for virtual functions, we modify the program of Fig. 10.1–Fig. 10.5 to incorporate virtual functions. Figure 10.8 and Fig. 10.9 are the header files for classes **Point** and **Circle**, respectively. Note that the only difference between these files and those of Fig. 10.1 and Fig. 10.3 is that we specify each class's **print** member function as **virtual** (line 17 of Fig. 10.8 and line 22 of Fig. 10.9). Because function **print** is **virtual** in class **Point**, class **Circle**'s **print** function overrides class **Point**'s. Now, if we aim a base-class **Point** pointer at a derived-class **Circle** object, and the program uses that pointer to call function **print**, the **Circle** object's **print** function will be invoked. There were no changes to the member-function implementations of classes **Point** and **Circle**, so we reuse the versions of Fig. 10.2 and Fig. 10.4.

```
1   // Fig. 10.8: point.h
2   // Point class definition represents an x-y coordinate pair.
3   #ifndef POINT_H
4   #define POINT_H
5
6   class Point {
7
8   public:
9       Point( int = 0, int = 0 ); // default constructor
10
11      void setX( int );   // set x in coordinate pair
12      int getX() const;   // return x from coordinate pair
13
14      void setY( int );   // set y in coordinate pair
15      int getY() const;   // return y from coordinate pair
16
17      virtual void print() const;   // output Point object
18
19   private:
20      int x;   // x part of coordinate pair
21      int y;   // y part of coordinate pair
22
23   }; // end class Point
24
25   #endif
```

Fig. 10.8 **Point** class header file declares **print** function as **virtual**.

```
1   // Fig. 10.9: circle.h
2   // Circle class contains x-y coordinate pair and radius.
3   #ifndef CIRCLE_H
4   #define CIRCLE_H
5
6   #include "point.h"   // Point class definition
7
8   class Circle : public Point {
9
```

Fig. 10.9 **Circle** class header file declares **print** function as **virtual**. (Part 1 of 2.)

```
10   public:
11
12      // default constructor
13      Circle( int = 0, int = 0, double = 0.0 );
14
15      void setRadius( double );   // set radius
16      double getRadius() const;   // return radius
17
18      double getDiameter() const;       // return diameter
19      double getCircumference() const;  // return circumference
20      double getArea() const;           // return area
21
22      virtual void print() const;       // output Circle object
23
24   private:
25      double radius;  // Circle's radius
26
27   }; // end class Circle
28
29   #endif
```

Fig. 10.9 `Circle` class header file declares `print` function as `virtual`. (Part 2 of 2.)

We modified Fig. 10.5 to create the program of Fig. 10.10. Lines 41–53 demonstrate again that a **Point** pointer aimed at a **Point** object can be used to invoke **Point** functionality, and a **Circle** pointer aimed at a **Circle** object can be used to invoke **Circle** functionality. Line 56 aims base-class pointer **pointPtr** at derived-class object **circle**. Note that when line 60 invokes member function **print** off the base-class pointer, the derived-class **Circle**'s **print** member function is invoked, so line 60 outputs different text than line 55 does in Fig. 10.5 (when member function **print** was not declared **virtual**). We see that declaring a member function **virtual** enables the program to determine which function to invoke based on the type of object to which the handle points, rather than on the type of the handle. The decision about which function to call is an example of *polymorphism*. Note that if **pointPtr** pointed to a **Point** object rather than pointed to a **Circle** object, class **Point**'s **print** function would have been invoked. Thus, the same message, in this case, **print**, sent to a variety of objects (off a base-class pointer) takes on "many forms"—hence, the term polymorphism.

```
1    // Fig. 10.10: fig10_10.cpp
2    // Introducing polymorphism, virtual functions and dynamic
3    // binding.
4    #include <iostream>
5
6    using std::cout;
7    using std::endl;
8    using std::fixed;
9
```

Fig. 10.10 Demonstrating polymorphism by invoking a derived-class virtual function via a base-class pointer to a derived-class object. (Part 1 of 3.)

```
10   #include <iomanip>
11
12   using std::setprecision;
13
14   #include "point.h"    // Point class definition
15   #include "circle.h"   // Circle class definition
16
17   int main()
18   {
19      Point point( 30, 50 );
20      Point *pointPtr = 0;
21
22      Circle circle( 120, 89, 2.7 );
23      Circle *circlePtr = 0;
24
25      // set floating-point numeric formatting
26      cout << fixed << setprecision( 2 );
27
28      // output objects point and circle using static binding
29      cout << "Invoking print function on point and circle "
30         << "\nobjects with static binding "
31         << "\n\nPoint: ";
32      point.print();           // static binding
33      cout << "\nCircle: ";
34      circle.print();          // static binding
35
36      // output objects point and circle using dynamic binding
37      cout << "\n\nInvoking print function on point and circle "
38         << "\nobjects with dynamic binding";
39
40      // aim base-class pointer at base-class object and print
41      pointPtr = &point;
42      cout << "\n\nCalling virtual function print with base-class"
43         << "\npointer to base-class object"
44         << "\ninvokes base-class print function:\n";
45      pointPtr->print();
46
47      // aim derived-class pointer at derived-class
48      // object and print
49      circlePtr = &circle;
50      cout << "\n\nCalling virtual function print with "
51         << "\nderived-class pointer to derived-class object "
52         << "\ninvokes derived-class print function:\n";
53      circlePtr->print();
54
55      // aim base-class pointer at derived-class object and print
56      pointPtr = &circle;
57      cout << "\n\nCalling virtual function print with base-class"
58         << "\npointer to derived-class object "
59         << "\ninvokes derived-class print function:\n";
60      pointPtr->print();  // polymorphism: invokes circle's print
61      cout << endl;
```

Fig. 10.10 Demonstrating polymorphism by invoking a derived-class virtual function via a base-class pointer to a derived-class object. (Part 2 of 3.)

```
62
63      return 0;
64
65  } // end main
```

```
Invoking print function on point and circle
objects with static binding

Point: [30, 50]
Circle: Center = [120, 89]; Radius = 2.70

Invoking print function on point and circle
objects with dynamic binding

Calling virtual function print with base-class
pointer to base-class object
invokes base-class print function:
[30, 50]

Calling virtual function print with
derived-class pointer to derived-class object
invokes derived-class print function:
Center = [120, 89]; Radius = 2.70

Calling virtual function print with base-class
pointer to derived-class object
invokes derived-class print function:
Center = [120, 89]; Radius = 2.70
```

Fig. 10.10 Demonstrating polymorphism by invoking a derived-class virtual function via a base-class pointer to a derived-class object. (Part 3 of 3.)

Despite the fact that a derived-class object also "is a" base-class object, the derived-class and base-class objects are indeed different. As we have discussed previously, derived-class objects can be treated as if they were base-class objects. This is a logical relationship, because the derived class contains all the members of the base class, but the derived class can have additional derived-class-only members. For this reason, aiming a derived-class pointer at a base-class object is not allowed without an explicit cast—such an assignment would leave the derived-class-only members undefined on the base-class object.

We have discussed four ways to aim base-class pointers and derived-class pointers at base-class objects and derived-class objects:

1. Aiming a base-class pointer at a base-class object is straightforward.

2. Aiming a derived-class pointer at a derived-class object is straightforward.

3. Aiming a base-class pointer at a derived-class object is safe, because the derived-class object *is an* object of its base class. However, this pointer can be used to invoke only base-class member functions. If this code refers to derived-class-only members through the base-class pointer, the compiler reports errors.

4. Aiming a derived-class pointer at a base-class object generates a compiler error. To avoid this error, the derived-class pointer first must be cast to a base-class

pointer explicitly. If the object to which the pointer points is not a derived-class object, this can be a dangerous operation. Section 10.9 demonstrates how to ensure that such a cast is performed only if the object is a derived-class object.

Common Programming Error 10.2

After aiming a base-class pointer at a derived-class object, attempting to reference derived-class-only members with the base-class pointer is a compilation error.

Common Programming Error 10.3

Treating a base-class object as a derived-class object can cause errors.

10.3 Polymorphism Examples

In this section, we discuss several examples of polymorphism. If class **Rectangle** is derived from class **Quadrilateral**, then a **Rectangle** object is a more specific version of a **Quadrilateral** object. Any operation (such as calculating the perimeter or the area) that can be performed on an object of class **Quadrilateral** also can be performed on an object of class **Rectangle**. Such operations also can be performed on other kinds of **Quadrilateral**s, such as **Square**s, **Parallelogram**s and **Trapezoid**s. When a program invokes a **virtual** function through a base-class (i.e., **Quadrilateral**) pointer or reference, C++ polymorphically chooses the correct function for the class from which the object was instantiated. We investigate this behavior in later examples.

Suppose that we design a video game that manipulates objects of many different types, including objects of classes **Martian**, **Venutian**, **Plutonian**, **SpaceShip** and **LaserBeam**. Also, imagine that each of these classes inherits from the common base class called **SpaceObject**, which contains member function **draw**. Each derived class implements this function. A screen-manager program would maintain a container (such as a **vector** of **SpaceObject**s) of pointers to objects of the various classes. To refresh the screen, the screen manager would periodically send each object the same message—namely, **draw**. However, each object responds in a unique way. For example, a **Martian** object might draw itself in red with the appropriate number of antennae. A **SpaceShip** object might draw itself as a bright, silver flying saucer. A **LaserBeam** object might draw itself as a bright red beam across the screen. Again, the same message (in this case, **draw**) sent to a variety of objects would have "many forms" of results—hence, the term *polymorphism*.

A polymorphic screen manager facilitates adding new classes to a system with minimal modifications to the system's code. Suppose that we want to add objects of class **Mercurian** to our video game. To do so, we must build a class **Mercurian** that inherits from **SpaceObject**, but provides its own definition of member function **draw**. Then, when objects of class **Mercurian** appear in the container, the programmer does not need to modify the code for the screen manager. The screen manager invokes member function **draw** on every object in the container, regardless of the object's type, so the new **Mercurian** objects simply "plug right in." Thus, without modifying the system (other than to build and include the classes themselves), programmers can use polymorphism to include additional classes that were not envisioned when the system was created.

With polymorphism, one function can cause different actions to occur, depending on the type of the object on which the function is invoked. This gives the programmer tremendous expressive capability.

Software Engineering Observation 10.4

*With **virtual** functions and polymorphism, the programmer can deal in generalities and let the execution-time environment concern itself with the specifics. The programmer can command a wide variety of objects to behave in manners appropriate to those objects without even knowing the types of those objects (as long as those objects belong to the same inheritance hierarchy and are being accessed off a common base-class pointer).*

Software Engineering Observation 10.5

Polymorphism promotes extensibility: Software written to invoke polymorphic behavior is written independently of the types of the objects to which messages are sent. Thus, new types of objects that can respond to existing messages can be incorporated into such a system without modifying the base system. Only client code that instantiates new objects must be modified to accommodate new types.

10.4 Type Fields and **switch** Structures

One way to determine the type of an object that is incorporated in a larger program is to use a **switch** structure. This allows us to distinguish among object types, then invoke an appropriate action for a particular object. For example, in a hierarchy of shapes in which each shape object has a **shapeType** attribute, a **switch** structure could check the object's **shapeType** to determine which **print** function to call.

However, using **switch** logic exposes programs to a variety of potential problems. For example, the programmer might forget to include a type test when one is warranted, or might forget to test all possible cases in a **switch** structure. When modifying a **switch**-based system by adding new types, the programmer might forget to insert the new cases in all relevant **switch** structures. Every addition or deletion of a class requires the modification of every **switch** structure in the system; tracking these statements down can be time consuming and error prone.

Software Engineering Observation 10.6

*Polymorphic programming can eliminate the need for unnecessary **switch** logic. By using the C++ polymorphism mechanism to perform the equivalent logic, programmers can avoid the kinds of errors typically associated with **switch** logic.*

Testing and Debugging Tip 10.2

An interesting consequence of using polymorphism is that programs take on a simplified appearance. They contain less branching logic and more simple, sequential code. This simplification facilitates testing, debugging and program maintenance.

10.5 Abstract Classes

When we think of a class as a type, we assume that programs will create objects of that type. However, there are cases in which it is useful to define classes for which the programmer never intends to instantiate any objects. Such classes are called *abstract classes*. Because such classes normally are used as base classes in inheritance hierarchies, we refer to such classes as *abstract base classes*. These classes cannot be used to instantiate objects, because, as we will soon see, abstract classes are incomplete. Derived classes must define the "missing pieces." We build programs with abstract classes in Section 10.6 and Section 10.9.

The purpose of an abstract class is to provide an appropriate base class from which other classes can inherit. Classes that can be used to instantiate objects are called *concrete classes*. Such classes provide implementations of every function they define. We could have an abstract base class **TwoDimensionalShape** and derive such concrete classes as **Square**, **Circle** and **Triangle**. We could also have an abstract base class **ThreeDimensionalShape** and derive such concrete classes as **Cube**, **Sphere** and **Cylinder**. Abstract base classes are too generic to define real objects; we need to be more specific before we can think of instantiating objects. For example, if someone tells you to "draw the shape," what shape would you draw? Concrete classes provide the specifics that make it reasonable to instantiate objects.

An inheritance hierarchy does not need to contain any abstract classes, but, as we will see, many good object-oriented systems have class hierarchies headed by abstract base classes. In some cases, abstract classes constitute the top few levels of the hierarchy. A good example of this is the shape hierarchy in Fig. 9.3, which begins with abstract base class **Shape**. On the next level of the hierarchy, we have two more abstract base classes, namely, **TwoDimensionalShape** and **ThreeDimensionalShape**. The next level of the hierarchy defines concrete classes for two-dimensional shapes (namely, **Circle**, **Square** and **Triangle**) and for three-dimensional shapes (namely, **Sphere**, **Cube** and **Tetrahedron**).

A class is made abstract by declaring one or more of its **virtual** functions to be "pure." A *pure **virtual** function* is one with an *initializer of = 0* in its declaration, as in

```
virtual void draw() const = 0;  // pure virtual function
```

Pure **virtual** functions normally do not provide implementations. Every concrete derived class must override all base-class pure **virtual** functions and provide concrete implementations of those functions. The difference between a **virtual** function and a pure **virtual** function is that a **virtual** function has an implementation and gives the derived class the option of overriding the function; by contrast, a pure **virtual** function does not provide an implementation and requires the derived class to override the function (for that derived class to be concrete).

Software Engineering Observation 10.7

*An abstract class defines a common public interface for the various classes in a class hierarchy. An abstract class typically contains one or more pure **virtual** functions that derived classes must override.*

Common Programming Error 10.4

Attempting to instantiate an object of an abstract class causes a compilation error.

Common Programming Error 10.5

*Failure to override a pure **virtual** function in a derived class then attempting to instantiate objects of that derived class is a compilation error.*

Software Engineering Observation 10.8

An abstract class must have at least one pure virtual function. An abstract class also can have data members and concrete functions (including constructors and destructors), which are subject to the normal rules of inheritance by derived classes.

Although we cannot instantiate objects of abstract base classes, we *can* use abstract base classes to declare pointers and references that can refer to objects of any concrete classes derived from these abstract classes. Programs typically use such pointers and references to manipulate such derived-class objects polymorphically.

Let us consider another application of polymorphism. A screen manager needs to display a variety of objects, including new types of objects that the programmer will add to the system after writing the screen manager. The system might need to display various shapes, such as **Circle**, **Triangle** or **Rectangle**, which are derived from abstract base class **Shape**. The screen manager uses **Shape *** pointers to manage the objects that are displayed. To draw any object (regardless of the level at which that object's class appears in the inheritance hierarchy), the screen manager uses a base-class pointer to the object to invoke the object's **draw** function, which is a pure **virtual** function in base class **Shape**; therefore, each derived class must implement function **draw**. Each **Shape** object in the inheritance hierarchy knows how to draw itself. The screen manager does not have to worry about the type of each object or whether the screen manager has ever encountered objects of that type.

Polymorphism is particularly effective for implementing layered software systems. In operating systems, for example, each type of physical device could operate quite differently from the others. Even so, commands to *read* or *write* data from and to devices may have a certain uniformity. The write message sent to a device-driver object needs to be interpreted specifically in the context of that device driver and how that device driver manipulates devices of a specific type. However, the write call itself really is no different from the write to any other device in the system—place some number of bytes from memory onto that device. An object-oriented operating system might use an abstract base class to provide an interface appropriate for all device drivers. Then, through inheritance from that abstract base class, derived classes are formed that all operate similarly. The capabilities (i.e., the **public** functions) offered by the device drivers are provided as pure **virtual** functions in the abstract base class. The implementations of these pure **virtual** functions are provided in the derived classes that correspond to the specific types of device drivers.

It is common in object-oriented programming to define an *iterator class* that can traverse all the objects in a container (such as an array). For example, a program can print a list of objects in a **vector** by creating an iterator object, then using the iterator to obtain the next element of the list each time the iterator is called. Iterators often are used in polymorphic programming to traverse an array or a linked list of pointers to objects from various levels of a hierarchy. The pointers in such a list are all base-class pointers. (Chapter 21, Standard Template Library, presents a thorough treatment of iterators.) A list of pointers to objects of base class **TwoDimensionalShape** could contain pointers to objects from classes **Square**, **Circle**, **Triangle** and so on. Using polymorphism to send a **draw** message, off a **TwoDimensionalShape *** pointer, to each object in the list would draw each object correctly on the screen.

10.6 Case Study: Inheriting Interface and Implementation

This section reexamines the **Point**, **Circle**, **Cylinder** hierarchy that we explored in Chapter 9. In this example, the hierarchy begins with abstract base class **Shape**, which defines the "interface" to the hierarchy—i.e., the set of functions that a program can invoke on all **Shape** objects. Class **Shape** provides four functions—**getArea**, **getVolume**,

getName and **print**. The diagram of Fig. 10.11 shows each of the four classes in the hierarchy and each of the four functions defined in class **Shape**. For each class, the diagram shows the desired results of each function. Note that class **Shape** specifies "**= 0**" for functions **getName** and **print**. We do this to indicate that **getName** and **print** are pure **virtual** functions. A default implementation does not make sense for each of these functions, because there is not enough information to determine what string **getName** should return or what **print** should output. Each subclass overrides these functions to provide appropriate implementations. Functions **getArea** and **getVolume** each have default implementations that return **0.0**. Class **Point** inherits these implementations—**Point**s indeed have an area of **0.0** and a volume of **0.0**. Class **Circle** inherits the default implementation of **getVolume**—**Circle**s indeed have a volume of **0.0**—and overrides function **getArea** to calculate the true area of a circle. Finally, class **Cylinder** overrides both **getArea** and **getVolume** to perform calculations appropriate for a cylinder.

Software Engineering Observation 10.9

A derived class can inherit interface or implementation from a base class. Hierarchies designed for implementation inheritance *tend to have their functionality high in the hierarchy— each new derived class inherits one or more member functions that were defined in a base class, and the new derived class uses the base-class definitions. Hierarchies designed for* interface inheritance *tend to have their functionality lower in the hierarchy—a base class specifies one or more functions that should be defined for each class in the hierarchy (i.e., they have the same signature), but the individual derived classes provide their own implementations of the function(s).*

The hierarchy in this example mechanically demonstrates the power of polymorphism. In the exercises, we explore a more substantial shape hierarchy. The **Shape** header file (Fig. 10.12) defines **virtual** functions **getArea** and **getVolume** (lines 15 and 18) and pure **virtual** functions **getName** and **print** (lines 21–22). All shapes have an area and a volume, so **virtual** functions **getArea** and **getVolume** return the shape's area and volume, respectively. The volume of two-dimensional shapes is always zero, whereas

	getArea	getVolume	getName	print
Shape	0.0	0.0	= 0	= 0
Point	0.0	0.0	"Point"	[x,y]
Circle	πr^2	0.0	"Circle"	center=[x,y]; radius=r
Cylinder	$2\pi r^2 + 2\pi rh$	$\pi r^2 h$	"Cylinder"	center=[x,y]; radius=r; height=h

Fig. 10.11 Defining the polymorphic interface for the **Shape** hierarchy classes.

three-dimensional shapes have a positive, nonzero volume. In the class **Shape** implementation (Fig. 10.13), virtual functions **getArea** (lines 10–14) and **getVolume** (lines 17–20) return zero, by default. Programmers override these functions in the derived concrete classes with appropriate implementations (see Fig. 10.11). We declare functions **getName** and **print** (lines 21–22 of Fig. 10.12) as pure virtual functions, so derived classes that inherit directly from **Shape** must implement these functions to become concrete classes.

```
1   // Fig. 10.12: shape.h
2   // Shape abstract-base-class definition.
3   #ifndef SHAPE_H
4   #define SHAPE_H
5
6   #include <string>  // C++ standard string class
7
8   using std::string;
9
10  class Shape {
11
12  public:
13
14     // virtual function that returns shape area
15     virtual double getArea() const;
16
17     // virtual function that returns shape volume
18     virtual double getVolume() const;
19
20     // pure virtual functions; overridden in derived classes
21     virtual string getName() const = 0; // return shape name
22     virtual void print() const = 0;     // output shape
23
24  }; // end class Shape
25
26  #endif
```

Fig. 10.12 Abstract base class **Shape** header file.

```
1   // Fig. 10.13: shape.cpp
2   // Shape class member-function definitions.
3   #include <iostream>
4
5   using std::cout;
6
7   #include "shape.h"  // Shape class definition
8
9   // return area of shape; 0.0 by default
10  double getArea() const
11  {
12     return 0.0;
13
14  }  // end function getArea
```

Fig. 10.13 Abstract base class **Shape**. (Part 1 of 2.)

```
15
16   // return volume of shape; 0.0 by default
17   double getVolume() const
18   {
19      return 0.0;
20
21   } // end function getVolume
```

Fig. 10.13 Abstract base class **Shape**. (Part 2 of 2.)

Class **Point** (Fig. 10.14–Fig. 10.15) inherits from abstract base class **Shape** and overrides pure virtual functions **getName** and **print**, which makes **Point** a concrete class. A point's area and volume are zero, so class **Point** does not override virtual base-class functions **getArea** and **getVolume**, thus inheriting **Shape**'s implementations of these functions. Note that in class **Point**'s header file (Fig. 10.14), we declared member functions **getName** and **print** as **virtual** (lines 20 and 22)—actually, placing the **virtual** keyword before these member functions is redundant. We defined them as

```
1    // Fig. 10.14: point.h
2    // Point class definition represents an x-y coordinate pair.
3    #ifndef POINT_H
4    #define POINT_H
5
6    #include "shape.h"  // Shape class definition
7
8    class Point : public Shape {
9
10   public:
11      Point( int = 0, int = 0 ); // default constructor
12
13      void setX( int );  // set x in coordinate pair
14      int getX() const;  // return x from coordinate pair
15
16      void setY( int );  // set y in coordinate pair
17      int getY() const;  // return y from coordinate pair
18
19      // return name of shape (i.e., "Point" )
20      virtual string getName() const;
21
22      virtual void print() const;  // output Point object
23
24   private:
25      int x;  // x part of coordinate pair
26      int y;  // y part of coordinate pair
27
28   }; // end class Point
29
30   #endif
```

Fig. 10.14 Point class header file.

virtual in base class **Shape**, so they remain **virtual** functions throughout the class hierarchy.

Figure 10.15 contains the member-function implementations for class **Point**. Lines 46–50 implement function **getName** to return the **string "Point"**. In addition, lines 53–57 implement function **print** to output the **Point**'s data. If we did not provide one or both of these implementations, class **Point** would have been an abstract class.

```cpp
1   // Fig. 10.15: point.cpp
2   // Point class member-function definitions.
3   #include <iostream>
4
5   using std::cout;
6
7   #include "point.h"    // Point class definition
8
9   // default constructor
10  Point::Point( int xValue, int yValue )
11     : x( xValue ), y( yValue )
12  {
13     // empty body
14
15  } // end Point constructor
16
17  // set x in coordinate pair
18  void Point::setX( int xValue )
19  {
20     x = xValue; // no need for validation
21
22  } // end function setX
23
24  // return x from coordinate pair
25  int Point::getX() const
26  {
27     return x;
28
29  } // end function getX
30
31  // set y in coordinate pair
32  void Point::setY( int yValue )
33  {
34     y = yValue; // no need for validation
35
36  } // end function setY
37
38  // return y from coordinate pair
39  int Point::getY() const
40  {
41     return y;
42
43  } // end function getY
44
```

Fig. 10.15 Point class implementation file. (Part 1 of 2.)

```
45   // override pure virtual function getName: return name of Point
46   string Point::getName() const
47   {
48      return "Point";
49
50   }  // end function getName
51
52   // override pure virtual function print: output Point object
53   void Point::print() const
54   {
55      cout << '[' << getX() << ", " << getY() << ']';
56
57   }  // end function print
```

Fig. 10.15 Point class implementation file. (Part 2 of 2.)

Class **Circle** (Fig. 10.16–Fig. 10.17) inherits from class **Point**. The **Circle** class header file (Fig. 10.16) declares additional member functions **setRadius** and **getRadius** (lines 15–16) for accessing the circle's radius. Class **Circle** also adds member functions **getDiameter** and **getCircumference** (lines 18–19) for obtaining the circle's diameter and circumference, respectively. We do not declare any of these functions **virtual**, so classes derived from class **Circle** cannot override them (although derived classes certainly can redefine them). We do declare member functions **getArea**, **getName** and **print virtual** as a matter of good practice—remember, these functions are all implicitly virtual, because they are virtual in base class **Point**.

```
1    // Fig. 10.16: circle.h
2    // Circle class contains x-y coordinate pair and radius.
3    #ifndef CIRCLE_H
4    #define CIRCLE_H
5
6    #include "point.h"  // Point class definition
7
8    class Circle : public Point {
9
10   public:
11
12      // default constructor
13      Circle( int = 0, int = 0, double = 0.0 );
14
15      void setRadius( double );  // set radius
16      double getRadius() const;  // return radius
17
18      double getDiameter() const;       // return diameter
19      double getCircumference() const;  // return circumference
20      virtual double getArea() const;   // return area
21
22      // return name of shape (i.e., "Circle")
23      virtual string getName() const;
24
```

Fig. 10.16 Circle class header file. (Part 1 of 2.)

```cpp
1   // Fig. 10.18: cylinder.h
2   // Cylinder class inherits from class Circle.
3   #ifndef CYLINDER_H
4   #define CYLINDER_H
5
6   #include "circle.h"   // Circle class definition
7
8   class Cylinder : public Circle {
9
10  public:
11
12     // default constructor
13     Cylinder( int = 0, int = 0, double = 0.0, double = 0.0 );
14
15     void setHeight( double );   // set Cylinder's height
16     double getHeight() const;   // return Cylinder's height
17
18     virtual double getArea() const;   // return Cylinder's area
19     virtual double getVolume() const; // return Cylinder's volume
20
21     // return name of shape (i.e., "Cylinder" )
22     virtual string getName() const;
23
24     virtual void print() const;   // output Cylinder
25
26  private:
27     double height;   // Cylinder's height
28
29  }; // end class Cylinder
30
31  #endif
```

Fig. 10.18 Cylinder class header file.

surface area (i.e., $2\pi r^2 + 2\pi rh$) and overrides member function **getVolume** (lines 41–45) to calculate the cylinder's volume ($\pi r^2 h$). Note that **Cylinder** function **getArea** invokes **Circle**'s **getArea** (line 35) to perform part of the area calculation; this is a nice example of code reuse. Member function **getName** (lines 48–52) overrides **Circle** function **getName**. If class **Cylinder** did not override this function, the class would have inherited **Circle** member function **getName**, which would have erroneously returned **"Circle"**. Similarly, **Cylinder** member function **print** (lines 55–60) overrides **Circle** function **print** to output information specific to a cylinder. Once again, note that **Cylinder**'s **print** function invokes **Circle**'s **print** (line 57) to output the **Circle** part of the **Cylinder**; this is another nice example of code reuse.

The program of Fig. 10.20 creates an object of each of the three concrete classes (**Point**, **Circle** and **Cylinder**) and manipulates those objects, first with static binding (lines 34–44), then polymorphically using a **vector** of **Shape** pointers. Lines 30–32 instantiate **Point** object **point**, **Circle** object **circle** and **Cylinder** object **cylinder**, respectively. Lines 34–44 then invoke member functions **getName** and **print** for objects **point**, **circle** and **cylinder** to output each object's class name and data (i.e., *x–y* coordinate pair, radius and height, depending on each object's type). Each

```cpp
1   // Fig. 10.19: cylinder.cpp
2   // Cylinder class inherits from class Circle.
3   #include <iostream>
4
5   using std::cout;
6
7   #include "cylinder.h"    // Cylinder class definition
8
9   // default constructor
10  Cylinder::Cylinder( int xValue, int yValue, double radiusValue,
11    double heightValue )
12    : Circle( xValue, yValue, radiusValue )
13  {
14     setHeight( heightValue );
15
16  } // end Cylinder constructor
17
18  // set Cylinder's height
19  void Cylinder::setHeight( double heightValue )
20  {
21     height = ( heightValue < 0.0 ? 0.0 : heightValue );
22
23  } // end function setHeight
24
25  // get Cylinder's height
26  double Cylinder::getHeight() const
27  {
28     return height;
29
30  } // end function getHeight
31
32  // override virtual function getArea: return Cylinder area
33  double Cylinder::getArea() const
34  {
35     return 2 * Circle::getArea() +            // code reuse
36        getCircumference() * getHeight();
37
38  } // end function getArea
39
40  // override virtual function getVolume: return Cylinder volume
41  double Cylinder::getVolume() const
42  {
43     return Circle::getArea() * getHeight();   // code reuse
44
45  } // end function getVolume
46
47  // override virtual function getName: return name of Cylinder
48  string Cylinder::getName() const
49  {
50     return "Cylinder";
51
52  }  // end function getName
53
```

Fig. 10.19 Cylinder class implementation file. (Part 1 of 2.)

```
54   // output Cylinder object
55   void Cylinder::print() const
56   {
57      Circle::print();   // code reuse
58      cout << "; height is " << getHeight();
59
60   } // end function print
```

Fig. 10.19 **Cylinder** class implementation file. (Part 2 of 2.)

member-function invocation in lines 34–44 is an example of static binding—at compile time, because we are using name handles (not pointers or references that could be set at execution time), the compiler can identify each object's type to determine which **getName** and **print** functions are called.

```
1    // Fig. 10.20: fig10_20.cpp
2    // Driver for shape, point, circle, cylinder hierarchy.
3    #include <iostream>
4
5    using std::cout;
6    using std::endl;
7    using std::fixed;
8
9    #include <iomanip>
10
11   using std::setprecision;
12
13   #include <vector>
14
15   using std::vector;
16
17   #include "shape.h"      // Shape class definition
18   #include "point.h"      // Point class definition
19   #include "circle.h"     // Circle class definition
20   #include "cylinder.h"   // Cylinder class definition
21
22   void virtualViaPointer( const Shape * );
23   void virtualViaReference( const Shape & );
24
25   int main()
26   {
27      // set floating-point number format
28      cout << fixed << setprecision( 2 );
29
30      Point point( 7, 11 );                    // create a Point
31      Circle circle( 22, 8, 3.5 );             // create a Circle
32      Cylinder cylinder( 10, 10, 3.3, 10 );    // create a Cylinder
33
34      cout << point.getName() << ": ";         // static binding
35      point.print();                           // static binding
36      cout << '\n';
```

Fig. 10.20 Demonstrating polymorphism via a hierarchy headed by an abstract base class. (Part 1 of 3.)

```
37
38      cout << circle.getName() << ": ";    // static binding
39      circle.print();                       // static binding
40      cout << '\n';
41
42      cout << cylinder.getName() << ": ";  // static binding
43      cylinder.print();                     // static binding
44      cout << "\n\n";
45
46      // create vector of three base-class pointers
47      vector< Shape * > shapeVector( 3 );
48
49      // aim shapeVector[0] at derived-class Point object
50      shapeVector[ 0 ] = &point;
51
52      // aim shapeVector[1] at derived-class Circle object
53      shapeVector[ 1 ] = &circle;
54
55      // aim shapeVector[2] at derived-class Cylinder object
56      shapeVector[ 2 ] = &cylinder;
57
58      // loop through shapeVector and call virtualViaPointer
59      // to print the shape name, attributes, area and volume
60      // of each object using dynamic binding
61      cout << "\nVirtual function calls made off "
62          << "base-class pointers:\n\n";
63
64      for ( int i = 0; i < shapeVector.size(); i++ )
65         virtualViaPointer( shapeVector[ i ] );
66
67      // loop through shapeVector and call virtualViaReference
68      // to print the shape name, attributes, area and volume
69      // of each object using dynamic binding
70      cout << "\nVirtual function calls made off "
71          << "base-class references:\n\n";
72
73      for ( int j = 0; j < shapeVector.size(); j++ )
74         virtualViaReference( *shapeVector[ j ] );
75
76      return 0;
77
78   } // end main
79
80   // make virtual function calls off a base-class pointer
81   // using dynamic binding
82   void virtualViaPointer( const Shape *baseClassPtr )
83   {
84      cout << baseClassPtr->getName() << ": ";
85
86      baseClassPtr->print();
87
88      cout << "\narea is " << baseClassPtr->getArea()
```

Fig. 10.20 Demonstrating polymorphism via a hierarchy headed by an abstract base class. (Part 2 of 3.)

```
89            << "\nvolume is " << baseClassPtr->getVolume()
90            << "\n\n";
91
92   } // end function virtualViaPointer
93
94   // make virtual function calls off a base-class reference
95   // using dynamic binding
96   void virtualViaReference( const Shape &baseClassRef )
97   {
98      cout << baseClassRef.getName() << ": ";
99
100     baseClassRef.print();
101
102     cout << "\narea is " << baseClassRef.getArea()
103          << "\nvolume is " << baseClassRef.getVolume() << "\n\n";
104
105   } // end function virtualViaReference
```

```
Point: [7, 11]
Circle: center is [22, 8]; radius is 3.50
Cylinder: center is [10, 10]; radius is 3.30; height is 10.00


Virtual function calls made off base-class pointers:

Point: [7, 11]
area is 0.00
volume is 0.00

Circle: center is [22, 8]; radius is 3.50
area is 38.48
volume is 0.00

Cylinder: center is [10, 10]; radius is 3.30; height is 10.00
area is 275.77
volume is 342.12


Virtual function calls made off base-class references:

Point: [7, 11]
area is 0.00
volume is 0.00

Circle: center is [22, 8]; radius is 3.50
area is 38.48
volume is 0.00

Cylinder: center is [10, 10]; radius is 3.30; height is 10.00
area is 275.77
volume is 342.12
```

Fig. 10.20 Demonstrating polymorphism via a hierarchy headed by an abstract base class. (Part 3 of 3.)

Line 47 then allocates **shapeVector**, which contains three **Shape** pointers. Line 50 aims **shapeVector[0]** at object **point**, line 53 aims **shapeVector[1]** at object **circle** and line 56 aims **shapeVector[2]** at object **cylinder**. The C++ compiler allows these assignments, because a **Point** is a **Shape**, a **Circle** is a **Shape** and a **Cylinder** is a **Shape**. Therefore, we can assign the addresses of **Point**, **Circle** and **Cylinder** objects to base class **Shape** pointers, even though **Shape** is an abstract class.

Next, a **for** structure (lines 64–65) traverses **shapeVector** and invokes function **virtualViaPointer** (lines 82–92) for each **shapeVector** element. Function **virtualViaPointer** receives in parameter **baseClassPtr** (of type **const Shape ***) the address stored in a **shapeVector** element. Each call to **virtualViaPointer** uses **baseClassPtr** to invoke **virtual** functions **getName** (line 84), **print** (line 86), **getArea** (line 88) and **getVolume** (line 89). Note that function **virtualViaPointer** does not contain any **Point**, **Circle** or **Cylinder** type information. The function knows only about type **Shape**. Therefore, at compile time, the compiler cannot know which concrete class' (i.e., **Point**, **Circle** or **Cylinder**) functions to call through **baseClassPtr**. Yet at execution time, each virtual-function invocation calls the function on the object to which **baseClassPtr** points at that time. The output illustrates that the appropriate functions for each class are indeed invoked. First, the string **"Point"** and the coordinates of the object **point** are output; the area and volume are both output as **0.00**. Next, the string **"Circle"**, the coordinates of the center of object **circle** and the radius of object **circle** are output; the area of **circle** is calculated and the volume is returned as **0.00**. Finally, the string **"Cylinder"**, the coordinates of the center of the base of object **cylinder**, the radius of object **cylinder** and the height of object **cylinder** are output; the area and volume of **cylinder** are calculated. All **virtual** function calls to **getName**, **print**, **getArea** and **getVolume** are resolved at run time with *dynamic binding* (also called *late binding*).

Finally, another **for** structure (lines 73–74) traverses **shapeVector** and invokes function **virtualViaReference** (lines 96–105) for each **shapeVector** element. Function **virtualViaReference** receives in its parameter **baseClassRef** (of type **const Shape &**), a reference formed by dereferencing the pointer stored in each **shapeVector** element (line 74). Each call to **virtualViaReference** invokes **virtual** functions **getName** (line 98), **print** (line 100), **getArea** (line 102) and **getVolume** (line 103) via reference **baseClassRef** to demonstrate that polymorphic processing can occur with base-class references as well. Each virtual-function invocation calls the function on the object to which **baseClassRef** refers at run time. This is another example of dynamic binding. The output produced using base-class references is identical to the output produced using base-class pointers.

10.7 Polymorphism, Virtual Functions and Dynamic Binding "Under the Hood"

C++ makes polymorphism easy to program. It is certainly possible to program for polymorphism in non-object-oriented languages such as C, but doing so requires complex and potentially dangerous pointer manipulations. This section discusses how C++ can implement polymorphism, virtual functions and dynamic binding internally. This will give you a solid understanding of how these capabilities really work. More importantly, it will help you appreciate the overhead of polymorphism—in terms of additional memory consumption and processor time. This will help you determine when to use polymorphism and when to avoid it. As you will see in Chapter 21, Standard Template Library (STL), the STL components were implemented without polymorphism and virtual functions—this was done to avoid execution-time overhead and achieve optimal performance to meet the unique requirements of the STL.

First, we will explain the data structures the C++ compiler builds at compile time to support polymorphism at execution time. Then we will show how an executing program uses these data structures to execute virtual functions and achieve the dynamic binding associated with polymorphism. Note that our discussion explains one possible implementation; this is not a language requirement.

When C++ compiles a class that has one or more virtual functions, it builds a *virtual function table (vtable)* for that class. An executing program uses the *vtable* to select the proper function implementation each time a virtual function of that class is called. Figure 10.21 illustrates the virtual function tables for classes **Shape**, **Point**, **Circle** and **Cylinder**.

In the *vtable* for class **Shape**, the first function pointer points to the implementation of function **getArea** for that class, namely, a function that returns an area of **0.0**. The second function pointer points to function **getVolume**, which also returns **0.0**. Functions **getName** and **print** are each pure **virtual**—they lack implementations, so their function pointers are each set to **0** (i.e., null pointer). Any class that has one or more **0** pointers in its *vtable* is an abstract class. Classes without any **0** *vtable* pointers (such as **Point**, **Circle** and **Cylinder**) are concrete classes.

Class **Point** inherits implementations of functions **getArea** and **getVolume** from class **Shape**, so the compiler simply sets these two function pointers in the **Point** *vtable* to be copies of the **getArea** and **getVolume** pointers in class **Shape**. Class **Point** overrides function **getName** to return the string **"Point"**, so the function pointer points to the **getName** function of class **Point**. **Point** also overrides **print**, so the corresponding function pointer points to the **Point** class function that prints the *x* and *y* coordinate values.

The **getArea** function pointer in the *vtable* for class **Circle** points to **Circle**'s **getArea** function that returns πr^2—this version overrides function **getArea** that was inherited indirectly from class **Shape**. The **getVolume** function pointer is simply copied from class **Point**—that pointer was previously copied into **Point** from **Shape**. The **getName** function pointer points to the **Circle** version of the function that returns the string **"Circle"**. The **print** function pointer points to **Circle**'s **print** function that prints the *x* and *y* coordinate values of the center of the circle and prints the radius.

The **getArea** function pointer in the *vtable* for class **Cylinder** points to **Cylinder**'s **getArea** function that calculates the surface area of the **Cylinder**, namely, $2\pi r^2 + 2\pi rh$—this version overrides **getArea** in class **Circle**. The **getVolume** function pointer points to **Cylinder**'s **getVolume** function that returns $\pi r^2 h$—this version overrides function **getVolume** that was inherited indirectly from class **Shape**. The **getName** function pointer points to **Cylinder**'s **getName** function that returns the string **"Cylinder"**. The **print** function pointer points to **Cylinder**'s **print** function that prints the *x* and *y* coordinate values of the center of the base of the cylinder and prints the radius and the height.

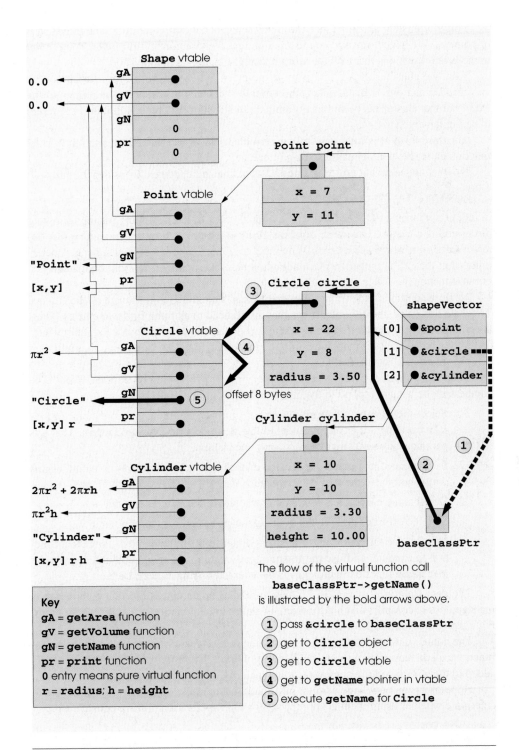

Fig. 10.21 Flow of control of a virtual function call.

Polymorphism is accomplished through an elegant data structure involving three levels of pointers. We have discussed one level—the function pointers in the *vtable*. These point to the actual functions that execute when a virtual function is invoked.

Now we consider the second level of pointers. Whenever an object of a class with **virtual** functions is instantiated, the compiler attaches to the object a pointer to the *vtable* for that class. This pointer is normally at the front of the object, but it is not required to be implemented that way.

The third level of pointer is simply the handle to the object that is receiving the virtual function call. This handle may also be a reference.

Now let us see how a typical **virtual** function call executes. Consider the call

```
baseClassPtr->getName()
```

in function **virtualViaPointer** (Fig. 10.20, lines 82–92). Assume for the following discussion that **baseClassPtr** contains **shapeVector[1]** (i.e., the address of object **circle** in **shapeVector**). When the compiler compiles this statement, it determines that the call is indeed being made via a base-class pointer and that **getName** is a virtual function.

Next, the compiler determines that **getName** is the third entry in each of the *vtables*. To locate this entry, the compiler notes that it will need to skip the first two entries. Thus, the compiler compiles an *offset* or *displacement* of eight bytes (four bytes for each pointer on today's popular 32-bit machines) into the machine-language object code that will execute the **virtual** function call.

Then the compiler generates code that performs the following operations, [*Note:* The numbers in the list correspond to the circled numbers in Fig. 10.21]:

1. Select the ith entry of **shapeVector** (in this case, the address of object **circle**), and pass it as an argument to function **virtualViaPointer**. This sets parameter **baseClassPtr** to point to **circle**.

2. Dereference that pointer to get to the **circle** object—which as you recall, begins with a pointer to the **Circle** *vtable*.

3. Dereference **circle**'s *vtable* pointer to get to the **Circle** *vtable*.

4. Skip the offset of eight bytes to select the **getName** function pointer.

5. Dereference the **getName** function pointer to form the name of the actual function to execute, and use the function call operator **()** to execute the appropriate **getName** function, which prints the character string **"Circle"**.

The data structures of Fig. 10.21 may appear to be complex, but this complexity is managed by the compiler and hidden from the programmer, making polymorphic programming straightforward in C++.

The pointer dereferencing operations and memory accesses that occur on every virtual function call do require some additional execution time. The *vtables* and the *vtable* pointers added to the objects require some additional memory.

Hopefully, you now have enough information about how virtual functions operate to determine whether using them is appropriate for each application you are considering.

Performance Tip 10.1

Polymorphism, as typically implemented with virtual functions and dynamic binding in C++, is efficient. Programmers may use these capabilities with nominal impact on performance.

Performance Tip 10.2

Virtual functions and dynamic binding enable polymorphic programming as opposed to **switch** *logic programming. C++ optimizing compilers normally generate code that runs at least as efficiently as hand-coded* **switch**-*based logic. One way or the other, the overhead of polymorphism is acceptable for most applications. But in some situations—real-time applications with stringent performance requirements, for example—the overhead of polymorphism may be too high.*

Software Engineering Observation 10.10

Dynamic binding enables independent software vendors (ISVs) to distribute software without revealing proprietary secrets. Software distributions can consist of only header files and object files. No source code needs to be revealed. Software developers can then use inheritance to derive new classes from those provided by the ISVs. Software that works with the classes the ISVs provide will continue to work with the derived classes and will use (via dynamic binding) the overridden virtual functions provided in these classes.

10.8 Virtual Destructors

A problem can occur when using polymorphism to process dynamically allocated objects of a class hierarchy. If an object with a nonvirtual destructor is destroyed explicitly by applying the **delete** operator to a base-class pointer to the object, the C++ standard specifies that the behavior is undefined.

There is a simple solution to this problem—declare the base-class destructor **virtual**. This makes all derived-class destructors virtual even though they do not have the same name as the base-class destructor. Now, if an object in the hierarchy is destroyed explicitly by applying the **delete** operator to a base-class pointer, the destructor for the appropriate class is called based on the object to which the base-class pointer points. Remember, when a derived-class object is destroyed, the base-class part of the derived-class object is also destroyed—the base-class destructor automatically executes after the derived-class destructor.

Good Programming Practice 10.2

If a class has virtual functions, provide a virtual destructor, even if one is not required for the class. Classes derived from this class may contain destructors that must be called properly.

Common Programming Error 10.6

Constructors cannot be virtual. Declaring a constructor **virtual** *is a syntax error.*

10.9 Case Study: Payroll System Using Polymorphism and Run-Time Type Information with dynamic_cast and typeid

Now we use virtual functions and polymorphism to perform payroll calculations based on the type of an employee. Consider the following problem statement:

A company pays its employees on a weekly basis. The company has four types of employees: salaried employees who are paid a fixed weekly salary regardless of the number of hours worked, hourly employees who are paid by the hour and receive overtime pay, commission employees who are paid a percentage of their sales and salaried-commission employees who receive a base salary plus a percentage of their sales. For this pay period, the company has decided to reward salaried-commission employees by adding 10% to their salaries. The company wants to implement a C++ application that performs its payroll calculations polymorphically.

We use a base class **Employee** to represent a "generic" employee. The classes that derive directly from **Employee** are **SalariedEmployee**, **CommissionEmployee** and **HourlyEmployee**. Class **BasePlusCommissionEmployee**—derived from **CommissionEmployee**—represents the last employee type. Figure 10.22 diagrams the inheritance hierarchy for our employee-payroll application. Note that abstract class *Employee* is italicized as per the convention of the UML.

An **earnings** function call certainly applies generically to all employees. But each employee's earnings calculation depends on the employee's class. So each class derives from base class **Employee**. We declare **earnings** as a pure virtual function in base class **Employee** (because in this class no specific implementation is appropriate), and each derived class overrides **earnings** with an appropriate implementation. To calculate an employee's earnings, the program aims a base-class pointer at that employee's object, then invokes its **earnings** function. We maintain a **vector** of base class **Employee** pointers to each **Employee** object. The program iterates through the **vector** and uses a base-class **Employee** pointer to invoke the **earnings** function for each employee object no matter what that employee's type is.

Let us consider the header file for class **Employee** (Fig. 10.23). The **public** member functions include a constructor that takes the first name, last name and social security number as arguments (line 13); *get* functions that return the first name, last name and social security number (lines 16, 19 and 22); *set* functions that set the first name, last name and social security number (lines 15, 18 and 21); pure virtual function **earnings** (line 25) and virtual function **print** (line 26). Why did we decide to declare function **earnings** as a pure virtual function? The answer is that it does not make sense to provide an implementation of this function in the **Employee** class. We cannot calculate the earnings for a generic employee—we first must know the specific **Employee** type before calculating the earnings. By declaring this function pure virtual, we indicate that each derived concrete class will provide an appropriate implementation of this function and that the program will be able to use base class **Employee** pointers to invoke **earnings** for any type of employee. Figure 10.24 contains the member-function implementations for class

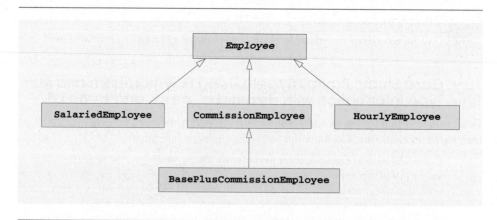

Fig. 10.22   Class hierarchy for the polymorphic employee-payroll application.

Employee. Note that the **Employee** constructor does not validate the social security number. An exercise in Chapter 15 asks you to validate a social security number to ensure that it is in the form **###-##-####**, where each # represents a digit.

```
1   // Fig. 10.23: employee.h
2   // Employee abstract base class.
3   #ifndef EMPLOYEE_H
4   #define EMPLOYEE_H
5
6   #include <string>  // C++ standard string class
7
8   using std::string;
9
10  class Employee {
11
12  public:
13     Employee( const string &, const string &, const string & );
14
15     void setFirstName( const string & );
16     string getFirstName() const;
17
18     void setLastName( const string & );
19     string getLastName() const;
20
21     void setSocialSecurityNumber( const string & );
22     string getSocialSecurityNumber() const;
23
24     // pure virtual function makes Employee abstract base class
25     virtual double earnings() const = 0;  // pure virtual
26     virtual void print() const;           // virtual
27
28  private:
29     string firstName;
30     string lastName;
31     string socialSecurityNumber;
32
33  }; // end class Employee
34
35  #endif // EMPLOYEE_H
```

Fig. 10.23 Employee class header file.

```
1   // Fig. 10.24: employee.cpp
2   // Abstract-base-class Employee member-function definitions.
3   // Note: No definitions are given for pure virtual functions.
4   #include <iostream>
5
6   using std::cout;
7   using std::endl;
8
9   #include "employee.h"  // Employee class definition
```

Fig. 10.24 Employee class implementation file. (Part 1 of 3.)

```
10
11    // constructor
12    Employee::Employee( const string &first, const string &last,
13       const string &SSN )
14       : firstName( first ),
15         lastName( last ),
16         socialSecurityNumber( SSN )
17    {
18       // empty body
19
20    } // end Employee constructor
21
22    // return first name
23    string Employee::getFirstName() const
24    {
25       return firstName;
26
27    } // end function getFirstName
28
29    // return last name
30    string Employee::getLastName() const
31    {
32       return lastName;
33
34    } // end function getLastName
35
36    // return social security number
37    string Employee::getSocialSecurityNumber() const
38    {
39       return socialSecurityNumber;
40
41    } // end function getSocialSecurityNumber
42
43    // set first name
44    void Employee::setFirstName( const string &first )
45    {
46       firstName = first;
47
48    } // end function setFirstName
49
50    // set last name
51    void Employee::setLastName( const string &last )
52    {
53       lastName = last;
54
55    } // end function setLastName
56
57    // set social security number
58    void Employee::setSocialSecurityNumber( const string &number )
59    {
60       socialSecurityNumber = number;   // should validate
61
62    } // end function setSocialSecurityNumber
```

Fig. 10.24 **Employee** class implementation file. (Part 2 of 3.)

```
63
64   // print Employee's information
65   void Employee::print() const
66   {
67      cout << getFirstName() << ' ' << getLastName()
68           << "\nsocial security number: "
69           << getSocialSecurityNumber() << endl;
70
71   } // end function print
```

Fig. 10.24 Employee class implementation file. (Part 3 of 3.)

Class **SalariedEmployee** (Fig. 10.25–Fig. 10.26) derives from class **Employee**. The public member functions (Fig. 10.25) include a constructor that takes a first name, a last name, a social security number and a weekly salary as arguments; a *set* function to assign a new value to data member **weeklySalary**; a *get* function to return **weeklySalary**'s value; a **virtual** function **earnings** that calculates a **SalariedEmployee**'s earnings and a **virtual** function **print** that outputs the employee's type, namely, **"salaried employee: "**. Note that in the implementation file (Fig. 10.26), the **SalariedEmployee** constructor cannot override the **Employee** constructor—the derived-class constructor still passes the first name, last name and social security number to the **Employee** constructor to initialize the base-class members (line 13). Also, note that virtual function **print** calls the base-class **Employee::print** function (line 44) to output the base class **Employee**-specific information (i.e., first name, last name and social security number).

```
1    // Fig. 10.25: salaried.h
2    // SalariedEmployee class derived from Employee.
3    #ifndef SALARIED_H
4    #define SALARIED_H
5
6    #include "employee.h"  // Employee class definition
7
8    class SalariedEmployee : public Employee {
9
10   public:
11      SalariedEmployee( const string &, const string &,
12         const string &, double = 0.0 );
13
14      void setWeeklySalary( double );
15      double getWeeklySalary() const;
16
17      virtual double earnings() const;
18      virtual void print() const;  // "salaried employee: "
19
20   private:
21      double weeklySalary;
22
23   }; // end class SalariedEmployee
24
25   #endif // SALARIED_H
```

Fig. 10.25 SalariedEmployee class header file.

```
33    // initialize vector with Employees
34    employees[ 0 ] = new SalariedEmployee( "John", "Smith",
35        "111-11-1111", 800.00 );
36    employees[ 1 ] = new CommissionEmployee( "Sue", "Jones",
37        "222-22-2222", 10000, .06 );
38    employees[ 2 ] = new BasePlusCommissionEmployee( "Bob",
39        "Lewis", "333-33-3333", 300, 5000, .04 );
40    employees[ 3 ] = new HourlyEmployee( "Karen", "Price",
41        "444-44-4444", 16.75, 40 );
42
43    // generically process each element in vector employees
44    for ( int i = 0; i < employees.size(); i++ ) {
45
46        // output employee information
47        employees[ i ]->print();
48
49        // downcast pointer
50        BasePlusCommissionEmployee *commissionPtr =
51            dynamic_cast < BasePlusCommissionEmployee * >
52                ( employees[ i ] );
53
54        // determine whether element points to base-salaried
55        // commission employee
56        if ( commissionPtr != 0 ) {
57            cout << "old base salary: $"
58                << commissionPtr->getBaseSalary() << endl;
59            commissionPtr->setBaseSalary(
60                1.10 * commissionPtr->getBaseSalary() );
61            cout << "new base salary with 10% increase is: $"
62                << commissionPtr->getBaseSalary() << endl;
63
64        } // end if
65
66        cout << "earned $" << employees[ i ]->earnings() << endl;
67
68    } // end for
69
70    // release memory held by vector employees
71    for ( int j = 0; j < employees.size(); j++ ) {
72
73        // output class name
74        cout << "\ndeleting object of "
75            << typeid( *employees[ j ] ).name();
76
77        delete employees[ j ];
78
79    } // end for
80
81    cout << endl;
82
83    return 0;
84
85 } // end main
```

Fig. 10.33 **Employee** class hierarchy driver program. (Part 2 of 3.)

```
salaried employee: John Smith
social security number: 111-11-1111
earned $800.00

commission employee: Sue Jones
social security number: 222-22-2222
earned $600.00

base-salaried commission employee: Bob Lewis
social security number: 333-33-3333
old base salary: $300.00
new base salary with 10% increase is: $330.00
earned $530.00

hourly employee: Karen Price
social security number: 444-44-4444
earned $670.00

deleting object of class SalariedEmployee
deleting object of class CommissionEmployee
deleting object of class BasePlusCommissionEmployee
deleting object of class HourlyEmployee
```

Fig. 10.33 **Employee** class hierarchy driver program. (Part 3 of 3.)

virtual in the base class, the system invokes the appropriate derived-class object's **print** function polymorphically. This function call is another example of dynamic binding—the virtual function is invoked through a base-class pointer, so the decision as to what function to invoke is deferred until run time.

In this example, we want to do some processing specific to objects of class **BasePlus-CommissionEmployee**; as we encounter these objects, we wish to increase by 10% their base salary. We process the employees generically (i.e., polymorphically); therefore, we cannot be certain as to which type of **Employee** is being manipulated at any given time. This creates a problem, because **BasePlusCommissionEmployee** employees must be identified so they can be paid properly. To accomplish this, we use operator *dynamic_cast* to help determine whether the type of each object is compatible with type **BasePlusCommissionEmployee**. Lines 50–52 dynamically downcast **employees[i]** from type **Employee *** to type **BasePlusCommissionEmployee ***. If the vector element points to a **BasePlusCommissionEmployee** object, then that object's address is assigned to **commissionPtr**; otherwise, **0** is assigned to **commissionPtr**.

If the value returned by the **dynamic_cast** in lines 50–52 is not **0**, the **if** structure (lines 56–64) performs the special processing required for the **BasePlusCommission-Employee** object. Lines 58, 59, 60 and 62 invoke **BasePlusCommissionEmployee** functions **getBaseSalary** and **setBaseSalary** to retrieve and update the employee's salary.

Line 66 invokes member function **earnings** on the object to which **employee[i]** points. Because we declared **earnings** as a virtual function in the base class, the program invokes the derived-class object's **earnings** function. This, too, uses dynamic binding.

The **for** loop (lines 71–79) displays each employee's object type and uses operator **delete** to deallocate the dynamic memory to which each vector element points. Operator

typeid[1] (line 75) returns a reference to an object of class ***type_info*** that contains the information about the type of its operand, including the name of that data type. When invoked, **type_info** member function ***name*** (line 75) returns a string that contains the type name (e.g., **class BasePlusCommissionEmployee**) of the argument passed to **typeid**. To use **typeid**, the program must include header file ***<typeinfo>*** (line 17).

SUMMARY

- With virtual functions and polymorphism, it becomes possible to design and implement systems that are more easily extensible. Programs can be written to process objects of types that may not exist when the program is under development.

- Polymorphic programming with virtual functions can eliminate the need for **switch** logic. The programmer can use the virtual function mechanism to perform the equivalent logic automatically, thus avoiding the kinds of errors typically associated with **switch** logic. Client code making decisions about object types and representations indicates poor class design.

- Derived classes can provide their own implementations of a base-class virtual function if necessary, but if they do not, the base class's implementation is used.

- If a virtual function is called by referencing a specific object by name and using the dot member-selection operator, the reference is resolved at compile time (this is called *static binding*); the virtual function that is called is the one defined for the class of that particular object.

- There are many situations in which it is useful to define abstract classes for which the programmer never intends to create objects. Because these are used only as base classes, we refer to them as abstract base classes. No objects of an abstract class may be instantiated.

- Classes from which objects can be instantiated are called concrete classes.

- A class is made abstract by declaring one or more of its virtual functions to be pure. A pure virtual function is one with an initializer of **= 0** in its declaration.

- If a class is derived from a class with a pure virtual function and that derived class does not supply a definition for that pure virtual function, then that virtual function remains pure in the derived class. Consequently, the derived class is also an abstract class.

- C++ enables polymorphism—the ability for objects of different classes related by inheritance to respond differently to the same member-function call.

- Polymorphism is implemented via virtual functions.

- When a request is made through a base-class pointer or reference to use a virtual function, C++ chooses the correct overridden function in the appropriate derived class associated with the object.

- Through the use of virtual functions and polymorphism, a member-function call can cause different actions depending on the type of the object receiving the call.

- Although we cannot instantiate objects of abstract base classes, we can declare pointers and references to objects of abstract base classes. Such pointers and references can be used to enable polymorphic manipulations of derived-class objects instantiated from concrete derived classes.

---

1. Operators **dynamic_cast** and **typeid** are part of C++'s *run-time type information* (*RTTI*) feature, which allows programmers to determine an object's type at run time. Some compilers, such as Microsoft Visual C++ 6, require that RTTI be enabled before it can be used in a program. To enable RTTI in Visual C++ 6, select **Project > Settings > C/C++**, and select **C++ Language** from the **Category** combo box. Then check **Enable Run-Time Type Information (RTTI)**. Consult your compiler's documentation to determine whether your compiler has similar requirements.

- Dynamic binding requires that at run time, the call to a virtual member function be routed to the virtual function version appropriate for the class. A virtual function table called the *vtable* is implemented as an array containing function pointers. Each class with virtual functions has a *vtable*. For each virtual function in the class, the *vtable* has an entry containing a function pointer to the version of the virtual function to use for an object of that class. The virtual function to use for a particular class could be the function defined in that class, or it could be a function inherited either directly or indirectly from a base class higher in the hierarchy.

- When a base class provides a virtual member function, derived classes can override the virtual function, but they do not have to override it. Thus, a derived class can use a base class' version of a virtual function, and this would be indicated in the *vtable*

- Each object of a class with virtual functions contains a pointer to the *vtable* for that class. The appropriate function pointer in the *vtable* is obtained and dereferenced to complete the call at execution time. This *vtable* lookup and pointer dereferencing require nominal run-time overhead.

- Any class that has one or more **0** pointers in its *vtable* is an abstract class. Classes without any **0** *vtable* pointers are concrete classes.

- New kinds of classes are regularly added to systems. New classes are accommodated by dynamic binding (also called late binding). The type of an object need not be known at compile time for a virtual-function call to be compiled. At run time, the appropriate member function will be called for the object to which the pointer points.

- Dynamic binding enables independent software vendors (ISVs) to distribute software without revealing proprietary secrets. Software distributions can consist of only header files and object files. No source code needs to be revealed. Software developers can then use inheritance to derive new classes from those provided by the ISVs. The software that works with the classes the ISVs provide will continue to work with the derived classes and will use (via dynamic binding) the overridden virtual functions provided in these classes.

- Declare the base-class destructor **virtual** if the class contains virtual functions. This makes all derived-class destructors virtual even though they do not have the same name as the base-class destructor. If an object in the hierarchy is destroyed explicitly by applying the **delete** operator to a base-class pointer to a derived-class object, the destructor for the appropriate class is called. After a derived-class destructor runs, the destructors for all of that class' base classes run all the way up the hierarchy—the root class' destructor runs last.

- Operator **dynamic_cast** checks the type of the object to which the pointer points, then determines whether this type has an *is–a* relationship with the type to which the pointer is being converted. If they have an *is–a* relationship, **dynamic_cast** returns the object's address. If not, **dynamic_cast** returns **0**.

- Operator **typeid** returns a reference to an object of class **type_info** that contains information about the data type of its operand, including the name of the data type. To use **typeid**, the program must include header file **<typeinfo>**.

- When invoked, **type_info** member function **name** returns the name of the type that the **type_info** object represents.

- Operators **dynamic_cast** and **typeid** are part of C++'s run-time type information (RTTI) feature, which allows a program to determine an object's type at run time.

TERMINOLOGY

abstract base class	class hierarchy
abstract class	concrete class
base-class virtual function	derived class

derived-class constructor
direct base class
displacement into *vtable*
downcasting
dynamic binding
dynamic_cast operator
early binding
eliminating **switch** statements
extensibility
implementation inheritance
independent software vendor (ISV)
indirect base class
inheritance
interface inheritance
late binding
name member function of class **type_info**
offset into *vtable*
override a pure virtual function
override a virtual function
pointer to a base class
pointer to a derived class

pointer to an abstract class
polymorphism
programming "in the general"
programming "in the specific"
pure virtual function (**= 0**)
reference to a base class
reference to a derived class
reference to an abstract class
RTTI (run-time type information)
run-time type information (RTTI)
static binding
switch logic
typeid operator
<typeinfo> header file
type_info class
virtual destructor
virtual function
virtual function table
vtable
vtable pointer

SELF-REVIEW EXERCISES

10.1   Fill in the blanks in each of the following statements:
   a) Treating a base-class object as a(n) _____ can cause errors.
   b) Polymorphism helps eliminate _____ logic.
   c) If a class contains at least one pure virtual function, it is a(n) _____ class.
   d) Classes from which objects can be instantiated are called _____ classes.
   e) Operator _____ can be used to downcast base-class pointers safely.
   f) Operator **typeid** returns a reference to a(n) _____ object.
   g) _____ involves using a base-class pointer or reference to invoke virtual functions on base-class and derived-class objects.
   h) Overridable functions are declared using keyword _____.
   i) Casting a base-class pointer to a derived-class pointer is called _____.

10.2   State whether each of the following is *true* or *false*. If *false*, explain why.
   a) All **virtual** functions in an abstract base class must be declared as pure **virtual** functions.
   b) Referring to a derived-class object with a base-class handle is dangerous.
   c) A class is made abstract by declaring that class **virtual**.
   d) If a base class declares a pure **virtual** function, a derived class must implement that function to become a concrete class.
   e) Polymorphic programming can eliminate the need for **switch** logic.

ANSWERS TO SELF-REVIEW EXERCISES

10.1   a) derived-class object.   b) **switch**.   c) abstract.   d) concrete.   e) **dynamic_cast**.
f) **type_info**. g) Polymorphism. h) **virtual**. i) downcasting.

10.2   a) False. An abstract base class can include virtual functions with implementations. b) False. Referring to a base-class object with a derived-class handle is dangerous. c) False. Classes are never declared **virtual**. Rather, a class is made abstract by including at least one pure virtual function in the class. d) True. e) True.

EXERCISES

10.3   How is it that polymorphism enables you to program "in the general" rather than "in the specific"? Discuss the key advantages of programming "in the general."

10.4   Discuss the problems of programming with **switch** logic. Explain why polymorphism can be an effective alternative to using **switch** logic.

10.5   Distinguish between inheriting interface and inheriting implementation. How do inheritance hierarchies designed for inheriting interface differ from those designed for inheriting implementation?

10.6   What are virtual functions? Describe a circumstance in which virtual functions would be appropriate.

10.7   Distinguish between static binding and dynamic binding. Explain the use of virtual functions and the *vtable* in dynamic binding.

10.8   Distinguish between virtual functions and pure virtual functions.

10.9   Suggest one or more levels of abstract base classes for the **Shape** hierarchy discussed in this chapter. (The first level is **Shape**, and the second level consists of the classes **TwoDimensionalShape** and **ThreeDimensionalShape**.)

10.10   How does polymorphism promote extensibility?

10.11   You have been asked to develop a flight simulator that will have elaborate graphical outputs. Explain why polymorphic programming would be especially effective for a problem of this nature.

10.12   Modify the payroll system of Fig. 10.23–Fig. 10.33 to include **private** data members **birthDate** (use class **Date** from Fig. 8.10–Fig. 8.11) to class **Employee**. Assume that payroll is processed once per month. Create a **vector** of **Employee** references to store the various employee objects. In a loop, calculate the payroll for each **Employee** (polymorphically), and add a $100.00 bonus to the person's payroll amount if this is the month in which the **Employee**'s birthday occurs.

10.13   Implement the **Shape** hierarchy shown in Fig. 9.3. Each **TwoDimensionalShape** should contain function **getArea** to calculate the area of the two-dimensional shape. Each **ThreeDimensionalShape** should have member functions **getArea** and **getVolume** to calculate the surface area and volume of the three-dimensional shape, respectively. Create a program that uses a **vector** of **Shape** pointers to objects of each concrete class in the hierarchy. The program should print the object to which each **vector** element points. Also, in the loop that processes all the shapes in the **vector**, determine whether each shape is a **TwoDimensionalShape** or a **ThreeDimensionalShape**. If a shape is a **TwoDimensionalShape**, display its area. If a shape is a **ThreeDimensionalShape**, display its area and volume

10.14   Develop a basic graphics package. Use the **Shape** class inheritance hierarchy from Chapter 9. Limit yourself to two-dimensional shapes such as squares, rectangles, triangles and circles. Interact with the user. Let the user specify the position, size, shape and fill characters to be used in drawing each shape. The user can specify more than one of the same shape. As you create each shape, place a **Shape *** pointer to each new **Shape** object into an array. Each class has its own **draw** member function. Write a polymorphic screen manager that walks through the array, sending **draw** messages to each object in the array to form a screen image. Redraw the screen image each time the user specifies an additional shape.

11

Templates

Objectives

- To be able to use function templates to create a group of related (overloaded) functions.
- To be able to distinguish between function templates and function-template specializations.
- To be able to use class templates to create a group of related types.
- To be able to distinguish between class templates and class-template specializations.
- To understand how to overload function templates.
- To understand the relationships among templates, friends, inheritance and static members.

Behind that outside pattern
the dim shapes get clearer every day.
It is always the same shape, only very numerous.
Charlotte Perkins Gilman

A Mighty Maze! but not without a plan.
Alexander Pope

Outline

11.1 Introduction
11.2 Function Templates
11.3 Overloading Function Templates
11.4 Class Templates
11.5 Class Templates and Nontype Parameters
11.6 Templates and Inheritance
11.7 Templates and Friends
11.8 Templates and **static** Members

Summary • Terminology • Self-Review Exercises • Answers to Self-Review Exercises • Exercises

11.1 Introduction

In this chapter, we discuss one of C++'s more powerful features, namely *templates*. *Function templates* and *class templates* enable programmers to specify, with a single code segment, an entire range of related (overloaded) functions—called *function-template specializations*—or an entire range of related classes—called *class-template specializations.*

We might write a single function template for an array-sort function, then have C++ generate separate function-template specializations that will sort **int** arrays, **float** arrays, arrays of strings and so on.

We discussed function templates in Chapter 3. For the benefit of those readers who skipped that treatment, we present an additional discussion and example in this chapter.

We might write a single class template for a stack class, then have C++ generate separate class-template specializations, such as a stack-of-**int** class, a stack-of-**float** class, a stack-of-**string** class and so on.

Note the distinction between templates and template specializations: Function templates and class templates are like stencils out of which we trace shapes; function-template specializations and class-template specializations are like the separate tracings that all have the same shape, but could, for example, be drawn in different colors.

Software Engineering Observation 11.1

Templates are one of C++'s most powerful capabilities for software reuse.

In this chapter, we present examples of a function template and a class template. We also consider the relationships between templates and other C++ features, such as overloading, inheritance, friends and **static** members.

The design and details of the template mechanisms discussed here are based on the work of Bjarne Stroustrup as presented in his paper, *Parameterized Types for C++*, and as published in the *Proceedings of the USENIX C++ Conference* held in Denver, Colorado, in October 1988.

This chapter is designed only as an introduction to the complex topic of templates. Chapter 21, Standard Template Library (STL), presents an in-depth treatment of the template container classes, iterators and algorithms of the STL. Chapter 21 contains dozens of live-code template-based examples illustrating more sophisticated template-programming techniques than those used here in Chapter 11.

11.2 Function Templates

Overloaded functions normally are used to perform *similar* operations on different types of data. If the operations are *identical* for each type, they can be performed more compactly and conveniently using *function templates*. The programmer writes a single function-template definition. Based on the argument types provided explicitly or inferred from calls to this function, the compiler generates separate object-code functions (i.e., function-template specializations) to handle each function call appropriately. In C, this task can be performed using macros created with the preprocessor directive **#define** (see Chapter 19, Preprocessor). However, *macros* can have serious side effects and do not enable the compiler to perform type checking. Function templates provide a compact solution, like macros, but enable full type checking.

Testing and Debugging Tip 11.1

Function templates, like macros, enable software reuse. Unlike macros, function templates help eliminate many types of errors through the scrutiny of full C++ type checking.

All function-template definitions begin with keyword **template** followed by a list of formal type parameters to the function template enclosed in *angle brackets (< and >)*; each formal type parameter must be preceded by either of the interchangeable keywords **class** or **typename**, as in

        template< class T >

or

        template< typename ElementType >

or

        template< class BorderType, class FillType >

The formal type parameters of a template definition are used to specify the *types* of the arguments to the function, to specify the return type of the function and to declare variables within the function. The function definition follows and is defined like any other function. Note that keywords **class** and **typename** used to specify function-template type parameters actually mean "any built-in type or user-defined type."

Common Programming Error 11.1

*Not placing **class** or **typename** before each formal type parameter of a function template is a syntax error.*

Let us examine function template **printArray** in Fig. 11.1, lines 9–17. Function template **printArray** declares (line 9) a single formal type parameter **T** (**T** can be any valid identifier) for the type of the array to be printed by function **printArray**; **T** is referred to as a *type parameter*. When the compiler detects a **printArray** function invocation in the program source code (e.g., lines 32, 37 and 42), the type of **printArray**'s first argument is substituted for **T** throughout the template definition, and C++ creates a complete function-template specialization for printing an array of the specified data type. Then, the newly created specialization is compiled. In Fig. 11.1, the compiler creates three

printArray specializations—one that expects an **int** array, one that expects a **double** array and one that expects a **char** array. For example, the function-template specialization for type **int** is

```
void printArray( const int *array, const int count )
{
   for ( int i = 0; i < count; i++ )
      cout << array[ i ] << " "

   cout << endl;

} // end function printArray
```

Every formal type parameter in a function-template definition (e.g., **T** in line 9) must appear in the function's parameter list at least once (e.g., **T** in line 10). The name of a formal type parameter can be used only once in the parameter list of a template header. Formal type parameter names among function templates need not be unique.

```
1   // Fig. 11.1: fig11_01.cpp
2   // Using template functions.
3   #include <iostream>
4
5   using std::cout;
6   using std::endl;
7
8   // function template printArray definition
9   template< class T >
10  void printArray( const T *array, const int count )
11  {
12     for ( int i = 0; i < count; i++ )
13        cout << array[ i ] << " ";
14
15     cout << endl;
16
17  } // end function printArray
18
19  int main()
20  {
21     const int aCount = 5;
22     const int bCount = 7;
23     const int cCount = 6;
24
25     int a[ aCount ] = { 1, 2, 3, 4, 5 };
26     double b[ bCount ] = { 1.1, 2.2, 3.3, 4.4, 5.5, 6.6, 7.7 };
27     char c[ cCount ] = "HELLO";   // 6th position for null
28
29     cout << "Array a contains:" << endl;
30
31     // call integer function-template specialization
32     printArray( a, aCount );
33
34     cout << "Array b contains:" << endl;
```

Fig. 11.1 Function-template specializations of function template **printArray**. (Part 1 of 2.)

```
35
36      // call double function-template specialization
37      printArray( b, bCount );
38
39      cout << "Array c contains:" << endl;
40
41      // call character function-template specialization
42      printArray( c, cCount );
43
44      return 0;
45
46   } // end main
```

```
Array a contains:
1 2 3 4 5
Array b contains:
1.1 2.2 3.3 4.4 5.5 6.6 7.7
Array c contains:
H E L L O
```

Fig. 11.1   Function-template specializations of function template `printArray`.
(Part 2 of 2.)

Figure 11.1 demonstrates function template **printArray**. The program begins by instantiating five-element **int** array **a**, seven-element **double** array **b** and six-element **char** array **c**. Then, the program outputs each array by calling **printArray**—once with a first argument **a** of type **int *** (line 32), once with a first argument **b** of type **double *** (line 37) and once with a first argument **c** of type **char *** (line 42). The call on line 32, for example, causes the compiler to infer that **T** is **int** and to instantiate a **printArray** function-template specialization, for which type parameter **T** is **int**. The call on line 37 causes the compiler to infer that **T** is **double** and to instantiate a second **printArray** function-template specialization, for which type parameter **T** is **double**. The call on line 42 causes the compiler to infer that **T** is **char** and to instantiate a third **printArray** function-template specialization, for which type parameter **T** is **char**. It is important to note that if **T** (line 9) represents a user-defined type, the first stream-insertion operator in line 13 must be overloaded for class **T**.

In this example, the template mechanism saves the programmer from having to write three separate overloaded functions with prototypes

```
void printArray( const int *, const int );
void printArray( const double *, const int );
void printArray( const char *, const int );
```

that all use the same code, except for type **T**.

Performance Tip 11.1

Although templates offer software-reusability benefits, remember that multiple function-template specializations and class-template specializations are instantiated in a program, despite the fact that the template is written only once. These copies can consume considerable memory.

11.3 Overloading Function Templates

Function templates and overloading are intimately related. The related function-template specializations generated from a function template all have the same name, so the compiler uses overloading resolution to invoke the proper function.

A function template may be overloaded in several ways. We can provide other function templates that specify the same function name but different function parameters. For example, function template **printArray** of Fig. 11.1 could be overloaded with another **printArray** function template with additional parameters **lowSubscript** and **highSubscript** to specify the portion of the array to output (see Exercise 11.4).

A function template also can be overloaded by providing non-template functions with the same function name but different function arguments. For example, function template **printArray** of Fig. 11.1 could be overloaded with a non-template version that specifically prints an array of character strings in neat, tabular format (see Exercise 11.5).

Common Programming Error 11.2

*If a template is invoked with a user-defined type, and if that template uses operators (e.g., **==**, **+**, **<=**) with objects of that class type, then those operators must be overloaded for the user-defined type. Forgetting to overload such operators causes errors.*

The compiler performs a matching process to determine what function to call when a function is invoked. First, the compiler tries to find and use a precise match in which the function names and argument types match those of the function call. If this fails, the compiler determines whether a function template is available that can be used to generate a function-template specialization with a precise match of function name and argument types. If such a function template is found, the compiler generates and uses the appropriate function-template specialization.

Common Programming Error 11.3

The compiler performs a matching process to determine what function to call when a function is invoked. If no match can be found, or if the matching process produces multiple matches (of equal rank), the compiler generates an error.

11.4 Class Templates

It is possible to understand the concept of a "stack" (a data structure into which we insert items at the top and retrieve those items in last-in-first-out order) independent of the type of the items being placed in the stack. However, to instantiate a stack, a data type must be specified. This creates a wonderful opportunity for software reusability. We need the means for describing the notion of a stack generically and instantiating classes that are type-specific versions of this generic class. C++ provides this capability through *class templates*, and the technique is called *generic programming*.

Software Engineering Observation 11.2

Class templates encourage software reusability by enabling type-specific versions of generic classes to be instantiated.

Class templates are called *parameterized types*, because they require one or more type parameters to specify how to customize a "generic class" template to form a class-template specialization.

The programmer who wishes to produce a variety of class-template specializations writes only one class-template definition. Each time the programmer needs an additional class-template specialization, the programmer uses a concise, simple notation, and the compiler writes the source code for the specialization the programmer requires. One **Stack** class template, for example, could thus become the basis for creating many **Stack** classes (such as "**Stack** of **double**," "**Stack** of **int**," "**Stack** of **char**," "**Stack** of **Employee**," etc.) used in a program.

Note the **Stack** class-template definition in Fig. 11.2. It looks like a conventional class definition, except that it is preceded by the header (line 6)

```
template< class T >
```

to specify a class-template definition with type parameter **T** that indicates the type of the **Stack** class to be created. The programmer need not specifically use identifier **T**—the programmer can use any valid identifier. The type of element to be stored on this **Stack** is mentioned generically as **T** throughout the **Stack** class header and member function definitions. In a moment, we show how **T** becomes associated with a specific type, such as **double** or **int**. There are two constraints for non-primitive data types used with this **Stack**: They must have a copy constructor, and they must support the assignment operator. If an object of the class used with this **Stack** contains dynamically allocated memory, the assignment operator should be overloaded for that type, as we saw in Chapter 8.

```
1   // Fig. 11.2: tstack1.h
2   // Stack class template.
3   #ifndef TSTACK1_H
4   #define TSTACK1_H
5
6   template< class T >
7   class Stack {
8
9   public:
10     Stack( int = 10 );   // default constructor (stack size 10)
11
12     // destructor
13     ~Stack()
14     {
15        delete [] stackPtr;
16
17     } // end ~Stack destructor
18
19     bool push( const T& );   // push an element onto the stack
20     bool pop( T& );          // pop an element off the stack
21
22     // determine whether Stack is empty
23     bool isEmpty() const
24     {
25        return top == -1;
26
27     } // end function isEmpty
```

Fig. 11.2   Class template **Stack**. (Part 1 of 3.)

```
28
29      // determine whether Stack is full
30      bool isFull() const
31      {
32         return top == size - 1;
33
34      } // end function isFull
35
36   private:
37      int size;      // # of elements in the stack
38      int top;       // location of the top element
39      T *stackPtr;   // pointer to the stack
40
41   }; // end class Stack
42
43   // constructor
44   template< class T >
45   Stack< T >::Stack( int s )
46   {
47      size = s > 0 ? s : 10;
48      top = -1;  // Stack initially empty
49      stackPtr = new T[ size ]; // allocate memory for elements
50
51   } // end Stack constructor
52
53   // push element onto stack;
54   // if successful, return true; otherwise, return false
55   template< class T >
56   bool Stack< T >::push( const T &pushValue )
57   {
58      if ( !isFull() ) {
59         stackPtr[ ++top ] = pushValue;  // place item on Stack
60         return true;  // push successful
61
62      } // end if
63
64      return false;  // push unsuccessful
65
66   } // end function push
67
68   // pop element off stack;
69   // if successful, return true; otherwise, return false
70   template< class T >
71   bool Stack< T >::pop( T &popValue )
72   {
73      if ( !isEmpty() ) {
74         popValue = stackPtr[ top-- ];  // remove item from Stack
75         return true;  // pop successful
76
77      } // end if
78
79      return false;  // pop unsuccessful
80
```

Fig. 11.2   Class template **Stack**. (Part 2 of 3.)

```
81    } // end function pop
82
83    #endif
```

Fig. 11.2   Class template **Stack**. (Part 3 of 3.)

The member-function definitions outside the class each begin with the header

```
template< class T >
```

(lines 44, 55 and 70). Thus, each definition resembles a conventional function definition, except that the **Stack** element type always is listed generically as type parameter **T**. The binary scope-resolution operator is used with the class-template name **Stack< T >** (lines 45, 56 and 71) to tie each member function definition to the class template's scope. In this case, the class name is **Stack< T >**. When **doubleStack** is instantiated as type **Stack< double >**, the **Stack** constructor function-template specialization uses **new** to create an array of elements of type **double** to represent the stack (line 49). The statement

```
stackPtr = new T[ size ];
```

in the **Stack** class-template definition is generated by the compiler in the class-template specialization **Stack< double >** as

```
stackPtr = new double[ size ];
```

Now, let us consider the driver (Fig. 11.3) that exercises the **Stack** class template. The driver begins by instantiating object **doubleStack** of size **5** (line 13). This object is declared to be of class **Stack< double >** (pronounced "**Stack** of **double**"). The compiler associates type **double** with type parameter **T** in the template to produce the source code for a **Stack** class of type **double**. Although the programmer does not see this source code, it is included in the program and compiled.

```
1    // Fig. 11.3: fig11_03.cpp
2    // Stack-class-template test program.
3    #include <iostream>
4
5    using std::cout;
6    using std::cin;
7    using std::endl;
8
9    #include "tstack1.h"   // Stack class template definition
10
11   int main()
12   {
13      Stack< double > doubleStack( 5 );
14      double doubleValue = 1.1;
15
16      cout << "Pushing elements onto doubleStack\n";
17
18      while ( doubleStack.push( doubleValue ) ) {
19         cout << doubleValue << ' ';
```

Fig. 11.3   Class template **Stack** test program. (Part 1 of 2.)

```
20          doubleValue += 1.1;
21
22     } // end while
23
24     cout << "\nStack is full. Cannot push " << doubleValue
25          << "\n\nPopping elements from doubleStack\n";
26
27     while ( doubleStack.pop( doubleValue ) )
28          cout << doubleValue << ' ';
29
30     cout << "\nStack is empty. Cannot pop\n";
31
32     Stack< int > intStack;
33     int intValue = 1;
34     cout << "\nPushing elements onto intStack\n";
35
36     while ( intStack.push( intValue ) ) {
37          cout << intValue << ' ';
38          ++intValue;
39
40     } // end while
41
42     cout << "\nStack is full. Cannot push " << intValue
43          << "\n\nPopping elements from intStack\n";
44
45     while ( intStack.pop( intValue ) )
46          cout << intValue << ' ';
47
48     cout << "\nStack is empty. Cannot pop\n";
49
50     return 0;
51
52 } // end main
```

```
Pushing elements onto doubleStack
1.1 2.2 3.3 4.4 5.5
Stack is full. Cannot push 6.6

Popping elements from doubleStack
5.5 4.4 3.3 2.2 1.1
Stack is empty. Cannot pop

Pushing elements onto intStack
1 2 3 4 5 6 7 8 9 10
Stack is full. Cannot push 11

Popping elements from intStack
10 9 8 7 6 5 4 3 2 1
Stack is empty. Cannot pop
```

Fig. 11.3 Class template **Stack** test program. (Part 2 of 2.)

Lines 18–22 invoke **push** to place the **double** values 1.1, 2.2, 3.3, 4.4 and 5.5 onto **doubleStack**. The **push** loop terminates when the driver attempts to **push** a sixth value onto **doubleStack** (which is full, because it was created to hold a maximum of

The predefined object **cin** is an **istream** instance and is said to be "connected to" (or attached to) the standard input device, which usually is the keyboard. The stream-extraction operator (**>>**) as used in the following statement causes a value for integer variable **grade** (assuming that **grade** has been declared as an **int** variable) to be input from **cin** to memory:

```
cin >> grade;   // data "flows" in the direction of the arrows
```

Note that the compiler determines the data type of **grade** and selects the appropriate overloaded stream-extraction operator. Assuming that **grade** has been declared properly, the stream-extraction operator does not require additional type information (as is the case, for example, in C-style I/O). The **>>** operator is overloaded to input data items of built-in types, strings and pointer values.

The predefined object **cout** is an **ostream** instance and is said to be "connected to" the standard output device, which usually is the display screen. The stream-insertion operator (**<<**), as used in the following statement, causes the value of variable **grade** to be output from memory to the standard output device:

```
cout << grade;  // data "flows" in the direction of the arrows
```

Note that the compiler also determines the data type of **grade** (assuming **grade** has been declared properly) and selects the appropriate stream-insertion operator, so the stream-insertion operator does not require additional type information. The **<<** operator is overloaded to output data items of built-in types, strings and pointer values.

The predefined object **cerr** is an **ostream** instance and is said to be "connected to" the standard error device. Outputs to object **cerr** are *unbuffered*, implying that each stream insertion to **cerr** causes its output to appear immediately—this is appropriate for notifying a user promptly about errors.

The predefined object **clog** is an instance of the **ostream** class and is said to be "connected to" the standard error device. Outputs to **clog** are *buffered*. This means that each insertion to **clog** could cause its output to be held in a buffer until the buffer is filled or until the buffer is flushed.[3]

C++ file processing uses class templates *basic_ifstream* (for file input), *basic_ofstream* (for file output) and *basic_fstream* (for file input and output). Each class template has a predefined template specialization that enables **char** I/O. C++ provides a set of **typedef**s that provide aliases for these template specializations. For example, the **typedef** *ifstream* represents a specialization of **basic_ifstream** that enables **char** input from a file. Similarly, **typedef** *ofstream* represents a specialization of **basic_ofstream** that enables **char** output to a file. Also, **typedef** *fstream* represents a specialization of **basic_fstream** that enables **char** input from, and output to, a file. Template **basic_ifstream** inherits from **basic_istream**, **basic_ofstream** inherits from **basic_ostream** and **basic_fstream** inherits from **basic_iostream**. The UML class diagram of Fig. 12.2 summarizes the various inheritance relationships of the I/O-related classes. The full stream-I/O class hierarchy provides most of the capabilities that programmers need. Consult the class-library reference for your C++ system for additional file-processing information.

---

3. Buffering is an I/O performance-enhancement technique discussed in operating systems courses.

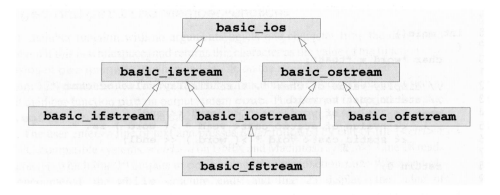

Fig. 12.2   Stream-I/O template hierarchy portion showing the main file-processing templates.

12.3 Stream Output

Formatted and unformatted output capabilities are provided by **ostream**. Capabilities for output include output of standard data types with the stream-insertion operator (**<<**); output of characters via the **put** member function; unformatted output via the **write** member function (Section 12.5); output of integers in decimal, octal and hexadecimal formats (Section 12.6.1); output of floating-point values with various precision (Section 12.6.2), with forced decimal points (Section 12.7.1), in scientific notation and in fixed notation (Section 12.7.5); output of data justified in fields of designated widths (Section 12.7.2); output of data in fields padded with specified characters (Section 12.7.3); and output of uppercase letters in scientific notation and hexadecimal notation (Section 12.7.6).

12.3.1 Output of **char *** Variables

C++ determines data types automatically, an improvement over C. Unfortunately, this feature sometimes "gets in the way." For example, suppose we want to print the value of a **char *** to a character string (i.e., the memory address of the first character of that string). However, the **<<** operator has been overloaded to print data of type **char *** as a null-terminated string. The solution is to cast the **char *** to a **void *** (in fact, this should be done to any pointer variable the programmer wishes to output as an address). Figure 12.3 demonstrates printing a **char *** variable in both string and address formats. Note that the address prints as a hexadecimal (base 16) number. We say more about controlling the bases of numbers in Section 12.6.1, Section 12.7.4, Section 12.7.5 and Section 12.7.7. [*Note:* The output of the program in Fig. 12.3 may differ among compilers.]

```
1   // Fig. 12.3: fig12_03.cpp
2   // Printing the address stored in a char * variable.
3   #include <iostream>
4
5   using std::cout;
6   using std::endl;
```

Fig. 12.3   Printing the address stored in a **char *** variable. (Part 1 of 2.)

```
30        // display x with plus sign
31        cout << showbase << setw( 10 ) << x << endl;
32
33        // display x with left justification
34        cout << left << setw( 10 ) << x << endl;
35
36        // display x as hex with internal justification
37        cout << internal << setw( 10 ) << hex << x << endl << endl;
38
39        cout << "Using various padding characters:" << endl;
40
41        // display x using padded characters (right justification)
42        cout << right;
43        cout.fill( '*' );
44        cout << setw( 10 ) << dec << x << endl;
45
46        // display x using padded characters (left justification)
47        cout << left << setw( 10 ) << setfill( '%' ) << x << endl;
48
49        // display x using padded characters (internal justification)
50        cout << internal << setw( 10 ) << setfill( '^' ) << hex
51           << x << endl;
52
53        return 0;
54
55   } // end main
```

```
10000 printed as int right and left justified
and as hex with internal justification.
Using the default pad character (space):
     10000
10000
0x    2710

Using various padding characters:
*****10000
10000%%%%
0x^^^^2710
```

Fig. 12.16   Using member function **fill** and stream manipulator **setfill** to change the padding character for fields larger than the values being printed. (Part 2 of 2.)

12.7.4 Integral Stream Base (dec, oct, hex, showbase)

C++ provides stream manipulators **dec**, **hex** and **oct** to specify that integers are to be displayed as decimal, hexadecimal and octal values, respectively. Stream insertions default to decimal if none of these manipulators is used. Integers prefixed with **0** (zero) are treated as octal values, integers prefixed with **0x** or **0X** are treated as hexadecimal values, and all other integers are treated as decimal values. Once a particular base is specified for a stream, all integers on that stream are processed using that base until a different base is specified or until the program terminates.

Stream manipulator **showbase** forces the base of an integral value to be output. Decimal numbers are output by default, octal numbers are output with a leading **0**, and hexadecimal numbers are output with either a leading **0x** or a leading **0X** (as we discuss in Section 12.7.6, stream manipulator **uppercase** determines which option is chosen). Figure 12.17 demonstrates the use of stream manipulator **showbase** to force an integer to print in decimal, octal and hexadecimal formats. To reset the **showbase** setting, output the stream manipulator *noshowbase*.

12.7.5 Floating-Point Numbers; Scientific and Fixed Notation (**scientific**, **fixed**)

Stream manipulators **scientific** and **fixed** control the output format of floating-point numbers. Stream manipulator **scientific** forces the output of a floating-point number in scientific format. Stream manipulator **fixed** forces a floating-point number to display a specific number of digits (as specified by member function **precision** or stream-manipulator **setprecision**) to the right of the decimal point. Without using another manipulator, the floating-point-number value determines the output format.

```
1   // Fig. 12.17: fig12_17.cpp
2   // Using stream-manipulator showbase.
3   #include <iostream>
4
5   using std::cout;
6   using std::endl;
7   using std::showbase;
8   using std::oct;
9   using std::hex;
10
11  int main()
12  {
13     int x = 100;
14
15     // use showbase to show number base
16     cout << "Printing integers preceded by their base:" << endl
17        << showbase;
18
19     cout << x << endl;         // print decimal value
20     cout << oct << x << endl;  // print octal value
21     cout << hex << x << endl;  // print hexadecimal value
22
23     return 0;
24
25  } // end main
```

```
Printing integers preceded by their base:
100
0144
0x64
```

Fig. 12.17 Stream-manipulator **showbase**.

Figure 12.18 demonstrates displaying floating-point numbers in fixed and scientific formats using stream manipulators **scientific** (line 22) and **fixed** (line 26). The exponent format in scientific notation might differ across different compilers.

12.7.6 Uppercase/Lowercase Control (**uppercase**)

Stream manipulator **uppercase** forces an uppercase **X** or **E** to be output with hexadecimal-integer values or with scientific-notation floating-point values, respectively (Fig. 12.19). Using stream manipulator **uppercase** causes all letters in a hexadecimal value to be uppercase. By default, the letters for hexadecimal values and the exponents in scientific-notation

```cpp
1   // Fig. 12.18: fig12_18.cpp
2   // Displaying floating-point values in system default,
3   // scientific and fixed formats.
4   #include <iostream>
5
6   using std::cout;
7   using std::endl;
8   using std::scientific;
9   using std::fixed;
10
11  int main()
12  {
13      double x = 0.001234567;
14      double y = 1.946e9;
15
16      // display x and y in default format
17      cout << "Displayed in default format:" << endl
18          << x << '\t' << y << endl;
19
20      // display x and y in scientific format
21      cout << "\nDisplayed in scientific format:" << endl
22          << scientific << x << '\t' << y << endl;
23
24      // display x and y in fixed format
25      cout << "\nDisplayed in fixed format:" << endl
26          << fixed << x << '\t' << y << endl;
27
28      return 0;
29
30  } // end main
```

```
Displayed in default format:
0.00123457      1.946e+009

Displayed in scientific format:
1.234567e-003   1.946000e+009

Displayed in fixed format:
0.001235        1946000000.000000
```

Fig. 12.18 Floating-point values displayed in default, scientific and fixed formats.

```
1   // Fig. 12.19: fig12_19.cpp
2   // Stream-manipulator uppercase.
3   #include <iostream>
4
5   using std::cout;
6   using std::endl;
7   using std::uppercase;
8   using std::hex;
9
10  int main()
11  {
12      cout << "Printing uppercase letters in scientific" << endl
13          << "notation exponents and hexadecimal values:" << endl;
14
15      // use std:uppercase to display uppercase letters;
16      // use std::hex to display hexadecimal values
17      cout << uppercase << 4.345e10 << endl << hex << 123456789
18          << endl;
19
20      return 0;
21
22  } // end main
```

```
Printing uppercase letters in scientific
notation exponents and hexadecimal values:
4.345E+010
75BCD15
```

Fig. 12.19 Stream manipulator **uppercase**.

floating-point values appear in lowercase. To reset the **uppercase** setting, output the stream-manipulator **nouppercase**.

12.7.7 Specifying Boolean Format (boolalpha)

C++ provides data type **bool**, whose values may be **false** or **true**, as a preferred alternative to the old style of using **0** to indicate **false** and nonzero to indicate **true**. A **bool** variable outputs as **0** or **1** by default, because the stream-insertion operator (**<<**) has been overloaded to display **bool**s as integers. However, we can use stream manipulator **boolalpha** to set the output stream to display **bool** values as the strings "**true**" and "**false**." Use stream manipulator **noboolalpha** to set the output stream to display **bool** values as integers (i.e., the default setting). The program of Fig. 12.20 demonstrates these stream manipulators. Line 16 displays the **bool** value, which line 13 sets to **true**, as an integer. Line 20 uses manipulator **boolalpha** to display the **bool** value as a string. Lines 23–24 then change the **bool**'s value and use manipulator **noboolalpha**, so line 27 can display the **bool** value as an integer. Line 31 uses manipulator **boolalpha** to display the **bool** value as a string.

Good Programming Practice 12.1

*Displaying **bool** values as **true** or **false**, rather than non-zero or **0**, respectively, makes program outputs clearer.*

```cpp
1   // Fig. 12.20: fig12_20.cpp
2   // Demonstrating stream-manipulators boolalpha and noboolalpha.
3   #include <iostream>
4
5   using std::cout;
6   using std::endl;
7   using std::cin;
8   using std::boolalpha;
9   using std::noboolalpha;
10
11  int main()
12  {
13     bool booleanValue = true;
14
15     // display default true booleanValue
16     cout << "booleanValue is " << booleanValue << endl;
17
18     // display booleanValue after using boolalpha
19     cout << "booleanValue (after using boolalpha) is "
20         << boolalpha << booleanValue << endl << endl;
21
22     cout << "switch booleanValue and use noboolalpha" << endl;
23     booleanValue = false; // change booleanValue
24     cout << noboolalpha << endl; // use noboolalpha
25
26     // display default false booleanValue after using noboolalpha
27     cout << "booleanValue is " << booleanValue << endl;
28
29     // display booleanValue after using boolalpha again
30     cout << "booleanValue (after using boolalpha) is "
31         << boolalpha << booleanValue << endl;
32
33     return 0;
34
35  } // end main
```

```
booleanValue is 1
booleanValue (after using boolalpha) is true

switch booleanValue and use noboolalpha

booleanValue is 0
booleanValue (after using boolalpha) is false
```

Fig. 12.20 Stream manipulators **boolalpha** and **noboolalpha**.

12.7.8 Setting and Resetting the Format State via Member-Function flags

Throughout Section 12.7, we have been using stream manipulators to change output-format characteristics. We now discuss how to return an output stream's format to its default state after having applied several manipulations. Member function *flags* without an argument returns the current format settings as a *fmtflags* data type (of namespace **ios_base**), which represents the *format state*. Member-function **flags** with a **fmtflags** argument sets the format state as specified by the argument and returns the prior state settings. The initial settings of the value that **flags** returns might differ across several systems. The program of Fig. 12.21 uses member function **flags** to save the stream's original format state (line 23), then restore the original format settings (line 31).

```cpp
1   // Fig. 12.21: fig12_21.cpp
2   // Demonstrating the flags member function.
3   #include <iostream>
4
5   using std::cout;
6   using std::endl;
7   using std::oct;
8   using std::scientific;
9   using std::showbase;
10  using std::ios_base;
11
12  int main()
13  {
14     int integerValue = 1000;
15     double doubleValue = 0.0947628;
16
17     // display flags value, int and double values (original format)
18     cout << "The value of the flags variable is: " << cout.flags()
19          << "\nPrint int and double in original format:\n"
20          << integerValue << '\t' << doubleValue << endl << endl;
21
22     // use cout flags function to save original format
23     ios_base::fmtflags originalFormat = cout.flags();
24     cout << showbase << oct << scientific; // change format
25
26     // display flags value, int and double values (new format)
27     cout << "The value of the flags variable is: " << cout.flags()
28          << "\nPrint int and double in a new format:\n"
29          << integerValue << '\t' << doubleValue << endl << endl;
30
31     cout.flags( originalFormat ); // restore format
32
33     // display flags value, int and double values (original format)
34     cout << "The restored value of the flags variable is: "
35          << cout.flags()
36          << "\nPrint values in original format again:\n"
37          << integerValue << '\t' << doubleValue << endl;
38
39     return 0;
40
41  } // end main
```

```
The value of the flags variable is: 513
Print int and double in original format:
1000       0.0947628                          (continued next page)
```

Fig. 12.21 **flags** member function. (Part 1 of 2.)

```
The value of the flags variable is: 012011
Print int and double in a new format:
01750    9.476280e-002

The restored value of the flags variable is: 513
Print values in original format again:
1000    0.0947628
```

Fig. 12.21 **flags** member function. (Part 2 of 2.)

12.8 Stream Error States

The state of a stream may be tested through bits in class **ios_base**. In a moment, we show how to test these bits, in the example of Fig. 12.22.

The **eofbit** is set for an input stream after end-of-file is encountered. A program can use member function **eof** to determine whether end-of-file has been encountered on a stream after an attempt to extract data beyond the end of the stream. The call

        cin.eof()

returns **true** if end-of-file has been encountered on **cin** and **false** otherwise.

The **failbit** is set for a stream when a format error occurs on the stream. For example, a format error occurs when the program is inputting integers and a non-digit character is encountered in the input stream. When such an error occurs, the characters are not lost. The **fail** member function reports whether a stream operation has failed; usually, recovering from such errors is possible.

The **badbit** is set for a stream when an error occurs that results in the loss of data. The **bad** member function reports whether a stream operation failed. Generally, such serious failures are nonrecoverable.

The **goodbit** is set for a stream if none of the bits **eofbit**, **failbit** or **badbit** is set for the stream.

The **good** member function returns **true** if the **bad**, **fail** and **eof** functions would all return **false**. I/O operations should be performed only on "good" streams.

The **rdstate** member function returns the error state of the stream. A call to **cout.rdstate**, for example, would return the state of the stream, which then could be tested by a **switch** statement that examines **eofbit**, **badbit**, **failbit** and **goodbit**. The preferred means of testing the state of a stream is to use member functions **eof**, **bad**, **fail** and **good**—using these functions does not require the programmer to be familiar with particular status bits.

The **clear** member function is used to restore a stream's state to "good," so that I/O may proceed on that stream. The default argument for **clear** is **goodbit**, so the statement

        cin.clear();

clears **cin** and sets **goodbit** for the stream. The statement

        cin.clear(ios::failbit)

- I/O mechanisms of the system move bytes from devices to memory and vice versa efficiently and reliably.
- C++ provides "low-level" and "high-level" I/O capabilities. Low-level I/O-capabilities specify that some number of bytes should be transferred device-to-memory or memory-to-device. High-level I/O is performed with bytes grouped into such meaningful units as integers, floats, characters, strings and programmer-defined types.
- C++ provides both unformatted-I/O and formatted-I/O operations. Unformatted-I/O transfers are fast, but process raw data that is difficult for people to use. Formatted I/O processes data in meaningful units, but requires extra processing time that can degrade the performance of high-volume data transfers.
- The **<iostream>** header file declares all stream-I/O operations.
- Header **<iomanip>** declares the parameterized stream manipulators.
- The **<fstream>** header declares file-processing operations.
- The **basic_istream** template supports stream-input operations.
- The **basic_ostream** template supports stream-output operations.
- The **basic_iostream** template supports both stream-input and stream-output operations.
- The **basic_istream** template and the **basic_ostream** template are each derived through single inheritance from the **basic_ios** template.
- The **basic_iostream** template is derived through multiple inheritance from both the **basic_istream** template and the **basic_ostream** template.
- The left-shift operator (**<<**) is overloaded to designate stream output and is referred to as the stream-insertion operator.
- The right-shift operator (**>>**) is overloaded to designate stream input and is referred to as the stream-extraction operator.
- The **istream** object **cin** is tied to the standard input device, normally the keyboard.
- The **ostream** object **cout** is tied to the standard output device, normally the screen.
- The **ostream** object **cerr** is tied to the standard error device. Outputs to **cerr** are unbuffered; each insertion to **cerr** appears immediately.
- The C++ compiler determines data types automatically for input and output.
- Addresses are displayed in hexadecimal format by default.
- To print the address in a pointer variable, cast the pointer to **void ***.
- Member function **put** outputs one character. Calls to **put** may be cascaded.
- Stream input is performed with the stream-extraction operator **>>**. This operator automatically skips whitespace characters in the input stream.
- The **>>** operator returns **false** after end-of-file is encountered on a stream.
- Stream extraction causes **failbit** to be set for improper input and **badbit** to be set if the operation fails.
- A series of values can be input using the stream-extraction operation in a **while** loop header. The extraction returns **0** when end-of-file is encountered.
- The **get** member function with no arguments inputs one character and returns the character; **EOF** is returned if end-of-file is encountered on the stream.
- Member function **get** with an argument of type **char** reference inputs one character. **EOF** is returned when end-of-file is encountered; otherwise, the **istream** object for which the **get** member function is being invoked is returned.

- Member function **get** with three arguments—a character array, a size limit and a delimiter (with default value newline)—reads characters from the input stream up to a maximum of limit - 1 characters and terminates, or terminates when the delimiter is read. The input string is terminated with a null character. The delimiter is not placed in the character array, but remains in the input stream.

- The **getline** member function operates like the three-argument **get** member function. The **getline** function removes the delimiter from the input stream, but does not store it in the string.

- Member function **ignore** skips the specified number of characters (the default is 1) in the input stream; it terminates if the specified delimiter is encountered (the default delimiter is **EOF**).

- The **putback** member function places the previous character obtained by a **get** on a stream back onto that stream.

- The **peek** member function returns the next character from an input stream, but does not extract (remove) the character from the stream.

- C++ offers type-safe I/O. If unexpected data is processed by the **<<** and **>>** operators, various error bits are set, which the user may test to determine whether an I/O operation succeeded or failed.

- Unformatted I/O is performed with member functions **read** and **write**. These input or output some number of bytes to or from memory, beginning at a designated memory address. They are input or output as raw bytes with no formatting.

- The **gcount** member function returns the number of characters input by the previous **read** operation on that stream.

- Member function **read** inputs a specified number of characters into a character array. **failbit** is set if fewer than the specified number of characters are read.

- To change the base in which integers output, use the manipulator **hex** to set the base to hexadecimal (base 16) or **oct** to set the base to octal (base 8). Use manipulator **dec** to reset the base to decimal. The base remains the same until changed explicitly.

- The parameterized stream manipulator **setbase** also sets the base for integer output. **setbase** takes one integer argument of **10**, **8** or **16** to set the base.

- Floating-point precision can be controlled using either the **setprecision** stream manipulator or the **precision** member function. Both set the precision for all subsequent output operations until the next precision-setting call. The **precision** member function with no argument returns the current precision value.

- Parameterized manipulators require the inclusion of the **<iomanip>** header file.

- Member function **width** sets the field width and returns the previous width. Values narrower than the field are padded with fill characters. The field-width setting applies only for the next insertion or extraction; the field width is set to **0** implicitly (subsequent values will be output as large as necessary). Values wider than a field are printed in their entirety. Function **width** with no argument returns the current width setting. Manipulator **setw** also sets the width.

- For input, the **setw** stream manipulator establishes a maximum string size; if a larger string is entered, the larger line is broken into pieces no larger than the designated size.

- Programmers may create their own stream manipulators.

- Stream manipulator **showpoint** forces a floating-point number to be output with a decimal point and with the number of significant digits specified by the precision.

- Stream manipulators **left** and **right** cause fields to be left-justified with padding characters to the right or right-justified with padding characters to the left.

- Stream manipulator **internal** indicates that a number's sign (or base when using stream manipulator **showbase**) should be left-justified within a field, its magnitude should be right-justified and intervening spaces should be padded with the fill character.

- Member function **fill** specifies the fill character to be used with stream manipulators **left**, **right** and **internal** (space is the default); the prior padding character is returned. Stream manipulator **setfill** also sets the fill character.

- Stream manipulators **oct**, **hex** and **dec** specify that integers are to be treated as octal, hexadecimal or decimal values, respectively. Integer output defaults to decimal if none of these bits is set; stream extractions process the data in the form the data is supplied.

- Stream manipulator **showbase** forces the base of an integral value to be output.

- Stream manipulator **scientific** is used to output a floating-point number in scientific format. Stream manipulator **fixed** is used to output a floating-point number with the precision specified by the **precision** member function.

- Stream manipulator **uppercase** forces an uppercase **X** or **E** to be output with hexadecimal integers or with scientific-notation floating-point values, respectively. When set, **uppercase** causes all letters in a hexadecimal value to be uppercase.

- Member function **flags** with no argument returns the **long** value of the current settings of the format state. Member function **flags** with a **long** argument sets the format state specified by the argument.

- The state of a stream may be tested through bits in class **ios_base**.

- The **eofbit** is set for an input stream after end-of-file is encountered during an input operation. The **eof** member function reports whether the **eofbit** has been set.

- The **failbit** is set for a stream when a format error occurs on the stream. The **fail** member function reports whether a stream operation has failed; it is normally possible to recover from such errors.

- The **badbit** is set for a stream when an error occurs that results in data loss. The **bad** member function reports whether such a stream operation failed. Such serious failures are normally nonrecoverable.

- The **good** member function returns true if the **bad**, **fail** and **eof** functions would all return **false**. I/O operations should be performed only on "good" streams.

- The **rdstate** member function returns the error state of the stream.

- Member function **clear** is used to restore a stream's state to "good," so that I/O may proceed on that stream.

- C++ provides the **tie** member function to synchronize **istream** and **ostream** operations to ensure that outputs appear before subsequent inputs.

TERMINOLOGY

bad member function of **basic_ios**	**clog**
badbit	**cout**
basic_fstream class template	**dec** stream manipulator
basic_ifstream class template	default fill character (space)
basic_ios class template	default precision
basic_iostream class template	end-of-file
basic_istream class template	**eof** member function of **basic_ios**
basic_ofstream class template	**eofbit**
basic_ostream class template	**fail** member function of **basic_ios**
boolalpha stream manipulator	**failbit**
cerr	field width
cin	fill character
clear member function of **basic_ios**	**fill** member function of **basic_ios**

fixed stream manipulator
flags member function of **ios_base**
fmtflags
format states
formatted I/O
fstream
gcount member function of
    basic_istream
get member function of **basic_istream**
getline member function of
    basic_istream
good member function of **basic_ios**
hex stream manipulator
high-level I/O
ifstream
ignore member function of
    basic_istream
in-memory formatting
internal stream manipulator
<iomanip> header file
ios_base class
iostream
istream
leading **0** (octal)
leading **0x** or **0X** (hexadecimal)
left justification
left stream manipulator
low-level I/O
noboolalpha stream manipulator
noshowbase stream manipulator
noshowpoint stream manipulator
noshowpos stream manipulator
noskipws stream manipulator
nouppercase stream manipulator
oct stream manipulator
ofstream
operator void * member function of
    basic_ios
operator! member function of
    basic_ios

ostream
output buffering
padding
parameterized stream manipulator
peek member function of **basic_istream**
precision member function of **ios_base**
predefined streams
put member function of **basic_ostream**
putback member function of
    basic_istream
rdstate member function of **basic_ios**
read member function of **basic_istream**
right justification
right stream manipulator
scientific stream manipulator
setbase stream manipulator
setfill stream manipulator
setprecision stream manipulator
setw stream manipulator
showbase stream manipulator
showpoint stream manipulator
showpos stream manipulator
skipws stream manipulator
stream input
stream manipulator
stream output
stream-extraction operator (**>>**)
stream-insertion operator (**<<**)
tie member function of **basic_ios**
typedef
type-safe I/O
unbuffered output
unformatted I/O
uppercase stream manipulator
programmer-defined streams
whitespace characters
width stream manipulator
write member function of
    basic_ostream

SELF-REVIEW EXERCISES

12.1   Answer each of the following:

    a)   Input/output in C++ occurs as _____ of bytes.

    b)   The stream manipulators that format justification are _____, _____ and _____.

    c)   Member function _____ can be used to set and reset format state.

    d)   Most C++ programs should include the _____ header file that contains the declarations required for all stream-I/O operations.

e) When using parameterized manipulators, the header file _____ must be included.

f) Header file _____ contains the declarations required for user-controlled file processing.

g) The **ostream** member function _____ is used to perform unformatted output.

h) Input operations are supported by _____.

i) Outputs to the standard error stream are directed to either the _____ or the _____ stream object.

j) Output operations are supported by _____.

k) The symbol for the stream-insertion operator is _____.

l) The four objects that correspond to the standard devices on the system include _____, _____, _____ and _____.

m) The symbol for the stream-extraction operator is _____.

n) The stream manipulators _____, _____ and _____ specify that integers should be displayed in octal, hexadecimal and decimal formats, respectively.

o) When used, the _____ stream manipulator causes positive numbers to display with a plus sign.

12.2 State whether the following are true or false. If the answer is false, explain why.

a) The stream member function **flags** with a **long** argument sets the **flags** state variable to its argument and returns its previous value.

b) The stream-insertion operator **<<** and the stream-extraction operator **>>** are overloaded to handle all standard data types—including strings and memory addresses (stream-insertion only)—and all programmer-defined data types.

c) The stream member function **flags** with no arguments resets the stream's format state.

d) The stream-extraction operator **>>** can be overloaded with an operator function that takes an **istream** reference and a reference to a programmer-defined type as arguments and returns an **istream** reference.

e) The stream-insertion operator **<<** can be overloaded with an operator function that takes an **istream** reference and a reference to a programmer-defined type as arguments and returns an **istream** reference.

f) Input with the stream-extraction operator **>>** always skips leading whitespace characters in the input stream, by default.

g) The stream member function **rdstate** returns the current state of the stream.

h) The **cout** stream normally is connected to the display screen.

i) The stream member function **good** returns **true** if the **bad**, **fail** and **eof** member functions all return **false**.

j) The **cin** stream normally is connected to the display screen.

k) If a nonrecoverable error occurs during a stream operation, the **bad** member function will return **true**.

l) Output to **cerr** is unbuffered and output to **clog** is buffered.

m) Stream manipulator **showpoint** forces floating-point values to print with the default six digits of precision unless the precision value has been changed, in which case floating-point values print with the specified precision.

n) The **ostream** member function **put** outputs the specified number of characters.

o) The stream manipulators **dec**, **oct** and **hex** affect only the next integer output operation.

p) By default, memory addresses are displayed as **long** integers.

12.3 For each of the following, write a single statement that performs the indicated task.

a) Output the string **"Enter your name: "**.

b) Use a stream manipulator that causes the exponent in scientific notation and the letters in hexadecimal values to print in capital letters.

c) Output the address of the variable **myString** of type **char ***.

d) Use a stream manipulator to ensure floating-point values print in scientific notation.

e) Output the address in variable **integerPtr** of type **int ***.

f) Use a stream manipulator such that, when integer values are output, the integer base for octal and hexadecimal values is displayed.

g) Output the value pointed to by **floatPtr** of type **float ***.

h) Use a stream member function to set the fill character to **'*'** for printing in field widths larger than the values being output. Write a separate statement to do this with a stream manipulator.

i) Output the characters **'O'** and **'K'** in one statement with **ostream** function **put**.

j) Get the value of the next character in the input stream without extracting it from the stream.

k) Input a single character into variable **charValue** of type **char**, using the **istream** member function **get** in two different ways.

l) Input and discard the next six characters in the input stream.

m) Use **istream** member function **read** to input 50 characters into **char** array **line**.

n) Read 10 characters into character array **name**. Stop reading characters if the **'.'** delimiter is encountered. Do not remove the delimiter from the input stream. Write another statement that performs this task and removes the delimiter from the input.

o) Use the **istream** member function **gcount** to determine the number of characters input into character array **line** by the last call to **istream** member function **read**, and output that number of characters, using **ostream** member function **write**.

p) Output the following values: **124**, **18.376**, **'Z'**, **1000000** and **"String"**.

q) Print the current precision setting, using a member function of object **cout**.

r) Input an integer value into **int** variable **months** and a floating-point value into **float** variable **percentageRate**.

s) Print **1.92**, **1.925** and **1.9258** separated by tabs and with **3** digits of precision, using a manipulator.

t) Print integer **100** in octal, hexadecimal and decimal, using stream manipulators.

u) Print integer **100** in decimal, octal and hexadecimal, using a stream manipulator to change the base.

v) Print **1234** right-justified in a **10**-digit field.

w) Read characters into character array **line** until the character **'z'** is encountered, up to a limit of **20** characters (including a terminating null character). Do not extract the delimiter character from the stream.

x) Use integer variables **x** and **y** to specify the field width and precision used to display the **double** value **87.4573**, and display the value.

12.4 Identify the error in each of the following statements and explain how to correct it.

a) **cout << "Value of x <= y is: " << x <= y;**

b) The following statement should print the integer value of **'c'**.
    cout << 'c';

c) **cout << ""A string in quotes"";**

12.5 For each of the following, show the output.

a) **cout << "12345" << endl;**
    cout.width(5);
    cout.fill('*');
    cout << 123 << endl << 123;

b) **cout << setw(10) << setfill('$') << 10000;**

c) **cout << setw(8) << setprecision(3) << 1024.987654;**

d) **cout << showbase << oct << 99 << endl << hex << 99;**

```
e) cout << 100000 << endl << showpos << 100000;
f) cout << setw( 10 ) << setprecision( 2 ) <<
        << scientific << 444.93738;
```

ANSWERS TO SELF-REVIEW EXERCISES

12.1   a) streams.   b) **left**, **right** and **internal**.   c) **flags**.   d) **<iostream>**.
e) **<iomanip>**.   f) **<fstream>**.   g) **write**.   h) **istream**.   i) **cerr** or **clog**.   j) **ostream**.
k) **<<**.   l) **cin**, **cout**, **cerr** and **clog**.   m) **>>**.   n) **oct**, **hex** and **dec**.   o) **showpos**.

12.2   a) True. b) False. The stream-insertion and stream-extraction operators are not overloaded
for all programmer-defined types. The programmer of a class must specifically provide the overloaded
operator functions to overload the stream operators for use with each programmer-defined type.
c) False. The stream member function **flags** with no arguments returns the current value of the
flags state variable. d) True. e) False. To overload the stream-insertion operator **<<**, the overloaded
operator function must take an **ostream** reference and a reference to a programmer-defined type as
arguments and return an **ostream** reference. f) True. g) True. h) True. i) True. j) False. The **cin**
stream is connected to the standard input of the computer, which normally is the keyboard. k) True.
l) True. m) True. n) False. The **ostream** member function **put** outputs its single-character argument. o) False. The stream manipulators **dec**, **oct** and **hex** set the output format state for integers to
the specified base until the base is changed again or the program terminates. p) False. Memory addresses are displayed in hexadecimal format by default. To display addresses as **long** integers, the address must be cast to a **long** value.

12.3   a) `cout << "Enter your name: ";`
b) `cout << uppercase;`
c) `cout << static_cast< void * >( myString );`
d) `cout << scientific;`
e) `cout << integerPtr;`
f) `cout << showbase;`
g) `cout << *floatPtr;`
h) `cout.fill( '*' );`
   `cout << setfill( '*' );`
i) `cout.put( 'O' ).put( 'K' );`
j) `cin.peek();`
k) `c = cin.get();`
   `cin.get( c );`
l) `cin.ignore( 6 );`
m) `cin.read( line, 50 );`
n) `cin.get( name, 10, '.' );`
   `cin.getline( name, 10, '.' );`
o) `cout.write( line, cin.gcount() );`
p) `cout << 124 << 18.376 << 'Z' << 1000000 << "String";`
q) `cout << cout.precision();`
r) `cin >> months >> percentageRate;`
s) `cout << setprecision( 3 ) << 1.92 << '\t'`
   `        << 1.925 << '\t' << 1.9258;`
t) `cout << oct << 100 << hex << 100 << dec << 100;`
u) `cout << 100 << setbase( 8 ) << 100 << setbase( 16 ) << 100;`
v) `cout << setw( 10 ) << 1234;`
w) `cin.get( line, 20, 'z' );`
x) `cout << setw( x ) << setprecision( y ) << 87.4573;`

stream-insertion operator should not be able to display the point if an input error occurred. The output format should be identical to the input format shown above. For negative imaginary values, a minus sign should be printed rather than a plus sign.

d) Write a **main** function that tests input and output of programmer-defined class **Complex**, using the overloaded stream-extraction and stream-insertion operators.

12.17 Write a program that uses a **for** structure to print a table of ASCII values for the characters in the ASCII character set from **33** to **126**. The program should print the decimal value, octal value, hexadecimal value and character value for each character. Use the stream manipulators **dec**, **oct** and **hex** to print the integer values.

12.18 Write a program to show that the **getline** and three-argument **get istream** member functions both end the input string with a string-terminating null character. Also, show that **get** leaves the delimiter character on the input stream, whereas **getline** extracts the delimiter character and discards it. What happens to the unread characters in the stream?

13

Exception Handling

Objectives

- To use **try**, **throw** and **catch** to detect, indicate and handle exceptions, respectively.
- To process uncaught and unexpected exceptions.
- To handle **new** failures.
- To use **auto_ptr** to prevent memory leaks.
- To understand the standard exception hierarchy.

I never forget a face, but in your case I'll make an exception.
Groucho (Julius Henry) Marx

No rule is so general, which admits not some exception.
Robert Burton

It is common sense to take a method and try it. If it fails, admit it frankly and try another. But above all, try something.
Franklin Delano Roosevelt

O! throw away the worser part of it,
And live the purer with the other half.
William Shakespeare

If they're running and they don't look where they're going
I have to come out from somewhere and catch them.
Jerome David Salinger

And oftentimes excusing of a fault
Doth make the fault the worse by the excuse.
William Shakespeare

To err is human, to forgive divine.
Alexander Pope

Outline

13.1	Introduction
13.2	Exception-Handling Overview
13.3	Other Error-Handling Techniques
13.4	Simple Exception-Handling Example: Divide by Zero
13.5	Rethrowing an Exception
13.6	Exception Specifications
13.7	Processing Unexpected Exceptions
13.8	Stack Unwinding
13.9	Constructors, Destructors and Exception Handling
13.10	Exceptions and Inheritance
13.11	Processing **new** Failures
13.12	Class **auto_ptr** and Dynamic Memory Allocation
13.13	Standard Library Exception Hierarchy

Summary • Terminology • Self-Review Exercises • Answers to Self-Review Exercises • Exercises

13.1 Introduction

In this chapter, we introduce *exception handling*. An *exception* is an indication of a problem that occurs during a program's execution. The name "exception" comes from the fact that, although a problem can occur, the problem occurs infrequently—if the "rule" is that a statement normally executes correctly, then the "exception to the rule" is that a problem occurs. Exception handling enables programmers to create applications that can resolve (or handle) exceptions. In many cases, handling an exception allows a program to continue executing as if no problem had been encountered. A more severe problem could prevent a program from continuing normal execution, instead requiring the program to notify the user of the problem before terminating in a controlled manner. The features presented in this chapter enable programmers to write robust and *fault-tolerant programs*. The style and details of C++ exception handling are based in part on the work of Andrew Koenig and Bjarne Stroustrup, as presented in their paper, "Exception Handling for C++ (revised)."[1]

The chapter begins with an overview of exception-handling concepts, then demonstrates basic exception-handling techniques. We show these techniques via an example that demonstrates handling an exception that occurs when a function attempts to divide by zero. We then discuss additional exception-handling issues, such as how to handle exceptions that occur in a constructor or destructor and how to handle exceptions that occur if operator **new** fails to allocate memory for an object. We conclude the chapter by introducing several classes that the C++ standard library provides for handling exceptions.

---

1. Koenig, A. and B. Stroustrup, "Exception Handling for C++ (revised)," *Proceedings of the Usenix C++ Conference*, p. 149–176, San Francisco, April 1990.

13.2 Exception-Handling Overview

Program logic frequently tests conditions that determine how program execution proceeds. Consider the following pseudocode:

> *Perform a task*
>
> *If the preceding task did not execute correctly*
>   *Perform error processing*
>
> *Perform next task*
>
> *If the preceding task did not execute correctly*
>   *Perform error processing*
>
> *...*

In this pseudocode, we begin by performing a task. We then test whether that task executed correctly. If not, we perform error processing. Otherwise, we restart the entire process and continue with the next task. Although this form of error handling works, intermixing program logic with error-handling logic can make the program difficult to read, modify, maintain and debug—especially in large applications. In fact, if many of the potential problems occur infrequently, intermixing program logic and error-handling logic can degrade a program's performance, because the program must test the error-handling logic to determine whether the next task can be performed.

Exception handling enables the programmer to remove error-handling code from the "main line" of the program's execution, which improves program clarity and enhances modifiability. Programmers can decide to handle any exceptions they choose—all exceptions, all exceptions of a certain type or all exceptions of a group of related types (e.g., exception types that belong to an inheritance hierarchy). Such flexibility reduces the likelihood that errors will be overlooked and thereby makes a program more robust.

Testing and Debugging Tip 13.1

Exception handling helps improve a program's fault tolerance. When it is easy to write error-processing code, programmers are more likely to use it.

Software Engineering Observation 13.1

Avoid using exception handling to handle potential errors in the conventional flow of control. Handling a larger number of exception cases can be cumbersome, and programs with a large number of exception cases can be difficult to read and maintain.

Exception handling is designed to process *synchronous errors*, which occur when a statement executes. Common examples of these errors are out-of-range array subscripts, arithmetic overflow (i.e., a value outside the representable range of values), division by zero, invalid function parameters and unsuccessful memory allocation (due to lack of memory). Exception handling is not designed to process errors associated with *asynchronous* events (e.g., disk I/O completions, network message arrivals, mouse clicks and keystrokes), which occur in parallel with, and independent of, the program's flow of control.

Good Programming Practice 13.1

For clarity, avoid using exception handling for purposes other than error handling.

With programming languages that do not support exception handling, programmers often delay writing error-processing code or sometimes forget to include it. This results in less robust software products. C++ enables the programmer to deal with exception handling easily from the inception of a project. However, the programmer must continue to incorporate an exception-handling strategy into software projects.

Software Engineering Observation 13.2

Try to incorporate an exception-handling strategy into a system from the inception of the design process. Including effective exception handling after a system has been implemented can be difficult.

Software Engineering Observation 13.3

In the past, programmers used many techniques to implement error-processing code. Exception handling provides a single, uniform technique for processing errors. This helps programmers working on large projects to understand each other's error-processing code.

The exception-handling mechanism also is useful for processing problems that occur when a program interacts with software elements, such as member functions, constructors, destructors and classes. Rather than handling problems internally, such software elements often use exceptions to notify programs when problems occur. This enables programmers to implement customized error handling for each application.

Performance Tip 13.1

When no exceptions occur, exception-handling code incurs little or no performance penalties. Thus, programs that implement exception handling operate more efficiently than do programs that intermix error-handling code with program logic.

Performance Tip 13.2

Exception handling should be used only for problems that occur infrequently. As a "rule of thumb," if a problem occurs at least 30% of the time when a particular statement executes, the program should test for the error inline; otherwise, the overhead of exception handling causes the program to execute more slowly.

Software Engineering Observation 13.4

Functions with common error conditions should return 0 or NULL (or other appropriate values) rather than throw exceptions. A program calling such a function can check the return value to determine success or failure of the function call.

Complex applications normally consist of predefined software components and application-specific components that use the predefined components. When a predefined component encounters a problem, that component needs a mechanism to communicate the problem to the application-specific component—the predefined component cannot know in advance how each application processes a problem that occurs. Exception handling simplifies combining software components and having them work together effectively by enabling predefined components to communicate problems to application-specific components, which can then process the problems in an application-specific manner.

Exception handling is geared to situations in which the function that detects an error is unable to handle it. Such a function *throws an exception*. There is no guarantee that there will be an *exception handler*—code that executes when the program detects an exception—to process that kind of exception. If there is, the exception handler *catches* and *handles* the exception. The result of an *uncaught exception* often yields adverse effects and might terminate program execution.

 Common Programming Error 13.1

Aborting a program component due to an uncaught exception could leave a resource—such as a file stream or an I/O device—in a state in which other programs are unable to acquire the resource. This is known as a "resource leak."

C++ provides **try** *blocks* to enable exception handling. A **try** block consists of keyword **try** followed by braces (**{}**) that define a block of code in which exceptions might occur. The **try** block encloses statements that might cause exceptions. At least one *catch block* (also called a *catch handler*) must immediately follow the **try** block. Each **catch** handler specifies in parentheses an exception parameter that represents the type of exception the **catch** handler can process. If an exception parameter includes a parameter name, the **catch** handler can use that parameter name to interact with a caught exception object.

The point in the program at which an exception occurs (i.e., the location where a function detects and throws an exception) is called the *throw point*. If an exception occurs in a **try** block, the **try** block *expires* (i.e., terminates immediately), and program control transfers to the first **catch** handler that follows the **try** block. C++ uses the *termination model of exception handling*, because the **try** block that encloses a thrown exception expires immediately when that exception occurs.[2] As with any other block of code, when a **try** block terminates, local variables defined in the block go out of scope. Next, the program searches for the first **catch** handler that can process the type of exception that occurred. The program locates the matching **catch** by comparing the thrown exception's type to each **catch**'s exception-parameter type until the program finds a match. A match occurs if the types are identical or if the thrown exception's type is a derived class of the exception-parameter type. When a match occurs, the code contained within the matching **catch** handler executes. When a **catch** handler finishes processing, local variables defined within the **catch** handler (including the **catch** parameter) go out of scope. Any remaining **catch** handlers that correspond to the **try** block are ignored, and execution resumes at the first line of code after the **try/catch** sequence.

If no exceptions occur in a **try** block, the program ignores the **catch** handler(s) for that block. Program execution resumes with the next statement after the **try/catch** sequence. If an exception that occurs in a **try** block has no matching **catch** handler, or if an exception occurs in a statement that is not in a **try** block, the function that contains the statement terminates immediately, and the program attempts to locate an enclosing **try** block in the calling function. This process is called *stack unwinding* (discussed in Section 13.8).

13.3 Other Error-Handling Techniques

We have discussed several ways to deal with exceptional situations prior to this chapter. The following summarizes these and other error-handling techniques:

---

2. Some languages use the *resumption model of exception handling*, in which, after the handling of the exception, control returns to the point at which the exception was thrown and execution resumes from that point.

- Ignore the exception. If an exception occurs, the program might fail as a result of the uncaught exception. This is devastating for commercial software products or for special-purpose software designed for mission-critical situations, but, for software developed for your own purposes, ignoring many kinds of errors is common.

- Abort the program. This, of course, prevents a program from running to completion and producing incorrect results. For many types of errors, this is appropriate, especially for nonfatal errors that enable a program to run to completion (potentially misleading the programmer to think that the program functioned correctly). This strategy also is inappropriate for mission-critical applications. Resource issues also are important here. If a program obtains a resource, the program should release that resource before program termination.

- Set error indicators. The problem with this approach is that programs might not check these error indicators at all points at which the errors could be troublesome.

- Test for the error condition, issue an error message and call **exit** (in **<cstdlib>**) to pass an appropriate error code to the program's environment.

- Use functions **setjump** and **longjump**. These **<csetjmp>** library functions enable the programmer to specify an immediate jump from a deeply nested function call to an error handler. Without using **setjump** or **longjump**, a program must execute several returns to exit the deeply nested function calls. Functions **setjump** and **longjump** are dangerous, because they unwind the stack without calling destructors for automatic objects. This can lead to serious problems.

- Certain specific kinds of errors have dedicated capabilities for handling them. For example, when operator **new** fails to allocate memory, it can cause a **new_handler** function to execute to handle the error. This function can be customized by supplying a function name as the argument to **set_new_handler**, as we discuss in Section 13.11.

13.4 Simple Exception-Handling Example: Divide by Zero

Let us consider a simple example of exception handling. The application in Fig. 13.1 uses **try** and **catch** to wrap code that might throw a "divide-by-zero" exception and to handle that exception, should one occur. The application enables the user to enter two integers, which are passed as arguments to function **quotient** (lines 28–37). This function divides the first number (**numerator**) by the second number (**denominator**). Assuming that the user does not specify **0** as the denominator for the division, function **quotient** returns the division result. However, if the user inputs a **0** value as the denominator, function **quotient** throws an exception.

In the Fig. 13.1 output, the first two lines show a successful calculation, and the next two lines show a failed calculation due to an attempt to divide by zero. Let us consider the user inputs and flow of program control that yield these outputs. The program begins after the user inputs values that represent the numerator and denominator (line 48). Line 53 passes these values to function **quotient** (lines 28–37), which either divides the integers and returns a result or throws an exception on an attempt to divide by zero. Note that a **try** block (lines 52–56) encloses the invocation of function **quotient**. As we discussed previously, a **try** block wraps code that might **throw** an exception. In this example, because the invocation to function **quotient** (line 53) can throw an exception, we enclose this function invocation in the **try** block.

```
1    // Fig. 13.1: fig13_01.cpp
2    // A simple exception-handling example that checks for
3    // divide-by-zero exceptions.
4    #include <iostream>
5
6    using std::cout;
7    using std::cin;
8    using std::endl;
9
10   #include <exception>
11
12   using std::exception;
13
14   // DivideByZeroException objects should be thrown by functions
15   // upon detecting division-by-zero exceptions
16   class DivideByZeroException : public exception {
17
18   public:
19
20      // constructor specifies default error message
21      DivideByZeroException::DivideByZeroException()
22         : exception( "attempted to divide by zero" ) {}
23
24   }; // end class DivideByZeroException
25
26   // perform division and throw DivideByZeroException object if
27   // divide-by-zero exception occurs
28   double quotient( int numerator, int denominator )
29   {
30      // throw DivideByZeroException if trying to divide by zero
31      if ( denominator == 0 )
32         throw DivideByZeroException(); // terminate function
33
34      // return division result
35      return static_cast< double >( numerator ) / denominator;
36
37   } // end function quotient
38
39   int main()
40   {
41      int number1;    // user-specified numerator
42      int number2;    // user-specified denominator
43      double result;  // result of division
44
45      cout << "Enter two integers (end-of-file to end): ";
46
```

Fig. 13.1   Exception-handling example that throws exceptions on attempts to divide by zero. (Part 1 of 2.)

```
47      // enable user to enter two integers to divide
48      while ( cin >> number1 >> number2 ) {
49
50         // try block contains code that might throw exception
51         // and code that should not execute if an exception occurs
52         try {
53            result = quotient( number1, number2 );
54            cout << "The quotient is: " << result << endl;
55
56         } // end try
57
58         // exception handler handles a divide-by-zero exception
59         catch ( DivideByZeroException &divideByZeroException ) {
60            cout << "Exception occurred: "
61               << divideByZeroException.what() << endl;
62
63         } // end catch
64
65         cout << "\nEnter two integers (end-of-file to end): ";
66
67      }  // end while
68
69      cout << endl;
70
71      return 0;  // terminate normally
72
73   }  // end main
```

```
Enter two integers (end-of-file to end): 100 7
The quotient is: 14.2857

Enter two integers (end-of-file to end): 100 0
Exception occurred: attempted to divide by zero

Enter two integers (end-of-file to end): ^Z
```

Fig. 13.1   Exception-handling example that throws exceptions on attempts to divide by zero. (Part 2 of 2.)

Let us consider the flow of control when the user inputs the numerator **100** and the denominator **7** (i.e., the first two lines of Fig. 13.1 output). In line 31, function **quotient** determines that the denominator does not equal zero, so line 35 performs the division and returns the result (**14.2857**) to line 53 as a **double** (the **static_cast** in line 35 ensures the proper return value type). Program control then continues sequentially from line 53, so line 54 displays the division result and line 56 reaches the end of the **try** block. Because the **try** block did not throw an exception, the program does not execute the statements contained in the **catch** handler (lines 59–63), and control continues to line 65 (the first line of code after the **catch** handler), which prompts the user to input two more integers.

Now let us consider a more interesting case in which the user inputs the numerator **100** and the denominator **0** (i.e., the third and fourth lines of Fig. 13.1 output). In line 31, **quotient** determines that the denominator equals zero, which indicates an attempt to divide by zero. Line 32 throws an exception, which we represent as an object of class

DivideByZeroException (lines 16–24). Class **DivideByZeroException** is a derived class of standard-library-class *exception* (defined in **<exception>**), which is the standard C++ base class for exceptions.

Note that, to throw an exception, line 32 uses keyword *throw* followed by an operand that represents the type of exception to throw. Normally, a **throw** statement specifies one operand. (In Section 13.5, we discuss how to use a **throw** statement that specifies no operands.) The operand of a **throw** can be of any type. If the operand is an object, we call it an *exception object*—in this example, the exception object is an object of type **DivideByZeroException**. However, a **throw** operand also can assume other values, such as the value of an expression (e.g., **throw x > 5**), or the value of an **int** (e.g., **throw 5**). The examples in this chapter focus exclusively on throwing exception objects.

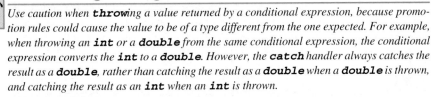

Common Programming Error 13.2

*Use caution when **throw**ing a value returned by a conditional expression, because promotion rules could cause the value to be of a type different from the one expected. For example, when throwing an **int** or a **double** from the same conditional expression, the conditional expression converts the **int** to a **double**. However, the **catch** handler always catches the result as a **double**, rather than catching the result as a **double** when a **double** is thrown, and catching the result as an **int** when an **int** is thrown.*

As part of throwing an exception, the **throw** operand is created and used to initialize the parameter in the **catch** handler, which we discuss momentarily. In this example, the **throw** statement in line 32 creates an object of class **DivideByZeroException**. The **DivideByZeroException** constructor (lines 21–22) passes to the **exception** base-class constructor a string that specifies the default error message for a **DivideByZeroException**. When line 32 throws the exception, function **quotient** exits immediately. Therefore, line 32 throws the exception before function **quotient** can perform the division in line 35. This is a central characteristic of exception handling: a function should throw an exception *before* the error has an opportunity to occur.

Because we decided to enclose the invocation of function **quotient** (line 53) in a **try** block, program control enters the **catch** block (lines 59–63) that immediately follows the **try** block. This **catch** block serves as the exception handler for the divide-by-zero exception. In general, when an exception is thrown within a **try** block, the exception is caught by a **catch** block that specifies the type matching the thrown exception. In this program, the **catch** block specifies that it catches **DivideByZeroException** objects—this type matches the object type thrown in function **quotient**. Actually, the **catch** handler catches a reference to the **DivideByZeroException** object created by function **quotient**'s **throw** statement (line 32).

Performance Tip 13.3

Catching an exception object by reference eliminates the overhead of copying the object that represents the thrown exception.

Good Programming Practice 13.2

Associating each type of run-time error with an appropriately named exception object improves program clarity.

The **catch** handler's body (lines 60–61) prints the associated error message returned by calling function *what* of base-class **exception**. This function returns the string that the **DivideByZeroException** constructor (lines 21–22) passed to the **exception** base-class constructor.

13.5 Rethrowing an Exception

It is possible that an exception handler, upon receiving an exception, might decide either that it cannot process that exception or that it can process the exception only partially. In such cases, the exception handler can defer the exception handling (or perhaps a portion of it) to another exception handler. In either case, the handler achieves this by *rethrowing* the exception via the statement

```
throw;
```

Regardless of whether a handler can process (even partially) an exception, the handler can rethrow the exception for further processing outside the handler. The next enclosing **try** block detects the rethrown exception, which the **catch** handler listed after that enclosing **try** block attempts to handle.

 Common Programming Error 13.3

*Executing an empty **throw** statement that is situated outside a **catch** handler causes a call to function **terminate**.*

The program of Fig. 13.2 demonstrates rethrowing an exception. In **main**'s **try** block (lines 38–43), line 40 calls function **throwException** (lines 13–33). Function **throwException** also contains a **try** block (lines 16–20), from which the **throw** statement at line 18 **throws** an instance of standard-library-class **exception**. Function **throwException**'s **catch** handler (lines 23–29) catches this exception, prints an error message (lines 24–25) and rethrows the exception (line 27). This terminates function **throwException** and returns control line 40 in the **try/catch** block in **main**. The **try** block terminates (so line 41 does not execute), and the **catch** block in **main** (lines 46–49) catches this exception and prints an error message (line 47).

```cpp
1   // Fig. 13.2: fig13_02.cpp
2   // Demonstrating exception rethrowing.
3   #include <iostream>
4
5   using std::cout;
6   using std::endl;
7
8   #include <exception>
9
10  using std::exception;
11
12  // throw, catch and rethrow exception
13  void throwException()
14  {
15      // throw exception and catch it immediately
16      try {
```

Fig. 13.2   Rethrowing an exception. (Part 1 of 2.)

```
17          cout << "  Function throwException throws an exception\n";
18          throw exception();  // generate exception
19
20     } // end try
21
22     // handle exception
23     catch ( exception &caughtException ) {
24          cout << "  Exception handled in function throwException"
25               << "\n  Function throwException rethrows exception";
26
27          throw;  // rethrow exception for further processing
28
29     } // end catch
30
31     cout << "This also should not print\n";
32
33  } // end function throwException
34
35  int main()
36  {
37     // throw exception
38     try {
39          cout << "\nmain invokes function throwException\n";
40          throwException();
41          cout << "This should not print\n";
42
43     } // end try
44
45     // handle exception
46     catch ( exception &caughtException ) {
47          cout << "\n\nException handled in main\n";
48
49     } // end catch
50
51     cout << "Program control continues after catch in main\n";
52
53     return 0;
54
55  } // end main
```

```
main invokes function throwException
  Function throwException throws an exception
  Exception handled in function throwException
  Function throwException rethrows exception

Exception handled in main
Program control continues after catch in main
```

Fig. 13.2   Rethrowing an exception. (Part 2 of 2.)

13.6 Exception Specifications

An *exception specification* (also called a **throw** *list*) enumerates a list of exceptions that a function can throw. For example, consider the function declaration

```
int someFunction( double value )
   throw ( ExceptionA, ExceptionB, ExceptionC )
{
   // function body
}
```

In this definition, the exception specification, which begins with keyword **throw** immediately following the closing parenthesis of the function's parameter list, indicates that function **someFunction** can throw exceptions of types **ExceptionA**, **ExceptionB** and **ExceptionC**. A function can throw only exceptions of the types indicated by the specification or exceptions of any type derived from these types. If the function **throw**s an exception that does not belong to a specified type, function **unexpected** is called.

A function with no exception specification can **throw** any exception. Placing **throw()**—an *empty exception specification*—after a function's parameter list states that the function does not **throw** exceptions. If the function attempts to **throw** an exception, function **unexpected** is invoked, which normally terminates the program. Section 13.7 shows that function **unexpected** can be customized by calling function **set_unexpected**.

Common Programming Error 13.4

*Throwing an exception that has not been declared in a function's exception specification causes a call to function **unexpected**.*

One interesting aspect of exception handling is that the compiler will not generate a syntax error if a function contains a **throw** expression for an exception not listed in the function's exception specification. An error occurs only when that function attempts to **throw** that exception at execution time.

13.7 Processing Unexpected Exceptions

Function **unexpected** calls the function registered with function **set_unexpected** (defined in header file **<exception>**). If no function has been registered in this manner, function **terminate** is called by default. Function **terminate** can be called in one of the five following ways: if a thrown exception cannot be caught; if the stack becomes corrupted during exception handling; if a call to function **unexpected** defaults to calling function **terminate**; if stack unwinding is initiated by an exception; and if a destructor attempts to **throw** an exception. Function **set_terminate** can specify the function to invoke when **terminate** is called. Otherwise, **terminate** calls **abort**.

Function **set_terminate** and function **set_unexpected** each return a pointer to the last function called by **terminate** and **unexpected**, respectively (0, the first time each is called). This enables the programmer to save the function pointer so it can be restored later. Functions **set_terminate** and **set_unexpected** take as arguments pointers to functions with **void** return types and no arguments.

If the last action of a programmer-defined termination function is not to exit a program, function **abort** will be called to end program execution after the other statements of the programmer-defined termination function are executed.

13.8 Stack Unwinding

When an exception is thrown but not caught in a particular scope, the function-call stack is unwound, and an attempt is made to **catch** the exception in the next outer **try/catch** block. Unwinding the function-call stack means that the function in which the exception was not caught terminates, all local variables in that function are destroyed and control returns to the statement that originally invoked that function. If a **try** block encloses that statement, an attempt is made to **catch** the exception. If a **try** block does not enclose that statement, stack unwinding occurs again. If no **catch** handler ever catches this exception, function **terminate** is called to terminate the program. The program of Fig. 13.3 demonstrates stack unwinding.

```cpp
1   // Fig. 13.3: fig13_03.cpp
2   // Demonstrating stack unwinding.
3   #include <iostream>
4
5   using std::cout;
6   using std::endl;
7
8   #include <stdexcept>
9
10  using std::runtime_error;
11
12  // function3 throws run-time error
13  void function3() throw ( runtime_error )
14  {
15     throw runtime_error( "runtime_error in function3" ); // fourth
16  }
17
18  // function2 invokes function3
19  void function2() throw ( runtime_error )
20  {
21     function3(); // third
22  }
23
24  // function1 invokes function2
25  void function1() throw ( runtime_error )
26  {
27     function2(); // second
28  }
29
30  // demonstrate stack unwinding
31  int main()
32  {
33     // invoke function1
34     try {
35        function1(); // first
36
37     } // end try
38
39     // handle run-time error
40     catch ( runtime_error &error ) // fifth
41     {
42        cout << "Exception occurred: " << error.what() << endl;
43
44     } // end catch
```

Fig. 13.3   Stack unwinding. (Part 1 of 2.)

```
45
46      return 0;
47
48  }  // end main
```

<pre>
Exception occurred: runtime_error in function3
</pre>

Fig. 13.3   Stack unwinding. (Part 2 of 2.)

In **main**, the **try** block (lines 34–37) calls **function1** (lines 25–28). Next, **function1** calls **function2** (lines 19–22), which in turn calls **function3** (lines 13–16). Line 15 of **function3** throws a ***runtime_error*** object (defined in header ***<stdexcept>***), which is the C++ standard base class for representing run-time errors. However, because no **try** block encloses the **throw** statement in line 15, stack unwinding occurs—**function3** terminates at line 15, then returns control to the statement in **function2** that invoked **function3** (i.e., line 21). Because no **try** block encloses line 21, stack unwinding occurs again—**function2** terminates at line 21 and returns control to the statement in **function1** that invoked **function2** (i.e., line 27). Because no **try** block encloses line 27, stack unwinding occurs one more time—**function1** terminates at line 27 and returns control to the statement in **main** that invoked **function1** (i.e., line 35). The **try** block of lines 34–37 encloses this statement, so the first matching **catch** handler located after this **try** block (line 40–44) catches and processes the exception.

13.9 Constructors, Destructors and Exception Handling

First, let us discuss an issue that we have mentioned but not yet resolved satisfactorily: What happens when an error is detected in a constructor? For example, how should an object's constructor respond when **new** fails and indicates that it was unable to allocate required memory for storing that object's internal representation? Because the constructor cannot return a value to indicate an error, we must choose an alternative means of indicating that the object has not been constructed properly. One scheme is to return the improperly constructed object and hope that anyone using the object would make appropriate tests to determine that the object exhibits an inconsistent state. Another scheme is to set some variable outside the constructor. Perhaps the best alternative is to require the constructor to **throw** an exception that contains the error information, thus offering an opportunity to handle the failure.

In addition, exceptions thrown by constructors cause destructors to be called for any objects built as part of the object being constructed before the exception is thrown. Destructors are called for every automatic object constructed in a **try** block before an exception is thrown. Stack unwinding is guaranteed to have been completed at the point that an exception handler begins executing. If a destructor invoked as a result of stack unwinding throws an exception, **terminate** is called.

If an object has member objects, and if an exception is thrown before the outer object is fully constructed, then destructors will be executed for the member objects that have been constructed prior to the occurrence of the exception. If an array of objects has been partially constructed when an exception occurs, only the destructors for the constructed array elements will be called.

An exception could preclude the operation of code that would normally release a resource, thus causing a resource leak. One technique to resolve this problem is to initialize a local object to acquire the resource. When an exception occurs, the destructor for that object will be invoked and can free the resource.

It is possible to **catch** exceptions thrown from destructors by enclosing the function that calls the destructor in a **try** block and providing a **catch** handler with the proper type. The thrown object's destructor executes after an exception handler completes execution.

13.10 Exceptions and Inheritance

Various exception classes can be derived from a common base class, as we discussed in Section 13.4, when we created class **DivideByZeroException** as a derived class of class **exception**. If a **catch** catches a pointer or reference to an exception object of a base-class type, it also can **catch** a pointer or reference to all objects of classes derived from that base class. This can allow for polymorphic processing of related errors.

Testing and Debugging Tip 13.2

*Using inheritance with exceptions enables an exception handler to **catch** related errors with concise notation. One approach is to **catch** each type of pointer or reference to a derived-class exception object individually, but a more concise approach is to **catch** pointers or references to base-class exception objects instead. Also, catching pointers or references to derived-class exception objects individually is error prone, especially if the programmer forgets to test explicitly for one or more of the derived-class pointer or reference types.*

13.11 Processing new Failures

The C++ standard specifies that, when operator **new** fails, it **throws** a **bad_alloc** exception (defined in header file **<new>**). However, some compilers are not compliant with the C++ standard and therefore use the version of **new** that returns **0** on failure. In this section, we present three examples of **new** failing. The first example returns **0** when **new** fails. The second and third examples use the version of **new** that **throws** a **bad_alloc** exception when **new** fails.

Figure 13.4 demonstrates **new** returning **0** on failure to allocate the requested amount of memory. The **for** structure at lines 13–30 should loop 50 times and, on each pass, allocate an array of 5,000,000 **double** values (i.e., 40,000,000 bytes, because a **double** is normally 8 bytes). The **if** structure at line 17 tests the result of each **new** operation to determine whether **new** allocated the memory successfully. If **new** fails and returns **0**, line 18 prints an error message, and the loop terminates.

```
1  // Fig. 13.4: fig13_04.cpp
2  // Demonstrating pre-standard new returning 0 when memory
3  // is not allocated.
4  #include <iostream>
5
6  using std::cout;
7
```

Fig. 13.4   **new** returning **0** on failure. (Part 1 of 2.)

```
 8   int main()
 9   {
10       double *ptr[ 50 ];
11
12       // allocate memory for ptr
13       for ( int i = 0; i < 50; i++ ) {
14           ptr[ i ] = new double[ 5000000 ];
15
16           // new returns 0 on failure to allocate memory
17           if ( ptr[ i ] == 0 ) {
18               cout << "Memory allocation failed for ptr[ "
19                   << i << " ]\n";
20
21               break;
22
23           } // end if
24
25           // successful memory allocation
26           else
27               cout << "Allocated 5000000 doubles in ptr[ "
28                   << i << " ]\n";
29
30       } // end for
31
32       return 0;
33
34   } // end main
```

```
Allocated 5000000 doubles in ptr[ 0 ]
Allocated 5000000 doubles in ptr[ 1 ]
Allocated 5000000 doubles in ptr[ 2 ]
Allocated 5000000 doubles in ptr[ 3 ]
Memory allocation failed for ptr[ 4 ]
```

Fig. 13.4   **new** returning **0** on failure. (Part 2 of 2.)

The output shows that the program performed only four iterations before **new** failed, and the loop terminated. Your output might differ based on the physical memory, disk space available for virtual memory on your system and the compiler used to compile the program.

Figure 13.5 demonstrates **new** throwing **bad_alloc** on failure to allocate the requested memory. The **for** structure (lines 22–26) inside the **try** block should loop 50 times and, on each pass, allocate an array of 5,000,000 **double** values. If **new** fails and throws a **bad_alloc** exception, the loop terminates, and the program continues in the exception-handling flow of control at line 31, where the **catch** handler catches and processes the exception. Lines 32–33 print the message **"Exception occurred:"** followed by the message returned from the base-class-**exception** version of function **what** (i.e., an exception-specific message, such as **"Allocation Failure"**). The output shows that the program performed only four iterations of the loop before **new** failed and threw the **bad_alloc** exception. Your output might differ based on the physical memory, disk space available for virtual memory on your system and the compiler you use to compile the program.

```cpp
1   // Fig. 13.5: fig13_05.cpp
2   // Demonstrating standard new throwing bad_alloc when memory
3   // cannot be allocated.
4   #include <iostream>
5
6   using std::cout;
7   using std::endl;
8
9   #include <new> // standard operator new
10
11  using std::bad_alloc;
12
13  int main()
14  {
15     double *ptr[ 50 ];
16
17     // attempt to allocate memory
18     try {
19
20        // allocate memory for ptr[ i ]; new throws bad_alloc
21        // on failure
22        for ( int i = 0; i < 50; i++ ) {
23           ptr[ i ] = new double[ 5000000 ];
24           cout << "Allocated 5000000 doubles in ptr[ "
25                << i << " ]\n";
26        }
27
28     } // end try
29
30     // handle bad_alloc exception
31     catch ( bad_alloc &memoryAllocationException ) {
32        cout << "Exception occurred: "
33             << memoryAllocationException.what() << endl;
34
35     } // end catch
36
37     return 0;
38
39  } // end main
```

```
Allocated 5000000 doubles in ptr[ 0 ]
Allocated 5000000 doubles in ptr[ 1 ]
Allocated 5000000 doubles in ptr[ 2 ]
Allocated 5000000 doubles in ptr[ 3 ]
Exception occurred: Allocation Failure
```

Fig. 13.5   **new** throwing **bad_alloc** on failure.

Compilers vary in their support for **new**-failure handling. Many C++ compilers return **0** by default when **new** fails. Some compilers support **new** throwing an exception if header file **<new>** (or **<new.h>**) is included. Other compilers throw **bad_alloc** by default, regardless of whether header file **<new>** is included. Consult the compiler documentation to determine the compiler's support for **new**-failure handling.

The C++ standard specifies that standard-compliant compilers can continue to use a version of **new** that returns **0** upon failure. For this purpose, header file **<new>** defines object ***nothrow*** (of type **nothrow_t**), which is used as follows:

```
double *ptr = new( nothrow ) double[ 5000000 ];
```

The preceding statement uses the version of **new** that does not throw **bad_alloc** exceptions (i.e., **nothrow**) to allocate an array of 5,000,000 **double**s.

Software Engineering Observation 13.5

*To make programs more robust, use the version of **new** that throws **bad_alloc** exceptions on failure.*

An additional feature for handling **new** failures is function ***set_new_handler*** (prototyped in standard header file **<new>**). This function takes as its argument a pointer to a function that takes no arguments and returns **void**. Essentially, this pointer points to the function that will be called if **new** fails. This provides the programmer with a uniform approach to handling all **new** failures, regardless of where a failure occurs in the program. Once **set_new_handler** registers a *new handler* in the program, operator **new** does not throw **bad_alloc** on failure; rather, it defers the error handling to the **new**-handler function.

If **new** allocates memory successfully, it returns a pointer to that memory. If **new** fails to allocate memory and **set_new_handler** did not register a **new**-handler function, **new** throws a **bad_alloc** exception. If **new** fails to allocate memory, and a **new**-handler function has been registered, the **new**-handler function is called. The C++ standard specifies that the **new**-handler function should perform one of the following tasks:

1. Make more memory available by deleting other dynamically allocated memory (or telling the user to close other applications) and return to operator **new** to attempt to allocate memory again.

2. Throw an exception of type **bad_alloc**.

3. Call function **abort** or **exit** (both found in header file **<cstdlib>**) to terminate the program.

Figure 13.6[3] demonstrates **set_new_handler**. Function **customNewHandler** (lines 14–18) prints an error message (line 16) then terminates the program via a call to **abort** (line 17). The output shows that the program performed only four iterations of the loop before **new** failed and invoked function **customNewHandler**. Your output might differ based on the physical memory, disk space available for virtual memory on your system and the compiler you use to compile the program.

---

3. The program of Fig. 13.6 works in Microsoft Visual C++ .NET, Borland C++ 5.5 and in GNU C++. The program does not work in Visual C++ 6, which, for backwards compatibility reasons, does not implement **set_new_handler**. In Visual C++ 6, function **_set_new_handler** provides similar functionality. For more information on this function, visit **msdn.microsoft.com/library/default.asp?url=/library/en-us/vccore98/HTML/_crt__set_new_handler.asp**.

```
1    // Fig. 13.6: fig13_06.cpp
2    // Demonstrating set_new_handler.
3    #include <iostream>
4
5    using std::cout;
6    using std::cerr;
7
8    #include <new>       // standard operator new and set_new_handler
9
10   using std::set_new_handler;
11
12   #include <cstdlib> // abort function prototype
13
14   void customNewHandler()
15   {
16      cerr << "customNewHandler was called";
17      abort();
18   }
19
20   // using set_new_handler to handle failed memory allocation
21   int main()
22   {
23      double *ptr[ 50 ];
24
25      // specify that customNewHandler should be called on failed
26      // memory allocation
27      set_new_handler( customNewHandler );
28
29      // allocate memory for ptr[ i ]; customNewHandler will be
30      // called on failed memory allocation
31      for ( int i = 0; i < 50; i++ ) {
32         ptr[ i ] = new double[ 5000000 ];
33
34         cout << "Allocated 5000000 doubles in ptr[ "
35              << i << " ]\n";
36
37      } // end for
38
39      return 0;
40
41   }  // end main
```

```
Allocated 5000000 doubles in ptr[ 0 ]
Allocated 5000000 doubles in ptr[ 1 ]
Allocated 5000000 doubles in ptr[ 2 ]
Allocated 5000000 doubles in ptr[ 3 ]
customNewHandler was called
```

Fig. 13.6   **set_new_handler** specifying the function to call when **new** fails.

13.12 Class `auto_ptr` and Dynamic Memory Allocation

A common programming practice is to allocate dynamic memory, assign the address of that memory to a pointer, use the pointer to manipulate the memory and deallocate the memory with **delete** when the memory is no longer needed. If an exception occurs after memory allocation but before the **delete** statement executes, a memory leak could occur. The C++ standard provides class template **auto_ptr** in header file ***<memory>*** to deal with this situation.

An object of class **auto_ptr** maintains a pointer to dynamically allocated memory. When an **auto_ptr** object goes out of scope, it performs a **delete** operation on its pointer data member. Class template **auto_ptr** provides operators ***** and **->** so that an **auto_ptr** object can be used just as a regular pointer variable is. Figure 13.7 demonstrates an **auto_ptr** object that points to a dynamically allocated object of class **Integer** (lines 12–48).

```
1   // Fig. 13.7: fig13_07.cpp
2   // Demonstrating auto_ptr.
3   #include <iostream>
4
5   using std::cout;
6   using std::endl;
7
8   #include <memory>
9
10  using std::auto_ptr; // auto_ptr class definition
11
12  class Integer {
13
14  public:
15
16     // Integer constructor
17     Integer( int i = 0 )
18        : value( i )
19     {
20        cout << "Constructor for Integer " << value << endl;
21
22     } // end Integer constructor
23
24     // Integer destructor
25     ~Integer()
26     {
27        cout << "Destructor for Integer " << value << endl;
28
29     } // end Integer destructor
30
31     // function to set Integer
32     void setInteger( int i )
33     {
34        value = i;
35
36     } // end function setInteger
37
38     // function to return Integer
39     int getInteger() const
40     {
```

Fig. 13.7 **auto_ptr** object manages dynamically allocated memory. (Part 1 of 2.)

```
41            return value;
42
43        } // end function getInteger
44
45     private:
46        int value;
47
48     };   // end class Integer
49
50     // use auto_ptr to manipulate Integer object
51     int main()
52     {
53        cout << "Creating an auto_ptr object that points to an "
54             << "Integer\n";
55
56        // "aim" auto_ptr at Integer object
57        auto_ptr< Integer > ptrToInteger( new Integer( 7 ) );
58
59        cout << "\nUsing the auto_ptr to manipulate the Integer\n";
60
61        // use auto_ptr to set Integer value
62        ptrToInteger->setInteger( 99 );
63
64        // use auto_ptr to get Integer value
65        cout << "Integer after setInteger: "
66             << ( *ptrToInteger ).getInteger()
67             << "\n\nTerminating program" << endl;
68
69        return 0;
70
71     }   // end main
```

```
Creating an auto_ptr object that points to an Integer
Constructor for Integer 7

Using the auto_ptr to manipulate the Integer
Integer after setInteger: 99

Terminating program
Destructor for Integer 99
```

Fig. 13.7   **auto_ptr** object manages dynamically allocated memory. (Part 2 of 2.)

Line 57 creates **auto_ptr** object **ptrToInteger** and initializes it with a pointer to a dynamically allocated **Integer** object that contains the value **7**. Line 62 uses the **auto_ptr** overloaded **->** operator to invoke function **setInteger** on the **Integer** object pointed to by **ptrToInteger**. Line 66 uses the **auto_ptr** overloaded ***** operator to dereference **ptrToInteger**, then uses the dot (**.**) operator to invoke function **getInteger** on the **Integer** object pointed to by **ptrToInteger**. Note that using the **auto_ptr ->** operator is just as effective as using the **auto_ptr *** and **.** operators—both approaches can be used to manipulate the **Integer** object data via an **auto_ptr**.

Because **ptrToInteger** is a local automatic variable in **main**, **ptrToInteger** is destroyed when **main** terminates. This forces a **delete** of the **Integer** object pointed to by **ptrToInteger**, which in turn calls the **Integer** class destructor. The memory that **Integer** occupies is released, regardless of how control leaves the block (e.g., by a **return** statement or by an exception). Most importantly, using this technique can prevent memory leaks. For example, suppose a function returns a pointer aimed at some object. Unfortunately, the function caller that receives this pointer might not **delete** the object, thus resulting in a memory leak. However, if the function returns an **auto_ptr** to the object, the object will be deleted automatically.

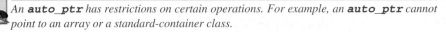

Software Engineering Observation 13.6

*An **auto_ptr** has restrictions on certain operations. For example, an **auto_ptr** cannot point to an array or a standard-container class.*

13.13 Standard Library Exception Hierarchy

Experience has shown that exceptions fall nicely into a number of categories. The C++ standard includes a hierarchy of exception classes. As we first discussed in Section 13.4, this hierarchy is headed by base-class **exception** (defined in header file **<exception>**), which contains **virtual** function **what**, which derived classes can override to issue appropriate error messages.

Immediate derived classes of base class **exception** include **runtime_error** and **logic_error** (both defined in header **<stdexcept>**), each of which has several derived classes. Also derived from **exception** are the exceptions thrown by C++ operators—for example, **bad_alloc** is thrown by **new** (Section 13.11), *bad_cast* is thrown by **dynamic_cast** (Chapter 10) and *bad_typeid* is thrown by **typeid** (Chapter 10). Including *bad_exception* in the **throw** list of a function means that, if an unexpected exception occurs, function **unexpected** can throw **bad_exception** rather than terminating the program's execution (by default) or calling another function specified by **set_unexpected**.

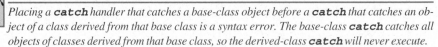

Common Programming Error 13.5

*Placing a **catch** handler that catches a base-class object before a **catch** that catches an object of a class derived from that base class is a syntax error. The base-class **catch** catches all objects of classes derived from that base class, so the derived-class **catch** will never execute.*

Class **logic_error** is the base class of several standard exception classes that indicate errors in program logic. For example, class *invalid_argument* indicates that an invalid argument was passed to a function. (Proper coding can, of course, prevent invalid arguments from reaching a function.) Class *length_error* indicates that a length larger than the maximum size allowed for the object being manipulated was used for that object. (We build programs that throw **length_error**s in Chapter 15, when we discuss **string**s.) Class *out_of_range* indicates that a value, such as a subscript into an array, exceeded its allowed range of values.

Class **runtime_error**, which we used briefly in Section 13.8, is the base class of several other standard exception classes that indicate errors that occur at execution time. For example, class *overflow_error* describes an arithmetic overflow error and class *underflow_error* describes an arithmetic underflow error.

Software Engineering Observation 13.7

*The standard **exception** hierarchy serves as a useful starting point for creating exceptions. Programmers can build programs that can **throw** standard exceptions, **throw** exceptions derived from the standard exceptions or **throw** their own exceptions not derived from the standard exceptions.*

Common Programming Error 13.6

*Programmer-defined exception classes need not be derived from class **exception**. Thus, writing **catch(exception anyException)** is not guaranteed to **catch** all exceptions a program could encounter.*

Testing and Debugging Tip 13.3

*To **catch** all exceptions potentially thrown in a **try** block, use **catch(...)**. Be aware that one weakness associated with catching exceptions in this manner is that the actual type of the caught exception is ambiguous. Another weakness is that, without a named parameter, there is no way to refer to the exception object inside the exception handler.*

Software Engineering Observation 13.8

*Use **catch(...)** to perform recovery that does not depend on the exception type (e.g., releasing common resources). The exception can be rethrown to alert more specific enclosing **catch** handlers.*

SUMMARY

- Some common examples of exceptions are an out-of-bounds array subscript, arithmetic overflow, division by zero, invalid function parameters and determining that there is insufficient memory to satisfy an allocation request by **new**.

- The spirit behind exception handling is to enable programs to **catch** and handle errors rather than letting them occur and suffering the consequences. With exception handling, if the programmer does not provide a means of handling an exception, the program will terminate; nonfatal errors normally allow a program to continue execution but produce incorrect results.

- Exception handling is designed for dealing with synchronous errors (i.e., errors that occur as the result of a program's execution).

- Exception handling is not designed to deal with asynchronous situations, such as network message arrivals, disk I/O completions, mouse clicks and the like.

- Exception handling typically is used in situations in which the error will be dealt with by a different part of the program (i.e., a different scope) from that which detected the error.

- Exceptions should not be used as a mechanism for specifying flow of control. Flow of control with conventional control structures generally is clearer and more efficient than with exceptions.

- Exception handling should be used to process exceptions from software components such as functions, libraries and widely used classes, wherever it does not make sense for those components to handle their own exceptions.

- Exception handling should be used on large projects to handle error processing in a uniform manner for the entire project.

- C++ exception handling is geared to situations in which the function that detects an error is unable to deal with it. Such a function will **throw** an exception. If the exception matches the type of the parameter in one of the **catch** blocks, the code for that **catch** block is executed. Otherwise, function **terminate** is called, which by default calls function **abort**.

- The programmer encloses in a **try** block the code that might generate an exception. The **try** block is immediately followed by one or more **catch** blocks. Each **catch** block defines an exception handler that specifies the type of exception it can catch and handle.

- Program control on a thrown exception leaves the **try** block and searches the **catch** blocks in order for an appropriate handler. If no exceptions are thrown in the **try** block, the exception handlers for that block are skipped, and the program resumes execution after the last **catch** block.

- Once an exception is thrown, the block in which the exception occurred terminates and control cannot return directly to the throw point.

- It is possible to communicate information to the exception handler from the point of the exception. That information is the type of the thrown object or information placed in the thrown object.

- The exceptions thrown by a particular function can be specified with an exception specification. An empty exception specification states that the function will not throw any exceptions.

- Exceptions are caught by the closest exception handler (for the **try** block from which the exception was thrown) specifying an appropriate type.

- As part of throwing an exception, the **throw** operand is created used to initialize the parameter in the exception handler, assuming that a proper exception handler exists.

- Errors are not always checked explicitly. A **try** block, for example, might appear to contain no error checking and include no **throw** statements, but code referenced in the **try** block could certainly cause error-checking code to execute.

- Exception handlers are contained in **catch** blocks. Each **catch** block starts with the keyword **catch**, followed by parentheses containing a type and an optional parameter name. This is followed by braces delineating the exception-handling code. When an exception is caught, the code in the **catch** block is executed. The **catch** handler defines its own scope.

- The parameter in a **catch** handler can be named or unnamed. If the parameter is named, the parameter can be referenced in the handler. If the parameter is unnamed (i.e., only a type is listed for the purpose of matching with the thrown object type or an ellipsis for all types), then the handler will ignore the thrown object. The handler can rethrow the object to an outer **try** block.

- It is possible to specify customized behavior to replace function **terminate** by creating another function to execute and providing that function's name as the argument in a **set_terminate** function call.

- It is possible that no handler will match a particular thrown object. This causes the search for a match to continue in an enclosing **try** block.

- The exception handlers are searched in order for an appropriate match. The first handler that yields a match is executed. When that handler finishes executing, control resumes with the first statement after the last **catch** block.

- The order of the exception handlers affects how an exception is handled.

- A derived-class object can be caught either by a handler specifying the derived-class type or by handlers specifying the types of any base classes of that derived class.

- Sometimes a program must process many closely related types of exceptions. Rather than providing separate exception classes and **catch** handlers for each, a programmer can provide a single exception class and **catch** handler for a group of exceptions.

- It is possible that, even though a precise match is available, a match requiring standard conversions will be made because that handler appears before the one that would result in a precise match.

- By default, if no handler is found for an exception, the program terminates.

- An exception handler cannot directly access variables in the scope of its **try** block. Information the handler needs normally is passed in the thrown object.

- A handler that catches a derived-class object should be placed before a handler that catches a base-class object.

- When an exception is caught, it is possible that resources might have been allocated but not yet released in the **try** block. The **catch** handler should release these resources.

- It is possible that a **catch** handler will decide that it cannot process an exception. In this case, the handler can rethrow the exception. A **throw** with no arguments rethrows the exception. If no exception was thrown to begin with, then the rethrow causes a call to **terminate**.

- Even if a handler can process an exception, and regardless of whether it does any processing on that exception, the handler can rethrow the exception for further processing outside the handler. A rethrown exception is detected by the next enclosing **try** block and is handled by an exception handler listed after that enclosing **try** block.

- Function **unexpected** calls a function specified with function **set_unexpected**. If no function has been specified in this manner, **terminate** is called by default.

- Function **terminate** can be called in various ways: explicitly; if a thrown exception cannot be caught; if the stack is corrupted during exception handling; as the default action on a call to **unexpected**; or if, during stack unwinding initiated by an exception, an attempt by a destructor to **throw** an exception causes **terminate** to be called.

- Header **<exception>** contains rototypes for **set_terminate** and **set_unexpected**.

- Functions **set_terminate** and **set_unexpected** return pointers to the last function called by **terminate** and **unexpected**, respectively (0, if they are being called for the first time). They enable the programmer to save the function pointer so it can be restored later.

- Functions **set_terminate** and **set_unexpected** take as arguments pointers to function with **void** return types and no arguments.

- If the last action of a programmer-defined termination function is not to exit a program, function **abort** will be called to end program execution after the other statements of the programmer-defined termination function are executed.

- An exception thrown outside a **try** block will cause the program to terminate.

- If a handler cannot be found after a **try** block, stack unwinding continues until an appropriate handler is found. If no handler is ultimately found, then **terminate** is called, which, by default, terminates the program with **abort**.

- Exception specifications list the exceptions that can be thrown from a function. A function can **throw** either the indicated exceptions, or derived types. If an exception not listed in the exception specification is thrown, **unexpected** is called.

- If a function **throw**s an exception of a particular class type, that function can also **throw** exceptions of all classes derived from that class with **public** inheritance.

- Exceptions thrown from constructors cause destructors to be called for all completed base-class objects and member objects of the object being constructed before the exception is thrown.

- If an array of objects has been partially constructed when an exception occurs, only the destructors for the fully constructed array elements will be called.

- Exceptions thrown from destructors can be caught by enclosing the function that calls the destructor in a **try** block and provide a **catch** handler with the proper type.

- The C++ standard specifies that, when **new** fails, it **throw**s a **bad_alloc** exception (**bad_alloc** is defined in header file **<new>**).

- Some compilers are not compliant with the C++ standard and still use the version of **new** that returns **0** on failure.

- Function **set_new_handler** (prototyped in header file **<new>**) takes as its argument a function pointer to a function that takes no arguments and returns **void**. The function pointer is registered as the function to call when **new** fails. Once a **new** handler is registered with **set_new_handler**, **new** will not throw **bad_alloc** on failure.

- An object of class **auto_ptr** maintains a pointer to dynamically allocated memory. When an **auto_ptr** object goes out of scope, it performs a **delete** operation on its pointer data member. Class template **auto_ptr** provides operators ***** and **->** so that an **auto_ptr** object can be used like a regular pointer variable.

- The C++ standard includes a hierarchy of exception classes headed by base class **exception** (defined in header file **<exception>**), which offers the service **what()** that is overridden in each derived class to issue an appropriate error message.

- Including **bad_exception** in the **throw** list of a function definition means that, if an unexpected exception occurs, function **unexpected** will throw **bad_exception** rather than terminating (by default) or calling another function specified with **set_unexpected**.

- Use **catch(...)** to **catch** all exceptions.

TERMINOLOGY

abort
auto_ptr
bad_alloc
bad_cast
bad_exception
bad_typeid
catch(...)
catch a group of exceptions
catch an exception
catch argument
catch block
dynamic_cast
empty exception specification
empty **throw** specification
enclosing **try** block
exception
exception declaration
exception handler
<exception> header file
exception list
exception object
exception specification
exceptional condition
exit
fault tolerance
function with no exception specification
handle an exception
handler for a base class
handler for a derived class
invalid_argument

length_error
logic_error
<memory> header file
mission-critical application
nested exception handlers
new_handler
<new> header file
nothrow
out_of_range
overflow_error
rethrow an exception
robustness
runtime_error
set_new_handler
set_terminate
set_unexpected
stack unwinding
<stdexcept> header file
terminate
throw an exception
throw an unexpected exception
throw expression
throw list
throw without arguments
throw point
try block
uncaught exception
underflow_error
unexpected

SELF-REVIEW EXERCISES

13.1   List five common examples of exceptions.

13.2   Give several reasons why exception-handling techniques should not be used for conventional program control.

13.3   Why are exceptions appropriate for dealing with errors produced by library functions?

13.4   What is a "resource leak?"

13.5   If no exceptions are thrown in a **try** block, where does control proceed to after the **try** block completes execution?

13.6   What happens if an exception is thrown outside a **try** block?

13.7   Give a key advantage and a key disadvantage of using **catch(...)**.

13.8   What happens if no **catch** handler matches the type of a thrown object?

13.9   What happens if several handlers match the type of the thrown object?

13.10   Why would a programmer specify a base-class type as the type of a **catch** handler, then **throw** objects of derived-class types?

13.11   Suppose a **catch** handler with a precise match to an exception object type is available. Under what circumstances might a different handler be executed for exception objects of that type?

13.12   Must throwing an exception cause program termination?

13.13   What happens when a **catch** handler **throw**s an exception?

13.14   What does the statement **throw;** do?

13.15   How does the programmer restrict the exception types that a function can throw?

13.16   What happens if a function **throw**s an exception of a type not allowed by the exception specification for the function?

13.17   What happens to the automatic objects that have been constructed in a **try** block when that block **throw**s an exception?

ANSWERS TO SELF-REVIEW EXERCISES

13.1   Insufficient memory to satisfy a **new** request, array subscript out of bounds, arithmetic overflow, division by zero, invalid function parameters.

13.2   (a) Exception handling is designed to handle infrequently occurring situations that often result in program termination, so compiler writers are not required to implement exception handling to perform optimally. (b) Flow of control with conventional control structures generally is clearer and more efficient than with exceptions. (c) Problems can occur because the stack is unwound when an exception occurs and resources allocated prior to the exception might not be freed. (d) The "additional" exceptions make it more difficult for the programmer to handle the larger number of exception cases.

13.3   It is unlikely that a library function will perform error processing that will meet the unique needs of all users.

13.4   A program that terminates abruptly could leave a resource in a state in which other programs would not be able to acquire the resource.

13.5   The exception handlers (in the **catch** blocks) for that **try** block are skipped and the program resumes execution after the last **catch** block.

13.6   An exception thrown outside a **try** block causes a call to **terminate**.

13.7   The form **catch(...)** catches any type of exception thrown in a **try** block. An advantage is all possible exception will be caught. A disadvantage is that the **catch** has no parameter, so it cannot reference information in the thrown object and cannot know the cause of the exception.

13.8   This causes the search for a match to continue in the next enclosing **try** block. As this process continues, it might eventually be determined that there is no handler in the program that matches the type of the thrown object; in this case, **terminate** is called, which by default calls **abort**. An alternative **terminate** function can be provided as an argument to **set_terminate**.

13.9   The first matching exception handler after the **try** block is executed.

13.10   This is a nice way to **catch** related types of exceptions.

13.11   A handler requiring standard conversions can appear before one with a precise match.

13.12   No, but it does terminate the block in which the exception is thrown.

13.13   The exception will be processed by a **catch** handler (if one exists) associated with the **try** block (if one exists) enclosing the **catch** handler that caused the exception.

13.14   It rethrows the exception.

13.15   Provide an exception specification listing the exception types that the function can throw.

13.16   Function **unexpected** is called.

13.17   Through the process of stack unwinding, destructors are called for each of these objects.

EXERCISES

13.18   List the various exceptional conditions that have occurred in programs throughout this text. List as many additional exceptional conditions as you can. For each of these, describe briefly how a program typically would handle the exception, using the exception-handling techniques discussed in this chapter. Some typical exceptions are division by zero, arithmetic overflow, array subscript out of bounds, exhaustion of the free store, etc.

13.19   Under what circumstances would the programmer not provide a parameter name when defining the type of the object that will be caught by a handler?

13.20   A program contains the statement

```
throw;
```

Where would you normally expect to find such a statement? What if that statement appeared in a different part of the program?

13.21   Under what circumstances would you use the following statement?

```
catch( ... ) { throw; }
```

13.22   Compare and contrast exception handling with the various other error-processing schemes discussed in the text.

13.23   List the advantages of exception handling over conventional means of error processing.

13.24   Provide reasons why exceptions should not be used as an alternative form of program control.

13.25   Describe a technique for handling related exceptions.

13.26   Until this chapter, we have found that dealing with errors detected by constructors can be awkward. Exception handling gives us a much better means of handling such errors. Consider a constructor for a **String** class. The constructor uses **new** to obtain space from the free store. Suppose

new fails. Show how you would deal with this without exception handling. Discuss the key issues. Show how you would deal with such memory exhaustion with exception handling. Explain why the exception-handling approach is superior.

13.27   Suppose a program **throw**s an exception and the appropriate exception handler begins executing. Now suppose that the exception handler itself **throw**s the same exception. Does this create infinite recursion? Write a program to check your observation.

13.28   Use inheritance to create a base exception class and various derived exception classes. Then show that a **catch** handler specifying the base class can **catch** derived-class exceptions.

13.29   Show a conditional expression that returns either a **double** or an **int**. Provide an **int** **catch** handler and a **double catch** handler. Show that only the **double catch** handler executes, regardless of whether the **int** or the **double** is returned.

13.30   Write a program designed to generate and handle a memory exhaustion error. Your program should loop on a request to create dynamic storage through operator **new**.

13.31   Write a program illustrating that all destructors for objects constructed in a block are called before an exception is thrown from that block.

13.32   Write a program illustrating that member object destructors are called for only those member objects that were constructed before an exception occurred.

13.33   Write a program that demonstrates how any exception is caught with **catch(...)**.

13.34   Write a program illustrating that the order of exception handlers is important. The first matching handler is the one that executes. Attempt to compile and run your program two different ways to show that two different handlers execute with two different effects.

13.35   Write a program that shows a constructor passing information about constructor failure to an exception handler after a **try** block.

13.36   Write a program that illustrates rethrowing an exception.

13.37   Write a program that illustrates that a function with its own **try** block does not have to catch every possible error generated within the **try**. Some exceptions can slip through to, and be handled in, outer scopes.

13.38   Write a program that **throw**s an exception from a deeply nested function and still has the **catch** handler following the **try** block enclosing the call chain catch the exception.

14

File Processing

Objectives

- To be able to create, read, write and update files.
- To become familiar with sequential-access file processing.
- To become familiar with random-access file processing.
- To be able to specify high-performance unformatted I/O operations.
- To understand the differences between formatted-data and raw-data file processing.
- To build a transaction-processing program using random-access file processing.

I read part of it all the way through.
Samuel Goldwyn

I can only assume that a "Do Not File" document is filed in a "Do Not File" file.
Senator Frank Church
Senate Intelligence Subcommittee Hearing, 1975

Outline

14.1   Introduction

14.2   The Data Hierarchy

14.3   Files and Streams

14.4   Creating a Sequential-Access File

14.5   Reading Data from a Sequential-Access File

14.6   Updating Sequential-Access Files

14.7   Random-Access Files

14.8   Creating a Random-Access File

14.9   Writing Data Randomly to a Random-Access File

14.10   Reading Data Sequentially from a Random-Access File

14.11   Example: A Transaction-Processing Program

14.12   Input/Output of Objects

Summary • Terminology • Self-Review Exercises • Answers to Self-Review Exercises • Exercises

14.1 Introduction

Storage of data in variables and arrays is temporary. *Files* are used for *data persistence*—permanent retention of large amounts of data. Computers store files on *secondary storage devices,* such as magnetic disks, optical disks and tapes. In this chapter, we explain how to build C++ programs that create, update and process data files. We consider both sequential-access files and random-access files. We compare formatted-data file processing and raw-data file processing. We examine techniques for input of data from, and output of data to, **string**s rather than files in Chapter 15.

14.2 The Data Hierarchy

Ultimately, all data items that digital computers process are reduced to combinations of zeros and ones. This occurs because it is simple and economical to build electronic devices that can assume two stable states—one state represents **0** and the other state represents **1**. It is remarkable that the impressive functions performed by computers involve only the most fundamental manipulations of **0**s and **1**s.

The smallest data item that computers support is called a *bit* (short for "*binary digit*"—a digit that can assume one of two values). Each data item, or bit, can assume either the value **0** or the value **1**. Computer circuitry performs various simple bit manipulations, such as examining the value of a bit, setting the value of a bit and reversing a bit (from **1** to **0** or from **0** to **1**).

Programming with data in the low-level form of bits is cumbersome. It is preferable to program with data in forms such as *decimal digits* (i.e., 0, 1, 2, 3, 4, 5, 6, 7, 8 and 9), *letters* (i.e., A through Z and a through z) and *special symbols* (i.e., $, @, %, &, *, (,), -, +, ", :, ?, / and many others). Digits, letters and special symbols are referred to as *characters.* The set of all characters used to write programs and represent data items on a particular computer is called that computer's *character set.* Because computers can process only **1**s and **0**s, every character in a computer's character set is represented as a pattern of **1**s and **0**s. *Bytes* are composed of eight bits. Programmers create programs and data items with characters; computers manipulate and process these characters as patterns of bits. For example, C++ provides data type **char**, which occupies one byte. C++ also provides data type **wchar_t**, which can occupy more than one byte (to support larger character sets, such as the *Unicode*® *character set*).

Just as characters are composed of bits, *fields* are composed of characters. A field is a group of characters that conveys some meaning. For example, a field consisting of upper-case and lowercase letters can represent a person's name.

Data items processed by computers form a *data hierarchy* (Fig. 14.1), in which data items become larger and more complex in structure as we progress from bits, to characters, to fields and to larger data structures.

Typically, a *record* (i.e., a **struct** or a **class** in C++) is composed of several fields (called data members in C++). In a payroll system, for example, a record for a particular employee might include the following fields:

1. Employee identification number

2. Name

3. Address

4. Hourly pay rate

5. Number of exemptions claimed

6. Year-to-date earnings

7. Amount of taxes withheld

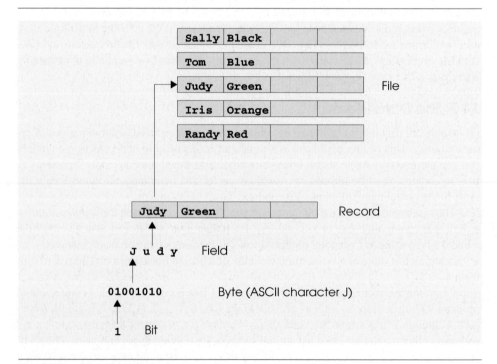

Fig. 14.1   Data hierarchy.

Thus, a record is a group of related fields. In the preceding example, each field is associated with the same employee. A *file* is a group of related records.[1] A company's payroll file normally contains one record for each employee. Thus, a payroll file for a small company might contain only 22 records, whereas a payroll file for a large company might contain 100,000 records. It is not unusual for a company to have many files, some containing millions, billions, or even trillions of characters of information.

To facilitate the retrieval of specific records from a file, at least one field in each record is chosen as a *record key*. A record key identifies a record as belonging to a particular person or entity and distinguishes that record from all other records. In the payroll record described previously, the employee identification number normally would be chosen as the record key.

There are many ways of organizing records in a file. A common type of organization is called a *sequential file*, in which records typically are stored in order by a record-key field. In a payroll file, records usually are placed in order by employee identification number. The first employee record in the file contains the lowest employee identification number, and subsequent records contain increasingly higher employee identification numbers.

Most businesses use many different files to store data. For example, a company might have payroll files, accounts-receivable files (listing money due from clients), accounts-payable files (listing money due to suppliers), inventory files (listing facts about all the items handled by the business) and many other types of files. A group of related files often are stored in a *database*. A collection of programs designed to create and manage databases is called a *database management system* (*DBMS*).

14.3 Files and Streams

C++ views each file as a sequence of bytes (Fig. 14.2). Each file ends either with an *end-of-file marker* or at a specific byte number recorded in a system-maintained, administrative data structure. When a file is *opened*, an object is created, and a stream is associated with the object. In Chapter 12, we saw that objects **cin**, **cout**, **cerr** and **clog** are created when **<iostream>** is included. The streams associated with these objects provide communication channels between a program and a particular file or device. For example, the **cin** object (standard-input stream object) enables a program to input data from the keyboard or from other devices, the **cout** object (standard-output stream object) enables a program to output data to the screen or other devices, and the **cerr** and **clog** objects (standard error stream objects) enable a program to output error messages to the screen or other devices.

0	1	2	3	4	5	6	7	8	9	...	n-1	
										...		end-of-file marker

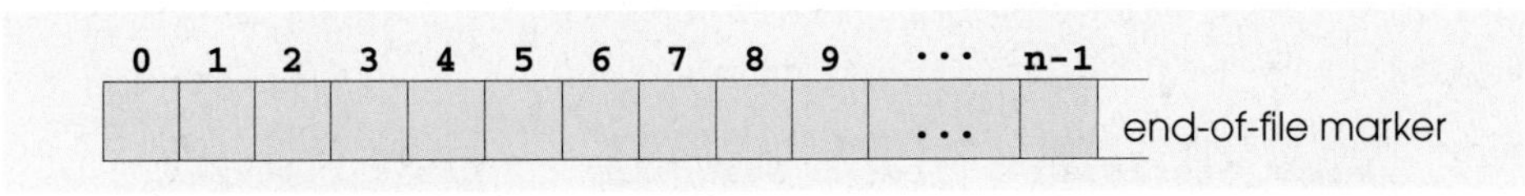

Fig. 14.2   C++'s view of a file of *n* bytes.

1. Generally, a file can contain arbitrary data in arbitrary formats. In some operating systems, a file is viewed as nothing more than a collection of bytes. In such an operating system, any organization of the bytes in a file (such as organizing the data into records) is a view created by the application programmer.

To perform file processing in C++, header files **<iostream>** and **<fstream>** must be included. Header **<fstream>** includes the definitions for the stream-class templates **basic_ifstream** (for file input), **basic_ofstream** (for file output) and **basic_fstream** (for file input and output). Each class template has a predefined template specialization that enables **char** I/O. In addition, the **fstream** library provides a set of **typedef**s that provide aliases for these template specializations. For example, the **typedef ifstream** represents a specialization of **basic_ifstream** that enables **char** input from a file. Similarly, **typedef ofstream** represents a specialization of **basic_ofstream** that enables **char** output to files. Also, **typedef fstream** represents a specialization of **basic_fstream** that enables **char** input from, and output to, files.

Files are opened by creating objects of these stream template specializations. These templates "derive" from class templates **basic_istream**, **basic_ostream** and **basic_iostream**, respectively. Thus, all member functions, operators and manipulators that belong to these templates (which we described in Chapter 12) also can be applied to file streams. Figure 14.3 summarizes the inheritance relationships of the I/O classes that we have discussed to this point.

14.4 Creating a Sequential-Access File

C++ imposes no structure on a file. Thus, a concept like that of a "record" does not exist in a C++ file. Therefore, the programmer must structure files to meet the application's requirements. In the following example, we see how the programmer can impose a simple record structure on a file.

Figure 14.4 creates a sequential-access file that might be used in an accounts-receivable system to help manage the money owed by a company's credit clients. For each client, the program obtains an account number, the client's name and the client's balance (i.e., the amount the client owes the company for goods and services received in the past). The data obtained for each client constitutes a record for that client. The account number serves as

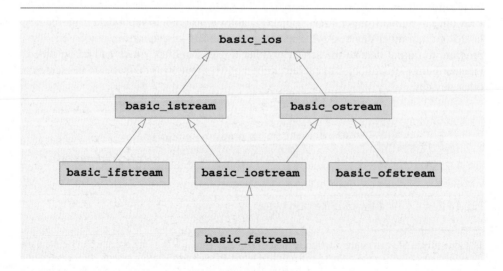

Fig. 14.3   Portion of stream I/O template hierarchy.

the record key in this application; that is, the program creates and maintains the file in account-number order. This program assumes the user enters the records in account-number order. In a comprehensive accounts-receivable system, a sorting capability would be provided for the user to enter records in any order—the records then would be sorted and written to the file.

```cpp
1   // Fig. 14.4: fig14_04.cpp
2   // Create a sequential file.
3   #include <iostream>
4
5   using std::cout;
6   using std::cin;
7   using std::ios;
8   using std::cerr;
9   using std::endl;
10
11  #include <fstream>
12
13  using std::ofstream;
14
15  #include <cstdlib>   // exit prototype
16
17  int main()
18  {
19     // ofstream constructor opens file
20     ofstream outClientFile( "clients.dat", ios::out );
21
22     // exit program if unable to create file
23     if ( !outClientFile ) {   // overloaded ! operator
24        cerr << "File could not be opened" << endl;
25        exit( 1 );
26
27     } // end if
28
29     cout << "Enter the account, name, and balance." << endl
30          << "Enter end-of-file to end input.\n? ";
31
32     int account;
33     char name[ 30 ];
34     double balance;
35
36     // read account, name and balance from cin, then place in file
37     while ( cin >> account >> name >> balance ) {
38        outClientFile << account << ' ' << name << ' ' << balance
39                      << endl;
40        cout << "? ";
41
42     } // end while
43
44     return 0;   // ofstream destructor closes file
45
46  } // end main
```

Fig. 14.4   Creating a sequential file.(Part 1 of 2.)

```
Enter the account, name, and balance.
Enter end-of-file to end input.
? 100 Jones 24.98
? 200 Doe 345.67
? 300 White 0.00
? 400 Stone -42.16
? 500 Rich 224.62
? ^Z
```

Fig. 14.4   Creating a sequential file.(Part 2 of 2.)

Let us examine this program. As stated previously, files are opened by creating **ifstream**, **ofstream** or **fstream** objects. In Fig. 14.4, the file is to be opened for output, so an **ofstream** object is created. Two arguments are passed to the object's constructor—the *filename* and the *file-open mode*. For an **ofstream** object, the file-open mode can be either **ios::out** to output data to a file or **ios::app** to append data to the end of a file (without modifying any data already in the file). Existing files opened with mode **ios::out** are *truncated*—all data in the file is discarded. If the specified file does not yet exist, then **ofstream** creates the file, using that filename.

Line 20 creates an **ofstream** object named **outClientFile** associated with the file **clients.dat** that is opened for output. The arguments **"clients.dat"** and **ios::out** are passed to the **ofstream** constructor, which opens the file. This establishes a "line of communication" with the file. By default, **ofstream** objects are opened for output, so line 20 could have executed the statement

```
        ofstream outClientFile( "clients.dat" );
```

to open **clients.dat** for output. Figure 14.5 lists the file-open modes.

Common Programming Error 14.1

*Use caution when opening an existing file for output (**ios::out**), especially when you want to preserve the file's contents, which will be discarded without warning.*

Mode	Description
ios::app	Append all output to the end of the file.
ios::ate	Open a file for output and move to the end of the file (normally used to append data to a file). Data can be written anywhere in the file.
ios::in	Open a file for input.
ios::out	Open a file for output.
ios::trunc	Discard the file's contents if they exist (this also is the default action for **ios::out**).
ios::binary	Open a file for binary (i.e., non-text) input or output.

Fig. 14.5   File open modes.

An **ofstream** object can be created without opening a specific file—a file can be attached to the object later. For example, the statement

```
ofstream outClientFile;
```

creates an **ofstream** object named **outClientFile**. The **ofstream** member function **open** opens a file and attaches it to an existing **ofstream** object as follows:

```
outClientFile.open( "clients.dat", ios::out );
```

 Common Programming Error 14.2

Not opening a file before attempting to reference it in a program will result in an error.

After creating an **ofstream** object and attempting to open it, the program tests whether the open operation was successful. The **if** structure at lines 23–27 uses the overloaded **ios** operator member function **operator!** to determine whether the open operation succeeded. The condition returns a **true** value if either the **failbit** or the **badbit** is set for the stream on the **open** operation. Some possible errors are attempting to open a nonexistent file for reading, attempting to open a file for reading without permission and opening a file for writing when no disk space is available.

If the condition indicates an unsuccessful attempt to open the file, line 24 outputs the error message "**File could not be opened**," and line 25 invokes function **exit** to terminate the program. The argument to **exit** is returned to the environment from which the program was invoked. Argument **0** indicates that the program terminated normally; any other value indicates that the program terminated due to an error. The calling environment (most likely the operating system) uses the value returned by **exit** to respond appropriately to the error.

Another overloaded **ios** operator member function—**operator void***—converts the stream to a pointer, so it can be tested as **0** (i.e., the null pointer) or nonzero (i.e., any other pointer value). If the **failbit** or **badbit** (see Chapter 12) has been set for the stream, **0** (**false**) is returned. The condition in the **while** structure of lines 37–42 invokes the **operator void*** member function on **cin** implicitly. The condition remains **true** as long as neither the **failbit** nor the **badbit** has been set for **cin**. Entering the end-of-file indicator sets the **failbit** for **cin**. The **operator void *** function can be used to test an input object for end-of-file instead of calling the **eof** member function explicitly on the input object.

If line 20 opened the file successfully, the program begins processing data. Lines 29–30 prompt the user to enter either the various fields for each record or the end-of-file indicator when data entry is complete. Figure 14.6 lists the keyboard combinations for entering end-of-file for various computer systems.

Computer system	Keyboard combination
UNIX systems	*<ctrl-d>* (on a line by itself)
IBM PC and compatibles	*<ctrl-z>* (sometimes followed by pressing *Enter*)

Fig. 14.6 End-of-file key combinations for various popular computer systems. (Part 1 of 2.)

```
54
55   // display single record from file
56   void outputLine( int account, const char * const name,
57      double balance )
58   {
59      cout << left << setw( 10 ) << account << setw( 13 ) << name
60           << setw( 7 ) << setprecision( 2 ) << right << balance
61           << endl;
62
63   } // end function outputLine
```

```
Account   Name       Balance
100       Jones        24.98
200       Doe         345.67
300       White         0.00
400       Stone       -42.16
500       Rich        224.62
```

Fig. 14.7   Reading and printing a sequential file.(Part 2 of 2.)

 Good Programming Practice 14.1

*Open a file for input only (using **ios::in**) if the file's contents should not be modified. This prevents unintentional modification of the file's contents and is an example of the principle of least privilege.*

Objects of class **ifstream** are opened for input by default. We could have used the statement

```
ifstream inClientFile( "clients.dat" );
```

to open **clients.dat** for input. Just as with an **ofstream** object, an **ifstream** object can be created without opening a specific file, because a file can be attached to it later.

The program uses the condition **!inClientFile** to determine whether the file was opened successfully before attempting to retrieve data from the file. Line 48 reads a set of data (i.e., a record) from the file. After the preceding line is executed the first time, **account** has the value **100**, **name** has the value **"Jones"** and **balance** has the value **24.98**. Each time line 48 executes, it reads another record from the file into the variables **account**, **name** and **balance**. Line 49 displays the records, using function **output-Line** (lines 56–63), which uses parameterized stream manipulators to format the data for display. When the end of file has been reached, the implicit call to **operator void*** in the **while** structure returns **false** (normally **operator void*** returns **true**), the **ifstream** destructor function closes the file and the program terminates.

To retrieve data sequentially from a file, programs normally start reading from the beginning of the file and read all the data consecutively until the desired data is found. It might be necessary to process the file sequentially several times (from the beginning of the file) during the execution of a program. Both the **istream** and the **ostream** provide member functions for repositioning the *file-position pointer* (the byte number of the next byte in the file to be read or written). These member functions are ***seekg*** ("seek get") for the **istream** and ***seekp*** ("seek put") for the **ostream**. Each **istream** object has a "get pointer," which indicates the byte number in the file from which the next input is to occur, and each **ostream** object has a "put pointer," which indicates the byte number in the file at which the next output should be placed. The statement

```
inClientFile.seekg( 0 );
```

repositions the file-position pointer to the beginning of the file (location **0**) attached to **in-ClientFile**. The argument to **seekg** normally is a **long** integer. A second argument can be specified to indicate the *seek direction*. The seek direction can be ***ios::beg*** (the default) for positioning relative to the beginning of a stream, ***ios::cur*** for positioning relative to the current position in a stream or ***ios::end*** for positioning relative to the end of a stream. The file-position pointer is an integer value that specifies the location in the file as a number of bytes from the file's starting location (this is occasionally referred to as the *offset* from the beginning of the file). Some examples of positioning the "get" file-position pointer are

```
// position to the nth byte of fileObject (assumes ios::beg)
fileObject.seekg( n );

// position n bytes forward in fileObject
fileObject.seekg( n, ios::cur );

// position n bytes back from end of fileObject
fileObject.seekg( n, ios::end );

// position at end of fileObject
fileObject.seekg( 0, ios::end );
```

The same operations can be performed using **ostream** member function **seekp**. Member functions ***tellg*** and ***tellp*** are provided to return the current locations of the "get" and "put" pointers, respectively. The following statement assigns the "get" file-position pointer value to variable **location** of type **long**:

```
location = fileObject.tellg();
```

Figure 14.8 enables a credit manager to display the account information for those customers with zero balances (i.e., customers who do not owe the company any money), credit balances (i.e., customers to whom the company owes money), and debit balances (i.e., customers who owe the company money for goods and services received in the past). The program displays a menu and allows the credit manager to enter one of three options to obtain credit information. Option 1 produces a list of accounts with zero balances. Option 2 produces a list of accounts with credit balances. Option 3 produces a list of accounts with debit balances. Option 4 terminates program execution. Entering an invalid option displays the prompt to enter another choice.

```
1   // Fig. 14.8: fig14_08.cpp
2   // Credit-inquiry program.
3   #include <iostream>
4
5   using std::cout;
6   using std::cin;
7   using std::ios;
```

Fig. 14.8 · Credit-inquiry program.(Part 1 of 5.)

```
 8   using std::cerr;
 9   using std::endl;
10   using std::fixed;
11   using std::showpoint;
12   using std::left;
13   using std::right;
14
15   #include <fstream>
16
17   using std::ifstream;
18
19   #include <iomanip>
20
21   using std::setw;
22   using std::setprecision;
23
24   #include <cstdlib>
25
26   enum RequestType { ZERO_BALANCE = 1, CREDIT_BALANCE,
27      DEBIT_BALANCE, END };
28   int getRequest();
29   bool shouldDisplay( int, double );
30   void outputLine( int, const char * const, double );
31
32   int main()
33   {
34      // ifstream constructor opens the file
35      ifstream inClientFile( "clients.dat", ios::in );
36
37      // exit program if ifstream could not open file
38      if ( !inClientFile ) {
39         cerr << "File could not be opened" << endl;
40         exit( 1 );
41
42      } // end if
43
44      int request;
45      int account;
46      char name[ 30 ];
47      double balance;
48
49      // get user's request (e.g., zero, credit or debit balance)
50      request = getRequest();
51
52      // process user's request
53      while ( request != END ) {
54
55         switch ( request ) {
56
57            case ZERO_BALANCE:
58               cout << "\nAccounts with zero balances:\n";
59               break;
60
```

Fig. 14.8   Credit-inquiry program.(Part 2 of 5.)

```
61            case CREDIT_BALANCE:
62               cout << "\nAccounts with credit balances:\n";
63               break;
64
65            case DEBIT_BALANCE:
66               cout << "\nAccounts with debit balances:\n";
67               break;
68
69         } // end switch
70
71         // read account, name and balance from file
72         inClientFile >> account >> name >> balance;
73
74         // display file contents (until eof)
75         while ( !inClientFile.eof() ) {
76
77            // display record
78            if ( shouldDisplay( request, balance ) )
79               outputLine( account, name, balance );
80
81            // read account, name and balance from file
82            inClientFile >> account >> name >> balance;
83
84         } // end inner while
85
86         inClientFile.clear();      // reset eof for next input
87         inClientFile.seekg( 0 ); // move to beginning of file
88         request = getRequest();   // get additional request from user
89
90      } // end outer while
91
92      cout << "End of run." << endl;
93
94      return 0; // ifstream destructor closes the file
95
96   } // end main
97
98   // obtain request from user
99   int getRequest()
100  {
101     int request;
102
103     // display request options
104     cout << "\nEnter request" << endl
105         << " 1 - List accounts with zero balances" << endl
106         << " 2 - List accounts with credit balances" << endl
107         << " 3 - List accounts with debit balances" << endl
108         << " 4 - End of run" << fixed << showpoint;
109
110     // input user request
111     do {
112        cout << "\n? ";
113        cin >> request;
```

Fig. 14.8   Credit-inquiry program.(Part 3 of 5.)

```
114
115       } while ( request < ZERO_BALANCE && request > END );
116
117       return request;
118
119   } // end function getRequest
120
121   // determine whether to display given record
122   bool shouldDisplay( int type, double balance )
123   {
124      // determine whether to display credit balances
125      if ( type == CREDIT_BALANCE && balance < 0 )
126         return true;
127
128      // determine whether to display debit balances
129      if ( type == DEBIT_BALANCE && balance > 0 )
130         return true;
131
132      // determine whether to display zero balances
133      if ( type == ZERO_BALANCE && balance == 0 )
134         return true;
135
136      return false;
137
138   } // end function shouldDisplay
139
140   // display single record from file
141   void outputLine( int account, const char * const name,
142      double balance )
143   {
144      cout << left << setw( 10 ) << account << setw( 13 ) << name
145         << setw( 7 ) << setprecision( 2 ) << right << balance
146         << endl;
147
148   } // end function outputLine
```

```
Enter request
 1 - List accounts with zero balances
 2 - List accounts with credit balances
 3 - List accounts with debit balances
 4 - End of run
? 1

Accounts with zero balances:
300        White            0.00

Enter request
 1 - List accounts with zero balances
 2 - List accounts with credit balances
 3 - List accounts with debit balances
 4 - End of run
? 2
```

continued at top of next page

Fig. 14.8   Credit-inquiry program.(Part 4 of 5.)

```
                                                            continued from previous page
Accounts with credit balances:
400          Stone              -42.16

Enter request
 1 - List accounts with zero balances
 2 - List accounts with credit balances
 3 - List accounts with debit balances
 4 - End of run
? 3

Accounts with debit balances:
100          Jones               24.98
200          Doe                345.67
500          Rich               224.62

Enter request
 1 - List accounts with zero balances
 2 - List accounts with credit balances
 3 - List accounts with debit balances
 4 - End of run
? 4
End of run.
```

Fig. 14.8   Credit-inquiry program.(Part 5 of 5.)

14.6 Updating Sequential-Access Files

Data that are formatted and written to a sequential-access file as shown in Section 14.4 cannot be modified without the risk of destroying other data in the file. For example, if the name "**White**" needs to be changed to "**Worthington**," the old name cannot be overwritten without corrupting the file. The record for **White** was written to the file as

        300 White 0.00

If this record were rewritten beginning at the same location in the file using the longer name, the record would be

        300 Worthington 0.00

The new record contains six more characters than the original record. Therefore, the characters beyond the second "**o**" in "**Worthington**" would overwrite the beginning of the next sequential record in the file. The problem is that, in the formatted input/output model using the insertion operator **<<** and the extraction operator **>>**, fields—and hence records—can vary in size. For example, values 7, 14, –117, 2074, and 27383 are all **int**s, which store the same number of "raw data" bytes internally. However, these integers become different-sized fields when output as formatted text (character sequences). Therefore, the formatted input/output model usually is not used to update records in place.

Such updating can be done awkwardly. For example, to make the preceding name change, the records before **300 White 0.00** in a sequential access file could be copied to a new file, the updated record then would be written to the new file, and the records after **300 White 0.00** would be copied to the new file. This requires processing every record in the file to update one record. If many records are being updated in one pass of the file, this technique can be acceptable.

14.7 Random-Access Files

So far, we have seen how to create sequential access files and search them to locate information. Sequential-access files are inappropriate for *instant-access applications*, in which a particular record must be located immediately. Common instant-access applications are airline-reservation systems, banking systems, point-of-sale systems, automated-teller machines and other kinds of *transaction-processing systems* that require rapid access to specific data. A bank might have hundreds of thousands (or even millions) of other customers, yet, when a customer uses an automated-teller machine, the program checks that customer's account in seconds for sufficient funds. This kind of instant access is made possible with *random-access files*. Individual records of a random-access file can be accessed directly (and quickly) without having to search other records.

As we have said, C++ does not impose structure on a file. So the application that wants to use random-access files must create them. A variety of techniques can be used to create random-access files. Perhaps the easiest method is to require that all records in a file be of the same fixed length. Using fixed-length records makes it easy for a program to calculate (as a function of the record size and the record key) the exact location of any record relative to the beginning of the file. We soon will see how this facilitates immediate access to specific records, even in large files.

Figure 14.9 illustrates C++'s view of a random-access file composed of fixed-length records (each record is 100 bytes long). A random-access file is like a railroad train with many cars—some empty and some with contents.

Data can be inserted into a random-access file without destroying other data in the file. Data stored previously also can be updated or deleted without rewriting the entire file. In the following sections, we explain how to create a random-access file, enter data, read the data both sequentially and randomly, update the data and delete data when no longer needed.

14.8 Creating a Random-Access File

The **ostream** member function **write** outputs a fixed number of bytes, beginning at a specific location in memory, to the specified stream. When the stream is associated with a file, function **write** writes the data at the location in the file specified by the "put" file-position pointer. The **istream** member function **read** inputs a fixed number of bytes from the specified stream to an area in memory beginning at a specified address. If the stream is associated with a file, function **read** inputs bytes at the location in the file specified by the "get" file-position pointer.

When writing an integer **number** to a file, instead of using the statement

```
outFile << number;
```

which could print as few as one digit or as many as 11 digits (10 digits plus a sign, each of which requires a single byte of storage) for a four-byte integer, we can use the statement

```
outFile.write( reinterpret_cast< const char * >( &number ),
   sizeof( number ) );
```

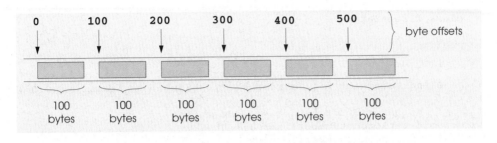

Fig. 14.9   C++ view of a random-access file.

which always writes four bytes (on a machine with four-byte integers). Function **write** expects data type **const char *** as its first argument; hence, we use operator **reinterpret_cast< const char * >** to convert the address of **number** to a **const char *** pointer. The second argument of **write** is an integer of type **size_t** specifying the number of bytes to be written. As we will see, **istream** function **read** then can be used to read the four bytes back into integer variable **number**.

If a program reads unformatted data (written by **write**), it must be compiled and executed on a system that is compatible with the program that wrote the data.

Random-access file-processing programs rarely write a single field to a file. Normally, they write one **struct** or **class** object at a time, as we show in the following examples.

Consider the following problem statement:

> *Create a credit-processing program capable of storing at most 100 fixed-length records for a company that can have up to 100 customers. Each record should consist of an account number that acts as the record key, a last name, a first name and a balance. The program should be able to update an account, insert a new account, delete an account and list all the account records in a formatted text file for printing.*

The next several sections introduce the techniques for creating this credit-processing program. Figure 14.12 illustrates opening a random-access file, defining the record format using an object of class **ClientData** (Fig. 14.10–Fig. 14.11) and writing data to the disk in binary format (Fig. 14.12 line 18 specifies binary mode **ios::binary**). This program initializes all 100 records of the file **"credit.dat"** with empty objects, using function **write**. Each empty object contains **0** for the account number, the null string (represented by empty quotation marks) for the last and first name and **0.0** for the balance. Each record is initialized with the amount of empty space in which the account data will be stored.

```
1   // Fig. 14.10: clientData.h
2   // Class ClientData definition used in Fig. 14.12-Fig. 14.15.
3   #ifndef CLIENTDATA_H
4   #define CLIENTDATA_H
5
6   #include <iostream>
7
8   using std::string;
9
```

Fig. 14.10 ClientData class header file.(Part 1 of 2.)

```
10   class ClientData {
11
12   public:
13
14      // default ClientData constructor
15      ClientData( int = 0, string = "", string = "", double = 0.0 );
16
17      // accessor functions for accountNumber
18      void setAccountNumber( int );
19      int getAccountNumber() const;
20
21      // accessor functions for lastName
22      void setLastName( string );
23      string getLastName() const;
24
25      // accessor functions for firstName
26      void setFirstName( string );
27      string getFirstName() const;
28
29      // accessor functions for balance
30      void setBalance( double );
31      double getBalance() const;
32
33   private:
34      int accountNumber;
35      char lastName[ 15 ];
36      char firstName[ 10 ];
37      double balance;
38
39   }; // end class ClientData
40
41   #endif
```

Fig. 14.10 **ClientData** class header file.(Part 2 of 2.)

```
1    // Fig. 14.11: ClientData.cpp
2    // Class ClientData stores customer's credit information.
3    #include <iostream>
4
5    using std::string;
6
7    #include <cstring>
8    #include "clientData.h"
9
10   // default ClientData constructor
11   ClientData::ClientData( int accountNumberValue,
12      string lastNameValue, string firstNameValue,
13      double balanceValue )
14   {
15      setAccountNumber( accountNumberValue );
16      setLastName( lastNameValue );
```

Fig. 14.11 **ClientData** class represents a customer's credit information.(Part 1 of 3.)

```
17       setFirstName( firstNameValue );
18       setBalance( balanceValue );
19
20    } // end ClientData constructor
21
22    // get account-number value
23    int ClientData::getAccountNumber() const
24    {
25       return accountNumber;
26
27    } // end function getAccountNumber
28
29    // set account-number value
30    void ClientData::setAccountNumber( int accountNumberValue )
31    {
32       accountNumber = accountNumberValue;
33
34    } // end function setAccountNumber
35
36    // get last-name value
37    string ClientData::getLastName() const
38    {
39       return lastName;
40
41    } // end function getLastName
42
43    // set last-name value
44    void ClientData::setLastName( string lastNameString )
45    {
46       // copy at most 15 characters from string to lastName
47       const char *lastNameValue = lastNameString.data();
48       int length = strlen( lastNameValue );
49       length = ( length < 15 ? length : 14 );
50       strncpy( lastName, lastNameValue, length );
51
52       // append null character to lastName
53       lastName[ length ] = '\0';
54
55    } // end function setLastName
56
57    // get first-name value
58    string ClientData::getFirstName() const
59    {
60       return firstName;
61
62    } // end function getFirstName
63
64    // set first-name value
65    void ClientData::setFirstName( string firstNameString )
66    {
67       // copy at most 10 characters from string to firstName
68       const char *firstNameValue = firstNameString.data();
69       int length = strlen( firstNameValue );
```

Fig. 14.11 **ClientData** class represents a customer's credit information.(Part 2 of 3.)

```
70          length = ( length < 10 ? length : 9 );
71          strncpy( firstName, firstNameValue, length );
72
73          // append new-line character to firstName
74          firstName[ length ] = '\0';
75
76      } // end function setFirstName
77
78      // get balance value
79      double ClientData::getBalance() const
80      {
81          return balance;
82
83      } // end function getBalance
84
85      // set balance value
86      void ClientData::setBalance( double balanceValue )
87      {
88          balance = balanceValue;
89
90      } // end function setBalance
```

Fig. 14.11 **ClientData** class represents a customer's credit information.(Part 3 of 3.)

In Fig. 14.12, lines 32–34 cause the **blankClient** to be written to the **credit.dat** file associated with **ofstream** object **outCredit**. Remember that operator **sizeof** returns the size in bytes of the object contained in parentheses (see Chapter 5). The first argument to function **write** on line 32 must be of type **const char ***. However, the data type of **&blankClient** is **ClientData ***. To convert **&blankClient** to **const char ***, line 33 uses the cast operator **reinterpret_cast** to convert the address of **blankClient** to a **const char ***, so the call to **write** compiles without issuing a syntax error.

```
1   // Fig. 14.12: fig14_12.cpp
2   // Creating a randomly accessed file.
3   #include <iostream>
4
5   using std::cerr;
6   using std::endl;
7   using std::ios;
8
9   #include <fstream>
10
11  using std::ofstream;
12
13  #include <cstdlib>
14  #include "clientData.h"   // ClientData class definition
15
16  int main()
17  {
18      ofstream outCredit( "credit.dat", ios::binary );
```

Fig. 14.12 Creating a random-access file sequentially.(Part 1 of 2.)

```
19
20       // exit program if ofstream could not open file
21       if ( !outCredit ) {
22          cerr << "File could not be opened." << endl;
23          exit( 1 );
24
25       } // end if
26
27       // create ClientData with no information
28       ClientData blankClient;
29
30       // output 100 blank records to file
31       for ( int i = 0; i < 100; i++ )
32          outCredit.write(
33             reinterpret_cast< const char * >( &blankClient ),
34             sizeof( ClientData ) );
35
36       return 0;
37
38    } // end main
```

Fig. 14.12 Creating a random-access file sequentially.(Part 2 of 2.)

14.9 Writing Data Randomly to a Random-Access File

Figure 14.13 writes data to the file **"credit.dat"** and uses the combination of **ostream** functions **seekp** and **write** to store data at exact locations in the file. Function **seekp** sets the "put" file-position pointer to a specific position in the file, then **write** outputs the data. Note that line 20 includes the header file **clientData.h** defined in Fig. 14.10, so the program can use **ClientData** objects.

Lines 62–63 position the "put" file-position pointer for object **outCredit** to the byte location calculated by

$$(\text{ client.getAccountNumber() - 1) * sizeof(ClientData)}$$

Because the account number is between 1 and 100, 1 is subtracted from the account number when calculating the byte location of the record. Thus, for record 1, the file-position pointer is set to byte 0 of the file. Note that line 29 uses the **ofstream** object **outCredit** to open the **credit.dat** file with file-open mode **ios::binary**.

```
1    // Fig. 14.13: fig14_13.cpp
2    // Writing to a random access file.
3    #include <iostream>
4
5    using std::cerr;
6    using std::endl;
7    using std::cout;
8    using std::cin;
9    using std::ios;
10
```

Fig. 14.13 Writing to a random-access file.(Part 1 of 3.)

```
11   #include <iomanip>
12
13   using std::setw;
14
15   #include <fstream>
16
17   using std::ofstream;
18
19   #include <cstdlib>
20   #include "clientData.h"   // ClientData class definition
21
22   int main()
23   {
24      int accountNumber;
25      char lastName[ 15 ];
26      char firstName[ 10 ];
27      double balance;
28
29      ofstream outCredit( "credit.dat", ios::binary );
30
31      // exit program if ofstream cannot open file
32      if ( !outCredit ) {
33         cerr << "File could not be opened." << endl;
34         exit( 1 );
35
36      } // end if
37
38      cout << "Enter account number "
39           << "(1 to 100, 0 to end input)\n? ";
40
41      // require user to specify account number
42      ClientData client;
43      cin >> accountNumber;
44      client.setAccountNumber( accountNumber );
45
46      // user enters information, which is copied into file
47      while ( client.getAccountNumber() > 0 &&
48         client.getAccountNumber() <= 100 ) {
49
50         // user enters last name, first name and balance
51         cout << "Enter lastname, firstname, balance\n? ";
52         cin >> setw( 15 ) >> lastName;
53         cin >> setw( 10 ) >> firstName;
54         cin >> balance;
55
56         // set record lastName, firstName and balance values
57         client.setLastName( lastName );
58         client.setFirstName( firstName );
59         client.setBalance( balance );
60
61         // seek position in file of user-specified record
62         outCredit.seekp( ( client.getAccountNumber() - 1 ) *
63            sizeof( ClientData ) );
```

Fig. 14.13   Writing to a random-access file.(Part 2 of 3.)

```
64
65        // write user-specified information in file
66        outCredit.write(
67           reinterpret_cast< const char * >( &client ),
68           sizeof( ClientData ) );
69
70        // enable user to specify another account number
71        cout << "Enter account number\n? ";
72        cin >> accountNumber;
73        client.setAccountNumber( accountNumber );
74
75     } // end while
76
77     return 0;
78
79  } // end main
```

```
Enter account number (1 to 100, 0 to end input)
? 37
Enter lastname, firstname, balance
? Barker Doug 0.00
Enter account number
? 29
Enter lastname, firstname, balance
? Brown Nancy -24.54
Enter account number
? 96
Enter lastname, firstname, balance
? Stone Sam 34.98
Enter account number
? 88
Enter lastname, firstname, balance
? Smith Dave 258.34
Enter account number
? 33
Enter lastname, firstname, balance
? Dunn Stacey 314.33
Enter account number
? 0
```

Fig. 14.13   Writing to a random-access file.(Part 3 of 3.)

14.10 Reading Data Sequentially from a Random-Access File

In the previous sections, we created a random-access file and wrote data to that file. In this section, we develop a program that reads the file sequentially and prints only those records that contain data. These programs produce an additional benefit. See if you can determine what it is; we will reveal it at the end of this section.

The **istream** function **read** inputs a specified number of bytes from the current position in the specified stream into an object. For example, lines 58–59 from Fig. 14.14 read the number of bytes specified by **sizeof(ClientData)** from the file associated with **ifstream** object **inCredit** and store the data in the **client** record. Note that function **read** requires a first argument of type **char ***. Since **&client** is of type **ClientData ***, **&client** must be cast to **char *** using the cast operator **reinterpret_cast**. Note that line 25 includes the header file **clientData.h** defined in Fig. 14.10, so the program can use **ClientData** objects.

Figure 14.14 reads every record in the **"credit.dat"** file sequentially, checks each record to determine whether it contains data, and displays formatted outputs for records containing data. The condition in line 51 uses the **ios** member function **eof** to determine when the end of file is reached and causes execution of the **while** structure to terminate. Also, if an error occurs when reading from the file, the loop terminates, because **inCredit** evaluates to **false**. The data input from the file is output by function **outputLine** (lines 68–76), which takes two arguments—an **ostream** object and a **clientData** structure to be output. The **ostream** parameter type is interesting because any **ostream** object (such as **cout**) or any object of a derived class of **ostream** (such as an object of type **ofstream**) can be supplied as the argument. This means that the same function can be used, for example, to perform output to the standard-output stream and to a file stream without writing separate functions.

```
1   // Fig. 14.14: fig14_14.cpp
2   // Reading a random access file.
3   #include <iostream>
4
5   using std::cout;
6   using std::endl;
7   using std::ios;
8   using std::cerr;
9   using std::left;
10  using std::right;
11  using std::fixed;
12  using std::showpoint;
13
14  #include <iomanip>
15
16  using std::setprecision;
17  using std::setw;
18
19  #include <fstream>
20
21  using std::ifstream;
22  using std::ostream;
23
24  #include <cstdlib>  // exit protoyype
25  #include "clientData.h"  // ClientData class definition
26
27  void outputLine( ostream&, const ClientData & );
28
29  int main()
30  {
31     ifstream inCredit( "credit.dat", ios::in );
32
```

Fig. 14.14 Reading a random-access file sequentially.(Part 1 of 2.)

```
33     // exit program if ifstream cannot open file
34     if ( !inCredit ) {
35        cerr << "File could not be opened." << endl;
36        exit( 1 );
37
38     } // end if
39
40     cout << left << setw( 10 ) << "Account" << setw( 16 )
41        << "Last Name" << setw( 11 ) << "First Name" << left
42        << setw( 10 ) << right << "Balance" << endl;
43
44     ClientData client; // create record
45
46     // read first record from file
47     inCredit.read( reinterpret_cast< char * >( &client ),
48        sizeof( ClientData ) );
49
50     // read all records from file
51     while ( inCredit && !inCredit.eof() ) {
52
53        // display record
54        if ( client.getAccountNumber() != 0 )
55           outputLine( cout, client );
56
57        // read next from file
58        inCredit.read( reinterpret_cast< char * >( &client ),
59           sizeof( ClientData ) );
60
61     } // end while
62
63     return 0;
64
65  } // end main
66
67  // display single record
68  void outputLine( ostream &output, const ClientData &record )
69  {
70     output << left << setw( 10 ) << record.getAccountNumber()
71            << setw( 16 ) << record.getLastName().data()
72            << setw( 11 ) << record.getFirstName().data()
73            << setw( 10 ) << setprecision( 2 ) << right << fixed
74            << showpoint << record.getBalance() << endl;
75
76  } // end outputLine
```

Account	Last Name	First Name	Balance
29	Brown	Nancy	-24.54
33	Dunn	Stacey	314.33
37	Barker	Doug	0.00
88	Smith	Dave	258.34
96	Stone	Sam	34.98

Fig. 14.14 Reading a random-access file sequentially.(Part 2 of 2.)

What about that additional benefit we promised? If you examine the output window, you will notice that the records are listed in sorted order (by account number). This is a consequence of how we stored these records in the file, using direct-access techniques. Compared to the bubble sort we used in Chapter 4, sorting using direct-access techniques is relatively fast. The speed is achieved by making the file large enough to hold every possible record that might be created. This of course means that the file could be occupied sparsely most of the time, resulting in a waste of storage. This is another example of the space-time trade-off: By using large amounts of space, we are able to develop a much faster sorting algorithm. Fortunately, the continuous reduction in price of storage units has made this less of an issue.

14.11 Example: A Transaction-Processing Program

We now present a substantial transaction-processing program (Fig. 14.15) using a random-access file to achieve "instant" access processing. The program maintains a bank's account information. The program updates existing accounts, adds new accounts, deletes accounts and stores a formatted listing of all current accounts in a text file. We assume that the program of Fig. 14.12 has been executed to create the file **credit.dat** and that the program of Fig. 14.13 has been executed to insert the initial data.

The program has five options (option 5 is for terminating the program). Option 1 calls function **printRecord** to store a formatted list of all the account information in a text file called **print.txt** that may be printed. Function **printRecord** (lines 115–152) takes an **fstream** object as an argument to be used to input data from the **credit.dat** file. Function **printRecord** invokes **istream** member function **read** (lines 147–148) and uses the sequential-file-access techniques of Fig. 14.14 to input data from **credit.dat**. Function **outputLine**, discussed in Section 14.10, is used to output the data to file **print.txt**. Note that **printRecord** uses **istream** member function **seekg** (line 132) to ensure that the file-position pointer is at the beginning of the file. After choosing Option 1, the **print.txt** file contains

```
Account      Last Name      First Name      Balance
29           Brown          Nancy            -24.54
33           Dunn           Stacey           314.33
37           Barker         Doug               0.00
88           Smith          Dave             258.34
96           Stone          Sam               34.98
```

Option 2 calls **updateRecord** (lines 155–199) to update an account. This function updates only an existing record, so the function first determines whether the specified record is empty. Lines 166–167 read data into object **client**, using **istream** member function **read**. Then line 170 compares the values returned by **getAccountNumber** of the **client** structure to zero to determine whether the record contains information. If this value is zero, lines 196–197 print a message that states that the record is empty. If the record contains information, line 171 displays the record, using function **outputLine**, line 176 inputs the transaction amount and lines 179–190 calculate the new balance and rewrite the record to the file. A typical output for Option 2 is

```
Enter account to update (1 - 100): 37
37         Barker              Doug                0.00

Enter charge (+) or payment (-): +87.99
37         Barker              Doug               87.99
```

Option 3 calls function **newRecord** (lines 202–251) to add a new account to the file. If the user enters an account number for an existing account, **newRecord** displays a message that the account exists (lines 248–249). This function adds a new account in the same manner as the program of Fig. 14.12. A typical output for Option 3 is

```
Enter new account number (1 - 100): 22
Enter lastname, firstname, balance
? Johnston Sarah 247.45
```

Option 4 calls function **deleteRecord** (lines 254–289) to delete a record from the file. Line 257 prompts the user to enter the account number. Only an existing record may be deleted, so, if the specified account is empty, line 287 displays an error message. If the account exists, lines 277–279 reinitialize that account by copying an empty record (**blankClient**) to the file. Line 281 displays a message to inform the user that the record has been deleted. A typical output for Option 4 is

```
Enter account to delete (1 - 100): 29
Account #29 deleted.
```

Note that line 44 opens the **credit.dat** file by creating an **fstream** object for reading and writing, using modes **ios::in** and **ios::out** "or-ed" together.

```
1   // Fig. 14.15: fig14_15.cpp
2   // This program reads a random access file sequentially, updates
3   // data previously written to the file, creates data to be placed
4   // in the file, and deletes data previously in the file.
5   #include <iostream>
6
7   using std::cout;
8   using std::cerr;
9   using std::cin;
10  using std::endl;
11  using std::ios;
12  using std::left;
13  using std::right;
14  using std::fixed;
15  using std::showpoint;
16
```

Fig. 14.15   Bank-account program.(Part 1 of 7.)

```
17  #include <fstream>
18
19  using std::ofstream;
20  using std::ostream;
21  using std::fstream;
22
23  #include <iomanip>
24
25  using std::setw;
26  using std::setprecision;
27
28  #include <cstdlib>        // exit prototype
29  #include "clientData.h"   // ClientData class definition
30
31  int enterChoice();
32  void printRecord( fstream& );
33  void updateRecord( fstream& );
34  void newRecord( fstream& );
35  void deleteRecord( fstream& );
36  void outputLine( ostream&, const ClientData & );
37  int getAccount( const char * const );
38
39  enum Choices { PRINT = 1, UPDATE, NEW, DELETE, END };
40
41  int main()
42  {
43     // open file for reading and writing
44     fstream inOutCredit( "credit.dat", ios::in | ios::out );
45
46     // exit program if fstream cannot open file
47     if ( !inOutCredit ) {
48        cerr << "File could not be opened." << endl;
49        exit ( 1 );
50
51     } // end if
52
53     int choice;
54
55     // enable user to specify action
56     while ( ( choice = enterChoice() ) != END ) {
57
58        switch ( choice ) {
59
60           // create text file from record file
61           case PRINT:
62              printRecord( inOutCredit );
63              break;
64
65           // update record
66           case UPDATE:
67              updateRecord( inOutCredit );
68              break;
69
```

Fig. 14.15   Bank-account program.(Part 2 of 7.)

```
70              // create record
71              case NEW:
72                  newRecord( inOutCredit );
73                  break;
74
75              // delete existing record
76              case DELETE:
77                  deleteRecord( inOutCredit );
78                  break;
79
80              // display error if user does not select valid choice
81              default:
82                  cerr << "Incorrect choice" << endl;
83                  break;
84
85          } // end switch
86
87          inOutCredit.clear(); // reset end-of-file indicator
88
89      } // end while
90
91      return 0;
92
93  } // end main
94
95  // enable user to input menu choice
96  int enterChoice()
97  {
98      // display available options
99      cout << "\nEnter your choice" << endl
100          << "1 - store a formatted text file of accounts" << endl
101          << "    called \"print.txt\" for printing" << endl
102          << "2 - update an account" << endl
103          << "3 - add a new account" << endl
104          << "4 - delete an account" << endl
105          << "5 - end program\n? ";
106
107     int menuChoice;
108     cin >> menuChoice; // receive choice from user
109
110     return menuChoice;
111
112 } // end function enterChoice
113
114 // create formatted text file for printing
115 void printRecord( fstream &readFromFile )
116 {
117     // create text file
118     ofstream outPrintFile( "print.txt", ios::out );
119
120     // exit program if ofstream cannot create file
121     if ( !outPrintFile ) {
122         cerr << "File could not be created." << endl;
```

Fig. 14.15 Bank-account program.(Part 3 of 7.)

```
123          exit( 1 );
124
125       } // end if
126
127       outPrintFile << left << setw( 10 ) << "Account" << setw( 16 )
128          << "Last Name" << setw( 11 ) << "First Name" << right
129          << setw( 10 ) << "Balance" << endl;
130
131       // set file-position pointer to beginning of record file
132       readFromFile.seekg( 0 );
133
134       // read first record from record file
135       ClientData client;
136       readFromFile.read( reinterpret_cast< char * >( &client ),
137          sizeof( ClientData ) );
138
139       // copy all records from record file into text file
140       while ( !readFromFile.eof() ) {
141
142          // write single record to text file
143          if ( client.getAccountNumber() != 0 )
144             outputLine( outPrintFile, client );
145
146          // read next record from record file
147          readFromFile.read( reinterpret_cast< char * >( &client ),
148             sizeof( ClientData ) );
149
150       } // end while
151
152    } // end function printRecord
153
154    // update balance in record
155    void updateRecord( fstream &updateFile )
156    {
157       // obtain number of account to update
158       int accountNumber = getAccount( "Enter account to update" );
159
160       // move file-position pointer to correct record in file
161       updateFile.seekg(
162          ( accountNumber - 1 ) * sizeof( ClientData ) );
163
164       // read first record from file
165       ClientData client;
166       updateFile.read( reinterpret_cast< char * >( &client ),
167          sizeof( ClientData ) );
168
169       // update record
170       if ( client.getAccountNumber() != 0 ) {
171          outputLine( cout, client );
172
173          // request user to specify transaction
174          cout << "\nEnter charge (+) or payment (-): ";
175          double transaction; // charge or payment
```

Fig. 14.15 Bank-account program.(Part 4 of 7.)

```
176         cin >> transaction;
177
178         // update record balance
179         double oldBalance = client.getBalance();
180         client.setBalance( oldBalance + transaction );
181         outputLine( cout, client );
182
183         // move file-position pointer to correct record in file
184         updateFile.seekp(
185             ( accountNumber - 1 ) * sizeof( ClientData ) );
186
187         // write updated record over old record in file
188         updateFile.write(
189             reinterpret_cast< const char * >( &client ),
190             sizeof( ClientData ) );
191
192     } // end if
193
194     // display error if account does not exist
195     else
196         cerr << "Account #" << accountNumber
197             << " has no information." << endl;
198
199 } // end function updateRecord
200
201 // create and insert record
202 void newRecord( fstream &insertInFile )
203 {
204     // obtain number of account to create
205     int accountNumber = getAccount( "Enter new account number" );
206
207     // move file-position pointer to correct record in file
208     insertInFile.seekg(
209         ( accountNumber - 1 ) * sizeof( ClientData ) );
210
211     // read record from file
212     ClientData client;
213     insertInFile.read( reinterpret_cast< char * >( &client ),
214         sizeof( ClientData ) );
215
216     // create record, if record does not previously exist
217     if ( client.getAccountNumber() == 0 ) {
218
219         char lastName[ 15 ];
220         char firstName[ 10 ];
221         double balance;
222
223         // user enters last name, first name and balance
224         cout << "Enter lastname, firstname, balance\n? ";
225         cin >> setw( 15 ) >> lastName;
226         cin >> setw( 10 ) >> firstName;
227         cin >> balance;
228
```

Fig. 14.15   Bank-account program.(Part 5 of 7.)

```
229        // use values to populate account values
230        client.setLastName( lastName );
231        client.setFirstName( firstName );
232        client.setBalance( balance );
233        client.setAccountNumber( accountNumber );
234
235        // move file-position pointer to correct record in file
236        insertInFile.seekp( ( accountNumber - 1 ) *
237           sizeof( ClientData ) );
238
239        // insert record in file
240        insertInFile.write(
241           reinterpret_cast< const char * >( &client ),
242           sizeof( ClientData ) );
243
244     } // end if
245
246     // display error if account previously exists
247     else
248        cerr << "Account #" << accountNumber
249           << " already contains information." << endl;
250
251  } // end function newRecord
252
253  // delete an existing record
254  void deleteRecord( fstream &deleteFromFile )
255  {
256     // obtain number of account to delete
257     int accountNumber = getAccount( "Enter account to delete" );
258
259     // move file-position pointer to correct record in file
260     deleteFromFile.seekg(
261        ( accountNumber - 1 ) * sizeof( ClientData ) );
262
263     // read record from file
264     ClientData client;
265     deleteFromFile.read( reinterpret_cast< char * >( &client ),
266        sizeof( ClientData ) );
267
268     // delete record, if record exists in file
269     if ( client.getAccountNumber() != 0 ) {
270        ClientData blankClient;
271
272        // move file-position pointer to correct record in file
273        deleteFromFile.seekp( ( accountNumber - 1 ) *
274           sizeof( ClientData ) );
275
276        // replace existing record with blank record
277        deleteFromFile.write(
278           reinterpret_cast< const char * >( &blankClient ),
279           sizeof( ClientData ) );
280
281        cout << "Account #" << accountNumber << " deleted.\n";
```

Fig. 14.15   Bank-account program.(Part 6 of 7.)

```
282
283      } // end if
284
285      // display error if record does not exist
286      else
287          cerr << "Account #" << accountNumber << " is empty.\n";
288
289   } // end deleteRecord
290
291   // display single record
292   void outputLine( ostream &output, const ClientData &record )
293   {
294       output << left << setw( 10 ) << record.getAccountNumber()
295              << setw( 16 ) << record.getLastName().data()
296              << setw( 11 ) << record.getFirstName().data()
297              << setw( 10 ) << setprecision( 2 ) << right << fixed
298              << showpoint << record.getBalance() << endl;
299
300   } // end function outputLine
301
302   // obtain account-number value from user
303   int getAccount( const char * const prompt )
304   {
305       int accountNumber;
306
307       // obtain account-number value
308       do {
309           cout << prompt << " (1 - 100): ";
310           cin >> accountNumber;
311
312       } while ( accountNumber < 1 || accountNumber > 100 );
313
314       return accountNumber;
315
316   } // end function getAccount
```

Fig. 14.15 Bank-account program.(Part 7 of 7.)

14.12 Input/Output of Objects

This chapter and Chapter 12 introduced C++'s object-oriented style of input/output. However, our examples concentrated on I/O of traditional data types rather than focusing on objects of user-defined types. In Chapter 8, we showed how to input and output objects using operator overloading. We accomplished object input by overloading the stream-extraction operator **>>** for the appropriate **istream**. We accomplished object output by overloading the stream-insertion operator **<<** for the appropriate **ostream**. In both cases, only an object's data members were input or output, and, in each case, they were in a format meaningful only for objects of that particular abstract data type. An object's member functions are available internally in the computer and are combined with the data values as these data are input via the overloaded stream-insertion operator.

When object data members are output to a disk file, we lose the object's type information. We store only data bytes, not type information, on a disk. If the program that reads this

Transaction file Account number	Transaction amount
100	27.14
300	62.11
400	100.56
900	82.17

14.9 Run the program of Exercise 14.7, using the files of test data created in Exercise 14.8. Print the new master file. Check that the accounts have been updated correctly.

14.10 It is possible (actually common) to have several transaction records with the same record key. This occurs because a particular customer might make several purchases and cash payments during a business period. Rewrite your accounts-receivable file-matching program of Exercise 14.7 to provide for the possibility of handling several transaction records with the same record key. Modify the test data of Exercise 14.8 to include the following additional transaction records:

Account number	Dollar amount
300	83.89
700	80.78
700	1.53

14.11 Write a series of statements that accomplish each of the following. Assume that we have defined class **Person** that contains **private** data members

```
char lastName[ 15 ];
char firstName[ 15 ];
char age[ 4 ];
```

and **public** member functions

```
// accessor functions for lastName
void setLastName( string );
string getLastName() const;

// accessor functions for firstName
void setFirstName( string );
string getFirstName() const;

// accessor functions for age
void setAge( string );
string getAge() const;
```

Also assume that any random-access files have been opened properly.
  a) Initialize the file **"nameage.dat"** with 100 records that store values **lastName = "unassigned"**, **firstName = ""** and **age = "0"**.
  b) Input 10 last names, first names and ages, and write them to the file.
  c) Update a record that already contains information. If the record does not contain information, inform the user **"No info"**.
  d) Delete a record that contains information by reinitializing that particular record.

14.12   You are the owner of a hardware store and need to keep an inventory that can tell you what different tools you have, how many of each you have on hand and the cost of each one. Write a program that initializes the random-access file **"hardware.dat"** to one hundred empty records, lets you input the data concerning each tool, enables you to list all your tools, lets you delete a record for a tool that you no longer have and lets you update *any* information in the file. The tool identification number should be the record number. Use the following information to start your file:

Record #	Tool name	Quantity	Cost
3	Electric sander	7	57.98
17	Hammer	76	11.99
24	Jig saw	21	11.00
39	Lawn mower	3	79.50
56	Power saw	18	99.99
68	Screwdriver	106	6.99
77	Sledge hammer	11	21.50
83	Wrench	34	7.50

14.13   Modify the telephone number word-generating program you wrote in Chapter 4 so that it writes its output to a file. This allows you to read the file at your convenience. If you have a computerized dictionary available, modify your program to look up the thousands of seven-letter words in the dictionary. Some of the interesting seven-letter combinations created by this program might consist of two or more words. For example, the phone number 8432677 produces "THEBOSS." Modify your program to use the computerized dictionary to check each possible seven-letter word to determine whether it is a valid one-letter word followed by a valid six-letter word, a valid two-letter word followed by a valid five-letter word and so on.

14.14   Write a program that uses the **sizeof** operator to determine the sizes in bytes of the various data types on your computer system. Write the results to the file **"datasize.dat"**, so that you may print the results later. The format for the results in the file should be

Data type	Size	Data type	Size
char	1	long int	4
unsigned char	1	unsigned long int	4
short int	2	float	4
unsigned short int	2	double	8
int	4	long double	16
unsigned int	4		

[*Note:* The sizes of the built-in data types on your computer might differ from those listed above.]

15

Class **string** and String Stream Processing

Objectives

- To use class **string** from the C++ standard library to treat strings as full-fledged objects.
- To assign, concatenate, compare, search and swap **string**s.
- To determine **string** characteristics.
- To find, replace and insert characters in a **string**.
- To convert **string**s to C-style strings.
- To use **string** iterators.
- To perform input from and output to **string**s in memory.

The difference between the almost-right word and the right word is really a large matter — it's the difference between the lightning bug and the lightning.
Mark Twain

I have made this letter longer than usual, because I lack the time to make it short.
Blaise Pascal

Mum's the word.
Miguel de Cervantes

Suit the action to the word, the word to the action; with this special observance, that you o'erstep not the modesty of nature.
William Shakespeare

Outline

15.1	Introduction
15.2	**string** Assignment and Concatenation
15.3	Comparing **strings**
15.4	Substrings
15.5	Swapping **strings**
15.6	**string** Characteristics
15.7	Finding Strings and Characters in a **string**
15.8	Replacing Characters in a **string**
15.9	Inserting Characters into a **string**
15.10	Conversion to C-Style **char *** Strings
15.11	Iterators
15.12	String Stream Processing

Summary • Terminology • Self-Review Exercises • Answers to Self-Review Exercises • Exercises

15.1 Introduction

The C++ template class **basic_string** provides typical string-manipulation operations such as copying, searching, etc. The template definition and all support facilities are defined in **namespace std**; these include the **typedef** statement

```
typedef basic_string< char > string;
```

that creates the alias type **string** for **basic_string< char >**. A **typedef** also is provided for the **wchar_t** type. Type **wchar_t**[1] stores characters (e.g., two-byte characters, four-byte characters, etc.) for supporting other character sets. We use **string** exclusively throughout this chapter. To use **string**s, include header file **<string>**.

A **string** object can be initialized with a constructor argument such as

```
string text( "Hello" );  // creates string from const char *
```

which creates a **string** containing the characters in **"Hello"** except, perhaps, the terminating **'\0'**, or with two constructor arguments as in

```
string name( 8, 'x' );  // string of 8 'x' characters
```

which creates a **string** containing eight **'x'** characters. Class **string** also provides a default constructor and a copy constructor.

---

1. Type **wchar_t** commonly is used to represent Unicode®, which does have 16-bit characters, but the size of **wchar_t** is not fixed by the standard. The Unicode Standard outlines a specification to produce consistent encoding of the world's characters and symbols. To learn more about the Unicode Standard, visit **www.unicode.org**.

A **string** also can be initialized via the alternate construction syntax in the definition of a **string** as in

```
string month = "March";  // same as: string month( "March" );
```

Remember that operator **=** in the preceding declaration is not an assignment; rather it is an implicit call to the **string** class constructor, which does the conversion.

Note that class **string** provides no conversions from **int** or **char** to **string** in a **string** definition. For example, the definitions

```
string error1 = 'c';
string error2( 'u' );
string error3 = 22;
string error4( 8 );
```

result in syntax errors. Note that assigning a single character to a **string** object is permitted in an assignment statement as in

```
string1 = 'n';
```

Common Programming Error 15.1

*Attempting to convert an **int** or **char** to a **string** via an assignment in a declaration or via a constructor argument is a syntax error.*

Unlike C-style **char *** strings, **string**s are not necessarily null terminated.[2] The length of a **string** is a data member of the **string** object and can be retrieved with member function **length**.[3] The subscript operator, **[]**, can be used with **string**s to access individual characters. Like C-style strings, **string**s have a first subscript of **0** and a last subscript of **length–1**.

Most **string** member functions take as arguments a starting subscript location and the number of characters on which to operate.

The stream extraction operator (**>>**) is overloaded to support **string**s. The statement

```
string stringObject;
cin >> stringObject;
```

reads a **string** from the standard input device. Input is delimited by whitespace characters. When a delimiter is encountered, the input operation is terminated. Function **getline** also is overloaded for **string**s. The statement

```
string string1;
getline( cin, string1 );
```

reads a **string** from the keyboard into **string1**. Input is delimited by a newline (**'\n'**).

15.2 **string** Assignment and Concatenation

Figure 15.1 demonstrates **string** assignment and concatenation. Line 8 includes header **string** for class **string**. The **string**s **string1**, **string2** and **string3** are cre-

---

2. The C++ standard provides only a description of the interface for class **string**—implementation is platform dependent.

3. Class **string** also provides member function **size**, which returns the same value as **length**.

ated in lines 14–17. Line 18 assigns **string1** to **string2**. After the assignment takes place, **string2** is a copy of **string1**. Line 19 uses member function *assign* to copy **string1** into **string3**. A separate copy is made (i.e., **string1** and **string3** are independent objects). Class **string** also provides an overloaded version of member function **assign** that copies a specified number of characters as in

```
myString.assign( stringObject, start, numberOfCharacters );
```

where **stringObject** is the **string** to be copied, **start** is the starting subscript and **numberOfCharacters** is the number of characters to copy.

```cpp
1   // Fig. 15.1: fig15_01.cpp
2   // Demonstrating string assignment and concatenation.
3   #include <iostream>
4
5   using std::cout;
6   using std::endl;
7
8   #include <string>
9
10  using std::string;
11
12  int main()
13  {
14     string string1( "cat" );
15     string string2;
16     string string3;
17
18     string2 = string1;          // assign string1 to string2
19     string3.assign( string1 );  // assign string1 to string3
20     cout << "string1: " << string1 << "\nstring2: " << string2
21          << "\nstring3: " << string3 << "\n\n";
22
23     // modify string2 and string3
24     string2[ 0 ] = string3[ 2 ] = 'r';
25
26     cout << "After modification of string2 and string3:\n"
27          << "string1: " << string1 << "\nstring2: " << string2
28          << "\nstring3: ";
29
30     // demonstrating member function at
31     for ( int i = 0; i < string3.length(); i++ )
32        cout << string3.at( i );
33
34     // declare string4 and string5
35     string string4( string1 + "apult" );
36     string string5;
37
38     // overloaded +=
39     string3 += "pet";              // create "carpet"
40     string1.append( "acomb" );     // create "catacomb"
```

Fig. 15.1   Demonstrating **string** assignment and concatenation. (Part 1 of 2.)

```
41
42        // append subscript locations 4 through end of string1 to
43        // create string "comb" (string5 was initially empty)
44        string5.append( string1, 4, string1.length() );
45
46        cout << "\n\nAfter concatenation:\nstring1: " << string1
47             << "\nstring2: " << string2 << "\nstring3: "
48             << string3 << "\nstring4: " << string4
49             << "\nstring5: " << string5 << endl;
50
51        return 0;
52
53   } // end main
```

```
string1: cat
string2: cat
string3: cat

After modification of string2 and string3:
string1: cat
string2: rat
string3: car

After concatenation:
string1: catacomb
string2: rat
string3: carpet
string4: catapult
string5: comb
```

Fig. 15.1   Demonstrating **string** assignment and concatenation. (Part 2 of 2.)

Line 24 uses the subscript operator to assign **'r'** to **string3[2]** (forming **"car"**) and to assign **'r'** to **string2[0]** (forming **"rat"**). The **string**s are then output.

Lines 31–32 output the contents of **string3** one character at a time using member function **at**. Member function **at** provides *checked access* (or *range checking*), i.e., going past the end of the **string** throws an **out_of_range** exception. (See Chapter 13 for a detailed discussion of exception handling.) Note that the subscript operator, **[ ]**, does not provide checked access. This is consistent with its use on arrays.

Common Programming Error 15.2

*Accessing a **string** subscript outside the bounds of the **string** using function **at** throws an **out_of_range** exception.*

Common Programming Error 15.3

*Accessing an element beyond the size of the **string** using the subscript operator is a logic error.*

String **string4** is declared (line 35) and initialized to the result of concatenating **string1** and **"apult"** using the overloaded addition operator, **+**, which for class **string** denotes concatenation. Line 39 uses the addition assignment operator, **+=**, to concatenate **string3** and **"pet"**. Line 40 uses member function **append** to concatenate **string1** and **"acomb"**.

Line 44 appends the string **"comb"** to empty **string string5**. An *empty* **string** is a **string** that does not contain any characters.

This member function is passed the **string** (**string1**) to retrieve characters from, the starting subscript in the **string** (**4**) and the number of characters to append (the value returned by **string1.length()**).

15.3 Comparing **strings**

Class **string** provides member functions for comparing **string**s. Figure 15.2 demonstrates class **string**'s comparison capabilities.

The program declares four **string**s with lines 14–17 and outputs each **string** (lines 19–21). The condition in line 24 tests **string1** against **string4** for equality using the overloaded equality operator. If the condition is **true**, **"string1 == string4"** is output. If the condition is **false**, the condition in line 27 is tested. All the **string** class overloaded operator functions demonstrated here as well as those not demonstrated here (**!=**, **<**, **>=** and **<=**) return **bool** values.

Line 34 uses **string** member function **compare** to compare **string1** to **string2**. Variable **result** is assigned **0** if the **string**s are equivalent, a positive number if **string1** is *lexicographically* greater than **string2** or a negative number if **string1** is lexicographically less than **string2**. Because a **string** starting with **'T'** is considered lexicographically greater than a string starting with **'H'**, so **result** is assigned a value greater than **0**, as is confirmed by the output.

```
1   // Fig. 15.2: fig15_02.cpp
2   // Demonstrating string comparison capabilities.
3   #include <iostream>
4
5   using std::cout;
6   using std::endl;
7
8   #include <string>
9
10  using std::string;
11
12  int main()
13  {
14     string string1( "Testing the comparison functions." );
15     string string2( "Hello" );
16     string string3( "stinger" );
17     string string4( string2 );
18
19     cout << "string1: " << string1 << "\nstring2: " << string2
20          << "\nstring3: " << string3 << "\nstring4: " << string4
21          << "\n\n";
22
```

Fig. 15.2   Comparing **strings**. (Part 1 of 3.)

```
Original string:
The values in any left subtree
are less than the value in the
parent node and the values in
any right subtree are greater
than the value in the parent node

Original string after erase:
The values in any left subtree
are less than the value in the


After first replacement:
The.values.in.any.left.subtree
are.less.than.the.value.in.the


After second replacement:
The;;alues;;n;;ny;;eft;;ubtree
are;;ess;;han;;he;;alue;;n;;he
```

Fig. 15.7   Demonstrating functions **erase** and **replace**. (Part 2 of 2.)

15.9 Inserting Characters into a **string**

Class **string** provides member functions for inserting characters into a **string**. Figure 15.8 demonstrates the **string insert** capabilities.

```cpp
1   // Fig. 15.8: fig15_08.cpp
2   // Demonstrating class string insert member functions.
3   #include <iostream>
4
5   using std::cout;
6   using std::endl;
7
8   #include <string>
9
10  using std::string;
11
12  int main()
13  {
14     string string1( "beginning end" );
15     string string2( "middle " );
16     string string3( "12345678" );
17     string string4( "xx" );
18
19     cout << "Initial strings:\nstring1: " << string1
20          << "\nstring2: " << string2 << "\nstring3: " << string3
21          << "\nstring4: " << string4 << "\n\n";
22
```

Fig. 15.8   Demonstrating the **string insert** member functions. (Part 1 of 2.)

```
23      // insert "middle" at location 10 in string1
24      string1.insert( 10, string2 );
25
26      // insert "xx" at location 3 in string3
27      string3.insert( 3, string4, 0, string::npos );
28
29      cout << "Strings after insert:\nstring1: " << string1
30           << "\nstring2: " << string2 << "\nstring3: " << string3
31           << "\nstring4: " << string4 << endl;
32
33      return 0;
34
35   } // end main
```

```
Initial strings:
string1: beginning end
string2: middle
string3: 12345678
string4: xx

Strings after insert:
string1: beginning middle end
string2: middle
string3: 123xx45678
string4: xx
```

Fig. 15.8　Demonstrating the **string insert** member functions. (Part 2 of 2.)

The program declares, initializes then outputs **string**s **string1**, **string2**, **string3** and **string4**. Line 24 uses **string** member function *insert* to insert **string2**'s content before element 10 of **string1**.

Line 27 uses **insert** to insert **string4** before **string3**'s element 3. The last two arguments specify the starting element of **string4** and the number of characters from **string4** that should be inserted.

15.10 Conversion to C-Style **char** * Strings

Class **string** provides member functions for converting **string**s to C-style strings. As mentioned earlier, unlike C-style strings, **string**s are not necessarily null terminated. These conversion functions are useful when a given function takes a C-style string as an argument. Figure 15.9 demonstrates conversion of **string**s to C-style strings.

```
1    // Fig. 15.9: fig15_09.cpp
2    // Converting to C-style strings.
3    #include <iostream>
4
5    using std::cout;
6    using std::endl;
7
```

Fig. 15.9　Converting **string**s to C-style strings and character arrays. (Part 1 of 2.)

```
 8   #include <string>
 9
10   using std::string;
11
12   int main()
13   {
14       string string1( "STRINGS" );
15       const char *ptr1 = 0;
16       int length = string1.length();
17       char *ptr2 = new char[ length + 1 ];   // including null
18
19       // copy characters from string1 into allocated memory
20       string1.copy( ptr2, length, 0 );
21       ptr2[ length ] = '\0';   // add null terminator
22
23       // output
24       cout << "string s is " << string1
25           << "\nstring1 converted to a C-Style string is "
26           << string1.c_str() << "\nptr1 is ";
27
28       // Assign to pointer ptr1 the const char * returned by
29       // function data(). NOTE: this is a potentially dangerous
30       // assignment. If string1 is modified, pointer ptr1 can
31       // become invalid.
32       ptr1 = string1.data();
33
34       // output each character using pointer
35       for ( int i = 0; i < length; i++ )
36          cout << *( ptr1 + i );      // use pointer arithmetic
37
38       cout << "\nptr2 is " << ptr2 << endl;
39       delete [] ptr2;
40       return 0;
41
42   }   // end main
```

```
string s is STRINGS
string1 converted to a C-Style string is STRINGS
ptr1 is STRINGS
ptr2 is STRINGS
```

Fig. 15.9   Converting **string**s to C-style strings and character arrays. (Part 2 of 2.)

The program declares a **string**, an **int** and two **char** pointers. The **string**
string1 is initialized to **"STRINGS"**, **ptr1** is initialized to **0** and **length** is initialized
to the length of **string1**. Memory of sufficient size to hold a C-style string equivalent of
string string1 is allocated dynamically and attached to pointer **char ptr2**.

Line 20 uses **string** member function *copy* to copy **string1** into the **char** array
pointed to by **ptr2**. Line 21 places a terminating null character in the array pointed to by
ptr2.

The first stream insertion (line 26) displays the null-terminated **const char ***
returned from *c_str* when **string string1** is converted to a C-style string.

Line 32 assigns the **const char * ptr1** a pointer returned by member function **data** to a non-null terminated C-style character array. Note that we do not modify **string string1** in this example. If **string1** were to be modified (e.g., the **string**'s dynamic memory changes its address due to a member function call such as **string1.insert(0, "abcd");**), **ptr1** could become invalid—which could lead to unpredictable results.

Lines 35–36 use pointer arithmetic to output the array pointed to by **ptr1**. In lines 38–39, the C-style string pointed to by **ptr2** is output and the memory allocated for **ptr2** is **delete**d to avoid a memory leak.

Common Programming Error 15.4

Not terminating the character array returned by **data** *with a null character can lead to execution-time errors.*

Good Programming Practice 15.1

Whenever possible, use the more robust **string***s rather than C-style strings.*

Common Programming Error 15.5

Converting **string***s that contain one or more null characters to C-style strings can cause logic errors, because null characters are interpreted as terminators for C-style strings.*

15.11 Iterators

Class **string** provides *iterators* for forward and backward traversal of **string**s. Iterators provide access to individual characters with syntax that is similar to pointer operations. Iterators are not range checked. Note that in this section we provide "mechanical examples" to demonstrate the use of iterators. We discuss more robust uses of iterators in Chapter 20. Figure 15.10 demonstrates iterators.

Lines 14–15 declare **string string1** and ***string::const_iterator iterator1***. A **const_iterator** is an iterator that cannot modify the container—in this case the **string**—through which it is iterating. Iterator **iterator1** is initialized to the beginning of **string1** with the **string** class member function *begin*. Two versions of **begin** exist—one that returns an ***iterator*** for iterating through a non-**const string** and a **const** version that returns a **const_iterator** for iterating through a **const string**. Line 17 outputs **string1**.

```
1   // Fig. 15.10: fig15_10.cpp
2   // Using an iterator to output a string.
3   #include <iostream>
4
5   using std::cout;
6   using std::endl;
7
8   #include <string>
9
10  using std::string;
11
```

Fig. 15.10 Using an iterator to output a **string**. (Part 1 of 2.)

```
12   int main()
13   {
14      string string1( "Testing iterators" );
15      string::const_iterator iterator1 = string1.begin();
16
17      cout << "string1 = " << string1
18           << "\n(Using iterator iterator1) string1 is: ";
19
20      // iterate through string
21      while ( iterator1 != string1.end() ) {
22         cout << *iterator1;   // dereference iterator to get char
23         ++iterator1;   // advance iterator to next char
24      } // end while
25
26      cout << endl;
27      return 0;
28
29   }  // end main
```

```
string1 = Testing iterators
(Using iterator iterator1) string1 is: Testing iterators
```

Fig. 15.10 Using an iterator to output a **string**. (Part 2 of 2.)

Lines 21–24 use the iterator **iterator1** to "walk through" **string1**. Class **string** member function **end** returns an iterator at the first position after the last element of **string1**. The contents of each element are printed by dereferencing the iterator much as you would dereference a pointer, and the iterator is advanced one position using operator **++**.

Class **string** provides member functions **rend** and **rbegin** for accessing individual **string** characters in reverse from the end of a **string** towards the beginning of a **string**. Member functions **rend** and **rbegin** can return *reverse_iterator*s and *const_reverse_iterator*s (based on whether the **string** is non-**const** or **const**). In the exercises, we ask the reader to write a program that demonstrate these capabilities. We will use iterators and reverse iterators more in Chapter 20.

Testing and Debugging Tip 15.1

*Use **string** member function **at** (rather than iterators) when you want the benefit of range checking.*

15.12 String Stream Processing

In addition to standard stream I/O and file stream I/O, C++ stream I/O includes capabilities for inputting from **string**s in memory and outputting to **string**s in memory. These capabilities often are referred to as *in-memory I/O* or *string stream processing*.

Input from a **string** is supported by class *istringstream*. Output to a **string** is supported by class *ostringstream*. The class names **istringstream** and **ostringstream** are actually aliases. These names are defined with the **typedef**s

```
typedef basic_istringstream< char > istringstream;
typedef basic_ostringstream< char > ostringstream;
```

Classes **basic_istringstream** and **basic_ostringstream** provide the same functionality as classes **istream** and **ostream** plus other member functions specific to in-memory formatting. Programs that use in-memory formatting must include the **<sstream>** and **<iostream>** header files.

One application of these techniques is data validation. A program can read an entire line at a time from the input stream into a **string**. Next, a validation routine can scrutinize the contents of the **string** and correct (or repair) the data, if necessary. Then the program can proceed to input from the **string**, knowing that the input data is in the proper format.

Outputting to a **string** is a nice way to take advantage of the powerful output formatting capabilities of C++ streams. Data can be prepared in a **string** to mimic the edited screen format. That **string** could be written to a disk file to preserve the screen image.

An **ostringstream** object uses a **string** object to store the data that are output. The **ostringstream** member function **str** returns a **string** copy of the **string**.

Figure 15.11 demonstrates an **ostringstream** object. The program creates **ostringstream** object **outputString** (line 18) and uses the stream-insertion operator to output a series of **string**s and numerical values to the object.

```
1   // Fig. 15.11: fig15_11.cpp
2   // Using a dynamically allocated ostringstream object.
3   #include <iostream>
4
5   using std::cout;
6   using std::endl;
7
8   #include <string>
9
10  using std::string;
11
12  #include <sstream>
13
14  using std::ostringstream;
15
16  int main()
17  {
18     ostringstream outputString;   // create ostringstream instance
19
20     string string1( "Output of several data types " );
21     string string2( "to an ostringstream object:" );
22     string string3( "\n          double: " );
23     string string4( "\n             int: " );
24     string string5( "\naddress of int: " );
25
26     double double1 = 123.4567;
27     int integer = 22;
28
29     // output strings, double and int to outputString
30     outputString << string1 << string2 << string3 << double1
31                  << string4 << integer << string5 << &integer;
32
```

Fig. 15.11 Using a dynamically allocated **ostringstream** object. (Part 1 of 2.)

```
33        // call str to output contents
34        cout << "outputString contains:\n" << outputString.str();
35
36        // add additional characters and call str to output string
37        outputString << "\nmore characters added";
38        cout << "\n\nafter additional stream insertions,\n"
39             << "outputString contains:\n" << outputString.str()
40             << endl;
41
42        return 0;
43
44   }  // end main
```

```
outputString contains:
Output of several data types to an ostringstream object:
        double: 123.457
           int: 22
address of int: 0012FE94

after additional stream insertions,
outputString contains:
Output of several data types to an ostringstream object:
        double: 123.457
           int: 22
address of int: 0012FE94
more characters added
```

Fig. 15.11 Using a dynamically allocated **ostringstream** object. (Part 2 of 2.)

Lines 30–31 output **string string1, string string2, string string3, double double1, string string4, int integer, string string5** and the address of **int integer**, all to **outputString** in memory. Line 34 uses the call **outputString.str()** to output a copy of the **string** created in lines 30–31. Line 37 demonstrates that more data can be appended to the **string** in memory by simply issuing another stream insertion operation to **outputString**. Lines 38–40 output **string outputString** after appending additional characters.

An **istringstream** object inputs data from a **string** in memory to program variables. The data is stored in an **istringstream** object as characters. Input from the **istringstream** object works identically to input from any file, in general, or from standard input, in particular. The end of the **string** is interpreted by the **istringstream** object as end-of-file.

Figure 15.12 demonstrates input from an **istringstream** object. Lines 18–19 create **string input** containing the data and **istringstream** object **inputString** constructed to contain the data in **string input**. The **string input** contains the data

```
Input test 123 4.7 A
```

which when read as input to the program consist of two strings (**"Input"** and **"test"**), an **int** value (**123**), a **double** value (**4.7**) and a **char** value (**'A'**). These characters are extracted to variables **string1**, **string2**, **integer**, **double1** and **character**, respectively, in lines 26–27.

```cpp
1   // Fig. 15.12: fig15_12.cpp
2   // Demonstrating input from an istringstream object.
3   #include <iostream>
4
5   using std::cout;
6   using std::endl;
7
8   #include <string>
9
10  using std::string;
11
12  #include <sstream>
13
14  using std::istringstream;
15
16  int main()
17  {
18      string input( "Input test 123 4.7 A" );
19      istringstream inputString( input );
20      string string1;
21      string string2;
22      int integer;
23      double double1;
24      char character;
25
26      inputString >> string1 >> string2 >> integer >> double1
27                  >> character;
28
29      cout << "The following items were extracted\n"
30           << "from the istringstream object:"
31           << "\nstring: " << string1
32           << "\nstring: " << string2
33           << "\n   int: " << integer
34           << "\ndouble: " << double1
35           << "\n  char: " << character;
36
37      // attempt to read from empty stream
38      long value;
39
40      inputString >> value;
41
42      // test stream results
43      if ( inputString.good() )
44          cout << "\n\nlong value is: " << value << endl;
45      else
46          cout << "\n\ninputString is empty" << endl;
47
48      return 0;
49
50  } // end main
```

Fig. 15.12 Demonstrating input from an **istringstream** object. (Part 1 of 2.)

```
The following items were extracted
from the istringstream object:
string: Input
string: test
   int: 123
double: 4.7
  char: A

inputString is empty
```

Fig. 15.12 Demonstrating input from an **istringstream** object. (Part 2 of 2.)

The data is then output in lines 29–35. The program attempts to read from **input-String** again in line 40. Because no data remain, the **if** condition (line 43) evaluates as **false** and the **else** part of the **if/else** structure is executed.

SUMMARY

- C++ template class **basic_string** provides typical string-manipulation operations such as copying, searching, etc.
- The **typedef** statement

      typedef basic_string< char > string;

  creates the type **string** for **basic_string< char >**. A **typedef** also is provided for the **wchar_t** type. Type **wchar_t** normally stores two-byte (16-bit) characters for supporting other character sets. The size of **wchar_t** is not fixed by the standard.
- To use **string**s, include C++ standard library header file **<string>**.
- Class **string** provides no conversions from **int** or **char** to **string**.
- Assigning a single character to a **string** object is permitted in an assignment statement.
- **string**s are not necessarily null terminated.
- Most **string** member functions take as arguments a starting subscript location and the number of characters on which to operate.
- Class **string** provides overloaded **operator=** and member function **assign** for **string** assignments.
- The subscript operator, **[]**, provides read/write access to any element of a **string**.
- **string** member function **at** provides checked access—going past either end of the **string** throws an **out_of_range** exception. The subscript operator (**[]**) does not provide checked access.
- Class **string** provides the overloaded **+** and **+=** operators and member function **append** to perform **string** concatenation.
- Class **string** provides overloaded **==**, **!=**, **<**, **>**, **<=** and **>=** operators for **string** comparisons.
- **string** function **compare** compares two **string**s (or substrings) and returns **0** if the **string**s are equal, a positive number if the first **string** is lexicographically greater than the second or a negative number if the first string is lexicographically less than the second.
- **string** member function **substr** retrieves a substring from a **string**.
- **string** member function **swap** swaps the contents of two **string**s.

- **string** member functions **size** and **length** return the size or length of a **string** (i.e., the number of characters currently stored in the **string**).

- **string** member function **capacity** returns the total number of characters that can be stored in the **string** without increasing the amount of memory allocated to the **string**.

- **string** member function **max_size** returns the maximum size a **string** can have.

- **string** member function **resize** changes the length of a **string**.

- Class **string** find functions **find**, **rfind**, **find_first_of**, **find_last_of**, **find_first_not_of** and **find_last_not_of** locate substrings or characters in a **string**.

- **string** member function **erase** deletes elements of a **string**.

- **string** member function **replace** replaces characters in a **string**.

- **string** member function **insert** inserts characters in a **string**.

- **string** member function **c_str** returns a **const char *** pointing to a null-terminated C-style character string that contains all the characters in a **string**.

- **string** member function **data** returns a **const char *** pointing to a non-null-terminated C-style character array that contains all the characters in a **string**.

- Class **string** provides member functions **end** and **begin** to iterate through individual elements.

- Class **string** provides member functions **rend** and **rbegin** for accessing individual **string** characters in reverse from the end of a **string** towards the beginning of a **string**.

- Input from a **string** is supported by type **istringstream**. Output to a **string** is supported by type **ostringstream**.

- **ostringstream** member function **str** returns a **string** copy of a **string**.

TERMINOLOGY

access member function of class **string**
at member function of class **string**
c_str member function of class **string**
capacity
capacity member function of class **string**
checked access
compare member function of class **string**
const_iterator
const_reverse_iterator
data member function of class **string**
empty member function of class **string**
empty string
equality operators: **==**, **!=**
erase member function of class **string**
find member function of class **string**
find_first_not_of member function of class **string**
find_first_of member function of class **string**
find_last_not_of member function of class **string**

find_last_of member function of class **string**
getline member function of class **string**
in-memory I/O
insert member function of class **string**
istringstream class
iterator
length member function of class **string**
length of a **string**
length_error exception
max_size member function of class **string**
maximum size of a **string**
operators: **+**, **+=**, **<<**, **>>**, **[]**
ostringstream class
out_of_range exception
range_error exception
rbegin member function of class **string**
relational operators: **>**, **<**, **>=**, **<=**
rend member function of class **string**
replace member function of class **string**
resize member function of class **string**

15.14 Write a program that inputs a **string** and prints the **string** backwards. Convert all uppercase characters to lowercase and all lowercase characters to uppercase.

15.15 Write a program that uses the comparison capabilities introduced in this chapter to alphabetize a series of animal names. Only uppercase letters should be used for the comparisons.

15.16 Write a program that creates a cryptogram out of a **string**. A cryptogram is a message or word where each letter is replaced with another letter. For example the **string**

> **The birds name was squawk**

might be scrambled to form

> **xms kbypo zhqs fho obrhfu**

Note that spaces are not scrambled. In this particular case, **'T'** was replaced with **'x'**, each **'a'** was replaced with **'h'**, etc. Uppercase letters become lowercase letters in the cryptogram. Use techniques similar to those in Exercise 15.7.

15.17 Modify Exercise 15.16 to allow users to solve the cryptogram. Users should input two characters at a time: The first character specifies a letter in the cryptogram, and the second letter specifies the replacement letter. If the replacement letter is correct, substitute the letter in the cryptogram with the replacement letter in uppercase.

15.18 Write a program that inputs a sentence and counts the number of palindromes in the sentence. A palindrome is a word that reads the same backwards and forwards. For example, **"tree"** is not a palindrome but **"noon"** is.

15.19 Write a program that counts the total number of vowels in a sentence. Output the frequency of each vowel.

15.20 Write a program that inserts the characters **"******"** in the exact middle of a **string**.

15.21 Write a program that erases the sequences **"by"** and **"BY"** from a **string**.

15.22 Write a program that inputs a line of text, replaces all punctuation marks with spaces and uses the C-string library function **strtok** to tokenize the **string** into individual words.

15.23 Write a program that inputs a line of text and prints the text backwards. Use iterators in your solution.

15.24 Write a recursive version of Exercise 15.23.

15.25 Write a program that demonstrates the use of the **erase** functions that take **iterator** arguments.

15.26 Write a program that generates the following from the **string "abcdefghijklm-nopqrstuvwxyz{"**:

```
            a
           bcb
          cdedc
         defgfed
        efghihgfe
       fghijkjihgf
      ghijklmlkjihg
     hijklmnonmlkjih
    ijklmnopqponmlkji
   jklmnopqrsrqponmlkj
  klmnopqrstutsrqponmlk
 lmnopqrstuvwvutsrqponml
mnopqrstuvwxyxwvutsrqponm
nopqrstuvwxyz{zyxwvutsrqpon
```

15.27 In Exercise 15.7, we asked you to write a simple encryption algorithm. Write a program that will attempt to decrypt a "rot13" message using simple frequency substitution. (Assume that you do not know the key.) The most frequent letters in the encrypted phrase should be substituted with the most commonly used English letters (a, e, i, o, u, s, t, r, etc.). Write the possibilities to a file. What made the code breaking easy? How can the encryption mechanism be improved?

15.28 Write a version of the bubble sort routine (Fig. 5.15) that sorts **string**s. Use function **swap** in your solution.

15.29 Modify class **Employee** in Fig. 10.23–Fig. 10.24 by adding **private** utility function called **isValidSocialSecurityNumber**. This member function should validate the format of a social security number (e.g., **###-##-####**, where **#** is a digit). If the format is valid, return **true**; otherwise return **false**.

16

Web Programming with CGI

Objectives

- To understand the Common Gateway Interface (CGI) protocol.
- To understand the Hypertext Transfer Protocol (HTTP) and to use HTTP headers.
- To understand a Web server's functionality.
- To introduce the Apache HTTP Server.
- To request documents from a Web server.
- To implement a simple CGI script.
- To send input to CGI scripts using XHTML forms.

This is the common air that bathes the globe.
Walt Whitman

The longest part of the journey is said to be the passing of the gate.
Marcus Terentius Varro

Railway termini... are our gates to the glorious and unknown. Through them we pass out into adventure and sunshine, to them, alas! we return.
E. M. Forster

There comes a time in a man's life when to get where he has to go—if there are no doors or windows—he walks through a wall.
Bernard Malamud

Outline

16.1   Introduction

16.2   HTTP Request Types

16.3   Multi-Tier Architecture

16.4   Accessing Web Servers

16.5   Apache HTTP Server

16.6   Requesting XHTML Documents

16.7   Introduction to CGI

16.8   Simple HTTP Transaction

16.9   Simple CGI Script

16.10   Sending Input to a CGI Script

16.11   Using XHTML Forms to Send Input

16.12   Other Headers

16.13   Case Study: An Interactive Web Page

16.14   Cookies

16.15   Server-Side Files

16.16   Case Study: Shopping Cart

16.17   Internet and Web Resources

Summary • Terminology • Self-Review Exercises • Answers to Self-Review Exercises • Exercises

16.1 Introduction

With the advent of the World Wide Web, the Internet gained tremendous popularity. This greatly increased the volume of requests users made for information from Web sites. It became evident that the degree of interactivity between the user and the Web site would be crucial. The power of the Web resides not only in serving content to users, but also in responding to requests from users and generating Web content dynamically.

In this chapter, we discuss specialized software—called a *Web server*—that responds to client (e.g., Web browser) requests by providing resources (e.g., XHTML[1] documents). For example, when users enter a *Uniform Resource Locator* (*URL*) address, such as **www.deitel.com**, into a Web browser, they are requesting a specific document from a Web server. The Web server maps the URL to a file on the server (or to a file on the server's network) and returns the requested document to the client. During this interaction, the Web server and the client communicate through the platform-independent *Hypertext Transfer Protocol* (*HTTP*), a protocol for transferring requests and files over the Internet (i.e., between Web servers and Web browsers).

---

1. The Extensible HyperText Markup Language (XHTML) has replaced the HyperText Markup Language (HTML) as the primary way of describing Web content. Readers not familiar with XHTML should read Appendix E, Introduction to XHTML, before reading this chapter.

Our Web-server discussion introduces the *Apache HTTP Server*. For illustration purposes, we use Internet Explorer to request documents and, later, to display content returned from "CGI scripts."

16.2 HTTP Request Types

HTTP defines several request types (also known as *request methods*), each of which specifies how a client makes requests from a server. The two most common are *get* and *post*. These request types retrieve and send client form data from and to a Web server. A form is an XHTML element that may contain text fields, radio buttons, check boxes and other graphical user interface components that allow users to enter data into a Web page. Forms can also contain hidden fields, not exposed as GUI components. A *get* request is used to send data to the server. A *post* request also is used to send data to the server. A *get* request sends form data as part of the URL (e.g., **www.searchsomething.com/search?query=***userquery*). In this fictitious request, the information following the **?** (**query=***userquery*) indicates user-specified input. For example, if the user performs a search on "Massachusetts," the last part of the URL would be **?query=Massachusetts**. A *get* request limits the *query string* (e.g., **query=Massachusetts**) to a predefined number of characters. This limit varies from server to server. If the query string exceeds this limit, a *post* request must be used.

Software Engineering Observation 16.1

The data sent in a post *request is not part of the URL and cannot be seen by users. Forms that contain many fields often are submitted via a* post *request. Sensitive form fields, such as passwords, usually are sent using this request type.*

An HTTP request often sends data to a *server-side form handler* that processes the data. For example, when a user participates in a Web-based survey, the Web server receives the information specified in the form as part of the request and processes the survey in the form handler.

Browsers often *cache* (save on a local disk) Web pages for quick reloading, to reduce the amount of data that the browser needs to download. However, browsers typically do not cache the responses to *post* requests, because subsequent *post* requests might not contain the same information. For example, users participating in a Web-based survey may request the same Web page. Each user's response changes the overall results of the survey, thus the information presented in the resulting Web page is different for each request.

Web browsers often cache the server's responses to *get* requests. A static Web page, such as a course syllabus, is cached in the event that the user requests the same resource again.

16.3 Multi-Tier Architecture

A Web server is part of a *multi-tier application*, sometimes referred to as an *n-tier* application. Multi-tier applications divide functionality into separate tiers (i.e., logical groupings of functionality). Tiers can be located on the same computer or on separate computers. Figure 16.1 presents the basic structure of a three-tier application.

The *information tier* (also called the *data tier* or the *bottom tier*) maintains data for the application. This tier typically stores data in a *relational database management system (RDBMS)*. For example, a retail store might have a database of product information, such

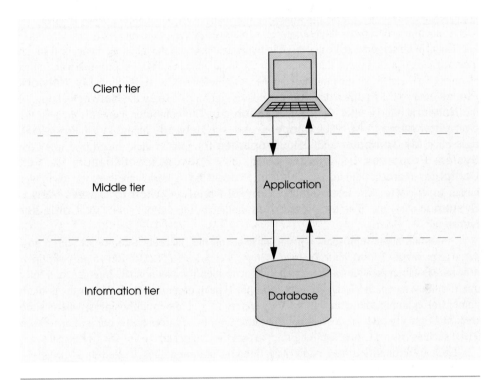

Fig. 16.1   Three-tier application model.

as descriptions, prices and quantities in stock. The same database also might contain customer information, such as user names for logging into the online store, billing addresses and credit-card numbers.

The *middle tier* implements *business logic* and *presentation logic* to control interactions between application clients and application data. The middle tier acts as an intermediary between data in the information tier and the application clients. The middle-tier *controller logic* processes client requests from the top tier (e.g., a request to view a product catalog) and retrieves data from the database. The middle-tier presentation logic then processes data from the information tier and presents the content to the client. In Web-based applications, the middle tier presentation logic typically presents content as XHTML documents.

Business logic in the middle tier enforces *business rule*s and ensures that data is reliable before updating the database or presenting data to a user. Business rules dictate how clients can and cannot access application data and how applications process data.

The *client tier*, or *top tier*, is the application's user interface. Users interact directly with the application through the user interface. The client interacts with the middle tier to make requests and to retrieve data from the information tier. The client then displays to the user the data retrieved from the middle tier.

16.4 Accessing Web Servers

To request documents from Web servers, users must know the URLs at which those documents reside. A URL contains a machine name (called a *host name*) on which the Web server resides. Users can request documents from *local Web servers* (i.e., ones residing on user's machines) or *remote Web servers* (i.e., ones residing on machines across a network).

Local Web servers can be accessed in two ways: through the machine name, or through **localhost**—a host name that references the local machine. We use **localhost** in this chapter. To determine the machine name in Windows Me, right-click **My Network Places**, and select **Properties** from the context menu to display the **Network** dialog. In the **Network** dialog, click the **Identification** tab. The computer name displays in the **Computer name:** field. Click **Cancel** to close the **Network** dialog. In Windows 2000, right click **My Computer** and select **Properties** from the context menu to display the **System Properties** dialog. In the dialog, click **Network Identification**. The **Full Computer Name:** field in the **System Properties** window displays the computer name. In Windows XP, select **Start > Control Panel > Switch to Classic View > System** to view the **System Properties** dialog. In the dialog, select the **Computer Name** tab.

A domain name represents a group of hosts on the Internet; it combines with a host name (e.g., **www**—World Wide Web) and a *top-level domain (TLD)* to form a *fully qualified host name*, which provides a user-friendly way to identify a site on the Internet. In a fully qualified host name, the TLD often describes the type of organization that owns the domain name. For example, the **com** TLD usually refers to a commercial business, whereas the **org** TLD usually refers to a non-profit organization. In addition, each country has its own TLD, such as **cn** for China, **et** for Ethiopia, **om** for Oman and **us** for the United States.

Each fully qualified host name is assigned a unique address called an *IP address*, which is much like the street address of a house. Just as people use street addresses to locate houses or businesses in a city, computers use IP addresses to locate other computers on the Internet. A *domain name system (DNS) server*, a computer that maintains a database of host names and their corresponding IP addresses, translates fully qualified host names to IP addresses. This translation is referred to as a *DNS lookup*. For example, to access the Deitel Web site, type the hostname (**www.deitel.com**) into a Web browser. The DNS server translates **www.deitel.com** into the IP address of the Deitel Web server (i.e., **63.110.43.82**). The IP address of **localhost** is always **127.0.0.1**.

16.5 Apache HTTP Server[2]

The Apache HTTP server, maintained by the Apache Software Foundation, is currently the most popular Web server because of its stability, cost, efficiency and portability. It is an open-source product that runs on Unix, Linux and Windows platforms.

To download the Apache HTTP server, visit **www.apache.org**.[3] For instructions on installing Apache, visit **www.deitel.com** After installing the Apache HTTP server, start the server by selecting the **Start** menu, then **Programs > Apache HTTP Server 2.0.39 > Control Apache Server > Start**. If the server starts successfully, a command-prompt window opens, and states that the service is starting (Fig. 16.2). To stop the Apache HTTP server, select **Start > Programs > Apache HTTP Server 2.0.39 > Control Apache Server > Stop**.

---

2. This section applies to Windows 98/NT/2000/Me/XP, Unix and Linux users.
3. In this chapter, we use version 2.0.39.

Fig. 16.2   Starting the Apache HTTP server.

16.6 Requesting XHTML Documents

This section shows how to request an XHTML document from the Apache HTTP server. In the Apache HTTP server directory structure, XHTML documents must be saved in the **htdocs** directory. On Windows platforms, the **htdocs** directory resides in **C:\Program Files\Apache Group\Apache**; on Linux platforms, the **htdocs** directory resides in the **/usr/local/httpd** directory.[4] Copy the **test.html** document from the Chapter 16 examples directory on the book's CD-ROM into the **htdocs** directory. To request the document, launch a Web browser, such as Internet Explorer, Netscape or equivalent and enter the URL in the **Address** field (i.e., **http://localhost/test.html**). Figure 16.3 shows the result of requesting **test.html**. [*Note*: In Apache, the root of the URL refers to the default directory, **htdocs**, so we do not enter the directory name in the **Address** field.]

16.7 Introduction to CGI

The *Common Gateway Interface (CGI)* is a standard for enabling applications (commonly called *CGI programs* or *CGI scripts*) to interact with Web servers and (indirectly) with clients (e.g., Web browsers). CGI is often used to generate *dynamic Web content* using client input, databases and other information services. A Web page is dynamic if its content is generated programmatically when the page is requested, unlike *static Web content*, which is not generated programmatically when the page is requested (i.e., the page already exists before the request is made). For example, we can use CGI to have a Web page ask users for their ZIP codes, then redirect users to another Web page that is specifically for people in

Fig. 16.3   Requesting **test.html** from Apache.

---

4. Linux users may already have apache installed by default. The **htdocs** directory may be found in a number of places depending on the Linux distribution.

that geographical area. In this chapter, we introduce the basics of CGI and use C++ to write our first CGI scripts.

The Common Gateway Interface is "common" in the sense that it is not specific to any particular operating system (such as Linux or Windows) or to any one programming language. CGI was designed to be used with virtually any programming language. Thus, CGI scripts can be written in C, C++, Perl, Python or Visual Basic without difficulty.

CGI was developed in 1993 by *NCSA (National Center for Supercomputing Applications—***www.ncsa.uiuc.edu**) for use with its popular *HTTPd Web server.* Unlike Web protocols and languages that have formal specifications, the initial concise description of CGI written by NCSA proved simple enough that CGI was adopted as an unofficial standard worldwide. CGI support was incorporated quickly into other Web servers, including Apache.

16.8 Simple HTTP Transaction

Before exploring how CGI operates, it is necessary to have a basic understanding of networking and how the World Wide Web works. In this section, we will examine the inner workings of the Hypertext Transfer Protocol (HTTP) and discuss what goes on behind the scenes when a browser requests and then displays a Web page. HTTP describes a set of *methods* and *headers* that allows clients and servers to interact and exchange information in a uniform and predictable way.

A Web page in its simplest form is an XHTML document, which is a plain text file that contains markings (*markup* or *elements*) that describe the structure of the data the document contains. For example, the XHTML

```
<title>My Web Page</title>
```

indicates to the browser that the text between the **<title>** *start element* and the **</title>** *end element* is the title of the Web page. XHTML documents also can contain *hypertext* information (usually called *hyperlinks*), which create links to other Web pages or to other locations on the same page. When a user activates a hyperlink (usually by clicking it with the mouse), the Web browser "follows" the hyperlink by loading the new Web page (or a different part of the same Web page).

Each XHTML file available for viewing over the Web has a *URL (Universal Resource Locator)* associated with it—an address of sorts. The URL contains information that directs a browser to the resource (most often a Web page) that the user wishes to access. For example, consider the URL

```
http://www.deitel.com/books/downloads.html
```

The **http://** indicates that the Web browser should request the resource using the Hypertext Transfer Protocol. The middle portion, **www.deitel.com**, is the *hostname* of the server. The hostname is the name of the computer where the resource resides; likewise, this computer is usually referred to as the *host*, because it houses and maintains the resource.

The name of the resource being requested, **/books/downloads.html** (an XHTML document), is the remainder of the URL. This portion of the URL specifies both the name of the resource (**downloads.html**) and its path (**/books**). The path could represent an actual directory in the Web server's file system. However, for security reasons, the path often is a *virtual directory*. In this case, the server translates the path into a real location on the server (or even on another computer), thus hiding the true location of the resource. In fact, it is even possible that the resource is created dynamically and does not reside anywhere on the server computer. As we will see, URLs also can be used to provide input to a program on the server.

Now we consider how a browser, when given a URL, performs a simple HTTP transaction to retrieve and display a Web page. Figure 16.4 illustrates the transaction in detail. The transaction is performed between a Web browser and a Web server.

In Step 1 of Fig. 16.4, the browser sends an HTTP request to the server. The request (in its simplest form) looks like the following:

```
GET /books/downloads.html HTTP/1.1
Host: www.deitel.com
```

The word **GET** is an *HTTP method,* that indicates the client wishes to retrieve a resource. The remainder of the request provides the name and path of the resource (an XHTML document) and the protocol's name and version number (**HTTP/1.1**).

Any server that understands HTTP (version 1.1) will be able to translate this request and respond appropriately. Step 2 of Fig. 16.4 shows the results of a successful request. The

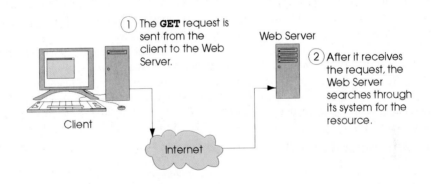

Fig. 16.4   Client interacting with server and Web server. Step 1: The *get* request,
                GET /books/downloads.htm HTTP/1.1. (Part 1 of 2.)

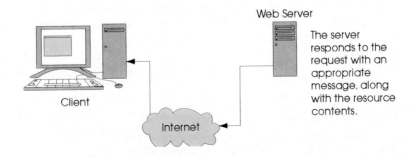

Fig. 16.4   Client interacting with server and Web server. Step 2: The HTTP response,
                HTTP/1.1 200 OK. (Part 2 of 2.)

server first responds with a line indicating the HTTP version, followed by a numeric code and a phrase describing the status of the transaction. For example,

```
HTTP/1.1 200 OK
```

indicates success;

```
HTTP/1.1 404 Not found
```

informs the client that the requested resource was not found on the server in the specified location.

The server then sends one or more *HTTP headers,* which provide information about the data being sent to the client. In this case, the server is sending an XHTML document, so the HTTP header reads

```
Content-Type: text/html
```

The information in the **Content-Type** header identifies the *MIME (Multipurpose Internet Mail Extensions) type* of the content. Each type of data sent from the server has a MIME type by which the browser determines how to process the data it receives. For example, the MIME type **text/plain** indicates that the data contains text that should be displayed without attempting to interpret any of the content as XHTML markup. Similarly, the MIME type **image/gif** indicates that the content is a GIF image. When this MIME type is received by the browser, it attempts to display the data as an image.

The headers are followed by a blank line, which indicates to the client that the server is finished sending HTTP headers. The server then sends the contents of the requested XHTML document (e.g., **downloads.html**). The connection is terminated when the transfer of the resource is complete. The client-side browser interprets the XHTML it receives and renders (or displays) the results.

16.9 Simple CGI Script

As long as an XHTML file on the server remains unchanged, its associated URL will display the same content in clients' browsers each time the file is accessed. For that content to change (e.g., to include new links or the latest company news), someone must alter the file manually on the server, probably with a text editor or Web-page-design software.

This need for manual change is a problem for Web page authors who want to create interesting and dynamic Web pages. To have a person continually alter a Web page is tedious. For example, if you want your Web page always to display the current date or weather conditions, the page would require continuous updating.

It is fairly straightforward to write a C++ program that outputs the current time and date (to the monitor of the local computer). In fact, this requires only a few lines of code:

```
time_t currentTime;     // time_t defined in <ctime>
time( &currentTime );

// asctime and localtime defined in <ctime>
cout << asctime( localtime( &currentTime ) );
```

C++ library function *localtime*, when passed a **time_t** variable (e.g., **current-Time**) returns a pointer to a structure containing the "broken-down" local time (i.e., days, hours, etc. are placed in individual structure members). Function **asctime**, which takes a pointer to a structure containing "broken-down" time, returns a string such as

Wed Jul 31 13:10:37 2002

What if we wish to send the current time to a client's browser window for display (rather than outputting it to the screen)? CGI makes this possible by allowing the server to redirect the output of a program to the Web server itself, sending the output to a client's browser. Redirection of output allows output (e.g., from a **cout** statement) to be sent somewhere other than the screen.

Figure 16.5 shows the full program listing for our first CGI script. Note that the program consists mainly of **cout** statements (lines 15–29). Until now, the output of **cout** always has been displayed on the screen. However, technically speaking, the default target for **cout** is *standard output*. When a C++ program is executed as a CGI script, the standard output is redirected by the Web server to the client Web browser. To execute the program, we placed the compiled C++ executable file in the Web server's **cgi-bin** directory. For the purpose of this chapter, we have changed the executable file extension from **.exe** to **.cgi**.[5] Assuming that the Web server is on your local computer, you can execute the script by typing

http://localhost/cgi-bin/localtime.cgi

in your browser's **Address** or **Location** field. If you are requesting this script from a remote Web server, you will need to replace **localhost** with the server's hostname or IP address.

```
1   // Fig. 16.5: localtime.cpp
2   // Displays the current date and time in a Web browser.
3
4   #include <iostream>
5
6   using std::cout;
7
8   #include <ctime>
9
10  int main()
11  {
12     time_t currentTime;   // variable for storing time
13
14     // output header
15     cout << "Content-Type: text/html\n\n";
16
17     // output XML declaration and DOCTYPE
18     cout << "<?xml version = \"1.0\"?>"
19          << "<!DOCTYPE html PUBLIC \"-//W3C//DTD XHTML 1.0 "
20          << "Transitional//EN\" \"http://www.w3.org/TR/xhtml1"
21          << "/DTD/xhtml1-transitional.dtd\">";
```

Fig. 16.5   First CGI script. (Part 1 of 2.)

5. On a server running Microsoft Windows, the executable may be run directly in **.exe** form.

```
22
23        time( &currentTime );   // store time in currentTime
24
25        // output html element and some of its contents
26        cout << "<html xmlns = \"http://www.w3.org/1999/xhtml\">"
27             << "<head><title>Current date and time</title></head>"
28             << "<body><p>" << asctime( localtime( &currentTime ) )
29             << "</p></body></html>";
30
31        return 0;
32
33   } // end main
```

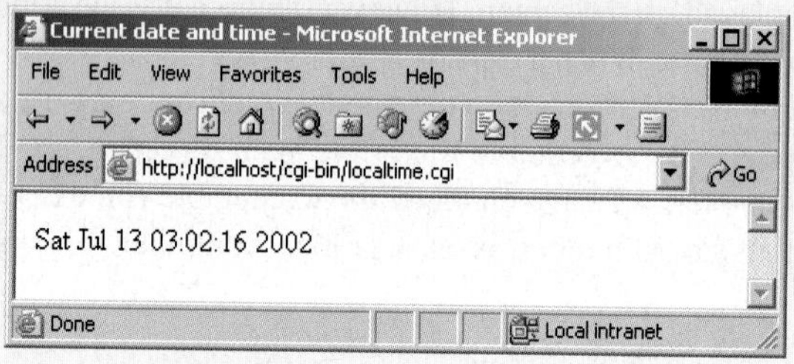

Fig. 16.5   First CGI script. (Part 2 of 2.)

The notion of standard output is similar to that of standard input, which we have seen frequently referenced with the expression **cin**. Just as standard input refers to the standard method of input into a program (normally, the keyboard), standard output refers to the standard method of output from a program (normally, the screen). It is possible to redirect (or *pipe*) standard output to another destination. Thus, in our CGI script, when we output an HTTP header (line 15) or XHTML elements (lines 18–21 and 26–29), the output is sent to the Web server, as opposed to the screen. The server sends that output to the client over HTTP, which interprets the headers and elements as if they were part of a normal server response to an XHTML document request.

Figure 16.6 illustrates this process in more detail. In Step 1, the client requests the resource named **localtime.cgi** from the server, just as it requested **downloads.html** in the previous example. If the server was not configured to handle CGI scripts, it might just return the contents of the C++ executable file to the client, as if it were any other document. However, based on the Web server configuration, the server executes **localtime.cgi** and sends the CGI program's output to the Web browser.

A properly configured Web server, however, will recognize that certain resources should be handled differently. For example, when the resource is a CGI script, the script must be executed by the server. A resource usually is designated as a CGI script in one of two ways: either it has a special filename extension (such as **.cgi** or **.exe**) or it is located in a specific directory (often **cgi-bin**). In addition, the server administrator must give permission explicitly for remote clients to be able to access and execute CGI scripts.[6]

---

6. If you are using the Apache HTTP Server and would like more information on configuration, consult the Apache home page at **www.apache.org**.

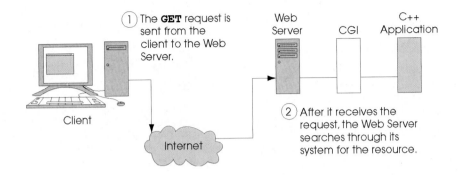

Fig. 16.6   Step 1: The *get* request, **GET /cgi-bin/localtime.cgi HTTP/ 1.1**. (Part 1 of 4.)

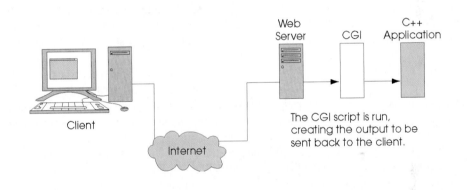

Fig. 16.6   Step 2: The Web server starts the CGI script. (Part 2 of 4.)

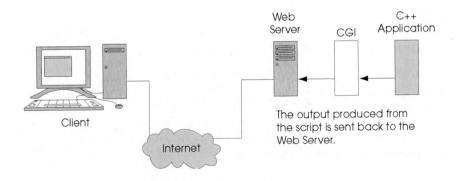

Fig. 16.6   Step 3: The output of the script is sent to the Web server. (Part 3 of 4.)

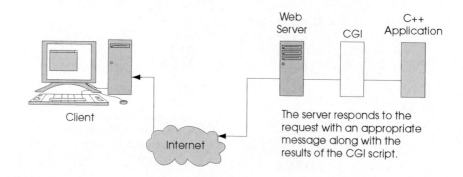

The server responds to the request with an appropriate message along with the results of the CGI script.

Fig. 16.6   Step 4: The HTTP response, **HTTP/1.1 200 OK**. (Part 4 of 4.)

In Step 2 of Fig. 16.6, the server recognizes that the resource is a CGI script and executes the script. In Step 3, the three **cout** statements (lines 15, 18–21 and 26–29 of Fig. 16.5) are executed, and the text is sent to the standard output and is returned to the Web server. Finally, in Step 4, the Web server adds a message to the output that indicates the status of the HTTP transaction (such as **HTTP/1.1 200 OK**, for success) and sends the entire output from the CGI program to the client.

The client-side browser then processes the XHTML output and displays the results. It is important to note that the browser is unaware of what has transpired on the server. In other words, as far as the browser is concerned, it requests a resource like any other and receives a response like any other. The client receives and interprets the script's output, just as if it were a simple, static XHTML document.

In fact, you can view the content that the browser receives by executing **localtime.cgi** from the command line, as we normally would execute any of the programs from the previous chapters. [*Note:* The file extension must be changed to **.exe** prior to executing from the command line on a system running Windows]. Figure 16.7 shows the output. For the purpose of this chapter, we formatted the output for readability.

```
Content-Type: text/html

<?xml version = "1.0"?>
<!DOCTYPE html PUBLIC "-//W3C//DTD XHTML 1.0 Transitional//EN"
   "http://www.w3.org/TR/xhtml1/DTD/xhtml1-transitional.dtd">

<html xmlns = "http://www.w3.org/1999/xhtml">
   <head>
      <title>Current date and time</title>
   </head>

   <body>
      <p>Mon Jul 15 13:52:45 2002</p>
   </body>
</html>
```

Fig. 16.7   Output of **localtime.cgi** when executed from the command line.

Notice that, with the CGI script, we must output the **Content-Type** header, whereas, for an XHTML document, the Web server would include the header.

To review, a CGI program prints the **Content-Type** header, a blank line and the data (XHTML, plain text, etc.) to standard output. The Web server retrieves this output, inserts the HTTP response to the beginning and delivers the content to the client. Later, we will see other content types that may be used in this manner, as well as other headers that may be used in addition to **Content-Type**.

The program of Figure 16.8 outputs the *environment variables* that the Web server provides when executing the CGI script. These variables contain information about the client and server environment, such as the type of Web browser being used and the location of the document on the server. Lines 15–24 initialize an array of **string** objects with the CGI environment variable names. Line 41 begins the XHTML table in which the data will be displayed.

Lines 45–48 output each row of the table. Let us examine each of these lines closely. Line 45 outputs an XHTML **<tr>** (table row) start tag, which indicates the beginning of a new table row. Line 48 outputs its corresponding **</tr>** end tag, which indicates the end of the row. Each row of the table contains two table cells. Each row contains the name of an environment variable and the data associated with that variable. The **<td>** start tag (line 45) begins a new table cell. The **for** loop (line 44) iterates through each of the 24 **string** objects. Each environment variable's name is output in the left table cell. The value associated with the environment variable is output by calling

```
1   // Fig. 16.8: environment.cpp
2   // Program to display CGI environment variables.
3   #include <iostream>
4
5   using std::cout;
6
7   #include <string>
8
9   using std::string;
10
11  #include <cstdlib>
12
13  int main()
14  {
15      string environmentVariables[ 24 ] = {
16          "COMSPEC", "DOCUMENT_ROOT", "GATEWAY_INTERFACE",
17          "HTTP_ACCEPT", "HTTP_ACCEPT_ENCODING",
18          "HTTP_ACCEPT_LANGUAGE", "HTTP_CONNECTION",
19          "HTTP_HOST", "HTTP_USER_AGENT", "PATH",
20          "QUERY_STRING", "REMOTE_ADDR", "REMOTE_PORT",
21          "REQUEST_METHOD", "REQUEST_URI", "SCRIPT_FILENAME",
22          "SCRIPT_NAME", "SERVER_ADDR", "SERVER_ADMIN",
23          "SERVER_NAME","SERVER_PORT","SERVER_PROTOCOL",
24          "SERVER_SIGNATURE","SERVER_SOFTWARE" };
25
26      // output header
27      cout << "Content-Type: text/html\n\n";
```

Fig. 16.8 Retrieving environment variables via function **getenv**. (Part 1 of 3.)

```
28
29       // output XML declaration and DOCTYPE
30       cout << "<?xml version = \"1.0\"?>"
31            << "<!DOCTYPE html PUBLIC \"-//W3C//DTD XHTML 1.0 "
32            << "Transitional//EN\" \"http://www.w3.org/TR/xhtml1"
33            << "/DTD/xhtml1-transitional.dtd\">";
34
35       // output html element and some of its contents
36       cout << "<html xmlns = \"http://www.w3.org/1999/xhtml\">"
37            << "<head><title>Environment Variables</title></head>"
38            << "<body>";
39
40       // begin outputting table
41       cout << "<table border = \"0\" cellspacing = \"2\">";
42
43       // iterate through environment variables
44       for ( int i = 0; i < 24; i++ )
45          cout << "<tr><td>" << environmentVariables[ i ]
46               << "</td><td>"
47               << getenv( environmentVariables[ i ].data() )
48               << "</td></tr>";
49
50       cout << "</table></body></html>";
51
52       return 0;
53
54    } // end main
```

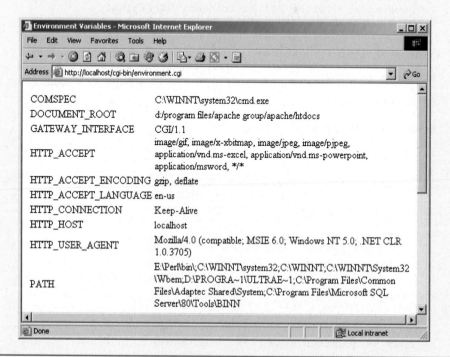

Fig. 16.8   Retrieving environment variables via function **getenv**. (Part 2 of 3.)

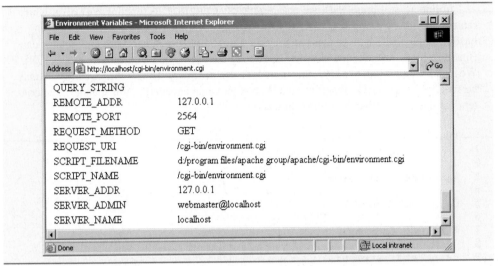

Fig. 16.8   Retrieving environment variables via function **getenv**. (Part 3 of 3.)

function **getenv** of **<cstdlib>** and passing it the string value returned from the function call **environmentVariables[i].data()**. Function **data** returns a C-style **char *** string containing the contents of the **environmentVariables[i] string**.

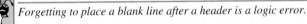

Common Programming Error 16.1

Forgetting to place a blank line after a header is a logic error.

16.10 Sending Input to a CGI Script

Though preset environment variables provide much information, we would like to be able to supply any type of data to our CGI scripts, such as a user's name or a search-engine query. The environment variable **QUERY_STRING** provides a mechanism to do just that. The **QUERY_STRING** variable contains information that is appended to a URL in a *get* request. For example, the URL

> **www.**_somesite_**.com/cgi-bin/script.cgi?state=California**

causes the Web browser to request a resource from **www.**_somesite_**.com**. The resource is a CGI script (**cgi-bin/script.cgi**). The Web server stores the data following the **?** (**state=California**) in the **QUERY_STRING** environment variable. The query string provides parameters that customize the request for a particular client. Note that the question mark is not part of the resource requested, nor is it part of the query string. It serves as a delimiter (or separator) between the two.

Figure 16.9 shows a simple example of a CGI script that reads data passed through the **QUERY_STRING**. Note that data in a query string can be formatted in a variety of ways. The CGI script reading the string must know how to interpret the formatted data. In the example in Fig. 16.9, the query string contains a series of name-value pairs delimited by ampersands (**&**), as in

> **name=Jill&age=22**

In line 15 of Figure 16.9, we pass **"QUERY_STRING"** to function **getenv**, which returns the query string and assigns it to **string** variable **query**. After outputting a header, some XHTML start tags and the title (lines 21–29), we test if **query** contains data (line 34). If not, we output a message instructing the user to add a query string to the URL. We also provide a link to a URL that includes a sample query string. Query-string data may be specified as part of a hyperlink in a Web page when encoded in this manner. The contents of the query string are output on line 42.

```
1   // Fig. 16.9: querystring.cpp
2   // Demonstrating QUERY_STRING.
3   #include <iostream>
4
5   using std::cout;
6
7   #include <string>
8
9   using std::string;
10
11  #include <cstdlib>
12
13  int main()
14  {
15     string query = getenv( "QUERY_STRING" );
16
17     // output header
18     cout << "Content-Type: text/html\n\n";
19
20     // output XML declaration and DOCTYPE
21     cout << "<?xml version = \"1.0\"?>"
22          << "<!DOCTYPE html PUBLIC \"-//W3C//DTD XHTML 1.0 "
23          << "Transitional//EN\" \"http://www.w3.org/TR/xhtml1"
24          << "/DTD/xhtml1-transitional.dtd\">";
25
26     // output html element and some of its contents
27     cout << "<html xmlns = \"http://www.w3.org/1999/xhtml\">"
28          << "<head><title>Name/Value Pairs</title></head>"
29          << "<body>";
30
31     cout << "<h2>Name/Value Pairs</h2>";
32
33     // if query contained no data
34     if ( query == "" )
35        cout << "Please add some name-value pairs to the URL "
36             << "above.<br/>Or try "
37             << "<a href=\"querystring.cgi?name=Joe&age=29\">"
38             << "this</a>.";
39
40     // user entered query string
41     else
42        cout << "<p>The query string is: " << query << "</p>";
43
```

Fig. 16.9   Reading input from **QUERY_STRING**. (Part 1 of 2.)

```
44        cout << "</body></html>";
45
46        return 0;
47
48  } // end main
```

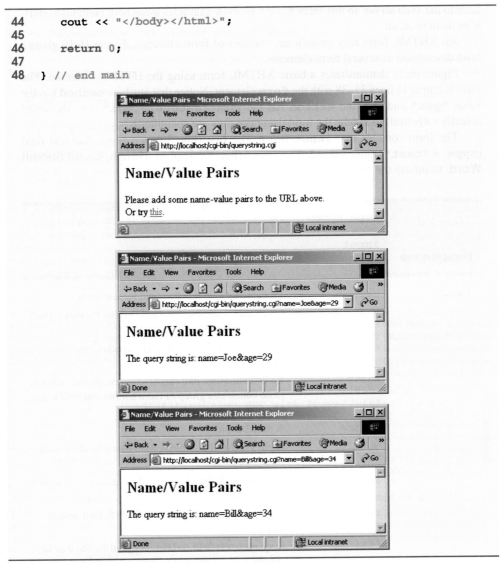

Fig. 16.9 Reading input from **QUERY_STRING**. (Part 2 of 2.)

16.11 Using XHTML Forms to Send Input

Having a client enter input directly into a URL is not a user-friendly approach. Fortunately, XHTML provides the ability to include *forms* on Web pages that provide a more intuitive way for users to input information to be sent to a CGI script.

The **form** element encloses an XHTML form. The **form** element generally takes two attributes. The first attribute is **action**, which specifies the action to take when the user submits the form. For our purposes, the **action** usually will be to call a CGI script to process the form's data. The second attribute used in the **form** element is **method**. The method attribute identifies the type of HTTP request to use when the browser submits the

```
54              // word was entered
55          else
56              cout << "<p>Your word is: " << wordString << "</p>";
57      }
58
59      cout << "</body></html>";
60
61      return 0;
62
63  } // end main
```

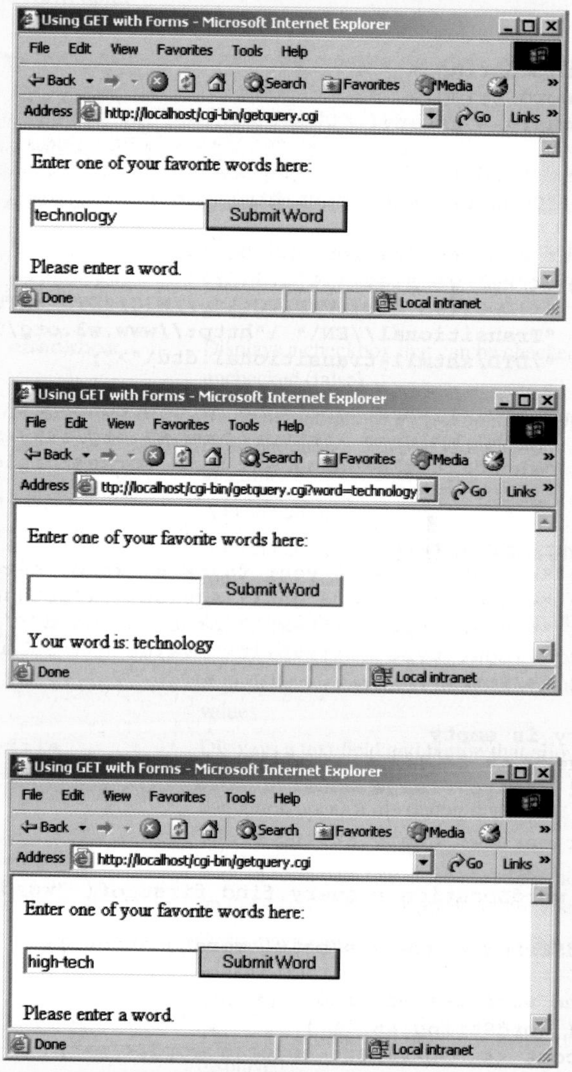

Fig. 16.11 Using **GET** with an XHTML form. (Part 2 of 3.)

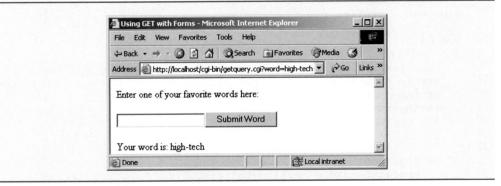

Fig. 16.11 Using **GET** with an XHTML form. (Part 3 of 3.)

The first time the script is executed, there should be no value in **QUERY_STRING** (unless the user has appended the query string to the URL). Once the user enters a word into the **word** field and presses **Submit Word**, the script is requested again. This time, the name of the input field (**word**) and the value entered by the user are placed in the **QUERY_STRING** variable by the browser. That is, if the user enters the word "**technology**" and presses the **Submit Word**, **QUERY_STRING** is assigned the value **word=technology** and the query string is appended to the URL in the browser window.

During the second execution of the script, the query string is decoded. Lines 46–48 in Fig. 16.11 search **query** for the first occurrence of **word=**, using **string** method **find_first_of**, which returns an integer value corresponding to the location in the **string** where the first match was found. A value of **5** is added to the location to move the position in the **string** to the first character of the user's favorite word. Method **substr** (line 48) returns the remainder of the **string** starting at the location specified by **wordLocation**, which is then assigned to **wordString**. Line 51 determines whether the user entered a word. If so, line 56 outputs the word entered by the user.

The two previous examples used *get* to pass data to the CGI scripts through an environment variable. Web browsers typically interact with Web servers by submitting forms using HTTP *post*. CGI programs read the contents of *post* requests using standard input. For comparison purposes, let us now reimplement the application of Fig. 16.11, using **POST** (as in Fig. 16.12). Notice that the code in the two figures is virtually identical. The XHTML form indicates that we are now using the **POST** method to submit the form data.

```
1   // Fig. 16.12: post.cpp
2   // Demonstrates POST method with XHTML form.
3   #include <iostream>
4
5   using std::cout;
6   using std::cin;
7
8   #include <string>
9
10  using std::string;
11
```

Fig. 16.12 Using **POST** with an XHTML form. (Part 1 of 4.)

```cpp
12   #include <cstdlib>
13
14   int main()
15   {
16      char postString[ 1024 ] = ""; // variable to hold POST data
17      string dataString = "";
18      string nameString = "";
19      string wordString = "";
20      int contentLength = 0;
21
22      // content was submitted
23      if ( getenv( "CONTENT_LENGTH" ) ) {
24         contentLength = atoi( getenv( "CONTENT_LENGTH" ) );
25
26         cin.read( postString, contentLength );
27         dataString = postString;
28      } // end if
29
30      // output header
31      cout << "Content-Type: text/html\n\n";
32
33      // output XML declaration and DOCTYPE
34      cout << "<?xml version = \"1.0\"?>"
35           << "<!DOCTYPE html PUBLIC \"-//W3C//DTD XHTML 1.0 "
36           << "Transitional//EN\" \"http://www.w3.org/TR/xhtml1"
37           << "/DTD/xhtml1-transitional.dtd\">";
38
39      // output XHTML element and some of its contents
40      cout << "<html xmlns = \"http://www.w3.org/1999/xhtml\">"
41           << "<head><title>Using POST with Forms</title></head>"
42           << "<body>";
43
44      // output XHTML form
45      cout << "<p>Enter one of your favorite words here:</p>"
46           << "<form method = \"post\" action = \"post.cgi\">"
47           << "<input type = \"text\" name = \"word\" />"
48           << "<input type = \"submit\" value = \"Submit Word\" />"
49           << "</form>";
50
51      // data was sent using POST
52      if ( contentLength > 0 ) {
53         int nameLocation =
54            dataString.find_first_of( "word=" ) + 5;
55
56         int endLocation = dataString.find_first_of( "&" ) - 1;
57
58         // retrieve entered word
59         wordString = dataString.substr( nameLocation,
60            endLocation - nameLocation );
61
62         // no data was entered in text field
63         if ( wordString == "" )
64            cout << "<p>Please enter a word.</p>";
```

Fig. 16.12   Using **POST** with an XHTML form. (Part 2 of 4.)

```
65
66          // output word
67          else
68              cout << "<p>Your word is: " << wordString << "</p>";
69
70      } // end if
71
72      // no data was sent
73      else
74          cout << "<p>Please enter a word.</p>";
75
76      cout << "</body></html>";
77
78      return 0;
79
80  } // end main
```

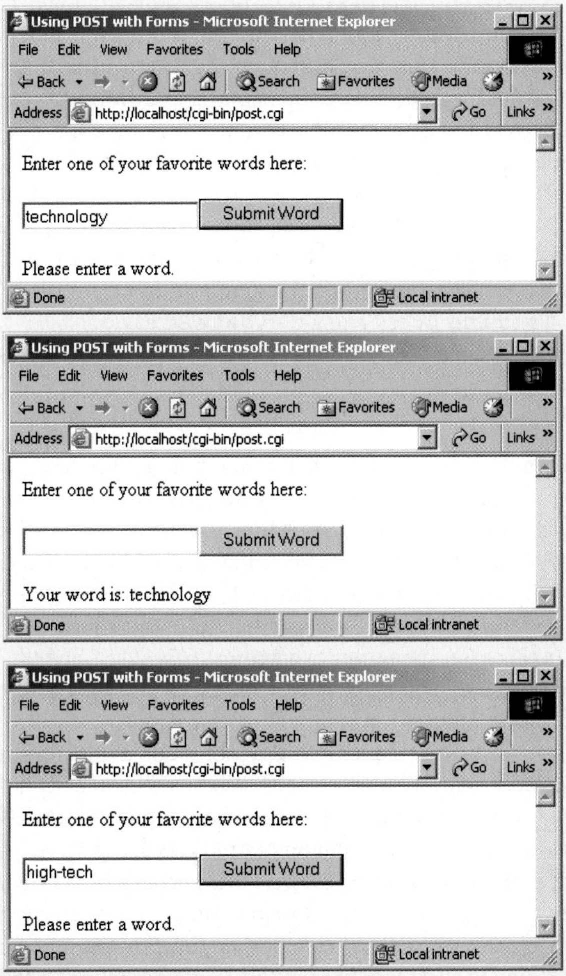

Fig. 16.12   Using **POST** with an XHTML form. (Part 3 of 4.)

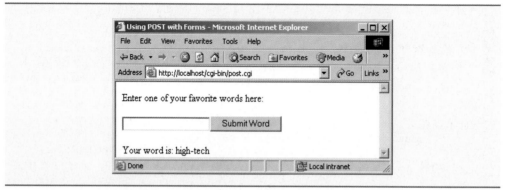

Fig. 16.12 Using **POST** with an XHTML form. (Part 4 of 4.)

The Web server sends *post* data to a CGI script via standard input. The data is encoded (i.e., formatted) just as in **QUERY_STRING** (that is, with name-value pairs connected by equals signs and ampersands), but the **QUERY_STRING** environment variable is not set. Instead, the **POST** method sets the environment variable **CONTENT_LENGTH**, to indicate the number of characters of data that were sent in the *post* requests.

The value of the **CONTENT_LENGTH** environment variable is used by the CGI script to process the correct amount of data. Line 23 determines whether **CONTENT_LENGTH** contains a value. Line 24 reads in the value and converts it to an integer by calling **<cstdlib>** function **atoi**. Line 26 calls function **cin.read** to read characters from standard input and stores the characters in array **postString**. Line 27 converts **post-String**'s data to a **string** by assigning it to **dataString**.

In earlier chapters, we read data from standard input using an expression such as

```
cin >> data;
```

The same approach might work in our CGI script as a replacement for the **cin.read** statement. Recall that **cin** reads data from standard input up to and including the first newline character, space or tab, whichever comes first. The CGI specification does not require a newline to be appended after the last name-value pair. Although some browsers append a newline or **EOF**, they are not required to do so. If **cin** is used with a browser that sends only the name-value pairs (as per the CGI specification), **cin** must wait for a newline that will never arrive. In this case, the server eventually "times out" and the CGI script terminates. Therefore, **cin.read** is preferred over **cin**, because the programmer can specify exactly how much data to read.

The CGI scripts from this section, while useful for explaining how *get* and *post* operate, do not include many of the features described in the CGI specification. For example, if we enter the words **didn't translate** into the text field and click the **submit** button, the script informs us that our word is **didn%27t+translate**.

What has happened here? Web browsers *URL encode* the XHTML form data they send. This means that spaces are replaced with plus signs, and other symbols (e.g., apostrophes) are translated into their ASCII value in hexadecimal format and preceded with a percent sign. URL encoding is necessary because URLs do not allow certain characters, such as spaces and apostrophes.

16.12 Other Headers

We mentioned in Section 16.9 that there are several HTTP headers in addition to the **Content-Type** header. A CGI script can supply other HTTP headers in addition to **Content-Type**. In most cases, the server passes these extra headers to the client without executing them. For example, the following *Refresh* *header* redirects the client to a new location after a specified amount of time:

> **Refresh:** "5; URL = http://www.deitel.com/newpage.html"

Five seconds after the Web browser receives this header, the browser requests the resource at the specified URL. Alternatively, the **Refresh** header can omit the URL, in which case it will refresh the current page after the given time has expired.

The CGI specification indicates that certain types of headers output by a CGI script are to be handled by the server, rather than be passed directly to the client. The first of these is the *Location* *header*. Like **Refresh**, **Location** redirects the client to a new location:

> **Location: http://www.deitel.com/newpage.html**

If used with a relative (or virtual) URL (i.e., **Location: /newpage.html**), the **Location** header indicates to the server that the redirection is to be performed on the server side without sending the **Location** header back to the client. In this case, it appears to the user as if the document rendered in their Web browser was the resource they requested.

The CGI specification also includes a *Status* *header*, which instructs the server to output a corresponding status header line (such as **HTTP/1.1 200 OK**). Normally, the server will send the appropriate status line to the client (adding, for example, the **200 OK** status line in most cases). However, CGI allows programmers to change the response status. For example, sending a

> **Status: 204 No Response**

header indicates that, although the request was successful, the client should not display a new page in the browser window. This header might be useful if you want to allow users to submit forms without relocating to a new page.

We have now covered the fundamentals of the CGI specification. To review, CGI allows scripts to interact with servers in three basic ways:

1. through the output of headers and content to the server via standard output;

2. by the server's setting of environment variables (including the URL-encoded **QUERY_STRING**) whose values are available within the script (via **getenv**); and

3. through **POST**ed, URL-encoded data that the server sends to the script's standard input.

16.13 Case Study: An Interactive Web Page

Figure 16.13 and Fig. 16.14 show the implementation of a simple interactive portal for the fictional Bug2Bug Travel Web site. The example queries the client for a name and password, then displays information about weekly travel specials based on the data entered. For simplicity, the example does not encrypt the data sent to the server.

Figure 16.13 displays the opening page. It is a static XHTML document containing a form that **POST**s data to the **portal.cgi** CGI script (line 16). The form contains one field each to collect the user's name (line 18) and the user's password (line 19). [*Note:* This XHTML document was placed in the document directory of the Web server.]

Figure 16.14 contains the CGI script. First, let us examine how the data is retrieved from standard input and stored in **string**s. The **string** library **find** function searches **dataString** (line 30) for an occurrence of **namebox=**. Function **find** returns a location in the string where **namebox=** was found. To retrieve the value associated with

```
1   <?xml version = "1.0"?>
2   <!DOCTYPE html PUBLIC "-//W3C//DTD XHTML 1.0 Transitional//EN"
3   "http://www.w3.org/TR/xhtml11/DTD/xhtml1-transitional.dtd">
4
5   <!-- Fig. 16.13: travel.html   -->
6   <!-- Bug2Bug Travel Homepage   -->
7
8   <html xmlns = "http://www.w3.org/1999/xhtml">
9      <head>
10        <title>Bug2Bug Travel</title>
11     </head>
12
13     <body>
14        <h1>Welcome to Bug2Bug Travel</h1>
15
16        <form method = "post" action = "/cgi-bin/portal.cgi">
17           <p>Please enter your name:</p>
18           <input type = "text" name = "namebox" />
19           <input type = "password" name = "passwordbox" />
20           <p>password is not encrypted</p>
21           <input type = "submit" name = "button" />
22        </form>
23
24     </body>
25  </html>
```

Fig. 16.13 Interactive portal to create a password-protected Web page.

namebox=—the value entered by the user—the position in the string moves forward **8** characters. Recall that a query string contains name-value pairs separated by equals signs and ampersands. To find the ending location for the data we wish to retrieve, we search for the **&** character on line 31. The program now contains an integer "pointing" to the starting location. The length of the entered word is determined by the calculation **endNamelocation - namelocation**. On lines 37–41, we assign the form-field values to variables **nameString** and **passwordString**. We use **nameString** in line 58 to output a personalized greeting to the user. The current weekly specials are displayed in lines 58–62. (In this example, we include this information as part of the script.)

If the member password is correct, additional specials are output (lines 66–67). If the password is incorrect, the client is informed that the password was invalid.

Note that we use a combination of a static Web page and a CGI script here. We could have incorporated the opening XHTML form and the processing of the data into a single CGI script, as we did in previous examples in this chapter. We ask the reader to do this in Exercise 16.8.

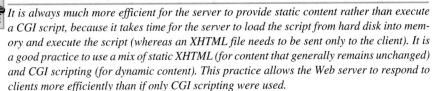

Performance Tip 16.1

It is always much more efficient for the server to provide static content rather than execute a CGI script, because it takes time for the server to load the script from hard disk into memory and execute the script (whereas an XHTML file needs to be sent only to the client). It is a good practice to use a mix of static XHTML (for content that generally remains unchanged) and CGI scripting (for dynamic content). This practice allows the Web server to respond to clients more efficiently than if only CGI scripting were used.

```cpp
1   // Fig. 16.14: portal.cpp
2   // Handles entry to Bug2Bug Travel.
3   #include <iostream>
4
5   using std::cout;
6   using std::cin;
7
8   #include <string>
9
10  using std::string;
11
12  #include <cstdlib>
13
14  int main()
15  {
16      char postString[ 1024 ] = "";
17      string dataString = "";
18      string nameString = "";
19      string passwordString = "";
20      int contentLength = 0;
21
22      // data was posted
23      if ( getenv( "CONTENT_LENGTH" ) )
24          contentLength = atoi( getenv( "CONTENT_LENGTH" ) );
25
```

Fig. 16.14 Interactive portal handler. (Part 1 of 3.)

```cpp
26        cin.read( postString, contentLength );
27        dataString = postString;
28
29        // search string for input data
30        int namelocation = dataString.find( "namebox=" ) + 8;
31        int endNamelocation = dataString.find( "&" );
32
33        int password = dataString.find( "passwordbox=" ) + 12;
34        int endPassword = dataString.find( "&button" );
35
36        // get values for name and password
37        nameString = dataString.substr( namelocation,
38           endNamelocation - namelocation );
39
40        passwordString = dataString.substr( password, endPassword -
41           password );
42
43        // output header
44        cout << "Content-Type: text/html\n\n";
45
46        // output XML declaration and DOCTYPE
47        cout << "<?xml version = \"1.0\"?>"
48             << "<!DOCTYPE html PUBLIC \"-//W3C//DTD XHTML 1.0 "
49             << "Transitional//EN\" \"http://www.w3.org/TR/xhtml1"
50             << "/DTD/xhtml1-transitional.dtd\">";
51
52        // output html element and some of its contents
53        cout << "<html xmlns = \"http://www.w3.org/1999/xhtml\">"
54             << "<head><title>Bug2Bug Travel</title></head>"
55             << "<body>";
56
57        // output specials
58        cout << "<h1>Welcome " << nameString << "!</h1>"
59             << "<p>Here are our weekly specials:</p>"
60             << "<ul><li>Boston to Taiwan ($875)</li>"
61             << "<li>San Diego to Hong Kong ($750)</li>"
62             << "<li>Chicago to Mexico City ($568)</li></ul>";
63
64        // password is correct
65        if ( passwordString == "coast2coast" )
66           cout << "<hr /><p>Current member special: "
67                << "Seattle to Tokyo ($400)</p>";
68
69        // password was incorrect
70        else
71           cout << "<p>Sorry. You have entered an incorrect "
72                << "password</p>";
73
74        cout << "</body></html>";
75        return 0;
76
77    } // end main
```

Fig. 16.14 Interactive portal handler. (Part 2 of 3.)

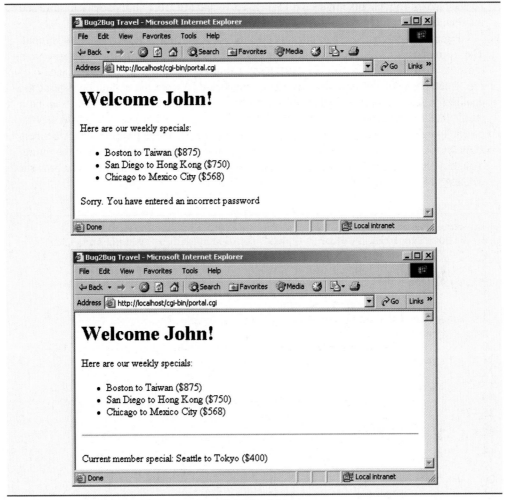

Fig. 16.14 Interactive portal handler. (Part 3 of 3.)

16.14 Cookies

In the last two sections, we discussed two ways in which information may be passed between programs (or executions of the same program) through a browser. This section concentrates on storing state information on the client computer with *cookies*. Cookies are essentially small text files that a Web server sends to your browser, which then writes the cookies onto your computer. Many Web sites use cookies to track a user's progress through their site (as in a shopping-cart application) or to help customize the site for an individual user.

Cookies do not break into your computer, nor do they erase your hard drive. However, they can be used to identify users and keep track of how often users visit a site or what users buy at a site. For this reason, cookies are considered to be a security and privacy concern. Popular Web browsers provide support for cookies. These browsers also allow users who are concerned about their privacy and security to disable this support. Most major Web sites use cookies. As a programmer, you should be aware of the possibility that cookies might be disabled by your clients. Figure 16.15, Fig. 16.16 and Fig. 16.17 use cookies to store and manipulate information about a user.

Figure 16.15 is an XHTML page that contains a form in which values are to be input. The form posts its information to **writecookie.cgi** (Fig. 16.16). This program retrieves the data contained in the **CONTENT_LENGTH** environment variable. Line 24 of Fig. 16.16 declares and initializes **string expires** to store the expiration date of the cookie (i.e., how long the cookie resides on the client's machine). This value can be a string, like the one in this example, or it can be a relative value. For instance, **+30d** sets the cookie to exist for 30 days. For the purposes of this chapter the expiration date is deliberately set to expire in 2010 to ensure that the program will run properly well into the future. You may set the expiration date of this example to any future date as needed. The browser deletes cookies when they expire.

```
1   <?xml version = "1.0"?>
2   <!DOCTYPE html PUBLIC "-//W3C//DTD XHTML 1.0 Transitional//EN"
3       "http://www.w3.org/TR/xhtml1/DTD/xhtml1-transitional.dtd">
4
5   <!-- Fig. 16.15: cookieform.html -->
6   <!-- Cookie Demonstration            -->
7
8   <html xmlns = "http://www.w3.org/1999/xhtml">
9       <head>
10          <title>Writing a cookie to the client computer</title>
11      </head>
12
13      <body>
14          <h1>Click Write Cookie to save your cookie data.</h1>
15
16          <form method = "post"
17              action = "/cgi-bin/writecookie.cgi">
18
19              <p>Name:<br />
20                  <input type = "text" name = "name" />
21              </p>
22
23              <p>Age:<br />
24                  <input type = "text" name = "age" />
25              </p>
26
27              <p>Favorite Color:<br />
28                  <input type = "text" name = "color" />
29              </p>
30
31              <p>
32                  <input type = "submit" name = "button" />
33              </p>
34          </form>
35
36      </body>
37  </html>
```

Fig. 16.15 XHTML document containing a form to post data to the server (Part 1 of 2.)

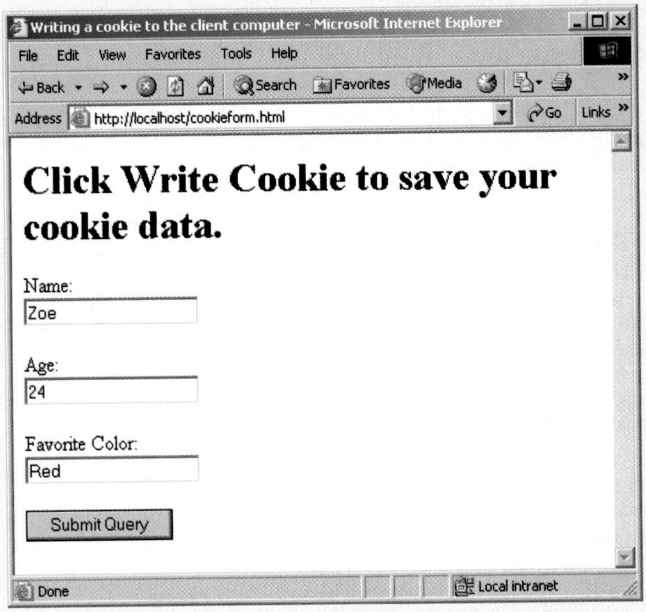

Fig. 16.15 XHTML document containing a form to post data to the server (Part 2 of 2.)

```cpp
1   // Fig. 16.16: writecookie.cpp
2   // Program to write a cookie to a client's machine.
3   #include <iostream>
4
5   using std::cout;
6   using std::cin;
7
8   #include <cstdlib>
9   #include <string>
10
11  using std::string;
12
13  int main()
14  {
15     char query[ 1024 ] = "";
16     string dataString = "";
17     string nameString = "";
18     string ageString = "";
19     string colorString = "";
20
21     int contentLength = 0;
22
23     // expiration date of cookie
24     string expires = "Friday, 14-MAY-10 16:00:00 GMT";
25
```

Fig. 16.16 Writing a cookie. (Part 1 of 3.)

```
26    // data was entered
27    if ( getenv( "CONTENT_LENGTH" ) ) {
28       contentLength = atoi( getenv( "CONTENT_LENGTH" ) );
29
30       // read data from standard input
31       cin.read( query, contentLength );
32       dataString = query;
33
34       // search string for data and store locations
35       int nameLocation = dataString.find( "name=" ) + 5;
36       int endName = dataString.find( "&" );
37
38       int ageLocation = dataString.find( "age=" ) + 4;
39       int endAge = dataString.find( "&color" );
40
41       int colorLocation = dataString.find( "color=" ) + 6;
42       int endColor = dataString.find( "&button" );
43
44       // get value for user's name
45       nameString = dataString.substr( nameLocation, endName -
46          nameLocation );
47
48       // get value for user's age
49       if ( ageLocation > 0 )
50          ageString = dataString.substr( ageLocation, endAge -
51             ageLocation );
52
53       // get value for user's favorite color
54       if ( colorLocation > 0 )
55          colorString = dataString.substr( colorLocation,
56             endColor - colorLocation );
57
58       // set cookie
59       cout << "Set-Cookie: Name=" << nameString << "age:"
60          << ageString << "color:" << colorString
61          << "; expires=" << expires << "; path=\n";
62
63    } // end if
64
65    // output header
66    cout << "Content-Type: text/html\n\n";
67
68    // output XML declaration and DOCTYPE
69    cout << "<?xml version = \"1.0\"?>"
70       << "<!DOCTYPE html PUBLIC \"-//W3C//DTD XHTML 1.0 "
71       << "Transitional//EN\" \"http://www.w3.org/TR/xhtml1"
72       << "/DTD/xhtml1-transitional.dtd\">";
73
74    // output html element and some of its contents
75    cout << "<html xmlns = \"http://www.w3.org/1999/xhtml\">"
76       << "<head><title>Cookie Saved</title></head>"
77       << "<body>";
78
```

Fig. 16.16   Writing a cookie. (Part 2 of 3.)

```
79        // output user's information
80        cout << "<p>The cookies have been set with the following"
81             << " data:</p>"
82             << "<p>Name: " << nameString   << "<br/></p>"
83             << "<p>Age:"   << ageString    << "<br/></p>"
84             << "<p>Color:" << colorString  << "<br/></p>"
85             << "<p>Click <a href=\"/cgi-bin/readcookie.cgi\">"
86             << "here</a> to read saved cookie data:</p>"
87             << "</body></html>";
88
89        return 0;
90
91   } // end main
```

Fig. 16.16   Writing a cookie. (Part 3 of 3.)

After obtaining the data from the form, the program creates a cookie (lines 59–61). In this example, we create a cookie by adding a line of text containing the name-value pairs of the posted data, delimited by a colon character (**:**). The line must be output before the header is written to the client. The line of text begins with the **Set-Cookie:** header, indicating that the browser should store the incoming data in a cookie. We set three attributes for the cookie: a name-value pair containing the data to be stored, a name-value pair containing the expiration date and a name-value pair containing the URL of the server domain (e.g., **www.deitel.com**) for which the cookie is valid. For this example, **path** is not set to any value, making the cookie readable from any server in the domain of the server that originally wrote the cookie. Lines 66–87 send a Web page indicating that the cookie has been written to the client.

Portability Tip 16.1

*Web browsers store the cookie information in a vendor-specific manner. For example, Internet Explorer stores cookies as text files in the **Temporary Internet Files** directory on the client's machine. Netscape stores its cookies in a single file named **cookies.txt**.*

Figure 16.17 reads the cookie written in Fig. 16.16 and displays the information. When a request is made from the client Web browser, the Web browser locates any cookies previously written by the server to which the request is being made. These cookies are sent by the browser as part of the request. On the server, the environment variable **HTTP_COOKIE** stores the client's cookies sent as part of the request. Line 20 calls function **getenv** with the **HTTP_COOKIE** environment variable as the first parameter. The value returned is stored in **dataString**. The name-value pairs are decoded and stored in strings on lines 23–36 according to the **name:value** encoding scheme used in Fig. 16.16. The contents of the cookie are output as a Web page on lines 39–58.

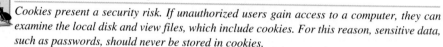

Software Engineering Observation 16.2

Cookies present a security risk. If unauthorized users gain access to a computer, they can examine the local disk and view files, which include cookies. For this reason, sensitive data, such as passwords, should never be stored in cookies.

```cpp
1   // Fig. 16.17: readcookie.cpp
2   // Program to read cookie data.
3   #include <iostream>
4
5   using std::cout;
6   using std::cin;
7
8   #include <cstdlib>
9   #include <string>
10
11  using std::string;
12
13  int main()
14  {
15     string dataString = "";
16     string nameString = "";
17     string ageString = "";
18     string colorString = "";
19
20     dataString = getenv( "HTTP_COOKIE" );
21
22     // search through cookie data string
23     int nameLocation = dataString.find( "Name=" ) + 5;
24     int endName = dataString.find( "age:" );
25
26     int ageLocation = dataString.find( "age:" ) + 4;
27     int endAge = dataString.find( "color:" );
28
29     int colorLocation = dataString.find( "color:" ) + 6;
30
31     // store cookie data in strings
32     nameString = dataString.substr( nameLocation, endName -
33        nameLocation );
34     ageString = dataString.substr( ageLocation, endAge -
35        ageLocation);
36     colorString = dataString.substr( colorLocation );
37
38     // output header
39     cout << "Content-Type: text/html\n\n";
40
```

Fig. 16.17   Program to read cookies from the client's computer. (Part 1 of 2.)

```
41      // output XML declaration and DOCTYPE
42      cout << "<?xml version = \"1.0\"?>"
43           << "<!DOCTYPE html PUBLIC \"-//W3C//DTD XHTML 1.0 "
44           << "Transitional//EN\" \"http://www.w3.org/TR/xhtml1"
45           << "/DTD/xhtml1-transitional.dtd\">";
46
47      // output html element and some of its contents
48      cout << "<html xmlns = \"http://www.w3.org/1999/xhtml\">"
49           << "<head><title>Read Cookies</title></head>"
50           << "<body>";
51
52      // data was found
53      if ( dataString != "" )
54          cout << "<h3>The following data is saved in a cookie on"
55               << " your computer</h3>"
56               << "<p>Name: "  << nameString  << "<br/></p>"
57               << "<p>Age: "   << ageString   << "<br/></p>"
58               << "<p>Color: " << colorString << "<br/></p>";
59
60      // no data was found
61      else
62          cout << "<p>No cookie data.</p>";
63
64      cout << "</body></html>";
65
66      return 0;
67
```

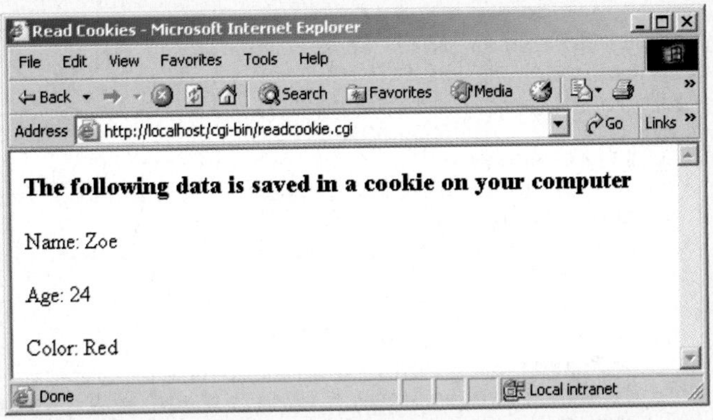

Fig. 16.17 Program to read cookies from the client's computer. (Part 2 of 2.)

16.15 Server-Side Files

The other mechanism by which to maintain state information is to create *server-side files* (i.e., files that are located on the server or on the server's network). This mechanism is a slightly more secure method by which to maintain vital information. In this mechanism, only someone with access and permission to change files on the server can alter files. Figure 16.18 and Fig. 16.19 ask users for contact information then store it on the server. The file that is created by the script is shown in Fig. 16.20.

The XHTML document in Fig. 16.18 posts the form data to the CGI script in Fig. 16.19. In the CGI script, lines 46–106 decode the parameters that were sent by the client. Line 123 creates an instance of the output file stream (**outFile**) that opens a file for appending. If the file **clients.txt** does not exist, it is created. Lines 132–136 output the personal information to the file. (See Fig. 16.20 for the contents of the file.) The remainder of the program outputs an XHTML document that summarizes the user's information.

There are a few important points to make about this program. First, we do not perform any validation on the data before writing the data to disk. Normally, the script would check for bad data, incomplete data, etc. Second, our file is located in the **cgi-bin** directory, which is publicly accessible. If someone knew the filename, it would be relatively easy to access someone else's contact information.

```
1   <?xml version = "1.0"?>
2   <!DOCTYPE html PUBLIC "-//W3C//DTD XHTML 1.0 Transitional//EN"
3   "http://www.w3.org/TR/xhtml1/DTD/xhtml1-transitional.dtd">
4
5   <!-- Fig. 16.18: savefile.html          -->
6   <!-- Form to input client information    -->
7
8   <html xmlns = "http://www.w3.org/1999/xhtml">
9      <head>
10        <title>Please enter your contact information</title>
11     </head>
12
13     <body>
14        <p>Please enter your information in the form below.</p>
15        <p>Note: You must fill in all fields.</p>
16        <form method = "post"
17           action = "/cgi-bin/savefile.cgi">
18           <p>
19              First Name:
20              <input type = "text" name = "firstname" size = "10" />
21              Last Name:
22              <input type = "text" name = "lastname" size = "15" />
23           </p>
24
25           <p>
26              Address:
27              <input type = "text" name = "address" size = "25" />
28              <br />
29              Town:
30              <input type = "text" name = "town" size = "10" />
31              State:
32              <input type = "text" name = "state" size = "2" />
33              <br/>
34              Zip Code:
35              <input type = "text" name = "zipcode" size = "5" />
36              Country:
37              <input type = "text" name = "country" size = "10" />
38           </p>
```

Fig. 16.18   XHTML document to read user's contact information. (Part 1 of 2.)

```
39              <p>
40                  E-mail Address:
41                  <input type = "text" name = "email" />
42              </p>
43                  <input type = "submit" value = "Enter" />
44                  <input type = "reset" value = "Clear" />
45          </form>
46      </body>
47  </html>
```

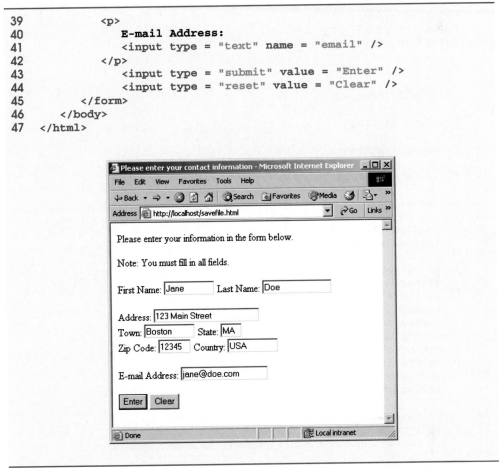

Fig. 16.18 XHTML document to read user's contact information. (Part 2 of 2.)

This script is not robust enough for deployment on the Internet, but it does provide an example of the use of server-side files to store information. Once the files are stored on the server, users cannot change the files unless they are allowed to do so by the server administrator. Thus, storing these files on the server is safer than storing user data in cookies. [*Note:* Many systems store user information in password-protected databases for higher levels of security.]

```
1   // Fig. 16.19: savefile.cpp
2   // Program to enter user's contact information into a
3   // server-side file.
4
5   #include <iostream>
6
7   using std::cerr;
```

Fig. 16.19 Creating a server-side file to store user data. (Part 1 of 5.)

```
8   using std::cout;
9   using std::cin;
10  using std::ios;
11
12  #include <fstream>
13
14  using std::ofstream;
15
16  #include <string>
17
18  using std::string;
19
20  #include <cstdlib>
21
22  int main()
23  {
24     char postString[ 1024 ] = "";
25     int contentLength = 0;
26
27     // variables to store user data
28     string dataString = "";
29     string firstname = "";
30     string lastname = "";
31     string address = "";
32     string town = "";
33     string state = "";
34     string zipcode = "";
35     string country = "";
36     string email = "";
37
38     // data was posted
39     if ( getenv( "CONTENT_LENGTH" ) )
40        contentLength = atoi( getenv( "CONTENT_LENGTH" ) );
41
42     cin.read( postString, contentLength );
43     dataString = postString;
44
45     // search for first '+' character
46     int charLocation = dataString.find( "+" );
47
48     // search for next '+' character
49     while ( charLocation < string::npos ) {
50        dataString.replace( charLocation, 1, " " );
51        charLocation = dataString.find( "+", charLocation + 1 );
52     } // end while
53
54     // find location of firstname
55     int firstStart  = dataString.find( "firstname=" ) + 10;
56     int endFirst = dataString.find( "&lastname" );
57
58     firstname = dataString.substr( firstStart,
59        endFirst - firstStart );
60
```

Fig. 16.19   Creating a server-side file to store user data. (Part 2 of 5.)

```
61      // find location of lastname
62      int lastStart = dataString.find( "lastname=" ) + 9;
63      int endLast = dataString.find( "&address" );
64
65      lastname = dataString.substr( lastStart,
66         endLast - lastStart );
67
68      // find location of address
69      int addressStart = dataString.find( "address=" ) + 8;
70      int endAddress = dataString.find( "&town" );
71
72      address = dataString.substr( addressStart,
73         endAddress - addressStart );
74
75      // find location of town
76      int townStart = dataString.find( "town=" ) + 5;
77      int endTown = dataString.find( "&state" );
78
79      town = dataString.substr( townStart, endTown - townStart);
80
81      // find location of state
82      int stateStart = dataString.find( "state=" ) + 6;
83      int endState = dataString.find( "&zipcode" );
84
85      state = dataString.substr( stateStart,
86         endState - stateStart );
87
88      // find location of zip code
89      int zipStart = dataString.find( "zipcode=" ) + 8;
90      int endZip = dataString.find( "&country" );
91
92      zipcode = dataString.substr( zipStart, endZip - zipStart );
93
94      // find location of country
95      int countryStart = dataString.find( "country=" ) + 8;
96      int endCountry = dataString.find( "&email" );
97
98      country = dataString.substr( countryStart,
99         endCountry - countryStart );
100
101     // find location of e-mail address
102     int emailStart = dataString.find( "email=" ) + 6;
103     int endEmail = dataString.find( "&submit" );
104
105     email = dataString.substr( emailStart,
106        endEmail - emailStart );
107
108     // output header
109     cout << "Content-Type: text/html\n\n";
110
```

Fig. 16.19 Creating a server-side file to store user data. (Part 3 of 5.)

```
111      // output XML declaration and DOCTYPE
112      cout << "<?xml version = \"1.0\"?>"
113           << "<!DOCTYPE html PUBLIC \"-//W3C//DTD XHTML 1.0 "
114           << "Transitional//EN\" \"http://www.w3.org/TR/xhtml1"
115           << "/DTD/xhtml1-transitional.dtd\">";
116
117      // output html element and some of its contents
118      cout << "<html xmlns = \"http://www.w3.org/1999/xhtml\">"
119           << "<head><title>Contact Information entered"
120           << "</title></head><body>";
121
122      // output to file
123      ofstream outFile( "clients.txt", ios::app );
124
125      // file was not opened properly
126      if ( !outFile ) {
127         cerr << "Error: could not open contact file.";
128         exit( 1 );
129      } // end if
130
131      // append data to clients.txt file
132      outFile << firstname << " " << lastname << "\n"
133              << address << "\n" << town << " "
134              << state << " " << country << " "
135              << zipcode << "\n" << email
136              << "\n\n";
137
138      // output data to user
139      cout << "<table><tbody>"
140           << "<tr><td>First Name:</td><td>"
141           << firstname << "</td></tr>"
142           << "<tr><td>Last Name:</td><td>"
143           << lastname << "</td></tr>"
144           << "<tr><td>Address:</td><td>"
145           << address << "</td></tr>"
146           << "<tr><td>Town:</td><td>"
147           << town << "</td></tr>"
148           << "<tr><td>State:</td><td>"
149           << state << "</td></tr>"
150           << "<tr><td>Zip Code:</td><td>"
151           << zipcode << "</td></tr>"
152           << "<tr><td>Country:</td><td>"
153           << country << "</td></tr>"
154           << "<tr><td>Email:</td><td>"
155           << email << "</td></tr>"
156           << "</tbody></table>"
157           << "</body>\n</html>\n";
158
159      return 0;
160
161   } // end main
```

Fig. 16.19 Creating a server-side file to store user data. (Part 4 of 5.)

Fig. 16.19 Creating a server-side file to store user data. (Part 5 of 5.)

```
Jane Doe
123 Main Street
Boston MA USA 12345
jane@doe.com
```

Fig. 16.20 Contents of **clients.txt** data file.

16.16 Case Study: Shopping Cart

Many businesses' Web sites contain shopping-cart applications, which allow customers to buy items conveniently on the Web. The sites record what the consumer wants to purchase and provide an easy, intuitive way to shop online. They do so by using an electronic shopping cart, just as people would use physical shopping carts in retail stores. As users add items to their shopping carts, the sites update the carts' contents. When users "check out," they pay for the items in their shopping carts. To see a real-world electronic shopping cart, we suggest going to the online bookstore **Amazon.com** (**www.amazon.com**).

The shopping cart implemented in this section (Fig. 16.21–Fig. 16.24) allows users to purchase books from a fictitious bookstore that sells four books (see Fig. 16.23). This example uses four scripts, two server-side files and cookies.

Figure 16.21 shows the first of these scripts, the login page. This script is the most complex of all the scripts in this section. The first **if** condition (line 39) determines whether data was posted to the program. The second **if** condition (line 70) determines whether the **dataString** was set (i.e., the decoding completed successfully). The first time we run this program, both conditions fail, so lines 75–86 output an XHTML form to the user, as shown in the first screen capture of Fig. 16.21. When the user fills out the form and clicks the **login** button, **login.cgi** is requested again.

```
1    // Fig. 16.21: login.cpp
2    // Program to output an XHTML form, verify the
3    // username and password entered, and add members.
4    #include <iostream>
5
6    using std::cerr;
7    using std::cout;
8    using std::cin;
9    using std::ios;
10
11   #include <fstream>
12
13   using std::ifstream;
14   using std::ofstream;
15
16   #include <string>
17
18   using std::string;
19
20   #include <cstdlib>
21
22   void header();
23   void writeCookie();
24
25   int main()
26   {
27      char query[ 1024 ] = "";
28      string dataString = "";
29
30      // strings to store username and password
31      string userName = "";
32      string passWord = "";
33      string newCheck = "";
34
35      int contentLength = 0;
36      int endPassword = 0;
37
38      // data was posted
39      if ( getenv( "CONTENT_LENGTH" ) ) {
40
41         // retrieve query string
42         contentLength = atoi( getenv( "CONTENT_LENGTH" ) );
43         cin.read( query, contentLength );
44         dataString = query;
45
46         // find username location
47         int userLocation = dataString.find( "user=" ) + 5;
48         int endUser = dataString.find( "&" );
49
50         // find password location
51         int passwordLocation = dataString.find( "password=" ) + 9;
52
53         endPassword = dataString.find( "&new" );
```

Fig. 16.21   Program that outputs a login page. (Part 1 of 7.)

```
54
55        // new membership requested
56        if ( endPassword > 0 )
57           passWord = dataString.substr( passwordLocation,
58              endPassword - passwordLocation );
59
60        // existing member
61        else
62           passWord = dataString.substr( passwordLocation );
63
64        userName = dataString.substr( userLocation, endUser -
65           userLocation );
66
67     } // end if
68
69     // no data was retrieved
70     if ( dataString == "" ) {
71        header();
72        cout << "<p>Please login.</p>";
73
74        // output login form
75        cout << "<form method = \"post\" "
76             << "action = \"/cgi-bin/login.cgi\"><p>"
77             << "User Name: "
78             << "<input type = \"text\" name = \"user\"/><br/>"
79             << "Password: "
80             << "<input type = \"password\" "
81             << "name = \"password\"/><br/>"
82             << "New? <input type = \"checkbox\""
83             << " name = \"new\" "
84             << "value = \"1\"/></p>"
85             << "<input type = \"submit\" value = \"login\"/>"
86             << "</form>";
87
88     } // end if
89
90     // process entered data
91     else {
92
93        // add new member
94        if ( endPassword > 0 ) {
95           string fileUsername = "";
96           string filePassword = "";
97           bool nameTaken = false;
98
99           // open password file
100          ifstream userData( "userdata.txt", ios::in );
101
102          // could not open file
103          if ( !userData ) {
104             cerr << "Could not open database.";
105             exit( 1 );
106          } // end if
```

Fig. 16.21   Program that outputs a login page. (Part 2 of 7.)

```
107
108        // read username and password from file
109        while ( userData >> fileUsername >> filePassword ) {
110
111            // name is already taken
112            if ( userName == fileUsername )
113                nameTaken = true;
114
115        } // end while
116
117        // user name is taken
118        if ( nameTaken ) {
119            header();
120            cout << "<p>This name has already been taken.</p>"
121                    << "<a href=\"/cgi-bin/login.cgi\">"
122                    << "Try Again</a>";
123        } // end if
124
125        // process data
126        else {
127
128            // write cookie
129            writeCookie();
130            header();
131
132            // open user data file
133            ofstream userData( "userdata.txt", ios::app );
134
135            // could not open file
136            if ( !userData ) {
137                cerr << "Could not open database.";
138                exit( 1 );
139            } // end if
140
141            // write user data to file
142            userData << "\n" << userName << "\n" << passWord;
143
144            cout << "<p>Your information has been processed."
145                    << "<a href=\"/cgi-bin/shop.cgi\">"
146                    << "Start Shopping</a></p>";
147
148        } // end else
149    } // end if
150
151    // search for password if entered
152    else {
153
154        // strings to store username and password from file
155        string fileUsername = "";
156        string filePassword = "";
157        bool authenticated = false;
158        bool userFound = false;
159
```

Fig. 16.21   Program that outputs a login page. (Part 3 of 7.)

```
160              // open password file
161              ifstream userData( "userdata.txt", ios::in );
162
163          // could not open file
164          if ( !userData ) {
165             cerr << "Could not open database.";
166             exit( 1 );
167          } // end if
168
169          // read in user data
170          while ( userData >> fileUsername >> filePassword ) {
171
172             // username and password match
173             if ( userName == fileUsername &&
174                passWord == filePassword )
175                authenticated = true;
176
177             // username was found
178             if ( userName == fileUsername )
179                userFound = true;
180          } // end while
181
182          // user is authenticated
183          if ( authenticated ) {
184             writeCookie();
185             header();
186
187             cout << "<p>Thank you for returning, "
188                  << userName << "!</p>"
189                  << "<a href=\"/cgi-bin/shop.cgi\">"
190                  << "Start Shopping</a>";
191          } // end if
192
193          // user not authenticated
194          else {
195             header();
196
197             // password is incorrect
198             if ( userFound )
199                cout << "<p>You have entered an incorrect "
200                     << "password. Please try again.</p>"
201                     << "<a href=\"/cgi-bin/login.cgi\">"
202                     << "Back to login</a>";
203
204             // user is not registered
205             else
206                cout << "<p>You are not a registered user.</p>"
207                     << "<a href=\"/cgi-bin/login.cgi\">"
208                     << "Register</a>";
209
210          } // end else
211       } // end else
212    } // end if
```

Fig. 16.21   Program that outputs a login page. (Part 4 of 7.)

```
213
214     cout << "</body>\n</html>\n";
215     return 0;
216
217  } // end main
218
219  // function to output header
220  void header()
221  {
222     // output header
223     cout << "Content-Type: text/html\n\n";
224
225     // output XML declaration and DOCTYPE
226     cout << "<?xml version = \"1.0\"?>"
227          << "<!DOCTYPE html PUBLIC \"-//W3C//DTD XHTML 1.0 "
228          << "Transitional//EN\" \"http://www.w3.org/TR/xhtml1"
229          << "/DTD/xhtml1-transitional.dtd\">";
230
231     // output html element and some of its contents
232     cout << "<html xmlns = \"http://www.w3.org/1999/xhtml\">"
233          << "<head><title>Login Page</title></head>"
234          << "<body>";
235
236  } // end header
237
238  // function to write cookie data
239  void writeCookie()
240  {
241     string expires = "Friday, 14-MAY-04 16:00:00 GMT";
242     cout << "Set-Cookie: CART=; expires="
243          << expires << "; path=\n";
244
245  } // end writeCookie
```

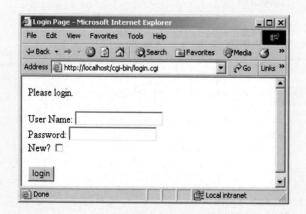

Fig. 16.21   Program that outputs a login page. (Part 5 of 7.)

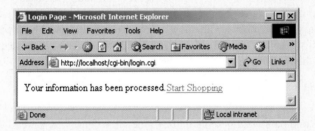

Fig. 16.21   Program that outputs a login page. (Part 6 of 7.)

Fig. 16.21   Program that outputs a login page. (Part 7 of 7.)

If the user checked the **New** checkbox on the Web page to create a new membership, the condition on line 94 evaluates to **true**. Next, we open **userdata.txt** (line 100)—the file that contains all the usernames and passwords. Lines 109–115 read through this file, comparing each username with the name entered. If the name is already in the list, lines 120–122 output a message to the user indicating that the name has been taken, and a link to the form is provided. Otherwise, the new user is added to the list. The file is opened again on line 133—this time for appending. Line 142 adds the new user information to **user-data.txt** in the format

```
Bernard
Jones
```

Each username and password is separated by a newline character. Lines 144–146 provide a hyperlink to the script of Fig. 16.22, which allows users to purchase items.

The last possible scenario for this script is for returning users (lines 152–211). This portion of the program executes when the user enters a name and password but does not select the **New** checkbox (i.e., the **else** of line 152 is evaluated). In this case, we assume that the user already has a username and password in **userdata.txt**. Lines 170–180 read through **userdata.txt** in an attempt to locate the username entered. If the username is found and the password entered is correct (lines 173–174), boolean variable **authenticated** is set to **true**. Line 183 determines whether the user has been authenticated. Function **writeCookie** is called to initialize the cookie and to remove existing data from prior sessions (line 184). The cookie, which is named **CART** (line 242), is used by other scripts to store book information. A message is output welcoming the user back to the Web site and providing a link to purchase books (**shop.cgi**) on lines 187–190.

If the user was not authenticated, the program determines whether the user was found (line 198). If the user was found but not authenticated, a message is output indicating that the password is invalid. A hyperlink is provided to the login page (**<a href="/cgi-bin/login.cgi">**), where the user can attempt to login again. If neither the username nor the password were found, an unregistered user has attempted to sign on (line 205). A message is output indicating that the user does not have the proper authorization to access the page, and lines 206–208 provide a link that allows the user to attempt another login.

Figure 16.22 uses the values in **catalog.txt** (Fig. 16.25) to output the items that the user can purchase. The **while** structure (lines 73–93) outputs a table containing the items. The last column for each row includes a button for adding the item to the shopping cart. Hidden form fields are specified for each book and its associated information. Lines 73–77 output the different values for each book, and lines 83–93 output a form containing **submit** buttons for purchasing books.

When a user purchases a book, the **viewcart.cgi** script is requested, and the ISBN for the book to be purchased is sent to the script. Figure 16.23 begins by reading the value of the cookie stored on the user's system on line 38. Any existing cookie data is stored in **string cookieString** (line 39). The entered ISBN number from the form of Fig. 16.22 is stored in **string isbnEntered** (line 54). The script determines whether the cart already contains data (line 65). If not, the **cookieString** is given the value of the entered ISBN number (line 66). If the cookie already contains data, the entered ISBN is appended to the existing cookie data (line 70). The new book is stored in the **CART** cookie on lines 73–74. The cart's contents are output in a table by calling function **outputBooks** (line 95).

```
1   // Fig. 16.22: shop.cpp
2   // Program to display available books.
3   #include <iostream>
4
5   using std::cerr;
6   using std::cout;
7   using std::cin;
8   using std::ios;
9
10  #include <istream>
11
12  #include <fstream>
13
14  using std::ifstream;
15  using std::ofstream;
16
17  #include <string>
18
19  using std::string;
20
21  #include <cstdlib>
22
23  void header();
24
25  int main()
26  {
27      // variables to store product information
28      char book[ 50 ] = "";
29      char year[ 50 ] = "";
30      char isbn[ 50 ] = "";
31      char price[ 50 ] = "";
32
33      string bookString = "";
34      string yearString = "";
35      string isbnString = "";
36      string priceString = "";
```

Fig. 16.22 CGI script that allows users to buy a book. (Part 1 of 3.)

```
37
38      bool nameTaken = false;
39
40      // open file for input
41      ifstream userData( "catalog.txt", ios::in );
42
43      // file could not be opened
44      if ( !userData ) {
45         cerr << "Could not open database.";
46         exit( 1 );
47      } // end if
48
49      header(); // output header
50
51      // output available books
52      cout << "<center><br/>Books available for sale<br/>"
53           << "<a href=\"/cgi-bin/logout.cgi\">Sign Out"
54           << "</a><br/><br/>"
55           << "<table border = \"1\" cellpadding = \"7\" >";
56
57      // file is open
58      while ( userData ) {
59
60         // retrieve data from file
61         userData.getline( book, 50 );
62         bookString = book;
63
64         userData.getline( year, 50 );
65         yearString = year;
66
67         userData.getline( isbn, 50 );
68         isbnString = isbn;
69
70         userData.getline( price, 50 );
71         priceString = price;
72
73         cout << "<tr>"
74              << "<td>" << bookString << "</td>"
75              << "<td>" << yearString << "</td>"
76              << "<td>" << isbnString << "</td>"
77              << "<td>" << priceString << "</td>";
78
79         // file is still open after reads
80         if ( userData )
81
82            // output form with buy button
83            cout << "<td><form method=\"post\" "
84                 << "action=\"/cgi-bin/viewcart.cgi\">"
85                 << "<input type=\"hidden\" name=\"add\""
86                 << "value=\"true\"/>"
87                 << "<input type=\"hidden\" name=\"isbn\""
88                 << "value=\"" << isbnString << "\"/>"
89                 << "<input type=\"submit\""
```

Fig. 16.22   CGI script that allows users to buy a book. (Part 2 of 3.)

```
90                       << "value=\"Buy\"/>\n"
91                       << "</form></td>\n";
92
93            cout << "</tr>\n";
94
95        } // end while
96
97        cout << "</table></center></body></html>";
98        return 0;
99    }
100
101    // function to output header information
102    void header()
103    {
104        // output header
105        cout << "Content-Type: text/html\n\n";
106
107        // output XML declaration and DOCTYPE
108        cout << "<?xml version = \"1.0\"?>"
109             << "<!DOCTYPE html PUBLIC \"-//W3C//DTD XHTML 1.0 "
110             << "Transitional//EN\" \"http://www.w3.org/TR/xhtml1"
111             << "/DTD/xhtml11-transitional.dtd\">";
112
113        // output html element and some of its contents
114        cout << "<html xmlns = \"http://www.w3.org/1999/xhtml\">"
115             << "<head><title>Login Page</title></head>"
116             << "<body>";
117    } // end header
```

Fig. 16.22   CGI script that allows users to buy a book. (Part 3 of 3.)

Figure 16.24 allows the user to log out of the shopping-cart application. This script outputs a message to the user and calls **writeCookie** (line 20), thus erasing the current information in the shopping cart.

```
1    // Fig. 16.23: viewcart.cpp
2    // Program to view books in the shopping cart.
3    #include <iostream>
4
5    using std::cerr;
6    using std::cout;
7    using std::cin;
8    using std::ios;
9
10   #include <istream>
11
12   #include <fstream>
13
14   using std::ifstream;
15   using std::ofstream;
16
```

Fig. 16.23   CGI script that allows users to view their carts' content. (Part 1 of 5.)

```
17   #include <string>
18
19   using std::string;
20
21   #include <cstdlib>
22
23   void outputBooks( const string &, const string & );
24
25   int main()
26   {
27      // variable to store query string
28      char query[ 1024 ] = "";
29      char *cartData; // variable to hold contents of cart
30
31      string dataString = "";
32      string cookieString = "";
33      string isbnEntered = "";
34      int contentLength = 0;
35
36      // retrieve cookie data
37      if ( getenv( "HTTP_COOKIE" ) ) {
38         cartData = getenv( "HTTP_COOKIE" );
39         cookieString = cartData;
40      } // end if
41
42      // data was entered
43      if ( getenv( "CONTENT_LENGTH" ) ) {
44         contentLength = atoi( getenv( "CONTENT_LENGTH" ) );
45         cin.read( query, contentLength );
46         dataString = query;
47
48         // find location of isbn value
49         int addLocation = dataString.find( "add=" ) + 4;
50         int endAdd = dataString.find( "&isbn" );
51         int isbnLocation = dataString.find( "isbn=" ) + 5;
52
53         // retrieve isbn number to add to cart
54         isbnEntered = dataString.substr( isbnLocation );
55
56         // write cookie
57         string expires = "Friday, 14-MAY-10 16:00:00 GMT";
58         int cartLocation = cookieString.find( "CART=" ) + 5;
59
60         // cookie exists
61         if ( cartLocation > 0 )
62            cookieString = cookieString.substr( cartLocation );
63
64         // no cookie data exists
65         if ( cookieString == "" )
66            cookieString = isbnEntered;
67
```

Fig. 16.23 CGI script that allows users to view their carts' content. (Part 2 of 5.)

```
68        // cookie data exists
69        else
70            cookieString += "," + isbnEntered;
71
72        // set cookie
73        cout << "Set-Cookie: CART=" << cookieString << "; expires="
74            << expires << "; path=\n";
75
76    } // end if
77
78    // output header
79    cout << "Content-Type: text/html\n\n";
80
81    // output XML declaration and DOCTYPE
82    cout << "<?xml version = \"1.0\"?>"
83        << "<!DOCTYPE html PUBLIC \"-//W3C//DTD XHTML 1.0 "
84        << "Transitional//EN\" \"http://www.w3.org/TR/xhtml1"
85        << "/DTD/xhtml1-transitional.dtd\">";
86
87    // output html element and some of its contents
88    cout << "<html xmlns = \"http://www.w3.org/1999/xhtml\">"
89        << "<head><title>Shopping Cart</title></head>"
90        << "<body><center>"
91        << "<p>Here is your current order:</p>";
92
93    // cookie data exists
94    if ( cookieString != "" )
95        outputBooks( cookieString, isbnEntered );
96
97    cout << "</body></html>\n";
98    return 0;
99
100 } // end main
101
102 // function to output books in catalog.txt
103 void outputBooks( const string &cookieRef, const string &isbnRef )
104 {
105    char book[ 50 ] = "";
106    char year[ 50 ] = "";
107    char isbn[ 50 ] = "";
108    char price[ 50 ] = "";
109
110    string bookString = "";
111    string yearString = "";
112    string isbnString = "";
113    string priceString = "";
114
115    // open file for input
116    ifstream userData( "catalog.txt", ios::in );
117
```

Fig. 16.23 CGI script that allows users to view their carts' content. (Part 3 of 5.)

```
118    // file could not be opened
119    if ( !userData ) {
120       cerr << "Could not open database.";
121       exit( 1 );
122    } // end if
123
124    // output link to log out and table to display books
125    cout << "<a href=\"/cgi-bin/logout.cgi\">Sign Out";
126    cout << "</a><br><br>";
127    cout << "<table border = 1 cellpadding = 7 >";
128
129    // file is open
130    while ( userData ) {
131
132       // retrieve book information
133       userData.getline( book, 50 );
134       bookString = book;
135
136       // retrieve year information
137       userData.getline( year, 50 );
138       yearString = year;
139
140       // retrieve isbn number
141       userData.getline( isbn, 50 );
142       isbnString = isbn;
143
144       // retrieve price
145       userData.getline( price, 50 );
146       priceString = price;
147
148       int match = cookieRef.find( isbn );
149
150       // match has been made
151       if ( match > 0 || isbnRef == isbnString ) {
152
153          // output table row with book information
154          cout << "<tr>"
155               << "<form method=\"post\""
156               << "action=\"/cgi-bin/viewcart.cgi\">"
157               << "<td>" << bookString << "</td>"
158               << "<td>" << yearString << "</td>"
159               << "<td>" << isbnString << "</td>"
160               << "<td>" << priceString << "</td>";
161
162       } // end if
163
164       cout << "</form></tr>";
165
166    } // end while
167
168    // output link to add more books
169    cout << "<a href=\"/cgi-bin/shop.cgi\">Back to book list</a>";
170 } // end outputBooks
```

Fig. 16.23 CGI script that allows users to view their carts' content. (Part 4 of 5.)

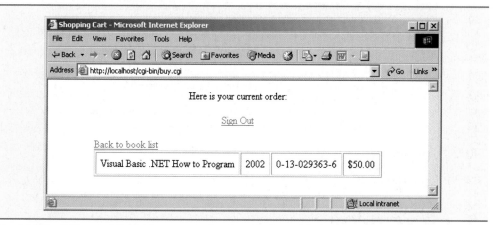

Fig. 16.23 CGI script that allows users to view their carts' content. (Part 5 of 5.)

Figure 16.25 shows the contents of the **catalog.txt** file. This file must reside in the same directory where the CGI scripts reside for this shopping-cart application to work correctly.

```
1   // Fig. 16.24: logout.cpp
2   // Program to log out of the system.
3   #include <iostream>
4
5   using std::cout;
6
7   #include <string>
8
9   using std::string;
10
11  #include <ctime>
12
13  #include <cstdlib>
14
15  void writeCookie();
16
17  int main()
18  {
19     // write the cookie
20     writeCookie();
21
22     // output header
23     cout << "Content-Type: text/html\n\n";
24
25     // output XML declaration and DOCTYPE
26     cout << "<?xml version = \"1.0\"?>"
27          << "<!DOCTYPE html PUBLIC \"-//W3C//DTD XHTML 1.0 "
28          << "Transitional//EN\"";
29
```

Fig. 16.24 Logout program. (Part 1 of 2.)

```
30        // output html element and its contents
31        cout << "<html xmlns = \"http://www.w3.org/1999/xhtml\">"
32             << "<head><title>Logged Out</title></head>"
33             << "<body>"
34             << "<center><p>You are now logged out<br>"
35             << "You will be billed accordingly<br>"
36             << "To login again, "
37             << "<a href=\"/cgi-bin/login.cgi\">click here</a>"
38             << "</body></html>\n";
39
40        return 0;
41
42    } // end main
43
44    // function to write cookie
45    void writeCookie()
46    {
47        // string containing expiration date
48        string expires = "Friday, 14-MAY-10 16:00:00 GMT";
49
50        // set cookie
51        cout << "Set-Cookie: CART=; expires=" << expires
52             << "; path=\n";
53
54    } // end writeCookie
```

Fig. 16.24 Logout program. (Part 2 of 2.)

16.17 Internet and Web Resources

Apache

www.apache.org
This is the product home page for the Apache HTTP server. Users may download Apache from this site.

www.apacheweek.com
This online magazine contains articles about Apache jobs, product reviews and other information concerning Apache software.

linuxtoday.com/stories/18780.html
This site contains an article about the Apache HTTP server and the platforms that support it. It also contains links to other Apache articles.

```
Visual Basic .NET How to Program
2002
0-13-029363-6
$50.00
C# How to Program
2002
0-13-062221-4
$49.95
C How to Program 3e
2001
0-13-089572-5
$50.00
Java How to Program 4e
2002
0-13-034151-7
$49.95
```

Fig. 16.25 Contents of `catalog.txt`.

CGI

www.gnu.org/software/cgicc/cgicc.html
This site contains a free open-source CGI library for creating CGI scripts in C++.

www.hotscripts.com
This site contains a rich collection of scripts for performing image manipulation, server administration, networking, etc. using CGI.

www.jmarshall.com/easy/cgi
This page contains a brief explanation of CGI for those with programming experience.

www.speakeasy.org/~cgires
This site contains a collection of CGI-related tutorials and scripts.

www.w3.org/CGI
This World Wide Web Consortium page discusses CGI security issues.

www.w3.org/Protocols
This World Wide Web Consortium site contains information on the HTTP specification and links to news, mailing lists and published articles.

SUMMARY

- Web servers respond to client requests by providing resources, such as XHTML documents.

- Web servers and clients communicate with each other via the platform-independent Hypertext Transfer Protocol (HTTP).

- The most common HTTP request types are *get* and *post*; these requests send client form data to a Web server.

- The *get* request sends form content as part of the URL; the *post* request attaches form contents to the end of an HTTP request. The data sent in a *post* request are not part of the URL and cannot be seen by the user.

- Browsers often cache Web pages for quick reloading. However, browsers typically do not cache the server's response to a *post* request, because the information might have changed.

- The information tier maintains data for the application in a database.

- A Web server is part of a multi-tier application—sometimes referred to as an *n*-tier application. A multi-tier application divides functionality into separate tiers. The three-tier application contains an information tier, a middle tier and a client tier.

- The middle tier implements business logic and presentation logic to control interactions between application clients and application data. A Web server is a middle-tier application.

- The client tier is the application's user interface. The client interacts with the middle tier to make requests and to retrieve data from the information tier. The client then displays data retrieved from the middle tier to the user.

- The Apache HTTP server, developed by the Apache Group, is the most popular Web server in use today. It runs on Windows and non-Windows platforms.

- A virtual directory is an alias for an existing directory on a local machine.

- The Common Gateway Interface (CGI) describes a set of protocols through which applications (commonly called CGI scripts or CGI programs) can interact with Web servers and interact (indirectly) with clients.

- CGI is "common" in the sense that it is not specific to any particular operating system (such as Linux or Windows) or to any one programming language.

- A Web page, in its simplest form, is nothing more than an XHTML document. This document is just a plain text file containing markings (markup or elements) that describe to a Web browser how to display and format the information in the document.

- Hypertext information creates links to different pages or to other portions of the same page.

- Any XHTML file available for viewing over the Internet has a URL (Universal Resource Locator) associated with it. The URL contains information that directs a browser to the resource that the user wishes to access.

- The hostname is the name of the computer where the resource resides and is translated into an IP address, which identifies the server on the Internet.

- To request a resource, the browser first sends an HTTP request message to the server. The server responds with a line indicating the HTTP version, followed by a numeric code and a phrase describing the status of the transaction. The server normally then sends one or more HTTP headers, which provide additional information about the data being sent. The header or set of headers is followed by a blank line, which indicates that the server finished sending HTTP headers. Then the server sends the contents of the requested resource, and the connection is terminated. The client-side browser interprets the XHTML it receives and displays the results.

- A properly configured Web server will recognize a CGI script and execute it. A resource usually is designated as a CGI script in one of two ways: Either it has a specific filename extension (such as **.cgi** or **.exe**), or it is located in a special directory (often **/cgi-bin**). The server administrator must give permission for remote clients to access and execute CGI scripts.

- When the server recognizes that the resource requested is a CGI script, the server executes the script. The output is piped to the Web server. Finally, the Web server adds an additional line to the output indicating the status of the HTTP transaction (such as **HTTP/1.1 200 OK**, for success) and sends the whole body of text to the client. The browser on the client side then interprets the output and displays the results appropriately.

- With a CGI script, programmers must include the **Content-Type** header explicitly, whereas with a normal XHTML document, the header would be added by the Web server.

- The CGI protocol for output to be sent to a Web browser consists of printing to standard output the **Content-Type** header, a blank line and the data (XHTML, plain text, etc.) to be output.

- CGI-enabled Web servers set environment variables that provide information about both the server's and the client's script-execution environment.

- The environment variable **QUERY_STRING** provides a mechanism that enables programmers to supply any sort of data to their CGI scripts. The **QUERY_STRING** variable contains information that is appended to a URL. A question mark character (**?**) delimits the resource requested from the query string.

- Data placed in a query string can be structured in a variety of ways, provided that the CGI script that reads the string knows how to interpret the encoded data.

- Forms provide another way for users to input information that is sent to a CGI script.

- The **<form>** element generally takes two attributes. The first attribute is **action**, which specifies the action to take when the user submits the form. The second attribute is **method**, which is either **GET** or **POST**.

- Using *get* with a form causes data to be passed to the CGI script through environment variable **QUERY_STRING**.

- The **POST** method enables CGI scripts to interact with servers via standard input.

- With **POST**, data is encoded just as with **QUERY_STRING**, but the **QUERY_STRING** environment variable is not set. Instead, the **POST** method sets the environment variable **CONTENT_LENGTH** to indicate the number of characters of data that are being sent or posted, then function **read** is used with **STDIN** to obtain the data.

- Web browsers encode the form data before it is sent. This means that spaces are replaced with plus signs, and certain other symbols (such as the apostrophe) are converted into their ASCII value equivalent and displayed in hexadecimal notation (preceded by a percent sign).

- A CGI script can supply HTTP headers in addition to **Content-Type**. In most cases, the server passes these extra headers to the client untouched.

- The CGI protocol indicates that certain types of headers output by a CGI script are to be handled by the server, rather than be passed directly to the client.

- Function **getenv** from library **<cstdlib>** returns a character array containing the value of the CGI environment variable passed to it.

TERMINOLOGY

action attribute of element form
Apache HTTP Server
asctime
<body> element
bottom tier
button type attribute for **input** element
cache
/cgi-bin directory
CGI (Common Gateway Interface)
.cgi file extension
CGI program
CGI script
CGI specification
checkbox type attribute for **input** element
client tier
CONTENT_LENGTH environment variable
Content-Type header
.cpp file extension
data tier

DNS lookup
domain name
domain name system (DNS)
dynamic vs. static Web content
dynamic Web content
Extensible HyperText Markup Language (XHTML)
file type attribute for **input** elements
filepath
form
form element
fully qualified host name
get (HTTP request)
getenv function of **<cstdlib>**
head element
hidden type attribute for **input** elements
host
hostname
htdocs directory

html element
HTTP (Hypertext Transfer Protocol)
HTTP connection
HTTP header
HTTP host
HTTP method
HTTP transaction
HTTP_USER_AGENT environment variable
HyperText Markup Language (HTML)
HyperText Transfer Protocol (HTTP)
image type attribute for input element
information tier
input element
IP address
local Web server
localhost
localtime
markup
method attribute of form element
middle tier
multi-tier application
n-tier application
open source
password type attribute for input element
pipe

post (HTTP request)
QUERY_STRING environment variable
radio type attribute for input element
redirect
remote Web server
request method
request type
reset type attribute for input element
select element
standard output
static Web content
submit type attribute for input element
text type attribute for input element
textarea element
title element
top tier
top-level domain (TLD)
URL (Universal Resource Locator)
virtual directory
Web server
XHTML
XHTML element
XHTML form
XHTML form element

SELF-REVIEW EXERCISES

16.1   Fill in the blanks in each of the following statements:
   a)   The two most common HTTP request types are _____ and _____.
   b)   Browsers often _____ Web pages for quick reloading.
   c)   In a three-tier application, a Web server is typically part of the _____ tier.
   d)   In the URL **http://www.deitel.com/books/downloads.htm**, the part that consists of **www.deitel.com** is the _____ of the server, where a client can find the desired resource.
   e)   A(n) _____ document is a text file containing markings that describe to a Web browser how to display and format the information in the document.
   f)   The environment variable _____ provides a mechanism for supplying data to CGI scripts.
   g)   A common way of reading input from the user is to implement _____.

16.2   State whether each of the following is *true* or *false*. If *false*, explain why.
   a)   Web servers and clients communicate with each other through the platform-independent HTTP.
   b)   Web servers often cache Web pages for reloading.
   c)   The information tier implements business logic to control the type of information that is presented to a particular client.
   d)   A dynamic Web page is a Web page that is not created programmatically.
   e)   We put data into a query string using a format that consists of a series of name-value pairs joined with exclamation points (**!**).

f) Using a CGI script is more efficient than using an XHTML document.

g) The *post* method of submitting form data is preferable when sending personal information to the Web server.

ANSWERS TO SELF-REVIEW EXERCISES

16.1   a) *get* and *post*. b) cache. c) middle. d) hostname. e) XHTML. f) **QUERY_STRING**. g) forms.

16.2   a) True. b) True. Web browsers often cache Web pages for quick reloading c) False. The middle tier implements business logic and presentation logic to control interactions between application clients and application data. d) False. A dynamic Web page is a Web page that is created programmatically. e) False. The pairs are joined with an ampersand (**&**). f) False. XHTML documents are more efficient than CGI scripts because XHTML documents do not need to be executed on the server side before they are output to the client. g) True.

EXERCISES

16.3   Define the following terms:
   a) HTTP.
   b) Multi-tier application.
   c) Request method.

16.4   Explain the difference between the *get* request type and the *post* request type. When is it ideal to use the *post* request type?

16.5   Write a CGI script that prints the squares of the integers from 1 to 10 on separate lines.

16.6   Write a CGI script that receives as input three numbers from the client and returns a statement indicating whether the three numbers could represent an equilateral triangle (all three sides are the same length), an isosceles triangle (two sides are the same length) or a right triangle (the square of one side is equal to the sum of the squares of the other two sides.)

16.7   Write a soothsayer script that allows the user to submit a question. When the question is submitted, the script should choose a random response from a list of vague answers and return a new page displaying the answer.

16.8   Modify the program of Fig. 16.14 to incorporate the opening XHTML form and the processing of the data into a single CGI script (i.e., combine the XHTML of Fig. 16.13 into the CGI script of Fig. 16.14.) When the CGI script is requested initially, the form should be displayed. When the form is submitted, the CGI script should execute.

16.9   Modify the shopping-cart application to enable users to remove items from the cart.

17

Data Structures

Objectives

- To be able to form linked data structures using pointers, self-referential classes and recursion.
- To be able to create and manipulate dynamic data structures such as linked lists, queues, stacks and binary trees.
- To understand various important applications of linked data structures.
- To understand how to create reusable data structures with class templates, inheritance and composition.

Much that I bound, I could not free;
Much that I freed returned to me.
Lee Wilson Dodd

'Will you walk a little faster?' said a whiting to a snail,
'There's a porpoise close behind us, and he's treading on my tail.'
Lewis Carroll

There is always room at the top.
Daniel Webster

Push on — keep moving.
Thomas Morton

I think that I shall never see
A poem lovely as a tree.
Joyce Kilmer

Outline

17.1 Introduction

17.2 Self-Referential Classes

17.3 Dynamic Memory Allocation and Data Structures

17.4 Linked Lists

17.5 Stacks

17.6 Queues

17.7 Trees

Summary • Terminology • Self-Review Exercises • Answers to Self-Review Exercises • Exercises • Special Section: Building Your Own Compiler

17.1 Introduction

We have studied fixed-size *data structures* such as single-subscripted arrays, double-subscripted arrays and **struct**s. This chapter introduces *dynamic data structures* that grow and shrink during execution. *Linked lists* are collections of data items "lined up in a row"— insertions and removals are made anywhere in a linked list. *Stacks* are important in compilers and operating systems: Insertions and removals are made only at one end of a stack—its *top*. *Queues* represent waiting lines; insertions are made at the back (also referred to as the *tail*) of a queue and removals are made from the front (also referred to as the *head*) of a queue. *Binary trees* facilitate high-speed searching and sorting of data, efficient elimination of duplicate data items, representation of file system directories and compilation of expressions into machine language. These data structures have many other interesting applications.

We will discuss the major types of data structures and implement programs that create and manipulate these data structures. We use classes, class templates, inheritance and composition to create and package these data structures for reusability and maintainability.

Studying this chapter is solid preparation for Chapter 21, Standard Template Library (STL). The STL is a major portion of the C++ Standard Library. The STL provides containers, iterators for traversing those containers and algorithms for processing the elements of those containers. You will see that the STL has taken each of the data structures we discuss in this chapter and packaged them into templatized classes. The STL code is carefully written to be portable, efficient and extensible. Once you understand the principles and construction of data structures as presented in this chapter, you will be able to make the best use of the prepackaged data structures, iterators and algorithms in the STL, a world-class set of components for helping realize the vision of software reuse.

The chapter examples are practical programs that you will be able to use in more advanced courses and in industry applications. The programs are especially heavy on pointer manipulation. The exercises include a rich collection of useful applications.

We encourage you to attempt the major project described in the special section entitled "Building Your Own Compiler." You have been using a compiler to translate your C++ programs to machine language so that you could execute these programs on your computer. In this project, you will actually build your own compiler. It will read a file of statements written in a simple, yet powerful, high-level language similar to early versions of the popular language BASIC. Your compiler will translate these statements into a file of Simpletron

Machine Language (SML) instructions—SML is the language you learned in the Chapter 5 special section, "Building Your Own Computer." Your Simpletron Simulator program will then execute the SML program produced by your compiler! Implementing this project using a heavily object-oriented approach will give you a wonderful opportunity to exercise most of what you have learned in this course. The special section carefully walks you through the specifications of the high-level language and describes the algorithms you will need to convert each type of high-level language statement into machine language instructions. If you enjoy being challenged, you might attempt the many enhancements to both the compiler and the Simpletron Simulator suggested in this chapter's exercises.

17.2 Self-Referential Classes

A *self-referential class* contains a pointer member that points to a class object of the same class type. For example, the definition

```
class Node {

public:
   Node( int );
   void setData( int );
   int getData() const;
   void setNextPtr( Node * );
   Node *getNextPtr() const;

private:
   int data;
   Node *nextPtr;

}; // end class Node
```

defines a type, **Node**. Type **Node** has two **private** data members—integer member **data** and pointer member **nextPtr**. Member **nextPtr** points to an object of type **Node**—another object of the same type as the one being declared here, hence the term "self-referential class." Member **nextPtr** is referred to as a *link*—i.e., **nextPtr** can be used to "tie" an object of type **Node** to another object of the same type. Type **Node** also has five member functions—a constructor that receives an integer to initialize member **data**, a **setData** function to set the value of member **data**, a **getData** function to return the value of member **data**, a **setNextPtr** function to set the value of member **nextPtr** and a **getNextPtr** function to return the value of member **nextPtr**.

Self-referential class objects can be linked together to form useful data structures such as lists, queues, stacks and trees. Figure 17.1 illustrates two self-referential class objects linked together to form a list. Note that a slash—representing a null (**0**) pointer—is placed in the link member of the second self-referential class object to indicate that the link does not point to another object. The slash is only for illustration purposes; it does not correspond to the backslash character in C++. A null pointer normally indicates the end of a data structure just as the null character (**'\0'**) indicates the end of a string.

Common Programming Error 17.1

*Not setting the link in the last node of a linked data structure to null (**0**) is a (possibly fatal) logic error.*

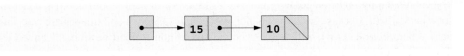

Fig. 17.1   Two self-referential class objects linked together.

17.3 Dynamic Memory Allocation and Data Structures

Creating and maintaining dynamic data structures requires dynamic memory allocation, which enables a program to obtain more memory at execution time to hold new nodes. When that memory is no longer needed by the program, the memory can be released so that it can be reused to allocate other objects in the future. The limit for dynamic memory allocation can be as large as the amount of available physical memory in the computer or the amount of available virtual memory in a virtual memory system. Often, the limits are much smaller because available memory must be shared among many programs.

Operators **new** and **delete** are essential to dynamic memory allocation. Operator **new** takes as an argument the type of the object being dynamically allocated and returns a pointer to an object of that type. For example, the statement

```
Node *newPtr = new Node( 10 );
```

allocates **sizeof(Node)** bytes, runs the **Node** constructor and stores a pointer to this memory in **newPtr**. If no memory is available, **new** throws a **bad_alloc** exception. The value **10** is the node's data.

The **delete** operator runs the **Node** destructor and deallocates memory allocated with **new**—the memory is returned to the system so that the memory can be reallocated in the future. To free memory dynamically allocated by the preceding **new**, use the statement

```
delete newPtr;
```

Note that **newPtr** itself is not deleted; rather the space **newPtr** points to is deleted. If **newPtr** has the value **0** (i.e., a pointer to nothing), the preceding statement has no effect.

The following sections discuss lists, stacks, queues and trees. The data structures presented in this chapter are created and maintained with dynamic memory allocation and self-referential classes.

Common Programming Error 17.2

Not returning dynamically allocated memory when it is no longer needed can cause the system to run out of memory prematurely. This is sometimes called a "memory leak."

17.4 Linked Lists

A *linked list* is a linear collection of self-referential class objects, called *nodes,* connected by pointer *links*—hence, the term "linked" list. A linked list is accessed via a pointer to the first node of the list. Subsequent nodes are accessed via the link-pointer member stored in each node. By convention, the link pointer in the last node of a list is set to null (zero) to mark the end of the list. Data are stored in a linked list dynamically—each node is created as necessary. A node can contain data of any type, including objects of other classes. If nodes contain base-class pointers or base-class references to base-class and derived-class objects related by inheritance, we can have a linked list of such nodes and use **virtual** function calls to process these objects polymorphically. Stacks and queues are also linear data structures and, as we will see, can be viewed as constrained versions of linked lists. Trees are nonlinear data structures.

Lists of data can be stored in arrays, but linked lists provide several advantages. A linked list is appropriate when the number of data elements to be represented at one time is unpredictable. Linked lists are dynamic, so the length of a list can increase or decrease as necessary. The size of a "conventional" C++ array, however, cannot be altered, because the array size is fixed at compile time. "Conventional" arrays can become full. Linked lists become full only when the system has insufficient memory to satisfy dynamic storage allocation requests.

Performance Tip 17.1

An array can be declared to contain more elements than the number of items expected, but this can waste memory. Linked lists can provide better memory utilization in these situations. Linked lists allow the program to adapt at run time.

Linked lists can be maintained in sorted order by inserting each new element at the proper point in the list. Existing list elements do not need to be moved.

Performance Tip 17.2

Insertion and deletion in a sorted array can be time consuming—all the elements following the inserted or deleted element must be shifted appropriately.

Performance Tip 17.3

The elements of an array are stored contiguously in memory. This allows immediate access to any array element because the address of any element can be calculated directly based on its position relative to the beginning of the array. Linked lists do not afford such immediate "direct access" to their elements.

Linked list nodes are normally not stored contiguously in memory. Logically, however, the nodes of a linked list appear to be contiguous. Figure 17.2 illustrates a linked list with several nodes.

Performance Tip 17.4

Using dynamic memory allocation (instead of arrays) for data structures that grow and shrink at execution time can save memory. Keep in mind, however, that pointers occupy space and that dynamic memory allocation incurs the overhead of function calls.

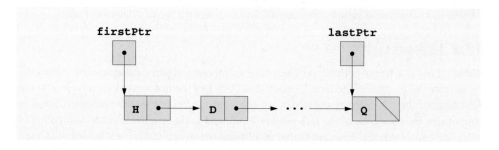

Fig. 17.2   A graphical representation of a list.

The program of Fig. 17.3–Fig. 17.5 uses a **List** class template (see Chapter 11 for information on class templates) to manipulate a list of integer values and a list of floating-point values. The driver program (Fig. 17.5) provides five options: 1) Insert a value at the beginning of the list, 2) insert a value at the end of the list, 3) delete a value from the front of the list, 4) delete a value from the end of the list and 5) terminate the list processing. A detailed discussion of the program follows. Exercise 17.20 asks you to implement a recursive function that prints a linked list backwards, and Exercise 17.21 asks you to implement a recursive function that searches a linked list for a particular data item.

The program uses class templates **ListNode** (Fig. 17.3) and **List** (Fig. 17.4). Encapsulated in each **List** object is a linked list of **ListNode** objects. Class **ListNode** (Fig. 17.3) contains private members **data** and **nextPtr** (lines 18–19), a constructor to initialize these members and function **getData** to return the data in a node. Member **data** stores a value of type **NODETYPE**, the type parameter passed to the class template. Member **nextPtr** stores a pointer to the next **ListNode** object in the linked list. Note that line 11 of the class declares class **List** as a friend of class **ListNode**. This makes all member functions of class **List** friends of class **ListNode** that can access the private members of **ListNode**s. Also, note that template notation is used in the friend declaration because **ListNode**s of a particular type can be processed only by a **List** of the same type (e.g., a **List** of **int** values manages **ListNode** objects that store **int** values).

Lines 27–28 of the **List** class template (Fig. 17.4) declare private data members **firstPtr** (a pointer to the first **ListNode** in a **List**) and **lastPtr** (a pointer to the last **ListNode** in a **List**). The default constructor (lines 36–43) initializes both pointers to **0** (null). The destructor (lines 46–67) ensures that all **ListNode** objects in a **List** object are destroyed when that **List** object is destroyed. The primary **List** functions are **insertAtFront** (lines 70–84), **insertAtBack** (lines 87–101), **removeFromFront** (lines 104–125) and **removeFromBack** (lines 128–158).

```
1    // Fig. 17.3: listnode.h
2    // Template ListNode class definition.
3    #ifndef LISTNODE_H
4    #define LISTNODE_H
5
6    // forward declaration of class List
7    template< class NODETYPE > class List;
8
9    template< class NODETYPE>
10   class ListNode {
11      friend class List< NODETYPE >; // make List a friend
12
13   public:
14      ListNode( const NODETYPE & );   // constructor
15      NODETYPE getData() const;       // return data in node
16
17   private:
18      NODETYPE data;                  // data
19      ListNode< NODETYPE > *nextPtr; // next node in list
20
21   }; // end class ListNode
```

Fig. 17.3   **ListNode** class-template definition. (Part 1 of 2.)

```
22
23   // constructor
24   template< class NODETYPE>
25   ListNode< NODETYPE >::ListNode( const NODETYPE &info )
26      : data( info ),
27        nextPtr( 0 )
28   {
29      // empty body
30
31   } // end ListNode constructor
32
33   // return copy of data in node
34   template< class NODETYPE >
35   NODETYPE ListNode< NODETYPE >::getData() const
36   {
37      return data;
38
39   } // end function getData
40
41   #endif
```

Fig. 17.3   ListNode class-template definition. (Part 2 of 2.)

```
1    // Fig. 17.4: list.h
2    // Template List class definition.
3    #ifndef LIST_H
4    #define LIST_H
5
6    #include <iostream>
7
8    using std::cout;
9
10   #include <new>
11   #include "listnode.h"   // ListNode class definition
12
13   template< class NODETYPE >
14   class List {
15
16   public:
17      List();        // constructor
18      ~List();       // destructor
19      void insertAtFront( const NODETYPE & );
20      void insertAtBack( const NODETYPE & );
21      bool removeFromFront( NODETYPE & );
22      bool removeFromBack( NODETYPE & );
23      bool isEmpty() const;
24      void print() const;
25
26   private:
27      ListNode< NODETYPE > *firstPtr;   // pointer to first node
28      ListNode< NODETYPE > *lastPtr;    // pointer to last node
29
```

Fig. 17.4   List class-template definition. (Part 1 of 5.)

```
30      // utility function to allocate new node
31      ListNode< NODETYPE > *getNewNode( const NODETYPE & );
32
33   }; // end class List
34
35   // default constructor
36   template< class NODETYPE >
37   List< NODETYPE >::List()
38      : firstPtr( 0 ),
39        lastPtr( 0 )
40   {
41      // empty body
42
43   } // end List constructor
44
45   // destructor
46   template< class NODETYPE >
47   List< NODETYPE >::~List()
48   {
49      if ( !isEmpty() ) {      // List is not empty
50         cout << "Destroying nodes ...\n";
51
52         ListNode< NODETYPE > *currentPtr = firstPtr;
53         ListNode< NODETYPE > *tempPtr;
54
55         while ( currentPtr != 0 ) {  // delete remaining nodes
56            tempPtr = currentPtr;
57            cout << tempPtr->data << '\n';
58            currentPtr = currentPtr->nextPtr;
59            delete tempPtr;
60
61         } // end while
62
63      } // end if
64
65      cout << "All nodes destroyed\n\n";
66
67   } // end List destructor
68
69   // insert node at front of list
70   template< class NODETYPE >
71   void List< NODETYPE >::insertAtFront( const NODETYPE &value )
72   {
73      ListNode< NODETYPE > *newPtr = getNewNode( value );
74
75      if ( isEmpty() )  // List is empty
76         firstPtr = lastPtr = newPtr;
77
78      else {  // List is not empty
79         newPtr->nextPtr = firstPtr;
80         firstPtr = newPtr;
81
82      } // end else
```

Fig. 17.4   **List** class-template definition. (Part 2 of 5.)

```
83
84   } // end function insertAtFront
85
86   // insert node at back of list
87   template< class NODETYPE >
88   void List< NODETYPE >::insertAtBack( const NODETYPE &value )
89   {
90      ListNode< NODETYPE > *newPtr = getNewNode( value );
91
92      if ( isEmpty() )  // List is empty
93         firstPtr = lastPtr = newPtr;
94
95      else {  // List is not empty
96         lastPtr->nextPtr = newPtr;
97         lastPtr = newPtr;
98
99      } // end else
100
101  } // end function insertAtBack
102
103  // delete node from front of list
104  template< class NODETYPE >
105  bool List< NODETYPE >::removeFromFront( NODETYPE &value )
106  {
107     if ( isEmpty() )  // List is empty
108        return false;  // delete unsuccessful
109
110     else {
111        ListNode< NODETYPE > *tempPtr = firstPtr;
112
113        if ( firstPtr == lastPtr )
114           firstPtr = lastPtr = 0;
115        else
116           firstPtr = firstPtr->nextPtr;
117
118        value = tempPtr->data;  // data being removed
119        delete tempPtr;
120
121        return true;  // delete successful
122
123     } // end else
124
125  } // end function removeFromFront
126
127  // delete node from back of list
128  template< class NODETYPE >
129  bool List< NODETYPE >::removeFromBack( NODETYPE &value )
130  {
131     if ( isEmpty() )
132        return false;  // delete unsuccessful
133
134     else {
135        ListNode< NODETYPE > *tempPtr = lastPtr;
```

Fig. 17.4   **List** class-template definition. (Part 3 of 5.)

```
136
137        if ( firstPtr == lastPtr )
138           firstPtr = lastPtr = 0;
139        else {
140           ListNode< NODETYPE > *currentPtr = firstPtr;
141
142           // locate second-to-last element
143           while ( currentPtr->nextPtr != lastPtr )
144              currentPtr = currentPtr->nextPtr;
145
146           lastPtr = currentPtr;
147           currentPtr->nextPtr = 0;
148
149        } // end else
150
151        value = tempPtr->data;
152        delete tempPtr;
153
154        return true;   // delete successful
155
156     } // end else
157
158 } // end function removeFromBack
159
160 // is List empty?
161 template< class NODETYPE >
162 bool List< NODETYPE >::isEmpty() const
163 {
164     return firstPtr == 0;
165
166 } // end function isEmpty
167
168 // return pointer to newly allocated node
169 template< class NODETYPE >
170 ListNode< NODETYPE > *List< NODETYPE >::getNewNode(
171    const NODETYPE &value )
172 {
173     return new ListNode< NODETYPE >( value );
174
175 } // end function getNewNode
176
177 // display contents of List
178 template< class NODETYPE >
179 void List< NODETYPE >::print() const
180 {
181     if ( isEmpty() ) {
182        cout << "The list is empty\n\n";
183        return;
184
185     } // end if
186
187     ListNode< NODETYPE > *currentPtr = firstPtr;
188
```

Fig. 17.4   **List** class-template definition. (Part 4 of 5.)

```
189    cout << "The list is: ";
190
191    while ( currentPtr != 0 ) {
192       cout << currentPtr->data << ' ';
193       currentPtr = currentPtr->nextPtr;
194
195    } // end while
196
197    cout << "\n\n";
198
199  } // end function print
200
201  #endif
```

Fig. 17.4   **List** class-template definition. (Part 5 of 5.)

Function **isEmpty** (lines 161–166) is called a *predicate function*—it does not alter the **List**; rather, it determines whether the **List** is empty (i.e., the pointer to the first node of the **List** is null). If the **List** is empty, **true** is returned; otherwise, **false** is returned. Function **print** (lines 178–199) displays the **List**'s contents. Utility function **getNewNode** (lines 169–175) returns a dynamically allocated **ListNode** object. This function is called from functions **insertAtFront** and **insertAtBack**.

 Good Programming Practice 17.1

Assign null (zero) to the link member of a new node. Pointers should be initialized before they are used.

The driver program (Fig. 17.5) uses function template **testList** to enable the user to manipulate objects of class **List**. Lines 81 and 85 create **List** objects for types **int** and **double**, respectively. Lines 82 and 86 invoke the **testList** function template with these **List** objects.

```
1    // Fig. 17.5: fig17_05.cpp
2    // List class test program.
3    #include <iostream>
4
5    using std::cin;
6    using std::endl;
7
8    #include <string>
9
10   using std::string;
11
12   #include "list.h"   // List class definition
13
14   // function to test a List
15   template< class T >
16   void testList( List< T > &listObject, const string &typeName )
17   {
18      cout << "Testing a List of " << typeName << " values\n";
```

Fig. 17.5   Manipulating a linked list. (Part 1 of 4.)

```
19
20      instructions();   // display instructions
21
22      int choice;
23      T value;
24
25      do {
26         cout << "? ";
27         cin >> choice;
28
29         switch ( choice ) {
30            case 1:
31               cout << "Enter " << typeName << ": ";
32               cin >> value;
33               listObject.insertAtFront( value );
34               listObject.print();
35               break;
36
37            case 2:
38               cout << "Enter " << typeName << ": ";
39               cin >> value;
40               listObject.insertAtBack( value );
41               listObject.print();
42               break;
43
44            case 3:
45               if ( listObject.removeFromFront( value ) )
46                  cout << value << " removed from list\n";
47
48               listObject.print();
49               break;
50
51            case 4:
52               if ( listObject.removeFromBack( value ) )
53                  cout << value << " removed from list\n";
54
55               listObject.print();
56               break;
57
58         } // end switch
59
60      } while ( choice != 5 );   // end do/while
61
62      cout << "End list test\n\n";
63
64   } // end function testList
65
66   // display program instructions to user
67   void instructions()
68   {
69      cout << "Enter one of the following:\n"
70           << "  1 to insert at beginning of list\n"
71           << "  2 to insert at end of list\n"
```

Fig. 17.5   Manipulating a linked list. (Part 2 of 4.)

```
72                << "  3 to delete from beginning of list\n"
73                << "  4 to delete from end of list\n"
74                << "  5 to end list processing\n";
75
76   } // end function instructions
77
78   int main()
79   {
80      // test List of int values
81      List< int > integerList;
82      testList( integerList, "integer" );
83
84      // test List of double values
85      List< double > doubleList;
86      testList( doubleList, "double" );
87
88      return 0;
89
90   } // end main
```

```
Testing a List of integer values
Enter one of the following:
  1 to insert at beginning of list
  2 to insert at end of list
  3 to delete from beginning of list
  4 to delete from end of list
  5 to end list processing
? 1
Enter integer: 1
The list is: 1

? 1
Enter integer: 2
The list is: 2 1

? 2
Enter integer: 3
The list is: 2 1 3

? 2
Enter integer: 4
The list is: 2 1 3 4

? 3
2 removed from list
The list is: 1 3 4

? 3
1 removed from list
The list is: 3 4
```

(continued next page)

Fig. 17.5   Manipulating a linked list. (Part 3 of 4.)

```
? 4
4 removed from list
The list is: 3

? 4
3 removed from list
The list is empty

? 5
End list test

Testing a List of double values
Enter one of the following:
  1 to insert at beginning of list
  2 to insert at end of list
  3 to delete from beginning of list
  4 to delete from end of list
  5 to end list processing
? 1
Enter double: 1.1
The list is: 1.1

? 1
Enter double: 2.2
The list is: 2.2 1.1

? 2
Enter double: 3.3
The list is: 2.2 1.1 3.3

? 2
Enter double: 4.4
The list is: 2.2 1.1 3.3 4.4

? 3
2.2 removed from list
The list is: 1.1 3.3 4.4

? 3
1.1 removed from list
The list is: 3.3 4.4

? 4
4.4 removed from list
The list is: 3.3

? 4
3.3 removed from list
The list is empty

? 5
End list test

All nodes destroyed

All nodes destroyed
```

Fig. 17.5   Manipulating a linked list. (Part 4 of 4.)

Over the next several pages, we discuss each of the member functions of class **List** in detail. Function **insertAtFront** (Fig. 17.4, lines 70–84) places a new node at the front of the list. The function consists of several steps:

1. Call function **getNewNode** (line 73), passing it **value**, which is a constant reference to the node value to be inserted.

2. Function **getNewNode** (lines 169–175) uses operator **new** to create a new list node and return a pointer to this newly allocated node, which is assigned to **newPtr** in **insertAtFront**.

3. If the list is empty (line 75), then both **firstPtr** and **lastPtr** are set to **newPtr** (line 76).

4. If the list is not empty (line 78), then the node pointed to by **newPtr** is threaded into the list by copying **firstPtr** to **newPtr->nextPtr** (line 79) so that the new node points to what used to be the first node of the list and copying **newPtr** to **firstPtr** (line 80) so that **firstPtr** now points to the new first node of the list.

Figure 17.6 illustrates function **insertAtFront**. Part a) of the figure shows the list and the new node before the **insertAtFront** operation. The dotted arrows in part b) illustrate the steps 2 and 3 of the **insertAtFront** operation that enable the node containing **12** to become the new list front.

Function **insertAtBack** (Fig. 17.4, lines 87–101) places a new node at the back of the list. The function consists of several steps:

1. Call function **getNewNode** (line 90), passing it **value**, which is a constant reference to the node value to be inserted.

2. Function **getNewNode** (lines 169–175) uses operator **new** to create a new list node and return a pointer to this newly allocated node, which is assigned to **newPtr** in **insertAtBack**.

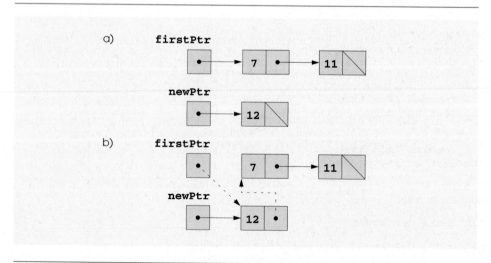

Fig. 17.6   Operation **insertAtFront** represented graphically.

3. If the list is empty (line 92), then both **firstPtr** and **lastPtr** are set to **newPtr** (line 93).

4. If the list is not empty (line 95), then the node pointed to by **newPtr** is threaded into the list by copying **newPtr** into **lastPtr->nextPtr** (line 96) so that the new node is pointed to by what used to be the last node of the list and copying **newPtr** to **lastPtr** (line 97) so that **lastPtr** now points to the new last node of the list.

Figure 17.7 illustrates an **insertAtBack** operation. Part a) of the figure shows the list and the new node before the operation. The dotted arrows in part b) illustrate the steps of function **insertAtBack** that enable a new node to be added to the end of a list that is not empty.

Function **removeFromFront** (Fig. 17.4, lines 104–125) removes the front node of the list and copies the node value to the reference parameter. The function returns **false** if an attempt is made to remove a node from an empty list (lines 107–108) and returns **true** if the removal is successful. The function consists of several steps:

1. Assign **tempPtr** the address to which **firstPtr** points (line 111). Eventually, **tempPtr** will be used to delete the node being removed.

2. If **firstPtr** is equal to **lastPtr** (line 113), i.e., if the list has only one element prior to the removal attempt, then set **firstPtr** and **lastPtr** to zero (line 114) to dethread that node from the list (leaving the list empty).

3. If the list has more than one node prior to removal, then leave **lastPtr** as is and set **firstPtr** to **firstPtr->nextPtr** (line 116), i.e., modify **firstPtr** to point to what was the second node prior to removal (and is the new first node now).

4. After all these pointer manipulations are complete, copy to reference parameter **value** the **data** member of the node being removed (line 118).

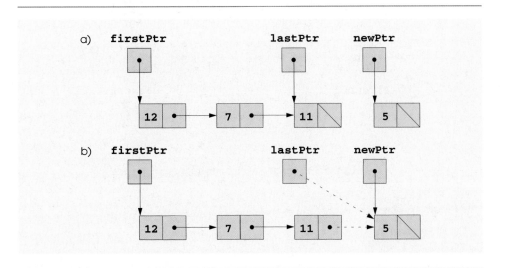

Fig. 17.7   Operation **insertAtBack** represented graphically.

5. Now **delete** the node pointed to by **tempPtr** (line 119).

6. Return **true**, indicating successful removal (line 121).

Figure 17.8 illustrates function **removeFromFront**. Part a) illustrates the list before the removal operation. Part b) shows actual pointer manipulations.

Function **removeFromBack** (Fig. 17.4, lines 128–158) removes the back node of the list and copies the node value to the reference parameter. The function returns **false** if an attempt is made to remove a node from an empty list (lines 131–132) and returns **true** if the removal is successful. The function consists of several steps:

1. Assign **tempPtr** the address to which **lastPtr** points (line 135). Eventually, **tempPtr** will be used to delete the node being removed.

2. If **firstPtr** is equal to **lastPtr** (line 137), i.e., if the list has only one element prior to the removal attempt, then set **firstPtr** and **lastPtr** to zero (line 138) to dethread that node from the list (leaving the list empty).

3. If the list has more than one node prior to removal, then assign **currentPtr** the address to which **firstPtr** points (line 140).

4. Now "walk the list" with **currentPtr** until it points to the node before the last node. This is done with a **while** loop (lines 143–144) that keeps replacing **currentPtr** by **currentPtr->nextPtr**, while **currentPtr->nextPtr** is not **lastPtr**.

5. Assign **lastPtr** to the address to which **currentPtr** points (line 146) to dethread the back node from the list.

6. Set **currentPtr->nextPtr** to zero (line 147) in the new last node of the list.

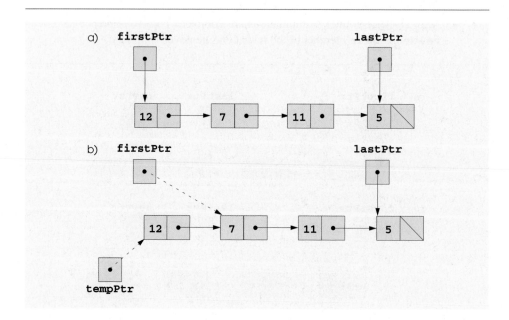

Fig. 17.8   Operation **removeFromFront** represented graphically.

7. After all the pointer manipulations are complete, copy to reference parameter **value** the **data** member of the node being removed (line 151).

8. Now **delete** the node pointed to by **tempPtr** (line 152).

9. Return **true** (line 154), indicating successful removal.

Figure 17.9 illustrates function **removeFromBack**. Part a) of the figure illustrates the list before the removal operation. Part b) of the figure shows the actual pointer manipulations.

Function **print** (lines 178–199) first determines whether the list is empty (line 181). If so, **print** prints **"The list is empty"** and returns (lines 182–183). Otherwise, it prints the data in the list. The function initializes **currentPtr** as a copy of **firstPtr** (line 187), then prints the string **"The list is: "** (line 189). While **currentPtr** is not null (line 191), **currentPtr->data** is printed (line 192) and **currentPtr** is assigned the value of **currentPtr->nextPtr** (line 193). Note that if the link in the last node of the list is not null, the printing algorithm will erroneously print past the end of the list. The printing algorithm is identical for linked lists, stacks and queues.

The kind of linked list we have been discussing is a *singly linked list*—the list begins with a pointer to the first node, and each node contains a pointer to the next node "in sequence." This list terminates with a node whose pointer member has the value 0. A singly linked list may be traversed in only one direction.

A *circular, singly linked list* begins with a pointer to the first node, and each node contains a pointer to the next node. The "last node" does not contain a 0 pointer; rather, the pointer in the last node points back to the first node, thus closing the "circle."

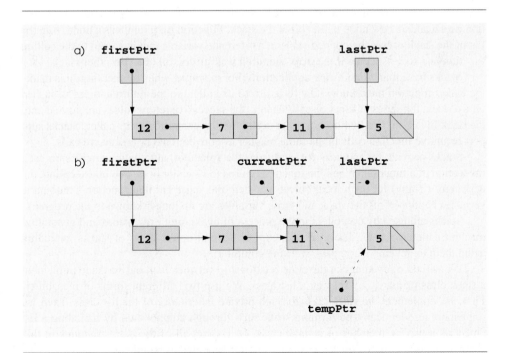

Fig. 17.9   Operation **removeFromBack** represented graphically.

A *doubly linked list* allows traversals both forwards and backwards. Such a list is often implemented with two "start pointers"—one that points to the first element of the list to allow front-to-back traversal of the list and one that points to the last element of the list to allow back-to-front traversal of the list. Each node has both a forward pointer to the next node in the list in the forward direction and a backward pointer to the next node in the list in the backward direction. If your list contains an alphabetized telephone directory, for example, a search for someone whose name begins with a letter near the front of the alphabet might begin from the front of the list. Searching for someone whose name begins with a letter near the end of the alphabet might begin from the back of the list.

In a *circular, doubly linked list*, the forward pointer of the last node points to the first node, and the backward pointer of the first node points to the last node, thus closing the "circle."

17.5 Stacks

In Chapter 11, Templates, we explained the notion of a stack class template with an under-lying array implementation. In this section, we use an underlying pointer-based linked-list implementation. We also discuss stacks in Chapter 21, Standard Template Library (STL).

A *stack* data structure allows nodes to be added to a stack and removed from a stack only at the top. For this reason, a stack is referred to as a *last-in, first-out (LIFO)* data struc-ture. One way to implement a stack is as a constrained version of a linked list. In such an implementation, the link member in the last node of the stack is set to null (zero) to indicate the bottom of the stack.

The primary member functions used to manipulate a stack are **push** and **pop**. Func-tion **push** adds a new node to the top of the stack. Function **pop** removes a node from the top of the stack, stores the popped value in a reference variable that is passed to the calling function and returns **true** if the **pop** operation was successful (**false** otherwise).

Stacks have many interesting applications. For example, when a function call is made, the called function must know how to return to its caller, so the return address is pushed onto a stack. If a series of function calls occurs, the successive return values are pushed onto the stack in last-in, first-out order so that each function can return to its caller. Stacks sup-port recursive function calls in the same manner as conventional nonrecursive calls.

Stacks provide the memory for, and store the values of, automatic variables on each invocation of a function. When the function returns to its caller or throws an exception, the destructor (if any) for each local object is called, the space for that function's automatic variables is popped off the stack and those variables are no longer known to the program.

Stacks are used by compilers in the process of evaluating expressions and generating machine language code. The exercises explore several applications of stacks, including using them to develop a complete working compiler.

We will take advantage of the close relationship between lists and stacks to implement a stack class primarily by reusing a list class. We use two different forms of reusability. First, we implement the stack class through private inheritance of the list class. Then we implement an identically performing stack class through composition by including a list object as a private member of a stack class. Of course, all of the data structures in this chapter, including these two stack classes, are implemented as templates to encourage fur-ther reusability.

The program of Fig. 17.10–Fig. 17.11 creates a **Stack** class template (Fig. 17.10) primarily through **private** inheritance of the **List** class template of Fig. 17.4. We want the **Stack** to have member functions **push** (lines 13–17), **pop** (lines 20–24), **isStack-Empty** (lines 27–31) and **printStack** (lines 34–38). Note that these are essentially the **insertAtFront**, **removeFromFront**, **isEmpty** and **print** functions of the **List** class template. Of course, the **List** class template contains other member functions (i.e., **insertAtBack** and **removeFromBack**) that we would not want to make accessible through the **public** interface to the **Stack** class. So when we indicate that the **Stack** class template is to inherit from the **List** class template, we specify **private** inheritance. This makes all the **List** class template's member functions **private** in the **Stack** class template. When we implement the **Stack**'s member functions, we then have each of these call the appropriate member function of the **List** class—**push** calls **insertAtFront** (line 15), **pop** calls **removeFromFront** (line 22), **isStackEmpty** calls **isEmpty** (line 29) and **printStack** calls **print** (line 36).

The stack class template is used in **main** (Fig. 17.11) to instantiate integer stack **intStack** of type **Stack< int >** (line 11). Integers 0 through 3 are pushed onto **intStack** (lines 16–20), then popped off **intStack** (lines 23–30). The program uses the **Stack** class template to create **doubleStack** of type **Stack< double >** (line 32). Values 1.1, 2.2, 3.3 and 4.4 are pushed onto **doubleStack** (lines 38–43), then popped off **doubleStack** (46–53).

```
1   // Fig. 17.10: stack.h
2   // Template Stack class definition derived from class List.
3   #ifndef STACK_H
4   #define STACK_H
5
6   #include "list.h"  // List class definition
7
8   template< class STACKTYPE >
9   class Stack : private List< STACKTYPE > {
10
11  public:
12     // push calls List function insertAtFront
13     void push( const STACKTYPE &data )
14     {
15        insertAtFront( data );
16
17     } // end function push
18
19     // pop calls List function removeFromFront
20     bool pop( STACKTYPE &data )
21     {
22        return removeFromFront( data );
23
24     } // end function pop
25
26     // isStackEmpty calls List function isEmpty
27     bool isStackEmpty() const
28     {
```

Fig. 17.10 **Stack** class-template definition. (Part 1 of 2.)

```
29            return isEmpty();
30
31      } // end function isStackEmpty
32
33      // printStack calls List function print
34      void printStack() const
35      {
36         print();
37
38      } // end function print
39
40   }; // end class Stack
41
42   #endif
```

Fig. 17.10 Stack class-template definition. (Part 2 of 2.)

```
1    // Fig. 17.11: fig17_11.cpp
2    // Template Stack class test program.
3    #include <iostream>
4
5    using std::endl;
6
7    #include "stack.h"   // Stack class definition
8
9    int main()
10   {
11      Stack< int > intStack;   // create Stack of ints
12
13      cout << "processing an integer Stack" << endl;
14
15      // push integers onto intStack
16      for ( int i = 0; i < 4; i++ ) {
17         intStack.push( i );
18         intStack.printStack();
19
20      } // end for
21
22      // pop integers from intStack
23      int popInteger;
24
25      while ( !intStack.isStackEmpty() ) {
26         intStack.pop( popInteger );
27         cout << popInteger << " popped from stack" << endl;
28         intStack.printStack();
29
30      } // end while
31
32      Stack< double > doubleStack;   // create Stack of doubles
33      double value = 1.1;
34
35      cout << "processing a double Stack" << endl;
```

Fig. 17.11   A simple stack program. (Part 1 of 3.)

```
36
37      // push floating-point values onto doubleStack
38      for ( int j = 0; j< 4; j++ ) {
39         doubleStack.push( value );
40         doubleStack.printStack();
41         value += 1.1;
42
43      } // end for
44
45      // pop floating-point values from doubleStack
46      double popDouble;
47
48      while ( !doubleStack.isStackEmpty() ) {
49         doubleStack.pop( popDouble );
50         cout << popDouble << " popped from stack" << endl;
51         doubleStack.printStack();
52
53      } // end while
54
55      return 0;
56
57   } // end main
```

```
processing an integer Stack
The list is: 0

The list is: 1 0

The list is: 2 1 0

The list is: 3 2 1 0

3 popped from stack
The list is: 2 1 0

2 popped from stack
The list is: 1 0

1 popped from stack
The list is: 0

0 popped from stack
The list is empty

processing a double Stack
The list is: 1.1

The list is: 2.2 1.1

The list is: 3.3 2.2 1.1

The list is: 4.4 3.3 2.2 1.1
```

(continued next page)

Fig. 17.11 A simple stack program. (Part 2 of 3.)

```
4.4 popped from stack
The list is: 3.3 2.2 1.1

3.3 popped from stack
The list is: 2.2 1.1

2.2 popped from stack
The list is: 1.1

1.1 popped from stack
The list is empty

All nodes destroyed

All nodes destroyed
```

Fig. 17.11   A simple stack program. (Part 3 of 3.)

Another way to implement a **Stack** class template is by reusing the **List** class template through composition. Figure 17.12 is a new implementation of the **Stack** class template that contains a **List< STACKTYPE >** object called **stackList** (line 43). This version of the **Stack** class template uses class **List** from Fig. 17.4. To test this class, use the driver program in Fig. 17.11, but include the new header file—**stackcomposition.h** in line 7 of that file. The output of the program is identical for both versions of class **Stack**.

```
1   // Fig. 17.12: stackcomposition.h
2   // Template Stack class definition with composed List object.
3   #ifndef STACKCOMPOSITION
4   #define STACKCOMPOSITION
5
6   #include "list.h"  // List class definition
7
8   template< class STACKTYPE >
9   class Stack {
10
11  public:
12     // no constructor; List constructor does initialization
13
14     // push calls stackList object's insertAtFront function
15     void push( const STACKTYPE &data )
16     {
17        stackList.insertAtFront( data );
18
19     } // end function push
20
21     // pop calls stackList object's removeFromFront function
22     bool pop( STACKTYPE &data )
23     {
24        return stackList.removeFromFront( data );
25
26     } // end function pop
```

Fig. 17.12 **Stack** class template with a composed **List** object. (Part 1 of 2.)

```
27
28     // isStackEmpty calls stackList object's isEmpty function
29     bool isStackEmpty() const
30     {
31         return stackList.isEmpty();
32
33     } // end function isStackEmpty
34
35     // printStack calls stackList object's print function
36     void printStack() const
37     {
38         stackList.print();
39
40     } // end function printStack
41
42 private:
43     List< STACKTYPE > stackList;   // composed List object
44
45 }; // end class Stack
46
47 #endif
```

Fig. 17.12 **Stack** class template with a composed **List** object. (Part 2 of 2.)

17.6 Queues

A *queue* is similar to a supermarket checkout line—the first person in line is serviced first, and other customers enter the line at the end and wait to be serviced. Queue nodes are removed only from the *head* of the queue and are inserted only at the *tail* of the queue. For this reason, a queue is referred to as a *first-in, first-out (FIFO)* data structure. The insert and remove operations are known as **enqueue** and **dequeue**.

Queues have many applications in computer systems. Most computers have only a single processor, so only one user at a time can be served. Entries for the other users are placed in a queue. Each entry gradually advances to the front of the queue as users receive service. The entry at the front of the queue is the next to receive service.

Queues are also used to support print spooling. A multiuser environment may have only a single printer. Many users may be generating outputs to be printed. If the printer is busy, other outputs may still be generated. These are "spooled" to disk (much as thread is wound onto a spool) where they wait in a queue until the printer becomes available.

Information packets also wait in queues in computer networks. Each time a packet arrives at a network node, it must be routed to the next node on the network along the path to the packet's final destination. The routing node routes one packet at a time, so additional packets are enqueued until the router can route them.

A file server in a computer network handles file access requests from many clients throughout the network. Servers have a limited capacity to service requests from clients. When that capacity is exceeded, client requests wait in queues.

The program of Fig. 17.13–Fig. 17.14 creates a **Queue** class template (Fig. 17.13) primarily through **private** inheritance of the **List** class template of Fig. 17.4. We want the **Queue** to have member functions **enqueue** (lines 13–17), **dequeue** (lines 20–24), **isQueueEmpty** (lines 27–31) and **printQueue** (lines 34–38). We note that these are

```
1    // Fig. 17.13: queue.h
2    // Template Queue class definition derived from class List.
3    #ifndef QUEUE_H
4    #define QUEUE_H
5
6    #include "list.h"   // List class definition
7
8    template< class QUEUETYPE >
9    class Queue : private List< QUEUETYPE > {
10
11   public:
12      // enqueue calls List function insertAtBack
13      void enqueue( const QUEUETYPE &data )
14      {
15         insertAtBack( data );
16
17      } // end function enqueue
18
19      // dequeue calls List function removeFromFront
20      bool dequeue( QUEUETYPE &data )
21      {
22         return removeFromFront( data );
23
24      } // end function dequeue
25
26      // isQueueEmpty calls List function isEmpty
27      bool isQueueEmpty() const
28      {
29         return isEmpty();
30
31      } // end function isQueueEmpty
32
33      // printQueue calls List function print
34      void printQueue() const
35      {
36         print();
37
38      } // end function printQueue
39
40   }; // end class Queue
41
42   #endif
```

Fig. 17.13 **Queue** class-template definition.

essentially the **insertAtBack**, **removeFromFront**, **isEmpty** and **print** functions of the **List** class template. Of course, the **List** class template contains other member functions (i.e., **insertAtFront** and **removeFromBack**) that we would not want to make accessible through the **public** interface to the **Queue** class. So when we indicate that the **Queue** class template is to inherit the **List** class template, we specify **private** inheritance. This makes all the **List** class template's member functions **private** in the **Queue** class template. When we implement the **Queue**'s member functions, we have each of these call the appropriate member function of the list class—**enqueue** calls **insert-**

AtBack (line 15), **dequeue** calls **removeFromFront** (line 22), **isQueueEmpty** calls **isEmpty** (line 29) and **printQueue** calls **print** (line 36).

Figure 17.14 uses the queue class template to instantiate integer queue **intQueue** of type **Queue< int >** (line 11). Integers 0 through 3 are enqueued to **intQueue** (lines 16–20), then dequeued from **intQueue** in first-in, first-out order (lines 23–30). Next, the program instantiates queue **doubleQueue** of type **Queue< double >** (line 32). Values 1.1, 2.2, 3.3 and 4.4 are enqueued to **doubleQueue** (lines 38–43), then dequeued from **doubleQueue** in first-in, first-out order (lines 46–53).

```
1   // Fig. 17.14: fig17_14.cpp
2   // Template Queue class test program.
3   #include <iostream>
4
5   using std::endl;
6
7   #include "queue.h"  // Queue class definition
8
9   int main()
10  {
11     Queue< int > intQueue;  // create Queue of ints
12
13     cout << "processing an integer Queue" << endl;
14
15     // enqueue integers onto intQueue
16     for ( int i = 0; i < 4; i++ ) {
17        intQueue.enqueue( i );
18        intQueue.printQueue();
19
20     } // end for
21
22     // dequeue integers from intQueue
23     int dequeueInteger;
24
25     while ( !intQueue.isQueueEmpty() ) {
26        intQueue.dequeue( dequeueInteger );
27        cout << dequeueInteger << " dequeued" << endl;
28        intQueue.printQueue();
29
30     } // end while
31
32     Queue< double > doubleQueue;  // create Queue of doubles
33     double value = 1.1;
34
35     cout << "processing a double Queue" << endl;
36
37     // enqueue floating-point values onto doubleQueue
38     for ( int j = 0; j< 4; j++ ) {
39        doubleQueue.enqueue( value );
40        doubleQueue.printQueue();
41        value += 1.1;
42
43     } // end for
```

Fig. 17.14 Queue-processing program. (Part 1 of 3.)

```
44
45      // dequeue floating-point values from doubleQueue
46      double dequeueDouble;
47
48      while ( !doubleQueue.isQueueEmpty() ) {
49         doubleQueue.dequeue( dequeueDouble );
50         cout << dequeueDouble << " dequeued" << endl;
51         doubleQueue.printQueue();
52
53      } // end while
54
55      return 0;
56
57   } // end main
```

```
processing an integer Queue
The list is: 0

The list is: 0 1

The list is: 0 1 2

The list is: 0 1 2 3

0 dequeued
The list is: 1 2 3

1 dequeued
The list is: 2 3

2 dequeued
The list is: 3

3 dequeued
The list is empty

processing a double Queue
The list is: 1.1

The list is: 1.1 2.2

The list is: 1.1 2.2 3.3

The list is: 1.1 2.2 3.3 4.4

1.1 dequeued
The list is: 2.2 3.3 4.4

2.2 dequeued
The list is: 3.3 4.4

3.3 dequeued
The list is: 4.4                                             (continued next page)
```

Fig. 17.14 Queue-processing program. (Part 2 of 3.)

```
4.4 dequeued
The list is empty

All nodes destroyed

All nodes destroyed
```

Fig. 17.14 Queue-processing program. (Part 3 of 3.)

17.7 Trees

Linked lists, stacks and queues are *linear data structures*. A tree is a nonlinear, two-dimensional data structure with special properties. Tree nodes contain two or more links. This section discusses *binary trees* (Fig. 17.15)—trees whose nodes all contain two links (none, one or both of which may be null). For the purposes of this discussion, refer to the nodes in Fig. 17.15. The *root node* (node **B**) is the first node in a tree. Each link in the root node refers to a *child* (nodes **A** and **D**). The *left child* (node **A**) is the root node of the *left subtree* (which contains only node **A**), and the *right child* (node **D**) is the root node of the *right subtree* (which contains nodes **D** and **C**). The children of a single node are called *siblings* (e.g., nodes **A** and **D** are siblings). A node with no children is called a *leaf node* (e.g., nodes **A** and **C** are leaf nodes). Computer scientists normally draw trees from the root node down—exactly the opposite of trees in nature.

This section discusses a special binary tree called a *binary search tree*. A binary search tree (with no duplicate node values) has the characteristic that the values in any left subtree are less than the value in its parent node, and the values in any right subtree are greater than the value in its parent node. Figure 17.16 illustrates a binary search tree with 12 values. Note that the shape of the binary search tree that corresponds to a set of data can vary, depending on the order in which the values are inserted into the tree.

The program of Fig. 17.17–Fig. 17.19 creates a binary search tree and traverses it (i.e., walks through all its nodes) three ways—using recursive *inorder, preorder* and *postorder traversals*.

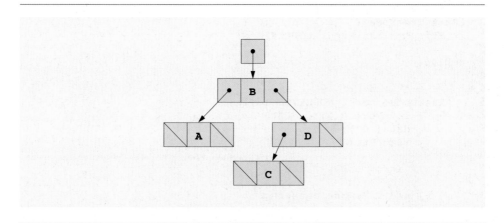

Fig. 17.15 A graphical representation of a binary tree.

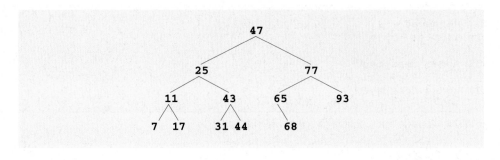

Fig. 17.16 A binary search tree.

We begin our discussion with the driver program (Fig. 17.19), then continue with the implementations of classes **TreeNode** (Fig. 17.17) and **Tree** (Fig. 17.18). Function **main** (Fig. 17.19) begins by instantiating integer tree **intTree** of type **Tree< int >** (line 16). The program prompts for 10 integers, each of which is inserted in the binary tree by calling **insertNode** (line 23). The program then performs preorder, inorder and postorder traversals (these are explained shortly) of **intTree** (lines 28, 31 and 34, respectively). The program then instantiates floating-point tree **doubleTree** of type **Tree< double >** (lines 36). The program prompts for 10 **double** values, each of which is inserted in the binary tree by calling **insertNode** (line 44). The program then performs preorder, inorder and postorder traversals of **doubleTree** (lines 49, 52 and 55, respectively).

```
1    // Fig. 17.17: treenode.h
2    // Template TreeNode class definition.
3    #ifndef TREENODE_H
4    #define TREENODE_H
5
6    // forward declaration of class Tree
7    template< class NODETYPE > class Tree;
8
9    template< class NODETYPE >
10   class TreeNode {
11      friend class Tree< NODETYPE >;
12
13   public:
14
15      // constructor
16      TreeNode( const NODETYPE &d )
17         : leftPtr( 0 ),
18           data( d ),
19           rightPtr( 0 )
20      {
21         // empty body
22
23      } // end TreeNode constructor
24
```

Fig. 17.17 **TreeNode** class-template definition. (Part 1 of 2.)

```
25      // return copy of node's data
26      NODETYPE getData() const
27      {
28         return data;
29
30      } // end getData function
31
32   private:
33      TreeNode< NODETYPE > *leftPtr;   // pointer to left subtree
34      NODETYPE data;
35      TreeNode< NODETYPE > *rightPtr;  // pointer to right subtree
36
37   }; // end class TreeNode
38
39   #endif
```

Fig. 17.17 **TreeNode** class-template definition. (Part 2 of 2.)

```
1    // Fig. 17.18: tree.h
2    // Template Tree class definition.
3    #ifndef TREE_H
4    #define TREE_H
5
6    #include <iostream>
7
8    using std::endl;
9
10   #include <new>
11   #include "treenode.h"
12
13   template< class NODETYPE >
14   class Tree {
15
16   public:
17      Tree();
18      void insertNode( const NODETYPE & );
19      void preOrderTraversal() const;
20      void inOrderTraversal() const;
21      void postOrderTraversal() const;
22
23   private:
24      TreeNode< NODETYPE > *rootPtr;
25
26      // utility functions
27      void insertNodeHelper(
28         TreeNode< NODETYPE > **, const NODETYPE & );
29      void preOrderHelper( TreeNode< NODETYPE > * ) const;
30      void inOrderHelper( TreeNode< NODETYPE > * ) const;
31      void postOrderHelper( TreeNode< NODETYPE > * ) const;
32
33   }; // end class Tree
34
```

Fig. 17.18 **Tree** class-template definition. (Part 1 of 4.)

```
35   // constructor
36   template< class NODETYPE >
37   Tree< NODETYPE >::Tree()
38   {
39      rootPtr = 0;
40
41   } // end Tree constructor
42
43   // insert node in Tree
44   template< class NODETYPE >
45   void Tree< NODETYPE >::insertNode( const NODETYPE &value )
46   {
47      insertNodeHelper( &rootPtr, value );
48
49   } // end function insertNode
50
51   // utility function called by insertNode; receives a pointer
52   // to a pointer so that the function can modify pointer's value
53   template< class NODETYPE >
54   void Tree< NODETYPE >::insertNodeHelper(
55      TreeNode< NODETYPE > **ptr, const NODETYPE &value )
56   {
57      // subtree is empty; create new TreeNode containing value
58      if ( *ptr == 0 )
59         *ptr = new TreeNode< NODETYPE >( value );
60
61      else  // subtree is not empty
62
63         // data to insert is less than data in current node
64         if ( value < ( *ptr )->data )
65            insertNodeHelper( &( ( *ptr )->leftPtr ), value );
66
67         else
68
69            // data to insert is greater than data in current node
70            if ( value > ( *ptr )->data )
71               insertNodeHelper( &( ( *ptr )->rightPtr ), value );
72
73            else  // duplicate data value ignored
74               cout << value << " dup" << endl;
75
76   } // end function insertNodeHelper
77
78   // begin preorder traversal of Tree
79   template< class NODETYPE >
80   void Tree< NODETYPE >::preOrderTraversal() const
81   {
82      preOrderHelper( rootPtr );
83
84   } // end function preOrderTraversal
85
```

Fig. 17.18 Tree class-template definition. (Part 2 of 4.)

```
86   // utility function to perform preorder traversal of Tree
87   template< class NODETYPE >
88   void Tree< NODETYPE >::preOrderHelper(
89      TreeNode< NODETYPE > *ptr ) const
90   {
91      if ( ptr != 0 ) {
92         cout << ptr->data << ' ';              // process node
93         preOrderHelper( ptr->leftPtr );        // go to left subtree
94         preOrderHelper( ptr->rightPtr );       // go to right subtree
95
96      } // end if
97
98   } // end function preOrderHelper
99
100  // begin inorder traversal of Tree
101  template< class NODETYPE >
102  void Tree< NODETYPE >::inOrderTraversal() const
103  {
104     inOrderHelper( rootPtr );
105
106  } // end function inOrderTraversal
107
108  // utility function to perform inorder traversal of Tree
109  template< class NODETYPE >
110  void Tree< NODETYPE >::inOrderHelper(
111     TreeNode< NODETYPE > *ptr ) const
112  {
113     if ( ptr != 0 ) {
114        inOrderHelper( ptr->leftPtr );        // go to left subtree
115        cout << ptr->data << ' ';             // process node
116        inOrderHelper( ptr->rightPtr );       // go to right subtree
117
118     } // end if
119
120  } // end function inOrderHelper
121
122  // begin postorder traversal of Tree
123  template< class NODETYPE >
124  void Tree< NODETYPE >::postOrderTraversal() const
125  {
126     postOrderHelper( rootPtr );
127
128  } // end function postOrderTraversal
129
130  // utility function to perform postorder traversal of Tree
131  template< class NODETYPE >
132  void Tree< NODETYPE >::postOrderHelper(
133     TreeNode< NODETYPE > *ptr ) const
134  {
135     if ( ptr != 0 ) {
136        postOrderHelper( ptr->leftPtr );      // go to left subtree
137        postOrderHelper( ptr->rightPtr );     // go to right subtree
138        cout << ptr->data << ' ';             // process node
```

Fig. 17.18 Tree class-template definition. (Part 3 of 4.)

```
139
140    } // end if
141
142 } // end function postOrderHelper
143
144 #endif
```

Fig. 17.18 **Tree** class-template definition. (Part 4 of 4.)

```
1  // Fig. 17.19: fig17_19.cpp
2  // Tree class test program.
3  #include <iostream>
4
5  using std::cout;
6  using std::cin;
7  using std::fixed;
8
9  #include <iomanip>
10 using std::setprecision;
11
12 #include "tree.h"  // Tree class definition
13
14 int main()
15 {
16    Tree< int > intTree;  // create Tree of int values
17    int intValue;
18
19    cout << "Enter 10 integer values:\n";
20
21    for( int i = 0; i < 10; i++ ) {
22       cin >> intValue;
23       intTree.insertNode( intValue );
24
25    } // end for
26
27    cout << "\nPreorder traversal\n";
28    intTree.preOrderTraversal();
29
30    cout << "\nInorder traversal\n";
31    intTree.inOrderTraversal();
32
33    cout << "\nPostorder traversal\n";
34    intTree.postOrderTraversal();
35
36    Tree< double > doubleTree;  // create Tree of double values
37    double doubleValue;
38
39    cout << fixed << setprecision( 1 )
40       << "\n\n\nEnter 10 double values:\n";
41
42    for ( int j = 0; j < 10; j++ ) {
43       cin >> doubleValue;
```

Fig. 17.19 Creating and traversing a binary tree. (Part 1 of 2.)

```
44            doubleTree.insertNode( doubleValue );
45
46    } // end for
47
48    cout << "\nPreorder traversal\n";
49    doubleTree.preOrderTraversal();
50
51    cout << "\nInorder traversal\n";
52    doubleTree.inOrderTraversal();
53
54    cout << "\nPostorder traversal\n";
55    doubleTree.postOrderTraversal();
56
57    cout << endl;
58
59    return 0;
60
61 } // end main
```

```
Enter 10 integer values:
50 25 75 12 33 67 88 6 13 68

Preorder traversal
50 25 12 6 13 33 75 67 68 88
Inorder traversal
6 12 13 25 33 50 67 68 75 88
Postorder traversal
6 13 12 33 25 68 67 88 75 50


Enter 10 double values:
39.2 16.5 82.7 3.3 65.2 90.8 1.1 4.4 89.5 92.5

Preorder traversal
39.2 16.5 3.3 1.1 4.4 82.7 65.2 90.8 89.5 92.5
Inorder traversal
1.1 3.3 4.4 16.5 39.2 65.2 82.7 89.5 90.8 92.5
Postorder traversal
1.1 4.4 3.3 16.5 65.2 89.5 92.5 90.8 82.7 39.2
```

Fig. 17.19   Creating and traversing a binary tree. (Part 2 of 2.)

Now we discuss the class-template definitions. We begin with the **TreeNode** class template (Fig. 17.17) that declares as its friend (line 11) the **Tree** class template (Fig. 17.18). Lines 33–35 declare a **TreeNode**'s private data—the node's **data** value, and pointers **leftPtr** (to the node's left subtree) and **rightPtr** (to the node's right subtree). The constructor (lines 16–23) sets **data** to the value supplied as a constructor argument and sets pointers **leftPtr** and **rightPtr** to zero (thus initializing this node to be a leaf node). Member function **getData** (lines 26–30) returns the **data** value.

The **Tree** class template (Fig. 17.18) has as **private** data **rootPtr** (line 24), a pointer to the root node of the tree. Lines 18–21 of the class declare the public member functions **insertNode** (that inserts a new node in the tree) and **preorderTraversal**,

inorderTraversal and **postorderTraversal**, each of which walks the tree in the designated manner. Each of these member functions calls its own separate recursive utility function to perform the appropriate operations on the internal representation of the tree. The **Tree** constructor initializes **rootPtr** to zero to indicate that the tree is initially empty.

The **Tree** class's utility function **insertNodeHelper** (lines 53–76) is called by **insertNode** (lines 44–49) to recursively insert a node into the tree. *A node can only be inserted as a leaf node in a binary search tree.* If the tree is empty, a new **TreeNode** is created, initialized and inserted in the tree (lines 58–59).

If the tree is not empty, the program compares the value to be inserted with the **data** value in the root node. If the insert value is smaller (line 64), the program recursively calls **insertNodeHelper** (line 65) to insert the value in the left subtree. If the insert value is larger (line 70), the program recursively calls **insertNodeHelper** (line 71) to insert the value in the right subtree. If the value to be inserted is identical to the data value in the root node, the program prints the message **" dup"** (line 74) and returns without inserting the duplicate value into the tree. Note that **insertNode** passes the address of **rootPtr** to **insertNodeHelper** (line 47) so it can modify the value stored in **rootPtr** (i.e., the address of the root node). To receive a pointer to **rootPtr** (which is also a pointer), **insertNodeHelper**'s first argument is declared as a pointer to a pointer to a **TreeNode**.

Each of the member functions **inOrderTraversal** (lines 101–106), **preOrder-Traversal** (lines 79–84) and **postOrderTraversal** (lines 123–128) traverses the tree and prints the node values. For the purpose of the following discussion, we use the binary search tree in Fig. 17.20.

Function **inOrderTraversal** invokes utility function **inOrderHelper** to perform the inorder traversal of the binary tree. The steps for an inorder traversal are:

1. Traverse the left subtree with an inorder traversal. (This is performed by the call to **inOrderHelper** at line 114).

2. Process the value in the node—i.e., print the node value (line 115).

3. Traverse the right subtree with an inorder traversal. (This is performed by the call to **inOrderHelper** at line 116).

The value in a node is not processed until the values in its left subtree are processed, because each call to **inOrderHelper** immediately calls **inOrderHelper** again with the pointer to the left subtree. The inorder traversal of the tree in Fig. 17.20 is

6 13 17 27 33 42 48

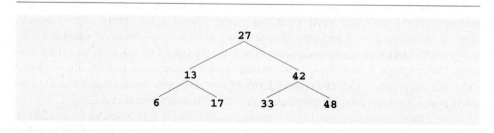

Fig. 17.20 A binary search tree.

Note that the inorder traversal of a binary search tree prints the node values in ascending order. The process of creating a binary search tree actually sorts the data—thus, this process is called the *binary tree sort*.

Function **preOrderTraversal** invokes utility function **preOrderHelper** to perform the preorder traversal of the binary tree. The steps for an preorder traversal are:

1. Process the value in the node (line 92).

2. Traverse the left subtree with a preorder traversal. (This is performed by the call to **preOrderHelper** at line 93).

3. Traverse the right subtree with a preorder traversal. (This is performed by the call to **preOrderHelper** at line 94).

The value in each node is processed as the node is visited. After the value in a given node is processed, the values in the left subtree are processed. Then the values in the right subtree are processed. The preorder traversal of the tree in Fig. 17.20 is

```
27  13  6  17  42  33  48
```

Function **postOrderTraversal** invokes utility function **postOrderHelper** to perform the postorder traversal of the binary tree. The steps for an postorder traversal are:

1. Traverse the left subtree with a postorder traversal. (This is performed by the call to **postOrderHelper** at line 136).

2. Traverse the right subtree with a postorder traversal. (This is performed by the call to **postOrderHelper** at line 137).

3. Process the value in the node (line 138).

The value in each node is not printed until the values of its children are printed. The **postOrderTraversal** of the tree in Fig. 17.20 is

```
6  17  13  33  48  42  27
```

The binary search tree facilitates *duplicate elimination*. As the tree is being created, an attempt to insert a duplicate value will be recognized, because a duplicate will follow the same "go left" or "go right" decisions on each comparison as the original value did when it was inserted in the tree. Thus, the duplicate will eventually be compared with a node containing the same value. The duplicate value may be discarded at this point.

Searching a binary tree for a value that matches a key value is also fast. If the tree is balanced, then each level contains about twice as many elements as the previous level. So a binary search tree with n elements would have a maximum of $\log_2 n$ levels; thus, a maximum of $\log_2 n$ comparisons would have to be made either to find a match or to determine that no match exists. This means, for example, that when searching a (balanced) 1000-element binary search tree, no more than 10 comparisons need to be made because $2^{10} > 1000$. When searching a (balanced) 1,000,000-element binary search tree, no more than 20 comparisons need to be made because $2^{20} > 1,000,000$.

In the exercises, algorithms are presented for several other binary tree operations such as deleting an item from a binary tree, printing a binary tree in a two-dimensional tree format and performing a level-order traversal of a binary tree. The level-order traversal of a binary tree visits the nodes of the tree row by row, starting at the root node level. On each level of the tree, the nodes are visited from left to right. Other binary tree exercises include allowing a binary search tree to contain duplicate values, inserting string values in a binary tree and determining how many levels are contained in a binary tree.

SUMMARY

- Self-referential classes contain members called links that point to objects of the same class type.
- Self-referential classes enable many objects to be linked together in stacks, queues, lists and trees.
- Dynamic memory allocation reserves a block of bytes in memory to store an object during program execution.
- A linked list is a linear collection of self-referential class objects.
- A linked list is a dynamic data structure—the length of the list increases or decreases as necessary.
- Linked lists can continue to grow until memory is exhausted.
- Linked lists provide a mechanism for insertion and deletion of data by pointer manipulation.
- A singly linked list begins with a pointer to the first node, and each node contains a pointer to the next node "in sequence." This list terminates with a node whose pointer member is 0. A singly linked list may be traversed in only one direction.
- A circular, singly linked list begins with a pointer to the first node, and each node contains a pointer to the next node. The pointer in the last node points to the first node, thus closing the "circle."
- A doubly linked list allows traversals both forwards and backwards. Each node has both a forward pointer to the next node in the list in the forward direction and a backward pointer to the next node in the list in the backward direction.
- In a circular, doubly linked list, the forward pointer of the last node points to the first node, and the backward pointer of the first node points to the last node, thus closing the "circle."
- Stacks and queues are constrained versions of linked lists.
- New stack nodes are added to a stack and are removed from a stack only at the top of the stack. For this reason, a stack is referred to as a last-in, first-out (LIFO) data structure.
- The link member in the last node of the stack is set to null (zero) to indicate the bottom of the stack.
- The primary operations used to manipulate a stack are **push** and **pop**. The **push** operation creates a new node and places it on the top of the stack. The **pop** operation removes a node from the top of the stack, deletes the memory that was allocated to that node and returns the popped value.
- In a queue data structure, nodes are removed from the head and added to the tail. For this reason, a queue is referred to as a first-in, first-out (FIFO) data structure. The add and remove operations are known as **enqueue** and **dequeue**.
- Trees are two-dimensional data structures requiring two or more links per node.
- Binary trees contain two links per node.
- The root node is the first node in the tree.
- Each of the pointers in the root node refers to a child. The left child is the first node in the left subtree, and the right child is the first node in the right subtree. The children of a node are called siblings. Any tree node that does not have any children is called a leaf node.
- A binary search tree has the characteristic that the value in the left child of a node is less than the value in its parent node, and the value in the right child of a node is greater than or equal to the value in its parent node. If there are no duplicate data values, the value in the right child is greater than the value in its parent node.
- An inorder traversal of a binary tree traverses the left subtree inorder, processes the value in the root node and then traverses the right subtree inorder. The value in a node is not processed until the values in its left subtree are processed.

- A preorder traversal processes the value in the root node, traverses the left subtree preorder then traverses the right subtree preorder. The value in each node is processed as the node is encountered.
- A postorder traversal traverses the left subtree postorder, traverses the right subtree postorder then processes the value in the root node. The value in each node is not processed until the values in both its subtrees are processed.

TERMINOLOGY

binary search tree
binary tree
binary tree sort
child node
children
circular, doubly linked list
circular, singly linked list
deleting a node
dequeue
double indirection
doubly linked list
duplicate elimination
dynamic data structures
dynamic memory allocation
enqueue
FIFO (first-in, first-out)
head of a queue
inorder traversal of a binary tree
inserting a node
leaf node
left child
left subtree
level-order traversal of a binary tree
LIFO (last-in, first-out)
linear data structure
linked list

node
nonlinear data structure
null pointer
parent node
pointer to a pointer
pop
postorder traversal of a binary tree
predicate function
preorder traversal of a binary tree
push
queue
right child
right subtree
root node
self-referential structure
siblings
singly linked list
sizeof
stack
subtree
tail of a queue
top
traversal
tree
visit a node

SELF-REVIEW EXERCISES

17.1 Fill in the blanks in each of the following:

a) A self-_____ class is used to form dynamic data structures that can grow and shrink at execution time

b) Operator _____ is used to dynamically allocate memory and construct an object; this operator returns a pointer to the object.

c) A _____ is a constrained version of a linked list in which nodes can be inserted and deleted only from the start of the list and node values are returned in last-in, first-out order.

d) A function that does not alter a linked list, but looks at the list to determine whether it is empty, is referred to as a _____function.

e) A queue is referred to as a _____ data structure because the first nodes inserted are the first nodes removed.

f) The pointer to the next node in a linked list is referred to as a _____.

g) Operator _____ is used to destroy an object and reclaim dynamically allocated memory.

h) A _____ is a constrained version of a linked list in which nodes can be inserted only at the end of the list and deleted only from the start of the list.

i) A _____ is a nonlinear, two-dimensional data structure that contains nodes with two or more links.

j) A stack is referred to as a _____ data structure because the last node inserted is the first node removed.

k) The nodes of a _____ tree contain two link members.

l) The first node of a tree is the _____ node.

m) Each link in a tree node points to a _____ or _____ of that node.

n) A tree node that has no children is called a _____ node.

o) The four traversal algorithms we mentioned in the text for binary search trees are _____, _____, _____ and _____.

17.2 What are the differences between a linked list and a stack?

17.3 What are the differences between a stack and a queue?

17.4 Perhaps a more appropriate title for this chapter would have been "Reusable Data Structures." Comment on how each of the following entities or concepts contributes to the reusability of data structures:

a) classes

b) class templates

c) inheritance

d) private inheritance

e) composition

17.5 Manually provide the inorder, preorder and postorder traversals of the binary search tree of Fig. 17.21.

ANSWERS TO SELF-REVIEW EXERCISES

17.1 a) referential. b) **new**. c) stack. d) predicate. e) first-in, first-out (FIFO). f) link. g) **delete**. h) queue. i) tree. j) last-in, first-out (LIFO). k) binary. l) root. m) child or subtree. n) leaf. o) inorder, preorder, postorder and level order.

17.2 It is possible to insert a node anywhere in a linked list and remove a node from anywhere in a linked list. Nodes in a stack may only be inserted at the top of the stack and removed from the top of a stack.

17.3 A queue has pointers to both its head and its tail so that nodes may be inserted at the tail and deleted from the head. A stack has a single pointer to the top of the stack, where both insertion and deletion of nodes are performed.

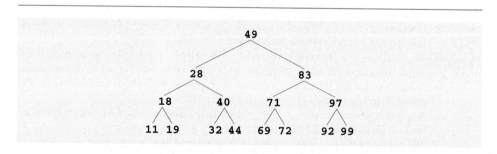

Fig. 17.21 A 15-node binary search tree.

17.4 a) Classes allow us to instantiate as many data structure objects of a certain type (i.e., class) as we wish.

  b) Class templates enable us to instantiate related classes—each based on different type parameters—we can then generate as many objects of each template class as we like.

  c) Inheritance enables us to reuse code from a base class in a derived class so that the derived-class data structure is also a base-class data structure (with public inheritance, that is).

  d) Private inheritance enables us to reuse portions of the code from a base class to form a derived-class data structure; because the inheritance is **private**, all **public** base-class member functions become **private** in the derived class. This enables us to prevent clients of the derived-class data structure from accessing base-class member functions that do not apply to the derived class.

  e) Composition enables us to reuse code by making a class object data structure a member of a composed class; if we make the class object a **private** member of the composed class, then the class object's **public** member functions are not available through the composed object's interface.

17.5 The inorder traversal is

   11 18 19 28 32 40 44 49 69 71 72 83 92 97 99

The preorder traversal is

   49 28 18 11 19 40 32 44 83 71 69 72 97 92 99

The postorder traversal is

   11 19 18 32 44 40 28 69 72 71 92 99 97 83 49

EXERCISES

17.6 Write a program that concatenates two linked list objects of characters. The program should include function **concatenate**, which takes references to both list objects as arguments and concatenates the second list to the first list.

17.7 Write a program that merges two ordered list objects of integers into a single ordered list object of integers. Function **merge** should receive references to each of the list objects to be merged and should return an object containing the merged list.

17.8 Write a program that inserts 25 random integers from 0 to 100 in order in a linked list object. The program should calculate the sum of the elements and the floating-point average of the elements.

17.9 Write a program that creates a linked list object of 10 characters and creates a second list object containing a copy of the first list, but in reverse order.

17.10 Write a program that inputs a line of text and uses a stack object to print the line reversed.

17.11 Write a program that uses a stack object to determine if a string is a palindrome (i.e., the string is spelled identically backwards and forwards). The program should ignore spaces and punctuation.

17.12 Stacks are used by compilers to help in the process of evaluating expressions and generating machine language code. In this and the next exercise, we investigate how compilers evaluate arithmetic expressions consisting only of constants, operators and parentheses.

Humans generally write expressions like **3 + 4** and **7 / 9** in which the operator (**+** or **/** here) is written between its operands—this is called *infix notation*. Computers "prefer" *postfix notation* in which the operator is written to the right of its two operands. The preceding infix expressions would appear in postfix notation as **3 4 +** and **7 9 /**, respectively.

To evaluate a complex infix expression, a compiler would first convert the expression to postfix notation and evaluate the postfix version of the expression. Each of these algorithms requires only a single left-to-right pass of the expression. Each algorithm uses a stack object in support of its operation, and in each algorithm the stack is used for a different purpose.

In this exercise, you will write a C++ version of the infix-to-postfix conversion algorithm. In the next exercise, you will write a C++ version of the postfix expression evaluation algorithm. Later in the chapter, you will discover that code you write in this exercise can help you implement a complete working compiler.

Write a program that converts an ordinary infix arithmetic expression (assume a valid expression is entered) with single-digit integers such as

```
(6 + 2) * 5 - 8 / 4
```

to a postfix expression. The postfix version of the preceding infix expression is

```
6 2 + 5 * 8 4 / -
```

The program should read the expression into character array **infix** and use modified versions of the stack functions implemented in this chapter to help create the postfix expression in character array **postfix**. The algorithm for creating a postfix expression is as follows:

1) Push a left parenthesis '(' onto the stack.
2) Append a right parenthesis ')' to the end of **infix**.
3) While the stack is not empty, read **infix** from left to right and do the following:
   If the current character in **infix** is a digit, copy it to the next element of **postfix**.
   If the current character in **infix** is a left parenthesis, push it onto the stack.
   If the current character in **infix** is an operator,
      Pop operators (if there are any) at the top of the stack while they have equal or higher precedence than the current operator, and insert the popped operators in **postfix**.
      Push the current character in **infix** onto the stack.
   If the current character in **infix** is a right parenthesis
      Pop operators from the top of the stack and insert them in **postfix** until a left parenthesis is at the top of the stack.
      Pop (and discard) the left parenthesis from the stack.

The following arithmetic operations are allowed in an expression:

+   addition
-    subtraction
*   multiplication
/   division
^   exponentiation
%   modulus

The stack should be maintained with stack nodes that each contain a data member and a pointer to the next stack node.

Some of the functional capabilities you may want to provide are:
a) function **convertToPostfix** that converts the infix expression to postfix notation
b) function **isOperator** that determines whether **c** is an operator
c) function **precedence** that determines whether the precedence of **operator1** is less than, equal to or greater than the precedence of **operator2** (the function returns -1, 0 and 1, respectively)
d) function **push** that pushes a value onto the stack
e) function **pop** that pops a value off the stack
f) function **stackTop** that returns the top value of the stack without popping the stack
g) function **isEmpty** that determines if the stack is empty
h) function **printStack** that prints the stack

17.13 Write a program that evaluates a postfix expression (assume it is valid) such as

```
6 2 + 5 * 8 4 / -
```

The program should read a postfix expression consisting of digits and operators into a character array. Using modified versions of the stack functions implemented earlier in this chapter, the program should scan the expression and evaluate it. The algorithm is as follows:

1) Append the null character (`'\0'`) to the end of the postfix expression. When the null character is encountered, no further processing is necessary.

2) While `'\0'` has not been encountered, read the expression from left to right.
   If the current character is a digit,
   Push its integer value onto the stack (the integer value of a digit character is its value in the computer's character set minus the value of `'0'` in the computer's character set).

   Otherwise, if the current character is an *operator*,
   Pop the two top elements of the stack into variables **x** and **y**.
   Calculate **y** *operator* **x**.
   Push the result of the calculation onto the stack.

3) When the null character is encountered in the expression, pop the top value of the stack. This is the result of the postfix expression.

Note: In step 2) above, if the operator is `'/'`, the top of the stack is **2** and the next element in the stack is **8**, then pop **2** into **x**, pop **8** into **y**, evaluate **8 / 2** and push the result, **4**, back onto the stack. This note also applies to operator `'-'`. The arithmetic operations allowed in an expression are

- **+** addition
- **–** subtraction
- ***** multiplication
- **/** division
- **^** exponentiation
- **%** modulus

The stack should be maintained with stack nodes that contain an **int** data member and a pointer to the next stack node. You may want to provide the following functional capabilities:

a) function **evaluatePostfixExpression** that evaluates the postfix expression

b) function **calculate** that evaluates the expression **op1 operator op2**

c) function **push** that pushes a value onto the stack

d) function **pop** that pops a value off the stack

e) function **isEmpty** that determines if the stack is empty

f) function **printStack** that prints the stack

17.14 Modify the postfix evaluator program of Exercise 17.13 so that it can process integer operands larger than 9.

17.15 (*Supermarket Simulation*) Write a program that simulates a checkout line at a supermarket. The line is a queue object. Customers (i.e., customer objects) arrive in random integer intervals of 1–4 minutes. Also, each customer is served in random integer intervals of 1–4 minutes. Obviously, the rates need to be balanced. If the average arrival rate is larger than the average service rate, the queue will grow infinitely. Even with "balanced" rates, randomness can still cause long lines. Run the supermarket simulation for a 12-hour day (720 minutes) using the following algorithm:

1) Choose a random integer between 1 and 4 to determine the minute at which the first customer arrives.

2) At the first customer's arrival time:
   Determine customer's service time (random integer from 1 to 4);
   Begin servicing the customer;
   Schedule arrival time of next customer (random integer 1 to 4 added to the current time).

3) For each minute of the day:

    If the next customer arrives,

        Say so,

        Enqueue the customer;

        Schedule the arrival time of the next customer;

    If service was completed for the last customer;

        Say so

        Dequeue next customer to be serviced

        Determine customer's service completion time

            (random integer from 1 to 4 added to the current time).

Now run your simulation for 720 minutes, and answer each of the following:

   a)   What is the maximum number of customers in the queue at any time?

   b)   What is the longest wait any one customer experiences?

   c)   What happens if the arrival interval is changed from 1–4 minutes to 1–3 minutes?

17.16   Modify the program of Fig. 17.17–Fig. 17.19 to allow the binary tree object to contain duplicates.

17.17   Write a program based on Fig. 17.17–Fig. 17.19 that inputs a line of text, tokenizes the sentence into separate words (you may want to use the **strtok** library function), inserts the words in a binary search tree and prints the inorder, preorder and postorder traversals of the tree. Use an OOP approach.

17.18   In this chapter, we saw that duplicate elimination is straightforward when creating a binary search tree. Describe how you would perform duplicate elimination using only a single-subscripted array. Compare the performance of array-based duplicate elimination with the performance of binary-search-tree-based duplicate elimination.

17.19   Write a function **depth** that receives a binary tree and determines how many levels it has.

17.20   (*Recursively Print a List Backwards*) Write a member function **printListBackwards** that recursively outputs the items in a linked list object in reverse order. Write a test program that creates a sorted list of integers and prints the list in reverse order.

17.21   (*Recursively Search a List*) Write a member function **searchList** that recursively searches a linked list object for a specified value. The function should return a pointer to the value if it is found; otherwise, null should be returned. Use your function in a test program that creates a list of integers. The program should prompt the user for a value to locate in the list.

17.22   (*Binary Tree Delete*) In this exercise, we discuss deleting items from binary search trees. The deletion algorithm is not as straightforward as the insertion algorithm. There are three cases that are encountered when deleting an item—the item is contained in a leaf node (i.e., it has no children), the item is contained in a node that has one child or the item is contained in a node that has two children.

If the item to be deleted is contained in a leaf node, the node is deleted and the pointer in the parent node is set to null.

If the item to be deleted is contained in a node with one child, the pointer in the parent node is set to point to the child node and the node containing the data item is deleted. This causes the child node to take the place of the deleted node in the tree.

The last case is the most difficult. When a node with two children is deleted, another node in the tree must take its place. However, the pointer in the parent node cannot be assigned to point to one of the children of the node to be deleted. In most cases, the resulting binary search tree would not adhere to the following characteristic of binary search trees (with no duplicate values): *The values in any left subtree are less than the value in the parent node, and the values in any right subtree are greater than the value in the parent node.*

Which node is used as a *replacement node* to maintain this characteristic? Either the node containing the largest value in the tree less than the value in the node being deleted, or the node containing the smallest value in the tree greater than the value in the node being deleted. Let us consider the node with the smaller value. In a binary search tree, the largest value less than a parent's value is located in the left subtree of the parent node and is guaranteed to be contained in the rightmost node of the subtree. This node is located by walking down the left subtree to the right until the pointer to the right child of the current node is null. We are now pointing to the replacement node, which is either a leaf node or a node with one child to its left. If the replacement node is a leaf node, the steps to perform the deletion are as follows:

1) Store the pointer to the node to be deleted in a temporary pointer variable (this pointer is used to delete the dynamically allocated memory).
2) Set the pointer in the parent of the node being deleted to point to the replacement node
3) Set the pointer in the parent of the replacement node to null.
4) Set the pointer to the right subtree in the replacement node to point to the right subtree of the node to be deleted.
5) Delete the node to which the temporary pointer variable points.

The deletion steps for a replacement node with a left child are similar to those for a replacement node with no children, but the algorithm also must move the child into the replacement node's position in the tree. If the replacement node is a node with a left child, the steps to perform the deletion are as follows:

1) Store the pointer to the node to be deleted in a temporary pointer variable.
2) Set the pointer in the parent of the node being deleted to point to the replacement node.
3) Set the pointer in the parent of the replacement node to point to the left child of the replacement node.
4) Set the pointer to the right subtree in the replacement node to point to the right subtree of the node to be deleted.
5) Delete the node to which the temporary pointer variable points.

Write member function **deleteNode**, which takes as its arguments a pointer to the root node of the tree object and the value to be deleted. The function should locate in the tree the node containing the value to be deleted and use the algorithms discussed here to delete the node. The function should print a message that indicates whether the value is deleted. Modify the program of Fig. 17.17–Fig. 17.19 to use this function. After deleting an item, call the **inOrder**, **preOrder** and **postOrder** traversal functions to confirm that the delete operation was performed correctly.

17.23 (*Binary Tree Search*) Write member function **binaryTreeSearch**, which attempts to locate a specified value in a binary search tree object. The function should take as arguments a pointer to the root node of the binary tree and a search key to be located. If the node containing the search key is found, the function should return a pointer to that node; otherwise, the function should return a null pointer.

17.24 (*Level-Order Binary Tree Traversal*) The program of Fig. 17.17–Fig. 17.19 illustrated three recursive methods of traversing a binary tree—inorder, preorder and postorder traversals. This exercise presents the *level-order traversal* of a binary tree in which the node values are printed level by level, starting at the root node level. The nodes on each level are printed from left to right. The level-order traversal is not a recursive algorithm. It uses a queue object to control the output of the nodes. The algorithm is as follows:

1) Insert the root node in the queue
2) While there are nodes left in the queue,
   Get the next node in the queue
   Print the node's value
   If the pointer to the left child of the node is not null
       Insert the left child node in the queue
   If the pointer to the right child of the node is not null
       Insert the right child node in the queue.

Write member function **levelOrder** to perform a level-order traversal of a binary tree object. Modify the program of Fig. 17.17–Fig. 17.19 to use this function. (*Note*: You will also need to modify and incorporate the queue-processing functions of Fig. 17.13 in this program.)

17.25 (*Printing Trees*) Write a recursive member function **outputTree** to display a binary tree object on the screen. The function should output the tree row by row, with the top of the tree at the left of the screen and the bottom of the tree toward the right of the screen. Each row is output vertically. For example, the binary tree illustrated in Fig. 17.21 is output as follows:

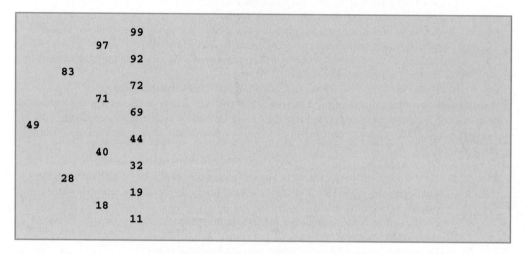

Note that the rightmost leaf node appears at the top of the output in the rightmost column and the root node appears at the left of the output. Each column of output starts five spaces to the right of the previous column. Function **outputTree** should receive an argument **totalSpaces** representing the number of spaces preceding the value to be output (this variable should start at zero so the root node is output at the left of the screen). The function uses a modified inorder traversal to output the tree—it starts at the rightmost node in the tree and works back to the left. The algorithm is as follows:

> While the pointer to the current node is not null
>> Recursively call **outputTree** with the right subtree of the current node and **totalSpaces** + 5
>> Use a **for** structure to count from 1 to **totalSpaces** and output spaces
>> Output the value in the current node
>> Set the pointer to the current node to point to the left subtree of the current node
>> Increment **totalSpaces** by 5.

SPECIAL SECTION—BUILDING YOUR OWN COMPILER

In Exercise 5.18 and Exercise 5.19, we introduced Simpletron Machine Language (SML) and you implemented a Simpletron computer simulator to execute programs written in SML. In this section, we build a compiler that converts programs written in a high-level programming language to SML. This section "ties" together the entire programming process. You will write programs in this new high-level language, compile these programs on the compiler you build and run the programs on the simulator you built in Exercise 5.19. You should make every effort to implement your compiler in an object-oriented manner.

17.26 (*The Simple Language*) Before we begin building the compiler, we discuss a simple, yet powerful, high-level language similar to early versions of the popular language BASIC. We call the language *Simple*. Every Simple *statement* consists of a *line number* and a Simple *instruction*. Line numbers must appear in ascending order. Each instruction begins with one of the following Simple *commands*: **rem**, **input**, **let**, **print**, **goto**, **if/goto** and **end** (see Fig. 17.22). All commands except **end** can be used repeatedly. Simple evaluates only integer expressions using the **+**, **-**, ***** and **/** operators. These operators have the same precedence as in C++. Parentheses can be used to change the order of evaluation of an expression.

Our Simple compiler recognizes only lowercase letters. All characters in a Simple file should be lowercase (uppercase letters result in a syntax error unless they appear in a **rem** statement, in which case they are ignored). A *variable name* is a single letter. Simple does not allow descriptive variable names, so variables should be explained in remarks to indicate their use in a program. Simple uses only integer variables. Simple does not have variable declarations—merely mentioning a variable name in a program causes the variable to be declared and initialized to zero automatically. The syntax of Simple does not allow string manipulation (reading a string, writing a string, comparing strings, etc.). If a string is encountered in a Simple program (after a command other than **rem**), the compiler generates a syntax error. The first version of our compiler will assume that Simple programs are entered correctly. Exercise 17.29 asks the student to modify the compiler to perform syntax error checking.

Simple uses the conditional **if/goto** statement and the unconditional **goto** statement to alter the flow of control during program execution. If the condition in the **if/goto** statement is true, control is transferred to a specific line of the program. The following relational and equality operators are valid in an **if/goto** statement: **<**, **>**, **<=**, **>=**, **==** and **!=**. The precedence of these operators is the same as in C++.

Let us now consider several programs that demonstrate Simple's features. The first program (Fig. 17.23) reads two integers from the keyboard, stores the values in variables **a** and **b** and computes and prints their sum (stored in variable **c**).

Command	Example statement	Description
rem	50 rem this is a remark	Text following **rem** is for documentation purposes and is ignored by the compiler.
input	30 input x	Display a question mark to prompt the user to enter an integer. Read that integer from the keyboard, and store the integer in **x**.
let	80 let u = 4 * (j - 56)	Assign **u** the value of **4 * (j - 56)**. Note that an arbitrarily complex expression can appear to the right of the equals sign.
print	10 print w	Display the value of **w**.
goto	70 goto 45	Transfer program control to line **45**.
if/goto	35 if i == z goto 80	Compare **i** and **z** for equality and transfer control to line **80** if the condition is true; otherwise, continue execution with the next statement.
end	99 end	Terminate program execution.

Fig. 17.22 Simple commands.

```
1    10 rem    determine and print the sum of two integers
2    15 rem
3    20 rem    input the two integers
4    30 input a
5    40 input b
6    45 rem
7    50 rem    add integers and store result in c
8    60 let c = a + b
9    65 rem
10   70 rem    print the result
11   80 print c
12   90 rem    terminate program execution
13   99 end
```

Fig. 17.23   Simple program that determines the sum of two integers.

The program of Fig. 17.24 determines and prints the larger of two integers. The integers are input from the keyboard and stored in **s** and **t**. The **if/goto** statement tests the condition **s >= t**. If the condition is true, control is transferred to line **90** and **s** is output; otherwise, **t** is output and control is transferred to the **end** statement in line **99** where the program terminates.

Simple does not provide a repetition structure (such as C++'s **for**, **while** or **do/while**). However, Simple can simulate each of C++'s repetition structures using the **if/goto** and **goto** statements. Figure 17.25 uses a sentinel-controlled loop to calculate the squares of several integers. Each integer is input from the keyboard and stored in variable **j**. If the value entered is the sentinel value **-9999**, control is transferred to line **99**, where the program terminates. Otherwise, **k** is assigned the square of **j**, **k** is output to the screen and control is passed to line **20**, where the next integer is input.

```
1    10 rem    determine the larger of two integers
2    20 input s
3    30 input t
4    32 rem
5    35 rem    test if s >= t
6    40 if s >= t goto 90
7    45 rem
8    50 rem    t is greater than s, so print t
9    60 print t
10   70 goto 99
11   75 rem
12   80 rem    s is greater than or equal to t, so print s
13   90 print s
14   99 end
```

Fig. 17.24   Simple program that finds the larger of two integers.

```
1    10 rem    calculate the squares of several integers
2    20 input j
3    23 rem
4    25 rem    test for sentinel value
5    30 if j == -9999 goto 99
```

Fig. 17.25   Calculate the squares of several integers. (Part 1 of 2.)

```
 6   33 rem
 7   35 rem    calculate square of j and assign result to k
 8   40 let k = j * j
 9   50 print k
10   53 rem
11   55 rem    loop to get next j
12   60 goto 20
13   99 end
```

Fig. 17.25 Calculate the squares of several integers. (Part 2 of 2.)

Using the sample programs of Fig. 17.23, Fig. 17.24 and Fig. 17.25 as your guide, write a Simple program to accomplish each of the following:

  a) Input three integers, determine their average and print the result.
  b) Use a sentinel-controlled loop to input 10 integers and compute and print their sum.
  c) Use a counter-controlled loop to input seven integers, some positive and some negative, and compute and print their average.
  d) Input a series of integers and determine and print the largest. The first integer input indicates how many numbers should be processed.
  e) Input 10 integers and print the smallest.
  f) Calculate and print the sum of the even integers from 2 to 30.
  g) Calculate and print the product of the odd integers from 1 to 9.

17.27 (*Building A Compiler; Prerequisite: Complete Exercises 5.18, 5.19, 17.12, 17.13 and 17.26*) Now that the Simple language has been presented (Exercise 17.26), we discuss how to build a Simple compiler. First, we consider the process by which a Simple program is converted to SML and executed by the Simpletron simulator (see Fig. 17.26). A file containing a Simple program is read by the compiler and converted to SML code. The SML code is output to a file on disk, in which SML instructions appear one per line. The SML file is then loaded into the Simpletron simulator, and the results are sent to a file on disk and to the screen. Note that the Simpletron program developed in Exercise 5.19 took its input from the keyboard. It must be modified to read from a file so it can run the programs produced by our compiler.

The Simple compiler performs two *passes* of the Simple program to convert it to SML. The first pass constructs a *symbol table* (object) in which every *line number* (object), *variable name* (object) and *constant* (object) of the Simple program is stored with its type and corresponding location in the final SML code (the symbol table is discussed in detail below). The first pass also produces the corresponding SML instruction object(s) for each of the Simple statements (object, etc.). As we will see, if

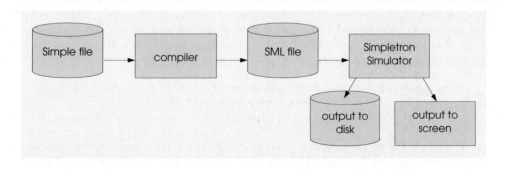

Fig. 17.26 Writing, compiling and executing a Simple language program.

the Simple program contains statements that transfer control to a line later in the program, the first pass results in an SML program containing some "unfinished" instructions. The second pass of the compiler locates and completes the unfinished instructions, and outputs the SML program to a file.

First Pass

The compiler begins by reading one statement of the Simple program into memory. The line must be separated into its individual *tokens* (i.e., "pieces" of a statement) for processing and compilation (standard library function **strtok** can be used to facilitate this task). Recall that every statement begins with a line number followed by a command. As the compiler breaks a statement into tokens, if the token is a line number, a variable or a constant, it is placed in the symbol table. A line number is placed in the symbol table only if it is the first token in a statement. The **symbolTable** object is an array of **tableEntry** objects representing each symbol in the program. There is no restriction on the number of symbols that can appear in the program. Therefore, the **symbolTable** for a particular program could be large. Make the **symbolTable** a 100-element array for now. You can increase or decrease its size once the program is working.

Each **tableEntry** object contains three members. Member **symbol** is an integer containing the ASCII representation of a variable (remember that variable names are single characters), a line number or a constant. Member **type** is one of the following characters indicating the symbol's type: **'C'** for constant, **'L'** for line number and **'V'** for variable. Member **location** contains the Simpletron memory location (**00** to **99**) to which the symbol refers. Simpletron memory is an array of 100 integers in which SML instructions and data are stored. For a line number, the location is the element in the Simpletron memory array at which the SML instructions for the Simple statement begin. For a variable or constant, the location is the element in the Simpletron memory array in which the variable or constant is stored. Variables and constants are allocated from the end of Simpletron's memory backwards. The first variable or constant is stored in location at **99**, the next in location at **98**, etc.

The symbol table plays an integral part in converting Simple programs to SML. We learned in Chapter 5 that an SML instruction is a four-digit integer composed of two parts—the *operation code* and the *operand*. The operation code is determined by commands in Simple. For example, the simple command **input** corresponds to SML operation code **10** (read), and the Simple command **print** corresponds to SML operation code **11** (write). The operand is a memory location containing the data on which the operation code performs its task (e.g., operation code **10** reads a value from the keyboard and stores it in the memory location specified by the operand). The compiler searches **symbolTable** to determine the Simpletron memory location for each symbol so the corresponding location can be used to complete the SML instructions.

The compilation of each Simple statement is based on its command. For example, after the line number in a **rem** statement is inserted in the symbol table, the remainder of the statement is ignored by the compiler because a remark is for documentation purposes only. The **input**, **print**, **goto** and **end** statements correspond to the SML *read*, *write*, *branch* (to a specific location) and *halt* instructions. Statements containing these Simple commands are converted directly to SML (note that a **goto** statement may contain an unresolved reference if the specified line number refers to a statement further into the Simple program file; this is sometimes called a forward reference).

When a **goto** statement is compiled with an unresolved reference, the SML instruction must be *flagged* to indicate that the second pass of the compiler must complete the instruction. The flags are stored in 100-element array **flags** of type **int** in which each element is initialized to **-1**. If the memory location to which a line number in the Simple program refers is not yet known (i.e., it is not in the symbol table), the line number is stored in array **flags** in the element with the same subscript as the incomplete instruction. The operand of the incomplete instruction is set to **00** temporarily. For example, an unconditional branch instruction (making a forward reference) is left as **+4000** until the second pass of the compiler. The second pass of the compiler is described shortly.

Compilation of **if/goto** and **let** statements is more complicated than other statements—
they are the only statements that produce more than one SML instruction. For an **if/goto**, the
compiler produces code to test the condition and to branch to another line if necessary. The result of
the branch could be an unresolved reference. Each of the relational and equality operators can be
simulated using SML's *branch zero* or *branch negative* instructions (or a combination of both).

For a **let** statement, the compiler produces code to evaluate an arbitrarily complex arithmetic
expression consisting of integer variables and/or constants. Expressions should separate each oper-
and and operator with spaces. Exercise 17.12 and Exercise 17.13 presented the infix-to-postfix conversion algorithm and the postfix evaluation algorithm used by compilers to evaluate expressions.
Before proceeding with your compiler, you should complete each of these exercises. When a compiler encounters an expression, it converts the expression from infix notation to postfix notation and
then evaluates the postfix expression.

How is it that the compiler produces the machine language to evaluate an expression containing
variables? The postfix evaluation algorithm contains a "hook" where the compiler can generate SML
instructions rather than actually evaluating the expression. To enable this "hook" in the compiler, the
postfix evaluation algorithm must be modified to search the symbol table for each symbol it encounters (and possibly insert it), determine the symbol's corresponding memory location and *push the
memory location onto the stack (instead of the symbol).* When an operator is encountered in the postfix expression, the two memory locations at the top of the stack are popped and machine language
for effecting the operation is produced using the memory locations as operands. The result of each
subexpression is stored in a temporary location in memory and pushed back onto the stack so the
evaluation of the postfix expression can continue. When postfix evaluation is complete, the memory
location containing the result is the only location left on the stack. This is popped and SML instructions are generated to assign the result to the variable at the left of the **let** statement.

Second Pass

The second pass of the compiler performs two tasks: Eesolve any unresolved references, and output
the SML code to a file. Resolution of references occurs as follows:

  a) Search the **flags** array for an unresolved reference (i.e., an element with a value other
     than **-1**).
  b) Locate the object in array **symbolTable**, containing the symbol stored in the **flags**
     array (be sure that the type of the symbol is **'L'** for line number).
  c) Insert the memory location from member **location** into the instruction with the un-
     resolved reference (remember that an instruction containing an unresolved reference has
     operand **00**).
  d) Repeat steps 1, 2 and 3 until the end of the **flags** array is reached.

After the resolution process is complete, the entire array containing the SML code is output to a disk
file with one SML instruction per line. This file can be read by the Simpletron for execution (after
the simulator is modified to read its input from a file). Compiling your first Simple program into an
SML file and then executing that file should give you a real sense of personal accomplishment.

A Complete Example

The following example illustrates a complete conversion of a Simple program to SML as it will be
performed by the Simple compiler. Consider a Simple program that inputs an integer and sums the
values from 1 to that integer. The program and the SML instructions produced by the first pass of the
Simple compiler are illustrated in Fig. 17.27. The symbol table constructed by the first pass is shown
in Fig. 17.28.

Most Simple statements convert directly to single SML instructions. The exceptions in this program are remarks, the **if/goto** statement in line **20** and the **let** statements. Remarks do not translate into machine language. However, the line number for a remark is placed in the symbol table in
case the line number is referenced in a **goto** statement or an **if/goto** statement. Line **20** of the

Simple program	SML location and instruction	Description
5 rem sum 1 to x	*none*	**rem** ignored
10 input x	00 +1099	read **x** into location **99**
15 rem check y == x	*none*	**rem** ignored
20 if y == x goto 60	01 +2098	load **y** (**98**) into accumulator
	02 +3199	sub **x** (**99**) from accumulator
	03 +4200	branch zero to unresolved location
25 rem increment y	*none*	**rem** ignored
30 let y = y + 1	04 +2098	load **y** into accumulator
	05 +3097	add **1** (**97**) to accumulator
	06 +2196	store in temporary location **96**
	07 +2096	load from temporary location **96**
	08 +2198	store accumulator in **y**
35 rem add y to total	*none*	**rem** ignored
40 let t = t + y	09 +2095	load **t** (**95**) into accumulator
	10 +3098	add **y** to accumulator
	11 +2194	store in temporary location **94**
	12 +2094	load from temporary location **94**
	13 +2195	store accumulator in **t**
45 rem loop y	*none*	**rem** ignored
50 goto 20	14 +4001	branch to location **01**
55 rem output result	*none*	**rem** ignored
60 print t	15 +1195	output **t** to screen
99 end	16 +4300	terminate execution

Fig. 17.27 SML instructions produced after the compiler's first pass.

Symbol	Type	Location
5	L	00
10	L	00
'x'	V	99
15	L	01
20	L	01
'y'	V	98
25	L	04

Fig. 17.28 Symbol table for program of Fig. 17.27. (Part 1 of 2.)

Symbol	Type	Location
30	L	04
1	C	97
35	L	09
40	L	09
't'	V	95
45	L	14
50	L	14
55	L	15
60	L	15
99	L	16

Fig. 17.28 Symbol table for program of Fig. 17.27. (Part 2 of 2.)

program specifies that if the condition **y == x** is true, program control is transferred to line **60**. Because line **60** appears later in the program, the first pass of the compiler has not as yet placed **60** in the symbol table (statement line numbers are placed in the symbol table only when they appear as the first token in a statement). Therefore, it is not possible at this time to determine the operand of the SML *branch zero* instruction at location **03** in the array of SML instructions. The compiler places **60** in location **03** of the **flags** array to indicate that the second pass completes this instruction.

We must keep track of the next instruction location in the SML array because there is not a one-to-one correspondence between Simple statements and SML instructions. For example, the **if/ goto** statement of line **20** compiles into three SML instructions. Each time an instruction is produced, we must increment the *instruction counter* to the next location in the SML array. Note that the size of Simpletron's memory could present a problem for Simple programs with many statements, variables and constants. It is conceivable that the compiler will run out of memory. To test for this case, your program should contain a *data counter* to keep track of the location at which the next variable or constant will be stored in the SML array. If the value of the instruction counter is larger than the value of the data counter, the SML array is full. In this case, the compilation process should terminate and the compiler should print an error message indicating that it ran out of memory during compilation. This serves to emphasize that although the programmer is freed from the burdens of managing memory by the compiler, the compiler itself must carefully determine the placement of instructions and data in memory, and must check for such errors as memory being exhausted during the compilation process.

A Step-by-Step View of the Compilation Process

Let us now walk through the compilation process for the Simple program in Fig. 17.27. The compiler reads the first line of the program

```
5 rem sum 1 to x
```

into memory. The first token in the statement (the line number) is determined using **strtok** (see Chapter 5 and Chapter 18 for a discussion of C++'s C-style string manipulation functions). The token returned by **strtok** is converted to an integer using **atoi** so the symbol **5** can be located in the symbol table. If the symbol is not found, it is inserted in the symbol table. Since we are at the beginning of the program and this is the first line, no symbols are in the table yet. So **5** is inserted into the symbol table as type **L** (line number) and assigned the first location in SML array (**00**). Although this line is a remark, a space in the symbol table is still allocated for the line number (in case it is referenced by a **goto** or an **if/goto**). No SML instruction is generated for a **rem** statement, so the instruction counter is not incremented.

The statement

        10 input x

is tokenized next. The line number **10** is placed in the symbol table as type **L** and assigned the first location in the SML array (**00** because a remark began the program so the instruction counter is currently **00**). The command **input** indicates that the next token is a variable (only a variable can appear in an **input** statement). Because **input** corresponds directly to an SML operation code, the compiler has to determine the location of **x** in the SML array. Symbol **x** is not found in the symbol table. So it is inserted into the symbol table as the ASCII representation of **x**, given type **V**, and assigned location **99** in the SML array (data storage begins at **99** and is allocated backwards). SML code can now be generated for this statement. Operation code **10** (the SML read operation code) is multiplied by 100, and the location of **x** (as determined in the symbol table) is added to complete the instruction. The instruction is then stored in the SML array at location **00**. The instruction counter is incremented by 1 because a single SML instruction was produced.

The statement

        15 rem   check y == x

is tokenized next. The symbol table is searched for line number **15** (which is not found). The line number is inserted as type **L** and assigned the next location in the array, **01** (remember that **rem** statements do not produce code, so the instruction counter is not incremented).

The statement

        20 if y == x goto 60

is tokenized next. Line number **20** is inserted in the symbol table and given type **L** with the next location in the SML array **01**. The command **if** indicates that a condition is to be evaluated. The variable **y** is not found in the symbol table, so it is inserted and given the type **V** and the SML location **98**. Next, SML instructions are generated to evaluate the condition. Since there is no direct equivalent in SML for the **if/goto**, it must be simulated by performing a calculation using **x** and **y** and branching based on the result. If **y** is equal to **x**, the result of subtracting **x** from **y** is zero, so the *branch zero* instruction can be used with the result of the calculation to simulate the **if/goto** statement. The first step requires that **y** be loaded (from SML location **98**) into the accumulator. This produces the instruction **01 +2098**. Next, **x** is subtracted from the accumulator. This produces the instruction **02 +3199**. The value in the accumulator may be zero, positive or negative. Since the operator is **==**, we want to *branch zero*. First, the symbol table is searched for the branch location (**60** in this case), which is not found. So **60** is placed in the **flags** array at location **03**, and the instruction **03 +4200** is generated (we cannot add the branch location, because we have not assigned a location to line **60** in the SML array yet). The instruction counter is incremented to **04**.

The compiler proceeds to the statement

        25 rem   increment y

The line number **25** is inserted in the symbol table as type **L** and assigned SML location **04**. The instruction counter is not incremented.

When the statement

        30 let y = y + 1

is tokenized, the line number **30** is inserted in the symbol table as type **L** and assigned SML location **04**. Command **let** indicates that the line is an assignment statement. First, all the symbols on the line are inserted in the symbol table (if they are not already there). The integer **1** is added to the symbol table as type **C** and assigned SML location **97**. Next, the right side of the assignment is converted from infix to postfix notation. Then the postfix expression (**y 1 +**) is evaluated. Symbol **y** is located in the symbol table, and its corresponding memory location is pushed onto the stack. Symbol **1** is also located in the symbol table, and its corresponding memory location is pushed onto the stack. When the operator **+** is encountered, the postfix evaluator pops the stack into the right operand of the operator, pops the stack again into the left operand of the operator and produces the SML instructions

> **04 +2098**   *(load **y**)*
> **05 +3097**   *(add **1**)*

The result of the expression is stored in a temporary location in memory (**96**) with instruction

> **06 +2196**   *(store temporary)*

and the temporary location is pushed on the stack. Now that the expression has been evaluated, the result must be stored in **y** (i.e., the variable on the left side of **=**). So the temporary location is loaded into the accumulator, and the accumulator is stored in **y** with the instructions

> **07 +2096**   *(load temporary)*
> **08 +2198**   *(store **y**)*

The reader will immediately notice that SML instructions appear to be redundant. We will discuss this issue shortly.

When the statement

> **35 rem   add y to total**

is tokenized, line number **35** is inserted in the symbol table as type **L** and assigned location **09**.

The statement

> **40 let t = t + y**

is similar to line **30**. The variable **t** is inserted in the symbol table as type **V** and assigned SML location **95**. The instructions follow the same logic and format as line **30**, and the instructions **09 +2095, 10 +3098, 11 +2194, 12 +2094** and **13 +2195** are generated. Note that the result of **t + y** is assigned to temporary location **94** before being assigned to **t** (**95**). Once again, the reader will note that the instructions in memory locations **11** and **12** appear to be redundant. Again, we will discuss this shortly.

The statement

> **45 rem   loop y**

is a remark, so line **45** is added to the symbol table as type **L** and assigned SML location **14**.

The statement

> **50 goto 20**

transfers control to line **20**. Line number **50** is inserted in the symbol table as type **L** and assigned SML location **14**. The equivalent of **goto** in SML is the *unconditional branch* (**40**) instruction that transfers control to a specific SML location. The compiler searches the symbol table for line **20** and finds that it corresponds to SML location **01**. The operation code (**40**) is multiplied by 100, and location **01** is added to it to produce the instruction **14 +4001**.

The statement

```
55 rem    output result
```

is a remark, so line **55** is inserted in the symbol table as type **L** and assigned SML location **15**.

The statement

```
60 print t
```

is an output statement. Line number **60** is inserted in the symbol table as type **L** and assigned SML location **15**. The equivalent of **print** in SML is operation code **11** (*write*). The location of **t** is determined from the symbol table and added to the result of the operation code multiplied by 100.

The statement

```
99 end
```

is the final line of the program. Line number **99** is stored in the symbol table as type **L** and assigned SML location **16**. The **end** command produces the SML instruction **+4300** (**43** is *halt* in SML), which is written as the final instruction in the SML memory array.

This completes the first pass of the compiler. We now consider the second pass. The **flags** array is searched for values other than **-1**. Location **03** contains **60**, so the compiler knows that instruction **03** is incomplete. The compiler completes the instruction by searching the symbol table for **60**, determining its location and adding the location to the incomplete instruction. In this case, the search determines that line **60** corresponds to SML location **15**, so the completed instruction **03 +4215** is produced, replacing **03 +4200**. The Simple program has now been compiled successfully.

To build the compiler, you will have to perform each of the following tasks:

a) Modify the Simpletron simulator program you wrote in Exercise 5.19 to take its input from a file specified by the user (see Chapter 14). The simulator should output its results to a disk file in the same format as the screen output. Convert the simulator to be an object-oriented program. In particular, make each part of the hardware an object. Arrange the instruction types into a class hierarchy using inheritance. Then execute the program polymorphically by telling each instruction to execute itself with an **executeInstruction** message.

b) Modify the infix-to-postfix conversion algorithm of Exercise 17.12 to process multi-digit integer operands and single-letter variable name operands. *Hint:* Standard library function **strtok** can be used to locate each constant and variable in an expression, and constants can be converted from strings to integers using standard library function **atoi** (**<csdtlib>**). (*Note:* The data representation of the postfix expression must be altered to support variable names and integer constants.)

c) Modify the postfix evaluation algorithm to process multidigit integer operands and variable name operands. Also, the algorithm should now implement the "hook" discussed previously so that SML instructions are produced rather than directly evaluating the expression. *Hint:* Standard library function **strtok** can be used to locate each constant and variable in an expression, and constants can be converted from strings to integers using standard library function **atoi**. (*Note:* The data representation of the postfix expression must be altered to support variable names and integer constants.)

d) Build the compiler. Incorporate parts (b) and (c) for evaluating expressions in **let** statements. Your program should contain a function that performs the first pass of the compiler and a function that performs the second pass of the compiler. Both functions can call other functions to accomplish their tasks. Make your compiler as object oriented as possible.

17.28 (*Optimizing the Simple Compiler*) When a program is compiled and converted into SML, a set of instructions is generated. Certain combinations of instructions often repeat themselves, usually in triplets called *productions*. A production normally consists of three instructions such as *load*, *add* and *store*. For example, Fig. 17.29 illustrates five of the SML instructions that were produced in the compilation of the program in Fig. 17.27. The first three instructions are the production that adds **1** to **y**. Note that instructions **06** and **07** store the accumulator value in temporary location **96** and load the value back into the accumulator so instruction **08** can store the value in location **98**. Often a production is followed by a load instruction for the same location that was just stored. This code can be *optimized* by eliminating the store instruction and the subsequent load instruction that operate on the same memory location, thus enabling the Simpletron to execute the program faster. Figure 17.30 illustrates the optimized SML for the program of Fig. 17.27. Note that there are four fewer instructions in the optimized code—a memory-space savings of 25%.

1	04	+2098	*(load)*
2	05	+3097	*(add)*
3	06	+2196	*(store)*
4	07	+2096	*(load)*
5	08	+2198	*(store)*

Fig. 17.29 Nonoptimized code from the program of Fig. 17.27.

Simple program	SML location and instruction		Description
5 rem sum 1 to x	*none*		**rem** ignored
10 input x	00	+1099	read **x** into location **99**
15 rem check y == x	*none*		**rem** ignored
20 if y == x goto 60	01	+2098	load **y** (**98**) into accumulator
	02	+3199	sub **x** (**99**) from accumulator
	03	+4211	branch to location **11** if zero
25 rem increment y	*none*		**rem** ignored
30 let y = y + 1	04	+2098	load **y** into accumulator
	05	+3097	add **1** (**97**) to accumulator
	06	+2198	store accumulator in **y** (**98**)
35 rem add y to total	*none*		**rem** ignored
40 let t = t + y	07	+2096	load **t** from location (**96**)
	08	+3098	add **y** (**98**) accumulator
	09	+2196	store accumulator in **t** (**96**)
45 rem loop y	*none*		**rem** ignored
50 goto 20	10	+4001	branch to location **01**
55 rem output result	*none*		**rem** ignored
60 print t	11	+1196	output **t** (**96**) to screen
99 end	12	+4300	terminate execution

Fig. 17.30 Optimized code for the program of Fig. 17.27.

Modify the compiler to provide an option for optimizing the Simpletron Machine Language code it produces. Manually compare the nonoptimized code with the optimized code, and calculate the percentage reduction.

17.29 (*Modifications to the Simple compiler*) Perform the following modifications to the Simple compiler. Some of these modifications may also require modifications to the Simpletron Simulator program written in Exercise 5.19.

a) Allow the modulus operator (**%**) to be used in **let** statements. Simpletron Machine Language must be modified to include a modulus instruction.

b) Allow exponentiation in a **let** statement using **^** as the exponentiation operator. Simpletron Machine Language must be modified to include an exponentiation instruction.

c) Allow the compiler to recognize uppercase and lowercase letters in Simple statements (e.g., **'A'** is equivalent to **'a'**). No modifications to the Simulator are required.

d) Allow **input** statements to read values for multiple variables such as **input x, y**. No modifications to the Simpletron Simulator are required.

e) Allow the compiler to output multiple values in a single **print** statement such as **print a, b, c**. No modifications to the Simpletron Simulator are required.

f) Add syntax-checking capabilities to the compiler so error messages are output when syntax errors are encountered in a Simple program. No modifications to the Simpletron Simulator are required.

g) Allow arrays of integers. No modifications to the Simpletron Simulator are required.

h) Allow subroutines specified by the Simple commands **gosub** and **return**. Command **gosub** passes program control to a subroutine, and command **return** passes control back to the statement after the **gosub**. This is similar to a function call in C++. The same subroutine can be called from many **gosub** commands distributed throughout a program. No modifications to the Simpletron Simulator are required.

i) Allow repetition structures of the form

```
for x = 2 to 10 step 2
    Simple statements
next
```

This **for** statement loops from **2** to **10** with an increment of **2**. The **next** line marks the end of the body of the **for**. No modifications to the Simpletron Simulator are required.

j) Allow repetition structures of the form

```
for x = 2 to 10
    Simple statements
next
```

This **for** statement loops from **2** to **10** with a default increment of **1**. No modifications to the Simpletron Simulator are required.

k) Allow the compiler to process string input and output. This requires the Simpletron Simulator to be modified to process and store string values. (*Hint*: Each Simpletron word can be divided into two groups, each holding a two-digit integer. Each two-digit integer represents the ASCII decimal equivalent of a character. Add a machine language instruction that will print a string beginning at a certain Simpletron memory location. The first half of the word at that location is a count of the number of characters in the string (i.e., the length of the string). Each succeeding half word contains one ASCII character expressed as two decimal digits. The machine language instruction checks the length and prints the string by translating each two-digit number into its equivalent character.)

l) Allow the compiler to process floating-point values in addition to integers. The Simpletron Simulator must also be modified to process floating-point values.

17.30 (*A Simple Interpreter*) An interpreter is a program that reads a high-level language program statement, determines the operation to be performed by the statement and executes the operation immediately. The high-level language program is not converted into machine language first. Interpreters execute slowly because each statement encountered in the program must first be deciphered. If statements are contained in a loop, the statements are deciphered each time they are encountered in the loop. Early versions of the BASIC programming language were implemented as interpreters.

Write an interpreter for the Simple language discussed in Exercise 17.26. The program should use the infix-to-postfix converter developed in Exercise 17.12 and the postfix evaluator developed in Exercise 17.13 to evaluate expressions in a **let** statement. The same restrictions placed on the Simple language in Exercise 17.26 should be adhered to in this program. Test the interpreter with the Simple programs written in Exercise 17.26. Compare the results of running these programs in the interpreter with the results of compiling the Simple programs and running them in the Simpletron Simulator built in Exercise 5.19.

17.31 (*Insert/Delete Anywhere in a Linked List*) Our linked list class template allowed insertions and deletions at only the front and the back of the linked list. These capabilities were convenient for us when we used private inheritance and composition to produce a stack class template and a queue class template with a minimal amount of code by reusing the list class template. Actually, linked lists are more general than those we provided. Modify the linked list class template we developed in this chapter to handle insertions and deletions anywhere in the list.

17.32 (*List and Queues without Tail Pointers*) Our implementation of a linked list (Fig. 17.3– Fig. 17.5) used both a **firstPtr** and a **lastPtr**. The **lastPtr** was useful for the **insertAt-Back** and **removeFromBack** member functions of the **List** class. The **insertAtBack** function corresponds to the **enqueue** member function of the **Queue** class. Rewrite the **List** class so that it does not use a **lastPtr**. Thus, any operations on the tail of a list must begin searching the list from the front. Does this affect our implementation of the **Queue** class (Fig. 17.13)?

17.33 Use the composition version of the stack program (Fig. 17.12) to form a complete working stack program. Modify this program to **inline** the member functions. Compare the two approaches. Summarize the advantages and disadvantages of inlining member functions.

17.34 (*Performance of Binary Tree Sorting and Searching*) One problem with the binary tree sort is that the order in which the data are inserted affects the shape of the tree—for the same collection of data, different orderings can yield binary trees of dramatically different shapes. The performance of the binary tree sorting and searching algorithms is sensitive to the shape of the binary tree. What shape would a binary tree have if its data were inserted in increasing order? in decreasing order? What shape should the tree have to achieve maximal searching performance?

17.35 (*Indexed Lists*) As presented in the text, linked lists must be searched sequentially. For large lists, this can result in poor performance. A common technique for improving list searching performance is to create and maintain an index to the list. An index is a set of pointers to various key places in the list. For example, an application that searches a large list of names could improve performance by creating an index with 26 entries—one for each letter of the alphabet. A search operation for a last name beginning with 'Y' would then first search the index to determine where the 'Y' entries begin and "jump into" the list at that point and search linearly until the desired name is found. This would be much faster than searching the linked list from the beginning. Use the **List** class of Fig. 17.3– Fig. 17.5 as the basis of an **IndexedList** class. Write a program that demonstrates the operation of indexed lists. Be sure to include member functions **insertInIndexedList**, **searchIn-dexedList** and **deleteFromIndexedList**.

18

Bits, Characters, Strings and Structures

Objectives

- To be able to create and use structures.
- To be able to pass structures to functions by value and by reference.
- To manipulate data with the bitwise operators and to create bit fields for storing data compactly.
- To be able to use the functions of the character-handling library **<cctype>**.
- To be able to use the string-conversion functions of the general-utilities library **<cstdlib>**.
- To be able to use the string-processing functions of the string-handling library **<cstring>**.
- To appreciate the power of function libraries as a means of achieving software reusability.

The same old charitable lie
Repeated as the years scoot by
Perpetually makes a hit—
"You really haven't changed a bit!"
Margaret Fishback

The chief defect of Henry King
Was chewing little bits of string.
Hilaire Belloc

Vigorous writing is concise. A sentence should contain no unnecessary words, a paragraph no unnecessary sentences.
William Strunk, Jr.

Outline

18.1   Introduction
18.2   Structure Definitions
18.3   Initializing Structures
18.4   Using Structures with Functions
18.5   `typedef`
18.6   Example: High-Performance Card-Shuffling and Dealing Simulation
18.7   Bitwise Operators
18.8   Bit Fields
18.9   Character-Handling Library
18.10   String-Conversion Functions
18.11   Search Functions of the String-Handling Library
18.12   Memory Functions of the String-Handling Library

Summary • Terminology • Self-Review Exercises • Answers to Self-Review Exercises • Exercises

18.1 Introduction

In this chapter, we say more about structures and discuss the manipulation of bits, characters and C-style strings. Many of the techniques we present are C-like and are included for the benefit of the C++ programmer who will work with C legacy code.

Structures may contain variables of many different data types—in contrast to arrays, which contain only elements of the same data type. This fact, and most of what we say about structures in the next several pages, applies to classes as well. Again, the major difference between structures and classes in C++ is that structure members default to **public** access and class members default to **private** access. We discuss how to declare structures, initialize them and pass them to functions. Then, we present a high-performance card-shuffling and dealing simulation in which we use structure objects to represent the cards.

18.2 Structure Definitions

Consider the following structure definition:

```
struct Card {
   char *face;
   char *suit;

}; // end struct Card
```

Keyword **struct** introduces the definition for structure **Card**. The identifier **Card** is the *structure name* and is used in C++ to declare variables of the *structure type* (in C, the type name of the preceding structure is **struct Card**). In this example, the structure type is **Card**. Data (and possibly functions—just as with classes) declared within the braces of the structure definition are the structure's *members*. Members of the same structure must have unique names, but two different structures may contain members of the same name without conflict. Each structure definition must end with a semicolon.

Common Programming Error 18.1

Forgetting the semicolon that terminates a structure definition is a syntax error.

The definition of **Card** contains two members of type **char ***—**face** and **suit**. Structure members can be variables of the basic data types (e.g., **int**, **double**, etc.) or aggregates, such as arrays and other structures. Data members in a single structure definition can be of many data types. For example, an **Employee** structure might contain character string members for the first and last names, an **int** member for the employee's age, a **char** member containing **'M'** or **'F'** for the employee's gender, a **double** member for the employee's hourly salary and so on.

A structure cannot contain an instance of itself. For example, a structure variable **Card** cannot be declared in the definition for structure **Card**. A pointer to a **Card** structure, however, can be included. A structure containing a member that is a pointer to the same structure type is referred to as a *self-referential structure*. We used a similar construct—self-referential classes—in Chapter 17 to build various kinds of linked data structures.

The preceding structure definition does not reserve any space in memory; rather, the definition creates a new data type that is used to declare structure variables. Structure variables are declared like variables of other types. The following declarations

```
Card oneCard;
Card deck[ 52 ];
Card *cardPtr;
```

declare **oneCard** to be a structure variable of type **Card**, **deck** to be an array with 52 elements of type **Card** and **cardPtr** to be a pointer to a **Card** structure. Variables of a given structure type can also be declared by placing a comma-separated list of the variable names between the closing brace of the structure definition and the semicolon that ends the structure definition. For example, the preceding declaration could have been incorporated into the **Card** structure definition as follows:

```
struct Card {
   char *face;
   char *suit;

} oneCard, deck[ 52 ], *cardPtr;
```

The structure name is optional. If a structure definition does not contain a structure name, variables of the structure type may be declared only between the closing right brace of the structure definition and the semicolon that terminates the structure definition.

Good Programming Practice 18.1

Provide a structure name when creating a structure type. The structure name is convenient for declaring new variables of the structure type later in the program and is required if the structure will be used in a function parameter declaration.

The only valid built-in operations that may be performed on structure objects are assigning a structure object to a structure object of the same type, taking the address (**&**) of a structure object, accessing the members of a structure object (see Chapter 6, Classes and

Data Abstraction) and using the **sizeof** operator to determine the size of a structure. As with classes, most operators can be overloaded to work with objects of a structure type.

Structure members are not necessarily stored in consecutive bytes of memory. Sometimes there are "holes" in a structure, because some computers store specific data types only on certain memory boundaries, such as half-word, word or double-word boundaries. A word is a standard memory unit used to store data in a computer—usually 2 bytes or 4 bytes. Consider the following structure definition in which structure objects **sample1** and **sample2** of type **Example** are declared:

```
struct Example {
    char c;
    int i;

} sample1, sample2;
```

A computer with 2-byte words might require that each of the members of **Example** be aligned on a word boundary (i.e., at the beginning of a word—this is machine dependent). Figure 18.1 shows a sample storage alignment for an object of type **Example** that has been assigned the character **'a'** and the integer **97** (the bit representations of the values are shown). If the members are stored beginning at word boundaries, there is a 1-byte hole (byte **1** in the figure) in the storage for objects of type **Example**. The value in the 1-byte hole is undefined. If the member values of **sample1** and **sample2** are in fact equal, the structures do not necessarily compare equally, because the undefined 1-byte holes are not likely to contain identical values.

Common Programming Error 18.2

Comparing structures is a syntax error.

Portability Tip 18.1

Because the size of data items of a particular type is machine dependent, and because storage alignment considerations are machine dependent, so too is the representation of a structure.

18.3 Initializing Structures

Structures can be initialized using initializer lists, as is done with arrays. For example, the declaration

```
Card oneCard = { "Three", "Hearts" };
```

creates **Card** variable **oneCard** and initializes member **face** to **"Three"** and member **suit** to **"Hearts"**. If there are fewer initializers in the list than members in the structure,

Byte	**0**		**1**	**2**	**3**
	01100001			00000000	01100001

Fig. 18.1   Possible storage alignment for a variable of type **Example**, showing an undefined area in memory.

the remaining members are initialized to **0**. Structure variables declared outside a function definition (i.e., externally) are initialized to **0** if they are not explicitly initialized in the external declaration. Structure variables may also be initialized in assignment statements by assigning a structure variable of the same type or by assigning values to the individual data members of the structure.

18.4 Using Structures with Functions

There are two ways to pass the information in structures to functions. You can either pass the entire structure or pass the individual members of a structure. By default, the data passes by value. Structures and their members can also be passed by reference by passing either references or pointers.

To pass a structure by reference, pass the address of the structure object or a reference to the structure object. Arrays of structures—like all other arrays—are passed by reference.

In Chapter 4, we stated that an array could be passed by value by using a structure. To pass an array by value, create a structure (or a class) with the array as a member, then pass an object of that structure (or class) type to a function by value. Because structure objects are passed by value, the array member, too, is passed by value.

Common Programming Error 18.3

Assuming that structures, like arrays, are passed by reference and trying to modify the caller's structure values in the called function is a logic error.

Performance Tip 18.1

Passing structures (and especially large structures) by reference is more efficient than passing structures by value (which requires the entire structure to be copied).

18.5 `typedef`

Keyword **typedef** provides a mechanism for creating synonyms (or aliases) for previously defined data types. Names for structure types are often defined with **typedef** to create shorter or more readable type names. For example, the statement

```
typedef Card *CardPtr;
```

defines the new type name **CardPtr** as a synonym for type **Card ***.

Good Programming Practice 18.2

Capitalize **typedef** *names to emphasize that these names are synonyms for other type names.*

Creating a new name with **typedef** does not create a new data type; **typedef** simply creates a new type name that can then be used in the program as an alias for an existing type name.

Synonyms for built-in data types can be created with **typedef**. For example, a program requiring 4-byte integers could use type **int** on one system and type **long int** on another system that has 2-byte integers. Programs designed for portability can use **typedef** to create an alias such as **Integer** for 4-byte integers. **Integer** can then be aliased to **int** on systems with 4-byte integers and can be aliased to **long int** on systems with 2-byte integers where **long int** values occupy 4 bytes. Then, to write portable programs, the programmer simply declares all 4-byte integer variables to be of type **Integer**.

Portability Tip 18.2

*Using **typedef** can help make a program more portable.*

18.6 Example: High-Performance Card-Shuffling and Dealing Simulation

The program in Fig. 18.2 is based on the card-shuffling and dealing simulation discussed in Chapter 5. The program represents the deck of cards as an array of structures and uses high-performance shuffling and dealing algorithms. The output is shown in Fig. 18.3.

```cpp
1    // Fig. 18.2: fig18_02.cpp
2    // Card shuffling and dealing program using structures.
3    #include <iostream>
4
5    using std::cout;
6    using std::cin;
7    using std::endl;
8    using std::left;
9    using std::right;
10
11   #include <iomanip>
12
13   using std::setw;
14
15   #include <cstdlib>
16   #include <ctime>
17
18   // Card structure definition
19   struct Card {
20      char *face;
21      char *suit;
22
23   }; // end structure Card
24
25   void fillDeck( Card * const, char *[], char *[] );
26   void shuffle( Card * const );
27   void deal( Card * const );
28
29   int main()
30   {
31      Card deck[ 52 ];
32      char *face[] = { "Ace", "Deuce", "Three", "Four",
33         "Five", "Six", "Seven", "Eight", "Nine", "Ten",
34         "Jack", "Queen", "King" };
35      char *suit[] = { "Hearts", "Diamonds", "Clubs", "Spades" };
36
37      srand( time( 0 ) );  // randomize
38
```

Fig. 18.2   High-performance card-shuffling and dealing simulation. (Part 1 of 2.)

```
39        fillDeck( deck, face, suit );
40        shuffle( deck );
41        deal( deck );
42
43        return 0;
44
45   } // end main
46
47   // place strings into Card structures
48   void fillDeck( Card * const wDeck,
49      char *wFace[], char *wSuit[] )
50   {
51      for ( int i = 0; i < 52; i++ ) {
52         wDeck[ i ].face = wFace[ i % 13 ];
53         wDeck[ i ].suit = wSuit[ i / 13 ];
54
55      } // end for
56
57   } // end function fillDeck
58
59   // shuffle cards
60   void shuffle( Card * const wDeck )
61   {
62      for ( int i = 0; i < 52; i++ ) {
63         int j = rand() % 52;
64         Card temp = wDeck[ i ];
65         wDeck[ i ] = wDeck[ j ];
66         wDeck[ j ] = temp;
67
68      } // end for
69
70   } // end function shuffle
71
72   // deal cards
73   void deal( Card * const wDeck )
74   {
75      for ( int i = 0; i < 52; i++ )
76         cout << right << setw( 5 ) << wDeck[ i ].face << " of "
77            << left << setw( 8 ) << wDeck[ i ].suit
78            << ( ( i + 1 ) % 2 ? '\t' : '\n' );
79
80   } // end function deal
```

Fig. 18.2 High-performance card-shuffling and dealing simulation. (Part 2 of 2.)

In the program, function **fillDeck** initializes the **Card** array in order with character strings representing Ace through King of each suit. The **Card** array is passed to function **shuffle**, where the high-performance shuffling algorithm is implemented. Function **shuffle** takes an array of 52 **Card** structures as an argument. The function loops through all 52 cards (array subscripts 0 to 51). For each card, a number between 0 and 51 is picked randomly. Next, the current **Card** structure and the randomly selected **Card** structure are swapped in the array. A total of 52 swaps are made in a single pass of the entire array, and the array of **Card** structures is shuffled! This algorithm does not suffer from indefinite

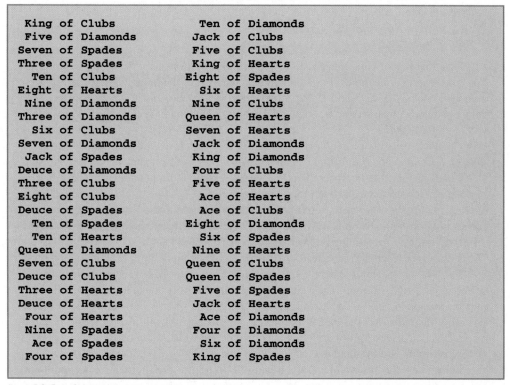

King of Clubs	Ten of Diamonds
Five of Diamonds	Jack of Clubs
Seven of Spades	Five of Clubs
Three of Spades	King of Hearts
Ten of Clubs	Eight of Spades
Eight of Hearts	Six of Hearts
Nine of Diamonds	Nine of Clubs
Three of Diamonds	Queen of Hearts
Six of Clubs	Seven of Hearts
Seven of Diamonds	Jack of Diamonds
Jack of Spades	King of Diamonds
Deuce of Diamonds	Four of Clubs
Three of Clubs	Five of Hearts
Eight of Clubs	Ace of Hearts
Deuce of Spades	Ace of Clubs
Ten of Spades	Eight of Diamonds
Ten of Hearts	Six of Spades
Queen of Diamonds	Nine of Hearts
Seven of Clubs	Queen of Clubs
Deuce of Clubs	Queen of Spades
Three of Hearts	Five of Spades
Deuce of Hearts	Jack of Hearts
Four of Hearts	Ace of Diamonds
Nine of Spades	Four of Diamonds
Ace of Spades	Six of Diamonds
Four of Spades	King of Spades

Fig. 18.3   Output for the high-performance card-shuffling and dealing simulation.

postponement like the shuffling algorithm presented in Chapter 5. Because the **Card** structures were swapped in place in the array, the high-performance dealing algorithm implemented in function **deal** requires only one pass of the array to deal the shuffled cards.

Common Programming Error 18.4

Forgetting to include the array subscript when referring to individual structures in an array of structures is an error.

18.7 Bitwise Operators

C++ provides extensive bit-manipulation capabilities for programmers who need to get down to the so-called "bits-and-bytes" level. Operating systems, test-equipment software, networking software and many other kinds of software require that the programmer communicate "directly with the hardware." In this and the next several sections, we discuss C++'s bit-manipulation capabilities. We introduce each of C++'s many bitwise operators, and we discuss how to save memory by using bit fields.

All data are represented internally by computers as sequences of bits. Each bit can assume the value **0** or the value **1**. On most systems, a sequence of 8 bits forms a *byte*— the standard storage unit for a variable of type **char**. Other data types are stored in larger numbers of bytes. Bitwise operators are used to manipulate the bits of integral operands (**char**, **short**, **int** and **long**; both **signed** and **unsigned**). Unsigned integers are normally used with the bitwise operators.

Portability Tip 18.3

Bitwise data manipulations are machine dependent.

Note that the bitwise operator discussions in this section show the binary representations of the integer operands. For a detailed explanation of the binary (also called base-2) number system, see Appendix C, Number Systems. Because of the machine-dependent nature of bitwise manipulations, some of these programs might not work on your system without modifications.

The bitwise operators are: *bitwise AND* (**&**), *bitwise inclusive OR* (**|**), *bitwise exclusive OR* (**^**), *left shift* (**<<**), *right shift* (**>>**) and *complement* (**~**). (Note that we have been using **&**, **<<** and **>>** for other purposes. This is a classic example of operator overloading.) The bitwise AND, bitwise inclusive OR and bitwise exclusive OR operators compare their two operands bit by bit. The bitwise AND operator sets each bit in the result to 1 if the corresponding bit in both operands is 1. The bitwise inclusive-OR operator sets each bit in the result to 1 if the corresponding bit in either (or both) operand(s) is 1. The bitwise exclusive-OR operator sets each bit in the result to 1 if the corresponding bit in exactly one operand is 1. The left-shift operator shifts the bits of its left operand to the left by the number of bits specified in its right operand. The right-shift operator shifts the bits in its left operand to the right by the number of bits specified in its right operand. The bitwise complement operator sets all **0** bits in its operand to **1** in the result and sets all **1** bits in its operand to **0** in the result. Detailed discussions of each bitwise operator appear in the following examples. The bitwise operators are summarized in Fig. 18.4.

When using the bitwise operators, it is useful to print values in their binary representation to illustrate the precise effects of these operators. Figure 18.5 prints an **unsigned** integer in its binary representation in groups of eight bits each.

Operator	Name	Description
&	bitwise AND	The bits in the result are set to **1** if the corresponding bits in the two operands are both **1**.
|	bitwise inclusive OR	The bits in the result are set to **1** if at least one of the corresponding bits in the two operands is **1**.
^	bitwise exclusive OR	The bits in the result are set to **1** if exactly one of the corresponding bits in the two operands is **1**.
<<	left shift	Shifts the bits of the first operand left by the number of bits specified by the second operand; fill from right with **0** bits.
>>	right shift with sign extension	Shifts the bits of the first operand right by the number of bits specified by the second operand; the method of filling from the left is machine dependent.
~	one's complement	All **0** bits are set to **1** and all **1** bits are set to **0**.

Fig. 18.4   Bitwise operators.

```
1   // Fig. 18.5: fig18_05.cpp
2   // Printing an unsigned integer in bits.
3   #include <iostream>
4
5   using std::cout;
6   using std::cin;
7   using std::endl;
8
9   #include <iomanip>
10
11  using std::setw;
12
13  void displayBits( unsigned );  // prototype
14
15  int main()
16  {
17     unsigned inputValue;
18
19     cout << "Enter an unsigned integer: ";
20     cin >> inputValue;
21     displayBits( inputValue );
22
23     return 0;
24
25  } // end main
26
27  // display bits of an unsigned integer value
28  void displayBits( unsigned value )
29  {
30     const int SHIFT = 8 * sizeof( unsigned ) - 1;
31     const unsigned MASK = 1 << SHIFT;
32
33     cout << setw( 10 ) << value << " = ";
34
35     for ( unsigned i = 1; i <= SHIFT + 1; i++ ) {
36        cout << ( value & MASK ? '1' : '0' );
37        value <<= 1;  // shift value left by 1
38
39        if ( i % 8 == 0 )  // output a space after 8 bits
40           cout << ' ';
41
42     } // end for
43
44     cout << endl;
45
46  } // end function displayBits
```

```
Enter an unsigned integer: 65000
    65000 = 00000000 00000000 11111101 11101000
```

Fig. 18.5   Printing an unsigned integer in bits.

Function **displayBits** (lines 28–46) uses the bitwise AND operator to combine variable **value** with constant **MASK**. Often, the bitwise AND operator is used with an operand called a *mask*—an integer value with specific bits set to **1**. Masks are used to hide some bits in a value while selecting other bits. In **displayBits**, line 31 assigns constant **MASK** the value **1 << SHIFT**. The value of constant **SHIFT** was calculated in line 30 with the expression

```
8 * sizeof( unsigned ) - 1
```

which multiplies the number of bytes an **unsigned** object requires in memory by **8** (the number of bits in a byte) to get the total number of bits required to store an **unsigned** object, then subtracts 1. The bit representation of **1 << SHIFT** on a computer that represents **unsigned** objects in four bytes of memory is

```
10000000 00000000 00000000 00000000
```

The left-shift operator shifts the value **1** from the low order (rightmost) bit to the high-order (leftmost) bit in **MASK**, and fills in **0** bits from the right. Line 36 determines whether a **1** or a **0** should be printed for the current leftmost bit of variable **value**. Assume that variable **value** contains **65000** (**00000000 00000000 11111101 11101000**). When **value** and **MASK** are combined using **&**, all the bits except the high-order bit in variable **value** are "masked off" (hidden), because any bit "ANDed" with **0** yields **0**. If the leftmost bit is **1**, **value & MASK** evaluates to

```
00000000 00000000 11111101 11101000    (value)
10000000 00000000 00000000 00000000    (MASK)
------------------------------------
00000000 00000000 00000000 00000000    (value & MASK)
```

which is interpreted as **false**, and **0** is printed. Then line 37 shifts variable **value** left by one bit with the expression **value <<= 1** (i.e., **value = value << 1**). These steps are repeated for each bit variable **value**. Eventually, a bit with a value of **1** is shifted into the leftmost bit position, and the bit manipulation is as follows:

```
11111101 11101000 00000000 00000000    (value)
10000000 00000000 00000000 00000000    (MASK)
------------------------------------
10000000 00000000 00000000 00000000    (value & MASK)
```

Because both left bits are **1**s, the result of the expression is nonzero (true) and a value of **1** is printed. Figure 18.6 summarizes the results of combining two bits with the bitwise AND operator.

Bit 1	Bit 2	Bit 1 & Bit 2
0	0	0
1	0	0
0	1	0
1	1	1

Fig. 18.6   Results of combining two bits with the bitwise AND operator (**&**).

Common Programming Error 18.5

*Using the logical AND operator (**&&**) for the bitwise AND operator (**&**) and vice versa is a logic error.*

The program of Fig. 18.7 demonstrates the bitwise AND operator, the bitwise inclusive OR operator, the bitwise exclusive OR operator and the bitwise complement operator. Function **displayBits** (lines 62–80) prints the **unsigned** integer values. The output is shown in Fig. 18.8.

```
1    // Fig. 18.7: fig18_07.cpp
2    // Using the bitwise AND, bitwise inclusive OR, bitwise
3    // exclusive OR and bitwise complement operators.
4    #include <iostream>
5
6    using std::cout;
7    using std::cin;
8
9    #include <iomanip>
10
11   using std::endl;
12   using std::setw;
13
14   void displayBits( unsigned );  // prototype
15
16   int main()
17   {
18      unsigned number1;
19      unsigned number2;
20      unsigned mask;
21      unsigned setBits;
22
23      // demonstrate bitwise &
24      number1 = 2179876355;
25      mask = 1;
26      cout << "The result of combining the following\n";
27      displayBits( number1 );
28      displayBits( mask );
29      cout << "using the bitwise AND operator & is\n";
30      displayBits( number1 & mask );
31
32      // demonstrate bitwise |
33      number1 = 15;
34      setBits = 241;
35      cout << "\nThe result of combining the following\n";
36      displayBits( number1 );
37      displayBits( setBits );
38      cout << "using the bitwise inclusive OR operator | is\n";
39      displayBits( number1 | setBits );
40
```

Fig. 18.7   Bitwise AND, bitwise inclusive-OR, bitwise exclusive-OR and bitwise complement operators. (Part 1 of 2.)

```
41     // demonstrate bitwise exclusive OR
42     number1 = 139;
43     number2 = 199;
44     cout << "\nThe result of combining the following\n";
45     displayBits( number1 );
46     displayBits( number2 );
47     cout << "using the bitwise exclusive OR operator ^ is\n";
48     displayBits( number1 ^ number2 );
49
50     // demonstrate bitwise complement
51     number1 = 21845;
52     cout << "\nThe one's complement of\n";
53     displayBits( number1 );
54     cout << "is" << endl;
55     displayBits( ~number1 );
56
57     return 0;
58
59  } // end main
60
61  // display bits of an unsigned integer value
62  void displayBits( unsigned value )
63  {
64     const int SHIFT = 8 * sizeof( unsigned ) - 1;
65     const unsigned MASK = 1 << SHIFT;
66
67     cout << setw( 10 ) << value << " = ";
68
69     for ( unsigned i = 1; i <= SHIFT + 1; i++ ) {
70        cout << ( value & MASK ? '1' : '0' );
71        value <<= 1;  // shift value left by 1
72
73        if ( i % 8 == 0 )  // output a space after 8 bits
74           cout << ' ';
75
76     } // end for
77
78     cout << endl;
79
80  } // end function displayBits
```

Fig. 18.7   Bitwise AND, bitwise inclusive-OR, bitwise exclusive-OR and bitwise complement operators. (Part 2 of 2.)

In Fig. 18.7, line 24 assigns **2179876355** (**10000001 11101110 01000110 00000011**) to variable **number1**, and line 25 assigns **1** (**00000000 00000000 00000000 00000001**) to variable **mask**. When **mask** and **number1** are combined using the bitwise AND operator (**&**) in the expression **number1 & mask** (line 30), the result is **00000000 00000000 00000000 00000001**. All the bits except the low-order bit in variable **number1** are "masked off" (hidden) by "ANDing" with constant **MASK**.

The bitwise inclusive-OR operator is used to set specific bits to 1 in an operand. In Fig. 18.7, line 33 assigns **15** (**00000000 00000000 00000000 00001111**) to variable **number1**, and line 34 assigns **241** (**00000000 00000000 00000000 11110001**) to

```
The result of combining the following
2179876355 = 10000001 11101110 01000110 00000011
         1 = 00000000 00000000 00000000 00000001
using the bitwise AND operator & is
         1 = 00000000 00000000 00000000 00000001

The result of combining the following
        15 = 00000000 00000000 00000000 00001111
       241 = 00000000 00000000 00000000 11110001
using the bitwise inclusive OR operator | is
       255 = 00000000 00000000 00000000 11111111

The result of combining the following
       139 = 00000000 00000000 00000000 10001011
       199 = 00000000 00000000 00000000 11000111
using the bitwise exclusive OR operator ^ is
        76 = 00000000 00000000 00000000 01001100

The one's complement of
     21845 = 00000000 00000000 01010101 01010101
is
4294945450 = 11111111 11111111 10101010 10101010
```

Fig. 18.8 Sample output for the program of Fig. 18.7.

variable **setBits**. When **number1** and **setBits** are combined using the bitwise OR operator in the expression **number1 | setBits** (line 39), the result is **255** (**00000000 00000000 00000000 11111111**). Figure 18.9 summarizes the results of combining two bits with the bitwise inclusive-OR operator.

Common Programming Error 18.6

Using the logical OR operator (| |) for the bitwise OR operator (|) and vice versa is a logic error.

The bitwise exclusive OR operator (^) sets each bit in the result to 1 if *exactly* one of the corresponding bits in its two operands is 1. In Fig. 18.7, lines 42–43 assign variables **number1** and **number2** the values **139** (**00000000 00000000 00000000 10001011**) and **199** (**00000000 00000000 00000000 11000111**), respectively. When these variables are combined with the exclusive-OR operator in the expression **number1 ^ number2** (line 48), the result is **00000000 00000000 00000000 01001100**. Figure 18.10 summarizes the results of combining two bits with the bitwise exclusive-OR operator.

Bit 1	Bit 2	Bit 1 | Bit 2
0	0	0
1	0	1
0	1	1
1	1	1

Fig. 18.9 Combining two bits with the bitwise inclusive-OR operator (|).

Bit 1	Bit 2	Bit 1 ^ Bit 2
0	0	0
1	0	1
0	1	1
1	1	0

Fig. 18.10 Combining two bits with the bitwise exclusive-OR operator (^).

The *bitwise* complement operator (~) sets all **1** bits in its operand to **0** in the result and sets all **0** bits to **1** in the result—otherwise referred to as "taking the *one's complement* of the value." In Fig. 18.7, line 51 assigns variable **number1** the value **21845** (**00000000 00000000 01010101 01010101**). When the expression **~number1** evaluates, the result is (**11111111 11111111 10101010 10101010**).

Figure 18.11 demonstrates the left-shift operator (**<<**) and the right-shift operator (**>>**). Function **displayBits** (lines 38–56) prints the **unsigned** integer values.

```
1   // Fig. 18.11: fig18_11.cpp
2   // Using the bitwise shift operators.
3   #include <iostream>
4
5   using std::cout;
6   using std::cin;
7   using std::endl;
8
9   #include <iomanip>
10
11  using std::setw;
12
13  void displayBits( unsigned );  // prototype
14
15  int main()
16  {
17      unsigned number1 = 960;
18
19      // demonstrate bitwise left shift
20      cout << "The result of left shifting\n";
21      displayBits( number1 );
22      cout << "8 bit positions using the left "
23          << "shift operator is\n";
24      displayBits( number1 << 8 );
25
26      // demonstrate bitwise right shift
27      cout << "\nThe result of right shifting\n";
28      displayBits( number1 );
29      cout << "8 bit positions using the right "
30          << "shift operator is\n";
31      displayBits( number1 >> 8 );
```

Fig. 18.11 Bitwise shift operators. (Part 1 of 2.)

```
32
33      return 0;
34
35   } // end main
36
37   // display bits of an unsigned integer value
38   void displayBits( unsigned value )
39   {
40      const int SHIFT = 8 * sizeof( unsigned ) - 1;
41      const unsigned MASK = 1 << SHIFT;
42
43      cout << setw( 10 ) << value << " = ";
44
45      for ( unsigned i = 1; i <= SHIFT + 1; i++ ) {
46         cout << ( value & MASK ? '1' : '0' );
47         value <<= 1;  // shift value left by 1
48
49         if ( i % 8 == 0 )  // output a space after 8 bits
50            cout << ' ';
51
52      } // end for
53
54      cout << endl;
55
56   } // end function displayBits
```

```
The result of left shifting
      960 = 00000000 00000000 00000011 11000000
8 bit positions using the left shift operator is
   245760 = 00000000 00000011 11000000 00000000

The result of right shifting
      960 = 00000000 00000000 00000011 11000000
8 bit positions using the right shift operator is
        3 = 00000000 00000000 00000000 00000011
```

Fig. 18.11 Bitwise shift operators. (Part 2 of 2.)

The left-shift operator (**<<**) shifts the bits of its left operand to the left by the number of bits specified in its right operand. Bits vacated to the right are replaced with **0**s; bits shifted off the left are lost. In the program of Fig. 18.11, line 17 assigns variable **number1** the value **960** (**00000000 00000000 00000011 11000000**). The result of left-shifting variable **number1** 8 bits in the expression **number1 << 8** (line 24) is **245760** (**00000000 00000011 11000000 00000000**).

The right-shift operator (**>>**) shifts the bits of its left operand to the right by the number of bits specified in its right operand. Performing a right shift on an **unsigned** integer causes the vacated bits at the left to be replaced by 0s; bits shifted off the right are lost. In the program of Fig. 18.11, the result of right-shifting **number1** in the expression **number1 >> 8** (line 31) is **3** (**00000000 00000000 00000000 00000011**).

Common Programming Error 18.7

The result of shifting a value is undefined if the right operand is negative or if the right operand is greater than or equal to the number of bits in which the left operand is stored.

Portability Tip 18.4

The result of right-shifting a signed value is machine dependent. Some machines fill with zeros and others use the sign bit.

Each bitwise operator (except the bitwise complement operator) has a corresponding assignment operator. These *bitwise assignment operators* are shown in Fig. 18.12 and are used in a similar manner to the arithmetic assignment operators introduced in Chapter 2.

Figure 18.13 shows the precedence and associativity of the operators introduced up to this point in the text. They are shown top to bottom in decreasing order of precedence.

Bitwise assignment operators	
&=	Bitwise AND assignment operator.
|=	Bitwise inclusive-OR assignment operator.
^=	Bitwise exclusive-OR assignment operator.
<<=	Left-shift assignment operator.
>>=	Right-shift with sign extension assignment operator.

Fig. 18.12 Bitwise assignment operators.

Operators	Associativity	Type
`::` (unary; right to left) `::` (binary; left to right)	left to right	highest
`()` `[]` `.` `->` `++` `--` `static_cast< type >()`	left to right	unary
`++` `--` `+` `-` `!` `delete` `sizeof` `*` `&` `new` `~`	right to left	unary
`*` `/` `%`	left to right	multiplicative
`+` `-`	left to right	additive
`<<` `>>`	left to right	shifting
`<` `<=` `>` `>=`	left to right	relational
`==` `!=`	left to right	equality
`&`	left to right	bitwise AND
`^`	left to right	bitwise XOR
`|`	left to right	bitwise OR
`&&`	left to right	logical AND
`||`	left to right	logical OR
`?:`	right to left	conditional
`=` `+=` `-=` `*=` `/=` `%=` `&=` `|=` `^=` `<<=` `>>=`	right to left	assignment
`,`	left to right	comma

Fig. 18.13 Operator precedence and associativity.

18.8 Bit Fields

C++ provides the ability to specify the number of bits in which an integral type or **enum** type member of a class or a structure is stored. Such a member is referred to as a *bit field*. Bit fields enable better memory utilization by storing data in the minimum number of bits required. Bit field members *must* be declared as an integral or **enum** data type.

Performance Tip 18.2

Bit fields help conserve storage.

Consider the following structure definition:

```
struct BitCard {
   unsigned face : 4;
   unsigned suit : 2;
   unsigned color : 1;

}; // end struct BitCard
```

The definition contains three **unsigned** bit fields—**face**, **suit** and **color**—used to represent a card from a deck of 52 cards. A bit field is declared by following an integral type or **enum** type member with a colon (**:**) and an integer constant representing the *width* of the field (i.e., the number of bits in which the member is stored). The width must be an integer constant between zero and the total number of bits used to store an **int** on your system.

The preceding structure definition indicates that member **face** is stored in 4 bits, member **suit** is stored in 2 bits and member **color** is stored in 1 bit. The number of bits is based on the desired range of values for each structure member. Member **face** stores values between **0** (Ace) and **12** (King)—4 bits can store a value between 0 and 15. Member **suit** stores values between **0** and **3** (0 = Diamonds, 1 = Hearts, 2 = Clubs, 3 = Spades)— 2 bits can store a value between 0 and 3. Finally, member **color** stores either **0** (Red) or **1** (Black)—1 bit can store either **0** or **1**.

The program in Fig. 18.14 (output shown in Fig. 18.15) creates array **deck** containing 52 **BitCard** structures (line 25). Function **fillDeck** inserts the 52 cards in the **deck** array, and function **deal** prints the 52 cards. Notice that bit field members of structures are accessed exactly as any other structure member is (lines 38–40 and 51–56). The member **color** is included as a means of indicating the card color on a system that allows color displays.

```
1   // Fig. 18.14: fig18_14.cpp
2   // Representing cards with bit fields in a struct.
3   #include <iostream>
4
5   using std::cout;
6   using std::endl;
7
8   #include <iomanip>
```

Fig. 18.14 Bit fields used to store a deck of cards. (Part 1 of 2.)

```
9
10   using std::setw;
11
12   // BitCard structure definition with bit fields
13   struct BitCard {
14      unsigned face : 4;    // 4 bits; 0-15
15      unsigned suit : 2;    // 2 bits; 0-3
16      unsigned color : 1;   // 1 bit; 0-1
17
18   }; // end struct BitBard
19
20   void fillDeck( BitCard * const );    // prototype
21   void deal( const BitCard * const );  // prototype
22
23   int main()
24   {
25      BitCard deck[ 52 ];
26
27      fillDeck( deck );
28      deal( deck );
29
30      return 0;
31
32   } // end main
33
34   // initialize BitCards
35   void fillDeck( BitCard * const wDeck )
36   {
37      for ( int i = 0; i <= 51; i++ ) {
38         wDeck[ i ].face = i % 13;
39         wDeck[ i ].suit = i / 13;
40         wDeck[ i ].color = i / 26;
41
42      } // end for
43
44   } // end function fillDeck
45
46   // output cards in two column format; cards 0-25 subscripted
47   // with k1 (column 1); cards 26-51 subscripted k2 (column 2)
48   void deal( const BitCard * const wDeck )
49   {
50      for ( int k1 = 0, k2 = k1 + 26; k1 <= 25; k1++, k2++ ) {
51         cout << "Card:" << setw( 3 ) << wDeck[ k1 ].face
52            << " Suit:" << setw( 2 ) << wDeck[ k1 ].suit
53            << " Color:" << setw( 2 ) << wDeck[ k1 ].color
54            << "    " << "Card:" << setw( 3 ) << wDeck[ k2 ].face
55            << " Suit:" << setw( 2 ) << wDeck[ k2 ].suit
56            << " Color:" << setw( 2 ) << wDeck[ k2 ].color
57            << endl;
58
59      } // end for
60
61   } // end function deal
```

Fig. 18.14 Bit fields used to store a deck of cards. (Part 2 of 2.)

```
Card:  0  Suit: 0  Color: 0    Card:  0  Suit: 2  Color: 1
Card:  1  Suit: 0  Color: 0    Card:  1  Suit: 2  Color: 1
Card:  2  Suit: 0  Color: 0    Card:  2  Suit: 2  Color: 1
Card:  3  Suit: 0  Color: 0    Card:  3  Suit: 2  Color: 1
Card:  4  Suit: 0  Color: 0    Card:  4  Suit: 2  Color: 1
Card:  5  Suit: 0  Color: 0    Card:  5  Suit: 2  Color: 1
Card:  6  Suit: 0  Color: 0    Card:  6  Suit: 2  Color: 1
Card:  7  Suit: 0  Color: 0    Card:  7  Suit: 2  Color: 1
Card:  8  Suit: 0  Color: 0    Card:  8  Suit: 2  Color: 1
Card:  9  Suit: 0  Color: 0    Card:  9  Suit: 2  Color: 1
Card: 10  Suit: 0  Color: 0    Card: 10  Suit: 2  Color: 1
Card: 11  Suit: 0  Color: 0    Card: 11  Suit: 2  Color: 1
Card: 12  Suit: 0  Color: 0    Card: 12  Suit: 2  Color: 1
Card:  0  Suit: 1  Color: 0    Card:  0  Suit: 3  Color: 1
Card:  1  Suit: 1  Color: 0    Card:  1  Suit: 3  Color: 1
Card:  2  Suit: 1  Color: 0    Card:  2  Suit: 3  Color: 1
Card:  3  Suit: 1  Color: 0    Card:  3  Suit: 3  Color: 1
Card:  4  Suit: 1  Color: 0    Card:  4  Suit: 3  Color: 1
Card:  5  Suit: 1  Color: 0    Card:  5  Suit: 3  Color: 1
Card:  6  Suit: 1  Color: 0    Card:  6  Suit: 3  Color: 1
Card:  7  Suit: 1  Color: 0    Card:  7  Suit: 3  Color: 1
Card:  8  Suit: 1  Color: 0    Card:  8  Suit: 3  Color: 1
Card:  9  Suit: 1  Color: 0    Card:  9  Suit: 3  Color: 1
Card: 10  Suit: 1  Color: 0    Card: 10  Suit: 3  Color: 1
Card: 11  Suit: 1  Color: 0    Card: 11  Suit: 3  Color: 1
Card: 12  Suit: 1  Color: 0    Card: 12  Suit: 3  Color: 1
```

Fig. 18.15 Sample output for the program of Fig. 18.14.

It is possible to specify an *unnamed bit field*, in which case the field is used as *padding* in the structure. For example, the structure definition uses an unnamed 3-bit field as padding—nothing can be stored in those three bits. Member **b** is stored in another storage unit.

```
struct Example {
    unsigned a : 13;
    unsigned   : 3;
    unsigned b : 4;

}; // end struct Example
```

An *unnamed bit field with a zero width* is used to align the next bit field on a new storage-unit boundary. For example, the structure definition

```
struct Example {
    unsigned a : 13;
    unsigned   : 0;
    unsigned b : 4;

}; // end struct Example
```

uses an unnamed **0**-bit field to skip the remaining bits (as many as there are) of the storage unit in which **a** is stored and align **b** on the next storage-unit boundary.

Portability Tip 18.5

Bit-field manipulations are machine dependent. For example, some computers allow bit fields to cross word boundaries, whereas others do not.

Common Programming Error 18.8

Attempting to access individual bits of a bit field as if they were elements of an array is a syntax error. Bit fields are not "arrays of bits."

Common Programming Error 18.9

Attempting to take the address of a bit field (the & operator may not be used with bit fields because they do not have addresses) is a syntax error.

Performance Tip 18.3

Although bit fields save space, using them can cause the compiler to generate slower-executing machine-language code. This occurs because it takes extra machine-language operations to access only portions of an addressable storage unit. This is one of many examples of the kinds of space-time trade-offs that occur in computer science.

18.9 Character-Handling Library

Most data are entered into computers as characters—including letters, digits and various special symbols. In this section, we discuss C++'s capabilities for examining and manipulating individual characters. In the remainder of the chapter, we continue the discussion of character-string manipulation that we began in Chapter 5.

The character-handling library includes several functions that perform useful tests and manipulations of character data. Each function receives a character—represented as an **int**—or **EOF** as an argument. Characters are often manipulated as integers. Remember that **EOF** normally has the value **-1** and that some hardware architectures do not allow negative values to be stored in **char** variables. Therefore, the character-handling functions manipulate characters as integers. Figure 18.16 summarizes the functions of the character-handling library. When using functions from the character-handling library, be sure to include the **<cctype>** header file.

Prototype	Description
int **isdigit**(int c)	Returns **true** if c is a digit and **false** otherwise.
int **isalpha**(int c)	Returns **true** if c is a letter and **false** otherwise.
int **isalnum**(int c)	Returns **true** if c is a digit or a letter and **false** otherwise.
int **isxdigit**(int c)	Returns **true** if c is a hexadecimal digit character and **false** otherwise. (See Appendix C, Number Systems, for a detailed explanation of binary numbers, octal numbers, decimal numbers and hexadecimal numbers.)
int **islower**(int c)	Returns **true** if c is a lowercase letter and **false** otherwise.
int **isupper**(int c)	Returns **true** if c is an uppercase letter; **false** otherwise.

Fig. 18.16 Character-handling library functions. (Part 1 of 2.)

Prototype	Description
int tolower(int c)	If **c** is an uppercase letter, **tolower** returns **c** as a lowercase letter. Otherwise, **tolower** returns the argument unchanged.
int toupper(int c)	If **c** is a lowercase letter, **toupper** returns **c** as an uppercase letter. Otherwise, **toupper** returns the argument unchanged.
int isspace(int c)	Returns **true** if **c** is a whitespace character—newline (**'\n'**), space (**' '**), form feed (**'\f'**), carriage return (**'\r'**), horizontal tab (**'\t'**), or vertical tab (**'\v'**)—and **false** otherwise
int iscntrl(int c)	Returns **true** if **c** is a control character and **false** otherwise.
int ispunct(int c)	Returns **true** if **c** is a printing character other than a space, a digit, or a letter and **false** otherwise.
int isprint(int c)	Returns **true** value if **c** is a printing character including space (**' '**) and **false** otherwise.
int isgraph(int c)	Returns **true** if **c** is a printing character other than space (**' '**) and **false** otherwise.

Fig. 18.16 Character-handling library functions. (Part 2 of 2.)

Figure 18.17 demonstrates functions *isdigit*, *isalpha*, *isalnum* and *isxdigit*. Function **isdigit** determines whether its argument is a digit (**0–9**). Function **isalpha** determines whether its argument is an uppercase letter (**A–Z**) or a lowercase letter (**a–z**). Function **isalnum** determines whether its argument is an uppercase letter, a lowercase letter or a digit. Function **isxdigit** determines whether its argument is a hexadecimal digit (**A–F**, **a–f**, **0–9**).

```
1   // Fig. 18.17: fig18_17.cpp
2   // Using functions isdigit, isalpha, isalnum and isxdigit.
3   #include <iostream>
4
5   using std::cout;
6   using std::endl;
7
8   #include <cctype>   // character-handling function prototypes
9
10  int main()
11  {
12     cout << "According to isdigit:\n"
13          << ( isdigit( '8' ) ? "8 is a" : "8 is not a" )
14          << " digit\n"
15          << ( isdigit( '#' ) ? "# is a" : "# is not a" )
16          << " digit\n";
```

Fig. 18.17 Character-handling functions **isdigit**, **isalpha**, **isalnum** and **isxdigit**. (Part 1 of 3.)

```
17
18        cout << "\nAccording to isalpha:\n"
19            << ( isalpha( 'A' ) ? "A is a" : "A is not a" )
20            << " letter\n"
21            << ( isalpha( 'b' ) ? "b is a" : "b is not a" )
22            << " letter\n"
23            << ( isalpha( '&' ) ? "& is a" : "& is not a" )
24            << " letter\n"
25            << ( isalpha( '4' ) ? "4 is a" : "4 is not a" )
26            << " letter\n";
27
28        cout << "\nAccording to isalnum:\n"
29            << ( isalnum( 'A' ) ? "A is a" : "A is not a" )
30            << " digit or a letter\n"
31            << ( isalnum( '8' ) ? "8 is a" : "8 is not a" )
32            << " digit or a letter\n"
33            << ( isalnum( '#' ) ? "# is a" : "# is not a" )
34            << " digit or a letter\n";
35
36        cout << "\nAccording to isxdigit:\n"
37            << ( isxdigit( 'F' ) ? "F is a" : "F is not a" )
38            << " hexadecimal digit\n"
39            << ( isxdigit( 'J' ) ? "J is a" : "J is not a" )
40            << " hexadecimal digit\n"
41            << ( isxdigit( '7' ) ? "7 is a" : "7 is not a" )
42            << " hexadecimal digit\n"
43            << ( isxdigit( '$' ) ? "$ is a" : "$ is not a" )
44            << " hexadecimal digit\n"
45            << ( isxdigit( 'f' ) ? "f is a" : "f is not a" )
46            << " hexadecimal digit" << endl;
47
48        return 0;
49
50   } // end main
```

```
According to isdigit:
8 is a digit
# is not a digit

According to isalpha:
A is a letter
b is a letter
& is not a letter
4 is not a letter

According to isalnum:
A is a digit or a letter
8 is a digit or a letter
# is not a digit or a letter
```

(continued next page)

Fig. 18.17 Character-handling functions **isdigit**, **isalpha**, **isalnum** and **isxdigit**. (Part 2 of 3.)

```
According to isxdigit:
F is a hexadecimal digit
J is not a hexadecimal digit
7 is a hexadecimal digit
$ is not a hexadecimal digit
f is a hexadecimal digit
```

Fig. 18.17 Character-handling functions **isdigit**, **isalpha**, **isalnum** and **isxdigit**. (Part 3 of 3.)

Figure 18.17 uses the conditional operator (**?:**) with each function to determine whether the string **" is a "** or the string **" is not a "** should be printed in the output for each character tested. For example, line 13 indicates that if **'8'** is a digit—i.e., if **isdigit** returns a true (nonzero) value—the string **"8 is a "** is printed. If **'8'** is not a digit (i.e., if **isdigit** returns **0**), the string **"8 is not a "** is printed.

The program of Fig. 18.18 demonstrates functions *islower*, *isupper*, *tolower* and *toupper*. Function **islower** determines whether its argument is a lowercase letter (**a-z**). Function **isupper** determines whether its argument is an uppercase letter (**A-Z**). Function **tolower** converts an uppercase letter to a lowercase letter and returns the lowercase letter. If the argument is not an uppercase letter, **tolower** returns the argument value. Function **toupper** converts a lowercase letter to an uppercase letter and returns the uppercase letter. If the argument is not a lowercase letter, **toupper** returns the argument value.

```
1   // Fig. 18.18: fig18_18.cpp
2   // Using functions islower, isupper, tolower and toupper.
3   #include <iostream>
4
5   using std::cout;
6   using std::endl;
7
8   #include <cctype>  // character-handling function prototypes
9
10  int main()
11  {
12      cout << "According to islower:\n"
13          << ( islower( 'p' ) ? "p is a" : "p is not a" )
14          << " lowercase letter\n"
15          << ( islower( 'P' ) ? "P is a" : "P is not a" )
16          << " lowercase letter\n"
17          << ( islower( '5' ) ? "5 is a" : "5 is not a" )
18          << " lowercase letter\n"
19          << ( islower( '!' ) ? "! is a" : "! is not a" )
20          << " lowercase letter\n";
21
```

Fig. 18.18 Character-handling functions **islower**, **isupper**, **tolower** and **toupper**. (Part 1 of 2.)

```
22        cout << "\nAccording to isupper:\n"
23             << ( isupper( 'D' ) ? "D is an" : "D is not an" )
24             << " uppercase letter\n"
25             << ( isupper( 'd' ) ? "d is an" : "d is not an" )
26             << " uppercase letter\n"
27             << ( isupper( '8' ) ? "8 is an" : "8 is not an" )
28             << " uppercase letter\n"
29             << ( isupper( '$' ) ? "$ is an" : "$ is not an" )
30             << " uppercase letter\n";
31
32        cout << "\nu converted to uppercase is "
33             << static_cast< char >( toupper( 'u' ) )
34             << "\n7 converted to uppercase is "
35             << static_cast< char >( toupper( '7' ) )
36             << "\n$ converted to uppercase is "
37             << static_cast< char >( toupper( '$' ) )
38             << "\nL converted to lowercase is "
39             << static_cast< char >( tolower( 'L' ) ) << endl;
40
41        return 0;
42
43     } // end main
```

```
According to islower:
p is a lowercase letter
P is not a lowercase letter
5 is not a lowercase letter
! is not a lowercase letter

According to isupper:
D is an uppercase letter
d is not an uppercase letter
8 is not an uppercase letter
$ is not an uppercase letter

u converted to uppercase is U
7 converted to uppercase is 7
$ converted to uppercase is $
L converted to lowercase is l
```

Fig. 18.18 Character-handling functions **islower**, **isupper**, **tolower** and **toupper**. (Part 2 of 2.)

Figure 18.19 demonstrates functions *isspace*, *iscntrl*, *ispunct*, *isprint* and *isgraph*. Function **isspace** determines whether its argument is a whitespace character, such as space (**' '**), form feed (**'\f'**), newline (**'\n'**), carriage return (**'\r'**), horizontal tab (**'\t'**) or vertical tab (**'\v'**). Function **iscntrl** determines whether its argument is a control character such as horizontal tab, vertical tab, form feed, alert (**'\a'**), backspace (**'\b'**), carriage return or newline. Function **ispunct** determines whether its argument is a printing character other than a space, digit or letter, such as **$**, **#**, **( )**, **[ ]**, **{ }**, **;**, **:** or **%**. Function **isprint** determines whether its argument is a character that can be displayed on the screen (including the space character). Function **isgraph** tests for the same characters as **isprint**; however, the space character is not included.

```cpp
1   // Fig. 18.19: fig18_19.cpp
2   // Using functions isspace, iscntrl, ispunct, isprint, isgraph.
3   #include <iostream>
4
5   using std::cout;
6   using std::endl;
7
8   #include <cctype>   // character-handling function prototypes
9
10  int main()
11  {
12     cout << "According to isspace:\nNewline "
13          << ( isspace( '\n' ) ? "is a" : "is not a" )
14          << " whitespace character\nHorizontal tab "
15          << ( isspace( '\t' ) ? "is a" : "is not a" )
16          << " whitespace character\n"
17          << ( isspace( '%' ) ? "% is a" : "% is not a" )
18          << " whitespace character\n";
19
20     cout << "\nAccording to iscntrl:\nNewline "
21          << ( iscntrl( '\n' ) ? "is a" : "is not a" )
22          << " control character\n"
23          << ( iscntrl( '$' ) ? "$ is a" : "$ is not a" )
24          << " control character\n";
25
26     cout << "\nAccording to ispunct:\n"
27          << ( ispunct( ';' ) ? "; is a" : "; is not a" )
28          << " punctuation character\n"
29          << ( ispunct( 'Y' ) ? "Y is a" : "Y is not a" )
30          << " punctuation character\n"
31          << ( ispunct( '#' ) ? "# is a" : "# is not a" )
32          << " punctuation character\n";
33
34     cout << "\nAccording to isprint:\n"
35          << ( isprint( '$' ) ? "$ is a" : "$ is not a" )
36          << " printing character\nAlert "
37          << ( isprint( '\a' ) ? "is a" : "is not a" )
38          << " printing character\n";
39
40     cout << "\nAccording to isgraph:\n"
41          << ( isgraph( 'Q' ) ? "Q is a" : "Q is not a" )
42          << " printing character other than a space\nSpace "
43          << ( isgraph( ' ' ) ? "is a" : "is not a" )
44          << " printing character other than a space" << endl;
45
46     return 0;
47
48  } // end main
```

Fig. 18.19 Character-handling functions **isspace**, **iscntrl**, **ispunct**, **isprint** and **isgraph**. (Part 1 of 2.)

```
According to isspace:
Newline is a whitespace character
Horizontal tab is a whitespace character
% is not a whitespace character

According to iscntrl:
Newline is a control character
$ is not a control character

According to ispunct:
; is a punctuation character
Y is not a punctuation character
# is a punctuation character

According to isprint:
$ is a printing character
Alert is not a printing character

According to isgraph:
Q is a printing character other than a space
Space is not a printing character other than a space
```

Fig. 18.19 Character-handling functions `isspace`, `iscntrl`, `ispunct`, `isprint` and `isgraph`. (Part 2 of 2.)

18.10 String-Conversion Functions

In Chapter 5, we discussed several of C++'s most popular character-string-manipulation functions. In the next several sections, we cover the remaining functions, including functions for converting strings to numeric values, functions for searching strings and functions for manipulating, comparing and searching blocks of memory.

This section presents the *string-conversion functions* from the *general-utilities library* `<cstdlib>`. These functions convert strings of characters to integer and floating-point values. Figure 18.20 summarizes the string-conversion functions. Note the use of **const** to declare variable **nPtr** in the function headers (read from right to left as "**nPtr** is a pointer to a character constant"). When using functions from the general-utilities library, be sure to include the `<cstdlib>` header file.

Prototype	Description
`double atof( const char *nPtr )`	Converts the string **nPtr** to **double**.
`int atoi( const char *nPtr )`	Converts the string **nPtr** to **int**.
`long atol( const char *nPtr )`	Converts the string **nPtr** to **long int**.
`double strtod( const char *nPtr, char **endPtr )`	
	Converts the string **nPtr** to **double**.

Fig. 18.20 String-conversion functions of the general-utilities library. (Part 1 of 2.)

Prototype	Description

```
long strtol( const char *nPtr, char **endPtr, int base )
```
                                               Converts the string **nPtr** to **long**.
```
unsigned long strtoul( const char *nPtr, char **endPtr, int base )
```
                                          Converts the string **nPtr** to **unsigned long**.

Fig. 18.20 String-conversion functions of the general-utilities library. (Part 2 of 2.)

Function *atof* (Fig. 18.21, line 12) converts its argument—a string that represents a floating-point number—to a **double** value. The function returns the **double** value. If the string cannot be converted—for example, if the first character of the string is not a digit—function **atof** returns zero.

Function *atoi* (Fig. 18.22, line 12) converts its argument—a string of digits that represents an integer—to an **int** value. The function returns the **int** value. If the string cannot be converted, function **atoi** returns zero.

```
1   // Fig. 18.21: fig18_21.cpp
2   // Using atof.
3   #include <iostream>
4
5   using std::cout;
6   using std::endl;
7
8   #include <cstdlib>   // atof prototype
9
10  int main()
11  {
12     double d = atof( "99.0" );
13
14     cout << "The string \"99.0\" converted to double is "
15          << d << "\nThe converted value divided by 2 is "
16          << d / 2.0 << endl;
17
18     return 0;
19
20  } // end main
```

```
The string "99.0" converted to double is 99
The converted value divided by 2 is 49.5
```

Fig. 18.21 String-conversion function **atof**.

```
1   // Fig. 18.22: fig18_22.cpp
2   // Using atoi.
3   #include <iostream>
```

Fig. 18.22 String-conversion function **atoi**. (Part 1 of 2.)

```
 4
 5   using std::cout;
 6   using std::endl;
 7
 8   #include <cstdlib>   // atoi prototype
 9
10   int main()
11   {
12      int i = atoi( "2593" );
13
14      cout << "The string \"2593\" converted to int is " << i
15           << "\nThe converted value minus 593 is " << i - 593
16           << endl;
17
18      return 0;
19
20   } // end main
```

```
The string "2593" converted to int is 2593
The converted value minus 593 is 2000
```

Fig. 18.22 String-conversion function **atoi**. (Part 2 of 2.)

Function *atol* (Fig. 18.23, line 12) converts its argument—a string of digits representing a long integer—to a **long** value. The function returns the **long** value. If the string cannot be converted, function **atol** returns zero. If **int** and **long** are both stored in 4 bytes, function **atoi** and function **atol** work identically.

```
 1   // Fig. 18.23: fig18_23.cpp
 2   // Using atol.
 3   #include <iostream>
 4
 5   using std::cout;
 6   using std::endl;
 7
 8   #include <cstdlib>   // atol prototype
 9
10   int main()
11   {
12      long x = atol( "1000000" );
13
14      cout << "The string \"1000000\" converted to long is " << x
15           << "\nThe converted value divided by 2 is " << x / 2
16           << endl;
17
18      return 0;
19
20   } // end main
```

```
The string "1000000" converted to long int is 1000000
The converted value divided by 2 is 500000
```

Fig. 18.23 String-conversion function **atol**.

Function ***strtod*** (Fig. 18.24) converts a sequence of characters representing a floating-point value to **double**. Function **strtod** receives two arguments—a string (**char ***) and a pointer to a string (i.e., a **char ****). The string contains the character sequence to be converted to **double**. The second argument enables **strtod** to modify a **char *** pointer in the calling function, such that the pointer points to the location of the first character after the converted portion of the string. Line 16 indicates that **d** is assigned the **double** value converted from **string** and that **&stringPtr** is assigned the location of the first character after the converted value (**51.2**) in **string**.

Function ***strtol*** (Fig. 18.25) converts to **long** a sequence of characters representing an integer. The function receives three arguments—a string (**char ***), a pointer to a string and an integer. The string contains the character sequence to convert. The second argument is assigned the location of the first character after the converted portion of the string. The integer specifies the *base* of the value being converted. Line 16 indicates that **x** is assigned the **long** value converted from **string**. The second argument, **&remainderPtr**, is assigned the remainder of **string** after the conversion. Using **NULL** for the second argument causes the remainder of the string to be ignored. The third argument, **0**, indicates that the value to be converted can be in octal (base 8), decimal (base 10) or hexadecimal (base 16).

In a call to function **strtol**, the base can be specified as zero or as any value between 2 and 36. (See Appendix C for a detailed explanation of the octal, decimal, hexadecimal and binary number systems). Numeric representations of integers from base 11 to base 36

```
1   // Fig. 18.24: fig18_24.cpp
2   // Using strtod.
3   #include <iostream>
4
5   using std::cout;
6   using std::endl;
7
8   #include <cstdlib>   // strtod prototype
9
10  int main()
11  {
12     double d;
13     const char *string1 = "51.2% are admitted";
14     char *stringPtr;
15
16     d = strtod( string1, &stringPtr );
17
18     cout << "The string \"" << string1
19          << "\" is converted to the\ndouble value " << d
20          << " and the string \"" << stringPtr << "\"" << endl;
21
22     return 0;
23
24  } // end main
```

```
The string "51.2% are admitted" is converted to the
double value 51.2 and the string "% are admitted"
```

Fig. 18.24 String-conversion function **strtod**.

use the characters A–Z to represent the values 10 to 35. For example, hexadecimal values can consist of the digits 0–9 and the characters A–F. A base-11 integer can consist of the digits 0–9 and the character A. A base-24 integer can consist of the digits 0–9 and the characters A–N. A base-36 integer can consist of the digits 0–9 and the characters A–Z.

Function **strtoul** (Fig. 18.26) converts to **unsigned long** a sequence of characters representing an **unsigned long** integer. The function works identically to function **strtol**. Line 16 indicates that **x** is assigned the **unsigned long** value converted from **string**. The second argument, **&remainderPtr**, is assigned the remainder of **string** after the conversion. The third argument, **0**, indicates that the value to be converted can be in octal, decimal or hexadecimal format.

```cpp
1   // Fig. 18.25: fig18_25.cpp
2   // Using strtol.
3   #include <iostream>
4
5   using std::cout;
6   using std::endl;
7
8   #include <cstdlib>   // strtol prototype
9
10  int main()
11  {
12     long x;
13     const char *string1 = "-1234567abc";
14     char *remainderPtr;
15
16     x = strtol( string1, &remainderPtr, 0 );
17
18     cout << "The original string is \"" << string1
19          << "\"\nThe converted value is " << x
20          << "\nThe remainder of the original string is \""
21          << remainderPtr
22          << "\"\nThe converted value plus 567 is "
23          << x + 567 << endl;
24
25     return 0;
26
27  } // end main
```

```
The original string is "-1234567abc"
The converted value is -1234567
The remainder of the original string is "abc"
The converted value plus 567 is -1234000
```

Fig. 18.25 String-conversion function **strtol**.

```cpp
1   // Fig. 18.26: fig18_26.cpp
2   // Using strtoul.
3   #include <iostream>
```

Fig. 18.26 String-conversion function **strtoul**. (Part 1 of 2.)

```
4
5    using std::cout;
6    using std::endl;
7
8    #include <cstdlib>   // strtoul prototype
9
10   int main()
11   {
12       unsigned long x;
13       const char *string1 = "1234567abc";
14       char *remainderPtr;
15
16       x = strtoul( string1, &remainderPtr, 0 );
17
18       cout << "The original string is \"" << string1
19            << "\"\nThe converted value is " << x
20            << "\nThe remainder of the original string is \""
21            << remainderPtr
22            << "\"\nThe converted value minus 567 is "
23            << x - 567 << endl;
24
25       return 0;
26
27   } // end main
```

```
The original string is "1234567abc"
The converted value is 1234567
The remainder of the original string is "abc"
The converted value minus 567 is 1234000
```

Fig. 18.26 String-conversion function **strtoul**. (Part 2 of 2.)

18.11 Search Functions of the String-Handling Library

This section presents the functions of the string-handling library used to search strings for characters and other strings. The functions are summarized in Fig. 18.27. Note that functions **strcspn** and **strspn** specify return type **size_t**. Type **size_t** is a type defined by the standard as the integral type of the value returned by operator **sizeof**.

Prototype	Description

```
char *strchr( const char *s, int c )
```
Locates the first occurrence of character **c** in string **s**. If **c** is found, a pointer to **c** in **s** is returned. Otherwise, a **NULL** pointer is returned.

```
char *strrchr( const char *s, int c )
```
Searches from the end of string **s** and locates the last occurrence of **c** in string **s**. If **c** is found, a pointer to **c** in string **s** is returned. Otherwise, a **NULL** pointer is returned.

Fig. 18.27 Search functions of the string-handling library. (Part 1 of 2.)

Prototype	Description

`size_t strspn( const char *s1, const char *s2 )`

Determines and returns the length of the initial segment of string **s1** consisting only of characters contained in string **s2**.

`char *strpbrk( const char *s1, const char *s2 )`

Locates the first occurrence in string **s1** of any character in string **s2**. If a character from string **s2** is found, a pointer to the character in string **s1** is returned. Otherwise, a **NULL** pointer is returned.

`size_t strcspn( const char *s1, const char *s2 )`

Determines and returns the length of the initial segment of string **s1** consisting of characters not contained in string **s2**.

`char *strstr( const char *s1, const char *s2 )`

Locates the first occurrence in string **s1** of string **s2**. If the string is found, a pointer to the string in **s1** is returned. Otherwise, a **NULL** pointer is returned.

Fig. 18.27 Search functions of the string-handling library. (Part 2 of 2.)

Portability Tip 18.6

*Type **size_t** is a system-dependent synonym for either type **unsigned long** or type **unsigned int***.

Function **strchr** searches for the first occurrence of a character in a string. If the character is found, **strchr** returns a pointer to the character in the string; otherwise, **strchr** returns **NULL**. The program of Fig. 18.28 uses **strchr** (lines 16 and 23) to search for the first occurrences of **'a'** and **'z'** in the string **"This is a test"**.

```
1   // Fig. 18.28: fig18_28.cpp
2   // Using strchr.
3   #include <iostream>
4
5   using std::cout;
6   using std::endl;
7
8   #include <cstring>   // strchr prototype
9
10  int main()
11  {
12      const char *string1 = "This is a test";
13      char character1 = 'a';
14      char character2 = 'z';
15
16      if ( strchr( string1, character1 ) != NULL )
17          cout << '\'' << character1 << "' was found in \""
18               << string1 << "\".\n";
19      else
```

Fig. 18.28 String-search function **strchr**. (Part 1 of 2.)

```
20          cout << '\'' << character1 << "' was not found in \""
21              << string1 << "\".\n";
22
23      if ( strchr( string1, character2 ) != NULL )
24          cout << '\'' << character2 << "' was found in \""
25              << string1 << "\".\n";
26      else
27          cout << '\'' << character2 << "' was not found in \""
28              << string1 << "\"." << endl;
29
30      return 0;
31
32   } // end main
```

```
'a' was found in "This is a test".
'z' was not found in "This is a test".
```

Fig. 18.28 String-search function **strchr**. (Part 2 of 2.)

Function **strcspn** (Fig. 18.29, line 18) determines the length of the initial part of the string in its first argument that does not contain any characters from the string in its second argument. The function returns the length of the segment.

Function **strpbrk** searches for the first occurrence in its first string argument of any character in its second string argument. If a character from the second argument is found, **strpbrk** returns a pointer to the character in the first argument; otherwise, **strpbrk** returns **NULL**. Line 16 of Fig. 18.30 locates the first occurrence in **string1** of any character from **string2**.

```
1    // Fig. 18.29: fig18_29.cpp
2    // Using strcspn.
3    #include <iostream>
4
5    using std::cout;
6    using std::endl;
7
8    #include <cstring>   // strcspn prototype
9
10   int main()
11   {
12       const char *string1 = "The value is 3.14159";
13       const char *string2 = "1234567890";
14
15       cout << "string1 = " << string1 << "\nstring2 = " << string2
16           << "\n\nThe length of the initial segment of string1"
17           << "\ncontaining no characters from string2 = "
18           << strcspn( string1, string2 ) << endl;
19
20       return 0;
21
22   } // end main
```

Fig. 18.29 String-search function **strcspn**. (Part 1 of 2.)

```
string1 = The value is 3.14159
string2 = 1234567890

The length of the initial segment of string1
containing no characters from string2 = 13
```

Fig. 18.29 String-search function **strcspn**. (Part 2 of 2.)

```
1   // Fig. 18.30: fig18_30.cpp
2   // Using strpbrk.
3   #include <iostream>
4
5   using std::cout;
6   using std::endl;
7
8   #include <cstring>   // strpbrk prototype
9
10  int main()
11  {
12     const char *string1 = "This is a test";
13     const char *string2 = "beware";
14
15     cout << "Of the characters in \"" << string2 << "\"\n'"
16          << *strpbrk( string1, string2 ) << '\''
17          << " is the first character to appear in\n\""
18          << string1 << '\"' << endl;
19
20     return 0;
21
22  } // end main
```

```
Of the characters in "beware"
'a' is the first character to appear in
"This is a test"
```

Fig. 18.30 String-search function **strpbrk**.

Function **strrchr** searches for the last occurrence of the specified character in a string. If the character is found, **strrchr** returns a pointer to the character in the string; otherwise, **strrchr** returns **0**. Line 19 of Fig. 18.31 searches for the last occurrence of the character **'z'** in the string **"A zoo has many animals including zebras"**.

```
1   // Fig. 18.31: fig18_31.cpp
2   // Using strrchr.
3   #include <iostream>
4
5   using std::cout;
6   using std::endl;
```

Fig. 18.31 String-search function **strrchr**. (Part 1 of 2.)

```
 7
 8   #include <cstring>   // strrchr prototype
 9
10   int main()
11   {
12      const char *string1 =
13         "A zoo has many animals including zebras";
14      int c = 'z';
15
16      cout << "The remainder of string1 beginning with the\n"
17           << "last occurrence of character '"
18           << static_cast< char >( c )   // print as char not int
19           << "' is: \"" << strrchr( string1, c ) << '\"' << endl;
20
21      return 0;
22
23   } // end main
```

```
The remainder of string1 beginning with the
last occurrence of character 'z' is: "zebras"
```

Fig. 18.31 String-search function **strrchr**. (Part 2 of 2.)

Function **strspn** (Fig. 18.32, line 19) determines the length of the initial part of the string in its first argument that contains only characters from the string in its second argument. The function returns the length of the segment.

Function **strstr** searches for the first occurrence of its second string argument in its first string argument. If the second string is found in the first string, a pointer to the location of the string in the first argument is returned. Line 18 of Fig. 18.33 uses **strstr** to find the string **"def"** in the string **"abcdefabcdef"**.

```
 1   // Fig. 18.32: fig18_32.cpp
 2   // Using strspn.
 3   #include <iostream>
 4
 5   using std::cout;
 6   using std::endl;
 7
 8   #include <cstring>   // strspn prototype
 9
10   int main()
11   {
12      const char *string1 = "The value is 3.14159";
13      const char *string2 = "aehils Tuv";
14
15      cout << "string1 = " << string1
16           << "\nstring2 = " << string2
17           << "\n\nThe length of the initial segment of string1\n"
18           << "containing only characters from string2 = "
19           << strspn( string1, string2 ) << endl;
```

Fig. 18.32 String-search function **strspn**. (Part 1 of 2.)

```
20
21      return 0;
22
23  } // end main
```

```
string1 = The value is 3.14159
string2 = aehils Tuv

The length of the initial segment of string1
containing only characters from string2 = 13
```

Fig. 18.32 String-search function **strspn**. (Part 2 of 2.)

```
1   // Fig. 18.33: fig18_33.cpp
2   // Using strstr.
3   #include <iostream>
4
5   using std::cout;
6   using std::endl;
7
8   #include <cstring>   // strstr prototype
9
10  int main()
11  {
12      const char *string1 = "abcdefabcdef";
13      const char *string2 = "def";
14
15      cout << "string1 = " << string1 << "\nstring2 = " << string2
16          << "\n\nThe remainder of string1 beginning with the\n"
17          << "first occurrence of string2 is: "
18          << strstr( string1, string2 ) << endl;
19
20      return 0;
21
22  } // end main
```

```
string1 = abcdefabcdef
string2 = def

The remainder of string1 beginning with the
first occurrence of string2 is: defabcdef
```

Fig. 18.33 String-search function **strstr**.

18.12 Memory Functions of the String-Handling Library

The string-handling library functions presented in this section facilitate manipulating, comparing and searching blocks of memory. The functions treat blocks of memory as arrays of bytes. These functions can manipulate any block of data. Figure 18.34 summarizes the memory functions of the string-handling library. In the function discussions, "object" refers to a block of data. [*Note:* The string-processing functions in prior sections operate on null-terminated character strings. The functions in this section operate on arrays of bytes. The null-character value (i.e., a byte containing 0) has no significance with the functions in this section.]

The pointer parameters to these functions are declared **void ***. In Chapter 5, we saw that a pointer to any data type can be assigned directly to a pointer of type **void ***. For this reason, these functions can receive pointers to any data type. Remember that a pointer of type **void *** cannot be assigned directly to a pointer to any data type. Because a **void *** pointer cannot be dereferenced, each function receives a size argument that specifies the number of characters (bytes) the function will process. For simplicity, the examples in this section manipulate character arrays (blocks of characters).

Function **memcpy** copies a specified number of characters (bytes) from the object pointed to by its second argument into the object pointed to by its first argument. The function can receive a pointer to any type of object. The result of this function is undefined if the two objects overlap in memory (i.e., are parts of the same object). The program of Fig. 18.35 uses **memcpy** (line 15) to copy the string in array **s2** to array **s1**.

Prototype	Description

void *memcpy(void *s1, const void *s2, size_t n)

> Copies **n** characters from the object pointed to by **s2** into the object pointed to by **s1**. A pointer to the resulting object is returned. The area from which characters are copied is not allowed to overlap the area to which characters are copied.

void *memmove(void *s1, const void *s2, size_t n)

> Copies **n** characters from the object pointed to by **s2** into the object pointed to by **s1**. The copy is performed as if the characters are first copied from the object pointed to by **s2** into a temporary array, and then copied from the temporary array into the object pointed to by **s1**. A pointer to the resulting object is returned. The area from which characters are copied is allowed to overlap the area to which characters are copied.

int memcmp(const void *s1, const void *s2, size_t n)

> Compares the first **n** characters of the objects pointed to by **s1** and **s2**. The function returns **0**, less than **0**, or greater than **0** if **s1** is equal to, less than or greater than **s2**, respectively.

void *memchr(const void *s, int c, size_t n)

> Locates the first occurrence of **c** (converted to **unsigned char**) in the first **n** characters of the object pointed to by **s**. If **c** is found, a pointer to **c** in the object is returned. Otherwise, **0** is returned.

void *memset(void *s, int c, size_t n)

> Copies **c** (converted to **unsigned char**) into the first **n** characters of the object pointed to by **s**. A pointer to the result is returned.

Fig. 18.34 Memory functions of the string-handling library.

```
1   // Fig. 18.35: fig18_35.cpp
2   // Using memcpy.
3   #include <iostream>
4
5   using std::cout;
6   using std::endl;
7
8   #include <cstring>   // memcpy prototype
9
10  int main()
11  {
12     char s1[ 17 ];
13     char s2[] = "Copy this string";
14
15     memcpy( s1, s2, 17 );
16
17     cout << "After s2 is copied into s1 with memcpy,\n"
18          << "s1 contains \"" << s1 << '\"' << endl;
19
20     return 0;
21
22  } // end main
```

```
After s2 is copied into s1 with memcpy,
s1 contains "Copy this string"
```

Fig. 18.35 Memory-handling function **memcpy**.

Function *memmove*, like **memcpy**, copies a specified number of bytes from the object pointed to by its second argument into the object pointed to by its first argument. Copying is performed as if the bytes are copied from the second argument to a temporary array of characters, and then copied from the temporary array to the first argument. This allows characters from one part of a string to be copied into another part of the same string.

Common Programming Error 18.10

*String-manipulation functions other than **memmove** that copy characters have undefined results when copying takes place between parts of the same string.*

The program in Fig. 18.36 uses **memmove** (line 16) to copy the last **10** bytes of array **x** into the first **10** bytes of array **x**.

```
1   // Fig. 18.36: fig18_36.cpp
2   // Using memmove.
3   #include <iostream>
4
5   using std::cout;
6   using std::endl;
7
8   #include <cstring>   // memmove prototype
9
```

Fig. 18.36 Memory-handling function **memmove**. (Part 1 of 2.)

```
10   int main()
11   {
12      char x[] = "Home Sweet Home";
13
14      cout << "The string in array x before memmove is: " << x;
15      cout << "\nThe string in array x after memmove is:  "
16           << static_cast< char * >( memmove( x, &x[ 5 ], 10 ) )
17           << endl;
18
19      return 0;
20
21   } // end main
```

```
The string in array x before memmove is: Home Sweet Home
The string in array x after memmove is:  Sweet Home Home
```

Fig. 18.36 Memory-handling function **memmove**. (Part 2 of 2.)

Function **memcmp** (Fig. 18.37, lines 21, 22 and 24) compares the specified number of characters of its first argument with the corresponding characters of its second argument. The function returns a value greater than zero if the first argument is greater than the second argument, zero if the arguments are equal, and a value less than zero if the first argument is less than the second argument.

```
1   // Fig. 18.37: fig18_37.cpp
2   // Using memcmp.
3   #include <iostream>
4
5   using std::cout;
6   using std::endl;
7
8   #include <iomanip>
9
10   using std::setw;
11
12   #include <cstring>   // memcmp prototype
13
14   int main()
15   {
16      char s1[] = "ABCDEFG";
17      char s2[] = "ABCDXYZ";
18
19      cout << "s1 = " << s1 << "\ns2 = " << s2 << endl
20           << "\nmemcmp(s1, s2, 4) = " << setw( 3 )
21           << memcmp( s1, s2, 4 ) << "\nmemcmp(s1, s2, 7) = "
22           << setw( 3 ) << memcmp( s1, s2, 7 )
23           << "\nmemcmp(s2, s1, 7) = " << setw( 3 )
24           << memcmp( s2, s1, 7 ) << endl;
```

Fig. 18.37 Memory-handling function **memcmp**. (Part 1 of 2.)

```
25
26      return 0;
27
28   } // end main
```

```
s1 = ABCDEFG
s2 = ABCDXYZ

memcmp(s1, s2, 4) =    0
memcmp(s1, s2, 7) = -1
memcmp(s2, s1, 7) =  1
```

Fig. 18.37 Memory-handling function **memcmp**. (Part 2 of 2.)

Function **memchr** searches for the first occurrence of a byte, represented as **unsigned char**, in the specified number of bytes of an object. If the byte is found in the object, a pointer to the byte in the object is returned; otherwise, the function returns **NULL**. Line 16 of Fig. 18.38 searches for the character (byte) **'r'** in the string **"This is a string"**.

Function **memset** copies the value of the byte in its second argument into a specified number of bytes of the object pointed to by its first argument. Line 16 in Fig. 18.39 uses **memset** to copy **'b'** into the first **7** bytes of **string1**.

```
1    // Fig. 18.38: fig18_38.cpp
2    // Using memchr.
3    #include <iostream>
4
5    using std::cout;
6    using std::endl;
7
8    #include <cstring>   // memchr prototype
9
10   int main()
11   {
12      char s[] = "This is a string";
13
14      cout << "The remainder of s after character 'r' "
15           << "is found is \""
16           << static_cast< char * >( memchr( s, 'r', 16 ) )
17           << '\"' << endl;
18
19      return 0;
20
21   } // end main
```

```
The remainder of s after character 'r' is found is "ring"
```

Fig. 18.38 Memory-handling function **memchr**.

```
1   // Fig. 18.39: fig18_39.cpp
2   // Using memset.
3   #include <iostream>
4
5   using std::cout;
6   using std::endl;
7
8   #include <cstring>   // memset prototype
9
10  int main()
11  {
12     char string1[ 15 ] = "BBBBBBBBBBBBBB";
13
14     cout << "string1 = " << string1 << endl;
15     cout << "string1 after memset = "
16          << static_cast< char * >( memset( string1, 'b', 7 ) )
17          << endl;
18
19     return 0;
20
21  } // end main
```

```
string1 = BBBBBBBBBBBBBB
string1 after memset = bbbbbbbBBBBBBB
```

Fig. 18.39 Memory-handling function **memset**.

SUMMARY

- Structures are collections of related variables (or aggregates) under one name.
- Structures can contain variables of different data types.
- Keyword **struct** begins every structure definition. Between the braces of the structure definition are the structure member declarations.
- Members of the same structure must have unique names.
- A structure definition creates a new data type that can be used to declare variables.
- A structure can be initialized with an initializer list by following the variable in the declaration with an equal sign and a comma-separated list of initializers enclosed in braces. If there are fewer initializers in the list than members in the structure, the remaining members are initialized to zero (or **NULL** for pointer members).
- Entire structure variables may be assigned to structure variables of the same type.
- A structure variable may be initialized with a structure variable of the same type.
- Structures variables and individual structure members are passed to functions by value.
- To pass a structure by reference, pass the address of the structure variable. An array of structures is passed by reference. To pass an array by value, create a structure with the array as a member.
- Creating a new type name with **typedef** does not create a new type; it creates a name that is synonymous to a type defined previously.
- The bitwise AND operator (**&**) takes two integral operands. A bit in the result is set to one if the corresponding bits in each of the operands are one.
- Masks are used to hide some bits while preserving others.

- The bitwise inclusive OR operator (**|**) takes two operands. A bit in the result is set to one if the corresponding bit in either operand is set to one.

- Each of the bitwise operators (except complement) has a corresponding assignment operator.

- The bitwise exclusive-OR operator (**^**) takes two operands. A bit in the result is set to one if exactly one of the corresponding bits in the two operands is set to 1.

- The left-shift operator (**<<**) shifts the bits of its left operand left by the number of bits specified by its right operand. Bits vacated to the right are replaced with **0**s.

- The right-shift operator (**>>**) shifts the bits of its left operand right by the number of bits specified in its right operand. Performing a right shift on an unsigned integer causes bits vacated at the left to be replaced by zeros. Vacated bits in signed integers can be replaced with zeros or ones—this is machine dependent.

- The bitwise complement operator (**~**) takes one operand and reverses its bits—this produces the one's complement of the operand.

- Bit fields reduce storage use by storing data in the minimum number of bits required. Bit-field members must be declared as **int** or **unsigned**.

- A bit field is declared by following an **unsigned** or **int** member name with a colon and the width of the bit field.

- The bit field width must be an integer constant between zero and the total number of bits used to store an **int** variable on your system

- If a bit field is specified without a name, the field is used as padding in the structure.

- An unnamed bit field with width **0** aligns the next bit field on a new machine word boundary.

- Function **islower** determines whether its argument is a lowercase letter (**a–z**). Function **isupper** determines whether its argument is an uppercase letter (**A–Z**).

- Function **isdigit** determines whether its argument is a digit (**0–9**).

- Function **isalpha** determines whether its argument is an uppercase (**A–Z**) or lowercase letter (**a–z**).

- Function **isalnum** determines whether its argument is an uppercase letter (**A–Z**), a lowercase letter (**a–z**), or a digit (**0–9**).

- Function **isxdigit** determines whether its argument is a hexadecimal digit (**A–F**, **a–f**, **0–9**).

- Function **toupper** converts a lowercase letter to an uppercase letter. Function **tolower** converts an uppercase letter to a lowercase letter.

- Function **isspace** determines whether its argument is one of the following whitespace characters: **' '** (space), **'\f'**, **'\n'**, **'\r'**, **'\t'** or **'\v'**.

- Function **iscntrl** determines whether its argument is one of the following control characters: **'\t'**, **'\v'**, **'\f'**, **'\a'**, **'\b'**, **'\r'** or **'\n'**.

- Function **ispunct** determines whether its argument is a printing character other than a space, a digit or a letter.

- Function **isprint** determines whether its argument is any printing character, including space.

- Function **isgraph** determines whether its argument is a printing character other than space.

- Function **atof** converts its argument—a string beginning with a series of digits that represents a floating-point number—to a **double** value.

- Function **atoi** converts its argument—a string beginning with a series of digits that represents an integer—to an **int** value.

- Function **atol** converts its argument—a string beginning with a series of digits that represents a long integer—to a **long** value.

- Function **strtod** converts a sequence of characters representing a floating-point value to **double**. The function receives two arguments—a string (**char ***) and a pointer to **char ***. The string contains the character sequence to be converted, and the pointer to **char *** is assigned the remainder of the string after the conversion.

- Function **strtol** converts a sequence of characters representing an integer to **long**. The function receives three arguments—a string (**char ***), a pointer to **char *** and an integer. The string contains the character sequence to be converted, the pointer to **char *** is assigned the remainder of the string after the conversion and the integer specifies the base of the value being converted.

- Function **strtoul** converts a sequence of characters representing an integer to **unsigned long**. The function receives three arguments—a string (**char ***), a pointer to **char *** and an integer. The string contains the character sequence to be converted, the pointer to **char *** is assigned the remainder of the string after the conversion and the integer specifies the base of the value being converted.

- Function **strchr** searches for the first occurrence of a character in a string. If the character is found, **strchr** returns a pointer to the character in the string; otherwise, **strchr** returns **NULL**.

- Function **strcspn** determines the length of the initial part of the string in its first argument that does not contain any characters from the string in its second argument. The function returns the length of the segment.

- Function **strpbrk** searches for the first occurrence in its first argument of any character that appears in its second argument. If a character from the second argument is found, **strpbrk** returns a pointer to the character; otherwise, **strpbrk** returns **NULL**.

- Function **strrchr** searches for the last occurrence of a character in a string. If the character is found, **strrchr** returns a pointer to the character in the string; otherwise, it returns **NULL**.

- Function **strspn** determines the length of the initial part of the string in its first argument that contains only characters from the string in its second argument and returns the length of the segment.

- Function **strstr** searches for the first occurrence of its second string argument in its first string argument. If the second string is found in the first string, a pointer to the location of the string in the first argument is returned.

- Function **memcpy** copies a specified number of characters from the object to which its second argument points into the object to which its first argument points. The function can receive a pointer to any object. The pointers are received by **memcpy** as **void** pointers and converted to **char** pointers for use in the function. Function **memcpy** manipulates the bytes of its argument as characters.

- Function **memmove** copies a specified number of bytes from the object pointed to by its second argument to the object pointed to by its first argument. Copying is accomplished as if the bytes are copied from the second argument to a temporary character array, and then copied from the temporary array to the first argument.

- Function **memcmp** compares the specified number of characters of its first and second arguments.

- Function **memchr** searches for the first occurrence of a byte, represented as **unsigned char**, in the specified number of bytes of an object. If the byte is found, a pointer to the byte is returned; otherwise, a **NULL** pointer is returned.

- Function **memset** copies its second argument, treated as an **unsigned char**, to a specified number of bytes of the object pointed to by the first argument.

TERMINOLOGY

^ bitwise exclusive-OR operator

^= bitwise exclusive-OR assignment operator

| bitwise inclusive-OR operator

|= bitwise inclusive-OR assignment operator

~ one's-complement operator

& bitwise AND operator

&= bitwise AND assignment operator	**memcmp**
<< left-shift operator	**memcpy**
<<= left-shift assignment operator	**memmove**
>> right-shift operator	**memset**
>>= right-shift assignment operator	one's complement
array of structures	padding
ASCII	pointer to a structure
atof	printing character
atoi	record
atol	right shift
bit field	search string
bitwise operators	self-referential structure
character code	shifting
character constant	space–time trade-offs
character set	**strchr**
complementing	**strcspn**
control character	string
<cctype>	string constant
<cstdlib>	string-conversion functions
<cstring>	string literal
delimiter	string processing
general-utilities library	**strpbrk**
hexadecimal digits	**strrchr**
initialization of structures	**strspn**
isalnum	**strstr**
isalpha	**strtod**
iscntrl	**strtol**
isdigit	**strtoul**
isgraph	**struct**
islower	structure assignment
isprint	structure initialization
ispunct	structure type
isspace	**tolower**
isupper	**toupper**
isxdigit	**typedef**
left shift	unnamed bit field
literal	whitespace characters
mask	width of a bit field
masking off bits	word processing
memchr	zero-width bit field

SELF-REVIEW EXERCISES

18.1   Fill in the blanks in each of the following:

a) A _____ is a collection of related variables under one name.

b) The bits in the result of an expression using the _____ operator are set to one if the corresponding bits in each operand are set to one. Otherwise, the bits are set to zero.

c) The variables declared in a structure definition are called its _____.

d) The bits in the result of an expression using the _____ operator are set to one if at least one of the corresponding bits in either operand is set to one. Otherwise, the bits are set to zero.

e) Keyword _____ introduces a structure declaration.

f) Keyword _____ is used to create a synonym for a previously defined data type.

g) The bits in the result of an expression using the _____ operator are set to one if exactly one of the corresponding bits in either operand is set to one. Otherwise, the bits are set to zero.

h) The bitwise AND operator **&** is often used to _____ bits, (i.e., to select certain bits from a bit string while zeroing others).

i) The name of the structure is referred to as the structure _____.

j) A structure member is accessed with either operator _____ or _____.

k) The _____ and _____ operators are used to shift the bits of a value to the left or to the right, respectively.

18.2   State whether each of the following is *true* or *false*. If *false*, explain why.

a) Structures may contain only one data type.

b) Members of different structures must have unique names.

c) Keyword **typedef** is used to define new data types.

d) Structures are always passed to functions by reference.

18.3   Write a single statement or a set of statements to accomplish each of the following:

a) Define a structure called **Part** containing **int** variable **partNumber** and **char** array **partName**, whose values may be as long as 25 characters.

b) Define **PartPtr** to be a synonym for the type **Part ***.

c) Declare variable **a** to be of type **Part**, array **b[10]** to be of type **Part** and variable **ptr** to be of type pointer to **Part**.

d) Read a part number and a part name from the keyboard into the members of variable **a**.

e) Assign the member values of variable **a** to element three of array **b**.

f) Assign the address of array **b** to the pointer variable **ptr**.

g) Print the member values of element three of array **b**, using the variable **ptr** and the structure pointer operator to refer to the members.

18.4   Find the error in each of the following:

a) Assume that **struct Card** has been defined as containing two pointers to type **char**—namely, **face** and **suit**. Also, the variable **c** has been declared to be of type **Card**, and the variable **cPtr** has been declared to be of type pointer to **Card**. Variable **cPtr** has been assigned the address of **c**.

```
cout << *cPtr.face << endl;
```

b) Assume that **struct Card** has been defined as containing two pointers to type **char**—namely, **face** and **suit**. Also, the array **hearts[13]** has been declared to be of type **Card**. The following statement should print the member **face** of element 10 of the array.

```
cout << hearts.face << endl;
```

c)
```
struct Person {
    char lastName[ 15 ];
    char firstName[ 15 ];
    int age;
}
```

d) Assume that variable **p** has been declared as type **Person** and that variable **c** has been declared as type **Card**.

```
p = c;
```

18.5   Write a single statement to accomplish each of the following. Assume that variables **c** (which stores a character), **x**, **y** and **z** are of type **int**; variables **d**, **e** and **f** are of type **double**; variable **ptr** is of type **char *** and arrays **s1[100]** and **s2[100]** are of type **char**.

    a) Convert the character stored in variable **c** to an uppercase letter. Assign the result to variable **c**.

    b) Determine if the value of variable **c** is a digit. Use the conditional operator as shown in Fig. 18.17–Fig. 18.19 to print **" is a "** or **" is not a "** when the result is displayed.

    c) Convert the string **"1234567"** to **long**, and print the value.

    d) Determine whether the value of variable **c** is a control character. Use the conditional operator to print **" is a "** or **" is not a "** when the result is displayed.

    e) Assign to **ptr** the location of the last occurrence of **c** in **s1**.

    f) Convert the string **"8.63582"** to **double**, and print the value.

    g) Determine whether the value of **c** is a letter. Use the conditional operator to print **" is a "** or **" is not a "** when the result is displayed.

    h) Assign to **ptr** the location of the first occurrence of **s2** in **s1**.

    i) Determine whether the value of variable **c** is a printing character. Use the conditional operator to print **" is a "** or **" is not a "** when the result is displayed.

    j) Assign to **ptr** the location of the first occurrence in **s1** of any character from **s2**.

    k) Assign to **ptr** the location of the first occurrence of **c** in **s1**.

    l) Convert the string **"-21"** to **int**, and print the value.

ANSWERS TO SELF-REVIEW EXERCISES

18.1   a) structure. b) bitwise AND (**&**). c) members. d) bitwise inclusive-OR (**|**). e) **struct**. f) **typedef**. g) bitwise exclusive-OR (**^**). h) mask. i) tag. j) structure member (**.**), structure pointer (**->**). k) left-shift operator (**<<**), right-shift operator (**>>**).

18.2   a) False. A structure can contain many data types.

    b) False. The members of separate structures can have the same names, but the members of the same structure must have unique names.

    c) False. **typedef** is used to define aliases for previously defined data types.

    d) False. Structures are always passed to functions by value.

18.3   a) `struct Part {`

```
          int partNumber;
          char partName[ 26 ];
     };
```

    b) `typedef Part * PartPtr;`

    c) `Part a, b[ 10 ], *ptr;`

    d) `cin >> a.partNumber >> a.partName;`

    e) `b[ 3 ] = a;`

    f) `ptr = b;`

    g) `cout << ( ptr + 3 )->partNumber << ' '`

```
               << ( ptr + 3 )->partName << endl;
```

18.4   a) Error: The parentheses that should enclose ***cPtr** have been omitted, causing the order of evaluation of the expression to be incorrect.

    b) Error: The array subscript has been omitted. The expression should be **hearts[10].face**.

    c) Error: A semicolon is required to end a structure definition.

    d) Error: Variables of different structure types cannot be assigned to one another.

18.5 a) `c = toupper( c );`
  b) `cout << '\'' << c << "\' "`
    `    << ( isdigit( c ) ? "is a" : "is not a" )`
    `    << " digit" << endl;`
  c) `cout << atol( "1234567" ) << endl;`
  d) `cout << '\'' << c << "\' "`
    `    << ( iscntrl( c ) ? "is a" : "is not a" )`
    `    << " control character" << endl;`
  e) `ptr = strrchr( s1, c );`
  f) `out << atof( "8.63582" ) << endl;`
  g) `cout << '\'' << c << "\' "`
    `    << ( isalpha( c ) ? "is a" : "is not a" )`
    `    << " letter" << endl;`
  h) `ptr = strstr( s1, s2 );`
  i) `cout << '\'' << c << "\' "`
    `    << ( isprint( c ) ? "is a" : "is not a" )`
    `    << " printing character" << endl;`
  j) `ptr = strpbrk( s1, s2 );`
  k) `ptr = strchr( s1, c );`
  l) `cout << atoi( "-21" ) << endl;`

EXERCISES

18.6   Provide the definition for each of the following structures and unions:

  a) Structure **Inventory**, containing character array **partName[30]**, integer **part-Number**, floating-point **price**, integer **stock** and integer **reorder**.

  b) A structure called **Address** that contains character arrays **streetAddress[25]**, **city[20]**, **state[3]** and **zipCode[6]**.

  c) Structure **Student**, containing arrays **firstName[15]** and **lastName[15]** and variable **homeAddress** of type **struct Address** from part (b).

  d) Structure **Test**, containing 16 bit fields with widths of 1 bit. The names of the bit fields are the letters **a** to **p**.

18.7   Consider the following structure definitions and variable declarations:

```
struct Customer {
   char lastName[ 15 ];
   char firstName[ 15 ];
   int customerNumber;

   struct {
      char phoneNumber[ 11 ];
      char address[ 50 ];
      char city[ 15 ];
      char state[ 3 ];
      char zipCode[ 6 ];
   } personal;

} customerRecord, *customerPtr;

customerPtr = &customerRecord;
```

Write a separate expression that accesses the structure members in each of the following parts:

a) Member **lastName** of structure **customerRecord**.
b) Member **lastName** of the structure pointed to by **customerPtr**.
c) Member **firstName** of structure **customerRecord**.
d) Member **firstName** of the structure pointed to by **customerPtr**.
e) Member **customerNumber** of structure **customerRecord**.
f) Member **customerNumber** of the structure pointed to by **customerPtr**.
g) Member **phoneNumber** of member **personal** of structure **customerRecord**.
h) Member **phoneNumber** of member **personal** of the structure pointed to by **customerPtr**.
i) Member **address** of member **personal** of structure **customerRecord**.
j) Member **address** of member **personal** of the structure pointed to by **customerPtr**.
k) Member **city** of member **personal** of structure **customerRecord**.
l) Member **city** of member **personal** of the structure pointed to by **customerPtr**.
m) Member **state** of member **personal** of structure **customerRecord.**
n) Member **state** of member **personal** of the structure pointed to by **customerPtr**.
o) Member **zipCode** of member **personal** of structure **customerRecord**.
p) Member **zipCode** of member **personal** of the structure pointed to by **customerPtr**.

18.8   Modify the program of Fig. 18.14 to shuffle the cards using a high-performance shuffle, as shown in Fig. 18.2. Print the resulting deck in two-column format, as in Fig. 18.3. Precede each card with its color.

18.9   Write a program that right-shifts an integer variable 4 bits. The program should print the integer in bits before and after the shift operation. Does your system place zeros or ones in the vacated bits?

18.10   If your computer uses 4-byte integers, modify the program of Fig. 18.5 so that it works with 4-byte integers.

18.11   Left-shifting an **unsigned** integer by 1 bit is equivalent to multiplying the value by 2. Write function **power2** that takes two integer arguments, **number** and **pow**, and calculates

   number * 2^pow

Use a shift operator to calculate the result. The program should print the values as integers and as bits.

18.12   The left-shift operator can be used to pack two character values into a 2-byte unsigned integer variable. Write a program that inputs two characters from the keyboard and passes them to function **packCharacters**. To pack two characters into an **unsigned** integer variable, assign the first character to the **unsigned** variable, shift the **unsigned** variable left by 8 bit positions and combine the **unsigned** variable with the second character using the bitwise inclusive-OR operator. The program should output the characters in their bit format before and after they are packed into the **unsigned** integer to prove that the characters are in fact packed correctly in the **unsigned** variable.

18.13   Using the right-shift operator, the bitwise AND operator and a mask, write function **unpackCharacters** that takes the **unsigned** integer from Exercise 18.12 and unpacks it into two characters. To unpack two characters from an **unsigned** 2-byte integer, combine the unsigned integer with the mask **65280** (**11111111 00000000**) and right-shift the result 8 bits. Assign the resulting value to a **char** variable. Then, combine the **unsigned** integer with the mask **255** (**00000000 11111111**). Assign the result to another **char** variable. The program should print the **unsigned** integer in bits before it is unpacked, then print the characters in bits to confirm that they were unpacked correctly.

18.14 If your system uses 4-byte integers, rewrite the program of Exercise 18.12 to pack 4 characters.

18.15 If your system uses 4-byte integers, rewrite the function **unpackCharacters** of Exercise 16.13 to unpack 4 characters. Create the masks you need to unpack the 4 characters by left-shifting the value 255 in the mask variable by 8 bits 0, 1, 2 or 3 times (depending on the byte you are unpacking).

18.16 Write a program that reverses the order of the bits in an **unsigned** integer value. The program should input the value from the user and call function **reverseBits** to print the bits in reverse order. Print the value in bits both before and after the bits are reversed to confirm that the bits are reversed properly.

18.17 Write a program that demonstrates passing an array by value. (Hint: Use a **struct**.) Prove that a copy was passed by modifying the array copy in the called function.

18.18 Write a program that inputs a character from the keyboard and tests the character with each function in the character-handling library. Print the value returned by each function.

18.19 The following program uses function **multiple** to determine whether the integer entered from the keyboard is a multiple of some integer **X**. Examine function **multiple**, then determine the value of **X**.

```
1    // Exercise 18.19: ex18_19.cpp
2    // This program determines if a value is a multiple of X.
3    #include <iostream>
4
5    using std::cout;
6    using std::cin;
7    using std::endl;
8
9    bool multiple( int );
10
11   int main()
12   {
13      int y;
14
15      cout << "Enter an integer between 1 and 32000: ";
16      cin >> y;
17
18      if ( multiple( y ) )
19         cout << y << " is a multiple of X" << endl;
20      else
21         cout << y << " is not a multiple of X" << endl;
22
23      return 0;
24
25   } // end main
26
27   // determine if num is a multiple of X
28   bool multiple( int num )
29   {
30      bool mult = true;
31
32      for ( int i = 0, mask = 1; i < 10; i++, mask <<= 1 )
33
34         if ( ( num & mask ) != 0 ) {
35            mult = false;
```

```
36            break;
37
38        } // end if
39
40      return mult;
41
42 } // end function multiple
```

18.20 What does the following program do?

```cpp
1  // Exercise 18.20: ex18_20.cpp
2  #include <iostream>
3
4  using std::cout;
5  using std::cin;
6  using std::endl;
7  using std::boolalpha;
8
9  bool mystery( unsigned );
10
11 int main()
12 {
13    unsigned x;
14
15    cout << "Enter an integer: ";
16    cin >> x;
17    cout << boolalpha
18         << "The result is " << mystery( x ) << endl;
19
20    return 0;
21
22 } // end main
23
24 // What does this function do?
25 bool mystery( unsigned bits )
26 {
27    const int SHIFT = 8 * sizeof( unsigned ) - 1;
28    const unsigned MASK = 1 << SHIFT;
29    unsigned total = 0;
30
31    for ( int i = 0; i < SHIFT + 1; i++, bits <<= 1 )
32
33       if ( ( bits & MASK ) == MASK )
34          ++total;
35
36    return !( total % 2 );
37
38 } // end function mystery
```

18.21 Write a program that inputs a line of text with **istream** member function **getline** (as in Chapter 12) into character array **s[100]**. Output the line in uppercase letters and lowercase letters.

18.22 Write a program that inputs four strings that represent integers, converts the strings to integers, sums the values and prints the total of the four values.

18.23   Write a program that inputs four strings that represent floating-point values, converts the strings to double values, sums the values and prints the total of the four values.

18.24   Write a program that inputs a line of text and a search string from the keyboard. Using function **strstr**, locate the first occurrence of the search string in the line of text, and assign the location to variable **searchPtr** of type **char ***. If the search string is found, print the remainder of the line of text beginning with the search string. Then, use **strstr** again to locate the next occurrence of the search string in the line of text. If a second occurrence is found, print the remainder of the line of text beginning with the second occurrence. {Hint: The second call to **strstr** should contain the expression **searchPtr + 1** as its first argument.)

18.25   Write a program based on the program of Exercise 16.24 that inputs several lines of text and a search string, then uses function **strstr** to determine the total number of occurrences of the string in the lines of text. Print the result.

18.26   Write a program that inputs several lines of text and a search character and uses function **strchr** to determine the total number of occurrences of the character in the lines of text.

18.27   Write a program based on the program of Exercise 16.26 that inputs several lines of text and uses function **strchr** to determine the total number of occurrences of each letter of the alphabet in the text. Uppercase and lowercase letters should be counted together. Store the totals for each letter in an array, and print the values in tabular format after the totals have been determined.

18.28   The chart in Appendix B shows the numeric code representations for the characters in the ASCII character set. Study this chart, and then state whether each of the following is *true* or *false*:
   a) The letter "**A**" comes before the letter "**B**."
   b) The digit "**9**" comes before the digit "**0**."
   c) The commonly used symbols for addition, subtraction, multiplication and division all come before any of the digits.
   d) The digits come before the letters.
   e) If a sort program sorts strings into ascending sequence, then the program will place the symbol for a right parenthesis before the symbol for a left parenthesis.

18.29   Write a program that reads a series of strings and prints only those strings beginning with the letter "**b**."

18.30   Write a program that reads a series of strings and prints only those strings that end with the letters "**ED**."

18.31   Write a program that inputs an ASCII code and prints the corresponding character. Modify this program so that it generates all possible three-digit codes in the range 000–255 and attempts to print the corresponding characters. What happens when this program is run?

18.32   Using the ASCII character chart in Appendix B as a guide, write your own versions of the character-handling functions in Fig. 18.16.

18.33   Write your own versions of the functions in Fig. 18.20 for converting strings to numbers.

18.34   Write your own versions of the functions in Fig. 18.27 for searching strings.

18.35   Write your own versions of the functions in Fig. 18.34 for manipulating blocks of memory.

18.36   *(Project: A Spelling Checker)* Many popular word-processing software packages have built-in spell checkers. We used spell-checking capabilities in preparing this book and discovered that, no matter how careful we thought we were in writing a chapter, the software was always able to find a few more spelling errors than we were able to catch manually.

In this project, you are asked to develop your own spell-checker utility. We make suggestions to help get you started. You should then consider adding more capabilities. You might find it helpful to use a computerized dictionary as a source of words.

Why do we type so many words with incorrect spellings? In some cases, it is because we simply do not know the correct spelling, so we make a "best guess." In some cases, it is because we transpose two letters (e.g., "defualt" instead of "default"). Sometimes we double-type a letter accidentally (e.g., "hanndy" instead of "handy"). Sometimes we type a nearby key instead of the one we intended (e.g., "biryhday" instead of "birthday"). And so on.

Design and implement a spell-checker program. Your program maintains an array **wordList** of character strings. You can either enter these strings or obtain them from a computerized dictionary.

Your program asks a user to enter a word. The program then looks up that word in the **wordList** array. If the word is present in the array, your program should print "**Word is spelled correctly.**"

If the word is not present in the array, your program should print "**Word is not spelled correctly.**" Then your program should try to locate other words in **wordList** that might be the word the user intended to type. For example, you can try all possible single transpositions of adjacent letters to discover that the word "default" is a direct match to a word in **wordList**. Of course, this implies that your program will check all other single transpositions, such as "edfault," "dfeault," "deafult," "defalut" and "defautl." When you find a new word that matches one in **wordList**, print that word in a message such as "**Did you mean "default?"**."

Implement other tests, such as the replacing of each double letter with a single letter and any other tests you can develop to improve the value of your spell checker.

19

Preprocessor

Objectives

- To use **#include** for developing large programs.
- To use **#define** to create macros and macros with arguments.
- To understand conditional compilation.
- To display error messages during conditional compilation.
- To use assertions to test if the values of expressions are correct.

Hold thou the good; define it well.
Alfred, Lord Tennyson

I have found you an argument; but I am not obliged to find you an understanding.
Samuel Johnson

A good symbol is the best argument, and is a missionary to persuade thousands.
Ralph Waldo Emerson

Conditions are fundamentally sound.
Herbert Hoover [December 1929]

The partisan, when he is engaged in a dispute, cares nothing about the rights of the question, but is anxious only to convince his hearers of his own assertions.
Plato

Outline

19.1   Introduction

19.2   The **#include** Preprocessor Directive

19.3   The **#define** Preprocessor Directive: Symbolic Constants

19.4   The **#define** Preprocessor Directive: Macros

19.5   Conditional Compilation

19.6   The **#error** and **#pragma** Preprocessor Directives

19.7   The **#** and **##** Operators

19.8   Line Numbers

19.9   Predefined Symbolic Constants

19.10 Assertions

Summary • Terminology • Self-Review Exercises • Answers to Self-Review Exercises • Exercises

19.1 Introduction

This chapter introduces the *preprocessor*. Preprocessing occurs before a program is compiled. Some possible actions are inclusion of other files in the file being compiled, definition of *symbolic constants* and *macros*, *conditional compilation* of program code and *conditional execution of preprocessor directives*. All preprocessor directives begin with **#**, and only whitespace characters may appear before a preprocessor directive on a line. Preprocessor directives are not C++ statements, so they do not end in a semicolon (**;**). Preprocessor directives are processed fully before compilation begins.

Common Programming Error 19.1

Placing a semicolon at the end of a preprocessor directive can lead to a variety of errors, depending on the type of preprocessor directive.

Software Engineering Observation 19.1

Many preprocessor features (especially macros) are more appropriate for C programmers than for C++ programmers. C++ programmers should familiarize themselves with the preprocessor, because they might need to work with C legacy code.

19.2 The #include Preprocessor Directive

The **#include** *preprocessor directive* has been used throughout this text. The **#include** directive causes a copy of a specified file to be included in place of the directive. The two forms of the **#include** directive are

```
#include <filename>
#include "filename"
```

The difference between these is the location the preprocessor searches for the file to be included. If the file name is enclosed in angle brackets (**<** and **>**)—used for *standard library header files*—the preprocessor searches for the specified file in an implementation-dependent manner, normally through predesignated directories. If the file name is enclosed in quotes, the preprocessor searches first in the same directory as the file being compiled, then in the same implementation-dependent manner as for a file name enclosed in angle brackets. This method is normally used to include programmer-defined header files.

The **#include** directive is used to include standard header files such as **<iostream>** and **<iomanip>**. The **#include** directive is also used with programs consisting of several source files that are to be compiled together. A *header file* containing declarations and definitions common to the separate program files is often created and included in the file. Examples of such declarations and definitions are classes, structures, unions, enumerations and function prototypes, constants and stream objects (e.g., **cin**).

19.3 The #define Preprocessor Directive: Symbolic Constants

The ***#define*** *preprocessor directive* creates *symbolic constants*—constants represented as symbols—and *macros*—operations defined as symbols. The **#define** preprocessor directive format is

> #define *identifier replacement-text*

When this line appears in a file, all subsequent occurrences (except those inside a string) of *identifier* in that file will be replaced by *replacement-text* before the program is compiled. For example,

> #define PI 3.14159

replaces all subsequent occurrences of the symbolic constant **PI** with the numeric constant **3.14159**. Symbolic constants enable the programmer to create a name for a constant and use the name throughout the program. Later, if the constant needs to be modified throughout the program, it can be modified once in the **#define** preprocessor directive—and when the program is recompiled, all occurrences of the constant in the program will be modified [*Note:* Everything to the right of the symbolic constant name replaces the symbolic constant.] For example, **#define PI = 3.14159** causes the preprocessor to replace every occurrence of **PI** with **= 3.14159**. This is the cause of many subtle logic and syntax errors. Redefining a symbolic constant with a new value is also an error. Note that **const** variables in C++ are preferred over symbolic constants. Constant variables have a specific data type and are visible by name to a debugger. Once a symbolic constant is replaced with its replacement text, only the replacement text is visible to a debugger. A disadvantage of **const** variables is that they might require a memory location of their data type size—symbolic constants do not require any additional memory.

Common Programming Error 19.2

Using symbolic constants in a file other than the file in which the symbolic constants are defined is a syntax error.

Good Programming Practice 19.1

Using meaningful names for symbolic constants helps make programs more self-documenting.

19.4 The #define Preprocessor Directive: Macros

[*Note:* This section is included for the benefit of C++ programmers who will need to work with C legacy code. In C++, macros can often be replaced by templates and inline functions.] A *macro* is an operation defined in a **#define** preprocessor directive. As with symbolic constants, the *macro-identifier* is replaced with the *replacement-text* before the program is compiled. Macros may be defined with or without *arguments*. A macro without arguments is processed like a symbolic constant. In a macro with arguments, the arguments are substituted in the replacement-text, then the macro is *expanded*—i.e., the replacement text replaces the *macro-identifier* and argument list in the program. [*Note:* There is no data type checking for macro arguments. A macro is used simply for text substitution.]

Consider the following macro definition with one argument for the area of a circle:

```
#define CIRCLE_AREA( x ) ( PI * ( x ) * ( x ) )
```

Wherever **CIRCLE_AREA(x)** appears in the file, the value of **x** is substituted for **x** in the replacement text, the symbolic constant **PI** is replaced by its value (defined previously) and the macro is expanded in the program. For example, the statement

```
area = CIRCLE_AREA( 4 );
```

is expanded to

```
area = ( 3.14159 * ( 4 ) * ( 4 ) );
```

Because the expression consists only of constants, at compile time the value of the expression can be evaluated, and the result is assigned to **area** at run time. The parentheses around each **x** in the replacement text and around the entire expression force the proper order of evaluation when the macro argument is an expression. For example, the statement

```
area = CIRCLE_AREA( c + 2 );
```

is expanded to

```
area = ( 3.14159 * ( c + 2 ) * ( c + 2 ) );
```

which evaluates correctly, because the parentheses force the proper order of evaluation. If the parentheses are omitted, the macro expansion is

```
area = 3.14159 * c + 2 * c + 2;
```

which evaluates incorrectly as

```
area = ( 3.14159 * c ) + ( 2 * c ) + 2;
```

because of the rules of operator precedence.

Common Programming Error 19.3

Forgetting to enclose macro arguments in parentheses in the replacement text is an error.

Macro **CIRCLE_AREA** could be defined as a function. Function **circleArea**, as in

```
double circleArea( double x ) { return 3.14159 * x * x; }
```

performs the same calculation as **CIRCLE_AREA**, but the overhead of a function call is associated with function **circleArea**. The advantages of **CIRCLE_AREA** are that macros insert code directly in the program—avoiding function overhead—and the program remains readable because **CIRCLE_AREA** is defined separately and named meaningfully. A disadvantage is that its argument is evaluated twice. Also, every time a macro appears in a program, the macro is expanded. If the macro is large, this produces an increase in program size. Thus, there is a trade-off between execution speed and program size (if disk space is low). Note that **inline** functions (see Chapter 3) are preferred to obtain the performance of macros and the software engineering benefits of functions.

Performance Tip 19.1

Macros can sometimes be used to replace a function call with **inline** *code prior to execution time. This eliminates the overhead of a function call. Inline functions are preferable to macros because they offer the type-checking services of functions.*

The following is a macro definition with two arguments for the area of a rectangle:

```
#define RECTANGLE_AREA( x, y )  ( ( x ) * ( y ) )
```

Wherever **RECTANGLE_AREA(x, y)** appears in the program, the values of **x** and **y** are substituted in the macro replacement text, and the macro is expanded in place of the macro name. For example, the statement

```
rectArea = RECTANGLE_AREA( a + 4, b + 7 );
```

is expanded to

```
rectArea = ( ( a + 4 ) * ( b + 7 ) );
```

The value of the expression is evaluated and assigned to variable **rectArea**.

The replacement text for a macro or symbolic constant is normally any text on the line after the identifier in the **#define** directive. If the replacement text for a macro or symbolic constant is longer than the remainder of the line, a backslash (****) must be placed at the end of each line of the macro (except the last line), indicating that the replacement text continues on the next line.

Symbolic constants and macros can be discarded using the **#undef** *preprocessor directive*. Directive **#undef** "undefines" a symbolic constant or macro name. The *scope* of a symbolic constant or macro is from its definition until it is either undefined with **#undef** or the end of the file is reached. Once undefined, a name can be redefined with **#define**.

Note that expressions with side effects (i.e., variable values are modified) should not be passed to a macro, because macro arguments may be evaluated more than once.

19.5 Conditional Compilation

Conditional compilation enables the programmer to control the execution of preprocessor directives and the compilation of program code. Each of the conditional preprocessor directives evaluates a constant integer expression that will determine whether the code will be compiled. Cast expressions, **sizeof** expressions and enumeration constants cannot be evaluated in preprocessor directives.

The conditional preprocessor construct is much like the **if** selection structure. Consider the following preprocessor code:

```
#ifndef NULL
    #define NULL 0
#endif
```

These directives determine if the symbolic constant **NULL** is already defined. The expression **defined(NULL)** evaluates to **1** if **NULL** is defined, and **0** otherwise. If the result is **0**, **!defined(NULL)** evaluates to **1**, and **NULL** is defined. Otherwise, the **#define** directive is skipped. Every **#if** construct ends with **#endif**. Directives *#ifdef* and *#ifndef* are shorthand for **#if defined(** *name* **)** and **#if !defined(** *name* **)**. A multiple-part conditional preprocessor construct may be tested using the **#elif** (the equivalent of **else if** in an **if** structure) and the **#else** (the equivalent of **else** in an **if** structure) directives.

During program development, programmers often find it helpful to "comment out" large portions of code to prevent it from being compiled. If the code contains C-style comments, **/*** and ***/** cannot be used to accomplish this task, because the first ***/** encountered would terminate the comment. Instead, the programmer can use the following preprocessor construct:

```
#if 0
    code prevented from compiling
#endif
```

To enable the code to be compiled, simply replace the value **0** in the preceding construct with the value **1**.

Conditional compilation is commonly used as a debugging aid. Output statements are often used to print variable values and to confirm the flow of control. These output statements can be enclosed in conditional preprocessor directives so the statements are compiled only until the debugging process is completed. For example,

```
#ifdef DEBUG
    cerr << "Variable x = " << x << endl;
#endif
```

causes the **cerr** statement to be compiled in the program if the symbolic constant **DEBUG** has been defined (**#define DEBUG**) before directive **#ifdef DEBUG**. When debugging is completed, the **#define** directive is removed from the source file and the output statements inserted for debugging purposes are ignored during compilation. In larger programs, it might be desirable to define several different symbolic constants that control the conditional compilation in separate sections of the source file.

Common Programming Error 19.4

Inserting conditionally compiled output statements for debugging purposes in locations where C++ currently expects a single statement can lead to syntax errors and logic errors. In this case, the conditionally compiled statement should be enclosed in a compound statement. Thus, when the program is compiled with debugging statements, the flow of control of the program is not altered.

19.6 The #error and #pragma Preprocessor Directives

The *#error directive*

```
#error tokens
```

prints an implementation-dependent message including the *tokens* specified in the directive. The tokens are sequences of characters separated by spaces. For example,

```
#error 1 - Out of range error
```

contains six tokens. In one popular C++ compiler, for example, when a **#error** directive is processed, the tokens in the directive are displayed as an error message, preprocessing stops and the program does not compile.

The **#pragma** *directive*

```
#pragma tokens
```

causes an implementation-defined action. A pragma not recognized by the implementation is ignored. A particular C++ compiler, for example, might recognize pragmas that enable the programmer to take advantage of that compiler's specific capabilities. For more information on **#error** and **#pragma**, see the documentation for your C++ implementation.

19.7 The # and ## Operators

The **#** and **##** preprocessor operators are available in C++ and ANSI C. The **#** operator causes a replacement-text token to be converted to a string surrounded by quotes. Consider the following macro definition:

```
#define HELLO( x ) cout << "Hello, " #x << endl;
```

When **HELLO(John)** appears in a program file, it is expanded to

```
cout << "Hello, " "John" << endl;
```

The string **"John"** replaces **#x** in the replacement text. Strings separated by whitespace are concatenated during preprocessing, so the above statement is equivalent to

```
cout << "Hello, John" << endl;
```

Note that the **#** operator must be used in a macro with arguments, because the operand of **#** refers to an argument of the macro.

The **##** operator concatenates two tokens. Consider the following macro definition:

```
#define TOKENCONCAT( x, y )  x ## y
```

When **TOKENCONCAT** appears in the program, its arguments are concatenated and used to replace the macro. For example, **TOKENCONCAT(O, K)** is replaced by **OK** in the program. The **##** operator must have two operands.

19.8 Line Numbers

The **#line** *preprocessor directive* causes the subsequent source code lines to be renumbered starting with the specified constant integer value. The directive

```
#line 100
```

starts line numbering from **100**, beginning with the next source code line. A file name can be included in the **#line** directive. The directive

```
#line 100 "file1.cpp"
```

indicates that lines are numbered from **100**, beginning with the next source code line and that the name of the file for the purpose of any compiler messages is **"file1.cpp"**. The directive could be used to help make the messages produced by syntax errors and compiler warnings more meaningful. The line numbers do not appear in the source file.

19.9 Predefined Symbolic Constants

There are six *predefined symbolic constants* (Fig. 19.1). The identifiers for each predefined symbolic constant begin and end with *two* underscores. These identifiers and the **defined** preprocessor operator (Section 19.5) cannot be used in **#define** or **#undef** directives.

19.10 Assertions

The **assert** *macro*—defined in the **<cassert>** header file—tests the value of an expression. If the value of the expression is **0** (false), then **assert** prints an error message and calls function **abort** (of the general utilities library—**<cstdlib>**) to terminate program execution. This is a useful debugging tool for testing whether a variable has a correct value. For example, suppose variable **x** should never be larger than **10** in a program. An assertion may be used to test the value of **x** and print an error message if the value of **x** is incorrect. The statement would be

    assert(x <= 10);

If **x** is greater than **10** when the preceding statement is encountered in a program, an error message containing the line number and file name is printed, and the program terminates. The programmer may then concentrate on this area of the code to find the error. If the symbolic constant **NDEBUG** is defined, subsequent assertions will be ignored. Thus, when assertions are no longer needed (i.e., when debugging is complete), the line

    #define NDEBUG

is inserted in the program file rather than deleting each assertion manually.

Most C++ compilers now include exception handling. C++ programmers prefer using exceptions rather than assertions. But assertions are still valuable for C++ programmers who work with C legacy code.

Symbolic constant	Description
__LINE__	The line number of the current source code line (an integer constant).
__FILE__	The presumed name of the source file (a string).
__DATE__	The date the source file is compiled (a string of the form `"Mmm dd yyyy"` such as `"Aug 19 2002"`).
__STDC__	Indicates whether the program conforms to the ANSI C standard. Contains value 1 if there is full conformance and is undefined otherwise.
__TIME__	The time the source file is compiled (a string literal of the form `"hh:mm:ss"`).
__TIMESTAMP__	The date and time of the last modification to the source file (a string of the form `"Ddd Mmm Date hh:mm:ss yyyy"`, such as `"Mon Aug 19 12:01:55 2002"`).

Fig. 19.1   The predefined symbolic constants.

SUMMARY

- All preprocessor directives begin with **#** and are processed before the program is compiled.

- Only whitespace characters may appear before a preprocessor directive on a line.

- The **#include** directive includes a copy of the specified file. If the file name is enclosed in quotes, the preprocessor begins searching in the same directory as the file being compiled for the file to be included. If the file name is enclosed in angle brackets (**<** and **>**), the search is performed in an implementation-defined manner.

- The **#define** preprocessor directive is used to create symbolic constants and macros.

- A symbolic constant is a name for a constant.

- A macro is an operation defined in a **#define** preprocessor directive. Macros may be defined with or without arguments.

- The replacement text for a macro or symbolic constant is any text remaining on the line after the identifier in the **#define** directive. If the replacement text for a macro or symbolic constant is too long to fit on one line, a backslash (****) is placed at the end of the line, indicating that the replacement text continues on the next line.

- Symbolic constants and macros can be discarded using the **#undef** preprocessor directive. Directive **#undef** "undefines" the symbolic constant or macro name.

- The scope of a symbolic constant or macro is from its definition until it is either undefined with **#undef** or the end of the file is reached.

- Conditional compilation enables the programmer to control the execution of preprocessor directives and the compilation of program code.

- The conditional preprocessor directives evaluate constant integer expressions. Cast expressions, **sizeof** expressions and enumeration constants cannot be evaluated in preprocessor directives.

- Every **#if** construct ends with **#endif**.

- Directives **#ifdef** and **#ifndef** are provided as shorthand for **#if defined**(*name*) and **#if !defined**(*name*).

- A multiple-part conditional preprocessor construct is tested with directives **#elif** and **#else**.

- The **#error** directive prints an implementation-dependent message that includes the tokens specified in the directive and terminates preprocessing and compiling.

- The **#pragma** directive causes an implementation-defined action. If the pragma is not recognized by the implementation, the pragma is ignored.

- The **#** operator causes a replacement text token to be converted to a string surrounded by quotes. The **#** operator must be used in a macro with arguments because the operand of **#** must be an argument of the macro.

- The **##** operator concatenates two tokens. The **##** operator must have two operands.

- The **#line** preprocessor directive causes the subsequent source code lines to be renumbered, starting with the specified constant integer value.

- There are six predefined symbolic constants. Constant **__LINE__** is the line number of the current source code line (an integer). Constant **__FILE__** is the presumed name of the file (a string). Constant **__DATE__** is the date the source file is compiled (a string). Constant **__TIME__** is the time the source file is compiled (a string). Note that each of the predefined symbolic constants begins and ends with two underscores.

- The **assert** macro—defined in the **<cassert>** header file—tests the value of an expression. If the value of the expression is **0** (false), then **assert** prints an error message and calls function **abort** to terminate program execution.

TERMINOLOGY

\ (backslash) continuation character	header file
abort	**#if**
argument	**#ifdef**
assert	**#ifndef**
<cassert>	**#include "filename"**
concatenation preprocessor operator **##**	**#include <filename>**
conditional compilation	**__LINE__**
conditional execution of preprocessor	**#line**
convert-to-string preprocessor directive	macro
<cstdio>	macro with arguments
<cstdlib>	operator **#**
__DATE__	**#pragma**
debugger	predefined symbolic constants
#define	preprocessing directive
directives	preprocessor
#elif	replacement text
#else	scope of a symbolic constant or macro
#endif	standard library header files
#error	symbolic constant
expand a macro	**__TIME__**
__FILE__	**#undef**

SELF-REVIEW EXERCISES

19.1   Fill in the blanks in each of the following:
a)   Every preprocessor directive must begin with _____.
b)   The conditional compilation construct may be extended to test for multiple cases by using the _____ and the _____ directives.
c)   The _____ directive creates macros and symbolic constants.
d)   Only _____ characters may appear before a preprocessor directive on a line.
e)   The _____ directive discards symbolic constant and macro names.
f)   The _____ and _____ directives are provided as shorthand notation for **#if defined(**_name_**)** and **#if !defined(**_name_**)**.
g)   _____ enables the programmer to control the execution of preprocessor directives and the compilation of program code.
h)   The _____ macro prints a message and terminates program execution if the value of the expression the macro evaluates is **0**.
i)   The _____ directive inserts a file in another file.
j)   The _____ operator concatenates its two arguments.
k)   The _____ operator converts its operand to a string.
l)   The character _____ indicates that the replacement text for a symbolic constant or macro continues on the next line.
m)   The _____ directive causes the source code lines to be numbered from the indicated value, beginning with the next source code line.

19.2   Write a program to print the values of the predefined symbolic constants **__LINE__**, **__FILE__**, **__DATE__**, **__TIME__** and **__TIMESTAMP__** listed in Fig. 19.1.

19.3   Write a preprocessor directive to accomplish each of the following:
a)   Define symbolic constant **YES** to have the value **1**.
b)   Define symbolic constant **NO** to have the value **0**.

c) Include the header file **common.h.** The header is found in the same directory as the file being compiled.

d) Renumber the remaining lines in the file, beginning with line number **3000**.

e) If symbolic constant **TRUE** is defined, undefine it, and redefine it as **1**. Do not use **#ifdef**.

f) If symbolic constant **TRUE** is defined, undefine it, and redefine it as **1**. Use the **#ifdef** preprocessor directive.

g) If symbolic constant **ACTIVE** is not equal to **0**, define symbolic constant **INACTIVE** as **0**. Otherwise, define **INACTIVE** as **1**.

h) Define macro **CUBE_VOLUME** that computes the volume of a cube (takes one argument).

ANSWERS TO SELF-REVIEW EXERCISES

19.1 a) **#.** b) **#elif, #else**. c) **#define**. d) whitespace. e) **#undef**. f) **#ifdef, #ifndef**.
g) Conditional compilation. h) **assert**. i) **#include**. j) **##**. k) **#**. l) ****. m) **#line**.

19.2   (See below.)

```
1   // ex19_02.cpp
2   // Self-review exercise 19.2 solution.
3   #include <iostream>
4
5   using std::cout;
6   using std::endl;
7
8   int main()
9   {
10      cout << "__LINE__  = " << __LINE__ << endl
11           << "__FILE__  = " << __FILE__ << endl
12           << "__DATE__  = " << __DATE__ << endl
13           << "__TIME__  = " << __TIME__ << endl
14           << "__TIMESTAMP__ = " << __TIMESTAMP__ << endl;
15
16      return 0;
17
18  } // end main
```

```
__LINE__  = 9
__FILE__  = c:\cpp4e\ch19\ex19_02.CPP
__DATE__  = Jul 17 2002
__TIME__  = 09:55:58
__TIMESTAMP__ = Wed Jul 17 09:55:58 2002
```

19.3   a) **#define** YES 1
        b) **#define** NO 0
        c) **#include** "common.h"
        d) **#line** 3000
        e) **#if defined(**TRUE**)**
               #undef TRUE
               #define TRUE 1
           #endif

f) `#ifdef` `TRUE`
     `#undef` `TRUE`
     `#define` `TRUE 1`
  `#endif`

g) `#if` `ACTIVE`
     `#define` `INACTIVE 0`
  `#else`
     `#define` `INACTIVE 1`
  `#endif`

h) `#define` `CUBE_VOLUME( x )   ( ( x ) * ( x ) * ( x ) )`

EXERCISES

19.4   Write a program that defines a macro with one argument to compute the volume of a sphere. The program should compute the volume for spheres of radii from 1 to 10 and print the results in tabular format. The formula for the volume of a sphere is

$$(\; 4.0 \; / \; 3 \;) \; * \; \pi \; * \; r^3$$

where π is `3.14159`.

19.5   Write a program that produces the following output:

```
The sum of x and y is 13
```

The program should define macro **SUM** with two arguments, **x** and **y**, and use **SUM** to produce the output.

19.6   Write a program that uses macro **MINIMUM2** to determine the smaller of two numeric values. Input the values from the keyboard.

19.7   Write a program that uses macro **MINIMUM3** to determine the smallest of three numeric values. Macro **MINIMUM3** should use macro **MINIMUM2** defined in Exercise 19.6 to determine the smallest number. Input the values from the keyboard.

19.8   Write a program that uses macro **PRINT** to print a string value.

19.9   Write a program that uses macro **PRINTARRAY** to print an array of integers. The macro should receive the array and the number of elements in the array as arguments.

19.10   Write a program that uses macro **SUMARRAY** to sum the values in a numeric array. The macro should receive the array and the number of elements in the array as arguments.

19.11   Rewrite the solutions to Exercise 19.4 to Exercise 19.10 as `inline` functions.

19.12   For each of the following macros, identify the possible problems (if any) when the preprocessor expands the macros:
  a) `#define SQR( x ) x * x`
  b) `#define SQR( x ) ( x * x )`
  c) `#define SQR( x ) ( x ) * ( x )`
  d) `#define SQR( x ) ( ( x ) * ( x ) )`

20

C Legacy Code Topics

Objectives

- To redirect keyboard input to come from a file and redirect screen output to a file.
- To write functions that use variable-length argument lists.
- To process command-line arguments.
- To process unexpected events within a program.
- To allocate memory dynamically for arrays, using C-style dynamic memory allocation.
- To resize memory dynamically allocated, using C-style dynamic memory allocation.

We'll use a signal I have tried and found far-reaching and easy to yell. Waa-hoo!
Zane Grey

It is quite a three-pipe problem.
Sir Arthur Conan Doyle

But yet an union in partition.
William Shakespeare

Outline

20.1   Introduction
20.2   Redirecting Input/Output on UNIX and DOS Systems
20.3   Variable-Length Argument Lists
20.4   Using Command-Line Arguments
20.5   Notes on Compiling Multiple-Source-File Programs
20.6   Program Termination with **exit** and **atexit**
20.7   The **volatile** Type Qualifier
20.8   Suffixes for Integer and Floating-Point Constants
20.9   Signal Handling
20.10 Dynamic Memory Allocation with **calloc** and **realloc**
20.11 The Unconditional Branch: **goto**
20.12 Unions
20.13 Linkage Specifications

Summary • Terminology • Self-Review Exercises • Answers to Self-Review Exercises • Exercises

20.1 Introduction

This chapter presents several topics not ordinarily covered in introductory courses. Many of the capabilities discussed here are specific to particular operating systems, especially UNIX and/or DOS. Much of the material is for the benefit of C++ programmers who will need to work with older C legacy code.

20.2 Redirecting Input/Output on UNIX and DOS Systems

Normally, the input to a program is from the keyboard (standard input), and the output from a program is displayed on the screen (standard output). On most computer systems—UNIX and DOS systems in particular—it is possible to *redirect* inputs to come from a file, and redirect outputs to be placed in a file. Both forms of redirection can be accomplished without using the file-processing capabilities of the standard library.

There are several ways to redirect input and output from the UNIX command line. Consider the executable file **sum** that inputs integers one at a time, keeps a running total of the values until the end-of-file indicator is set, then prints the result. Normally the user inputs integers from the keyboard and enters the end-of-file key combination to indicate that no further values will be input. With input redirection, the input can be stored in a file. For example, if the data are stored in file **input**, the command line

```
$ sum < input
```

causes program **sum** to be executed; the *redirect input symbol (<)* indicates that the data in file **input** (instead of the keyboard) are to be used as input by the program. Redirecting input on a DOS system is performed identically.

Note that **$** is the UNIX command-line prompt. (Some UNIX systems use a **%** prompt.) Redirection is an operating-system function, not another C++ feature.

The second method of redirecting input is *piping*. A *pipe (|)* causes the output of one program to be redirected as the input to another program. Suppose program **random** outputs a series of random integers; the output of **random** can be "piped" directly to program **sum** using the UNIX command line

```
$ random | sum
```

This causes the sum of the integers produced by **random** to be calculated. Piping can be performed in UNIX and DOS.

Program output can be redirected to a file by using the *redirect output symbol (>)*. (The same symbol is used for UNIX and DOS.) For example, to redirect the output of program **random** to a new file called **out**, use

```
$ random > out
```

Finally, program output can be appended to the end of an existing file by using the *append output symbol (>>)*. (The same symbol is used for UNIX and DOS.) For example, to append the output from program **random** to file **out** created in the preceding command line, use the command line

```
$ random >> out
```

20.3 Variable-Length Argument Lists[1]

It is possible to create functions that receive an unspecified number of arguments. An ellipsis (**...**) in a function's prototype indicates that the function receives a variable number of arguments of any type. Note that the ellipsis must always be placed at the end of the parameter list, and there must be at least one argument before the ellipsis. The macros and definitions of the *variable arguments header **<cstdarg>*** (Fig. 20.1) provide the capabilities necessary to build functions with variable-length argument lists.

Identifier	Description
va_list	A type suitable for holding information needed by macros **va_start**, **va_arg** and **va_end**. To access the arguments in a variable-length argument list, an object of type **va_list** must be declared.
va_start	A macro that is invoked before the arguments of a variable-length argument list can be accessed. The macro initializes the object declared with **va_list** for use by the **va_arg** and **va_end** macros.

Fig. 20.1   The type and the macros defined in header **<cstdarg>**. (Part 1 of 2.)

---

1. In C++, programmers use function overloading to accomplish much of what C programmers accomplish with variable-length argument lists.

Identifier	Description
va_arg	A macro that expands to an expression of the value and type of the next argument in the variable-length argument list. Each invocation of **va_arg** modifies the object declared with **va_list** so that the object points to the next argument in the list.
va_end	A macro that performs termination housekeeping in a function whose variable-length argument list was referred to by the **va_start** macro.

Fig. 20.1   The type and the macros defined in header **<cstdarg>**. (Part 2 of 2.)

Figure 20.2 demonstrates function **average** that receives a variable number of arguments. The first argument of **average** is always the number of values to be averaged, and the remainder of the arguments must all be of type **double**.

Function **average** uses all the definitions and macros of header **<cstdarg>**. Object **list**, of type **va_list**, is used by macros **va_start**, **va_arg** and **va_end** to process the variable-length argument list of function **average**. The function invokes **va_start** to initialize object **list** for use in **va_arg** and **va_end**. The macro receives two arguments—object **list** and the identifier of the rightmost argument in the argument list before the ellipsis—**count** in this case (**va_start** uses **count** here to determine where the variable-length argument list begins).

```
1   // Fig. 20.2: fig20_02.cpp
2   // Using variable-length argument lists.
3   #include <iostream>
4
5   using std::cout;
6   using std::endl;
7   using std::ios;
8
9   #include <iomanip>
10
11  using std::setw;
12  using std::setprecision;
13  using std::setiosflags;
14  using std::fixed;
15
16  #include <cstdarg>
17
18  double average( int, ... );
19
20  int main()
21  {
22      double double1 = 37.5;
23      double double2 = 22.5;
24      double double3 = 1.7;
25      double double4 = 10.2;
26
```

Fig. 20.2   Using variable-length argument lists. (Part 1 of 2.)

```
27        cout << fixed << setprecision( 1 ) << "double1 = "
28             << double1 << "\ndouble2 = " << double2 << "\ndouble3 = "
29             << double3 << "\ndouble4 = " << double4 << endl
30             << setprecision( 3 )
31             << "\nThe average of double1 and double2 is "
32             << average( 2, double1, double2 )
33             << "\nThe average of double1, double2, and double3 is "
34             << average( 3, double1, double2, double3 )
35             << "\nThe average of double1, double2, double3"
36             << " and double4 is "
37             << average( 4, double1, double2, double3, double4 )
38             << endl;
39
40        return 0;
41
42   } // end main
43
44   // calculate average
45   double average( int count, ... )
46   {
47        double total = 0;
48        va_list list;  // for storing information needed by va_start
49
50        va_start( list, count );
51
52        // process variable length argument list
53        for ( int i = 1; i <= count; i++ )
54           total += va_arg( list, double );
55
56        // end the va_start
57        va_end( list );
58
59        return total / count;
60
61   } // end function average
```

```
double1 = 37.5
double2 = 22.5
double3 = 1.7
double4 = 10.2

The average of double1 and double2 is 30.000
The average of double1, double2, and double3 is 20.567
The average of double1, double2, double3 and double4 is 17.975
```

Fig. 20.2   Using variable-length argument lists. (Part 2 of 2.)

Next, function **average** repeatedly adds the arguments in the variable-length argument list to the **total**. The value to be added to **total** is retrieved from the argument list by invoking macro **va_arg**. Macro **va_arg** receives two arguments—object **list** and the type of the value expected in the argument list (**double** in this case)—and returns the value of the argument. Function **average** invokes macro **va_end** with object **list** as an argument before returning. Finally, the average is calculated and returned to **main**. Note that we used only **double** arguments for the variable-length portion of the argument list. Actually, any data type or a mixture of data types can be used as long as the proper type is specified each time **va_arg** is used.

Common Programming Error 20.1

Placing an ellipsis in the middle of a function parameter list is a syntax error. An ellipsis may only be placed at the end of the parameter list.

20.4 Using Command-Line Arguments

On many systems—DOS and UNIX in particular—it is possible to pass arguments to **main** from a command line by including parameters **int argc** and **char *argv[]** in the parameter list of **main**. Parameter **argc** receives the number of command-line arguments. Parameter **argv** is an array of **char ***'s pointing to strings in which the actual command-line arguments are stored. Common uses of command-line arguments include printing the arguments, passing options to a program and passing filenames to a program.

Figure 20.3 copies a file into another file one character at a time. The executable file for the program is called **copyFile** (i.e., the executable name for the file). A typical command line for the **copyFile** program on a UNIX system is

```
$ copyFile input output
```

This command line indicates that file **input** is to be copied to file **output**. When the program executes, if **argc** is not **3** (**copyFile** counts as one of the arguments), the program prints an error message and terminates (lines 17–18). Otherwise, array **argv** contains the strings **"copyFile"**, **"input"** and **"output"**. The second and third arguments on the command line are used as file names by the program. The files are opened by creating **ifstream** object **inFile** and **ofstream** object **outFile** (lines 21and 30). If both files are opened successfully, characters are read from file **input** with member function **get** and written to file **output** with member function **put** until the end-of-file indicator for file **input** is set (lines 40–46). Then the program terminates. The result is an exact copy of file **input**. Note that not all computer systems support command-line arguments as easily as UNIX and DOS. Some Macintosh and VMS systems, for example, require special settings for processing command-line arguments. See the manuals for your system for more information on command-line arguments.

```cpp
1   // Fig. 20.3: fig20_03.cpp
2   // Using command-line arguments
3   #include <iostream>
4
5   using std::cout;
6   using std::endl;
7   using std::ios;
8
9   #include <fstream>
10
11  using std::ifstream;
12  using std::ofstream;
```

Fig. 20.3   Using command-line arguments. (Part 1 of 2.)

```
13
14    int main( int argc, char *argv[] )
15    {
16       // check number of command-line arguments
17       if ( argc != 3 )
18          cout << "Usage: copyFile infile_name outfile_name" << endl;
19
20       else {
21          ifstream inFile( argv[ 1 ], ios::in );
22
23          // input file could not be opened
24          if ( !inFile ) {
25             cout << argv[ 1 ] << " could not be opened" << endl;
26             return -1;
27
28          }  // end if
29
30          ofstream outFile( argv[ 2 ], ios::out );
31
32          // output file could not be opened
33          if ( !outFile ) {
34             cout << argv[ 2 ] << " could not be opened" << endl;
35             inFile.close();
36             return -2;
37
38          } // end if
39
40          char c = inFile.get(); // read first character
41
42          while ( inFile ) {
43             outFile.put( c );    // output character
44             c = inFile.get();    // read next character
45
46          }  // end while
47       }  // end else
48
49       return 0;
50
51    }  // end main
```

Fig. 20.3   Using command-line arguments. (Part 2 of 2.)

20.5 Notes on Compiling Multiple-Source-File Programs

As stated earlier in the text, it is normal to build programs that consist of multiple source files (see Chapter 6, Classes and Data Abstraction). There are several considerations when creating programs in multiple files. For example, the definition of a function must be entirely contained in one file—it cannot span two or more files.

In Chapter 3, we introduced the concepts of storage class and scope. We learned that variables declared outside any function definition are of storage class **static** by default and are referred to as global variables. Global variables are accessible to any function defined in the same file after the variable is declared. Global variables also are accessible to functions in other files; however, the global variables must be declared in each file in which they are used. For example, if we define global integer variable **flag** in one file, and refer to it in a second file, the second file must contain the declaration

```
extern int flag;
```

prior to the variable's use in that file. In the preceding declaration, the storage class specifier **extern** indicates to the compiler that variable **flag** is defined either later in the same file or in a different file. The compiler informs the linker that unresolved references to variable **flag** appear in the file. (The compiler does not know where **flag** is defined, so it lets the linker attempt to find **flag**.) If the linker cannot locate a definition of **flag**, a linker error is reported. If a proper global definition is located, the linker resolves the references by indicating where **flag** is located.

Performance Tip 20.1

Global variables increase performance because they can be accessed directly by any function—the overhead of passing data to functions is eliminated.

Software Engineering Observation 20.1

Global variables should be avoided unless application performance is critical, because they violate the principle of least privilege, and they make software difficult to maintain.

Just as **extern** declarations can be used to declare global variables to other program files, function prototypes can be used to declare functions in other program files. (The **extern** specifier is not required in a function prototype.) This is accomplished by including the function prototype in each file in which the function is invoked, then compiling the files together. Function prototypes indicate to the compiler that the specified function is defined either later in the same file or in a different file. The compiler does not attempt to resolve references to such a function—that task is left to the linker. If the linker cannot locate a function definition, an error is generated.

As an example of using function prototypes to extend the scope of a function, consider any program containing the preprocessor directive **#include <cstring>**. This directive includes in a file the function prototypes for functions such as **strcmp** and **strcat**. Other functions in the file can use **strcmp** and **strcat** to accomplish their tasks. The **strcmp** and **strcat** functions are defined for us separately. We do not need to know where they are defined. We are simply reusing the code in our programs. The linker resolves our references to these functions. This process enables us to use the functions in the standard library.

Software Engineering Observation 20.2

Creating programs in multiple source files facilitates software reusability and good software engineering. Functions may be common to many applications. In such instances, those functions should be stored in their own source files, and each source file should have a corresponding header file containing function prototypes. This enables programmers of different applications to reuse the same code by including the proper header file and compiling their application with the corresponding source file.

Portability Tip 20.1

Some systems do not support global variable names or function names of more than 6 characters. This should be considered when writing programs that will be ported to multiple platforms.

It is possible to restrict the scope of a global variable or function to the file in which it is defined. The storage class specifier **static**, when applied to a file scope variable or a function, prevents it from being used by any function that is not defined in the same file. This is referred to as *internal linkage*. Global variables (except those that are **const**) and functions that are not preceded by **static** in their definitions have *external linkage*—they can be accessed in other files if those files contain proper declarations and/or function prototypes.

The global variable declaration

```
static double pi = 3.14159;
```

creates variable **pi** of type **double**, initializes it to **3.14159** and indicates that **pi** is known only to functions in the file in which it is defined.

The **static** specifier is commonly used with utility functions that are called only by functions in a particular file. If a function is not required outside a particular file, the principle of least privilege should be enforced by using **static**. If a function is defined before it is used in a file, **static** should be applied to the function definition. Otherwise, **static** should be applied to the function prototype.

When building large programs from multiple source files, compiling the program becomes tedious if making small changes to one file means that the entire program must be recompiled. Many systems provide special utilities that recompile only the modified program file. On UNIX systems, the utility is called **make**. Utility **make** reads a file called **makefile** that contains instructions for compiling and linking the program. Systems such as Borland C++ and Microsoft Visual C++ for PCs provide **make** utilities and "projects." For more information on **make** utilities, see the manual for your particular system.

20.6 Program Termination with **exit** and **atexit**

The general utilities library (**<cstdlib>**) provides methods of terminating program execution other than a conventional return from function **main**. Function **exit** forces a program to terminate as if it executed normally. The function often is used to terminate a program when an error is detected in the input or if a file to be processed by the program cannot be opened. Function **atexit** *registers* a function in the program to be called when the program terminates by reaching the end of **main** or when **exit** is invoked.

Function **atexit** takes a pointer to a function (i.e., the function name) as an argument. Functions called at program termination cannot have arguments and cannot return a value.

Function **exit** takes one argument. The argument is normally the symbolic constant **EXIT_SUCCESS** or **EXIT_FAILURE**. If **exit** is called with **EXIT_SUCCESS**, the implementation-defined value for successful termination is returned to the calling environment. If **exit** is called with **EXIT_FAILURE**, the implementation-defined value for unsuccessful termination is returned. When function **exit** is invoked, any functions previously registered with **atexit** are invoked in the reverse order of their registration, all streams associated with the program are flushed and closed, and control returns to the host environment. Figure 20.4 tests functions **exit** and **atexit**. The program prompts the user to determine whether the program should be terminated with **exit** or by reaching the end of **main**. Note that function **print** is executed at program termination in each case.

```
1    // Fig. 20.4: fig20_04.cpp
2    // Using the exit and atexit functions
3    #include <iostream>
4
5    using std::cout;
6    using std::endl;
7    using std::cin;
8
9    #include <cstdlib>
10
11   void print();
12
13   int main()
14   {
15      atexit( print );          // register function print
16
17      cout << "Enter 1 to terminate program with function exit"
18           << "\nEnter 2 to terminate program normally\n";
19
20      int answer;
21      cin >> answer;
22
23      // exit if answer is 1
24      if ( answer == 1 ) {
25         cout << "\nTerminating program with function exit\n";
26         exit( EXIT_SUCCESS );
27
28      }  // end if
29
30      cout << "\nTerminating program by reaching the end of main"
31           << endl;
32
33      return 0;
34
35   }  // end main
36
37   // display message before termination
38   void print()
39   {
40      cout << "Executing function print at program termination\n"
41           << "Program terminated" << endl;
42
43   }  // end function print
```

```
Enter 1 to terminate program with function exit
Enter 2 to terminate program normally
2

Terminating program by reaching the end of main
Executing function print at program termination
Program terminated
```

Fig. 20.4   Using functions **exit** and **atexit**. (Part 1 of 2.)

```
Enter 1 to terminate program with function exit
Enter 2 to terminate program normally
1

Terminating program with function exit
Executing function print at program termination
Program terminated
```

Fig. 20.4   Using functions **exit** and **atexit**. (Part 2 of 2.)

20.7 The `volatile` Type Qualifier

The *volatile* type qualifier is applied to a definition of a variable that may be altered from outside the program (i.e., the variable is not completely under the control of the program). Thus, the compiler cannot perform optimizations (such as speeding program execution or reducing memory consumption, for example) that depend on "knowing that a variable's behavior is influenced only by program activities the compiler can observe."

20.8 Suffixes for Integer and Floating-Point Constants

C++ provides integer and floating-point suffixes for specifying the types of integer and floating-point constants. The integer suffixes are: **u** or **U** for an **unsigned** integer, **l** or **L** for a **long** integer, and **ul** or **UL** for an **unsigned long** integer. The following constants are of type **unsigned**, **long** and **unsigned long**, respectively:

```
174u
8358L
28373ul
```

If an integer constant is not suffixed, its type is **int**; if the constant cannot be stored in an **int** it is stored in a **long**.

The floating-point suffixes are **f** or **F** for a **float** and **l** or **L** for a **long double**. The following constants are of type **long double** and **float**, respectively:

```
3.14159L
1.28f
```

A floating-point constant that is not suffixed is of type **double**. A constant with an improper suffix results in either a compiler warning or an error.

20.9 Signal Handling

An unexpected event, or *signal*, can terminate a program prematurely. Some unexpected events include *interrupts* (pressing *Ctrl+C* on a UNIX or DOS system), *illegal instructions*, *segmentation violations, termination orders from the operating system* and *floating-point exceptions* (division by zero or multiplying large floating-point values). The *signal-handling library* provides function *signal* to *trap* unexpected events. Function **signal** receives two arguments—an integer signal number and a pointer to the signal-handling function. Signals can be generated by function *raise*, which takes an integer signal number as an argument. Figure 20.5 summarizes the standard signals defined in header file **<csignal>**. The next example demonstrates functions **signal** and **raise**.

Figure 20.6 traps an interactive signal (**SIGINT**) with function **signal**. The program calls **signal** with **SIGINT** and a pointer to function **signalHandler**. (Remember that the name of a function is a pointer to the function.) Now, when a signal of type **SIGINT** occurs, function **signalHandler** is called, a message is printed and the user is given the option to continue normal execution of the program. If the user wishes to continue execution, the signal handler is reinitialized by calling **signal** again (some systems require the signal handler to be reinitialized), and control returns to the point in the program at which the signal was detected. In this program, function **raise** is used to simulate an interactive signal. A random number between **1** and **50** is chosen. If the number is **25**, then **raise** is called to generate the signal. Normally, interactive signals are initiated outside the program. For example, pressing *Ctrl+C* during program execution on a UNIX or DOS system generates an interactive signal that terminates program execution. Signal handling can be used to trap the interactive signal and prevent the program from terminating.

Signal	Explanation
SIGABRT	Abnormal termination of the program (such as a call to **abort**).
SIGFPE	An erroneous arithmetic operation, such as a divide by zero or an operation resulting in overflow.
SIGILL	Detection of an illegal instruction.
SIGINT	Receipt of an interactive attention signal.
SIGSEGV	An invalid access to storage.
SIGTERM	A termination request sent to the program.

Fig. 20.5   Signals defined in header **<csignal>**.

```
1   // Fig. 20.6: fig20_06.cpp
2   // Using signal handling
3   #include <iostream>
4
5   using std::cout;
6   using std::cin;
7   using std::endl;
8
9   #include <iomanip>
10
11  using std::setw;
12
13  #include <csignal>
14  #include <cstdlib>
15  #include <ctime>
16
17  void signalHandler( int );
```

Fig. 20.6   Using signal handling. (Part 1 of 3.)

```
18
19   int main()
20   {
21      signal( SIGINT, signalHandler );
22      srand( time( 0 ) );
23
24      // create and output random numbers
25      for ( int i = 1; i <= 100; i++ ) {
26         int x = 1 + rand() % 50;
27
28         // raise SIGINT when x is 25
29         if ( x == 25 )
30            raise( SIGINT );
31
32         cout << setw( 4 ) << i;
33
34         // output endl when i is a multiple of 10
35         if ( i % 10 == 0 )
36            cout << endl;
37
38      }  // end for
39
40      return 0;
41
42   }  // end main
43
44   // handles signal
45   void signalHandler( int signalValue )
46   {
47      cout << "\nInterrupt signal (" << signalValue
48           << ") received.\n"
49           << "Do you wish to continue (1 = yes or 2 = no)? ";
50
51      int response;
52
53      cin >> response;
54
55      // check for invalid responses
56      while ( response != 1 && response != 2 ) {
57         cout << "(1 = yes or 2 = no)? ";
58         cin >> response;
59
60      }  // end while
61
62      // determine if it is time to exit
63      if ( response != 1 )
64         exit( EXIT_SUCCESS );
65
66      // call signal and pass it SIGINT and address of signalHandler
67      signal( SIGINT, signalHandler );
68
69   }  // end function signalHandler
```

Fig. 20.6 Using signal handling. (Part 2 of 3.)

```
  1   2   3   4   5   6   7   8   9  10
 11  12  13  14  15  16  17  18  19  20
 21  22  23  24  25  26  27  28  29  30
 31  32  33  34  35  36  37  38  39  40
 41  42  43  44  45  46  47  48  49  50
 51  52  53  54  55  56  57  58  59  60
 61  62  63  64  65  66  67  68  69  70
 71  72  73  74  75  76  77  78  79  80
 81  82  83  84  85  86  87  88  89  90
 91  92  93  94  95  96  97  98  99
Interrupt signal (2) received.
Do you wish to continue (1 = yes or 2 = no)? 1
 100
```

```
  1   2   3   4
Interrupt signal (2) received.
Do you wish to continue (1 = yes or 2 = no)? 2
```

Fig. 20.6   Using signal handling. (Part 3 of 3.)

20.10 Dynamic Memory Allocation with `calloc` and `realloc`

In Chapter 7, we discussed C++-style dynamic memory allocation with **new** and **delete**. C++ programmers should use **new** and **delete**, rather than C's functions **malloc** and **free** (header **<cstdlib>**). However, most C++ programmers will find themselves reading a great deal of C legacy code, and therefore we include this additional discussion on C-style dynamic memory allocation.

The general utilities library (**<cstdlib>**) provides two other functions for dynamic memory allocation—**calloc** and **realloc**. These functions can be used to create and modify *dynamic arrays*. As shown in Chapter 5, Pointers and Strings, a pointer to an array can be subscripted like an array. Thus, a pointer to a contiguous portion of memory created by **calloc** can be manipulated as an array. Function **calloc** dynamically allocates memory for an array and initializes the memory to zeroes. The prototype for **calloc** is

```
void *calloc( size_t nmemb, size_t size );
```

It receives two arguments—the number of elements (**nmemb**) and the size of each element (**size**)—and initializes the elements of the array to zero. The function returns a pointer to the allocated memory or a null pointer (**0**) if the memory is not allocated.

Function **realloc** changes the size of an object allocated by a previous call to **malloc**, **calloc** or **realloc**. The original object's contents are not modified, provided that the memory allocated is larger than the amount allocated previously. Otherwise, the contents are unchanged up to the size of the new object. The prototype for **realloc** is

```
void *realloc( void *ptr, size_t size );
```

Function **realloc** takes two arguments—a pointer to the original object (**ptr**) and the new size of the object (**size**). If **ptr** is **0**, **realloc** works identically to **malloc**. If

size is **0** and **ptr** is not **0**, the memory for the object is freed. Otherwise, if **ptr** is not **0** and size is greater than zero, **realloc** tries to allocate a new block of memory. If the new space cannot be allocated, the object pointed to by **ptr** is unchanged. Function **realloc** returns either a pointer to the reallocated memory or a null pointer.

20.11 The Unconditional Branch: goto

Throughout the text we have stressed the importance of using structured programming techniques to build reliable software that is easy to debug, maintain and modify. In some cases, performance is more important than strict adherence to structured-programming techniques. In these cases, some unstructured programming techniques may be used. For example, we can use **break** to terminate execution of a repetition structure before the loop continuation condition becomes false. This saves unnecessary repetitions of the loop if the task is completed before loop termination.

Another instance of unstructured programming is the *goto statement*—an unconditional branch. The result of the **goto** statement is a change in the flow of control of the program to the first statement after the *label* specified in the **goto** statement. A label is an identifier followed by a colon. A label must appear in the same function as the **goto** statement that refers to it. Figure 20.7 uses **goto** statements to loop 10 times and print the counter value each time. After initializing **count** to **1**, the program tests **count** to determine whether it is greater than **10**. (The label **start** is skipped, because labels do not perform any action.) If so, control is transferred from the **goto** to the first statement after the label **end**. Otherwise, **count** is printed and incremented, and control is transferred from the **goto** to the first statement after the label **start**.

```cpp
1   // Fig. 20.7: fig20_07.cpp
2   // Using goto.
3   #include <iostream>
4
5   using std::cout;
6   using std::endl;
7
8   #include <iomanip>
9
10  using std::left;
11  using std::setw;
12
13  int main()
14  {
15     int count = 1;
16
17     start:  // label
18
19        // goto end when count exceeds 10
20        if ( count > 10 )
21           goto end;
22
23        cout << setw( 2 ) << left << count;
```

Fig. 20.7   Using **goto**. (Part 1 of 2.)

```
24          ++count;
25
26          // goto start on line 17
27          goto start;
28
29     end:   // label
30
31          cout << endl;
32
33          return 0;
34
35   }   // end main
```

```
1   2   3   4   5   6   7   8   9   10
```

Fig. 20.7   Using **goto**. (Part 2 of 2.)

In Chapter 2, we stated that only three control structures are required to write any program—sequence, selection and repetition. When the rules of structured programming are followed, it is possible to create deeply nested control structures from which it is difficult to escape efficiently. Some programmers use **goto** statements in such situations as a quick exit from a deeply nested structure. This eliminates the need to test multiple conditions to escape from a control structure.

Performance Tip 20.2

*The **goto** statement can be used to exit deeply nested control structures efficiently.*

Software Engineering Observation 20.3

*The **goto** statement should be used only in performance-oriented applications. The **goto** statement is unstructured and can lead to programs that are more difficult to debug, maintain and modify.*

20.12 Unions

A *union* (defined with keyword **union**) is a region of memory that, over time, can contain objects of a variety of types. However, at any moment, a **union** can contain a maximum of one object, because the members of a **union** share the same storage space. It is the programmer's responsibility to ensure that the data in a **union** is referenced with a member name of the proper data type.

Common Programming Error 20.2

*The result of referencing a **union** member other than the last one stored is undefined. It treats the stored data as a different type.*

Portability Tip 20.2

*If data are stored in a **union** as one type and referenced as another type, the results are implementation-dependent.*

At different times during a program's execution, some objects might not be relevant, while one other object is—so a **union** shares the space instead of wasting storage on objects that are not being used. The number of bytes used to store a **union** must be at least enough to hold the largest member.

Performance Tip 20.3

*Using **union**s conserves storage.*

Portability Tip 20.3

*The amount of storage required to store a **union** is implementation-dependent.*

A **union** is declared in the same format as a **struct** or a **class**. For example,

```
union Number {
    int x;
    double y;
};
```

indicates that **Number** is a **union** type with members **int x** and **double y**. The **union** definition must precede all functions in which it will be used.

Software Engineering Observation 20.4

*As with a **struct** or a **class** declaration, a **union** declaration simply creates a new type. Placing a **union** or **struct** declaration outside any function does not create a global variable.*

The only valid built-in operations that can be performed on a **union** are assigning a **union** to another **union** of the same type, taking the address (**&**) of a **union** and accessing **union** members using the structure member operator (**.**) and the structure pointer operator (**->**). **union**s cannot be compared.

Common Programming Error 20.3

*Comparing **union**s is a syntax error, because the compiler does not know which member of each is active and hence which member of one to compare to which member of the other.*

A **union** is similar to a class in that it can have a constructor to initialize any of its members. A **union** that has no constructor can be initialized with another **union** of the same type, with an expression of the type of the first member of the **union** or with an initializer (enclosed in braces) of the type of the first member of the **union**. **union**s can have other member functions, such as destructors, but a **union**'s member functions cannot be declared **virtual**. The members of a **union** are **public** by default.

Common Programming Error 20.4

*Initializing a **union** in a declaration with a value or an expression whose type is different from the type of the **union**'s first member is a syntax error.*

A **union** cannot be used as a base class in inheritance (i.e., classes cannot be derived from **union**s). **union**s can have objects as members only if these objects do not have a constructor, a destructor or an overloaded assignment operator. None of a **union**'s data members can be declared **static**.

Figure 20.8 uses the variable **value** of type **union Number** to display the value stored in the **union** as both an **int** and a **double**. The program output is implementation-depen-

```
1   // Fig. 20.8: fig20_08.cpp
2   // An example of a union.
3   #include <iostream>
4
5   using std::cout;
6   using std::endl;
7
8   // define union Number
9   union Number {
10     int integer1;
11     double double1;
12
13  };  // end union Number
14
15  int main()
16  {
17     Number value;  // union variable
18
19     value.integer1 = 100;  // assign 100 to member integer1
20
21     cout << "Put a value in the integer member\n"
22          << "and print both members.\nint:    "
23          << value.integer1 << "\ndouble: " << value.double1
24          << endl;
25
26     value.double1 = 100.0;  // assign 100.0 to member double1
27
28     cout << "Put a value in the floating member\n"
29          << "and print both members.\nint:    "
30          << value.integer1 << "\ndouble: " << value.double1
31          << endl;
32
33     return 0;
34
35  }  // end main
```

```
Put a value in the integer member
and print both members.
int:    100
double: -9.25596e+061
Put a value in the floating member
and print both members.
int:    0
double: 100
```

Fig. 20.8   Printing the value of a **union** in both member data types.

dent. The program output shows that the internal representation of a **double** value can be quite different from the representation of an **int**.

An *anonymous* **union** is a **union** without a type name that does not attempt to define objects or pointers before its terminating semicolon. Such a **union** does not create a type, but does create an unnamed object. An anonymous **union**'s members may be accessed directly in the scope in which the anonymous **union** is declared just as are any other local variable—there is no need to use the dot (**.**) or arrow (**->**) operators.

Anonymous **union**s have some restrictions. Anonymous **union**s can contain only data members. All members of an anonymous **union** must be **public**. And an anonymous **union** declared globally (i.e., at file scope) must be explicitly declared **static**. Figure 20.9 illustrates the use of an anonymous **union**.

```cpp
1   // Fig. 20.9: fig20_09.cpp
2   // Using an anonymous union.
3   #include <iostream>
4
5   using std::cout;
6   using std::endl;
7
8   int main()
9   {
10      // declare an anonymous union
11      // members integer1, double1 and charPtr share the same space
12      union {
13         int integer1;
14         double double1;
15         char *charPtr;
16
17      };  // end anonymous union
18
19      // declare local variables
20      int integer2 = 1;
21      double double2 = 3.3;
22      char *char2Ptr = "Anonymous";
23
24      // assign value to each union member
25      // successively and print each
26      cout << integer2 << ' ';
27      integer1 = 2;
28      cout << integer1 << endl;
29
30      cout << double2 << ' ';
31      double1 = 4.4;
32      cout << double1 << endl;
33
34      cout << char2Ptr << ' ';
35      charPtr = "union";
36      cout << charPtr << endl;
37
38      return 0;
39
40   }  // end main
```

```
1 2
3.3 4.4
Anonymous union
```

Fig. 20.9   Using an anonymous **union**.

20.13 Linkage Specifications

It is possible from a C++ program to call functions written and compiled with a C compiler. As stated in Section 3.20, C++ specially encodes function names for type-safe linkage. C, however, does not encode its function names. Thus, a function compiled in C will not be recognized when an attempt is made to link C code with C++ code, because the C++ code expects a specially encoded function name. C++ enables the programmer to provide *linkage specifications* to inform the compiler that a function was compiled on a C compiler and to prevent the name of the function from being encoded by the C++ compiler. Linkage specifications are useful when large libraries of specialized functions have been developed, and the user either does not have access to the source code for recompilation into C++ or does not have time to convert the library functions from C to C++.

To inform the compiler that one or several functions have been compiled in C, write the function prototypes as follows:

```
extern "C" function prototype      // single function

extern "C"    // multiple functions
{
    function prototypes
}
```

These declarations inform the compiler that the specified functions are not compiled in C++, so name encoding should not be performed on the functions listed in the linkage specification. These functions can then be linked properly with the program. C++ environments normally include the standard C libraries and do not require the programmer to use linkage specifications for those functions.

SUMMARY

- On many systems—UNIX and DOS systems in particular—it is possible to redirect input to a program and output from a program. Input is redirected from the UNIX and DOS command lines using the redirect input symbol (**<**) or by using a pipe (**|**). Output is redirected from the UNIX and DOS command lines using the redirect output symbol (**>**) or the append output symbol (**>>**). The redirect output symbol simply stores the program output in a file, and the append output symbol appends the output to the end of a file.

- The macros and definitions of the variable arguments header **<cstdarg>** provide the capabilities necessary to build functions with variable-length argument lists.

- An ellipsis (**...**) in a function prototype indicates that the function receives a variable number of arguments.

- Type **va_list** is suitable for holding information needed by macros **va_start**, **va_arg** and **va_end**. To access the arguments in a variable-length argument list, an object of type **va_list** must be declared.

- Macro **va_start** is invoked before the arguments of a variable-length argument list can be accessed. The macro initializes the object declared with **va_list** for use by macros **va_arg** and **va_end**.

- Macro **va_arg** expands to an expression of the value and type of the next argument in the variable-length argument list. Each invocation of **va_arg** modifies the **va_list** object so that the object points to the next argument in the list.

- Macro **va_end** facilitates a normal return from a function whose variable argument list was referred to by the **va_start** macro.

- On many systems—DOS and UNIX in particular—it is possible to pass command-line arguments to **main** by including in **main**'s parameter list the parameters **int argc** and **char *argv[]**. Parameter **argc** is the number of command-line arguments. Parameter **argv** is an array of **char ***'s containing the command-line arguments.

- The definition of a function must be entirely contained in one file—it cannot span two or more files.

- Global variables must be declared in each file in which they are used.

- Function prototypes can be used to declare functions in other program files. (The **extern** specifier is not required in a function prototype.) This is accomplished by including the function prototype in each file in which the function is invoked, then compiling the files together.

- The storage class specifier **static**, when applied to a file scope variable or a function, prevents it from being used by any function that is not defined in the same file. This is referred to as internal linkage. Global variables and functions that are not preceded by **static** in their definitions have external linkage—they can be accessed in other files if those files contain proper declarations and/or function prototypes.

- The **static** specifier is commonly used with utility functions that are called only by functions in a particular file. If a function is not required outside a particular file, the principle of least privilege should be enforced by using **static**.

- When building large programs from multiple source files, compiling the program becomes tedious if making small changes to one file means that the entire program must be recompiled. Many systems provide special utilities that recompile only the modified program file. On UNIX systems, the utility is called **make**. Utility **make** reads a file called **makefile** that contains instructions for compiling and linking the program.

- Function **exit** forces a program to terminate as if it had executed normally.

- Function **atexit** registers a function in a program to be called upon normal termination of the program—i.e., either when the program terminates by reaching the end of **main**, or when **exit** is invoked.

- Function **atexit** takes a pointer to a function (i.e., a function name) as an argument. Functions called at program termination cannot have arguments and cannot return a value.

- Function **exit** takes one argument—normally the symbolic constant **EXIT_SUCCESS** or the symbolic constant **EXIT_FAILURE**. If **exit** is called with **EXIT_SUCCESS**, the implementation-defined value for successful termination is returned to the calling environment. If **exit** is called with **EXIT_FAILURE**, the implementation-defined value for unsuccessful termination is returned.

- When function **exit** is invoked, any functions registered with **atexit** are invoked in the reverse order of their registration, all streams associated with the program are flushed and closed and control returns to the host environment.

- The **volatile** qualifier is used to prevent optimizations of a variable, because it can be modified from outside the program's scope.

- C++ provides integer and floating-point suffixes for specifying the types of integer and floating-point constants. The integer suffixes are **u** or **U** for an **unsigned** integer, **l** or **L** for a **long** integer and **ul** or **UL** for an **unsigned long** integer. If an integer constant is not suffixed, its type is determined by the first type capable of storing a value of that size (first **int**, then **long int**). The floating-point suffixes are **f** or **F** for a **float** and **l** or **L** for a **long double**. A floating-point constant that is not suffixed is of type **double**.

- The signal-handling library provides the capability to register a function to trap unexpected events with function **signal**. Function **signal** receives two arguments—an integer signal number and a pointer to the signal handling function.

- Signals can also be generated with function **raise** and an integer argument.

- The general-utilities library (**cstdlib**) provides functions **calloc** and **realloc** for dynamic memory allocation. These functions can be used to create dynamic arrays.

- Function **calloc** receives two arguments—the number of elements (**nmemb**) and the size of each element (**size**)—and initializes the elements of the array to zero. The function returns a pointer to the allocated memory or if the memory is not allocated, the function returns a null pointer.

- Function **realloc** changes the size of an object allocated by a previous call to **malloc**, **calloc** or **realloc**. The original object's contents are not modified, provided that the amount of memory allocated is larger than the amount allocated previously.

- Function **realloc** takes two arguments—a pointer to the original object (**ptr**) and the new size of the object (**size**). If **ptr** is null, **realloc** works identically to **malloc**. If **size** is **0** and the pointer received is not null, the memory for the object is freed. Otherwise, if **ptr** is not null and **size** is greater than zero, **realloc** tries to allocate a new block of memory for the object. If the new space cannot be allocated, the object pointed to by **ptr** is unchanged. Function **realloc** returns either a pointer to the reallocated memory or a null pointer.

- The result of the **goto** statement is a change in the program's flow of control. Program execution continues at the first statement after the label in the **goto** statement.

- A label is an identifier followed by a colon. A label must appear in the same function as the **goto** statement that refers to it.

- A **union** is a data type whose members share the same storage space. The members can be almost any type. The storage reserved for a **union** is large enough to store its largest member. In most cases, **union**s contain two or more data types. Only one member, and thus one data type, can be referenced at a time.

- A **union** is declared in the same format as a structure.

- A **union** can be initialized only with a value of the type of its first member.

- C++ enables the programmer to provide linkage specifications to inform the compiler that a function was compiled on a C compiler and to prevent the name of the function from being encoded by the C++ compiler.

- To inform the compiler that one or several functions have been compiled in C, write the function prototypes as follows:

```
extern "C" function prototype   // single function

extern "C"    // multiple functions
{
    function prototypes
}
```

These declarations inform the compiler that the specified functions are not compiled in C++, so name encoding should not be performed on the functions listed in the linkage specification. These functions can then be linked properly with the program.

- C++ environments normally include the standard C libraries and do not require the programmer to use linkage specifications for those functions.

TERMINOLOGY

append output symbol **>>**

argv

atexit

calloc

command-line arguments

const

<csignal>

<cstdarg>

dynamic arrays

event

exit

EXIT_FAILURE

EXIT_SUCCESS

extern "C"

extern storage class specifier

external linkage

float suffix (**f** or **F**)

floating-point exception

free

goto statement

I/O redirection

illegal instruction

internal linkage

interrupt

long double suffix (**l** or **L**)

long integer suffix (**l** or **L**)

make

makefile

malloc

pipe **|**

piping

raise

realloc

redirect input symbol **<**

redirect output symbol **>**

segmentation violation

signal

signal-handling library

static storage class specifier

trap

union

unsigned integer suffix (**u** or **U**)

unsigned long integer suffix (**ul** or **UL**)

va_arg

va_end

va_list

va_start

variable-length argument list

volatile

SELF-REVIEW EXERCISES

20.1 Fill in the blanks in each of the following:

a) Symbol _____ redirects input data from the keyboard to come from a file.

b) The _____ symbol is used to redirect the screen output to be placed in a file.

c) The _____ symbol is used to append the output of a program to the end of a file.

d) A _____ is used to direct the output of a program as the input of another program.

e) An _____ in the parameter list of a function indicates that the function can receive a variable number of arguments.

f) Macro _____ must be invoked before the arguments in a variable-length argument list can be accessed.

g) Macro _____ is used to access the individual arguments of a variable-length argument list.

h) Macro _____ performs termination housekeeping in a function whose variable argument list was referred to by macro **va_start**.

i) Argument _____ of **main** receives the number of arguments in a command line.

j) Argument _____ of **main** stores command-line arguments as character strings.

k) The UNIX utility _____ reads a file called _____ that contains instructions for compiling and linking a program consisting of multiple source files. The utility recompiles a file only if the file has been modified since it was last compiled.

l) Function _____ forces a program to terminate execution.

m) Function _____ registers a function to be called upon normal termination of the program.

n) An integer or floating-point _____ can be appended to an integer or floating-point constant to specify the exact type of the constant.

o) Function _____ can be used to register a function to trap unexpected events.

p) Function _____ generates a signal from within a program.

q) Function _____ dynamically allocates memory for an array and initializes the elements to zero.

r) Function _____ changes the size of a block of dynamically allocated memory.

s) A _____ is an entity containing a collection of variables that occupy the same memory, but at different times.

t) The _____ keyword is used to introduce a union definition.

ANSWERS TO SELF-REVIEW EXERCISES

20.1 a) redirect input (`<`). b) redirect output (`>`). c) append output (`>>`). d) pipe (`|`). e) ellipsis (`...`). f) `va_start`. g) `va_arg`. h) `va_end`. i) `argc`. j) `argv`. k) `make`, `makefile`. l) `exit`. m) `atexit`. n) suffix. o) `signal`. p) `raise`. q) `calloc`. r) `realloc`. s) union. t) `union`.

EXERCISES

20.2 Write a program that calculates the product of a series of integers that are passed to function **product** using a variable-length argument list. Test your function with several calls, each with a different number of arguments.

20.3 Write a program that prints the command-line arguments of the program.

20.4 Write a program that sorts an integer array into ascending order or descending order. The program should use command-line arguments to pass either argument **-a** for ascending order or **-d** for descending order. [*Note*: This is the standard format for passing options to a program in UNIX.]

20.5 Read the manuals for your system to determine what signals are supported by the signal-handling library (`<csignal>`). Write a program with signal handlers for the signals **SIGABRT** and **SIGINT**. The program should test the trapping of these signals by calling function **abort** to generate a signal of type **SIGABRT** and by pressing *Ctrl+C* to generate a signal of type **SIGINT**.

20.6 Write a program that dynamically allocates an array of integers. The size of the array should be input from the keyboard. The elements of the array should be assigned values input from the keyboard. Print the values of the array. Next, reallocate the memory for the array to half of the current number of elements. Print the values remaining in the array to confirm that they match the first half of the values in the original array.

20.7 Write a program that takes two file names as command-line arguments, reads the characters from the first file one at a time and writes the characters in reverse order to the second file.

20.8 Write a program that uses **goto** statements to simulate a nested looping structure that prints a square of asterisks as shown in Fig. 20.10. The program should use only the following three output statements:

```
cout << '*';
cout << ' ';
cout << endl;
```

```
*****
*   *
*   *
*   *
*****
```

Fig. 20.10 Sample output for Exercise 20.8.

20.9   Provide the definition for **union Data** containing **char charcter1**, **short short1**, **long long1**, **float float1** and **double double1**.

20.10   Create **union Integer** with members **char charcter1**, **short short1**, **int integer1** and **long long1**. Write a program that inputs values of type **char, short, int** and **long** and stores the values in **union** variables of type **union Integer**. Each **union** variable should be printed as a **char**, a **short**, an **int** and a **long**. Do the values always print correctly?

20.11   Create **union FloatingPoint** with members **float float1, double double1** and **long double longDouble**. Write a program that inputs values of type **float, double** and **long double** and stores the values in **union** variables of type **union FloatingPoint**. Each **union** variable should be printed as a **float**, a **double** and a **long double**. Do the values always print correctly?

20.12   Given the **union**

```
union A {
    double y;
    char *zPtr;
};
```

which of the following are correct statements for initializing the **union**?

a) **A p = B;   // B is of same type as A**
b) **A q = x;   // x is a double**
c) **A r = 3.14159;**
d) **A s = { 79.63 };**
e) **A t = { "Hi There!" };**
f) **A u = { 3.14159, "Pi" };**
g) **A v = { y = −7.843, zPtr = &x };**

Standard Template Library (STL)

Objectives

- To be able to use the template STL containers, container adapters and "near containers."
- To be able to program with the dozens of STL algorithms.
- To understand how algorithms use iterators to access the elements of STL containers.
- To become familiar with the STL resources available on the Internet and the World Wide Web.

The shapes a bright container can contain!
Theodore Roethke

Journey over all the universe in a map.
Miguel de Cervantes

O! thou hast damnable iteration, and art indeed able to corrupt a saint.
William Shakespeare

That great dust heap called "history."
Augustine Birrell

The historian is a prophet in reverse.
Friedrich von Schlegel

Attempt the end, and never stand to doubt;
Nothing's so hard but search will find it out.
Robert Herrick

Push on — keep moving.
Thomas Morton

Outline

21.1   Introduction to the Standard Template Library (STL)

       21.1.1   Introduction to Containers

       21.1.2   Introduction to Iterators

       21.1.3   Introduction to Algorithms

21.2   Sequence Containers

       21.2.1   `vector` Sequence Container

       21.2.2   `list` Sequence Container

       21.2.3   `deque` Sequence Container

21.3   Associative Containers

       21.3.1   `multiset` Associative Container

       21.3.2   `set` Associative Container

       21.3.3   `multimap` Associative Container

       21.3.4   `map` Associative Container

21.4   Container Adapters

       21.4.1   `stack` Adapter

       21.4.2   `queue` Adapter

       21.4.3   `priority_queue` Adapter

21.5   Algorithms

       21.5.1   `fill`, `fill_n`, `generate` and `generate_n`

       21.5.2   `equal`, `mismatch` and `lexicographical_compare`

       21.5.3   `remove`, `remove_if`, `remove_copy` and `remove_copy_if`

       21.5.4   `replace`, `replace_if`, `replace_copy` and `replace_copy_if`

       21.5.5   Mathematical Algorithms

       21.5.6   Basic Searching and Sorting Algorithms

       21.5.7   `swap`, `iter_swap` and `swap_ranges`

       21.5.8   `copy_backward`, `merge`, `unique` and `reverse`

       21.5.9   `inplace_merge`, `unique_copy` and `reverse_copy`

       21.5.10   Set Operations

       21.5.11   `lower_bound`, `upper_bound` and `equal_range`

Outline

21.5.12 Heapsort

21.5.13 `min` and `max`

21.5.14 Algorithms Not Covered in This Chapter

21.6   Class `bitset`

21.7   Function Objects

21.8   STL Internet and Web Resources

Summary • Terminology • Self-Review Exercises • Answers to Self-Review Exercises • Exercises • Recommended Reading

21.1 Introduction to the Standard Template Library (STL)

Throughout this book, we have discussed the importance of software reuse. Recognizing that many data structures and algorithms commonly were used by C++ programmers, the C++ standard committee added the *Standard Template Library (STL)* to the C++ Standard Library. The STL defines powerful, template-based, reusable components that implement many common data structures and algorithms used to process those data structures. The STL offers proof of concept for generic programming with templates—introduced in Chapter 11, Templates and demonstrated in detail in Chapter 17, Data Structures.

The STL was developed by Alexander Stepanov and Meng Lee at Hewlett-Packard and is based on their research in the field of generic programming, with significant contributions from David Musser. As you will see, STL is cleverly conceived and is designed for performance and flexibility.

This chapter introduces the STL and discusses its three key components—*containers* (popular templatized data structures), *iterators* and *algorithms*. The STL containers are data structures capable of storing objects of any data type. We will see that there are three container categories—*first-class containers*, *adapters* and *near containers*.

Performance Tip 21.1

For any particular application, several different STL containers might be appropriate. Select the most appropriate container that achieves the best performance (i.e., balance of speed and size) for that application. Efficiency was a crucial consideration in STL's design.

Performance Tip 21.2

Standard Library capabilities are implemented to operate efficiently across many applications. For some applications with unique performance requirements, it might be necessary to write your own customized implementations.

Each STL container has associated member functions. A subset of these member functions is defined in all STL containers. We illustrate most of this common functionality in our examples of STL containers **vector** (a dynamically resizable array), **list** (a linked list) and **deque** (a double-ended queue). We introduce container-specific functionality in examples for each of the other STL containers.

STL iterators, which have properties similar to those of pointers, are used by programs to manipulate the STL-container elements. In fact, standard arrays can be manipulated as STL containers, using standard pointers as iterators. We will see that manipulating containers with iterators is convenient and provides tremendous expressive power when combined with STL algorithms—in some cases, reducing many lines of code to a single statement. There are five categories of iterators that we discuss in Section 21.1.2 and use throughout this chapter.

STL algorithms are functions that perform such common data manipulations as searching, sorting and comparing elements (or entire data structures). There are approximately 70 algorithms implemented in the STL. Most of these algorithms use iterators to access container elements. Each algorithm has minimum requirements for the types of iterators that can be used with the algorithm. We will see that each first-class container supports specific iterator types, some of which are more powerful than others. A container's supported iterator type determines whether the container can be used with a specific algorithm. Iterators encapsulate the mechanism used to access container elements. This encapsulation enables many of the STL algorithms to be applied to several containers without regard for the underlying container implementation. As long as a container's iterators support the minimum requirements of the algorithm, then the algorithm can process that container's elements. This also enables programmers to create new algorithms that can process the elements of multiple different container types.

Software Engineering Observation 21.1

The STL approach allows general programs to be written so that the code does not depend on the underlying container. Such a programming style is called generic programming.

In Chapter 17, we studied data structures. We built linked lists, queues, stacks and trees. We carefully wove link objects together with pointers. Pointer-based code is complex, and the slighest omission or oversight can lead to serious memory-access violations and memory-leak errors with no compiler complaints. Implementing additional data structures, such as deques, priority queues, sets and maps. requires substantial additional work. In addition, if many programmers on a large project implement similar containers and algorithms for different tasks, the code becomes difficult to modify, maintain and debug. An advantage of the STL is that programmers can reuse the STL containers, iterators and algorithms to implement common data representations and manipulations. This reuse results in substantial development-time and resource savings.

Software Engineering Observation 21.2

Avoid reinventing the wheel; program with the reusable components of the C++ Standard Library. STL includes many of the most popular data structures as containers and provides various popular algorithms programs use to process data in these containers.

Testing and Debugging Tip 21.1

When programming pointer-based data structures and algorithms, we must do our own debugging and testing to be sure our data structures, classes and algorithms function properly. It is easy to make errors when manipulating pointers at this low a level. Memory leaks and memory-access violations are common in such custom code. For most programmers, and for most of the applications they will need to write, the prepackaged, templatized data structures of the STL are sufficient. Using the STL helps programmers reduce testing and debugging time. One caution is that, for large projects, template compile time can be significant.

This chapter is meant to be an introduction to the STL. It is by no means complete or comprehensive. However, it is a friendly, accessible chapter that should convince you of the value of the STL and encourage further study. We use the same "live-code approach" that we have used throughout the book. This might be one of the most important chapters in the book for you in terms of your appreciation of software reuse.

21.1.1 Introduction to Containers

The STL container types are shown in Fig. 21.1. The containers are divided into three major categories—*sequence containers*, *associative containers* and *container adapters*.

The sequence containers (sometimes are referred to as *sequential containers*) represent linear data structures, such as vectors and linked lists. Associative containers are non-linear containers that typically can locate elements stored in the containers quickly. Such containers can store sets of values or *key/value pairs*. The sequence containers and associative containers are collectively referred to as the *first-class containers*. As we saw in Chapter 17, stacks and queues actually are constrained versions of sequential containers. For this reason, STL implements stacks and queues as container adapters that enable a program to view a sequential container in a constrained manner. There are four other container types that are considered "near-containers"—C-like arrays (discussed in Chapter 4), **string**s (discussed in Chapter 15), **bitset**s for maintaining sets of flag values and **valarray**s for performing high-speed mathematical vector operations (this last class is optimized for computation performance and is not as flexible as the first-class containers). These four types are

Standard Library container class	Description
Sequence Containers	
vector	rapid insertions and deletions at back
	direct access to any element
deque	rapid insertions and deletions at front or back
	direct access to any element
list	doubly linked list, rapid insertion and deletion anywhere
Associative Containers	
set	rapid lookup, no duplicates allowed
multiset	rapid lookup, duplicates allowed
map	one-to-one mapping, no duplicates allowed, rapid key-based lookup
multimap	one-to-many mapping, duplicates allowed, rapid key-based lookup
Container Adapters	
stack	last-in-first-out (LIFO)
queue	first-in-first-out (FIFO)
priority_queue	highest priority element is always the first element out

Fig. 21.1   Standard Library container classes.

considered "near containers" because they exhibit capabilities similar to those of the first-class containers, but do not support all the first-class-container capabilities.

STL was carefully designed so that the containers provide similar functionality. There are many generic operations, such as member-function **size**, that apply to all containers, and other operations that apply to subsets of similar containers. This encourages extensibility of the STL with new classes. Figure 21.2 describes the functions common to all Standard Library containers. [*Note:* Overloaded operators **operator<**, **operator<=**, **operator>**, **operator>=**, **operator==** and **operator!=** are not provided for **priority_queue**s.]

Common member functions for all STL containers	Description
default constructor	A constructor to provide a default initialization of the container. Normally, each container has several constructors that provide different initialization methods for the container.
copy constructor	A constructor that initializes the container to be a copy of an existing container of the same type.
destructor	Destructor function for cleanup after a container is no longer needed.
empty	Returns **true** if there are no elements in the container; otherwise, returns **false**.
max_size	Returns the maximum number of elements for a container.
size	Returns the number of elements currently in the container.
operator=	Assigns one container to another.
operator<	Returns **true** if the first container is less than the second container; otherwise, returns **false**.
operator<=	Returns **true** if the first container is less than or equal to the second container; otherwise, returns **false**.
operator>	Returns **true** if the first container is greater than the second container; otherwise, returns **false**.
operator>=	Returns **true** if the first container is greater than or equal to the second container; otherwise, returns **false**.
operator==	Returns **true** if the first container is equal to the second container; otherwise, returns **false**.
operator!=	Returns **true** if the first container is not equal to the second container; otherwise, returns **false**.
swap	Swaps the elements of two containers.
Functions that are only found in first-class containers	
begin	The two versions of this function return either an **iterator** or a **const_iterator** that refers to the first element of the container.

Fig. 21.2   STL container common functions. (Part 1 of 2.)

Common member functions for all STL containers	Description
end	The two versions of this function return either an **iterator** or a **const_iterator** that refers to the next position after the end of the container.
rbegin	The two versions of this function return either a **reverse_iterator** or a **const_reverse_iterator** that refers to the last element of the container.
rend	The two versions of this function return either a **reverse_iterator** or a **const_reverse_iterator** that refers to the position before the first element of the container.
erase	Erases one or more elements from the container.
clear	Erases all elements from the container.

Fig. 21.2   STL container common functions. (Part 2 of 2.)

The header files for each of the Standard Library containers are shown in Fig. 21.3. The contents of these header files are all in **namespace std**.[1]

Figure 21.4 shows the common **typedef**s (to create synonyms or aliases for lengthy type names) found in first-class containers. These **typedef**s are used in generic declarations of variables, parameters to functions and return values from functions. For example, **value_type** in each container is always a **typedef** that represents the type of value stored in the container.

Standard Library container header files	
<vector>	
<list>	
<deque>	
<queue>	Contains both **queue** and **priority_queue**.
<stack>	
<map>	Contains both **map** and **multimap**.
<set>	Contains both **set** and **multiset**.
<bitset>	

Fig. 21.3   Standard Library container header files.

---

1. Some older C++ compilers do not support the new-style header files. Many of these compilers provide their own versions of the header-file names. See your compiler documentation for more information on the STL support your compiler provides.

typedef	Description
value_type	The type of element stored in the container.
reference	A reference to the type of element stored in the container.
const_reference	A constant reference to the type of element stored in the container. Such a reference can only be used for *reading* elements in the container and for performing **const** operations.
pointer	A pointer to the type of element stored in the container.
iterator	An iterator that points to the type of element stored in the container.
const_iterator	A constant iterator that points to the type of element stored in the container and can be used only to *read* elements.
reverse_iterator	A reverse iterator that points to the type of element stored in the container. This type of iterator is for iterating through a container in reverse.
const_reverse_iterator	A constant reverse iterator that points to the type of element stored in the container and can be used only to *read* elements. This type of iterator is for iterating through a container in reverse.
difference_type	The type of the result of subtracting two iterators that refer to the same container (**operator-** is not defined for iterators of **list**s and associative containers).
size_type	The type used to count items in a container and index through a sequence container (cannot index through a **list**).

Fig. 21.4 **typedef**s found in first-class containers.

Performance Tip 21.3

*STL generally avoids inheritance and **virtual** functions in favor of using generic programming with templates to achieve better execution-time performance.*

Portability Tip 21.1

Programming with STL will enhance the portability of your code.

When preparing to use an STL container, it is important to ensure that the type of element being stored in the container supports a minimum set of functionality. When an element is inserted into a container, a copy of that element is made. For this reason, the element type should provide its own copy constructor and assignment operator. [*Note:* This is required only if default memberwise copy and default memberwise assignment do not perform a proper copy and assignment operations for the element type.] Also, the associative containers and many algorithms require elements to be compared. For this reason, the element type should provide an equality operator (**==**) and a less-than operator (**<**).

Software Engineering Observation 21.3

The equality and less-than operators are technically not required for the elements stored in a container unless the elements need to be compared. However, when creating code from a template, some pre-standard compilers require all parts of the template to be defined, whereas other compilers require only the parts of the template that are actually used in the program.

21.1.2 Introduction to Iterators

Iterators have many features in common with pointers and are used to point to the elements of first-class containers (and for a few other purposes, as we will see). Iterators hold state information sensitive to the particular containers on which they operate; thus, iterators are implemented appropriately for each type of container. Nevertheless, certain iterator operations are uniform across containers. For example, the dereferencing operator (*****) dereferences an iterator so that you can use the element to which it points. The **++** operation on an iterator moves the iterator to the next element of the container (much as incrementing a pointer into an array aims the pointer at the next element of the array).

STL first-class containers provide member functions **begin()** and **end()**. Function **begin()** returns an iterator pointing to the first element of the container. Function **end()** returns an iterator pointing to the first element past the end of the container (an element that doesn't exist). If iterator **i** points to a particular element, then **++i** points to the "next" element and ***i** refers to the element pointed to by **i**. The iterator resulting from **end()** can be used only in an equality or inequality comparison to determine whether the "moving iterator" (**i** in this case) has reached the end of the container.

We use an object of type **iterator** to refer to a container element that can be modified. We use an object of type **const_iterator** to refer to a container element that cannot be modified.

We use iterators with *sequences* (also called *ranges*). These sequences can be in containers, or they can be *input sequences* or *output sequences*. The program of Fig. 21.5 demonstrates input from the standard input (a sequence of data for input into a program), using an **istream_iterator**, and output to the standard output (a sequence of data for output from a program), using an **ostream_iterator**. The program inputs two integers from the user at the keyboard and displays the sum of the integers.[2]

```
1   // Fig. 21.5: fig21_05.cpp
2   // Demonstrating input and output with iterators.
3   #include <iostream>
4
5   using std::cout;
6   using std::cin;
7   using std::endl;
```

Fig. 21.5   Input and output stream iterators. (Part 1 of 2.)

---

2. The examples in this chapter precede each use of an STL function and each definition of an STL container object with the "**std::**" prefix rather than placing the **using** statements at the beginning of the program, as was shown in most prior examples. Differences in compilers and the complex code generated when using STL, make it difficult to construct a proper set of **using** statements that enable the programs to compile without errors. To allow these programs to compile on the widest variety of platforms, we chose the "**std::**" prefix approach.

```
8
9    #include <iterator>  // ostream_iterator and istream_iterator
10
11   int main()
12   {
13      cout << "Enter two integers: ";
14
15      // create istream_iterator for reading int values from cin
16      std::istream_iterator< int > inputInt( cin );
17
18      int number1 = *inputInt;  // read int from standard input
19      ++inputInt;               // move iterator to next input value
20      int number2 = *inputInt;  // read int from standard input
21
22      // create ostream_iterator for writing int values to cout
23      std::ostream_iterator< int > outputInt( cout );
24
25      cout << "The sum is: ";
26      *outputInt = number1 + number2;  // output result to cout
27      cout << endl;
28
29      return 0;
30
31   } // end main
```

```
Enter two integers: 12 25
The sum is: 37
```

Fig. 21.5   Input and output stream iterators. (Part 2 of 2.)

Line 16 creates an **istream_iterator** that is capable of extracting (inputting) **int** values in a type-safe manner from the standard input object **cin**. Line 18 dereferences iterator **inputInt** to read the first integer from **cin** and assigns that integer to **number1**. Note that the dereferencing operator ***** applied to **inputInt** gets the value from the stream associated with **inputInt**; this is similar to dereferencing a pointer. Line 19 positions iterator **inputInt** to the next value in the input stream. Line 20 inputs the next integer from **inputInt** and assigns it to **number2**.

Line 23 creates an **ostream_iterator** that is capable of inserting (outputting) **int** values in the standard output object **cout**. Line 26 outputs an integer to **cout** by assigning to ***outputInt** the sum of **number1** and **number2**. Notice the use of the dereferencing operator ***** to use ***outputInt** as an *lvalue* in the assignment statement. If you want to output another value using **outputInt**, the iterator must be incremented with **++** (both preincrement and postincrement can be used).

Testing and Debugging Tip 21.2

The ***** *(dereferencing) operator of any* **const** *iterator returns a* **const** *reference to the container element, thus disallowing the use of non-***const** *member functions.*

Common Programming Error 21.1

Attempting to dereference an iterator positioned outside its container is a runtime logic error. In particular, the iterator returned by **end()** *cannot be dereferenced or incremented.*

Common Programming Error 21.2

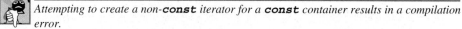

*Attempting to create a non-**const** iterator for a **const** container results in a compilation error.*

Figure 21.6 shows the categories of iterators used by the STL. Each category provides a specific set of functionality.

Figure 21.7 illustrates the hierarchy of iterator categories. As you follow the hierarchy from top to bottom, each iterator category supports all the functionality of the categories above it in the figure. Thus the "weakest" iterator types are at the top and the most powerful iterator type is at the bottom. Note that this is not an inheritance hierarchy.

Category	Description
input	Used to read an element from a container. An input iterator can move only in the forward direction (i.e., from the beginning of the container to the end of the container) one element at a time. Input iterators support only one-pass algorithms—the same input iterator cannot be used to pass through a sequence twice.
output	Used to write an element to a container. An output iterator can move only in the forward direction one element at a time. Output iterators support only one-pass algorithms—the same output iterator cannot be used to pass through a sequence twice.
forward	Combines the capabilities of input and output iterators and retains their position in the container (as state information).
bidirectional	Combines the capabilities of a forward iterator with the ability to move in the backward direction (i.e., from the end of the container toward the beginning of the container). Bidirectional iterators support multi-pass algorithms.
random access	Combines the capabilities of a bidirectional iterator with the ability to directly access any element of the container, i.e., to jump forward or backward by an arbitrary number of elements.

Fig. 21.6   Iterator categories.

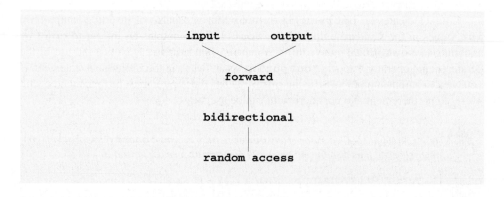

Fig. 21.7   Iterator category hierarchy.

The iterator category that each container supports determines whether that container can be used with specific algorithms in the STL. Containers that support random-access iterators can be used with all algorithms in the STL. As we will see, pointers into arrays can be used in place of iterators in most STL algorithms, including those that require random-access iterators. Figure 21.8 shows the iterator category supported by each of the STL containers. Note that only **vector**s, **deque**s, **list**s, **set**s, **multiset**s, **map**s and **multimap**s (i.e., the first-class containers) are traversable with iterators.

Software Engineering Observation 21.4

Using the "weakest iterator" that yields acceptable performance helps produce maximally reusable components.

Figure 21.9 shows the predefined iterator **typedef**s that are found in the class definitions of the STL containers. Not every **typedef** is defined for every container. We use **const** versions of the iterators for traversing read-only containers. We use reverse iterators to traverse containers in the reverse direction.

Container	Type of iterator supported
Sequence containers	
vector	random access
deque	random access
list	bidirectional
Associative containers	
set	bidirectional
multiset	bidirectional
map	bidirectional
multimap	bidirectional
Container adapters	
stack	no iterators supported
queue	no iterators supported
priority_queue	no iterators supported

Fig. 21.8   Iterator types supported by each Standard Library container.

Predefined **typedef**s for iterator types	Direction of ++	Capability
iterator	forward	read/write
const_iterator	forward	read
reverse_iterator	backward	read/write
const_reverse_iterator	backward	read

Fig. 21.9   Iterator **typedef**s.

Figure 21.10 shows some operations that can be performed on each iterator type. Note that the operations for each iterator type include all operations preceding that type in the figure. Note also that, for input iterators and output iterators, it is not possible to save the iterator, then use the saved value later.

Iterator operation	Description
All iterators	
++p	preincrement an iterator
p++	postincrement an iterator
Input iterators	
*p	dereference an iterator (for use as an *rvalue*)
p = p1	assign one iterator to another
p == p1	compare iterators for equality
p != p1	compare iterators for inequality
Output iterators	
*p	dereference an iterator (for use as an *lvalue*)
p = p1	assign one iterator to another
Forward iterators	Forward iterators provide all the functionality of both input iterators and output iterators.
Bidirectional iterators	
--p	predecrement an iterator
p--	postdecrement an iterator
Random-access iterators	
p += i	Increment the iterator **p** by **i** positions.
p -= i	Decrement the iterator **p** by **i** positions.
p + i	Results in an iterator positioned at **p** incremented by **i** positions.
p - i	Results in an iterator positioned at **p** decremented by **i** positions.
p[i]	Return a reference to the element offset from **p** by **i** positions
p < p1	Return **true** if iterator **p** is less than iterator **p1** (i.e., iterator **p** is before iterator **p1** in the container); otherwise, return **false**.
p <= p1	Return **true** if iterator **p** is less than or equal to iterator **p1** (i.e., iterator **p** is before iterator **p1** or at the same location as iterator **p1** in the container); otherwise, return **false**.

Fig. 21.10 Iterator operations for each type of iterator. (Part 1 of 2.)

Iterator operation	Description
p > p1	Return **true** if iterator **p** is greater than iterator **p1** (i.e., iterator **p** is after iterator **p1** in the container); otherwise, return **false**.
p >= p1	Return **true** if iterator **p** is greater than or equal to iterator **p1** (i.e., iterator **p** is after iterator **p1** or at the same location as iterator **p1** in the container); otherwise, return **false**.

Fig. 21.10   Iterator operations for each type of iterator. (Part 2 of 2.)

21.1.3 Introduction to Algorithms

A crucial aspect of the STL is that it provides algorithms that can be used generically across a variety of containers. STL provides many algorithms you will use frequently to manipulate containers. Inserting, deleting, searching, sorting and others are appropriate for some or all of the STL containers.

STL includes approximately 70 standard algorithms. We provide live-code examples of most of these and summarize the others in tables. The algorithms operate on container elements only indirectly through iterators. Many algorithms operate on sequences of elements defined by pairs of iterators—a first iterator pointing to the first element of the sequence and a second iterator pointing to one element past the last element of the sequence. Also, it is possible to create your own new algorithms that operate in a similar fashion so they can be used with the STL containers and iterators.

Algorithms often return iterators that indicate the results of the algorithms. Algorithm **find()**, for example, locates an element and returns an iterator to that element. If the element is not found, **find()** returns the **end()** iterator, which can be tested to determine whether an element was not found (the return of **end()** assumes a search of the entire container). The **find()** algorithm can be used with any STL container. STL algorithms create yet another opportunity for reuse. Using the rich collection of popular algorithms can save programmers much time and effort.

If an algorithm uses less powerful iterators, the algorithm can also be used with containers that support more powerful iterators. Some algorithms demand powerful iterators; e.g., **sort** demands random-access iterators.

Software Engineering Observation 21.5

STL is implemented concisely. Until now, class designers would have associated the algorithms with the containers by making the algorithms member functions of the containers. STL takes a different approach. The algorithms are separated from the containers and operate on elements of the containers only indirectly through iterators. This separation makes it easier to write generic algorithms applicable to many container classes.

Software Engineering Observation 21.6

STL is extensible. It is straightforward to add new algorithms and to do so without changes to STL containers.

Software Engineering Observation 21.7

STL algorithms can operate on STL containers and on pointer-based, C-like arrays.

Portability Tip 21.2

Because STL algorithms process containers only indirectly through iterators, one algorithm can often be used with many different containers.

Figure 21.11 shows many of the *mutating-sequence algorithms*—i.e., the algorithms that result in modifications of the containers to which the algorithms are applied.

Figure 21.12 shows many of the non-mutating-sequence algorithms—i.e., the algorithms that do not result in modifications of the containers to which the algorithms are applied.

Figure 21.13 shows the numerical algorithms of the header file **<numeric>**.

Mutating-sequence algorithms		
`copy`	`remove`	`reverse_copy`
`copy_backward`	`remove_copy`	`rotate`
`fill`	`remove_copy_if`	`rotate_copy`
`fill_n`	`remove_if`	`stable_partition`
`generate`	`replace`	`swap`
`generate_n`	`replace_copy`	`swap_ranges`
`iter_swap`	`replace_copy_if`	`transform`
`partition`	`replace_if`	`unique`
`random_shuffle`	`reverse`	`unique_copy`

Fig. 21.11 Mutating-sequence algorithms.

Non-mutating-sequence algorithms		
`adjacent_find`	`find`	`find_if`
`count`	`find_each`	`mismatch`
`count_if`	`find_end`	`search`
`equal`	`find_first_of`	`search_n`

Fig. 21.12 Non-mutating sequence algorithms.

Numerical algorithms from header file `<numeric>`	
`accumulate`	`partial_sum`
`inner_product`	`adjacent_difference`

Fig. 21.13 Numerical algorithms from header file **<numeric>**.

21.2 Sequence Containers

The C++ Standard Template Library provides three sequence containers—**vector**, *list* and *deque*. Class **vector** and class **deque** both are based on arrays. Class **list** implements a linked-list data structure similar to our **List** class presented in Chapter 17, but more robust.

One of the most popular containers in the STL is **vector**. Class **vector** is a refinement of the kind of "smart" **Array** class we created in Chapter 8. A **vector** can change size dynamically. Unlike C and C++ "raw" arrays (see Chapter 4), **vector**s can be assigned to one another. This is not possible with pointer-based, C-like arrays, because those array names are constant pointers and cannot be the targets of assignments. Just as with C arrays, **vector** subscripting does not perform automatic range checking, but class **vector** does provide this capability via member function **at**.

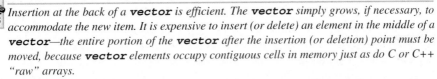

Performance Tip 21.4

*Insertion at the back of a **vector** is efficient. The **vector** simply grows, if necessary, to accommodate the new item. It is expensive to insert (or delete) an element in the middle of a **vector**—the entire portion of the **vector** after the insertion (or deletion) point must be moved, because **vector** elements occupy contiguous cells in memory just as do C or C++ "raw" arrays.*

Figure 21.2 presented the operations common to all the STL containers. Beyond these operations, each container typically provides a variety of other capabilities. Many of these capabilities are common to several containers. However, these operations are not always equally efficient for each container. The programmer must choose the container most appropriate for the application.

Performance Tip 21.5

*Applications that require frequent insertions and deletions at both ends of a container normally use a **deque** rather than a **vector**. Although we can insert and delete elements at the front and back of both a **vector** and a **deque**, class **deque** is more efficient than **vector** for doing insertions and deletions at the front.*

Performance Tip 21.6

*Applications with frequent insertions and deletions in the middle and/or at the extremes of a container normally use a **list**, due to its efficient implementation of insertion and deletion anywhere in the data structure.*

In addition to the common operations described in Fig. 21.2, the sequence containers have several other common operations—**front** to return a reference to the first element in the container, **back** to return a reference to the last element in the container, **push_back** to insert a new element at the end of the container and **pop_back** to remove the last element of the container.

21.2.1 **vector** Sequence Container

Class **vector** provides a data structure with contiguous memory locations.[3] This enables efficient, direct access to any element of a vector via the subscript operator **[]**, exactly as with a C or C++ "raw" array. Class **vector** is most commonly used when the data in the container must be sorted and easily accessible via a subscript. When a **vector**'s memory is exhausted, the **vector** allocates a larger contiguous area of memory, copies the original elements into the new memory and deallocates the old memory.

Performance Tip 21.7

*Choose the **vector** container for the best random-access performance.*

Performance Tip 21.8

*Objects of class **vector** provide rapid indexed access with the overloaded subscript operator **[]** because they are stored in contiguous storage like a C or C++ raw array.*

Performance Tip 21.9

It is faster to insert many elements at once than one at a time

An important part of every container is the type of iterator it supports. This determines which algorithms can be applied to the container. A **vector** supports random-access iterators—i.e., all iterator operations shown in Fig. 21.10 can be applied to a **vector** iterator. All STL algorithms can operate on a **vector**. The iterators for a **vector** are normally implemented as pointers to elements of the **vector**. Each of the STL algorithms that take iterator arguments requires those iterators to provide a minimum level of functionality. If an algorithm requires a forward iterator, for example, that algorithm can operate on any container that provides forward iterators, bidirectional iterators or random-access iterators. As long as the container supports the algorithm's minimum iterator functionality, the algorithm can operate on the container.

Figure 21.14 illustrates several functions of the **vector** class template. Many of these functions are available in every Standard Library first-class container. You must include header file **<vector>** to use class **vector**.

```
1   // Fig. 21.14: fig21_14.cpp
2   // Demonstrating standard library vector class template.
3   #include <iostream>
4
5   using std::cout;
6   using std::cin;
7   using std::endl;
8
9   #include <vector>   // vector class-template definition
10
11  // prototype for function template printVector
12  template < class T >
13  void printVector( const std::vector< T > &integers2 );
14
15  int main()
16  {
17      const int SIZE = 6;
```

Fig. 21.14 Standard Library **vector** class template. (Part 1 of 3.)

---

3. Contiguous memory is not actually guaranteed by the C++ standard. However, the C++ standard committee is leaning toward making contiguous memory a requirement for class **vector**.

```
18       int array[ SIZE ] = { 1, 2, 3, 4, 5, 6 };
19
20       std::vector< int > integers;
21
22       cout << "The initial size of integers is: "
23            << integers.size()
24            << "\nThe initial capacity of integers is: "
25            << integers.capacity();
26
27       // function push_back is in every sequence collection
28       integers.push_back( 2 );
29       integers.push_back( 3 );
30       integers.push_back( 4 );
31
32       cout << "\nThe size of integers is: " << integers.size()
33            << "\nThe capacity of integers is: "
34            << integers.capacity();
35
36       cout << "\n\nOutput array using pointer notation: ";
37
38       for ( int *ptr = array; ptr != array + SIZE; ++ptr )
39          cout << *ptr << ' ';
40
41       cout << "\nOutput vector using iterator notation: ";
42       printVector( integers );
43
44       cout << "\nReversed contents of vector integers: ";
45
46       std::vector< int >::reverse_iterator reverseIterator;
47
48       for ( reverseIterator = integers.rbegin();
49            reverseIterator!= integers.rend();
50            ++reverseIterator )
51          cout << *reverseIterator << ' ';
52
53       cout << endl;
54
55       return 0;
56
57   } // end main
58
59   // function template for outputting vector elements
60   template < class T >
61   void printVector( const std::vector< T > &integers2 )
62   {
63      std::vector< T >::const_iterator constIterator;
64
65      for ( constIterator = integers2.begin();
66           constIterator != integers2.end();
67           constIterator++ )
68         cout << *constIterator << ' ';
69
70   } // end function printVector
```

Fig. 21.14   Standard Library **vector** class template. (Part 2 of 3.)

```
The initial size of v is: 0
The initial capacity of v is: 0
The size of v is: 3
The capacity of v is: 4

Contents of array a using pointer notation: 1 2 3 4 5 6
Contents of vector v using iterator notation: 2 3 4
Reversed contents of vector v: 4 3 2
```

Fig. 21.14   Standard Library **vector** class template. (Part 3 of 3.)

Line 20 defines an instance called **integers** of class **vector** that stores **int** values. When this object is instantiated, an empty **vector** is created with size 0 (i.e., the number of elements stored in the **vector**) and capacity 0 (i.e., the number of elements that can be stored without allocating more memory to the **vector**).

Lines 23 and 25 demonstrate the **size** and **capacity** functions; each initially returns 0 for **vector v** in this example. Function **size**—available in every container— returns the number of elements currently stored in the container. Function **capacity** returns the number of elements that can be stored in the **vector** before the **vector** dynamically resizes itself to accommodate more elements.

Lines 28–30 use function **push_back**—available in all sequence containers—to add an element to the end of the **vector**. If an element is added to a full **vector**, the **vector** increases its size—some STL implementations have the **vector** double its size.

Performance Tip 21.10

*It can be wasteful to double the size of a **vector** when more space is needed. For example, a full **vector** of 1,000,000 elements resizes to accommodate 2,000,000 elements when a new element is added. This leaves 999,999 elements unused. Programmers can use **re-size()** to control space usage better.*

Lines 32 and 34 use **size** and **capacity** to illustrate the new size and capacity of the **vector** after the **push_back** operations. Function **size** returns 3—the number of elements added to the **vector**. Function **capacity** returns 4, indicating that we can add one more element without allocating more memory for the **vector**. When we added the first element, the size of **integers** became 1 and the capacity of **integers** became 1. When we added the second element, the size of **integers** became 2 and the capacity of **integers** became 2. When we added the third element, the size of **integers** became 3 and the capacity of **integers** became 4. If we add two more elements, the size of **integers** would be 5 and the capacity would be 8. The capacity doubles each time the total space allocated to the **vector** is full and another element is added.

Lines 38–39 demonstrate how to output the contents of an array using pointers and pointer arithmetic. Line 42 calls function **printVector** (defined at lines 60–70) to output the contents of a **vector** using iterators. Function template **printVector** receives a **const** reference to a **vector** (**integers2**) as its argument. Line 63 defines a **const_iterator** called **constIterator** that iterates through the **vector** and outputs its contents. A **const_iterator** enables the program to read the elements of the **vector**, but does not allow the program to modify the elements. The **for** structure at lines 65–68 initializes **constIterator** using **vector** member function **begin**, which returns a **const_iterator** to the first element in the **vector**—there is another version of **begin** that returns an **iterator** that can be used for non-**const** containers. Note that a **const_iterator** is returned because the identifier **integers2** was declared **const** in the parameter list of function **printVector**. The loop continues as long as **constIterator** has not reached the end of the **vector**. This is determined by comparing **constIterator** to the result of **integers2.end()**, which returns an iterator indicating the location after the last element of the **vector**. If **constIterator** is equal to this value, the end of the **vector** has been reached. Functions **begin** and **end** are available for all first-class containers. The body of the loop dereferences iterator **constIterator** to get the value in the current element of the **vector**. Remember that the iterator acts like a pointer to the element and that operator * is overloaded to return the value of the element. The expression **constIterator++** (line 67) positions the iterator to the next element of the **vector**.

Testing and Debugging Tip 21.4

Only random-access iterators support **<**. *It is better to use* **!=** *and* **end()** *to test for end of container.*

Line 46 declares a **reverse_iterator** that can be used to iterate through a **vector** backwards. All first-class containers support this type of iterator.

Lines 48–51 use a **for** structure similar to that in function **printVector** to iterate through the **vector**. In this loop, functions **rbegin** (i.e., the iterator for the starting point for iterating in reverse through the container) and **rend** (i.e., the iterator for the ending point for iterating in reverse through the container) delineate the range of elements to output in reverse. As with functions **begin** and **end**, **rbegin** and **rend** can return a **const_reverse_iterator** or a **reverse_iterator** based on whether or not the container is constant.

Figure 21.15 illustrates functions that enable retrieval and manipulation of the elements of a **vector**. Line 17 uses an overloaded **vector** constructor that takes two iterators as arguments to initialize **integers**. Remember that pointers into an array can be used as iterators. Line 17 initializes **integers** with the contents of integer array **a** from location **a** up to—but not including—location **a + SIZE**.

```
1   // Fig. 21.15: fig21_15.cpp
2   // Testing Standard Library vector class template
3   // element-manipulation functions.
4   #include <iostream>
5
6   using std::cout;
7   using std::endl;
8
9   #include <vector>      // vector class-template definition
10  #include <algorithm>   // copy algorithm
11
12  int main()
13  {
14     const int SIZE = 6;
```

Fig. 21.15 Standard Library **vector** class template element-manipulation functions. (Part 1 of 3.)

```
15        int array[ SIZE ] = { 1, 2, 3, 4, 5, 6 };
16
17        std::vector< int > integers( array, array + SIZE );
18        std::ostream_iterator< int > output( cout, " " );
19
20        cout << "Vector integers contains: ";
21        std::copy( integers.begin(), integers.end(), output );
22
23        cout << "\nFirst element of integers: " << integers.front()
24             << "\nLast element of integers: " << integers.back();
25
26        integers[ 0 ] = 7;       // set first element to 7
27        integers.at( 2 ) = 10;   // set element at position 2 to 10
28
29        // insert 22 as 2nd element
30        integers.insert( integers.begin() + 1, 22 );
31
32        cout << "\n\nContents of vector integers after changes: ";
33        std::copy( integers.begin(), integers.end(), output );
34
35        // access out-of-range element
36        try {
37           integers.at( 100 ) = 777;
38
39        } // end try
40
41        // catch out_of_range exception
42        catch ( std::out_of_range outOfRange ) {
43           cout << "\n\nException: " << outOfRange.what();
44
45        } // end catch
46
47        // erase first element
48        integers.erase( integers.begin() );
49        cout << "\n\nVector integers after erasing first element: ";
50        std::copy( integers.begin(), integers.end(), output );
51
52        // erase remaining elements
53        integers.erase( integers.begin(), integers.end() );
54        cout << "\nAfter erasing all elements, vector integers "
55             << ( integers.empty() ? "is" : "is not" ) << " empty";
56
57        // insert elements from array
58        integers.insert( integers.begin(), array, array + SIZE );
59        cout << "\n\nContents of vector integers before clear: ";
60        std::copy( integers.begin(), integers.end(), output );
61
62        // empty integers; clear calls erase to empty a collection
63        integers.clear();
64        cout << "\nAfter clear, vector integers "
65             << ( integers.empty() ? "is" : "is not" ) << " empty";
66
```

Fig. 21.15 Standard Library **vector** class template element-manipulation functions. (Part 2 of 3.)

```
67        cout << endl;
68
69        return 0;
70
71    } // end main
```

```
Vector integers contains: 1 2 3 4 5 6
First element of integers: 1
Last element of integers: 6

Contents of vector integers after changes: 7 22 2 10 4 5 6

Exception: invalid vector<T> subscript

Vector integers after erasing first element: 22 2 10 4 5 6
After erasing all elements, vector integers is empty

Contents of vector integers before clear: 1 2 3 4 5 6
After clear, vector integers is empty
```

Fig. 21.15 Standard Library **vector** class template element-manipulation functions. (Part 3 of 3.)

Line 18 defines an **ostream_iterator** called **output** that can be used to output integers separated by single spaces via **cout**. An **ostream_iterator< int >** is a type-safe output mechanism that outputs only values of type **int** or a compatible type. The first argument to the constructor specifies the output stream, and the second argument is a string specifying separator characters for the values output—in this case, a space character. We use the **ostream_iterator** to output the contents of the **vector** in this example.

Line 21 uses algorithm *copy* from the Standard Library to output the entire contents of **vector integers** to the standard output. Algorithm **copy** copies each element in the container starting with the location specified by the iterator in its first argument and up to—but not including—the location specified by the iterator in its second argument. The first and second arguments must satisfy input iterator requirements—they must be iterators through which values can be read from a container. Also, applying **++** to the first iterator must eventually cause the first iterator to reach the second iterator argument in the container. The elements are copied to the location specified by the output iterator (i.e., an iterator through which a value can be stored or output) specified as the last argument. In this case, the output iterator is an **ostream_iterator** (**output**) that is attached to **cout**, so the elements are copied to the standard output. To use the algorithms of the Standard Library, you must include the header file **<algorithm>**.

Lines 23–24 use functions **front** and **back** (available for all sequence containers) to determine the first and last element of the **vector**, respectively.

Common Programming Error 21.3

*The **vector** must not be empty; otherwise, results of the **front** and **back** functions are undefined.*

Lines 26–27 illustrate two ways to subscript through a **vector** (that also can be used with the **deque** containers). Line 26 uses the subscript operator that is overloaded to return either a reference to the value at the specified location or a constant reference to that value, depending on whether the container is constant. Function **at** (line 27)performs the same operation with one additional feature—bounds checking. Function **at** first checks the value supplied as an argument and determines whether it is in the bounds of the **vector**. If not, function **at** throws an **out_of_bounds** exception (as demonstrated in lines 36–45). Figure 21.16 shows some of the STL exception types. (The Standard Library exception types are discussed in Chapter 13, Exception Handling.)

Line 30 uses one of the three **insert** functions provided by each sequence container. Line 30 inserts the value 22 before the element at the location specified by the iterator in the first argument. In this example, the iterator is pointing to the second element of the **vector**, so 22 is inserted as the second element and the original second element becomes the third element of the **vector**. Other versions of **insert** allow inserting multiple copies of the same value starting at a particular position in the container, or inserting a range of values from another container (or array), starting at a particular position in the original container.

Lines 48 and 53 use the two **erase** functions that are available in all first-class containers. Line 48 indicates that the element at the location specified by the iterator argument should be removed from the container (in this example, the element at the beginning of the **vector**). Line 53 specifies that all elements in the range starting with the location of the first argument up to—but not including—the location of the second argument should be erased from the container. In this example, all the elements are erased from the **vector**. Line 55 uses function **empty** (available for all containers and adapters) to confirm that the **vector** is empty.

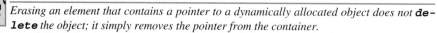

Common Programming Error 21.4

*Erasing an element that contains a pointer to a dynamically allocated object does not **de-lete** the object; it simply removes the pointer from the container.*

Line 58 demonstrates the version of function **insert** that uses the second and third arguments to specify the starting location and ending location in a sequence of values (possibly from another container; in this case, from array of integers **array**) that should be inserted into the **vector**. Remember that the ending location specifies the position in the sequence after the last element to be inserted; copying is performed up to—but not including—this location.

Finally, line 63 uses function **clear** (found in all first-class containers) to empty the **vector**. This function calls the version of **erase** used in line 53 to empty the **vector**.

STL exception types	Description
out_of_range	Indicates when subscript is out of range—e.g., when an invalid subscript is specified to **vector** member function **at**.
invalid_argument	Indicates an invalid argument was passed to a function.
length_error	Indicates an attempt to create too long a container, **string**, etc.
bad_alloc	Indicates that an attempt to allocate memory with **new** (or with an allocator) failed because not enough memory was available.

Fig. 21.16 STL exception types.

[*Note:* There are other functions that are common to all containers and common to all sequence containers that have not yet been covered. We will cover most of these in the next few sections. We will also cover many functions that are specific to each container.]

21.2.2 **list** Sequence Container

The **list** sequence container provides an efficient implementation for insertion and deletion operations at any location in the container. If most of the insertions and deletions occur at the ends of the container, the **deque** data structure (Section 21.2.3) provides a more efficient implementation. Class **list** is implemented as a doubly linked list—every node in the **list** contains a pointer to the previous node in the **list** and to the next node in the **list**. This enables class **list** to support bidirectional iterators that allow the container to be traversed both forwards and backwards. Any algorithm that requires input, output, forward or bidirectional iterators can operate on a **list**. Many of the **list** member functions manipulate the elements of the container as an ordered set of elements.

In addition to the member functions of all STL containers in Fig. 21.2 and the common member functions of all sequence containers discussed in Section 21.5, class **list** provides eight other member functions—**splice**, **push_front**, **pop_front**, **remove**, **unique**, **merge**, **reverse** and **sort**. Several of these member functions are **list**-optimized implementations of STL algorithms presented in Section 21.5. Figure 21.17 demonstrates several features of class **list**. Remember that many of the functions presented in Fig. 21.14–Fig. 21.15 can be used with class **list**. Header file **<list>** must be included to use class **list**.

```
1   // Fig. 21.17: fig21_17.cpp
2   // Standard library list class template test program.
3   #include <iostream>
4
5   using std::cout;
6   using std::endl;
7
8   #include <list>        // list class-template definition
9   #include <algorithm>   // copy algorithm
10
11  // prototype for function template printList
12  template < class T >
13  void printList( const std::list< T > &listRef );
14
15  int main()
16  {
17      const int SIZE = 4;
18      int array[ SIZE ] = { 2, 6, 4, 8 };
19
20      std::list< int > values;
21      std::list< int > otherValues;
22
23      // insert items in values
24      values.push_front( 1 );
```

Fig. 21.17 Standard Library **list** class template. (Part 1 of 4.)

```
25        values.push_front( 2 );
26        values.push_back( 4 );
27        values.push_back( 3 );
28
29        cout << "values contains: ";
30        printList( values );
31
32        values.sort();   // sort values
33
34        cout << "\nvalues after sorting contains: ";
35        printList( values );
36
37        // insert elements of array into otherValues
38        otherValues.insert( otherValues.begin(),
39           array, array + SIZE );
40
41        cout << "\nAfter insert, otherValues contains: ";
42        printList( otherValues );
43
44        // remove otherValues elements and insert at end of values
45        values.splice( values.end(), otherValues );
46
47        cout << "\nAfter splice, values contains: ";
48        printList( values );
49
50        values.sort();   // sort values
51
52        cout << "\nAfter sort, values contains: ";
53        printList( values );
54
55        // insert elements of array into otherValues
56        otherValues.insert( otherValues.begin(),
57           array, array + SIZE );
58        otherValues.sort();
59
60        cout << "\nAfter insert, otherValues contains: ";
61        printList( otherValues );
62
63        // remove otherValues elements and insert into values
64        // in sorted order
65        values.merge( otherValues );
66
67        cout << "\nAfter merge:\n   values contains: ";
68        printList( values );
69        cout << "\n   otherValues contains: ";
70        printList( otherValues );
71
72        values.pop_front();   // remove element from front
73        values.pop_back();    // remove element from back
74
75        cout << "\nAfter pop_front and pop_back:"
76             << "\n   values contains: ";
77        printList( values );
```

Fig. 21.17 Standard Library **list** class template. (Part 2 of 4.)

```
78
79      values.unique();   // remove duplicate elements
80
81      cout << "\nAfter unique, values contains: ";
82      printList( values );
83
84      // swap elements of values and otherValues
85      values.swap( otherValues );
86
87      cout << "\nAfter swap:\n   values contains: ";
88      printList( values );
89      cout << "\n   otherValues contains: ";
90      printList( otherValues );
91
92      // replace contents of values with elements of otherValues
93      values.assign( otherValues.begin(), otherValues.end() );
94
95      cout << "\nAfter assign, values contains: ";
96      printList( values );
97
98      // remove otherValues elements and insert into values
99      // in sorted order
100     values.merge( otherValues );
101
102     cout << "\nAfter merge, values contains: ";
103     printList( values );
104
105     values.remove( 4 );   // remove all 4s
106
107     cout << "\nAfter remove( 4 ), values contains: ";
108     printList( values );
109
110     cout << endl;
111
112     return 0;
113
114  } // end main
115
116  // printList function template definition; uses
117  // ostream_iterator and copy algorithm to output list elements
118  template < class T >
119  void printList( const std::list< T > &listRef )
120  {
121     if ( listRef.empty() )
122        cout << "List is empty";
123
124     else {
125        std::ostream_iterator< T > output( cout, " " );
126        std::copy( listRef.begin(), listRef.end(), output );
127
128     } // end else
129
130  } // end function printList
```

Fig. 21.17 Standard Library **list** class template. (Part 3 of 4.)

```
values contains: 2 1 4 3
values after sorting contains: 1 2 3 4
After insert, otherValues contains: 2 6 4 8
After splice, values contains: 1 2 3 4 2 6 4 8
After sort, values contains: 1 2 2 3 4 4 6 8
After insert, otherValues contains: 2 4 6 8
After merge:
   values contains: 1 2 2 2 3 4 4 4 6 6 8 8
   otherValues contains: List is empty
After pop_front and pop_back:
   values contains: 2 2 2 3 4 4 4 6 6 8
After unique, values contains: 2 3 4 6 8
After swap:
   values contains: List is empty
   otherValues contains: 2 3 4 6 8
After assign, values contains: 2 3 4 6 8
After merge, values contains: 2 2 3 3 4 4 6 6 8 8
After remove( 4 ), values contains: 2 2 3 3 6 6 8 8
```

Fig. 21.17 Standard Library **list** class template. (Part 4 of 4.)

Lines 20–21 instantiate two **list** objects capable of storing integers. Lines 24–25 use function **push_front** to insert integers at the beginning of **values**. Function **push_front** is specific to classes **list** and **deque** (not to **vector**). Lines 26–27 use function **push_back** to insert integers at the end of **values**. Remember that function **push_back** is common to all sequence containers.

Line 32 uses **list** member function **sort** to arrange the elements in the **list** in ascending order. [*Note:* This is different from the **sort** in the STL algorithms.] There is a second version of function **sort** that allows the programmer to supply a binary predicate function that takes two arguments (values in the list), performs a comparison and returns a **bool** value indicating the result. This function determines the order in which the elements of the **list** are sorted. This version could be particularly useful for a **list** that stores pointers rather than values. [*Note:* We demonstrate a unary predicate function in Fig. 21.28. A unary predicate function takes a single argument, performs a comparison using that argument and returns a **bool** value indicating the result.]

Line 45 uses **list** function **splice** to remove the elements in **otherValues** and insert them into **values** before the iterator position specified as the first argument. There are two other versions of this function. Function **splice** with three arguments allows one element to be removed from the container specified as the second argument from the location specified by the iterator in the third argument. Function **splice** with four arguments uses the last two arguments to specify a range of locations that should be removed from the container in the second argument and placed at the location specified in the first argument.

After the inserting of more elements in **list otherValues** and the sorting of both **values** and **otherValues**, line 65 uses **list** member function **merge** to remove all elements of **otherValues** and insert them in sorted order into **values**. Both **list**s must be sorted in the same order before this operation is performed. A second version of **merge** enables the programmer to supply a predicate function that takes two arguments (values in the list) and returns a **bool** value. The predicate function specifies the sorting order used by **merge**.

Line 72 uses **list** function **pop_front** to remove the first element in the **list**. Line 73 uses function **pop_back** (available for all sequence containers) to remove the last element in the **list**.

Line 79 uses **list** function **unique** to remove duplicate elements in the **list**. The **list** should be in sorted order (so that all duplicates are side by side) before this operation is performed, to guarantee that all duplicates are eliminated. A second version of **unique** enables the programmer to supply a predicate function that takes two arguments (values in the list) and returns a **bool** value specifying whether two elements are equal.

Line 85 uses function **swap** (available to all containers) to exchange the contents of **values** with the contents of **otherValues**.

Line 93 uses **list** function **assign** to replace the contents of **values** with the contents of **otherValues** in the range specified by the two iterator arguments. A second version of **assign** replaces the original contents with copies of the value specified in the second argument. The first argument of the function specifies the number of copies. Line 105 uses **list** function **remove** to delete all copies of the value **4** from the **list**.

21.2.3 deque Sequence Container

Class **deque** provides many of the benefits of a **vector** and a **list** in one container. The term **deque** (pronounced "deek") is short for "double-ended queue." Class **deque** is implemented to provide efficient indexed access (using subscripting) for reading and modifying its elements, much like a **vector**. Class **deque** is also implemented for efficient insertion and deletion operations at its front and back, much like a **list** (although a **list** is also capable of efficient insertions and deletions in the middle of the **list**). Class **deque** provides support for random-access iterators, so **deque**s can be used with all STL algorithms. One of the most common uses of a **deque** is to maintain a first-in-first-out queue of elements. In fact, a **deque** is the default underlying implementation for the queue adaptor (Section 21.4.2).

Additional storage for a **deque** can be allocated at either end of the **deque** in blocks of memory that are typically maintained as an array of pointers to those blocks.[4] Due to the non-contiguous memory layout of a **deque**, a **deque** iterator must be more intelligent than the pointers that are used to iterate through **vector**s or pointer-based arrays.

Performance Tip 21.11

*In several implementations, once a storage block is allocated for a **deque**, the block is not deallocated until the **deque** is destroyed. This makes the operation of a **deque** more efficient than if memory were repeatedly allocated, deallocated and reallocated. But this means that the **deque** is more likely to use memory inefficiently (than a **vector**, for example).*

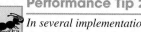
Performance Tip 21.12

*Insertions and deletions in the middle of a **deque** are optimized to minimize the number of elements copied, to maintain the illusion that the elements of the **deque** are contiguous.*

Class **deque** provides the same basic operations as class **vector**, but adds member functions **push_front** and **pop_front** to allow insertion and deletion at the beginning of the **deque**, respectively.

---

4. This is an implementation-specific detail, not a requirement of the C++ standard.

Figure 21.18 demonstrates features of class **deque**. Remember that many of the functions presented in Fig. 21.14, Fig. 21.15 and Fig. 21.17 also can be used with class **deque**. Header file **<deque>** must be included to use class **deque**.

```cpp
1   // Fig. 21.18: fig21_18.cpp
2   // Standard library class deque test program.
3   #include <iostream>
4
5   using std::cout;
6   using std::endl;
7
8   #include <deque>        // deque class-template definition
9   #include <algorithm>    // copy algorithm
10
11  int main()
12  {
13     std::deque< double > values;
14     std::ostream_iterator< double > output( cout, " " );
15
16     // insert elements in values
17     values.push_front( 2.2 );
18     values.push_front( 3.5 );
19     values.push_back( 1.1 );
20
21     cout << "values contains: ";
22
23     // use subscript operator to obtain elements of values
24     for ( int i = 0; i < values.size(); ++i )
25        cout << values[ i ] << ' ';
26
27     values.pop_front();   // remove first element
28
29     cout << "\nAfter pop_front, values contains: ";
30     std::copy( values.begin(), values.end(), output );
31
32     // use subscript operator to modify element at location 1
33     values[ 1 ] = 5.4;
34
35     cout << "\nAfter values[ 1 ] = 5.4, values contains: ";
36     std::copy( values.begin(), values.end(), output );
37
38     cout << endl;
39
40     return 0;
41
42  } // end main
```

```
values contains: 3.5 2.2 1.1
After pop_front, values contains: 2.2 1.1
After values[ 1 ] = 5.4, values contains: 2.2 5.4
```

Fig. 21.18 Standard Library **deque** class template.

Line 13 instantiates a **deque** that can store **double** values. Lines 17–19 use functions **push_front** and **push_back** to insert elements at the beginning and end of the **deque**. Remember that **push_back** is available for all sequence containers, but **push_front** is available only for class **list** and class **deque**.

The **for** structure at lines 24–25 uses the subscript operator to retrieve the value in each element of the **deque** for output. Note that the condition uses function **size** to ensure that we do not attempt to access an element outside the bounds of the **deque**.

Line 27 uses function **pop_front** to demonstrate removing the first element of the **deque**. Remember that **pop_front** is available only for class **list** and class **deque** (not for class **vector**).

Line 33 uses the subscript operator to create an *lvalue*. This enables values to be assigned directly to any element of the **deque**.

21.3 Associative Containers

The STL's associative containers provide direct access to store and retrieve elements via *keys* (often called *search keys*). The four associative containers are **multiset**, **set**, **multimap** and **map**. Each associative container maintains its keys in sorted order. Iterating through an associative container traverses it in the sort order for that container. Classes **multiset** and **set** provide operations for manipulating sets of values where the values are the keys—there is not a separate value associated with each key. The primary difference between a **multiset** and a **set** is that a **multiset** allows duplicate keys and a **set** does not. Classes **multimap** and **map** provide operations for manipulating values associated with keys (these values are sometimes referred to as *mapped values*). The primary difference between a **multimap** and a **map** is that a **multimap** allows duplicate keys with associated values to be stored and a **map** allows only unique keys with associated values. In addition to the common member functions of all containers presented in Fig. 21.2, all associative containers also support several other member functions, including **find**, **lower_bound**, **upper_bound** and **count**. Examples of each of the associative containers and the common associative container member functions are presented in the next several subsections.

21.3.1 **multiset** Associative Container

The **multiset** associative container provides fast storage and retrieval of keys and allows duplicate keys. The ordering of the elements is determined by a *comparator function object*. For example, in an integer **multiset**, elements can be sorted in ascending order by ordering the keys with comparator function object **less< int >**. The data type of the keys in all associative containers must support comparison properly based on the comparator function object specified—keys sorted with **less< T >** must support comparison with **T::operator<**. If the keys used in the associative containers are of programmer-defined data types, those types must supply the appropriate comparison operators. A **multiset** supports bidirectional iterators (but not random-access iterators).

Performance Tip 21.13

*For performance reasons, **multiset**s and **set**s are typically implemented as so-called red–black binary search trees. With this internal representation, the binary search tree tends to be balanced, thus minimizing average search times.*

Figure 21.19 demonstrates the **multiset** associative container for a **multiset** of integers sorted in ascending order. Header file **<set>** must be included to use class **multiset**. Containers **multiset** and **set** provide the same member functions.

```
1   // Fig. 21.19: fig21_19.cpp
2   // Testing Standard Library class multiset
3   #include <iostream>
4
5   using std::cout;
6   using std::endl;
7
8   #include <set>  // multiset class-template definition
9
10  // define short name for multiset type used in this program
11  typedef std::multiset< int, std::less< int > > ims;
12
13  #include <algorithm>  // copy algorithm
14
15  int main()
16  {
17     const int SIZE = 10;
18     int a[ SIZE ] = { 7, 22, 9, 1, 18, 30, 100, 22, 85, 13 };
19
20     ims intMultiset;  // ims is typedef for "integer multiset"
21     std::ostream_iterator< int > output( cout, " " );
22
23     cout << "There are currently " << intMultiset.count( 15 )
24         << " values of 15 in the multiset\n";
25
26     intMultiset.insert( 15 );  // insert 15 in intMultiset
27     intMultiset.insert( 15 );  // insert 15 in intMultiset
28
29     cout << "After inserts, there are "
30         << intMultiset.count( 15 )
31         << " values of 15 in the multiset\n\n";
32
33     // iterator that cannot be used to change element values
34     ims::const_iterator result;
35
36     // find 15 in intMultiset; find returns iterator
37     result = intMultiset.find( 15 );
38
39     if ( result != intMultiset.end() ) // if iterator not at end
40        cout << "Found value 15\n";     // found search value 15
41
42     // find 20 in intMultiset; find returns iterator
43     result = intMultiset.find( 20 );
44
45     if ( result == intMultiset.end() )     // will be true hence
46        cout << "Did not find value 20\n"; // did not find 20
47
```

Fig. 21.19 Standard Library **multiset** class template. (Part 1 of 2.)

```
48       // insert elements of array a into intMultiset
49       intMultiset.insert( a, a + SIZE );
50
51       cout << "\nAfter insert, intMultiset contains:\n";
52       std::copy( intMultiset.begin(), intMultiset.end(), output );
53
54       // determine lower and upper bound of 22 in intMultiset
55       cout << "\n\nLower bound of 22: "
56            << *( intMultiset.lower_bound( 22 ) );
57       cout << "\nUpper bound of 22: "
58            << *( intMultiset.upper_bound( 22 ) );
59
60       // p represents pair of const_iterators
61       std::pair< ims::const_iterator, ims::const_iterator > p;
62
63       // use equal_range to determine lower and upper bound
64       // of 22 in intMultiset
65       p = intMultiset.equal_range( 22 );
66
67       cout << "\n\nequal_range of 22:"
68            << "\n    Lower bound: " << *( p.first )
69            << "\n    Upper bound: " << *( p.second );
70
71       cout << endl;
72
73       return 0;
74
75    } // end main
```

```
There are currently 0 values of 15 in the multiset
After inserts, there are 2 values of 15 in the multiset

Found value 15
Did not find value 20

After insert, intMultiset contains:
1 7 9 13 15 15 18 22 22 30 85 100

Lower bound of 22: 22
Upper bound of 22: 30

equal_range of 22:
   Lower bound: 22
   Upper bound: 30
```

Fig. 21.19 Standard Library **multiset** class template. (Part 2 of 2.)

Line 11 uses a **typedef** to create a new type name (alias) for a **multiset** of integers ordered in ascending order, using the function object **less< int >**. This new type (**ims**) is then used to instantiate an integer **multiset** object, **intMultiset** (line 20).

 Good Programming Practice 21.1

*Use **typedef**s to make code with long type names (such as **multiset**s) easier to read.*

The output statement at line 23 uses function **count** (available to all associative containers) to count the number of occurrences of the value **15** currently in the **multiset**.

Lines 26–27 use one of the three versions of function **insert** to add the value **15** to the **multiset** twice. A second version of **insert** takes an iterator and a value as arguments and begins the search for the insertion point from the iterator position specified. A third version of **insert** takes two iterators as arguments that specify a range of values to add to the **multiset** from another container.

Line 37 uses function **find** (available to all associative containers) to locate the value **15** in the **multiset**. Function **find** returns an **iterator** or a **const_iterator** pointing to the earliest location at which the value is found. If the value is not found, **find** returns an **iterator** or a **const_iterator** equal to the value returned by a call to **end**. Line 43 demonstrates this case.

Line 49 uses function **insert** to insert the elements of array **a** into the **multiset**. At line 52, the **copy** algorithm copies the elements of the **multiset** to the standard output. Note that the elements are displayed in ascending order.

Lines 56 and 58 use functions *lower_bound* and *upper_bound* (available in all associative containers) to locate the earliest occurrence of the value **22** in the **multiset** and the element *after* the last occurrence of the value **22** in the **multiset**. Both functions return **iterator**s or **const_iterator**s pointing to the appropriate location or the iterator returned by **end** if the value is not in the **multiset**.

Line 61 instantiates an instance of class **pair** called **p**. Objects of class **pair** are used to associate pairs of values. In this example, the contents of a **pair** are two **const_iterator**s for our integer-based **multiset**. The purpose of **p** is to store the return value of **multiset** function *equal_range* that returns a **pair** containing the results of both a **lower_bound** and an **upper_bound** operation. Type **pair** contains two **public** data members called *first* and *second*.

Line 65 uses function **equal_range** to determine the **lower_bound** and **upper_bound** of **22** in the **multiset**. Lines 68–69 use **p.first** and **p.second**, respectively, to access the **lower_bound** and **upper_bound**. We dereferenced the iterators to output the values at the locations returned from **equal_range**.

21.3.2 set Associative Container

The **set** associative container is used for fast storage and retrieval of unique keys. The implementation of a **set** is identical to that of a **multiset**, except that a **set** must have unique keys. Therefore, if an attempt is made to insert a duplicate key into a **set**, the duplicate is ignored; because this is the intended mathematical behavior of a set, we do not identify it as a common programming error. A **set** supports bidirectional iterators (but not random-access iterators). Figure 21.20 demonstrates a **set** of **double**s. Header file **<set>** must be included to use class **set**.

Line 11 uses **typedef** to create a new type name (**double_set**) for a set of **double** values ordered in ascending order, using the function object **less< double >**.

Line 20 uses the new type **double_set** to instantiate object **doubleSet**. The constructor call takes the elements in array **a** between **a** and **a + SIZE** (i.e., the entire array) and inserts them into the **set**. Line 24 uses algorithm **copy** to output the contents of the **set**. Notice that the value **2.1**—which appeared twice in array **a**—appears only once in **doubleSet**. This is because container **set** does not allow duplicates.

```
1   // Fig. 21.20: fig21_20.cpp
2   // Standard library class set test program.
3   #include <iostream>
4
5   using std::cout;
6   using std::endl;
7
8   #include <set>
9
10  // define short name for set type used in this program
11  typedef std::set< double, std::less< double > > double_set;
12
13  #include <algorithm>
14
15  int main()
16  {
17     const int SIZE = 5;
18     double a[ SIZE ] = { 2.1, 4.2, 9.5, 2.1, 3.7 };
19
20     double_set doubleSet( a, a + SIZE );
21     std::ostream_iterator< double > output( cout, " " );
22
23     cout << "doubleSet contains: ";
24     std::copy( doubleSet.begin(), doubleSet.end(), output );
25
26     // p represents pair containing const_iterator and bool
27     std::pair< double_set::const_iterator, bool > p;
28
29     // insert 13.8 in doubleSet; insert returns pair in which
30     // p.first represents location of 13.8 in doubleSet and
31     // p.second represents whether 13.8 was inserted
32     p = doubleSet.insert( 13.8 ); // value not in set
33
34     cout << "\n\n" << *( p.first )
35        << ( p.second ? " was" : " was not" ) << " inserted";
36
37     cout << "\ndoubleSet contains: ";
38     std::copy( doubleSet.begin(), doubleSet.end(), output );
39
40     // insert 9.5 in doubleSet
41     p = doubleSet.insert( 9.5 );   // value already in set
42
43     cout << "\n\n" << *( p.first )
44        << ( p.second ? " was" : " was not" ) << " inserted";
45
46     cout << "\ndoubleSet contains: ";
47     std::copy( doubleSet.begin(), doubleSet.end(), output );
48
49     cout << endl;
50
51     return 0;
52
53  } // end main
```

Fig. 21.20 Standard Library **set** class template. (Part 1 of 2.)

```
doubleSet contains: 2.1 3.7 4.2 9.5

13.8 was inserted
doubleSet contains: 2.1 3.7 4.2 9.5 13.8

9.5 was not inserted
doubleSet contains: 2.1 3.7 4.2 9.5 13.8
```

Fig. 21.20   Standard Library **set** class template. (Part 2 of 2.)

Line 27 defines a **pair** consisting of a **const_iterator** for a **double_set** and a **bool** value. This object stores the result of a call to **set** function **insert**.

Line 32 uses function **insert** to place the value **13.8** in the **set**. The returned **pair**, **p**, contains an iterator **p.first** pointing to the value **13.8** in the **set** and a **bool** value that is **true** if the value was inserted and **false** if the value was not inserted (because it was already in the **set**). In this case, **13.8** was not in the set, so it was inserted. Line 41 attempts to insert **9.5**, which is already in the set. The output of lines 43–44 shows that **9.5** was not inserted.

21.3.3 multimap Associative Container

The **multimap** associative container is used for fast storage and retrieval of keys and associated values (often called *key/value pairs*). Many of the methods used with **multiset**s and **set**s are also used with **multimap**s and **map**s. The elements of **multimap**s and **map**s are **pair**s of keys and values instead of individual values. When inserting into a **multimap** or **map**, a **pair** object that contains the key and the value is used. The ordering of the keys is determined by a comparator function object. For example, in a **multimap** that uses integers as the key type, keys can be sorted in ascending order by ordering the keys with comparator function object **less< int >**. Duplicate keys are allowed in a **multimap**, so multiple values can be associated with a single key. This is often called a one-to-many relationship. For example, in a credit-card transaction-processing system, one credit-card account can have many associated transactions; in a university, one student can take many courses, and one professor can teach many students; in the military, one rank (like "private") has many people. A **multimap** supports bidirectional iterators (but not random-access iterators). As with **multiset**s and **set**s, **multimap**s are typically implemented as a red–black binary search tree in which the nodes of the tree are key/value **pair**s. Figure 21.21 demonstrates the **multimap** associative container. Header file **<map>** must be included to use class **multimap**.

```
1   // Fig. 21.21: fig21_21.cpp
2   // Standard library class multimap test program.
3   #include <iostream>
4
5   using std::cout;
6   using std::endl;
7
```

Fig. 21.21   Standard Library **multimap** class template. (Part 1 of 2.)

```
8    #include <map>  // map class-template definition
9
10   // define short name for multimap type used in this program
11   typedef std::multimap< int, double, std::less< int > > mmid;
12
13   int main()
14   {
15      mmid pairs;
16
17      cout << "There are currently " << pairs.count( 15 )
18           << " pairs with key 15 in the multimap\n";
19
20      // insert two value_type objects in pairs
21      pairs.insert( mmid::value_type( 15, 2.7 ) );
22      pairs.insert( mmid::value_type( 15, 99.3 ) );
23
24      cout << "After inserts, there are "
25           << pairs.count( 15 )
26           << " pairs with key 15\n\n";
27
28      // insert five value_type objects in pairs
29      pairs.insert( mmid::value_type( 30, 111.11 ) );
30      pairs.insert( mmid::value_type( 10, 22.22 ) );
31      pairs.insert( mmid::value_type( 25, 33.333 ) );
32      pairs.insert( mmid::value_type( 20, 9.345 ) );
33      pairs.insert( mmid::value_type( 5, 77.54 ) );
34
35      cout << "Multimap pairs contains:\nKey\tValue\n";
36
37      // use const_iterator to walk through elements of pairs
38      for ( mmid::const_iterator iter = pairs.begin();
39            iter != pairs.end(); ++iter )
40         cout << iter->first << '\t'
41              << iter->second << '\n';
42
43      cout << endl;
44
45      return 0;
46
47   } // end main
```

```
There are currently 0 pairs with key 15 in the multimap
After inserts, there are 2 pairs with key 15

Multimap pairs contains:
Key       Value
5         77.54
10        22.22
15        2.7
15        99.3
20        9.345
25        33.333
30        111.11
```

Fig. 21.21 Standard Library **multimap** class template. (Part 2 of 2.)

Performance Tip 21.14

A **multimap** *is implemented to efficiently locate all values paired with a given key.*

Line 11 uses **typedef** to define alias **mmid** for a **multimap** type in which the key type is **int**, the type of a key's associated value is **double** and the elements are ordered in ascending order. Line 15 uses the new type to instantiate a **multimap** called **pairs**. Line 17 uses function **count** to determine the number of key/value pairs with a key of **15**.

Line 21 uses function **insert** to add a new key/value pair to the **multimap**. The expression **mmid::value_type(15, 2.7)** creates a **pair** object in which **first** is the key (**15**) of type **int** and **second** is the value (**2.7**) of type **double**. The type **mmid::value_type** is defined in line 11 as part of the **typedef** for the **multimap**. Line 22 inserts another **pair** object, in which the key is **15** and the value is **99.3**. Then lines 24–26 output the number of pairs with key **15**.

Lines 29–33 insert five additional **pair**s into the **multimap**. The **for** structure at lines 38–41 outputs the contents of the **multimap**, including both keys and values. Lines 41–42 use the **const_iterator** called **iter** to access the members of the **pair** in each element of the **multimap**. Notice in the output that the keys appear in ascending order.

21.3.4 map Associative Container

The **map** associative container is used for fast storage and retrieval of unique keys and associated values. Duplicate keys are not allowed in a **map**, so only a single value can be associated with each key. This is called a *one-to-one mapping*. For example, a company that uses unique employee numbers, such as 100, 200 and 300, might have a **map** that associates employee numbers with their telephone extensions—4321, 4115 and 5217, respectively. With a **map** you specify the key and get back the associated data quickly. A **map** is commonly called an *associative array*. Providing the key in a **map**'s subscript operator **[]** locates the value associated with that key in the **map**. Insertions and deletions can be made anywhere in a **map**.

Figure 21.22 demonstrates the **map** associative container. Figure 21.22 uses the same features as Fig. 21.21 and demonstrates the subscript operator. Header file **<map>** must be included to use class **map**. Lines 36 and 39 use the subscript operator of class **map**. When the subscript is a key that is already in the **map** (line 36), the operator returns a reference to the associated value. When the subscript is a key that is not in the **map** (line 39), the operator inserts the key in the **map** and returns a reference that can be used to associate a value with that key. Line 36 replaces the value for the key **25** (previously **33.333** as specified in line 22) with a new value, **9999.99**. Line 39 inserts a new key/value **pair** (called *creating an association*) in the **map**.

```
1   // Fig. 21.22: fig21_22.cpp
2   // Standard library class map test program.
3   #include <iostream>
4
5   using std::cout;
6   using std::endl;
```

Fig. 21.22 Standard Library **map** class template. (Part 1 of 3.)

```
7
8    #include <map>  // map class-template definition
9
10   // define short name for map type used in this program
11   typedef std::map< int, double, std::less< int > > mid;
12
13   int main()
14   {
15      mid pairs;
16
17      // insert eight value_type objects in pairs
18      pairs.insert( mid::value_type( 15, 2.7 ) );
19      pairs.insert( mid::value_type( 30, 111.11 ) );
20      pairs.insert( mid::value_type( 5, 1010.1 ) );
21      pairs.insert( mid::value_type( 10, 22.22 ) );
22      pairs.insert( mid::value_type( 25, 33.333 ) );
23      pairs.insert( mid::value_type( 5, 77.54 ) ); // dupe ignored
24      pairs.insert( mid::value_type( 20, 9.345 ) );
25      pairs.insert( mid::value_type( 15, 99.3 ) ); // dupe ignored
26
27      cout << "pairs contains:\nKey\tValue\n";
28
29      // use const_iterator to walk through elements of pairs
30      for ( mid::const_iterator iter = pairs.begin();
31           iter != pairs.end(); ++iter )
32         cout << iter->first << '\t'
33              << iter->second << '\n';
34
35      // use subscript operator to change value for key 25
36      pairs[ 25 ] = 9999.99;
37
38      // use subscript operator insert value for key 40
39      pairs[ 40 ] = 8765.43;
40
41      cout << "\nAfter subscript operations, pairs contains:"
42           << "\nKey\tValue\n";
43
44      for ( mid::const_iterator iter2 = pairs.begin();
45           iter2 != pairs.end(); ++iter2 )
46         cout << iter2->first << '\t'
47              << iter2->second << '\n';
48
49      cout << endl;
50
51      return 0;
52
53   } // end main
```

```
pairs contains:
Key     Value
5       1010.1
10      22.22                              (continued next page)
```

Fig. 21.22 Standard Library **map** class template. (Part 2 of 3.)

```
15        2.7
20        9.345
25        33.333
30        111.11

After subscript operations, pairs contains:
Key       Value
5         1010.1
10        22.22
15        2.7
20        9.345
25        9999.99
30        111.11
40        8765.43
```

Fig. 21.22 Standard Library **map** class template. (Part 3 of 3.)

21.4 Container Adapters

The STL provides three *container adapters*—**stack**, **queue** and **priority_queue**. Adapters are not first-class containers, because they do not provide the actual data-structure implementation in which elements can be stored and because adapters do not support iterators. The benefit of an adapter class is that the programmer can choose an appropriate underlying data structure. All three adapter classes provide member functions *push* and *pop* that properly insert an element into each adapter data structure and properly remove an element from each adapter data structure. The next several subsections provide examples of the adapter classes.

21.4.1 stack Adapter

Class **stack** enables insertions into and deletions from the underlying data structure at one end (commonly referred to as a *last-in-first-out* data structure). A **stack** can be implemented with any of the sequence containers: **vector**, **list** and **deque**. This example creates three integer stacks, using each of the sequence containers of the Standard Library as the underlying data structure to represent the **stack**. By default, a **stack** is implemented with a **deque**. The **stack** operations are **push** to insert an element at the top of the **stack** (implemented by calling function **push_back** of the underlying container), **pop** to remove the top element of the **stack** (implemented by calling function **pop_back** of the underlying container), *top* to get a reference to the top element of the **stack** (implemented by calling function **back** of the underlying container), **empty** to determine whether the **stack** is empty (implemented by calling function **empty** of the underlying container) and **size** to get the number of elements in the **stack** (implemented by calling function **size** of the underlying container).

Performance Tip 21.15

*Each of the common operations of a **stack** is implemented as an **inline** function that calls the appropriate function of the underlying container. This avoids the overhead of a second function call.*

Performance Tip 21.16

*For the best performance, use class **deque** or **vector** as the underlying container for a* **stack***.*

Figure 21.23 demonstrates the **stack** adapter class. Header file **<stack>** must be included to use class **stack**.

Lines 19, 22 and 25 instantiate three integer stacks. Line 19 specifies a **stack** of integers that uses the default **deque** container as its underlying data structure. Line 22 specifies a **stack** of integers that uses a **vector** of integers as its underlying data structure. Line 25 specifies a **stack** of integers that uses a **list** of integers as its underlying data structure.

```cpp
1   // Fig. 21.23: fig21_23.cpp
2   // Standard library adapter stack test program.
3   #include <iostream>
4
5   using std::cout;
6   using std::endl;
7
8   #include <stack>      // stack adapter definition
9   #include <vector>     // vector class-template definition
10  #include <list>       // list class-template definition
11
12  // popElements function-template prototype
13  template< class T >
14  void popElements( T &stackRef );
15
16  int main()
17  {
18      // stack with default underlying deque
19      std::stack< int > intDequeStack;
20
21      // stack with underlying vector
22      std::stack< int, std::vector< int > > intVectorStack;
23
24      // stack with underlying list
25      std::stack< int, std::list< int > > intListStack;
26
27      // push the values 0-9 onto each stack
28      for ( int i = 0; i < 10; ++i ) {
29          intDequeStack.push( i );
30          intVectorStack.push( i );
31          intListStack.push( i );
32
33      } // end for
34
35      // display and remove elements from each stack
36      cout << "Popping from intDequeStack: ";
37      popElements( intDequeStack );
38      cout << "\nPopping from intVectorStack: ";
39      popElements( intVectorStack );
```

Fig. 21.23 Standard Library **stack** adapter class. (Part 1 of 2.)

```
40        cout << "\nPopping from intListStack: ";
41        popElements( intListStack );
42
43        cout << endl;
44
45        return 0;
46
47   } // end main
48
49   // pop elements from stack object to which stackRef refers
50   template< class T >
51   void popElements( T &stackRef )
52   {
53        while ( !stackRef.empty() ) {
54           cout << stackRef.top() << ' ';    // view top element
55           stackRef.pop();                   // remove top element
56
57        } // end while
58
59   } // end function popElements
```

```
Popping from intDequeStack: 9 8 7 6 5 4 3 2 1 0
Popping from intVectorStack: 9 8 7 6 5 4 3 2 1 0
Popping from intListStack: 9 8 7 6 5 4 3 2 1 0
```

Fig. 21.23 Standard Library **stack** adapter class. (Part 2 of 2.)

Lines 29–31 each use function **push** (available in each adapter class) to place an integer on top of each **stack**.

Function **popElements** (lines 50–59) pops the elements off each **stack**. Line 54 uses **stack** function **top** to retrieve the top element of the **stack** for output. Function **top** does not remove the top element. Line 55 uses function **pop** (available in each adapter class) to remove the top element of the **stack**. Function **pop** does not return a value.

21.4.2 queue Adapter

Class **queue** enables insertions at the back of the underlying data structure and deletions from the front of the underlying data structure (commonly referred to as a *first-in-first-out* data structure). A **queue** can be implemented with STL data structure **list** or **deque**. By default, a **queue** is implemented with a **deque**. The common **queue** operations are **push** to insert an element at the back of the **queue** (implemented by calling function **push_back** of the underlying container), **pop** to remove the element at the front of the **queue** (implemented by calling function **pop_front** of the underlying container), **front** to get a reference to the first element in the **queue** (implemented by calling function **front** of the underlying container), **back** to get a reference to the last element in the **queue** (implemented by calling function **back** of the underlying container), **empty** to determine whether the **queue** is empty (implemented by calling function **empty** of the underlying container) and **size** to get the number of elements in the **queue** (implemented by calling function **size** of the underlying container).

Performance Tip 21.17

*Each of the common operations of a **queue** is implemented as an **inline** function that calls the appropriate function of the underlying container. This avoids the overhead of a second function call.*

Performance Tip 21.18

*For the best performance, use class **deque** as the underlying container for a **queue**.*

Figure 21.24 demonstrates the **queue** adapter class. Header file **<queue>** must be included to use a **queue**.

Line 12 instantiates a **queue** that stores **double** values. Lines 15–17 use function **push** to add elements to the **queue**. The **while** structure at lines 21–25 uses function **empty** (available in all containers) to determine whether the **queue** is empty (line 21).

```cpp
1   // Fig. 21.24: fig21_24.cpp
2   // Standard library adapter queue test program.
3   #include <iostream>
4
5   using std::cout;
6   using std::endl;
7
8   #include <queue>   // queue adapter definition
9
10  int main()
11  {
12     std::queue< double > values;
13
14     // push elements onto queue values
15     values.push( 3.2 );
16     values.push( 9.8 );
17     values.push( 5.4 );
18
19     cout << "Popping from values: ";
20
21     while ( !values.empty() ) {
22        cout << values.front() << ' ';   // view front element
23        values.pop();                     // remove element
24
25     } // end while
26
27     cout << endl;
28
29     return 0;
30
31  } // end main
```

```
Popping from values: 3.2 9.8 5.4
```

Fig. 21.24 Standard Library **queue** adapter class templates.

While there are more elements in the **queue**, line 22 uses **queue** function **front** to read (but not remove) the first element in the **queue** for output. Line 23 removes the first element in the **queue** with function **pop** (available in all adapter classes).

21.4.3 `priority_queue` Adapter

Class **priority_queue** provides functionality that enables insertions in sorted order into the underlying data structure and deletions from the front of the underlying data structure. A **priority_queue** can be implemented with STL data structures **vector** or **deque**. By default, a **priority_queue** is implemented with a **vector** as the underlying data structure. When adding elements to a **priority_queue**, the elements are inserted in priority order such that the highest-priority element (i.e., the largest value) will be the first element removed from the **priority_queue**. This is usually accomplished by using a sorting technique called *heapsort* that always maintains the largest value (i.e., highest priority) at the front of the data structure—such a data structure is called a *heap*. The comparison of elements is performed with comparator function object **less< T >** by default, but the programmer can supply a different comparator.

The common **priority_queue** operations are **push** to insert an element at the appropriate location based on priority order of the **priority_queue** (implemented by calling function **push_back** of the underlying container, then reordering the elements using heapsort), **pop** to remove the highest-priority element of the **priority_queue** (implemented by calling function **pop_back** of the underlying container after removing the top element of the heap), **top** to get a reference to the top element of the **priority_queue** (implemented by calling function **front** of the underlying container), **empty** to determine whether the **priority_queue** is empty (implemented by calling function **empty** of the underlying container) and **size** to get the number of elements in the **priority_queue** (implemented by calling function **size** of the underlying container).

Performance Tip 21.19

Each of the common operations of a **priority_queue** *is implemented as an* **inline** *function that calls the appropriate function of the underlying container. This avoids the overhead of a second function call.*

Performance Tip 21.20

For the best performance, use class **vector** *as the underlying container for a* **priority_queue**.

Figure 21.25 demonstrates the **priority_queue** adapter class. Header file **<queue>** must be included to use class **priority_queue**.

```
1   // Fig. 21.25: fig21_25.cpp
2   // Standard library adapter priority_queue test program.
3   #include <iostream>
4
5   using std::cout;
6   using std::endl;
```

Fig. 21.25 Standard Library **priority_queue** adapter class. (Part 1 of 2.)

```
7
8   #include <queue>   // priority_queue adapter definition
9
10  int main()
11  {
12     std::priority_queue< double > priorities;
13
14     // push elements onto priorities
15     priorities.push( 3.2 );
16     priorities.push( 9.8 );
17     priorities.push( 5.4 );
18
19     cout << "Popping from priorities: ";
20
21     while ( !priorities.empty() ) {
22        cout << priorities.top() << ' ';   // view top element
23        priorities.pop();                   // remove top element
24
25     } // end while
26
27     cout << endl;
28
29     return 0;
30
31  } // end main
```

```
Popping from priorities: 9.8 5.4 3.2
```

Fig. 21.25 Standard Library **priority_queue** adapter class.   (Part 2 of 2.)

Line 12 instantiates a **priority_queue** that stores **double** values and uses a **vector** as the underlying data structure. Lines 15–17 use function **push** to add elements to the **priority_queue**. The **while** structure at lines 21–25 uses function **empty** (available in all containers) to determine whether the **priority_queue** is empty (line 21). While there are more elements, line 22 uses **priority_queue** function **top** to retrieve the highest-priority element in the **priority_queue** for output. Line 23 removes the highest-priority element in the **priority_queue** with function **pop** (available in all adapter classes).

21.5 Algorithms

Until STL, class libraries of containers and algorithms were essentially incompatible among vendors. Early container libraries generally used inheritance and polymorphism, with the associated overhead of **virtual** function calls. Early libraries built the algorithms into the container classes as class behaviors. STL separates the algorithms from the containers. This makes it much easier to add new algorithms. STL is implemented for efficiency. It avoids the overhead of **virtual** function calls. With STL, the elements of containers are accessed through iterators. The next several subsections demonstrate many of the STL algorithms.

Software Engineering Observation 21.8

STL algorithms do not depend on the implementation details of the containers on which they operate. As long as the container's (or array's) iterators satisfy the requirements of the algorithm, STL algorithms can work on C-style, pointer-based arrays, on STL containers and on user-defined data structures.

Software Engineering Observation 21.9

Algorithms can be added easily to the STL without modifying the container classes.

21.5.1 `fill`, `fill_n`, `generate` and `generate_n`

Figure 21.26 demonstrates algorithms `fill`, `fill_n`, `generate` and `generate_n`. Functions `fill` and `fill_n` set every element in a range of container elements to a specific value. Functions `generate` and `generate_n` use a *generator function* to create values for every element in a range of container elements. The generator function takes no arguments and returns a value that can be placed in an element of the container.

```cpp
1   // Fig. 21.26: fig21_26.cpp
2   // Standard library algorithms fill, fill_n, generate
3   // and generate_n.
4   #include <iostream>
5
6   using std::cout;
7   using std::endl;
8
9   #include <algorithm>   // algorithm definitions
10  #include <vector>      // vector class-template definition
11
12  char nextLetter();     // prototype
13
14  int main()
15  {
16     std::vector< char > chars( 10 );
17     std::ostream_iterator< char > output( cout, " " );
18
19     // fill chars with 5s
20     std::fill( chars.begin(), chars.end(), '5' );
21
22     cout << "Vector chars after filling with 5s:\n";
23     std::copy( chars.begin(), chars.end(), output );
24
25     // fill first five elements of chars with As
26     std::fill_n( chars.begin(), 5, 'A' );
27
28     cout << "\n\nVector chars after filling five elements"
29        << " with As:\n";
30     std::copy( chars.begin(), chars.end(), output );
31
32     // generate values for all elements of chars with nextLetter
33     std::generate( chars.begin(), chars.end(), nextLetter );
```

Fig. 21.26 Algorithms `fill`, `fill_n`, `generate` and `generate_n`. (Part 1 of 2.)

```
34
35        cout << "\n\nVector chars after generating letters A-J:\n";
36        std::copy( chars.begin(), chars.end(), output );
37
38        // generate values for first five elements of chars
39        // with nextLetter
40        std::generate_n( chars.begin(), 5, nextLetter );
41
42        cout << "\n\nVector chars after generating K-O for the"
43             << " first five elements:\n";
44        std::copy( chars.begin(), chars.end(), output );
45
46        cout << endl;
47
48        return 0;
49
50   } // end main
51
52   // returns next letter in the alphabet (starts with A)
53   char nextLetter()
54   {
55        static char letter = 'A';
56        return letter++;
57
58   } // end function nextLetter
```

```
Vector chars after filling with 5s:
5 5 5 5 5 5 5 5 5 5

Vector chars after filling five elements with As:
A A A A A 5 5 5 5 5

Vector chars after generating letters A-J:
A B C D E F G H I J

Vector chars after generating K-O for the first five elements:
K L M N O F G H I J
```

Fig. 21.26 Algorithms `fill`, `fill_n`, `generate` and `generate_n`. (Part 2 of 2.)

Line 20 uses function **fill** to place the character **'5'** in every element of **vector chars** from **chars.begin()** up to, but not including, **chars.end()**. Note that the iterators supplied as the first and second argument must be at least forward iterators (i.e., they can be used for both input from a container and output to a container in the forward direction).

Line 26 uses function **fill_n** to place the character **'A'** in the first five elements of **vector chars**. The iterator supplied as the first argument must be at least an output iterator (i.e., it can be used for output to a container in the forward direction). The second argument specifies the number of elements to fill. The third argument specifies the value to place in each element.

Line 33 uses function **generate** to place the result of a call to generator function **nextLetter** in every element of **vector chars** from **chars.begin()** up to, but not including, **chars.end()**. The iterators supplied as the first and second arguments must be at least forward iterators. Function **nextLetter** (defined at lines 53–58) begins with the character **'A'** maintained in a **static** local variable. The statement at line 56 increments the value of **letter** and returns the old value of **letter** each time **next-Letter** is called.

Line 40 uses function **generate_n** to place the result of a call to generator function **nextLetter** in five elements of **vector chars**, starting from **chars.begin()**. The iterator supplied as the first argument must be at least an output iterator.

21.5.2 equal, mismatch and lexicographical_compare

Figure 21.27 demonstrates comparing sequences of values for equality using algorithms **equal**, **mismatch** and **lexicographical_compare**.

```cpp
1   // Fig. 21.27: fig21_27.cpp
2   // Standard library functions equal,
3   // mismatch and lexicographical_compare.
4   #include <iostream>
5
6   using std::cout;
7   using std::endl;
8
9   #include <algorithm>    // algorithm definitions
10  #include <vector>       // vector class-template definition
11
12  int main()
13  {
14     const int SIZE = 10;
15     int a1[ SIZE ] = { 1, 2, 3, 4, 5, 6, 7, 8, 9, 10 };
16     int a2[ SIZE ] = { 1, 2, 3, 4, 1000, 6, 7, 8, 9, 10 };
17
18     std::vector< int > v1( a1, a1 + SIZE );
19     std::vector< int > v2( a1, a1 + SIZE );
20     std::vector< int > v3( a2, a2 + SIZE );
21
22     std::ostream_iterator< int > output( cout, " " );
23
24     cout << "Vector v1 contains: ";
25     std::copy( v1.begin(), v1.end(), output );
26     cout << "\nVector v2 contains: ";
27     std::copy( v2.begin(), v2.end(), output );
28     cout << "\nVector v3 contains: ";
29     std::copy( v3.begin(), v3.end(), output );
30
31     // compare vectors v1 and v2 for equality
32     bool result =
33        std::equal( v1.begin(), v1.end(), v2.begin() );
```

Fig. 21.27 Algorithms **equal**, **mismatch** and **lexicographical_compare**. (Part 1 of 2.)

```
34
35        cout << "\n\nVector v1 " << ( result ? "is" : "is not" )
36           << " equal to vector v2.\n";
37
38        // compare vectors v1 and v3 for equality
39        result = std::equal( v1.begin(), v1.end(), v3.begin() );
40        cout << "Vector v1 " << ( result ? "is" : "is not" )
41           << " equal to vector v3.\n";
42
43        // location represents pair of vector iterators
44        std::pair< std::vector< int >::iterator,
45                   std::vector< int >::iterator > location;
46
47        // check for mismatch between v1 and v3
48        location =
49           std::mismatch( v1.begin(), v1.end(), v3.begin() );
50
51        cout << "\nThere is a mismatch between v1 and v3 at "
52           << "location " << ( location.first - v1.begin() )
53           << "\nwhere v1 contains " << *location.first
54           << " and v3 contains " << *location.second
55           << "\n\n";
56
57        char c1[ SIZE ] = "HELLO";
58        char c2[ SIZE ] = "BYE BYE";
59
60        // perform lexicographical comparison of c1 and c2
61        result = std::lexicographical_compare(
62           c1, c1 + SIZE, c2, c2 + SIZE );
63
64        cout << c1
65           << ( result ? " is less than " :
66                " is greater than or equal to " )
67           << c2 << endl;
68
69        return 0;
70
71    } // end main
```

```
Vector v1 contains: 1 2 3 4 5 6 7 8 9 10
Vector v2 contains: 1 2 3 4 5 6 7 8 9 10
Vector v3 contains: 1 2 3 4 1000 6 7 8 9 10

Vector v1 is equal to vector v2.
Vector v1 is not equal to vector v3.

There is a mismatch between v1 and v3 at location 4
where v1 contains 5 and v3 contains 1000

HELLO is greater than or equal to BYE BYE
```

Fig. 21.27 Algorithms **equal**, **mismatch** and **lexicographical_compare**.
(Part 2 of 2.)

Lines 32–33 use function **equal** to compare two sequences of values for equality. Each sequence need not necessarily contain the same number of elements—**equal** returns **false** if the sequences are not of the same length. Function **operator==** performs the comparison of the elements. In this example, the elements in **vector v1** from **v1.begin()** up to, but not including, **v1.end()** are compared to the elements in **vector v2** starting from **v2.begin()**. In this example, **v1** and **v2** are equal. The three iterator arguments must be at least input iterators (i.e., they can be used for input from a sequence in the forward direction). Line 39 uses function **equal** to compare **vector**s **v1** and **v3**, which are not equal.

There is another version of function **equal** that takes a binary predicate function as a fourth parameter. The binary predicate function receives the two elements being compared and returns a **bool** value indicating whether the elements are equal. This can be useful in sequences that store objects or pointers to values rather than actual values, because you can define one or more comparisons. For example, you can compare **Employee** objects for age, Social Security number, or location rather than comparing entire objects. You can compare what pointers refer to rather than comparing the pointer contents (i.e., the addresses stored in the pointers).

Lines 44–49 begin by instantiating a **pair** of iterators called **location** for a **vector** of integers. This object stores the result of the call to **mismatch** (line 49). Function **mismatch** compares two sequences of values and returns a **pair** of iterators indicating the location in each sequence of the mismatched elements. If all the elements match, the two iterators in the **pair** are equal to the last iterator for each sequence. The three iterator arguments must be at least input iterators. Line 52 determines the actual location of the mismatch in the **vector**s with the expression **location.first - v1.begin()**. The result of this calculation is the number of elements between the iterators (this is analogous to pointer arithmetic that we studied in Chapter 5). This corresponds to the element number in this example, because the comparison is performed from the beginning of each **vector**. As with function **equal**, there is another version of function **mismatch** that takes a binary predicate function as a fourth parameter.

Lines 61–62 use function **lexicographical_compare** to compare the contents of two character arrays. This function's four iterator arguments must be at least input iterators. As you know, pointers into arrays are random-access iterators. The first two iterator arguments specify the range of locations in the first sequence. The last two iterator arguments specify the range of locations in the second sequence. While iterating through the sequences, if the element in the first sequence is less than the corresponding element in the second sequence, the function returns **true**. If the element in the first sequence is greater than or equal to the element in the second sequence, the function returns **false**. This function can be used to arrange sequences lexicographically. Typically, such sequences contain strings.

21.5.3 remove, remove_if, remove_copy and remove_copy_if

Figure 21.28 demonstrates removing values from a sequence with algorithms **remove**, **remove_if**, **remove_copy** and **remove_copy_if**.

Line 28 uses function **remove** to eliminate all elements with the value **10** in the range from **v.begin()** up to, but not including, **v.end()** from **v**. The first two iterator arguments must be forward iterators so that the algorithm can modify the elements in the sequence. This function does not modify the number of elements in the **vector** or destroy the eliminated elements, but it does move all elements that are not eliminated toward the beginning of the **vector**. The function returns an iterator positioned after the last **vector** element that was not deleted. Elements from the iterator position to the end of the **vector** have undefined values (in this example, each "undefined" position has value 0).

Line 41 uses function **remove_copy** to copy all elements that do not have the value **10** in the range from **v2.begin()** up to, but not including, **v2.end()** from **v2**. The elements are placed in **c**, starting at position **c.begin()**. The iterators supplied as the first two arguments must be input iterators. The iterator supplied as the third argument must be an output iterator so that the element being copied can be inserted into the copy location. This function returns an iterator positioned after the last element copied into **vector c**. Note, on line 34, the use of the vector constructor that receives the number of elements in the **vector** and the initial values of those elements.

```
1    // Fig. 21.28: fig21_28.cpp
2    // Standard library functions remove, remove_if,
3    // remove_copy and remove_copy_if.
4    #include <iostream>
5
6    using std::cout;
7    using std::endl;
8
9    #include <algorithm>    // algorithm definitions
10   #include <vector>       // vector class-template definition
11
12   bool greater9( int );  // prototype
13
14   int main()
15   {
16      const int SIZE = 10;
17      int a[ SIZE ] = { 10, 2, 10, 4, 16, 6, 14, 8, 12, 10 };
18
19      std::ostream_iterator< int > output( cout, " " );
20
21      std::vector< int > v( a, a + SIZE );
22      std::vector< int >::iterator newLastElement;
23
24      cout << "Vector v before removing all 10s:\n   ";
25      std::copy( v.begin(), v.end(), output );
26
27      // remove 10 from v
28      newLastElement = std::remove( v.begin(), v.end(), 10 );
29
30      cout << "\nVector v after removing all 10s:\n   ";
31      std::copy( v.begin(), newLastElement, output );
32
33      std::vector< int > v2( a, a + SIZE );
34      std::vector< int > c( SIZE, 0 );
35
```

Fig. 21.28   Algorithms **remove**, **remove_if**, **remove_copy** and **remove_copy_if**. (Part 1 of 3.)

```
36      cout << "\n\nVector v2 before removing all 10s "
37          << "and copying:\n    ";
38      std::copy( v2.begin(), v2.end(), output );
39
40      // copy from v2 to c, removing 10s in the process
41      std::remove_copy( v2.begin(), v2.end(), c.begin(), 10 );
42
43      cout << "\nVector c after removing all 10s from v2:\n    ";
44      std::copy( c.begin(), c.end(), output );
45
46      std::vector< int > v3( a, a + SIZE );
47
48      cout << "\n\nVector v3 before removing all elements"
49          << "\ngreater than 9:\n    ";
50      std::copy( v3.begin(), v3.end(), output );
51
52      // remove elements greater than 9 from v3
53      newLastElement =
54          std::remove_if( v3.begin(), v3.end(), greater9 );
55
56      cout << "\nVector v3 after removing all elements"
57          << "\ngreater than 9:\n    ";
58      std::copy( v3.begin(), newLastElement, output );
59
60      std::vector< int > v4( a, a + SIZE );
61      std::vector< int > c2( SIZE, 0 );
62
63      cout << "\n\nVector v4 before removing all elements"
64          << "\ngreater than 9 and copying:\n    ";
65      std::copy( v4.begin(), v4.end(), output );
66
67      // copy elements from v4 to c2, removing elements greater
68      // than 9 in the process
69      std::remove_copy_if(
70          v4.begin(), v4.end(), c2.begin(), greater9 );
71
72      cout << "\nVector c2 after removing all elements"
73          << "\ngreater than 9 from v4:\n    ";
74      std::copy( c2.begin(), c2.end(), output );
75
76      cout << endl;
77
78      return 0;
79
80  } // end main
81
82  // determine whether argument is greater than 9
83  bool greater9( int x )
84  {
85      return x > 9;
86
87  } // end greater9
```

Fig. 21.28 Algorithms **remove**, **remove_if**, **remove_copy** and
remove_copy_if. (Part 2 of 3.)

```
Vector v before removing all 10s:
   10 2 10 4 16 6 14 8 12 10
Vector v after removing all 10s:
   2 4 16 6 14 8 12

Vector v2 before removing all 10s and copying:
   10 2 10 4 16 6 14 8 12 10
Vector c after removing all 10s from v2:
   2 4 16 6 14 8 12 0 0 0

Vector v3 before removing all elements
greater than 9:
   10 2 10 4 16 6 14 8 12 10
Vector v3 after removing all elements
greater than 9:
   2 4 6 8

Vector v4 before removing all elements
greater than 9 and copying:
   10 2 10 4 16 6 14 8 12 10
Vector c2 after removing all elements
greater than 9 from v4:
   2 4 6 8 0 0 0 0 0 0
```

Fig. 21.28 Algorithms **remove**, **remove_if**, **remove_copy** and **remove_copy_if**. (Part 3 of 3.)

Lines 53–54 use function **remove_if** to delete all those elements in the range from **v3.begin()** up to, but not including, **v3.end()** from **v3** for which our user-defined unary predicate function **greater9** returns **true**. Function **greater9** (defined at lines 83–87) returns **true** if the value passed to it is greater than 9; otherwise, it returns **false**. The iterators supplied as the first two arguments must be forward iterators so that the algorithm can modify the elements in the sequence. This function does not modify the number of elements in the **vector**, but it does move to the beginning of the **vector** all elements that are not eliminated. This function returns an iterator positioned after the last element in the **vector** that was not deleted. All elements from the iterator position to the end of the **vector** have undefined values.

Lines 69–70 use function **remove_copy_if** to copy all those elements in the range from **v4.begin()** up to, but not including, **v4.end()** from **v4** for which the unary predicate function **greater9** returns **true**. The elements are placed in **c2**, starting at position **c2.begin()**. The iterators supplied as the first two arguments must be input iterators. The iterator supplied as the third argument must be an output iterator so that the element being copied can be inserted into the copy location. This function returns an iterator positioned after the last element copied into **c2**.

21.5.4 **replace**, **replace_if**, **replace_copy** and **replace_copy_if**

Figure 21.29 demonstrates replacing values from a sequence using algorithms **replace**, **replace_if**, **replace_copy** and **replace_copy_if**.

```cpp
1   // Fig. 21.29: fig21_29.cpp
2   // Standard library functions replace, replace_if,
3   // replace_copy and replace_copy_if.
4   #include <iostream>
5
6   using std::cout;
7   using std::endl;
8
9   #include <algorithm>
10  #include <vector>
11
12  bool greater9( int );
13
14  int main()
15  {
16     const int SIZE = 10;
17     int a[ SIZE ] = { 10, 2, 10, 4, 16, 6, 14, 8, 12, 10 };
18
19     std::ostream_iterator< int > output( cout, " " );
20
21     std::vector< int > v1( a, a + SIZE );
22     cout << "Vector v1 before replacing all 10s:\n   ";
23     std::copy( v1.begin(), v1.end(), output );
24
25     // replace 10s in v1 with 100
26     std::replace( v1.begin(), v1.end(), 10, 100 );
27
28     cout << "\nVector v1 after replacing 10s with 100s:\n   ";
29     std::copy( v1.begin(), v1.end(), output );
30
31     std::vector< int > v2( a, a + SIZE );
32     std::vector< int > c1( SIZE );
33
34     cout << "\n\nVector v2 before replacing all 10s "
35          << "and copying:\n   ";
36     std::copy( v2.begin(), v2.end(), output );
37
38     // copy from v2 to c1, replacing 10s with 100s
39     std::replace_copy(
40        v2.begin(), v2.end(), c1.begin(), 10, 100 );
41
42     cout << "\nVector c1 after replacing all 10s in v2:\n   ";
43     std::copy( c1.begin(), c1.end(), output );
44
45     std::vector< int > v3( a, a + SIZE );
46
47     cout << "\n\nVector v3 before replacing values greater"
48          << " than 9:\n   ";
49     std::copy( v3.begin(), v3.end(), output );
50
51     // replace values greater than 9 in v3 with 100
52     std::replace_if( v3.begin(), v3.end(), greater9, 100 );
```

Fig. 21.29 Algorithms **replace**, **replace_if**, **replace_copy** and **replace_copy_if**. (Part 1 of 2.)

```
53
54      cout << "\nVector v3 after replacing all values greater"
55             << "\nthan 9 with 100s:\n   ";
56      std::copy( v3.begin(), v3.end(), output );
57
58      std::vector< int > v4( a, a + SIZE );
59      std::vector< int > c2( SIZE );
60
61      cout << "\n\nVector v4 before replacing all values greater "
62             << "than 9 and copying:\n   ";
63      std::copy( v4.begin(), v4.end(), output );
64
65      // copy v4 to c2, replacing elements greater than 9 with 100
66      std::replace_copy_if(
67         v4.begin(), v4.end(), c2.begin(), greater9, 100 );
68
69      cout << "\nVector c2 after replacing all values greater "
70             << "than 9 in v4:\n   ";
71      std::copy( c2.begin(), c2.end(), output );
72
73      cout << endl;
74
75      return 0;
76
77   } // end main
78
79   // determine whether argument is greater than 9
80   bool greater9( int x )
81   {
82      return x > 9;
83
84   } // end function greater9
```

```
Vector v1 before replacing all 10s:
   10 2 10 4 16 6 14 8 12 10
Vector v1 after replacing 10s with 100s:
   100 2 100 4 16 6 14 8 12 100

Vector v2 before replacing all 10s and copying:
   10 2 10 4 16 6 14 8 12 10
Vector c1 after replacing all 10s in v2:
   100 2 100 4 16 6 14 8 12 100

Vector v3 before replacing values greater than 9:
   10 2 10 4 16 6 14 8 12 10
Vector v3 after replacing all values greater
than 9 with 100s:
   100 2 100 4 100 6 100 8 100 100

Vector v4 before replacing all values greater than 9 and copying:
   10 2 10 4 16 6 14 8 12 10
Vector c2 after replacing all values greater than 9 in v4:
   100 2 100 4 100 6 100 8 100 100
```

Fig. 21.29 Algorithms **replace**, **replace_if**, **replace_copy** and
          replace_copy_if. (Part 2 of 2.)

```
67
68        // calculate cube of each element in v;
69        // place results in cubes
70        std::transform(
71           v.begin(), v.end(), cubes.begin(), calculateCube );
72
73        cout << "\n\nThe cube of every integer in Vector v is:\n";
74        std::copy( cubes.begin(), cubes.end(), output );
75
76        cout << endl;
77
78        return 0;
79
80     } // end main
81
82     // determine whether argument is greater than 9
83     bool greater9( int value )
84     {
85        return value > 9;
86
87     } // end function greater9
88
89     // output square of argument
90     void outputSquare( int value )
91     {
92        cout << value * value << ' ';
93
94     } // end function outputSquare
95
96     // return cube of argument
97     int calculateCube( int value )
98     {
99        return value * value * value;
100
101    } // end function calculateCube
```

```
Vector v before random_shuffle: 1 2 3 4 5 6 7 8 9 10
Vector v after random_shuffle: 5 4 1 3 7 8 9 10 6 2

Vector v2 contains: 100 2 8 1 50 3 8 8 9 10
Number of elements matching 8: 3
Number of elements greater than 9: 3

Minimum element in Vector v2 is: 1
Maximum element in Vector v2 is: 100

The total of the elements in Vector v is: 55

The square of every integer in Vector v is:
25 16 1 9 49 64 81 100 36 4

The cube of every integer in Vector v is:
125 64 1 27 343 512 729 1000 216 8
```

Fig. 21.30 Mathematical algorithms of the Standard Library. (Part 3 of 3.)

Line 40 uses function **count** to count the elements with the value **8** in the range from **v2.begin()** up to, but not including, **v2.end()** in **v2**. This function requires its two iterator arguments to be at least input iterators.

Line 45 uses function **count_if** to count those elements in the range from **v2.begin()** up to, but not including, **v2.end()** in **v2** for which the predicate function **greater9** returns **true**. Function **count_if** requires its two iterator arguments to be at least input iterators.

Line 51 uses function **min_element** to locate the smallest element in the range from **v2.begin()** up to, but not including, **v2.end()** in **v2**. The function returns an input iterator located at the smallest element or, if the range is empty, returns the iterator itself. The function requires its two iterator arguments to be at least input iterators. A second version of this function takes as its third argument a binary function that compares the elements in the sequence. The binary function takes two arguments and returns a **bool** value.

Good Programming Practice 21.2

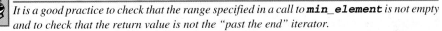

*It is a good practice to check that the range specified in a call to **min_element** is not empty and to check that the return value is not the "past the end" iterator.*

Line 55 uses function **max_element** to locate the largest element in the range from **v2.begin()** up to, but not including, **v2.end()** in **v2**. The function returns an input iterator located at the largest element. The function requires its two iterator arguments to be at least input iterators. A second version of this function takes as its third argument a binary predicate function that compares the elements in the sequence. The binary function takes two arguments and returns a **bool** value.

Line 59 uses function **accumulate** (the template of which is in header file **<numeric>**) to sum the values in the range from **v.begin()** up to, but not including, **v.end()** in **v**. The function's two iterator arguments must be at least input iterators. A second version of this function takes as its third argument a general function that determines how elements are accumulated. The general function must take two arguments and return a result. The first argument to this function is the current value of the accumulation. The second argument is the value of the current element in the sequence being accumulated. For example, to accumulate the sum of the squares of every element, you could use the function

```
int sumOfSquares( int accumulator, int currentValue )
{
    return accumulator + currentValue * currentValue;
}
```

that receives the previous total as its first argument (**accumulator**) and the new value to square and add to the total as its second argument (**currentValue**). When the function is called, it squares **currentValue**, adds **currentValue** to **accumulator** and returns the new total.

Line 64 uses function **for_each** to apply a general function to every element in the range from **v.begin()** up to, but not including, **v.end()** in **v**. The general function should take the current element as an argument and should not modify that element. Function **for_each** requires its two iterator arguments to be at least input iterators.

Lines 70–71 use function **transform** to apply a general function to every element in the range from **v.begin()** up to, but not including, **v.end()** in **v**. The general function (the fourth argument) should take the current element as an argument, should not modify the element and should return the **transform**ed value. Function **transform** requires its first two iterator arguments to be at least input iterators and its third argument to be at least an output iterator. The third argument specifies where the **transform**ed values should be placed. Note that the third argument can equal the first.

21.5.6 Basic Searching and Sorting Algorithms

Figure 21.31 demonstrates some basic searching and sorting capabilities of the Standard Library, including **find**, **find_if**, **sort** and **binary_search**.

```
1   // Fig. 21.31: fig21_31.cpp
2   // Standard library search and sort algorithms.
3   #include <iostream>
4
5   using std::cout;
6   using std::endl;
7
8   #include <algorithm>   // algorithm definitions
9   #include <vector>      // vector class-template definition
10
11  bool greater10( int value );   // prototype
12
13  int main()
14  {
15     const int SIZE = 10;
16     int a[ SIZE ] = { 10, 2, 17, 5, 16, 8, 13, 11, 20, 7 };
17
18     std::vector< int > v( a, a + SIZE );
19     std::ostream_iterator< int > output( cout, " " );
20
21     cout << "Vector v contains: ";
22     std::copy( v.begin(), v.end(), output );
23
24     // locate first occurrence of 16 in v
25     std::vector< int >::iterator location;
26     location = std::find( v.begin(), v.end(), 16 );
27
28     if ( location != v.end() )
29        cout << "\n\nFound 16 at location "
30             << ( location - v.begin() );
31     else
32        cout << "\n\n16 not found";
33
34     // locate first occurrence of 100 in v
35     location = std::find( v.begin(), v.end(), 100 );
36
37     if ( location != v.end() )
38        cout << "\nFound 100 at location "
39             << ( location - v.begin() );
40     else
41        cout << "\n100 not found";
42
```

Fig. 21.31 Basic searching and sorting algorithms of the Standard Library. (Part 1 of 2.)

```
43     // locate first occurrence of value greater than 10 in v
44     location = std::find_if( v.begin(), v.end(), greater10 );
45
46     if ( location != v.end() )
47        cout << "\n\nThe first value greater than 10 is "
48             << *location << "\nfound at location "
49             << ( location - v.begin() );
50     else
51        cout << "\n\nNo values greater than 10 were found";
52
53     // sort elements of v
54     std::sort( v.begin(), v.end() );
55
56     cout << "\n\nVector v after sort: ";
57     std::copy( v.begin(), v.end(), output );
58
59     // use binary_search to locate 13 in v
60     if ( std::binary_search( v.begin(), v.end(), 13 ) )
61        cout << "\n\n13 was found in v";
62     else
63        cout << "\n\n13 was not found in v";
64
65     // use binary_search to locate 100 in v
66     if ( std::binary_search( v.begin(), v.end(), 100 ) )
67        cout << "\n100 was found in v";
68     else
69        cout << "\n100 was not found in v";
70
71     cout << endl;
72
73     return 0;
74
75  } // end main
76
77  // determine whether argument is greater than 10
78  bool greater10( int value )
79  {
80     return value > 10;
81
82  } // end function greater10
```

```
Vector v contains: 10 2 17 5 16 8 13 11 20 7

Found 16 at location 4
100 not found

The first value greater than 10 is 17
found at location 2

Vector v after sort: 2 5 7 8 10 11 13 16 17 20

13 was found in v
100 was not found in v
```

Fig. 21.31 Basic searching and sorting algorithms of the Standard Library. (Part 2 of 2.)

Line 26 uses function **find** to locate the value **16** in the range from **v.begin()** up to, but not including, **v.end()** in **v**. The function requires its two iterator arguments to be at least input iterators. The function returns an input iterator that either is positioned at the first element containing the value or indicates the end of the sequence (as is the case in line 35).

Line 44 uses function **find_if** to locate the first value in the range from **v.begin()** up to, but not including, **v.end()** in **v** for which the unary predicate function **greater10** returns **true**. Function **greater10** (defined at lines 78–82) takes an integer and returns a **bool** value indicating whether the integer argument is greater than 10. Function **find_if** requires its two iterator arguments to be at least input iterators. The function returns an input iterator that either is positioned at the first element containing a value for which the predicate function returns **true** or indicates the end of the sequence.

Line 54 uses function **sort** to arrange the elements in the range from **v.begin()** up to, but not including, **v.end()** in **v** in ascending order. The function requires its two iterator arguments to be random-access iterators. A second version of this function takes a third argument that is a binary predicate function taking two arguments that are values in the sequence and returning a **bool** indicating the sorting order—if the return value is **true**, the two elements being compared are in sorted order.

Common Programming Error 21.5

*Attempting to **sort** a container by using an iterator other than a random-access iterator is a syntax error. Function **sort** requires a random-access iterator.*

Line 60 uses function **binary_search** to determine whether the value 13 is in the range from **v.begin()** up to, but not including, **v.end()** in **v**. The sequence of values must be sorted in ascending order first. Function **binary_search** requires its two iterator arguments to be at least forward iterators. The function returns a **bool** indicating whether the value was found in the sequence. Line 66 demonstrates a call to function **binary_search** in which the value is not found. A second version of this function takes a fourth argument that is a binary predicate function taking two arguments that are values in the sequence and returning a **bool**. The predicate function returns **true** if the two elements being compared are in sorted order.

21.5.7 swap, iter_swap and swap_ranges

Figure 21.32 demonstrates algorithms **swap**, **iter_swap** and **swap_ranges** for swapping elements.

```
1   // Fig. 21.32: fig21_32.cpp
2   // Standard library algorithms iter_swap, swap and swap_ranges.
3   #include <iostream>
4
5   using std::cout;
6   using std::endl;
7
8   #include <algorithm>   // algorithm definitions
9
10  int main()
11  {
```

Fig. 21.32 Demonstrating **swap**, **iter_swap** and **swap_ranges**. (Part 1 of 2.)

```
12      const int SIZE = 10;
13      int a[ SIZE ] = { 1, 2, 3, 4, 5, 6, 7, 8, 9, 10 };
14      std::ostream_iterator< int > output( cout, " " );
15
16      cout << "Array a contains:\n   ";
17      std::copy( a, a + SIZE, output );
18
19      // swap elements at locations 0 and 1 of array a
20      std::swap( a[ 0 ], a[ 1 ] );
21
22      cout << "\nArray a after swapping a[0] and a[1] "
23            << "using swap:\n   ";
24      std::copy( a, a + SIZE, output );
25
26      // use iterators to swap elements at locations
27      // 0 and 1 of array a
28      std::iter_swap( &a[ 0 ], &a[ 1 ] );
29      cout << "\nArray a after swapping a[0] and a[1] "
30            << "using iter_swap:\n   ";
31      std::copy( a, a + SIZE, output );
32
33      // swap elements in first five elements of array a with
34      // elements in last five elements of array a
35      std::swap_ranges( a, a + 5, a + 5 );
36
37      cout << "\nArray a after swapping the first five elements\n"
38            << "with the last five elements:\n   ";
39      std::copy( a, a + SIZE, output );
40
41      cout << endl;
42
43      return 0;
44
45   } // end main
```

```
Array a contains:
   1 2 3 4 5 6 7 8 9 10
Array a after swapping a[0] and a[1] using swap:
   2 1 3 4 5 6 7 8 9 10
Array a after swapping a[0] and a[1] using iter_swap:
   1 2 3 4 5 6 7 8 9 10
Array a after swapping the first five elements
with the last five elements:
   6 7 8 9 10 1 2 3 4 5
```

Fig. 21.32 Demonstrating **swap**, **iter_swap** and **swap_ranges**. (Part 2 of 2.)

Line 20 uses function **swap** to exchange two values. In this example, the first and second elements of array **a** are exchanged. The function takes as arguments references to the two values being exchanged.

Line 28 uses function **iter_swap** to exchange the two elements. The function takes two forward-iterator arguments (in this case, pointers to elements of an array) and exchanges the values in the elements to which the iterators refer.

Line 35 uses function **swap_ranges** to exchange the elements in the range from **a** up to, but not including, **a + 5** with the elements beginning at position **a + 5**. The function requires three forward iterator arguments. The first two arguments specify the range of elements in the first sequence that will be exchanged with the elements in the second sequence starting from the iterator in the third argument. In this example, the two sequences of values are in the same array, but the sequences can be from different arrays or containers.

21.5.8 `copy_backward`, `merge`, `unique` and `reverse`

Figure 21.33 demonstrates STL algorithms **copy_backward**, **merge**, **unique** and **reverse**.

```
1   // Fig. 21.33: fig21_33.cpp
2   // Standard library functions copy_backward, merge,
3   // unique and reverse.
4   #include <iostream>
5
6   using std::cout;
7   using std::endl;
8
9   #include <algorithm>  // algorithm definitions
10  #include <vector>      // vector class-template definition
11
12  int main()
13  {
14     const int SIZE = 5;
15     int a1[ SIZE ] = { 1, 3, 5, 7, 9 };
16     int a2[ SIZE ] = { 2, 4, 5, 7, 9 };
17
18     std::vector< int > v1( a1, a1 + SIZE );
19     std::vector< int > v2( a2, a2 + SIZE );
20
21     std::ostream_iterator< int > output( cout, " " );
22
23     cout << "Vector v1 contains: ";
24     std::copy( v1.begin(), v1.end(), output );
25     cout << "\nVector v2 contains: ";
26     std::copy( v2.begin(), v2.end(), output );
27
28     std::vector< int > results( v1.size() );
29
30     // place elements of v1 into results in reverse order
31     std::copy_backward( v1.begin(), v1.end(), results.end() );
32
33     cout << "\n\nAfter copy_backward, results contains: ";
34     std::copy( results.begin(), results.end(), output );
35
36     std::vector< int > results2( v1.size() + v2.size() );
37
```

Fig. 21.33 Demonstrating **copy_backward**, **merge**, **unique** and **reverse**. (Part 1 of 2.)

```
38        // merge elements of v1 and v2 into results2 in sorted order
39        std::merge( v1.begin(), v1.end(), v2.begin(), v2.end(),
40           results2.begin() );
41
42        cout << "\n\nAfter merge of v1 and v2 results2 contains:\n";
43        std::copy( results2.begin(), results2.end(), output );
44
45        // eliminate duplicate values from results2
46        std::vector< int >::iterator endLocation;
47        endLocation =
48           std::unique( results2.begin(), results2.end() );
49
50        cout << "\n\nAfter unique results2 contains:\n";
51        std::copy( results2.begin(), endLocation, output );
52
53        cout << "\n\nVector v1 after reverse: ";
54
55        // reverse elements of v1
56        std::reverse( v1.begin(), v1.end() );
57
58        std::copy( v1.begin(), v1.end(), output );
59
60        cout << endl;
61
62        return 0;
63
64    } // end main
```

```
Vector v1 contains: 1 3 5 7 9
Vector v2 contains: 2 4 5 7 9

After copy_backward, results contains: 1 3 5 7 9

After merge of v1 and v2 results2 contains:
1 2 3 4 5 5 7 7 9 9

After unique results2 contains:
1 2 3 4 5 7 9

Vector v1 after reverse: 9 7 5 3 1
```

Fig. 21.33 Demonstrating **copy_backward**, **merge**, **unique** and **reverse**.
(Part 2 of 2.)

Line 31 uses function **copy_backward** to copy elements in the range from
v1.begin() up to, but not including, **v1.end()** in **v1**, placing the elements in
results by starting from the element before **results.end()** and working toward the
beginning of the **vector**. The function returns an iterator positioned at the last element
copied into the **results** (i.e., the beginning of **results**, because we are going backwards). The elements are placed in **results** in the same order as **v1**. This function
requires three bidirectional iterator arguments (iterators that can be incremented and decremented to iterate forwards and backwards through a sequence, respectively). The main dif-

ference between **copy** and **copy_backward** is that the iterator returned from **copy** is positioned *after* the last element copied and the iterator returned from **copy_backward** is positioned *at* the last element copied (which is really the first element in the sequence). Also, **copy** requires two input iterators and an output iterator as argument.

Lines 39–40 use function **merge** to combine two sorted ascending sequences of values into a third sorted ascending sequence. The function requires five iterator arguments. The first four arguments must be at least input iterators and the last argument must be at least an output iterator. The first two arguments specify the range of elements in the first sorted sequence (**v1**), the second two arguments specify the range of elements in the second sorted sequence (**v2**) and the last argument specifies the starting location in the third sequence (**results2**) where the elements will be merged. A second version of this function takes as its sixth argument a binary predicate function that specifies the sorting order.

Note that line 36 creates vector **results2** with the number of elements **v1.size()** **+ v2.size()**. Using the **merge** function as shown here requires that the sequence where the results are stored be at least the size of the two sequences being merged. If you do not want to allocate the number of elements for the resulting sequence before the **merge** operation, you can use the following statements:

```
std::vector< int > results2();
std::merge ( v1.begin(), v1.end(), v2.begin(), v2.end(),
   std::back_inserter( results2 ) );
```

The argument **std::back_inserter(results2)** uses function template *back_inserter* (header file **<iterator>**) for the container **results2**. A **back_inserter** calls the container's default **push_back** function to insert an element at the end of the container. More importantly, if an element is inserted into a container that has no more elements available, the container grows in size. Thus, the number of elements in the container does not have to be known in advance. There are two other inserters— *front_inserter* (to insert an element at the beginning of a container specified as its argument) and *inserter* (to insert an element before the iterator supplied as its second argument in the container supplied as its first argument).

Lines 47–48 use function **unique** on the sorted sequence of elements in the range from **results2.begin()** up to, but not including, **results2.end()** in **results2**. After this function is applied to a sorted sequence with duplicate values, only a single copy of each value remains in the sequence. The function takes two arguments that must be at least forward iterators. The function returns an iterator positioned after the last element in the sequence of unique values. The values of all elements in the container after the last unique value are undefined. A second version of this function takes as a third argument a binary predicate function specifying how to compare two elements for equality.

Line 56 uses function **reverse** to reverse all the elements in the range from **v1.begin()** up to, but not including, **v1.end()** in **v1**. The function takes two arguments that must be at least bidirectional iterators.

21.5.9 **inplace_merge**, **unique_copy** and **reverse_copy**

Figure 21.34 demonstrates STL algorithms **inplace_merge**, **unique_copy** and **reverse_copy**.

```
1   // Fig. 21.34: fig21_34.cpp
2   // Standard library algorithms inplace_merge,
3   // reverse_copy and unique_copy.
4   #include <iostream>
5
6   using std::cout;
7   using std::endl;
8
9   #include <algorithm>    // algorithm definitions
10  #include <vector>       // vector class-template definition
11  #include <iterator>     // back_inserter definition
12
13  int main()
14  {
15     const int SIZE = 10;
16     int a1[ SIZE ] = { 1, 3, 5, 7, 9, 1, 3, 5, 7, 9 };
17     std::vector< int > v1( a1, a1 + SIZE );
18
19     std::ostream_iterator< int > output( cout, " " );
20
21     cout << "Vector v1 contains: ";
22     std::copy( v1.begin(), v1.end(), output );
23
24     // merge first half of v1 with second half of v1 such that
25     // v1 contains sorted set of elements after merge
26     std::inplace_merge( v1.begin(), v1.begin() + 5, v1.end() );
27
28     cout << "\nAfter inplace_merge, v1 contains: ";
29     std::copy( v1.begin(), v1.end(), output );
30
31     std::vector< int > results1;
32
33     // copy only unique elements of v1 into results1
34     std::unique_copy(
35        v1.begin(), v1.end(), std::back_inserter( results1 ) );
36
37     cout << "\nAfter unique_copy results1 contains: ";
38     std::copy( results1.begin(), results1.end(), output );
39
40     std::vector< int > results2;
41
42     cout << "\nAfter reverse_copy, results2 contains: ";
43
44     // copy elements of v1 into results2 in reverse order
45     std::reverse_copy(
46        v1.begin(), v1.end(), std::back_inserter( results2 ) );
47
48     std::copy( results2.begin(), results2.end(), output );
49
50     cout << endl;
51
52     return 0;
```

Fig. 21.34 Demonstrating **inplace_merge**, **unique_copy** and **reverse_copy**. (Part 1 of 2.)

```
53
54   } // end main
```

```
Vector v1 contains: 1 3 5 7 9 1 3 5 7 9
After inplace_merge, v1 contains: 1 1 3 3 5 5 7 7 9 9
After unique_copy results1 contains: 1 3 5 7 9
After reverse_copy, results2 contains: 9 9 7 7 5 5 3 3 1 1
```

Fig. 21.34 Demonstrating **inplace_merge**, **unique_copy** and **reverse_copy**. (Part 2 of 2.)

Line 26 uses function **inplace_merge** to merge two sorted sequences of elements in the same container. In this example, the elements from **v1.begin()** up to, but not including, **v1.begin() + 5** are merged with the elements from **v1.begin() + 5** up to, but not including, **v1.end()**. This function requires its three iterator arguments to be at least bidirectional iterators. A second version of this function takes as a fourth argument a binary predicate function for comparing elements in the two sequences.

Lines 34–35 use function **unique_copy** to make a copy of all the unique elements in the sorted sequence of values from **v1.begin()** up to, but not including, **v1.end()**. The copied elements are placed into vector **results1**. The first two arguments must be at least input iterators and the last argument must be at least an output iterator. In this example, we did not preallocate enough elements in **results1** to store all the elements copied from **v1**. Instead, we use function **back_inserter** (defined in header file **<iterator>**) to add elements to the end of **v1**. The **back_inserter** uses class **vector**'s capability to insert elements at the end of the **vector**. Because the **back_inserter** inserts an element rather than replacing an existing element's value, the **vector** is able to grow to accommodate additional elements. A second version of the **unique_copy** function takes as a fourth argument a binary predicate function for comparing elements for equality.

Lines 45–46 use function **reverse_copy** to make a reversed copy of the elements in the range from **v1.begin()** up to, but not including, **v1.end()**. The copied elements are inserted into **results2** using a **back_inserter** object to ensure that the **vector** can grow to accommodate the appropriate number of elements copied. Function **reverse_copy** requires its first two iterator arguments to be at least bidirectional iterators and its third iterator argument to be at least an output iterator.

21.5.10 Set Operations

Figure 21.35 demonstrates Standard Library functions **includes**, **set_difference**, **set_intersection**, **set_symmetric_difference** and **set_union** for manipulating sets of sorted values. To demonstrate that Standard Library functions can be applied to arrays and containers, this example uses only arrays (remember, a pointer into an array is a random-access iterator).

Lines 27 and 33 call function **includes** in the conditions of **if** structures. Function **includes** compares two sets of sorted values to determine whether every element of the second set is in the first set. If so, **includes** returns **true**; otherwise, **includes** returns **false**. The first two iterator arguments must be at least input iterators and must describe the first set of values. In line 27, the first set consists of the elements from **a1** up to, but not

```
1   // Fig. 21.35: fig21_35.cpp
2   // Standard library algorithms includes, set_difference,
3   // set_intersection, set_symmetric_difference and set_union.
4   #include <iostream>
5
6   using std::cout;
7   using std::endl;
8
9   #include <algorithm>   // algorithm definitions
10
11  int main()
12  {
13     const int SIZE1 = 10, SIZE2 = 5, SIZE3 = 20;
14     int a1[ SIZE1 ] = { 1, 2, 3, 4, 5, 6, 7, 8, 9, 10 };
15     int a2[ SIZE2 ] = { 4, 5, 6, 7, 8 };
16     int a3[ SIZE2 ] = { 4, 5, 6, 11, 15 };
17     std::ostream_iterator< int > output( cout, " " );
18
19     cout << "a1 contains: ";
20     std::copy( a1, a1 + SIZE1, output );
21     cout << "\na2 contains: ";
22     std::copy( a2, a2 + SIZE2, output );
23     cout << "\na3 contains: ";
24     std::copy( a3, a3 + SIZE2, output );
25
26     // determine whether set a2 is completely contained in a1
27     if ( std::includes( a1, a1 + SIZE1, a2, a2 + SIZE2 ) )
28        cout << "\n\na1 includes a2";
29     else
30        cout << "\n\na1 does not include a2";
31
32     // determine whether set a3 is completely contained in a1
33     if ( std::includes( a1, a1 + SIZE1, a3, a3 + SIZE2 ) )
34        cout << "\na1 includes a3";
35     else
36        cout << "\na1 does not include a3";
37
38     int difference[ SIZE1 ];
39
40     // determine elements of a1 not in a2
41     int *ptr = std::set_difference( a1, a1 + SIZE1,
42        a2, a2 + SIZE2, difference );
43
44     cout << "\n\nset_difference of a1 and a2 is: ";
45     std::copy( difference, ptr, output );
46
47     int intersection[ SIZE1 ];
48
49     // determine elements in both a1 and a2
50     ptr = std::set_intersection( a1, a1 + SIZE1,
51        a2, a2 + SIZE2, intersection );
52
```

Fig. 21.35 **set** operations of the Standard Library. (Part 1 of 2.)

```
53        cout << "\n\nset_intersection of a1 and a2 is: ";
54        std::copy( intersection, ptr, output );
55
56        int symmetric_difference[ SIZE1 ];
57
58        // determine elements of a1 that are not in a2 and
59        // elements of a2 that are not in a1
60        ptr = std::set_symmetric_difference( a1, a1 + SIZE1,
61           a2, a2 + SIZE2, symmetric_difference );
62
63        cout << "\n\nset_symmetric_difference of a1 and a2 is: ";
64        std::copy( symmetric_difference, ptr, output );
65
66        int unionSet[ SIZE3 ];
67
68        // determine elements that are in either or both sets
69        ptr = std::set_union( a1, a1 + SIZE1,
70           a3, a3 + SIZE2, unionSet );
71
72        cout << "\n\nset_union of a1 and a3 is: ";
73        std::copy( unionSet, ptr, output );
74
75        cout << endl;
76
77        return 0;
78
79   } // end main
```

```
a1 contains: 1 2 3 4 5 6 7 8 9 10
a2 contains: 4 5 6 7 8
a3 contains: 4 5 6 11 15

a1 includes a2
a1 does not include a3

set_difference of a1 and a2 is: 1 2 3 9 10

set_intersection of a1 and a2 is: 4 5 6 7 8

set_symmetric_difference of a1 and a2 is: 1 2 3 9 10

set_union of a1 and a3 is: 1 2 3 4 5 6 7 8 9 10 11 15
```

Fig. 21.35   set operations of the Standard Library. (Part 2 of 2.)

including, **a1 + SIZE1**. The last two iterator arguments must be at least input iterators and must describe the second set of values. In this example, the second set consists of the elements from **a2** up to, but not including, **a2 + SIZE2**. A second version of function **includes** takes a fifth argument that is a binary predicate function for comparing elements for equality.

Lines 41–42 use function **set_difference** to find the elements from the first set of sorted values that are not in the second set of sorted values (both sets of values must be in ascending order). The elements that are different are copied into the fifth argument (in this case, the array **difference**). The first two iterator arguments must be at least input iterators for the first set of values. The next two iterator arguments must be at least input iterators for the second set of values. The fifth argument must be at least an output iterator indicating where to store a copy of the values that are different. The function returns an output iterator positioned immediately after the last value copied into the set to which the fifth argument points. A second version of function **set_difference** takes a sixth argument that is a binary predicate function indicating the order in which the elements were originally sorted. The two sequences must be sorted using the same comparison function.

Lines 50–51 use function **set_intersection** to determine the elements from the first set of sorted values that are in the second set of sorted values (both sets of values must be in ascending order). The elements common to both sets are copied into the fifth argument (in this case, array **intersection**). The first two iterator arguments must be at least input iterators for the first set of values. The next two iterator arguments must be at least input iterators for the second set of values. The fifth argument must be at least an output iterator indicating where to store a copy of the values that are the same. The function returns an output iterator positioned immediately after the last value copied into the set to which the fifth argument points. A second version of function **set_intersection** takes a sixth argument that is a binary predicate function indicating the order in which the elements were originally sorted. The two sequences must be sorted using the same comparison function.

Lines 60–61 use function **set_symmetric_difference** to determine the elements in the first set that are not in the second set and the elements in the second set that are not in the first set (both sets of values must be in ascending order). The elements that are different are copied from both sets into the fifth argument (in this case, the array **symmetric_difference**). The first two iterator arguments must be at least input iterators for the first set of values. The next two iterator arguments must be at least input iterators for the second set of values. The fifth argument must be at least an output iterator indicating where to store a copy of the values that are different. The function returns an output iterator positioned immediately after the last value copied into the set to which the fifth argument points. A second version of function **set_symmetric_difference** takes a sixth argument that is a binary predicate function indicating the order in which the elements were originally sorted. The two sequences must be sorted using the same comparison function.

Lines 69–70 use function **set_union** to create a set of all the elements that are in either or both of the two sorted sets (both sets of values must be in ascending order). The elements are copied from both sets into the fifth argument (in this case the array **unionSet**). Elements that appear in both sets are only copied from the first set. The first two iterator arguments must be at least input iterators for the first set of values. The next two iterator arguments must be at least input iterators for the second set of values. The fifth argument must be at least an output iterator indicating where to store the copied elements. The function returns an output iterator positioned immediately after the last value copied into the set to which the fifth argument points. A second version of function **set_union** takes a sixth argument that is a binary predicate function indicating the order in which the elements were originally sorted. The two sequences must be sorted using the same comparison function.

21.5.11 `lower_bound`, `upper_bound` and `equal_range`

Figure 21.36 demonstrates Standard Library functions `lower_bound`, `upper_bound` and `equal_range`.

Line 24 uses function `lower_bound` to find the first location in a sorted sequence of values at which the third argument could be inserted in the sequence such that the sequence would still be sorted in ascending order. The first two iterator arguments must be at least forward iterators. The third argument is the value for which to determine the lower bound. The function returns a forward iterator pointing to the position at which the insert can occur. A second version of function `lower_bound` takes as a fourth argument a binary predicate function indicating the order in which the elements were originally sorted.

Line 31 uses function **upper_bound** to find the last location in a sorted sequence of values at which the third argument could be inserted in the sequence such that the sequence would still be sorted in ascending order. The first two iterator arguments must be at least forward iterators. The third argument is the value for which to determine the upper bound. The function returns a forward iterator pointing to the position at which the insert can occur. A second version of function **upper_bound** takes as a fourth argument a binary predicate function indicating the order in which the elements were originally sorted.

Line 40 uses function **equal_range** to return a **pair** of forward iterators containing the combined results of performing both a **lower_bound** and an **upper_bound** operation. The first two iterator arguments must be at least forward iterators. The third argument is the value for which to locate the equal range. The function returns a **pair** of forward iterators for the lower bound (**eq.first**) and upper bound (**eq.second**), respectively.

Functions `lower_bound`, `upper_bound` and `equal_range` are often used to locate insertion points in sorted sequences. Line 52 uses `lower_bound` to locate the first point at which **5** can be inserted in order in **v**. Line 61 uses **upper_bound** to locate the last point at which **7** can be inserted in order in **v**. Line 71 uses **equal_range** to locate the first and last points at which **5** can be inserted in order in **v**.

```
1   // Fig. 21.36: fig21_36.cpp
2   // Standard library functions lower_bound, upper_bound and
3   // equal_range for a sorted sequence of values.
4   #include <iostream>
5
6   using std::cout;
7   using std::endl;
8
9   #include <algorithm>   // algorithm definitions
10  #include <vector>      // vector class-template definition
11
12  int main()
13  {
14     const int SIZE = 10;
15     int a1[] = { 2, 2, 4, 4, 4, 6, 6, 6, 6, 8 };
16     std::vector< int > v( a1, a1 + SIZE );
17     std::ostream_iterator< int > output( cout, " " );
18
```

Fig. 21.36 Algorithms `lower_bound`, `upper_bound` and `equal_range`. (Part 1 of 3.)

```
19      cout << "Vector v contains:\n";
20      std::copy( v.begin(), v.end(), output );
21
22      // determine lower-bound insertion point for 6 in v
23      std::vector< int >::iterator lower;
24      lower = std::lower_bound( v.begin(), v.end(), 6 );
25
26      cout << "\n\nLower bound of 6 is element "
27          << ( lower - v.begin() ) << " of vector v";
28
29      // determine upper-bound insertion point for 6 in v
30      std::vector< int >::iterator upper;
31      upper = std::upper_bound( v.begin(), v.end(), 6 );
32
33      cout << "\nUpper bound of 6 is element "
34          << ( upper - v.begin() ) << " of vector v";
35
36      // use equal_range to determine both the lower- and
37      // upper-bound insertion points for 6
38      std::pair< std::vector< int >::iterator,
39                 std::vector< int >::iterator > eq;
40      eq = std::equal_range( v.begin(), v.end(), 6 );
41
42      cout << "\nUsing equal_range:\n"
43          << "    Lower bound of 6 is element "
44          << ( eq.first - v.begin() ) << " of vector v";
45      cout << "\n   Upper bound of 6 is element "
46          << ( eq.second - v.begin() ) << " of vector v";
47
48      cout << "\n\nUse lower_bound to locate the first point\n"
49          << "at which 5 can be inserted in order";
50
51      // determine lower-bound insertion point for 5 in v
52      lower = std::lower_bound( v.begin(), v.end(), 5 );
53
54      cout << "\n   Lower bound of 5 is element "
55          << ( lower - v.begin() ) << " of vector v";
56
57      cout << "\n\nUse upper_bound to locate the last point\n"
58          << "at which 7 can be inserted in order";
59
60      // determine upper-bound insertion point for 7 in v
61      upper = std::upper_bound( v.begin(), v.end(), 7 );
62
63      cout << "\n   Upper bound of 7 is element "
64          << ( upper - v.begin() ) << " of vector v";
65
66      cout << "\n\nUse equal_range to locate the first and\n"
67          << "last point at which 5 can be inserted in order";
68
69      // use equal_range to determine both the lower- and
70      // upper-bound insertion points for 5
```

Fig. 21.36 Algorithms **lower_bound**, **upper_bound** and **equal_range**. (Part 2 of 3.)

```
71          eq = std::equal_range( v.begin(), v.end(), 5 );
72
73      cout << "\n   Lower bound of 5 is element "
74           << ( eq.first - v.begin() ) << " of vector v";
75      cout << "\n   Upper bound of 5 is element "
76           << ( eq.second - v.begin() ) << " of vector v"
77           << endl;
78
79      return 0;
80
81  } // end main
```

```
Vector v contains:
2 2 4 4 4 6 6 6 6 8

Lower bound of 6 is element 5 of vector v
Upper bound of 6 is element 9 of vector v
Using equal_range:
   Lower bound of 6 is element 5 of vector v
   Upper bound of 6 is element 9 of vector v

Use lower_bound to locate the first point
at which 5 can be inserted in order
   Lower bound of 5 is element 5 of vector v

Use upper_bound to locate the last point
at which 7 can be inserted in order
   Upper bound of 7 is element 9 of vector v

Use equal_range to locate the first and
last point at which 5 can be inserted in order
   Lower bound of 5 is element 5 of vector v
   Upper bound of 5 is element 5 of vector v
```

Fig. 21.36 Algorithms **lower_bound**, **upper_bound** and **equal_range**. (Part 3 of 3.)

21.5.12 Heapsort

Figure 21.37 demonstrates the Standard Library functions for performing the heapsort sorting algorithm. Heapsort is a sorting algorithm in which an array of elements is arranged into a special binary tree called a *heap*. The key features of a heap are that the largest element is always at the top of the heap and the values of the children of any node in the binary tree are always less than or equal to that node's value. A heap arranged in this manner is often called a *maxheap*. Heapsort is generally discussed in computer science courses called "Data Structures" and "Algorithms."

Line 24 uses function **make_heap** to take a sequence of values in the range from **v.begin()** up to, but not including, **v.end()** and create a heap that can be used to produce a sorted sequence. The two iterator arguments must be random-access iterators, so this function will work only with arrays, **vector**s and **deque**s. A second version of this function takes as a third argument a binary predicate function for comparing values.

```
1    // Fig. 21.37: fig21_37.cpp
2    // Standard library algorithms push_heap, pop_heap,
3    // make_heap and sort_heap.
4    #include <iostream>
5
6    using std::cout;
7    using std::endl;
8
9    #include <algorithm>
10   #include <vector>
11
12   int main()
13   {
14      const int SIZE = 10;
15      int a[ SIZE ] = { 3, 100, 52, 77, 22, 31, 1, 98, 13, 40 };
16      std::vector< int > v( a, a + SIZE ), v2;
17      std::ostream_iterator< int > output( cout, " " );
18
19      cout << "Vector v before make_heap:\n";
20      std::copy( v.begin(), v.end(), output );
21
22      // create heap from vector v
23      std::make_heap( v.begin(), v.end() );
24
25      cout << "\nVector v after make_heap:\n";
26      std::copy( v.begin(), v.end(), output );
27
28      // sort elements of v with sort_heap
29      std::sort_heap( v.begin(), v.end() );
30
31      cout << "\nVector v after sort_heap:\n";
32      std::copy( v.begin(), v.end(), output );
33
34      // perform the heapsort with push_heap and pop_heap
35      cout << "\n\nArray a contains: ";
36      std::copy( a, a + SIZE, output );
37
38      cout << endl;
39
40      // place elements of array a into v2 and
41      // maintain elements of v2 in heap
42      for ( int i = 0; i < SIZE; ++i ) {
43         v2.push_back( a[ i ] );
44         std::push_heap( v2.begin(), v2.end() );
45         cout << "\nv2 after push_heap(a[" << i << "]): ";
46         std::copy( v2.begin(), v2.end(), output );
47
48      } // end for
49
50      cout << endl;
51
52      // remove elements from heap in sorted order
53      for ( int j = 0; j < v2.size(); ++j ) {
```

Fig. 21.37 Using Standard Library functions to perform a heapsort. (Part 1 of 2.)

```
54              cout << "\nv2 after " << v2[ 0 ] << " popped from heap\n";
55              std::pop_heap( v2.begin(), v2.end() - j );
56              std::copy( v2.begin(), v2.end(), output );
57
58       } // end for
59
60       cout << endl;
61
62       return 0;
63
64    } // end main
```

```
Vector v before make_heap:
3 100 52 77 22 31 1 98 13 40
Vector v after make_heap:
100 98 52 77 40 31 1 3 13 22
Vector v after sort_heap:
1 3 13 22 31 40 52 77 98 100

Array a contains: 3 100 52 77 22 31 1 98 13 40

v2 after push_heap(a[0]): 3
v2 after push_heap(a[1]): 100 3
v2 after push_heap(a[2]): 100 3 52
v2 after push_heap(a[3]): 100 77 52 3
v2 after push_heap(a[4]): 100 77 52 3 22
v2 after push_heap(a[5]): 100 77 52 3 22 31
v2 after push_heap(a[6]): 100 77 52 3 22 31 1
v2 after push_heap(a[7]): 100 98 52 77 22 31 1 3
v2 after push_heap(a[8]): 100 98 52 77 22 31 1 3 13
v2 after push_heap(a[9]): 100 98 52 77 40 31 1 3 13 22

v2 after 100 popped from heap
98 77 52 22 40 31 1 3 13 100
v2 after 98 popped from heap
77 40 52 22 13 31 1 3 98 100
v2 after 77 popped from heap
52 40 31 22 13 3 1 77 98 100
v2 after 52 popped from heap
40 22 31 1 13 3 52 77 98 100
v2 after 40 popped from heap
31 22 3 1 13 40 52 77 98 100
v2 after 31 popped from heap
22 13 3 1 31 40 52 77 98 100
v2 after 22 popped from heap
13 1 3 22 31 40 52 77 98 100
v2 after 13 popped from heap
3 1 13 22 31 40 52 77 98 100
v2 after 3 popped from heap
1 3 13 22 31 40 52 77 98 100
v2 after 1 popped from heap
1 3 13 22 31 40 52 77 98 100
```

Fig. 21.37   Using Standard Library functions to perform a heapsort. (Part 2 of 2.)

Line 30 uses function **sort_heap** to sort a sequence of values in the range from **v.begin()** up to, but not including, **v.end()** that are already arranged in a heap. The two iterator arguments must be random-access iterators. A second version of this function takes as a third argument a binary predicate function for comparing values.

Line 45 uses function **push_heap** to add a new value into a heap. We take one element of array **a** at a time, append that element to the end of **vector v2** and perform the **push_heap** operation. If the appended element is the only element in the **vector**, the **vector** is already a heap. Otherwise, function **push_heap** rearranges the elements of the **vector** into a heap. Each time **push_heap** is called, it assumes that the last element currently in the **vector** (i.e., the one that is appended before the **push_heap** function call) is the element being added to the heap and that all other elements in the **vector** are already arranged as a heap. The two iterator arguments to **push_heap** must be random-access iterators. A second version of this function takes as a third argument a binary predicate function for comparing values.

Line 56 uses **pop_heap** to remove the top heap element. This function assumes that the elements in the range specified by its two random-access iterator arguments are already a heap. Repeatedly removing the top heap element results in a sorted sequence of values. Function **pop_heap** swaps the first heap element (**v2.begin()**, in this example) with the last heap element (the element before **v2.end() - i**, in this example), then ensures that the elements up to, but not including, the last element still form a heap. Notice in the output that, after the **pop_heap** operations, the **vector** is sorted in ascending order. A second version of this function takes as a third argument a binary predicate function for comparing values.

21.5.13 **min** and **max**

Algorithms **min** and **max** determine the minimum of two elements and the maximum of two elements, respectively. Figure 21.38 demonstrates **min** and **max** for **int** and **char** values.[5]

```
1   // Fig. 21.38: fig21_38.cpp
2   // Standard library algorithms min and max.
3   #include <iostream>
4
5   using std::cout;
6   using std::endl;
7
8   #include <algorithm>
9
10  int main()
11  {
12     cout << "The minimum of 12 and 7 is: "
13          << std::min( 12, 7 );
```

Fig. 21.38 Algorithms **min** and **max**.   (Part 1 of 2.)

---

5. Microsoft's Visual C++ 6 compiler does not support the STL **min** and **max** algorithms, because they conflict with functions by the same name in the Microsoft Foundation Classes (MFC)—Microsoft's reusable classes for creating Windows applications. Figure 21.38 was compiled with Borland C++.

```
14        cout << "\nThe maximum of 12 and 7 is: "
15           << std::max( 12, 7 );
16        cout << "\nThe minimum of 'G' and 'Z' is: "
17           << std::min( 'G', 'Z' );
18        cout << "\nThe maximum of 'G' and 'Z' is: "
19           << std::max( 'G', 'Z' ) << endl;
20
21        return 0;
22
23     } // end main
```

```
The minimum of 12 and 7 is: 7
The maximum of 12 and 7 is: 12
The minimum of 'G' and 'Z' is: G
The maximum of 'G' and 'Z' is: Z
```

Fig. 21.38   Algorithms **min** and **max**.   (Part 2 of 2.)

21.5.14 Algorithms Not Covered in This Chapter

Figure 21.39 discusses the algorithms that are not covered in this chapter.

Algorithm	Description
inner_product	
	Calculate the sum of the products of two sequences by taking corresponding elements in each sequence, multiplying those elements and adding the result to a total.
adjacent_difference	
	Beginning with the second element in a sequence, calculate the difference (using operator **–**) between the current and previous elements, and store the result. The first two input iterator arguments indicate the range of elements in the container and the third output iterator argument indicates where the results should be stored. A second version of this algorithm takes as a fourth argument a binary function to perform a calculation between the current element and the previous element.
partial_sum	
	Calculate a running total (using operator **+**) of the values in a sequence. The first two input iterator arguments indicate the range of elements in the container and the third output iterator argument indicates where the results should be stored. A second version of this algorithm takes as a fourth argument a binary function that performs a calculation between the current value in the sequence and the running total.

Fig. 21.39   Algorithms not covered in this chapter. (Part 1 of 3.)

Algorithm	Description
`nth_element`	
	Use three random-access iterators to partition a range of elements. The first and last arguments represent the range of elements. The second argument is the partitioning element's location. After this algorithm executes, all elements to the left of the partitioning element are less than that element and all elements to the right of the partitioning element are greater than or equal to that element. A second version of this algorithm takes as a fourth argument a binary comparison function.
`partition`	
	This algorithm is similar to `nth_element`, but it requires less powerful bidirectional iterators, making it more flexible than `nth_element`. Algorithm `partition` requires two bidirectional iterators indicating the range of elements to partition. The third element is a unary predicate function that helps partition the elements so that all elements in the sequence for which the predicate is **true** are to the left (toward the beginning of the sequence) of all elements for which the predicate is **false**. A bidirectional iterator is returned indicating the first element in the sequence for which the predicate returns **false**.
`stable_partition`	
	This algorithm is similar to `partition` except that elements for which the predicate function returns **true** are maintained in their original order and elements for which the predicate function returns **false** are maintained in their original order.
`next_permutation`	
	Next lexicographical permutation of a sequence.
`prev_permutation`	
	Previous lexicographical permutation of a sequence.
`rotate`	
	Use three forward iterator arguments to rotate the sequence indicated by the first and last argument by the number of positions indicated by subtracting the first argument from the second argument. For example, the sequence 1, 2, 3, 4, 5 rotated by two positions would be 4, 5, 1, 2, 3.
`rotate_copy`	
	This algorithm is identical to `rotate` except that the results are stored in a separate sequence indicated by the fourth argument—an output iterator. The two sequences must have the same number of elements.

Fig. 21.39 Algorithms not covered in this chapter. (Part 2 of 3.)

Algorithm	Description
adjacent_find	
	This algorithm returns an input iterator indicating the first of two identical adjacent elements in a sequence. If there are no identical adjacent elements, the iterator is positioned at the **end** of the sequence.
partial_sort	
	Use three random-access iterators to sort part of a sequence. The first and last arguments indicate the sequence of elements. The second argument indicates the ending location for the sorted part of the sequence. By default, elements are ordered using operator **<** (a binary predicate function can also be supplied). The elements from the second argument iterator to the end of the sequence are in an undefined order.
partial_sort_copy	
	Use two input iterators and two random-access iterators to sort part of the sequence indicated by the two input iterator arguments. The results are stored in the sequence indicated by the two random-access iterator arguments. By default, elements are ordered using operator **<** (a binary predicate function can also be supplied). The number of elements sorted is the smaller of the number of elements in the result and the number of elements in the original sequence.
stable_sort	
	The algorithm is similar to **sort** except that all equal elements are maintained in their original order.

Fig. 21.39   Algorithms not covered in this chapter. (Part 3 of 3.)

21.6 Class **bitset**

Class **bitset** makes it easy to create and manipulate *bit sets*. Bit sets are useful for representing a set of bit flags. **bitset**s are fixed in size at compile time. The declaration

        bitset< size > b;

creates **bitset b**, in which every bit is initially **0**. The statement

        b.set(bitNumber);

sets bit **bitNumber** of **bitset b** "on." The expression **b.set()** sets all bits in **b** "on." The statement

        b.reset(bitNumber);

sets bit **bitNumber** of **bitset b** "off." The expression **b.reset()** sets all bits in **b** "off." The statement

        b.flip(bitNumber);

"flips" bit **bitNumber** of **bitset b** (e.g., if the bit is on, **flip** sets it off). The expression **b.flip()** flips all bits in **b**. The statement

```
b[ bitNumber ];
```

returns a reference to the bit **bitNumber** of **bitset b**. Similarly,

```
b.at( bitNumber );
```

performs range checking on **bitNumber** first. Then, if **bitNumber** is in range, **at** returns a reference to the bit. Otherwise, **at** throws an **out_of_range** exception. The statement

```
b.test( bitNumber );
```

performs range checking on **bitNumber** first. Then, if **bitNumber** is in range, **test** returns **true** if the bit is on, **false** if the bit is off. Otherwise, **test** throws an **out_of_range** exception. The expression

```
b.size()
```

returns the number of bits in **bitset b**. The expression

```
b.count()
```

returns the number of bits that are set in **bitset b**. The expression

```
b.any()
```

returns **true** if any bit is set in **bitset b**. The expression

```
b.none()
```

returns **true** if none of the bits is set in **bitset b**. The expressions

```
b == b1
b != b1
```

compare the two **bitset**s for equality and inequality, respectively.

Each of the bitwise assignment operators **&=**, **|=** and **^=** can be used to combine **bitset**s. For example,

```
b &= b1;
```

performs a bit-by-bit logical AND between **bitset**s **b** and **b1**. The result is stored in **b**. Bitwise logical OR and bitwise logical XOR are performed by

```
b |= b1;
b ^= b2;
```

The expression

```
b >>= n;
```

shifts the bits in **bitset b** right by **n** positions. The expression

```
b <<= n;
```

shifts the bits in **bitset b** left by **n** positions. The expressions

```
      b.to_string()
      b.to_ulong()
```

convert **bitset b** to a **string** and an **unsigned long**, respectively.

Figure 21.40 revisits the Sieve of Eratosthenes for finding prime numbers that we discussed in Exercise 4.29. A **bitset** is used instead of an array to implement the algorithm. The program displays all the prime numbers from 2 to 1023, then allows the user to enter a number to determine whether that number is prime.

Line 20 creates a **bitset** of **size** bits (**size** is 1024 in this example). We ignore the bits at positions 0 and 1 in this program. By default, all the bits in the **bitset** are set "off."

```
1   // Fig. 21.40: fig21_40.cpp
2   // Using a bitset to demonstrate the Sieve of Eratosthenes.
3   #include <iostream>
4
5   using std::cin;
6   using std::cout;
7   using std::endl;
8
9   #include <iomanip>
10
11  using std::setw;
12
13  #include <bitset>    // bitset class definition
14  #include <cmath>     // sqrt prototype
15
16  int main()
17  {
18     const int size = 1024;
19     int value;
20     std::bitset< size > sieve;
21
22     sieve.flip();
23
24     // perform Sieve of Eratosthenes
25     int finalBit = sqrt( sieve.size() ) + 1;
26
27     for ( int i = 2; i < finalBit; ++i )
28
29        if ( sieve.test( i ) )
30
31           for ( int j = 2 * i; j < size; j += i )
32              sieve.reset( j );
33
34     cout << "The prime numbers in the range 2 to 1023 are:\n";
35
36     // display prime numbers in range 2-1023
37     for ( int k = 2, counter = 0; k < size; ++k )
38
39        if ( sieve.test( k ) ) {
40           cout << setw( 5 ) << k;
```

Fig. 21.40 Class **bitset** and the Sieve of Eratosthenes. (Part 1 of 2.)

```
41
42            if ( ++counter % 12 == 0 )
43               cout << '\n';
44
45         } // end outer if
46
47      cout << endl;
48
49      // get value from user to determine whether value is prime
50      cout << "\nEnter a value from 1 to 1023 (-1 to end): ";
51      cin >> value;
52
53      while ( value != -1 ) {
54
55         if ( sieve[ value ] )
56            cout << value << " is a prime number\n";
57         else
58            cout << value << " is not a prime number\n";
59
60         cout << "\nEnter a value from 2 to 1023 (-1 to end): ";
61         cin >> value;
62
63      } // end while
64
65      return 0;
66
67   } // end main
```

```
The prime numbers in the range 2 to 1023 are:
    2     3     5     7    11    13    17    19    23    29    31    37
   41    43    47    53    59    61    67    71    73    79    83    89
   97   101   103   107   109   113   127   131   137   139   149   151
  157   163   167   173   179   181   191   193   197   199   211   223
  227   229   233   239   241   251   257   263   269   271   277   281
  283   293   307   311   313   317   331   337   347   349   353   359
  367   373   379   383   389   397   401   409   419   421   431   433
  439   443   449   457   461   463   467   479   487   491   499   503
  509   521   523   541   547   557   563   569   571   577   587   593
  599   601   607   613   617   619   631   641   643   647   653   659
  661   673   677   683   691   701   709   719   727   733   739   743
  751   757   761   769   773   787   797   809   811   821   823   827
  829   839   853   857   859   863   877   881   883   887   907   911
  919   929   937   941   947   953   967   971   977   983   991   997
 1009  1013  1019  1021

Enter a value from 1 to 1023 (-1 to end): 389
389 is a prime number

Enter a value from 2 to 1023 (-1 to end): 88
88 is not a prime number

Enter a value from 2 to 1023 (-1 to end): -1
```

Fig. 21.40 Class **bitset** and the Sieve of Eratosthenes. (Part 2 of 2.)

Lines 25–32 determine all the prime numbers from 2 to 1023. The integer **finalBit** is used to determine when the algorithm is complete. The basic algorithm is that a number is prime if it has no divisors other than 1 and itself. Starting with the number 2, once we know a number is prime, we can eliminate all multiples of that number. The number 2 is divisible only by 1 and itself, so it is prime. Therefore, we can eliminate 4, 6, 8 and so on. The number 3 is divisible only by 1 and itself. Therefore, we can eliminate all multiples of 3 (keep in mind that all even numbers have already been eliminated).

21.7 Function Objects

Function objects and function adapters are provided to make STL more flexible. A *function object* contains a function that can be treated syntactically and semantically as a function using **operator()**. STL's function objects and function adapters are defined in header **<functional>**. A function object can also encapsulate data with the enclosed function. The standard function objects are **inline**d for performance. STL function objects are shown in Fig. 21.41.

Figure 21.42 demonstrates the **accumulate** numeric algorithm (discussed in Fig. 20.30) to calculate the sum of the squares of the elements in a **vector**. The fourth argument to **accumulate** is a binary function object or a function pointer to a binary function that takes two arguments and returns a result. Function **accumulate** is demonstrated twice—once with a function pointer to a binary function, and once with a function object.

STL function objects	Type
divides< T >	arithmetic
equal_to< T >	relational
greater< T >	relational
greater_equal< T >	relational
less< T >	relational
less_equal< T >	relational
logical_and< T >	logical
logical_not< T >	logical
logical_or< T >	logical
minus< T >	arithmetic
modulus< T >	arithmetic
negate< T >	arithmetic
not_equal_to< T >	relational
plus< T >	arithmetic
multiplies< T >	arithmetic

Fig. 21.41 Function objects in the Standard Library.

```
1    // Fig. 21.42: fig21_42.cpp
2    // Demonstrating function objects.
3    #include <iostream>
4
5    using std::cout;
6    using std::endl;
7
8    #include <vector>        // vector class-template definition
9    #include <algorithm>     // copy algorithm
10   #include <numeric>       // accumulate algorithm
11   #include <functional>    // binary_function definition
12
13   // binary function adds square of its second argument and
14   // running total in its first argument, then returns sum
15   int sumSquares( int total, int value )
16   {
17      return total + value * value;
18
19   } // end function sumSquares
20
21   // binary function class template defines overloaded operator()
22   // that adds suare of its second argument and running total in
23   // its first argument, then returns sum
24   template< class T >
25   class SumSquaresClass : public std::binary_function< T, T, T > {
26
27   public:
28
29      // add square of value to total and return result
30      const T operator()( const T &total, const T &value )
31      {
32         return total + value * value;
33
34      } // end function operator()
35
36   }; // end class SumSquaresClass
37
38   int main()
39   {
40      const int SIZE = 10;
41      int array[] = { 1, 2, 3, 4, 5, 6, 7, 8, 9, 10 };
42
43      std::vector< int > integers( array, array + SIZE );
44
45      std::ostream_iterator< int > output( cout, " " );
46
47      int result = 0;
48
49      cout << "vector v contains:\n";
50      std::copy( integers.begin(), integers.end(), output );
51
52      // calculate sum of squares of elements of vector integers
53      // using binary function sumSquares
```

Fig. 21.42 Binary function object. (Part 1 of 2.)

```
54    result = std::accumulate( integers.begin(), integers.end(),
55       0, sumSquares );
56
57    cout << "\n\nSum of squares of elements in integers using "
58       << "binary\nfunction sumSquares: " << result;
59
60    // calculate sum of squares of elements of vector integers
61    // using binary-function object
62    result = std::accumulate( integers.begin(), integers.end(),
63       0, SumSquaresClass< int >() );
64
65    cout << "\n\nSum of squares of elements in integers using "
66       << "binary\nfunction object of type "
67       << "SumSquaresClass< int >: " << result << endl;
68
69    return 0;
70
71 } // end main
```

```
vector v contains:
1 2 3 4 5 6 7 8 9 10

Sum of squares of elements in integers using binary
function sumSquares: 385

Sum of squares of elements in integers using binary
function object of type SumSquaresClass< int >: 385
```

Fig. 21.42 Binary function object. (Part 2 of 2.)

Lines 15–19 define a function **sumSquares** that squares its second argument **value**, adds that square and its first argument **total** and returns the sum. Function **accumulate** will pass each of the elements of the sequence over which it iterates as the second argument to **sumSquares** in the example. On the first call to **sumSquares**, the first argument will be the initial value of the **total** (which is supplied as the third argument to **accumulate**; **0** in this program). All subsequent calls to **sumSquares** receive as the first argument the running sum returned by the previous call to **sumSquares**. When **accumulate** completes, it returns the sum of the squares of all the elements in the sequence.

Lines 24–36 define a class **SumSquaresClass** that inherits from class **binary_function** (in header file **<functional>**). Classes that inherit from **binary_function** define the overloaded **operator()** function with two arguments. Class **SumSquaresClass** is used to define function objects for which the overloaded **operator()** functions perform the same task as function **sumSquares**. The three type parameters (**T**) to the template **binary_function** are the type of the first argument to **operator()**, the type of the second argument to **operator()** and the return type of **operator()**, respectively. Function **accumulate** will pass the elements of the sequence over which it iterates as the second argument to function **operator()** of the object of class **SumSquaresClass** that is passed to the **accumulate** algorithm. On the first call to **operator()**, the first argument will be the initial value of the **total** (which is supplied as the third argument to **accumulate**: **0** in this program). All subsequent calls to **operator()** receive as the first argument the result returned by the previous call to **operator()**. When **accumulate** completes, it returns the sum of the squares of all the elements in the sequence.

Lines 54–55 call function **accumulate** with a pointer to function **sumSquares** as its last argument.

The statement at lines 62–63 call function **accumulate** with an object of class **SumSquaresClass** as the last argument. The expression **SumSquaresClass< int >()** creates an instance of class **SumSquaresClass** that is passed to **accumulate**, which sends the object the message (invokes the function) **operator()**. The statement could be written as two separate statements, as follows:

```
SumSquaresClass< int > sumSquaresObject;
result = accumulate(
    v.begin(), v.end(), 0, sumSquaresObject );
```

The first line defines an object of class **SumSquaresClass**. That object is then passed to function **accumulate** and is sent the message **operator()**.

Software Engineering Observation 21.10

Unlike function pointers, a function object can also encapsulate data.

21.8 STL Internet and Web Resources

The following is a collection of Internet and World Wide Web STL resources. These sites include tutorials, references, FAQs, articles, books, interviews and software.

Tutorials

www.cs.brown.edu/people/jak/programming/stl-tutorial/tutorial.html
This STL tutorial is organized by examples, philosophy, components and extending STL. You will find code examples using the STL components, useful explanations and helpful diagrams.

web.ftech.net/~honeyg/articles/eff_stl.htm
This STL tutorial provides information on the STL components, containers, stream and iterator adaptors, transforming and selecting values, filtering and transforming values and objects.

www.xraylith.wisc.edu/~khan/software/stl/os_examples/examples.html
This site is helpful for people just learning about the STL. You will find an introduction to the STL and ObjectSpace STL Tool Kit examples.

References

www.sgi.com/tech/stl
The Silicon Graphics Standard Template Library Programmer's Guide is a useful resource for STL information. You can download the STL from this site and find the latest information, design documentation and links to other STL resources.

www.cs.rpi.edu/projects/STL/stl/stl.html
This is the Standard Template Library Online Reference Home Page from Rensselaer Polytechnic Institute. You will find detailed explanations of the STL, as well as links to other useful resources for information about the STL.

www.dinkumware.com/refcpp.html
This site contains useful information about the ANSI/ISO Standard C++ Library; it includes extensive information about the Standard Template Library.

Articles, Books and Interviews

www.byte.com/art/9510/sec12/art3.htm

The *Byte Magazine* site has a copy of an article on the STL written by Alexander Stepanov. Stepanov, one of the creators of the Standard Template Library, provides information on the use of the STL in generic programming.

ANSI/ISO C++ Standard

www.ansi.org

You can purchase a copy of the C++ standard document from this site.

Software

www.cs.rpi.edu/~musser/stl-book

The RPI STL site includes information on how STL differs from other C++ libraries and on how to compile programs that use STL. The site lists the STL files and provides example programs that use STL, STL Container Classes and STL Iterator Categories. It also provides an STL-compatible compiler list, FTP sites for STL source code and related materials.

www.cs.rpi.edu/~wiseb/stl-borland.html

"Using the Standard Template Library with Borland C++." This site is a useful reference for people using the Borland C++ compiler. The author has sections on warnings and incompatibilities.

msdn.microsoft.com/visualc

This is the Microsoft Visual C++ home page. Here you can find the latest Visual C++ news, updates, technical resources, samples and downloads.

www.borland.com/cbuilder

This is the Borland C++Builder home page. Here you can find a variety of C++ resources, including several C++ newsgroups, information on the latest product enhancements, FAQs and many other resources for programmers using C++Builder.

SUMMARY

- Using STL can save considerable time and effort and result in higher-quality programs.

- The choice of what Standard Library container to use in a particular application is based on performance considerations.

- STL containers are all templates so that you can tailor them to hold the type of data relevant to your particular applications.

- STL includes many popular data structures as containers and provides many algorithms that programs use to process data in these containers.

- STL containers are in three major categories—*sequence containers*, *associative containers* and *container adapters*. The sequence containers and associative containers are collectively referred to as the *first-class containers*.

- Four other types are considered "near containers" because they exhibit capabilities similar to those of the first-class containers, but do not support all the capabilities of first-class containers—array, **string**, **bitset** and **valarray**.

- A **vector** provides rapid insertion and deletion at the back of the **vector** and direct access to any element. **vector**s support random-access iterators.

- A **deque** provides rapid insertion and deletion at the front or back of the **deque** and direct access to any element. **deque**s support random-access iterators.

- A **list** provides rapid insertion and deletion anywhere in the **list** and supports bidirectional iterators.

- **set**s provide rapid key lookup. No duplicate keys are allowed. **set**s support bidirectional iterators.

- A **multiset** provides rapid lookup of a key. Duplicate keys are allowed. **multiset**s support bidirectional iterators.

- A **map** provides rapid lookup of a key and its corresponding "mapped" value. No duplicate keys are allowed (i.e., a one-to-one mapping is specified). **map**s support bidirectional iterators.

- A **multimap** provides rapid lookup of a key and its corresponding "mapped" values. Duplicate keys are allowed (i.e., a one-to-many mapping). **multimap**s support bidirectional iterators.

- A **stack** provides a last-in-first-out (LIFO) data structure.

- A **queue** provides a first-in-first-out (FIFO) data structure.

- A **priority_queue** provides a first-in-first-out (FIFO) data structure with the highest-priority item always at the front of the **priority_queue**.

- STL has been carefully designed so that the containers provide similar functionality. There are many generic operations that apply to all containers and other operations that apply to subsets of similar containers. This contributes to the extensibility of the STL.

- STL avoids **virtual** functions in favor of using generic programming with templates, to achieve better execution-time performance.

- It is important to ensure that the type of element being stored in an STL container meets the constraints of the template, which normally require that the type provide a copy constructor, an assignment operator and—for associative containers—a less-than operator (**<**).

- Iterators are used with sequences that might be in containers or might be input sequences or output sequences.

- Input iterators are used to read an element from a container. An input iterator can move only in the forward direction (i.e., from the beginning of the container to the end of the container), one element at a time. Input iterators support only one-pass algorithms.

- Output iterators are used to write an element to a container. An output iterator can move only in the forward direction, one element at a time. Output iterators support only one-pass algorithms.

- Forward iterators combine the capabilities of input and output iterators. Forward iterators support multi-pass algorithms.

- Bidirectional iterators combine the capabilities of a forward iterator with the ability to move in the backward direction.

- Random-access iterators have the capabilities of bidirectional iterators and the ability to access any element of the container directly.

- The category of iterator supported by each container determines whether that container can be used with specific algorithms in the STL. Containers that support random-access iterators can be used with all algorithms in the STL.

- Pointers into arrays can be used in place of iterators in all STL algorithms.

- STL has approximately 70 standard algorithms. Mutating-sequence algorithms result in modifications to container elements. Non-mutating-sequence algorithms do not modify container elements.

- Functions **fill** and **fill_n** set every element in a range of container elements to a specific value.

- Functions **generate** and **generate_n** use a generator function to create values for every element in a range of container elements.

- Function **equal** compares two sequences of values for equality.

- Function **mismatch** compares two sequences of values and returns a **pair** of iterators indicating the location in each sequence of the mismatched elements. If all the elements match, the **pair** contains the result of function **end** for each sequence.

- Function **lexicographical_compare** compares the contents of two sequences to determine whether one sequence is less than another sequence (similar to a string comparison).

- Functions **remove** and **remove_copy** delete all elements in a sequence that match a specified value. Functions **remove_if** and **remove_copy_if** delete all elements in a sequence for which the unary predicate function passed to the functions returns **true**.

- Functions **replace** and **replace_copy** replace all elements in a sequence that match a specified value. Functions **replace_if** and **replace_copy_if** replace with a new value all elements in a sequence for which the unary predicate function passed to the functions returns **true**.

- Function **random_shuffle** reorders the elements in a sequence randomly.

- Function **count** counts the elements with the specified value in a sequence. Function **count_if** counts the elements in a sequence for which the supplied unary predicate function returns **true**.

- Function **min_element** locates the smallest element in a sequence. Function **max_element** locates the largest element in a sequence.

- Function **accumulate** sums the values in a sequence. A second version of this function receives a pointer to a general function that takes two arguments and returns a result. The general function determines how the elements in a sequence are accumulated.

- Function **for_each** applies a general function to every element in a sequence. The general function takes one argument (that it should not modify) and returns **void**.

- Function **transform** applies a general function to every element in a sequence. The general function takes one argument (that it can modify) and returns the **transform**ed result.

- Function **find** locates an element in a sequence and, if the element is found, returns an iterator to the element; otherwise, **find** returns an iterator indicating the end of the sequence. Function **find_if** locates the first element for which the supplied unary predicate function returns **true**.

- Function **sort** arranges the elements in a sequence in sorted order (ascending order by default, or in the order indicated by a supplied binary predicate function).

- Function **binary_search** determines whether an element is in a sorted sequence.

- Function **swap** exchanges two values.

- Function **iter_swap** exchanges two values referred to by iterators.

- Function **swap_ranges** exchanges the elements in two sequences of elements.

- Function **copy_backward** copies elements in a sequence and places the elements in another sequence, starting from the last element in the second sequence and working toward the beginning of the second sequence.

- Function **merge** combines two sorted ascending sequences into a third sorted sequence. Note that **merge** also works on unsorted sequences, but would not produce a sorted sequence.

- A **back_inserter** uses the container's default capability for inserting an element at the end of the container. When an element is inserted into a container that has no more elements available, the container grows in size. There are two other inserters—**front_inserter** and **inserter**. A **front_inserter** inserts an element at the beginning of a container (specified as its argument), and an **inserter** inserts an element before the iterator supplied as its second argument in the container supplied as its first argument.

- Function **unique** removes all duplicates from a sorted sequence.

- Function **reverse** reverses all the elements in a sequence.

- Function **inplace_merge** merges two sorted sequences of elements in the same container.

- Function **unique_copy** makes a copy of all the unique elements in a sorted sequence. Function **reverse_copy** makes a reversed copy of the elements in a sequence.

- Function **includes** compares two sorted sets of values to try to find if every element of the second set is in the first set. If so, **includes** returns **true**; otherwise, **includes** returns **false**.
- Function **set_difference** finds the elements from the first set of sorted values that are not in the second set of sorted values (both sets of values must be in ascending order using the same comparison function).
- Function **set_intersection** finds the elements from the first set of sorted values that are in the second set of sorted values (both sets of values must be in ascending order using the same comparison function).
- Function **set_symmetric_difference** determines the elements in the first set that are not in the second set and the elements in the second set that are not in the first set (both sets of values must be in ascending order using the same comparison function).
- Function **set_union** creates a set of all the elements that are in either or both of the two sorted sets (both sets of values must be in ascending order using the same comparison function).
- Function **lower_bound** finds the first location in a sorted sequence at which the third argument can be inserted in the sequence, yet leave the sequence still sorted in ascending order.
- Function **upper_bound** finds the last location in a sorted sequence at which the third argument could be inserted in the sequence, yet leave the sequence still be sorted in ascending order.
- Function **equal_range** returns a **pair** of forward iterators containing the combined results of performing both a **lower_bound** and an **upper_bound** operation.
- Heapsort is a sorting algorithm in which an array of elements is arranged into a special binary tree called a heap. The key features of a heap are that the largest element is always at the top of the heap and that the values of the children of any node in the binary tree are always less than or equal to that node's value. A heap arranged in this manner is often called a maxheap.
- Function **make_heap** takes a sequence of values and creates a heap that can be used to produce a sorted sequence.
- Function **sort_heap** sorts a sequence of values that are already arranged in a heap.
- Function **push_heap** adds a new value into a heap. **push_heap** assumes that the last element currently in the container is the element being added to the heap and that all other elements in the container are already arranged as a heap. Function **pop_heap** removes the top element of the heap. This function assumes that the elements are already arranged as a heap.
- Function **min** finds the minimum of two values. Function **max** finds the maximum of two values.
- Class **bitset** makes it easy to create and manipulate bit sets. Bit sets are useful for representing a set of boolean flags. **bitset**s are fixed in size at compile time.

TERMINOLOGY

accumulate()
adapter
adjacent_difference()
adjacent_find()
<algorithm>
assign()
assignment
associative array
associative container
back()
begin()

bidirectional iterator
binary_search()
const_iterator
const_reverse_iterator
container
container adapter classes
copy()
copy_backward()
count()
count_if()
creating an association

`<deque>`
deque sequence container
deque<T>
deque<T>::iterator
empty()
end()
equal()
equal_range()
erase()
fill()
fill_n()
find()
first-class containers
first-in-first-out (FIFO)
for_each()
forward iterator
front()
`<functional>`
function object
generate()
generate_n()
generic programming
inplace_merge()
input iterator
insert()
istream_iterator
iterator
`<iterator>`
iter_swap()
last-in-first-out (LIFO)
lexicographical_compare()
`<list>`
list sequence container
lower_bound()
make_heap()
`<map>`
map associative container
max()
max_element()
max_size()
merge()
min()
min_element()
mismatch()
multimap associative container
multiset associative container
mutating-sequence algorithm
namespace std
non-mutating-sequence algorithm
nth_element

`<numeric>`
one-to-one mapping
operator!=()
operator<()
operator<=()
operator==()
operator>()
operator>=()
ostream_iterator
output iterator
partial_sort()
partial_sort_copy()
partial_sum()
partition()
platform-independent class libraries
platform-specific class libraries
pop()
pop_back()
pop_front()
pop_heap()
priority_queue container adapter class
push()
push_back()
push_front
push_heap()
queue container adapter class
random-access iterator
random_shuffle()
range
rbegin()
remove()
remove_copy()
remove_copy_if()
remove_if()
rend()
replace()
replace_copy()
replace_copy_if()
replace_if()
reverse iterator
reverse the contents of a container
reverse()
reverse_copy()
reverse_iterator
rotate()
rotate_copy()
sequence
sequence container
sequential container
`<set>`

set associative container	**string**
set_difference()	**string()**
set_intersection()	**struct less<T>**
set_symmetric_difference()	**swap()**
set_union()	**swap_range()**
size()	**top()**
size_type	**transform()**
sort()	**unique()**
sorting algorithm	**upper_bound()**
sort_heap()	**value_type**
<stack>	**valarray**
stack container adapter class	**<vector>**
Standard Template Library (STL)	**vector** sequence container

SELF-REVIEW EXERCISES

21.1   (T/F) The STL makes abundant use of inheritance and **virtual** functions.

21.2   The two types of STL containers are sequence containers and _____ containers.

21.3   The five main iterator types are _____, _____, _____, _____ and _____.

21.4   (T/F) A pointer is a generalized form of iterator.

21.5   (T/F) STL algorithms can operate on C-like pointer-based arrays.

21.6   (T/F) STL algorithms are encapsulated as member functions within each container class.

21.7   (T/F) The **remove** algorithm does not decrease the size of the **vector** from which elements are being removed.

21.8   The three STL container adapters are _____, _____ and _____.

21.9   (T/F) Container member function **end()** yields the position of the last element of the container.

21.10   STL algorithms operate on container elements indirectly, using _____.

21.11   The **sort** algorithm requires a _____ iterator.

ANSWERS TO SELF-REVIEW EXERCISES

21.1   False. These were avoided for performance reasons.

21.2   Associative.

21.3   Input, output, forward, bidirectional, random access.

21.4   False. It is actually vice versa.

21.5   True.

21.6   False. STL algorithms are not member functions. They operate indirectly on containers, through iterators.

21.7   True.

21.8   **stack**, **queue**, **priority_queue**.

21.9   False. It actually yields the position just after the end of the container.

21.10   Iterators.

21.11   Random-access.

EXERCISES

21.12 Write a function template **palindrome** that takes **vector** parameter and returns **true** or **false** according to whether the **vector** does or does not read the same forwards as backwards (e.g., a **vector** containing 1, 2, 3, 2, 1 is a palindrome, but a **vector** containing 1, 2, 3, 4 is not).

21.13 Modify Fig. 21.29, the Sieve of Eratosthenes, so that, if the number the user inputs into the program is not prime, the program displays the prime factors of the number. Remember that a prime number's factors are only 1 and the prime number itself. Every non-prime number has a unique prime factorization. For example, the factors of 54 are 2, 3, 3 and 3. When these values are multiplied together, the result is 54. For the number 54, the prime factors output should be 2 and 3.

21.14 Modify Exercise 21.13 so that, if the number the user inputs into the program is not prime, the program displays the prime factors of the number and the number of times that prime factor appears in the unique prime factorization. For example, the output for the number 54 should be

> **The unique prime factorization of 54 is: 2 * 3 * 3 * 3**

RECOMMENDED READING

Ammeraal, L. *STL for C++ Programmers.* New York, NY: John Wiley, 1997.

Glass, G. and B. Schuchert. *The STL <Primer>.* Upper Saddle River, NJ: Prentice Hall PTR, 1995.

Henricson, M. and E. Nyquist. *Industrial Strength C++: Rules and Recommendations.* Upper Saddle River, NJ: Prentice Hall, 1997.

Josuttis, N. *The C++ Standard Library: A Tutorial and Handbook.* Reading, MA: Addison-Wesley, 1999.

Koenig, A. and B. Moo. *Ruminations on C++.* Reading, MA: Addison-Wesley, 1997.

Musser, D. R. and A. A. Stepanov. "Algorithm-Oriented Generic Libraries," *Software Practice and Experience* Vol. 24, No. 7, July 1994.

Musser, D. R. and A. Saini. *STL Tutorial and Reference Guide: C++ Programming with the Standard Template Library.* Reading, MA: Addison-Wesley, 1996.

Meyers, S. *Effective STL: 50 Specific Ways to Improve Your Use of the Standard Template Library.* Reading, MA: Addison-Wesley, 2001.

Nelson, M. *C++ Programmer's Guide to the Standard Template Library.* Foster City, CA: Programmer's Press, 1995.

Pohl, I. *C++ Distilled: A Concise ANSI/ISO Reference and Style Guide.* Reading, MA: Addison-Wesley, 1997.

Pohl, I. *Object-Oriented Programming Using C++, Second Edition.* Reading, MA: Addison-Wesley, 1997.

Robson, R. *Using the STL: The C++ Standard Template Library.* New York, NY: Springer Verlag, 2000.

Schildt, H. *STL Programming from the Ground Up.* Osborne McGraw-Hill, 1999.

Stroustrup, B. "Making a **vector** Fit for a Standard," *The C++ Report* October 1994.

Stroustrup, B. *The Design and Evolution of C++.* Reading, MA: Addison-Wesley, 1994.

Stroustrup, B. *The C++ Programming Language, Third Edition.* Reading, MA: Addison-Wesley, 1997.

Stepanov, A. and M. Lee. "The Standard Template Library," *Internet Distribution* 31 October 1995 **<www.cs.rpi.edu/~musser/doc.ps>**.

Vilot, M. J. "An Introduction to the Standard Template Library," *The C++ Report* Vol. 6, No. 8, October 1994.

22

Other Topics

Objectives

- To use **const_cast** and **reinterpret_cast**.
- To understand the concept of **namespace**s.
- To understand operator keywords.
- To understand **explicit** constructors.
- To use **mutable** members in **const** objects.
- To understand and use class-member pointer operators **.*** and **->*.**
- To use multiple inheritance.
- To understand the role of **virtual** base classes in multiple inheritance.

What's in a name? that which we call a rose
By any other name would smell as sweet.
William Shakespeare

O Diamond! Diamond! thou little knowest the mischief done!
Sir Isaac Newton

The die is cast.
Julius Caesar

Outline

22.1   Introduction
22.2   `const_cast` Operator
22.3   `reinterpret_cast` Operator
22.4   `namespaces`
22.5   Operator Keywords
22.6   `explicit` Constructors
22.7   `mutable` Class Members
22.8   Pointers to Class Members (`.*` and `->*`)
22.9   Multiple Inheritance
22.10   Multiple Inheritance and `virtual` Base Classes
22.11   Closing Remarks

Summary • Terminology • Self-Review Exercises • Answers to Self-Review Exercises • Exercises

22.1 Introduction

We now consider some additional C++ features including, cast operators, **namespace**s, operator keywords and multiple inheritance. We also discuss pointer-to-class-member operators and **virtual** base classes.

22.2 `const_cast` Operator

C++ provides the ***const_cast*** operator for casting away **const** or **volatile** qualification. Figure 22.1 demonstrates the use of **const_cast**.

```
1   // Fig. 22.1: fig22_01.cpp
2   // Demonstrating operator const_cast.
3   #include <iostream>
4
5   using std::cout;
6   using std::endl;
7
8   // class ConstCastTest definition
9   class ConstCastTest {
10  public:
11     void setNumber( int );
12     int getNumber() const;
13     void printNumber() const;
14  private:
15     int number;
16  };  // end class ConstCastTest
17
```

Fig. 22.1   Demonstrating operator **const_cast**. (Part 1 of 2.)

```
18   // set number
19   void ConstCastTest::setNumber( int num ) { number = num; }
20
21   // return number
22   int ConstCastTest::getNumber() const { return number; }
23
24   // output number
25   void ConstCastTest::printNumber() const
26   {
27      cout << "\nNumber after modification: ";
28
29      // cast away const-ness to allow modification
30      const_cast< ConstCastTest * >( this )->number--;
31
32      cout << number << endl;
33
34   }  // end printNumber
35
36   int main()
37   {
38      ConstCastTest test;   // create ConstCastTest instance
39
40      test.setNumber( 8 );  // set private data number to 8
41
42      cout << "Initial value of number: " << test.getNumber();
43
44      test.printNumber();
45      return 0;
46
47   }  // end main
```

```
Initial value of number: 8
Number after modification: 7
```

Fig. 22.1 Demonstrating operator **const_cast**. (Part 2 of 2.)

Lines 9–16 define class **ConstCastTest**, which contains three member functions and **private** variable **number**. Two of the member functions are declared **const**. Function **setNumber** sets **number**'s value. Function **getNumber** returns **number**'s value.

The **const** member function **printNumber** modifies **number**'s value in line 30. In **const** member function **printNumber**, the data type of the **this** pointer is **const ConstCastTest ***. The preceding statement casts away the "**const**-ness" of the **this** pointer with operator **const_cast**. The type of the **this** pointer for the remainder of that statement is now **ConstCastTest ***. This allows **number** to be modified. Operator **const_cast** cannot be used to directly cast away a constant variable's "**const**-ness."

22.3 reinterpret_cast Operator

C++ provides the **reinterpret_cast** operator for *nonstandard casts* (e.g., casting from one pointer type to a different pointer type, etc.). Operator **reinterpret_cast** cannot be used for standard casts (i.e., **double** to **int**, etc.). Figure 22.2 demonstrates the use of the **reinterpret_cast** operator.

The program declares an integer and a pointer. Pointer **ptr** is initialized to the address of **x**. Line 14 uses operator **reinterpret_cast** to cast **ptr** (of type **int ***) to **char ***. The address returned is dereferenced.

Testing and Debugging Tip 22.1

*It is easy to use **reinterpret_cast** to perform dangerous manipulations that could lead to serious execution-time errors.*

Portability Tip 22.1

*Using **reinterpret_cast** can cause programs to behave differently on different platforms.*

22.4 namespaces

A program includes many identifiers defined in different scopes. Sometimes a variable of one scope will "overlap" (i.e., collide) with a variable of the same name in a different scope, potentially creating a problem. Such overlapping can occur at many levels. Identifier overlapping occurs frequently in third-party libraries that happen to use the same names for global identifiers (such as functions). When this occurs, compiler errors usually are generated.

Good Programming Practice 22.1

Avoid beginning identifiers with the underscore character, which can lead to linker errors.

```cpp
1   // Fig. 22.2: fig22_02.cpp
2   // Demonstrating operator reinterpret_cast.
3   #include <iostream>
4
5   using std::cout;
6   using std::endl;
7
8   int main()
9   {
10      int x = 120;
11      int *ptr = &x;
12
13      // use reinterpret_cast to cast from int * to char *
14      cout << *reinterpret_cast< char * >( ptr ) << endl;
15
16      return 0;
17
18  }  // end main
```

```
x
```

Fig. 22.2   Demonstrating operator **reinterpret_cast**.

The C++ standard attempts to solve this problem with ***namespace***s. Each **namespace** defines a scope where identifiers and variables are placed. To use a **namespace** *member*, either the member's name must be qualified with the **namespace** name and the binary scope resolution operator (**::**), as in

> *namespace_name***::***member*

or else a **using** statement must occur before the name is used; typically, **using** statements are placed at the beginning of the file in which members of the **namespace** are used. For example, the statement

> **using namespace** *namespace_name***;**

at the beginning of a source code file specifies that members of **namespace** *namespace_name* can be used in the file without preceding each member with the *namespace_name* and the scope resolution operator (**::**).

Testing and Debugging Tip 22.2

*Precede a member with its **namespace** name and the scope resolution operator (**::**) if the possibility exists of a scoping conflict.*

Not all **namespace**s are guaranteed to be unique. Two third-party vendors might inadvertently use the same **namespace**. Figure 22.3 demonstrates the use of **namespace**s.

```
1   // Fig. 22.3: fig22_03.cpp
2   // Demonstrating namespaces.
3   #include <iostream>
4
5   using namespace std;   // use std namespace
6
7   int integer1 = 98;   // global variable
8
9   // create namespace Example
10  namespace Example {
11
12     // declare two constants and one variable
13     const double PI = 3.14159;
14     const double E = 2.71828;
15     int integer1 = 8;
16
17     void printValues();   // prototype
18
19     // nested namespace
20     namespace Inner {
21
22        // define enumeration
23        enum Years { FISCAL1 = 1990, FISCAL2, FISCAL3 };
24
25     } // end Inner
26
27  } // end Example
```

Fig. 22.3   Demonstrating the use of **namespace**s. (Part 1 of 2.)

```
28
29   // create unnamed namespace
30   namespace {
31      double doubleInUnnamed = 88.22;   // declare variable
32
33   } // end unnamed namespace
34
35   int main()
36   {
37      // output value doubleInUnnamed of unnamed namespace
38      cout << "doubleInUnnamed = " << doubleInUnnamed;
39
40      // output global variable
41      cout << "\n(global) integer1 = " << integer1;
42
43      // output values of Example namespace
44      cout << "\nPI = " << Example::PI << "\nE = "
45          << Example::E << "\ninteger1 = "
46          << Example::integer1 << "\nFISCAL3 = "
47          << Example::Inner::FISCAL3 << endl;
48
49      Example::printValues();   // invoke printValues function
50
51      return 0;
52
53   } // end main
54
55   // display variable and constant values
56   void Example::printValues()
57   {
58      cout << "\nIn printValues:\ninteger1 = "
59          << integer1 << "\nPI = " << PI << "\nE = "
60          << E << "\ndoubleInUnnamed = " << doubleInUnnamed
61          << "\n(global) integer1 = " << ::integer1
62          << "\nFISCAL3 = " << Inner::FISCAL3 << endl;
63
64   } // end printValues
```

```
doubleInUnnamed = 88.22
(global) integer1 = 98
PI = 3.14159
E = 2.71828
integer1 = 8
FISCAL3 = 1992

In printValues:
integer1 = 8
PI = 3.14159
E = 2.71828
doubleInUnnamed = 88.22
(global) integer1 = 98
FISCAL3 = 1992
```

Fig. 22.3 Demonstrating the use of **namespace**s. (Part 2 of 2.)

Line 5 informs the compiler that **namespace std** is being used. The contents of header file **<iostream>** are all defined as part of **namespace std**. [*Note: Most C++ programmers consider it poor practice to write a **using** statement such as line 5 because the entire contents of the **namespace** are included.*]

The **using namespace** statement specifies that members of a **namespace** will be used frequently throughout a program. This allows the programmer access to all the members of the **namespace** and to write more concise statements such as

```
cout << "double1 = " << double1;
```

rather than

```
std::cout << "double1 = " << double1;
```

Without line 5, every **cout** and **endl** in Fig. 22.3 would have to be qualified with **std::**. The **using namespace** statement can be used for predefined **namespace**s (e.g., **std**) or programmer-defined **namespace**s.

Lines 10–27 use the keyword **namespace** to define **namespace Example**. The body of a **namespace** is delimited by braces (**{}**). Unlike class bodies, **namespace** bodies do not end in semicolons. **Example**'s members consist of two constants (**PI** and **E**), an **int** (**integer1**), a function (**printValues**) and a *nested **namespace*** (**Inner**). Note that member **integer1** has the same name as global variable **integer1** (line 7). Variables that have the same name must have different scopes—otherwise syntax errors occur. A **namespace** can contain constants, data, classes, nested **namespace**s, functions, etc. Definitions of **namespace**s must occupy the global scope or be nested within other **namespace**s.

Lines 30–33 create an *unnamed* **namespace** containing the member **doubleInUnnamed**. Unnamed **namespace** members occupy the *global **namespace***, are accessible directly and do not have to be qualified with a **namespace** name. *Global variables* are also part of the global **namespace** and are accessible in all scopes following the declaration in the file.

Software Engineering Observation 22.1

*Each separate compilation unit has its own unique unnamed **namespace**, i.e., the unnamed **namespace** replaces the **static** linkage specifier.*

Line 38 outputs the value of **doubleInUnnamed**. Member **doubleInUnnamed** is directly accessible as part of the unnamed **namespace**. Line 41 outputs the value of global variable **integer1**. Lines 44–47 output the values of **PI**, **E**, **integer1** and **FISCAL3**. **PI**, **E** and **integer1** are **Example** members and are therefore qualified with **Example::**. Member **integer1** must be qualified because a global variable has the same name. Otherwise, the global variable's value is output. **FISCAL3** is a member of nested **namespace Inner** and is qualified with **Example::Inner::**.

Function **printValues** is a member of **Example** and can access other members of the same **namespace** directly without using a **namespace** qualifier. The **cout** on lines 58–62 outputs **integer1**, **PI**, **E**, **doubleInUnnamed**, global variable **integer1** and **FISCAL3**. Notice that **PI** and **E** are not qualified with **Example**, **doubleInUnnamed** is still accessible, the global version of **integer1** has been qualified with the unary scope resolution operator (**::**) and **FISCAL3** has been qualified with **Inner::**. When accessing members of a nested **namespace**, the members must be qualified with the **namespace** name (unless the member is being used inside the nested **namespace**).

Keyword **using** also can be used to allow an individual **namespace** member to be used. For example, the line

```
using Example::PI;
```

would allow **PI** to be used without **namespace** qualification. This is done typically when only one **namespace** member is frequently used. Namespaces can be aliased. For example the statement

```
namespace CPPHTP4E = CPlusPlusHowToProgram4E;
```

creates the alias **CPPHTP4E** for **CPlusPlusHowToProgram4E**.

Common Programming Error 22.1

*Placing **main** in a **namespace** is a syntax error.*

Software Engineering Observation 22.2

*Ideally, in large programs, every entity should be declared in a class, function, block or **namespace**. This helps clarify every entity's role.*

22.5 Operator Keywords

The C++ standard provides *operator keywords* (Fig. 22.4) that can be used in place of several C++ operators. Operator keywords can be useful for keyboards that do not support certain characters such as **!**, **&**, **^**, **~**, **|**, etc.

Operator	Operator keyword	Description
Logical operator keywords		
&&	and	logical AND
||	or	logical OR
!	not	logical NOT
Inequality operator keyword		
!=	not_eq	inequality
Bitwise operator keywords		
&	bitand	bitwise AND
|	bitor	bitwise inclusive OR
^	xor	bitwise exclusive OR
~	compl	bitwise complement
Bitwise assignment operator keywords		
&=	and_eq	bitwise AND assignment

Fig. 22.4   Operator keywords as alternatives to operator symbols. (Part 1 of 2.)

Operator	Operator keyword	Description
`|=`	**`or_eq`**	bitwise inclusive OR assignment
`^=`	**`xor_eq`**	bitwise exclusive OR assignment

Fig. 22.4   Operator keywords as alternatives to operator symbols. (Part 2 of 2.)

Figure 22.5 demonstrates the use of the operator keywords. This program was compiled with Microsoft Visual C++, which requires the header file **`<iso646.h>`** to use the operator keywords. Other compilers might differ, so check documentation for your compiler to determine which header file to include. (It is possible that the compiler will not require any header file to use these keywords.)

The program declares and initializes two integers, **a** and **b**. Logical and bitwise operations are performed with **a** and **b** using the various operator keywords. The result of each operation is output.

```
1   // Fig. 22.5: fig22_05.cpp
2   // Demonstrating operator keywords.
3   #include <iostream>
4
5   using std::cout;
6   using std::endl;
7   using std::boolalpha;
8
9   #include <iso646.h>
10
11  int main()
12  {
13     int a = 2;
14     int b = 3;
15
16     cout << boolalpha
17          <<    "   a and b: " << ( a and b )
18          << "\n    a or b: " << ( a or b )
19          << "\n     not a: " << ( not a )
20          << "\na not_eq b: " << ( a not_eq b )
21          << "\na bitand b: " << ( a bitand b )
22          << "\na bit_or b: " << ( a bitor b )
23          << "\n   a xor b: " << ( a xor b )
24          << "\n   compl a: " << ( compl a )
25          << "\na and_eq b: " << ( a and_eq b )
26          << "\n a or_eq b: " << ( a or_eq b )
27          << "\na xor_eq b: " << ( a xor_eq b ) << endl;
28
29     return 0;
30
31  }  // end main
```

Fig. 22.5   Demonstrating the operator keywords. (Part 1 of 2.)

```
    a and b: true
     a or b: true
      not a: false
a not_eq b: false
a bitand b: 3
a bit_or b: 3
    a xor b: 0
   compl a: -4
a and_eq b: 3
 a or_eq b: 3
a xor_eq b: 1
```

Fig. 22.5   Demonstrating the operator keywords. (Part 2 of 2.)

22.6 `explicit` Constructors

In Chapter 8, Operator Overloading, we discussed that any constructor that is called with one argument can be used by the compiler to perform an *implicit conversion* in which the type received by the constructor is converted to an object of the class in which the constructor is defined. The conversion is automatic and the programmer need not use a cast operator. In some situations, implicit conversions are undesirable or error-prone. For example, our **Array** class in Fig. 22.6 defines a constructor that takes a single **int** argument. The intent of this constructor is to create an **Array** object containing the number of elements specified by the **int** argument. However, this constructor can be misused by the compiler to perform an implicit conversion. The program (Fig. 22.6, Fig. 22.7 and Fig. 22.8) uses a class similar to that of class **Array** in Chapter 8 to demonstrate an improper implicit conversion.

```
1   // Fig 22.6: array.h
2   // Simple class Array (for integers).
3   #ifndef ARRAY_H
4   #define ARRAY_H
5
6   #include <iostream>
7
8   using std::ostream;
9
10  // class Array definition
11  class Array {
12     friend ostream &operator<<( ostream &, const Array & );
13  public:
14     Array( int = 10 );   // default/conversion constructor
15     ~Array();            // destructor
16  private:
17     int size; // size of the array
18     int *ptr; // pointer to first element of array
19
20  };  // end class Array
21
22  #endif  // ARRAY_H
```

Fig. 22.6   Single-argument constructors and implicit conversions—**array.h**.

```
1   // Fig 22.7: array.cpp
2   // Member function definitions for class Array.
3   #include <iostream>
4
5   using std::cout;
6   using std::ostream;
7
8   #include <new>
9
10  #include "array.h"
11
12  // default constructor for class Array (default size 10)
13  Array::Array( int arraySize )
14  {
15     size = ( arraySize < 0 ? 10 : arraySize );
16     cout << "Array constructor called for "
17         << size << " elements\n";
18
19     // create space for array
20     ptr = new int[ size ];
21
22     // initialize array elements to zeroes
23     for ( int i = 0; i < size; i++ )
24       ptr[ i ] = 0;
25
26  }  // end constructor
27
28  // destructor for class Array
29  Array::~Array() { delete [] ptr; }
30
31  // overloaded stream insertion operator for class Array
32  ostream &operator<<( ostream &output, const Array &arrayRef )
33  {
34     for ( int i = 0; i < arrayRef.size; i++ )
35        output << arrayRef.ptr[ i ] << ' ' ;
36
37     return output;    // enables cout << x << y;
38
39  }  // end operator<<
```

Fig. 22.7 Single-argument constructors and implicit conversions—**array.cpp**.

```
1   // Fig 22.8: fig22_08.cpp
2   // Driver for simple class Array.
3   #include <iostream>
4
5   using std::cout;
6
7   #include "array.h"
8
9   void outputArray( const Array & );
```

Fig. 22.8 Single-argument constructors and implicit conversions—**fig22_08.cpp**. (Part 1 of 2.)

```
10
11   int main()
12   {
13      Array integers1( 7 );
14
15      outputArray( integers1 );    // output Array integers1
16
17      outputArray( 15 );   // convert 15 to an Array and output
18
19      return 0;
20
21   }  // end main
22
23   // print array contents
24   void outputArray( const Array &arrayToOutput )
25   {
26      cout << "The array received contains:\n"
27           << arrayToOutput << "\n\n";
28
29   }  // end outputArray
```

```
Array constructor called for 7 elements
The array received contains:
0 0 0 0 0 0 0

Array constructor called for 15 elements
The array received contains:
0 0 0 0 0 0 0 0 0 0 0 0 0 0 0
```

Fig. 22.8 Single-argument constructors and implicit conversions—**fig22_08.cpp**.
(Part 2 of 2.)

Line 13 in **main** instantiates **Array** object **integers1** and calls the single argument constructor with the **int** value **7** to specify the number of elements in the **Array**. The **Array** constructor outputs a line of text indicating that the **Array** constructor was called and the number of elements that were allocated in the **Array**. Line 15 calls function **outputArray** (defined in lines 24–29) to output the contents of the **Array**. Function **outputArray** receives as its argument a **const Array &** to the **Array**, then outputs the **Array** using the overloaded stream insertion operator **<<**. Line 17 calls function **outputArray** with the **int** value **15** as an argument. There is no function **outputArray** that takes an **int** argument, so the compiler checks class **Array** to determine whether there is a conversion constructor that can convert an **int** into an **Array**. Because class **Array** provides a conversion constructor, the compiler uses that constructor to create a temporary **Array** object containing **15** elements and passes the temporary **Array** object to function **outputArray** to output the **Array**. The output shows that the **Array** conversion constructor was called for a **15**-element **Array** and the contents of the **Array** were output.

C++ provides the keyword *explicit* to suppress implicit conversions via conversion constructors. A constructor that is declared **explicit** cannot be used in an implicit conversion. The next program (Fig. 22.9, Fig. 22.10 and Fig. 22.11) demonstrates an **explicit** constructor.

```
1   // Fig. 22.9: array.h
2   // Simple class Array (for integers).
3   #ifndef ARRAY_H
4   #define ARRAY_H
5
6   #include <iostream>
7
8   using std::ostream;
9
10  // class Array definition
11  class Array {
12     friend ostream &operator<<( ostream &, const Array & );
13  public:
14     explicit Array( int = 10 );  // default constructor
15     ~Array();                     // destructor
16  private:
17     int size; // size of the array
18     int *ptr; // pointer to first element of array
19
20  };  // end class Array
21
22  #endif  // ARRAY_H
```

Fig. 22.9 Demonstrating an **explicit** constructor—**array.h**.

```
1   // Fig. 22.10: array.cpp
2   // Member function definitions for class Array.
3   #include <iostream>
4
5   using std::cout;
6   using std::ostream;
7
8   #include <new>
9
10  #include "array.h"
11
12  // default constructor for class Array (default size 10)
13  Array::Array( int arraySize )
14  {
15     size = ( arraySize < 0 ? 10 : arraySize );
16     cout << "Array constructor called for "
17        << size << " elements\n";
18
19     // create space for array
20     ptr = new int[ size ];
21
22     // initialize array elements to zeroes
23     for ( int i = 0; i < size; i++ )
24        ptr[ i ] = 0;
25
26  }  // end constructor
27
```

Fig. 22.10 Demonstrating an **explicit** constructor—**array.cpp**. (Part 1 of 2.)

```
28   // destructor for class Array
29   Array::~Array() { delete [] ptr; }
30
31   // overloaded insertion operator for class Array
32   ostream &operator<<( ostream &output, const Array &arrayRef )
33   {
34      for ( int i = 0; i < arrayRef.size; i++ )
35         output << arrayRef.ptr[ i ] << ' ' ;
36
37      return output;     // enables cout << x << y;
38
39   } // end operator<<
```

Fig. 22.10 Demonstrating an **explicit** constructor—**array.cpp**. (Part 2 of 2.)

The only modification to the program composed of Fig. 22.6, Fig. 22.7 and Fig. 22.8 was the addition of the keyword **explicit** to the declaration of the single-argument constructor at line 14. When the program is compiled, the compiler produces an error message indicating that the integer value passed to **outputArray** at line 18 cannot be converted to a **const Array &**. The compiler error message is shown in the output window. Line 20 illustrates how to create an **Array** of **15** elements and pass it to **outputArray** using the **explicit** constructor.


```
1    // Fig. 22.11: fig22_11.cpp
2    // Driver for simple class Array.
3    #include <iostream>
4
5    using std::cout;
6
7    #include "array.h"
8
9    void outputArray( const Array & );
10
11   int main()
12   {
13      Array integers1( 7 );
14
15      outputArray( integers1 );    // output Array integers1
16
17      // ERROR: construction not allowed
18      outputArray( 15 );  // convert 15 to an Array and output
19
20      outputArray( Array( 15 ) ); // must use constructor
21
22      return 0;
23
24   } // end main
25
```

Fig. 22.11 Demonstrating an **explicit** constructor—**fig22_11.cpp**.
(Part 1 of 2.)

```
26   // display array contents
27   void outputArray( const Array &arrayToOutput )
28   {
29      cout << "The array received contains:\n"
30           << arrayToOutput << "\n\n";
31
32   } // end outputArray
```

```
c:\cpp4e\ch22\FIG22_09_10_11\Fig22_11.cpp(18) : error C2664:
'outputArray' : cannot convert parameter 1 from 'const int' to
'const class Array &'
Reason: cannot convert from 'const int' to 'const class Array'
No constructor could take the source type, or constructor overload
resolution was ambiguous
Error executing cl.exe.

test.exe - 1 error(s), 0 warning(s)
```

Fig. 22.11 Demonstrating an **explicit** constructor—**fig22_11.cpp**.
(Part 2 of 2.)

Common Programming Error 22.2

*Attempting to invoke an **explicit** constructor for an implicit conversion is a syntax error.*

Common Programming Error 22.3

*Using the **explicit** keyword on data members or member functions other than a single-argument constructor is a syntax error.*

Software Engineering Observation 22.3

*Use the **explicit** keyword on single-argument constructors that should not be used by the compiler to perform implicit conversions.*

22.7 mutable Class Members

In Section 22.2, we introduced the **const_cast** operator, which allowed "**const**-ness" to be cast away. C++ provides the storage-class specifier *mutable* as an alternative to **const_cast**. A **mutable** data member is always modifiable, even in a **const** member function or **const** object. This reduces the need to cast away "**const**-ness."

Portability Tip 22.2

*The effect of attempting to modify an object that was defined as constant, regardless of whether that modification was made possible by a **const_cast** or C-style cast, varies among compilers.*

Both **mutable** and **const_cast** allow a data member to be modified; they are used in different contexts. For a **const** object with no **mutable** data members, operator **const_cast** must be used every time a member is to be modified. This greatly reduces the chance of a member being accidentally modified because the member is not permanently modifiable. Operations involving **const_cast** are typically hidden in a member function's implementation. The user of a class might not be aware that a member is being modified.

Software Engineering Observation 22.4

__mutable__ members are useful in classes that have "secret" implementation details that do not contribute to the logical value of an object.

Figure 22.12 demonstrates using a **mutable** member. The program defines class **TestMutable** (lines 9–17), which contains a constructor, two functions and **private mutable** data member **value**. Line 12 defines function **modifyValue** as a **const** member function that increments **mutable** data member **value**. Normally, a **const** member function cannot modify data members unless the object on which the function operates—i.e., to one to which **this** points—is cast (using **const_cast**) to a non-**const** type. Because **value** is **mutable**, this **const** function is able to modify the data. Member function **getValue** (line 13) is a **const** function that returns **value**. Note that **getValue** can change **value** because **value** is **mutable**.

Line 21 declares **const TestMutable** object **test** and initializes it to **99**. Line 23 outputs the contents of **value**. Line 25 calls the **const** member function **modifyValue** to add one to **value**. Note that both **test** and **modifyValue** are **const**. Line 26 outputs the contents of **value** (**100**) to prove that the **mutable** data member was indeed modified.

```
1   // Fig. 21.12: fig21_12.cpp
2   // Demonstrating storage class specifier mutable.
3   #include <iostream>
4
5   using std::cout;
6   using std::endl;
7
8   // class TestMutable definition
9   class TestMutable {
10  public:
11     TestMutable( int v = 0 ) { value = v; }
12     void modifyValue() const { value++; }
13     int getValue() const { return value; }
14  private:
15     mutable int value;   // mutable member
16
17  };  // end class TestMutable
18
19  int main()
20  {
21     const TestMutable test( 99 );
22
23     cout << "Initial value: " << test.getValue();
24
25     test.modifyValue();     // modifies mutable member
26     cout << "\nModified value: " << test.getValue() << endl;
27
28     return 0;
29
30  }  // end main
```

Fig. 22.12 Demonstrating a **mutable** data member. (Part 1 of 2.)

Initial value: 99
Modified value: 100

Fig. 22.12 Demonstrating a **mutable** data member. (Part 2 of 2.)

22.8 Pointers to Class Members (. * and ->*)

C++ provides the **.*** and **->*** operators for accessing class members. Pointers to class members are not the same kind of pointers we have discussed previously. Attempting to use the **->** or ***** operator with a pointer to a class member generates syntax errors. Figure 22.13 demonstrates the pointer-to-class-member operators.

Common Programming Error 22.4

*Attempting to use the **->** or ***** operator with a pointer to a class member is a syntax error.*

```
1   // Fig. 22.13 : fig22_13.cpp
2   // Demonstrating operators .* and ->*.
3   #include <iostream>
4
5   using std::cout;
6   using std::endl;
7
8   // class Test definition
9   class Test {
10  public:
11     void function() { cout << "function\n"; }
12     int value;  // public data member
13  };  // end class Test
14
15  void arrowStar( Test * );
16  void dotStar( Test * );
17
18  int main()
19  {
20     Test test;
21
22     test.value = 8;       // assign value 8
23     arrowStar( &test );   // pass address to arrowStar
24     dotStar( &test );     // pass address to dotStar
25
26     return 0;
27
28  }  // end main
29
30  // access member function of Test object using ->*
31  void arrowStar( Test *testPtr )
32  {
33     // declare function pointer
34     void ( Test::*memPtr )() = &Test::function;
35
```

Fig. 22.13 Demonstrating the **.*** and **->*** operators. (Part 1 of 2.)

```
36          // invoke function indirectly
37          ( testPtr->*memPtr )();
38
39      }   // end arrowStar
40
41      // access members of Test object data member using .*
42      void dotStar( Test *testPtr2 )
43      {
44          int Test::*vPtr = &Test::value;    // declare pointer
45
46          cout << ( *testPtr2 ).*vPtr << endl;   // access value
47
48      }   // end dotStar
```

```
function
8
```

Fig. 22.13 Demonstrating the `.*` and `->*` operators. (Part 2 of 2.)

Common Programming Error 22.5

Declaring a member function pointer without enclosing the pointer name in parentheses is a syntax error.

Common Programming Error 22.6

Declaring a member function pointer without preceding the pointer name with a class name followed by the scope resolution operator (::) is a syntax error.

The program declares class **Test**, which provides **public** member function **function** and **public** data member **value**. Function **function** outputs **"function"**. Lines 15–16 prototype functions **arrowStar** and **dotStar**. In lines 20 and 22, object **test** is instantiated, and data member **value** of **test** is set to **8**. Lines 23–24 call functions **arrowStar** and **dotStar**; each call passes the address of **test**.

Line 34 in function **arrowStar** declares and initializes **memPtr** as a pointer to a member of class **Test** that is a function with a **void** return type and no parameters. We start by examining the left side of the assignment. First, **void** is the member function's return type. The empty parentheses indicate that this member function takes no arguments. The other set of parentheses specify a pointer **memPtr**, which points to a member of class **Test**. The parentheses around **Test::*memPtr** are required. [*Note:* **memPtr** is a standard function pointer if **Test::** is not specified.] Next we examine the side value of the assignment.

The right side of the assignment uses the address operator (**&**) to get the address of the member function called **function** (which must return **void** and take no arguments). Pointer **memPtr** is initialized to this offset. Note that both the left side and the right side of the assignment in line 34 do not refer to any specific object. Only the class name is used with the binary scope resolution operator (::). Without the **&Test::**, the right side of the assignment in line 34 is a function pointer. Line 37 invokes the member function stored in **memPtr** (i.e., **function**), using the **->*** operator. Line 44 declares and initializes **vPtr** as a pointer to an **int** data member of class **Test**. The right side of the assignment specifies the name of the data member **value**. Note that, without the **Test::**, **vPtr** becomes an **int *** pointer to the address of **int value**.

Line 46 uses the **.*** operator to access the member named in **vPtr**. Note that, in client code, we can use only pointer-to-member operators for accessible members. In this example, both **value** and **function** are **public**.

Common Programming Error 22.7

Placing space(s) between the two characters of **.*** *or* **->*** *is a syntax error.*

Common Programming Error 22.8

Reversing the order of the symbols in **.*** *or* **->*** *is a syntax error.*

22.9 Multiple Inheritance

So far in this book, we have discussed single inheritance, in which each class is derived from exactly one base class. A class may be derived from more than one base class; such derivation is called *multiple inheritance*. Multiple inheritance means that a derived class inherits the members of several base classes. This powerful capability encourages interesting forms of software reuse, but can cause a variety of ambiguity problems.

Good Programming Practice 22.2

Multiple inheritance is a powerful capability when used properly. Multiple inheritance should be used when an "is a" relationship exists between a new type and two or more existing types (i.e., type A "is a" type B and type A "is a" type C).

Consider the multiple-inheritance example (Fig. 22.14, Fig. 22.15, Fig. 22.16, Fig. 22.17, Fig. 22.18). Class **Base1** contains one **protected** data member—**int value**. **Base1** contains a constructor that sets **value** and **public** member function **getData** that returns **value**.

Class **Base2** is similar to class **Base1**, except that its **protected** data is **char letter**. **Base2** also has a **public** member function **getData**, but this function returns the value of **char letter**.

Class **Derived** is inherited from both class **Base1** and class **Base2** through multiple inheritance. **Derived** has **private** data member **double real** and has **public** member function **getReal** that reads the value of **double real**.

Note how straightforward it is to indicate multiple inheritance by following the colon (**:**) after **class Derived** with a comma-separated list of base classes. Note also that constructor **Derived** explicitly calls base-class constructors for each of its base classes, **Base1** and **Base2**, through the member-initializer syntax. Again, base-class constructors are called in the order that the inheritance is specified, not in the order in which their constructors are mentioned. And if the base-class constructors are not explicitly called in the member initializer list, their default constructors will be called implicitly.

```
1   // Fig. 22.14: base1.h
2   // Definition of class Base1
3   #ifndef BASE1_H
4   #define BASE1_H
5
```

Fig. 22.14 Demonstrating multiple inheritance—**base1.h**. (Part 1 of 2.)

```
6   // class Base1 definition
7   class Base1 {
8   public:
9      Base1( int parameterValue ) { value = parameterValue; }
10     int getData() const { return value; }
11
12  protected:      // accessible to derived classes
13     int value;   // inherited by derived class
14
15  };  // end class Base1
16
17  #endif  // BASE1_H
```

Fig. 22.14 Demonstrating multiple inheritance—**base1.h**. (Part 2 of 2.)

```
1   // Fig. 22.15: base2.h
2   // Definition of class Base2
3   #ifndef BASE2_H
4   #define BASE2_H
5
6   // class Base2 definition
7   class Base2 {
8   public:
9      Base2( char characterData ) { letter = characterData; }
10     char getData() const { return letter; }
11
12  protected:        // accessible to derived classes
13     char letter;   // inherited by derived class
14
15  };  // end class Base2
16
17  #endif  // BASE2_H
```

Fig. 22.15 Demonstrating multiple inheritance—**base2.h**.

```
1   // Fig. 22.16: derived.h
2   // Definition of class Derived which inherits
3   // multiple base classes (Base1 and Base2).
4   #ifndef DERIVED_H
5   #define DERIVED_H
6
7   #include <iostream>
8
9   using std::ostream;
10
11  #include "base1.h"
12  #include "base2.h"
13
14  // class Derived definition
15  class Derived : public Base1, public Base2 {
16     friend ostream &operator<<( ostream &, const Derived & );
```

Fig. 22.16 Demonstrating multiple inheritance—**derived.h**. (Part 1 of 2.)

```
17
18    public:
19       Derived( int, char, double );
20       double getReal() const;
21
22    private:
23       double real;     // derived class's private data
24
25    };   // end class Derived
26
27    #endif   // DERIVED_H
```

Fig. 22.16 Demonstrating multiple inheritance—**derived.h**. (Part 2 of 2.)

```
1    // Fig. 22.17: derived.cpp
2    // Member function definitions for class Derived
3    #include "derived.h"
4
5    // constructor for Derived calls constructors for
6    // class Base1 and class Base2.
7    // use member initializers to call base-class constructors
8    Derived::Derived( int integer, char character, double double1 )
9       : Base1( integer ), Base2( character ), real( double1 ) { }
10
11   // return real
12   double Derived::getReal() const { return real; }
13
14   // display all data members of Derived
15   ostream &operator<<( ostream &output, const Derived &derived )
16   {
17      output << "    Integer: " << derived.value
18             << "\n  Character: " << derived.letter
19             << "\nReal number: " << derived.real;
20
21      return output;    // enables cascaded calls
22
23   }  // end operator<<
```

Fig. 22.17 Demonstrating multiple inheritance—**derived.cpp**.

The overloaded stream-insertion operator for **Derived** uses dot notation off the derived object **derived** to print **value**, **letter** and **real**. This operator function is a **friend** of **Derived**, so **operator<<** can directly access **private** data member **real** of **Derived**. Also, because this operator is a **friend** of a derived class, it can access the **protected** members **value** and **letter** of **Base1** and **Base2**, respectively.

Now let us examine the driver program in **main**. We create object **base1** of class **Base1** and initialize it to **int** value **10**. We create object **base2** of class **Base2** and initialize it to **char** value **'Z'**. Then, we create object **derived** of class **Derived** and initialize it to contain **int** value **7**, **char** value **'A'** and **double** value **3.5**.

The contents of each of the base-class objects is printed by calling the **getData** member function for each object. Even though there are two **getData** functions, the calls are not ambiguous, because they refer directly to the object **b1** version of **getData** and the object **b2** version of **getData**.

Next, we print the contents of **Derived** object **derived** with static binding. But here we do have an ambiguity problem, because this object contains two **getData** functions, one inherited from **Base1** and one inherited from **Base2**. This problem is easy to solve by using the binary scope resolution operator as in **derived.Base1::get-Data()** to print the **int** in **value** and **derived.Base2::getData()** to print the **char** in **letter**. The **double** value in **real** is printed without ambiguity with the call **derived.getReal()**. Next, we demonstrate that the *is a* relationships of single inheritance also apply to multiple inheritance. We assign the address of derived object **derived** to base-class pointer **base1Ptr**, and we print **int value** by invoking **Base1** member function **getData** off **base1Ptr**. We then assign the address of derived object **derived** to base-class pointer **base2Ptr**, and we print **char letter** by invoking **Base2** member function **getData** off **base2Ptr**.

```
1   // Fig. 22.18: fig22_18.cpp
2   // Driver for multiple inheritance example.
3   #include <iostream>
4
5   using std::cout;
6   using std::endl;
7
8   #include "base1.h"
9   #include "base2.h"
10  #include "derived.h"
11
12  int main()
13  {
14     Base1 base1( 10 ), *base1Ptr = 0;  // create Base1 object
15     Base2 base2( 'Z' ), *base2Ptr = 0; // create Base2 object
16     Derived derived( 7, 'A', 3.5 );    // create Derived object
17
18     // print data members of base-class objects
19     cout << "Object base1 contains integer "
20          << base1.getData()
21          << "\nObject base2 contains character "
22          << base2.getData()
23          << "\nObject derived contains:\n" << derived << "\n\n";
24
25     // print data members of derived-class object
26     // scope resolution operator resolves getData ambiguity
27     cout << "Data members of Derived can be"
28          << " accessed individually:"
29          << "\n    Integer: " << derived.Base1::getData()
30          << "\n  Character: " << derived.Base2::getData()
31          << "\nReal number: " << derived.getReal() << "\n\n";
32
33     cout << "Derived can be treated as an "
34          << "object of either base class:\n";
35
```

Fig. 22.18 Demonstrating multiple inheritance—**fig22_18.cpp**. (Part 1 of 2.)

```
36        // treat Derived as a Base1 object
37        base1Ptr = &derived;
38        cout << "base1Ptr->getData() yields "
39             << base1Ptr->getData() << '\n';
40
41        // treat Derived as a Base2 object
42        base2Ptr = &derived;
43        cout << "base2Ptr->getData() yields "
44             << base2Ptr->getData() << endl;
45
46        return 0;
47
48   }  // end main
```

```
Object base1 contains integer 10
Object base2 contains character Z
Object derived contains:
    Integer: 7
  Character: A
Real number: 3.5

Data members of Derived can be accessed individually:
    Integer: 7
  Character: A
Real number: 3.5

Derived can be treated as an object of either base class:
base1Ptr->getData() yields 7
base2Ptr->getData() yields A
```

Fig. 22.18 Demonstrating multiple inheritance—**fig22_18.cpp**. (Part 2 of 2.)

This example showed the mechanics of multiple inheritance in a simple example and introduced a simple ambiguity problem. Multiple inheritance is a complex topic dealt with in more detail in advanced C++ texts.

Software Engineering Observation 22.5

Multiple inheritance is a powerful feature, but it can introduce complexity into a system. Great care is required in the design of a system to use multiple inheritance properly; it should not be used when single inheritance will do the job.

22.10 Multiple Inheritance and `virtual` Base Classes

In Section 22.9, we discussed multiple inheritance, the process by which one class inherits from two or more classes. Multiple inheritance is used, for example, in the C++ standard library to form class **iostream** (Fig. 22.19).

Class **ios** is the base class for both **ostream** and **istream**, each of which is formed with single inheritance. Class **iostream** inherits from both **ostream** and **istream**. This enables objects of class **iostream** to provide the functionality of both **istream**s and **ostream**s. In multiple-inheritance hierarchies, the situation described in Fig. 22.19 is referred to as *diamond* inheritance.

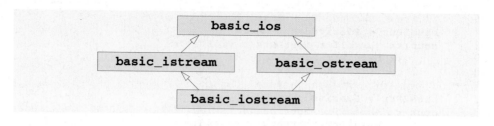

Fig. 22.19 Multiple inheritance to form class **iostream**.

Because classes **ostream** and **istream** each inherit from **ios**, a potential problem exists for **iostream**. Class **iostream** could contain duplicate *base-class objects* (e.g., **ios** is inherited into both **ostream** and **istream**). A problem could arise when an **iostream** pointer is upcast to an **ios** pointer. Two **ios** subobjects could exist. Which would then be used? Such a situation would be ambiguous and would result in a syntax error. Figure 22.20 demonstrates this kind of ambiguity, but through implicit conversion rather than upcasting; of course, **iostream** does not really suffer from the problem we mentioned. In this section, we will explain how using **virtual** base classes solves the problem of duplicate subobjects.

```
1  // Fig. 22.20: fig22_20.cpp
2  // Attempting to polymorphically call a function that is
3  // multiply inherited from two base classes.
4  #include <iostream>
5
6  using std::cout;
7  using std::endl;
8
9  // class Base definition
10 class Base {
11 public:
12    virtual void print() const = 0;   // pure virtual
13
14 };  // end class Base
15
16 // class DerivedOne definition
17 class DerivedOne : public Base {
18 public:
19
20    // override print function
21    void print() const { cout << "DerivedOne\n"; }
22
23 };  // end class DerivedOne
24
25 // class DerivedTwo definition
26 class DerivedTwo : public Base {
27 public:
28
```

Fig. 22.20 Attempting to call a multiply inherited function polymorphically. (Part 1 of 2.)

```
29      // override print function
30      void print() const { cout << "DerivedTwo\n"; }
31
32   };   // end class DerivedTwo
33
34   // class Multiple definition
35   class Multiple : public DerivedOne, public DerivedTwo {
36   public:
37
38      // qualify which version of function print
39      void print() const { DerivedTwo::print(); }
40
41   };     // end class Multiple
42
43   int main()
44   {
45      Multiple both;    // instantiate Multiple object
46      DerivedOne one;   // instantiate DerivedOne object
47      DerivedTwo two;   // instantiate DerivedTwo object
48
49      // create array of base-class pointers
50      Base *array[ 3 ];
51
52      array[ 0 ] = &both;    // ERROR--ambiguous
53      array[ 1 ] = &one;
54      array[ 2 ] = &two;
55
56      // polymorphically invoke print
57      for ( int i = 0; i < 3; i++ )
58         array[ i ] -> print();
59
60      return 0;
61
62   }   // end main
```

```
c:\cpp4e\ch22\fig22_20_21\fig22_20.cpp(52) : error C2594: '=' :
ambiguous conversions from 'class Multiple *' to 'class Base *'
Error executing cl.exe.

test.exe - 1 error(s), 0 warning(s)
```

Fig. 22.20 Attempting to call a multiply inherited function polymorphically. (Part 2 of 2.)

The program defines class **Base**, which contains pure **virtual** function **print**. Classes **DerivedOne** and **DerivedTwo** **public**ly inherit from **Base** and override **print**. Class **DerivedOne** and class **DerivedTwo** each contain a **Base** "subobject."

Class **Multiple** multiply inherits from **DerivedOne** and **DerivedTwo**. Function **print** is overridden to call **DerivedTwo**'s **print**. Note the qualification to specify which subobject version to call.

In **main**, an object of each class in the hierarchy is created. An array of **Base *** pointers also is declared. Each array element is initialized to the address of an object. An error occurs when the address of **both** (of multiply inherited type **Multiple**) is implicitly converted to **Base ***. Object **both** contains duplicate subobjects inherited from **Base** and this, of course, makes calls to function **print** ambiguous. A **for** loop is written to call **print** for each of the objects pointed to by **array**, polymorphically.

The problem of duplicate subobjects is resolved with **virtual** inheritance. When a base class is inherited as **virtual**, only one subobject will appear in the derived class—a process called *virtual base class* inheritance. Figure 22.21 revises the program of Fig. 22.20 to use a **virtual** base class.

Class **Base** is defined and contains pure **virtual** function **print**. Class **DerivedOne** inherits from **Base** with the line

```
class DerivedOne : virtual public Base {
```

and class **DerivedTwo** inherits from **Base** with the line

```
class DerivedTwo : virtual public Base {
```

```
1   // Fig. 22.21: fig22_21.cpp
2   // Using virtual base classes.
3   #include <iostream>
4
5   using std::cout;
6   using std::endl;
7
8   // class Base definition
9   class Base {
10  public:
11
12     // implicit default constructor
13
14     virtual void print() const = 0; // pure virtual
15
16  };  // end Base class
17
18  // class DerivedOne definition
19  class DerivedOne : virtual public Base {
20  public:
21
22     // implicit default constructor calls
23     // Base default constructor
24
25     // override print function
26     void print() const { cout << "DerivedOne\n"; }
27
28  };  // end DerivedOne class
29
30  // class DerivedTwo definition
31  class DerivedTwo : virtual public Base {
32  public:
33
```

Fig. 22.21 Using **virtual** base classes. (Part 1 of 2.)

```
34      // implicit default constructor calls
35      // Base default constructor
36
37      // override print function
38      void print() const { cout << "DerivedTwo\n"; }
39
40   }; // end DerivedTwo class
41
42   // class Multiple definition
43   class Multiple : public DerivedOne, public DerivedTwo {
44   public:
45
46      // implicit default constructor calls
47      // DerivedOne and DerivedTwo default constructors
48
49      // qualify which version of function print
50      void print() const { DerivedTwo::print(); }
51
52   }; // end Multiple class
53
54   int main()
55   {
56      Multiple both;    // instantiate Multiple object
57      DerivedOne one;   // instantiate DerivedOne object
58      DerivedTwo two;   // instantiate DerivedTwo object
59
60      // declare array of base-class pointers and initialize
61      // each element to a derived-class type
62      Base *array[ 3 ];
63
64      array[ 0 ] = &both;
65      array[ 1 ] = &one;
66      array[ 2 ] = &two;
67
68      // polymorphically invoke function print
69      for ( int i = 0; i < 3; i++ )
70         array[ i ]->print();
71
72      return 0;
73
74   }  // end main
```

```
DerivedTwo
DerivedOne
DerivedTwo
```

Fig. 22.21 Using **virtual** base classes. (Part 2 of 2.)

Both classes inherit from **Base**—each contains one subobject from **Base**. Class **Multiple** inherits from both **DerivedOne** and **DerivedTwo**. Only one subobject of **Base** is inherited into class **Multiple**. The compiler now allows conversion to occur (**Multiple *** to **Base ***). In **main**, an object is created for each class in the hierarchy. An array of **Base** pointers is also declared. Each **array** element is initialized to the address of an object. Note that the upcast from **both**'s address to **Base *** is now permitted. A **for** loop walks along **array** and polymorphically calls **print** for each object.

Designing hierarchies with **virtual** base classes is straightforward if default constructors are used for base classes. The previous two examples use compiler-generated default constructors. If a **virtual** base class provides a constructor, the design becomes more complicated because the *most derived class* must initialize the **virtual** base class.

In our two examples, **Base**, **DerivedOne**, **DerivedTwo** and **Multiple** are each the most derived class. If creating a **Base** object, **Base** is the most derived class. If creating a **DerivedOne** (or **DerivedTwo**) object, **DerivedOne** (or **DerivedTwo**) is the most derived class. If creating a **Multiple** object, **Multiple** is the most derived class. No matter how far down the hierarchy a class is, it is therefore the most derived class and responsible for initializing the **virtual** base class.

Software Engineering Observation 22.6

*Providing a default constructor for **virtual** base classes simplifies hierarchy design.*

22.11 Closing Remarks

We sincerely hope you have enjoyed learning C++ and object-oriented programming from our book. The future seems clear. We wish you success in pursuing it!

We would greatly appreciate your comments, criticisms, corrections and suggestions for improving the text. Please address all correspondence to our e-mail address:

    deitel@deitel.com

Good luck!

SUMMARY

- The **const_cast** operator casts away the **const**-ness of objects.
- The **reinterpret_cast** operator is provided for nonstandard casts between unrelated types.
- Each **namespace** defines a scope where identifiers and variables are placed. To use a **namespace** member, either the member's name must be qualified with the **namespace** name and the binary scope resolution operator (**::**) or a **using** statement must occur before the name is used.
- A **namespace** can contain constants, data, classes, nested **namespace**s, functions, etc. Definitions of **namespace**s must occupy the global scope or be nested within other **namespace**s.
- Unnamed **namespace** members occupy the global **namespace**.
- The C++ standard provides operator keywords that can be used in place of several C++ operators.
- C++ provides the keyword **explicit** to suppress implicit conversions via conversion constructors. A constructor that is declared **explicit** cannot be used in an implicit conversion.
- A **mutable** data member is modifiable in a **const** member function or **const** object.
- C++ provides the **.*** and **->*** operators to access class members via pointers to those members.
- Multiple inheritance is the process of deriving a class from two or more classes.
- Multiple inheritance can create duplicate subobjects that can be resolved with **virtual** inheritance. When a base class is inherited as **virtual**, only one subobject will appear in the derived class—a process called **virtual** base-class inheritance.

TERMINOLOGY

.* operator
->* operator
and operator keyword
and_eq operator keyword
anonymous **namespace**
bitand operator keyword
bitor operator keyword
compl operator keyword
const_cast operator
diamond inheritance
explicit keyword
explicit conversion
global **namespace**
global variables
implicit conversion
most derived class
multiple inheritance

mutable keyword
namespace keyword
nested **namespace**
not operator keyword
not_eq operator keyword
operator keywords
or operator keyword
or_eq operator keyword
pointer to class member operator
pointer to data member
pointer to member function
reinterpret_cast operator
subobject
using a **namespace**
virtual base class
xor operator keyword
xor_eq operator keyword

SELF-REVIEW EXERCISES

22.1 Fill in the blanks for each of the following:
   a) The _____ operator qualifies a member with its namespace.
   b) The _____ operator allows an object's "**const**-ness" to be cast away.
   c) The _____ operator allows conversions between nonstandard types.

22.2 State which of the following are *true* and which are *false*. If a statement is *false*, explain why.
   a) **namespace**s are guaranteed to be unique.
   b) **namespace**s cannot have **namespace**s as members.
   c) Keyword **explicit** can be applied only to member functions.

ANSWERS TO SELF-REVIEW EXERCISES

22.1 a) binary scope resolution (**::**). b) **const_cast**. c) **reinterpret_cast**.

22.2 a) False. Programmers might inadvertently choose the **namespace** already in use.
   b) False. **namespace**s can be nested.
   c) False. Keyword **explicit** may be applied to single-argument constructors only.

EXERCISES

22.3 Fill in the blanks for each of the following:
   a) Keyword _____ specifies that a **namespace** or **namespace** member is being used.
   b) Operator _____ is the operator keyword for logical OR.
   c) Storage specifier _____ allows a member of a **const** object to be modified.

22.4 Write a **namespace**, **Currency**, that defines constant members **ONE**, **TWO**, **FIVE**, **TEN**, **TWENTY**, **FIFTY** and **HUNDRED**. Write two short programs that use **Currency**. One program should make all constants available and the other program should only make **FIVE** available.

22.5 Write a program that uses the **reinterpret_cast** operator to cast different pointer types to **int**. Do any conversions result in syntax errors?

22.6   Write a program that demonstrates upcasting from a derived class to a base class. Use the **static_cast** operator to perform the upcast. How does this compare to your results in Exercise 22.5?

22.7   Write a program that creates an **explicit** constructor that takes two arguments. Does the compiler permit this? Remove **explicit** and attempt an implicit conversion. Does the compiler permit this?

22.8   What is the benefit of an **explicit** constructor?

22.9   Write a program that creates a class containing two constructors. One constructor should take a single **int** argument. The second constructor should take one **char *** argument. Write a driver program that constructs several different objects, each object having a different type passed into the constructor. Do not use **explicit**. What happens? Now use **explicit** only for the constructor that takes one **int**. What happens?

22.10   Given the **namespace**s in Fig. 22.22, determine whether each statement is *true* or *false*. Explain any *false* answers.
   a)   Variable **kilometers** is accessible within **namespace Data**.
   b)   Object **string1** is accessible within **namespace Data**.
   c)   Constant **POLAND** is not accessible within **namespace Data**.
   d)   Constant **GERMANY** is accessible within **namespace Data**.
   e)   Function **function** is accessible to **namespace Data**.
   f)   Namespace **Data** is accessible to **namespace CountryInformation**.
   g)   Object **map** is accessible to **namespace CountryInformation**.
   h)   Object **string1** is accessible within **namespace RegionalInformation**.

22.11   Compare and contrast **mutable** and **const_cast**. Give at least one example of when one might be preferred over the other. [*Note*: This exercise does not require any code to be written.]

22.12   Write a program that uses **const_cast** to modify a **const** variable. [*Hint:* Use a pointer in your solution to point to the **const** identifier.]

22.13   What problem do **virtual** base classes solve?

```
1    namespace CountryInformation {
2       using namespace std;
3       enum Countries { POLAND, SWITZERLAND, GERMANY,
4                        AUSTRIA, CZECH_REPUBLIC };
5       int kilometers;
6       string string1;
7
8       namespace RegionalInformation {
9          short getPopulation();  // assume definition exists
10         MapData map;      // assume definition exists
11      }  // end RegionalInformation
12   }  // end CountryInformation
13
14   namespace Data {
15      using namespace CountryInformation::RegionalInformation;
16      void *function( void *, int );
17   }  // end Data
```

Fig. 22.22 namespaces for Exercise 22.10.

22.14 Write a program that uses **virtual** base classes. The class at the top of the hierarchy should provide a constructor that takes at least one argument (i.e., do not provide a default constructor). What challenges does this present for the inheritance hierarchy?

22.15 Find the error(s) in each of the following. When possible, explain how to correct each error.

a)
```
namespace Name {
    int x;
    int y;
    mutable int z;
};
```

b)
```
int integer = const_cast< int >( double );
```

c)
```
namespace PCM( 111, "hello" );    // construct namespace
```

d)
```
explicit int x = 99;
```

Operator Precedence Chart

Operators are shown in decreasing order of precedence from top to bottom.

Operator	Type	Associativity
::	binary scope resolution	left to right
::	unary scope resolution	
()	parentheses	left to right
[]	array subscript	
.	member selection via object	
->	member selection via pointer	
++	unary postincrement	
--	unary postdecrement	
typeid	run-time type information	
dynamic_cast< *type* >	run-time type-checked cast	
static_cast< *type* >	compile-time type-checked cast	
reinterpret_cast< *type* >	cast for non-standard conversions	
const_cast< *type* >	cast away **const**-ness	
++	unary preincrement	right to left
--	unary predecrement	
+	unary plus	
-	unary minus	
!	unary logical negation	
~	unary bitwise complement	*(this level of*
(*type*)	C-style unary cast	*precedence*
sizeof	determine size in bytes	*continued on*
&	address	*next page)*

Fig. A.1 Operator precedence chart. (Part 1 of 2.)

Operator	Type	Associativity

`*`
`new`
`new[]`
`delete`
`delete[]`
	dereference
	dynamic memory allocation
	dynamic array allocation
	dynamic memory deallocation
	dynamic array deallocation
		(this level of precedence continued from previous page)

`.*` `->*`	pointer to member via object pointer to member via pointer	left to right

`*`
`/`
`%`
	multiplication
	division
	modulus
		left to right

`+` `-`	addition subtraction	left to right
`<<` `>>`	bitwise left shift bitwise right shift	left to right

`<`
`<=`
`>`
`>=`
	relational less than
	relational less than or equal to
	relational greater than
	relational greater than or equal to
		left to right

`==` `!=`	relational is equal to relational is not equal to	left to right
`&`	bitwise AND	left to right
`^`	bitwise exclusive OR	left to right
`|`	bitwise inclusive OR	left to right
`&&`	logical AND	left to right
`||`	logical OR	left to right
`?:`	ternary conditional	right to left

`=`
`+=`
`-=`
`*=`
`/=`
`%=`
`&=`
`^=`
`|=`
`<<=`
`>>=`
	assignment
	addition assignment
	subtraction assignment
	multiplication assignment
	division assignment
	modulus assignment
	bitwise AND assignment
	bitwise exclusive OR assignment
	bitwise inclusive OR assignment
	bitwise left-shift assignment
	bitwise right-shift assignment
		right to left

`,`	comma	left to right

Fig. A.1   Operator precedence chart. (Part 2 of 2.)

ASCII Character Set

	0	1	2	3	4	5	6	7	8	9
0	nul	soh	stx	etx	eot	enq	ack	bel	bs	ht
1	nl	vt	ff	cr	so	si	dle	dc1	dc2	dc3
2	dc4	nak	syn	etb	can	em	sub	esc	fs	gs
3	rs	us	sp	!	"	#	$	%	&	`
4	(	)	*	+	,	-	.	/	0	1
5	2	3	4	5	6	7	8	9	:	;
6	<	=	>	?	@	A	B	C	D	E
7	F	G	H	I	J	K	L	M	N	O
8	P	Q	R	S	T	U	V	W	X	Y
9	Z	[	\	]	^	_	'		a	b	c
10	d	e	f	g	h	i	j	k	l	m
11	n	o	p	q	r	s	t	u	v	w
12	x	y	z	{	|	}	~	del		

Fig. B.1 ASCII character set.

The digits at the left of the table are the left digits of the decimal equivalent (0–127) of the character code, and the digits at the top of the table are the right digits of the character code. For example, the character code for "**F**" is 70, and the character code for "**&**" is 38.

Number Systems

Objectives

- To understand basic number systems concepts such as base, positional value and symbol value.
- To understand how to work with numbers represented in the binary, octal and hexadecimal number systems
- To be able to abbreviate binary numbers as octal numbers or hexadecimal numbers.
- To be able to convert octal numbers and hexadecimal numbers to binary numbers.
- To be able to convert back and forth between decimal numbers and their binary, octal and hexadecimal equivalents.
- To understand binary arithmetic and how negative binary numbers are represented using two's complement notation.

Here are only numbers ratified.
William Shakespeare

Nature has some sort of arithmetic-geometrical coordinate system, because nature has all kinds of models. What we experience of nature is in models, and all of nature's models are so beautiful.
It struck me that nature's system must be a real beauty, because in chemistry we find that the associations are always in beautiful whole numbers—there are no fractions.
Richard Buckminster Fuller

Outline

C.1   Introduction

C.2   Abbreviating Binary Numbers as Octal Numbers and Hexadecimal Numbers

C.3   Converting Octal Numbers and Hexadecimal Numbers to Binary Numbers

C.4   Converting from Binary, Octal or Hexadecimal to Decimal

C.5   Converting from Decimal to Binary, Octal or Hexadecimal

C.6   Negative Binary Numbers: Two's Complement Notation

Summary • Terminology • Self-Review Exercises • Answers to Self-Review Exercises • Exercises

C.1 Introduction

In this appendix, we introduce the key number systems that programmers use, especially when they are working on software projects that require close interaction with "machine-level" hardware. Projects like this include operating systems, computer networking software, compilers, database systems and applications requiring high performance.

When we write an integer such as 227 or –63 in a program, the number is assumed to be in the *decimal (base 10) number system*. The *digits* in the decimal number system are 0, 1, 2, 3, 4, 5, 6, 7, 8 and 9. The lowest digit is 0 and the highest digit is 9—one less than the *base*, 10. Internally, computers use the *binary (base 2) number system*. The binary number system has only two digits, namely 0 and 1. Its lowest digit is 0 and its highest digit is 1—one less than the base, 2. Fig. C.1 summarizes the digits used in the binary, octal, decimal and hexadecimal number systems.

As we will see, binary numbers tend to be much longer than their decimal equivalents. Programmers who work in assembly languages and in high-level languages that enable programmers to reach down to the "machine level" find it cumbersome to work with binary numbers. So two other number systems—the *octal number system (base 8)* and the *hexadecimal number system (base 16)*—are popular, primarily because they make it convenient to abbreviate binary numbers.

In the octal number system, the digits range from 0 to 7. Because both the binary number system and the octal number system have fewer digits than the decimal number system, their digits are the same as the corresponding digits in decimal.

The hexadecimal number system poses a problem because it requires sixteen digits—a lowest digit of 0 and a highest digit with a value equivalent to decimal 15 (one less than the base, 16). By convention, we use the letters A through F to represent the hexadecimal digits corresponding to decimal values 10 through 15. Thus, in hexadecimal, we can have numbers like 876 consisting solely of decimal-like digits, numbers like 8A55F consisting of digits and letters and numbers like FFE consisting solely of letters. Occasionally, a hexadecimal number spells a common word such as FACE or FEED—this can appear strange to programmers accustomed to working with numbers. Fig. C.2 summarizes each of the number systems.

Each of these number systems uses *positional notation*—each position in which a digit is written has a different *positional value*. For example, in the decimal number 937 (the 9, the 3 and the 7 are referred to as *symbol values*), we say that the 7 is written in the *ones position*, the 3 is written in the *tens position* and the 9 is written in the *hundreds position*. Notice that each of these positions is a power of the base (base 10) and that these powers begin at 0 and increase by 1 as we move left in the number (Fig. C.3).

Binary digit	Octal digit	Decimal digit	Hexadecimal digit
0	0	0	0
1	1	1	1
	2	2	2
	3	3	3
	4	4	4
	5	5	5
	6	6	6
	7	7	7
		8	8
		9	9
			A (decimal value of 10)
			B (decimal value of 11)
			C (decimal value of 12)
			D (decimal value of 13)
			E (decimal value of 14)
			F (decimal value of 15)

Fig. C.1   Digits of the binary, octal, decimal and hexadecimal number systems.

Attribute	Binary	Octal	Decimal	Hexadecimal
Base	2	8	10	16
Lowest digit	0	0	0	0
Highest digit	1	7	9	F

Fig. C.2   Comparison of the binary, octal, decimal and hexadecimal number systems.

Positional values in the decimal number system			
Decimal digit	9	3	7
Position name	Hundreds	Tens	Ones
Positional value	100	10	1
Positional value as a power of the base (10)	10^2	10^1	10^0

Fig. C.3   Positional values in the decimal number system.

For longer decimal numbers, the next positions to the left would be the *thousands position* (10 to the 3rd power), the *ten-thousands position* (10 to the 4th power), the *hundred-thousands position* (10 to the 5th power), the *millions position* (10 to the 6th power), the *ten-millions position* (10 to the 7th power) and so on.

In the binary number 101, we say that the rightmost 1 is written in the *ones position*, the 0 is written in the *twos position*, and the leftmost 1 is written in the *fours position*. Notice that each of these positions is a power of the base (base 2) and that these powers begin at 0 and increase by 1 as we move left in the number (Fig. C.4).

For longer binary numbers, the next positions to the left would be the *eights position* (2 to the 3rd power), the *sixteens position* (2 to the 4th power), the *thirty-twos position* (2 to the 5th power), the *sixty-fours position* (2 to the 6th power) and so on.

In the octal number 425, we say that the 5 is written in the *ones position*, the 2 is written in the *eights position*, and the 4 is written in the *sixty-fours position*. Notice that each of these positions is a power of the base (base 8) and that these powers begin at 0 and increase by 1 as we move left in the number (Fig. C.5).

For longer octal numbers, the next positions to the left would be the *five-hundred-and-twelves position* (8 to the 3rd power), the *four-thousand-and-ninety-sixes position* (8 to the 4th power), the *thirty-two-thousand-seven-hundred-and-sixty eights position* (8 to the 5th power) and so on.

In the hexadecimal number 3DA, we say that the A is written in the *ones position*, the D is written in the *sixteens position*, and the 3 is written in the *two-hundred-and-fifty-sixes position*. Notice that each of these positions is a power of the base (base 16) and that these powers begin at 0 and increase by 1 as we move left in the number (Fig. C.6).

Positional values in the binary number system

Binary digit	1	0	1
Position name	Fours	Twos	Ones
Positional value	4	2	1
Positional value as a power of the base (2)	2^2	2^1	2^0

Fig. C.4   Positional values in the binary number system.

Positional values in the octal number system

Decimal digit	4	2	5
Position name	Sixty-fours	Eights	Ones
Positional value	64	8	1
Positional value as a power of the base (8)	8^2	8^1	8^0

Fig. C.5   Positional values in the octal number system.

Positional values in the hexadecimal number system			
Decimal digit	**3**	**D**	**A**
Position name	Two-hundred-and-fifty-sixes	Sixteens	Ones
Positional value	**256**	**16**	**1**
Positional value as a power of the base (16)	16^2	16^1	16^0

Fig. C.6   Positional values in the hexadecimal number system.

For longer hexadecimal numbers, the next positions to the left would be the *four-thousand-and-ninety-sixes position* (16 to the 3rd power), the *sixty-five-thousand-five-hundred-and-thirty-sixes position* (16 to the 4th power) and so on.

C.2 Abbreviating Binary Numbers as Octal Numbers and Hexadecimal Numbers

The main use of octal and hexadecimal numbers in computing is for abbreviating lengthy binary representations. Fig. C.7 demonstrates that lengthy binary numbers can be expressed more concisely in number systems with higher bases than in the binary number system.

Decimal number	Binary representation	Octal representation	Hexadecimal representation
0	0	0	0
1	1	1	1
2	10	2	2
3	11	3	3
4	100	4	4
5	101	5	5
6	110	6	6
7	111	7	7
8	1000	10	8
9	1001	11	9
10	1010	12	A
11	1011	13	B
12	1100	14	C
13	1101	15	D
14	1110	16	E
15	1111	17	F
16	10000	20	10

Fig. C.7   Decimal, binary, octal and hexadecimal equivalents.

A particularly important relationship that both the octal number system and the hexadecimal number system have to the binary system is that the bases of octal and hexadecimal (8 and 16 respectively) are powers of the base of the binary number system (base 2). Consider the following 12-digit binary number and its octal and hexadecimal equivalents. See whether you can determine how this relationship makes it convenient to abbreviate binary numbers in octal or hexadecimal. The answer follows the numbers.

Binary Number	Octal equivalent	Hexadecimal equivalent
100011010001	4321	8D1

To see how the binary number converts easily to octal, simply break the 12-digit binary number into groups of three consecutive bits each, and write those groups over the corresponding digits of the octal number as follows:

100	011	010	001
4	3	2	1

Notice that the octal digit you have written under each group of thee bits corresponds precisely to the octal equivalent of that 3-digit binary number shown in Fig. C.7.

The same kind of relationship can be observed in converting numbers from binary to hexadecimal. In particular, break the 12-digit binary number into groups of four consecutive bits each, and write those groups over the corresponding digits of the hexadecimal number as follows:

1000	1101	0001
8	D	1

Notice that the hexadecimal digit you wrote under each group of four bits corresponds precisely to the hexadecimal equivalent of that 4-digit binary number shown in Fig. C.7.

C.3 Converting Octal Numbers and Hexadecimal Numbers to Binary Numbers

In the previous section, we saw how to convert binary numbers to their octal and hexadecimal equivalents by forming groups of binary digits and simply rewriting these groups as their equivalent octal digit values or hexadecimal digit values. This process may be used in reverse to produce the binary equivalent of a given octal or hexadecimal number.

For example, the octal number 653 is converted to binary simply by writing the 6 as its 3-digit binary equivalent 110, the 5 as its 3-digit binary equivalent 101 and the 3 as its 3-digit binary equivalent 011 to form the 9-digit binary number 110101011.

The hexadecimal number FAD5 is converted to binary simply by writing the F as its 4-digit binary equivalent 1111, the A as its 4-digit binary equivalent 1010, the D as its 4-digit binary equivalent 1101 and the 5 as its 4-digit binary equivalent 0101 to form the 16-digit 1111101011010101.

C.4 Converting from Binary, Octal or Hexadecimal to Decimal

Because we are accustomed to working in decimal, it is often convenient to convert a binary, octal, or hexadecimal number to decimal to get a sense of what the number is "really" worth. Our diagrams in Section C.1 express the positional values in decimal. To convert a number to decimal from another base, multiply the decimal equivalent of each digit by its positional value, and sum these products. For example, the binary number 110101 is converted to decimal 53 as shown in Fig. C.8.

To convert octal 7614 to decimal 3980, we use the same technique, this time using appropriate octal positional values as shown in Fig. C.9.

To convert hexadecimal AD3B to decimal 44347, we use the same technique, this time using appropriate hexadecimal positional values as shown in Fig. C.10.

C.5 Converting from Decimal to Binary, Octal or Hexadecimal

The conversions of the last section follow naturally from the positional-notation conventions. Converting from decimal to binary, octal or hexadecimal also follows these conventions.

Suppose we wish to convert decimal 57 to binary. We begin by writing the positional values of the columns right to left until we reach a column whose positional value is greater than the decimal number. We do not need that column, so we discard it. Thus, we first write

Positional values: **64   32   16   8   4   2   1**

Converting a binary number to decimal

Positional values:	32	16	8	4	2	1
Symbol values:	1	1	0	1	0	1
Products:	1*32=32	1*16=16	0*8=0	1*4=4	0*2=0	1*1=1
Sum:	= 32 + 16 + 0 + 4 + 0 + 1 = 53					

Fig. C.8   Converting a binary number to decimal.

Converting an octal number to decimal

Positional values:	512	64	8	1
Symbol values:	7	6	1	4
Products	7*512=3584	6*64=384	1*8=8	4*1=4
Sum:	= 3584 + 384 + 8 + 4 = 3980			

Fig. C.9   Converting an octal number to decimal.

Converting a hexadecimal number to decimal

Positional values:	4096	256	16	1
Symbol values:	A	D	3	B
Products	A*4096=40960	D*256=3328	3*16=48	B*1=11
Sum:	= 40960 + 3328 + 48 + 11 = 44347			

Fig. C.10   Converting a hexadecimal number to decimal.

Then we discard the column with positional value 64, leaving

Positional values: **32   16   8   4   2   1**

Next, we work from the leftmost column to the right. We divide 32 into 57 and observe that there is one 32 in 57 with a remainder of 25, so we write 1 in the 32's column. We divide 16 into 25 and observe that there is one 16 in 25 with a remainder of 9 and write 1 in the 16's column. We divide 8 into 9 and observe that there is one 8 in 9 with a remainder of 1. The next two columns both produce the quotient zero when their positional values are divided into 1, so we write 0s in the 4 and 2 columns. Finally, 1 into 1 is 1, so we write 1 in the 1's column. This yields

Positional values: **32   16   8   4   2   1**
Symbol values: **1   1   1   0   0   1**

and thus decimal 57 is equivalent to binary 111001.

To convert decimal 103 to octal, we begin by writing the positional values of the columns until we reach a column whose positional value is greater than the decimal number. We do not need that column, so we discard it. Thus, we first write

Positional values: **512 64   8   1**

Then we discard the column with positional value 512, yielding

Positional values: **64   8   1**

Next we work from the leftmost column to the right. We divide 64 into 103 and observe that there is one 64 in 103 with a remainder of 39, so we write 1 in the 64's column. We divide 8 into 39 and observe that there are four 8s in 39 with a remainder of 7 and write 4 in the 8's column. Finally, we divide 1 into 7 and observe that there are seven 1s in 7 with no remainder, so we write 7 in the 1's column. This yields

Positional values: **64   8   1**
Symbol values: **1   4   7**

and thus decimal 103 is equivalent to octal 147.

To convert decimal 375 to hexadecimal, we begin by writing the positional values of the columns until we reach a column whose positional value is greater than the decimal number. We do not need that column, so we discard it. Thus, we first write

Positional values: **4096 256 16   1**

Then we discard the column with positional value 4096, yielding

Positional values: **256 16   1**

Next we work from the leftmost column to the right. We divide 256 into 375 and observe that there is one 256 in 375 with a remainder of 119, so we write 1 in the 256 column. We divide 16 into 119 and observe that there are seven 16s in 119 with a remainder of 7 and write 7 in the 16's column. Finally, we divide 1 into 7 and observe that there are seven 1s in 7 with no remainder, so we write 7 in the 1's column. This yields

Positional values: **256 16   1**
Symbol values: **1   7   7**

and thus decimal 375 is equivalent to hexadecimal 177.

C.6 Negative Binary Numbers: Two's Complement Notation

The discussion in this appendix has been focussed on positive numbers. In this section, we explain how computers represent negative numbers using *two's complement notation*. First we explain how the two's complement of a binary number is formed, then we show why it represents the negative value of the given binary number.

Consider a machine with 32-bit integers. Suppose

```
int value = 13;
```

The 32-bit representation of **value** is

```
00000000 00000000 00000000 00001101
```

To form the negative of **value** we first form its *one's complement* by applying C++'s bit-wise complement operator (**~**), which is also called the *bitwise NOT operator*:

```
onesComplementOfValue = ~value;
```

Internally, **~value** is now **value** with each of its bits reversed—ones become zeros and zeros become ones, as follows:

```
value:
00000000 00000000 00000000 00001101

~value  (i.e., value's one's complement):
11111111 11111111 11111111 11110010
```

To form the two's complement of **value**, we simply add one to **value**'s one's complement. Thus,

```
Two's complement of value:
11111111 11111111 11111111 11110011
```

Now if this is in fact equal to –13, we should be able to add it to binary 13 and obtain the result 0. Let us try this:

```
 00000000 00000000 00000000 00001101
+11111111 11111111 11111111 11110011
------------------------------------
 00000000 00000000 00000000 00000000
```

The carry bit coming out of the leftmost column is discarded, and we indeed get zero as the result. If we add the one's complement of a number to the number, the result would be all 1s. The key to getting a result of all zeros is that the two's complement is 1 more than the one's complement. The addition of 1 causes each column to add to 0 with the carry 1. The carry keeps moving leftward until it is discarded from the leftmost bit, and hence the resulting number is all zeros.

Computers actually perform a subtraction such as

```
x = a - value;
```

by adding the two's complement of **value** to **a**, as follows:

```
x = a + ( ~value + 1 );
```

Suppose **a** is 27 and **value** is 13 as before. If the two's complement of **value** is actually the negative of **value**, then adding the two's complement of **value** to **a** should produce the result 14. Let us try this:

```
a  (i.e., 27)        00000000 00000000 00000000 00011011
+(~value + 1)       +11111111 11111111 11111111 11110011
                    -------------------------------------
                     00000000 00000000 00000000 00001110
```

which is indeed equal to 14.

SUMMARY

- When we write an integer such as 19 or 227 or –63 in a program, the number is automatically assumed to be in the decimal (base 10) number system. The digits in the decimal number system are 0, 1, 2, 3, 4, 5, 6, 7, 8 and 9. The lowest digit is 0 and the highest digit is 9—one less than the base, 10.

- Internally, computers use the binary (base 2) number system. The binary number system has only two digits, namely, 0 and 1. Its lowest digit is 0 and its highest digit is 1—one less than the base, 2.

- The octal number system (base 8) and the hexadecimal number system (base 16) are popular primarily because they make it convenient to abbreviate binary numbers.

- The digits of the octal number system range from 0 to 7.

- The hexadecimal number system poses a problem because it requires sixteen digits—a lowest digit of 0 and a highest digit with a value equivalent to decimal 15 (one less than the base, 16). By convention, we use the letters A through F to represent the hexadecimal digits corresponding to decimal values 10 through 15.

- Each number system uses positional notation—each position in which a digit is written has a different positional value.

- A particularly important relationship that both the octal number system and the hexadecimal number system have to the binary system is that the bases of octal and hexadecimal (8 and 16 respectively) are powers of the base of the binary number system (base 2).

- To convert an octal number to a binary number, simply replace each octal digit with its three-digit binary equivalent.

- To convert a hexadecimal number to a binary number, simply replace each hexadecimal digit with its four-digit binary equivalent.

- Because we are accustomed to working in decimal, it is convenient to convert a binary, octal or hexadecimal number to decimal to get a sense of the number's "real" worth.

- To convert a number to decimal from another base, multiply the decimal equivalent of each digit by its positional value, and sum these products.

- Computers represent negative numbers using two's complement notation.

- To form the negative of a value in binary, first form its one's complement by applying C++'s bitwise complement operator (~). This reverses the bits of the value. To form the two's complement of a value, simply add one to the value's one's complement.

TERMINOLOGY

base	base 16 number system
base 2 number system	binary number system
base 8 number system	bitwise complement operator (~)
base 10 number system	conversion

decimal number system	one's complement notation
digit	positional notation
hexadecimal number system	positional value
negative value	symbol value
octal number system	two's complement notation

SELF-REVIEW EXERCISES

C.1   The bases of the decimal, binary, octal and hexadecimal number systems are _____, _____, _____ and _____ respectively.

C.2   In general, the decimal, octal and hexadecimal representations of a given binary number contain (more/fewer) digits than the binary number contains.

C.3   (True/False) A popular reason for using the decimal number system is that it forms a convenient notation for abbreviating binary numbers simply by substituting one decimal digit per group of four binary bits.

C.4   The (octal/hexadecimal/decimal) representation of a large binary value is the most concise (of the given alternatives).

C.5   (True/False) The highest digit in any base is one more than the base.

C.6   (True/False) The lowest digit in any base is one less than the base.

C.7   The positional value of the rightmost digit of any number in either binary, octal, decimal or hexadecimal is always _____.

C.8   The positional value of the digit to the left of the rightmost digit of any number in binary, octal, decimal, or hexadecimal is always equal to _____.

C.9   Fill in the missing values in this chart of positional values for the rightmost four positions in each of the indicated number systems:

decimal	1000	100	10	1
hexadecimal	...	256	...	...
binary	...	...	...	...
octal	512	64	8	1

C.10   Convert binary **110101011000** to octal and to hexadecimal.

C.11   Convert hexadecimal **FACE** to binary.

C.12   Convert octal **7316** to binary.

C.13   Convert hexadecimal **4FEC** to octal. [*Hint*: First convert 4FEC to binary then convert that binary number to octal.]

C.14   Convert binary **1101110** to decimal.

C.15   Convert octal **317** to decimal.

C.16   Convert hexadecimal **EFD4** to decimal.

C.17   Convert decimal **177** to binary, to octal and to hexadecimal.

C.18   Show the binary representation of decimal **417**. Then show the one's complement of **417**, and the two's complement of **417**.

C.19   What is the result when the one's complement of a number is added to itself?

SELF-REVIEW ANSWERS

C.1   **10, 2, 8, 16**.

C.2   Fewer.

C.3   False.

C.4   Hexadecimal.

C.5   False. The highest digit in any base is one less than the base.

C.6   False. The lowest digit in any base is zero.

C.7   **1** (the base raised to the zero power).

C.8   The base of the number system.

C.9   Fill in the missing values in this chart of positional values for the rightmost four positions in each of the indicated number systems:

decimal	**1000**	**100**	**10**	**1**
hexadecimal	**4096**	**256**	**16**	**1**
binary	**8**	**4**	**2**	**1**
octal	**512**	**64**	**8**	**1**

C.10   Octal **6530**; Hexadecimal **D58**.

C.11   Binary **1111 1010 1100 1110**.

C.12   Binary **111 011 001 110**.

C.13   Binary **0 100 111 111 101 100; Octal 47754**.

C.14   Decimal **2+4+8+32+64=110**.

C.15   Decimal **7+1*8+3*64=7+8+192=207**.

C.16   Decimal **4+13*16+15*256+14*4096=61396**.

C.17   Decimal **177**
to binary:

```
256 128 64 32 16 8 4 2 1
128 64 32 16 8 4 2 1
(1*128)+(0*64)+(1*32)+(1*16)+(0*8)+(0*4)+(0*2)+(1*1)
10110001
```

to octal:

```
512 64 8 1
64 8 1
(2*64)+(6*8)+(1*1)
261
```

to hexadecimal:

```
256 16 1
16 1
(11*16)+(1*1)
(B*16)+(1*1)
B1
```

C.18   Binary:

```
512 256 128 64 32 16 8 4 2 1
256 128 64 32 16 8 4 2 1
(1*256)+(1*128)+(0*64)+(1*32)+(0*16)+(0*8)+(0*4)+(0*2)+
(1*1)
110100001
```

One's complement: **001011110**
Two's complement: **001011111**
Check: Original binary number + its two's complement

```
110100001
001011111
----------
000000000
```

C.19   Zero.

EXERCISES

C.20   Some people argue that many of our calculations would be easier in the base **12** number system because **12** is divisible by so many more numbers than **10** (for base **10**). What is the lowest digit in base **12**? What might the highest symbol for a digit in base **12** be? What are the positional values of the rightmost four positions of any number in the base **12** number system?

C.21   How is the highest symbol value in the number systems we discussed related to the positional value of the first digit to the left of the rightmost digit of any number in these number systems?

C.22   Complete the following chart of positional values for the rightmost four positions in each of the indicated number systems:

```
decimal   1000    100     10      1
base 6    ...     ...     6       ...
base 13   ...     169     ...     ...
base 3    27      ...     ...     ...
```

C.23   Convert binary **100101111010** to octal and to hexadecimal.

C.24   Convert hexadecimal **3A7D** to binary.

C.25   Convert hexadecimal **765F** to octal. [*Hint*: First convert **765F** to binary, then convert that binary number to octal.]

C.26   Convert binary **1011110** to decimal.

C.27   Convert octal **426** to decimal.

C.28   Convert hexadecimal **FFFF** to decimal.

C.29   Convert decimal **299** to binary, to octal and to hexadecimal.

C.30   Show the binary representation of decimal **779**. Then show the one's complement of **779** and the two's complement of **779**.

C.31   What is the result when the two's complement of a number is added to itself?

C.32   Show the two's complement of integer value **-1** on a machine with 32-bit integers.

C++ Internet and Web Resources

This appendix contains a list of C++ resources that are available on the Internet and the World Wide Web. These resources include FAQs (Frequently Asked Questions), tutorials, links to the ANSI/ISO C++ standard, information about popular C++ compilers and access to free compilers, demos, books, tutorials, software tools, articles, interviews, conferences, journals and magazines, online courses, newsgroups and career resources. For additional information about the American National Standards Institute (ANSI) and its activities related to C++, visit **www.ansi.org**.

D.1 Resources

www.cplusplus.com
This site contains information about the history and development of C++ as well as tutorials, documentation, reference material, source code and forums.

www.possibility.com/Cpp/CppCodingStandard.html
The *C++ Coding Standard* site examines the C++ standard and the standardizing process. The site includes such topics as standards enforcement, formatting, portability and documentation and offers links to additional C++ Web resources.

help-site.com/cpp.html
Help-site.com provides links to C++ resources on the Web, including tutorials and a C++ FAQ.

www.glenmccl.com/tutor.htm
This reference site discusses topics such as object-oriented design and writing robust code. The site provides introductions to C++ language topics, including keyword **static**, data type **bool**, namespaces, the Standard Template Library and memory allocation.

www.programmersheaven.com/zone3/cat353
This site offers an extensive collection of free C++ libraries.

www.programmersheaven.com/zone3
This site provides links to articles, tutorials, development tools and source code.

www.hal9k.com/cug
The *C/C++ Users Group (CUG)* site contains C++ resources, journals, shareware and freeware.

www.devx.com
DevX is a comprehensive resource for programmers that provides the latest news, tools and techniques for various programming languages. The *C++ Zone* offers tips, discussion forums, technical help and online newsletters.

www.cprogramming.com
This site contains interactive tutorials, quizzes, articles, journals, compiler downloads, book recommendations and free source code.

www.eecs.utoledo.edu/~cwinner/c.html
This site provides links to tutorials, compilers, FAQs, source code, C++ reference material and career-related sites for C++ programmers.

www.acm.org/crossroads/xrds3-2/ovp32.html
The Association for Computing Machinery's (ACM) site offers a comprehensive listing of C++ resources, including recommended texts, journals and magazines, published standards, newsletters, FAQs and newsgroups.

www.vb-bookmark.com/vbCpp.html
The C++ Bookmark site contains links to class libraries, development environments, source code, tutorials, compilers, seminars, magazines and user groups.

www.comeaucomputing.com/resources
Comeau Computing's site links to technical discussions, FAQs (including one devoted to templates), user groups, newsgroups and an online C++ compiler.

www.exciton.cs.rice.edu/CppResources
The site provides a document that summarizes the technical aspects of C++. The site also discusses the differences between Java and C++.

www.accu.informika.ru/resources/public/terse/cpp.htm
The Association of C & C++ Users (ACCU) site contains links to C++ tutorials, articles, developer information, discussions and book reviews.

noyce.ucdavis.edu/CDFgroup/CPPPAGE.htm
This site links to tutorials, information about C++ libraries and information about the GNU Compiler Collection.

www.cuj.com
The *C/C++ User's Journal* is an online magazine that contains articles, tutorials and downloads. The site features news about C++, forums and links to information about development tools.

directory.google.com/Top/Computers/Programming/Languages/C++/Resources/Directories
Google's C++ resources directory ranks the most useful C++ sites.

www.compinfo-center.com/c++.htm
This site provides links to C++ FAQs, newsgroups and magazines.

www.apl.jhu.edu/~paulmac/c++-references.html
This site contains book reviews and recommendations for introductory, intermediate and advanced C++ programmers and links to online C++ resources, including books, magazines and tutorials.

www.enteract.com/~bradapp/links/cplusplus-links.html
This site divides links into categories, including Resources and Directories, Projects and Working Groups, Libraries, Training, Tutorials, Publications and Coding Conventions.

www.codeproject.com
Articles, code snippets, user discussions, books and news about C++, C# and .NET programming are available at this site.

www.austinlinks.com/CPlusPlus
Quadralay Corporation's site links to numerous C++ resources, including Visual C++/MFC Libraries, C++ programming information, C++ career resources and a list of tutorials and other online tools for learning C++.

www.csci.csusb.edu/dick/c++std
Links to the ANSI/ISO C++ Standard and the **comp.std.c++** Usenet group are available at this site.

www.research.att.com/~bs/homepage.html
This is the home page for Bjarne Stroustrup, designer of the C++ programming language. This site provides a list of C++ resources, FAQs and other useful C++ information.

D.2 Tutorials

www.rdw.tec.mn.us/msc/index.shtml
Minnesota State College-Southeast Technical offers online C++ courses for credit.

library.advanced.org/3074
This tutorial is designed for Pascal programmers who want to learn C++.

ftp://rtfm.mit.edu/pub/usenet/news.answers/C-faq/learn-c-cpp-today
This site provides detailed descriptions of several C++ tutorials that are available on the Web. The site also contains information about various C++ compilers.

www.cprogramming.com/tutorial.html
This site offers a step-by-step tutorial, with sample code, that covers file I/O, recursion, binary trees, template classes and more.

www.programmersheaven.com/zone3/cat34
Free tutorials that are appropriate for many skill levels are available at this site.

www.eecs.utoledo.edu/~cwinner/c.html
This site offers links to tutorials, compilers, FAQs, source code, C++ reference material and career-related Web sites for C++ programmers.

www.programmershelp.co.uk/c++.php
This site contains free online courses and a comprehensive list of C++ tutorials. This site also provides FAQs, downloads and other resources.

www.codeproject.com/script/articles/beginners.asp
This site lists tutorials and articles available for C++ beginners.

development.freeservers.com/c_cpp
This site contains C++ tutorials, articles, games, sample programs, development tools and links to other C++ resources.

www.eng.hawaii.edu/Tutor/Make
This site provides a tutorial that describes how to create makefiles.

www.cpp-home.com
Free tutorials, discussions, chat rooms, articles, compilers, forums and online quizzes related to C++ are available at this site. The C++ tutorials overview such topics as ActiveX/COM, MFC and graphics.

www.codebeach.com
Code Beach contains source code, tutorials, books and links to major programming languages, including C++, Java, ASP, Visual Basic, XML, Python, Perl and C#.

www.kegel.com/academy/tutorials.html
This site provides links to tutorials on C, C++ and assembly languages.

www.intelinfo.com/newly_researched_free_training/C++.html
This site has a comprehensive list of free tutorials on the Web, with brief descriptions.

D.3 FAQs

www.faqs.org/faqs/by-newsgroup/comp/comp.lang.c++.html
This site consists of links to FAQs and tutorials gathered from the **Comp.Lang.C++** newsgroup.

www.eskimo.com/~scs/C-faq/top.html
This C FAQ list contains topics such as pointers, memory allocation and strings.

www.technion.ac.il/technion/tcc/usg/Ref/C_Programming.html
This site contains C/C++ programming references, including FAQs and tutorials.

www.faqs.org/faqs/by-newsgroup/comp/comp.compilers.html
This site contains a list of FAQs generated in the **comp.compilers** newsgroup.

D.4 Visual C++

msdn.microsoft.com/visualc
Microsoft's Visual C++ page provides information about the latest release of Visual C++ .NET.

www.aul.fiu.edu/tech/visualc.html
This site contains articles, tutorials, FAQs and newsgroups on Visual C++ and information on C/C++.

www.vb-bookmark.com/VisualCPP.html
The *Visual Basic/Visual C++ Bookmark* site contains source code, usergroups, tips and Visual C++ programming information.

www.programmershelp.co.uk/c++visc.php
This site contains links to various resources on Visual C++, including source code, development tools and articles.

www.freeprogrammingresources.com/visualcpp.html
This site contains free programming resources for Visual C++ programmers, including tutorials and sample programming applications.

www.mvps.org/vcfaq
The *Most Valuable Professional (MVP)* site contains a Visual C++ FAQ.

www.onesmartclick.com/programming/visual-cpp.html
This site contains Visual C++ tutorials, online books, tips, tricks, FAQs and debugging.

D.5 Newsgroups

www.phoaks.com/comp/lang/c++/index.html
This site is a resource for information related to the **comp.lang.c++** newsgroup.

kom.net/~dbrick/newspage/comp.lang.c++.html
Visit this site to connect to newsgroups related to the **comp.lang.c++** hierarchy.

ai.kaist.ac.kr/~ymkim/Program/c++.html
This site offers tutorials, libraries, popular compilers, FAQs and newsgroups, including **comp.lang.c++**.

pent21.infosys.tuwien.ac.at/cetus/
oo_c_plus_plus.html#oo_c_plus_plus_general_newsgroups
This site features a list of general C++ newsgroups.

D.6 Compilers and Development Tools

msdn.microsoft.com/visualc
The *Microsoft Visual C++* site provides product information, overviews, supplemental materials and ordering information for the Visual C++ compiler.

www.borland.com/bcppbuilder
This is a link to the *Borland C++ Builder 6*. A free command-line version is available for download.

www.thefreecountry.com/developercity/ccompilers.shtml
This site lists free C and C++ compilers for a variety of operating systems.

www.faqs.org/faqs/by-newsgroup/comp/comp.compilers.html
This site lists FAQs generated within the **comp.compilers** newsgroup.

www.ncf.carleton.ca/%7Ebg283
The *Miracle C compiler*, a DOS-based C++ compiler, is available at this site. The compiler is free for download, and the source code is available for a registration fee.

www.compilers.net
Compilers.net is designed to help users locate compilers.

sunset.backbone.olemiss.edu/%7Ebobcook/eC
This C++ compiler is designed for Pascal programmers who want to transition to C++.

developer.intel.com/software/products/compilers/c60
The *Intel C++ compiler* is available at this site.

www.kai.com/C_plus_plus
This site offers the *Kai C++ compiler* for a 30-day free trial.

www.symbian.com/developer/development/cppdev.html
Symbian provides a C++ Developer's Pack and links to various resources, including code and development tools for C++ programmers (particularly those working with the Symbian operating system).

www.winwarelinks.com/apps/development/cplusplus.htm
This site contains resources for C++ development tools and software applications.

D.7 Standard Template Library

Tutorials

www.cs.brown.edu/people/jak/programming/stl-tutorial/tutorial.html
This STL tutorial is organized by examples, philosophy, components and extending STL. You will find code examples using the STL components, useful explanations and helpful diagrams.

web.ftech.net/~honeyg/articles/eff_stl.htm
An STL tutorial available at this site provides information on the STL components, containers, stream and iterator adaptors, transforming and selecting values, filtering and transforming values and objects.

www.xraylith.wisc.edu/~khan/software/stl/os_examples/examples.html
This site is helpful for people just learning about the STL. You will find an introduction to the STL and ObjectSpace STL Tool Kit examples.

References

www.sgi.com/tech/stl
The Silicon Graphics Standard Template Library Programmer's Guide is a useful resource for STL information. You can download STL source code from this site, and find the latest information, design documentation and links to other STL resources.

`www.cs.rpi.edu/projects/STL/stl/stl.html`

This is the *Standard Template Library Online Reference* home page from Rensselaer Polytechnic Institute. You will find detailed explanations of the STL as well as links to other useful resources for information about the STL.

`www.dinkumware.com/refcpp.html`

This site contains useful information about the ANSI/ISO Standard C++ Library and contains information about the Standard Template Library.

Articles, Books and Interviews

`www.byte.com/art/9510/sec12/art3.htm`

The *Byte Magazine* site has a copy of an article written by one of the creators of the Standard Template Library, Alexander Stepanov, that provides information on the use of the STL in generic programming.

ANSI/ISO C++ Standard

`www.ansi.org`

You can purchase a copy of the C++ Standard from this site.

Software

`www.cs.rpi.edu/~musser/stl-book`

The RPI STL site includes information on how STL differs from other C++ libraries and on how to compile programs that use STL. A list of STL include files, example programs that use STL, STL Container Classes, and STL Iterator Categories are available. The site also provides an STL-compatible compiler list, FTP sites for STL source code and related materials.

`www.cs.rpi.edu/~wiseb/stl-borland.html`

This site is a reference for Borland C++ compiler users. The site includes sections on warnings and incompatibilities.

Good Programming Practice E.1

*Assign documents file names that describe their functionality. This practice can help you identify documents faster. It also helps people who want to link to a page, by giving them an easy-to-remember name. For example, if you are writing an XHTML document that contains product information, you might want to call it **products.html**.*

Machines running specialized software called a *Web server* store XHTML documents. Clients (e.g., Web browsers) request specific *resources*, such as XHTML documents, from the Web server. For example, typing **www.deitel.com/books/downloads.htm** into a Web browser's address field requests **downloads.htm** from the Web server running at **www.deitel.com**. This document is located in a directory named **books**.

E.3 First XHTML Example

In this appendix, we present XHTML markup and provide screen captures that show how Internet Explorer renders (i.e., displays) the XHTML. Every XHTML document we show has line numbers for the reader's convenience. These line numbers are not part of the XHTML documents.

Our first example (Fig. E.1) is an XHTML document named **main.html** that displays the message **Welcome to XHTML!** in the browser. The key line in the program is line 14, which tells the browser to display **Welcome to XHTML!** Now let us consider each line of the program.

```
1   <?xml version = "1.0"?>
2   <!DOCTYPE html PUBLIC "-//W3C//DTD XHTML 1.0 Strict//EN"
3      "http://www.w3.org/TR/xhtml1/DTD/xhtml1-strict.dtd">
4
5   <!-- Fig. E.1: main.html -->
6   <!-- Our first Web page. -->
7
8   <html xmlns = "http://www.w3.org/1999/xhtml">
9      <head>
10        <title>Our first Web page</title>
11     </head>
12
13     <body>
14        <p>Welcome to XHTML!</p>
15     </body>
16  </html>
```

Fig. E.1   First XHTML example.

Lines 1–3 are required in XHTML documents to conform with proper XHTML syntax. Lines 5–6 are *XHTML comments*. XHTML document creators insert comments to improve markup readability and to describe the content of a document. Comments also help other people read and understand an XHTML document's markup and content. Comments do not cause the browser to perform any action when the user loads the XHTML document into the Web browser to view the document. XHTML comments always start with **<!--** and end with **-->**. Each of our XHTML examples includes comments that specify the figure number and file name and provide a brief description of the example's purpose. Subsequent examples include comments in the markup, especially to highlight new features.

Good Programming Practice E.2

Place comments throughout your markup. Comments help other programmers understand the markup, assist in debugging and list useful information that you do not want the browser to render. Comments also help you understand your own markup when you revisit a document for modifications or updates in the future.

XHTML markup contains text that represents the content of a document and *elements* that specify a document's structure. Some important elements of an XHTML document include the **html** element, the **head** element and the **body** element. The **html** element encloses the *head section* (represented by the **head** *element*) and the *body section* (represented by the **body** *element*). The head section contains information about the XHTML document, such as the *title* of the document. The head section also can contain special document-formatting instructions called *style sheets* and client-side programs called *scripts* for creating dynamic Web pages. The body section contains the page's content that the browser displays when the user visits the Web page.

XHTML documents delimit an element with *start* and *end* tags. A start tag consists of the element name in angle brackets (e.g., **<html>**). An end tag consists of the element name preceded by a **/** in angle brackets (e.g., **</html>**). In this example, lines 8 and 16 define the start and end of the **html** element. Note that the end tag on line 16 has the same name as the start tag, but is preceded by a **/** inside the angle brackets. Many start tags define *attributes* that provide additional information about an element. Browsers can use this additional information to determine how to process the element. Each attribute has a *name* and a *value*, separated by an equal sign (**=**). Line 8 specifies a required attribute (**xmlns**) and value (**http://www.w3.org/1999/xhtml**) for the **html** element in an XHTML document.

Common Programming Error E.1

Not enclosing attribute values in either single or double quotes is a syntax error.

Common Programming Error E.2

Using uppercase letters in an XHTML element or attribute name is a syntax error.

An XHTML document divides the **html** element into two sections—head and body. Lines 9–11 define the Web page's head section with a **head** element. Line 10 specifies a **title** element. This is called a *nested element*, because it is enclosed in the **head** element's start and end tags. The **head** element also is a nested element, because it is enclosed in the **html** element's start and end tags. The **title** element describes the Web page. Titles usually appear in the *title bar* at the top of the browser window and also as the text identifying a page when users add the page to their list of **Favorites** or **Bookmarks**, which enable users to return to their favorite sites. Search engines (i.e., sites that allow users to search the Web) also use the `title` for cataloging purposes.

Good Programming Practice E.3

Indenting nested elements emphasizes a document's structure and promotes readability.

Common Programming Error E.3

XHTML does not permit tags to overlap—a nested element's end tag must appear in the document before the enclosing element's end tag. For example, the nested XHTML tags `<head><title>hello</head></title>` *cause a syntax error, because the enclosing* **head** *element's ending* `</head>` *tag appears before the nested* **title** *element's ending* `</title>` *tag.*

Good Programming Practice E.4

Use a consistent `title` *naming convention for all pages on a site. For example, if a site is named "Bailey's Web Site," then the* `title` *of the main page might be "Bailey's Web Site—Links." This practice can help users better understand the Web site's structure.*

Line 13 opens the document's **body** element. The body section of an XHTML document specifies the document's content, which may include text and tags.

Some tags, such as the *paragraph tags* (`<p>` and `</p>`) in line 14, mark up text for display in a browser. All text placed between the `<p>` and `</p>` tags form one paragraph. When the browser renders a paragraph, a blank line usually precedes and follows paragraph text.

This document ends with two closing tags (lines 15–16). These tags close the **body** and **html** elements, respectively. The ending `</html>` tag in an XHTML document informs the browser that the XHTML markup is complete.

To view this example in Internet Explorer, perform the following steps:

1. Copy the Appendix E examples onto your machine (these examples are available on the CD-ROM that accompanies this book).

2. Launch Internet Explorer, and select **Open...** from the **File** Menu. This displays the **Open** dialog.

3. Click the **Open** dialog's **Browse...** button to display the **Microsoft Internet Explorer** file dialog.

4. Navigate to the directory containing the Appendix E examples, and select the file **main.html**; then click **Open**.

5. Click **OK** to have Internet Explorer (or any other browser) render the document. Other examples are opened in a similar manner.

At this point, your browser window should appear similar to the sample screen capture shown in Fig. E.1.

E.4 Headers

Some text in an XHTML document might be more important than other text. For example, the text in this section is considered more important than a footnote. XHTML provides six *headers*, called *header elements*, for specifying the relative importance of information. Figure E.2 demonstrates these elements (**h1** through **h6**).

```
1   <?xml version = "1.0"?>
2   <!DOCTYPE html PUBLIC "-//W3C//DTD XHTML 1.0 Strict//EN"
3      "http://www.w3.org/TR/xhtml1/DTD/xhtml1-strict.dtd">
4
5   <!-- Fig. E.2: header.html -->
6   <!-- XHTML headers.        -->
7
8   <html xmlns = "http://www.w3.org/1999/xhtml">
9      <head>
10         <title>XHTML headers</title>
11      </head>
12
13      <body>
14
15         <h1>Level 1 Header</h1>
16         <h2>Level 2 header</h2>
17         <h3>Level 3 header</h3>
18         <h4>Level 4 header</h4>
19         <h5>Level 5 header</h5>
20         <h6>Level 6 header</h6>
21
22      </body>
23   </html>
```

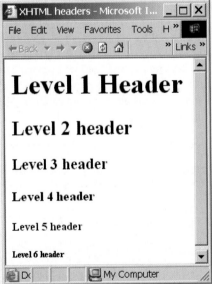

Fig. E.2   Header elements **h1** through **h6**.

Header element **h1** (line 15) is considered the most significant header and is rendered in a larger font than the other five headers (lines 16–20). Each successive header element (i.e., **h2**, **h3**, etc.) is rendered in a smaller font.

Portability Tip E.1

The text size used to display each header element can vary significantly between browsers.

Look-and-Feel Observation E.1

Placing a header at the top of every XHTML page helps viewers understand the purpose of each page.

Look-and-Feel Observation E.2

Use larger headers to emphasize more important sections of a Web page.

E.5 Linking

One of the most important XHTML features is the *hyperlink,* which references (or *links* to) other resources, such as XHTML documents and images. In XHTML, both text and images can act as hyperlinks. Web browsers typically underline text hyperlinks and color their text blue by default, so that users can distinguish hyperlinks from plain text. In Fig. E.3, we create text hyperlinks to four different Web sites. Line 17 introduces the **<strong>** tag. Browsers typically display text marked up with **<strong>** in a bold font.

Links are created using the **a** (*anchor*) *element.* Line 21 defines a hyperlink that links the text **Deitel** to the URL assigned to attribute **href**, which specifies the location of a linked resource, such as a Web page, a file or an e-mail address. This particular anchor element links to a Web page located at **http://www.deitel.com**. When a URL does not indicate a specific document on the Web site, the Web server returns a default Web page. This page often is called **index.html**; however, most Web servers can be configured to to use any file as the default Web page for the site. (Open **http://www.deitel.com** in one browser window and **http://www.deitel.com/index.html** in a second browser window to confirm that they are identical.) If the Web server cannot locate a requested document, the server returns an error indication to the Web browser, and the browser displays an error message to the user.

```
1   <?xml version = "1.0"?>
2   <!DOCTYPE html PUBLIC "-//W3C//DTD XHTML 1.0 Strict//EN"
3       "http://www.w3.org/TR/xhtml1/DTD/xhtml1-strict.dtd">
4
5   <!-- Fig. E.3: links.html      -->
6   <!-- Introduction to hyperlinks. -->
7
8   <html xmlns = "http://www.w3.org/1999/xhtml">
9      <head>
10        <title>Introduction to hyperlinks</title>
11     </head>
12
13     <body>
14
15        <h1>Here are my favorite sites</h1>
16
17        <p><strong>Click a name to go to that page.</strong></p>
18
```

Fig. E.3   Linking to other Web pages. (Part 1 of 2.)

```
19          <!-- create four text hyperlinks -->
20          <p>
21             <a href = "http://www.deitel.com">Deitel</a>
22          </p>
23
24          <p>
25             <a href = "http://www.prenhall.com">Prentice Hall</a>
26          </p>
27
28          <p>
29             <a href = "http://www.yahoo.com">Yahoo!</a>
30          </p>
31
32          <p>
33             <a href = "http://www.usatoday.com">USA Today</a>
34          </p>
35
36       </body>
37    </html>
```

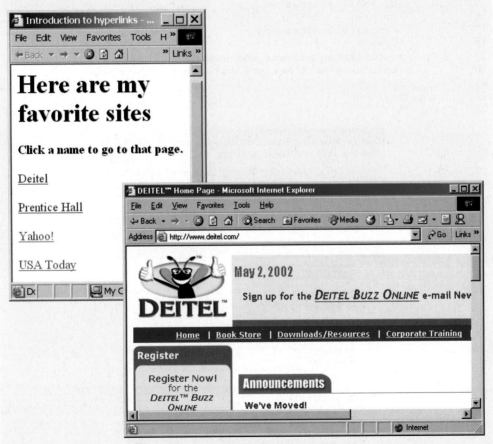

Fig. E.3   Linking to other Web pages. (Part 2 of 2.)

Anchors can link to e-mail addresses through a ***mailto:*** URL. When someone clicks this type of anchored link, most browsers launch the default e-mail program (e.g., Outlook Express) to enable the user to write an e-mail message to the linked address. Figure E.4 demonstrates this type of anchor.

```
1   <?xml version = "1.0"?>
2   <!DOCTYPE html PUBLIC "-//W3C//DTD XHTML 1.0 Strict//EN"
3       "http://www.w3.org/TR/xhtml1/DTD/xhtml1-strict.dtd">
4
5   <!-- Fig. E.4: contact.html   -->
6   <!-- Adding email hyperlinks. -->
7
8   <html xmlns = "http://www.w3.org/1999/xhtml">
9      <head>
10         <title>Adding e-mail hyperlinks</title>
11      </head>
12
13      <body>
14
15         <p>My email address is
16            <a href = "mailto:deitel@deitel.com">
17               deitel@deitel.com
18            </a>
19            . Click the address and your browser will
20            open an e-mail message and address it to me.
21         </p>
22      </body>
23   </html>
```

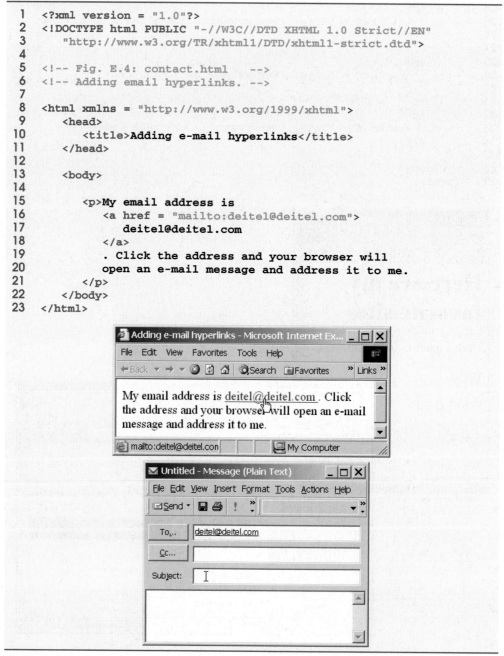

Fig. E.4   Linking to an e-mail address.

Lines 17–19 contain an e-mail link. The form of an e-mail anchor is **<a href = "mailto:***emailaddress***">...</a>**. In this case, we link to the e-mail address **deitel@deitel.com**.

E.6 Images

The examples discussed so far demonstrated how to mark up documents that contain only text. However, most Web pages contain both text and images. In fact, images are an equal and essential part of Web-page design. The two most popular image formats used by Web developers are Graphics Interchange Format (GIF) and Joint Photographic Experts Group (JPEG) images. Users can create images, using specialized pieces of software, such as Adobe PhotoShop Elements and Jasc Paint Shop Pro (**www.jasc.com**). Images may also be acquired from various Web sites, such as **gallery.yahoo.com**. Figure E.5 demonstrates how to incorporate images into Web pages.

Good Programming Practice E.5

Always include the **width** *and the* **height** *of an image inside the* **<img>** *tag. When the browser loads the XHTML file, it will know immediately from these attributes how much screen space to provide for the image and will lay out the page properly, even before it downloads the image.*

Performance Tip E.1

Including the **width** *and* **height** *attributes in an* **<img>** *tag will help the browser load and render pages faster.*

```
1   <?xml version = "1.0"?>
2   <!DOCTYPE html PUBLIC "-//W3C//DTD XHTML 1.0 Strict//EN"
3      "http://www.w3.org/TR/xhtml1/DTD/xhtml1-strict.dtd">
4
5   <!-- Fig. E.5: picture.html    -->
6   <!-- Adding images with XHTML. -->
7
8   <html xmlns = "http://www.w3.org/1999/xhtml">
9      <head>
10         <title>Adding images in XHTML</title>
11      </head>
12
13      <body>
14
15         <p>
16            <img src = "cool8se.jpg" height = "238" width = "181"
17               alt = "An imaginary landscape." />
18
19            <img src = "fish.jpg" height = "238" width = "181"
20               alt = "A picture of a fish swimming." />
21         </p>
22
23      </body>
24   </html>
```

Fig. E.5   Placing images in XHTML files. (Part 1 of 2.)

Fig. E.5   Placing images in XHTML files. (Part 2 of 2.)

Common Programming Error E.4

Entering new dimensions for an image that change its inherent width-to-height ratio might distort the appearance of the image. For example, if your image is 200 pixels wide and 100 pixels high, you should ensure that any new dimensions have a 2:1 width-to-height ratio.

Lines 16–17 use an **img** element to insert an image in the document. The image file's location is specified with the **img** element's **src** attribute. In this case, the image is located in the same directory as this XHTML document, so only the image's file name is required. Optional attributes **width** and **height** specify the image's width and height, respectively. The document author can scale an image by increasing or decreasing the values of the image **width** and **height** attributes. If these attributes are omitted, the browser uses the image's actual width and height. Images are measured in *pixels* ("picture elements"), which represent dots of color on the screen. The image in Fig. E.5 is **181** pixels wide and **238** pixels high.

Every **img** element in an XHTML document has an **alt** attribute. If a browser cannot render an image, the browser displays the **alt** attribute's value. A browser might not be able to render an image for several reasons. It might not support images—as is the case with a *text-based browser* (i.e., a browser that can display only text)—or the client may have disabled image viewing to reduce download time. Figure E.5 shows Internet Explorer rendering the **alt** attribute's value when a document references a nonexistent image file (**fish.jpg**).

The **alt** attribute is important for creating *accessible* Web pages for users with disabilities, especially those with vision impairments and text-based browsers. Specialized software called a *speech synthesizer* often is used by people with disabilities. Such software applications "speak" the **alt** attribute's value so that the user knows what the browser is displaying.

Some XHTML elements (called *empty elements*) contain only attributes and do not mark up text (i.e., text is not placed between the start and end tags). Empty elements (e.g., **img**) must be terminated, either by using the *forward slash character* (**/**) inside the closing right angle bracket (**>**) of the start tag or by explicitly including the end tag. When using the forward slash character, we add a space before the forward slash to improve readability (as shown at the ends of lines 17 and 20). Rather than using the forward slash character, lines 19–20 could be written with a closing **</img>** tag as follows:

```
<img src = "cool8se.jpg" height = "238" width = "181"
    alt = "An imaginary landscape."></img>
```

By using images as hyperlinks, Web developers can create graphical Web pages that link to other resources. In Fig. E.6, we create six different image hyperlinks.

Lines 16–19 create an *image hyperlink* by nesting an **img** element within an anchor (**a**) element. The value of the **img** element's **src** attribute value specifies that this image (**links.jpg**) resides in a directory named **buttons**. The **buttons** directory and the XHTML document are in the same directory. Images from other Web documents also can be referenced (after obtaining permission from the document's owner) by setting the **src** attribute to the name and location of the image.

```
1   <?xml version = "1.0"?>
2   <!DOCTYPE html PUBLIC "-//W3C//DTD XHTML 1.0 Strict//EN"
3       "http://www.w3.org/TR/xhtml1/DTD/xhtml1-strict.dtd">
4
5   <!-- Fig. E.6: nav.html           -->
6   <!-- Using images as link anchors. -->
7
8   <html xmlns = "http://www.w3.org/1999/xhtml">
9       <head>
10          <title>Using images as link anchors</title>
11      </head>
12
13      <body>
14
15          <p>
16              <a href = "links.html">
17                  <img src = "buttons/links.jpg" width = "65"
18                      height = "50" alt = "Links Page" />
19              </a><br />
20
21              <a href = "list.html">
22                  <img src = "buttons/list.jpg" width = "65"
23                      height = "50" alt = "List Example Page" />
24              </a><br />
25
26              <a href = "contact.html">
27                  <img src = "buttons/contact.jpg" width = "65"
28                      height = "50" alt = "Contact Page" />
29              </a><br />
30
```

Fig. E.6   Using images as link anchors. (Part 1 of 2.)

```
31              <a href = "header.html">
32                  <img src = "buttons/header.jpg" width = "65"
33                      height = "50" alt = "Header Page" />
34              </a><br />
35
36              <a href = "table.html">
37                  <img src = "buttons/table.jpg" width = "65"
38                      height = "50" alt = "Table Page" />
39              </a><br />
40
41              <a href = "form.html">
42                  <img src = "buttons/form.jpg" width = "65"
43                      height = "50" alt = "Feedback Form" />
44              </a><br />
45          </p>
46
47      </body>
48  </html>
```

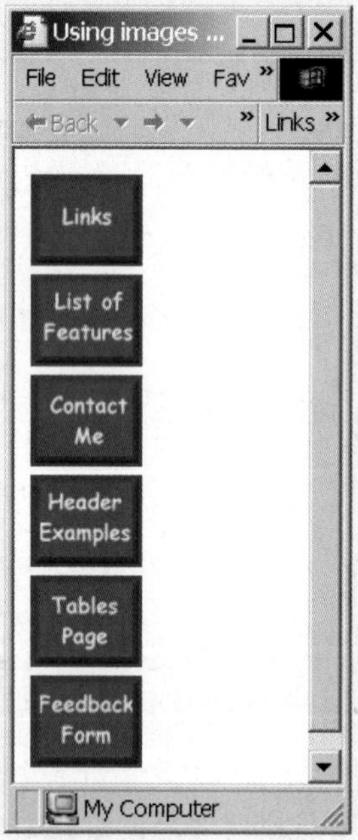

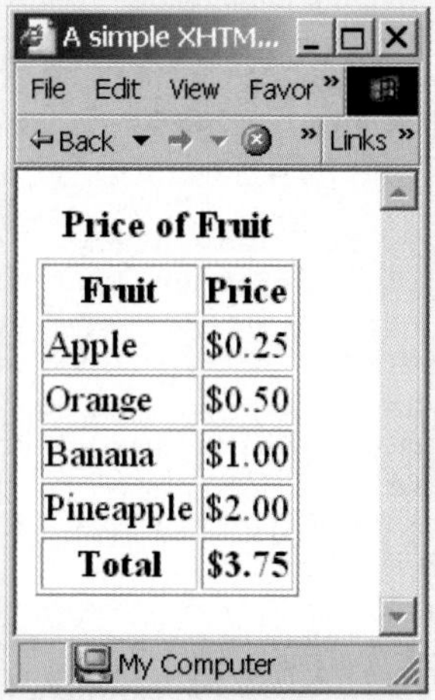

Fig. E.6   Using images as link anchors. (Part 2 of 2.)

On line 19, we introduce the **br** *element*, which most browsers render as a *line break*. Any markup or text following a **br** element is rendered on the next line. Like the **img** element, **br** is an example of an empty element terminated with a forward slash. We add a space before the forward slash to enhance readability.

E.7 Special Characters and More Line Breaks

When marking up text, certain characters or symbols (e.g., **<**) might be difficult to embed directly into an XHTML document. Some keyboards do not provide these symbols, or the presence of these symbols could cause syntax errors. For example, the markup

```
<p>if x < 10 then increment x by 1</p>
```

results in a syntax error, because it uses the less-than character (**<**), which is reserved for start tags and end tags such as **<p>** and **</p>**. XHTML provides *special characters* or *entity references* (in the form **&***code***;**) for representing these characters. We could correct the previous line by writing

```
<p>if x &lt; 10 then increment x by 1</p>
```

which uses the special character **<** for the less-than symbol.

Figure E.7 demonstrates how to use special characters in an XHTML document. For a list of special characters, see Appendix F. Lines 26–27 contain other special characters, which are expressed either as word abbreviations (e.g., **&amp** for ampersand and **&copy** for copyright) or as *hexadecimal (hex)* values (e.g., **&** is the hexadecimal representation of **&**). Hexadecimal numbers are base-16 numbers—digits in a hexadecimal number have values from 0 to 15 (a total of 16 different values). The letters A–F represent the hexadecimal digits corresponding to decimal values 10–15. Thus, in hexadecimal notation, we can have numbers like 876 consisting solely of decimal-like digits, numbers like DA19F consisting of digits and letters, and numbers like DCB consisting solely of letters. We discuss hexadecimal numbers in detail in Appendix C.

In lines 33–35, we introduce three new elements. Most browsers render the ***del*** element as strike-through text. With this format, users can easily indicate document revisions. To *superscript* text (i.e., raise text on a line with a decreased font size) or *subscript* text (i.e., lower text on a line with a decreased font size), use the ***sup*** and ***sub*** elements, respectively. We also use special characters **<** for a less-than sign and ***¼*** for the fraction 1/4 (line 37).

```
1   <?xml version = "1.0"?>
2   <!DOCTYPE html PUBLIC "-//W3C//DTD XHTML 1.0 Strict//EN"
3      "http://www.w3.org/TR/xhtml1/DTD/xhtml1-strict.dtd">
4
5   <!-- Fig. E.7: contact2.html      -->
6   <!-- Inserting special characters. -->
7
8   <html xmlns = "http://www.w3.org/1999/xhtml">
9      <head>
10        <title>Inserting special characters</title>
11     </head>
12
13     <body>
14
```

Fig. E.7   Inserting special characters into XHTML. (Part 1 of 2.)

```
15          <!-- special characters are    -->
16          <!-- entered using form &code; -->
17          <p>
18              Click
19              <a href = "mailto:deitel@deitel.com">here
20              </a> to open an e-mail message addressed to
21              deitel@deitel.com.
22          </p>
23
24          <hr /> <!-- inserts a horizontal rule -->
25
26          <p>All information on this site is <strong>&copy;</strong>
27              Deitel <strong>&amp;</strong> Associates, Inc. 2003.</p>
28
29          <!-- to strike through text use <del> tags     -->
30          <!-- to subscript text use <sub> tags          -->
31          <!-- to superscript text use <sup> tags        -->
32          <!-- these tags are nested inside other tags -->
33          <p><del>You may download 3.14 x 10<sup>2</sup>
34              characters worth of information from this site.</del>
35              Only <sub>one</sub> download per hour is permitted.</p>
36
37          <p>Note: <strong>&lt; &frac14;</strong> of the information
38              presented here is updated daily.</p>
39
40      </body>
41  </html>
```

Inserting special characters - Microsoft Internet Explorer

File   Edit   View   Favorites   Tools   Help

← Back ▾ → ▾ ⊗ ⊡ ⌂ | ◻Search ⌧Favorites ⌧Media ⊗ | ⧉▾ ⊜ ⊠ ▾ ⊟   » Links »

Click here to open an e-mail message addressed to deitel@deitel.com.

All information on this site is © Deitel & Associates, Inc. 2003.

~~You may download 3.14 x 10^2 characters worth of information from this site.~~
Only $_{one}$ download per hour is permitted.

Note: < ¼ of the information presented here is updated daily.

Done   My Computer

Fig. E.7   Inserting special characters into XHTML. (Part 2 of 2.)

In addition to special characters, this document introduces a *horizontal rule*, indicated by the **<hr />** tag in line 24. Most browsers render a horizontal rule as a horizontal line. The **<hr />** tag also inserts a line break above and below the horizontal line.

E.8 Unordered Lists

Up to this point, we have presented basic XHTML elements and attributes for linking to resources, creating headers, using special characters and incorporating images. In this section, we discuss how to organize information on a Web page using lists. Later in the appendix, we introduce another feature for organizing information, called a table. Figure E.8 displays text in an *unordered list* (i.e., a list that does not order its items by letter or number). The *unordered list element **ul*** creates a list in which each item begins with a bullet (called a *disc*).

Each entry in an unordered list (element ***ul*** in line 20) is an ***li*** (*list item*) element (lines 23, 25, 27 and 29). Most Web browsers render these elements with a line break and a bullet symbol indented from the beginning of the new line.

E.9 Nested and Ordered Lists

Lists may be nested to represent hierarchical relationships, as in an outline format. Figure E.9 demonstrates nested lists and *ordered lists* (i.e., list that order their items by letter or number).

```
1   <?xml version = "1.0"?>
2   <!DOCTYPE html PUBLIC "-//W3C//DTD XHTML 1.0 Strict//EN"
3      "http://www.w3.org/TR/xhtml1/DTD/xhtml1-strict.dtd">
4
5   <!-- Fig. E.8: links2.html              -->
6   <!-- Unordered list containing hyperlinks. -->
7
8   <html xmlns = "http://www.w3.org/1999/xhtml">
9      <head>
10        <title>Unordered list containing hyperlinks</title>
11     </head>
12
13     <body>
14
15        <h1>Here are my favorite sites</h1>
16
17        <p><strong>Click on a name to go to that page.</strong></p>
18
19        <!-- create an unordered list -->
20        <ul>
21
22           <!-- add four list items -->
23           <li><a href = "http://www.deitel.com">Deitel</a></li>
24
25           <li><a href = "http://www.w3.org">W3C</a></li>
26
27           <li><a href = "http://www.yahoo.com">Yahoo!</a></li>
28
29           <li><a href = "http://www.cnn.com">CNN</a></li>
30
31        </ul>
32
33     </body>
34  </html>
```

Fig. E.8   Unordered lists in XHTML. (Part 1 of 2.)

Fig. E.8   Unordered lists in XHTML. (Part 2 of 2.)

The first ordered list begins in line 33. Attribute **type** specifies the *sequence type* (i.e., the set of numbers or letters used in the ordered list). In this case, setting **type** to **"I"** specifies upper-case roman numerals. Line 47 begins the second ordered list and sets attribute **type** to **"a"**, specifying lowercase letters for the list items. The last ordered list (lines 71–75) does not use attribute **type**. By default, the list's items are enumerated from one to three.

A Web browser indents each nested list to indicate a hierarchal relationship. By default, the items in the outermost unordered list (line 18) are preceded by *discs*. List items nested inside the unordered list of line 18 are preceded by *circles*. Although not demonstrated in this example, subsequent nested list items are preceded by *squares*. Unordered list items can be explicitly set to discs, circles or squares by setting the **ul** element's **type** attribute to **"disc"**, **"circle"** or **"square"**, respectively.

E.10 Basic XHTML Tables

This section presents the XHTML *table*—a frequently used feature that organizes data into rows and columns. Our first example (Fig. E.10) uses a table with six rows and two columns to display price information for fruit.

```
1   <?xml version = "1.0"?>
2   <!DOCTYPE html PUBLIC "-//W3C//DTD XHTML 1.0 Transitional//EN"
3       "http://www.w3.org/TR/xhtml1/DTD/xhtml1-transitional.dtd">
4
5   <!-- Fig. E.9: list.html                         -->
6   <!-- Advanced Lists: nested and ordered. -->
7
8   <html xmlns = "http://www.w3.org/1999/xhtml">
9      <head>
10        <title>Advanced lists</title>
11     </head>
12
13     <body>
14
```

Fig. E.9   Nested and ordered lists in XHTML. (Part 1 of 3.)

```
15          <h1>The Best Features of the Internet</h1>
16
17          <!-- create an unordered list -->
18          <ul>
19             <li>You can meet new people from countries around
20                the world.</li>
21
22             <li>
23                You have access to new media as it becomes public:
24
25                <!-- start nested list, use modified bullets -->
26                <!-- list ends with closing </ul> tag          -->
27                <ul>
28                   <li>New games</li>
29                   <li>
30                      New applications
31
32                      <!-- ordered nested list -->
33                      <ol type = "I">
34                         <li>For business</li>
35                         <li>For pleasure</li>
36                      </ol>
37
38                   </li>
39
40                   <li>Around the clock news</li>
41                   <li>Search engines</li>
42                   <li>Shopping</li>
43                   <li>
44                      Programming
45
46                      <!-- another nested ordered list -->
47                      <ol type = "a">
48                         <li>XML</li>
49                         <li>Java</li>
50                         <li>XHTML</li>
51                         <li>Scripts</li>
52                         <li>New languages</li>
53                      </ol>
54
55                   </li>
56
57                </ul> <!-- ends nested list started in line 27 -->
58
59             </li>
60
61             <li>Links</li>
62             <li>Keeping in touch with old friends</li>
63             <li>It is the technology of the future!</li>
64
65          </ul>    <!-- ends unordered list started in line 18 -->
66
67          <h1>My 3 Favorite <em>CEOs</em></h1>
```

Fig. E.9   Nested and ordered lists in XHTML. (Part 2 of 3.)

```
68
69          <!-- ol elements without type attribute have -->
70          <!-- numeric sequence type (i.e., 1, 2, ...) -->
71          <ol>
72              <li>Lawrence J. Ellison</li>
73              <li>Steve Jobs</li>
74              <li>Michael Dell</li>
75          </ol>
76
77      </body>
78  </html>
```

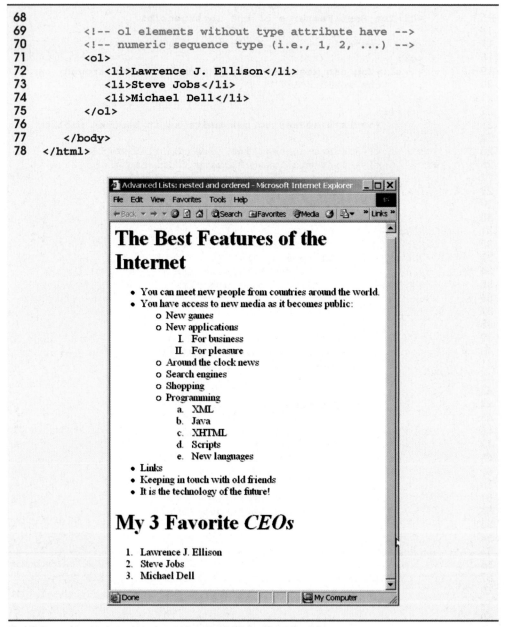

Fig. E.9   Nested and ordered lists in XHTML. (Part 3 of 3.)

Tables are defined with the **table** element. Lines 16–18 specify the start tag for a table element that has several attributes. The ***border*** attribute specifies the table's border width in pixels. To create a table without a border, set **border** to **"0"**. This example assigns attribute **width "40%"**, to set the table's width to 40 percent of the browser's width. A developer can also set attribute **width** to a specified number of pixels.

As its name implies, attribute **summary** (line 17) describes the table's contents. Speech devices use this attribute to make the table more accessible to users with visual impairments. The **caption** element (line 22) describes the table's content and helps text-based browsers interpret the table data. Text inside the **<caption>** tag is rendered above the table by most browsers. Attribute **summary** and element **caption** are two of many XHTML features that make Web pages more accessible to users with disabilities.

```
1   <?xml version = "1.0"?>
2   <!DOCTYPE html PUBLIC "-//W3C//DTD XHTML 1.0 Strict//EN"
3      "http://www.w3.org/TR/xhtml1/DTD/xhtml1-strict.dtd">
4
5   <!-- Fig. E.10: table1.html  -->
6   <!-- Creating a basic table. -->
7
8   <html xmlns = "http://www.w3.org/1999/xhtml">
9      <head>
10         <title>Creating a basic table</title>
11      </head>
12
13      <body>
14
15         <!-- the <table> tag begins table -->
16         <table border = "1" width = "40%"
17            summary = "This table provides information about
18               the price of fruit">
19
20            <!-- <caption> tag summarizes table's   -->
21            <!-- contents to help visually impaired -->
22            <caption><strong>Price of Fruit</strong></caption>
23
24            <!-- <thead> is first section of table -->
25            <!-- it formats table header area       -->
26            <thead>
27               <tr> <!-- <tr> inserts one table row -->
28                  <th>Fruit</th> <!-- insert heading cell -->
29                  <th>Price</th>
30               </tr>
31            </thead>
32
33            <!-- all table content is enclosed within <tbody> -->
34            <tbody>
35               <tr>
36                  <td>Apple</td> <!-- insert data cell -->
37                  <td>$0.25</td>
38               </tr>
39
40               <tr>
41                  <td>Orange</td>
42                  <td>$0.50</td>
43               </tr>
44
```

Fig. E.10   XHTML table. (Part 1 of 2.)

```
45              <tr>
46                  <td>Banana</td>
47                  <td>$1.00</td>
48              </tr>
49
50              <tr>
51                  <td>Pineapple</td>
52                  <td>$2.00</td>
53              </tr>
54          </tbody>
55
56          <!-- <tfoot> is last section of table -->
57          <!-- it formats table footer          -->
58          <tfoot>
59              <tr>
60                  <th>Total</th>
61                  <th>$3.75</th>
62              </tr>
63          </tfoot>
64
65      </table>
66
67      </body>
68  </html>
```

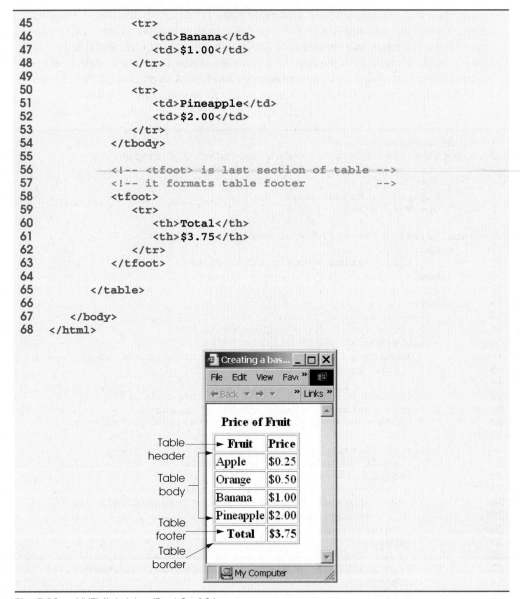

Fig. E.10   XHTML table. (Part 2 of 2.)

 Testing and Debugging Tip E.1

Try resizing the browser window to see how the width of the window affects the width of the table.

A table has three distinct sections—*head*, *body* and *foot*. The head section (or *header cell*) is defined with a **thead** element (lines 26–31), which contains header information, such as column names. Each **tr** element (lines 27–30) defines an individual *table row*. The columns in the head section are defined with **th** elements. Most browsers center text formatted by **th** (table header column) elements and display it in bold. Table header elements are nested inside table row elements.

The body section, or *table body*, contains the table's primary data. The table body (lines 34–54) is defined in a **tbody** element. *Data cells* contain individual pieces of data and are defined with **td** (*table data*) elements.

The foot section (lines 58–63) is defined with a *tfoot* (table foot) element and represents a footer. Text commonly placed in the footer includes calculation results and footnotes. Like other sections, the foot section can contain table rows and each row can contain columns.

E.11 Intermediate XHTML Tables and Formatting

In the previous section, we explored the structure of a basic table. In Fig. E.11, we enhance our discussion of tables by introducing elements and attributes that allow the document author to build more complex tables.

Common Programming Error E.5

*When using **colspan** and **rowspan** to adjust the size of table data cells, keep in mind that the modified cells will occupy more than one column or row; other rows or columns of the table must compensate for the extra rows or columns spanned by individual cells. If you do not, the formatting of your table will be distorted, and you could inadvertently create more columns and rows than you originally intended.*

The table begins on line 17. Element *colgroup* (lines 22–27) groups and formats columns. The *col* element (line 26) specifies two attributes in this example. The *align* attribute determines the alignment of text in the column. The *span* attribute determines how many columns the *col* element formats. In this case, we set **align**'s value to **"right"** and **span**'s value to **"1"** to right-align text in the first column (the column containing the picture of the camel in the sample screen capture).

Table cells are sized to fit the data they contain. Document authors can create larger data cells by using attributes *rowspan* and *colspan*. The values assigned to these attributes specify the number of rows or columns occupied by a cell. The **th** element at lines 36–39 uses the attribute **rowspan = "2"** to allow the cell containing the picture of the camel to use two vertically adjacent cells (thus the cell *spans* two rows). The **th** element at lines 42–45 uses the attribute **colspan = "4"** to widen the header cell (containing **Camelid comparison** and **Approximate as of 9/2002**) to span four cells.

Line 42 introduces attribute *valign*, which aligns data vertically and may be assigned one of four values—**"top"** aligns data with the top of the cell, **"middle"** vertically centers data (the default for all data and header cells), **"bottom"** aligns data with the bottom of the cell and **"baseline"** ignores the fonts used for the row data and sets the bottom of all text in the row on a common *baseline* (i.e., the horizontal line to which each character in a word is aligned).

```
1    <?xml version = "1.0"?>
2    <!DOCTYPE html PUBLIC "-//W3C//DTD XHTML 1.0 Strict//EN"
3       "http://www.w3.org/TR/xhtml1/DTD/xhtml1-strict.dtd">
4
```

Fig. E.11   Complex XHTML table. (Part 1 of 3.)

```
5   <!-- Fig. E.11: table2.html        -->
6   <!-- Intermediate table design. -->
7
8   <html xmlns = "http://www.w3.org/1999/xhtml">
9      <head>
10        <title>Intermediate table design</title>
11     </head>
12
13     <body>
14
15        <h1>Table Example Page</h1>
16
17        <table border = "1">
18           <caption>Here is a more complex sample table.</caption>
19
20           <!-- <colgroup> and <col> tags are -->
21           <!-- used to format entire columns -->
22           <colgroup>
23
24              <!-- span attribute determines how  -->
25              <!-- many columns <col> tag affects -->
26              <col align = "right" span = "1" />
27           </colgroup>
28
29           <thead>
30
31              <!-- rowspans and colspans merge specified    -->
32              <!-- number of cells vertically or horizontally   -->
33              <tr>
34
35                 <!-- merge two rows -->
36                 <th rowspan = "2">
37                    <img src = "camel.gif" width = "205"
38                       height = "167" alt = "Picture of a camel" />
39                 </th>
40
41                 <!-- merge four columns -->
42                 <th colspan = "4" valign = "top">
43                    <h1>Camelid comparison</h1><br />
44                    <p>Approximate as of 9/2002</p>
45                 </th>
46              </tr>
47
48              <tr valign = "bottom">
49                 <th># of Humps</th>
50                 <th>Indigenous region</th>
51                 <th>Spits?</th>
52                 <th>Produces Wool?</th>
53              </tr>
54
55           </thead>
56
```

Fig. E.11   Complex XHTML table. (Part 2 of 3.)

```
57              <tbody>
58
59                  <tr>
60                      <th>Camels (bactrian)</th>
61                      <td>2</td>
62                      <td>Africa/Asia</td>
63                      <td rowspan = "2">Llama</td>
64                      <td rowspan = "2">Llama</td>
65                  </tr>
66
67                  <tr>
68                      <th>Llamas</th>
69                      <td>1</td>
70                      <td>Andes Mountains</td>
71                  </tr>
72
73              </tbody>
74
75          </table>
76
77      </body>
78  </html>
```

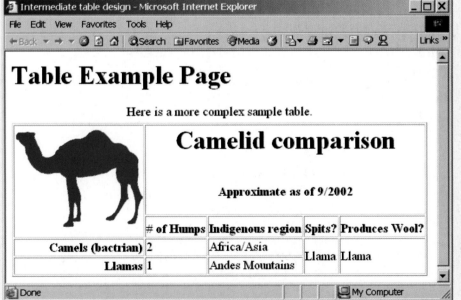

Fig. E.11   Complex XHTML table. (Part 3 of 3.)

E.12 Basic XHTML Forms

When browsing Web sites, users often need to provide information such as e-mail addresses, search keywords and zip codes. XHTML provides a mechanism, called a *form*, for collecting such user information.

Data that users enter on a Web page normally is sent to a Web server that provides access to a site's resources (e.g., XHTML documents or images). These resources are located either on the same machine as the Web server or on a machine that the Web server can access through the network. When a browser requests a Web page or file that is located on a server, the server processes the request and returns the requested resource. A request contains the name and path of the desired resource and the method of communication (called a *protocol*). XHTML documents use the Hypertext Transfer Protocol (HTTP).

Figure E.12 sends the form data to the Web server, which passes the form data to a *CGI* (*Common Gateway Interface*) script (i.e., a program) written in C++, C, Perl or some other language. The script processes the data received from the Web server and typically returns information to the Web server. The Web server then sends the information in the form of an XHTML document to the Web browser. [*Note*: This example demonstrates client-side functionality. If the form is submitted (by clicking **Submit Your Entries**), an error occurs.]

```
1   <?xml version = "1.0"?>
2   <!DOCTYPE html PUBLIC "-//W3C//DTD XHTML 1.0 Strict//EN"
3      "http://www.w3.org/TR/xhtml1/DTD/xhtml1-strict.dtd">
4
5   <!-- Fig. E.12: form.html   -->
6   <!-- Form design example 1. -->
7
8   <html xmlns = "http://www.w3.org/1999/xhtml">
9      <head>
10         <title>Form design example 1</title>
11      </head>
12
13      <body>
14
15         <h1>Feedback Form</h1>
16
17         <p>Please fill out this form to help
18            us improve our site.</p>
19
20         <!-- <form> tag begins form, gives -->
21         <!-- method of sending information -->
22         <!-- and location of form scripts  -->
23         <form method = "post" action = "/cgi-bin/formmail">
24
25            <p>
26
27               <!-- hidden inputs contain non-visual -->
28               <!-- information                      -->
29               <input type = "hidden" name = "recipient"
30                  value = "deitel@deitel.com" />
31
32               <input type = "hidden" name = "subject"
33                  value = "Feedback Form" />
```

Fig. E.12   Simple form with hidden fields and a text box. (Part 1 of 2.)

```
34
35                    <input type = "hidden" name = "redirect"
36                       value = "main.html" />
37            </p>
38
39            <!-- <input type = "text"> inserts text box -->
40            <p>
41               <label>Name:
42                  <input name = "name" type = "text" size = "25"
43                     maxlength = "30" />
44               </label>
45            </p>
46
47            <p>
48
49               <!-- input types "submit" and "reset" -->
50               <!-- insert buttons for submitting    -->
51               <!-- and clearing form's contents      -->
52               <input type = "submit" value =
53                  "Submit Your Entries" />
54
55               <input type = "reset" value =
56                  "Clear Your Entries" />
57            </p>
58
59         </form>
60
61      </body>
62   </html>
```

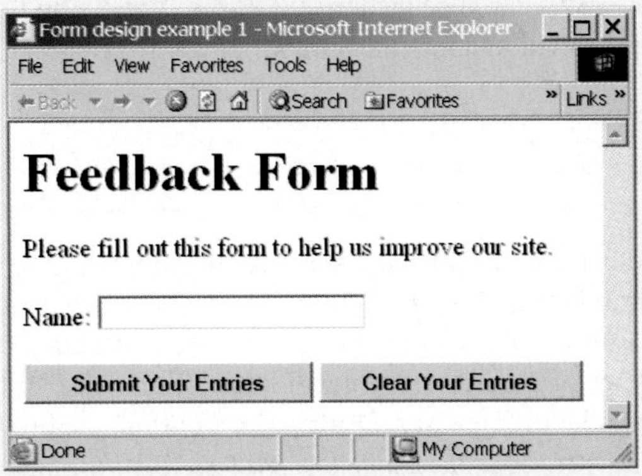

Fig. E.12   Simple form with hidden fields and a text box. (Part 2 of 2.)

Forms can contain visual and non-visual components. Visual components include clickable buttons and other graphical user interface components with which users interact. Non-visual components, called *hidden inputs*, store any data that the document author specifies, such as e-mail addresses and XHTML document file names that act as links. The form begins on line 23 with the **form** element. Attribute **method** specifies how the form's data is sent to the Web server.

Using **method = "post"** appends form data to the browser request, which contains the protocol (i.e., HTTP) and the requested resource's URL. Scripts located on the Web server's computer (or on a computer accessible through the network) can access the form data sent as part of the request. For example, a script may take the form information and update an electronic mailing list. The other possible value, **method = "get"**, appends the form data directly to the end of the URL. For example, the URL **/cgi-bin/formmail** might have the form information **name = bob** appended to it.

The **action** attribute in the **<form>** tag specifies the URL of a script on the Web server; in this case, it specifies a script that e-mails form data to an address. Most Internet Service Providers (ISPs) have a script like this on their site; ask the Web-site system administrator how to set up an XHTML document to use the script correctly.

Lines 29–36 define three **input** elements that specify data to provide to the script that processes the form (also called the *form handler*). These three **input** elements have **type** attribute **"hidden"**, which allows the document author to send form data that is not entered by a user to a script.

The three hidden inputs are an e-mail address to which the data will be sent, the e-mail's subject line and a URL where the browser will be redirected after submitting the form. Two other **input** attributes are **name**, which identifies the **input** element, and **value**, which provides the value that will be sent (or posted) to the Web server.

Good Programming Practice E.6

*Place hidden **input** elements at the beginning of a form, immediately after the opening **<form>** tag. This placement allows document authors to locate hidden **input** elements quickly.*

We introduce another **type** of **input** in lines 38–39. The **"text"** input inserts a *text box* into the form. Users can type data in text boxes. The **label** element (lines 37–40) provides users with information about the **input** element's purpose.

Common Programming Error E.6

*Forgetting to include a **label** element for each form element is a design error. Without these labels, users cannot determine the purpose of individual form elements.*

The **input** element's **size** attribute specifies the number of characters visible in the text box. Optional attribute **maxlength** limits the number of characters input into the text box. In this case, the user is not permitted to type more than **30** characters into the text box.

There are two types of **input** elements in lines 52–56. The **"submit"** input element is a button. When the user presses a **"submit"** button, the browser sends the data in the form to the Web server for processing. The **value** *attribute* sets the text displayed on the button (the default value is **Submit**). The **"reset"** input element allows a user to reset all **form** elements to their default values. The **value** attribute of the **"reset"** **input** element sets the text displayed on the button (the default value is **Reset**).

E.13 More Complex XHTML Forms

In the previous section, we introduced basic forms. In this section, we introduce elements and attributes for creating more complex forms. Figure E.13 contains a form that solicits user feedback about a Web site.

The ***textarea*** element (lines 42–44) inserts a multiline text box, called a *textarea*, into the form. The number of rows is specified with the ***rows*** *attribute* and the number of columns (i.e., characters) is specified with the ***cols*** *attribute*. In this example, the **textarea** is four rows high and 36 characters wide. To display default text in the text area, place the text between the **<textarea>** and **</textarea>** tags. Default text can be specified in other **input** types, such as textboxes, by using the **value** attribute.

The ***"password"*** input in lines 52–53 inserts a password box with the specified **size**. A password box allows users to enter sensitive information, such as credit card numbers and passwords, by "masking" the information input with asterisks. The actual value input is sent to the Web server, not the asterisks that mask the input.

Lines 60–78 introduce the *checkbox* **form** element. Checkboxes enable users to select from a set of options. When a user selects a checkbox, a check mark appears in the check box. Otherwise, the checkbox remains empty. Each ***"checkbox"*** **input** creates a new checkbox. Checkboxes can be used individually or in groups. Checkboxes that belong to a group are assigned the same **name** (in this case, **"thingsliked"**).

We continue our discussion of forms by presenting a third example that introduces several more form elements from which users can make selections (Fig. E.14). In this example, we introduce two new **input** types. The first type is the *radio button* (lines 90–113), specified with type **"radio"**. Radio buttons are similar to checkboxes, except that only one radio button in a group of radio buttons may be selected at any time. All radio buttons in a group have the same **name** attribute; they are distinguished by their different **value** attributes. The attribute–value pair ***checked = "checked"*** (line 92) indicates which radio button, if any, is selected initially. The **checked** attribute also applies to checkboxes.

```
1   <?xml version = "1.0"?>
2   <!DOCTYPE html PUBLIC "-//W3C//DTD XHTML 1.0 Strict//EN"
3       "http://www.w3.org/TR/xhtml1/DTD/xhtml1-strict.dtd">
4
5   <!-- Fig. E.13: form2.html   -->
6   <!-- Form design example 2. -->
7
8   <html xmlns = "http://www.w3.org/1999/xhtml">
9       <head>
10          <title>Form design example 2</title>
11      </head>
12
13      <body>
14
15          <h1>Feedback Form</h1>
16
17          <p>Please fill out this form to help
18             us improve our site.</p>
19
20          <form method = "post" action = "/cgi-bin/formmail">
21
22              <p>
23                  <input type = "hidden" name = "recipient"
24                      value = "deitel@deitel.com" />
```

Fig. E.13   Form with textareas, password boxes and checkboxes. (Part 1 of 3.)

```
25
26              <input type = "hidden" name = "subject"
27                 value = "Feedback Form" />
28
29              <input type = "hidden" name = "redirect"
30                 value = "main.html" />
31          </p>
32
33          <p>
34             <label>Name:
35                <input name = "name" type = "text" size = "25" />
36             </label>
37          </p>
38
39          <!-- <textarea> creates multiline textbox -->
40          <p>
41             <label>Comments:<br />
42                <textarea name = "comments" rows = "4"
43                   cols = "36">Enter your comments here.
44                </textarea>
45             </label></p>
46
47          <!-- <input type = "password"> inserts -->
48          <!-- textbox whose display is masked    -->
49          <!-- with asterisk characters           -->
50          <p>
51             <label>E-mail Address:
52                <input name = "email" type = "password"
53                   size = "25" />
54             </label>
55          </p>
56
57          <p>
58             <strong>Things you liked:</strong><br />
59
60             <label>Site design
61             <input name = "thingsliked" type = "checkbox"
62                value = "Design" /></label>
63
64             <label>Links
65             <input name = "thingsliked" type = "checkbox"
66                value = "Links" /></label>
67
68             <label>Ease of use
69             <input name = "thingsliked" type = "checkbox"
70                value = "Ease" /></label>
71
72             <label>Images
73             <input name = "thingsliked" type = "checkbox"
74                value = "Images" /></label>
75
76             <label>Source code
```

Fig. E.13   Form with textareas, password boxes and checkboxes. (Part 2 of 3.)

```
77                    <input name = "thingsliked" type = "checkbox"
78                       value = "Code" /></label>
79                 </p>
80
81                 <p>
82                    <input type = "submit" value =
83                       "Submit Your Entries" />
84
85                    <input type = "reset" value =
86                       "Clear Your Entries" />
87                 </p>
88
89              </form>
90
91           </body>
92        </html>
```

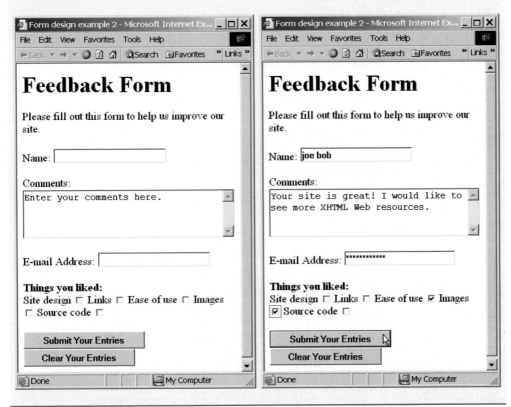

Fig. E.13   Form with textareas, password boxes and checkboxes. (Part 3 of 3.)

Common Programming Error E.7

*When your **form** has several checkboxes with the same **name**, you must make sure that they have different **value**s, or the scripts running on the Web server will not be able to distinguish between them.*

Common Programming Error E.8

*When using a group of radio buttons in a form, forgetting to set the **name** attributes to the same name is a logic error that lets the user select all of the radio buttons at the same time.*

The **select** element (lines 123–136) provides a drop-down list from which the user can select an item. The **name** attribute identifies the drop-down list. The **option** element (lines 124–135) adds items to the drop-down list. The **option** element's **selected** attribute specifies which item initially is displayed as the selected item in the **select** element.

```
1   <?xml version = "1.0"?>
2   <!DOCTYPE html PUBLIC "-//W3C//DTD XHTML 1.0 Strict//EN"
3       "http://www.w3.org/TR/xhtml1/DTD/xhtml1-strict.dtd">
4
5   <!-- Fig. E.14: form3.html  -->
6   <!-- Form design example 3. -->
7
8   <html xmlns = "http://www.w3.org/1999/xhtml">
9       <head>
10          <title>Form design example 3</title>
11      </head>
12
13      <body>
14
15          <h1>Feedback Form</h1>
16
17          <p>Please fill out this form to help
18             us improve our site.</p>
19
20          <form method = "post" action = "/cgi-bin/formmail">
21
22              <p>
23                  <input type = "hidden" name = "recipient"
24                     value = "deitel@deitel.com" />
25
26                  <input type = "hidden" name = "subject"
27                     value = "Feedback Form" />
28
29                  <input type = "hidden" name = "redirect"
30                     value = "main.html" />
31              </p>
32
33              <p>
34                  <label>Name:
35                      <input name = "name" type = "text" size = "25" />
36                  </label>
37              </p>
38
39              <p>
40                  <label>Comments:<br />
```

Fig. E.14   Form including radio buttons and drop-down lists. (Part 1 of 4.)

```
41              <textarea name = "comments" rows = "4"
42                  cols = "36"></textarea>
43          </label>
44      </p>
45
46      <p>
47          <label>E-mail Address:
48              <input name = "email" type = "password"
49                  size = "25" />
50          </label>
51      </p>
52
53      <p>
54          <strong>Things you liked:</strong><br />
55
56          <label>Site design
57              <input name = "thingsliked" type = "checkbox"
58                  value = "Design" />
59          </label>
60
61          <label>Links
62              <input name = "thingsliked" type = "checkbox"
63                  value = "Links" />
64          </label>
65
66          <label>Ease of use
67              <input name = "thingsliked" type = "checkbox"
68                  value = "Ease" />
69          </label>
70
71          <label>Images
72              <input name = "thingsliked" type = "checkbox"
73                  value = "Images" />
74          </label>
75
76          <label>Source code
77              <input name = "thingsliked" type = "checkbox"
78                  value = "Code" />
79          </label>
80
81      </p>
82
83      <!-- <input type = "radio" /> creates one radio   -->
84      <!-- button. The difference between radio buttons -->
85      <!-- and checkboxes is that only one radio button -->
86      <!-- in a group can be selected.                  -->
87      <p>
88          <strong>How did you get to our site?:</strong><br />
89
90          <label>Search engine
91              <input name = "howtosite" type = "radio"
92                  value = "search engine" checked = "checked" />
93          </label>
```

Fig. E.14   Form including radio buttons and drop-down lists. (Part 2 of 4.)

```
94
95            <label>Links from another site
96               <input name = "howtosite" type = "radio"
97                  value = "link" />
98            </label>
99
100           <label>Deitel.com Web site
101              <input name = "howtosite" type = "radio"
102                 value = "deitel.com" />
103           </label>
104
105           <label>Reference in a book
106              <input name = "howtosite" type = "radio"
107                 value = "book" />
108           </label>
109
110           <label>Other
111              <input name = "howtosite" type = "radio"
112                 value = "other" />
113           </label>
114
115        </p>
116
117        <p>
118           <label>Rate our site:
119
120              <!-- <select> tag presents a drop-down -->
121              <!-- list with choices indicated by      -->
122              <!-- <option> tags                        -->
123              <select name = "rating">
124                 <option selected = "selected">Amazing</option>
125                 <option>10</option>
126                 <option>9</option>
127                 <option>8</option>
128                 <option>7</option>
129                 <option>6</option>
130                 <option>5</option>
131                 <option>4</option>
132                 <option>3</option>
133                 <option>2</option>
134                 <option>1</option>
135                 <option>Awful</option>
136              </select>
137
138           </label>
139        </p>
140
141        <p>
142           <input type = "submit" value =
143              "Submit Your Entries" />
144
145           <input type = "reset" value = "Clear Your Entries" />
146        </p>
```

Fig. E.14   Form including radio buttons and drop-down lists. (Part 3 of 4.)

```
147
148        </form>
149
150      </body>
151  </html>
```

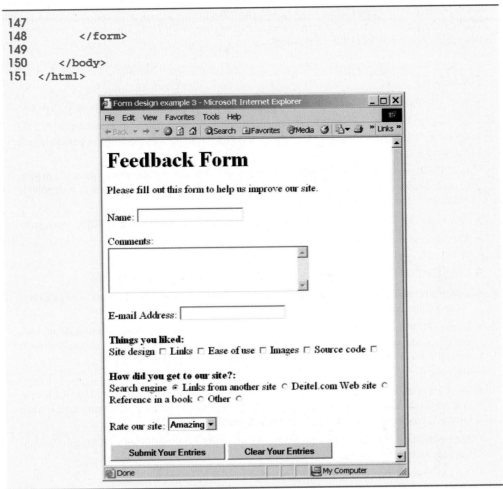

Fig. E.14   Form including radio buttons and drop-down lists. (Part 4 of 4.)

E.14 Internet and World Wide Web Resources

www.w3.org/TR/xhtml1
The *XHTML 1.0 Recommendation* contains general information, information on compatibility issues, document type definition information, definitions, terminology and much more relating to XHTML.

www.xhtml.org
XHTML.org provides XHTML development news and links to other XHTML resources, which include books and articles.

www.w3schools.com/xhtml/default.asp
The *XHTML School* provides XHTML quizzes and references. This page also contains links to X–HTML syntax, validation and document type definitions.

hotwired.lycos.com/webmonkey/00/50/index2a.html
This site provides an article about XHTML. Key sections of the article overview XHTML and discuss tags, attributes and anchors.

wdvl.com/Authoring/Languages/XML/XHTML
The Web Developers' Virtual Library provides an introduction to XHTML. This site also contains articles, examples and links to other technologies.

SUMMARY

- XHTML (Extensible Hypertext Markup Language) is a markup language for creating Web pages.

- A key issue when using XHTML is the separation of the presentation of a document (i.e., the document's appearance when rendered by a browser) from the structure of the information in the document.

- In XHTML, text is marked up with elements, delimited by tags that are names contained in pairs of angle brackets. Some elements may contain additional markup called attributes, which provide additional information about the element.

- A machine that runs specialized piece of software called a Web server stores XHTML documents.

- XHTML documents that are syntactically correct are guaranteed to render properly. XHTML documents that contain syntax errors might not display properly.

- Every XHTML document contains a start `<html>` tag and an end `</html>` tag.

- Comments in XHTML always begin with `<!--` and end with `-->`. The browser ignores all text inside a comment.

- Every XHTML document contains a **head** element, which generally contains information, such as a title, and a **body** element, which contains the page content. Information in the **head** element generally is not rendered in the display window but could be made available to the user through other means.

- The **title** element names a Web page. The title usually appears in the colored bar (called the title bar) at the top of the browser window and also appears as the text identifying a page when users add your page to their list of **Favorites** or **Bookmarks**.

- The body of an XHTML document is the area in which the document's content is placed. The content may include text and tags.

- All text placed between the `<p>` and `</p>` tags form one paragraph.

- XHTML provides six headers (**h1** through **h6**) for specifying the relative importance of information. Header element **h1** is considered the most significant header and is rendered in a larger font than the other five headers. Each successive header element (i.e., **h2**, **h3**, etc.) is rendered in a smaller font.

- Web browsers typically underline text hyperlinks and color them blue by default.

- The `<strong>` tag usually causes a browser to render text in a bold font.

- Users can insert links with the **a** (anchor) element. The most important attribute for the **a** element is **href**, which specifies the resource (e.g., page, file, e-mail address) being linked.

- Anchors can link to an e-mail address using a **mailto** URL. When someone clicks this type of anchored link, most browsers launch the default e-mail program (e.g., Outlook Express) to initiate e-mail messages to the linked addresses.

- The **img** element's **src** attribute specifies an image's location. Optional attributes **width** and **height** specify the image width and height, respectively. Images are measured in pixels ("picture elements"), which represent dots of color on the screen.

- The **alt** attribute makes Web pages more accessible to users with disabilities, especially those with vision impairments.

- Some XHTML elements are empty elements, contain only attributes and do not mark up text. Empty elements (e.g., **img**) must be terminated, either by using the forward slash character (**/**) or by explicitly writing an end tag.

- The **br** element causes most browsers to render a line break. Any markup or text following a **br** element is rendered on the next line.

- XHTML provides special characters or entity references (in the form **&**code**;**) for representing characters that cannot be marked up.

- Most browsers render a horizontal rule, indicated by the **<hr />** tag, as a horizontal line. The **hr** element also inserts a line break above and below the horizontal line.

- The unordered list element **ul** creates a list in which each item in the list begins with a bullet symbol (called a disc). Each entry in an unordered list is an **li** (list item) element. Most Web browsers render these elements with a line break and a bullet symbol at the beginning of the line.

- Lists may be nested to represent hierarchical data relationships.

- Attribute **type** specifies the sequence type (i.e., the set of numbers or letters used in the ordered list).

- XHTML tables mark up tabular data and are one of the most frequently used features in XHTML.

- The **table** element defines an XHTML table. Attribute **border** specifies the table's border width, in pixels. Tables without borders set this attribute to **"0"**.

- Element **summary** summarizes the table's contents and is used by speech devices to make the table more accessible to users with visual impairments.

- Element **caption** describe's the table's content. The text inside the **<caption>** tag is rendered above the table in most browsers.

- A table can be split into three distinct sections: head (**thead**), body (**tbody**) and foot (**tfoot**). The head section contains information such as table titles and column headers. The table body contains the primary table data. The table foot contains information such as footnotes.

- Element **tr**, or table row, defines individual table rows. Element **th** defines a header cell. Text in **th** elements usually is centered and displayed in bold by most browsers. This element can be present in any section of the table.

- Data within a row are defined with **td**, or table data, elements.

- Element **colgroup** groups and formats columns. Each **col** element can format any number of columns (specified with the **span** attribute).

- The document author has the ability to merge data cells with the **rowspan** and **colspan** attributes. The values assigned to these attributes specify the number of rows or columns occupied by the cell. These attributes can be placed inside any data-cell tag.

- XHTML provides forms for collecting information from users. Forms contain visual components, such as buttons that users click. Forms may also contain non-visual components, called hidden inputs, which are used to store any data, such as e-mail addresses and XHTML document file names used for linking.

- A form begins with the **form** element. Attribute **method** specifies how the form's data is sent to the Web server.

- The **"text"** input inserts a text box into the form. Text boxes allow the user to input data.

- The **input** element's **size** attribute specifies the number of characters visible in the **input** element. Optional attribute **maxlength** limits the number of characters input into a text box.

- The **"submit"** input submits the data entered in the form to the Web server for processing. Most Web browsers create a button that submits the form data when clicked. The **"reset"** input allows a user to reset all **form** elements to their default values.

- The **textarea** element inserts a multiline text box, called a text area, into a form. The number of rows in the text area is specified with the **rows** attribute and the number of columns (i.e., characters) is specified with the **cols** attribute.

- The **"password"** input inserts a password box into a form. A password box allows users to enter sensitive information, such as credit-card numbers and passwords, by "masking" the information input with another character. Asterisks are the masking character used for password boxes. The actual value input is sent to the Web server, not the asterisks that mask the input.

- The checkbox input allows the user to make a selection. When the checkbox is selected, a check mark appears in the checkbox. Otherwise, the checkbox is empty. Checkboxes can be used individually and in groups. Checkboxes that are part of the same group have the same **name**.

- A radio button is similar in function and use to a checkbox, except that only one radio button in a group can be selected at any time. All radio buttons in a group have the same **name** attribute value and have different attribute **value**s.

- The **select** input provides a drop-down list of items. The **name** attribute identifies the drop-down list. The **option** element adds items to the drop-down list. The **selected** attribute, like the **checked** attribute for radio buttons and checkboxes, specifies which list item is displayed initially.

TERMINOLOGY

<!--...--> (XHTML comment)
a element (**<a>...</a>**)
action attribute
alt attribute
& (& special character)
anchor
angle brackets (**< >**)
attribute
body element
border attribute
br (line break) element
browser request
<caption> tag
checkbox
checked attribute
col element
colgroup element
cols attribute
colspan attribute
comments in XHTML
© (© special character)
disc
element
e-mail anchor
empty tag
form
form element
head element
header
header cell
header elements (**h1** through **h6**)

height attribute
hexadecimal code
hidden input element
<hr /> tag (horizontal rule)
href attribute
.htm (XHTML file-name extension)
.html (XHTML file-name extension)
<html> tag
hyperlink
image hyperlink
img element
input element
level of nesting
<li> (list item) tag
linked document
mailto: URL
markup language
maxlength attribute
method attribute
name attribute
nested list
nested tag
ol (ordered list) element
p (paragraph) element
password box
"radio" (attribute value)
rows attribute (**textarea**)
rowspan attribute (**tr**)
selected attribute
size attribute (**input**)
special character

src attribute (**img**)
\<strong\> tag
sub element
subscript
superscript
syntax
table element
tag
tbody element
td element
text editor
textarea
textarea element
tfoot (table foot) element
\<thead\>...\</thead\>
title element
tr (table row) element

type attribute
unordered-list element (**ul**)
valign attribute (**th**)
value attribute
Web page
Web server
width attribute
World Wide Web (WWW)
XHTML (Extensible Hypertext Markup
    Language)
XHTML comment
XHTML form
XHTML markup
XHTML tag
XML declaration
xmlns attribute

XHTML
Special Characters

The table of Fig. F.1 shows many commonly used XHTML special characters—called *character entity references* by the World Wide Web Consortium. For a complete list of character entity references, see the site

www.w3.org/TR/REC-html40/sgml/entities.html

Character	XHTML encoding	Character	XHTML encoding
non-breaking space	` `	ê	`&#234;`
§	`&#167;`	ì	`&#236;`
©	`&#169;`	í	`&#237;`
®	`&#174;`	î	`&#238;`
π	`&#188;`	ñ	`&#241;`
∫	`&#189;`	ò	`&#242;`
Ω	`&#190;`	ó	`&#243;`
à	`&#224;`	ô	`&#244;`
á	`&#225;`	õ	`&#245;`
â	`&#226;`	÷	`&#247;`
ã	`&#227;`	ù	`&#249;`
å	`&#229;`	ú	`&#250;`
ç	`&#231;`	û	`&#251;`
è	`&#232;`	•	`&#8226;`
é	`&#233;`	™	`&#8482;`

Fig. F.1   XHTML special characters.

Bibliography

Alhir, S. *UML in a Nutshell*. Cambridge, MA: O'Reilly & Associates, Inc., 1998.

Allison, C. "Text Processing I." *The C Users Journal* Vol. 10, No. 10, October 1992, 23–28.

Allison, C. "Text Processing II." *The C Users Journal* Vol. 10, No. 12, December 1992, 73–77.

Allison, C. "Code Capsules: A C++ Date Class, Part I," *The C Users Journal* Vol. 11, No. 2, February 1993, 123–131.

Allison, C. "Conversions and Casts." *The C/C++ Users Journal* Vol. 12, No. 9, September 1994, 67–85.

Almarode, J. "Object Security." *Smalltalk Report* Vol. 5, No. 3 November/December 1995, 15–17.

American National Standard, Programming Language C++. (ANSI Document ISO/IEC 14882), New York, NY: American National Standards Institute, 1998.

Anderson, A. E. and W. J. Heinze. *C++ Programming and Fundamental Concepts*. Englewood Cliffs, NJ: Prentice Hall, 1992.

Baker, L. *C Mathematical Function Handbook*. New York, NY: McGraw Hill, 1992.

Bar-David, T. *Object-Oriented Design for C++*. Englewood Cliffs, NJ: Prentice Hall, 1993.

Beck, K. "Birds, Bees, and Browsers–Obvious Sources of Objects." *The Smalltalk Report* Vol. 3, No. 8, June 1994,13.

Becker, P. "Shrinking the Big Switch Statement." *Windows Tech Journal* Vol. 2, No. 5, May 1993, 26–33.

Becker, P. "Conversion Confusion." *C++ Report* October 1993, 26–28.

Berard, E. V. *Essays on Object-Oriented Software Engineering: Volume I*. Englewood Cliffs, NJ: Prentice Hall, 1992.

Binder, R. V. "State-Based Testing." *Object Magazine* Vol. 5, No. 4, August 1995, 75–78.

Binder, R. V. "State-Based Testing: Sneak Paths and Conditional Transitions." *Object Magazine* Vol. 5, No. 6, October 1995, 87–89.

Blum, A. *Neural Networks in C++: An Object-Oriented Framework for Building Connectionist Systems*. New York, NY: John Wiley & Sons, 1992.

Booch, G. *Object-Oriented Analysis and Design, Second Edition*. Reading, MA: Addison-Wesley, 1994.

Booch, G. *Object Solutions: Managing the Object-Oriented Project*. Reading, MA: Addison-Wesley, 1996.

Booch, G. *Object-Oriented Design with Applications, Third Edition*. Reading: MA: Addison-Wesley, 2003.

Booch, G., Rumbaugh, J. and I. Jacobson. *The Unified Modeling Language User Guide*. Reading, MA: Addison-Wesley, 1999.

Cargill, T. *Programming Style*. Reading, MA: Addison-Wesley, 1992.

Carroll, M. D. and M. A. Ellis. *Designing and Coding Reusable C++*. Reading, MA: Addison-Wesley, 1995.

Coplien, J. O. and D. C. Schmidt. *Pattern Languages of Program Design*. Reading, MA: Addison-Wesley, 1995.

Deitel, H. M. *Operating Systems, Second Edition*. Reading, MA: Addison-Wesley, 1990.

Deitel, H. M. and P. J. Deitel. *Java How to Program, Fourth Edition*. Upper Saddle River, NJ: Prentice Hall, 2002.

Deitel, H. M. and P. J. Deitel. *C How to Program, Third Edition*. Upper Saddle River, NJ: Prentice Hall, 2000.

Deitel, H. M. and P. J. Deitel. *The Java Multimedia Cyber Classroom, Fourth Edition*. Upper Saddle River, NJ: Prentice Hall, 2002.

Duncan, R. "Inside C++: Friend and Virtual Functions, and Multiple Inheritance." *PC Magazine* 15 October 1991, 417–420.

Ellis, M. A. and B. Stroustrup. *The Annotated C++ Reference Manual*. Reading, MA: Addison-Wesley, 1990.

Embley, D. W., B. D. Kurtz and S. N. Woodfield. *Object-Oriented Systems Analysis: A Model-Driven Approach*. Englewood Cliffs, NJ: Yourdon Press, 1992.

Entsminger, G. and B. Eckel. *The Tao of Objects: A Beginner's Guide to Object-Oriented Programming*. New York, NY: Wiley Publishing, 1990.

Firesmith, D.G. and B. Henderson-Sellers. "Clarifying Specialized Forms of Association in UML and OML." *Journal of Object-Oriented Programming* May 1998: 47–50.

Flamig, B. *Practical Data Structures in C++*. New York, NY: John Wiley & Sons, 1993.

Fowler, M. and K. Scott. *UML Distilled: Applying the Standard Object Modeling Language*. Reading, MA: Addison-Wesley, 1997.

Gamma, E., R. Helm, R. Johnson and J. Vlissides, *Design Patterns: Elements of Reusable Object-Oriented Software*. Reading, MA: Addison-Wesley, 1995.

Gehani, N. and W. D. Roome. *The Concurrent C Programming Language*. Summit, NJ: Silicon Press, 1989.

Giancola, A. and L. Baker. "Bit Arrays with C++." *The C Users Journal* Vol. 10, No. 7, July 1992, 21–26.

Glass, G. and B. Schuchert. *The STL <Primer>*. Upper Saddle River, NJ: Prentice Hall PTR, 1995.

Gooch, T. "Obscure C++." *Inside Microsoft Visual C++* Vol. 6, No. 11, November 1995, 13–15.

Hansen, T. L. *The C++ Answer Book*. Reading, MA: Addison-Wesley, 1990.

Henricson, M. and E. Nyquist. *Industrial Strength C++: Rules and Recommendations*. Upper Saddle River, NJ: Prentice Hall, 1997.

International Standard: Programming Languages—C++. ISO/IEC 14882:1998. New York, NY: American National Standards Institute, 1998.

Jacobson, I. "Is Object Technology Software's Industrial Platform?" *IEEE Software Magazine* Vol. 10, No. 1, January 1993, 24–30.

Jaeschke, R. *Portability and the C Language.* Indianapolis, IN: Sams Publishing, 1989.

Johnson, L.J. "Model Behavior." *Enterprise Development* May 2000: 20–28.

Josuttis, N. *The C++ Standard Library: A Tutorial and Reference.* Boston, MA: Addison-Wesley, 1999.

Kernighan, B. W. and D. M. Ritchie. *The C Programming Language, Second Edition.* Englewood Cliffs, NJ: Prentice Hall, 1988.

Knight, A. "Encapsulation and Information Hiding." *The Smalltalk Report* Vol. 1, No. 8 June 1992, 19–20.

Koenig, A. "What is C++ Anyway?" *Journal of Object-Oriented Programming* April/May 1991, 48–52.

Koenig, A. "Implicit Base Class Conversions." *The C++ Report* Vol. 6, No. 5, June 1994, 18–19.

Koenig, A. and B. Stroustrup. "Exception Handling for C++ (Revised)," *Proceedings of the USENIX C++ Conference,* San Francisco, CA, April 1990.

Koenig, A. and B. Moo. *Ruminations on C++: A Decade of Programming Insight and Experience.* Reading, MA: Addison-Wesley, 1997.

Kruse, R. L., B. P. Leung and C. L. Tondo. *Data Structures and Program Design in C.* Englewood Cliffs, NJ: Prentice Hall, 1991.

Langer, A. and K. Kreft. *Standard C++ IOStreams and Locales: Advanced Programmer's Guide and Reference.* Reading, MA: Addison-Wesley, 2000.

Lejter, M., S. Meyers and S. P. Reiss. "Support for Maintaining Object-Oriented Programs," *IEEE Transactions on Software Engineering* Vol. 18, No. 12, December 1992, 1045–1052.

Lippman, S. B. *C++ Primer, Third Edition,* Reading, MA: Addison-Wesley, 1998.

Lorenz, M. *Object-Oriented Software Development: A Practical Guide.* Englewood Cliffs, NJ: Prentice Hall, 1993.

Lorenz, M. "A Brief Look at Inheritance Metrics." *The Smalltalk Report* Vol. 3, No. 8 June 1994, 1, 4–5.

Martin, J. *Principles of Object-Oriented Analysis and Design.* Englewood Cliffs, NJ: Prentice Hall, 1993.

Martin, R. C. *Designing Object-Oriented C++ Applications Using the Booch Method.* Englewood Cliffs, NJ: Prentice Hall, 1995.

Matsche, J. J. "Object-Oriented Programming in Standard C." *Object Magazine* Vol. 2, No. 5, January/February 1993, 71–74.

McCabe, T. J. and A. H. Watson. "Combining Comprehension and Testing in Object-Oriented Development." *Object Magazine* Vol. 4, No. 1, March/April 1994, 63–66.

McLaughlin, M. and A. Moore. "Real-Time Extensions to the UML." *Dr. Dobb's Journal* December 1998: 82–93.

Melewski, D. "UML Gains Ground." *Application Development Trends* October 1998: 34–44.

Melewski, D. "UML: Ready for Prime Time?" *Application Development Trends* November 1997: 30–44.

Melewski, D. "Wherefore and What Now, UML?" *Application Development Trends* December 1999: 61–68.

Meyer, B. *Object-Oriented Software Construction, Second Edition.* Englewood Cliffs, NJ: Prentice Hall, 1997.

Meyer, B. *Eiffel: The Language.* Englewood Cliffs, NJ: Prentice Hall, 1992.

Meyer, B. and D. Mandrioli. *Advances in Object-Oriented Software Engineering.* Englewood Cliffs, NJ: Prentice Hall, 1992.

Meyers, S. "Mastering User-Defined Conversion Functions." *The C/C++ Users Journal* Vol. 13, No. 8, August 1995, 57–63.

Meyers, S. *More Effective C++: 35 New Ways to Improve Your Programs and Designs.* Reading, MA: Addison-Wesley, 1996.

Meyers, S. *Effective C++: 50 Specific Ways to Improve Your Programs and Designs, Second Edition.* Reading, MA: Addison-Wesley, 1998.

Meyers, S. *Effective STL: 50 Specific Ways to Improve Your Use of the Standard Template Library.* Reading, MA: Addison-Wesley, 2001.

Muller, P. *Instant UML.* Birmingham, UK: Wrox Press Ltd, 1997.

Murray, R. *C++ Strategies and Tactics.* Reading, MA: Addison-Wesley, 1993.

Musser, D. R. and A. A. Stepanov. "Algorithm-Oriented Generic Libraries." *Software Practice and Experience* Vol. 24, No. 7, July 1994.

Musser, D. R., G. J. Derge and A. Saini. *STL Tutorial and Reference Guide: C++ Programming with the Standard Template Library, Second Edition.* Reading, MA: Addison-Wesley, 2001.

Nelson, M. *C++ Programmer's Guide to the Standard Template Library.* New York, NY: Wiley Publishing, 1995.

Nerson, J. M. "Applying Object-Oriented Analysis and Design." *Communications of the ACM,* Vol. 35, No. 9, September 1992, 63–74.

Nierstrasz, O., S. Gibbs and D. Tsichritzis. "Component-Oriented Software Development." *Communications of the ACM* Vol. 35, No. 9, September 1992, 160–165.

Perry, P. "UML Steps to the Plate." *Application Development Trends* May 1999: 33–36.

Pinson, L. J. and R. S. Wiener. *Applications of Object-Oriented Programming.* Reading, MA: Addison-Wesley, 1990.

Pittman, M. "Lessons Learned in Managing Object-Oriented Development." *IEEE Software Magazine* Vol. 10, No. 1, January 1993, 43–53.

Plauger, P. J. *The Standard C Library.* Englewood Cliffs, NJ: Prentice Hall, 1992.

Plauger, D. "Making C++ Safe for Threads." *The C Users Journal* Vol. 11, No. 2, February 1993, 58–62.

Pohl, I. *C++ Distilled: A Concise ANSI/ISO Reference and Style Guide.* Reading, MA: Addison-Wesley, 1997.

Pohl, I. *Object-Oriented Programming Using C++, Second Edition.* Reading, MA: Addison-Wesley, 1997.

Press, W. H., S. A. Teukolsky, W. T. Vetterling and B. Flannery. *Numerical Recipes in C, Second Edition.* Cambridge, MA: Cambridge University Press, 1992.

Prieto-Diaz, R. "Status Report: Software Reusability." *IEEE Software* Vol. 10, No. 3, May 1993, 61–66.

Prince, T. "Tuning Up Math Functions." *The C Users Journal* Vol. 10, No. 12, December 1992.

Prosise, J. "Wake Up and Smell the MFC: Using the Visual C++ Classes and Applications Framework." *Microsoft Systems Journal* Vol. 10, No. 6, June 1995, 17–34.

Rabinowitz, H. and C. Schaap. *Portable C.* Englewood Cliffs, NJ: Prentice Hall, 1990.

Reed, D. R. "Moving from C to C++." *Object Magazine* Vol. 1, No. 3, September/October 1991, 46–60.

Ritchie, D. M. "The UNIX System: The Evolution of the UNIX Time-Sharing System." *AT&T Bell Laboratories Technical Journal* Vol. 63, No. 8, Part 2, October 1984, 1577–1593.

Ritchie, D. M., S. C. Johnson, M. E. Lesk and B. W. Kernighan. "UNIX Time-Sharing System: The C Programming Language." *The Bell System Technical Journal* Vol. 57, No. 6, Part 2, July/August 1978, 1991–2019.

Rosler, L. "The UNIX System: The Evolution of C—Past and Future." *AT&T Laboratories Technical Journal* Vol. 63, No. 8, Part 2, October 1984, 1685–1699.

Robson, R. *Using the STL: The C++ Standard Template Library.* New York, NY: Springer Verlag, 2000.

Rubin, K. S. and A. Goldberg. "Object Behavior Analysis." *Communications of the ACM* Vol. 35, No. 9, September 1992, 48–62.

Rumbaugh, J., M. Blaha, W. Premerlani, F. Eddy and W. Lorensen. *Object-Oriented Modeling and Design.* Englewood Cliffs, NJ: Prentice Hall, 1991.

Rumbaugh, J., Jacobson, I. and G. Booch. *The Unified Modeling Language Reference Manual.* Reading, MA: Addison-Wesley, 1999.

Saks, D. "Inheritance." *The C Users Journal* May 1993, 81–89.

Schildt, H. *STL Programming from the Ground Up.* Berkeley, CA: Osborne McGraw-Hill, 1999.

Schlaer, S. and S. J. Mellor. *Object Lifecycles: Modeling the World in States.* Englewood Cliffs, NJ: Prentice Hall, 1992.

Schmuller, J. *Sam's Teach Yourself UML in 24 Hours.* Indianapolis: Macmillan Computer Publishing, 1999.

Sedgwick, R. *Algorithms in C++.* Reading, MA: Addison-Wesley, 1992.

Sessions, R. *Class Construction in C and C++: Object-Oriented Programming.* Englewood Cliffs, NJ: Prentice Hall, 1992.

Skelly, C. "Pointer Power in C and C++." *The C Users Journal* Vol. 11, No. 2, February 1993, 93–98.

Smith, J. D. *Reusability & Software Construction in C & C++.* New York, NY: John Wiley & Sons, 1990.

Snyder, A. "The Essence of Objects: Concepts and Terms." *IEEE Software Magazine* Vol. 10, No. 1, January 1993, 31–42.

Stepanov, A. and M. Lee. "The Standard Template Library." 31 October 1995 **<www.cs.rpi.edu/~musser/doc.ps>**.

Stroustrup, B. "The UNIX System: Data Abstraction in C." *AT&T Bell Laboratories Technical Journal* Vol. 63, No. 8, Part 2, October 1984, 1701–1732.

Stroustrup, B. "What is Object-Oriented Programming?" *IEEE Software* Vol. 5, No. 3, May 1988, 10–20.

Stroustrup, B. "Parameterized Types for C++." *Proceedings of the USENIX C++ Conference* Denver, CO, October 1988.

Stroustrup, B. "Why Consider Language Extensions?: Maintaining a Delicate Balance." *The C++ Report* September 1993, 44–51.

Stroustrup, B. "Making a **vector** Fit for a Standard." *The C++ Report* October 1994.

Stroustrup, B. *The Design and Evolution of C++*. Reading, MA: Addison-Wesley, 1994.

Stroustrup, B. *The C++ Programming Language, Special Third Edition*. Reading, MA: Addison-Wesley, 2000.

Taligent's Guide to Designing Programs: Well-Mannered Object-Oriented Design in C++. Reading, MA: Addison-Wesley, 1994.

Taylor, D. *Object-Oriented Information Systems: Planning and Implementation*. New York, NY: John Wiley & Sons, 1992.

Tondo, C. L. and S. E. Gimpel. *The C Answer Book*. Englewood Cliffs, NJ: Prentice Hall, 1989.

Unified Modeling Language Specification: Version 1.4. Framingham, MA: Object Management Goup (OMG), 2001.

Urlocker, Z. "Polymorphism Unbounded." *Windows Tech Journal* Vol. 1, No. 1, January 1992, 11–16.

Van Camp, K. E. "Dynamic Inheritance Using Filter Classes." *The C/C++ Users Journal* Vol. 13, No. 6, June 1995, 69–78.

Vilot, M. J. "An Introduction to the Standard Template Library." *The C++ Report* Vol. 6, No. 8, October 1994.

Voss, G. *Object-Oriented Programming: An Introduction*. Berkeley, CA: Osborne McGraw-Hill, 1991.

Voss, G. "Objects and Messages." *Windows Tech Journal* February 1993, 15–16.

Wang, B. L. and J. Wang. "Is a Deep Class Hierarchy Considered Harmful?" *Object Magazine* Vol. 4, No. 7, November/December 1994, 35–36.

Weisfeld, M. "An Alternative to Large Switch Statements." *The C Users Journal* Vol. 12, No. 4, April 1994, 67–76.

Weiskamp, K. and B. Flamig. *The Complete C++ Primer, Second Edition*. Orlando, FL: Academic Press, 1993.

Wiebel, M., and S. Halladay. "Using OOP Techniques Instead of *switch* in C++." *The C Users Journal* Vol. 10, No. 10, October 1993, 105–112.

Wiener, R. S. and L. J. Pinson. *An Introduction to Object-Oriented Programming and C++*. Reading, MA: Addison-Wesley, 1988.

Wilde, N. and R. Huitt. "Maintenance Support for Object-Oriented Programs." *IEEE Transactions on Software Engineering* Vol. 18, No. 12, December 1992, 1038–1044.

Wilde, N., P. Matthews and R. Huitt. "Maintaining Object-Oriented Software." *IEEE Software Magazine* Vol. 10, No. 1, January 1993, 75–80.

Wilson, G. V. and P. Lu. *Parallel Programming Using C++*. Cambridge, MA: MIT Press, 1996.

Wilt, N. "Templates in C++." *The C Users Journal* May 1993, 33–51.

Wirfs-Brock, R., B. Wilkerson and L. Wiener. *Designing Object-Oriented Software*. Englewood Cliffs, NJ: Prentice Hall PTR, 1990.

Wyatt, B. B., K. Kavi and S. Hufnagel. "Parallelism in Object-Oriented Languages: A Survey." *IEEE Software* Vol. 9, No. 7, November 1992, 56–66.

Yamazaki, S., K. Kajihara, M. Ito and R. Yasuhara. "Object-Oriented Design of Telecommunication Software." *IEEE Software Magazine* Vol. 10, No. 1, January 1993, 81–87.

Index

Symbols

-- unary operator 99
! (logical NOT) 124, 126, 1190
!= (inequality operator) 35, 36, 550, 1190
preprocessor operator 22, 1054, 1059
preprocessor operator 1059
$ Unix command line prompt 1067
% modulus operator 31
% prompt 1067
& (address operator) 322, 323, 1190
& and * operators as inverses 324
& character 907
& in a parameter list 213
& to declare reference 211
&& (logical AND operator) 124, 125, 205, 1190
&= (bitwise AND assignment operator) 1169, 1190
¼ entity reference 1249
< entity reference 1249
( ) function call operator 175
* (pointer dereference operator) 323
* operator 31
+ operator 29, 31
++ operator 99
++ operator on an iterator 1098
+= operator 98, 550, 854
.* operator 1199, 1201

.h header file 180, 181
/ operator 31
// single-line comment 22
:: (binary scope resolution operator) 497
:: (unary scope resolution operator) 217, 1189, 1200
< (less-than operator) 35
<< left shift 29
<< operator 23
<= (less-than-or-equal-to operator) 35
<cstring> 362
<list> 1113
<string> 588
<typeinfo> header file 714
<vector> 592
= operator 29, 31, 126
== (equality operator) 35, 126, 550
> (greater-than operator) 35
-> (member selection via pointer) 1199
->* operator 1199
>= (greater-than-or-equal-to operator) 35
>> right shift 30
?: (ternary conditional operator) 78, 205
\ backslash-character escape sequence 24
\" double-quote-character escape sequence 24

\a alert 24
\n (newline) escape sequence 24
\r carriage-return 24
\t tab 24, 159
^ (bitwise exclusive OR operator) 1190
^= (bitwise exclusive OR assignment operator) 1169, 1191
| 1190
|= (bitwise inclusive OR assignment operator) 1169, 1191
|| (logical OR operator) 124, 125, 205, 1190
|| (logical OR) operator truth table 125
"object speak" xxxvii
"object think" xxxvii
'\0' 360
'\n' 360

Numerics

0 pointer 959
0X 755
0x 755
12-hour clock format 408
24-hour clock format 408

A

a element 1242, 1247

abbreviated assignment operator
    99
abbreviating assignment
    expressions 98
abort 790, 796, 1060, 1076
abort a program 784
absolute value 173
abstract class 663, 680, 681, 682,
    696
abstract data type (ADT) 411, 413,
    502, 504
abstraction 40, 611
access a global variable 217
access class member 418
access function 426, 427
access member off handle 418
access non-**static** class data
    members and member
    functions 500
access **private** member of a
    class 424
access privilege 331, 335
access structure member 418,
    1002
access the caller's data 211
access violation 54, 362, 1093
Accessing an object's members
    through each type of object
    handle 419
accessing **union** members 1081
accessor member function 426
accounts receivable file 811
accounts receivable program 847
accounts receivable system 812
accumulate 1104, 1172, 1174
accumulated output 29
accumulator 387, 388
action 3, 77, 79, 82, 227, 502
action attribute 1262
action attribute (**form**) 897,
    898
action expression 74, 77, 78, 83,
    108, 117, 121
action-label 228
action-oriented 41
action state 74, 130
action state symbol 74
action/decision model of
    programming 77, 78
activation 301
activation bar 303
activity 74, 301
activity diagram 73, 74, 76, 78, 82,
    108, 130, 229, 230, 296, 374
    do/while structure 121
    for structure 108

if structure 77
if/else structure 78
sequence structure 73
switch structure 118
while structure 82
activity diagram that models the
    elevator's logic for
    responding to button presses
    230
actor 139
Ada 13
adapter 1128
add a new account to a file 835
add an integer to a pointer 341
addition 5, 30, 31, 32
addition assignment operator (**+=**)
    98
Addition program 26
address (**&**) of a structure 1002
address of a bit field 1020
address operator (**&**) 322, 325,
    336, 548, 1200
addressable storage unit 1020
adjacent_difference
    1104, 1166
adjacent_find 1104, 1168
"administrative" section of the
    computer 6
aggregate data type 406
Aiming a derived-class pointer at a
    base-class object 671
airline reservation system 311,
    824
alert escape sequence (**'a'**) 24
alert escape sequence (**'a'**) 1024
algebraic expression 32
<algorithm> 182, 1111
algorithm 54, 72, 77, 78, 83, 89,
    943, 1092, 1103, 1133
algorithms **copy_backward**,
    merge, **unique** and
    reverse 1152
algorithms **equal**, **mismatch**
    and
    **lexicographical_com
    pare** 1136
algorithms **fill**, **fill_n**,
    generate and
    generate_n 1134
algorithms **inplace_merge**,
    unique_copy and
    reverse_copy 1155
algorithms **lower_bound**,
    upper_bound and
    equal_range 1160
algorithms **min** and **max** 1165

algorithms of the STL 719
algorithms **remove**,
    remove_if,
    remove_copy and
    remove_copy_if 1139
algorithms **replace**,
    replace_if,
    replace_copy and
    replace_copy_if 1142
algorithms separated from
    container 1103
algorithms **swap**, **iter_swap**
    and **swap_ranges** 1150
alias 213, 323, 325, 870
alias for a type 1096
alias for the name of an object 445
alignment 1003
allocate dynamic memory 797
allocate memory 182, 495
allocator 1112
alphabetizing strings 367
alt attribute 1246
alter the flow of control 122
ALU 5
ambiguity problem 1201, 1204
American National Standards
    Committee on Computers
    and Information Processing
    (X3) 9
American National Standards
    Institute (ANSI) 3, 504
American Standard Code for
    Information Interchange
    (ASCII) 367
analysis 42
analysis phase 374
Analytical Engine 13
and operator keyword 1190
and_eq operator keyword 1190
"ANDed" 1010
angle brackets (**<** and **>**) 222, 720,
    1054
anonymous **union** 1082
ANSI 3, 9
ANSI C 9, 20
ANSI/ISO 9899: 1990 9
ANSI/ISO C++ Standard 21,
    1175, 1176, 1232, 1235
any 1169
Apache HTTP server 882, 884,
    886
Apache Software Foundation 884
append 855
append data to a file 814
append output symbol (**>>**) 1067
Apple Computer 7

approximation of floating-point numbers 93
arbitrary range of subscripts 504
argc 1070
argument 171
argument coercion 179
argument for a macro 1056
arguments in correct order 175
arguments passed to member-object constructors 479
argv[] 1070
arithmetic 17
arithmetic and logic unit (ALU) 5
arithmetic assignment operator 98, 99
arithmetic average 278
arithmetic calculation 31
arithmetic mean 32
arithmetic operator 31
arithmetic overflow 781
arithmetic overflow error 800
arithmetic underflow error 800
"arity" of an operator 549
ARPA 18
ARPAnet 18, 19
array 253, 254, 334, 504, 505, 946
array assignment 504
array bounds 266, 267
array bounds checking 266
Array class 557
Array class definition with overloaded operators 557
Array class member-function and **friend** function definitions 558
Array class test program 561
array comparison 504
array initializer list 258
array input/output 504
array name 344, 345
array name as a constant pointer to beginning of array 334, 344, 345
array notation 345
array of pointers to functions 358, 395
array of strings 349
array size 272
array-sort function 719
array-subscript operator ([]) 564
array subscripting 334, 345
arrays and functions 273
arrays as full-fledged objects 256
arrays passed by reference 276
arrays that know their size 504
arrow 67, 74

arrow member selection operator (->) 407, 408, 418
arrow operator (->) 491
arrowhead 301
ASCII (American Standard Code for Information Interchange) 116, 360, 367, 744
ASCII character set 68
ASCII decimal equivalent of a character 998
asctime function 888, 890
assembler 8
assembly language 7
assert 1060
<assert.h> header file 181
assign 1117
assign one iterator to another 1102
assigned the value of 36
assigning a structure to a structure of the same type 1002
assigning a **union** to another **union** of the same type 1081
Assigning addresses of base-class and derived-class objects to base-class and derived-class pointers 669
assigning character strings to **string** objects 578
assigning class objects 426, 449
assignment operator (=) 29, 39, 102, 448, 547, 548, 1097
assignment operator (arithmetic) 98
assignment statement 29, 101
assignment-operator function 566
associate from left-to-right 102
associate from right-to-left 39, 102, 116
association 42, 142, 143, 1126
association between classes 142
associations between classes in a class diagram 142
associative array 1126
associative container 1094, 1097, 1101, 1119, 1122
associativity 39, 126, 127
associativity not changed by overloading 549
associativity of operators 32
asterisk (*) 31, 165
asynchronous event 781
at 854, 870, 1105, 1112, 1169
at member function of class **string** 854
AT&T 14

atexit function 1073, 1074
atof function 1026
atoi function 912, 993, 996, 1026, 1027
atol function 1026
Attempting to call a multiply inherited function polymorphically 1206
Attempting to modify a constant pointer to constant data 335
Attempting to modify a constant pointer to nonconstant data 334
Attempting to modify data through a nonconstant pointer to constant data 333
attribute 40, 41, 142, 225, 296, 374, 405, 411
attribute name 226
attribute of an element 1239
attribute type 226
attributes of a variable 192
auto 192, 193
auto_ptr 797, 798, 799
auto_ptr object goes out of scope 798
auto_ptr object manages dynamically allocated memory 798
auto_ptr overloaded * operator 799
auto_ptr overloaded -> operator 799
automated teller machine 824
automatic array 258
automatic array initialization 270
automatic local array 270
automatic local object 436
automatic local variable 193, 196, 214
automatic object 784, 792
automatic storage class 193, 253, 272
automatic variable 960
automatically destroyed 196
automobile 168
average 32, 92, 278
average calculation 83
average of several integers 164
averaging calculation 89
avoid repeating code 433
aware of 648

B

B 8

Babbage, Charles 13
back 1105, 1111, 1130
back_inserter 1154, 1156
backslash (****) 23, 1057
backslash (****) escape sequence 24
backslash zero 267
backward pointer 960
backwards traversal 869
bad_exception 800
bad member function 766
bad_alloc exception 793, 794, 796, 800, 945, 1112
bad_cast exception 800
bad_exception 800
bad_typeid exception 800
badbit 744, 766, 815
balanced tree 977
Bank account program 835
banking system 824
bar chart 165, 262
base-2 number system 1008
base-8 number system 755
base-10 number system 173, 755
base-16 number system 755
base case(s) 199, 204, 206
base class 610, 611, 613, 650, 654, 713
base-class **catch** 800
base-class constructor 629, 642
base-class default constructor 629
base class **Employee** 700
base-class exception 800
base-class member accessibility in derived class 649
base-class pointer (or reference type) 695, 700, 945
base-class pointer to a derived-class object 699
base-class **private** member 614
base-class reference 678, 695, 945
base *e* 173
base specified for a stream 760
base-class member function redefined in a derived class 636
baseline 1257
BasePlusCommission-Employee class header file 709
BasePlusCommission-Employee class implementation file 710
BASIC (Beginner's All-Purpose Symbolic Instruction Code) 11, 943, 987, 999

basic searching and sorting algorithms of the Standard Library 1148
basic_fstream template 742, 812
basic_ifstream template 742, 812
basic_ios template 741
basic_iostream template 741, 812
basic_istream template 741, 812
basic_istringstream class 870, 871
basic_ofstream template 742, 812
basic_ostream template 812
basic_ostringstream class 870, 871
basic_string 851
basics of computers 4
batch 6
batch processing 6
BCPL 8
begin 1095, 1098, 1108, 1109
begin iterator 869
Beginner's All-Purpose Symbolic Instruction Code (BASIC) 11, 943, 987, 999
beginning of a file 818
beginning of a stream 819
behavior 40, 41, 139, 405, 411, 503
bell 24
Bell class header file 453, 519
Bell class implementation file 519
Bell Laboratories 9
bibliography 21
bidirectional iterator 1100, 1101, 1106, 1113, 1119, 1122, 1124, 1153, 1154, 1156, 1167
bidirectional-iterator operation 1102
binary 162
binary arithmetic operator 93
binary comparison function 1167
binary digit 809
binary function 1166, 1172
binary function object 1172, 1173
binary integer 162
binary number 1020
binary number system 1029
binary operator 29, 31, 126
binary operator **+** 31

binary predicate function 1116, 1138, 1147, 1150, 1154, 1158, 1159, 1162, 1168
binary scope resolution operator (**::**) 217, 416, 497, 1187, 1200, 1204
binary search 283, 285, 286
binary search of a sorted array 286
binary search tree 969, 976, 977, 984
binary tree 943, 969, 970, 1162
binary tree delete 984
binary tree search 985
binary tree sort 977, 999
binary tree with duplicates 984
binary_search 1148, 1150
bit 809, 1001
bit field 1007, 1017, 1019
bit-field manipulation 1020
bit field member of structure 1017
bit fields save space 1020
bit fields used to store a deck of cards 1017
bit manipulation 809, 1007
bitand operator keyword 1190
bitor operator keyword 1190
"bits-and-bytes" level 1007
<bitset> 182, 1096
bitset 1094, 1168, 1169, 1170
bitwise AND (**&**) 1008
bitwise AND assignment operator (**&=**) 1016, 1190
bitwise AND operator (**&**) 1008, 1010, 1011, 1012, 1048
Bitwise AND, bitwise inclusive-OR, bitwise exclusive-OR and bitwise complement operators 1011
bitwise assignment operator 1016, 1169, 1190
bitwise complement operator (**~**) 1011, 1014, 1016, 1190
bitwise exclusive OR assignment operator (**^=**) 1016
bitwise exclusive OR operator (**^**) 1008, 1011, 1013, 1014, 1190, 1191
bitwise inclusive OR assignment operator (**|=**) 1016
bitwise inclusive OR operator (**|**) 1008, 1011, 1012, 1013, 1190, 1191
bitwise left-shift operator (**<<**) 547, 1014
bitwise operator 1007, 1008, 1016
bitwise operator keyword 1190

bitwise OR 1169
bitwise right-shift operator (**>>**) 547
bitwise shift operator 1014
blank 76, 165
blank line 28, 88
block 80, 81, 92, 176, 193, 195, 196
block is active 193
block is exited 193
block of data 1036
block of memory 1036, 1079, 1117
block scope 195
blueprint 406
body element 1239, 1240
body of a class definition 411
body of a function 23, 24
body of a loop 81, 82, 103, 108, 167
body section 1239
Bohm, C. 73, 132
"bombing" 88
Booch, Grady 43
bool data type 76
bool value **false** 76
bool value **true** 76
boolalpha stream manipulator 763
Boolean UML type 226
border attribute 1254
Borland C++ 15, 220, 1073, 1176
boss 171
bottom of a stack 960
bottom tier 882
boundary of a storage unit 1019
bounds checking 266
box 67
br (line break) element 1248
braces (**{}**) 24, 38, 80, 81, 92, 117
braces in a **do/while** structure 120
bracket (**[]**) 255
branch negative 991
branch zero instruction 991, 994
break statement 117, 119, 122, 167, 1079
break statement exiting a **for** structure 122
browser 909, 910
browser request 1260
"brute force" computing 166
bubble sort 277, 309, 336, 355
bubble sort using function pointers 355

bubble sort with call-by-reference 336
bubbleSort function 336, 338
bucket sort 317
buffer fills 768
buffer is filled 742
buffer is flushed 742
buffered output 742
buffered standard error stream 740
buffering 768
building a compiler 989
building-block appearance 130
building-block approach 10
"building blocks" 41
Building class header file 456, 511
Building class implementation file 512
building your own compiler 943, 986
built-in data type 503, 504
"bull's-eye" 229
business logic 883
business rule 883
business software 13
button attribute value (**type**) 898
Button class header file 653
Button class implementation file 653
Byron, Lord 13
byte 1007
byte offset 825

C

C 8
.C extension 15
C legacy code 469, 1054, 1056, 1060, 1066, 1078
C-like array 1094
C programming language 1237
C-style **char *** strings 867
C-style dynamic memory allocation 1078
C-style pointer-based array 1134
C-style string 867
C# programming language 12
C++ 7, 8, 20, 886, 888
C++ career resource 1232
C++ compiler 15, 1232
C++ development environment 16
C++ enhancements to C 4
C++ environment 16
C++ executable 890
C++ How to Program 4

C++ language 20
C++ Multimedia Cyber Classroom
     Fourth Edition 3, 4
C++ preprocessor 15, 22
C++ programming environment 170
C++ programming language 14
C++ resource 21, 1232
C++ resources on the Web 1230
C++ standard library 10, 170
C++ standard library header file 180
c_str member function of class **string** 868
cache 882
calculate a salesperson's earnings 158
calculate the value of π 166
calculation 6, 31, 73
calendar time 187
call stack 334
called function 170
calling environment 815
calling function (caller) 171, 175
calling functions by reference 325
calloc function 1078
cannot return a value from a constructor 412
capacity 1108
capacity of a **string** 859
caption element 1255
card dealing algorithm 355
card game 350
card shuffling and dealing simulation 350, 352, 1001, 1005
career resource 1232
carriage return (**'\r'**) 24, 1021, 1024
CART cookie 929
cascaded assignment 579
cascading **+=** operators 579
cascading member function call 491, 492
Cascading member function calls 494
Cascading Style Sheets (CSS) 20
case label 113, 117, 118, 195
case sensitive 27
case study: **Date** class 582
case study: **String** class 569
casino 182, 188
<cassert> header file 181, 1060
cast 343

cast away "**const**-ness" 1185
cast expression 1057
cast operator 89, 92, 180, 343,
    568, 1184, 1192
cast variable visible in debugger
    1055
casting 344
cast-operator function 568
cataloging 450
catch a base class object 800
catch all exceptions 801
catch block (or handler) 783,
    787, 792, 793
catch related errors 793
catch(...) 801
catch(exception e) 801
<cctype> header file 181, 331,
    1020
CD-ROM 4
ceil 172
central processing unit (CPU) 6
centralized control 19
CERN 19
cerr (standard error unbuffered)
    17, 740, 741, 811
<cfloat> header file 181
.cgi 889
CGI (Common Gateway
    Interface) 885, 1260
.cgi file extension 890
CGI protocol 886
CGI script 885, 889, 890, 895,
    906, 1262
cgi-bin directory 889, 890, 916
chaining 29
char 27, 116, 180, 867, 1007
char * 361
char * returned by **data** 895
char ** 1029
character 360, 809, 1001
character array 267, 347, 361, 554,
    867
character array as a string 268
character code 367
character constant 360
character entity reference 56
character handling library function
    1020
character manipulation 171
character presentation 182
character sequence 823
character set 68, 119, 367, 809
character string 256, 267
character-string manipulation
    1020

character's numerical
    representation 116
character-handling functions
    isdigit, **isalpha**,
    isalnum and **isxdigit**
    1021
character-handling functions
    islower, **isupper**,
    tolower and **toupper**
    1023
character-handling functions
    isspace, **iscntrl**,
    ispunct, **isprint** and
    isgraph 1025
character-handling library
    function 1021
characters represented as numeric
    codes 367
checkbox 1263
checkbox attribute value
    (**type**) 898
checked access 854
checked attribute 1263
checkerboard pattern 67, 162
checkout line in a supermarket 983
child 969
child node 984
Chinese 503
cin (standard input stream) 17,
    28, 740, 741, 811, 815, 890
cin.clear 766
cin.eof 745, 766
cin.get 116, 746
cin.getline 362
cin.tie 768
circle 1252
Circle class contains an *x-y*
    coordinate and a radius 619
Circle class test program 621
Circle class that inherits from
    class **Point** 667, 688
Circle3 class that inherits from
    class **Point2** 627
Circle4 class that inherits from
    class **Point3** but does not
    use **protected** data 634
Circle5 class inherits from
    class **Point4** 645
CircleTest demonstrates class
    Circle functionality 621
CircleTest4 demonstrates
    class **Circle4**
    functionality 636
circular include 457
circular include problem 522
circular, doubly linked list 960

circular, singly-linked list 959
clarity 3, 20, 28, 265
class 4, 10, 41, 133, 253, 1055
class 170, 222, 405, 411, 720,
    810
class **Array** 557
class average on a quiz 83
class-average problem 83, 89
class-average problem with
    sentinel-controlled
    repetition 89
class-average program with
    counter-controlled repetition
    84
class **bitset** and the Sieve of
    Eratosthenes 1170
class **Complex** 601
class definition 411
class development 556
class diagram xxxviii, 47, 141,
    225, 226, 296, 374, 451, 453,
    457
class diagram showing attributes
    226
class diagram that includes
    attributes and operations
    298, 452
class **Employee** 700
class hierarchy 681, 699, 996
class **HugeInt** 604
class libraries 15, 113, 171, 420,
    450
class library 649
class members default to **pri-
    vate** access 1001
class Node 944
class **Polynomial** 608
class **RationalNumber** 607
class scope 195, 416, 418
class-scope variable is hidden 418
class **string** 569
class template 719, 723, 947, 975
class-template **auto_ptr** 798
class-template definition 724
class template scope 726
class-template specialization 719,
    723
class template **Stack** 724, 726
Class **Time** definition 411
class's data members 416
class's implementation 416
class's interface 416
class's member functions 416
class's object code 420
class's source code 420
classic C 9

clear member function 766, 1096
client 507, 913, 916
client code 680
client computer 7, 909
client object 296
client of a class 412, 417, 420, 440
client of a queue 505
client tier 883, 938
client/server computing 7
clients.txt 916
<climits> header file 181
Clock class header file 454, 514
Clock class implementation file 514
clog (standard error buffered) 740, 741, 811
close 816
close a stream 1073
<cmath> header file 172, 179, 181
COBOL (COmmon Business Oriented Language) 13, 1237
code walkthrough xxxviii, 48, 509
coefficient 608
coin tossing 183, 245
col element 1257
colgroup element 1257
collaboration 225, 372
collaboration diagram 372
collaboration diagram for loading and unloading passengers 373
collection classes 505
colon (**:**) 195, 297, 479, 1079, 1201
cols attribute 1263
colspan attribute 1257
column 289
column heading 256
column subscript 289
com (top level domain) 884
combining control structures in two ways 127
comma operator (**,**) 106, 205
comma-separated list 27, 39, 106, 171, 175, 321
comma-separated list of base classes 1201
comma-separated list of arguments 171
command-and-control software systems 13
command line 1066

command-line argument 349, 1070
command-line prompt 1067
comment (**//**) 22, 28, 1239
commercial application 13
commercial data processing 847
commission worker 166
CommissionEmployee class header file 707
CommissionEmployee class implementation file 708
Common Gateway Interface (CGI) 885, 1260
Common Programming Error 10
commonality among classes 374
commutative 551
commutative operation 551
comp.lang.c 1233
comparator function object 1119, 1124
comparator function object **less** 1119, 1132
compare 855
compare iterators 1102
comparing blocks of memory 1036
comparing strings 362, 365
comparing **string**s 855
comparing **union**s 1081
comparisons in a bubble sort 278
compilation error 24
compilation of **if/goto** statement in compiler simulator 991
compilation phase 24
compilation process for a Simple program 993
compilation unit 1189
compile 15, 420
compile error 24
compile-time error 24
compiler 8, 16, 24, 92, 960, 998
compiler generates SML instruction 991
compiler optimization 1075
compiler option 21
compiling 8, 943, 1072
compiling a multiple-source-file program 1071
compl operator keyword 1190
complement operator (**~**) 1008
complete elevator-simulator class diagram that incorporates inheritance 652
Complex class 465, 601

Complex class member-function definitions 602
complex condition 124
complex number 465, 601
component 41, 42, 170, 450
component member of a class 460
component object 456
component-oriented software development 504
composition 143, 417, 478, 509, 511, 610, 611, 613, 648, 964
composition symbol 143
compound interest 110, 165, 166, 168
compound-interest calculation with **for** 110, 111
compound statement 80, 176
computation 4
computer 4
computer-assisted instruction (CAI) 245
Computer name: field 884
computer network 7, 965
computer networking 7
computer program 5
computer programmer 5
computer simulator 390
computerized dictionary 849
computing the sum of the elements of an array 261
concatenate 854
concatenate two linked list objects 981
concatenated string 579
concatenating strings 365
concatenation 29
concept 503
concrete class 681
condition 34, 76, 78, 121, 123, 228
conditional compilation 1054, 1057
conditional execution of activities 301
conditional execution of preprocessor directive 1054
conditional expression 78, 79, 787
conditional operator (**?:**) 78, 79
conditional preprocessor directive 1057
conditionally compiled output statement 1058
confusing equality (**==**) and assignment (**=**) operators 36
confusing equality (**==**) and assignment (**=**) operators 127

conserving memory 193
consistent state 415, 430, 431, 440
const 210, 213, 273, 275, 470,
    554, 1055
const char * 332
const class member 509
const int * const 335
const member function 469
const member function on a
    const object 473
const member function on a
    non-**const** object 473
const object 260, 469, 473
const object must be initialized
    260
const objects and **const**
    member functions 473
const pointer 556
const qualifier 329, 1184
const reference 410
const type qualifier applied to an
    array parameter 275
const variable 478
const variables must be
    initialized 260
const version of **operator[]**
    567
const with function parameters
    330
const_cast operator 1184,
    1197
const_iterator 869, 1095,
    1096, 1097, 1098, 1101,
    1102, 1108, 1122, 1124,
    1126
const_reference 1097
const_reverse_iterator
    870, 1096, 1097, 1101, 1109
constant 172, 989
constant integral expression 119
constant pointer 344, 489
constant pointer to an integer
    constant 335
constant pointer to constant data
    331, 335
constant pointer to nonconstant
    data 331, 334
constant reference 213, 566
constant variable 259, 261
"**const**-ness" 1197
constraint 144, 145
constructed inside out 484
constructor 412, 430, 453
Constructor and destructor call
    order 647
constructor call 430

constructor called recursively 565
constructor in a **union** 1081
Constructor with default
    arguments 433
constructors and destructors called
    automatically 435
constructors cannot be **virtual**
    699
contact.html 1244, 1249
container 54, 182, 869, 943, 1092,
    1094, 1133
container adapter 1094, 1101,
    1128
container class 427, 485, 505, 564,
    719, 730, 1094
Content-type header 893, 905
CONTENT_LENGTH environment
    variable 904
continue statement 122, 167,
    168
continue statement terminating
    a single iteration of a **for**
    structure 123
control character 1024
control structure 72, 73, 75, 77, 78,
    429, 1080
control-structure nesting 75
control-structure stacking 75, 129
control variable 105
control-variable name 106
controller 138, 143
controlling expression 117
controlling the printing of trailing
    zeros and decimal points for
    doubles 756
converge on the base case 206
conversational computing 29
conversion between a built-in type
    and a class 579
conversion constructor 568, 577,
    579, 1194
conversion operator 568
conversions among built-in types
    568
conversions among built-in types
    by cast 568
convert among user-defined types
    and built-in types 568
convert between types 568
convert lowercase letters 181
Converting a string to uppercase
    331
converting between classes and
    built-in types 426
converting from a higher data type
    to a lower data type 180

Converting **string**s to C-style
    strings and character arrays
    867
convertToUppercase 331
cookie 52, 909, 910, 921
cookieform.html 910
copy 868, 1104, 1111
copy a string using array notation
    347
copy a string using pointer
    notation 347
copy constructor 450, 564, 565,
    567, 1095, 1097
copy constructors in pass-by-value
    parameter passing 579
copy of the argument 330
copy_backward 1104, 1152
copying overhead 408
copying strings 347, 363
correct in a mathematical sense
    128
correct number of arguments 175
correction 17
correctly initializing and using a
    constant variable 260
corrupted stack 790
cos 172
cosine 172
count 1104, 1119, 1122, 1144,
    1169
count_if 1104, 1144, 1147
counter 83, 88, 95, 159, 193
counter-controlled repetition 83,
    84, 86, 94, 95, 102, 103, 206
counter-controlled repetition with
    the **for** structure 104
counter variable 85
counting loop 104
counting up by one 86
cout (**<<**) (the standard output
    stream) 17, 23, 26, 29, 740,
    741, 811, 889
cout.put 744
cout.write 748
.cpp extension 15
CPU 6, 16, 17
"craft valuable classes" 42
crafting valuable classes 417
Craps simulation 188, 192, 250
"crashing" 88
create new data type 503, 504
create object dynamically 455
create your own data type 30
CreateAndDestroy class
    definition 436

CreateAndDestroy class
member function definitions
437
creating a random access file 824
Creating a sequential file 813
Creating a structure, setting its
members and printing the
structure 408
creating an association 1126
creating and destroying objects
dynamically 303
Creating and traversing a binary
tree 974
Credit inquiry program 819
credit limit on a charge account
157
credit processing program 825
crossword puzzle generator 402
cryptogram 878
<csdtlib> header file 796
<csetjmp> 784
<csignal> header file 1076
CSS (Cascading Style Sheets) 20
<cstdio> header file 181
<cstdlib> header file 181, 182,
895, 904, 1026, 1073, 1078
<cstring> header file 181, 580
<ctime> header file 181, 188,
889
<ctrl>-d 116, 815
ctrl key 116
<ctrl>-z 116, 754, 815
Ctrl+C 1075
<cstdlib> header file 183
<ctype.h> header file 181
cubeByReference 326, 327
cubeByValue 325
current position in a stream 819
cursor 24
customized code 173
customized function 174
.cxx extension 15
cylinder 689
Cylinder class header file 690
Cylinder class implementation
file 691
Cylinder class inherits from
class **Circle4** and
redefines member function
getArea 639

D

dangerous pointer manipulation
695
dangling **else** problem 161

dangling pointer 566, 578, 579
dangling reference 214
data 5
data abstraction 4, 469, 502, 556
data-analysis program 279, 282
data hierarchy 809, 810
data member 41, 406, 411, 416
data member function of class
string 895
data members normally **private**
412
data persistence 809
data representation 503
data structures 54, 253, 943, 1092
data tier 882
data type 502
data type **bool** 76
data type **int** 27
data typing 9
data validation 426
database 811
database management system
(DBMS) 811
Date class 466, 479, 582
Date class definition with
overloaded increment
operators 582
Date class member function
definitions 480
Date class member-function and
friend-function
definitions 583
Date class test program 586
__**DATE**__ predefined symbolic
constant 1060
__**STDC**__ predefined symbolic
constant 1060
date source file is compiled 1060
DBMS (database management
system) 811
deallocate memory 495, 797
deallocates memory allocated with
new 945
debug 13, 20
debugger 1055
debugging 186, 1239
debugging aid 1058
debugging tool 1060
DEC PDP-11 9
DEC PDP-7 computer 9
dec stream manipulator 750, 755,
760
decimal (base 10) number system
755, 1029, 1030
decimal digit 809
decimal number 166, 760, 1020

decimal point 89, 93, 112, 743,
756
decimal point in a floating-point
number 172
decision 3, 76, 77, 133
decision path 229
decision symbol 76
deck of cards 349, 350
declaration 27, 72
declarations of parameters 175
declare a reference 459
declaring a **static** member
function **const** 502
decrement a control variable 102
decrement a pointer 341
decrement operator 99, 581
decrypter 877
dedicated communications line 18
deeply nested structure 132
default access for **struct**
members is **public** 426
default access mode for class is
private 424
default argument 215, 216, 217,
430
Default arguments to a function
216
default arguments with
constructors 430
default case 113, 117, 118,
119, 185
default constructor 431, 484, 563,
565, 585, 629, 728, 1095
default delimiter 748
default function argument 433
default memberwise assignment
449, 548, 1097
default memberwise copy 565,
1097
default precision 93
default to decimal 760
default to **public** access 1001
defensive programming 106
#define 1057, 1060
#define NDEBUG 1060
#define PI 3.14159 1055
#define preprocessor directive
424, 1055
!defined 1058
defined 1058
definite repetition 83
definition 102
deitel@deitel.com 4
del element 1249
delay loop 107

delete 495, 509, 566, 798, 800, 1078

delete [] (dynamic array deallocation) 497

delete a record from a file 835

delete operator 699, 945

deleting an item from a binary tree 977

deleting dynamically allocated memory 502

delimiter 895

delimiter (with default value '**\n**') 746

delimiter character 362, 368

Demonstrating a **mutable** data member 1198

Demonstrating an **explicit constructor** 1195

demonstrating class template **Stack** 724, 726

Demonstrating function **substr** 858

Demonstrating functions **erase** and **replace** 865

Demonstrating input from an **istringstream** object 873

Demonstrating multiple inheritance 1201

Demonstrating operator **const_cast** 1184

Demonstrating operator **reinterpret_cast** 1186

Demonstrating **set_new_handler** 797

Demonstrating **string** assignment and concatenation 853

Demonstrating the **.*** and **->*** operators 1199

Demonstrating the operator keywords 1191

Demonstrating the **string find** member functions 862

Demonstrating the **string insert** functions 866

Demonstrating the use of **namespace**s 1187

DeMorgan's Laws 166

<deque> header file 182, 1096, 1118

deque sequence container 1092, 1101, 1105, 1111, 1113, 1116, 1117, 1128, 1129

dequeue 965

dequeue operation 505

dereference a **0** pointer 323

dereference a **const** iterator 1099

dereference a pointer 323, 326, 331

dereference an iterator 1098, 1099, 1102

dereference an iterator positioned outside its container 1099

dereferencing operator (*****) 323

derive one class from another 417

derived class 610, 611, 613, 648, 651, 700

derived-class **catch** 800

derived-class destructor 699

descriptive words and phrases in problem statement 225

design 42

design process 374

destroy object 509

destroying objects dynamically 303

destructor 416, 435, 453, 1095

destructor calls in reverse order of constructor calls 435

destructor overloading 435

destructor receives no parameters and returns no value 416, 435

destructors cannot be overloaded 416

dethread a node from a list 958

diagnostics that aid program debugging 181

dialogue 29

diameter 76, 77

diamond 67, 74, 76, 143, 167

diamond inheritance 1205

diamond symbol 229

dice game 188

dictionary 849

Die-rolling program using an array instead of **switch** 263

difference_type 1097

digit 27, 360

direct access 946

direct base class 610

directly reference a value 321

disc 1251, 1252

disk 5, 6, 15, 17, 989

disk drive 739

disk file 996

disk I/O completion 781

disk space 794, 796, 815

display screen 739, 742

distributed client/server applications 7

distributed computing 7

divide and conquer 170, 173

divide by zero 17, 88, 1075

DivideByZeroException 787

divides< T > 1172

division 5, 31, 32, 93

division by zero is undefined 503

DNS (domain name server) 884

DNS lookup 884

do action-label 229

do/while repetition structure 120, 121, 133

document a program 22

dollar amount 112

domain name 884

domain name server (DNS) 884

Door class header file 455, 522

Door class implementation file 522

DOS 1066, 1075

dot operator (**.**) 407, 408, 418, 491, 674, 799

dotted line 74

double 111, 172, 179, 1075

double-array subscripting 601

double-ended queue 1117

double quote 23, 24

double selection 132

double-selection structure 74, 95, 113

double-subscripted array representation of a deck of cards 350

double-subscripted array 289, 290, 292, 293, 295, 312, 349, 943

double-subscripted array manipulations 293

double-subscripted array representation of a deck of cards 350

double-word boundary 1003

"doubly initializing" member objects 485

doubly linked list 1094, 1113

doubly-linked list 960

downcasting 671

drawing a shape 673

dummy value 86

duplicate base-class object 1206

duplicate elimination 943, 977, 984

duplicate key 1119, 1124

duplicate node value 969

dynamic array 1078

dynamic binding 663, 674, 695, 698
dynamic content 11
dynamic creation of objects 461
dynamic data structure 253, 320, 943
dynamic memory 797
dynamic memory allocation 945, 946, 1078
dynamic memory management 495
dynamic object management 509
dynamic vs. static Web content 885, 888
dynamic Web content 885, 888
dynamic_cast 800
dynamic_cast operator 713
dynamically allocate and deallocate storage 435
dynamically allocate array of integers 564, 1088
dynamically allocated memory 502, 699, 798
dynamically allocated memory for an array 1078
dynamically allocated storage 449, 450, 565, 569, 578
dynamically creates exact amount of space 485

E

EBCDIC (Extended Binary Coded Decimal Interchange Code) 367
edit 15
edit phase 17
editing a file 15
editor 15, 16
Eight Queens 316
Eight Queens: brute-force approaches 316
element of an array 253
element of chance 182
Elevator class header file 461, 528
Elevator class implementation file 530
Elevator simulation 405, 511
ElevatorButton class header file 457, 524, 654
ElevatorButton class implementation file 525
ElevatorButton class member-function definitions 655

#elif 1058
ellipsis (**...**) in a function prototype 1067, 1068
else 77, 81
emacs 15
emacs text editor 1237
e-mail (electronic mail) 18, 1245
e-mail anchor 1245
embedded parentheses 32
Employee class 479, 485
Employee class definition showing composition 481
Employee class definition with a static data member to track the number of **Employee** objects in memory 498
Employee class header file 701
Employee class hierarchy driver program 711
Employee class implementation file 701
Employee class member function definitions, including constructor with a member-initializer list 482
Employee class member-function definitions 499
empty 1095, 1130, 1131, 1132
empty element 1247, 1248
empty exception specification 790
empty function parameter list 209
empty member function of **string** 591
empty quotation marks 825
empty space 825
empty statement 81
empty **string** 855, 861
encapsulate 41
encapsulation 417, 448, 485
encrypted integer 163
encrypter 877
encryption 163, 877, 879
end 1096, 1098, 1099, 1109, 1168
end iterator 1103
end line 29
end of a sequence 1150
end of a stream 819
end of a string 944
"end of data entry" 86
end-of-file 116, 117, 361, 766, 816
end-of-file indicator 815, 816, 1070
end-of-file key combination 816, 1066
end of **main** 24
end Simple command 987, 990

end tag 1239
#endif preprocessor directive 1058, 424
endl 29, 93
end-of-file marker 811
English-like abbreviations 8
enqueue 965
enqueue operation 505
Enter key 28, 117, 119
entity reference 1249
entry point 128
enum keyword 190
enumeration 190, 1055
enumeration constant 191, 1057
environment 171
environment.cpp 893
EOF 745, 748, 1020
eof member function 745, 766, 767
eofbit 766
equal 1104, 1136, 1138
equal to 35
equal_to 1172
equal_range 1122, 1160
Equality and relational operators 36
equality operator (**==**) 34, 35, 36, 556, 1097
equality operators (**==** and **!=**) 76, 124
equation of straight line 33
erase 1096, 1112
erase member function of class **string** 865
Erroneous attempt to initialize a constant of a built-in data type by assignment 476
#error preprocessor directive 1058
error 17
error bit 748
error checking 171
error detected in a constructor 792
error message 17
error-processing code 782
error state of a stream 744, 766, 767
escape character 23
escape early from a loop 122
escape sequence 23, 25, 159
evaluating a postfix expression 983
evaluating expressions 960, 981
evaluation algorithm 996
even integer 164
event 227

examination-results problem 96
Examples
    Accessing an object's
       members through each type
       of object handle 419
    Activity diagram that models
       the elevator's logic for
       responding to button presses
       230
    Addition program 26
    Aiming a derived-class pointer
       at a base-class object 671
    Algorithms copy_backward,
       merge, unique and reverse
       1152
    Algorithms equal, mismatch
       and lexicographical_compare
       1136
    Algorithms **min** and **max**
       1165
    Algorithms **swap**,
       iter_swap and
       swap_ranges 1150
    Array class definition with
       overloaded operators 557
    Array class member-
       function and friend-function
       definitions 558
    Array class test program 561
    Array of pointers to functions
       358
    associations between classes
       in a class diagram 142
    Attempting to call a multiply
       inherited function
       polymorphically 1206
    Attempting to modify a
       constant pointer to constant
       data 335
    Attempting to modify a
       constant pointer to
       nonconstant data 334
    Attempting to modify data
       through a nonconstant
       pointer to constant data 333
    auto_ptr object manages
       dynamically allocated
       memory 798
    Bank account program 835
    BasePlusCommission-
       Employee class header file
       709
    BasePlusCommission-
       Employee class
       implementation file 710

Examples (cont.)
    Basic searching and sorting
       algorithms of the Standard
       Library 1148
    Bell class header file 453,
       519
    Bell class implementation
       file 519
    Binary function object 1173
    Binary search of a sorted array
       286
    Bit fields used to store a deck
       of cards 1017
    Bitwise AND, bitwise
       inclusive-OR, bitwise
       exclusive-OR and bitwise
       complement operators 1011
    Bitwise shift operators 1014
    break statement exiting a
       for structure 122
    Bubble sort with call-by-
       reference 336
    Building class header file
       456, 511
    Building class
       implementation file 512
    Button class header file 653
    Button class implementation
       file 653
    Cascading member function
       calls 491, 494
    CGI script that allows users to
       buy a book 929
    CGI script that allows users to
       view the contents of their
       shopping carts 931
    Character arrays processed as
       strings 268
    Character-handling functions
       isdigit, **isalpha**,
       isalnum and **isxdigit**
       1021
    Character-handling functions
       islower, **isupper**,
       tolower and **toupper**
       1023
    Character-handling functions
       isspace, **iscntrl**,
       ispunct, **isprint** and
       isgraph 1025
    Circle class contains an *x-y*
       coordinate and a radius 619
    Circle class test program
       621
    Circle class that inherits
       from class **Point** 667, 688

Examples (cont.)
    Circle3 class that inherits
       from class **Point2** 627
    Circle4 class that inherits
       from class **Point3** but does
       not use **protected** data
       634
    Circle5 class inherits from
       class **Point4** 645
    CircleTest4 demonstrates
       class **Circle4** functionality
       636
    Class **bitset** and the Sieve
       of Eratosthenes 1170
    Class diagram showing
       attributes 226
    Class diagram that includes
       attributes and operations 298,
       452
    Class **Time** definition**Time**
       411
    Class-average problem with
       sentinel-controlled repetition
       89
    Class-average program with
       counter-controlled repetition
       84
    Clock class header file 454,
       514
    Clock class implementation
       file 514
    Collaboration diagram for
       loading and unloading
       passengers 373
    CommissionEmployee
       class header file 707
    CommissionEmployee
       class implementation file 708
    Comparing **string**s 855
    complete elevator-simulator
       class diagram that
       incorporates inheritance 652
    Complex class definition 601
    Complex class member-
       function definitions 602
    Complex numbers 603
    Complex XHTML table 1257
    Compound interest
       calculations with **for** 111
    Computing the sum of the
       elements of an array 261
    const objects and **const**
       member functions 473
    const type qualifier applied
       to an array parameter 275

Examples (cont.)

const variables must be initialized 260

Constructor and destructor call order 647

Constructor with default arguments 433

contact.html 1244, 1249

continue statement terminating a single iteration of a **for** structure 123

Controlling the printing of trailing zeros and decimal points for **double**s 756

Converting a string to uppercase 331

Converting **string**s to C-style strings and character arrays 867

Correctly initializing and using a constant variable 260

Counter-controlled repetition with the **for** structure 104

Craps simulation 188

CreateAndDestroy class definition 436

CreateAndDestroy class member function definitions 437

Creating a sequential file 813

Creating a server-side file to store user data 917

Creating a structure, setting its members and printing the structure 408

Creating and traversing a binary tree 974

Credit inquiry program 819

Cylinder class header file 690

Cylinder class implementation file 691

Cylinder class inherits from class **Circle4** and redefines member function **getArea** 639

Date class definition 479

Date class definition with overloaded increment operators 582

Date class member function definitions 480

Date class member-function and friend-function definitions 583

Date class test program 586

Examples (cont.)

Default arguments to a function 216

Default memberwise assignment 449

Demonstrating a **mutable** data member 1198

Demonstrating an **explicit** constructor 1195

Demonstrating class template **Stack** 724, 726

Demonstrating function **substr** 858

Demonstrating functions **erase** and **replace** 865

Demonstrating **inplace_merge**, **unique_copy** and **reverse_copy** 1155

Demonstrating input from an **istringstream** object 873

Demonstrating **lower_bound**, **upper_bound** and **equal_range** 1160

Demonstrating multiple inheritance 1201

Demonstrating operator **const_cast** 1184

Demonstrating operator **reinterpret_cast** 1186

Demonstrating **set_new_handler** 797

Demonstrating Standard Library functions **fill**, **fill_n**, **generate** and **generate_n** 1134

Demonstrating Standard Library functions **remove**, **remove_if**, **remove_copy** and **remove_copy_if** 1139

Demonstrating Standard Library functions **replace**, **replace_if**, **replace_copy** and **replace_copy_if** 1142

Demonstrating **string** assignment and concatenation 853

Demonstrating the **.*** and **->*** operators 1199

Demonstrating the operator keywords 1191

Examples (cont.)

Demonstrating the **string find** member functions 862

Demonstrating the **string insert** functions 866

Demonstrating the use of **namespace**s 1187

Die-rolling program using an array instead of **switch** 263

do/while structure 121

Door class header file 455, 522

Door class implementation file 522

Double-subscripted array manipulations 293

Elevator class header file 461, 528

Elevator class implementation file 530

Elevator simulation 511

ElevatorButton class header file 457, 524, 654

ElevatorButton class implementation file 525

ElevatorButton class member-function definitions 655

Employee class definition showing composition 481

Employee class definition with a static data member to track the number of **Employee** objects in memory 498

Employee class header file 701

Employee class hierarchy driver program 711

Employee class implementation file 701

Employee class member function definitions, including constructor with a member-initializer list 482

Employee class member-function definitions 499

Equality and relational operators 36

Erroneous attempt to initialize a constant of a built-in data type by assignment 476

Exception-handling example that throws exceptions on attempts to divide by zero 785

Examples (cont.)

Factorial calculations with a recursive function 200

Fibonacci numbers generated with a recursive function 202

fig20_02.cpp 1068

fig20_03.cpp 1070

fig20_04.cpp 1074

fig20_06.cpp 1076

fig20_07.cpp 1079

fig20_08.cpp 1082

fig20_09.cpp 1083

First CGI script 889

flags member function of **ios_base** 765

Floating-point values displayed in default, scientific and fixed format 762

Floor class header file 459, 535

Floor class implementation file 536

FloorButton class header file 458, 526, 656

FloorButton class implementation file 526

FloorButton class member-function definitions 656

Form including radio buttons and drop-down lists 1266

form.html 1260

form2.html 1263

form3.html 1266

Friends can access **private** members of class 486

full class diagram for elevator simulation 144

Functions that take no arguments 208

Generating values to be placed into elements of an array 259

get, **put** and **eof** member functions 745

Header elements **h1** through **h6** 1241

header.html 1241

High-performance card-shuffling and dealing simulation 1005

Histogram printing program 262

HourlyEmployee class header file 705

Examples (cont.)

HourlyEmployee class implementation file 705

HTML/XHTML special characters 1274

Huge integers 607

Implementation class definition 506

Implementing a proxy class 508

Inheritance examples 612, 613

Inheritance hierarchy for university **CommunityMembers** 613

Initializing a reference 213

Initializing an array's elements to zeros and printing the array 256

Initializing multidimensional arrays 290

Initializing the elements of an array with a declaration 257

inline function to calculate the volume of a cube 210

Input and output stream iterators 1098

Input of a string using **cin** with stream extraction contrasted with input using **cin.get** 746

Inputting character data using **cin** member function **getline** 747

Inserting special characters into XHTML 1249

Interactive portal handler 907

Interactive portal to create a password-protected Web page 906

Interface class definition 507

Interface class member-function definitions 507

Left justification and right justification with stream-manipulators **left** and **right** 757

Light class header file 456, 520

Light class implementation file 520

Linear search of an array 284

Linking to an e-mail address 1244

Linking to other Web pages 1242

Examples (cont.)

links.html 1242

List class-template definition 948

list of nouns in problem statement 140

list.html 1252

ListNode class-template definition 947

Logout program for the shopping cart example 935

main.html 1238

Manipulating a linked list 952

Mathematical algorithms of the Standard Library 1144

Member initializer used to initialize a constant of a built-in data type 475

Member-object initializers 483

Memory-handling function **memchr** 1040

Memory-handling function **memcmp** 1039

Memory-handling function **memcpy** 1038

Memory-handling function **memmove** 1038

Memory-handling function **memset** 1041

Modified list of verb phrases for classes in the system 371

multiplicity values 143

Multipurpose sorting program using function pointers 355

Name mangling to enable type-safe linkage 221

nav.html 1247

Nested and ordered lists in XHTML 1252

Nested control structures: Examination-results problem 96

new returning **0** on failure 793

new throwing **bad_alloc** on failure 795

Non-**friend**/non-member functions cannot access **private** members 488

object diagram of empty building 145

Overloaded function definitions 219

Overloaded stream-insertion and stream-extraction operators 552

Examples (cont.)

Pass-by-reference with a pointer argument used to cube a variable's value 327

Pass-by-value used to cube a variable's value 326

Passing arguments by value and by reference 212

Passing arrays and individual array elements to functions 273

Person class header file 454, 538

Person class implementation file 539

picture.html 1245

Placing images in XHTML files 1245

Point class implementation file 686

Point class represents an *x-y* coordinate pair 616, 665

Point class test program 617

Point/Circle/Cylinder hierarchy test program 640

Point2 class represents an *x-y* coordinate pair as **protected** data 625

Point3 class uses member functions to manipulate its **private** data 632

Point4 base class contains a constructor and a destructor 643

Pointer operators **&** and ***** 323

Precision of floating-point values 751

Preincrementing and postincrementing 100

Printing a string one character at a time using a nonconstant pointer to constant data 332

Printing an integer with internal spacing and plus sign 758

Printing an unsigned integer in bits 1009

Printing on multiple lines with a single statement using **cout** 25

Printing on one line with separate statements using **cout** 25

Printing **string** characteristics 859

Examples (cont.)

Printing the address stored in a **char *** variable 743

Printing the value of a **union** in both member data types 1082

Private base-class data cannot be accessed from derived class 623

private members of a class are not accessible outside the class 425

Program that outputs a login page 922

programmer-defined function **square** 174

Programmer-defined **maximum** function 177

Protected base-class data can be accessed from derived class 629

Queue class-template definition 966

Queue-processing program 967

Randomizing the die-rolling program 186

Reading a random-access file sequentially 832

Reading and printing a sequential file 817

Reading cookies from the client's computer 914

Reading input from **QUERY_STRING** 896

Referencing array elements with the array name and with pointers 345

representing a class in the UML 142

Rethrowing an exception 788

Retrieving environment variables via function **getenv** 893

Returning a reference to a **private** data member 446

Rolling a six-sided die 6000 times 184

SalariedEmployee class header file 703

SalariedEmployee class implementation file 704

SalesPerson class definition 427

SalesPerson class member function definitions 428

Examples (cont.)

Scheduler class header file 458, 515

Scheduler class implementation file 516

Scoping example 196

Sequence diagram for scheduling process 302

Sequence diagram that models the steps the building repeats during the simulation 300

Set and *get* functions manipulating an object's **private** data 443

Set of recursive calls to method **Fibonacci** 205

set operations of the Standard Library 1157

Shifted, scaled integers produced by **1 + rand() % 6** 183

Signals defined in header **<csignal>** 1076

Simple form with hidden fields and a text box 1260

Single-argument constructors and implicit conversions 1192

sizeof operator used to determine standard data type sizes 340

sizeof operator when applied to an array name returns the number of bytes in the array 339

Sorting an array with bubble sort 277

Stack class-template definition 961

Stack class-template definition with a composed **List** object 964

Stack test program 962

Stack unwinding 791

Standard library class **string** 588

Standard library class **vector** 592

Standard Library **deque** class template 1118

Standard Library **list** class template 1113

Standard Library **map** class template 1126

Standard Library **multimap** class template 1124

Examples (cont.)

Standard Library **multiset** class template 1120

Standard Library **priority_queue** adapter class 1132

Standard Library **queue** adapter class templates 1131

Standard Library **set** class template 1123

Standard Library **stack** adapter class 1129

Standard Library **vector** class template 1106

Standard Library **vector** class template element-manipulation functions 1109

statechart diagram for class **Elevator** 228

statechart diagram for classes **FloorButton** and **ElevatorButton** 228

static array initialization and automatic array initialization 270

static data member tracking the number of objects of a class 498, 501

strcat and **strncat** 365

strcmp and **strncmp** 366

strcpy and **strncpy** 364

Stream manipulator **showbase** 761

Stream manipulators **boolalpha** and **noboolalpha** 764

Stream manipulators **hex**, **oct**, **dec** and **setbase** 750

String class definition with operator overloading 569

String class member-function and friend-function definitions 571

String class test program 574

String copying using array notation and pointer notation 347

String-search function **strcspn** 1033

strlen 370

strtok 368

Student-poll-analysis program 265

Summation with **for** 109

Examples (cont.)

Survey-data analysis program 279

switch structure testing multiple letter grade values 114

table1.html 1255

table2.html 1258

Testing error states 767

Text printing program 22

this pointer used implicitly and explicitly to access an object's members 490

Time abstract data type implementation as a class 413

Time class containing a constructor with default arguments 431

Time class definition 421

Time class definition modified to enable cascaded member-function calls 491

Time class definition with *set* and *get* functions 440

Time class member function definitions 421

Time class member function definitions including a constructor that takes arguments 431

Time class member function definitions, including **const** member functions 471

Time class member function definitions, including *set* and *get* functions 441

Time class with **const** member functions 471

Tree class-template definition 971

TreeNode class-template definition 970

Unary scope resolution operator 217

Unformatted I/O using the **read**, **gcount** and **write** member functions 749

Uninitialized local reference causes a syntax error 214

Unordered lists in XHTML 1251

use-case diagram for elevator system 139

User-defined, nonparameterized stream manipulators 754

Examples (cont.)

Using a dynamically allocated **ostringstream** object 871

Using a function template 223

Using an anonymous **union** 1083

Using an iterator to output a **string** 869

Using command-line arguments 1070

Using function **swap** to swap two **string**s 858

Using functions **exit** and **atexit** 1074

Using **GET** with an XHTML form 899

Using **goto** 1079

Using images as link anchors 1247

Using member function **fill** and stream manipulator **setfill** to change the padding character for fields larger than the values being printed 759

Using member functions **get**, **put** and **eof** 745

Using **POST** with an XHTML form 901

Using signal handling 1076

Using Standard Library functions to perform a heapsort 1163

Using stream manipulator **uppercase** 763

Using template functions 721

Using variable-length argument lists 1068

Using **virtual** base classes 1208

Utility function demontration 429

verb phrases for each class in simulator 297

width member function of class **ios_base** 753

Writing a cookie 911

XHTML document containing a form to post data to the server 910

XHTML document to read user's contact information 916

XHTML table 1255

<exception> 182, 787, 790, 800
exception 780
exception 800
exception class 800
exception classes derived from common base class 793
exception handler 780, 782
exception handling 182
Exception-handling example that throws exceptions on attempts to divide by zero 785
exception not listed in exception specification 790
exception object 787
exception specification 789
exception standard base class 787
exceptional condition 118
.exe 889, 890, 892
executable image 17
executable statement 28, 72
execute a program 15, 16, 17
execution-time error 17
execution-time overhead 696
exhaust memory 202
exit 228
exit 784, 796
exit a deeply-nested structure 1080
exit a function 24
exit a loop 167
exit a program 790
exit action 229
exit function 436, 815, 1073, 1074
exit point 128
EXIT_FAILURE constant 1073
EXIT_SUCCESS constant 1073
exp 173
expand a macro 1056
expires attribute 910
explicit constructor 1194, 1195
explicit conversion 92
explicit keyword 1194, 1196
explicit use of the **this** pointer 489
exponent 608
exponential "explosion" of calls 205
exponential complexity 205
exponential function 173
exponentiation 34, 110
expression 76, 78, 92, 106, 172

extend the base programming language 504
Extended Binary Coded Decimal Interchange Code (EBCDIC) 367
extensibility 680, 1103
extensibility of C++ 555
extensibility of STL 1095
Extensible HyperText Markup Language (XHTML) 20, 52, 881, 886, 1237
extensible language 202, 267, 412, 504
Extensible Markup Language (XML) 20
extern "C" 1084
extern keyword 192, 194, 1072
external declaration 1004
external linkage 1073
extract commonality 650

F

F floating-point suffix 1075
f floating-point suffix 1075
fabs 173
face values of cards 350
factorial 163, 165, 199, 200, 202
Factorial calculations with a recursive function 200
fail member function 766
failbit 744, 748, 766, 815
false 34, 74, 76, 77, 78, 81, 206, 763
FAQs 1232
fatal error 17, 88, 323, 392
fatal logic error 88
Fibonacci numbers generated with a recursive function 202
Fibonacci series 202, 205
field 810
field width 113, 256, 749, 752
fields larger than values being printed 759
FIFO 505, 965, 1094, 1117, 1130
fig20_02.cpp 1068
fig20_03.cpp 1070
fig20_04.cpp 1074
fig20_06.cpp 1076
fig20_07.cpp 1079
fig20_08.cpp 1082
fig20_09.cpp 1083
file 809, 811, 818
file as a collection of bytes 811
file attribute value (**type**) 898
file of n bytes 811

file open mode 814, 816
__FILE__ predefined symbolic constant 1060
file processing 740, 742, 847
file scope 195, 418, 497, 732, 1083
file server 7
file system directory 943
filename 814, 816, 1059
filename extension 15
file-position pointer 818, 829, 834
file-processing class 743
fill 1104, 1134
fill character 408, 749, 752, 758, 759
fill member function 757, 759
fill_n 1104, 1134
final state 74, 129
final value of a control variable 102, 108
find 1103, 1104, 1119, 1122, 1148
find member function of class **string** 862, 863, 864
find_each 1104
find_end 1104
find_first_not_of member function of class **string** 864
find_first_of 1104
find_first_of member function of class **string** 864, 901
find_if 1104, 1148
find_last_of member function of class **string** 864
finding strings and characters in a **string** 862
first 1122, 1124
first-class container 1096, 1098, 1101, 1109, 1112
first-in first-out (FIFO) 505, 965, 1094, 1117, 1130
first pass of Simple compiler 990, 991, 993, 996
first refinement 87, 95, 351
fixed 93
fixed format 762
fixed notation 743
fixed-point format 93
fixed-point notation 756
fixed-point value 113
fixed stream manipulator 756, 761
fixed word size 503
flag 86, 990

flags member function 764, 765
flags member function of
   ios_base 765
flight simulator 717
float 27, 92, 180, 1075
<float.h> header file 181
floating point 751, 756, 762
floating-point arithmetic 547
floating-point constant not
   suffixed 1075
floating-point division 92
floating-point exception 1075
floating-point number 86, 89, 92,
   93
floating-point number in scientific
   format 761
floating-point size limit 181
floating-point values displayed in
   default, scientific and fixed
   format 762
floor 173, 242
Floor class header file 459, 535
Floor class implementation file
   536
FloorButton class header file
   458, 526, 656
FloorButton class
   implementation file 526
FloorButton class member-
   function definitions 656
flow of control 39, 82
flow of control in the **if/else**
   structure 78
flow of control of a **virtual**
   function call 697
flush a stream 1073
flush buffer 768
flush output buffer 29
flushing stream 749
fmod function 173
fmtflags data type 764
for map 1126
for repetition structure 104, 105,
   106, 108, 133
for repetition structure example
   108
for structure activity diagram
   108
for_each 1144, 1147
force a decimal point 93, 743
forcing a plus sign 758
form 897, 1237, 1259
form element 1261
form feed (**'\f'**) 1021, 1024
form XHTML element
   (**<form>...</form>**) 897

formal type parameter 222, 224,
   728
formal type parameter in a
   function template definition
   721
formal type parameters of a
   template definition 720
format error 766
format of floating-point numbers
   in scientific format 762
format state 749, 765
format-state stream manipulators
   755
formatted data file processing 809
formatted input/output 740, 823
formatted text 823
formatting 749
formulating algorithms 83, 86
FORTRAN (FORmula
   TRANslator) 13, 1237
Fortran (FORmula TRANslator)
   progamming language 13,
   1237
forward declaration 457, 459, 507,
   522
forward iterator 1100, 1106, 1144,
   1150, 1151, 1152, 1154,
   1167
forward iterator operation 1102
forward pointer 960
forward reference 990
forward slash (**/**) 227, 1247
fraction 607
fractional part 92
free fucntion 1078
free memory 945
friend function 412, 415, 424,
   426, 430, 439, 443, 485, 549,
   550, 557, 568, 613, 649, 719,
   731
friend functions to enhance
   performance 485
friend of a derived class 1203
friends are not member
   functions 486
Friends can access **private**
   members of class 486
friendship granted, not taken 486
friendship not symmetric 486
friendship not transitive 486
front 1105, 1111, 1130
front of a queue 505
front_inserter 1154
<fstream> header file 181, 742,
   812, 814, 834, 835
<fstream.h> header file 181

full class diagram for elevator
   simulation 144
Full Computer Name: field 884
fully qualified host name 884
function 10, 17, 23, 41, 133, 171,
   173, 178, 406
function adapter 1172
function argument 172
function body 176
function call 171, 176
function-call operator **()** 581
function call operator **()** 698
function-call overhead 209, 579
function call stack 334
function-call stack 790
function definition 174, 176, 195
function definition as a function
   prototype 175
function header 190, 338
function name 171, 174, 194, 355,
   1072, 1073
function object 1119, 1124, 1172,
   1175
function object can encapsulate
   data 1175
function object **less< int >**
   1119, 1121
function object **less< T >** 1124,
   1132
function overhead 1057
function overloading 219, 412,
   739, 1067
function parameter as a local
   variable 176
function pointer 355, 696, 698,
   1172, 1175, 1200
function prototype 111, 175, 176,
   178, 179, 195, 208, 211, 327,
   420, 485, 1055, 1067, 1072,
   1084
function prototype for **rand** in
   <cstdlib> 183
function prototype for **srand** in
   <cstdlib> 186
function prototype for **time** in
   <ctime> 188
function prototype scope 195
function-prototype scope 195
function prototypes are mandatory
   178
function **raise** 1075
function scope 195, 418
function-scope variable 418
function signature 179
function template 222, 223, 719
function template **max** 250

function template **min** 250

function-template specialization 719

function template(s) 719, 720, 723

function that calls itself 198

function that takes no arguments 208

<functional> header file 182, 1172, 1174

functional structure of a program 24

functionalization 5

functionalizing a program 173, 207

functions as building blocks 173

functions for manipulating data in the standard library containers 182

functions should be small 176

functions with empty parameter lists 208

G

gallery.yahoo.com 1245

gambling casino 182

game of "guess the number" 246

game of chance 188

game of craps 188, 192

game playing 182

"garbage" value 85

Gates, Bill 11

gcd 248

gcount 749

general class average problem 86

general utilities library **<cstdlib>** 1026, 1060, 1073, 1078

generalities 680

generate 1104, 1134, 1136

generate_n 1104, 1134, 1136

Generating values to be placed into elements of an array 259

generator function 1134

generic algorithm 1103

generic class 723

generic programming 723, 1092, 1093, 1097, 1176, 1235

get member function 745, 746

get member function 426, 439, 440, 445

get pointer 818

get request type 882, 887, 1262

get the value of **private** data member 426

get, **put** and **eof** member functions 745

getenv function 894, 895, 896, 905

getline function 362, 747, 852

getquery.cgi 898

getquery.cpp 899

gets the value of 36

GIF (Graphics Interchange Format) 1245

global function 425, 731

global identifier 1186

global **namespace** 1189

global object constructor 436

global scope 437, 1189

global variable 194, 195, 196, 198, 217, 272, 1071, 1072, 1189

golden mean 202

golden ratio 202

good member function 766

Good Programming Practice 10, 20

goodbit 766

gosub 998

goto elimination 73

goto statement 73, 195, 1079

goto statement in Simple 987, 988, 990

goto-less programming 73

grade point average 165

graph 165

graph information 262

graphical representation of a binary tree 969

Graphics Interchange Format (GIF) 1245

graphics package 717

greater than 35

greater than or equal to 35

greater<T> 1172

greater_equal 1172

greatest common divisor (GCD) 245, 248

gross pay 158

group of related fields 811

guard condition 76, 77, 78, 83, 108, 117, 121, 227, 229

H

h1 header element 1240

h6 header element 1240

half word 998, 1003

halt in SML 996

handle 535

handle on an object 418, 451, 452, 455

hangman 877

hardcopy printer 17

hardware 3, 5

hardware platform 9

"has-a" relationship (composition) 611

head 1239

head element 1239

head of a queue 943, 965

head section 1239

header 913, 1240

header cell 1256

header element 1240

header file 47, 180, 181, 420, 424, 451, 649, 699, 1054, 1072, 1104, 1106, 1111, 1113, 1118, 1120, 1122, 1126, 1129, 1131, 1132, 1147, 1154, 1156

header file **<csignal>** 1076

header file **<memory>** 798

header file **<new>** 793, 795

header file **<stdexcept>** 800

header file name enclosed in angle brackets 423

header file name enclosed in quotes 423

header files xxxviii

header.html 1241

heap 1132, 1162, 1165

heapsort 1132, 1162

height attribute 1246

Hejlsberg, Anders 12

helper function 427

help-site.com 1230

Hewlett-Packard 1092

hex stream manipulator 750, 755, 760

hexadecimal 166, 743, 760, 762, 1030

hexadecimal (base-16) number 743, 750, 755, 760, 1029

hexadecimal integer 323

hexadecimal notation 743

hexadecimal number system 1020

hexadecimal value 1249

hidden attribute value (**type**) 898

hide an internal data representation 505

hide implementation 502, 507

hide implementation detail 171, 502

hide names in outer scope 196

hide **private** data from clients 420

hiding 485

hiding implementation 417

hierarchical boss function/worker function relationship 172

hierarchical form of management 171

hierarchy of exception classes 800

hierarchy of shapes 680

high-level language 8, 9

highest level of precedence 32

"highest" type 180

high-level I/O 739

high-performance card-shuffling and dealing simulation 1005

histogram 165, 262, 282

histogram-printing program 262

horizontal rule 56, 1250

horizontal tab (`'\t'`) 24, 1021, 1024

host 886

host environment 1073

host object 479

hostname 886

`hotwired.lycos.com/ webmonkey/00/50/ index2a.html` 1269

HourlyEmployee class header file 705

HourlyEmployee class implementation file 705

how the system should be constructed 139

hr element 1250

href attribute 1242

htdocs directory 885

.html (XHTML file name extension) 1237

HTML (HyperText Markup Language) 881, 1237

html element 1239

HTTP (Hypertext Transfer Protocol) 881, 882, 886

HTTP (version 1.1) 887

HTTP header 888

HTTP method 887

HTTP transaction 892

Huge 607

Huge integer 607

HugeInt class 604

HugeInteger class 467

hybrid language 9, 443

hyperlink 928, 1242

HyperText Markup Language (HTML) 881, 1237

Hypertext Transfer Protocol (HTTP) 881, 886

hypotenuse 166

hypotenuse 237, 243

I

IBM 7, 13

IBM PC compatible systems 754

IBM Personal Computer 7, 754

IDE (integrated development environment) 12

Identification tab in the **Network** dialog 884

identifier 27, 74, 195

identifiers for variable names 192

identify the classes 140

IE (Internet Explorer) 1237, 1246

#if 1058

if single-selection structure 74, 76, 77, 132, 133

if structure 34, 38

if structure activity diagram 77

if/else double-selection structure 74, 77, 78, 132

if/else structure activity diagram 78

if/goto statement in Simple 987, 988, 991, 994

#ifdef preprocessor directive 1058

#ifndef preprocessor directive 1058, 424

ifstream 742, 812, 814, 816, 818, 831, 1070

ifstream constructor function 816

ignore 554, 748

ignore the return character 510

illegal instruction 1075

image attribute value (**type**) 898

image hyperlink 1247

image/gif MIME type 888

images in Web pages 1245

img element 1246, 1247

implementation 299

Implementation class definition 506

implementation details, hidden 406

implementation file 507

implementation inheritance 683

implementation of a class 420

implementation of a function 700

implementation of a member function changes 433

Implementing a proxy class 508

implicit compiler-defined conversion between built-in types 579

implicit conversion 92, 578, 1192, 1194, 1197, 1206

implicit conversions via conversion constructors 1194

implicit conversions with single-argument constructors 1192

implicit first argument 489

implicit handle 418

implicit pointer 485

implicit, user-defined conversions 578

implicitly **virtual** 674

imprecision of floating-point numbers 112

improper implicit conversion 1192

in-memory formatting 871

in-memory I/O 870

#include 1054

include a header file 420, 424

#include <cstring> 1072

#include 1054

#include "filename" 1054

#include <iomanip> 93

#include <iostream> 22

#include preprocessor directive 178, 181, 420, 1054

includes 1156, 1158

increment a control variable 102, 107, 108

increment a pointer 341

increment an iterator 1102

increment and decrement operators 100

increment operator 99, 581

increment the instruction counter 993

indefinite postponement 351

indefinite repetition 86

indentation 38, 39, 76, 77, 80, 104

independent software vender (ISV) 699

independent software vendor (ISV) 10, 420, 649, 699

index 254

indexed access 1117

indexed list 999

indirect base class 612

indirection 321

indirection operator (*****) 323, 325

indirectly reference a value 321
ineqality operator (**!=**) 556
inequality 1190
inequality operator keyword 1190
infinite loop 82, 92, 107, 163, 202
infinite recursion 565
infix arithmetic expression 982
infix notation 981
infix-to-postfix conversion
    algorithm 982, 991, 996
infix-to-postfix converter 999
information hiding 41, 195, 336,
    406, 415, 502
information tier 882, 937
inherit implementation 717
inherit interface 681, 717
inheritance 41, 143, 412, 417, 418,
    461, 469, 610, 613, 648, 649,
    650, 663, 699, 719, 996,
    1133
inheritance example 612
inheritance hierarchy 674, 682
Inheritance hierarchy for
    university **Communi-
    tyMember**s 613
inheritance relationships of
    I/O-related classes 742
inheritance relationships of the I/
    O-related classes 812
Inheritance to exploit
    commonality among classes
    374
inheriting interface versus
    inheriting implementation
    717
initial state 74, 129, 227
initial value for an attribute 227
initial value of a control variable
    102, 105
initialization phase 87
initialize a constant of a built-in
    data type 475
initialize a pointer 322
initialize pointer to **0** (null) 947
initialize to a consistent state 431
initialize to zero 84
initialize with an assignment
    statement 476
initializer 257, 430
initializer list 257, 258, 361
initializer of = **0** for pure
    virtual function 681
initializing a pointer declared
    const 335
Initializing a reference 213

initializing an array's elements to
    zeros and printing the array
    256
initializing class objects 426, 430
initializing multidimensional
    arrays 290
initializing the elements of an
    array with a declaration 257
inline function 209, 210, 416,
    551, 567, 580, 999, 1056,
    1057, 1128, 1131, 1132,
    1172
inline function definition 420
inline function to calculate the
    volume of a cube 210
inner block 195
inner_product 1104, 1166
innermost pair of parentheses 32
inorder traversal 969, 986
inOrderTraversal 976
inplace_merge 1154, 1155
input 990
input a line of text 747
Input and output stream iterators
    1098
input data 17
input device 5
input element 1262
input from string in memory 182
input iterator 1100, 1102, 1138,
    1139, 1144, 1147, 1154,
    1158, 1159, 1168
input line of text into an array 362
input of a string using **cin** with
    stream extraction contrasted
    with input using **cin.get**
    746
input/output (I/O) 171, 739
input/output library functions 181
input/output of objects 841
input/output operations 74
input/output stream header file
    <iostream> 22
input sequence 1098
input Simple command 987
input stream 744, 746
input stream iterator 1098
input-stream iterator 1098
input stream object (**cin**) 26, 28
input XHTML element 898
inputting character data using **cin**
    member-function **getline**
    747
inputting from **string**s in
    memory 870

INRIA (Institut National de
    Recherche en Informatique
    et Automatique) 20
insert 1112, 1122, 1126
insert member function of class
    string 866, 867
inserter 1154
insertion 505, 943
insertion at back of **vector** 1105
instant-access application 824
instant access processing 834
instantiate 41, 406
Institut National de Recherche en
    Informatique et
    Automatique (INRIA) 20
instruction 16, 17
instruction counter 993
instruction execution cycle 390
int 23, 28, 179
int & 211
int * 327
int * const 329
int operands promoted to
    float 92
integer 23, 27, 162
integer arithmetic 547
integer division 31, 92
integer promotion 92
integerPower 243
integers prefixed with **0** (octal)
    760
integers prefixed with **0x** or **0X**
    (hexadecimal) 760
IntegerSet class 545
integral size limit 181
integrated development
    environment (IDE) 12
integrity of an internal data
    structure 505
interaction 370, 371, 374, 451
interaction among objects 372
interactive attention signal 1076
interactive computing 29
interactive signal 1076
interchangeability of arrays and
    pointers 347
interest on deposit 168
interest rate 110, 165
interface 41, 663
Interface class definition 507
Interface class member-
    function definitions 507
interface inheritance 683
interface of a class 406, 412, 420
interface remains the same 445
internal character string 578

internal linkage 1073
internal representation of a
    string 569
internal spacing 758
internal stream manipulator
    391, 755, 758
International Organization for
    Standardization (ISO) 3, 9,
    504
Internet 18, 21
Internet Explorer (IE) 1237, 1246
Internet Protocol (IP) 19
Internet Service Provider (ISP)
    1262
Internet STL resources 1175
interpreter program 8
interrupt 1075
interrupt handler 362
Intranet 10, 11, 14, 18, 19
intToFloat 237
invalid access to storage 1076
invalid_argument 800
invalid_argument exception
    1112
invoke a function 171, 175
invoking a non-**const** member
    function on a **const** object
    470
<iomanip.h> header file 93,
    181
<iomanip> header file 181, 740,
    750, 1055
ios::app 814
ios::ate 814
ios::beg 819
ios::binary 814, 829
ios class 1205
ios::cur 819
ios::end 819
ios::in 814, 818, 835
ios::out 814, 835
ios::trunc 814
ios_base base class 766
<iostream> header file 22, 181,
    740, 741, 1055, 1189
iostream class 742, 1205, 1206
<iostream.h> header file 181
<iostream> header file 812
<iostream.h> header file 116
IP 19
IP address 889
"is a" 1201, 1203
"is a" relationship (inheritance)
    611, 648
is-a relationship 679
isalnum 1020, 1021

isalpha 1020, 1021
iscntrl 1021, 1024
isdigit 1020, 1021, 1023
isEmpty predicate function 427
isFull predicate function 427
isgraph function 1021, 1024
islower function 331, 1020,
    1023
ISP (Internet Service Provider)
    1262
isprint function 1021, 1024
ispunct function 1021, 1024
isspace function 1021, 1024
istream class 741, 742, 818,
    824, 831, 834, 841, 871,
    1205, 1206
istream member function
    ignore 554
istream_iterator 1098,
    1099
istringstream class 870,
    872, 873
isupper function 1020, 1023
ISV (independent software
    vender) 699
isxdigit function 1020, 1021
iter_swap 1104, 1150
iteration 83, 206
iterative solution 199, 206
<iterator> 1154, 1156
<iterator> header file 182
iterator 505, 682, 719, 869, 870
iterator 54, 1092, 1095, 1096,
    1097, 1098, 1101, 1122
iterator-category hierarchy 1100
iterator class 485, 682
iterator object 505
iterator operation 1102
iterator pointing to first element
    past the end of container
    1098
iterator to the next element of a
    container 1098
iterator **typedef** 1101

J

Jacobson, Ivar 43
Jacopini, G. 73, 132
Japanese 503
Java 11, 14
*Java How to Program: Fifth
    Edition* 11
job 6
Joint Photographic Experts Group
    (JPEG) 1245

justified field 759

K

Keio University 20
Kemeny, John 11
Kernighan and Ritchie C 9
key 877, 1119
key/value pair 1124, 1126
keyboard 5, 6, 17, 28, 116, 119,
    388, 739, 742, 811, 1066
keyboard input 91
keyword 74, 75
keyword **template** 720
KIS ("keep it simple") 20
Knight's Tour 313
Knight's Tour: brute-force
    approaches 315
Knight's Tour: closed-tour test
    316
"knows a" relationship 648
Koenig, Andrew 780
Kurtz, Thomas 11

L

L floating-point suffix 1075
l floating-point suffix 1075
L integer suffix 1075
l integer suffix 1075
label 195
label specified in a **goto**
    statement 1079
labels in a **switch** structure 195
Laboratory for Computer Science
    18
language interoperability 13
large object 213
large programs 170
largest element of a collection 601
last-in first-out (LIFO) data
    structure 502, 723, 728, 960,
    1094, 1128
last-in-first-out order 723, 728
late binding 695
leading **0** 761
leading **0x** and leading **0X** 761
leaf node 984
Lee, Meng 1092
left brace (**{**) 23, 26
left child 969
left justification 77, 113, 352, 757,
    758

left justification and right justification with stream-manipulators **left** and **right** 757

left node 976

left-shift assignment operator 1016

left-shift operator (**<<**) 741, 1008, 1014, 1015, 1048, 547

left side of an assignment 128, 254, 445, 564

left stream manipulator 113, 755, 757

left subtree 969, 975, 976, 977, 984

left-to-right pass of an expression 982

left to right evaluation 32, 33

left value 128

legacy C code 1056

legacy code 4, 330, 1060, 1066, 1078

length member function of class **string** 852

length of a string 267, 361, 857

length of a substring 581

length_error 800

length_error exception 859, 1112

less_equal<T> 1172

less than 35

less than or equal to 35

less< double > 1122

less< int > 1119, 1121, 1124

less<T> 1172

less-than operator (**<**) 1097

let statement in Simple 987, 991, 999

letter 809

level of indentation 78

level-order traversal of a binary tree 977, 985

lexicographical permutator 1167

lexicographical_compare 1136, 1138

<li> (list item) tag 1251

libraries 16

licensing class 450

lifeline 300, 301

LIFO 502, 723, 728, 960, 1094, 1128

Light class header file 456, 520

Light class implementation file 520

limerick 398

<limits> header file 182

<limits.h> header file 181

line 33

line number 987, 989, 990, 1060

line of communication with a file 814, 816

line of text 747

__LINE__ predefined symbolic constant 1060

#line preprocessor directive 1059

line with an arrowhead 301

linear data structure 946, 969

linear search of an array 283, 284, 285

link 15, 16, 944, 969

link to a class's object code 420

linkage 192, 1189

linkage specification 1084

linked data structure 407

linked list 505, 943, 945, 946, 947, 952, 959

linked list class template 999

linker 16, 1072

linker error 1186

linker link 17

linking 16, 1073

links 145

links.html 1242

links2.html 1251

Linux 884

<list> 1096

<list> header file 182

list 944, 1128

list 1092, 1097, 1101, 1105

List class template 947, 961, 964, 965

List class-template definition 948

list of nouns in problem statement 140

list processing 947

list searching performance 999

list sequence container 1113

list.html 1252

List< STACKTYPE > 964

ListNode class-template definition 947

literal 28

live-code approach 3, 1094

load 15

loader 16

loading 17

local area network (LAN) 7

local automatic object 437

local variable 85, 173, 193, 194, 196, 334, 1083

<locale> header file 182

localhost 884, 889

localtime function 888, 890

localtime.cgi 890, 892

localtime.cpp 889

Location header 905

location in memory 30

log 173

log10 173

$\log_2 n$ levels in a binary search tree with n elements 977

logarithm 173

logic error 36, 85

logic_error 800

logical AND (**&&**) 124, 166, 1011, 1190

logical decision 4

logical NOT (**!**) 124, 126, 166, 1190

logical operator 124

logical operator keyword 1190

logical OR (**||**) 124, 166, 1013, 1190

logical unit 5

logical_and 1172

logical_not 1172

logical_or 1172

login.cgi 921

login.cpp 922

Logo language 312

logout.cpp 935

long 119, 179, 1075

long double 180, 1075

long int 119, 180, 201

loop 81, 83, 88

loop-continuation condition 103, 105, 108, 120, 121

loop-continuation condition fails 206

loop-continuation test 167

loop counter 102

loop iteration 83

loop nested within a loop 95

looping structure 74, 81

loss of data 766

Lovelace, Lady Ada 13

lower_bound 1119, 1122, 1160

lowercase letter 1020, 1023

lowercase letters 27, 68, 75, 181, 331

"lowest type" 180

low-level I/O capabilitY 739

lvalue ("left value") 128, 213, 254, 322, 323, 445, 564, 568, 580, 1102, 1119

*lvalue*s as *rvalue*s 128

M

m-by-n array 289
machine-dependent 7, 323, 342, 503
machine language 7, 8, 193, 991
machine-language code 113, 960
machine-language programming 387
Macintosh 754, 816
macro 180, 720, 1067, 1068
macro argument 1056
macro definition 1059
macro expansion 1057
macros defined in header **<cst-darg>** 1067
magic number 261
magnetic disk 809
magnitude 758
magnitude right-justified 755
mail-order house 165
mailto: URL 1244
main 23, 24, 26, 30, 174, 1073
main.html 1238
maintenance of software 15
make utility 1073
"make your point" 188
make_heap 1162
makefile 1073
malloc function 1078
mandatory function prototype 178
mangled function name 220
Manhattan 168
Manipulating a linked list 952
manipulating individual characters 1020
manipulator 113, 812
"manufacturing" section of the computer 5
map 1094, 1096, 1101, 1119, 1124, 1126
<map> header file 182, 1096, 1126
mapped value 1119
markup 886
markup language 52, 55, 1237
mask 1010
"masked off" 1010
Massachusetts Institute of Technology (MIT) 20
math library 172, 181
math library function 111, 171, 172, 236
math library function **sqrt** 179
<math.h> header file 181
mathematical algorithm 1144

mathematical algorithms of the Standard Library 1144
mathematical calculation 171
mathematical class 547
mathematical computation 13
max function 1165
max_element function 1144, 1147
max_size function 1095
maxheap 1162
maximum 177
maximum length of a string 861
maxlength attribute 1262
mean 32, 278
meaningful name 176
mechanics of multiple inheritance 1205
median 278, 282
member 407
member access operator (**.**) 407
member-access specifier 411, 486
member access specifier **public** 411
member function 41, 406, 411, 412, 416
member function call 547
member function calls for **const** objects 470
member function calls often concise 417
member function defined in a class definition 416
member function inlined 416
member functions normally **public** 412
member functions that take no arguments 417
member-initialization syntax 509, 529
member initializer 474, 475, 476, 566, 578
member initializer for a **const** data member 478
member-initializer list 476, 479, 482, 512, 1201
member-initializer syntax 475
Member initializer used to initialize a constant of a built-in data type 475
member-object initializer 483
Member-object initializers 483
member object's default constructor 484, 485
member selection operator (**.**) 407, 418, 491, 674, 799
members of a structure 407

memberwise assignment 448, 548
memberwise copy 565
memchr 1040
memchr function 1037, 1040
memcmp function 1037, 1039
memcpy 1038
memcpy function 1037
memmove function 1037, 1038
<memory> header file 182
memory 5, 16, 17, 27, 30, 193, 794, 796, 798
memory access violation 54
memory-access violation 1093
memory address 320, 743
memory consumption 696
memory functions of the string handling library 1037
memory leak 54, 798, 800, 869, 945, 1093
memory location 30, 84
memory not allocated 1078
memory unit 5
<memory> 798
memory-handling function **memchr** 1040
memory-handling function **memcmp** 1039
memory-handling function **memcpy** 1038
memory-handling function **memmove** 1038
memory-handling function **memset** 1041
memset function 1037, 1040
menu driven system 358
merge 1113, 1116, 1152, 1154
merge symbol 82
merge two ordered list objects 981
merging of decision paths 229
message 41, 296, 301, 303, 370, 547
message number 372
message sent to an object 411
method 41, 406, 411
method = "get" 1262
method = "post" 1262
method attribute 1261
method attribute (**form**) 897
metric conversion program 402
MFC 14
microprocessor chip technology 18
Microsoft MFC (Microsoft Foundation Classes) 14
Microsoft Visual C++ 15, 1073, 1176, 1191

Microsoft Visual C++ home page 1234
Microsoft Windows 116
Microsoft's Windows-based systems 7
middle tier 883, 938
middle value 282
mileage obtained by automobiles 157
military format 408
MIME (Multipurpose Internet Mail Extensions) 888
MIME type 888
MIME type **image/gif** 888
MIME type **text/html** 888
MIME type **text/plain** 888
min 1165
min_element 1144, 1147
minus 1172
minus sign (-) indicating private visibility 451
mismatch 1104, 1136, 1138
mission critical 784
MIT (Massachusetts Institute of Technology) 20
MIT's Project Mac 18
mode 278, 282
model 141, 390
model an interaction 374
model of a simulation 138
modeling 41
modifiability 415
modifications to the Simple compiler 998
Modified list of verb phrases for classes in the system 371
modify a constant pointer 334
modify address stored in pointer variable 334
modularize a program 173
module in C++ 170
modulus 31, 32
modulus operator (%) 31, 67, 162, 183, 188
modulus<T> 1172
monetary calculation 112
monetary format 182
most derived class 1210
mouse 5
multidimensional array 290
multimap associative container 1094, 1096, 1101, 1119, 1124, 1126
multiple 243

multiple inheritance 41, 610, 612, 741, 1201, 1202, 1203, 1204, 1205
multiple inheritance demonstration 1201
multiple of another number 32
multiple-selection structure 74, 113
multiple source file 420
multiple-source-file program 1071, 1072
multiple-statement body 38
multiple-subscripted array 289, 292
multiplication 5, 31, 32
multiplicative operators *, /, % 93
multiplicity 142, 143
multiplicity values 143
multiplies<T> 1172
multiprocessor 6
multiprogramming 6
Multipurpose Internet Mail Extensions (MIME) 888
Multipurpose sorting program using function pointers 355
multiset 1094, 1096, 1101, 1119, 1122, 1124
multitasking 13
multi-tier application 882, 938
multiuser environment 965
Musser, David 1092
mutable data member 192, 1197, 1198
mutable demonstration 1198
mutating-sequence algorithm 1104
My Network Places 884

N

name attribute 1262
name decoration 219
name function of class **type_info** 714
name handle 418, 500
name mangling 219
Name mangling to enable type-safe linkage 221
name of a control variable 102
name of a function 171
name of a source file 1060
name of a variable 30, 192
name of an array 254, 325
name of an attribute 1239
name of operation 297
name/value pair 913

named constant 259
namespace keyword 1187, 1189
namespace member 1187
namespace qualifier 1189
namespaces 1187
natural language of a computer 7
natural logarithm 173
nav.html 1247
NCSA (the National Center for Supercomputing Applications) 886
NDEBUG 1060
near container 1094
negate<T> 1172
nested block 195
nested building block 133
nested control structure 94, 131, 1080
Nested control structures: Examination-results problem 96
nested element 1239
nested **for** structure 292
nested function call 784
nested **if/else** structure 79, 80
nested list 1251
nested **namespace** 1189
nested parentheses 32, 34
nesting 77, 78, 104, 133
nesting rule 131
.NET platform 12
Netscape 1237
Network and **Dialup Connections** explorer 884
network connection 739
Network dialog 884
Network Identification 884
network message arrival 781
Network Neighborhood 884
network node 965
network of networks 19
new 495, 509, 566, 945, 1078, 1112
<new> 793, 795
new block of memory 1079
new calls the constructor 496
new fails 784, 792
new failure handler 795, 796
<new.h> 795
new returning **0** on failure 793, 796
new stream manipulator 754
new throwing **bad_alloc** on failure 794, 795
new_handler 784

newline (`'\n'`) 23, 24, 29, 38,
    360, 744, 1024
newline character 119
nickname 323, 325
noboolalpha stream
    manipulator 763
node 945
non-member function to overload
    an operator 551
non-member, **friend** function
    554, 556
non-member, non-**friend**
    function 549
non-**static** member function
    568
non-**const** member function 474
non-**const** member function
    called on a **const** object
    473
non-**const** member function on a
    non-**const** object 473
nonconstant pointer to constant
    data 330, 332, 333
nonconstant pointer to
    nonconstant data 330
non-contiguous memory layout of
    a deque 1117
nondestructive read 30
nonfatal error 17, 178, 784
Non-**friend**/non-member
    functions cannot access
    private members 488
nonlinear, two-dimensional data
    structure 969
nonmodifiable function code 418
nonmutating sequence algorithm
    1104
nonparameterized stream
    manipulator 93
nonrecoverable failure 766
nonstandard cast 1185
non-**static** member function
    489, 500
non-type parameter 730
non-type template size parameter
    730
nonzero treated as **true** 127
noshowbase stream
    manipulator 755, 761
noshowpoint stream
    manipulator 756
noshowpos stream manipulator
    391, 756, 758
noskipws stream manipulator
    755
not equal 35

not operator keyword 1190
not_eq operator keyword 1190
not_equal_to<T> 1172
note 74
Notepad text editor 1237
nothrow 796
nothrow_t 796
noun 14, 140, 141, 225
nouns in a system specification 41
nouns in problem statement 168
nouns in the problem statement
    225, 374
nouppercase stream
    manipulator 756, 763
nth_element 1167
n-tier application 882, 938
NULL 321, 1029, 1031, 1032
null (**0**) 363, 944
null character (`'\0'`) 267, 332,
    348, 360, 361, 363, 369, 749,
    944, 983
null pointer (**0**) 815, 944, 985,
    1078
null statement 81
null string 825
null-terminated string 268, 349,
    743, 867
number of arguments 175
number of elements in an array
    339
<numeric> 1104, 1147
numerical algorithm 1104, 1172
numerical data type limit 182

O

object 4, 9, 14, 40, 41, 133, 406
object "speak" 405
object "think" 405
object-based programming (OBP)
    469
object code 15, 16, 420
Object Constraint Language
    (OCL) 145
object creation 303
object diagram 145, 300
object diagram of empty building
    145
object file 699
object handle 419, 500
object interact 405
object leaves scope 435
Object Management Group
    (OMG) 43
object module 420
object of a derived class 664, 668

object of a derived class is
    instantiated 642
object orientation 40
object-orientation 405
object oriented 41
object oriented analysis and design
    (OOAD) 42, 43
object-oriented analysis and
    design (OOAD) process 42
object-oriented analysis phase 138
object-oriented design (OOD) 40,
    133, 138, 168, 370, 486
object-oriented language 14
object-oriented programming
    (OOP) 4, 5, 9, 21, 41, 43,
    133, 173, 370, 412, 469, 610,
    663, 673
"object speak" 40, 63
"object think" 40
object's *vtable* pointer 698
object-oriented design (OOD)
    xxxvii, 296, 405, 451
objects contain only data 418
ObjectSpace STL Tool Kit
    example 1175, 1234
oct stream manipulator 750, 755,
    760
octal (base 8) number system 166,
    760, 1029
octal (base-8) number system 750,
    755
octal number 743, 760, 1020, 1030
odd integer 164
odd number 167
off-by-one error 86, 105, 106, 255
offset 698, 825
offset from the beginning of a file
    819
offset to a pointer 344
ofstream 742, 812, 814, 815,
    816, 818, 828, 829, 832,
    1070
"old-style" header files 181
OMG (Object Management
    Group) 43
one-pass algorithm 1100
one-to-many mapping 1094
one-to-many relationship 1124
one-to-one mapping 1094, 1126
one-to-one relationship 142
one-to-two relationship 142, 143
one's complement 1008, 1014
online C++ courses for credit 1232
OOAD (object oriented analysis
    and design) 42, 43

OOD (object-oriented design) 296, 405, 451

OOP (object oriented programming) 4, 5, 9, 21, 41, 43, 133, 173, 370, 412, 469, 610, 663, 673

open a file for input 814

open a file for output 814

open a nonexistent file 815

open source 884

opened 811

operand 29, 31, 78, 387, 990

operating system 6, 7, 9, 362, 815

operation 40, 142, 296, 300, 374

operation code 387, 990

operation implemented as function 225

operations allowed on data 503

operator 98

operator- 1097

operator + 1166

operator += 854

operator < 1168

operator << 763

operator associativity 127

operator function 550

operator keyword 1184, 1190, 1191

operator keyword 548

operator keywords demonstration 1191

operator overloading 30, 222, 410, 547, 739, 1008

operator precedence 32, 102, 127, 1016

operator precedence chart 39, 1214

operator void* 768, 815, 818

operator! member function 555, 768, 815

operator!= member function 567, 1095

operator() member function 601, 1172, 1174, 1175

operator+ member function 548

operator++ member function 581, 582, 587

operator++(int) member function 582

operator< 580, 1095

operator<< 554, 564, 577, 608

operator<= 1095

operator= member function 566, 1095

operator== member function 567, 580, 1095, 1138

operator> member function 1095

operator>= member function 580, 1095

operator>> member function 553, 554, 564, 577

operator[]
  const version 567

operators
  arithmetic 99
  decrement 100
  increment 100

operators **.*** and **->*** 1199

operators that can be overloaded 549

operators that must be non-members 554

opinion poll 278

optical disk 809

optimization 1075

optimizations on constants 470

optimized code 997

optimizing compiler 113, 194, 470

optimizing the simple compiler 996

or operator keyword 1190

or_eq operator keyword 1191

order in which actions should execute 72, 83

order in which constructors and destructors are called 438, 453

order in which destructors are called 436

order in which operators are applied to their operands 204

order of evaluation 205

order of evaluation of operators 32, 66

ordered list 1251, 1252

org (top level domain) 884

original format setting 765

ostream class 741, 742, 749, 819, 824, 829, 832, 841

ostream_iterator 1098, 1099

ostringstream class 870, 871

other character sets 851

out-of-range array subscript 781

out-of-range element 564, 580

out of scope 198

out_of_bounds exception 1112

out_of_range exception 800, 854, 1112, 1169

outCredit 829

outer block 195

outer **for** structure 292

output a floating-point value 756

output buffering 768

output data 17

output data items of built-in type 742

output device 5

output format of floating-point number 761

output iterator 1100, 1102, 1135, 1144, 1156, 1159, 1166, 1167

output of **char *** variables 743

output of character 743

output of floating-point value 743

output of integer 743

output of standard data type 743

output of uppercase letter 743

output sequence 1098

output stream 1111

output stream iterator 1098

output-stream iterator 1098

output to string in memory 182

output unit 5

outputting to **string**s in memory 870

oval 67

overflow 781, 1076

overflow error 503

overflow_error 800

overhead of a function call 567, 1057

overhead of call-by-value 410

overhead of **virtual** function 1133

overload a **const** member function with a non-**const** version 470

overload a member function 418

overload an operator as a non-member, non-**friend** function 551

overload equality operator 410

overload the **<<** operator 410

overload the addition operator (**+**) 548

overload unary operator **!** 555

overloaded **+=** concatenation operator 579

overloaded **<<** operator 551, 580

overloaded **[]** operator 564

overloaded addition-assignment
operator (+=) 586
overloaded assignment (=)
operator 564, 566, 577, 578
overloaded binary operator 549
overloaded cast-operator function
568
overloaded concatenation operator
579
overloaded constructor 430
overloaded equality operator (==)
564, 567, 580
overloaded function 219, 720, 722
overloaded function definition 219
overloaded function-call operator
() 581
overloaded increment operator
582
overloaded inequality operator
563, 567
overloaded less-than operator 580
overloaded negation operator 580
overloaded operator += 586
overloaded **operator[]**
member function 567
overloaded output operator 842
overloaded postincrement
operator 586
overloaded preincrement operator
586
overloaded stream-insertion and
stream-extraction operator
552
overloaded stream-insertion
operator 841, 1203
overloaded string-concatenation
operator 579
overloaded subscript operator 564,
567, 580, 601
overloaded unary operator 549
overloading 30, 219, 412, 719
overloading + 550
overloading += 550
overloading << and >> 222
overloading an assignment
operator 550
overloading binary operator +=
555
overloading binary operators 555
overloading function call operator
() 581
overloading function-call operator
() 601
overloading operators 222
overloading postincrement
operator 587

overloading postincrementing
operator 582
overloading predecrement and
postdecrement operators 582
overloading preincrement and
postincrement operators 582
overloading resolution 723
overloading stream-insertion and
stream-extraction operators
552, 563, 564, 577, 585, 586
overloading template functions
723
overloading the stream-insertion
operator << 841
oxymoron 259

P

π 166
p (paragraph) element 1240
packaging code as a function 173
packet 18, 965
packet switching 18
pad with specified character 743
padding 1019
padding character 752, 755, 757,
759
padding in a structure 1019
page layout software 360
Paint Shop Pro 1245
pair 1122, 1138
pair of braces {} 38
pair of iterators 1103
palindrome 981
palindrome function 1182
paper 5
parallelogram 611
parameter 173, 175, 193, 916
parameter declaration 175
parameter-list 175
parameter names in function
prototypes for
documentation 179
parameterized stream manipulator
93, 113, 740, 750, 754, 818
parameterized type 735
parameters in functions 176
parent node 969, 984
parentheses operator (()) 32, 93
parentheses to force order of
evaluation 39
partial_sort 1168
partial_sort_copy 1168
partial_sum 1104, 1166
partition 1104, 1167
partitioning element 1167

partitioning step 394
Pascal 13, 1232
Pascal, Blaise 13
pass a structure 1004
pass a structure call-by-reference
1004
pass-by-reference 211, 272, 273,
320, 326, 327, 329, 336
pass-by-reference with a pointer
argument used to cube a
variable's value 327
pass-by-reference with pointers
213, 325
pass-by-reference with references
325
pass-by-value 211, 272, 325, 326,
327, 328, 336
pass-by-value used to cube a
variable's value 326
pass large-size arguments as
const references 410
pass size of an array 272, 338
passing a filename to a program
1070
passing an array element 273
passing an entire array 273
passing an object by value 450
Passing arguments by value and
by reference 212
passing arrays and individual array
elements to functions 273
passing arrays to functions 272,
282
passing large objects 213
passing options to a program 350,
1070
password attribute value
(**type**) 898
password box 1263
password-protected database 917
"past the end" iterator 1147
path attribute in cookies 913
path to a resource 886
pattern of **1**s and **0**s 810
payroll file 811
payroll program 8
payroll system 810
peek member function 748
percent sign (**%**) (modulus
operator) 31
perfect number 244
performance 10
performance of binary tree sorting
and searching 999
Performance Tips 10
permutation 1167

Person class header file 454, 538
Person class implementation file 539
personal computer 4
personal computing 7
Peter Minuit problem 113, 168
phase 87
PhoneNumber class 608
PhotoShop Elements 1245
PI 1055, 1056
Pi 67
picture.html 1245
pieceworker 166
pig Latin 398
pipe 890
pipe (|) 1067
piping 1067
pixel 1246
Plauger, P.J. 10
playing card 350
plus sign 758
plus sign (**+**) indicating public visibility 451
plus<T> 1172
Point class implementation file 686
Point class represents an *x-y* coordinate pair 616, 665
Point class test program 617
point-of-sale system 824
Point/Circle/Cylinder hierarchy test program 640
Point2 class represents an *x-y* coordinate pair as **protected** data 625
Point3 class uses member functions to manipulate its **private** data 632, 643
pointer 320, 341
pointer 1097
pointer arithmetic 331, 341, 342, 343, 345, 1108
pointer arithmetic is machine dependent 342
pointer arithmetic on a character array 342
pointer assignment 343
pointer-based strings 360
pointer comparison 344
pointer dereferencing operator (*****) 408
pointer exercise 393
pointer expression 341, 344
pointer handle 418
pointer link 945
pointer manipulation 695, 943

pointer notation 345
pointer operators **&** and ***** 323
pointer subtraction 341
pointer to a function 355, 357, 1073
pointer to a structure 334
pointer to an object 416
pointer-to-class-member operators 1184
pointer to **void** (**void ***) 343
pointer values as hexadecimal integers 323
pointer variable 798
pointer/offset notation 344
pointer/subscript notation 345
pointers and array subscripting 344, 345
pointers and arrays 344
pointers declared **const** 334
pointers to dynamically allocated storage 491, 567
PointTest class demonstrates class **Point** functionality 617
poker playing program 385
polymorphic exception processing 793
polymorphic programming 680, 682, 698
polymorphic screen manager 679
polymorphically invoking functions in a derived class 1206
polymorphism 119, 469, 650, 663, 676, 679, 996, 1133
polymorphism and references 696
polymorphism as an alternative to **switch** logic 717
polynomial 35
Polynomial class 608
pop 728, 960, 1128, 1130, 1132, 1133
pop_back 1105, 1117, 1128, 1132
pop_front 1113, 1117, 1119, 1130
pop_heap 1165
portability 20
Portability Tips 10, 20
portable 9
portable code 10
portable language 20
portal.cgi 906
portal.cpp 907
position number 253
positional value 162

positioning relative to the current position in a stream 731
post request type 882, 901, 1262
post.cpp 901
postdecrement 101, 581
postdecrement operator 99
postfix evaluation algorithm 991, 996
postfix evaluator 995, 999
postfix expression 983, 996
postfix expression evaluation algorithm 982
postfix notation 981
postincrement 100, 101, 581, 586
postincrement an iterator 1102
postincrement operator 99
postorder traversal 969, 984, 985
postOrderTraversal 977
pow function 34, 110, 113, 173
power 173
power 151
precedence 32, 34, 39, 101, 107, 126, 204, 344
precedence chart 39
precedence not changed by overloading 549
precedence of the conditional operator 78
precision 93, 743, 749, 751
precision 751
precision member function 761
precision of floating-point values 751
precision setting 751
precompiled object file 507
predecrement 101, 581
predecrement operator 99
predefined **namespace**s 1189
predefined symbolic constant 1060
predicate function 427, 952, 1116, 1138, 1141, 1144, 1147, 1150, 1154, 1158, 1159, 1162, 1167
preincrement 101, 581, 586
preincrement operator 99
preincrementing and postincrementing 100
preorder traversal 969
preOrderTraversal 977
"pre-packaged" classes 171
prepackaged data structure 943
"pre-packaged" functions 170
preprocess 15
preprocessor 15, 16, 178, 1054

preprocessor directive **#define** 720

preprocessor directives 15, 22, 26, 424

presentation logic 883

presentation of a document 1237

prev_permutation 1167

prevent class objects from being copied 567

prevent header files from being included more than once 424

prevent memory leak 800

prevent one class object from being assigned to another 567

primary memory 5, 17

prime 244

prime factorization 1182

prime number 1170

primitive data type promotion 92

principal 110, 168

principle of least privilege 193, 276, 327, 330, 338, 349, 420, 469, 470, 818, 1072, 1073, 1102

print a line of text 21

print a linked list backwards 947

print a list backwards 984

print Simple command 987, 990

print spooling 965

printArray function template 720

printer 17, 739, 965

printing a binary tree in a two-dimensional tree format 977

Printing a string one character at a time using a nonconstant pointer to constant data 332

printing a tree 986

printing an integer with internal spacing and plus sign 758

printing an unsigned integer in bits 1009

printing character other than a space, digit or letter 1024

printing character other than space 1021

printing character, including space 1021

printing dates 400

Printing on multiple lines with a single statement using **cout** 25

Printing on one line with separate statements using **cout** 25

Printing **string** characteristics 859

printing the address stored in a **char** * variable 743

Printing the value of a **union** in both member data types 1082

priority_queue adapter class 1094, 1095, 1096, 1101, 1128, 1132, 1133

private 411, 412, 424, 426

private base class 648

Private base-class data cannot be accessed from derived class 623

private data member 439, 446

private function 297

private inheritance 610, 613, 648, 961

private inheritance as an alternative to composition 648

private libraries 16

private member function 412, 426

private members of a base class 613

private members of a class are not accessible outside the class 425

private static data member 498

probability 183

procedural programming language 41, 406

procedure 72

processing phase 87

processing unit 5

product of odd integers 165

productivity 18

program 5

program control 72

program development environment 15

program-development tool 76, 98

program in the general 663, 717

program in the specific 663

program termination 437, 1073

programmer 5

programmer-defined function 174, 177, 192

programmer-defined function **square** 174

programmer-defined header file 181, 423

Programmer-defined **maximum** function 177

programmer-defined termination function 790

programmer-defined type 406

programming environment 171

programming language 7

project 1073

Project Mac 18

promotion 92

promotion hierarchy for built-in data types 180

promotion rule 179

prompt 28, 91, 1067

prompting message 768

proprietary class 649

protected 412, 418, 424, 614, 653

protected base class 648

Protected base-class data can be accessed from derived class 629

protected inheritance 610, 613, 648

protection mechanism 450

prototype 178

proxy class 420, 506, 508

pseudo-random number 186

pseudocode 42, 72, 76, 77, 94

pseudocode algorithm 89

public 411, 424, 453

public base class 648

public behavior 412

public data 412

public function 297

public inheritance 610, 613

public interface 420, 425

public member function 412, 439

public member of a derived class 613

public static class member 497

public static member function 498

punctuation mark 368

pure procedure 418

pure **virtual** function 681, 695, 700

purpose of the program 22

push 727, 728, 960, 1128, 1130, 1131, 1132

push memory location on the stack 991

push_back 1105, 1108, 1116, 1119, 1128, 1130, 1132, 1154

push_front 1113, 1116

push_heap 1165

put file position pointer 824, 829

put member function 743, 744, 745

put pointer 819

putback member function 748

Pythagorean triple 166

Q

Quadralay Corporation's Web site 1232

qualityPoints 245

query function 439

query string 882, 896

QUERY_STRING environment variable 895, 901

querystring.cpp 896

queue 505, 943, 944, 946, 959, 965

queue 1094, 1096, 1101, 1128, 1130, 1131, 1132

queue adapter class template 1131

queue class 505

Queue class-template definition 966

queue grows infinitely 983

<queue> header file 182, 1096, 1131, 1132

queue in a computer network 965

queue object 983

Queue-processing program 967

quicksort 394

quotation mark 23

R

RAD (rapid application development) 12, 450

radian 172

radio 1263

radio attribute value (**type**) 898

radius of a circle 163

raise to a power 151, 173

rand function 182, 183, 310

RAND_MAX symbolic constant 182, 188

random-access file 809, 824, 825, 831, 834

random-access iterator 1100, 1101, 1106, 1109, 1117, 1119, 1138, 1144, 1150, 1156, 1162, 1165, 1167, 1168

random-access iterator operations 1102

random integers in range 1 to 6 183

random interval 983

random number 186, 263

random-number generation 146, 263

random-number generator 516

random_shuffle 1104, 1144

random-access file 832

randomizing 186

Randomizing the die-rolling program 186

range 1147

range checking 426, 556, 854, 1105

rapid application development (RAD) 12, 450

Rational 466

Rational Software Corporation 43, 138

Rational Unified Process ™ 138

RationalNumber class 607

raw array 504

raw data 823

raw data processing 809

rbegin 1096, 1109

rbegin member function of class **string** 870

RDBMS (relational database management system) 882

read 824, 831, 834

read data sequentially from a file 816

read member function 748

readability 22, 76, 95, 176, 1239

readcookie.cpp 914

Reading a random-access file sequentially 832

Reading and printing a sequential file 817

real number 89

realloc 1078

reassign a reference 214

receiving object 296

"receiving" section of the computer 5

reclaim the dynamic storage 566

record 810, 812, 834, 848

record format 825

record key 811, 848

recover from errors 766

Rectangle 467

rectangle symbol 301

recursion 198, 206, 247

recursion examples and exercises 206

recursion step 199, 204

recursive binary search 207, 283, 318

recursive binary tree insert 207

recursive call 199, 204

recursive Eight Queens 207, 318

recursive evaluation 200

recursive factorial function 207

recursive Fibonacci function 207

recursive function 198, 947

recursive function call 960

recursive greatest common divisor 207

recursive inorder traversal of a binary tree 207

recursive linear search 207, 284, 318

recursive linked list delete 207

recursive linked list insert 207

recursive maze traversal 207

recursive multiply two integers 207

recursive postorder traversal of a binary tree 207

recursive preorder traversal of a binary tree 207

recursive quicksort 207

recursive selection sort 207, 317

recursive solution 206

recursive step 394

recursive sum of two integers 207

recursive Towers of Hanoi 207

recursive utility function 976

recursively calculate minimum value in an array 207

recursively check if a string is a palindrome 207

recursively determine whether a string is a palindrome 317

recursively print a linked list backwards 207

recursively print a list backwards 984

recursively print a string backwards 207, 318

recursively print an array 207, 318

recursively print an array backwards 207

recursively print backwards a
    string input at the keyboard
    207
recursively printing keyboard
    inputs in reverse 207
recursively raising an integer to an
    integer power 207
recursively search a linked list 207
recursively search a list 984
recursively sum the elements of an
    array 207
redirect input symbol < 1066
redirect input/output on Unix and
    DOS systems 1066
redirect inputs to come from a file
    1066
redirect output of one program to
    input of another program
    1067
redirect output symbol > 1067
redirect output to a file 1066
redirecting input on a DOS system
    1066
reducing program development
    time 171
redundant parentheses 34, 124
reentrant code 418
reference 320, 739, 1097
reference argument 325
reference handle 457
reference must be initialized when
    it is declared 457
reference parameter 211, 213
reference to a constant 213
reference to a **private** data
    member 445
reference to an automatic variable
    214
reference to an **int** 211
reference to an object 416
reference to constant data 334
references and polymorphism 695
references must be initialized 214
references vs. pointers 451
referencing array elements 345
referencing array elements with
    the array name and with
    pointers 345
refinement process 87
Refresh header 905
register 192, 193, 194
register a function with **atexit**
    1073
reinterpret_cast
    demonstration 1186

reinterpret_cast operator
    825, 828, 832, 1185, 1186
reinventing the wheel 10, 171
relational database management
    system (RDBMS) 882
relational operator 34, 35, 36
relational operators >, <, >=, and
    <= 105, 124
reliable software 1079
rem statement in Simple 987, 990
remainder after integer division 31
remark 995
removal 943
remove 1104, 1113, 1117, 1138,
    1139
remove_copy 1104, 1138, 1139
remove_copy_if 1104, 1138,
    1139, 1141
remove_if 1104, 1138, 1139
rend 1096, 1109
rend member function of class
    string 870
repeatability of function **rand**
    186
repeating code 173
repetition 75, 132, 133
repetition structure 73, 81, 88, 988
    do/while 120, 121, 133
    for 104, 105, 106, 108, 133
    while 81, 82, 103, 120, 133
repetition terminates 81, 82
replace 1104, 1141, 1142
replace == operator with = 127
replace member function of
    class **string** 865
replace_copy 1104, 1141,
    1142, 1144
replace_copy_if 1104,
    1141, 1142, 1144
replace_if 1104, 1141, 1142
replacement node 984, 985
replacement text 1056, 1059
replacement text for a macro or
    symbolic constant 1057
representation of data members
    445
representing a class in the UML
    142
request 913
request method 882
requirement 20, 42, 138
reserved keyword 75
reset 1168
reset attribute value (**type**)
    898
resource leak 783, 793

restore a stream's state to "good"
    766
result of an uncaught exception
    783
resumption model of exception
    handling 783
rethrow an exception 788, 806
Rethrowing an exception 788
return a result 177
return a value 23
return an integer result 175
Return key 28
return statement 24, 171, 175,
    177, 199, 998
return type 175
return type defined **void** 175
return type in a function header
    178
return type of a function 179
return type of an operation 297
Returning a reference to a
    private data member 446
reusability 133, 174, 338, 722, 723
reusable componentry 14, 450
reusable software component 9
reuse 417
"reuse, reuse, reuse" 42
reused 42
reusing components 15
reverse 1104, 1113, 1152, 1154
reverse order of bits in
    unsigned integer 1049
reverse_copy 1104, 1154,
    1155, 1156
reverse_iterator 1096,
    1097, 1101, 1109
Richards, Martin 8
right brace (**}**) 23, 24, 30
right child 969
right justification 113, 352, 755,
    757
right operand 23
right shift (**>>**) 1008
right shift with sign extension
    assignment operator 1016
right-shifting a signed value is
    machine dependent 1016
right stream manipulator 755,
    757
right subtree 975, 976, 977, 984
right to left associativity 39
right triangle 163, 166
right value 128
rightmost (trailing) argument 215
rightmost node of a subtree 985

right-shift operator (**>>**) 547, 741, 1008, 1015, 1048
rise-and-shine algorithm 72
Ritchie, D. 9
robust application 780
Rogue Wave 14
roles 144
rollDice 190
rolling a die 184
Rolling a six-sided die 6000 times 184
rolling two dice 188, 190, 311
root node 969, 976
root node of the left subtree 969
root node of the right subtree 969
rotate 1104, 1167
rotate_copy 1104, 1167
rounded rectangle 227
rounding 93
rounding numbers 173
row subscript 289
rows 289
rows attribute (**textarea**) 1263
rowspan attribute (**tr**) 1257
RTTI (run-time type information) 664, 714
RTTI run-time type information 182, 664, 714
rule of thumb 124
rules for forming structured programs 129
rules of operator precedence 32
Rumbaugh, James 43
run-time type information (RTTI) 182, 664, 714
running total 87
runtime error 17
runtime_error 800
rvalue ("right value") 128, 1102 213, 564, 568

S

SalariedEmployee class header file 703
SalariedEmployee class implementation file 704
SalesPerson class definition 427
SalesPerson class member function definitions 428
savefile.cpp 917
savefile.html 916
savings account 110

SavingsAccount class 545
scalable 261
scalar 272, 336
scale 261
scaling 184
scaling factor 184, 188
scanning images 5
Scheduler class header file 458, 515
Scheduler class implementation file 516
scientific 762
scientific format 762
scientific notation 93, 743
scientific notation floating-point value 762
scientific stream manipulator 756, 761
scope 106, 416, 1071, 1186
scope of a symbolic constant or macro 1057
scope of an identifier 192, 194
scope resolution operator (**::**) 408, 497, 1187, 1189, 1200, 1204
scope-resolution operator (**::**) 726, 731
scoping conflict 1187
scoping example 196
screen 5, 6, 17, 22
screen cursor 24
screen-manager program 679
screen output 996
script 1239
scrutinize any attempt to modify data 439
scrutinize data 415
search 1104
search a linked list 947, 999
search engine 1240
search functions of the string handling library 1031
search key 284, 285, 1119
search_n 1104
searching 505, 943, 1148
searching algorithm 1148
searching array 283
searching blocks of memory 1036
searching performance 999
searching strings 362, 1026
second 1122
second-degree polynomial 34, 35
second pass of Simple compiler 996
second refinement 87, 88, 96, 351
secondary storage 17

secondary storage device 15, 809
secondary storage unit 6
"secret" implementation details 1198
security 450, 914, 916
security hole 915
security issues involving the Common Gateway Interface 937
seed 187
seed function **rand** 186
seek direction 819
seek get 818
seek put 818
seekg 818, 834
seekp 818, 829
segmentation violation 1075
select a substring 581
select XHTML element (**form**) 898
selected attribute 1266
selection 75, 131, 132
selection structure 73, 76
self-assignment 491, 566, 578
self-documentation 27
self-referential class 944, 945
self-referential structure 407, 1002
semicolon (**;**) 23, 38, 81, 176, 407, 430, 1054
semicolon at the end of a function prototype 178
semicolon that terminates a structure definition 1002
send message using a reference 457
sending object 296
sentinel-controlled loop 988
sentinel-controlled repetition 86, 88, 89, 91
sentinel value 86, 88, 116
separate interface from implementation 420
sequence 75, 130, 132, 1150, 1152, 1154, 1166, 1167
sequence container 1094, 1101, 1105, 1112, 1116
sequence diagram 300, 301, 303, 372, 374, 451, 459
sequence diagram for scheduling process 302
sequence diagram that models the steps the building repeats during the simulation 300
sequence of integers 164
sequence of messages 372
sequence of random numbers 186

sequence structure 73
sequence-structure activity
    diagram 73
sequence type 1252
sequential-access file 809, 811,
    812, 816, 823
sequential container 1094
sequential execution 73
sequential file 813, 817
server 917
server object 296
server-side file 915, 917, 921
server-side form handler 882
service 297
`<set>` 1096, 1120, 1122
`<set>` header file 182
`set` 1094, 1101, 1119, 1122, 1168
Set and *get* functions manipulating
    an object's `private` data
    443
`set` associative container 1122
`set_difference` 1156, 1158
set function 426, 439, 440, 443,
    445, 485
`set_intersection` 1156,
    1159
`set_new_handler` 784, 796
Set of recursive calls to method
    `Fibonacci` 205
`set` operations of the Standard
    Library 1157
`set_symmetric_differen`
    `ce` 1156, 1159
`set_terminate` 790
set the value of a `private` data
    member 426
`set_unexpected` 790, 800
`set_new_handler` 796
`set_union` 1156, 1159
`setbase` stream manipulator
    750
`Set-Cookie:` HTTP header
    913
`setfill` parameterized stream
    manipulator 391, 408, 757,
    759
`setprecision` 93, 112, 751
`setw` parameterized stream
    manipulator 113, 256, 361,
    554, 752, 753, 757
Shakespeare, William 399
shape class hierarchy 613, 614,
    661
shape of a tree 999
share the resources of a computer
    6

sheer brute force 166
shift a range of numbers 184
shifted, scaled integers 184
Shifted, scaled integers produced
    by `1 + rand() % 6` 183
shifting value 188
"shipping" section of the computer
    5
`shop.cgi` 928
`shop.cpp` 929
shopping cart application 909, 921
`short` 119, 179
short-circuit evaluation 126
`short int` 119
`showbase` stream manipulator
    755, 761
`showpoint` stream manipulator
    93, 756
`showpos` stream manipulator
    391, 756, 758
shrink-wrapped software 649
shuffle 350
shuffle cards 1048
shuffling algorithm 1006
side effect 720
side effect of an expression 194,
    204, 211
sides of a right triangle 163
sides of a square 166
sides of a triangle 163
Sieve of Eratosthenes 317, 1170,
    1182
`SIGABRT` 1076
`SIGFPE` 1076
`SIGILL` 1076
`SIGINT` 1076
sign extension 1008
sign left justified 755
signal 1075
signal handler 1076
signal handling 1076
signal handling library 1075
signal number 1075
`signal` to trap unexpected
    events 1075
signal value 86
signals defined in header `<csig-`
    `nal>` 1076
signature 179, 219, 581, 582
`SIGSEGV` 1076
`SIGTERM` 1076
silicon chip 3
Silicon Graphics Standard
    Template Library
    Programmer's Guide 1175,
    1234

simple CGI script 888
Simple command 987
simple condition 124, 125
Simple interpreter 999
Simple language 987
Simple Machine Language 387,
    989
Simple statement 987
simplest activity diagram 130
Simpletron Machine Language
    (SML) 396, 943, 986, 989,
    998
Simpletron memory location 998
Simpletron Simulator 397, 944,
    989, 996, 998
Simula 14
simulated deck of cards 350
simulated pass-by-reference 273
simulation 372, 390, 510
Simulation: Tortoise and the Hare
    386
simulator xxxvii, 45, 138, 225
`sin` 173
sine 173
single-argument constructor 568,
    577, 1192, 1193, 1196
Single-argument constructors and
    implicit conversions 1192
single entry point 128
single-entry/single-exit control
    structure 75, 77, 129
single exit point 128
single inheritance 610, 1204, 1205
single-line comment 22
single quote (`'`) character 360
single selection 132
single-selection `if` structure 74,
    76, 80
single-selection structure 113
single-subscripted array 329, 330,
    338
singly-linked list 959
sinking sort 277
six-sided die 183
`size` 1095, 1108, 1130, 1154,
    1169, 1170
`size` attribute (`input`) 1262
`size` member function of class
    `string` 852
`size` member function of `vec-`
    `tor` 595
size of a `string` 859
size of a structure 1003
size of a variable 30, 192
size of an array 268, 338
`size_t` 338, 825

size_type 1097
sizeof 339, 340, 418, 489, 829,
    945, 1031, 1057
sizeof array name 338
sizeof operator 849, 1003
sizeof operator used to
    determine standard data type
    sizes 340
sizeof operator when applied to
    an array name returns the
    number of bytes in the array
    339
sizes of the built-in data type 849
skip remainder of **switch**
    structure 122
skip remaining code in loop 123
skipping whitespace 749, 755
skipws stream manipulator 755
small diamond symbol 229
smaller integer sizes 120
smallest 237
smallest of several integers 165
Smalltalk 9
"smart" **Array** 1105
"smart array" 267
SML 387, 989
SML branch zero instruction 993
SML operation code 387
"sneakernet" 7
software 3, 5
software asset 42, 417
Software Engineering
    Observation 10
software reuse 10, 24, 48, 133,
    173, 417, 610, 648, 719, 720,
    722, 723, 943, 1201
software simulator 133
solid circle 74
solid circle with an attached
    arrowhead 227
solid diamond 143
solid line with an arrowhead 229
sort 1113, 1116, 1148, 1168
sort function 719
sorting 505, 813, 943, 1148
sorting algorithm 1148
sorting an array with bubble sort
    277
sorting arrays 276
sorting order 1150, 1154
sorting strings 182
source code 420, 649
source-code file 420
source-code form 1237
source file 1072
space (' ') 27

space cannot be allocated 1079
space-time tradeoff 834
spaces for padding 759
span attribute 1257
speaking to a computer 5
special character 27, 360, 1249
Special Section: Building Your
    Own Compiler 986
Special Section: Building Your
    Own Computer 387
special symbol 809
specific 680
speech device 1255
speech synthesizer 1246
spelling checker 1051
spiral 202
splice 1113, 1116
spool to disk 965
spooling 965
sqrt function 172, 173
square 162, 1252
square bracket 227
square function 180
square root 172, 173, 751
squares of several integers 988
srand 186, 188
srand(time(0)) 187
src attribute (**img**) 1246, 1247
<sstream> header file 182, 871
stable_partition 1104,
    1167
stable_sort 1168
Stack 724
<stack> 1096, 1129
<stack> header file 182
stack 502, 505, 723, 726, 790, 943,
    944, 946, 959, 962
stack adapter class 1094, 1101,
    1128, 1129
stack class 719
Stack class template 724, 730,
    964
stack class template 960, 999
Stack class-template definition
    961
Stack class-template definition
    with a composed **List**
    object 964
stack corrupted 790
stack-of-**float** class 719
stack-of-**int** class 719
stack-of-**string** class 719
Stack test program 962
Stack unwinding 791
stack unwinding 783, 784, 790,
    792

Stack< double > 726, 728, 961
stack<int> 728
Stack<T> 726, 728
stacked building block 133
stacking 75, 77, 78, 133
stacks implemented with arrays
    502
stacks used by compilers 981
"standalone" unit 7
standard algorithm 1103
standard cast 1186
standard class libraries 504
standard data type size 340
standard error stream (**cerr**) 17
standard exception classes 800
standard **exception** hierarchy
    801
standard format 408
standard input 28, 890, 1066
standard-input stream (**cin**) 740
standard input stream object 811
standard library 170
standard library algorithm 182
Standard library class **string**
    485, 588
Standard library class **vector**
    592
Standard Library container class
    1094
Standard Library container header
    file 1096
Standard Library **deque** class
    template 1118
standard library exception
    hierarchy 800
standard library header file 181,
    1054
Standard Library **list** class
    template 1113
Standard Library **map** class
    template 1126
Standard Library **multimap**
    class template 1124
Standard Library **multiset**
    class template 1120
Standard Library
    priority_queue
    adapter class 1132
Standard Library **queue** adapter
    class template 1131
Standard Library **set** class
    template 1123
Standard Library **stack** adapter
    class 1129
Standard Library **vector** class
    template 1106

Standard Library **vector** class
     template element-
     manipulation functions 1109
standard output 889, 1066
standard output object (**cout**) 23,
     811
standard-output object (**cout**)
     740
standard signal 1076
standard stream library 740
Standard Template Library (STL)
     54, 182, 503, 696, 719, 1092
Standard Template Library Online
     Reference Home Page 1175,
     1235
Standard Template Library
     Programmer's Guide 1175,
     1234
Standard Template Library with
     Borland C++ 1176
standardized function 173
"standardized, interchangeable
     parts" 42
start tag 1239
state 40, 227
state bit 744
state diagram 227
state transition 228
statechart diagram 227, 229, 296,
     374
statechart diagram for class
     Elevator 228
statechart diagram for classes
     FloorButton and
     ElevatorButton 228
statement 21, 23
statement spread over several lines
     39
statement terminator (;) 23
statements in braces 176
states of class **Elevator** 296
static 192, 194, 214, 1073,
     1081, 1083
static array initialization 270
static array initialization and
     automatic array initialization
     270
static binding 674, 692, 1204
static_cast<int> 116
static class member 509
static class variable 497
static data member 498, 732
static data member tracking
     the number of objects of a
     class 501

static data members save
     storage 497
static linkage specifier 1189
static local object 436, 437
static local variable 196, 198,
     269, 1136
static member 497, 500
static storage class 193, 195
static Web content 885
static_cast<*type*> 102, 127,
     255
status bit 766
Status header 905
std namespace 1189
std::cin 26, 28
std::cout 23
std::endl 29
<stdexcept> header file 182
<stdexcept> 800
<stdio.h> header file 181
<stdlib.h> header file 181
Stepanov, Alexander 1092, 1176,
     1235
stepwise refinement 351
STL (Standard Template Library)
     54, 182, 503, 696, 719, 1092
STL container function 1096
STL exception type 1112
STL in generic programming
     1176, 1235
STL Reference 1175, 1234
STL Software 1176, 1235
STL tutorial 1175, 1234
storage alignment 1003
storage class 192, 194, 1071
storage class specifier 192
storage unit 1020
storage-unit boundary 1019
str member function 871, 872
straight-line form 32, 33
straight-time 158
strcat and **strncat** functions
     365
strcat function 363, 365, 1072
strcmp and **strncmp** functions
     366
strcmp function 363, 365, 366,
     367, 1072
strcpy and **strncpy** 364
strcpy function 363, 364
strcspn function 1031, 1033
stream base 750
stream class 812
stream-extraction operator **>>**
     ("get from") 26, 28, 38, 222,
     547, 552, 564, 742, 744, 841

stream I/O class hierarchy 812
stream input 741, 744
stream input/output 22
stream-insertion operator **<<** ("put
     to") 23, 25, 29, 222, 547,
     552, 564, 741, 743, 816,
     1203
stream manipulator 29, 93, 113,
     749, 754, 758, 818
stream-manipulator **showbase**
     761
stream manipulators **boolalpha**
     and **noboolalpha** 764
stream of bytes 739
stream of characters 23
stream operation failed 766
stream output 741
string 347, 360
string 485, 588, 893, 910, 929,
     1094
string array 349
string array **suit** 349
string assignment 852, 853
string being tokenized 369
string class 485, 504, 548, 591,
     852
string class copy constructor
     852
String class definition with
     operator overloading 569
string class from the standard
     library 182
String class member-function
     and **friend**-function
     definitions 571
String class test program 574
string comparison 855
string concatenation 852
string constant 360
string-conversion function 1026
String-conversion function **atof**
     1027
String-conversion function **atoi**
     1027
String-conversion function **atol**
     1028
String-conversion function
     strtod 1029
String-conversion function
     strtol 1030
String-conversion function
     strtoul 1030
string copying 347
string copying using array notation
     and pointer notation 347
string data type 504

string find member function 862

<string> header file 182

string input and output 998

string insert member function 866

string is a constant pointer 361

string length 369

string literal 28, 267, 268, 360, 361

string manipulation 171, 993

string of characters 23

string processing 320

String-search function **strchr** 1032

strcspn 1033

String-search function **strpbrk** 1034

String-search function **strrchr** 1034

String-search function **strspn** 1035

String-search function **strstr** 1036

string stream processing 870

<string.h> header file 181

string::const_iterator 869

string::npos 864

<string> header file 851

string-conversion function **atof** 1027

string-conversion function **atoi** 1027

string-conversion function **atol** 1028

string-conversion function **strtod** 1029

string-conversion function **strtol** 1030

string-conversion function **strtoul** 1030

strings as full-fledged objects 256, 360

string-search function **strchr** 1032

string-search function **strcspn** 1033

string-search function **strpbrk** 1034

string-search function **strrchr** 1034

string-search function **strspn** 1035

string-search function **strstr** 1036

strlen function 363, 369, 370

strncat function 363, 365

strncmp function 363, 365, 366, 367

strncpy function 363, 364

strong element 1242

Stroustrup, Bjarne 9, 14, 719, 780, 1232

strpbrk function 1032, 1033

strrchr function 1031, 1034

strspn function 1032, 1035

strstr function 1032, 1035

strtod function 1026, 1029

strtok function 363, 368

strtol function 1027, 1029, 1030

strtoul function 1027, 1030

struct keyword 406, 407, 810, 825, 943, 1001, 1081

structure 253, 320, 334, 406, 1001, 1055

structure definition 406, 407, 1001, 1002, 1017

structure member 1001

structure member operator (**.**) 1081

structure members default to **private** access 1001

structure name 1001, 1002

structure tag 407

structure type 407, 1001, 1003

structured program 129

structured programming 3, 4, 5, 9, 13, 14, 21, 39, 40, 71, 73, 123, 405, 503, 1079

structured-programming summary 128

structured systems analysis and design 14

structures are ordinarily passed by value 410

student-poll-analysis program 265

style sheet 1239

sub element 1249

submit attribute value (**type**) 898

subobject 1207

subproblem 199

subscript 254, 1249

subscript operator 1119

subscript operator **[]** 854

subscript operator **[]** used with **string**s 852

subscript operator of map 1126

subscript out of range 1112

subscript range checking 504

subscript through a **vector** 1112

subscripted name of an array element 272

subscripted name used as an *rvalue* 564

subscripting 1117

subscripting with a pointer and an offset 345

substr member function of class **string** 857, 858, 901

substr member function of **string** 591

substring 581

substring length 581

substring of a **string** 857

subtract an integer from a pointer 341

subtract one pointer from another 341

subtraction 5, 31, 32

suit values of cards 349

sum of the elements of an array 261

summary attribute 1255

summation with **for** 109

sup element 1249

supercomputer 5

supermarket checkout line 965

supermarket simulation 983

superscript 1249

suppression of symbols in a diagram 142

survey 264, 266, 278

survey-data analysis program 279, 282

swap 278

swap 336, 1095, 1104, 1117, 1150

swap member function of class **string** 858

swap two **string**s 858

swap_ranges 1104, 1150

swapping **string**s 858

switch logic 119, 680, 714

switch multiple-selection structure 113, 117, 132, 842

switch multiple-selection structure activity diagram with **break** statements 118

switch structure testing multiple letter grade values 114

symbol 851

symbol table 989, 993, 994

symbolic constant 1054, 1055, 1056, 1057, 1060

symbolic constant **NDEBUG** 1060

symbolic constant **PI** 1056

symmetric key encryption 877
synchronize operation of an
     istream and an **ostream**
     768
synchronous error 781
synonym 323, 325
syntax checking 998
syntax error 24
system box 139
System Properties window
     884
system requirement 138

T

tab 38
tab escape sequence \t 76, 119,
     159
Tab key 24
tab stop 24
table body 1257
table data 1257
table element 1254
table head element 1256
table of values 289
table row 1256
tabular format 256
tail of a list 999
tail of a queue 943, 965
tail pointer 999
tails 183
tan 173
tangent 173
task 6
tbody (table body) element 1257
TCP (Transmission Control
     Protocol) 19
TCP/IP 19
td element 1257
telephone 163
telephone number word
     generating program 849
tellg function 819
tellp function 819
template 719, 943, 947, 960, 1056
template 75
template **auto_ptr** 798
template class 851
template definition 223, 720
template function 223, 721
template keyword 222, 720
templates and friends 731
templates and inheritance 731
Temporary Internet Files
     directory 913
temporary location 992, 995

temporary object 568
temporary **String** object 579
temporary value 92, 180
terminal 6
terminate 17
terminate 790
terminate a loop 88
terminate a program 796, 1073
terminate a repetition structure
     1079
terminate normally 815
terminate successfully 24
terminating condition 200, 266
terminating execution 505
terminating null character, **'\0'**,
     of a string 267, 269, 361,
     362, 363, 369, 485, 868
terminating right brace (**}**) of a
     block 195
terminating right brace (**}**) of the
     class definition 424
termination housekeeping 435
termination model of exception
     handling 783
termination order from the
     operating system 1075
termination phase 87
termination request sent to the
     program 1076
termination test 206
ternary conditional operator (**?:**)
     205, 550
test 13, 20
test 1169
test character 181
test state bits after an I/O operation
     744
testing an item for membership
     505
Testing and Debugging Tip 10
Testing error states 767
text analysis 399
text attribute value (**type**) 898
text-based browser 1246
text box 1262
text editor 360, 816, 1237
text file 834
Text printing program 22
text substitution 1056
text/html MIME type 888
text/plain MIME type 888
textarea XHTML element
     898, 1263
tfoot (table foot) element 1257
th (table header column) element
     1256

The C Programming Language 9
thead (table head) tag 1256
Thinking About Objects 4, 21, 405
third refinement 352
this pointer 485, 489, 491, 500,
     550, 566
this pointer used explicitly 489
this pointer used implicitly and
     explicitly to access an
     object's members 490
Thompson, Ken 8
throughput 6
throw 785
throw a conditional expression
     787
throw an exception 782
throw an **int** 787
throw exceptions derived from
     standard exceptions 801
throw exceptions not derived
     from standard exceptions
     801
throw list 789
throw point 783
throw standard exceptions 801
throw statement 788
throw() exception specification
     790
thrown object's destructor 793
TicTacToe 467
tie 768
tilde character (**~**) 416, 435
Time 411
time 187
time-and-a-half 158, 166
Time class 413, 466
Time class containing a
     constructor with default
     arguments 431
Time class definition 421
Time class definition modified to
     enable cascaded member-
     function calls 491
Time class definition with *set* and
     get functions 440
Time class member function
     definitions 421
Time class member function
     definitions, including a
     constructor that takes
     arguments 431
Time class member function
     definitions, including
     const member functions
     471

Time class member function
definitions, including *set* and
get functions 441
Time class with **const** member
functions 471
__TIME__ predefined symbolic
constant 1060
__TIMESTAMP__ predefined
symbolic constant 1060
time source file is compiled 1060
<time.h> header file 181
time_t type 888, 889
timesharing 6, 14
title bar 1239
title element 1239
title of a document 1239
title XHTML element (**<ti-
tle>…</title>**) 886
TLD (top-level domain) 884
token 363, 368, 993, 995
tokenize a sentence into separate
words 984
tokenizing strings 362, 368
tolower function 1021, 1023
top 87
top 1128, 1130, 1133
top-down, stepwise refinement 5,
86, 87, 89, 94, 351
top-level domain (TLD) 884
top of a stack 943, 960
top tier 883
Tortoise and the Hare 386
total 83, 87, 193
toupper function 331, 1021,
1023
Towers of Hanoi 246, 247
tr (table row) element 1256
traditional C 9
trailing zero 93, 172, 756
transaction 847
transaction file 847
transaction processing 1124
transaction processing program
834
transaction processing system 824
transaction record 848
transfer of control 73
transform 1104, 1144, 1147
transition 74, 227
transition arrow 74, 76, 78, 82, 83
translate 15
translation 7
translator program 8
Transmission Control Protocol
(TCP) 19
transmit securely 163

trapezoid 611
travel.html 906
traversal 869
traversals forwards and backwards
960
traverse a binary tree 969, 977
traverse the left subtree 976
traverse the right subtree 976
traversing a container 943
tree 505, 944, 969, 977
Tree class template 975
Tree class-template definition
971
tree sort 977
Tree<int> 970
TreeNode class-template
definition 970
trigonometric cosine 172
trigonometric sine 173
trigonometric tangent 173
tripleByReference 250
tripleCallByValue 250
true 34, 74, 76, 77, 78, 79, 80,
103
truncate 31, 92, 485, 814
truncate fractional part of a
double 179
truth table 125
  ! (logical NOT) operator 126
  && (logical AND) operator
125
  || (logical OR) operator 125
try block 783, 788, 792
try block expires 783
Turing Machine 73
turtle graphics 312
12-hour clock format 408
24-hour clock format 408
two largest values 159
two levels of refinement 89
two-to-one relationship 142
tying an output stream to an input
stream 768
type attribute 1252, 1262
type checking 720, 1056, 1057
type field 842
type information 841
type of a variable 30, 192
type of the **this** pointer 489
type parameter 222, 223, 224, 720,
724, 730
type qualifier 275
type-safe I/O 739
type-safe linkage 219, 1084
type_info class 714

typedef 741, 851, 870, 1004,
1096, 1121, 1126
typedefs in first-class
containers 1097
typeid 800
typeid operator 714
<typeinfo> header file 182
typeless language 9
typename 222, 720

U

U integer suffix 1075
u integer suffix 1075
ul element 1251
UL integer suffix 1075
ul integer suffix 1075
ultimate operator overloading
exercise 600
UML
  activity diagram 73, 74, 76, 78,
    82, 108
  arrow 74
  diamond 76
  dotted line 74
  final state 74
  guard condition 76
  merge symbol 82
  note 74
  solid circle 74
UML (Unified Modeling
  Language) 40, 42, 43, 73
UML class diagram xxxviii, 47,
  451
UML Partner 43
UML specification 143
UML specifications document 44
the UML 40, 43
unary decrement operator (**--**) 99
unary increment operator (**++**) 99
unary operator 93, 126, 322
unary operator overload 555
unary-operator overload 549
unary plus (**+**) and minus (**-**)
operators 93
unary predicate function 1116,
  1141, 1144
unary scope resolution operator
  (**::**) 217
unbuffered output 742
unbuffered standard-error stream
  740
unconditional branch 1079
unconditional branch **goto** 1079
unconditional branch instruction
  995

unconditional **goto** statement in Simple 987
#undef preprocessor directive 1057, 1060
undefined area in memory 1003
undefined value 85
underflow_error 800
underlying container 1128
underlying data structure 1132
underscore (_) 27
unexpected 790, 800
unexpected event 1075
unformatted I/O 739, 740, 748
unformatted I/O using the **read**, **gcount** and **write** member functions 749
unformatted output 743, 744
Unicode 810, 851
Unified Modeling Language (UML) 40, 42, 43, 73
The Unified Modeling Language User Guide 44
Uniform Resource Locator (URL) 881
unincremented copy of an object 587
uninitialized data 410
Uninitialized local reference causes a syntax error 214
uninitialized variable 85
union 1080, 1081
union constructor 1081
union functions cannot be **virtual** 1081
union with no constructor 1081
unique 1104, 1113, 1152, 1154
unique_copy 1104, 1154, 1156
unique key 1119, 1122, 1126
unique_copy 1155
United States Department of Defense (DOD) 13
University of Illinois at Urbana-Champaign 18
Unix 7, 8, 14, 116, 754, 815, 884, 1070, 1073, 1075
Unix command line 1066, 1067
unnamed bit field 1019
unnamed bit field with a zero width 1019
unnamed object 1082
unoptimized code 997
unordered list element (**ul**) 1251
unresolved reference 991, 1072
unsigned 180, 186, 1075
unsigned char 180
unsigned int 180, 186, 338

unsigned integer in bits 1009
unsigned long 180, 202, 1030, 1075
unsigned long int 180, 201
unsigned short 180
unsigned short int 180
unspecified number of arguments 1067
unsuccessful termination 1073
untie an input stream from an output stream 768
unwinding the function call stack 791
upcast 1210
upcasting 1206
update a record 848
update records in place 823
upper_bound 1119, 1122, 1160
uppercase letter 27, 68, 181, 331, 1020
uppercase letter (**A-Z**) 1023
uppercase stream manipulator 756, 761, 762
URL (Uniform Resource Locator) 881, 886
URL (Universal Resource Locator) 886
use case 139, 146, 374
use-case diagram 139
use-case diagram for elevator system 139
USENIX C++ Conference 719
user-defined type 41, 191, 406, 568
user interface 883
userdata.txt 928
user-defined, nonparameterized stream manipulator 754
"uses a" relationship 648
using 37, 59
Using a dynamically allocated **ostringstream** object 871
Using a function template 223
Using a **static** data member to maintain a count of the number of objects of a class 498
Using an anonymous **union** 1083
Using an iterator to output a **string** 869
using arrays instead of **switch** 263
Using command-line arguments 1070

Using function **swap** to swap two **string**s 858
Using functions **exit** and **atexit** 1074
Using **goto** 1079
using member function **fill** and stream manipulator **setfill** to change the padding character for fields larger than the values being printed 759
using namespace 1189
Using signal handling 1076
using Standard Library functions to perform a heapsort 1163
using statement 1187
using stream manipulator **uppercase** 763
using template functions 721
Using variable-length argument lists 1068
Using **virtual** base classes 1208
<utility> header file 181
Utility function 429
utility function 426, 516, 518, 529
utility make 1073

V

va_arg macro 1067, 1068
va_end macro 1067, 1068
va_list macro 1067, 1068
va_start macro 1067, 1068
valarray macro 1094
validate a function call 178
validation 871
validity checking 440, 445
valign attribute (**th**) 1257
value 29
value attribute 1262
value of a variable 30, 192
value of an attribute 1239
value_type 1096, 1097, 1126
variable 27, 41, 172, 406
variable-length argument list 1068
variable name 987
VAX VMS 816
vector 548, 588, 592, 1092, 1101, 1105, 1108, 1128, 1129, 1132
vector class template 1106
<vector> header file 182, 1096, 1106
verb 296, 374, 406
verb phrase 296, 299, 371, 374

verb phrases for each class in simulator 297
verbs in a problem statement 168
verbs in a system specification 41
vertical spacing 76, 104
vertical tab ('v') 1021, 1024
vi 15
vi text editor 1237
video I/O 740
viewcart.cgi 929
viewcart.cpp 931
virtual base classes 1184, 1206, 1208
virtual base-class destructor 699
virtual destructor 699
virtual directory 886
virtual function 663
virtual function 674, 696, 698, 699, 713, 1081, 1097, 1133, 1207
virtual function call 698
virtual function call illustrated 697
virtual function in a base class 713
virtual function table (*vtable*) 696
virtual inheritance 1208
virtual memory 794, 796, 945
virtual memory operating systems 14
Visual C++ home page 1234
visualizing recursion 207
VMS 1070
void 208
void * 343, 1037
void parameter list 175
void return type 179
volatile qualifier 1075, 1184
volume of a cube 210
vtable 696, 698
vtable pointer 698

W

W3C (World Wide Web Consortium) 20
W3C Candidate Recommendation 20
W3C host 20
W3C Proposed Recommendation 20
W3C Recommendation 20
W3C Working Draft 20
waiting line 505

walk a list 958
"walk off" either end of an array 556
"warehouse" section of the computer 6
warning 24
wchar_t 740, 851
"weakest" iterator type 1100, 1101
Web browser 913
Web server 881, 886, 909, 1238, 1260
Web site 3
what function of class **exception** 787, 794
when interactions occur 372
which objects participate an interactions 372
while repetition struc ture 81, 82, 103, 120, 133
while structure activity diagram 82
whitespace 744, 745, 746, 749, 1059
whitespace character 38, 76, 119, 268, 1021, 1024, 1054
whole number 27
whole/part relationship 143
width 752, 753
width attribute 1246, 1254
width implicitly set to 0 752
width member function of class **ios_base** 753
width of a bit field 1017
width of random number range 188
width setting 752
width-to-height ratio 1246
Wiltamuth, Scott 12
Win32 API (Windows 32-bit Application Programming Interface) 12
Windows 116
Windows 2000 884
Windows 32-bit Application Programming Interface (Win32 API) 12
Wirth, Nicklaus 13
word 387, 1003
word boundary 1003
word equivalent of a check amount 401
word processing 360, 400
Wordpad 1237
worker 171
workflow 73
workstation 7

World Wide Web 4, 19
World Wide Web Consortium (W3C) 20
World Wide Web resources 1175
wraparound 587
write 743, 748, 749, 824, 829
writecookie.cgi 910
writecookie.cpp 911
writing data randomly to a random access file 829
www.apache.org 890
www.deitel.com 3, 4, 884, 1242
www.jasc.com 1245
www.omg.org 44
www.unicode.org 851
www.w3.org 20
www.w3.org/markup 1237
www.w3.org/TR/xhtml1 1269
www.w3schools.com/ xhtml/default.asp 1269
www.xhtml.org 1269

X

X3J11 technical committee 9
Xerox's Palo Alto Research Center (PARC) 9
XHTML (Extensible HyperText Markup Language) 20, 52, 881, 886, 1237
XHTML comment 1239
XHTML document 56
XHTML form 897, 1259
XHTML list 56
XHTML Recommendation 1269
XHTML special character 1274.
XHTML table 56
XHTML tag 890
XML (Extensible Markup Language) 20
xor 144
xor operator keyword 1190
xor_eq operator keyword 1191

Z

zero-based counting 106
zeros and ones 809
zeroth element 253

End-User License Agreement for Microsoft Software

IMPORTANT-READ CAREFULLY: This Microsoft End-User License Agreement ("EULA") is a legal agreement between you (either an individual or a single entity) and Microsoft Corporation for the Microsoft software products included in this package, which includes computer software and may include associated media, printed materials, and "online" or electronic documentation ("SOFTWARE PRODUCT"). The SOFTWARE PRODUCT also includes any updates and supplements to the original SOFTWARE PRODUCT provided to you by Microsoft. By installing, copying, downloading, accessing or otherwise using the SOFTWARE PRODUCT, you agree to be bound by the terms of this EULA. If you do not agree to the terms of this EULA, do not install, copy, or otherwise use the SOFTWARE PRODUCT.

SOFTWARE PRODUCT LICENSE

The SOFTWARE PRODUCT is protected by copyright laws and international copyright treaties, as well as other intellectual property laws and treaties. The SOFTWARE PRODUCT is licensed, not sold.

1. GRANT OF LICENSE. This EULA grants you the following rights:

   1.1 License Grant. Microsoft grants to you as an individual, a personal nonexclusive license to make and use copies of the SOFTWARE PRODUCT for the sole purposes of evaluating and learning how to use the SOFTWARE PRODUCT, as may be instructed in accompanying publications or documentation. You may install the software on an unlimited number of computers provided that you are the only individual using the SOFTWARE PRODUCT.

   1.2 Academic Use. You must be a "Qualified Educational User" to use the SOFTWARE PRODUCT in the manner described in this section. To determine whether you are a Qualified Educational User, please contact the Microsoft Sales Information Center/One Microsoft Way/Redmond, WA 98052-6399 or the Microsoft subsidiary serving your country. If you are a Qualified Educational User, you may either:

(i)   exercise the rights granted in Section 1.1, OR

(ii)   if you intend to use the SOFTWARE PRODUCT solely for instructional purposes in connection with a class or other educational program, this EULA grants you the following alternative license models:

(A)   Per Computer Model. For every valid license you have acquired for the SOFTWARE PRODUCT, you may install a single copy of the SOFTWARE PRODUCT on a single computer for access and use by an unlimited number of student end users at your educational institution, provided that all such end users comply with all other terms of this EULA, OR

(B)   Per License Model. If you have multiple licenses for the SOFTWARE PRODUCT, then at any time you may have as many copies of the SOFTWARE PRODUCT in use as you have licenses, provided that such use is limited to student or faculty end users at your educational institution and provided that all such end users comply with all other terms of this EULA. For purposes of this subsection, the SOFTWARE PRODUCT is "in use" on a computer when it is loaded into the temporary memory (i.e., RAM) or installed into the permanent memory (e.g., hard disk, CD ROM, or other storage device) of that computer, except that a copy installed on a network server for the sole purpose of distribution to other computers is not "in use". If the anticipated number of users of the SOFTWARE PRODUCT will exceed the number of applicable licenses, then you must have a reasonable mechanism or process in place to ensure that the number of persons using the SOFTWARE PRODUCT concurrently does not exceed the number of licenses.

2.   DESCRIPTION OF OTHER RIGHTS AND LIMITATIONS.

- Limitations on Reverse Engineering, Decompilation, and Disassembly. You may not reverse engineer, decompile, or disassemble the SOFTWARE PRODUCT, except and only to the extent that such activity is expressly permitted by applicable law notwithstanding this limitation.

- Separation of Components. The SOFTWARE PRODUCT is licensed as a single product. Its component parts may not be separated for use on more than one computer.

- Rental. You may not rent, lease or lend the SOFTWARE PRODUCT.

- Trademarks. This EULA does not grant you any rights in connection with any trademarks or service marks of Microsoft.

- Software Transfer. The initial user of the SOFTWARE PRODUCT may make a one-time permanent transfer of this EULA and SOFTWARE PRODUCT only directly to an end user. This transfer must include all of the SOFTWARE PRODUCT (including all component parts, the media and printed materials, any upgrades, this EULA, and, if applicable, the Certificate of Authenticity). Such transfer may not be by way of consignment or any other indirect transfer. The transferee of such one-time transfer must agree to comply with the terms of this EULA, including the obligation not to further transfer this EULA and SOFTWARE PRODUCT.

- No Support. Microsoft shall have no obligation to provide any product support for the SOFTWARE PRODUCT.

- Termination. Without prejudice to any other rights, Microsoft may terminate this EULA if you fail to comply with the terms and conditions of this EULA. In such event, you must destroy all copies of the SOFTWARE PRODUCT and all of its component parts.

3. COPYRIGHT. All title and intellectual property rights in and to the SOFTWARE PRODUCT (including but not limited to any images, photographs, animations, video, audio, music, text, and "applets" incorporated into the SOFTWARE PROD-UCT), the accompanying printed materials, and any copies of the SOFTWARE PRODUCT are owned by Microsoft or its suppliers. All title and intellectual property rights in and to the content which may be accessed through use of the SOFT-WARE PRODUCT is the property of the respective content owner and may be protected by applicable copyright or other intellectual property laws and treaties. This EULA grants you no rights to use such content. All rights not expressly granted are reserved by Microsoft.

4. BACKUP COPY. After installation of one copy of the SOFTWARE PROD-UCT pursuant to this EULA, you may keep the original media on which the SOFTWARE PRODUCT was provided by Microsoft solely for backup or archival purposes. If the original media is required to use the SOFTWARE PRODUCT on the COMPUTER, you may make one copy of the SOFTWARE PRODUCT solely for backup or archival purposes. Except as expressly pro-vided in this EULA, you may not otherwise make copies of the SOFTWARE PRODUCT or the printed materials accompanying the SOFTWARE PROD-UCT.

5. U.S. GOVERNMENT RESTRICTED RIGHTS. The SOFTWARE PROD-UCT and documentation are provided with RESTRICTED RIGHTS. Use, duplication, or disclosure by the Government is subject to restrictions as set forth in subparagraph (c)(1)(ii) of the Rights in Technical Data and Computer Software clause at DFARS 252.227-7013 or subparagraphs (c)(1) and (2) of the Commercial Computer Software-Restricted Rights at 48 CFR 52.227-19, as applicable. Manufacturer is Microsoft Corporation/One Microsoft Way/ Redmond, WA 98052-6399.

6. EXPORT RESTRICTIONS. You agree that you will not export or re-export the SOFTWARE PRODUCT, any part thereof, or any process or service that is the direct product of the SOFTWARE PRODUCT (the foregoing collectively referred to as the "Restricted Components"), to any country, person, entity or end user subject to U.S. export restrictions. You specifically agree not to export or re-export any of the Restricted Components (i) to any country to which the U.S. has embargoed or restricted the export of goods or services, which currently include, but are not necessarily limited to Cuba, Iran, Iraq, Libya, North Korea, Sudan and Syria, or to any national of any such country, wherever located, who intends to transmit or transport the Restricted Compo-nents back to such country; (ii) to any end-user who you know or have reason to know will utilize the Restricted Components in the design, development or

production of nuclear, chemical or biological weapons; or (iii) to any end-user who has been prohibited from participating in U.S. export transactions by any federal agency of the U.S. government. You warrant and represent that neither the BXA nor any other U.S. federal agency has suspended, revoked, or denied your export privileges.

7. NOTE ON JAVA SUPPORT. THE SOFTWARE PRODUCT MAY CONTAIN SUPPORT FOR PROGRAMS WRITTEN IN JAVA. JAVA TECHNOLOGY IS NOT FAULT TOLERANT AND IS NOT DESIGNED, MANUFAC-TURED, OR INTENDED FOR USE OR RESALE AS ON-LINE CONTROL EQUIPMENT IN HAZARDOUS ENVIRONMENTS REQUIRING FAIL-SAFE PERFORMANCE, SUCH AS IN THE OPERATION OF NUCLEAR FACILITIES, AIRCRAFT NAVIGATION OR COMMUNICATION SYS-TEMS, AIR TRAFFIC CONTROL, DIRECT LIFE SUPPORT MACHINES, OR WEAPONS SYSTEMS, IN WHICH THE FAILURE OF JAVA TECH-NOLOGY COULD LEAD DIRECTLY TO DEATH, PERSONAL INJURY, OR SEVERE PHYSICAL OR ENVIRONMENTAL DAMAGE.

MISCELLANEOUS

If you acquired this product in the United States, this EULA is governed by the laws of the State of Washington.

If you acquired this product in Canada, this EULA is governed by the laws of the Province of Ontario, Canada. Each of the parties hereto irrevocably attorns to the jurisdiction of the courts of the Province of Ontario and further agrees to commence any litigation which may arise hereunder in the courts located in the Judicial District of York, Province of Ontario.

If this product was acquired outside the United States, then local law may apply.

Should you have any questions concerning this EULA, or if you desire to contact Microsoft for any reason, please contact

Microsoft, or write: Microsoft Sales Information Center/One Microsoft Way/Redmond, WA 98052-6399.

LIMITED WARRANTY

LIMITED WARRANTY. Microsoft warrants that (a) the SOFTWARE PRODUCT will perform substantially in accordance with the accompanying written materials for a period of ninety (90) days from the date of receipt, and (b) any Support Services provided by Microsoft shall be substantially as described in applicable written materials provided to you by Microsoft, and Microsoft support engineers will make commercially reasonable efforts to solve any problem. To the extent allowed by applicable law, implied warranties on the SOFTWARE PRODUCT, if any, are limited to ninety (90) days. Some states/jurisdictions do not allow limitations on duration of an implied warranty, so the above limitation may not apply to you.

CUSTOMER REMEDIES. Microsoft's and its suppliers' entire liability and your exclusive remedy shall be, at Microsoft's option, either (a) return of the price paid, if any, or (b) repair or replacement of the SOFTWARE PRODUCT that does not meet Microsoft's Limited Warranty and that is returned to Microsoft with a copy of your receipt. This Limited Warranty is void if failure of the SOFTWARE PRODUCT has resulted from accident, abuse, or misapplication. Any replacement SOFTWARE PRODUCT will be warranted for the remainder of the original warranty period or thirty (30) days, whichever is longer. Outside the United States, neither these remedies nor any product support services offered by Microsoft are available without proof of purchase from an authorized international source.

NO OTHER WARRANTIES. TO THE MAXIMUM EXTENT PERMITTED BY APPLICABLE LAW, MICROSOFT AND ITS SUPPLIERS DISCLAIM ALL OTHER WARRANTIES AND CONDITIONS, EITHER EXPRESS OR IMPLIED, INCLUDING, BUT NOT LIMITED TO, IMPLIED WARRANTIES OR CONDITIONS OF MER-CHANTABILITY, FITNESS FOR A PARTICULAR PURPOSE, TITLE AND NON-INFRINGEMENT, WITH REGARD TO THE SOFTWARE PRODUCT, AND THE PROVISION OF OR FAILURE TO PROVIDE SUPPORT SERVICES. THIS LIMITED WARRANTY GIVES YOU SPECIFIC LEGAL RIGHTS. YOU MAY HAVE OTHERS, WHICH VARY FROM STATE/JURISDICTION TO STATE/JURISDICTION.

LIMITATION OF LIABILITY. TO THE MAXIMUM EXTENT PERMITTED BY APPLICABLE LAW, IN NO EVENT SHALL MICROSOFT OR ITS SUPPLIERS BE LIABLE FOR ANY SPECIAL, INCIDENTAL, INDIRECT, OR CONSEQUENTIAL DAMAGES WHATSOEVER (INCLUDING, WITHOUT LIMITATION, DAMAGES FOR LOSS OF BUSINESS PROFITS, BUSINESS INTERRUPTION, LOSS OF BUSI-NESS INFORMATION, OR ANY OTHER PECUNIARY LOSS) ARISING OUT OF THE USE OF OR INABILITY TO USE THE SOFTWARE PRODUCT OR THE FAILURE TO PROVIDE SUPPORT SERVICES, EVEN IF MICROSOFT HAS BEEN ADVISED OF THE POSSIBILITY OF SUCH DAMAGES. IN ANY CASE, MICROSOFT'S ENTIRE LIABILITY UNDER ANY PROVISION OF THIS EULA SHALL BE LIMITED TO THE GREATER OF THE AMOUNT ACTUALLY PAID BY YOU FOR THE SOFTWARE PRODUCT OR U.S.$5.00; PROVIDED, HOWEVER, IF YOU HAVE ENTERED INTO A MICROSOFT SUPPORT SERVICES AGREEMENT, MICROSOFT'S ENTIRE LIABILITY REGARDING SUPPORT SERVICES SHALL BE GOVERNED BY THE TERMS OF THAT AGREEMENT. BECAUSE SOME STATES/JURISDICTIONS DO NOT ALLOW THE EXCLUSION OR LIMITATION OF LIA-BILITY, THE ABOVE LIMITATION MAY NOT APPLY TO YOU.

0495 Part No. 64358

The DEITEL™
Suite of Products...

JavaBeans™ (EJB) and design patterns into a production-quality system that allows developers to benefit from the leverage and platform independence Java 2 Enterprise Edition provides. The book also features the development of a complete, end-to-end e-business solution using advanced Java technologies. Additional topics include Swing, Java 2D and 3D, XML, design patterns, CORBA, Jini™, JavaSpaces™, Jiro™, Java Management Extensions (JMX) and Peer-to-Peer networking with an introduction to JXTA. This textbook also introduces the Java 2 Micro Edition (J2ME™) for building applications for handheld and wireless devices using MIDP and MIDlets. Wireless technologies covered include WAP, WML and i-mode.

Visual C++ .NET How to Program

Coming Fall 2002

BOOK / CD-ROM

©2003, 1600 pp., paper (0-13-437377-4)

Visual C++® .NET How to Program provides a comprehensive introduction to building Visual C++ applications for Microsoft's new .NET Framework. The book begins with a strong foundation in introductory and intermediate programming principles, including control structures, functions, arrays, pointers, strings, classes and data abstraction, inheritance, virtual methods, polymorphism, I/O, exception handling, file processing, data structures and more. The book discusses program development with the Microsoft® Visual Studio® .NET integrated development environment (IDE) and shows how to edit, compile and debug applications with the IDE. The book then explores more sophisticated .NET application-development topics in detail. Key topics include: creating reusable software components with assemblies, modules and dynamic link libraries; using classes from the Framework Class Library (FCL); building graphical user interfaces (GUIs) with the FCL; implementing multithreaded applications; building networked applications; manipulating databases with ADO .NET and creating XML Web services. The first 75% of the book covers programming with Microsoft's new managed-code approach. The five chapters in the last quarter of the book focus on programming with unmanaged code in Visual C++ .NET. These chapters demonstrate how to use "attributed programming" to simplify common tasks (such as connecting to databases) and to improve code readability; how to integrate managed- and unmanaged-code software components; and how to use ATL Server to create Web-based applications and Web services with unmanaged code. The book features LIVE-CODE ™ examples that highlight crucial .NET-programming concepts and demonstrate Web services at work. Substantial introductions to XML and XHTML also are included.

C# How to Program

BOOK / CD-ROM

©2002, 1568 pp., paper (0-13-062221-4)

An exciting new addition to the How to Program series, *C# How to Program* provides a comprehensive introduction to Microsoft's new object-oriented language. C# builds on the skills already mastered by countless C++ and Java programmers, enabling them to create powerful Web applications and components—ranging from XML-based Web services on Microsoft's .NET platform to middle-tier business objects and system-level applications. *C# How to Program* begins with a strong foundation in the introductory and intermediate programming principles students will need in industry. It then explores such essential topics as object-oriented programming and exception handling. Graphical user interfaces are extensively covered, giving readers the tools to build compelling and fully interactive programs. Internet technologies such as XML, ADO .NET and Web services are also covered as well as topics including regular expressions, multithreading, networking, databases, files and data structures.

Visual Basic .NET How to Program Second Edition

BOOK / CD-ROM

©2002, 1400 pp., paper (0-13-029363-6)

Teach Visual Basic .NET programming from the ground up! This introduction of Microsoft's .NET Framework marks the beginning of major revisions to all of Microsoft's programming languages. This book provides a comprehensive introduction to the next version of Visual Basic—Visual Basic .NET—featuring extensive updates and increased functionality. *Visual Basic .NET How to Program, Second Edition* covers introductory programming techniques as well as more advanced topics, featuring enhanced treatment of developing Web-based applications. Other topics discussed include an extensive treatment of XML and wireless applications, databases, SQL and ADO .NET, Web forms, Web services and ASP .NET.

C How to Program Third Edition

BOOK / CD-ROM

©2001, 1253 pp., paper (0-13-089572-5)

Highly practical in approach, the Third Edition of the world's best-selling C text introduces the fundamentals of structured programming and software engineering and gets up to speed quickly. This comprehensive book not only covers the full C language, but also reviews library functions and introduces object-based and object-oriented programming in C++ and Java. The Third Edition includes a new 346-page introduction to Java 2 and the basics of GUIs, and the 298-page introduction to C++ has been updated to be consistent with the most current ANSI/ISO C++ standards. Plus, icons throughout the book point out valuable programming tips such as Common Programming Errors, Portability Tips and Testing and Debugging Tips.

Getting Started with Microsoft® Visual C++™ 6 with an Introduction to MFC

BOOK / CD-ROM

©2000, 163 pp., paper
(0-13-016147-0)

Internet & World Wide Web How to Program, Second Edition

BOOK / CD-ROM

©2002, 1428 pp., paper
(0-13-030897-8)

The revision of this groundbreaking book in the Deitels' *How to Program Series* offers a thorough treatment of programming concepts that yield visible or audible results in Web pages and Web-based applications. This book discusses effective Web-based design, server- and client-side scripting, multitier Web-based applications development, ActiveX® controls and electronic commerce essentials. This book offers an alternative to traditional programming courses using markup languages (such as XHTML, Dynamic HTML and XML) and scripting languages (such as JavaScript, VBScript, Perl/CGI, Python and PHP) to teach the fundamentals of programming "wrapped in the metaphor of the Web."

Updated material on **www·deitel·com** and **www·prenhall·com/deitel** provides additional resources for instructors who want to cover Microsoft® or non-Microsoft technologies. The Web site includes an extensive treatment of Netscape® 6 and alternate versions of the code from the Dynamic HTML chapters that will work with non-Microsoft environments as well.

Wireless Internet & Mobile Business How to Program

©2002, 1292 pp., paper
(0-13-062226-5)

While the rapid expansion of wireless technologies, such as cell phones, pagers and personal digital assistants (PDAs), offers many new opportunities for businesses and programmers, it also presents numerous challenges related to issues such as security and standardization. This book offers a thorough treatment of both the management and technical aspects of this growing area, including coverage of current practices and future trends. The first half explores the business issues surrounding wireless technology and mobile business, including an overview of existing and developing communi-

cation technologies and the application of business principles to wireless devices. It also discusses location-based services and location-identifying technologies, a topic that is revisited throughout the book. Wireless payment, security, legal and social issues, international communications and more are also discussed. The book then turns to programming for the wireless Internet, exploring topics such as WAP (including 2.0), WML, WMLScript, XML, XHTML™, wireless Java programming (J2ME)™, Web Clipping and more. Other topics covered include career resources, wireless marketing, accessibility, Palm™, PocketPC, Windows CE, i-mode, Bluetooth, MIDP, MIDlets, ASP, Microsoft .NET Mobile Framework, BREW™, multimedia, Flash™ and VBScript.

Python How to Program

BOOK / CD-ROM

©2002, 1376 pp., paper
(0-13-092361-3)

This exciting new book provides a comprehensive introduction to Python—a powerful object-oriented programming language with clear syntax and the ability to bring together various technologies quickly and easily. This book covers introductory-programming techniques and more advanced topics such as graphical user interfaces, databases, wireless Internet programming, networking, security, process management, multithreading, XHTML, CSS, PSP and multimedia. Readers will learn principles that are applicable to both systems development and Web programming. The book features the consistent and applied pedagogy that the *How to Program Series* is known for, including the Deitels' signature LIVE-CODE™ Approach, with thousands of lines of code in hundreds of working programs; hundreds of valuable programming tips identified with icons throughout the text; an extensive set of exercises, projects and case studies; two-color four-way syntax coloring and much more.

e-Business & e-Commerce for Managers

©2001, 794 pp., cloth
(0-13-032364-0)

This comprehensive overview of building and managing e-businesses explores topics such as the decision to bring a business online, choosing a business model, accepting payments, marketing strategies and security, as well as many other important issues (such as career resources). The book features Web resources and online demonstrations that supplement the text and direct readers to additional materials. The book also includes an appendix that develops a complete

Web-based shopping-cart application using HTML, JavaScript, VBScript, Active Server Pages, ADO, SQL, HTTP, XML and XSL. Plus, company-specific sections provide "real-world" examples of the concepts presented in the book.

XML How to Program

BOOK / CD-ROM

©2001, 934 pp., paper (0-13-028417-3)

This book is a comprehensive guide to programming in XML. It teaches how to use XML to create customized tags and includes chapters that address standard custom-markup languages for science and technology, multimedia, commerce and many other fields. Concise introductions to Java, JavaServer Pages, VBScript, Active Server Pages and Perl/CGI provide readers with the essentials of these programming languages and server-side development technologies to enable them to work effectively with XML. The book also covers cutting-edge topics such as XSL, DOM™ and SAX, plus a real-world e-commerce case study and a complete chapter on Web accessibility that addresses Voice XML. It includes tips such as Common Programming Errors, Software Engineering Observations, Portability Tips and Debugging Hints. Other topics covered include XHTML, CSS, DTD, schema, parsers, XPath, XLink, namespaces, XBase, XInclude, XPointer, XSLT, XSL Formatting Objects, JavaServer Pages, XForms, topic maps, X3D, MathML, OpenMath, CML, BML, CDF, RDF, SVG, Cocoon, WML, XBRL and BizTalk™ and SOAP™ Web resources.

Perl How to Program

BOOK / CD-ROM

©2001, 1057 pp., paper (0-13-028418-1)

This comprehensive guide to Perl programming emphasizes the use of the Common Gateway Interface (CGI) with Perl to create powerful, dynamic multi-tier Web-based client/server applications. The book begins with a clear and careful introduction to programming concepts at a level suitable for beginners, and proceeds through advanced topics such as references and complex data structures. Key Perl topics such as regular expressions and string manipulation are covered in detail. The authors address important and topical issues such as object-oriented programming, the Perl database interface (DBI), graphics and security. Also included is a treatment of XML, a bonus chapter introducing the Python programming language, supplemental material on career resources and a complete chapter on Web accessibility. The text includes tips such as Common Programming Errors, Software Engineering Observations, Portability Tips and Debugging Hints.

e-Business & e-Commerce How to Program

BOOK / CD-ROM

©2001, 1254 pp., paper (0-13-028419-X)

This innovative book explores programming technologies for developing Web-based e-business and e-commerce solutions, and covers e-business and e-commerce models and business issues. Readers learn a full range of options, from "build-your-own" to turnkey solutions. The book examines scores of the top e-businesses (examples include Amazon, eBay, Priceline, Travelocity, etc.), explaining the technical details of building successful e-business and e-commerce sites and their underlying business premises. Learn how to implement the dominant e-commerce models—shopping carts, auctions, name-your-own-price, comparison shopping and bots/ intelligent agents—by using markup languages (HTML, Dynamic HTML and XML), scripting languages (JavaScript, VBScript and Perl), server-side technologies (Active Server Pages and Perl/CGI) and database (SQL and ADO), security and online payment technologies. Updates are regularly posted to **www·deitel·com** and the book includes a CD-ROM with software tools, source code and live links.

www·deitel·com/newsletter/subscribe·html

BOOK/MULTIMEDIA PACKAGES

Complete Training Courses

Each complete package includes the corresponding *How to Program Series* book and interactive multimedia CD-ROM Cyber Classroom. *Complete Training Courses* are perfect for anyone interested Web and e-commerce programming. They are affordable resources for college students and professionals learning programming for the first time or reinforcing their knowledge.

Each *Complete Training Course* is compatible with Windows 95, Windows 98, Windows NT and Windows 2000 and includes the following features:

Intuitive Browser-Based Interface

You'll love the *Complete Training Courses'* new browser-based interface, designed to be easy and accessible to anyone who's ever used a Web browser. Every *Complete Training Course* features the full text, illustrations and program listings of its corresponding *How to Program* book—all in full color—with full-text searching and hyperlinking.

Further Enhancements to the Deitels' Signature LIVE-CODE™ Approach

Every code sample from the main text can be found in the interactive, multimedia, CD-ROM-based *Cyber Classrooms* included in the *Complete Training Courses*. Syntax coloring of code is included for the *How to Program* books that are published in full color. Even the recent two-color and one-color books use effective multi-way syntax shading. The *Cyber Classroom* products always are in full color.

Audio Annotations

Hours of detailed, expert audio descriptions of thousands of lines of code help reinforce concepts.

Easily Executable Code

With one click of the mouse, you can execute the code or save it to your hard drive to manipulate using the programming environment of your choice. With selected *Complete Training Courses*, you can also load all of the code into a development environment such as Microsoft® Visual C++™, enabling you to modify and execute the programs with ease.

Abundant Self-Assessment Material

Practice exams test your understanding with hundreds of test questions and answers in addition to those found in the main text. Hundreds of self-review questions, all with answers, are drawn from the text; as are hundreds of programming exercises, half with answers.

www.phptr.com/phptrinteractive

Sign up now for the new *DEITEL™ Buzz Online* newsletter at:

BOOK/MULTIMEDIA PACKAGES

The Complete C++ Training Course, Fourth Edition
(0-13-100252-X)

The Complete C# Training Course
(0-13-064584-2)

The Complete e-Business & e-Commerce Programming Training Course
(0-13-089549-0)

The Complete Internet & World Wide Web Programming Training Course, Second Edition
(0-13-089550-4)

The Complete Java™ 2 Training Course, Fourth Edition
(0-13-064931-7)

The Complete Perl Training Course
(0-13-089552-0)

The Complete Python Training Course
(0-13-067374-9)

The Complete Visual Basic 6 Training Course
(0-13-082929-3)

You can run the hundreds of Visual Basic programs with the click of a mouse and automatically load them into Microsoft®'s Visual Basic® 6 Working Model edition software, allowing you to modify and execute the programs with ease.

The Complete Visual Basic .NET Training Course, Second Edition
(0-13-042530-3)

The Complete Wireless Internet & Mobile Business Programming Training Course
(0-13-062335-0)

The Complete XML Programming Training Course
(0-13-089557-1)

All of these ISBNs are retail ISBNs. College and university instructors should contact your local Prentice Hall representative or write to cs@prenhall.com for the corresponding student edition ISBNs.

If you would like to purchase the Cyber Classrooms separately...

Prentice Hall offers Multimedia Cyber Classroom CD-ROMs to accompany the *How to Program* series texts for the topics listed at right. If you have already purchased one of these books and would like to purchase a stand-alone copy of the corresponding *Multimedia Cyber Classroom,* you can make your purchase at the following Web site:

www.informit.com/cyberclassrooms

For **C++ Multimedia Cyber Classroom, 4/E**, ask for product number 0-13-100253-8

For **C# Multimedia Cyber Classroom**, ask for product number 0-13-064587-7

For **e-Business & e-Commerce Cyber Classroom**, ask for product number 0-13-089540-7

For **Internet & World Wide Web Cyber Classroom, 2/E**, ask for product number 0-13-089559-8

For **Java Multimedia Cyber Classroom, 4/E**, ask for product number 0-13-064935-X

For **Perl Multimedia Cyber Classroom**, ask for product number 0-13-089553-9

For **Python Multimedia Cyber Classroom**, ask for product number 0-13-067375-7

For **Visual Basic 6 Multimedia Cyber Classroom**, ask for product number 0-13-083116-6

For **Visual Basic .NET Multimedia Cyber Classroom, 2/E**, ask for product number 0-13-065193-1

For **XML Multimedia Cyber Classroom**, ask for product number 0-13-089555-5

For **Wireless Internet & m-Business Programming Multimedia Cyber Classroom,** ask for product number 0-13-062337-7

e-LEARNING • www.InformIT.com/deitel

Deitel & Associates, Inc. has partnered with Prentice Hall's parent company, Pearson PLC, and its information technology Web site, **InformIT.com**, to launch the Deitel InformIT kiosk at **www.InformIT.com/deitel**. The Deitel InformIT kiosk contains information on the continuum of Deitel products, including:

- **Free informational articles**
- **Deitel e-Matter**
- **Books and e-Books**
- **Web-based training**
- **Instructor-led training by Deitel & Associates**
- *Complete Training Courses/Cyber Classrooms*

Deitel & Associates is also contributing to two separate weekly InformIT e-mail newsletters.

The first is the InformIT promotional newsletter, which features weekly specials and discounts on Pearson publications. Each week a new Deitel™ product is featured along with information about our corporate instructor-led training courses and the opportunity to read about upcoming issues of our own e-mail newsletter, the DEITEL™ BUZZ ONLINE.

The second newsletter is the InformIT editorial newsletter, which contains approximately 50 new articles per week on various IT topics, including programming, advanced computing, networking, security, databases, creative media, business, Web development, software engineering, operating systems and more. Deitel & Associates contributes 2-3 articles per week pulled from our extensive existing content base or material being created during our research and development process.

Both of these publications are sent to over 750,000 registered users worldwide (for opt-in registration, visit **www.InformIT.com**).

e-LEARNING • from Deitel & Associates, Inc.

Cyber Classrooms, Web-Based Training and Course Management Systems

DEITEL is committed to continuous research and development in e-Learning.

We are pleased to announce that we have incorporated examples of Web-based training, including a five-way Macromedia® Flash™ animation of a `for` loop in Java™, into the *Java 2 Multimedia Cyber Classroom, 4/e* (which is included in *The Complete Java 2 Training Course, 4/e*). Our instructional designers and Flash animation team are developing additional simulations that demonstrate key programming concepts.

We are enhancing the Multimedia Cyber Classroom products to include more audio, pre- and post-assessment questions and Web-based labs with solutions for the benefit of professors and students alike. In addition, our Multimedia Cyber Classroom products, currently available in CD-ROM format, are being ported to Pearson's CourseCompass course-management system—*a powerful e-platform for teaching and learning*. Many Deitel materials are available in WebCT, Blackboard and CourseCompass formats for colleges, and will soon be available for various corporate learning management systems.

Sign up now for the new *DEITEL™ BUZZ Online* **newsletter at:**
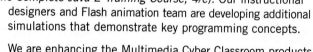

Future Publications

Here are some new titles we are considering for 2002/2003 release:

Computer Science Series: *Operating Systems 3/e, Data Structures in C++, Data Structures in Java, Theory and Principles of Database Systems.*

Database Series: *Oracle, SQL Server, MySQL.*

Internet and Web Programming Series: *Open Source Software Development: Apache, Linux, MySQL and PHP.*

Programming Series: *Flash™.*

.NET Programming Series: *ADO .NET with Visual Basic .NET, ASP .NET with Visual Basic .NET, ADO .NET with C#, ASP .NET with C#.*

Object Technology Series: *OOAD with the UML, Design Patterns, Java™ and XML.*

Advanced Java™ Series: *JDBC, Java 2 Enterprise Edition, Java Media Framework (JMF), Java Security and Java Cryptography (JCE), Java Servlets, Java2D and Java3D, JavaServer Pages™ (JSP), JINI and Java 2 Micro Edition™ (J2ME).*

DEITEL™ BUZZ ONLINE Newsletter

The Deitel and Associates, Inc. free opt-in newsletter includes:

- Updates and commentary on industry trends and developments
- Resources and links to articles from our published books and upcoming publications.
- Information on the Deitel publishing plans, including future publications and product-release schedules
- Support for instructors
- Resources for students
- Information on Deitel Corporate Training

To sign up for the Deitel™ Buzz Online newsletter, visit `www.deitel.com /newsletter/subscribe.html`.

E-Books

We are committed to providing our content in traditional print formats and in emerging electronic formats, such as e-books, to fulfill our customers' needs. Our R&D teams are currently exploring many leading-edge solutions.

Visit `www.deitel.com` and read the DEITEL™ BUZZ ONLINE for periodic updates.

Turn the page to find out more about Deitel & Associates!

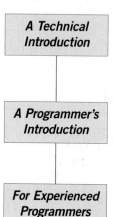